COLLINS
FAMILY COOKERY

DESSERT

COLLINS
FAMILY
COOKERY

by

ELIZABETH CRAIG

15 COLOUR PLATES
AND 144 PHOTOGRAPHS
WITH
40 LINE DECORATIONS
BY GORDON F. HUNTLY

COLLINS
LONDON AND GLASGOW

FIRST PUBLISHED 1957
LATEST REPRINT 1973

ISBN 0 00 435136 3
PRINTED IN GREAT BRITAIN BY
COLLINS CLEAR-TYPE PRESS

ACKNOWLEDGEMENTS

I wish to acknowledge the generous co-operation of a number of firms and organisations. Some of them helped me to establish my experimental kitchen without which it would have been difficult to prepare this book. Others have contributed photographs and information.

The American Department of Agriculture (Bureau of Home Economics)
The British Electrical Development Association
Cadbury Brothers Ltd.
Alfred Bird & Sons, Consumer Service
The English Electric Company Ltd.
Fillerys (Great Britain) Ltd.
H. Fisher (Oldham) Ltd.
T. J. Green & Company Ltd.
Hague and McKenzie Ltd.
The Herring Board
The Jackson Electric Stove Company Ltd.
Kenwood Electrics Ltd.
Richard Klinger Ltd.
T. Wall & Sons Ltd.
Millard Brothers Ltd.
Moffats Overseas Ltd.
North Thames Gas Board
Platers and Stampers Ltd.
W. & M. Pumphrey Ltd.
Radiation Ltd.
Mrs. M. K. Smith
Smiths English Clocks Ltd.
Vernons Industries Ltd.
George Wostenholm & Son Ltd.
Woman's Journal
Yorkshire Post

CONTENTS

ILLUSTRATIONS

COLOUR

BLACK AND WHITE

FOREWORD

As a lover of good food, I am glad that my wife has written this book, for it should help keep alive the art of cooking, an art which, I fear, is slowly dying. The ingenuity of the processors of food, aided by the skill of the food chemists, yearly makes it easier for the lazy or overburdened housewife to serve a palatable meal without contributing much culinary skill of her own. But there will never be a satisfactory pre-fabrication of perfectly cooked food of a variety infinite enough to suit the most critical and capricious palates. For that, you must consult Elizabeth Craig.

ARTHUR MANN

Let me present to you my latest cookery book. I have tried to make it as comprehensive as possible, and I hope it will be as useful to the housewife who does her own cooking as to the hostess who employs a cook, to the young bride starting housekeeping, as to the experienced housewife who so often writes asking for something new.

This is not a conventional cookery book just as I am not a conventional cook. It is a collection of recipes created by me, handed down to me, and passed on to me by friends and readers.

I have prepared this book with the needs in mind of those of you who write to me from all parts of the world. I hope that within its covers you will find the answers to many of your problems.

LONDON

General Information

When analysing the contents of this book, I want you to remember that I have tried to give you not only recipes for standard British fare, but recipes popular with housewives in other lands, as judging from my post bag these are in constant demand. Some of the recipes in this book are economical, others expensive. I have had to cater for all needs. Generally speaking, they are planned for 4-6 persons, according to size of servings, but I have included a few for two, and also a few for large numbers.

This is not an austerity cookery book. When compiling it I have kept ever before me the need to perpetuate recipes that are what they claim to be, not a pallid imitation due to a shortage of this or that. To those who jib at the general use of butter, I venture to suggest that, when butter is short, margarine can be substituted, though it does not impart as good a flavour. To others who gasp at savoury dishes containing six eggs, for example, I wish to draw attention to the fact that many of these recipes are intended for six persons. If catering for fewer, you can adapt the recipes to suit.

Cooking Times: It is impossible to give exact times for cooking, either in the oven or on top of the stove. Although I have stated a time in practically every case, it is only approximate for various reasons: a cake, for example, baked in a small deep tin will take longer to cook than when baked in a wide tin not so deep, and the position in the oven may also affect the time. To make certain that your food is properly baked, follow exactly the instructions of the manufacturer of your cooker regarding the time and temperature required.

When reading this cookery book, you will find at the beginning of each section, a guide to that section, and sometimes a reference to other sections, together with all information you require when following the recipes.

EQUIPPING THE KITCHEN

The ideal kitchen is U-shaped with a compact working centre through which household traffic cannot pass. In this kitchen, the sink is installed below the window at the centre of the U, with the refrigerator at one side, and the stove at the other. The alternative is an L-shaped kitchen with equipment installed in order of use.

No matter the shape, the kitchen should be light and airy, and planned so that work can be done as quickly and efficiently as possible without discomfort.

Have a preparation centre, cook-stove and sink following each other, and plenty of cupboard space, to take equipment, close to the centre at which it is required.

KITCHEN FURNITURE

Every modern kitchen should have built-in units. These should include wall storage cupboards, a kitchen cabinet, one or more dressers and a table which can be moved on castors according to requirements.

Kitchen Cabinet : You need a model to take ingredients required daily in the preparation of food with a cupboard below to hold large cooking vessels, such as the mixing-bowls, colander, and sieves.

Kitchen Dressers : Choose a dresser or dressers either with a Formica, porcelain or stainless steel top. Dressers give you extra counter space. Choose a model fitted entirely with drawers, or one fitted with a large cupboard below and two drawers above, or one of each, according to your needs.

Wall Storage Cupboards : Stream-line these cupboards round your kitchen at the same level, above your dresser or dressers, stove, etc. The one above the stove should be lined below with asbestos.

Chairs and/or Stools : Choose wooden chairs enamelled to tone with colour scheme, or buy deal chairs and have them enamelled to match. Select a stool covered with rexine to match the colour scheme. If not eating in the kitchen, choose only one chair.

Clock : Have an electric clock installed on the wall where it can be easily seen, but not above refrigerator or stove. If preferred, choose from the many attractive kitchen clocks available to match all colour schemes. Don't forget to invest in a minute timer which, if set for time required, will ring a bell at zero hour.

Housemaid's Cupboard : Have housemaid's cupboard in kitchens if there is no other storage space available. Choose one to match your kitchen furniture, or one of plain deal, and have it enamelled to tone. Store in it, besides the usual brushes, polishes, etc., an electric vacuum cleaner, and an electric floor polisher if you have polished floors.

Radio : Not an essential, but if you have music while you work, working time passes more quickly.

Sewing Machine : If kitchen is large enough, it is a good idea to furnish a little corner for mending and sewing.

TO CHOOSE LARGE EQUIPMENT

Choose all large equipment, except the refrigerator, with working surfaces suited to your height. The pull-out lap board in the kitchen cabinet you select, should have a working surface 26 inches from the floor, to allow you to sit down when you want to prepare food. If it hasn't you should invest in one table of this height, or have a table adjusted for seated work. All dressers, cooker, sink and table should be of uniform height, 30-36 inches from the floor, according to what suits you.

Preparation Centre : This can be a movable table, or a dresser with a Formica, stainless steel or porcelain top.

COOKER

Whether you prefer cooking by gas or electricity, choose a model thermostatically controlled, and give preference to a design with a large grill.

Electric Cooker : All electric cookers include means of boiling, grilling, and baking and roasting, each operation being controlled by a separate switch. Thus each operation referred to can be performed separately, or two or three simultaneously.

Boiler Plates: Always control the heat of the boiling plate by the available heat switch. Never reduce heat by using an asbestos mat. There are three types of boiling plates in general use :

(1) *Radiant:* Any type of pan can be used on this plate, but it should be of the same diameter as the plate, and should have a well-fitting lid. (2) *The Enclosed or Solid Type:* This is made of cast iron with the top surface ground over. The pans used on this plate should also have ground bases to ensure sufficient conduction of the heat from plate to the pan. An advantage of this type is that the solid model retains heat so that the current can be switched off before the cooking on the plate is completed. (3) This consists of a thick ribbon-like element placed on a fire-clay former. This type of plate is particularly valuable for boiling small quantities of liquid, for example, milk.

Grill Boiler: This is an enclosed boiling plate with a flat upper surface on which you can boil. The heating elements are so arranged that the heat is also thrown down upon food placed in the grill pan on the runners below, so that pans can be heated on top, or the contents cooked, while grilling proceeds below. When the boiling plate only is required, a deflector plate is placed in position to reflect all the heat upwards, and so prevent it being thrown down into the heat cupboard or grill pan. Always keep deflector plate shining clean. Many cookers also have an eye-level grill.

Oven: To obtain the best results from baking or roasting in an electric oven, follow the manufacturers' instructions for the required setting of the thermostat dial given in accompanying chart.

Oven Grill: To grill in oven, set control to 500° F. unless otherwise instructed on your cooker chart. Turn top element to " High " or " Full." Do not put the food to be grilled in the oven until the coils are red. It is not necessary to heat the oven while grilling. Use only the top element. Leave the door open about 2 inches if desired.

Gas Cooker : If you wish to cook by gas, see that your cooker, when it arrives, is accompanied by an instruction card, baking sheet or tray, a grill pan and grill grid, and a meat tin. The instruction card will give you all the information you require about heating up the cooker, cooking times, shelf positions, and thermostat settings. Hang card close to cooker for reference.

Boiling Burners: They are usually of different sizes : the small ones for simmering, medium-sized for general work, and large ones for really quick boiling. In some cookers the burners are all the same size. Where they are of different size, it is generally more economical to use the smaller burners in preference to the large ones, as they use less gas.

Oil Cookers : You have a choice between the flat-wicked, blue-flamed, and the wickless oil stoves. Before deciding, carefully examine all types with an eye to the amount of space it has to fill, and the number in family. Keep perfectly clean, and trim wicks carefully. You will find these cookers an inexpensive alternative to solid fuel cookers. They must not be allowed to stand in a draught.

Solid Fuel Cookers : These cookers are very satisfactory, and will give years of service at moderate running cost. Housewives who use them will be quite independent of the vagaries that we, who rely on electricity or gas, sometimes have to endure, so long as a store of fuel is always on hand. They are particularly valuable for country homes to which electricity and gas are not supplied. They burn night and day, so that the country housewife can start cooking breakfast without having to light a fire.

SINK

Stainless steel, cast in one piece with the draining board, is the most hygienic as there are no joins in which either particles of food or dirty water can lodge. If your kitchen is large enough, select a double-bowled, double draining board model, with stainless steel bowls and draining boards, and with porcelain enamelled cupboards below. This is an ideal arrangement, as it allows you to wash in one bowl and rinse in the other. An alternative you might prefer is to have a single bowl sink, with a draining board on the left, and an electric dish washer on the right, with a second draining board beyond ; or you can still have a double sink, and the dish washer in addition. If possible choose a sink with a folding down top. The best models have sunken containers at the back for holding soap.

REFRIGERATOR

Try to secure a model with rounded edges and enamelled in the same shade or shades as your cooker and kitchen furniture. It should have interior lighting that goes off and on automatically as you open or shut the door, stainless steel shelves or racks, a frozen storage compartment containing three freezing trays, large enough to take moulds, 1 or 2 Humi-dors, a meat keeper, and storage containers graduated in size. Should you live in a part of the country where neither gas nor electricity is available, choose an oil refrigerator.

WATER HEATER

If your hot water supply in the kitchen is not automatic, install an electric storage heater or a gas boiler which will provide constant hot water for washing up and laundry work, or have an electric immersion heater fixed in your tank or cylinder. This will also give you an automatic supply of constant hot water.

SMALL ELECTRIC EQUIPMENT

Coffee Percolator : Choose a model with a non-drip spout, a cool plastic handle, and, if possible, a design that keeps your coffee hot until you are ready to serve it.

Food Warmer or Hot Plate : This is ideal for keeping food warm. It should be placed on a table in front of the hatch, or in dining-room.

Kettle : This appliance enables you to boil water quickly anywhere and at any time, merely by connecting up to a wall plug and switching on. Have it fixed so that it can be used either in the kitchen or in the dining-room.

Mixer : No kitchen is complete without an electric mixer. With its help, you can turn out mayonnaise, minced fish, meat and vegetables, and fruit and vegetable juices, grind coffee beans and knead bread. It is the housewife's best friend.

Table Cooker : This is handy when you want to prepare a meal at table. Some models are equipped so that you can bake, boil, fry, grill, steam, stew, roast or toast, as well as poach eggs in the poacher. Another is so constructed that you can turn it on to a fireproof plate, and cook whatever is on the plate. There are also small table grillers which can be used for frying and toasting, and serve if required, as hot plates.

Toaster : If you haven't a table cooker, you need a toaster. Choose a design that pops out toast when it is ready.

Waffle Iron: Take your choice between a round and an oblong waffle iron, and have it fixed so that it can be used either in the kitchen or in the dining-room.

POTS AND PANS

1 stock pot.
3 frying-pans, 4-, 8-, and 10-inch, in aluminium.
1 pan for deep frying, with basket, and timbale irons.
1 shallow aluminium stew pan.
1 aluminium egg poacher.
1 steam-cooker with lip on bottom pan for replenishing.
1 pressure cooker, designed for use as a cooker, and for table use.
1 aluminium waterless cooker.
1 enamel tea-kettle.
1 large or small skillet.
3 saucepans with lids, 1, 1½ and 2 pint sizes.
1 omelet pan, aluminium.
1 fish-kettle, aluminium.
2 double boilers, 1 small and 1 large.
1 girdle with folding handle and swivel, in aluminium or cast iron.
1 deep aluminium soup pan.
1 vegetable steamer.
1 bain marie.

Store this equipment in bottom of kitchen dresser, and in wall storage cupboard above dresser. It pays to get the non-stick kind.

BAKING EQUIPMENT

1 covered roasting pan and trivet.
2 loaf tins, small and medium.
1 Swiss roll tin, 10 by 8 inches.
1 slab cake tin, 6 by 6, 7 by 7, or 8 by 8 inches.
2 open roasting tins, 8 by 12, and 10 by 15 inches.
3 sandwich tins, 6 inches.
2 sandwich tins 9 inches, and 2 cake tins (8 and 9 inches).
1 Yorkshire pudding tin.

MARKETING AND STORING

To be able to shop wisely, so that you make every shilling spent on food yield the maximum return in value received, you need to know not only the characteristics of fresh foods in their prime, but signs of their deterioration. You must also bear in mind when each fruit and each vegetable is in season, in order to buy the finest quality at the lowest price.

HINTS FOR THE SHOPPER

(1) Patronise shops noted for their cleanliness, for the high quality of their goods, and their service.

(2) Shop personally when possible, pay cash, and carry your purchases home when you can.

(3) Ignore cheap lines if they show signs of damage or deterioration.

(4) Examine larder daily. Make out a list of what is required, including food necessary for the following day.

(5) Inspect pantry or store room weekly. When any article is taken from it, make a note of it on a slate kept on a hook on the wall, and replace this item the next time you go shopping.

DAIRY PRODUCTS

All dairy products should be stored at a temperature to prevent cream or milk souring, and fats becoming rancid. The ideal temperature, 42-45° F., can be obtained in a refrigerator. If not available, store, covered, in the larder at elbow or lower level.

Cream : Choose light or coffee cream for serving with coffee or fruit, and thick or whipping cream which contains more fat, for whipping. Store, covered, in the coldest part of the refrigerator or larder.

Eggs: Brown- and white-shelled equally good. Buy fresh for storing in refrigerator. If to be stored in a larder, place in an egg rack in the coldest and darkest part, which is nearest the floor. A fresh egg when broken has no odour, its yolk is rounded, and the white is thickish. If stale, the white is thin and sometimes faintly coloured, and the yolk is flat instead of round.

Fats (butter, lard, margarine, etc.) : Buy them all wrapped. Store in refrigerator, near the top if possible. If you haven't a refrigerator, store in covered container, or wrapped, in the coldest and darkest part of your larder.

Milk : Buy only T.B. tested milk, Jersey for preference. Allow 1 quart for each child and 1 pint for each adult per day, for all purposes. Wipe caps and bottles with a clean cloth. Place on an upper shelf in refrigerator. If you haven't a refrigerator, store in the coldest and darkest part of the larder. Always keep covered.

GROCERIES

To save yourself endless trouble, buy the type of groceries that will store well in as large quantities as possible. The ideal way to shop for groceries is to stock up once a month in non-perishable items. Buy perishables, such as bacon and cheese, once a week. Here is a list of groceries you should keep in stock. Add to them according to taste :

Bacon : Choose for breakfast streaky, back or gammon, according to taste, with deep pink and white firm fat. Store, covered, in coldest and darkest part of your larder.

Biscuits : Buy in small quantities, in packages rather than loose, and store

23

in air-tight tins ; if consumption is large, buy in tins. You should always have a store of biscuits and pretzels to serve with cheese ; biscuits to serve with cocktails ; macaroons ; ratafias for trifles ; sweet biscuits to serve with coffee ; sponge fingers for charlotte russes ; and ice wafers to serve with ice cream.

Cereals (barley, ground rice, oatmeal, rice, sago, semolina and tapioca) : Buy in large quantities only if catering for large numbers. Store in air-tight tins in pantry or store room. Must be kept dry.

Barley : Choose for thickening broths, etc.

Ground Rice : Choose for puddings, cold moulds, or as a substitute for semolina, etc.

Oatmeal : Choose for porridge, stuffings, biscuits, etc. Use quickly.

Rice : Choose Patna, for curries and risottos, and Carolina or Java for puddings, thickening broths, etc. Use " Speedi " or minute rice when a rice dish is wanted in a hurry.

Sago : Choose for thickening broths or for puddings.

Semolina : Use for making gnocchi and other meatless dishes, and for milk puddings, etc.

Tapioca : Use for thickening broths, and for puddings, etc., and the minute variety when speed is an important factor.

Cheese : You should always have in store some Cheddar and some Parmesan cheese. Select hard cheeses, such as Cheddar, Dutch, whole and grated Parmesan, or Samsoe for culinary use. When cheese is wanted for the table, buy Cheddar, Dutch and a choice of soft cheese and semi-hard cheese of the blue variety, or processed cheese. Brie, Camembert, Chambourcy, Gervais and Petit Suisse are popular members of the cream cheese family. Danish blue, Gorgonzola, Roquefort and Stilton represent the blue. Edam and American processed cheese are popular not only for table use, but for cubing for apéritif parties. If spreads are wanted, choose cream or sour milk cheese, or double cream. Wrap cream, double cream, sour milk (cottage) or processed cheese in greaseproof paper, folding the edges under so that the cheese is completely enclosed. Place in a covered dish. Store on upper shelf of refrigerator. Wrap blue cheese and Gruyère cheese in tin foil or waxed paper. Store on a plate in the coolest part of your larder, or in a covered dish, with the lid slightly tilted or cheese will develop mould. Store a wedge of cheese that has been cut, in a clean cloth moistened with vinegar water. Allow 1 tablespoon vinegar to $\frac{1}{4}$ pint of water. Rinse and wring out cloth before using. Wrap parcel in greaseproof paper. If to be kept longer than for 6 or 7 days, moisten cloth when dry as before, and wrap cheese.

Coffee : If you have a coffee grinder, buy freshly-roasted beans and grind your own. Otherwise, have it ground at the shop, or buy coffee packed in vacuum tins. Keep closely covered or it will lose its flavour and aroma.

Dried Fruits (apricots, currants, prunes, raisins, sultanas, etc.) : Buy in small quantities as they do not keep indefinitely. Liable to ferment if allowed to become damp. Wash before cooking. Choose Valencia raisins for cakes and puddings, and Muscatel raisins for dessert. Use within 2 to 3 months.

Flour : *Cornflour:* Choose for thickening sauces, for blancmanges, and for adding to plain flour in the proportion of 1 oz. to 7 oz. of plain flour when a very light cake batter is wanted.
Plain Flour: Choose plain flour of a reliable brand for sponge cakes and for making biscuits and pastry with raising agent, if suggested. Use within 2 to 3 months, or it may become musty.
Self-raising Flour: Include self-raising flour in stock. It saves you the trouble of sifting a raising agent with plain flour when time is precious. Keep perfectly dry or raising qualities may be affected.
Wholemeal Flour: Buy in a very small quantity unless making wholemeal bread frequently. Has high food value. Buy in small quantities and use within a week or two.
Store each variety of flour in a tin or bin in a dry, airy cupboard.

Italian Pastas : Genoa is the best. Store in tightly-covered tins in dry, airy cupboard or pantry.
Macaroni, Noodles and Spaghetti: Choose for savoury dishes, etc.
Vermicelli: Choose when wanting to thicken broths or soups, etc.

Nuts (almonds, cashew, desiccated coconut, ground almonds, pistachio and walnuts, etc.) : Buy in small quantities, or they may become rancid. Store on the lower shelf in a dry cupboard, in tightly-closed tins.

Pulses (butter and haricot beans, dried and split green peas, lentils) : Buy and store like cereals.

Raising Agents (baking powder, bicarbonate of soda, cream of tartar, golden raising powder) : Buy all in small quantities. Keep closely covered. Label varieties bought loose very clearly. Store in a dry place.

Salt : Buy kitchen salt for using in kitchen, as well as celery and garlic salt. If salt is in block form, crush it with a rolling pin and pack it in a tightly-closed storage jar. Store all salts in a dry cupboard or they will become damp.

Seasonings (curry powder and paste, mustard (dry, seeds and Continental), paprika, peppercorns (black and white), pepper (black, cayenne, coralline and white)) : Buy all seasonings in small quantities. Keep tightly covered or they will deteriorate.

Spices (allspice, anise (ground), caraway seeds, cinnamon (ground and sticks), cloves, coriander (ground and whole), ginger (ground and root), mace (ground and blades), mixed spice, nutmeg (whole)) : Buy in small quantities. Store in a tightly-closed tin.

Sugar : Buy in large quantities when possible. Store icing sugar whether packaged or loose, in tightly-covered jars or tins, as air and damp causes it to " lump." Keep all sugar dry.

Brown (Barbados, Demerara, light brown, etc.) : Choose for sweetening gingerbread mixtures, spiced steamed puddings, stewed apples and apple sauce, etc. Beat light brown up with butter or margarine and spread on bread for children.

Caster: Choose when a fine sugar is wanted for cake-making, etc., for dredging cakes and pastry, and for serving with fruit, etc.

Granulated: Choose for general purposes.

Loaf: Choose for sweetening tea, and for preserving.

SUGAR FOR COFFEE : Sugar candy or Demerara.

Tea (Ceylon, China, Indian) : If buying in packets, store in tightly-closed tin.

Bottled Goods : Buy large bottles of bottled goods in daily use, such as olive oil and vinegar. Store in a dark cupboard.

Beverages: Order soft drinks monthly. Keep tightly-corked. Store in pantry.

Colourings and Essences: Keep tightly-corked in a dark cupboard. (Carmine or cochineal, amber and sap green colourings, essential ; almond, anchovy, lemon, rennet and vanilla essences, essential.)

Fruit (apricots, cherries, fruit salad, etc.) : Choose size giving two or more helpings to each member of family.

Olive Oil: Store in the dark. If catering for large numbers, better to buy by the gallon.

Pickles: Capers, dill, gherkins, olives (queen or stuffed), onions (cocktail), mixed, etc. : Store in a dark, airy cupboard.

Salad Dressings: Mayonnaise and salad cream.

Sauces: Anchovy, Soy, tomato and Worcester sauce.

Vinegars: Chilli, cider, pure malt, tarragon, white and wine vinegar.

Canned Goods : Reject any cans of food sold in tins with dents or bulges. Choose well-known brands. Store on a low shelf in the pantry. Once a can has been opened, it is safe to leave the food in can from meal to meal or overnight, if it can be placed in a refrigerator or an ice box. Do not leave until the edge of can begins to rust and so fouls the contents. When buying for storage purposes, you should write the date on a label, so that the oldest cans are used first. Always follow manufacturer's instructions given on cans for use of contents. " BLOWN CANS " : If the end of a can bulges outwards due to pressure inside, and cannot readily be pressed back to the flat position, the can is said to be " blown." Blown or leaking cans should always be thrown away.

LENGTH OF TIME TO STORE CANNED GOODS

FISH AND MEATS : 4 or 5 years.

FRUIT AND FRUIT JUICES : 1 year, or slightly longer.

GOLDEN SYRUP, HONEY AND TREACLE: Do not store indefinitely or they may crystallise.

MILK (Dried) : 1 year. Once opened, should be used within a few weeks.

MILK (Evaporated) : About 3 years.

MILK (Sweetened Condensed) : 8 or 9 months. Can be used after longer storage, but may be sugary.

PRESERVED IN LACQUERED CANS (honey, jam, jellies, marmalade) : 3 years.

SOUPS : 2 or 3 years.

VEGETABLES : 2 years at least.

THE STORE ROOM

This may either be a pantry off the kitchen, or a small room near by ; if catering for large numbers, you will require both. The ideal faces the north. Equip it with as many shelves as it will take. Air store room daily. Scrub shelves and floor weekly, but do not close the door until perfectly dry. Keep all your reserve of kitchen stationery, linen, dusters, house flannels, chamois leathers, mops, etc., in a drawer or drawers in store room. Once a week, replenish kitchen cabinet from store room.

LARDER

The ideal larder has shelves fixed an inch from the walls so that steam cannot condense in the crevices. Scrub out larder weekly and wipe shelves daily with a damp cloth to gather up dust. Never brush larder. Keep all food covered. Place all semi-perishable foods, such as bananas and melons, in the larder. Wrap melons or they will spoil the flavour of other fresh foods near by. If you have no refrigerator, use porous containers for dairy produce.

TO STORE IN A REFRIGERATOR

It isn't possible to lay down drastic laws about where to store food in a refrigerator as makes differ in construction, but there are certain rules to be observed in all refrigerators.

(1) Set to maintain a temperature of about 45° F.

(2) Keep everything covered to prevent loss of moisture and frost forming on the frozen storage compartment.

(3) Before storing food, remove wrappings, and place in clean containers or in plastic bags, cellophane envelopes, or greaseproof paper.

(4) Allow hot foods and liquids to cool to room temperature before placing in refrigerator.

(5) Wipe milk and cream caps and bottles before storing.

(6) Don't crowd dishes together. Air must circulate.

If your refrigerator handbook does not go fully into the storage of food, the following notes will help you :

Dairy Foods :

Cream and Milk: Place next to freezing compartment. Pour out only as much as you require at one time. Never pour any back into bottle.

Eggs : Store only as required for current use in a container to prevent evaporation. If you haven't a suitable one, wash eggs, cover with cold water, stand for 12 hours, then store in refrigerator towards the bottom. If you have to switch on to the coldest temperature, remove eggs until temperature is reduced or they will crack.

Fats: Store in covered container, or wrap in greaseproof paper. Place on an upper shelf. Remove only what is needed at one time.

Fish : Wash and trim. Wrap loosely in greaseproof paper or in thin plastic material to prevent smell affecting other food. Store in meat keeper if not in use. Otherwise place as near to freezing compartment as possible. (It will keep fresh for at least 24 hours.) If wanted stored for a longer period, place in freezing compartment. If cooked, leave until quite cold, then store in a bowl or jar with a fairly close cover.

Game and Poultry : Clean, wash and dry. Wrap loosely in greaseproof or waxed paper. Place on shelf below freezing compartment.

Meat : Unwrap. If to be sliced or chopped, don't slice or chop until just before cooking. Fold lightly in greaseproof paper or thin plastic material, leaving ends open. Store at once in meat keeper or near freezing compartment. Wrap minced meat loosely in greaseproof paper and store in freezing compartment. Cook within 24 hours of purchase. Place cooked meat in a plastic or refrigerator bag and wrap in greaseproof paper. Store in meat keeper, or place in a covered dish and store below freezing compartment.

Frozen Foods : Place in wrappings, still frozen, in freezing compartment. Defrost meat and fruit at normal kitchen temperature. If left wrapped in refrigerator, a medium-sized roast or a chicken will take about 2 days to defrost.

Fruit : Store all fruit in bottom of refrigerator to check ripening, except melon and pineapple. Place them, closely wrapped, in refrigerator when to be chilled. Wrap the citric fruits in greaseproof paper to prevent smells spreading.

Vegetables : Wash and thoroughly clean all greens. Wash and dry cucumbers and tomatoes. Trim off any damaged or inedible parts. Shake well and store in vegetable container.

TO KEEP YOUR REFRIGERATOR IN ORDER

Do not let frost build up on freezing compartment to great thickness, or it will choke refrigeration. Defrost when the frost is nearly $\frac{1}{4}$ inch thick. Once a fortnight should be often enough for this operation, but in hot, humid weather it may be necessary to defrost every ten days or even once a week. To defrost, turn cold controller to defrosting position. Switch off. See that drip tray is empty and in place. Leave refrigerator until all signs of frost have disappeared, except for emptying the drip tray when necessary, then start cleaning.

(1) Wash fittings with tepid soda water. Rinse in clean warm water. Wipe dry.

(2) Wash the inside with warm soda water, allowing 2 teaspoons bicarbonate of soda, or a teaspoon of washing soda, to a quart of water. If you haven't any soda, add a few drops of ammonia to water. Wipe with a cloth wrung out of clean warm water, then dry.

(3) Replace fittings. Fill ice trays and replace.

Polish the outside after washing and drying with a good furniture cream.

FLAVOURINGS

The success of many a dish depends on its flavouring. A soupçon of garlic, for example, transforms any savoury salad. A dash of sherry lifts clear soup out of the commonplace. There is only one point to remember about flavouring with extracts or essences, herbs, spices, wines, etc. Act with caution.

ESSENCES

Cakes and sponge puddings are usually flavoured with vanilla or lemon essence, although if butter is used as an ingredient, neither a cake nor a sponge pudding should require any flavouring. Almond and orange, pineapple, and rose essences are the best for egg and butter-sponge cakes and puddings. Equal quantity of lemon and vanilla, and almond, lemon and vanilla make a delicious flavouring both for cakes and iced puddings. Equal quantity of orange and rose essence is a good combination for a white sponge cake. Vanilla essence is most popular with egg or milk puddings, and for cakes containing walnuts, as well as for flavouring whipped cream and desserts. Be careful to follow instructions given with essences, as different brands vary in strength.

MUSHROOM ESSENCE

Pick mushrooms on a dry day. Remove half the stems, cutting them level with the flaps. Peel and break into pieces. Spread out on large platters. Sprinkle with a little salt. Stand for 3 hours, then mash with a plated or silver fork. (Do not use steel.) Leave for 12 hours. Mash mushrooms with the back of a wooden spoon, then strain off the liquid that oozes from them. Place in an enamel saucepan. Bring to boil. Simmer gently till reduced to half the quantity. Leave till quite cold. Pour into sterilised bottles. Cork and seal with wax.

SPICED WINE ESSENCE

Pour a bottle of inexpensive white wine into a fire-proof jar or casserole. Strain in the juice of 4 lemons. Add ½ pint of vinegar, ½ lb. of salt, 2 oz. white pepper, 1 oz. dried parsley, and 1 drachm each of ground basil, cloves, mace, nutmeg and thyme. Cover and place in a moderate oven, 350° F. When boiling, lower to simmering heat, about 300° F. Simmer gently for 4 hours, then strain through blotting paper, or muslin. Bottle and cork. When required, flavour with 3 or 4 drops to a pint of liquid.

FLAVOURING LIQUEURS AND WINES

Liqueurs and wines too are little used in the kitchen in English-speaking countries. Note that, in flavouring, they should be used with restraint.

LIQUEURS FOR FLAVOURING

Apricot brandy	Cherry brandy	Kirsch
Aurum	Cognac	Maraschino
Bénédictine	Cointreau	Marnique
Cerasella	Curaçao	Parfait Amour
Chartreuse	Grand Marnier	Tia Maria

Use any of these liqueurs for flavouring fruit cocktails, fruit and wine cups, and for icings in place of essences, in ice cream sauce, and fruit compôtes, etc.

Fruit Cocktails or Grapefruit: To flavour, add 1 teaspoon liqueur to each portion.

Fruit Jellies: Allow ¼ gill liqueur to a quart jelly, or 1¼ tablespoons to a pint jelly.

WINES FOR FLAVOURING

Burgundy	Madeira	Tarragona
Champagne	Marsala	Vermouth
Claret	Port wine	White wines
Italian Vermouth	Sherry	

First Course :
Appetiser (Olives) : Rinse with Madeira or Sherry.
Melon Cocktail: Flavour with Madeira, 1 teaspoon per portion.
Oysters: Bathe in Champagne and return to their shells.
Shellfish Cocktail: Flavour with Sherry or Madeira, 1 teaspoon per portion.
Soup (clear or cream) : Madeira, Marsala or Sherry, allowing 1 to 2 teaspoons per portion.
Fish : Flavour with white wine, Australian Hock, Graves or Spanish white wine, unless otherwise instructed in recipe, and unless tomatoes figure among ingredients, when Madeira or Sherry as well as the foregoing can be used. Red-fleshed fish, such as salmon, can be cooked with red wine as well as with white.
Meat : *Beef, Lamb and Mutton:* Cook with Claret or Burgundy.
Pork: Cook with Sherry.
Veal: Cook with Claret.
Ham: Cook with Champagne, Claret or Port wine.

Poultry and Game : There is no hard and fast rule about the choice of wine for flavouring dishes of poultry or game. When making a casserole of

EGGS

Baked, boiled, scrambled, poached and stuffed eggs. *See pages* 59, 64, 63, *and* 79-80.

FISH
Lobster Thermidor, Dressed Crab, and Cabbage Pond. *See pages* 171, 166-167 *and* 778.

chicken or duck without following any special recipe, use Madeira or Sherry, or Marsala. When preparing a cream or soufflé of game or poultry, choose Madeira or Sherry unless making soufflé with a strongly-flavoured game such as hare or venison, when Claret or Port wine is to be preferred. Flavour gravy to accompany any roast game with Madeira, Port or Sherry, and bread sauce to accompany game with Madeira or Sherry. Try young grouse stuffed with brown bread-crumbs, soaked in Port wine, and roasted, cooking birds upside down.

Hot and Cold Puddings : Madeira, Marsala, Port wine, Sherry and Vermouth as well as Rum are invaluable for flavouring puddings.

Sweet Sauces : Madeira and Sherry, as well as Brandy and Rum, are generally used for flavouring hard sauces to serve with Christmas and other fruit puddings.

Flavouring Oils : These are generally used for flavouring candies or sweets. Only a few drops necessary.

Oil of Aniseed	Oil of Lemon
Oil of Caraway	Oil of Lime
Oil of Cloves	Oil of Peppermint

Flavouring Syrups : Use for flavouring cold sweets, ice creams, and fruit cups, fruit cocktails, etc.

Blackcurrant	Maple	Pomegranate
Grenadine	Maraschino	Rose Hip
Kirsch	Mulberry	

Flavouring Vinegars : Use for flavouring salad dressings.

Chervil	Pure Malt	Tarragon
Chilli	Shallot	Wines

Flavouring Vegetables :

Garlic: Rub a cut clove of garlic round the inside of a salad bowl before mixing salad, or a cube of bread, known as a " chapon," and toss the chapon with the salad, then remove before serving to give the soupçon of garlic that is so popular. If a stronger flavour is wanted, peel and bruise a clove with the flat of a knife, and add to dressing before coating salad. Remove if liked before serving salad.

Horseradish: Scrape the white fleshy roots, then grate. Mix with vinegar to moisten. Serve as a condiment with fish, particularly oysters, and meat. Add young, tender leaves to salad greens.

Mushroom: Though not really a vegetable, usually classed with vegetables. The sliced, peeled stalks are useful for flavouring sauces, soups and brown stock. The peelings, if washed, can be used with the stalks in this way. When fresh mushrooms are not available, substitute soaked dried mushrooms.

Onion: Spanish are milder and sweeter than other varieties. When not available, and a mild flavour of onion is wanted, par-boil other varieties, changing the water once or twice before using onion. When a faint piquant

31

flavour of onion is wanted, use the minced foliage of *chives*. They impart a tantalising flavour to salads and salad dressings, savoury omelets, scrambled eggs, root vegetable salads, etc. When adding chives, it is not necessary to add parsley. Use both the green and the white part, finely chopped, of *spring onions* in green and root salads, as well as for garnishing salads.

Shallots (Eschalots) : The shallot has a more delicate flavour than an onion. Use in place of onion, particularly in salads.

MISCELLANEOUS FLAVOURINGS

Angelica : Candy stems before the plant flowers. Use for decorating and flavouring cakes, and for decorating cold sweets. Boil leaves and stalks, and treat as salad.

Bay Leaf : Use a bit of fresh or dried bay leaf for flavouring court bouillon, sauces, soups and stews, etc.

Elderflower Blossom : Use for flavouring apple or gooseberry jelly, fruit cups and fruit syrups.

Flavouring Waters : Use for flavouring almond paste, marzipan, cake batters, etc.

    Orange Flower Water   Rose Water

Grated Orange or Lemon Rind : Use for flavouring cakes and puddings, etc. Use snippets of lemon rind for flavouring cocktails and cups.

Salts : Use *coarse salt* (common or kitchen) for flavouring any savoury dish, and either *table salt* for table use, or *rock salt*. Serve the latter in a salt mill. Use *bay salt* for pickling. When celery is out of season, and the flavour is wanted in a dish, salt with *celery salt*, or add a little in addition to common salt. Use *garlic salt* for imparting a garlic flavour when garlic is not available, and *onion salt* in the same way.

Scented Geranium Leaves : Use for flavouring fruit jellies or for garnishing fruit cups and punches.

Scented Rose Leaves : Add to cream. Soak till flavoured to taste, then remove leaves. Serve cream with fruit, or whip for decorating.

CULINARY HERBS

If you don't grow your own herbs so that you can pick them fresh when required, and dry and store them for winter use, then buy the following, which are the most popular in modern cookery, giving choice to those packed in bottles or tins.

Anise : Use seeds for decorating sweet rolls and coffee cakes, and the leaves for garnishing salads. Add to ingredients for spiced cakes and most liquorice products. Also an ingredient of curry powder.

Balm : Use the foliage for flavouring fruit and wine cups. In the old days it was freely used for flavouring sauces, soups and stews.

Borage : An indispensable ingredient of claret cup and other wine cups, as well as of Pimms No. 1. The flowers can be added to salads, not only for their cucumber flavour, but also for decoration. Candy borage flowers also.

Caraway : Use dried seeds for flavouring rye bread, cream cheese, green cabbage, sauerkraut, etc.

Chervil : Use minced as a flavouring for stuffed eggs or spinach soup, and the foliage in mixed green salads, and as a garnish for aspics, brawns, and many cold entrées.

Dill : Use seeds for flavouring pickled cucumbers and spiced vinegar for cucumber pickles, and add a pinch to sauerkraut, or to Russian borsch.

Fennel : Use blanched foliage for salads. Add to Court-bouillon when boiling fish, and for garnishing fish dishes.

Marjoram : One of the ingredients of bouquet garnis, of mixed herbs, and of fines herbes. Use crushed for flavouring sausages and sausage meat, and lamb, fish sauces and roast pork, etc.

Mint : Use for flavouring jelly to serve with cold lamb, for garnishing orange salad, flavouring new potatoes and green peas, or for making into mint sauce to serve with roast lamb, garnishing fruit cocktails and cups, etc.

Parsley : Use sprigs for flavouring stocks, sauces and soups, etc., and for garnishing. Mince leaves for adding to stuffings, omelets, scrambled eggs, salads, and for garnishing.

Rosemary : Use in a bouquet garni. Pick tender fresh leaves and stems for flavouring fish and meat sauces, and stews, particularly veal. Use with sage for flavouring roast pork. Decorate cider and claret cup with the flowers.

Sage : Use this strongly-flavoured herb sparingly when making any dish of pork or in a stuffing for duck, goose or pork. In the United States, it is used in tomato dishes, and for flavouring string beans, and cream or sour milk cheese.

Savory : One of the ingredients of a bouquet garni. Use also for flavouring bean, lentil and split pea purée, hamburger steaks, stuffing for roast veal, broad and string beans, and French dressing.

Sweet Basil : The foliage is frequently used for flavouring sauces, ragouts

and soups, particularly mock turtle, tomato and vegetable. If the flavour
liked, it can be added to tomato juice and fish cocktails, omelet, meat cake
stewed liver, all tomato dishes, and fish or vegetable salads, etc. Sometime
the tips are added to fruit and wine cup for garnish, as well as to salads.

Tarragon : This is one of the most valuable herbs. Mince and use f
flavouring egg dishes, green salads, savoury jellies, fish sauces and cocktai
tomato juice and soup, melted butter to serve with fish, and chicken dishe
Use sprigs for flavouring vinegar.

Thyme (Common and Lemon) : A sprig of thyme is one of the ingredier
of a bouquet garni. Use sprigs for flavouring veal stock, and crushed thyr
for flavouring sauces, soups, stuffings, etc.

Aux Fines Herbes : This expression usually refers to an omelet made wi
a mixture of finely-minced herbs, such as equal quantity of chervil or parsle
mixed with minced chives to taste, but the mixture can be added to taste
fish and meat stuffing, casseroles and stews as well. Use any combination
herbs you like, such as parsley and basil with chives, or parsley, tarragon ar
watercress with chives.

Here is another version : Mince $\frac{1}{2}$ medium-sized onion. Place in a sma
basin. Trim and mince 2 spring onions and $\frac{1}{2}$ small leek, and place with onio
Finely chop 2 sprigs of parsley, and 2-4 leaves of marjoram, according
taste. Mix well.

Bouquet Garni : This is a bouquet of herbs used for flavouring stoc
sauces, soups, stews, etc., frequently combined with a bay leaf. Use ar
combination of herbs you have, tied if liked in a small muslin bag :

(1) $\frac{1}{2}$ a bay leaf, 1 sprig marjoram, 2 sprigs parsley, 2 sprigs thyme.
(2) 1 bay leaf, 2 sprigs parsley, 1 sprig lemon thyme, 1 sprig commo
thyme.
(3) 1 sprig marjoram, 1 sprig parsley, 1 sprig lemon thyme.
(4) Place in a small muslin bag : foliage off 1 stick celery, $\frac{1}{4}$ bay lea
1 sprig thyme, 2 or 3 sprigs parsley, 1 young carrot cut lengthwi
in two, 1 trimmed young leek, and a slice of hamburg parsley if yo
grow it. Use for flavouring stock.

Bouquet of Dried Herbs : If you do not grow your own herbs, and cann
obtain fresh ones, make a bouquet of dried herbs. Tie 1 bay leaf and 3 clov
in a small cheesecloth bag with $\frac{1}{2}$ teaspoon crushed dried thyme and $\frac{1}{2}$ teaspoo
dried basil. When wanted for flavouring, place bag in 2 cups of stock, c
water flavoured with a meat cube and vegetables. Boil for 5 minutes, the
remove and wash and dry bag, and use it again after boiling. The bag shou
only be $1\frac{1}{2}$-2 inches square.

Mixed Herbs : A combination of herbs in general use for flavourin
omelets, scrambled eggs, stuffings, meat and poultry dishes, etc.

Powdered Herbs : To save time when cooking, it is a good idea blend your own herb powder with dried bay leaf and spices according to taste, and sieve and bottle it ready for use.

(1) Powder equal quantity of dried basil, marjoram, parsley and thyme with 2 dried bay leaves. Weigh. Add salt, pepper and powdered dried lemon peel in the proportion of 1 saltspoon each of salt and lemon peel, and $\frac{1}{2}$ teaspoon pepper to each oz. of mixed herbs. Rub through a wire sieve, then bottle and cork.

(2) HERB POWDER :

1 oz. dried lemon thyme	$\frac{1}{4}$ oz. dried parsley
1 oz. sweet dried basil	1 oz. dried savory
1 oz. marjoram sweet dried	$\frac{1}{2}$ oz. dried lemon peel

Place the herbs in a mortar. Mince and add lemon peel. Pound thoroughly, then rub through a wire sieve. Pack in bottles. Cork tightly.

(3) HERB AND SPICE POWDER :

$\frac{1}{2}$ oz. dried bay leaves	$\frac{1}{4}$ oz. dried grated lemon peel
$1\frac{1}{2}$ oz. dried marjoram	$\frac{1}{4}$ oz. cayenne pepper
$1\frac{1}{2}$ oz. dried sweet basil	$\frac{1}{2}$ oz. grated nutmeg
$1\frac{1}{2}$ oz. dried thyme	$\frac{1}{2}$ oz. ground mace
1 oz. dried savory	1 oz. ground peppercorns
1 peeled clove garlic	1 oz. whole cloves

Place the herbs with the bay leaves in a mortar. Mince garlic and add with lemon peel. Pound on a board, then remove to a basin. Add the spices. Pound again on board. Stir into herbs. Rub through a wire sieve. Bottle and cork. When required for flavouring, allow 1 teaspoon of the powder to 1 quart of liquid.

SPICES

Allspice Berries (sometimes known as Jamaica Pepper) : Use for flavouring stock, in pickling, etc.
Ground: Use for flavouring cakes, curries and puddings.

Cassia : Aromatic bark resembling cinnamon in flavour. Use in pickling and for flavouring puddings.
Ground: Popular spice for mincemeat and for using in biscuits, cakes and puddings in combination with allspice, clove and cinnamon.

Cayenne Pepper : Very hot ground pepper. Used for " pepping up " fish, game, meat dishes, sauces, and savouries, also for garnishing appetisers and snacks.

Celery Seed : Use for flavouring soups, stews, stocks, fish dishes, potato salad, paprika cheese, for spreads, and in pickling and salad dressings, etc.

Chilli Peppers :
Whole: Included in pickling spices.
Broken: Use in stew and soups that require strong seasonings.

Chilli Powder : Use for flavouring fish cocktail sauces, highly-spiced meat dishes and gravies, scrambled eggs, etc.

Cinnamon :
Sticks: Include in pickling spices, spiced vinegars, etc.
Ground: Use for flavouring spiced cakes and puddings, etc.

Cloves :
Whole: Use in sweet pickles, certain stewed fruits, and for garnishing and flavouring baked ham, etc.
Ground: Use in spiced biscuits, cakes and puddings.

Coriander :
Whole: Use for mixed pickles.
Ground: Use for flavouring buns, biscuits, gingerbread, curry powder, poultry stuffings, sausage meat, etc.

Cumin Seeds : Use in curries and for flavouring certain cheese.

Curry Powder : Blend of several spices : ginger, turmeric, coriander, pepper, etc., flavoured with garlic. Use for making curried game, meat, fish, poultry, etc., and for flavouring French dressing, etc.

Ginger :
Root: Use in pickling, chutneys, preserves, and for flavouring stewed dried fruits.
Ground: Include in spices for gingerbread and spiced biscuits, buns, cakes and puddings.

Mace :
Blades: Use in pickling, preserving, flavouring stewed cherries, etc.
Ground: Use for flavouring all rich fruit cakes, puddings, mince meat, chocolate dishes, white sauce, etc.

Mixed Spice : Buy whole for pickling, and ground for using in spiced cakes, biscuits, puddings, etc.

Mustard :
Ground Mustard Seed: Use for flavouring salad dressings, gravies, sauces, meat dishes, etc.
Whole: Use in pickles, chutneys and piquant sauces.

Nutmeg (Grated) : Use for flavouring puddings, sauces and spinach, and for garnishing custard, junkets and milk puddings.

Paprika (Sweet Pepper) : Use for flavouring cream or sour milk cheese, mayonnaise for dressing root vegetable salads, French dressing to be used with fish, and tomato condiments and tomato juice.

Pepper (Black and White) :
Whole: Use peppercorns for flavouring pickles and stock for soup and sauces, etc.

Ground: Use for seasoning gravies, sauces, fish and meat dishes, etc.
Mignonette: Crushed white peppercorns, resembling mignonette seeds.

Turmeric : Use in mustard pickles, and curry powder.

GRAVY SPICE

¼ lb. freshly-ground black pepper	1 oz. grated nutmeg
6 oz. dry salt	1 oz. ground cinnamon
¼ oz. freshly-ground ginger	

Mix ingredients well together. Rub twice through a fine sieve. Store in small, tightly-corked jars. To use, allow ¼-½ teaspoon of gravy spice to about ¾ pint of gravy.

PREPARATION DEFINITIONS

Aspic : A well-seasoned savoury jelly made from rich stock, or fish, game or poultry essence or from water, flavoured meat extract, or tomato juice set with gelatine.

To Bard : To place thin slices of fat bacon over the breast of a bird. All dry birds, such as guinea fowl and ptarmigan, should be barded before roasting. (If all game and poultry is barded, no basting is required.) Bacon should be ¼ inch thick and be slit here and there. Tie it on with string.

To Blanch : This usually means to cook in boiling water for a few minutes, then to plunge into cold. Again, it may mean pouring boiling water over food, then cold-dipping. The object is to whiten, or to facilitate peeling.

Croquettes : Chopped, ground, or minced cooked food bound usually with thick white sauce. Generally egged and crumbed and fried.

To Cut and Fold In : To mix in with a light cut, then with an over and over motion. Always fold in one way. Usually referring to beaten egg white or whipped cream which have to be folded into other ingredients. Do not beat when folding. Motion must be light.

To " Glacer " : To coat with a thin sugar syrup, cooked to crack stage, 275-300° F., or to brush pastry with broken egg white or water, and dredge with caster sugar when half baked.

To Glaze : To coat cold savoury dishes with aspic or meat glaze, or to coat pastry with beaten egg yolk, sometimes diluted with equal quantity of water.

Julienne : Usually refers to vegetables cut into thin match-like strips.

To Knead : Is to press back dough, then press forwards, folding it over on itself until it is smooth.

To Lard : To insert thin strips of fat about the size of a match, known as " lardoons," into meat. Cut soft fat pork in thin slices, then in strips, about the size of a match. Place the strips in turn between the slits of a larding needle, then drive the needle into the meat, making a stitch ½ inch wide. Now draw the fat through the stitch so that the ends of the lardoon stand up above the meat. Insert lardoons in rows. Larding is usually employed on lean pieces of meat to be baked or braised. This improves the flavour of the meat and makes it more nutritive.

To Marinate : To saturate with French dressing or vinegar. Fish, meat and ingredients of root salads are sometimes marinated. Stand fish or meat for 2 or 3 hours, and vegetables for 1 hour unless otherwise instructed, until the food has absorbed the flavour and most of the moisture, turning once or twice at regular intervals.

To Mask : To coat completely with cream, jelly, mayonnaise, or a sauce, etc.

To Pipe : To ornament with a syringe and fancy tube.

To Render : To heat fat slowly until it melts off collective tissue, such as rendering lard.

To Scald : To heat liquid to a temperature just below boiling point, at which bubbles appear round sides of surface. It also can mean to lower food into boiling liquid for a moment or two.

To Score : To make narrow, horizontal or perpendicular lines over a surface, or to cut, as in the case of ham fat on ham to be baked, lines to form diamonds.

To Skewer : (1) To run pieces of meat, such as bacon and kidney, on skewers for baking. (2) To use skewers in the trussing of game, meat and poultry. Skewers are large metal or wooden pins.

To Tammy : Literally means to strain sauce through a tamis, a worsted cloth, prepared for the purpose.

COOKING DEFINITIONS

À la King : Food, such as chicken, shrimps, etc., served in a rich cream sauce, sometimes flavoured with sherry and usually enriched with mushrooms, egg yolks, etc.

To Barbecue : An American definition of cooking meat, etc., on a spit or on a rack over coals, and usually basting it with a highly-seasoned sauce.

To Baste : To ladle melted fat or other liquid as instructed, over baked or roasted meat or other food while cooking, so as to keep from drying out or burning.

To Braise : This implies two operations : (1) To brown meat by baking, frying or grilling it, called searing. (2) To simmer it in a small amount of liquid in a covered fireproof dish or saucepan at a low temperature till tender. Method generally used for cuts of meat not suitable for roasting.

To Broil or Grill : To cook under direct heat, or over hot charcoal or coals. Chops, steaks, young chicken, etc., usually cooked in this way.

To Caramelize : To heat sugar until it melts and turns into a caramel brown syrup.

To Coddle : To cook very gently just below boiling point. Usually applied to eggs.

To Deep or French Fry : To cook in a large amount of hot fat till golden brown.

To Devil : To prepare food with hot seasoning. Grill or bake.

Fireless Cooking : To cook by means of stored heat in a fireless cooker or hay box.

To Pan-Broil : To cook in a hot frying pan, sometimes dry, sometimes lightly greased to prevent burning.

To Par-boil : To cook food until only partially tender in boiling water, as the preliminary to a second method of cooking.

To Pasteurize : To partially sterilize a liquid, usually milk, at a temperature of 140-180° F., in order to arrest fermentation, and destroy certain pathogenic organisms.

To Poach : To cook gently in liquid just below boiling point, *i.e.* eggs.

To Pre-Cook : To cook food partially as the preliminary to another method of cooking, such as cooking fruit in syrup before bottling.

To Reduce : To cook a liquid to a smaller quantity in an uncovered pan.

To Roast : To cook uncovered in a baking tin in dry heat in an oven. Word means the same as bake, but whereas " bake " is generally applied to breads, cakes, puddings, savoury pies, etc., the word "roast" is more often applied than baked to game, meat and poultry.

To Scallop : Usually refers to baking creamed fish, game, meat or poultry in a greased fireproof dish.

To Scramble : To stir mixture while cooking until it thickens, such as beaten eggs, etc.

To Sear : To cook food rapidly at a high temperature till a crust is formed on the upper surface to seal in the juices. Generally refers to joints. This process can be followed either in a frying pan, in the oven, or under the grill.

To Shirr : To break eggs into a fireproof dish, then add cream as a rule and bake.

To Sterilize : To kill bacteria, usually by boiling in water, or heating in the oven. Process refers usually to preservation of food.

FRENCH CULINARY TERMS

À la Bourgeoise : In homely style.

À la Broche : To roast on a spit.

À la Carte : Dishes prepared to order.

À la Florentine : Usually refers to fish served on spinach, then coated with sauce mornay and browned in oven, or under grill.

À la Jardinière : With diced mixed vegetables.

À la Julienne : With vegetable garnish in thin strips.

À la Minute : Something cooked in the quickest possible way, such as Entrecôte à la Minute.

À la Mirabelle : Small yellow plums.

À la Serviette : To serve wrapped in a napkin.

À la Soubise : Flavoured with onion.

À la Vinaigrette : Coated or served with sauce made of oil, vinegar, herbs, etc.

Appétissants : Small, savoury tit-bits.

Atelats : Skewers for decorating entrées and joints.

Au Bleu : Fish dipped in vinegar at boiling point for $\frac{1}{2}$ a minute, then cold-dipped in iced water and poached. Salmon and trout usually treated in this way. Sometimes vinegar is omitted, and fish is cooked in white wine.

Au Gratin : Usually applied to a scalloped savoury dish covered with crumbs, moistened butter, and sometimes mixed with equal quantity of cheese, then browned.

Au Maigre : Dishes without meat. Usually associated with Lent.

Au Naturel : Dish served either without cooking, or very plainly cooked with no trimmings.

Au Jus : Served with the accompanying gravy consisting of the juice of the game, meat or vegetable, etc.

Ballotine : Small galantines usually made of game or poultry.

Bavaroise : Bavarian cream.

Béchamel : Standard French white sauce, usually flavoured onion or shallot and cloves or mace.

Beignets : Fritters.

Bisque : (1) Rich cream soup usually made from a purée of shellfish. (2) Rich frozen ice cream usually containing nuts.

Blanquette : Usually made with chicken or veal and a white sauce enriched with cream or egg yolks.

Bouchée : Small puff paste patties. Traditional size is a mouthful.

Boudin : A very small French black sausage.

Bouquet Garni : A small bunch of savoury herbs, sometimes called a fagot or faggot.

Cannelons : Small rolls of pastry stuffed with minced meat.

Carte de Jour : Daily bill of fare.

Chantilly : A dish in which cream, plain or whipped, and sweetened and flavoured with vanilla essence, is one of the ingredients.

Chapon : A small piece of bread rubbed with garlic and tossed in salads to impart flavouring, then removed.

Chaudfroid : Term given to savoury dishes, such as cutlets, boiled chicken, etc., masked with cold sauce, and usually garnished with truffles and aspic jelly.

Demi-Glace : Brown sauce (Espagnole) diluted with additional stock, then boiled to a glazing consistency and strained. Flavour with Marsala or sherry before using.

Demi-Tasse : A small cup of after-dinner coffee.

En Brochette : Grilled and served from skewers.

En Cocotte : Dish cooked in small earthenware ramekins or shells. Usually baked.

En Coquille : In shell-shaped ramekins.

En Papillottes : Cooked in paper envelopes.

En Tasse : Served in a cup, usually soup.

En Terrine : Served in a china pot. Usually pâtés and potted meats.

Entrecôte : French name for a steak cut from the middle part of loin or rib of beef.

Entrée : Strictly speaking, it is a small portion of food served as a separate course before the main course at a formal dinner or banquet. Usually served with a sauce. At family meals, the main course can be an entrée.

Escalope : Thin round veal steaks, sometimes called " Collops."

Estragon : Tarragon.

Feuilletage : Puff paste.

Flambé : Food coated with spirits and lit, such as plum pudding.

Fleurons : Half-moons of puff pastry used for garnishing.

Fondue : Swiss preparation of melted cheese.

Fricassée : White stew of chicken, rabbit or veal.

Fumet : Essence of fish, game, etc.

Grenadins : Small slices of veal larded and braised.

Macédoine : A mixture of fruit or vegetables, cut in even-shaped discs. Sometimes applied to jellied fruit or a fruit salad flavoured liqueur.

Parmentier : Flavoured or cooked with potato.

Piquer : To lard.

Poeller : Method of braising meat in a fireproof earthenware pan over charcoal.

Purée : A heavy, smooth, very thick pulp made by passing cooked food through a sieve. Usually refers to purée of fruit, vegetables, or to a soup.

Quenelles : Forcemeat composed of fish, meat, poultry and eggs, etc., shaped in balls, ovals or small " eggs," and poached in hot stock or water. Used as an entrée, or for garnishing soup or entrées.

Ragoût : A rich seasoned meat stew.

Savarin : A light spongy yeast cake named after Brillat-Savarin, in the shape of a ring.

Suprême : The best portion of a dish or the most delicate, *i.e.* Suprême de Volaille, the breast of chicken.

Timbale : Timbale-shaped moulds of baked unsweetened custard combined with minced cooked chicken, fish or vegetables.

Tournedos : Small fillets of beef sliced from the undercut of fillet. Cut in neat rounds. Grilled or fried and garnished. Serve as an entrée.

Velouté : This means velvet-like.

THINGS YOU STILL NEED TO KNOW

Here are some definitions you still need to know:

Antipasto : Italian appetiser or hors d'oeuvre.

Apéritif : A dry fortified wine, such as dry sherry or Vermouth, or a cocktail.

Appetiser : Usually a tiny individual portion of food daintily served with apéritifs, or as a first course, such as a canapé, or caviare.

Batter : A creamy mixture of flour and liquid that can be dropped from a spoon, or poured. Generally used for coating.

Bombe Glacée : A melon-shaped or round iced pudding lined with one variety of ice cream, and filled with another.

Cobbler : A variety of pie cooked in a deep pie dish and covered with a rich baking powder dough. Sometimes the dough covers the sides of pie dish as well, but not the bottom.

Compote : Several varieties of fruit poached in syrup.

Devils : Fish roes, kidneys, legs of poultry, mushrooms, fish, steaks, etc., can be devilled. To devil, highly season the meat, gashing any legs before rubbing in the Devil Paste. Coat meat with the paste as given.

Devil Paste : Mix 1 teaspoon Worcester sauce with ¼ teaspoon made mustard, 1 teaspoon chutney, ¼ teaspoon curry powder, pinch of salt, dash of cayenne pepper, and 1 oz. butter, melted.

Goulash : Thick Hungarian beef or veal stew flavoured with paprika and cooked with vegetables.

Pilau : Spiced rice cooked with fish, meat or poultry.

Raspings : Either sifted breadcrumbs, baked till brown, or stale bread and crusts browned in oven then crushed. Use for coating boiled hams, moulds and sprinkling over certain savoury dishes.

Risotto : Italian dish of rice and fish, meat or poultry, generally flavoured with onion or shallot and sometimes saffron or tomato, or both. Can be served in place of fish at dinner, or as a main course at lunch or supper.

To Clarify Butter : Melt butter in a saucepan without stirring. Skim and pour off the pure butter, leaving any sediment behind. Use for baking purposes in cakes, buns, etc., for greasing cake and other tins, and for covering potted meats and pastes.

To Clarify Fat : Put any trimmings of fat from meat and dripping to be clarified in a saucepan. Place it over a moderate heat, and, when melted, strain into a clean pan. For every 3 lb., add ¼ teaspoon bicarbonate of soda and 1 pint of water. Boil till the water has evaporated and the fat is clear. Skim when cool and strain into a jar.

To Fry Onion Rings : Slice peeled onions thinly, beginning at the root end. Divide into rings. Toss in seasoned flour. Shake and fry till brown in smoking hot fat. Drain before using.

To Fry Parsley : Wash, stalk and dry parsley, then place in a wire basket and fry in deep smoking hot fat for 1 minute. Drain on paper before serving as a garnish.

To Make Bacon Curls or Rolls : Remove rind and any bone, and cut in pieces 1½ by 3 inches in size. (The bacon should be very thin.) Roll up loosely. Run on to a skewer and bake, fry or grill till cooked. Useful garnish for roast chicken, turkey, veal, and scrambled eggs, etc.

To Make Breadcrumbs :
Dried: Put pieces of stale bread or any crusts left over from making sandwiches or toast in a moderate oven. Bake till crisp and pale brown. Crush them on a baking board with a rolling pin. Put through a wire sieve and store when cold in an airtight tin.

Fried: Melt a piece of butter in a frying pan or a baking tin. Add fresh breadcrumbs, requiring to be fried or baked. Allow 2 teaspoons butter to 1 cup of crumbs. Sprinkle with salt and pepper to taste and either fry or bake until a rich brown, turning occasionally in the process. Use with roast game.

To Make Browning : Place ½ lb. loaf sugar and ¼ pint water in an iron saucepan. Boil without a cover until the syrup turns the colour of coffee. Cool. Bottle and use for adding to gravy, stews or soups to darken the liquid. NOTE : Be careful not to cook till it burns.

To Make Croûtes : Used for supporting an entrée. Size depends on size of dish used in serving. When possible, make the croûtes large enough to take the food, for example, sweetbreads, or large enough to take a bird such as grouse. They should be about ¾ inch thick, unless a preference is shown for thicker ones. When wanted to support an entrée, make them 2 inches thick.

To Make Glaze : For ham, tongue, etc., put ¼ gill water, ¼ oz. gelatine and ¼ oz. meat extract into a saucepan. Stir till boiling and slightly thick. Wipe ham or tongue with a cloth wrung out of hot water before brushing with glaze. A richer flavoured glaze can be obtained by cooking 2 quarts of stock until reduced to nearly ¼ pint, skimming it frequently.

To Make Liquid Caramel : Place 1 lb. caster or loaf sugar and ¾ pint of water in an iron saucepan. Heat slowly, without stirring, till mixture begins to colour, then stir occasionally until you get it the shade you want. Amber or light brown is the usual shade. If, by mistake, you get it very dark, keep it for using as browning.

To Make Praline : Melt ¼ lb. caster sugar in an iron saucepan till a rich brown. Add the same quantity of chopped blanched almonds or other nuts, and a few drops of lemon juice. Turn quickly on to a buttered or oiled tin. Leave till hard, then chop. Use for ice cream, etc.

To Prepare Onion Juice: Slice the root off an onion. Squeeze onion on a squeezer kept for the purpose.

To Prepare Roux : Blond, brown and white. Cook equal quantities of butter and flour in a saucepan over the heat. If *blond* is wanted, slightly brown the mixture. If *brown*, cook till rich nut brown. If *white*, cook without browning. 1 heaped tablespoon roux thickens 1 pint of liquid. It can be made in a large quantity and, if kept closely covered, it will keep good a long time.

To Use a Vanilla Pod : Infuse the pod in milk, leaving it in until the milk is nicely flavoured with vanilla, then remove. Dry, dip in caster sugar, and store in a caster sugar jar until required again. Milk can be used for puddings and cakes, etc. The sugar becomes flavoured also.

To Whip Cream and Eggs : Whisk or beat in a cool place till frothy. Whip cream gently to start with. If required for piping, should be stiff enough to keep its shape. Sweeten and flavour when cream begins to thicken. To stiffen cream for a cake filling, stir 1 teaspoon gelatine, dissolved in 2 tablespoons of milk, into every ½ pint of cream before whipping.

MEASURING TOOLS

Use household scales and measuring spoons, or measuring cups and spoons. It is quicker to weigh a large quantity of an ingredient on scales than to measure it in cups.

THE ELIZABETH CRAIG MEASURING CUP

There is much confusion about what size cup is meant when cup measurements are given in recipes. I use in my recipes, the " Elizabeth Craig " measuring cup. The cup measurement as marked in this cup is equal to one average-sized teacup, or an American ½ pint (8 fluid oz., that is, 2 fluid oz. less than the English ½ pint). It is the same size cup as is used all over the American continent, besides elsewhere abroad, and it has been used here almost exclusively for many years. This cup gives three sets of measurements : (1) Parts of a cup. (2) Liquid ounces. (3) Parts of half a pint. When following my recipes, you measure up to the cup mark, not to the rim of the cup, when a cup of anything is required.

Measuring Spoons : 1 set of measuring spoons : tablespoon, dessertspoon, teaspoon, ½ teaspoon and ¼ teaspoon.

HOW TO MEASURE

All measurements given in this book are level unless otherwise stated.

To measure accurately when following recipes, level off ingredients in cups (if using a teacup) and spoons. When a rounded or heaped cup or spoon is required, I have stated this in the ingredients.

To Measure Dry Ingredients (using a cup) : When measuring dry ingredients in my standard measuring cup, fill up to the ridge marked " 1 Cup," and shake level with it. If using an average-sized teacup, and a cup of anything is required, fill up to the rim and level off ingredient with a palette knife.

To Measure Liquids (using a cup) : Simply fill up to the ridge marked " 1 Cup," or to quantity required.

To Measure Dry Ingredients (with spoon) : Take a slightly heaped spoonful of ingredient, and slide a palette knife across the top, taking care not to press ingredient. The result will be a level spoonful of ingredient. To measure ½ a spoonful (if you haven't a measuring spoon for this purpose), divide ingredient through the middle, lengthwise if spoon is oval shaped, crosswise if round, and carefully scoop out one half. To obtain ¼ spoonful, measure ½ spoonful, then divide remaining half in two crosswise, and carefully scoop out half.

NOTE : Sift flours and icing sugar before measuring.

To Measure Liquids (with spoon) : Fill spoon up to the rim—not to over-flowing—with a spoonful as required. To save waste, particularly where essences are concerned, it is safer to use measuring spoons than parts of a spoon.

To Weigh Sticky Ingredients (honey, syrup or treacle) : First weigh basin or saucepan, then place on scales the additional weight required, then pour in ingredient. (To measure in a cup or spoon, first heat cup or spoon.)

What is a Pinch ? As much as can be held between the thumb and forefinger. A " good pinch " is double this quantity.

USEFUL MEASURES

HOMELY

Few grains	=	Less than ⅛ teaspoon
1 yeast cake	=	1 oz. baker's yeast
Weight of an egg	=	Approximately 2 oz.
1 2-lb. loaf of bread		Yields 29 slices
Walnut of fat, etc.	=	Approximately ¼ oz.

AVOIRDUPOIS TABLE

16 drachms	=	1 oz.
16 oz.	=	1 pound (lb.)
14 lb.	=	1 stone
28 lb.	=	1 quarter (qr.)
4 quarters	=	1 hundredweight (cwt.)
20 cwt.	=	1 ton

LIQUID MEASURE

60 drops	=	1 teaspoon
1 wineglass	=	½ gill
1 gill	=	¼ pint
4 gills	=	1 pint (pt.)
2 pints	=	1 quart (qt.)
4 quarts	=	1 gallon (gall.)

SPOON AND CUP TABLE

1 saltspoon	approximates	½ teaspoon
1 teaspoon	,,	½ dessertspoon
1 dessertspoon	,,	½ tablespoon
1 breakfast cup	,,	½ pint
1 teacup	,,	8 fluid ounces (ozs.)

CONTINENTAL EQUIVALENTS

Fluid: The Continental measure for liquids is a litre. 1 pint of liquid equals approximately ½ a litre, accurately .57 of a litre. 1 quart equals approximately 1 and 1/7th of a litre, accurately 1.14.

Solid: The Continental measure for solids is a gram.

1 oz.	=	28.32	grams
4 oz.	=	113·4	grams
8 oz.	=	226·8	grams
1 lb.	=	453·6	grams
2·2 lb. or 2 lb. 3½ oz.	=	1,000	grams, or 1 kilogram

TABLE OF EQUIVALENTS

Ingredient	*Approximate Equivalent to 1 Measuring Cup*	*Approximate Equivalent to 1 Tablespoon*
Almonds, ground	¼ lb.	⅓ oz.
Arrowroot	5 oz.	¼ oz.
Barley, pearl	½ lb.	1 oz.
Breadcrumbs, dried	6 oz.	½ oz.
" stale	2 oz.	½ oz.
Cheese, grated	4 oz.	¼ oz.
Cocoa	¼ lb.	¼ oz.
Coconut, desiccated	¼ lb.	¼ oz.
Coffee, ground	¼ lb.	¼ oz.
Cornflour	5 oz.	¼ oz.
(Curry powder, Raising Agents and Spices: 1 teaspoon = ⅛ of an oz.)		
Custard Powder	¼ lb.	¼ oz.
Dried Fruit (except stone fruit)	6 oz.	
Fats	½ lb.	½ oz.
Flour	¼ lb.	¼ oz.
Gelatine, powdered		½ oz.
Jam, Honey, Syrup and Treacle	¾ lb.	¾ oz.
Minced Meat	½ lb.	½ oz.
Nuts, chopped	¼ lb.	¼ oz.
Oatmeal, medium grain	6 oz.	⅓ oz.
Rice	½ lb.	¾ oz.
Sago and Semolina	6 oz.	½ oz.
Sugar, brown (closely packed)	7 oz.	About ½ oz.
" caster	½ lb.	½ oz.
" granulated	7½ oz.	About ½ oz.
" icing	5 oz.	Fully ¼ oz.
Tapioca	6 oz.	½ oz.

MISCELLANEOUS

1 lb. bacon	Yields	15-20 slices
1 lb. chocolate	"	About 3 cups grated
1 square chocolate	=	1 oz.
½ pint cream	Enough	For 8-10 cups of coffee
½ pint cream, whipped	"	For 10 desserts (2 tablespoons each)
1 medium-sized lemon	Yields	2-3 tablespoons juice and 1 rounded teaspoon grated rind
16 marshmallows	=	¼ lb.
1 medium-sized orange	Yields	½ cup juice and ¾ tablespoon rind
8 lumps of sugar	=	1 oz.

COOKING TEMPERATURES

Method of Cooking	*Temperature Fahrenheit*
Stewing - - - - -	165° F.
Simmering - - - - -	180° F.
Boiling - - - - -	212° F.
Jellying - - - - -	220-222° F.

FRYING TABLE

(Deep Fat)

Food	Fat Temperature	Oil Temperature	Bread Test
Uncooked mixtures - - (Doughnuts and fritters)	360-375° F.	375-385° F.	1 minute
Chops, egged and crumbed	385° F.	385° F.	40 seconds
Cooked mixtures - - (Croquettes, fish cakes, etc.)	375-385° F.	385° F.	40 seconds
Fish - - - -	375° F.	375° F.	1 minute
Onions - - - -	360-375° F.	375° F.	1 minute
*Potatoes - - - (crisps, chips, straws, etc.)	390° F.	395° F.	20 seconds

* I prefer to fry by the "two step" method : (1) 375° F. till soft and starting to brown. Drain on absorbent paper. (2) Fry at 390° F. till brown.

Bread Test : Use this test when you have no thermometer to test temperature. Drop an inch square of bread into hot fat or oil. If it browns at specified time, fat or oil is at right temperature for frying. If it browns in less time, cool fat or oil and test again. If it takes longer, heat a little and test again.

COOKING IN THE OVEN

To cook successfully in the oven, you must be able to depend on the temperature required. This means that you have to use an oven with a heat regulator or one fitted with a thermometer. To help you to get perfect results, I am appending a table giving temperatures Fahrenheit and an indication of the general terms used to describe these temperatures in this book.

If you cook by gas, it is necessary to work out the equivalent oven setting for your own cooker, preferably from its handbook, as these still vary considerably from one cooker to another. A rough and ready conversion may be done from the descriptions Very Slow, Slow, etc., which are given with the temperature Fahrenheit in each recipe. However, more exact equivalents can be worked out from the Gas Council approved list of temperatures and equivalents given overleaf in the right hand column of the table.

To use your oven successfully, follow instructions given in your book as to where to place food that requires slow cooking, quick cooking, etc. Generally, food cooks quicker at the top than at the bottom. Large dishes, such as pies and puddings, as well as joints, etc., are placed in the centre of the oven, but, as all ovens are not heated in the same way, follow instructions given with your cooker to get perfect results.

Pre-heat oven according to instructions, either for length of time required, or until regulator indicates temperature has been reached.

APPROXIMATE OVEN TEMPERATURES

Recipe description	Degrees Fahrenheit	Gas Cooker setting	Degrees Fahrenheit
Very Slow	250°	$\frac{1}{4}$	225°
		$\frac{1}{2}$	250°
Slow	300°	1	275°
Moderately Slow ⎫	335°	2	300°
Fairly Slow ⎭		3	325°
Moderate	350°	4	350°
Moderately Hot	375°	5	375°
	400°	6	400°
Fairly Hot	425°	7	425°
Hot	450°	8	450°
Very Hot	500°	9	475°

PLANNING BALANCED MEALS

A properly balanced diet is necessary to build up healthy bodies, provide new energy, regulate bodily processes and furnish resistance against disease. To be able to plan such a diet, you need to learn at least the ABC of food values. The various classes or groups of food, and what part each should play in a normal daily diet, are detailed below.

CLASS 1 : Breads made from wholemeal, or a combination of white flour and wholemeal, and cereals, such as oatmeal and those made from whole wheat, furnish iron and vitamin B.

CLASS 2 : Milk (fresh, buttermilk, skimmed milk, etc.), milk products and cheese, furnish calcium, protein, phosphorus, iodine and vitamins A, B and G.

CLASS 3 : Fish (canned and quick frozen), game, meat (including offal), poultry and pulses, furnish protein, iron and vitamins B and G.

CLASS 4 : Butter and fortified margarine, furnish energy and a certain amount of calcium, iron and vitamin A.

CLASS 5 : Eggs furnish protein, iron and a certain amount of vitamins A, B and G.

CLASS 6 : Green leafy and yellow vegetables (raw, cooked, frozen or canned), furnish vitamin A, and a certain amount of calcium and iron, and vitamins B, C and G.

CLASS 7 : Grapefruit, lemons, oranges, pineapple and tomatoes (fresh or canned), furnish vitamins B and C.

CLASS 8 : All vegetables, excluding those in Class 6 (fresh, canned or quick frozen), and all fruits except those in Class 7, furnish iron and vitamins.

FUNCTION AND SOURCE OF FOOD MATERIALS

The function of food materials is to build and maintain healthy bodies. That is why it is essential that each of the following are included in the daily diet.

Calcium is necessary for bone, glands, muscles, nerves and teeth. It is supplied by almonds, cheese, dried beans and peas, figs and dates, all fish, egg yolk, milk, olives, green and leafy vegetables, etc.

Fats furnish energy, heat and a bedding for muscles and nerves. Supplied by butter, cheese, cod liver oil, chocolate, cream, egg yolks, lard, margarine, fat meat and poultry, oily fish, nuts, olives, avocado pears, etc.

Iodine : This is essential, as a shortage would cause glandular troubles. Supplied by fish liver oils, fresh or canned fish of all kinds and iodized salt.

Iron helps to make blood. Supplied by cocoa, dried beans, peas, lentils, dates and prunes, almonds, egg yolk, liver, currants and raisins, green and leafy vegetables, whole wheat, oysters, treacle, etc.

Phosphorus is necessary to build strong bones, muscles, etc. Supplied by almonds, cashew nuts, cheese, dried beans, peas, lentils, chocolate, egg yolk, all salt water fish, liver, meat and poultry, etc.

Protein : Plenty of protein is absolutely essential. Without it growth would be impossible. Primarily a body-building material, it also is one of the three sources of energy, and is absolutely necessary for the maintenance of body tissues. Supplied by cheese, eggs, all fish and sea food, all grains, game, meat and poultry, milk, and dishes made from one or more of these foods.

Sugars furnish energy, heat and fat. Supplied by dried fruits, beetroot, sweet chocolate, honey, jam, jellies, syrups, treacle and sugar.

Starches furnish energy, heat and fat. Supplied by all pulses, grains and flours, corn, cornflour, rice, tapioca, potatoes, Jerusalem artichokes, vegetable marrows, and all nuts, etc.

Vitamin A : Necessary for growth and for maintenance of good health, it strengthens resistance to infectious diseases, especially of the ears, eyes, nose, lungs and throat. It is also claimed to prevent night blindness. Supplied by carrots, green salads and leafy vegetables, dark green leaves of salads and vegetables, tomatoes, egg yolks, fish liver oils, butter, cream, margarine, milk, kidney and liver, etc.

Vitamin B : Required for growth and general good health, it stimulates appetite, and protects brain tissues and nerves, etc. Helps digestion also. Supplied by green leafy vegetables, egg yolks, whole grain cereals and flours, lean meat, pork, kidney, liver, pulses, peanuts, grapefruit, oranges, pineapple, peas, potatoes, etc.

Vitamin C (ascorbic acid) : This increases resistance to infection, promotes growth and helps to maintain sound teeth. Supplied by citrus fruits, fresh or canned pineapple, green salads, tomatoes, asparagus, cabbage, peas, bananas, melon, potatoes, turnip, etc.

Vitamin D prevents rickets in children and assists in building and maintaining strong bones and teeth. Supplied by egg yolk, cereals, fish liver oil, sardines, salmon, liver, etc.

Vitamin G promotes growth and good bodily health. Helps the digestive system and keeps old age at bay. Supplied by green salads and green leafy vegetables, whole wheat cereals and bread, lean meat, kidney and liver, egg yolks, yeast, etc.

Body Cleansers : These include roughage (the name given to parts of food not digested in the usual way), minerals, vitamins and water. *Roughage* is important because it supplies the essential bulk to prevent constipation, and helps to counteract conditions due to over-refined foods. Supplied by whole wheat bread, coarse cereals, unpeeled fruit, vegetable fibres, green salads, prunes, etc. Minerals, vitamins and water are all necessary to regulate certain bodily processes. Water and other liquids, such as buttermilk, cocoa, coffee, tea, non-alcoholic drinks, soups, and watery fruits and vegetables all supply liquids necessary for building and repairing body tissues, for the elimination of waste products, for regulating body temperatures, etc.

HOW TO BUILD A MENU

There are two ways of planning a menu :
(1) Plan menus for a week, then go shopping for immediate needs.
(2) Shop before you plan.
To plan a perfect menu, you must consider the character, colour, flavour and texture of the various courses. They should contrast. You should also plan a balanced menu without including any one food more than once, and see that you note the correct accompaniments to each dish.

Character : Never compose a menu only from dried courses, or only from wet courses. By this, I mean do not start dinner with potted shrimps, follow with baked, fried or grilled meat, and end with fritters, pancakes, or a steamed pudding. This is an example of a dry meal. In the same way, do not start with a soup, follow with a casserole or stew of game, meat or poultry and end with a fruit salad or stewed fruit and custard. This is an example of a wet meal. You must try, when possible, to follow a wet course with a dry, or a dry with a wet.

A good example of a perfect family menu is : Broth, followed by a baked, fried or grilled main course with suitable accompaniments, and fruit and cream, or a creamy sweet, or baked pudding. Always serve sauce with a dry meat course, such as fish and meat cakes, baked or steamed fish, or meat loaf, dried fish, etc., and when serving a soft savoury dish for lunch, such as a baked cheese pudding, risotto, or spaghetti, it should be accompanied by a crisp green salad just as a cream soup or a purée requires fried croûtons.

Colour : Choose courses of contrasting colours, but if necessary to have two courses of the same colour following, garnish one with a contrasting colour to avoid similarity. Never compose a menu of only brown or only white courses. An example of a badly chosen menu is : cream of chicken soup ; sole with a cream sauce ; boiled chicken with rice, mashed potatoes and cauliflower ; vanilla ice cream. If you substitute salmon and sauce tartare for the sole, and strawberry tartlets for the sweet, the meal will look and be more appetising. I would also substitute green peas for cauliflower. Always remember that a splash of colour provided by garnish also tempts the appetite.

Flavour : Do not let a distinct flavour, such as tomato, figure in two courses. For example, if serving tomato soup, do not garnish a fish or meat course with tomatoes, or coat a fish or meat loaf, etc., with tomato sauce.

Texture : If starting lunch or dinner with a cream soup, do not end it with a creamy sweet, or, if serving a steamed steak and kidney pudding, do not end with a steamed sweet pudding, and so on.

Accompaniments : When choosing accompaniments to the main course, remember that rich savoury dishes, such as roast duck, goose or pork, need the accompaniment of an acid sauce to aid digestion. Flat-tasting fish, such as cod, haddock, turbot, whiting, etc., require a piquant sauce such as caper, tartare or tomato. Again, certain puddings, such as steamed batter or sponge puddings, need a contrasting accompaniment. Give them a lemon sauce, or syrup or honey sharpened with lemon juice. Fruit compôtes, salads and stewed fruit do not make a complete course unless accompanied by cream, custard sauce, junket or a milk mould. The accompaniments are fully dealt with in each section.

SAMPLE DAILY MENUS FOR EACH SEASON

When studying these menus, please note that I am taking it for granted that cereal, if liked, honey or marmalade and tea or coffee will be served at breakfast, and that toast or rolls, or both, will be served at lunch or supper and dinner.

Spring :

BREAKFAST

Orange Juice
Ham Omelet
Crisp Toast
Butter

LUNCHEON OR SUPPER

FAMILY	FORMAL
Tomato Juice	Egg Mayonnaise
Scallops of Fish	Grilled Trout
Lettuce Salad	Lettuce and Cucumber Salad
Steamed Rhubarb	Lemon Chiffon Pie
Custard Sauce	Biscuits and Cheese
Madeleines	Watercress

AFTERNOON TEA

Cress Sandwiches
Drop Scones
Cherry Cake,
Shortbread Biscuits

DINNER

FAMILY	FORMAL
Vegetable Broth	Cream of Tomato
Baked Meat Loaf	Asparagus
Tomato Sauce	Melted Butter
Roast Potatoes, Green Peas	Grilled Spring Chicken
Apple Fritters	Sauce Tartare
Lemon Sauce	Chip Potatoes, Fried Mushrooms
	*Fruit Salad

*If a savoury is preferred to a sweet, serve either fried herring roes or potted
shrimps on toast, and end with fresh fruit.*

Summer :

BREAKFAST

Grapefruit
Scrambled Egg on Toast
Hot Brioches

LUNCHEON OR SUPPER

FAMILY	FORMAL
Sardines and Potato Salad	Hors d'oeuvre
Baked Stuffed Tomatoes	Salmon Mayonnaise
Vanilla Ice Cream	Potato and Cucumber Salad
Hot Chocolate Sauce	Strawberry Sundae
	Vanilla Wafers

AFTERNOON TEA

Cucumber Sandwiches
Tomato Sandwiches
Devonshire Splits
Chocolate Layer Cake
Florentines

DINNER

FAMILY
Iced Melon
Boiled Chicken with Rice
Buttered String Beans
Summer Pudding
Custard Sauce

FORMAL
Jellied Madrilène Soup
Roast Duckling
Apple Sauce
New Potatoes, Green Peas
Lettuce and Orange Salad
Raspberry Tartlets

Autumn :

BREAKFAST

Pineapple Juice
Fried Sausage Cakes
Fried Bananas
Crisp Toast
Hot Rolls

LUNCHEON OR SUPPER

FAMILY
Fish Pie
Stewed Apples
Custard Sauce
Biscuits and Cheese
Celery

FORMAL
Shrimp Cocktail
Grilled Lamb Cutlets
Maître d'Hôtel Butter
Creamed Potatoes, Fried Tomatoes
Blackberry Flan

AFTERNOON TEA

Wild Duck Sandwiches
Watercress Sandwiches
Hot Buttered Scones
Gingerbread Layer Cake
Kisses or Queen Cakes

DINNER

FAMILY
Brown Onion Soup
Stuffed Vegetable Marrow
Mashed Potatoes, Cauliflower
Topsy Turvy Apple Cake
Custard Sauce

FORMAL
Kidney Soup
Sole Meunière
Roast Partridges
Potato Straws, Heart of Lettuce Salad
Pear Melba

Winter :

BREAKFAST

Baked Apple or Stewed Prunes
Bacon and Egg
Waffles
Butter and Honey

LUNCHEON OR SUPPER

FAMILY
Tomato Soup
Bobitie
Jacket Potatoes, Pickled Beetroot
Queen's Pudding

FORMAL
Quiche Lorraine
Stewed Kidneys
Boiled Noodles, Green Peas
Chocolate Bavarois
Biscuits and Cheese
Celery

AFTERNOON TEA

Toasted Crumpets
Mushroom Sandwiches
Currant Bread and Butter
Maids of Honour
Dundee Cake

DINNER

FAMILY
Cream of Mushroom Soup
Fried Croûtons
Casserole of Chicken
Mashed Potatoes, Cabbage
Apple Betty
Custard Sauce

FORMAL
Chicken Noodle Soup
Lobster Thermidor
Grilled Medallions of Steak
Béarnaise Sauce
Chip Potatoes, Grilled Mushrooms
Cream Caramel

Breakfast Dishes

Light Breakfast: Fruit or fruit juice ; cereal, if liked ; rolls or toast, or rolls and toast ; butter and honey or marmalade ; coffee or tea.

Substantial Breakfast: Fruit or fruit juice ; cereal ; savoury course ; rolls or toast, or rolls and toast ; tea or coffee (milk for young children).

To speed up a cooked cereal, such as oatmeal, soak it overnight in the amount of liquid required to cook it, or partly cook it so that it can be finished off in the top of a double boiler while you are preparing the rest of the meal, in the morning.

FRUIT IN THE MENU

Breakfast is the best time to introduce vitamin C food in the shape of citrus fruits which are richest in these vitamins. Allow $\frac{1}{2}$ cup or $\frac{1}{4}$ pint grapefruit or orange juice, or $\frac{1}{2}$ a grapefruit, fresh or canned, per person. Tomato juice also provides vitamin C, but you need to allow 1 cup or $\frac{1}{2}$ pint if you wish to provide as much vitamin C.

Any other fruits may be used for breakfast. Give young children a combination of stewed apples, figs or prunes with a suitable cereal, such as creamed rice or semolina, occasionally in place of a fresh fruit course and a cereal.

PORRIDGE

To make perfect porridge, you need fresh medium or coarse oatmeal bought straight from the mill. There is a variety half-way between coarse and fine, known as medium meal, which is preferred by many people. Porridge can also be made with bere-meal.

SCOTTISH OATMEAL PORRIDGE

1 pint cold water   2 tablespoons oatmeal   1 small saltspoon salt

Pour the water into the porridge pot. Bring to boiling point. Sprinkle oatmeal in from your left hand while you stir with the right. (If you add it quickly, it will form lumps.) Stir steadily till boiling, cover saucepan and draw to the side of stove, or reduce heat under pan as low as possible so that the porridge can simmer very gently. Cook for about 10 minutes, until the oatmeal has swollen, stirring frequently, then add salt. Simmer very gently for 15-20 minutes longer. *For 2 persons.*

CEREALS FOR FOUR PERSONS

Farina : Bring 2 pints water to the boil in the top of a double boiler over direct heat. Add 2 teaspoons salt. Gradually stir in $\frac{1}{2}$ pint farina. Stir constantly until thick and boiling. Cook over boiling water from $\frac{1}{2}$-$\frac{3}{4}$ hour, stirring occasionally.

Oat : Mix 1 cup rolled oats with $\frac{1}{2}$ cup coarse oatmeal in the top of a double boiler. Slowly stir in 4 cups boiling water. Cover. Cook over boiling water for 20 minutes to $\frac{1}{2}$ hour, stirring occasionally. Season with salt.

Rice : Rinse and drain 1 cup rice. Place in a double boiler. Cover with boiling water. Add a teaspoon of salt and stir till boiling. Boil for 10 minutes, stirring occasionally, then slip pan into the top of bottom container. Stir in 1 pint milk. Cover closely and cook over boiling water till milk is absorbed, stirring occasionally. Serve with milk. If liked, add 1 cup halved stoned dates after milk and rice have boiled.

Boiled Rice: (1) Sprinkle boiled rice with grape-nuts. Serve with golden syrup or top milk. (2) Serve with sliced banana and top milk.

Cereal and Fruit: Stir sliced dates, raisins soaked in fruit juice overnight and drained, into any cooked cereal just before serving, or serve cooked cereals with stewed apricots, figs, pears or prunes.

Cereal and Fresh Fruit: Spoon ripe berries, slices of banana, or sliced fresh peaches, over creamed rice, farina or semolina, or frozen fruit can be defrosted and used for the same purpose.

Flakes and Fresh Fruit: Pick over, rinse and drain 1 lb. blackcurrants, loganberries or raspberries. Place in an enamel saucepan. Add $\frac{1}{4}$ pint water. Cover and stew gently till tender. Sweeten to taste. Chill in a glass dish. Apples and other fruit may be used in same way. Serve with cereal flakes and cream. *For 4 persons.*

Grape-nuts and Bananas: Peel and slice bananas lengthwise. Sprinkle grape-nuts over each length. Serve with caster sugar and thin cream.

EGGS FOR BREAKFAST

BAKED OR SHIRRED EGGS (Oeufs sur le Plat)

To Bake Eggs with Butter: Grease a shallow-eared, round fireproof dish. Break in one egg, then another, taking care to keep the yolks whole. Season with salt and pepper to taste. Fleck with butter. Place on a baking sheet. Bake in a moderate oven, 350° F., for 5 to 15 minutes, until set to taste. If liked, garnish the dish at opposite sides with a wedge of tomato, seasoned and brushed with melted butter, after adding the eggs, but before baking.

To Bake Eggs with Cream; Place 1 tablespoon cream in each buttered ramekin. Break an egg into it. Season with salt and pepper to taste. Place on a baking sheet. Bake in a moderate oven, 350° F., for 15-20 minutes, until eggs are set.

BAKED EGGS AND BACON

Allow 1 rasher of bacon and 1 egg for each person. Remove rind from bacon. Grill very lightly, then line a muffin tin with each rasher. Break 1 egg at a time into a cup, then slip into a lined muffin tin. Bake in a moderate oven, 350° F., for 10-12 minutes, until eggs are set to taste. Serve each on a round of hot buttered toast or fried bread.

EGG NESTS ON TOAST (Oeufs en Chemise)

6 new-laid eggs
3½ teaspoons salt
6 small rounds of toast
1½ tablespoons butter

Separate yolks and whites of eggs, putting whites into a basin and keeping the yolks whole in their half shell till required. Add salt to whites, and beat to a stiff froth. Toast the rounds of bread. Dip the edges in hot water and spread rounds with butter. Place them on a baking sheet. Heap egg whites on toast. Make a hollow in the centre of each white and put ¼ teaspoon butter in it, then drop an egg yolk into each. Cook for 3 minutes in a moderate oven, 350° F., and serve immediately. *For 6 persons.*

TO BOIL EGGS

Choose new-laid when possible, and boil in one of the following ways :

(1) Bring enough water to the boil to completely cover eggs when inserted. If part of an egg is left uncovered, this part will not be fully cooked. Place an egg in a tablespoon. Slip gently off spoon into the water. Boil for 3-5 minutes, according to taste. A soft-boiled egg needs 3 minutes ; a firm egg, 5 minutes.

(2) This is sometimes called " coddling ". Slip eggs into boiling water. Let the water come to a rapid boil again. Cover pan with lid. Draw to the side where the water will keep hot but not boil, or even simmer. Stand for 8-10 minutes.

(3) Place eggs in a saucepan of cold water. Bring slowly to the boil. Remove

at once if wanted soft-boiled. Otherwise cover and remove pan from stove and leave eggs for 3-5 minutes before serving.

HINTS ON BOILING EGGS

(1) When boiling eggs fresh from the nest, allow a little longer in each case.

(2) Always remove eggs from refrigerator some time before boiling them, so that they will be at room temperature when you are ready to cook them.

TO FRY EGGS

To Fry Without Turning: Allow 1 tablespoon (½ oz.) butter, lard, bacon fat or olive oil for each egg. Heat in a frying-pan large enough to take all the eggs comfortably. Break one egg at a time into a cup and slip into the hot fat or oil. Fry slowly until the whites are set, spooning the fat or oil over the yolks as they cook. Remove each with a slice, allowing fat to drain back into pan. Slip each on to a round of hot buttered toast or fried bread.

To Fry on Both Sides: Turn eggs when whites are lightly set, and brown on the other side. Serve as above.

To Fry the French Way: Double the quantity of fat and fry one egg at a time. Break egg into a saucer. Tilt frying-pan so that the hot fat or oil runs to one side, and slip in egg. Spoon the white up round the yolk, when the white will gradually fry into the shape of a nest with the yolk in the centre. White will be firm, but yolk soft.

To Fry the Scottish Way: Follow first method, but cover pan. Fry for about 4 minutes when the steam will have cooked the top of the eggs, covering them with a snowy film.

OMELETS (Omelettes)

There are two kinds of omelets : (1) The English Omelet, (2) The French Omelet. The first has the yolks and whites beaten separately which results in a fluffy omelet, while for the second, the yolks and whites are beaten together.

RULES FOR OMELET-MAKING

(1) Eggs should be absolutely fresh.

(2) The fat or oil must be hot.

(3) Omelet should be served the moment it is ready and eaten at once, or it falls flat.

OMELET PAN

The omelet needs a thick frying-pan with a smooth level surface. Keep this pan entirely for omelet-making. A pan made of aluminium, a copper-lined pan, or a steel pan make the best omelets. Choose a pan suitable for the size of omelet you generally make, allowing a 6-inch pan for a 2-egg omelet. If your pan is too large, the omelet will be too thin and a little tough. If the pan is too small, the omelet may be under-cooked. It must be scrupulously clean or the egg will stick. If your omelet pan is new, it should be seasoned before using.

To SEASON PAN : Melt a walnut of lard in pan. Heat until it turns light brown. Pour fat off, then wipe pan thoroughly with clean kitchen paper. Sprinkle pan with a little salt and rub this vigorously over the pan with a pad of kitchen paper. Turn out the salt, then wipe thoroughly with a clean cloth. The pan is now ready for use.

To CLEAN PAN : If you rub the pan with salt as suggested and wipe it with a clean cloth afterwards, that will normally keep it in perfect order. If you haven't made an omelet for some time, I would give your pan the salt treatment before cooking one again.

To HEAT PAN : Choose the hot plate or ring that is as near to the size of the omelet pan as possible. Place pan over low heat, so that the whole pan gradually heats through. When hot enough to melt the fat, add fat or oil, and heat until fat stops sizzling, and oil shows signs of a faint blue smoke.

INGREDIENTS FOR AN OMELET

Fat : Clarified butter or unsalted margarine best, but bacon fat can be used. Allow $\frac{1}{4}$-$\frac{1}{2}$ oz. fat to each egg. *Oil:* Allow $\frac{3}{4}$ tablespoon for 2 eggs, 1 tablespoon for 3 eggs.

Eggs : Absolutely fresh. Allow 2 eggs per person for an ideal-sized omelet, but when eggs are scarce, allow 3 for two persons.

Liquid if Used : Water gives a lighter omelet than milk. Allow in the proportion of 1 teaspoon-1 tablespoon per egg, according to taste. Tomato juice or stock can be substituted for the water or milk.

ENGLISH OMELET (Omelette, Soufflé)

3 fresh eggs
Salt and pepper to taste
2 tablespoons tepid water or milk
¾ oz. clarified butter

Basic Recipe: Separate yolks and whites of eggs. Beat yolks till creamy and honey-coloured. Add salt and pepper to taste and liquid. Heat omelet pan and add butter. Beat egg whites to a stiff froth. Fold into egg yolks. Tilt pan until the butter flows round the inside edge. When hot, pour in mixture gently. Cook over brisk heat two or three minutes by which time the omelet should be golden brown below. Slip into the top of a moderate oven, and cook until risen and delicately browned on top. Remove at once. Fold in two and slide out on to a hot plate or dish, with the help of a spatula if necessary. Garnish with parsley. *For 2 persons.*

To Finish Cooking Under Grill: If oven is not in use, finish cooking and brown delicately under grill.

To Vary: Spread with any hot savoury filling before folding.

(1) Beat 1 or 1½ teaspoons minced parsley or chives, or half parsley and half chives, into egg yolks.

(2) Add 2 oz. creamed cooked fish, 3 oz. mushrooms sliced and fried, 1 dessertspoon minced parsley and minced chives, to the egg yolks.

To Vary English Omelet: (3) Before folding, slip in 2 or 3 tablespoons of fried mushrooms, chopped fried bacon and tomato, or creamed smoked haddock.

FRENCH OMELET (Omelette à la Française)

If you want to make a real French omelet, rub the inside of your basin with a cut clove of garlic before adding eggs.

1-1½ oz. butter
4 eggs
Water to taste
Salt and pepper to taste

Basic Recipe; Heat pan. Add butter. Break each egg into a cup, then slip into a basin. Add water, allowing 1½-2 tablespoons, according to taste, then salt and pepper to taste. Beat only till yolks and whites are blended. When butter stops sizzling, gently pour the mixture into pan. With the handle in your left hand, tilt the pan up and down, or lift the edge of mixture as it sets, to allow the running egg to flow underneath. (Don't stir it round and round or the omelet will be more like scrambled eggs.) Keep the pan moving all the time while you are cooking. When lightly set on top, but still creamy, roll over from the handle end and slip on to hot plate or dish, loosening if necessary with a palette knife. Serve at once, garnished with parsley. *For 2 persons.*

VARIATIONS

Asparagus : Cut up enough left-over asparagus tips to give you ¼ pint. Melt 2 oz. butter. Heat till it stops sizzling. Add asparagus. Stir lightly till hot, then add egg mixture. Follow basic recipe.

Bacon : Remove rinds from 3 rashers of lean bacon. Cube bacon. Fry till crisp in the butter. Add ½ teaspoon minced parsley and ½ teaspoon minced chives to egg mixture. Pour into hot fat and bacon. Follow basic recipe, being careful with the salt.

Croûtons : Fry 1 heaped tablespoon diced bread in 1½ oz. butter, till crisp, then stir in egg mixture. Follow basic recipe.

Herb (Aux Fines Herbes) : Add ½ teaspoon minced parsley, 1 teaspoon minced chives and ½ teaspoon minced chervil, or ¼ teaspoon crushed tarragon or thyme to the egg mixture. Double the parsley if liked. Follow basic recipe.

Kidney : Blanch and skin a sheep's kidney and cut into dice. Fry in 1½ oz. butter. Add egg mixture. Follow basic recipe.

Mushroom : Peel and slice 3 oz. mushrooms. Fry in 1½ oz. butter. Add egg mixture and follow basic recipe.

Parsley : Add 1 teaspoon minced parsley to egg mixture before cooking.

Shrimp : Heat 2 tablespoons peeled shrimps in 1½ oz. butter. Add egg mixture. Follow basic recipe.

Tomato : Scald, peel and remove seeds from 3 firm tomatoes. Cut into quarters, then halve the quarters. Heat 1½ tablespoons olive oil in omelet pan. Add tomatoes. Fry gently for 5 minutes. Drain off oil. Stir tomatoes into egg mixture. Follow basic recipe.

TO POACH EGGS

Choose fresh eggs, but don't attempt to poach a new-laid egg. Eggs need to be at least 1½ days old to poach successfully. You need a deep frying-pan or a shallow saucepan and a perforated ladle or skimmer. Fill pan three-quarters full with water, measuring water. Add salt in the proportion of ½ teaspoon to 1 quart of water. Bring water to boiling point. Break egg into a saucer without breaking the yolk. Slip it gently into the water. Add all other eggs to be poached in the same way, then remove pan from stove. Cover. Keep hot at side of stove until eggs are set to taste in 3-4 minutes. If by cooking in this way, some of the yolk still remains yellow, spoon the water over it carefully until coated with a white film. If you prefer, keep the pan on the stove over very low heat so that the water remains below boiling point. When ready, remove with a perforated ladle or skimmer. Drain any water back into pan and place each egg on a round of hot buttered toast or fried bread. Season with pepper to taste.

NOTE : If you find poaching eggs by either of the above methods difficult, brush the inside of muffin rings with melted butter. Place the rings in the water and slip an egg into each, when the water is at boiling point, or use an " egg poacher."

To Vary: Butter a ramekin for each egg required. Separate each yolk and white of egg. Beat white till stiff. Place in ramekin. Slip the yolk into the centre. It must be whole. Lower into pan of water at boiling point. Cover. Leave until set. Slip a pat of butter on top. Season with salt and pepper. Serve in ramekins.

HINTS ON POACHING EGGS

(1) To avoid any chance of egg sticking to bottom of pan, brush pan with olive oil before adding water.

(2) Remove any scum that may arise when poaching in an uncovered pan.

(3) To help to keep eggs in shape, add 1 teaspoon of lemon juice, or a dessertspoon vinegar to a pint of water, or in this proportion no matter the amount of water required.

(4) Poach in milk or tomato juice of the same temperature as the water, using only enough to come half-way up the egg.

(5) Never let the liquid boil after adding the egg.

BATTERED EGGS

Poach as many eggs as you require, then dry each gently in a cloth. Drop 2 or 3 sprigs of parsley into a pan of deep frying fat. Heat fat. Remove parsley. Dip 1 egg at a time into seasoned batter, then slip into fat and fry till golden. Sprinkle with a few drops of lemon juice. Serve at once garnished with parsley.

NEWHAVEN POACHED EGGS (Oeufs Pochés, Newhaven)

6 fish cakes
6 poached eggs
¼ pint cream or mushroom sauce
Pimiento as required

Use fish cakes made from haddock, halibut, sole or smoked fish. Arrange on hot individual plates. Place a poached egg on top of each. Pour sauce over. Garnish each with a cross of pimiento. *For 6 persons.*

SNOWCAPS (Oeufs à la Neige)

2 sheep's kidneys
½ oz. butter
2 tablespoons minced bacon or ham
2 medium-sized peeled tomatoes
Salt and pepper to taste
4 rounds fried bread
4 poached eggs

Dip kidneys in boiling water. Skin and remove cores. Chop roughly and fry in butter for a minute or two till tender. Add bacon or ham. Fry for another minute, then add tomato, salt and pepper to taste. Cook till tomatoes are soft, then spread mixture over croûtes of bread. Top each with a perfectly poached egg. Serve at once on a hot dish. Garnish with paprika. *For 4 persons.*

TO SCRAMBLE EGGS

There are two important points to remember when making scrambled eggs :
(1) They should be cooked very slowly.
(2) They should be stirred constantly.

Basic Recipe: To each egg allow ¼ oz. butter and from 1-2 tablespoons milk, according to taste, and salt and pepper to taste. Choose a fairly strong saucepan of a suitable size.

Break each egg into a cup, and then slip into a basin. Melt butter in a saucepan with half the milk, but do not allow to boil. Beat eggs. Add remainder of milk and seasoning. Beat till blended. Pour into saucepan. Stir over low heat until the mixture begins to set, and " clots." Remove from stove. Stir till creamy. Dish up.

To Serve : (1) Pile on a hot dish. Serve garnished with triangles of fried bread or hot buttered toast, points upwards, and allowing one or two per person. Sprinkle with minced chives or parsley.

(2) Serve on rounds or squares of fried bread or hot buttered toast. Garnish with minced chives, parsley, or paprika.

(3) Cut the crusts off one slice of bread per person. Butter bread on one side and press each slice, buttered side upwards, into a buttered muffin tin, so that the four points are uppermost. Bake in a hot oven, 450° F., for

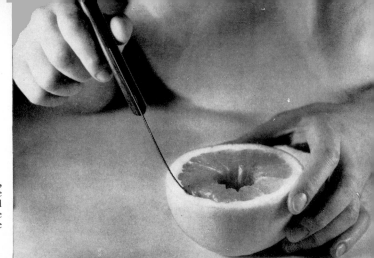

To prepare Grapefruit, first remove membrane in centre with a curved knife, then separate sections and remove pulp from the rind.

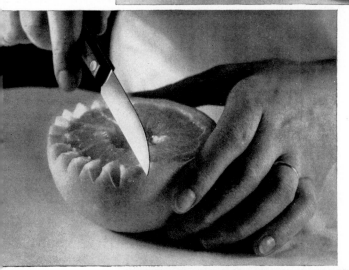

If liked, "vandyke" round edge of rind with a short, sharp knife, then dredge fruit with castor sugar.

Garnish fruit with petals of fresh or frosted mint. *See page 74.*

Serve Fruit Cocktails in squat glasses, placing each on a small plate covered with a paper doily *See pages 73-74.*

Serve Fish Cocktails in squat glasses lined with crisp lettuce leaves. *See page* 71-72.

Serve Jellied Chicken Bouillon in soup cups. *See page* 94.

Arrange any Stuffed Tomato Salads on a bed of crisp lettuce leaves. *See page* 462.

10-15 minutes. Meanwhile, scramble eggs. Pile into each case. Garnish with minced parsley.

To Vary: Add to eggs before scrambling, minced chives or parsley to taste, crushed herbs to taste, or ½ oz. chopped ham or tongue to each egg.

WHEN MAKING SCRAMBLED EGGS WITH 4 EGGS

Chez Moi : Follow basic recipe, but stir 2 tablespoons minced cold ham, flaked Finnan haddock, or 1 each of minced cold chicken and tongue in with the eggs, or add 2 rashers bacon, roughly chopped and fried till crisp, just before eggs begin to set.

Chicken Liver Scramble : Allow 1 cooked, finely-minced liver and add with the eggs. Follow basic recipe.

Mushroom Scramble : Follow basic recipe, adding ¼ lb. chopped cooked mushrooms, or sliced drained bottled mushrooms, after butter is melted.

Pimiento Scramble : Add 1 tablespoon minced pimiento with salt and pepper to egg mixture.

Tomato Scramble : Substitute stewed tomatoes, or tomatoes fried in bacon fat, for the milk when mixing and cooking the eggs.

CHIPOLATA SCRAMBLE (Oeufs Brouillés aux Saucissons)

6 chipolata sausages
1 egg
2 egg yolks
3 tablespoons milk
2 oz. butter
½ teaspoon minced parsley
Pinch of herbs
Salt and pepper to taste
4 slices hot buttered toast

Parboil, skin and mash sausages. Beat egg with yolks, and stir into sausages. Add milk, butter, parsley, herbs, salt and pepper to taste. Place in a saucepan and stir till thickened. Serve piled up on toasts. *For 4 persons.*

TO STEAM EGGS

Butter the cups of an egg poacher. Break an egg into a cup, then slip one at a time into each poacher cup. Place in pan with boiling water below. Cover. Steam for about 3 minutes, or until eggs are as lightly or firmly cooked as required. Loosen the edges with a palette knife. Serve on rounds of buttered toast or fried bread. Dredge lightly with minced parsley or chives. *Allow 1 egg per person.*

To Vary: Spread toast or fried bread first with bloater or kipper paste, and keep warm while you steam the eggs.

If You Haven't an Egg Poacher: Butter as many ramekins as you want. Sprinkle lightly with salt and pepper, and slip an egg into each. Sprinkle top slightly with salt and pepper. Lower into a frying-pan of boiling water coming half-way up the sides of the ramekins. Cover. Let the water simmer for 2 or 3 minutes until the eggs are set to taste. *Allow 1 egg per person.*

BENEDICT EGGS

3 eggs
3 rashers bacon
3 oven scones
Salt, pepper and paprika to taste

Steam eggs. While they are cooking, remove rind from bacon and grill bacon. Toast halved scones and butter them. Slip an egg on three of the halves of scones. Season to taste. Place bacon on remaining half scones. *For 3 persons.*

BACON, HAM, KIDNEY, LIVER AND SAUSAGES

Bacon or ham and eggs is a dish that is known all over the world to be the standard main course on the British breakfast table. Usually the bacon or ham is fried, but sometimes it is grilled. It is not necessary, however, to serve eggs always with bacon or ham. Either can be associated with fried or grilled kidneys, liver, sausages or sausage cakes.

BREAKFAST FRIES OR GRILLS

Fried or Grilled Bacon or Ham with: (1) Fried bread and fried or grilled mushrooms or tomatoes.
(2) Bread or corn fritters.
Fried or Grilled Kidney with: (1) Curls of grilled bacon.
(2) Topped with maître d'hôtel butter. Serve on fried bread.
Fried Calf's, Lamb's or Sheep's Liver with: fried bacon and mushrooms or tomatoes.
Fried or Grilled Sausages with: (1) Fried or grilled bacon and fried apple slices, fried mushrooms, or fried tomatoes.
(2) Corn fritters, corn pancakes or waffles.
(3) Fried bacon and potato cakes.
Fried or Grilled Sausage Cakes: Fry or grill sausage cakes and arrange in a circle round a hot dish. Place a dessertspoon of fried apple on the top of each. Fill the centre with scrambled eggs garnished with paprika or minced parsley.
Bacon and Eggs: Serve with fried bananas, mushrooms or tomatoes, or with fried bread or corn fritters.

To Fry Bacon: Choose streaky, back or gammon rashers as you prefer. The back rashers are the choicest. Remove rind with a pair of scissors. Place either in a cold or slightly-heated frying-pan side by side. Cook slowly till the fat becomes clear, turning frequently, otherwise the bacon won't be evenly cooked. Dish up in overlapping slices. Keep hot. Fry bread, mushrooms, tomatoes, eggs, or other accompaniments in the bacon fat.

To Grill Bacon: Remove rinds. Place rashers side by side on the grill rack. Slip grill rack in grill pan. Place under hot grill. Cook until the fat turns clear, turning frequently, then continue to grill to taste, allowing 2-2½ minutes on each side.

To Fry Liver : Wash in tepid salted water. Dry thoroughly. Cut into slices about ¼ inch thick. Dip in seasoned flour. Fry lightly on both sides in bacon dripping.

Mixed Breakfast Grill : 1 streaky rasher ; 1 sausage ; 1 sheep's kidney ; 1 mushroom ; 1 tomato. *For 1 person.*

GRILLED LIVER AND BACON (Foie de Veau au Lard)

1 lb. calves' liver
2 tablespoons melted butter
Pepper to taste
3 halved rashers of bacon
1 tablespoon minced parsley
6 tablespoons fried croûtons

Cut liver into slices ¼ inch thick. Gash here and there with a sharp knife. Brush with melted butter. Place side by side on the oiled bars of a grill rack. Slip under grill. Grill slowly till half cooked, then season with pepper to taste, and finish cooking. Arrange in overlapping slices on a hot dish. Garnish with grilled bacon or curls of bacon. Throw parsley into remainder of butter in grill pan. Heat and pour over liver. Garnish with fried croûtons. *For 6 persons.*

FISH FOR BREAKFAST

The smoked varieties of fish are more suitable for breakfast than the fresh.

Made-up Fish Dishes Suitable for Breakfast:
Fish cakes ; creamed fish ; fried cod's roe ; creamed smoked haddock ; curried prawns ; kedgeree ; Scotch kedgeree ; smoked haddock with tomatoes; etc. *See* FISH SECTION *for other suitable recipes.*

BAKED SMOKED HADDOCK

2 medium-sized haddocks
2 tablespoons milk
½ cup stale breadcrumbs
Black pepper to taste
Salt as required
1 oz. butter

Dip fish for a moment or two in boiling water, then skin and drain. Dip in milk, then in crumbs. Place side by side in a well greased fireproof dish. Season with black pepper and salt as required. Dab with butter. Bake in a moderately hot oven, 375° F, for about 20 minutes, basting with the butter at half-time. Dish up. Garnish if liked with grilled curls of bacon, otherwise sprinkle with melted butter. *For 4 persons.*

FISH TOASTS (Croûtes de Poisson)

1 lb. boiled smoked haddock or canned salmon
1 oz. butter

Weigh haddock free from skin and bone. (If using salmon, drain thoroughly and remove any skin or bone.) Melt butter in a saucepan. Add

2 tablespoons flour
1 pint hot milk
Salt and pepper to taste
2 chopped hard-boiled eggs

flour. Stir till smooth. Stir in milk gradually. Cook till smooth. Flake and add fish. Season to taste. Stir till piping hot, then add eggs. Serve on hot buttered toast or fried bread. (If preferred, add only the whites, and garnish the toasts with the sieved egg yolk.) *For 6 persons.*

FRIED HERRINGS, SCOTS WAY (Harengs, Ecossaise)

Clean fish and remove backbones carefully. Season with salt and pepper to taste. Dip in medium oatmeal. Press it gently into the flesh, then stand for a little while before cooking. Melt enough butter to cover the bottom of a frying-pan. Fry fish on skin side first, then on the other, till oatmeal is crisp and golden brown. Fry the roes, dipped in flour, alongside. Serve herrings, each with a little fried roe and a pat of unsalted butter on top. *Allow 1 or 2 per person.*

STEWED OR CREAMED SMOKED HADDOCK

If using an Arbroath haddock, place it in a shallow dish. Cover with boiling water. Leave till cool, then the skin and bone will come away easily. If using a Finnan or Moray Firth haddock, halve or cut into 4 fillets, according to size. Cover with boiling water. Stand till cool, then remove skin. Bone only if liked. Melt 1 oz. butter in a saucepan. Stir in ½ oz. flour. When frothy, stir in ½ pint hot milk by degrees. Stir till smooth and boiling. Add fish. Season with black pepper and salt as required. Cover and simmer for 3 or 4 minutes, till creamy, then add 2 chopped hard-boiled eggs. Serve with hot toast. *For 2 or 4 persons, depending on size.*

BREAKFAST CAKES

There are quite a number of savoury cakes that can be substituted for fried bread or toast as an accompaniment to bacon or sausages. For other suitable savoury cakes, for example, corn fritters, potato cakes, *see the* VEGETABLE SECTION.

BREAD FRITTERS (Beignets de Pain)

2 oz. flour
Pinch of salt
2 teaspoons melted butter
½ gill tepid water
1 egg white
4 slices bread

Sift flour into a basin with the salt. Make a hollow in centre. Add butter. Stir till smooth, then gradually beat in the water. Beat egg white till stiff and fold in. Remove crusts from bread. Dip each slice in milk, then into the batter. Fry in deep smoking hot fat till golden brown. Drain on absorbent paper. Serve as a garnish to 8 rashers of fried or grilled bacon. *For 4 persons.*

HAM CRISPS (Sandwiches de Jambon)

½ lb. cold boiled ham
¼ teaspoon made mustard
8 slices stale bread
2 cups milk
2 beaten eggs
2 oz. butter

Put ham through a meat grinder with a fine knife. Stir in mustard. Make into 4 sandwiches with the stale bread. Press each firmly. Stir milk into eggs. Beat slightly. Dip each sandwich in this mixture. Melt butter in a frying pan. Add sandwiches. Fry till brown below, then turn and fry on the other side. Serve hot, garnished if liked with slices of fried tomato, or fried mushrooms. *For 4 persons.*

HAM PANCAKES (Crêpes de Jambon)

5 oz. flour
Salt and pepper to taste
½ teaspoon baking powder
2 beaten eggs
½ pint milk
¼ lb. chopped boiled ham
1 teaspoon minced parsley

Sift flour, salt, pepper and baking powder into a basin. Make a hollow in the centre. Stir in eggs, diluted with half the milk. Beat well. Stir in remainder of milk, ham, parsley and more seasoning if required. Cover the bottom of a frying-pan with melted fat. Fry the batter by pouring it from a tablespoon in rounds into the hot fat, keeping rounds about an inch apart. When golden brown below, turn and brown on other side. Serve with fried or grilled sausages, or garnish with fried mushrooms or fried halved tomatoes. *For 2 or 3 persons.*

RICE PANCAKES (Crêpes de Riz)

2 oz. flour
½ teaspoon salt
½ teaspoon baking powder
4 tablespoons milk
1 beaten egg
2 cups boiled rice

Sift flour with salt and baking powder into a basin. Gradually stir in remaining ingredients. Melt enough fat in a frying-pan to cover the bottom. Drop batter from a tablespoon in rounds about 1 inch apart. Fry till golden brown below, then turn and brown on other side. Serve as an accompaniment to fried or grilled bacon or pork sausages. *For 4 persons.*

HAM WAFFLES

2 cups sifted flour
¼ teaspoon bicarbonate of soda
2 teaspoons baking powder
½ teaspoon salt
1 tablespoon sugar
2 separated eggs
1¾ cups sour milk
⅛ cup melted butter
¼ cup minced ham

Sift flour with bicarbonate of soda, baking powder and salt into a basin. Add sugar. Mix egg yolks with milk. Beat well, then mix in butter. Beat into flour mixture. Beat till you get a smooth batter. Gently fold in stiffly beaten egg whites. Pour into waffle iron. Sprinkle with the minced ham. Close iron and cook. If liked, sugar may be omitted. *For 4 persons.*

Appetisers

Appetisers are tantalizing kickshaws that pique the appetite.

Nowadays they are nearly as popular in Britain as they are in France. One of the reasons for this is that by serving a cold course at the beginning of a meal, the cook is given time to put the finishing touches to the next course which can only be undertaken at the last minute.

The secret of providing an attractive appetiser as a first course is to offer a selection of piquant titbits, known as hors d'oeuvres, that will stimulate the appetite. It's not even necessary to offer a choice of the latter. You can start with an individual hors d'oeuvre, if you prefer, such as tomatoes filled with a game, meat or poultry salad, or with smoked salmon, or a smoked trout, etc.

When selecting from the recipes I am giving, remember to adapt the quantity or size of appetiser according to the number of courses to follow. This is important. If a three-course meal, allow more hors d'oeuvres than you would for a formal dinner party or banquet consisting of 5 or 6 courses.

CAVIARE

Beluga is the best, but it does not carry well. It comes from a fish called Beluga, a member of the sturgeon family. Its eggs are large and grey. Sevruga, the next best, is of the same colour, but the eggs are smaller. There are many other varieties of caviare, such as the roe of the sturgeon proper which varies in colour from grey to black. Red caviare is made from the roe of any fish, but most frequently of the grey mullet or sea carp.

To Serve Caviare: (1) Chill. If sold in a pot, place pot on a plate covered with a lace paper doily. Serve with a bone spoon. If sold in a tin, turn it out into a chilled glass dish. Serve like potted caviare. When the weather is hot, better to imbed pot or tin in a bowl of cracked ice. Garnish with butterflies or wedges of lemon. Serve with Melba toast, butter balls and cayenne pepper, if liked.

FISH COCKTAILS (Coupes de Poisson)

Fish cocktails make an appetising and attractive first course, especially in hot weather. Make heart of lettuce leaves into individual nests or cups on serving plates, or line large tulip-shaped glasses with them. Fill with dressed fish. Sprinkle lightly with cayenne pepper or paprika to taste. Serve in orange or tomato shells, scalloped round edges with scissors, if preferred.

Fish for Cocktails: Crab, crawfish, crayfish, halibut, lobster, mussels, oysters, prawns, salmon, scallops, shrimps and turbot.

To Prepare Fish: All the fish cocktails given are made from cooked fish, except the mussel and oyster. Shred crab. Dice or flake crawfish, crayfish, halibut, lobster, salmon, scallops and turbot, but be sure to remove the beard from the scallops after cooking them. Leave the mussels, oysters, prawns and shrimps whole, but beard oysters. If liked, sprinkle with pepper or paprika and lemon juice. Coat with cocktail sauce. Chill.

To Garnish Fish Cocktails: Crab : use the smallest claws. Crawfish and Lobster : use coral when present. *To garnish any fish cocktail:* Plant a sprig of chervil, fennel, parsley, or a tip of celery foliage in the centre of each. When serving fish cocktails in the shells of oranges or tomatoes, put a wreath of fennel, mustard and cress, smilax or watercress tips round the base.

Fish Required: 1½ cups prepared fish. *For 6 persons.*

Sauce Required: 1 cup sauce. *For 6 persons.*

HORSERADISH SAUCE (Sauce de Raifort Froide)

2 tablespoons grated horse-radish
2 tablespoons lemon juice
¼ pint tomato ketchup
5 tablespoons chilli sauce
1 teaspoon chopped chives or green pepper
Dash of salt

Mix ingredients in order given. Chill thoroughly and use. *For 4 or 5 cocktails.*

TARRAGON MAYONNAISE SAUCE (Sauce d'Estragon)

¼ pint mayonnaise
2 tablespoons tomato ketchup
1 tablespoon chilli sauce
1 teaspoon lemon juice
1 tablespoon tarragon vinegar
Dash of tabasco
Dash of celery salt

Mix ingredients in order given. Chill thoroughly and use. *For 6 cocktails.*

SCALLOP COCKTAIL

Allow 1 boiled scallop to each cocktail. Cut in small pieces the size of a prawn. Chill. Place in cocktail glasses lined with lettuce leaves. Coat with cocktail sauce to taste.

SEAFOOD COCKTAILS (Coupes de Poissons Assorties)

These are sometimes made with a mixture of shellfish, or with a combination of shellfish and halibut, salmon or turbot.

(1) Mix 1 cup diced, boiled halibut with $\frac{1}{2}$ cup prawns. Coat with 1 cup cocktail sauce.

(2) Mix 1 cup flaked boiled salmon with $\frac{1}{2}$ cup picked shrimps. Coat with 1 cup cocktail sauce.

(3) Mix 1 cup diced boiled turbot with $\frac{1}{2}$ cup shredded crab. Coat with 1 cup cocktail sauce.

(4) Mix $\frac{3}{4}$ lb. flaked boiled salmon with 2 oz. prawns and 2 oz. picked shrimps. Coat with $\frac{1}{4}$ pint sauce tartare. If liked, add 2 or 3 tablespoons diced peeled cucumber. *For 6 persons.*

NOTE : Always remove the black thread on the back of prawns before using.

FRUIT CUP COCKTAILS (Coupes de Fruit)

Fruit cup cocktails can be served as a first course at lunch, dinner or supper in place of soup. The success of them depends on their being well chilled and on the combination of fruit used. They are specially welcome in the spring and summer months. If a mixed cocktail is wanted, be sure to choose a judicious mixture of both bitter and sweet fruit, such as grapefruit and pineapple ; grapefruit, strawberries and tinned peaches ; and grapefruit and cantaloup melon. A fruit cocktail should be rather sharp in flavour and not syrupy. When planning your menus, be careful not to end with dessert when starting with a fruit cocktail. Allow $\frac{1}{2}$ cup per person. Chill well. Serve in grapefruit or cocktail glasses or in " shells " made from grapefruit or large oranges.

To Garnish: Place a maraschino cherry, a blackberry, raspberry or strawberry, or 1 teaspoon grated pineapple in the centre of each glass of cocktail, or use a sprig of fresh mint, one or two petals of frosted mint, or a cherry frozen in lemon juice. In the latter case, add no lemon juice to the fruit cocktail. It is also possible to garnish cocktails by arranging berries, cherries, or small grapes in a design on top of each cocktail.

If liked, substitute a vine leaf, or a spray of maidenhair, for the doily on the plates.

APPLE COCKTAILS (Coupes de Pomme)

2 cups apple juice
3 tablespoons lemon or orange juice

Chill the apple juice. Add lemon juice or orange juice and gingerale. Dip rims of 6 large cocktail glasses in lemon or orange juice, then in caster

1 pint chilled gingerale
¼ pint diced dessert apple
6 chopped glacé cherries

sugar. Divide apple equally between the glasses, then divide the apple juice mixture. Sprinkle with the chopped cherries. Serve at once. *For 6 persons.*

AVOCADO COCKTAIL VINAIGRETTE

Chill firm avocados, then peel and slice. Soak for about 5 minutes in chilled French dressing. Serve in lettuce nests on individual plates. Sprinkle with cayenne pepper or mint. *Allow 1 avocado between 2 or 4 persons.*

CARMEN COCKTAILS (Coupes à la Carmen)

2 cups grapefruit sections
2 teaspoons caster sugar
1 teaspoon lemon juice
2 cups small strawberries
8 sprigs fresh mint (small)

Place the grapefruit sections in a basin. Sprinkle with caster sugar, then lemon juice. Chill. Divide equally between 8 sundae glasses. Lightly stir ¼ cup chilled strawberries into each cocktail. Plant a sprig of mint in the centre. If liked, a teaspoon of kirsch, curacao, Grand Marnier or Maraschino can be added to each cocktail just before serving. *For 8 persons.*

GOOSEBERRY COCKTAILS (Coupes de Groseilles)

3 cups bottled or dessert goose-berries
1 tablespoon pineapple syrup
1 cup grapefruit juice
Dash of brandy if liked
6 maraschino cherries

If using fresh gooseberries, top, tail and wash. Mix pineapple syrup with the grapefruit juice. Add to berries. Chill. Add brandy. Divide equally between 6 cocktail glasses. Sprinkle with chopped cherries. *For 6 persons.*

HONEY DEW COCKTAILS (Coupes de Melon à la Menthe)

Large honeydew melon
1 bunch mint
4 tablespoons caster sugar
1 cup boiling water

Scoop out the flesh of the melon with a potato ball cutter. Wash and dry the mint thoroughly. Chop finely without crushing it. Cover with sugar and water. Stand for half an hour. Strain and pour over melon balls. Leave till cold. Serve very cold with a few drops of Créme de Menthe poured over each cocktail. *For 6 persons.*

MELON COCKTAILS (Coupes de Melon)

1 cup melon balls
1 firm sweet apple
2 tablespoons maraschino syrup
1 cup seeded, skinned grapes
1 or 2 grains salt
6 maraschino cherries

With a potato ball cutter, cut out melon balls and apple balls. Place in a basin. Add syrup, grapes and salt. Chill well. Divide equally between 6 grapefruit glasses. Garnish each with a cherry. Add 1 teaspoon Grand Marnier to each cocktail. *For 6 persons.*

PINEAPPLE COCKTAILS (Coupes d'Anana)

1 cup diced fresh pineapple
Caster sugar to taste
Juice of ½ lemon
½ cup small strawberries
Dash of brandy or Grand Marnier

Peel and remove eyes from pineapple, then cut all the fruit away from the stem. Dice. Place in a basin. Sprinkle with caster sugar to taste and stand for 12 hours. Chill. Hull and rinse berries. Halve if large. Divide equally between 4 cocktail glasses. Sprinkle to taste with brandy or Grand Marnier. *For 4 persons.*

UGLI COCKTAILS

2 large uglis
Juice of 1 lemon
Dash of Kirsch or Maraschino

Peel fruit. Halve and with a sharp knife, carefully remove pulp from sections into a basin. Add lemon juice, Kirsch or Maraschino to taste and divide equally between 6 fruit cocktail glasses. Garnish with a maraschino cherry and a sprig of frosted or fresh mint. Chill and serve. *For 6 persons.*

To Vary: Remove sections from uglis and squeeze off juice. Add lemon juice and Kirsch or Maraschino to taste and serve in cocktail glasses as a fruit juice cocktail.

GRAPEFRUIT

Grapefruit should always be served chilled. Halve with a stainless knife. Sprinkle with 1 heaped teaspoon caster sugar.

For Breakfast: Chill in refrigerator overnight.

For Lunch or Dinner: Place a Maraschino cherry in the centre of each, or fill the hollows with grated pineapple or a fresh berry in season, or place a tiny sprig of fresh mint or two petals of frosted mint in the centre.

To Prepare Grapefruit: Wash and dry grapefruit. Cut in half. With a curved knife, separate flesh from the membrane and from the skin. Remove core or pithy skins with scissors. Sprinkle with sugar to taste. Chill.

If grapefruit is not of a good shape, loosen pulp from membrane with a grapefruit knife and scrape out pulp with a pointed grapefruit spoon as well as the juice from the sections. Sweeten to taste. Chill. Serve in grapefruit glasses, or in china containers sold for this purpose. Another way of serving grapefruit is to prepare it in its shell and then place it in a silver container lined with packed ice.

MELON (Melon)

Wrap melons in kitchen paper or tie in a cellophane bag, then chill in an ice box or in a refrigerator. Halve if small. If large, cut in wedges. Remove seeds and any stringy portions. If small, serve each half on individual plates, and place a tablespoon of cracked ice or fresh berries on each portion. Pass round with the melon a dish of ground ginger and a sugar sifter.

Cantaloup, Honeydew or Tiger Melons: Chill and wipe melon. Halve, then remove seeds. Cut in wedges. Serve arranged in a circle, peel side downwards, on a large glass or silver dish, or on a fruit plate lined with ferns or geranium leaves. Serve with ground ginger and sugar.

Water Melon: Chill for 12 to 24 hours. Wipe. Remove a slice from each end. Halve lengthwise, then cut in wedges. Serve like cantaloup melon.

OYSTERS (Huîtres)

Do not open oysters until they are required. As soon as you bring them home, slip them into a basin of cold water. Add two handfuls of fine oatmeal, and use oysters as you want them. Wash, scrub and dry shells, then, with a cloth in your left hand, take up one oyster at a time, with its deep shell downwards. Insert a sharp knife between the edges of the shells, at the valve side, and cut through. Line serving plates with cracked ice, then arrange 4 or 6 oysters on each plate, in the deep shells, with small ends of shells to the centre. Place two fingers or a quarter of lemon on the ice in the centre of each plate, and decorate with a sprig of parsley, if liked. If oysters are chilled in an ice box or refrigerator for 15 minutes before serving, it is not necessary to serve them on ice-lined plates. *Allow 4 to 6 per person.*

Accompaniments to Oysters: Arrange thin brown bread and butter in slices overlapping each other on a plate lined with a lace paper doily. Serve also with oyster crackers, tabasco and cayenne pepper, and with tarragon or chilli vinegar, if liked.

TO VARY SERVICE OF OYSTERS

(1) Put a scalloped lemon shell coated with tomato cocktail sauce in the centre of each plate, or use a squat glass for the sauce.

(2) Season oysters to taste with lemon juice, salt and tabasco. Place in scalloped grapefruit shells. Garnish each portion with grated horseradish. Serve on plates lined with lace paper doilies.

(3) *Oyster Iceberg:* Take a large oblong of clear ice and, with a hot iron, melt a hollow in the centre large enough to hold oysters you wish to serve. Drain water off as fast as the ice melts. Place the prepared block of ice on a dish lined with a folded table napkin. Arrange sprigs of parsley and quarters of lemon, or maidenhair fern and lemon, round the base. Open oyster shells and turn oysters into the hollow in " iceberg." Serve at once with cocktail sauce.

PATES (Pâtés)

Pâtés are always a popular first course. They are served alone or as part of a mixed hors d'oeuvre. You can buy the most succulent pâté de foie gras in terrines. Serve pâtes chilled and sliced with Melba toast, butter balls and cut lemon, if liked. If served from a terrine, place on a plate lined with a lace paper doily and garnish with parsley. If turned out, garnish with watercress and radish roses.

CHICKEN LIVER PATE (Pâté de Foie de Volaille)

½ lb. chicken livers
1 egg
1 oz. butter or margarine
1 medium-sized onion
Salt and pepper to taste
½ teaspoon crushed dried herbs

Wash the livers. Drop in boiling salted water. Simmer gently till cooked through. Drain well. Chop finely and place in a bowl. Boil eggs till hard, then shell and chop coarsely. Melt fat in a small frying-pan. Peel and chop onion and add to fat. Fry slowly until soft and clear, then add liver and egg. Season to taste with salt and pepper, and add herbs, if liked. Beat until blended. Shape into a little loaf or pack into a terrine. Chill before serving.

CHICKEN AND DUCK PATES (Pâté à la Lyons)

3 chicken livers
3 duck livers
1 tablespoon butter
1 tablespoon minced onion
Salt and pepper to taste
1 dessertspoon chopped truffle
1 teaspoon brandy or sherry

Wipe livers with a damp cloth. Melt butter in a frying-pan. Add livers. Fry slowly till cooked, turning occasionally. Remove from pan. Fry onion till clear and soft, and put through a sieve with the liver. If liked, add 1 tablespoon chopped boiled ham before sieving. If too dry, add a little more butter, but cream it before beating into the purée. Season to taste with salt and pepper. Stir in truffle, and gradually beat in brandy or sherry. Pour into a meat jar or pot. Run clarified butter over the top. Chill before serving.

DUCK, GOOSE AND PORK PATE (Pâté à l'Avignon)

1 duck's liver
1 goose's liver
8 oz. streaky pork
3 truffles
Salt and pepper to taste
Pinch of ground mace
1 teaspoon port wine

Wipe livers with a damp cloth. Put pork through a meat grinder. Peel and quarter truffles. Chop peelings. Season pork with salt, pepper and ground mace, and stir in wine and truffle peelings. Grease the bottom of a small fireproof dish. Spread half pork over bottom. Sprinkle with the quartered truffles. Add the goose liver. Season to taste with salt and pepper. Cover with the duck liver, then with remainder of pork. Cover closely. Place in a baking tin containing enough warm water to come an inch up side of dish. Bake in a slow oven, 300° F., for about 1½ hours. Remove from stove. Leave till tepid, then uncover and weight down. Drain off gravy. Fill up with melted goose or pork fat. When required, scrape off fat, then turn out and remove remainder of fat. Coat with aspic or meat jelly, if liked. Chill and serve.

MOCK FOIE GRAS (Pâté de Veau)

1 calf's liver
1 calf's tongue
½ cup melted butter or margarine
¼ teaspoon cayenne pepper
¼ teaspoon ground cloves

Wash the liver and tongue. Place each in a separate saucepan. Cover with slightly salted water. Cover and simmer gently till tender. Remove from pan. Leave till cold and firm. Slice liver, then pound in a mortar, gradually

1 dessertspoon Worcester sauce
1 teaspoon made mustard
1 teaspoon onion juice
1 tablespoon Madeira or sherry

adding the butter or margarine as you pound. If you add it too quickly the mixture may curdle. When into a smooth paste, add all the seasonings and the onion juice, then the wine. Pack a layer firmly into a jar. Pare and cut up the tongue into small slivers. Arrange some slivers over pâté. Cover with another layer of pâté and fill up with pâté and tongue in this way. Pack down firmly. When jars are almost full, run a layer of clarified butter over the top of each. Cover and store in a cool place till required.

POTTED SHRIMPS (Crevettes au Beurre)

Chill. Serve either from the carton in which they are sold, or from the pot in which you have potted them, with Melba toast, and butter, or on a croûte of crisply fried bread. Garnish with cayenne pepper.

PRAWNS (Crevettes)

Serve without shelling, suspended round the rim of a glass bowl filled with ice. Decorate ice with fingers of lemon and parsley. Serve with mayonnaise. Allow 8 to 10 prawns per person.

Another way is to fill a large salad bowl with cracked ice, and sink a smaller bowl of the same shape in the centre filled with prawns. If liked, sink an even smaller bowl or a scalloped grapefruit shell of mayonnaise inside that. Garnish with watercress and poise slit halved slices of lemon on rim of bowl, allowing one per person.

SMOKED SALMON (Saumon Fumé)

Allow 1½ oz. of thinly sliced smoked salmon, cut across the grain, per person. Arrange overlapping each other on a dish lined with a lace paper doily or serve directly on to individual plates. Garnish with sprigs of parsley or fennel, and lemon butterflies. Serve with Melba toast and butter balls. Sometimes arranged in rolls or cornucopias on plates. If liked, chop salmon. Pile on canapés of fried bread about 3 inches across. Sprinkle lightly with paprika and lemon juice.

MIXED HORS D'OEUVRES (Hors d'Oeuvres Variés)

Give at least four varieties of hors d'oeuvre. Here is an example : Egg mayonnaise, sardines, potato salad, and pickled cabbage. If five are wanted, include sliced smoked salmon, liver sausage or pâté. If six, add either smoked fillets of herring to the assortment or Avocado, Russian or tomato salad.

To Serve: Place each variety in a separate compartment of an hors d'oeuvre dish, or, if you haven't got one, use a large round platter and arrange each variety according to taste. You may serve the hors d'oeuvre on individual plates, or in a group of small dishes so that people can help themselves. Serve with hot croissants, fresh crisp rolls heated, or Melba toast and butter balls.

Garnishes : Celery foliage, sprigs of chervil, radish roses, sprigs of parsley, chopped chives, paprika, slivers of red and green peppers, mustard and cress and watercress.

Relishes : Black, green or stuffed olives, crisp celery sticks, pickled onions, spring onions, sour and sweet pickled gherkins, trimmed crisp radishes. Arrange dishes of one or more relishes on the table when serving an hors d'oeuvre course, such as celery and olives, radishes and spring onions, gherkins and pickled onions.

Portions per Head : Allow 1 sardine or 1 fillet of smoked herring, 1 or 2 slices liver sausage or salami, or one of each and 2 heaped tablespoons potato salad or 1 of potato salad and 1 of Russian salad, if a second salad is served, and a tablespoon pickled beetroot or red cabbage per person. Introduce a tablespoon egg mayonnaise, a wafer of smoked salmon or a tablespoon of baked beans in tomato sauce when a larger variety is wanted.

SINGLE HORS D'OEUVRES

Pass single hors d'oeuvres round on a platter, or serve on individual plates.

BASQUE SALAD (Salade à la Basque)

½ can tunny fish
½ cup canned green peas
1 small sliced beetroot
Mayonnaise as required
2 peeled tomatoes

Flake fish and toss with peas and beetroot in mayonnaise to coat. Serve in an hors d'oeuvre dish as an individual course. Garnish with slices of tomato. *For 4 persons.*

HERRING SALAD (Salade d'Harengs)

4 fillets soused herring
6 cold boiled potatoes
½ cup diced beetroot
2 pickled gherkins
Salt and black pepper to taste
Vinegar to moisten
4 tablespoons mayonnaise
Lettuce & chives or parsley

Cut herring into dice. Dice potatoes. Add to herring with beetroot. Slice and chop gherkins, and add to salad with salt and black pepper to taste. Sprinkle with vinegar, then coat with mayonnaise. Serve in a salad bowl lined with lettuce leaves. Garnish with minced chives or parsley. Serve as a single hors d'oeuvre. *For 4 persons.*

ASPARAGUS WITH EGGS (Asperges au Diable)

24 boiled asparagus stalks
2 devilled eggs
4 teaspoons tomato mayonnaise
Vinaigrette sauce as required

Arrange cold boiled asparagus in 4 bundles in the shape of a cross, with the ends to the centre. Cut the eggs in halves lengthwise, then stuff. See page 79. Place a half egg between each bundle of asparagus with its pointed end to the centre. Top each with a teaspoon of tomato mayonnaise. Fill centre of dish with sprigs of watercress. Serve with Vinaigrette Sauce.

ASPARAGUS WITH HOLLANDAISE SAUCE
(Asperges à l'Hollandaise)

36 boiled asparagus stalks
6 strips pimiento
½ pint Hollandaise sauce

Arrange asparagus in bundles of 6 round the platter with tips to the outside. " Tie " each bundle together round the centre with a narrow strip of pimento, tucking the ends below. Fill a shallow butter or jam dish with the sauce. Place in centre of dish. Chill. Cover rim of sauce dish with sprigs of watercress. Dredge sauce lightly with paprika. *For 6 persons.*

EGG AND SARDINE MOUSSE (Mousse d'Oeufs à la Bretonne)

3 hard-boiled eggs
1 dozen small sardines
1 walnut butter
Salt and pepper to taste
Pinch of celery salt
½ teaspoon onion juice
Cream as required
6 rounds of bread, 2 inches across

Shell and chop eggs. Rub through a sieve. Bone sardines. Rub through a sieve. Cream butter and gradually beat in egg and sardine purée. Season with salt, pepper and celery salt to taste. Stir in onion juice, and cream as required. Fry rounds of bread in butter, hot oil or bacon fat till crisp and gold on both sides. Drain on paper. When cold, force purée in a pyramid on centre of each canapé. If liked, scald and peel 2 firm tomatoes about 1½ inches across. Thinly remove blossom ends and stalk ends and cut remaining tomato in 3 equal-thick slices. Place a slice on each canapé. Force purée on top. Dredge lightly with minced chives or parsley. *For 6 persons.*

STUFFED EGGS (Oeufs Farcis)

Cut 4 hard-boiled eggs in halves lengthwise. Remove yolks. Combine with one of the following fillings :

Caviare Filling : Crush egg yolks with a fork. Mix with 1 teaspoon chopped chives or onion, ½ teaspoon lemon juice, 1 tablespoon caviare, and thick cream to moisten. Stuff egg whites. Sprinkle with finely chopped capers or black or green olives, or dredge lightly with paprika. Serve each half on a crisp lettuce leaf. *Allow 2 per person.*
If preferred, substitute mayonnaise for cream. Substitute watercress for chives or onion and flavour with onion juice.

Crab Filling : Crush yolks with a fork. Add ½ teaspoon dry mustard, ½ teacup shredded crab, 1 dessertspoon chopped green pepper, ½ teacup finely chopped celery, and about 4 tablespoons mayonnaise to moisten. Stuff egg whites, piling them high with the mixture. Arrange each on an oval slice of fried bread. Garnish with chopped chives.

Fish Filling : Fill egg whites with chopped, boned sardines, flaked tuna fish, or chopped freshly boiled salmon mixed with chopped anchovies to taste. Season to taste. Mash the yolks with mayonnaise to moisten. Cover the filling with this mixture. Sprinkle lightly with cayenne pepper and minced chives or parsley. Serve each on an oval of fried bread to fit. *Allow 1 stuffed egg per person.*

Vegetable Filling : Rub yolks through a sieve. Mix ½ cup sliced cooked shredded French or runner beans with 1 tablespoon shredded boiled carrot, 1 tablespoon shredded boiled beetroot, about 2 tablespoons mayonnaise, salt, cayenne pepper and paprika to taste. If liked, substitute celery for the carrots. Pat mixture into egg white shells. Sprinkle with the yolks and very finely chopped chives or parsley.

NEWHAVEN CANAPES (Canapés à la Newhaven)

1 fillet of cooked smoked herring
1 peeled cooking apple
2 cold boiled potatoes
1 tablespoon shredded celery
3 tablespoons minced beetroot
French dressing as required
8 canapés
8 cooked button mushrooms

Chop herring. Core and chop apple. Slice and chop potatoes. Mix till blended. Stir in celery and beetroot, and French dressing to moisten. Divide equally between 8 canapés of toast or fried bread. Dredge lightly with paprika. Top each with a fried mushroom in centre. *For 8 persons.*

SOUSED FISH ROES (Laitances à la Vinaigrette)

1 lb. fish roes
1 sliced medium sized carrot
2 chopped celery stalks
1 sliced medium sized onion
1 bay leaf
2 sprigs parsley
6 black peppercorns
2 cloves
1 blade mace
Vinegar or white wine and water

Wash roes and place in a greased shallow fireproof dish. Sprinkle with the carrot, celery stalks, onion, bay leaf, parsley, peppercorns, cloves and mace. Cover with equal quantity of vinegar or white wine and water. Bake in a moderate oven, 350° F., till cooked through. Time depends on the size of the roes. Cool. Serve on individual plates, arranging roes on top of small mound of potato salad. Garnish with watercress. *For 6 persons.*

SNAILS (Escargots)

The snails that fatten in the vineyards of Burgoyne are considered the finest. It is usually this variety which is imported into Britain, and sold ready to eat. Serve half a dozen per person, with crisp French bread or rolls, or Melba toast and butter.

STUFFED TOMATOES (Tomates Farcies)

To Prepare for Stuffing: Wash 6 large firm tomatoes. Remove a slice from the top of each tomato and carefully scrape out the pulp without breaking the shells. Sprinkle inside with salt and pepper. Turn upside down on a rack to drain and chill. Fill with poultry or meat salad, or one of the following :

CHICKEN LIVER STUFFING (Farce de Foie de Volaille)

½ cup chopped cooked chicken liver or sweetbreads
1 teaspoon minced onion
½ clove garlic
1 chopped hard-boiled egg
1 tablespoon finely shredded celery
Salt and cayenne pepper to taste
1 chopped stuffed olive

Mix liver or sweetbreads with the onion. Chop and add garlic, egg, celery, salt and pepper to taste, and olive, then mix with cream or mayonnaise. Pack into tomatoes. Ornament filling with the prongs of a fork. Arrange on crisp heart of lettuce leaves. Garnish with mustard and cress, or watercress, and stuffed olives, if liked.

MUSHROOM STUFFING (Farce de Champignons)

1 lb. minced peeled mushrooms
Juice of 1 lemon
Salt and pepper to taste
5 oz. chopped boiled or steamed potatoes
¼ pint cold cooked green peas
1 heaped teaspoon minced parsley
1 teaspoon chopped fennel
½ teaspoon chopped tarragon

Prepare tomatoes for stuffing, and rub inside with salt and garlic. Fry the mushrooms in butter for preference, otherwise in hot oil, and drain well. Add lemon juice and salt and pepper to taste. Stir in potatoes and leave until cold. Add mushrooms, peas, parsley, fennel and tarragon. Stir until blended, then stir in mayonnaise to moisten. Chill. Stuff tomatoes. Dredge with paprika.

SHELLFISH STUFFING (Farce de Coquillage)

1 cup flaked crab, chopped crawfish or lobster
4 tablespoons chopped hard-boiled egg
2 tablespoons shredded lettuce heart

Mix shellfish with egg and lettuce heart. Coat with mayonnaise. Stuff tomato shells. Garnish filling with chopped gherkin or green pepper. *For 4 tomato shells.*

Soups

Uncooked meat is the basis of all good stocks. Good stock is the basis of all good soups, except meatless (maigre). Stock is also required for the foundation of many gravies and sauces, and for using in certain made-up dishes.

CLASSES OF STOCKS

Brown : Brown stock is generally made from shin of beef and cracked bones. If wanted for consommé, knuckle of veal or a calf's foot must be added because beef lacks the gelatinous substance that characterises good consommé. Chicken stock may be used as part of the liquid required. When a rich brown stock is wanted, allow $\frac{1}{4}$ lb. ham, 2 lb. shin of beef, 2 lb. knuckle of veal to 2 quarts water.

Fish : Fish stock is usually made from water and any variety of fish, except those of the oily class, and trimmings of fish, fish heads or shellfish. Any dark skin must be removed before using fish for stock.

Game : Game stock can be made from carcases of game or joints of boned game and second brown stock, unless a rich game stock is wanted for game consommé, when chicken or veal stock should be used in place of the second brown stock.

Vegetable (Brown and White) **:** This is made from vegetables and water, and can be light or dark, depending upon the vegetables used. Mushroom stalks and peelings can be added to enrich the colour and flavour.

White : Should be made with any white meat, such as chicken, rabbit, turkey or veal (with or without their bones), or calf's head or feet. When a rich white stock is wanted, use a combination of chicken, rabbit, turkey, veal and a calf's foot.

Stock can also be made from bones or carcases, or both. Beef or mutton bones provide a good stock for kidney, potato, tomato or vegetable soup, etc. The trimmings of neck of lamb provide excellent stock for barley or Scotch broth, or any other soup for which lamb or mutton on their bones are required. Veal bones, the carcase of a chicken, or both, make a good stock for cream soups. The well-scrubbed shank of a ham gives you good stock for bean, dried green pea, lentil or split pea soup.

HINTS ON STOCK MAKING

1. *Suitable Meat:* Beef: leg and shin: lamb: neck: mutton: scrag end: knuckle of veal.
Never use pork for making stock. Chop meat into inch cubes and remove any fat before putting it into a stock pot.

2. Allow 1 quart cold water to each pound of meat and bones and 1 quart extra.

3. Allow 2/3 lean meat and 1/3 bones when possible. Chop or saw bones very small before using.

4. Allow 1 clove, 4 peppercorns, $\frac{1}{2}$ bay leaf, 1 small sprig parsley, $\frac{1}{4}$ lb. onion, 1 sprig thyme, 1 stick celery, 1 trimmed leek, 1 medium-sized carrot and 1 thick slice parsnip and turnip to 1 lb. of meat and bone and 2 quarts cold water, when brown stock is wanted. Omit parsnip and turnip for white stock.

5. If a very dark stock is wanted, melt a piece of marrow fat and fry and brown a third of the meat, turning frequently, after soaking the meat and bones in cold water for 1 hour. Place meat in stock pot. Pour 2 or 3 tablespoons of the soaking water into the frying pan. Bring to boil, and strain into stock pot, or fry the vegetables in a little melted fat before adding water to pan.

6. Keep stock well skimmed as the scum rises, or the colour will be poor. When ready, strain and cool quickly. A cake of fat will form on top. Leave this till stock is required, then loosen round edge with a knife and remove carefully. Remove any fat that still remains by wiping stock with a piece of butter muslin wrung out of hot water. Clarify fat and use for frying.

7. If stock is required as soon as made, skim off fat with a spoon, then remove any that remains by drawing a piece of paper over the surface.

8. Never leave stock in a saucepan overnight.

To Store Stock : To store stock so that it will keep for several days, pour into a freshly-scalded jar or basin, cool and either store in refrigerator, or in larder. If in larder, it should be boiled up every day during the warm weather, but only every other day during the remainder of the year.

BONE STOCK

2 lb. raw bones and meat trim-
    mings
1 teaspoon salt
Water or vegetable water as
    required
2 onions
1 stick celery
1 carrot
1 leek
3 cloves
1 teaspoon black pepper
1 blade mace
1 sprig parsley
1 sprig thyme

Chop up the bones and put them with any trimmings of meat, into a saucepan and add salt. (A
leg of mutton bone, or the bones of any joint, the
trimmings of cutlets, a bone from bacon or a piece
of bacon rind, all give a nice flavour to the stock.)
Cover bones well with water or vegetable water.
Simmer for 4 hours. Prepare vegetables and add
with spices and herbs. Simmer 2 hours longer.
Strain through a hair sieve into a basin.

BROWN STOCK

2 lb. shin of beef
½ lb. raw bones
2 quarts cold water
½ teaspoon salt
1 stick celery
1 carrot
1 thick slice turnip
1 onion
1 sprig parsley
6 peppercorns
1 bay leaf

Put meat and bones in a stock pot. Cover with
the cold water and stand for 1 hour. Bring
slowly to boil. Add salt and skim at once. Cover
and simmer for 2-3 hours. Prepare vegetables.
Add with all the other ingredients to stock pot.
Cover and simmer gently for 2 hours, or until
bones are clean. Strain through a hair sieve into
a basin.

SECOND BROWN STOCK: Make as brown stock, using the same meat and
bones over again, but with fresh vegetables and other ingredients. Any odd
cooked or uncooked bones, or scraps of meat, can be added before vegetables.

BROWN VEGETABLE STOCK

1½ cups kidney beans
½ bay leaf
1 clove
1 sprig parsley
Black pepper to taste
Salt to taste
1 cup chopped peeled potato
½ cup sliced celery
2 slices parsnip or turnip
¼ cup sliced onion or ¾ cup
    leek
¾ cup sliced carrot
2½ quarts cold water

Rinse beans in a colander under the cold water
tap. Place in soup pan. Add bay leaf, clove,
parsley, seasonings. Fry vegetables in 1½ tablespoons margarine till fat is absorbed and they are
slightly browned. Add to other ingredients in
pan with the water. Bring to boil. Simmer
gently in an uncovered saucepan, *without* stirring,
for 4 hours, if you want clear stock. If not,
cover saucepan. Season with salt and pepper
again, if liked. Strain without mashing into a
basin. Boil up again before using. Flavour
with vegetable extract, if liked.

WHITE VEGETABLE STOCK: Use white pepper. Omit carrot and substitute
chopped cauliflower, without the stalks, for the beans. Follow above method,
but omit frying of vegetables.

FISH STOCK

2 lb. bones and trimmings of any white fish
2 medium-sized onions or shallots
½ leek
2 slices carrot
2 sprigs parsley
1 sprig chervil
1 teaspoon salt
2 white peppercorns
¼ pint white wine
2 quarts water
Squeeze lemon juice

Place fish bones and trimmings in saucepan. Prepare and slice onions or shallots. Add with sliced leek, carrot, parsley, chervil, and a sprig fennel, if possible, salt, peppercorns and wine to other ingredients in pan. Bring slowly to boil. Cook until reduced to half the quantity, when liquid should be slightly syrupy. Add water. Bring to boil. Skim well. Cook for ½ hour. Add lemon juice and strain into a basin. Use when a fish stock is wanted for fish dishes or for a fish sauce.

GAME STOCK

Fresh carcases of game
1 quart second brown stock
Vegetables and seasonings as in brown stock

Follow method for brown stock by placing carcase and bones in a stock pot. Cover with cold water and stand for 1 hour. Bring slowly to boil. Add salt and skim at once. Cover closely and simmer for 2 to 3 hours. Prepare vegetables. Add with all other ingredients to stock pot. Cover and simmer for 2 hours, or until bones are clean. Strain into a basin.

GAME STOCK FOR CONSOMME

1 old pheasant or 2 partridges
2 oz. butter or margarine
1 medium-sized onion
1 medium-sized carrot
½ leek
1 stick celery
4 mushrooms
3 quarts chicken or veal stock
1 sprig parsley
1 sprig thyme
12 black peppercorns
1 dessertspoon salt

Wash pheasant or partridges inside and out under cold water tap. Dry and cut into joints. Break carcase. Melt fat in a saucepan. Add game. Fry, turning occasionally, until light brown all over. Prepare and slice vegetables and mushrooms. Add to fat in pan, when the game has been cooking for 10 minutes, then fry slowly for another 10 minutes, turning birds occasionally and stirring vegetables occasionally. Add stock. Bring slowly to boil. Skim well. Add parsley, thyme, peppercorns and salt. Simmer gently, uncovered, for 3 hours.

GIBLET STOCK

1 set chicken giblets
1 teaspoon salt
1 small onion
1 medium-sized carrot
1 leek
1 stick celery
1 sprig parsley
½ bay leaf
2 cloves
2 white peppercorns
1 blade mace

Cut gall bladder very carefully away from the liver so as not to break it ; if you do, the liver will have a bitter taste. Slit open the gizzard and remove the inside. Cover feet with boiling water. Cook for 5 or 10 minutes, then remove nails and scrape off skin. Wash feet, gizzard, heart, neck and the tips of the wings after removing from bird, in salted cold water, then drain. Place giblets in a saucepan. If able to get 1 lb.

1 quart water knuckle of veal, add as well. Season with salt. Prepare vegetables and add. Add herbs and spices, then the water. If you have any second stock, you'll have a richer giblet stock, if you substitute the second stock for the water. Bring slowly to boil. Skim and simmer very gently for 3 hours uncovered.

WHITE STOCK

4 lbs. raw chicken, rabbit or veal
1/4 cup diced celery
1/4 cup chopped onion
1 sliced leek
1/4 cup diced carrot
2 blades mace
6 white peppercorns
1 teaspoon salt
2 sprigs parsley
1 sprig lemon thyme
1/2 bay leaf
5 pints cold water

This stock can be made, if preferred, with an old fowl in place of the chicken, rabbit or veal. Cut meat in small pieces. Place in a saucepan with a snippet of lemon peel, the mace, seasonings, and herbs. Cover with the water to a depth of 2 inches. Stand for 1/2 hour. Bring slowly to boil. Skim well. Simmer gently for 4 hours, skimming as required. Add vegetables after 2 hours. Strain through a hair sieve. Remove fat when cold.

SOUP GARNISHES

Some garnishes are added to soup, either just before serving, such as minced chives or parsley, or passed round in a dainty dish, such as grated cheese with Minestrone soup. Others are cooked in the soup, such as dumplings, macaroni, noodles, spaghetti, and other forms of Italian paste.

ALMOND BALLS (Boules d'Amandes)

2 eggs
Salt and pepper to taste
1/2 teaspoon minced parsley
6 grated blanched almonds
1/2 teaspoon baking powder
Flour as required

Separate yolks and whites of eggs. Beat yolks till blended. Stir in salt, pepper, parsley, almonds, baking powder and enough flour to make a stiff batter. Beat well. Beat egg whites till stiff. Fold into batter. Test one out in boiling soup. To do this, drop batter from a teaspoon into soup, and cover. Cook steadily for 10 minutes. If the ball breaks in boiling, stir a little more flour into the batter before dropping the balls into the boiling soup 10 minutes before they are required. Cover and cook steadily till ready. *For 6 persons.*

Almond Croûtons (Croûtes d'Amandes) : Remove crusts from 4 thin slices of bread. Brush with melted butter or margarine. Cut into rounds 1½ inches across. With same cutter, remove 3 " almonds " from each round. Bake in a moderate oven, 350° F., till pale brown. Pass round with soup. *For 4 persons.*

Alphabet : Buy tiny macaroni letters of the alphabet and allow ¼ cup to enough bouillon for 6 persons. When bouillon boils, add letters. Cover and cook for 5 minutes before serving.

86

CHEESE DUMPLINGS (Boules de Fromage)

2 eggs
2 tablespoons grated Parmesan cheese
1½ tablespoons stale bread-crumbs
Pinch of paprika
¼ teaspoon minced chives or parsley or crushed herbs
Pinch of salt

Separate yolks and whites of eggs. Beat egg yolks. Stir in cheese, crumbs, paprika, chives, parsley or herbs, and salt. Beat egg whites till stiff. Drop batter from a teaspoon into simmering bouillon. Cover. Cook from 1 to 2 minutes. *For 6 persons.*

Cheesettes : Dip ½-inch squares of bread into 1 beaten egg blended with ¾ tablespoon melted margarine or butter. Roll in grated cheese. Bake a little apart in a greased baking tin in a rather hot oven, 425° F., until pale brown. Serve with cream of artichoke, cauliflower, or tomato. *Allow 6 per portion.*

CRACKER BALLS (Boules de Biscuit)

1 oz. butter or margarine
1 beaten egg
Grated nutmeg and ground ginger to taste
Salt and pepper to taste
1 teaspoon minced parsley
About 6 tablespoons cracker crumbs

Stir fat into egg. Add nutmeg, ginger, salt and pepper, parsley and enough of the crumbs to make into a firm paste. With lightly floured hands, make into balls the size of marbles. Drop into boiling soup or broth 10 minutes before serving. *For 6 persons.*

CHEESE CUSTARD (Crème de Fromage)

4 egg yolks
¾ cup milk
¼ teaspoon salt
1 tablespoon grated Parmesan cheese

Beat egg yolks. Stir in milk and salt, then the cheese. Strain into a shallow oiled mould. Cover with oiled paper, then place in a pan of hot water. Bring slowly to boiling point. Lower heat. Cook at simmering point for half-hour, or till set when a knife is inserted in the centre. Leave in mould till cold. Turn out gently. Cut into crescents, diamonds, dice or rounds with a vegetable cutter. Serve in clear soups. *For 6 persons.*

EGG CUSTARD (Garniture Royale)

2 egg yolks
1 dessertspoon milk
Pinch of salt
Dust of cayenne pepper

Beat yolks. Stir in milk and seasoning. Strain into a well-greased cup or small mould. Stand on a fold of paper in a saucepan. Add enough cold water to come half-way up container. Lay a piece of greased paper on top, then cover with lid. Bring water slowly to the boil. Lower heat or draw pan to one side. Poach until custard is firm in centre when tested with a knife. Leave in container until slightly cool, then turn out gently on to a wet paper. When cold, cut in thin slices with a wet knife. Cut into fancy shapes with a vegetable cutter. Wash gently in 2 or 3 changes of hot water, then stand in cold water till required. Colour with a few drops of cochineal before cooking, if liked. *For 6 persons.*

GREEN PEA CUSTARD (Crème de Légumes)

1 cup cooked green peas
Pinch of celery salt
Pinch of salt
Pinch of grated nutmeg
Pinch of paprika
2 egg yolks
1 egg
½ cup stock

Rub peas through a sieve. Stir in celery salt, salt, nutmeg and paprika. Beat egg yolks slightly with the egg. Stir in stock. Gradually beat into purée. Pour into a greased sandwich tin, about 7 inches across. Stand in a saucepan of hot water coming half-way up the side of tin. Bake in a moderate oven, 350° F., for about 25 minutes, until set when tested in centre with a knife. Remove from oven. Leave until cold. Cut in dice. Use for garnishing any consommé. *For 12 persons.*

KNEDLIKY (Boules à la Prague)

½ lb. skinned fillet of fish
1 hard-boiled egg yolk
1 egg
¾ oz. butter
1½ teaspoons minced parsley
Pinch of grated lemon rind
1 bread roll
Milk as required
Salt and pepper to taste

Cut up fillet. Place in a mortar. Add egg yolk. Pound fillet and egg yolk together till blended. Break egg into another basin. Add butter, parsley, lemon rind, and roll soaked in milk for 5 minutes, then drained, the prepared fish, salt and pepper to taste, and enough breadcrumbs to make a mixture you can shape into dumplings. It must not be too stiff. Mix till blended. With floured hands, mould small portions into dumplings the size of walnuts. Throw into rapidly boiling water. Cover. Boil for 5 to 7 minutes. Drain. Use with fish or vegetable broths. *For 6 persons.*

TOMATO CUSTARD (Crème de Tomates)

2 eggs
1 medium sized tomato
Pinch of salt
Pinch of cayenne pepper
Few drops of carmine

Beat eggs only till blended. Halve tomato. Rub pulp through a hair sieve. Add salt, pepper and carmine. Rub again through sieve. Finish off as described under " Egg Custard." Use for garnishing any consommé. *For 6 persons.*

EGG BALLS (Boules d'Oeufs)

2 hard-boiled egg yolks
Salt and pepper to taste
1 egg white
1 tablespoon seasoned flour
¾ oz. butter

Rub yolks through a sieve into a basin. Stir in salt and pepper and enough egg white to slightly moisten. Shape into balls about ¾ inch across. Roll in flour. Melt butter and add balls. Fry till pale brown, turning occasionally. Add to soup before dishing up. *For 5 persons.*

EINLAUF

3 tablespoons flour
Pinch of salt
1 beaten egg
¼ cup cold water

Sift flour and salt into a basin. Beat egg. Add water. Stir till blended. Stir in flour and salt. Beat till smooth. Pour slowly from the end of a dessertspoon into boiling bouillon. Cover. Cook for 2 to 3 minutes. Add 1 teaspoon chopped parsley. *For 6 persons.*

FORCEMEAT BALLS (Boulettes de Godiveau)

1 oz. shredded suet
1 minced, cooked hare liver
2 oz. breadcrumbs
1 teaspoon minced parsley
¼ teaspoon minced lemon peel
¼ teaspoon crushed herbs
Salt and black pepper to taste
1 beaten egg as required

Place suet in a basin. Add hare liver, crumbs, parsley, lemon peel, herbs, salt and pepper to taste and enough egg to bind. With floured hands, shape into "marbles." Either poach in salted simmering water or stock for 7 minutes, or fry in a little clarified fat till pale gold. Add to hare soup just before serving. *For 6 persons.*

FRENCH CROUTONS (Croûtons Français)

Cut out tiny rounds of bread about the size of a sixpence. Fry in a little hot fat on both sides till pale gold. Brush one side of each with slightly beaten egg white. Dip this side in finely minced tongue or truffles. Arrange in a circle on a plate covered with a paper doily. Serve with cream of mushroom soup. *Allow 5 or 6 per portion.*

FRIED CROUTONS (Croûtons frits)

Cut bread ¼ inch thick, then into strips ¼ inch wide. Cut strips into ¼ inch squares. Place in a frying basket. Lower into deep smoking hot fat. Fry till light brown, then drain well on absorbent paper. Serve on a plate lined with a lace paper doily with cream soups and purées. *Allow 6 to 7 per portion.*

FRITTER BEANS (La Pluie d'Or)

1 egg
½ teaspoon salt
2 oz. flour
3 dessertspoons milk or stock

Beat egg till blended. Stir in salt, flour and milk or stock. Beat well. Run through a strainer into hot deep fat. Fry till golden brown. Remove at once. Drain on absorbent paper. Add to broths. *For 6 persons.*

MARROW BALLS FOR CLEAR SOUP (Boules de Moelle)

2 tablespoons marrow fat
1 beaten egg
Salt and pepper to taste
Sieved breadcrumbs to stiffen

Melt marrow in a saucepan. Turn into a basin. Beat till creamy. Stir in egg. Season to taste. Add enough breadcrumbs to make mixture stiff enough to mould. Shape into small balls the size of a large marble. Place gently in a saucepan of boiling water. Boil till light and fluffy. Serve with consommés, allowing 3 or 4 per portion.

CHICKEN, GAME, RABBIT OR VEAL (Quenelles de Viande)

¼ lb. chicken, game, rabbit or veal
¼ oz. butter
1 oz. warmed flour
½ gill chicken, game, rabbit or veal stock

Wipe meat thoroughly with a damp cloth. If using veal, remove any fat and skin before weighing. Chop up meat. Pass twice through a meat grinder. Melt butter in a saucepan. Add flour and stock. Stir till smooth and boiling, and thick.

½ egg
Salt and pepper to taste
Pinch of ground mace

Remove from stove. Place the meat with the sauce in a mortar. Beat egg and add with salt and pepper to taste, and mace. Pound to a paste, then rub through a fine wire sieve. Shape into quenelles with the help of two wet teaspoons. To do this, fill one teaspoon with the mixture, then cover with another teaspoon of mixture, pressing the two together. Place side by side in a greased frying pan. Almost cover them with boiling water. Lay a greased paper on top. Poach very slowly for about 10 minutes, basting occasionally with the water, until firm. Remove carefully to a heated cloth. Add to consommé or bouillon, *allowing 2 per portion.*

Salad Garnishes : Boiled onion rings, strips of raw celery, diced boiled carrot and macaroni. Suitable for vegetable bouillon.

SUET DUMPLINGS (Boules à la Paysanne)

1 oz. shredded suet or dripping
¼ lb. self-raising flour
1 level teaspoon salt
1 tablespoon minced parsley
¼ lb. sausage meat or corned beef
Water or stock as required

Mix all dry ingredients together. Mix with enough stock or water to make a stiff dough. Make into 8 equal-sized balls, rolling with floured hands. Add to boiling broth. Cover. Simmer for 20 minutes. *For 4 persons.*

Soup Accompaniments : Sometimes an accompaniment is passed round with soup, such as grated cheese, hot cheese corkscrews, cheese straws, Melba toast, pulled bread, or garlic bread, etc., in place of garnishing consommé or bouillon with dumplings. For example :

CHEESE CORKSCREWS (Soupirs de Fromage)

½ lb. flaky, rough puff or shortcrust pastry
Grated cheese as required
Salt, cayenne pepper and paprika to taste

Roll pastry out on a lightly floured board to ¼ inch thickness, in the shape of an oblong. Sprinkle half thickly with grated cheese, then with salt, cayenne pepper and paprika to taste. Fold in two. Sprinkle the half again with cheese and cayenne pepper. Fold and roll out into a strip ¼ inch thick. Cut into short strips about 3 inches long, and ¼ inch wide. Dip in grated Parmesan cheese. Twist into corkscrews. To do this, hold one end with one hand and twist the strip away from you with the other. Bake side by side in a greased baking tin, a little apart, in a hot oven, 450° F., till crisp and golden.

DEVILLED CRUSTS (Diablotins)

1 bread roll
½ oz. butter
2 tablespoons grated Gruyère cheese
Cayenne pepper to taste

Cut roll into strips about ⅛ inch thick. Spread each slice with butter. Sprinkle with cheese. Season with cayenne pepper to taste. Place side by side on a buttered baking sheet. Bake in a hot oven, 450° F., until golden in 8-10 minutes. Serve with any clear soup on a plate covered with a lace paper doily.

PUFFETTES (Biscuits de l'Air)

¼ lb. flour
¾ teaspoon salt
1 tablespoon butter or margarine
Milk as required

Sift flour and salt into a basin. Lightly rub in fat. Stir in enough milk to make a very stiff dough. Knead till smooth. Shape into small equal-sized balls. Roll each one out into a thin wafer. Place a little apart on a greased baking sheet sprinkled with flour then shaken to remove any superfluous flour. Bake in a hot oven, 450° F., until puffy and pale gold.

Pulled Bread: With a fork, pull pieces of bread about the size of a plover's egg from a new loaf. Dip in milk. Place side by side in a baking tin. Bake in a moderately hot oven, 375° F., till golden. Serve in a hot dish lined with a folded napkin.

SUNPUFFS (Pouffes d'Or)

½ cup mayonnaise
¼ teaspoon minced parsley
Paprika to taste
½ egg white
Biscuits as required

Place mayonnaise in a basin. Stir in parsley and paprika. Beat egg white to a stiff froth. Fold into mayonnaise. Pile on round unsweetened biscuits. Cook under grill for 1 minute, or till puffy and golden. Serve at once on a hot dish lined with a paper doily. *For 3 persons.*

CLASSES OF SOUP

There are roughly 6 classes of soup : (1) Bouillon. (2) Broth. (3) Consommé. (4) Cream Soup. (5) Fish Soup. (6) Purée.

The average broth is simply a bouillon with the addition of vegetables and usually a cereal, dumplings, or some form of Italian paste as well.

HINTS ON SOUP MAKING

(1) Once soup comes to the boil, let it simmer steadily unless otherwise instructed in recipe. If boiled too fast it will become cloudy.

(2) Season all soups that need long simmering very slightly at the beginning. Complete seasoning if necessary when nearly ready. If soup should turn out too salt, add a halved raw potato. Simmer gently till potato is soft but unbroken, then remove it.

(3) If you allow soup thickened with egg, or egg and cream, to come to the boil, it will curdle.

(4) Serve hot soups in heated plates or cups and cold soups, really chilled.

COLOURING FOR SOUPS

Use a white-lined saucepan and a wooden spoon for delicately coloured and white soups and chicken or veal stock. When a recipe calls for frying the vegetables, do not allow them to turn colour for white and light soups. To improve the colour of brown soups, use brown stock and brown roux. Wash and add onion peelings when making stock for brown soups. To enrich the colour of mock lobster bisque, cream of tomato soup, and fish soups, such as crayfish, lobster, etc., which should be pink, add very carefully a drop or two of carmine or cochineal. Add to any green cream soup, such as green pea, a drop or two of green vegetable colouring, if necessary.

THICKENINGS FOR SOUPS

Cereals or Italian Pastes: Allow 2 oz. cereals or Italian paste to 1 quart soup. Add to soups according to time they take to cook.

Eggs: Beat egg yolk or yolks with a little cream or milk. Strain into soup slowly, stirring constantly, and quickly, but do not allow to boil again.

Flour, Cornflour or Arrowroot: Blend with milk for cream soups or stock or water for brown soups, till creamy, then stir into boiling soup. Cook for a moment or two, stirring contantly.

Roux: Add to soup, allowing 1 heaped tablespoon roux to 1 pint soup. Stir till boiling. *See page 45.*

BOUILLONS AND BROTHS

" Bouillon " is generally the name given to unclarified beef, chicken, or veal stock. When stock is rich, it can be jellied ; when not rich enough it can be stiffened with gelatine. Unclarified stock is still bouillon when vegetables and sometimes a garnish, such as dumplings, pearl barley or rice, are added, but then usually goes under the name of "Broth." Broth can also be made with mutton, poultry, calves' feet, sheep's head, etc.

BEEF BOUILLON (Bouillon de Boeuf)

BASIC RECIPE
2½ lb. gravy beef
3 pints cold water
1 lb. marrow bones
10 peppercorns
½ tablespoon salt
¼ cup diced turnip
¼ cup diced celery
¼ cup diced carrot
¼ cup diced onion
¼ cup diced parsnip

Wipe meat. Cut half of it into inch squares and place in a saucepan. Add water. Cover and stand for ½ an hour. Remove marrow fat from bones. Melt fat in a frying-pan, and brown the remainder of meat, then turn it and the bones into saucepan. Place on stove. Bring to boiling point. Skim carefully, then simmer, barely moving, for 6 hours. Add peppercorns, salt, and prepared vegetables. Simmer for 1 hour. Strain. Leave till cool, then skim. Serve in soup cups. *Allow ¼ pint per person.*

BEEF AND TOMATO BOUILLON (Bouillon de Tomates)

3 cups sieved tomatoes
½ teaspoon salt
1½ teaspoons caster sugar
3 cloves
1 slice onion
3 cups beef stock
Golden dumplings
1 heaped teaspoon minced parsley

Use stewed or canned tomatoes. Place in a saucepan. Add salt, sugar, cloves and onion. Cover and simmer for 5 minutes. Strain through a piece of muslin. Pour liquid into saucepan. Add beef stock. Bring to boil. Garnish with golden dumplings and parsley or with diced, cooked vegetables in season. *For 4 persons.*

CELERY BOUILLON (Bouillon de Céleri)

3 cups clarified white stock
Salt and pepper to taste
Celery salt and paprika to taste
2-3 tablespoons whipped cream
2-3 teaspoons minced parsley

Heat stock and season to taste with salt, pepper, celery salt and paprika. Serve in hot soup cups. Flavour cream with parsley. Divide cream equally between cups. Dredge lightly with paprika. Serve at once. *For 4 persons.*

CHICKEN BOUILLON (Bouillon de Volaille)

1 large chicken
1 teaspoon salt
3 quarts cold water
1 medium-sized carrot
1 medium-sized turnip
1 medium-sized onion
1 small stick celery
2 cloves
Salt and pepper to taste

Cut chicken into joints, and place with the carcase in a saucepan. Add salt and water. Bring to boil and skim. Let soup simmer gently until all scum has risen and is removed. Peel, slice and add vegetables. Add cloves. Simmer for 2 hours. Season to taste, and clarify. *Allow ¼ pint per person.* Serve with hot cheese corkscrews.

Beef Bouillon : Measure out quantity of soup required into a saucepan, after clarifying. Flavour to taste with Madeira or sherry. Pour into soup cups, filling them to within half an inch of the rims. Cool and stand in refrigerator till set.

JELLIED BEEF BOUILLON (Bouillon de Boeuf en Gelée)

1½ lb. shin of beef
1 tablespoon butter
3 quarts cold water
1½ lb. knuckle of veal
Half a marrow bone
3 medium-sized onions
3 scraped carrots
1 slice turnip
9 peppercorns
Pinch of celery salt
1 bay leaf
1 sprig parsley
1 tablespoon salt

Cut beef into cubes. Melt butter in a saucepan. Add beef. Fry till brown. Add water, knuckle of veal, cut in pieces, and marrow bone. Heat slowly to boiling point. Cover and simmer gently for 5 hours. Skim. Add sliced, peeled onions, sliced carrots, turnip, and remaining ingredients. Cover and simmer for 2 hours. Strain through a piece of muslin. Cool. Remove fat. Chill until jellied. Spoon into soup cups. This gives you from 1½ to 2 quarts of bouillon.

93

JELLIED CHICKEN BOUILLON (Bouillon de Volaille en Gelée)

1½ pints jellied chicken bouillon
1½ teaspoons minced parsley

The bouillon should be rich enough to form a jelly. Melt jelly in a saucepan. Stir in minced parsley. Turn into a wet enamelled baking dish. Leave till cold, then serve in soup cups, either beaten slightly with a fork or cut into cubes. *For 4 persons.*

JELLIED MUSHROOM BOUILLON
(Bouillon de Champignons en Gelée)

½ lb. mushrooms
½ medium-sized onion
1 quart beef or chicken stock
1 clove
Celery salt to taste
Salt and pepper to taste
2 tablespoons powdered gelatine
Whipped cream as required

Wipe mushrooms with a damp cloth, then place in a saucepan. Cut onion in slices. Add with stock, clove, celery salt and salt and pepper to taste. Simmer gently, uncovered, until mushrooms are tender, then remove from stove. Dissolve gelatine in the stock and strain. Chill. Whip lightly with a fork. Serve in cups. Decorate each portion with a heaped teaspoon of whipped cream. Dredge cream lightly with paprika, if liked. *For 6 persons.*

JELLIED TOMATO BOUILLON (Bouillon de Tomates, Frappé)

1 pint rich white stock
1 slice onion
¼ teaspoon celery salt
1½ tablespoons powdered gelatine
½ gill cold water
Salt and pepper to taste
1 tablespoon lemon juice
½ pint tomato juice
Cream and paprika or parsley

Pour stock into a saucepan. Add onion and celery salt. Bring to boil. Strain into a basin. Soften gelatine in 2 tablespoons of the cold water. Add to stock. Stir till dissolved. Add remainder of water, salt and pepper to taste, and lemon and tomato juice. Pour into soup cups. Chill. Top each portion with a teaspoon of whipped cream. Sprinkle with paprika or minced parsley. *For 5 persons.*

CROUTE-AU-POT

2 quarts beef and veal stock
1 medium-sized carrot
1 small turnip
½ cabbage
2 oz. butter
Salt and pepper to taste
Pinch of grated nutmeg
2 dinner rolls
2 teaspoons finely chopped chives or parsley

Remove any fat from stock; it need not be clarified, unless liked. Prepare carrot, turnip and cabbage. Cut carrot and turnip into small round slices and shred cabbage. Melt butter in a saucepan. Add vegetables. Cover and cook slowly for 10 minutes. Season with salt, pepper and nutmeg. (If vegetables are old, par-boil and drain well before frying.) Simmer, uncovered, for about ½ hour, skimming occasionally. Meanwhile, slice roll thinly and bake in a moderate oven, 350° F., until golden brown on both sides. Place in soup tureen. Add soup and chives or parsley. Re-season if necessary. Serve at once. *For 8 persons.*

HOTCH POTCH (Potage à l'Écossaise)

1 lb. neck mutton
Salt to taste
4 pints water
1 small turnip
2 onions (par-boiled)
1 stick celery
2 medium-sized carrots
½ lettuce
1 medium cauliflower
½ pint green peas
1 teaspoon sugar
Pepper to taste

Place mutton, salt and water in saucepan. Bring to boil. Skim carefully as soon as water boils. Wash and prepare vegetables. Cut them up small. Break cauliflower into sprigs. Add all the vegetables to soup except cauliflower and peas. Cook very gently for 1½ hours. Add cauliflower sprigs, peas, sugar and pepper. Cook gently half an hour longer. Remove mutton. Serve as a second course, masked with white sauce and chopped capers, and accompanied by mashed potatoes and glazed young carrots. Dish up soup. *For 6 persons.*

JULIENNE BROTH (Potage à la Julienne)

1 large scraped carrot
1 small peeled turnip
½ head celery
2 prepared leeks
1 medium-sized peeled onion
2 oz. butter
1½ quarts boiling beef stock
Salt and pepper to taste
1 teaspoon caster sugar
2 sprigs chervil
2 sprigs tarragon
1 lettuce

Dice carrot, turnip, celery, leeks and onion. Melt butter in a saucepan. Add prepared vegetables. Fry till lightly browned, stirring frequently. Add stock, salt, pepper and sugar. Skim off all fat, then add washed, chopped chervil and tarragon. Remove stalk from lettuce and separate leaves. Wash thoroughly and shred. Drain and add to soup. Boil for 5 minutes. *For 6 or 8 persons.*

LEEK BROTH (Potage de Poireaux)

6 medium-sized leeks
1 oz. butter or margarine
1 quart stock or water
2 oz. vermicelli
Salt and pepper to taste
¾ pint milk

Remove roots and outer skin from leeks. Trim off ends of leaves. Wash leeks thoroughly, then cut into thin slices. Wash in two or three more waters before draining, to make sure that all grit is removed. Melt fat in a saucepan. Add leeks. Cover and simmer for 15 minutes, stirring occasionally. Add water or stock, and boil for 30 minutes with lid on pan. Add crushed vermicelli. Cover and simmer for 15 minutes longer. Uncover. Season to taste with salt and pepper. Stir in milk, brought almost to the boil. Re-season if necessary. *For 6 persons.*

SCOTCH BROTH (Potage à l'Écossaise)

2 lb. neck of mutton
1 quart water
1 medium-sized carrot
1 medium-sized onion
½ small turnip
1 tablespoon pearl barley
¼ teaspoon pepper
1 teaspoon salt
1 tablespoon minced parsley

The scrag end of a neck of mutton will do if it is first soaked in warm water to draw out the blood. Cut meat into pieces about 2 inches square. If the butcher has not cut it into small joints, chop bones in half. Put the pieces into a clean saucepan with the cold water. Well wash and peel carrot, onion and turnip, and cut them into dice about the size of a pea. Put these into the saucepan. Add pearl barley, pepper and salt. Bring very gently to boil and skim well. Draw to side of stove. Simmer very gently for 2½ hours. On no account let the soup boil hard or the meat will be tough. Immediately before serving remove all bones and add parsley. Serve with meat in tureen. If mutton is to be a separate course, do not cut up before making soup. ½ cup green peas can be added 15 minutes before serving, if liked. *For 3 or 4 persons.*

TRIPE BROTH (Potage de Tripe)

6 oz. cooked honeycomb tripe
2 tablespoons margarine
2 tablespoons minced onion
1½ tablespoons flour
2 quarts white stock
1 cup diced potato
4 tablespoons diced celery
½ cup diced carrot
1 saltspoon Worcester sauce
½ tablespoon minced parsley
Salt and pepper to taste

Wash, dry and cut tripe into small pieces. Melt margarine in a frying-pan. Add onion. Fry slowly till golden brown. Stir in flour. Add tripe, and stock (made from chicken or veal bones, or turkey bones, or a carcase). Bring to boil. Simmer very slowly for 1½ hours with lid on. Add remainder of ingredients. Cover and simmer gently for 1¼ hours. Season to taste. *For 6 persons.*

CLEAR SOUPS (Consommés)

Clear soups are generally prepared only for luncheon, dinner or supper parties.

There are some clear soups which demand a mixture of brown and white clear stock, and others that require a mixture of rich brown and white clear stock and tomato juice.

The most suitable meat for consommé is the aitchbone, buttock piece, or the top of the leg and the ribs. To prepare meat, bone it, then crack the bones and put with the meat in saucepan or stock pot with the cold water required. Carefully skim as the water approaches boiling point. Do not add salt, vegetables or any flavourings until water is at full boil, then simmer gently in uncovered pan for about 5 hours, when stock is ready for straining and clarifying.

The garnish, from which consommé takes its name, is usually placed in the bottom of soup cups or tureen, and the consommé is poured over it, but sometimes garnish is added to the consommé when dished up.

To Flavour Consommés : Add 1 teaspoon Madeira, Marsala or sherry per portion just before serving, unless any other wine is suggested in recipe.

Quantities to Allow (¼ pint per person) : In the following recipes I have given a rough idea of the number of persons each soup will serve when wanted for a party, because these soups, as I have already said, are generally prepared only for parties. It is impossible to be exact about the amount of yield, as the quantity depends to a certain extent on what you consider is " simmering." I have therefore tried to plan each recipe so that the yield is a little more than is actually required for the number of persons given, so that you should not be short. One or two of the soups are designed for large parties as you will see.

Serve Clear Soups, garnished with parsley, in soup cups. *See page* 97.

Garnish Beef Bouillon with small boiled and drained noodles. *See page* 92.

Beef and Tomato Bouillon, garnished with cooked vegetables in season. *See page* 93.

FISH AND CHIPS

(*Top left*) Ingredients required for Fish and Chips. *See pages* 125 *and* 431. (*Top right*) Peeled potatoes cut in chips, soaked and dried and ready for deep-frying. *See page* 431. (*Bottom left*) Brush fillets of fish, dipped in seasoned flour, in beaten egg, then coat with sieved breadcrumbs. *See pages* 124 *and* 125. (*Bottom right*) Fried Fillets of Fish and Fried Chips ready for serving. *See pages* 125 *and* 126.

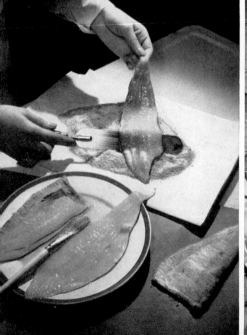

CLEAR SOUP (Consommé)

BASIC RECIPE
2 quarts unclarified beef stock
1 lb. shin of beef
2 tablespoons cold water
1 medium-sized carrot
1 slice turnip
1 medium-sized onion
1 sprig parsley
½ bay leaf
6 black peppercorns
4 white peppercorns
2 cloves
Whites and shells of 2 eggs
1 lump sugar
1 glass sherry

Remove all fat from stock. Mince meat finely. Stir in water. Pour stock into a saucepan. Add beef mixture. Halve carrot and add with turnip. Slice onion and add with parsley, bay leaf, peppercorns and cloves. Beat egg whites slightly. Wash egg shells and remove inner skin. Crush shells. Add to egg whites. Turn into soup. Whisk over stove until stock comes almost to boiling point, then simmer *very gently* for 20 minutes. Remove from stove. Stand for 5 minutes. Strain through butter-muslin, 2 or 3 thicknesses of cheese cloth, or a jelly bag, dipped in scalding water and wrung dry, without breaking the scum formed on top. Pour into a clean saucepan. Add sugar. Bring almost to boiling point, but do not allow to boil or it will cloud. Add sherry and any garnish required. Serve at once. If stock is very rich and well seasoned, only add beef, egg shells and egg whites. Strain as soon as the soup comes to boiling point. Reheat and use. *For 15 or 16 persons.*

Clear Asparagus Soup (Consommé d'Asperges) : Heat clarified beef stock in saucepan, allowing ¼ pint per person. Serve in hot soup cups. Garnish each portion with 4 hot asparagus tips and a dust of finely minced parsley.

Clear Soup with Spinach (Consommé aux Epinards) : Colour 1 quart boiling clarified stock with beetroot juice to taste. Garnish with spinach custard dice made from ½ lb. spinach and ½ beaten egg. *For 8 persons.*

Clear Noodle Soup (Consommé aux Nouilles) : Add 2 tablespoons of boiled square noodles to 1 quart boiling clarified stock. *For 8 persons.*

Clear Soup, Aux Oeufs (Consommé aux Oeufs) : Beat white of one egg to a stiff froth. Season with paprika. Divide equally between 6 hot soup cups. Divide 1½ pints hot clarified stock between the cups. *For 6 persons.*

Clear Green Pea Soup (Consommé aux Petits Pois) : Boil ½ pint green peas in salted water till tender. Drain. Add to 5 gills hot clarified stock, flavoured Madeira or sherry to taste. *For 5 persons.*

CLEAR BROWN SOUP (Consommé à la Brunoise)

1 medium-sized carrot
½ small turnip
1 teaspoon chopped onion or shallot
½ leek
½ small stick celery
¾ oz. butter or margarine
1 quart hot clarified stock

Prepare vegetables : cut carrot, the red part only, into small dice. Dice onion or shallot, leek and celery. Melt butter or margarine in a saucepan. Add prepared vegetables. Stew gently for 3 or 4 minutes. Add ½ pint stock. Simmer gently until the vegetables are cooked. Cook peas and beans in boiling salted water until tender. When

1 dessertspoon green peas
1 dessertspoon small diced French beans
1 teaspoon minced chervil

the vegetables are all ready, add remainder of stock and drained peas and beans. Bring almost to boiling point. Pour into heated soup cups. Sprinkle with chervil. *For 7 or 8 persons.*

CLEAR SOUP, CELESTINE (Consommé à la Célestine)

1 oz. flour
Salt and pepper to taste
1 egg
¼ pint milk
1 teaspoon melted butter
1 walnut butter
2 quarts clarified stock

Season flour to taste with salt and pepper, then make into a smooth batter by adding slightly beaten egg and milk by degrees. Beat well, then stir in melted fat. Melt butter or margarine in an omelet pan and cook batter like very thin pancakes. When well browned on each side, drain on kitchen paper and trim edges to make cakes square. Cut into inch-wide strips, then crosswise into match-like strips. Place in the bottom of soup tureen or soup cups. Heat stock. Pour over garnish. *For 14 to 16 persons.*

CLEAR SOUP, DUCHESSE (Consommé à la Duchesse)

1 quart clarified chicken stock
¾ oz. sago
¼ pint diced boiled chicken breast
1 dessertspoon minced chives or parsley
Salt and pepper to taste

Heat clarified stock until boiling. Sprinkle in the sago. Simmer for ¼ hour. Add chicken and chives or parsley, and a tablespoon of sherry if the stock was not flavoured with sherry. Season if necessary. *For 7 or 8 persons.*

CLEAR SOUP, ITALIENNE (Consommé à l'Italienne)

1½ oz. spaghetti, shell macaroni or noodles
2¼ pints hot clarified stock
Grated Parmesan cheese

Put spaghetti or other paste in a saucepan of boiling water. Cook till soft. Drain well. Separate noodles under cold water tap. Drain well. Heat stock till boiling. Add cooked paste and serve. Pass round a dish of grated Parmesan cheese with this soup. *For 8 persons.*

CLEAR SOUP, JARDINIÈRE (Consommé à la Jardinière)

2 small peeled carrots
2 slices turnip
½ small cucumber
1 quart clarified stock
Salt to taste

Prepare carrots and turnip. Wash cucumber. Cut vegetables with a round vegetable cutter about the size and shape of green peas. Boil separately in a little salted water until tender, but not broken. Drain well. Heat stock with salt to taste. Add vegetables. Simmer for a moment or two, then serve. Sometimes tiny sprigs of boiled cauliflower are added as well and the soup flavoured delicately with sherry. *For 7 or 8 persons.*

CLEAR JULIENNE SOUP (Consommé à la Julienne)

1 medium-sized carrot
2 small slices turnip

Peel vegetables. Cut in Julienne strips, from 1 to 1½ inches long and ⅛ inch thick. Melt fat in a

½ leek
1 small onion
½ stick celery
1 cabbage leaf
2 or 3 French beans
1 oz. butter or margarine
Pinch of sugar
2¼ pints clarified stock
Salt and pepper to taste
1 oz. cooked peas

saucepan. Add vegetables. Sprinkle with the sugar. Cook for 3 or 4 minutes, stirring gently all the time, then add stock. Bring to simmering point. Simmer gently for ½ hour. Season to taste with salt and pepper, then add peas. *For 8 persons.*

CLEAR MADRILENE SOUP (Consommé à la Madrilène)

2 cups chicken stock
2 cups beef stock
2 cups canned tomatoes
1 cup chopped carrots
1 medium-sized onion, chopped
½ cup chopped leeks
Salt and pepper to taste

Bring stocks and vegetables to a boil. Cover. Simmer for 1 hour, adding salt and pepper when partially cooked. Strain and clarify as follows : Combine egg white and the crushed shells of 1 egg with 2 tablespoons cold water. Add to the cold soup stock. Heat slowly to boiling point, stirring constantly. Remove from heat. Add ¼ cup cold water and let settle. Strain through 2 thicknesses of butter muslin or a jelly bag. This makes 1½ pints clear soup. Garnish with diced, cooked carrot and cooked peas, each cooked separately. *For 6 persons.*

Jellied Madrilène Soup (Consommé Madrilène, Froid) : Allow ¾ tablespoon powdered gelatine to 2 cups Madrilène Consommé. Soften gelatine in 2 tablespoons water for 4 or 5 minutes. Stir in half the soup. When gelatine is dissolved, stir in remainder of soup. Season to taste with salt. Pour into soup cups. Chill until set. Whip soup in cups and serve. *For 4 persons.*

CLEAR MOCK TURTLE SOUP (Consommé de Tortue Fausse)

½ calf's head
4 quarts chicken or veal stock
1 stick celery
1 medium-sized carrot
1 medium-sized onion
1 sprig parsley
1 sprig thyme
1 sprig marjoram
8 black peppercorns
4 white peppercorns
1 lb. shin of beef
1 tablespoon cold water
3 egg whites
3 egg shells
1 dessertspoon salt
1 glass sherry

Wash head. Remove meat and cut in pieces. Take out tongue and brains. If brains are left in the head (as they are sometimes sold separately), remove. Chop bones. Place meat and bones in a large saucepan. Add stock. Bring to boil, then skim well. Simmer very gently for 3 hours. Strain stock into a basin. Leave till cold, then remove all the fat. Prepare and slice vegetables. Place in a clean saucepan with the stock. Add herbs and peppercorns. Mince beef finely. Mix it with the cold water. Add to stock. Whisk egg whites. Remove inner lining from shells and crush shells. Add egg whites and shells to stock. Whisk all together over stove till at boiling point. Draw pan to one side. Simmer *very gently* for 20 minutes. Add salt and sherry, and a squeeze of lemon juice, if liked. Simmer for 5 minutes. Strain and reheat. *For 10 to 12 persons.*

CLEAR MULLIGATAWNY SOUP (Consommé à l'Indienne)

1 teaspoon curry paste
1 tablespoon curry powder
1/4 pint cold water
4 oz. lean shredded beef
1 medium-sized onion
1 small carrot
1 small apple
1 quart brown stock
1 egg white
1 egg shell
Salt to taste
Juice of 1 lemon
2 oz. diced cooked chicken
2 or 3 tablespoons cooked rice

Mix curry paste and powder with the water. Add beef. Soak for 1/4 hour. Place in a rinsed saucepan. Peel vegetables and apple and slice into stock. Add slightly beaten egg white and crushed egg shell after removing inner skin. Whisk till almost boiling. Add salt to taste. Draw pan to side of stove. Cover. Stand for 15 minutes. Strain. Reheat in a clean saucepan almost to boiling point. Add lemon juice, diced chicken and rice. If a milder flavoured mulligatawny soup is wanted, halve quantity of curry powder. Sometimes boiled rice is passed round separately. *For 6 persons.*

CLEAR TOMATO SOUP (Consommé de Tomates)

2 quarts stock
8 large ripe tomatoes
1 teaspoon sugar
1 strip bacon rind
A few drops tarragon vinegar
1 teaspoon strained lemon juice
1 teaspoon beef extract
Eggs and white wine as required
Seasoning if necessary
2 tablespoons custard garnish
A few drops of carmine

Place stock in a saucepan. Wash and add tomatoes. Stir in sugar, bacon rind, or a bacon bone if preferred, vinegar, lemon juice and beef extract. Bring to boil. Simmer for 1 hour, then strain and leave till cold. Remove any fat, and measure. To each quart, allow the shells and whites of 4 eggs and 1/2 gill white wine. Remove inner lining from egg shells. Beat egg whites slightly. Pour stock into a clean saucepan. Add egg shells and whites, wine, and a drop or two of carmine. Bring to boil, whisking constantly.

Simmer very gently for 1/4 hour. Strain. Reheat and add tomato custard dice. *For 8 persons.*

CLEAR SOUP, TOLEDO (Consommé à la Toledo)

1 quart clarified brown stock
1 cooked medium-sized carrot
1 tablespoon yellow custard crescents
1 tablespoon white custard dice

Bring stock to boiling point. Cut carrot into small stars. With a half-moon vegetable cutter, cut out yellow custard. Add with white custard dice and carrot to stock. *For 6 or 7 persons.*

CLEAR SOUP, VERT PRE (Consommé Vert Pré)

1 quart clarified stock
2 tablespoons tapioca
1 tablespoon diced French beans
1 tablespoon asparagus tips
1 tablespoon green peas
6 spinach leaves
Salt and pepper to taste

Bring stock to boil. Sprinkle in tapioca. Simmer for 1/4 hour. Cook beans, asparagus tips and peas separately in boiling salted water. Shred spinach leaves finely and cook in a little of the stock. When vegetables are ready, drain and place in a soup tureen. Season. Strain stock over. *For 7 or 8 persons.*

CREAM SOUPS

There are two kinds of cream soups. One made with white stock and one without stock. The latter is suitable for vegetarians. It can be flavoured with vegetable extract if liked. Sometimes beaten egg yolks are added to thicken the soup. Their addition increases the protein content. Cream soups containing egg yolks provide a valuable course at a vegetarian meal, when meat is deficient, or in any meal lacking in proteins. Cream soups should be of the consistency of "single cream." Cream is usually added at the last moment when a rich cream soup is wanted.

Quantity to Allow : 1¼ gills per person. Adapt quantities to suit if a second helping may be required.

CREAM SOUP

BASIS RECIPE:
3 cups minced raw vegetables
1 pint vegetable water, or white stock
1 bay leaf
5 peppercorns
5 allspice berries
1 sliced onion
3 tablespoons butter
3 tablespoons flour
1 pint hot milk
Salt and pepper to taste
Fried croûtons

Place vegetables in a saucepan with the vegetable water or stock, bay leaf, peppercorns, allspice berries and onion. Bring slowly to the boil. Cover. Simmer until tender in about 20 minutes, then rub through a sieve. Melt butter in a saucepan. Add flour. Stir until frothy, then gradually stir in the milk. Stir until smooth and boiling. Simmer gently for 2 or 3 minutes over low heat, stirring constantly, then strain the stock. Gradually stir into the white sauce. Season with salt and pepper to taste, and, if too thick, thin with additional hot milk. Serve with fried croûtons. *For 6 persons.*

To Vary: Substitute 1½ cups of cooked green peas and ½ cup cooked carrot for raw vegetables given.

Cream of Fish: Substitute 1 cup minced canned, or flaked, boiled halibut, salmon or tunny fish for the 3 cups vegetables given in basic recipe.

CREAM OF ARTICHOKES (Crème à la Palestine)

2 lb. Jerusalem artichokes
Squeeze lemon juice
1 small stick celery
1 leek
1 oz. butter
1½ pints white stock
¾ pint milk
½ oz. flour
Salt and pepper to taste
Whipped cream

Wash and peel artichokes. Put into water with lemon juice. Wash celery and leek and cut into small pieces. Melt butter in a saucepan. Add artichokes, celery and leek and stir over the fire for a few minutes. Add stock and boil till vegetables are tender. Rub through a wire sieve and return to pan. Mix milk gradually with flour, then add to soup with salt and pepper. Serve garnished with whipped cream. *For 6 or 7 persons.*

CREAM OF BARLEY (Crème d'Orge)

½ cup pearl barley
1 slice onion
2 quarts chicken or veal stock

Rinse barley and place with onion in a saucepan. Add half stock. Bring to boil. Cover and boil for ¾ hour. Uncover and add remainder of stock.

Salt and pepper to taste
2 egg yolks
1 cup hot cream
Fried croûtons

Cover and simmer till tender. Strain into the top of a double boiler. Season to taste with salt and pepper. Beat egg yolks. Stir in hot cream by degrees. When thoroughly blended, stir mixture into hot stock in double boiler, adding only a little at a time and stirring constantly until thick. Serve with fried croûtons. *For 6 persons.*

CREAM OF CAULIFLOWER (Crème de Chou-fleur)

1 fairly large cauliflower
1 quart white stock
1 oz. flour
2 beaten egg yolks
½ cup hot milk
1 lump sugar
Grated nutmeg
Salt and pepper to taste
1 oz. butter, melted
Cheesettes or minced parsley

Break cauliflower up into sprigs. Soak in salt and water for ½ hour. Heat stock in another pan. Stir in flour, and when frothy, add stock. Stir till soup boils. Throw in cauliflower sprigs. Boil with lid off till quite tender. Press through a hair sieve. Reheat. Stir in beaten yolks diluted with ½ cup hot milk, but not boiling, sugar, and seasonings. Add butter and stir till thick. Garnish with cheesettes or parsley. *For 6 persons.*

CREAM OF CELERIAC (Crème de Céleri-rave)

1 oz. butter or margarine
1 lb. sliced celeriac
1 sliced leek
1 tablespoon chopped onion
2 tablespoons chopped potato
1 pint chicken or veal stock
Salt and pepper to taste
½ oz. flour
½ pint milk
3 tablespoons cream
1 tablespoon grated cheese
Fried croûtons

Melt fat. Add vegetables. Fry slowly for 5 minutes, stirring occasionally. Add stock and salt and pepper to taste. Cover. Simmer gently until vegetables are tender. Rub through a sieve. Rinse saucepan. Pour soup into it. Mix flour smoothly to a cream with a little of the milk, then stir in remainder of milk. Add to soup. Stir until boiling. Season again if necessary. Stir in cream and cheese. Re-season if necessary. Garnish with fried croûtons. *For 4 persons.*

CREAM OF CHEESE (Crème de Fromage)

½ pint milk
½ pint well seasoned white stock
2 large slices onion
1 tablespoon butter
1 tablespoon flour
1 egg yolk
¼ cup grated cheese
2 heaped teaspoons parsley
½ teaspoon salt
Celery salt
Pepper to taste
Pinch of ground mace

Pour milk and stock into a saucepan. Bring to boil. Add onion. Stand till well flavoured, then strain. Melt butter in top of a double boiler. Stir in flour and, when mixture is smooth and frothy, stir in milk and stock by degrees, being careful not to add it all at once. Stir liquid constantly until it comes to the boil and thickens. Draw pan to one side. Stand for a moment. Beat egg yolk and stir in quickly. Return pan to stove. Cook soup for 1 minute over pan of hot water, stirring constantly, then stir in grated cheese and parsley. Season. Beat with egg beater for a moment or two. *For 3 persons.*

CREAM OF CHESTNUTS (Crème de Marrons)

24 large chestnuts
3 oz. butter
1½ pints chicken stock
1 teaspoon caster sugar
¼ pint white sauce
¼ pint cream
Salt and pepper to taste
Celery salt to taste
Minced chervil, chives or parsley

Slit chestnuts at each end. Place in a saucepan. Cover with boiling water. Boil steadily for 10 minutes, then remove outer and inner shells. Melt butter in a saucepan. Add chestnuts. Fry slowly for 5 minutes, but do not allow to brown. Add stock. Bring to boil. Cover and simmer till chestnuts are tender. Rub through a hair sieve. Rinse pan. Reheat soup. Add sugar, then stir a little into the white sauce to thin it down. Pour back into soup, stirring constantly. Add cream by degrees, stirring constantly over slow heat, then season to taste with salt and pepper and celery salt. Garnish with chervil, chives or parsley. *For 6 persons.*

NOTE : If wanted for a party, omit white sauce, and use ½ pint cream, or float a teaspoon of whipped cream on each portion.

CREAM OF CHICKEN (Crème de Volaille)

2 oz. butter
1 tablespoon flour
1½ pints chicken stock
½ pint milk
Salt and pepper to taste
Grated nutmeg to taste
2 sprigs parsley
1 stick celery
1 sprig thyme
½ bay leaf
1 egg yolk
½ gill cream
Minced parsley

Melt butter in a saucepan. Add flour. Stir till well mixed, and frothy, then gradually stir in chicken stock and milk. When smooth and boiling, season to taste. Add parsley, celery, thyme and bay leaf. Cover pan. Cook steadily for 45 minutes, then rub through a fine sieve. Return soup to saucepan. Beat egg yolk in the cream in top of a double boiler, over boiling water, until hot, then gradually stir into soup, but don't allow to boil again. Garnish with minced parsley. *For 4 persons.*

Cream of Curry : Add 1 heaped teaspoon curry powder with the parsley.

CREAM OF CORN (Crème de Maïs)

1 can sweet corn
1 pint white stock
1 pint hot milk
1 slice onion
1 teaspoon salt
Pepper and paprika to taste
2 tablespoons butter
2 tablespoons flour
6 heaped teaspoons whipped cream

Put corn and stock on to boil in a saucepan. Cook for 20 minutes, stirring frequently. Rub through a hair sieve. Scald milk with onion, then strain milk into corn purée. Season to taste. Melt butter in saucepan. Stir in flour, and when it bubbles, add purée. Stir till boiling. Add a little sherry if liked, but in that case be careful not to boil again. Garnish with whipped cream. *For 6 persons.*

CREAM OF CUCUMBER (Crème de Concombre)

2 tablespoons butter
2 large cucumbers
2 tablespoons flour

Melt butter in a saucepan. Peel, slice and seed cucumbers. Add to butter. Cover and simmer for 10 minutes. Stir in flour and gradually dilute with

3 cups chicken or veal stock
2 cups milk
1 slice onion
1 blade mace
3 or 4 tablespoons cream
2 eggs yolks
2 tablespoons whipped cream

stock. Bring to boil, then add milk, slowly heated in another saucepan, with the onion and mace, then strained. Rub through a sieve. Reheat, still stirring, till soup comes to boil. Draw pan to side of stove. Stir in cream and egg yolks. Reheat, stirring until slightly thickened, but do not allow to boil. Season to taste. Garnish with whipped cream. *For 4 persons.*

CREAM OF GREEN PEAS (Crème de Pois Verts)

1 quart shelled peas and their pods
1 teaspoon sugar
2 sprigs mint
1 quart chicken or veal stock
2 small peeled onions
1 sprig parsley
½ pint water
1 oz. butter
1 oz. flour
1 pint milk
Salt and pepper to taste
Fried croûtons

Throw peas into boiling, salted water, enough to cover. Add sugar, mint, and cook for 20 minutes. Strain, reserving 2 tablespoons, and pass the remainder with the mint through a hair sieve to give you a purée. Put washed pea pods in another saucepan with stock, onions, parsley and water. Cook, uncovered, stirring occasionally, until tender. Rub pods and stock through a hair sieve until all the soft green substance inside the pods has gone into the stock. Stir pea purées together. Melt butter in a saucepan. Stir in flour, and when frothy, gradually stir in first the milk, then the purée. Keep stirring till boiling. Season to taste with pepper and salt. Serve garnished with reserved peas, or put all the peas into the soup and serve with croûtons of fried bread. *For 6 persons.*

CREAM OF LENTILS (Crème de Lentilles)

½ lb. lentils
1 onion
2 rashers streaky bacon
1 quart water or white stock
Salt and pepper to taste
½ cup milk
1 teaspoon minced mint
Fried croûtons

Rinse lentils. Soak in cold water to cover for 24 hours. Drain well. Turn into a saucepan. Add peeled and sliced onion, bacon, and water or stock. Bring to boil. Cover. Simmer gently till lentils are tender, when season to taste. Strain stock into a clean saucepan. Rub lentils through a sieve into soup. Bring to boiling point. Remove saucepan from heat. Stir in milk and heat again, but do not allow to boil. Add mint. Garnish with fried croûtons. *For 6 persons.*

CREAM OF LETTUCE (Crème de Laitue)

1 lb. lettuce leaves
½ lb. sorrel
2 oz. butter
1 medium-sized peeled onion
1 sprig parsley
1 sprig chervil
1 quart chicken stock
1½ oz. flour
½ pint milk
2 eggs yolks
Salt and pepper to taste

Wash and dry lettuce and sorrel leaves. Melt butter in a saucepan. Slice in onion, and add leaves, parsley and chervil. Cook for 5 minutes, stirring frequently. Add stock. Stir till boiling. Simmer for 20 minutes. Rub through a fine sieve. Return to pan. Stir in flour creamed with milk. Bring to boiling point and boil for 5 minutes, stirring constantly. Remove pan from heat. Beat egg yolks in a basin. Stir in salt, pepper to taste

½ gill cream
Whipped cream
allow to boil. Serve in cups.

and cream, then add a little soup. Stir into soup in pan, and keep stirring till piping hot, but don't allow to boil. Serve in cups. Garnish with whipped cream. *For 6 persons.*

CREAM OF MUSHROOMS (Crème de Champignons)

8 oz. mushrooms
1 quart white stock
1 slice onion
1 blade mace
2 cloves
4 white peppercorns
2 tablespoons butter
2 tablespoons flour
1 cup cream
Salt and pepper to taste
Whipped cream

Wipe, peel and chop mushrooms. Pour stock into saucepan. Add onion, mushrooms, mace, cloves and peppercorns. Cover. Bring to boil. Simmer for 20 minutes. Rub through a sieve. Reheat. Melt butter in a saucepan. Stir in flour. When it froths, dilute with a little soup and cream. Keep stirring, gradually adding remainder of soup. Season to taste. Serve in cups. Garnish each portion with whipped cream. *For 4 persons.*

CREAM OF POTATO (Crème de Pommes de Terre)

3 medium-sized peeled potatoes
1 quart milk
2 slices onion
3 tablespoons butter
2 tablespoons flour
1 tablespoon minced parsley
Salt and pepper to taste
Cayenne pepper to taste
Celery salt to taste
Minced chives or parsley

egg whisk before serving. *persons.*

Cook potatoes till soft in usual way. Drain and rub through sieve. Heat milk and onion in pan. Remove onion from milk. Add milk to potatoes, and melt butter in a saucepan. Stir in flour, then gradually stir in hot milk mixture. Cook for 5 minutes. Add parsley. Season to taste with salt, pepper, cayenne pepper and celery salt to taste. If soup is too thick for your taste, dilute with a little hot milk. If wanted frothy, beat with an egg whisk before serving. Garnish with minced chives or parsley. *For 6 persons.*

CREAM OF SPINACH (Crème d'Épinards)

2 quarts spinach
3 oz. fresh butter
Pinch grated nutmeg
1 teaspoon salt
2 quarts white stock
1 teaspoon caster sugar
Fried croûtons

Wash and boil spinach in its own juice. There should be a pint of it when cooked, chopped and mashed into a fine paste. Place in saucepan with butter, nutmeg, and salt. Cook for 10 minutes, stirring constantly. Add stock. Boil up. Rub through a sieve. Reheat and stir in 2 or 3 pats of butter and sugar before serving. Serve with fried croûtons. *For 7 or 8 persons.*

CREAM OF TOMATOES (Crème de Tomates)

1½ lb. tomatoes
1 slice onion
1 saltspoon ground mace
1 saltspoon pepper
1 clove garlic
1 quart milk
1 tablespoon butter

Wash tomatoes and place in a saucepan with onion, mace, pepper and garlic. Cook for 5 minutes. Heat milk in a double boiler. Add butter and flour, kneaded together. Stir till sauce is smooth and slightly thickened. Sieve tomatoes into a basin. Reheat. Add soda. Stir a minute, then

2 tablespoons flour
1/2 teaspoon baking soda
1 saltspoon celery salt
Paprika or cheesettes

gradually stir in the hot white sauce, but do not allow to boil. Add celery salt. Serve in hot soup cups. Sprinkle lightly with paprika or serve with cheesettes. *For 4 persons.*

CREAM OF VEAL (Crème de Veau)

4 pints veal stock
2 oz. cornflour
1 cup milk
1/4 pint cream
2 egg yolks
Salt, pepper and celery salt to taste
Minced chives or parsley

Strain stock into a saucepan. Dissolve cornflour in a little of the cold milk. Stir in remainder of milk and pour into stock. Stir till boiling. Mix cream with egg yolks in a basin. Stir in quickly a cup of boiling soup, then mix soup, cream and yolks quickly with soup in saucepan. Stir till very hot, but not boiling. Season to taste. Garnish with minced chives or parsley. *For 8 persons.*

CREAM OF WATERCRESS (Crème de Cresson)

2 large bunches watercress
1 quart white stock or water
1/2 teaspoon salt
1 lb. potatoes
1 oz. butter
1 oz. flour
Pepper to taste
Fried croûtons

Pick over watercress. Place in a colander or sieve and toss under cold water tap till perfectly clean. Leave till dry, then chop finely. Pour stock or water into a saucepan. Add salt. Peel and chop potatoes and add to water. Cover and simmer till tender. Place a colander over a basin and pour in potato water. Rub potatoes through a sieve. Melt butter in a saucepan. Stir in flour, and when frothy, pour in potato water, stirring all the time. When smooth, add potato purée. Cover and simmer for 30 minutes. Add pepper to taste, and watercress. Cover and simmer for 5 minutes. Serve with fried croûtons. *For 4 persons.*

DUTCH CREAM SOUP (Crème Hollandaise)

1 small cucumber
2 small carrots
1 oz. butter or margarine
3/4 oz. flour
1 1/2 pints chicken or veal stock
2 egg yolks
1/4 pint cream
4 tablespoons boiled green peas
1/2 teaspoon minced tarragon
1/2 teaspoon minced parsley
Salt and pepper to taste
Whipped cream

Prepare cucumber and carrots, then cut into rounds with a vegetable cutter ; there should be between 1 1/2 and 2 gills altogether. Place in a saucepan. Cover with boiling salted water. Simmer until tender. Strain thoroughly. Melt fat. Stir in flour. Gradually stir in stock. Stir until boiling. Skim and boil for 2 or 3 minutes, stirring constantly. Beat egg yolks. Gradually beat in cream. When blended, stir very gradually into stock and cook over low heat until thick, stirring constantly, but do not allow to boil. Add cucumber, carrot and green peas, and 2 tablespoons sliced cooked French beans, if liked. Stir until boiling, then add tarragon and parsley. Season to taste with salt and pepper. Garnish with whipped cream. *For 4 persons.*

FISH SOUPS

Fish soups, some of which are known as bisques, are usually a combination of sieved cooked fish, fish stock and white sauce. They are most popular during Lent, but can be served at any time of the year.

Garnishes : Minced chervil, chives, fennel or parsley ; some of the fish ; fried croûtons ; paprika ; or whipped cream.

Accompaniments : Oyster crackers ; salted crackers ; pretzels ; small cream crackers ; small cheese biscuits brushed with melted butter, salted and heated.

Quantity to Allow : About 1½ gills per person.

CREAM OF CRAB (Crème de Crabe)

1 lb. flaked crab
3 pints hot milk
3 hard-boiled eggs
Pinch of allspice
½ teaspoon dry mustard
Salt and pepper to taste
1 tablespoon butter or margarine
2 small lemons
3 tablespoons thick cream

Place the crab in top of a double boiler. Add milk, shelled eggs, allspice, mustard and salt and pepper to taste. Cover and cook over low heat for 12 minutes, then rub through a sieve. Reheat. Uncover and add fat. Wash, dry and cut the lemons into thin slices. Place in heated soup tureen. Add soup. Whip and float cream on top. If serving in cups, divide whipped cream equally between portions. *For 6 or 8 persons.*

CREAM OF LOBSTER (Crème d'Homard)

1 lobster (2 lb.)
1 pint fish stock
1 cup medium white sauce
Salt and pepper to taste
1 heaped teaspoon minced parsley or chervil
Whipped cream flavoured paprika

Break up lobster. Remove all meat from shell and claws. Bring to boil. Boil for 25 minutes. Strain into a basin. Add stock. Return to saucepan. Cut lobster into small pieces. Add to stock. Gradually stir in sauce. Stir until piping hot. Add salt and pepper to taste and parsley or chervil. Garnish with paprika cream. *For 4 persons.*

CREAM OF OYSTER (Crème d'Huîtres)

1 pint small shelled oysters
1 pint thin white sauce
Salt and cayenne pepper to taste
Pinch of ground mace
1 heaped teaspoon minced chives or parsley
Oyster crackers

Pick over the oysters, removing any bits of shell. Place in a saucepan. Strain in liquid. Cook until the edges curl and the oysters " plump " out. Add to sauce. Season to taste with salt and cayenne pepper, and mace. Garnish with minced chives or parsley. Serve with oyster crackers. *For 3 persons.*

CREAM OF SALMON (Crème de Saumon)

1 cup canned salmon
2 tablespoons butter or margarine
2 tablespoons flour
1 quart hot milk
1 teaspoon salt
Pepper to taste
1 teaspoon minced parsley
Fried croûtons

Drain off oil from salmon, and turn on to a dish. Remove any skin and bones, then flake and rub fish through a sieve. Melt fat. Stir in flour by degrees, and then a cup of the milk gradually. Stir till smooth and add remainder of milk. Stir till boiling. Add salmon. Season to taste. Add parsley. Serve with fried croûtons. *For 5 or 6 persons.*

SCALLOP STEW (Soupe de Pétoncles, Américaine)

1½ pints hot milk
2 tablespoons butter
1 teaspoon sugar
¼ teaspoon Worcester sauce
Salt and pepper to taste
1 lb. scallops
Dash of paprika
½ pint thick cream
1 dessertspoon minced parsley

Pour milk into the top of a double boiler. Add butter, sugar, Worcester sauce and salt and pepper to taste. Wash scallops. Remove beards and any black portions. Rinse scallops well. Chop finely and place in boiler. Bring to boil and cook for 5 minutes stirring constantly. Stir in cream. Repeat but do not allow to boil. Add paprika and parsley. *For 6 persons.*

PUREES

A purée is a soup made of vegetables, or of lentils, dried beans, or peas and vegetables rubbed through a sieve and served with fried croûtons. If a very smooth purée is wanted, " bind " with creamed arrowroot, cornflour or flour. These nourishing soups are most welcome in cold weather. They are generally served with fried croûtons. If preferred they can be garnished otherwise.

Quantity to Allow : About 1½ gills per person.

VEGETABLE PUREE (Purée de Légumes)

BASIS RECIPE
2 oz. butter, dripping or margarine
2 lb. prepared vegetables to taste
2 peeled medium-sized onions
1 quart stock
Flour and milk as required
Salt and pepper to taste

Melt fat in a saucepan. Slice vegetables thinly and add. Cover. Cook very slowly for 10 minutes, shaking pan occasionally. Add stock, or half stock and half water, or use water flavoured with a meat cube or extract. Cover. Simmer gently till vegetables are soft. Rub through a hair sieve. Measure purée. Rinse saucepan. Add purée. Cream flour with milk, allowing ½ oz.

flour and ¼ pint milk to each pint of soup. Stir till blended. Cook for 5 to 10 minutes, stirring constantly. Season with salt and pepper. If adding cream, allow 1 tablespoon to each pint of soup. Reheat, but don't allow to come to the boil. *For 5 or 6 persons.*

Artichoke and Mushroom Purée : Substitute 1½ lb. Jerusalem artichokes, and $\frac{1}{2}$ lb. mushrooms for mixed vegetables if a strong mushroom flavour is wanted, otherwise allow only 6 oz. mushrooms.

ASPARAGUS PUREE (Purée d'Asperges)

1 quart chicken or veal stock
12 stalks asparagus
2 oz. butter
2 oz. flour
1/4 pint milk
1 egg yolk
Salt and pepper to taste

Remove fat from stock. Pour stock into a saucepan. Add prepared asparagus. Cover and simmer till asparagus is tender. Remove asparagus and cut off tips and rub as much of the stalks through a sieve as will go. Add to stock. Melt butter in a saucepan. Stir in flour. When frothy, add asparagus purée and stock. Stir till boiling. Add half milk. Simmer for 3 minutes. Beat egg yolk. Stir in remainder of milk. Remove pan from fire and strain egg and milk into soup, stirring constantly. Season to taste with salt and pepper. Add asparagus tips. Serve at once in a hot soup tureen. If soup is too thick, thin down with milk before adding egg yolk. When using canned asparagus, substitute the liquid for half the stock. *For 4 or 6 persons.*

BEAN AND LENTIL PUREE (Purée Duboys)

1 cup haricot beans
1 cup lentils
1½ quarts water or stock
1 medium-sized carrot
1 medium-sized potato
1 stick celery
1 handful sorrel
1 dessertspoon butter
Salt and pepper to taste
1/2 cup hot cream
Fried croûtons

Wash beans and lentils. Place in a colander under the cold water tap. Drain well. Place in saucepan. Add water or stock. Bring to boil. Cover and simmer gently until nearly tender. Prepare carrot, potato and celery. Cut into slices. Add to beans and lentils in pan. Cover and simmer until tender. Meanwhile wash sorrel thoroughly. Place in a saucepan with butter. Cook slowly, stirring frequently, until soft, then pour in soup. Stir until boiling, then rub through a hair sieve. Rinse saucepan. Add purée. Stir until boiling. If the flavour of sorrel is not sharp enough, add a drop or two of vinegar. Season to taste with salt and pepper. Stir in cream, but do not allow to boil. Serve with fried croûtons. *For 6 persons.*

BEAN AND TOMATO PUREE (Purée à la Condé)

1/2 lb. haricot beans
1 quart white stock
1 oz. butter or margarine
1 onion
1/4 medium-sized turnip
1 small carrot
1/4 pint tomato purée
Salt and pepper to taste
1/4 pint cream

Soak beans in a basin of water overnight. Drain and place in saucepan with stock. Cover tightly. Boil for 30 minutes, tightly covered. Melt fat in another saucepan. Dice and add vegetables. Stir for 5 minutes. Add to the beans and stock. Cover saucepan. Simmer for 2 hours. Rub soup through a wire sieve. Turn purée into rinsed pan. Add tomato purée. Season to taste with salt and pepper. Heat till piping hot. Heat cream slightly, then pour into a hot soup tureen. Stir in purée. *For 6 persons.*

BELGIAN TOMATO PUREE (Purée de Tomates à la Belgique)

White stock as required
1 large prepared leek
1½ lb. tomatoes
2 large prepared peeled potatoes
3 sticks celery
2 medium-sized carrots
1 thick slice bread
Pinch caster sugar
Salt and pepper to taste
2 pats fresh butter
1 egg yolk
2 tablespoons cold water

Measure 1 pint of stock into a saucepan, or you can use left-over chicken or veal gravy, diluted with water. Slice and add leek. Wash, and slice in tomatoes. Slice and add potatoes. Wash, scrape and slice in celery. Scrape, wash and slice in carrots. Add a pinch of salt. Bring to the boil. Add bread and sugar. Skim, cover and simmer gently for 1 hour. Stir occasionally or the vegetables may adhere to the bottom of the pan. When tender, rub through sieve. Thin to taste with extra boiling stock. Bring to boil. Season to taste with salt and pepper. Just before serving, stir in butter, and egg yolk, beaten and mixed with water. Stir till creamy, but do not allow to boil after adding egg yolk. If liked, you can float a teaspoon of whipped cream on each portion. *For 6 persons.*

CABBAGE AND POTATO PUREE
(Purée de Chou à la Fermière)

1 small cabbage
1 oz. butter or margarine
3 bacon rinds
1 peeled medium-sized onion
4 sliced medium-sized potatoes
1 quart water
1 ham bone
½ pint milk
Salt and pepper to taste

Wash cabbage and remove stalks. Trim and shred cabbage. Melt fat in a soup pan. Add bacon rinds and slice in onion. Cook for 3 minutes, turning occasionally. Add potatoes, water and ham bone. Cover and simmer till vegetables are soft. Rub through a sieve. Reheat purée. Add milk. Season with salt and pepper to taste. Stir till piping hot. *For 5 or 6 persons.*

CELERY PUREE (Purée de Céleri)

3 heads celery
1 medium-sized onion
1 oz. butter or margarine
1 quart white stock
1 pint milk
Salt and pepper to taste
½ gill cream
Fried croûtons

Trim and wash celery. Remove any stalks that are damaged. Slice remainder thinly. Peel and chop onion. Melt fat in a saucepan and add celery and onion. Fry slowly for 3 or 4 minutes, stirring frequently. Add stock and half the milk. Bring to boil. Simmer gently until celery is tender. Rub through a sieve. Rinse saucepan. Add purée. Stir in remainder of milk. Season with salt and pepper to taste. Heat to boiling point and stir in cream. Serve with fried croûtons. *For 6 persons.*

CREOLE GREEN PEA PUREE (Purée de Pois à la Créole)

1½ pints green peas
1 medium-sized peeled onion
2 sprigs parsley
1½ pints white stock
1½ pints milk

Place peas in a saucepan. Add minced peeled onion and minced parsley. Boil in stock till tender. Rub through a sieve. Rinse out pan and pour in purée. Stir in milk, brought just to

Salt and pepper to taste
Fried croûtons

boiling point. Season to taste. Serve with fried croûtons. *For 6 persons.*

LENTIL AND TOMATO PUREE (Purée à la Westmorland)

1½ cups lentils
¼ teaspoon baking soda
2 quarts cold water
½ cup celery leaves
¼ pint canned tomatoes
2 tablespoons minced onion
1 teaspoon sugar
Salt and pepper to taste
2 tablespoons butter or margarine
3 small tablespoons flour
1 pint milk
Fried croûtons

Rinse lentils in a colander. Drain well. Soak overnight in cold water to cover. Strain. Rinse again. Place in a saucepan. Add soda, cold water, celery leaves, tomatoes, onion and sugar. Bring to boil. Cover and simmer gently until tender, then rub through a sieve fine enough to retain tomato seeds. Season to taste with salt and pepper. Measure. There should be 2 quarts. If not, add water or stock to make up that amount. Melt butter or margarine in a saucepan. Add flour. Stir till frothy, then stir in milk. Stir till boiling. Gradually stir in purée, but do not allow to boil. When piping hot, serve with fried croûtons. *For 8 persons.*

POTATO PUREE (Purée de Pommes de terre)

2 tablespoons butter or margarine
2 teaspoons chopped onion
2 dessertspoons minced celery
½ lb. sliced potatoes
1½ quarts boiling beef stock
1 tablespoon flour
½ teaspoon salt
Pepper to taste
Fried croûtons

Melt half the fat in a saucepan. Add onion and celery. Simmer for 10 minutes. Add potatoes. Cover and cook for 3 minutes. Add stock. Bring to boil. Cover. Simmer for 1 hour. Rub through a sieve. Rinse saucepan. Melt remainder of fat. Stir in flour, then gradually stir in potato purée. Bring to boil. Season with salt and pepper. Serve with fried croûtons. *For 6 persons.*

SPLIT PEA PUREE (Purée, Egyptienne)

½ lb. split peas
1½ oz. butter, margarine or dripping
1 peeled onion
1 stick celery
1 small peeled carrot
1 small peeled turnip
1 quart ham bone stock
Salt and pepper to taste
Fried croûtons

Soak peas in cold water to cover overnight. Melt fat in a saucepan. Drain peas and add with diced onion, celery, carrot and turnip. Stir over fire for 5 minutes, taking care that the vegetables do not brown, then add stock and season to taste with salt and pepper. Boil up gently and skim. Simmer until peas are tender. Sieve. Reheat. Serve with fried croûtons. *For 4 persons.*

MISCELLANEOUS SOUPS

COCK-A-LEEKIE

1 old fowl
1 good mutton bone
8 or 10 leeks

Place fowl and mutton bone on to boil with water to cover. Skim when water comes to boil, then cover and simmer for 3 hours. Clean and trim

12 prunes, soaked overnight in cold water
Salt and pepper to taste

leeks. Remove green stalks, and slit white stems. Wash stems well. Cut into inch slices. Add to stock. Simmer for 1½ hours. Add stoned prunes ½ hour before soup is ready. Season to taste. Remove fowl and mutton bone. Serve fowl separately, either covered with sauce, or as a salad or curry. Reserve one breast for chopping and adding to soup. *For 6 or 7 persons.*

CREOLE LETTUCE SOUP (Soupe de Laitue à la Créole)

2 quarts white stock
2 small lettuces
1½ tablespoons butter
1 lump sugar
1 tablespoon wine vinegar
Salt and pepper to taste
1 teaspoon flour
2 slices bread
1 egg
¼ pint cream

Remove any fat from stock. Pour stock into pan. Bring to boil. Simmer until reduced to 2½ pints. Wash, drain, and chop lettuce leaves. Melt 1 tablespoon of the butter in a saucepan. Add lettuce, sugar and vinegar. Cook slowly, stirring constantly, until lettuce is soft, then add stock. Season to taste with salt and pepper. Mix flour to a paste with remainder of butter. Add to soup with a dash of cayenne pepper if liked. Stir till soup boils. Remove from stove. Remove crusts from bread. Cut bread into dice. Place in the bottom of a soup tureen, or divide equally between soup cups or plates. Beat egg. Stir in cream by degrees. Mix well and add a little of the soup. Stir into soup. Return pan to stove. Stir till at boiling point but don't allow to boil. Garnish with whipped cream, if liked. *For 10 persons.*

FRENCH ONION SOUP (Soupe à l'Oignon, Française)

6 medium-sized onions
3 tablespoons butter
1 quart beef stock
Salt and pepper to taste
6 slices French bread
½ cup grated Parmesan cheese

Slice onions. Melt butter in a heavy saucepan. Add onions and fry slowly for about 20 minutes, or until pale brown, stirring frequently so that the slices are evenly cooked. Add stock. Bring to boil. Simmer ¼ hour. Season to taste with salt and pepper. Serve in hot soup cups. Toast or fry bread in butter or fat. Float one on each portion. Sprinkle it with Parmesan cheese. *For 6 persons.*

GOOD WIFE SOUP (Potage à la Bonne Femme)

1 lettuce
2 leeks
2 sorrel leaves
2 sprigs chervil
2 sprigs tarragon
1 inch cucumber
2 oz. butter
1 quart white stock
1 small potato
3 egg yolks
¼ pint cream
1 French roll
Salt and pepper to taste

Separate lettuce leaves. Wash lettuce. Trim and wash leeks. Wash sorrel and shred lettuce and sorrel leaves finely. Chop chervil, tarragon and cucumber. Melt butter in a saucepan. Add prepared vegetables and herbs. Stir over low heat till fat is absorbed, but do not allow to brown. Add stock. Peel and chop potato into small round slices. Add. Simmer till vegetables are tender. Beat egg yolks. Gradually stir in cream. Stir slowly into soup. Cook over stove, stirring constantly, until thick, but do not allow

Garnish fresh Herrings fried in Salt with wedges of lemon. *See page* 141.

Fish Pie, covered with Potato Flaky Pastry. *See page* 520.

Baked Stuffed Herring, garnished with lemon butterflies. Serve with potato crisps. *See pages* 140-141.

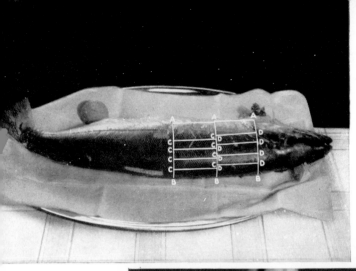

To carve Boiled Salmon, first make cuts across the fish from A - B, as illustrated. *See page* 185.

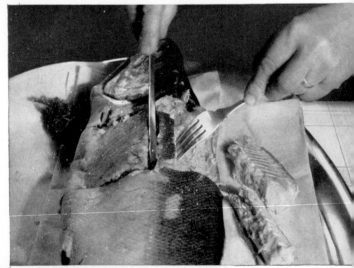

To carve neat portions of Salmon, remove the slices at right angles. *See page* 185.

Remove head and tail ends from Soles before carving. *See page* 185.

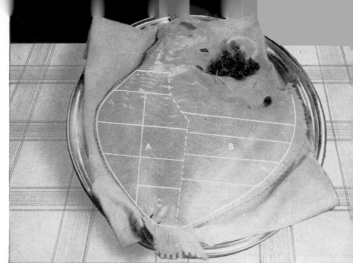

Carve large Turbot in squares. *See page* 184.

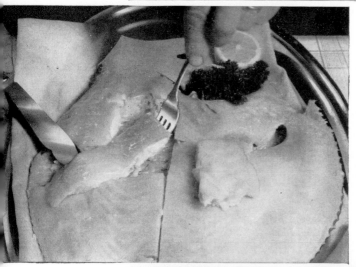

Make an incision from the middle of small Turbot before carving as illustrated. *See page* 184.

Cut Herring, Mackerel and Trout along the back of the spine before carving as illustrated. *See page* 186.

Garnish Chicken, Ham and Tongue Loaf with slices of tomato and sprigs of watercress. Serve with Devilled Eggs. *See* pages 322-323.

Serve Crab and Cucumber Salad, garnished heart of lettuce leaves, green peas and radish roses. *See page* 476-477.

Garnish Salmon Mousse with a wreath of radish slices on top and a wreath of watercress round the base. *See page* 150.

to boil. Slice roll. Toast in oven till dry, then place in bottom of soup tureen. Season to taste. Pour soup over. *For 6 persons.*

GRAVY SOUP (Potage de Boeuf)

1½ lb. shin of beef
1½ quarts water or stock
1 carrot
½ turnip
1 medium-sized onion
1 stick celery
1 oz. butter or dripping
2 bay leaves
1 tablespoon cornflour
Salt and pepper to taste

Wipe meat and cut into dice, then place in a saucepan. Add cold water or stock. Cover and bring to boil. Prepare vegetables. Slice and fry carrot, turnip, onion and celery in smoking hot fat till brown, then add to soup with bay leaves. Simmer for 3 hours, then rub through a sieve. Dissolve cornflour in 3 tablespoons stock or water. Stir into soup and boil for 4 minutes, stirring constantly. Season to taste. *For 6 persons.*

HARE SOUP (Soupe de Lièvre)

1 fresh brown hare
2 oz. butter
3 oz. lean bacon or ham bone
2 medium-sized onions
1 carrot
4 shallots
2 oz. flour
2 quarts stock
2 teaspoons salt
3 cloves
1 blade mace
12 peppercorns
1 bay leaf
¼ teaspoon sugar
½ pint port wine
Egg balls as required

Skin hare. Dip a cloth in tepid water and wipe it carefully all over, changing the water if necessary. Remove the eyes. Cut up hare to where ribs begin. Clean, remove and skin kidneys and liver. Wring a cloth out of fresh water and wash all the inside of the hare perfectly clean, specially the skinny parts. Break the diaphragm and let the blood run into a clean dry basin. Remove and rinse the heart in a little water and strain water into the blood. Joint hare, dividing bones at one chop to avoid splintering. Keep some of the best joints to cook as cutlets or fillets or in a pie. Put butter, and bacon, freed from rind and cut small, into a large strong pot. When smoking hot, add peeled and sliced onions, scraped and sliced carrot and peeled shallots. Fry for 2 minutes, stirring all the time. If the bacon is fat, use less butter. Dip each joint in the flour. Fry on both sides to a soft dark brown. Sprinkle in remaining flour. Add stock. If water has to be used, add 2 lb. shin of beef, one scraped head of celery, washed and diced, 2 tablespoons chopped and peeled turnip. Add salt. Bring slowly to boil, then skim carefully. Add cloves, mace, peppercorns, bay leaf and sugar. Simmer very slowly for 2 or 3 hours, if young. If old, for 4 hours. When tender, strain soup through a hair sieve. Cool. Meanwhile remove meat from the bones and pass it through meat grinder. Pound well in a mortar, moistening it with a little stock. Now rub through a hair sieve. Return strained stock to saucepan. Bring to boil. Place 3 or 4 tablespoons sieved meat into a basin and thin it down gradually with some hot stock. Do not add a lot of stock at once or the soup will lump and curdle. Mix meat and stock to a smooth paste, then thin down with more soup to a creamy consistency and turn into a saucepan. Stir constantly till boiling, then add ½ pint of port gradually, more seasoning, if required, and a dash of cayenne. Draw pan to side of stove, and, when soup is off the boil, strain in blood. Stir in carefully until soup looks brown. Reheat, stirring constantly, but do not boil. Serve garnished with egg balls. *For 7 or 8 persons.*

LIVER AND MUSHROOM SOUP (Crème de Foie de Veau)

3 tablespoons butter
8 oz. chopped calves' liver
1 cup chopped peeled mushrooms
1 sprig parsley
Salt and pepper to taste
1 quart beef stock
1 tablespoon flour
1 cup thin cream

Melt half the butter in a saucepan. Add liver, mushrooms and parsley. Fry slowly for 5 minutes. Add ½ teaspoon salt and pepper to taste, and the stock. Cover and bring to boil. Lower to simmering heat. Cover pan and simmer for 20 minutes, or until tender. Melt remainder of butter in a small saucepan. Stir in flour, and when frothy, stir in a little of the soup liquor by degrees until you have added about ½ pint. Stir till boiling, then add by degrees to the soup, stirring constantly. Stir in cream by degrees. Cook over low heat for 5 minutes, stirring constantly. Re-season if necessary. *For 6 persons.*

MILK SOUP (Potage au Lait)

1 medium-sized onion
1 leek
½ celery stick
1 oz. butter
1 oz. flour
1 pint chicken or veal stock
Salt and pepper to taste
1 pint top milk or thin cream

Peel onion. Trim and wash leek. Scrape and wash celery. Slice vegetables thinly. Melt butter in a saucepan. Add vegetables. Fry slowly until the butter is absorbed without allowing them to brown. Stir in flour and stock. Keep stirring until boiling. Simmer gently for 20 minutes. Rub through a hair sieve. Reheat. Season with salt and pepper to taste, then stir in milk. Bring almost to boiling point before serving. *For 4 or 5 persons.*

MINESTRONE SOUP (Potage à l'Italienne)

1 small scraped carrot
1 small peeled onion
2 prepared leeks
1 small peeled turnip
1 cleaned celery stick
3 tablespoons olive oil
2 quarts weak beef or chicken stock
Salt and pepper to taste
½ saltspoon powdered saffron
1 oz. spaghetti
1 oz. rice
1 small peeled potato
1 large peeled tomato
1 tablespoon minced parsley

Cut prepared vegetables into dice. Heat olive oil in a saucepan. Add carrot, onion, leeks, turnip and celery. Cook slowly for 10 minutes, stirring occasionally. Add stock. Cover and bring to boil. Skim. Add salt, pepper and saffron. Cover and simmer for ¾ hour. Break spaghetti into 1½-inch pieces and add with rice. Bring to boil. Boil for 20 minutes. Dice potato and tomato and add. Boil gently for 25 minutes. Add parsley. Serve with a dish of grated Parmesan or Gruyère cheese. *For 8 or 9 persons.*

MOCK TURTLE SOUP (Potage de Tortue Fausse)

½ calf's head
Salt and pepper to taste
Paprika to taste

Prepare calf's head and place in a saucepan. Cover with cold water. Bring to boil. Add salt, pepper and paprika. Slice onions and carrots.

2 peeled onions
2 scraped carrots
½ cup sieved tomatoes
Butter as required
Flour as required
1 teaspoon grated lemon rind
½ teaspoon lemon juice

Add with tomatoes. Cover and simmer for 3 hours. Strain. Melt butter in a saucepan. Stir in flour and thin with 2 cups of the stock, allowing 1 tablespoon butter and 2 tablespoons flour to each quart of prepared stock. Bring to boil, stirring constantly, and boil till smooth. Stir in remainder of stock. Add grated lemon rind, strained lemon juice, and ¼ cup sherry, if liked, and diced calf's head. *For 6 or 8 persons.*

MULLIGATAWNY SOUP (Potage à l'Indienne)

2 peeled onions
1 scraped carrot
½ head celery
4 apples
1 oz. lean ham
2 oz. butter
1 oz. flour
1 dessertspoon curry paste
1 oz. curry powder
1 teaspoon sugar
2 quarts stock
½ lb. cold chicken
Juice ½ lemon

Prepare vegetables and cut into dice. Peel and chop apples. Cut ham into small pieces. Fry all in butter for 3 minutes. Add flour, curry paste and powder and all other ingredients, except chicken and lemon juices. Stir till boiling. Simmer till vegetables are quite tender, then rub through a sieve. Reheat. Add chicken and lemon juice. Serve with about 2 cups boiled rice passed round in a separate dish. If you stir in ¼ pint cream, this greatly improves soup. *For 6 or 7 persons.*

OXTAIL SOUP (Potage de Queue de Boeuf)

3½ lb. oxtail
1 oz. butter or dripping
¾ lb. lean beef
3 quarts water
1 tablespoon salt
1 small turnip
1 large onion
3 medium-sized carrots
1 tablespoon diced celery
¼ cup diced celeriac
1 dessertspoon flour

Split oxtail and cut into small pieces. Melt fat. Fry tail lightly. Put meat and prepared oxtail in soup pan. Pour over water. Add salt. Bring slowly to boil. Cook slowly but steadily for 4 hours. Add vegetables, all cleaned and diced. Boil 1 hour longer till stock is reduced to half its original quantity. Strain but reserve carrot and turnip. Melt fat in a saucepan. Add flour. Stir until brown. Gradually pour in a cup of soup stock. Stir this into remaining stock. Add carrot and turnip. Reheat. Serve with toast. *For 7 or 8 persons.*

QUEEN'S SOUP (Potage à la Reine)

1 scraped carrot
1 peeled onion
2 oz. bacon
1 old fowl
2 quarts chicken stock
2 oz. butter or chicken fat
Salt and cayenne pepper to taste
1 cup boiled or canned peas

Slice carrot and onion. Dice bacon, and truss chicken. Place in a saucepan. Add half the stock. Cover and cook slowly till bird is tender. Remove chicken. Take off skin. Remove meat from bones and put through a meat grinder. Pound to a paste in a mortar with butter or fat. Season to taste with salt and cayenne pepper. Rub through a sieve. Scrape purée into a saucepan. Strain in chicken stock. Stir in reserved stock. Boil up. Simmer for 10 minutes. Reheat. Season and add peas. *For 8 or 10 persons.*

RUSSIAN BEET SOUP (Milchik)

6 beetroots
2 pints white stock
Salt and pepper to taste
1 teaspoon vinegar *or*
2 tablespoons Madeira or sherry
Whipped cream as required

Wash and slice beetroot into a saucepan. Boil, in the usual way, in cold salted water to cover. Drain. Rub through a fine sieve. Rinse saucepan. Add purée and salt. Season with salt and pepper. Bring to boil. Boil for $\frac{1}{4}$ hour. Stir in vinegar or wine. Garnish with whipped cream. *For 6 persons.*

SCOTCH KIDNEY SOUP (Potage de Rognon, Ecossaise)

1 ox kidney
2 oz. flour
2 oz. butter
1 peeled onion
2 quarts stock
1 scraped carrot
1 small sliced turnip
Salt and pepper to taste
1 teaspoon Worcester sauce

Wipe and remove fat from kidney. Cut kidney into small pieces. Roll in flour. Melt butter in a saucepan. Add chopped onion and kidney. Brown both, then stir in stock and bring slowly to boil, skimming when necessary. Dice and add carrot and turnip. Cover and simmer gently for 3 hours. Pour into a sieve. Remove kidney and rub soup through. Melt a pat of butter in a saucepan. Stir in flour left over after flouring kidney. Add soup by degrees, and stir till boiling. Add kidney. Season to taste. Stir in Worcester sauce. Reheat and serve. *For 8 or 9 persons.*

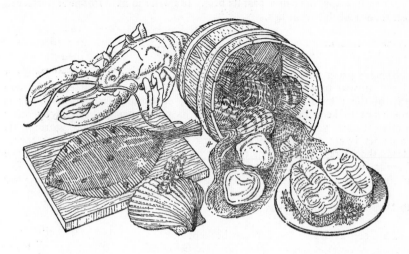

Fish

Fish is a valuable food, though less satisfying and less stimulating than butchers' meat. Low in carbohydrates and fats, it is an ideal food for people of sedentary occupations, and for those who are unable to take exercise, such as aged people and invalids.

Generally rich in proteins and vitamins A, B and D, fish is a source of calcium, iron and phosphorus. Herrings are a cheap source of protein and fat. They also supply vitamins A and D. All oily fish, such as eel, mackerel, mullet, pilchards, salmon, sardines, sprats, sturgeon and tunny fish, are excellent sources of fat and vitamins A and D. The molluscs, which include mussels and oysters, have not only a high vitamin but an iodine content and are easily digested when raw, but the crustaceans, including crabs, lobsters, etc., though equally nutritious, are not so digestible owing to their high fat content. White fish, sometimes known as "lean fish," cod, hake, plaice, sole, etc., have their fat confined to the liver, so are more digestible than oily fish and therefore more suitable for invalids and convalescents. On the other hand, they are not so nutritious because they contain less tissue forming protein than oily fish.

TO CHOOSE FISH

If there's a good choice, first plan dish, then select accordingly, making sure that the fish is fresh and in season. When buying fillets, see that the flesh is firm and supple, not flabby, and that the smell is fresh and slightly saline. Never choose any that smell of ammonia. The same thing applies to whole fish with this addition : they should have bright eyes, bright red gills, and firm bright scales. If eyes are dull, gills are dark maroon red and the scales break easily away, the fish is past its best. It's wiser to have frozen or preserved fish than doubtful fresh fish.

TO STORE FISH

Remove paper wrappings from fish, then wipe with a damp cloth. Re-wrap closely in wax paper, or place in a plastic bag. Place, if possible, in the drip tray of the refrigerator, or in a container, or chilling compartment. It is important to keep fish covered to avoid its odour being absorbed by other foods. Unless you wish to serve with heads on, remove before storing. If container is not available, cover fish first with damp butter-muslin or cheese cloth, then wrap in wax paper. Lay on a plate. Store directly under the freezing unit of the refrigerator. If you haven't a refrigerator, place on ice. If ice is not available, place in a cold cellar, or in the coldest part of your larder, in a draught if possible, or in a meat safe. Lay a meat cover on top to keep off flies and insects.

To Keep Fish : Some fish can be kept better than others. The oily class should be eaten as soon as possible after being caught. If it has to be kept, prepare it for cooking, then rinse and wipe dry. Place in the refrigerator, or on ice, or store in cellar, larder or meat safe as already described. If you haven't a refrigerator, white fish of the brill, turbot or halibut variety can be safely kept for a day or two, but the cod, haddock, hake, whiting varieties should be rubbed over with salt, if not to be cooked at once, or cleaned, cut into steaks, and fried lightly in a little hot oil. Finish cooking when required. Surplus herring, mackerel, salmon, skate, smelts, sprats can be soused or pickled.

To Test Doubtful Fish: Smell the backbone ; it's along the backbone that fish first show signs of decomposition. Another test is to place in a basin of cold fresh water. If the fish floats, it is not fit to eat.

Frozen Fish : If purchased in its frozen form, it should be placed, unopened, in a covered container in the refrigerator if possible, or on ice, and left for about 7 to 10 hours to thaw out. If to be used soon, place in cold water. Soak for 2 or 3 hours, but this is not so good a method as to allow it to thaw itself out, as frozen fish loses some of its flavour while soaking. If no refrigerator is available, do not buy frozen fish unless you wish to use it at once, as it will soon decompose once it has thawed out. Cook " quick frozen " fish at once without thawing, but allow a little longer than you would when cooking fresh fish or thaw at room temperature. Dry all frozen fish with a cloth before cooking. *" Quick frozen " fish must be kept in a frozen state unless cooked the day it is bought.*

Smoked Fish : Unwrap and re-wrap in greaseproof or wax paper. Store in larder. Don't place smoked fish, except smoked salmon, to chill in refrigerator. Use within a day or two. Kippers should be stored just below chilling point. They soon contract mould if stored in a refrigerator.

TO CLEAN FISH

Most housewives prefer to buy fish ready for cooking. This means that it is cleaned, split and boned, made into fillets or dressed to your taste by the fishmonger. It is most important that fish should be cleaned thoroughly before starting to prepare it for the table. Make certain that any fish that is to be served with the skin on has no scales left on. Remove scales carefully with the back of a knife. If any congealed blood has been left inside the fish, rub inside with a soft brush or cloth dipped in salt. This will remove any fine black skin as well as the blood. Should you want to leave the head on fish, be sure to remove the eyes at this stage. To do so, cut the skin round the sockets. Press your thumb behind each eye in turn and push it out.

To Scale: Scrape from tail to head against scales with the back of knife. Rinse knife and fish frequently during operation.

To Clean Flat Fish: Lay scaled fish on a board or paper-covered table. If to be skinned, do so now. With a sharp knife make a transverse cut under the gills on the dark side. Remove insides without breaking the membrane that holds them together. Rinse insides. Rub with brush or cloth dipped in salt to remove any fine black skin, or blood remaining in cavities. Remove fins and gills—but not the fins of a gelatinous fish such as the turbot. If fish is not to be served whole, remove the head with the gills, and remove or trim tail according to taste. Lastly, rinse fish thoroughly in cold water, both inside and out. Dry with a cloth.

Round Fish : This is the class of fish which swim back uppermost, such as haddock, mackerel, whiting, etc. Lay scaled fish on board or paper-covered table. With a sharp knife make an incision or slit in the underside of fish, from just below head to half-way to the tail. Remove insides, then rinse inside. Rub with brush or cloth dipped in salt to remove any fine black skin or blood remaining in cavities. Remove fins and gills, and head if liked. Rinse fish thoroughly inside and out in cold water. Dry with a cloth.

Small Fish (such as sardines, smelts, etc.) : Make a small slit just below the gills. Remove insides through gills. Wash carefully, then remove fins and tails.

Whitebait: Do not remove insides.

Fish Cutlets, Steaks and Fillets : Scale or skin if required. Wipe carefully with a piece of butter-muslin or cheese cloth wrung out of cold water.

Fish Roes : Remove from small fish. Rinse and replace when fish is to be baked or grilled with roe inside. If fish is large, remove and rinse roe and cook separately. If the roe is cooked inside large fish, fish will be overdone when the roe is ready.

Flat Fish (whole) : After removing fins, wash and dry fish. Place on a board with the tail towards you and the dark side uppermost. Make a crosswise cut $\frac{1}{2}$ inch above tail. Insert your right thumb between the skin and the flesh at this point, and pass it up the right side towards the head. Repeat this on the other side with your left thumb. Gripping the tail of the fish down on the board with your left hand, dip your right fingers in a little salt and grasping the loosened skin at the root of the tail, draw it sharply off towards the head. Turn fish, and remove the white skin by the same procedure. Sometimes you will find it necessary to ease it off with a blunt knife.

Flat Fish (fillets) : If fillets are wanted, it is best to fillet before skinning. Place fillets on a board, skin side downwards. Dip fingers in salt. Now, gripping the tail end of the skin firmly with the left fingers, separate the flesh by short horizontal strokes from side to side with a sharp wet knife, keeping the flat of the knife pressed against the fish, and the edge close to the skin. Do this quickly and lightly.

Round Fish : Wash and dry fish. Place fish on board with the tail towards you. Cut off a narrow strip over and along backbone close to the back fins. Now make an incision across fish just below head, and gradually loosen the skin below head with the point of a sharp knife. Now dip your left fingers in salt and, beginning to loosen skin on one side, gently pull the skin down towards the tail, pressing flesh down with a knife in the right hand. Turn fish over and repeat process.

To Bone Fish for Stuffing : When boning fish, you must see that you handle flesh carefully so as not to break the flakes. Scale and clean fish. Skin if wanted, then split fish down the abdomen. Remove insides. Rinse. Lay on board covered with paper. Starting at the tail, slip knife under the flesh and cut off the flesh close to the bone along one side, scraping it gently as you cut it clean away from the bone and pressing knife against bone. Turn fish over on its other side and remove flesh in the same way. Now pick out or remove the backbone with your fingers or scissors, and the bones along both sides, all in one piece. Pick out any remaining bones with fingers or tweezers, or as many as possible. Rinse carefully in cold fresh water. Drain thoroughly. Stuff. Sew the edges together and cook fish as required.

To Fillet Fish : A little practice is necessary to fillet neatly. Fillets of fish are solid slices of fish free of bones. Sometimes skinned on both sides. If to be rolled up into " coronets " or " turbans," and the skin is left on one side, roll up with the skin outside. These slices are cut from each side of the backbone. Flat fish have four fillets and round fish two. If the fillets in either case are large, cut them into two or three smaller fillets slantwise. Always examine fillets before cooking to make certain that no tiny bones have been left in the flesh. All bones must be removed before cooking.

Flat Fish: First of all, make a straight long cut down the centre of the body from head to tail. The easiest way to fillet flat fish is to remove the fillet from the left-hand side on the upper side of the fish with a sharp, broad-bladed knife, then turn fish round before removing the second fillet. You work towards the tail for the left-hand fillet, and towards the head for the right-hand one. Remove fins as closely as possible, then cut round the head and tail, but don't remove them. Now make a cut through flesh along the side of the backbone to the tail. Next draw the point of your knife over the bone, under the flesh, and neatly remove the fillets on each side with long strokes. You may have to work your knife backwards and forwards to get them off without breaking them. Turn fish on other side and repeat treatment.

Round Fish: Wash, dry and remove heads. Cut off fins. Make an incision down the centre back, right to the bone, with a sharp knife, then, with the tail towards you, cut along the abdomen. Cut flesh cleanly from the bones with long strokes so as not to break up the fleshy tissue, working from head to tail and pressing knife against bone as you cut. Turn fish, this time with head towards you, and remove second fillet in the same way.

To Prepare Fish Steaks : Choose large fish from 4 to 6 lb. in weight, for making into steaks. When cleaning, do not skin as the skin holds flesh together. Cut in parallel slices across and right through the backbone, $\frac{1}{2}$ to $1\frac{1}{2}$ inches thick, according to taste and to how they are to be cooked.

TO COOK FISH

To be able to serve fish in perfection, do not over-cook it. Fish should be cooked only long enough to coagulate the protein. You can generally tell when it is ready by examining the flesh next to the bone. If it shows signs of coming away from bone, remove from stove at once.

TO MAKE A MARINADE FOR FISH

2 saltspoons salt
1 teaspoon minced parsley
$\frac{1}{2}$ bay leaf
Freshly ground pepper to taste
1 sprig thyme
1 clove
1 small blade mace
2 teaspoons minced onion
3 tablespoons salad oil
3 tablespoons vinegar

For Fish to be Baked or Boiled: Mix flavouring and seasoning together. Stir in oil, then vinegar. Pour over fish. Soak for at least 1 hour, turning twice during that period. Can be soaked for 2 hours if fish is thick, when it should be gashed thrice across the sides about $\frac{1}{4}$ inch deep, and about $\frac{3}{4}$ inch apart, if marinating whole fish. *For Fish to be Fried or Grilled:* Substitute a sprig of parsley for minced parsley and 4 slices onion for minced onion. Add a sprig of tarragon. Remove sprig of parsley and onion before cooking fish.

BAKED STUFFED FISH (Poisson farci au four)

Choose round fish, such as codling, haddock, etc., 3 to 5 lb. in weight. Remove head, if liked. If left on, remove eyes, and clean sockets. Trim or remove tail. Rub with a wet cloth dipped in salt both inside and out, then rinse and dry. Fill cavity with stuffing. Sew up with needle and thread. Either make three gashes through the skin on each side to keep fish shapely while cooking, or truss into the shape of a letter " S " with a skewer. Place on a greased rack. Brush with melted fat. If gashed, sprinkle the gashes well with melted fat. If not gashed, cover with strips of bacon, or dab all over with butter, and baste frequently while baking. Bake, uncovered, for $\frac{3}{4}$ to 1 hour, according to thickness, in a moderately hot oven, 375° F.

BAKED FISH AU GRATIN (Poisson au gratin)

Clean, wash and skin any medium-sized flat fish. Remove head, and trim fins and tail. Mix 1 teaspoon each of minced mushrooms and parsley with a pinch minced onion. Sprinkle half this mixture on a shallow buttered " gratin " fireproof dish. Score each side of fish from the centre back to the fins in oblique lines. Season one side with salt and pepper. Sprinkle with lemon juice. Lay fish in dish, seasoned side downwards. Season top with salt and pepper to taste. Sprinkle with a few drops lemon juice. Spread with remainder of parsley mixture. Coat lightly with dried breadcrumbs. Sprinkle with melted butter to moisten. Bake in a moderate oven, 350° F., for 15 to 20 minutes. Serve from dish, with tomato sauce, or dish up and stir $\frac{1}{4}$ pint Bercy or parsley sauce into the strained liquor from dish. Serve either in a hot sauce-boat. *For 2 persons.*

BAKED STUFFED FILLETS (Filets de Poisson farcis au four)

Use fillet of cod, haddock, plaice, sole, etc. Season prepared fillet with salt and pepper to taste. Spread stuffing evenly over the side from which the skin has been taken. Fold in two, or roll from head to tail, or pair fillets with stuffing, if liked. Place in a shallow buttered fireproof dish. Place a pat of butter on each fillet. Cover with buttered paper. Bake in a moderate oven, 350° F., for 20 to 30 minutes. If liked, pour $\frac{1}{2}$ to 1 gill of milk ($\frac{1}{4}$ pint) into tin before baking.

BAKED FILLETS, PROVENÇALE (Filets de Poisson, Provençale)

3 oz. sliced mushrooms
3 tablespoons butter
Salt and pepper to taste
Pinch of celery salt
1½ cups stale breadcrumbs
4 to 5 tablespoons hot milk
3 large fillets of fish

Fry mushrooms slowly in half the butter for 3 minutes. Add salt, pepper, celery salt, breadcrumbs and milk. Stir till blended. Divide fillets, each into 2 strips about 1½ inches wide. Grease muffin tins with butter. Line each tin with a strip of fish. Pack stuffing in centre of each. Cover with buttered paper. Bake in a moderate oven, 350° F., for about 20 minutes, then remove paper. Dab with remaining butter. Bake for 8 minutes longer till pale brown. Turn out carefully with a flexible knife. *For 6 persons.*

BAKED STUFFED FISH STEAKS
(Tranches de Poisson farcies au four)

Choose middle cut of cod, hake, halibut, or turbot, etc., when possible, 1½ to 2 inches thick. This is the best part for stuffing, as the flap helps to keep it in. (Tail can also be stuffed if boned.) Bake, in a moderately hot oven, 400° F., for about $\frac{1}{2}$ hour, basting every 10 minutes with $\frac{1}{2}$ oz. butter dissolved in 2 tablespoons boiling water, flavoured with 1 teaspoon lemon juice, and seasoned to taste.

Sauces to Serve with Baked Fish : Serve Hollandaise or Tartare sauce with a non-oily fish, such as cod, haddock, hake, John Dory, etc. Serve anchovy, fennel, mushroom, or mustard sauce with herring, mackerel and other oily fish.

TO BOIL AND POACH FISH

Only large fish, or large cuts of fish, can be "boiled," as it is called. To have fish boiled perfectly, *simmer* very slowly or poach in salted water, water and wine, or in a court bouillon, until cooked.

COURT BOUILLON

2 quarts water
2 tablespoons lemon juice or vinegar
1/4 cup sliced carrot
1/4 cup sliced celery
2-3 tablespoons sliced onion
1/2 bay leaf
2 cloves
6 crushed black peppercorns
2 sprigs parsley
1 clove garlic if liked
2 or 3 allspice berries
1 sprig thyme
1 1/2 teaspoons salt

If liked, equal quantity of white wine and water can be used instead of all water. Bring water, or water and wine, to boil. Add lemon juice or vinegar and remaining ingredients. Skim. Simmer very gently for 1 hour, when it is ready for use.

To Cook Fish in Court Bouillon: Rub fish all over with lemon juice to keep firm and white. Place fish on rack and lower into bouillon. There should be enough to cover fish by about an inch. If a fish kettle is not available, tie in butter muslin or cheesecloth and lay on a fireproof plate at the bottom of a large saucepan. Cover with lid or oiled paper. Bring to simmering point. Skim. Cook at this temperature on top of stove, or in the oven, till fish is tender and shows signs of coming away from bone, allowing 6 to 10 minutes per lb. and 6 to 10 minutes over, depending on whether fish or steaks are thin or thick. Drain thoroughly and dish up.

To Oven-Boil or Oven-Poach Fish : Place in greased or oiled baking dish or tin. Barely cover with fish stock, court bouillon, or just water, then with greased or oiled paper. Cook very gently in a slow oven, then serve like fish boiled or poached on top of stove.

TO POACH FISH

This method prevents fish breaking when cooked. Measure enough cold water into fish-kettle to cover fish by about an inch when added. To each quart of water required, add the following before the fish : 2 level teaspoons salt, 2 teaspoons vinegar, 1 scraped and washed medium-sized carrot, cut in slices, 1 small sliced peeled onion, or 2 halved peeled shallots, 1 sprig each of parsley and thyme, 1 clove and 1/2 bay leaf. Bring all to simmering point. Simmer for 5 to 10 minutes. Remove from stove. Leave till tepid. Wrap all delicate fish, such as salmon and trout, in butter-muslin or oiled paper, as they break very easily in cooking. Don't add any vinegar when cooking salmon. Place prepared fish gently on an oiled or greased rack, and lower rack into kettle. Leave pan uncovered. Bring to a very slow simmer. Cook for time required. Thick fish takes about 10 to 15 minutes, thin fish about 8 minutes.

When ready, flesh should separate easily from bones. Drain carefully. Serve on a hot dish, lined with a folded napkin or lace paper doily. Garnish with sprigs of fennel or parsley, and lemon fingers.

Sauces to Serve with Boiled or Poached Fish: Anchovy, caper, egg, fennel, Hollandaise, parsley, shrimp or Tartare.

TO CURRY FISH

Any firm fish or fillets of firm fish can be curried.

CURRIED WHITE FISH (Kari de Poisson)

BASIC RECIPE
1 lb. solid fish
1 peeled onion
1 oz. butter or margarine
1 cored peeled apple
1 dessertspoon lemon juice
2½ teaspoons curry powder
1 chopped peeled tomato
1¼ tablespoons flour
2 cups boiled rice

Clean and place fish in a saucepan. Cover with water. Bring to boil and simmer till ready, in about 10 minutes, then leave till cool, and weigh free from skin and bone. Chop onion. Melt fat in a frying pan. Add onion and fry slowly till clear, then add apple. Stir for a moment or two. Remove from stove. Add strained lemon juice, curry powder, tomato, flour and ¼ pint of the fish liquor. Cover and simmer for 15 minutes, or longer, until you obtain a thickish sauce. Flake and add fish. Bring again to boil. Place in a hot dish in a border of boiled rice. Serve with chutney. *For 2 or 3 persons.*

TO FRY FISH

1. *Batter:* Season fish with salt and pepper, and flavour to taste with lemon juice. Dip in one of the following batters, beaten egg and crumbs, or flour:

THIN BATTER

2 oz. flour
Salt and pepper to taste
Tepid water

Mix flour with salt and pepper. Stir in enough water to give you the consistency of thin cream. To coat with this batter, dip fillets, steaks or small whole fish, thoroughly dried, in the batter, then cover carefully with sieved or finely dried breadcrumbs.

THICK BATTER

¼ lb. flour
Salt and pepper to taste
1 beaten egg
Tepid milk or water

Mix flour with salt and pepper to taste. Stir in egg, and enough tepid milk or water to make a stiff batter. This batter should coat back of a spoon thickly. If flour is of poor quality, sift ½ teaspoon baking powder with flour or substitute self-raising flour.

2. *Egg and Crumb:* Season crumbs with salt and pepper, allowing 1 teaspoon salt and ¼ teaspoon pepper to ¾ pint crumbs. Use either dried or sieved stale breadcrumbs, crushed vermicelli, corn or wheat flakes. Place crumbs or flakes on a sheet of paper. Wipe fillets with a damp cloth. Beat 1 egg slightly with 1 tablespoon cold water. Lift fillets with a broad-bladed knife, and place in

the mixture, one at a time. Dredge top with the egg. Lift to allow any surplus egg to run back on to the plate, then gently place in crumbs. Toss crumbs over the fish and gently pat with a knife to make crumbs adhere to fish. Shake lightly to remove any extra crumbs before cooking. Remove to a plate covered with kitchen paper. Fillets coated in this way can be deep or shallow fried, oven-fried and baked. Better to stand for a little while before frying.

3. *Flour:* Dip fish in flour seasoned with salt, pepper and paprika, if liked. If flesh is at all soft, dip in seasoned flour, then in milk, and again in flour, crumbs or medium oatmeal before frying. Use oatmeal when frying herring or mackerel. Fry at once. Flour coating is generally used for shallow frying. Gudgeon, smelts, sprats, whiting and whitebait only need to be dipped in seasoned flour before frying, in oil for preference.

TEMPERATURES FOR FRYING

FAT (Butter, clarified dripping, margarine, lard)	Fish Cakes and Croquettes	380-390° F.	for 1 minute
	Fillets of Fish	370-375° F.	for 4-6 minutes
	Small Whole Fish	370-375° F.	for 3-5 minutes
OIL:	Fish Cakes and Croquettes	385° F.	for 1 minute
	Fillets of Fish	375° F.	for 4-6 minutes
	Small Whole Fish	375° F.	for 3-5 minutes

NOTE : Always clarify dripping to be used for frying. If any water remains in the unclarified fat, it will sputter when heated. Strain off after frying fish and store for use again.

To Deep or French Fry (*Equipment Required*) : Use a deep frying-pan with a frying-basket when available, otherwise, a deep strong saucepan into which frying-basket will fit ; a spoon, preferably perforated ; and a broad-bladed knife.
Method: Heat at least 1 lb., preferably 1½ lb., lard, clarified dripping, or oil till smoking hot. The pan must be large enough to allow fat to come half-way up the sides only. If pan is too shallow, fat may boil over. Lower prepared fish into fat or oil. If fillets, place skin side downwards, to prevent curling up. There should only be one layer in the basket. Only fry a few pieces of fish at one time. If too many are added, the temperature of fat or oil will be reduced and the fish will absorb the fat and become soggy. Cook till golden brown. Drain on soft kitchen or absorbent paper.

To Shallow or Dry Fry (Sautéing) : Cod, hake, halibut, or turbot steaks, small thick fish, such as smelts, small trout ; fillets of flat fish and small flat fish. Heat fat or oil in a frying-pan to the depth of ⅛ to ¼ inch thick till smoking hot. Fry prepared fish till brown below. Turn with a broad-bladed knife, and brown on second side. Drain on soft kitchen or absorbent paper.

To Oven-Fry : Season prepared fish fillets or steaks, or whole flat fish, with salt and pepper to taste. Sprinkle with cooking oil. Roll in fine dried crumbs. Place in a well-oiled baking tin or dish. Bake in a fairly hot oven, 425° F., till crisp and golden. Drain on soft kitchen or absorbent paper.

To Serve Fried Fish : Arrange on a flat hot dish. Garnish with sprigs of fennel, fresh or fried parsley and lemon butterflies or wedges. Omit lemon when fish is to be served with mayonnaise or sauce Tartare or tomato salad.

Sauces to Serve with Fried Fish : Anchovy, Hollandaise, Meunière, mustard, shrimp, Tartare, or tomato, etc.

TO GRILL FISH

This is a method of cooking fish greatly neglected in Britain. Grilled fish is more digestible than fried fish. To grill with an electric griller, switch on at " High " for 2 minutes before starting operations. With a gas one, turn flame on full for 4 minutes. Lower heat as required, according to thickness and size of fish.

To prepare fish, cut large ones, such as cod, haddock, salmon, etc., in steaks about 1 to 1½ inches thick, and cut deep gashes equal distance apart, on both sides of small fish, such as bloaters, herring, mackerel, etc., to allow heat to penetrate flesh. If grilling a fish without much flavour, or a dry fish, soak it in a marinade for at least 1 hour, turning every 20 minutes, before draining and grilling. Delicate fish, such as red mullet or trout, can be wrapped in buttered paper before grilling, but must be grilled under low heat, otherwise paper will catch fire. Small soles and plaice can also be grilled in this way. Turn frequently when cooking. Dust fish with seasoned flour, then dredge with melted fat or oil. To grill fish, heat grill as suggested. Place fish on a hot greased or oiled griller. Slip under grill quickly, allowing 2 to 6 inches space between fish and grill heat. Lower heat and grill slowly till brown on both sides, turning once. If fish is thick, turn twice. Use a fish slice, and handle fish carefully or flesh might break. Do not test with a fork. If not certain whether fish is cooked or not, gently insert the back of a small knife close to the bone. If fish contains roe, grill roes separately, then insert with a knife, for if roes are left in, the fish will be cooked while roes are still half raw. To grill split fish, place, skin side downwards, on a well-oiled or greased griller. Grill slowly for 6 to 10 minutes, about 6 inches from heat, till fish is nicely browned. Baste freely. Turn and grill on skin side till skin is crisp. Sprinkle with a little melted butter or margarine before serving.

To Grill Fish Steaks: Rinse steaks, 1 to 1½ inches thick, and dry thoroughly. Trim if required. Season with salt and pepper to taste. Flavour with a few drops lemon juice or tarragon vinegar. Brush with melted butter or cooking oil. Dredge lightly with flour, if liked. When grill is heated, place steaks side by side on greased or oiled griller. Slip under grill, about 2 inches from heat. Reduce heat slightly. If liked, cover with strips of bacon. Cook for 2 or 3 minutes, then turn. Cook again for 2 or 3 minutes, then turn again. Continue cooking in this way until fish comes slightly away from bone, when the fish will be creamy looking. It should take 10 to 15 minutes, depending on thickness. Steaks ½ to 1 inch thick take 6 to 10 minutes. Steaks 1 to 1½ inches thick take 10 to 15 minutes.

To Serve: Arrange on a flat hot dish lined with a lace paper doily. Garnish with fried parsley and lemon. Serve with Hollandaise sauce or Maître d'Hôtel butter. Sometimes I serve grilled mushrooms or tomatoes with grilled fish steaks.

To Grill Fillets: Brush fillets with melted butter, margarine or oil. Place. skin side downwards, on griller. Grill about 4 to 5 inches from grill, according to thickness, for 3 to 5 minutes on one side. Season with salt and pepper to taste. Sprinkle with a drop or two of lemon juice, then turn. Baste with melted fat or oil. Season and sprinkle with lemon juice and finish grilling.

To Pan-Grill : Heat frying-pan to hissing point. Rub with a piece of suet or with any piece of fat very sparingly. Sear prepared fish on each side. Lower heat and finish pan-grilling, turning occasionally, and draining off any fat, otherwise fish will be fried. This method is suitable only for oily fish, such as herrings, mackerel, salmon, etc., and cured fish like kippers.

TO STEAM FISH

Prepare as for boiling. Tie fish in muslin before steaming. If you haven't a steamer, after washing and wiping dry, place on a greased or oiled plate. Fleck here and there with tiny bits of butter or margarine. Cover with greased or oiled paper, then with lid. Stand on top of a pan of boiling water. Allow to steam from 12 to 30 minutes, according to thickness and variety.

To Serve: Sprinkle with the liquid from fish ; or coat with a sauce made partly with milk and partly with the fish liquor. Serve with boiled potatoes and green peas or a green salad.

If steaming fillets, they can be rolled up and packed into a basin and seasoned carefully before steaming. If following this method for fillets, cover basin tightly with greased paper and steam for 10 to 12 minutes.

TO STEW FISH

Prepare fish as for boiling or steaming. Place in a shallow enamelled saucepan. Add enough fish stock or half stock and half milk to come up to the top of fish. Cover. Simmer very gently until fish is creamy-looking. Fish can also be stewed in fireproof ware in a very slow oven, 275° F. to 300° F. In France, a fish stew is called a " Matelote." Here is the recipe :

MATELOTE OF FISH (Matelote de Poisson)

2 lb. eel or other fish
3 oz. butter
1 lb. minced onions
1 oz. flour
1 pint white stock or wine
1/4 lb. small onions
1/2 lb. mushrooms
Salt and pepper to taste
Bouquet garni
2 cloves
1 blade mace
Dash cayenne pepper

Any fish can be used for this method of cooking. Eel is very popular on the Continent, cut into chunks about 2 inches long. Cut other fish into small steaks, about 2 inches long, and allow 2 chunks or steaks per head. Melt butter in a saucepan. Add minced onions. Fry until pale gold. Stir in flour. When frothy, stir in white stock or wine. Peel and add small onions whole. Peel, slice and add mushrooms with salt and pepper to taste, bouquet garni, cloves, mace and

2 egg yolks
Fried croûtons

cayenne pepper. (If liked, a little grated nutmeg and a pinch of ground ginger and cinnamon can be added.) Cover pan. Simmer slowly for ¾ hour, then add fish. Uncover. Simmer for 15 minutes. Remove pan from stove. Arrange fish in a deep hot dish. Beat egg yolks. Add to sauce, stirring until thick, but do not allow to boil. Garnish with croûtons of bread fried in butter. In some parts of France, ½ gill Burgundy is set on fire and stirred into the sauce just before adding the egg yolks. *For 4 persons.*

GEFUELLTER FISH

3 lb. fish
2 peeled medium-sized onions
1 slice bread
Salt and pepper to taste
1 egg
1 cup cold water
¼ celeriac

Clean a 3-lb. fish thoroughly, then remove the skin whole, and bone fish. Put 1 onion through the meat grinder with the flesh of the fish. Add bread. Soak in cold water to cover for 5 minutes, then squeeze dry. Stir in salt and pepper to taste, egg and water. Beat until smooth. Thoroughly wash fish skin in salt water. Drain well and pack with the mixture. Season outside with salt and pepper to taste. Place on rack of fish-kettle. Add fish bones and sliced remaining onion. Slice celeriac and add. Cover with boiling water. Cook rapidly for 2 or 3 minutes, then lower heat and simmer for about 1 hour, until filling is cooked through. Dish up fish carefully. *For 6 persons.*

TO PLANK FISH

This method of cooking fish is very popular in the United States. Bone a large flat fish. Season with salt and pepper to taste. Brush with melted butter. Place on grid or griller, skin side downwards, and grill for 5 minutes. Remove to a hot buttered plank, made for the purpose, of ash, hickory or oak. The skin should be placed next to the wood. Season with paprika to taste. Brush again with melted butter. Place in a fairly hot oven, 425° F. and bake until brown, then lower heat. Bake until cooked through, then force mashed potatoes, enriched with milk and butter and seasoned to taste, in a trail, or rose design, round the edges. Bake until potatoes are golden brown. Sprinkle with melted butter and minced chives or parsley. Serve from plank, or on a hot flat dish. *For 4 persons.*

TO SCALLOP FISH (Coquilles de Poisson)

BASIC RECIPE
2 cups flaked cooked fish
3½ oz. butter
4 tablespoons flour
1½ cups milk
Salt and pepper to taste
Paprika and cayenne pepper to taste
2 teaspoons minced parsley

Remove skin and bone from fish before flaking. Melt 2½ oz. butter in a saucepan. Add flour. Stir till smooth, then add milk. Cook till smooth and thick, stirring constantly. Season to taste with salt, pepper, paprika and cayenne pepper. Lightly stir in parsley and fish. Brush 5 scallop shells with melted butter. Divide mixture equally between them. Smooth over top with a palette

Boned brisket of Beef
trussed ready for brais-
ing. *See pages* 193-194.

Tenderize Steak for
grilling as illustrated,
or sprinkle with meat
tenderizer.

How to slit and stuff
thick Pork Chops for
grilling.

Fried Hamburg Steak can also be served with beans and garnished sippets of toast. *See page* 209.

Garnish Pot Roast of Beef with cooked root vegetables, and dumplings if liked. *See page* 210.

Use grilled mushroom and sausages for garnishing Fried Cake made of meat, sausage meat or venison.

½ cup stale breadcrumbs
Grated cheese to taste

knife. Sprinkle with crumbs, then with grated cheese to taste. Dab with remainder of butter. Bake in a moderate oven, 350° F., for 20 minutes. *For 5 persons.*

To Vary: Flavour sauce to taste with anchovy essence and a pinch of ground mace, or substitute cheese sauce, flavoured with dry mustard to taste, for the parsley sauce. If liked, ¼ cup crumbs mixed with ¼ cup grated cheese can be used for coating.

SAUCES FOR FISH

Here is a list of some of the sauces suitable for serving with fish cooked in the usual ways. If any specific sauce is required to go with any particular dish, it will be given or suggested in the recipe.

Baked Fish : Asparagus, cucumber, Hollandaise, Maître d'Hôtel butter, mushroom, Tartare, tomato, etc.

Baked Stuffed Fish : Hollandaise or Tartare with a non-oily fish, such as cod, haddock, hake or John Dory. Anchovy, fennel, mushroom or mustard with herring, mackerel and other oily fish.

Boiled or Steamed Fish : Admiral, ambassador, anchovy, asparagus, caper, celery, cucumber, curry, egg, fennel, gooseberry, Hollandaise, lemon, lobster, mayonnaise, Mornay, mussel, mustard, oyster, parsley, shrimp, Suprême, Tartare, tomato, etc.

Fried or Grilled Fish : Anchovy butter, black butter, caper, cucumber, egg and parsley, fennel, Hollandaise, horse-radish cream, Maître d'Hôtel butter, Meunière, mushroom, mustard, Suprême, Tartare, tomato mayonnaise, tomato, etc.

STUFFINGS FOR FISH

Here are some stuffings to choose from when you want to stuff fish before baking unless any other filling is suggested in recipe.

Celery	Crab	Cucumber	Egg
Herb	Lobster	Mushroom	Onion
Oyster	Parsley	Roe	Shrimp
		Whiting, etc.	

GARNISHES FOR FISH

Anchovy Fillets: For fish loaves, fish mayonnaise, aspic of fish, etc.
Asparagus Tips: Boiled, tied in bundles with a belt of pimiento, if liked. For creamed fish.
Beetroot Cups : Containing mayonnaise, Hollandaise or Tartare sauce. For boiled or steamed fish.
Capers: Chopped or whole. Use for garnishing mayonnaise of fish.
Chervil: Sprigs or minced. For fish in aspic.

Chives: Minced. **For** creamed fish.

Crayfish: Use for dressed fish dishes and fish salads.

Cucumber: Cut in slices. For creamed fish dishes.

Egg: Hard-boiled. Slices or chopped whites and sieved yolks. For creamed fish or fish Mornay.

Fennel: Minced for creamed fish. Sprigs for boiled or steamed.

Lemon: Butterflies, slices and wedges. For fried or grilled fish.

Lemon Baskets : Containing mayonnaise, Hollandaise or Tartare sauce. For boiled or steamed fish.

Lemon Slices: Dipped in paprika or minced parsley. For fried or grilled fish.

Lobster Coral, Claws and Feelers: Use with any lobster dish or salad.

Mussel Shells (Stuffed) : Use for garnishing any hot baked whole fish or fillets, or, if liked, for fish salads.

Parsley: Fresh or fried sprigs. For baked, fried or grilled fish. Minced. For creamed fish or fish Mornay.

Pastry (Fleurons) : For creamed fish.

Prawns and *Shrimps:* Use to garnish smoked salmon, or any light sauce for coating hot fish.

Quenelles: For dressed fish.

Smoked Salmon (chopped) : Use for fish salads, canapés of fish, etc.

Watercress: Sprigs. Use for garnishing fish salads and cold fish dishes.

QUANTITIES REQUIRED

Fish : Allow ½ lb. fish with bone per person, or 6 oz. fish without bone.
Sauce : Allow ¼ to ½ gill sauce per person when serving sauce with fish.

Anchovies (Anchois) (*Seasonable, June-September*) : A small herring-like fish, more celebrated when cured than fresh. Caught in nets in the English Channel and in the Mediterranean. Foundation of many famous relishes and sauces. *To Fry Anchovies* (Anchois frits) : Dip in batter, allowing 1 cup to 12 anchovies. Drop into deep hot fat. Fry until golden. Drain on absorbent paper. Garnish with fried parsley and lemon. Serve as an hors d'oeuvre.

Barbel (Barbeau) (*Seasonable, October-January*) : A fresh-water fish seldom eaten in England. The French call it " Little Carp." Coarse and woolly and insipid flesh that needs to be disguised, when cooked, by a good sauce. *To Cook:* Soak in salted water for 2 hours. Rinse and dry, then cook in " Court Bouillon for Fresh Water Fish " for ½ hour, until tender. Serve hot with anchovy or caper sauce, or cold with mayonnaise, or Vinaigrette sauce and potato salad.

BARBEL BONNE FEMME (Barbeau à la Bonne Femme)

1 medium-sized barbel
Salt and pepper to taste
1 heaped teaspoon minced parsley
2 teaspoons chopped shallots
2 oz. mushrooms
2 tablespoons stale breadcrumbs

Clean fish. Brush a large baking dish or tin lavishly with melted butter or margarine. Season fish on both sides with salt and pepper. Mix parsley with shallots and sprinkle over. Wipe, peel, and slice mushrooms thinly. Place on top of fish, then sprinkle with breadcrumbs. Mix

Strained juice ½ lemon
½ gill cider or white wine

lemon juice with the cider or wine, and sprinkle carefully over the fish, so as not to disturb the coating. Bake in a slow oven, 300° F., until fish shows signs of coming away from the bone in about ½ hour, basting frequently with stock. *For 2 or 3 persons.*

Bass (Bar) (*Seasonable, May-September*) : There are many varieties of this spiny-finned fish. European species, known as " Loup de mer " (wolf of the sea, or sea bass), considered culinary delicacy. Caught in estuaries during spawning season. *To Cook:* Scrape, scale, clean and wash, then poach. Serve hot with caper or shrimp sauce and boiled potatoes, or cold with anchovy or Tartare sauce. Good dipped in seasoned flour or medium oatmeal and fried till brown on each side. Medium-sized and large bass can be cooked by any recipe given under " Salmon," and small bass can be fried, grilled or cooked by any recipe given for " Trout."

Bream (Brème) (*Seasonable, July-March*) : Fresh water or carp bream.

Sea Bream (*Seasonable, February-November*) : Fresh water bream is very tasteless, but can be prepared and served like carp. Sea bream is a very delicate fish. Clean, but do not scale. Wash and dry. Grill or make into fish cakes or pie. Fillet and fry like haddock. *To Grill Sea Bream:* Clean, but do not scale. Wash and dry. Remove fins. Make two gashes on each side. Soak in a marinade for ½ hour, basting occasionally with the liquor. Sometimes sea bream is wrapped in greased paper before grilling. Baste frequently in either case with melted butter until ready. Serve with melted butter sauce, flavoured with lemon juice and minced parsley to taste. *Baked Stuffed Sea Bream:* Clean fish, but do not scale. Stuff with any fish forcemeat and sew up. Place in a greased baking dish or tin. Bake in a moderate oven, 350° F., for about ¾ hour, basting occasionally with melted butter or margarine. Serve with anchovy, caper or tomato sauce.

BAKED SEA BREAM (Brème, St. Jacques)

1 sea bream (2 lb. in weight)
1 tablespoon butter
1 teaspoon anchovy sauce
1 teaspoon tomato sauce
1 teaspoon minced parsley
1 minced shallot
1 tablespoon chopped mushrooms
¼ pint stock

Clean, wash and arrange sea bream in a greased baking dish. Melt butter. Stir in sauces. Pour over fish. Sprinkle in parsley, shallot and mushrooms. Add stock. Bake for 20 minutes, basting frequently, then gently remove fillets of sea bream to hot serving dish. Pour sauce over fish. *For 4 persons.*

Brill (Barbue) (*Seasonable, June-April*) : This flat fish, available in some places all the year round, looks like a broad sole. The flesh has a yellowish tone. Boil whole or cut into slices. Serve with caper, lobster, Hollandaise, melted butter or shrimp sauce. Fry whole or filleted, boil and scallop or cook au gratin. If wished to be served whole, follow any recipe given for turbot. If fillets are wanted, follow any recipes given for fillets of sole.

BRILL WITH MORNAY SAUCE (Barbue à la Mornay)

1 brill (3 lb. in weight)
Salt and pepper to taste
2½ oz. butter
1½ oz. flour
¾ pint milk
1½ oz. grated Parmesan cheese
¼ pint cream

Fillet and skin brill. Cut each fillet into 2 or 3 pieces. Place in a well-buttered shallow fireproof dish. Sprinkle with salt and pepper to taste. Cover with a well-buttered paper or with the cover of dish. If the latter, dab fillets with tiny pats of butter before covering. Bake in a moderate oven, 350° F., for about 10 minutes. Melt butter in a saucepan. Stir in flour and when frothy, stir in milk. When smooth and boiling, simmer for 5 minutes, stirring constantly. Add cheese. Stir till melted. Strain into a fresh saucepan. Stir in cream, and re-season, if liked. Pour over fillets. Brown under grill or on top of oven. *For 6 persons.*

Carp (Carpe) (*Seasonable, October–February*) : Carp is sometimes called the " Queen of Rivers." Its family includes a large number of other fish from barbel, fresh-water bream, chub, dace, dudgeon, to minnow, roach and tench. These fish are sometimes known as " mud fish." The soft roe of the carp is a great delicacy and its tongue is highly prized. On the Continent, carps' heads are frequently bought for the sake of the tongue. Carp is one of the traditional dishes served in Germany on Christmas and New Year's Eve. Usually braised or stewed in fillets or steaks. *To Clean:* Rub with salt. Place the sharp point of a knife between scales and the skin at the tail of the fish. Pass knife gently along back up to the head, dividing scales carefully from the skin. In this way, you can remove the whole of the scales in one piece from each side. When scaled, make a small incision in tail over the bladder. Pull out gills and the inside with the aid of a knife, taking care not to disturb or break the gall as you remove it or the flesh will taste bitter. Soak in salt water and vinegar for 2 hours to draw out the blood. Soak in fresh water for ½ hour, then dry with a cloth. *To Boil or Poach:* Wrap in cheese cloth or butter muslin. Tie the ends. Place in a saucepan. Cover with salted boiling water. Add a slice of onion, a sprig parsley and 1 tablespoon vinegar. Cover. Simmer till ready, allowing 10 minutes per lb. Serve like any boiled or poached fish.

FILLETS OF CARP, MARLENE (Carpe à la Marlène)

4 small carp
Salt and pepper to taste
Ground mace to taste
1 dessertspoon minced parsley
1 cup white wine
1 bouquet garni
1 onion
2 cloves
Small stick horseradish
1 cup cream
2 egg yolks
Fried carp roe

Wash and split carp. Divide into fillets. Sprinkle with salt, pepper and mace to taste. Place in shallow saucepan. Cover with cold water. Add parsley, wine and bouquet garni. Peel onion and insert cloves. Add with a 2-inch stick of horseradish to pan. Bring to simmering point. Simmer very gently for about an hour, then remove fillets. Strain liquor carefully into another saucepan. Bring to boil and remove from stove. Gradually stir in cream or top milk. Return to stove. Stir until at boiling point, then remove from stove again. Stir for a moment or two, then gradually stir in egg yolks mixed with a tablespoon or two of additional cream. When piping hot, pour over carp. Garnish with fried roe. *For 4 persons.*

Char (*Seasonable, February-October*) : A delicious member of the trout family with rich red fatty flesh. Best in autumn. In Britain it is peculiar to the lakes of Cumberland and the lochs of Scotland. *To Cook:* Grill, pot and serve cold, or treat by any recipe given for trout. *To Grill Char:* Wash and dry with a soft cloth. Dredge with seasoned flour. Brush with melted butter or olive oil. Grill gently for 10 to 15 minutes, depending on size, turning occasionally. Serve with a piquant sauce. Allow 1 medium-sized char for 2 persons.

Chub (Chabot) (*Seasonable, November-March*) : A fresh-water fish belonging to carp family. Roe is best part. *To Cook:* Must be cooked fresh. Can be treated by any recipe given for carp. Wash, then soak in a marinade. Cut in slices and poach. Serve with anchovy, caper or Tartare sauce.

Coalfish (Colin) (*Seasonable in winter*) : First cousin of cod. Known in northern districts as " saithe." Wash and treat like cod. Sometimes called " rock salmon."

Cod (Cabillaud) (*Seasonable, October-January, but obtainable all the year round*) : Best cod are round and plump near the tail. *To Clean Cod:* Remove gills and inside of fish. Wash in fresh water. If to be cooked in steaks, or if half cod is to be cooked for making into fish cakes, kedgeree, or fish pies, etc., then soak in fresh water for $\frac{1}{2}$ hour. *To Cook:* It's wisest not to cook a cod whole, as the part round the shoulders is much thicker than round the tail, with the result that when the tail is cooked, the shoulders will still be half-raw. Boil and steam head and shoulders or middle cut. Cut remainder into steaks. or fillet, and fry or grill, etc. *To Boil Cod:* Cleanse thoroughly the head and shoulders. Rub salt over inside and thick part. Stand for about $1\frac{1}{2}$ hours, Rinse. Wrap head and shoulders or middle cut in cheese cloth or butter muslin. Place on a rack in fish kettle. Cover with tepid salted water, allowing 5 oz. salt to a gallon water. Add also $\frac{1}{2}$ bay leaf, 2 cloves, 1 blade mace, 1 sprig parsley, and 1 tablespoon vinegar. Bring to simmering point. Skim carefully. Simmer gently until fin comes out when gently pulled, in about $\frac{1}{2}$ hour. Drain well. Garnish with lemon. Serve with anchovy, caper, oyster, parsley or shrimp sauce. In the olden days, grated horse-radish was sometimes served with boiled cod. *To Fry Cod Steaks:* The tail-end is usually chosen. Cut 1 inch thick. Wipe dry. Dip in seasoned flour, oatmeal or cornmeal. Shallow-fry, or dip steaks in batter and deep-fry. Garnish with fennel or parsley sprigs. Serve with anchovy sauce or melted butter.

BAKED COD STEAKS À LA FRANCAISE
(Cabillaud à la Française)

3 cod steaks
Salt and pepper to taste
3 tablespoons butter

Have steaks cut about 1 lb. each in weight. Season on both sides with salt and pepper to taste. Melt half the butter in a frying pan with a short handle.

½ gill white wine
¼ pint water
2 tablespoons flour
1 hard-boiled egg
1 egg yolk
2 tablespoons cream

Place steaks in pan, side by side. Add wine and water. Cover with a thinly buttered round of paper. Bring liquid to boil. Boil for 5 minutes. Place in a moderate oven, 350° F. Bake for 20 minutes. Remove from oven. Remove paper. Arrange steaks side by side on a hot dish. Keep hot. Melt remainder of butter in a saucepan. Stir in flour. When frothy, stir in strained fish liquor. Stir till boiling and smooth, then shell, chop and add egg. Season again with salt and pepper. Boil for 3 minutes. Cool slightly. Mix egg yolk to a cream with the cream. Add to sauce, stirring constantly, but do not allow to boil. Season again if necessary. When cooked, pour at once over steaks. Garnish with minced parsley. *For 6 persons.*

Cod's Roe : This can usually be bought boiled or raw. *To Boil:* Wash and tie in butter muslin. Place in saucepan. Cover with boiling salted water. Add 3 or 4 peppercorns and a sprig of parsley. Simmer gently until tender, in ¼ to ¾ hour, according to thickness. Remove. Unwrap. Cool. Serve sliced and fried. Roe can also be egged and crumbed before frying. *Allow* 1 *lb. for* 3 *or* 4 *persons.* *To Fry:* Dip in seasoned flour, or in fine oatmeal. Fry in hot bacon dripping or butter until golden brown. Sometimes I add chopped onion or shallot, allowing 1 tablespoon to 1 lb. cod's roe, to the fat before frying. When roe is brown below, I turn it and heap onion on top. Cover and finish cooking. Dish up. Stir in evaporated milk, just enough to coat the slices, not to provide a sauce. Garnish with minced parsley and lemon. *Allow* 1 *lb. for* 3 *or* 4 *persons*, according to taste.

CREAMED COD'S ROE (Laitance de Cabillaud à la Crème)

1 large cod's roe
2 tablespoons vinegar
3 tablespoons butter
Flour as required
1 teaspoon minced onion
4 tablespoons cream
Salt and pepper to taste

Bring cod's roe to boil in hot water to cover, mixed with the vinegar. Simmer gently for 1 hour. Drain off water. Place on a flat dish and weigh down. When cold, cut into thick slices. Melt butter in a frying pan. Dip roe slices in flour. Fry onion lightly, then add roe, and fry till golden brown on both sides. Arrange in a hot dish. Stir cream gradually into butter remaining in pan. Season to taste with salt and pepper. Mask roe with sauce. Serve at once. *For 4 or 6 persons.*

Conger Eel (*Seasonable all the year round*): Larger than the fresh-water variety with coarser flesh, but wholesome and nourishing. Best in autumn. Basis of a famous soup in Channel Isles. Made into pies on the Cornish coast. Choose small for preference. *To Cook:* Make soup of the head and tail. Slice middle cut and bake, boil, fry, stew or make into pies. Can also be cooked by any recipes given for cod. *To Fry:* Dip equal-thick slices of eel in seasoned flour, then egg and crumb. Fry in hot oil till golden. Serve hot with anchovy, shrimp or tomato sauce. Garnish with lemon. *Allow* 2 *lb. for* 4 *or* 5 *persons.*

STEWED CONGER EEL (Ragoût d'Anguille de Mer)

½ pint water
3 slices conger eel
2 slices onion
1 sprig parsley
1 sprig thyme
½ bay leaf
1 blade mace
2 cloves
Salt and pepper to taste
1 oz. butter
1 oz. flour
¼ pint milk
Minced capers, paprika or parsley

Bring water to boil in shallow saucepan. Add eel, onion, herbs, mace, cloves and salt and pepper to taste. Cover and simmer gently for 20 minutes. Melt butter in a small saucepan. Add flour. Stir until frothy, and cook until thoroughly blended, stirring constantly. Strain in stock from fish. When smooth and boiling, stir in milk. Season to taste again. Dish up eel. Coat with sauce. Sprinkle lightly with minced capers, paprika or parsley. Serve with creamed or mashed potatoes. *For 3 persons.*

To Vary Stewed Eels: Substitute cider for water and milk.

Dabs (Limandes) (*Seasonable most of the year, according to district*) : Small flat fish belonging to plaice family, but better flavoured. Sometimes known in England as a " Thames flounder." Were largely used for making " souchet " —a famous fish soup—at one time. *To Cook:* Fry or grill small ones. If large, remove black skin and fillet. Egg and crumb and fry. Serve with potato chips and sauce Tartare. Cook fillets by any recipe given for plaice or sole. Dabs are greatly improved by soaking in salted water for ½ hour before cooking.

Dace (Vandorse) (*Seasonable, June-December*) : Fresh water fish. Scarcely worth cooking. Clean. Soak in salted water for 2 or 3 hours. *To Cook:* Wipe dry and fry, grill or poach. Serve with claret sauce or melted butter, flavoured with lemon juice and cayenne pepper.

Dogfish or Huss (Rousette) (*Seasonable most of the year, best in winter*) : Inexpensive fish. Economical, as it has no bones except the backbone. Usually salted without head or fins. *To Cook:* Place in a casserole with cold water, salt to taste, spices, etc., allowing 1½ gills cold water, 1 teaspoon salt, 2 peppercorns, 1 bay leaf, and 2 cloves to 1 lb. huss or dogfish. Cover and bake in a moderate oven, 350° F., for 20 minutes. Drain. Serve with ½ pint egg and parsley sauce. *For 3 persons.*

Eels (fresh water) (Anguille) (*best in the winter, obtainable all the year round*) : Must be eaten fresh. Most nutritious. Thames eels best flavoured. Soak in salt water. Skin before cleaning. Tie a piece of string round the neck, then cut skin round neck just below string and loosen with a pair of scissors. Holding the head with one hand, pull skin off with the other—in the way in which you would pull a glove off your hand. Now clean. First remove fins with a pair of scissors, then rip open belly almost to tail and remove guts and inside fats without breaking the gall. Carefully remove all the blood. Flush inside with plenty of water, and be sure to wear gloves when doing this if you have a cut on your hands, as eel blood has been known to be poisonous, so you must not let it enter any wound in your finger. Soak in salt water for 30 minutes, then rinse in plenty of fresh water. Wipe dry. Place on a chopping

board and remove backbone. Cut into steaks for cooking. *To Cook:* Boil
fry, grill or stew.

To Fry Eels (Anguille frite) : Clean. Cut into 3-inch steaks. Wipe dry
Mix slightly beaten egg with 1½ tablespoons water. Dip steaks first in bread
crumbs, then in egg, and again in crumbs. Fry in deep hot fat for 3 to 5
minutes. Serve garnished with lemon and fried parsley.

JELLIED EELS (Anguilles en Gelée)

1½ lb. eels
1 medium-sized onion
1 clove
1 blade mace
½ bay leaf
1 sprig parsley
1 sprig thyme
6 peppercorns
2 tablespoons wine vinegar
3 sheets gelatine
Salt and pepper to taste

Prepare eels and cut into equal-sized chunks
Place in a saucepan. Add peeled onion, stuck
with clove, mace, bay leaf, parsley, thyme
peppercorns, vinegar and cold water to cover
Cover pan, and bring to boil. Simmer till eels
are tender. Drain fish well. Remove to a shallow
dish. Add gelatine to stock. Season to taste.
Stir till dissolved. Strain through jelly bag and
pour over fish. Chill. Serve with Vinaigrette
sauce. *For 4 persons.*

STEWED EELS (Anguilles à l'Anglaise)

2 lb. eels
½ pint bone stock
¼ pint port wine
3 allspice berries
1 blade mace
2 cloves
3 slices lemon
1 small peeled onion
Salt and pepper to taste
1 oz. butter
1 oz. flour
1 glass claret or sherry
1 dessertspoon mushroom
ketchup

Wash and skin eels. Cut into steaks 3 inches long
Place in a shallow stew pan. Add stock, wine,
allspice berries, mace, cloves, lemon, onion and
salt and pepper to taste. Cover. Simmer slowly
for about ¾ hour, or until tender, then dish up
carefully. Melt butter in a saucepan. Add flour.
Strain in stock and stir until smooth and boiling.
Boil for 10 minutes, then add claret or sherry and
ketchup. If preferred, substitute cream for the
claret or sherry and ketchup. Arrange eel steaks
in a circle, one piece overlapping another. Strain
sauce over. *For 5 or 6 persons.*

Flounders (*Obtainable all year round, but best November-March*) : In olden
days these Thames flounders (also called lemon soles) were the basis of a famous
fish soup called " Waterzoei," which, I understand, is of Flemish origin, though
in Belgium, fresh water fish, such as barbel, carp, eels, perch, roach and tench,
are used in its place. Very digestible. Flat-shaped like plaice, but darker in
colour. Clean and cook like plaice.

Garfish (Orphie) (*Seasonable, September to March*) : Cook like eels and
conger eels.

Grayling (Ombre) (*Seasonable, July-December*) : Smooth-scaled fresh water
fish. Cucumber flavour. Cousin of trout. *To Bake Grayling:* Place seasoned
fish side by side in a shallow, well-buttered fireproof dish. Place a pat of butter
on each. Cover. Bake in a moderate oven, 350° F., for ¾ hour, then strain

off liquid. Cream ½ oz. flour with cold water and stir in fish stock. Stir until boiling. Season with salt and pepper to taste. Pour over fish. Sometimes melted butter is diluted to taste with the stock and poured over instead of thickening sauce. *Allow 1 medium-sized grayling for 2 persons.* *To Fry :* Scale and skin fish carefully, then remove fins and scales, but leave on heads. Wash and wipe dry. Season with salt and pepper. Dip in flour. Fry in hot dripping or lard about ¾ inch deep until cooked below, in about ½ minute, then turn carefully and fry on other side. Drain on absorbent paper. Serve with fried parsley and melted butter. *Allow 1 medium-sized grayling for 2 persons.* *To Grill:* Dip cleaned seasoned grayling in olive oil. Grill for 2 or 3 minutes on one side, then turn and grill on other. Keep turning carefully and grilling until cooked through. Dish up. Sprinkle with strained lemon juice. Garnish with parsley. *For 2 persons.*

Gudgeon (Goujon) (*Seasonable, June-November*) : A member of the carp family. Flesh has a good flavour, and is firm and digestible. Very celebrated in France. Frequently used as a garnish. *To Clean:* Don't scale. Remove inside and gills. Cleanse thoroughly under running water. Soak in salted water for 2 hours. Wipe dry. *To Cook:* Treat like smelts. Dip in seasoned flour, then egg and crumb. Fry until golden brown in deep hot fat. Serve garnished with fried parsley.

Gurnet (Gurnard) (Grondin) (*Seasonable, February-September*) : Good flavoured fish with firm white flesh. There are many members of the gurnet family. The red gurnet, or " sea cuckoo," so-called because of the noise it makes, is the best. Cleanse and dry fish thoroughly. Remove fins and gills. If wanted filleted, run the edge of a sharp knife along the edge of the spine and lift the flesh from the bone, then cut into fillets. *To Cook:* Bake, or stuff and bake, or fillet and dip in batter, or egg and crumb, and fry for about 10 minutes. *To Boil:* Clean and simmer medium-sized fish in salted water to cover for about ½ hour. Serve with anchovy, parsley or piquant sauce or melted butter. *Allow 1 medium-sized gurnet for 3 persons.*

BAKED GURNET (Grondin au four)

1 small gurnets
2 chopped shallot
2 tablespoons chopped mushrooms
Salt and pepper to taste
1 dessertspoon lemon juice
3 tablespoons white wine
1 oz. butter
2 tablespoons browned breadcrumbs
Lemon and parsley

Clean and skin gurnets. Cut off heads and fins. Score fish across three times on each side. Sprinkle with shallot, mushrooms, salt and pepper to taste and lemon juice. Lay side by side in a well-buttered deep fireproof dish. Pour wine over fish, and dab with butter. Lay a thickly buttered paper over them. Bake in a moderately hot oven, 400° F., until they are cooked, basting them frequently with the wine. About 5 minutes before they are done, sprinkle the browned breadcrumbs on top to allow them to get thoroughly hot. Garnish with lemon and parsley. If preferred, the wine may be omitted, and milk or fish stock substituted. Serve from dish. *For 2 persons.*

Haddock (Eglefin) (*Seasonable, August-February, best in winter*): One of the cheapest and most useful fish. Medium-sized preferable, as small ones are bony. The best come from Devon, Cornwall and Dublin Bay. *To Cook:* Bake, or stuff and bake, boil, grill, curry, or fillet and fry. Use cold boiled haddock for made-up fish dishes.

BAKED HADDOCK WITH CHEESE SAUCE
(Eglefin au gratin)

2 lb. fillet of haddock
1½ tablespoons melted butter
  or margarine
Salt and pepper to taste
1 teaspoon flour
½ cup top off milk
1 cup grated cheese
¼ teaspoon mustard
Tomato catsup as required

Cut fillets in two crosswise. Arrange in a shallow greased fireproof dish, side by side. Brush with butter or margarine. Season with salt and pepper, and paprika if available. Stir flour into remainder of margarine in saucepan. Add milk and stir till smooth and boiling. Add cheese, mustard and salt and pepper to taste. Stir over low heat till cheese is melted. Pour over fish. Make a pattern with a thin streak of tomato catsup on top of sauce. Bake in a moderately hot oven, 375° F., from 20 to 30 minutes. Serve with mashed, creamed or boiled new potatoes, and green peas or runner or French beans, if wanted for a main course at dinner. *For 5 persons.*

JELLIED HADDOCK (Eglefin en Gelée)

4 slices haddock
¾ pint water
½ teaspoon salt
2 teaspoons meat extract
¼ pint vinegar
1 oz. powdered gelatine
2 firm tomatoes
1 hard-boiled egg

Wash haddock. Place in a deep baking dish with water, salt, meat extract and vinegar. Bake from 15 to 20 minutes. Strain liquid into a basin. Leave till cold. Soak gelatine for 5 minutes, then turn into a small saucepan. Stir over low heat till gelatine is dissolved. Remove from stove. Stir into strained stock. Scald, peel and chill tomatoes, then cut each into 4 slices. Arrange between fish slices. Strain liquid over fish and tomatoes. Leave till set. Cut egg white into narrow fingers and arrange like petals of a flower in the centre with the coarsely sieved yolk in the centre of " fingers." Serve with new potato salad, flavoured with minced chives or spring onion. *For 4 persons.*

Jellied Hake (Merluche en gelée): Follow above recipe, substituting 4 slices hake for the haddock.

Hake (Merluche) (*Seasonable all the year round, best September-April*): Coarse member of cod family. Preparation simplified on account of easily detached backbone. Cheap and digestible. *To Bone Hake:* Clean fish in usual way, then take hold of backbone, from where it starts, between your right finger and thumb, then slide finger and thumb along edge of bone down body as far as it has to be boned. You can then remove bone. Remove fins, and you have a completely boned fish which is particularly useful when you have to cater for invalids, children or old people. *To Cook:* Boil or steam whole or in large " cuts." Serve with anchovy, brown caper, Tartare or tomato sauce. Divide into steaks and fry or grill. Bake, or stuff and bake. Curry when cold, or make into fish cakes, pies, puddings, etc. Follow any recipe suggested for cod or halibut.

BAKED HAKE (Merluche au four)

1 small onion
3 teaspoons minced parsley
8 slices hake
Juice 1 lemon
Salt, pepper and paprika to taste
¼ lb. mushrooms
¼ lb. stale breadcrumbs
2 oz. butter or margarine
½ gill white wine

Peel and mince onion. Mix with parsley. Sprinkle half the mixture over a shallow, well-buttered fireproof dish big enough to hold steaks side by side. Arrange fish on top. Sprinkle with remainder of mixture, lemon juice, and salt, pepper and paprika to taste. Cover with sliced mushrooms and breadcrumbs. Dab with butter or margarine. Pour in wine at the side. Bake for 25 minutes in a moderate oven, 350° F. *For 4 persons.*

Halibut (Fletan) (*Seasonable all the year, best August-April*): A very large flat fish, sometimes called " workhouse turbot." Very digestible. Cheaper than turbot as a rule, and delicately flavoured. Middle cut is best. Should be eaten as fresh as possible. Choose thick, plump fish. *To Cook:* Choose head and shoulders or middle cut for preference. Tail is somewhat insipid. Chicken halibut (*Seasonable, March-October*), weighing about 3 to 5 lb., are best filleted and fried. Bake, boil, fry or steam, and serve, or cook by any recipe suggested for turbot.

CASSEROLE OF HALIBUT (Casserole de Flétan)

2 peeled onions
3 large carrots
1 cup sliced celery
3 oz. butter
2 lb. halibut
Salt and pepper to taste
1 tablespoon lemon juice
1 tablespoon minced parsley

Mince onions. Scrape and mince carrots. Place onion, carrot, and celery in a saucepan. Cover with boiling salted water. Cover and simmer for 20 minutes. Meanwhile, melt butter in another pan. Add halibut. Brown slightly below, then turn and brown on the other side. Lift carefully into a shallow casserole or other covered fireproof dish. Add butter from pan. Sprinkle with salt and pepper to taste, then with lemon juice. Add boiled, drained vegetables and a cup of the vegetable water. Cover closely. Bake in a moderate oven, 350° F., for ½ hour. Remove to serving dish with a skimmer. Arrange vegetables round. Pour liquor into a saucepan. Thicken to taste with cornflour blended with a little vegetable water. Boil up. Stir in parsley. Pour over fish. *For 6 persons.*

HALIBUT SOUFFLE (Soufflé de Flétan)

½ lb. raw halibut
2 anchovy fillets
1 oz. butter
2 oz. flour
¼ pint milk
Salt and cayenne pepper to taste
3 eggs

Wipe and cut halibut, weighed without bone, into shreds. Add the anchovy fillets. Place fish and fillets in a mortar and pound until smooth. Rub through a wire sieve. Melt butter in a saucepan. Stir in flour. When frothy, stir in milk. Keep stirring until sauce thickens, then turn into a mortar. Add fish purée, salt and cayenne pepper

¼ pint cream
1 teaspoon minced parsley
Sauce to taste

to taste and 1 egg. Pound well, then add another egg. Pound and add last egg. Half whip cream and fold it into mixture. Add parsley. Place in a buttered mould. Cover with buttered greaseproof paper. Steam gently for 45 minutes. Turn out carefully on to a hot dish. Serve with parsley, Hollandaise, tomato or any other sauce to taste. Pour part over and serve remainder in a hot sauce-boat. *For 3 or 4 persons.*

Herring (Hareng) (*Seasonable all the year round, best May-November*): One of the cheapest and most nutritious fish. Soft roed herrings considered best. Loch Fyne herring considered a delicacy in Britain.

There are two ways of boning a herring : (1) Slit under-side neatly down the middle. Flatten out on board with the cut side down, then lightly press down the middle with your fingers. This will make the bone come out without damaging the flesh. Turn fish on to its back and gently pull the backbone out with your fingers. If you are careful, most of the small bones will come away with it. Pick out remainder. This is the best way to bone herrings that are to be stuffed. If there are roes inside, remove, wash and reserve them for a savoury. (2) Run your finger or knife inside fish and alongside the backbone, opening it out so that it lies flat. Break the backbone near the tail and lift it out with as many small bones as will come with it. Remove tail and also the small hard fins at the belly, then with a knife, lift out any small bones left in the fish. *To Cook:* Grill or bone and fry in oatmeal for breakfast. Boil in water or white wine, or stuff and bake for lunch or supper. Pickle or " pot " and serve cold with potato salad as a first course at luncheon or part of an hors d'oeuvre course at dinner. *To Boil Herrings* (Harengs bouillis) : (1) Clean. Cook slowly in boiling salted water sharpened with vinegar for about 10 minutes. Serve with boiled potatoes and mustard sauce. (2) Clean. Simmer slowly in wine for about 5 minutes. Leave in wine until cold. Serve as an hors d'oeuvre course, dressed with olive oil sharpened with vinegar, and garnished with chopped onion or shallot and paprika.

Cream Sauce for Boiled Herrings: Heat 6 tablespoons thick cream in a saucepan. Stir in salt and pepper to taste. Stir until boiling, then gradually add 2 oz. unsalted butter and the strained juice of ½ lemon. When blended, pour over fish.

To Grill Loch Fyne Herrings: Clean, split, then fillet. Season with salt and pepper to taste. Brush insides with melted butter. Make a sandwich of two fillets, and hold in place with tiny skewers. Brush with melted butter and grill. Remove skewers and serve.

BAKED STUFFED HERRINGS (Harengs farcis au four)

4 herrings
1 small onion
½ cup breadcrumbs
1 large soft roe
½ teaspoon mixed herbs
1 teaspoon minced parsley
Salt and pepper to taste

Remove heads. Clean and wash fish. Split open and remove backbones. To make the stuffing, chop onion finely. Add breadcrumbs, roe, herbs, parsley, seasoning, mushrooms and butter. Mix well. Sprinkle underside of each herring with salt and pepper and spread on a little of the stuffing.

2 chopped mushrooms
1 teaspoon melted butter

Roll up. Tie with coarse white cotton. Place in a greased pie-dish. Cover with greaseproof paper. Bake for 15 minutes, then remove paper and allow to brown. If preferred, instead of rolling up fish, spread the insides with stuffing, then fold the fish back into shape and bake as before. Potatoes in their jackets and hot baked beetroot (served with melted butter sauce) may be cooked at the same time. Serve if preferred with fried potato crisps and a green salad. *For 4 persons.*

FRIED HERRINGS WITH YELLOW SAUCE
(Harengs, Hollandaises)

5 large fresh herrings
3 oz. butter
1 tablespoon flour
¼ pint sour cream
Salt and pepper to taste
Lemon and parsley

Clean, wash, and dry herrings. Melt butter in a frying-pan. Dip herrings in flour. Place in pan when butter starts to turn colour. Fry slowly until brown below, then turn and brown on other side. Remove to a hot dish. Stir in sour cream. Season to taste with salt and pepper. Coat herrings with the sauce. Garnish with lemon and sprigs of parsley. *For 5 persons.*

GRILLED HERRINGS (Harengs grillés)

6 fresh herrings
Salt and pepper to taste

Prepare fish, removing scales, fins, and heads, then split up cavity and clean well in cold water. Make 3 slits on each side to backbone, about 1½ inches apart. Rinse and dry. Season with salt and pepper to taste. Brush on both sides with melted butter or bacon dripping. Grease and heat grill. Grill from 10 to 15 minutes, depending on size, turning three times and basting frequently with melted fat. Serve garnished with lemon, parsley and a pat of Maître d'Hôtel butter, and with mustard sauce. *For 3 or 6 persons.*

HERRINGS FRIED IN SALT (Harengs frits au Sel)

There is so much oil in the flesh of a herring that it is quite possible to fry it without any other fat. Use only a strong thick frying-pan. (A thin one will burn.) Sprinkle pan with salt. Heat gently at first, shaking the pan occasionally. Continue heating until pan is very hot, then lay in herrings, previously scaled, cleaned, washed and dried. Fry on each side for 4 to 5 minutes, until golden brown and crisp. Serve at once. Garnish with wedges of lemon. *Allow 1 herring per person.*

HERRING'S ROES AU GRATIN (Laitances de Harengs au gratin)

15 soft roes
1 tablespoon minced onion
½ oz. butter
2 tablespoons chopped mushrooms
Salt and cayenne pepper to taste
Pinch grated nutmeg
1 dessertspoon minced parsley

Wash all roes thoroughly in cold water containing a dash of lemon juice, then put into boiling water to firm them. Drain and wipe dry. Fry onion slowly in butter until transparent. Add mushrooms. Fry for a minute or two, then add roes, salt and cayenne pepper and nutmeg. Cook slowly until roes are heated. Place in layers in a greased

Breadcrumbs as required
½ gill sherry
1 tablespoon melted glaze
fireproof dish. Sprinkle each layer thinly with parsley and breadcrumbs. Add sherry to melted glaze and pour over roes. Sprinkle again thinly with stale breadcrumbs mixed with chopped parsley to taste. Moisten with melted butter. Bake in a moderate oven, 350° F., for 12 minutes. Serve as a luncheon or supper dish.

John Dory (St. Pierre or Dorée) (*Seasonable all the year round: best September-February*) : A delicious fish. Name taken from the colour of skin which is gilded or dorée. These dorys are caught off the southern coast. *To Clean:* Cut off fins. Remove gills. Split boned fish along breast from where remove inside. Wash as little as possible. Cover. Liver is very delicate but dissolves quickly if fish is kept some time. *To Cook:* Good boiled or steamed. Serve with anchovy, caper, lobster, or shrimp sauce and melted butter. Stuff and bake whole, or fillet and stuff and bake. You can also fillet and dip in batter and fry until golden brown. Serve with sauce Tartare. Treat in any way suggested for turbot. The larger the John Dory is the better. *To Boil:* Cleanse thoroughly and remove fins, but not the head. Place in a fish-kettle. Cover with warm water. Add salt to taste. Bring slowly almost to boiling point. Simmer gently for ¼ hour, or until fish shows signs of coming away from bone. Drain well. Serve on a hot dish in a folded napkin. Garnish with lemon butterflies and sprigs of parsley.

SPANISH DORY (Dorée, Espagnole)

1 medium-sized John Dory
3 dessertspoons olive oil
Salt and pepper to taste
2 large peeled onions
3 dessertspoons salad oil
3 dessertspoons vinegar
Scale, clean, wash, dry and cut fish into equal-sized slices. Dry. Measure frying oil into frying-pan. When smoking hot, add fish slices carefully. Fry, turning occasionally, till golden brown on both sides. Season well with salt and pepper. Place in a shallow fireproof dish. Cut onions into thin slices and fry till crisp. Arrange on top of fish. Heat oil and vinegar. Pour over fish. Stand overnight. Serve cold with a green salad. *For 4 persons.*

Lampreys (Lamproie) (*Seasonable, February-Mid-June*) : Eel-like fish. Two varieties. The smaller are more commonly known as " lampreys." Best fish caught in the Severn. They are delicate, rare and rich, but are indigestible. *To Clean:* Clean like eels, but do not skin. Rinse in hot water. Remove head, tails and gills. Take out the cartilage and the string on either side of fish, down the back. Dry thoroughly. Drain for 3 or 4 hours. *To Cook:* Bake, boil, fry, jug, pot, roast, stew, or fillet and fry. *To Stew* (Ragoût de Lamproie) : Rub a medium-sized lamprey with salt. Wash in warm water, then prepare as described above. Season with salt, pepper and grated nutmeg. Cut into pieces about 3 inches long. Place in a shallow saucepan. Add 4 small peeled onions, 12 button mushrooms, 1 bay leaf, 1 tablespoon minced parsley, 1 strip thin lemon rind, ¾ pint boiling white stock and ½ gill sherry. Bring to simmering point. Simmer gently until cooked in about 1¼ to 1½ hours. Dish up. Thicken gravy with a pat of butter creamed with flour. Stir until boiling. Boil for 3 or 4 minutes, stirring constantly. Sprinkle

with juice ½ lemon. Strain sauce over fish. Garnish with cut lemon˙
For 4 persons.

Ling (Morno) (*Seasonable, September-April*) : Largest member of the cod family. Usually split and dried. Flesh rather coarse and unpalatable unless fish is young. *To Cook:* Bake, fry, or make into a pie or curry. Can be cooked by any recipe given for cod.

BAKED LING (Morno au four)

4 lb. sliced ling
Flour as required
2 dessertspoons salt
½ teaspoon white pepper
1 saltspoon ground mace
3 oz. unsalted butter
1 tablespoon flour
½ pint milk
Sippets of toast for garnish

Dip ling in flour. Season with salt, pepper and ground mace. Place in a greased pie-dish. Divide butter into tiny pieces and sprinkle over fish. Cream flour with a little of the milk, then stir in rest of milk. Pour over fish. Bake in a slow oven, 325° F., for about 50 minutes to 1 hour. Serve garnished with sippets of toast. *For 6 persons.*

Mackerel (Maquereau) (*Seasonable, October-July: best March-July*): A beautifully formed and coloured sea fish. Excellent for breakfast during the spring and early summer. Often sold smoked in parts of Europe and America. If not able to eat fresh, pickle or souse it. *To Cook:* Most popular grilled and served with Maître d'Hôtel or tarragon butter, or fennel or gooseberry sauce. Bake, boil, fry, grill, pickle, pot, souse, etc., or treat by any recipe given for herring. *To Bake* (Maquereau roti) : Split, clean and head and tail. Dry. Place side by side in a small, greased baking dish. Season with salt and pepper. Dot over with dripping, allowing ½ tablespoon to each medium-sized fish. Add enough milk to cover. Bake in a hot oven, 400° F., for 25 minutes. If preferred, stuff and bake covered with a can of tomatoes instead of milk. *To Boil:* Wash, clean, and remove heads and insides. If there are roes, wash and replace them. Tie in a piece of cheesecloth or butter muslin. Place in a shallow pan. Cover with cold salted water, allowing 1 oz. salt to 1 quart water. Simmer gently for 10-15 minutes. Serve with melted butter or margarine, seasoned and flavoured with minced parsley. *To Fry:* Split down back. Clean. Carefully scrape out all the black from inside. Drain. Melt enough fat to grease frying-pan. Add fish. Fry till brown. Turn and fry on other side. Serve with fennel or gooseberry sauce, or like boiled mackerel.

MACKEREL AUX FINES HERBES (Maquereaux aux Fines Herbes)

12 button mushrooms
4 chopped peeled shallots
1 dessertspoon minced parsley
1 dessertspoon minced chervil
1 teaspoon minced tarragon
Salt and pepper to taste
2 medium-sized mackerel

Grease a shallow fireproof dish with butter. Wipe and slice mushrooms. Mix with shallots, parsley, chervil and tarragon. Cover the bottom of dish with this mixture. Season with salt and pepper to taste. Fillet mackerel. Place on top. Sprinkle with crumbs. Add stock or wine. Dab here and

Stale breadcrumbs as required
¼ pint white stock or wine
1 tablespoon butter
Squeeze lemon juice

there with butter. Bake in a slow oven, 300° F., for about 15-20 minutes, basting half time. Sprinkle with lemon juice. *For 2 persons.*

OLD ENGLISH MACKEREL (Maquereax à l'Anglaise)

2 mackerel
½ cup green gooseberries
1½ tablespoons butter
1 teaspoon chopped chervil
1 teaspoon chopped tarragon
Salt and pepper to taste
¼ pint water
3 or 4 slices onion
1 cup thick cream
Pinch grated nutmeg
½ pint green gooseberries

Clean mackerel. Mix the gooseberries with 1¼ tablespoons of the butter, chervil, tarragon and salt and pepper to taste. Divide mixture between mackerel and stuff. Place fish carefully in a shallow greased fireproof dish side by side. Add water and remainder of butter, and onion slices. Cover and cook until fish show signs of coming away from the bones. Remove fish. Dry carefully with a hot cloth. Dish up. Heat the cream with the nutmeg. Stir in hot sieved boiled green gooseberries to taste. Season with salt and pepper. Pour over fish. Serve with new or mashed potatoes. *For 2 persons.*

Megrim (Flet) : A coarse member of the turbot family. Cook like dabs and other flat fish.

Mullet—Grey (Mulet) *(obtainable all the year round—best, July-October)*: Small fish caught at the mouth of rivers. Abounds on south coast. *To Cook:* Bake, boil, grill, or roast when large. Can be cooked like salmon. If small, cook like whiting. When boiled, serve with Hollandaise sauce. Can be filleted and fried.

GRILLED GREY MULLETS (Mulets grillés)

4 medium-sized grey mullet
Salt and pepper to taste
3 tablespoons salad oil
2 bay leaves
2 tablespoons vinegar
2 or 3 sprigs parsley
1 or 2 slices onion

Scale, wash, clean and wipe mullet dry. Gash on both sides nearly ¼ inch deep, as when preparing herring for grilling. Place side by side in a shallow dish. Sprinkle with all other ingredients mixed together. Soak for 1 hour, turning at half time and basting occasionally with marinade. Place on a greased or oiled grill. Grill like herring. Serve with mustard sauce. If preferred, fry two finely chopped shallots in 1 oz. butter, then add ½ gill white wine, 2 or 3 tablespoons white stock, and 5 or 6 chopped mushrooms. Simmer for 15 minutes. Skim off fat. Stir in 1 teaspoon minced parsley or chives. Pour over fish. *For 4 persons.*

Mullet—Red (Rouget) *(seasonable all the year round—best, April-October)*: Soon deteriorates, so should be used as soon as possible. *To Clean:* Handle fish lightly. Do not scrape. Wipe off scales with a damp piece of muslin. Remove eyes and fins with a pair of scissors. Pull out gills and all that comes with them. Rinse, but be sure to retain liver. *To Cook:* Bake, grill or stew whole. If very large, fillet and bake or stew. Sometimes red mullet is soaked in hot melted butter, seasoned with salt and pepper, before grilling. Again, it is soaked in olive oil. *To Bake Red Mullet* (Rouget rôti) : Clean, wash and wipe dry. Fold each fish in oiled or buttered paper, carefully closing the ends to keep in the juice that comes from the fish. Place, side by side, in a greased baking dish or shallow baking tin. Bake in a moderate oven, 350° F., for 20 to 25 minutes, depending on size. Dish up in paper cases. Serve with anchovy, Bearnaise or Italian sauce. *To Fry* (Rouget frit) : Dip cleaned small mullet in seasoned flour. Fry, in enough hot butter to cover bottom of pan, very slowly for about ¼ hour. Dish up. Sprinkle with parsley and lemon juice to taste. Boil up 1 tablespoon unsalted butter in the pan until it turns colour, then strain over fish.

NOTE : Some Continental cooks stuff mullet with breadcrumbs, chopped shallot and fennel, moistened butter, before frying, grilling or cooking, wrapped in oiled paper.

RED MULLET WITH TOMATO SAUCE (Rougets, Espagnols)

2 tablespoons melted butter
2 thinly sliced peeled onions
3 thin slices lemon
Salt and pepper to taste
6 small red mullet
¾ lb. ripe tomatoes
1½ tablespoons olive oil
1 peeled clove garlic
Pinch cayenne pepper

Pour the butter into a flat fireproof dish. Arrange slices of onion and lemon in the bottom. Sprinkle with salt and pepper to taste and put the cleaned fish on top. Cover fish with buttered paper. Cook slowly over an asbestos mat, turning the dish round occasionally till the onions become clear. Wash, scald and peel tomatoes. Cut in slices. Place in a saucepan with the oil, garlic, onion slices. Cover. Cook very slowly for ½ an hour. Season to taste with salt and pepper. Cover again and cook until all the liquid is evaporated. Rub through a sieve, and spread over fish. Sprinkle lightly with cayenne pepper. Bake in a moderate oven, 350° F., for about 10 minutes. *For 6 persons.*

Perch (Perche) (*Seasonable, June-February*) : One of the best and most common of our fresh-water fish. Perch taken from running water is better than fish taken from lakes and canals. Very difficult to scale. *To Clean:* Scale and remove spines from back. There are two ways of scaling it : either plunge it for 2 to 3 minutes in boiling water and then scale, or boil it and scale afterwards. Wash in hot water and remove fins and gills. Soak for 2 to 3 hours, in salted water before cooking, to get rid of the muddy flavour. Dry thoroughly. *To Cook:* Soak in salted water for 2 to 3 hours. When large, cut into steaks, season, egg and crumb, or dip in batter, and fry in deep smoking hot fat or oil. When small, dip in seasoned flour. Fry in boiling oil for 5 minutes. Drain on crumpled paper. Serve with parsley and lemon. Can also be baked, boiled, grilled, potted or stewed.

POTTED PERCH (Terrine de Perches)

6 medium-sized perch
Salt to taste
4 peppercorns
2 allspice berries

Clean and remove gills, heads, tails, and scales. Pack closely into a greased pie-dish. Sprinkle with salt. Place the peppercorns, berries, bay leaf, ginger, and chilli pepper in a small muslin bag.

½ bay leaf
¼ inch root ginger
1 chilli pepper
5 oz. unsalted butter

Beat them with a mallet to crush them as far as possible and place on top of fish. Slice butter over. Cover closely. Bake in a slow oven, 300° F., for about 2 hours, then remove bag. Serve as part of an hors d'oeuvre, or as a cold luncheon dish with potato salad.

Pike (Brochet) (*Seasonable, September-March*) : Commonly called a "jack." Young pike are known as "pickerels." Roe is sometimes made into caviare. In some countries, the roe is salted and dried. *To Cook:* Bake, boil, fry, grill, roast or stew. Serve fried or grilled with horseradish sauce.

STEWED PIKE (Ragoût de Brochet)

3 lbs. fillet of pike
4 medium-sized onions
4 oz. butter
1 teaspoon paprika
½ pint sour cream
Salt and pepper to taste

Wipe fillets with a damp cloth. Season with salt and pepper. Peel and slice onions. Melt butter in a shallow saucepan. Fry onion slowly till clear. Stir in paprika and cream. Season to taste. Add fillets. Cover pan. Stew slowly for about 35 minutes. Dish up and strain sauce over. *For 6 persons.*

Pilchards (Royans) (*Seasonable, July-March*) : Sometimes known as "gypsy herring." Caught off the coasts of Devon and Cornwall. Oilier than herring. Cook by any recipes given for herring. In Cornwall, sometimes split and boned. Season with salt and pepper to taste. Brush insides with melted butter. Make a sandwich of two fillets, and hold in place with tiny skewers. Brush with melted butter and grill.

Plaice (Plie) (*Seasonable, May-December, obtainable all the year round*) : Known on the Sussex coast as "diamond plaice," because of the little orange diamonds on its back. The best are sometimes called "Dover plaice." They are caught between Folkestone and Hastings. One of the least esteemed of the flat fish. Rather flavourless and watery. *To Cook:* Best filleted. Dip fillets in seasoned flour, or egg and crumb, and fry. Whole fish can also be treated by any recipe given for sole, or can be substituted for sole when it is unobtainable. Some cooks hold that the flavour is improved if you salt the fish or fillets slightly and lay them between the folds of a dry cloth for ½ hour before cooking.

BAKED STUFFED PLAICE (Plie farcie au four)

3 plaice
3 minced shallots
1 teaspoon minced parsley
½ teaspoon beef extract
1 oz. butter
3 teaspoons lemon juice
½ pint white wine if liked
Seasoned breadcrumbs as required

Choose plaice weighing about 1 lb. each. Skin both sides, then make a cut from head to tail in the thick side of fish. Mix shallots, parsley, beef extract, butter and lemon juice to a paste. Raise the fillets from bone with a sharp knife. Push a little of the mixture under each raised fillet, then place fish in a lightly buttered shallow fireproof baking dish and pour wine over. Sprinkle breadcrumbs on top. Dab with one or two tiny pats of butter. Bake in a moderate oven, 350° F., for about 30 minutes. Serve from dish. *For 6 persons.*

PLAICE FAVOURITE (Plie Favorite)

4 fillets plaice
1 minced shallot
2 tomatoes
1 glass white wine
1 oz. butter
Salt and pepper to taste
¼ pint picked shrimps
1 teaspoon minced parsley
2 tablespoons cream

Butter a fireproof dish. Place fillets in it length-wise, leaving a space in the centre. Chop shallot. (Use a small onion if shallot is not available.) Scald, peel and chop tomatoes and mix with shallot. Place in the middle of fish. Pour wine over. Dab with tiny bits of butter. Season with salt and pepper to taste. Cover with buttered paper. Bake in a moderate oven for 10 minutes, then place shrimps on top of filling. Cover with freshly buttered paper. Bake for another 5 minutes. Carefully drain liquid into a saucepan. Add parsley. Boil up for 2 minutes. Draw pan to side of fire. Stir in cream. Pour over fish. *For 2 or 4 persons, depending on size of fillets.*

Roach (Gardon) (*Seasonable, September-March*) : Small fish belonging to carp family, seldom more than 1½ lbs. in weight. It usually inhabits gently flowing streams. White flesh, but tail red after being cooked. Best fried. Can also be baked or grilled like grayling. *To Fry* (Gardon frite) : Wash and dry thoroughly. Dredge with seasoned flour. Fry in a little hot fat until flesh shows signs of leaving bone. Drain on absorbent paper. Arrange on a hot dish. Garnish with parsley. Serve with anchovy sauce.

Rock Salmon (*Seasonable, September-May*) : Another name for coalfish. Wash and treat like cod.

Salmon (Saumon) (*Seasonable, February-August*) (King of fish) : Best salmon caught in Scottish rivers and in the Severn. The sooner the salmon is cooked after it is caught the better. Cheapest in July and August. *To Cook:* Boil, poach, or steam whole. Bake, fry, grill or stew cutlets or steaks. Middle cut is best. Can also be potted, pickled or smoked. *To Boil a Middle Cut or Tail:* Weigh fish. Season and wrap in oiled paper. Place in a pan in hot, salted water to cover, allowing 1 teaspoon salt to 1 pint water. Bring to simmering point. Skim if required. Simmer very gently, allowing 10 minutes to the pound. Serve with mayonnaise or Tartare sauce and boiled new potatoes. *To Boil a Six-pounder:* Season to taste. Wrap in butter muslin or cheese cloth. Simmer very gently for about ¾ hour. Drain well. Serve with caper sauce. Garnish with parsley and lemon. *To Cook Salmon for Serving Cold:* Scale, wash and rub whole fish, middle cut, or tail piece with lemon juice inside and out. Place on a rack in a fish-kettle. Add court bouillon, cold water, or half water and half wine to cover, 1 sprig parsley, 1 sprig fennel if possible, and 1 sprig thyme, 1 slice lemon and 1 tablespoon vinegar. Bring slowly to full boil. Cover closely and remove from stove. Leave in liquid until cool, then chill. *To Crimp and Boil Salmon:* Crimping should be done before the muscles of the fish become rigid. *To Crimp:* Remove the gills and the inside, opening fish as little as possible. Make deep gashes on both sides of the body with a sharp knife, about 2 inches apart. Plunge fish at once into very cold water. Leave for 2 hours, changing water at half-hour intervals. Place enough cold water in a fish-kettle to cover salmon entirely. Add salt, allowing 6 oz. to 4 quarts water. Bring quickly to boil. Skim carefully, then put in fish. Simmer gently, allowing less time than when boiling salmon that is not crimped. The time will depend on the thickness. Serve with lobster sauce. *To Grill:* Brush dried inch-thick steaks with seasoned olive oil or melted butter. Grease grill. Grill for 6 minutes on each side, turning gently at half time. Baste occasionally. Spread if liked with anchovy or Maître d'Hôtel butter. Serve with boiled new potatoes and Tartare sauce. Garnish with lemon or parsley.

CHAUDFROID OF SALMON (Chaudfroid de Saumon)

3 firm tomatoes
¼ pint aspic jelly
1½ gills well-seasoned white sauce
2 teaspoons lemon juice
½ gill cream
6 small cutlets salmon
Capers to garnish
Mustard and cress

Scald tomatoes in boiling water for a few seconds. Drain off water. Cover with cold water. Stand 2 minutes. Peel. Melt jelly in top of a double boiler. Make sauce. When cooked, take off and stir in melted jelly and strain in lemon juice. Strain through a very fine strainer into a basin. Stir in cream. Cut boiled or steamed middle cut of salmon cutlets in halves. Bone and skin and coat with sauce. Arrange side by side on a flat dish. Garnish each with a row of capers. Slice tomatoes and place tomato slices round fillets. Garnish each slice with a little mustard and cress. *For 6 persons.*

COLLARED SALMON (Saumon Mariné)

1 small plump salmon
Salt and white pepper to taste
Cayenne pepper and ground mace to taste
Bay leaves, peppercorns, cloves and allspice berries
Vinegar and water as required

There are various ways of collaring salmon. In the olden days, the salmon was spread with an elaborate stuffing before it was rolled up. This is a simpler method. Only half a salmon is required for one dish, so either make two dishes, or use remaining half boiled or in any way you choose. Prepare salmon for collaring. Remove head and tail. Wash and scale, then split in two lengthwise. Bone. Rinse and dry thoroughly. Weigh. Allow the following spices for 4 lb. fillet : 2 teaspoons salt, ½ teaspoon white pepper, pinch cayenne pepper and mace. Mix well and sprinkle over fillet. Roll up. Bind firmly with boiled string. Place in a shallow saucepan just large enough to hold fish, bay leaves, peppercorns, cloves, allspice berries, vinegar and water, allowing 1 pint water and 1½ gills vinegar, 2 bay leaves, 6 black peppercorns, 2 cloves, ½ teaspoon allspice berries, and salt to taste. Pour vinegar and water into pan. Add remainder of ingredients, then place in fish. Cover closely. Simmer very gently for about 1 hour or until cooked through. Remove and curl round inside of a large bowl or soufflé dish. Leave the stock until cold. Strain over salmon.

PICKLED OR SOUSED SALMON (Saumon en Marinade)

4 lb. boiled salmon
1 pint salmon stock
1 pint vinegar
1 oz. peppercorns
1 oz. allspice berries
3 bay leaves
1 tablespoon salt

Bone salmon. Place in a deep baking dish. Mix salmon stock and vinegar together. When quite cold, pour over fish. Place peppercorns and allspice here and there in dish. Add bay leaves, and sprinkle with salt. (If not enough liquid to cover fish entirely, add more fish liquor and vinegar in equal quantities.) Soak for 15 hours. Serve for supper or as a luncheon dish. *For 12 persons.*

QUENELLES OF SALMON (Quenelles de Saumon)

6 oz. prepared salmon
3 oz. butter
1/4 lb. panada
Salt and cayenne pepper to taste
1 large egg
2 egg yolks

Remove the skin from a thick slice of salmon. Scrape flesh from bone with a spoon. Rub through a fine sieve on to a plate. Weigh out 6 oz. Place in a mortar. Pound with the butter and panada till smoothly blended. Season with salt and cayenne pepper to taste. Gradually stir in the whole egg, then the yolks. Pound again till blended. Chill till required. Shape like small eggs with 2 wet dessertspoons. Poach in boiling salted water, or, if preferred, steam in quenelle moulds.

RUSSIAN SALMON LOAF (Pain de Saumon à la Russe)

1 lb. boiled salmon
3/4 oz. butter
1 dessertspoon flour
1 teaspoon dry mustard
Dash cayenne pepper
1/4 oz. caster sugar
1/2 pint milk
2 beaten egg yolks
4 tablespoons vinegar
1/4 oz. powdered gelatine
Slices of cucumber

Remove any skin and bone from salmon. Flake salmon. Melt butter. Sift in flour, mustard and cayenne pepper. Add sugar. Stir in melted butter and milk. Boil for a few minutes, stirring constantly. Cool, then add egg yolks. Turn into top of a double boiler and cook, stirring constantly, till thick. Allow to get cold, then stir in vinegar and the gelatine soaked in cold water to cover for 5 minutes. Add salmon. Mix well and pour into a wet mould. When set, turn out. Serve garnished with overlapping slices of cucumber, accompanied by sauce Tartare or mayonnaise. *For 5 persons.*

ICED SALMON CREAMS (Crèmes de Saumon, glacées)

1 lb. boiled salmon
1/4 pint milk
Salt and pepper to taste
1/4 teaspoon paprika
1/2 teaspoon French mustard
1 1/2 tablespoons melted butter
2 beaten egg yolks
3 tablespoons cold water
1/2 tablespoon powdered gelatine
1/4 gill wine vinegar

Drain salmon. Carefully remove any skin and bone. Flake fish. Place milk, salt, pepper, paprika and mustard, diluted with some of the milk, in a double boiler. Stir over boiling water till hot. Add butter and egg yolks, mixed with half the cold water. Cook in double boiler till thick. Add gelatine, soaked in remainder of cold water for 5 minutes, then dissolved. Chill. Stir in flaked salmon and vinegar. Turn into wet

Endive, sliced cucumber and eggs

dariole moulds. Chill. Turn out on to a dish. Garnish with curly endive, sliced cucumber and devilled eggs, yolks moistened mayonnaise, and dredged paprika. *For 6 or 8 persons.*

SALMON LOAF (Pain de Saumon, Américain)

1 can salmon
¼ cup milk
¾ cup soft breadcrumbs
2 eggs, separated
Salt and pepper to taste
2 tablespoons melted butter
Juice ½ lemon
1 teaspoon minced parsley
½ teaspoon onion juice

Turn out salmon on to a shallow dish. Remove skin and bones. Heat milk and stir in enough bread crumbs to make a paste. Stir into salmon with egg yolks, seasonings, and other ingredients. Beat egg whites till stiff. Fold into mixture. Put into a well-oiled mould. Bake in a hot oven, 425° F., for 35 minutes. Turn out. Serve hot with tomato sauce, or cold with sauce Tartare. *For 6 persons.*

SALMON MOUSSE, À LA REINE
(Mousse de Saumon à la Reine)

½ pint aspic jelly
1 truffle
½ lb. boiled salmon
3 tablespoons white sauce
Salt and pepper to taste
¼ oz. powdered gelatine
¼ pint whipped cream
1 egg white
Slices cucumber, lettuce leaves and radish roses

To prepare mould, place on cracked ice in a basin and coat the inside well with a thin layer of liquid aspic jelly. Cut truffle into fancy shapes. Arrange in a design on top of the jelly lining when set. If liked, sprinkle bottom of mould lightly with finely minced parsley before making a design with the truffle. Leave till set. To make mousse, weigh salmon, freed from skin and bone, then place in a mortar. Pound it well with a pestle, and stir in sauce by degrees. Season to taste with salt and pepper. Pound again till well mixed. (If wanted a rich salmon pink, pound in a few drops of cochineal.) Rub through a fine wire sieve into a basin. Stir in 1½ gills of the aspic jelly and the gelatine, softened in cold water to cover, then dissolved in remainder of aspic jelly, melted in a saucepan. When blended, lightly fold in the whipped cream and stiffly whisked egg white. Pour into prepared mould. Leave till set and chilled. Turn out on to a glass dish. Garnish round mousse with sliced cucumber, crisp lettuce leaves and radish roses. *For 6 persons.*

SALMON SOUFFLE (Soufflés de Saumon)

1 oz. butter
1 oz. flour
¼ pint hot milk
3 separated eggs
¼ lb. cooked salmon
Salt and cayenne pepper to taste
A few drops of anchovy essence

Melt butter in a saucepan. Stir in flour, then milk. When smooth and boiling, allow to cool slightly, then beat in one egg yolk at a time till all are mixed in. Put salmon through a meat grinder, then rub through a sieve. Season to taste with salt, cayenne pepper and anchovy essence. Stir into sauce. Re-season if necessary.

Fold in lightly frothed egg whites. Fill buttered soufflé dish or mould two-thirds full. Cover with buttered paper. Steam very gently for 45 minutes. Serve with anchovy or egg sauce, sharpened with lemon juice. *For 2 persons.*

ICED SALMON SOUFFLES (Soufflés de Saumon glacés)

¼ lb. canned salmon
1 teaspoon powdered gelatine
Anchovy essence or chopped capers
Salt and cayenne pepper to taste
2 egg whites
½ gill thick cream
Whole capers to decorate

Flake and rub salmon through a sieve. Dissolve gelatine in about a teaspoon of liquid drained from salmon and stir into salmon. Add anchovy essence or chopped capers and salt and cayenne pepper to taste. Beat egg whites till stiff. Fold into mixture. Whip cream and fold in about half of it. Pour into 4 individual soufflé dishes. When set and chilled, decorate each with remainder of cream and crown with a caper. *For 4 persons.*

Sardines (Sardines) : Some say that the sardines are the young of the herrings, but more generally accepted as young pilchards. *To Cook:* Grill on one side for 1 minute, then turn and grill on the other side. Season with salt and pepper to taste. Sprinkle with melted butter and minced parsley. *Allow 3 or 4 per person.* They can also be fried in butter for 2 or 3 minutes.

Shad (Alose) : Very popular in France and Germany. Known in Germany as " May fish." The American shad is very superior to the European variety. In the U.S.A. the roe is considered a great delicacy, either fresh or canned. Usually caught up rivers when they come to spawn. *To Cook:* Fillet and fry. Serve with anchovy, caper or mustard sauce, or Maître d'Hôtel butter. Soak in a marinade, basting frequently, for 2 hours. Grill like herring. Serve with caper or mustard sauce. Shad weighing about 2 lb. takes ½ hour to grill. In France, grilled shad is served with sorrel purée. Shad can also be boiled and served with caper, Hollandaise or lobster sauce.

Shad Roes (Laitances d'Alose) : Wash thoroughly, then par-boil. Place in a saucepan. Add 1 quart boiling water, 1 teaspoon salt and 1 tablespoon lemon juice. Cover. Simmer gently for about 10 minutes. Remove with a skimmer. Place in a basin of cold water. Leave for a minute or two, then drain well. Peel off the membrane. *To Fry:* Dip in seasoned flour. Fry in hot oil or butter until golden brown below, then turn and brown on other side. Serve garnished Maître d'Hôtel butter and grilled curls of bacon. Can be egged and crumbed and fried until golden in deep fat or oil. *To Grill:* Brush with melted butter. Season with salt and pepper. Cook under a slow grill until golden on top, then turn and brown on other side. Takes 4 to 10 minutes, according to thickness. Baste with melted butter while cooking. Sprinkle with lemon juice before serving. Garnish with Maître d'Hôtel butter and grilled curls of bacon. *Fresh or Canned Shad Roe:* Season 3 tablespoons flour. Dip a hard-boiled roe or a drained canned roe in the flour. Fry until brown below in melted butter, then turn. Add 1 heaped teaspoon minced onion to the fat. Cover. Cook slowly until brown below and onion is clear. Dish up. Add 2 or 3 tablespoons cream to the butter. Stir quickly until blended, then spoon over roe. Serve with new potatoes and green peas.

Skate (Raie) (*Seasonable, October-August*) : Several varieties know as thornbacks, rays and tinkers. Thornbacks considered best. Flesh coarse. but palatable. Very nutritious. Flesh of the wing or fin is the best part. Usually sold crimped. Very popular in France. Young skate are called " maids." Unwholesome out of season. If kept for a day or two before cooking, they will be more tender. *To Clean:* Wash and rub with salt. Rinse well. Remove tail. Pull off fins. Hang in a cool larder. *To Cook:* Boil or poach. Also delicious baked, fried or grilled. Steep in cold water for 1 hour before using. *To Fry:* (1) Soak fillets of skate in cold water to cover with 1 tablespoon vinegar, 6 peppercorns, and a sprig of parsley, for 1 hour. Drain. Dry. Dip in seasoned flour. Egg and crumb. Fry in hot oil or dripping to cover until golden brown. Drain. Serve with hot sauce tartare. (2) Wash and dry 1 lb. skate cutlets. Soak in marinade for 2 to 3 hours. Drain well. Dip in seasoned flour, then in butter. Fry in deep smoking hot fat for about 5 minutes until golden brown. Drain on absorbent paper. Garnish with lemon and parsley. Serve with black butter or caper sauce. *To Poach:* Poach in salted water to cover for ½ to 1 hour, according to size. Drain. Serve with caper or shrimp sauce.

BOILED SKATE WITH BLACK BUTTER
(Raie au Beurre Noire)

1 lb. skate
2 oz. butter
1 tablespoon wine vinegar
Salt and pepper to taste
1 teaspoon minced parsley
1 teaspoon minced capers

Simmer skate gently in court bouillon, allowing about 15 minutes. When ready, remove skate carefully. Drain well. Arrange on a hot dish. Melt butter until dark brown, but not black. Remove from stove. Stir in vinegar gradually. Season to taste with salt and pepper. Coat fish with this black butter. Sprinkle with parsley and capers. In Provence, the skate liver is fried and used as a garnish for this dish. *For 2 persons.*

Skate Liver (Foie de Raie) : Considered a great delicacy. *To Cook:* Skate liver can be made into an excellent sauce for skate : Boil liver in strongly salted water till quite firm. Cut into small pieces. Place in a saucepan with ½ pint butter sauce. Season to taste with salt and pepper and a dash of vinegar. Bring quickly to boiling point. Serve hot with skate.

Smelt (Eperlan) (*Seasonable, October-May*) : A delicious little fish, known in Scotland as " sperlings." Often used as a garnish. *To Clean:* Handle carefully. The gourmet never washes smelts, only wipes them with a damp cloth. Make a tiny cut with scissors just below the gills, then gently press out the entrails. Rinse carefully, taking care not to damage flesh. If you insist on mashing them, pull out gills so that the entrails come away at the same time. *To Bake:* Remove fins from 12 smelts. Clean and dry. Season to taste with salt and pepper. Place side by side in a greased fireproof dish. Sprinkle with lemon juice to taste, then with 3 tablespoons sieved breadcrumbs mixed with 1 teaspoon minced parsley and flavoured, if liked, with a few drops of anchovy essence. Sprinkle over fish, then melt 2 oz. butter and sprinkle over. Cover with greased paper. Bake for about ¼ hour in a moderate oven,

350° F. *To Fry:* Dredge with seasoned flour. Melt ½ oz. butter. Beat 2 egg yolks. Stir into butter. Dip smelts in this, then in sieved stale breadcrumbs. Fry in boiling fat, then drain on absorbent paper. Arrange like a star on a hot dish. Serve with shrimp sauce. Garnish with fried parsley.

POTTED SMELTS (Terrine d'Eperlans)

6 dozen smelts
2 tablespoons salt
1 oz. allspice berries
1 oz. black peppercorns
1 oz. whole cloves
2 cups olive oil
4 cups malt vinegar
2 cups tarragon vinegar

Clean smelts. Remove heads and tails. Pack in layers in small deep earthenware or stone pots, with salt in between. Tie spices in a muslin bag and place here and there among the fish. Cover with oil and vinegars. Bake for 4 hours in a moderate oven, 350° F. These potted smelts will keep for a month or two if closely covered.

SMELTS À LA MEUNIERE (Eperlans à la Meunière)

Split and bone smelts, if liked. Score 4 or 5 gashes on each side with a sharp knife. Sprinkle with lemon juice and salt and pepper to taste. Stand for 15 minutes. Dip in flour. Melt for 6 smelts 1 tablespoon butter in a small frying-pan. Fry on both sides till golden and cooked through. Dish up. Sprinkle with lemon juice and minced parsley. Melt another tablespoon butter and coat fish. *Allow 2 or 3 smelts per person.*

Smelts au Beurre Noire : Fry as described. Coat with beurre noire. Garnish with sprigs of parsley.

SMELTS ESPAGNOL (Eperlans, Espagnols)

6 smelts
Salt and pepper to taste
Squeeze lemon juice
1 teaspoon onion juice
1 pimiento
1 tablespoon grated Parmesan cheese
Egg and crumb
¼ pint tomato sauce
1½ cups mayonnaise
3 tablespoons chopped olives

Wipe smelts with a damp cloth, then split and bone. Place on a shallow plate. Sprinkle with salt and pepper to taste and lemon and onion juice. Cover. Stand for 7 minutes, then turn and stand for another 7 minutes. Rub pimiento through a fine sieve. Stir in cheese. Spread insides of smelts with stuffing. Roll up. Fasten with tiny wooden skewers. Crumb, then egg and crumb. Fry in deep smoking hot fat until golden brown. Serve with tomato sauce mixed gradually with mayonnaise and olives. *For 4 persons.*

Snoek : Known also as " barracouta." Imported to Britain from South Africa in cans. They are sold in ½ lb. cans, some plain and some packed in tomato sauce. *To Cook:* Remove from can and remove any bones. Make into fish cakes, pies or kedgeree. Scallop with cheese sauce, etc.

Sole (Sole) (*Seasonable all the year round, best April-January*) : King of flat fish. The best soles are caught off the coast of Dover and known as Dover soles. Some consider the Dover sole to be second to the turbot in excellence, and others that the Dover sole comes first. Sometimes known as a sea-partridge. Flesh delicate and firm. If cooked as soon as caught, they are in perfection, but they can be kept for a day without spoiling. Soles with roes are rather insipid. They should be filleted. Lemon soles, rounder and wider than Dover soles, are good for eating, but inferior in flavour and texture. Torbay soles, sometimes known as witches or flukes, can be cooked by any of the following recipes, for any soles can be used in these recipes, except where I have stipulated Dover soles. Slips are small soles, suitable for flouring and frying for breakfast. *To Clean :* Soles should be cleaned 2 hours before cooking if possible. Remove gills. Make a small opening in belly. Remove insides, leaving roe, then detach skin at the back of the head and pull it all off the fish together. Remove fins. Rinse and drain thoroughly. *To Fillet :* Cut round the edge of the fish next to the fins and make a long deep incision down the centre of the back. Pass the blade of a knife between the bone and the flesh, from incision outwards, and gradually work off in one fillet. Repeat to remove second fillet on the same side, then turn and remove fillets on the other side in the same way. *To Cook:* Large soles can be cooked like turbot. Slips are best fried or grilled whole. Soles in general are best baked, boiled, fried or grilled and garnished with lemon.

FILLETS OF SOLE, BONNE FEMME
(Filets de Sole, Bonne Femme)

1½ lb. Dover sole
3 peppercorns
1 clove peeled garlic
1 slice onion
½ pint water
½ gill white wine
1 sprig parsley
1 sprig fennel
2 sprigs chervil
4 oz. mushrooms
2 oz. butter
Salt and pepper to taste
¾ oz. flour
½ gill milk
1 tablespoon cream
¼ pint Hollandaise sauce

Skin and fillet sole. Wash and dry. Arrange fillets side by side in a well-buttered fireproof dish. Put the fish bones and trimmings in a saucepan with peppercorns, garlic, onion, water, wine and herbs. Bring slowly to the boil, and simmer for ½ hour. Strain over fillets. Cover with buttered paper. Cook in a moderate oven, 350° F., for ¼ hour. Wash mushrooms in cold water sharpened with lemon juice. Slice. Melt 1 oz. of the butter in a saucepan. Add mushrooms and salt and pepper to taste. Cover with buttered paper then with lid. Stew gently for 5 or 6 minutes, stirring constantly. To make sauce : Melt remainder of butter in a saucepan. Remove pan from stove. Season to taste, and stir in flour. Stir until blended, then gradually stir in ½ gill of the fish stock. Return to stove. Cook until thick, stirring occasionally, then gradually stir in milk. Stir again until boiling, then remove from stove and add cream. Arrange fillets on a hot dish. Coat smoothly with the sauce. Sprinkle with mushrooms. Coat with the Hollandaise sauce. Brown slowly under the grill or in the top of an oven. *For 4 persons.*

FILLETS OF SOLE, DUGLERE (Filets de Sole, Duglère)

1 sole (1 lb. in weight)
Salt and pepper to taste
1 chopped shallot

Fillet sole. Wipe with a damp cloth. Season with salt and pepper to taste, then place side by side in a small buttered shallow baking dish.

2 tomatoes
1 glass white wine
1 oz. melted butter
2 tablespoons cream
1 teaspoon minced parsley

Arrange shallot and peeled and quartered tomatoes round. Sprinkle with white wine. Bake in a moderate oven, 350° F., for about ¼ hour. Remove to a hot dish. Strain stock into a saucepan. Cook until reduced to half its quantity. Stir in butter and cream. Mask fish with sauce and sprinkle with parsley. *For 2 persons.*

FILLETS OF SOLE, FLORENTINE (Filets de Sole, Florentine)

1 large sole (1 lb. in weight)
Salt and pepper to taste
¼ pint water
4 tablespoons cooked spinach
1 small cup Mornay sauce
1½ tablespoons grated Parmesan cheese

Fillet the sole, then fold the fillets in two and place in a small buttered tin. Season with salt and pepper to taste and pour in the water. Cover and cook in a moderate oven, 350° F., for about 15 minutes, or till cooked right through. Drain well. Mash the spinach with butter, and salt and pepper to taste. Line a hot fireproof dish with it. Lay the fillets on top. Pour the sauce over. Sprinkle with grated cheese. Bake in a hot oven till golden brown, or brown under grill. *For 2 persons.*

FILLETS OF SOLE, MORNAY (Filets de Sole, Mornay)

1½ lb. Dover sole
Squeeze lemon juice
1 bay leaf
3 tablespoons water
½ pint milk
1 slice onion
1 peeled clove of garlic
4 black peppercorns
2 oz. butter
¾ oz. flour
Salt and black pepper to taste
1½ oz. grated Parmesan cheese
2 tablespoons cream

Skin and fillet sole. Rinse and dry well. Fold under both ends and place in a shallow, well-buttered fireproof dish. Add lemon juice, bay leaf, and water. Place sole carcase on top. Bake in a moderate oven, 350° F., for 15 minutes. Pour milk into a saucepan. Add onion, clove of garlic and peppercorns. Bring slowly to boil. Melt half the butter in another saucepan. Remove from stove. Add flour and salt and black pepper to taste. Strain in heated milk. Stir till boiling. Add cheese, cream and the remainder of butter, bit by bit, stirring after each addition. Simmer for a minute or two. Dish up fillets on a flat hot dish. Cover with sauce. Sprinkle with additional grated Parmesan cheese to taste. Brown in a hot oven, or under a grill. Serve with mashed potatoes and green peas or fried mushrooms. *For 4 persons.*

FILLETS OF SOLE, ST. RAPHAEL (Filets de Sole, St. Raphael)

4 peeled medium-sized tomatoes
3 tablespoons butter
1 tablespoon minced onion
6 oz. chopped mushrooms
1 tablespoon minced parsley
¾ pint fish stock
¼ pint white wine
Salt and pepper to taste
1½ lb. fillets of sole

Chop tomatoes. Melt butter in a shallow saucepan. Add tomato, onion, mushroom and parsley. Cook lightly, stirring occasionally, in the butter for 2 minutes, then pour in the stock. Add wine and seasoning to taste. Add fillets. Cover and simmer gently for 5 to 10 minutes, depending on thickness of fillets. When tender, remove fillets to a hot dish, arranging them side by side. Boil sauce quickly until reduced to ½ pint. Pour over fish. Serve with mashed or boiled new potatoes. *For 6 persons.*

SCALLOPS OF SOLE AU PARMESAN
(Coquilles de Sole au Parmesan)

1 large sole
½ gill cider
½ gill water
Salt and pepper to taste
¾ pint white sauce
3 tablespoons grated Parmesan cheese
¼ lb. sliced peeled mushrooms
½ teaspoon minced parsley
Breadcrumbs and butter as required

Fillet sole and place fillets in saucepan. Mix cider and water and pour over fish. Season with salt and pepper to taste. Cover and simmer for about 5 minutes, then remove fillets. Butter 6 large scallop shells. Flake fish into sauce. Add cheese, and mushrooms lightly fried. Stir in parsley. Divide mixture equally between scallop shells. Cover with a layer of bread-crumbs. Dab with butter. Bake till brown in the top of a moderate oven. Sometimes I omit the crumbs and cut thin slices of banana which I lay on top, and brush them with melted butter before baking. *For 6 persons.*

SOLE À LA MEUNIERE (Sole à la Meunière)

Allow 1 small sole or 1 fillet, 4 to 6 oz. in weight, per person. Melt 2 oz. butter in a frying-pan. Season sole with salt and black pepper to taste. Dust with flour. When butter is at boiling point, put in fish or fillets. Fry for ½ minute, then turn and fry on other side for ½ minute. Fry slowly, turning carefully until cooked right through. Dish up. Sprinkle with lemon juice. Coat with hot melted butter. Sprinkle with minced parsley. Garnish with sprigs of parsley or lemon butterflies.

SOLE À LA PORTUGAISE (Sole à la Portugaise)

1 large sole
1 oz. butter
1 teaspoon minced parsley
5 or 6 drops anchovy essence
Salt and pepper to taste
1 large Spanish onion
1 large tomato
4 tablespoons stale bread-crumbs
3 tablespoons grated cheese
¼ pint tomato sauce

Wash, skin and remove fins, tail and head of fish. Work butter and parsley on a plate with a knife and beat in anchovy essence. Make a slit down the centre of fish. Lift flesh a little at each side of incision to form a pocket. Stuff with ¾ of the mixture. Spread remainder of mixture in the bottom of a shallow, buttered fireproof dish. Place fish on top. Season to taste. Peel and slice onion and tomato. Place slices alternately down the centre of the fish. Mix breadcrumbs with cheese and sprinkle on top. Pour sauce round. Cover with a lid or sheet of buttered paper. Place in a hot oven, 450° F. Switch to low. Bake for 10 minutes. Uncover and bake for 3 or 4 minutes. Serve with new potatoes, or alone. *For 2 persons.*

SOLE VERONIQUE (Filets de Sole, Véronique)

4 fillets Dover sole
2 sliced onions
1 clove garlic
Juice 1 lemon
Salt and pepper to taste
Sprig parsley

Wash and dry fillets. Turn the two ends under. Place side by side in a shallow well-buttered fireproof dish. Arrange onion on top. Peel and mince garlic finely and sprinkle over onion, then strain in lemon juice. Season to taste. Lay parsley,

Sprig thyme
Sprig chervil
Sprig fennel
Bay leaf
½ pint white wine
½ gill water
2 oz. butter
¾ oz. flour
½ gill milk
1 tablespoon cream
½ lb. muscatel grapes
1 tablespoon melted butter
1 heaped teaspoon minced parsley

thyme, chervil, fennel, and bay leaf on top. Mix white wine with water. Sprinkle over. Cover with greased paper. Cook in a moderate oven, 350° F., for 15 to 20 minutes till cooked through. Carefully remove herbs from fillets and dish fillets up. Keep warm while making sauce. Melt half butter in a small saucepan. Remove pan from stove. Stir in flour. When smooth, stir in 1½ gills fish liquor, then return pan to stove. Stir till thick and boiling. Gradually add milk. Stir again till boiling, then remove from stove and stir in the cream and remainder of butter. Cover grapes with boiling water. Stand for a moment or two then skin and seed. Pour melted butter into a shallow saucepan. Add grapes. Season with salt and pepper to taste. Add parsley. Shake over slow heat till warm. Pour sauce over fillets. Garnish with grapes. Sometimes the dish is put under the grill for a few moments before garnishing with grapes. *For 4 persons.*

Sprats (Sprats) (*Seasonable in England, November-March ; in Scotland, May-June*) : Resemble herring. Abundant in the Firth of Forth. Sometimes smoked. *To Cook:* Dry and dip in seasoned flour or batter. Fry in smoking hot fat or oil. Drain thoroughly on absorbent paper. You can grill and serve them with mustard sauce. *To Dry-Fry:* Clean, wash and dry smelts on a cloth. Heat frying-pan only slightly. Sprinkle with salt, about 1 tablespoon. Lay sprats in pan, side by side. Sprinkle with cayenne pepper and lemon juice. Fry gently for 3 or 4 minutes. Turn gently and carefully. Sprinkle with a little more lemon juice. Fry gently for 4 minutes. *To Grill:* Clean and wash sprats. Wipe dry. Rub hot griller with block suet. Dredge sprats with seasoned flour. Grill for 2 or 3 minutes. Allow 1 lb. for 4 persons. Serve with brown bread and butter and lemon fingers. *To Pot:* Follow recipe given for potted smelts. *Pickled Sprats* (Sprats en Matelote) : Clean and behead sprats. Place in a pie dish. Cover with equal quantity of vinegar and water. Add allspice berries, black peppercorns, salt, bay leaves and sliced peeled onions, allowing ¼ tablespoon allspice berries, ½ oz. peppercorns, 1 rounded teaspoon salt, 2 or 3 bay leaves and 1 sliced peeled onion to 1 quart vinegar required. Cover dish. Bake in a moderate oven, 350° F., for about 20 minutes to ½ hour.

Sturgeon (Esturgeon) (*Seasonable, August-March*) : Called a Royal fish on account of the fact that in olden days it had to be sent to the reigning sovereign. Firm, well-flavoured flesh, not unlike veal. Belly resembles pork. Not often met with in Britain. Sterlet is the most highly prized species. Caviare is made from the roe. Very popular in France. *To Cook:* Can be baked and boiled and served with Hollandaise sauce, braised or roasted and served like veal with purée of sorrel. Cook like scallops of veal by frying in butter, or grill. *To Boil:* Cut in slices about 1 in. thick. Place in boiling water. Add 1 sprig parsley, ½ bay leaf, 2 cloves, 6 peppercorns, 1 small peeled onion, 1 teaspoon salt and ½ tablespoon vinegar. Boil slowly, allowing ½ hour per lb. Dish up in folded napkin. Garnish with parsley and serve with anchovy or lobster sauce.

BAKED STURGEON (Esturgeon au four)

2 lb. middle cut sturgeon
Salt and cayenne pepper to taste
1 heaped teaspoon minced parsley
1 heaped teaspoon minced onion or shallot
Juice of ½ lemon
½ pint white wine
¼ lb. butter

Clean and skin fish. Place in a large greased baking dish. Sprinkle with salt and pepper to taste and the herbs, lemon juice and wine. Dab with butter. Bake in a moderate oven, 350° F., basting frequently, for 1 to 1¼ hours, depending on thickness. Serve from dish. *For 6 persons.*

Tench (Tanche) (*Seasonable, October-June, obtainable all the year round*) : Fresh-water fish allied to carp family, but richer and better flavoured. More of a pond than river fish. On the Continent, tench are kept in tanks. *To Clean:* Twist into the shape of a letter S, and scrape upwards from the belly to the back. Remove gills and open belly. Take out inside and wash clean. Rub fish with lemon juice and stand for 1 hour. Some people soak in boiling water for a few minutes before scaling and gutting. Wipe fish. *To Cook:* Grill whole. or fillet, egg and crumb and fry. Serve with anchovy or shrimp sauce. Or fry like small perch. You can follow any recipes given for trout.

MATELOTE OF TENCH (Matelote de Tanches)

2 medium-sized tench
1 tablespoon chopped onion
½ carrot
2 or 3 slices turnip
1 sprig parsley
1 sprig thyme
1 bay leaf
1 blade mace
3 cloves
½ pint white stock
2 glasses port wine
6 allspice berries
Salt and pepper to taste

Prepare tench for cooking as described. Place on a drainer or rack of small fish kettle. Add onion, carrot, turnip, parsley, thyme, bay leaf, mace, cloves, white stock, wine, allspice berries and salt and pepper to taste. Cover closely. Simmer very gently for about half hour. Drain well. Dish up. Serve with Matelote sauce poured over, or with mussel sauce. *For 6 persons.*

Trout (Truite) : Seasons vary according to the rivers from which they are caught, but you can usually reckon from February-September ; in their prime, June-August. River trout are in their prime in August. There are various kinds of trout ; the ordinary river trout, sea trout, etc., but the salmon trout is considered the best. Some are migratory, such as sea trout and salmon trout, and others not, such as lake trout. *To Clean:* Trout sometimes served with scales on. Clean like salmon. *To Cook:* Fry or grill small trout. Simmer larger trout in a good court bouillon. Should be cooked as soon as possible after catching, as the flesh soon deteriorates. Pickle or souse like herrings.

If *Trout au Bleu* is wanted, do not scale trout. Place in a dish of vinegar to cover. (In France, the fish is placed in boiling vinegar as soon as killed then simmered in white wine only.) Remove from vinegar when skin has turned blue. Place in hot court bouillon, made with half water and half wine. Bring to boil. Draw pan to side of stove. Cover tightly. Stand for 5 minutes, then drain fish carefully and dish up. *To Fry:* Either dip in seasoned flour and fry in butter when starting to brown, turning trout very gently when brown below, then season them, or egg and crumb and fry in deep hot fat until golden brown. If preferred, trout can be filleted before frying, or split down the centre and boned before frying. *To Grill Trout* (Truite grillée) : Clean trout. There are two ways of preparing them for grilling : one is to gash them two or three times down the back or score them down the side with knife and season flesh with salt and pepper to taste, and the other is to split and bone them and close them again after seasoning. Brush with melted butter or olive oil. Place in a well-greased or oiled grill pan. Grill slowly for about 10 to 20 minutes, turning carefully as they break easily. Baste frequently with butter in pan. Slip a pat of Maître d'Hôtel butter inside each. Garnish with lemon and fried sprigs of parsley. *To Pot Trout* (Terrine de Truites) : Clean and dry 1 dozen small trout. Season with salt. Stand for 10 hours. Dry. Mix 1 chopped onion and 4 white peppercorns with ½ oz. cloves, ¼ oz. cayenne pepper, and ¼ teaspoon ground mace. Sprinkle this mixture over trout. Place, backs downwards, in an earthenware jar. Cover with 2 lbs. clarified butter. Place in a very slow oven, 275° F., and bake for 3 to 4 hours. If the butter does not cover trout, add more to give a covering layer ¼ inch deep. Cover jars and keep in refrigerator or larder until required. *To Cook Rainbow Trout:* Clean and wipe trout dry. Season inside with salt and pepper to taste. Gash down backbone 2 inches apart. Sprinkle fish with salt and pepper to taste. Coat with seasoned flour. Shake to remove superfluous flour. Place in a hot, generously-buttered fireproof dish over an asbestos mat. Fry slowly until golden brown below, then slip into the oven and brown on top, basting with butter. Serve from dish garnished with lemon and fried parsley.

BAKED STUFFED TROUT (Truites farcies, au four)

6 medium-sized trout
Cucumber stuffing
3 tablespoons water
1 tablespoon vinegar
1 sprig thyme
1 spring onion
1 sprig parsley
¼ teaspoon salt
Dash pepper
1 oz. butter
1 teaspoon flour
8 drops anchovy essence
6 capers
1 teaspoon lemon juice

Empty and scale trout. Fill with cucumber stuffing. (If preferred, trout can be filleted, and the fillets sandwiched together with the stuffing before baking.) Measure water into a saucepan. Add vinegar, thyme, onion, parsley, and salt and pepper to taste. (If you haven't any thyme, use a pinch of crushed herbs.) Simmer for 5 minutes. Strain liquor into a shallow baking dish or tin. Add trout, arranging side by side. Cover with greased or oiled paper. Bake in a moderate oven, 350° F., for 20 to 30 minutes, depending on size. Remove to a hot dish. Mix butter to a paste with flour. Add to liquor in dish or tin. Stir till boiling. Add anchovy essence, capers and lemon juice. Boil for 5 minutes. Pour round fish. Serve with boiled potatoes. *For 6 persons.*

SCOTCH WAY WITH RIVER TROUT (Truites Ecossaises)

4 river trout
Salt and pepper to taste
2 oz. medium-sized oatmeal

Split, clean, bone and rinse trout. Sprinkle with salt and pepper to taste on both sides. Flatten with a broad-bladed knife. Turn oatmeal on to

2 oz. butter
Sprigs parsley and cut lemon
a sheet of kitchen paper, and coat the trout on both sides. Melt butter in a frying-pan. When smoking hot, add trout. Fry till brown below, then turn and brown on other side. Drain on absorbent paper. Arrange on a hot dish. Garnish with sprigs of parsley and cut lemon. *For 2 persons.*

TROUT AU BEURRE NOIRE (Truite au Beurre Noire)

Clean, wash and wipe dry. Dip in flour. Fry in a little hot butter or cooking fat, till cooked, turning gently. Season with salt and pepper to taste and dish up. Add a walnut of butter for each fish to frying-pan. Cook till slightly brown. Sprinkle trout with minced parsley then coat with the cooked butter. Garnish with quarters of lemon.

Tunny Fish (Tuna or Thon) (*Seasonable, June-December*): Belongs to mackerel family. Flesh delicate—somewhat resembling veal. It is usually sold canned in oil in Britain and served as an hors d'oeuvre as it comes from the can, or it is made into a salad. On the Continent, fresh tunny is popular braised and served with green peas, or grilled and served with purée of sorrel, or cut into steaks and fried in oil. If obtainable fresh in England, boil or grill and serve with Maître d'Hôtel sauce. Canned tunny makes appetising canapé spreads and sandwich fillings.

SCALLOPED TUNNY FISH (Coquilles de Thon)

Mix 2 cups parsley sauce with grated cheese to taste. Flake 1 can tunny fish. Stir lightly into sauce with 2 tablespoons cooked green peas. Season to taste. Grease 6 scallop shells. Fill with mixture. Sprinkle with stale bread-crumbs, then with melted butter to moisten. Bake till golden.

If liked, serve, instead of baking in scallop shells, on rounds or squares of hot fried bread or buttered toast. The point to remember when preparing it is to keep the flakes whole. Don't stir until into a paste.

To Vary : If liked, substitute chopped fried mushrooms for the peas, or $1\frac{1}{2}$ tablespoons chopped green pepper.

Turbot (Turbot) (*Seasonable all the year round, best March-August*): Known as the " Pheasant of the Sea." Considered finest flat fish. In olden days called " King of Lent." Flesh white, delicate and deliciously flavoured. Dogger Bank turbot are the finest. *To Clean:* Remove gills carefully. Make an incision at the back of the fish close to the head, from where remove inside. Wash well with salted water. Do not remove the fins. They are considered a delicacy. Rub fish over with a cut lemon before cooking. *To Cook:* Usually served boiled or steamed with Hollandaise, lobster, oyster or shrimp sauce. A properly cooked turbot should have firm, curd-like flesh. A small turbot, known as " chicken turbot," can be boiled or steamed whole, or filleted and treated like sole. Follow any recipes given for halibut. *To Boil* (Turbot bouilli) : Prepare and wipe a medium-sized turbot, or 2 lb. middle cut, thoroughly with a damp cloth. Trim fins but do not remove them as the

Serve Chicken or Beef Croquettes in a mushroom ring, garnished buttered green peas. *See pages* 333, *and* 255.

Arrange Stewed Ox Kidney in a border of boiled cut macaroni, garnished minced parsley and sippets of toast. *See page* 247.

Aspic of Ham, set in a flan case. Garnish with young boiled carrots, coated French dressing, and curly endive.

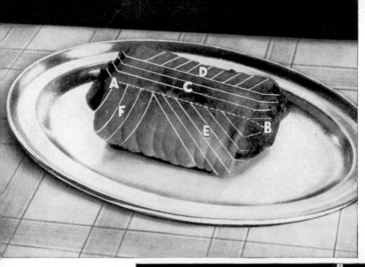

Saddle of Mutton, marked for carving. *See page* 238

Cut along the spinal bone until the knife touches the bone. *See page* 238.

Cutting the Saddle crosswise on the slant yields good slices of fat and lean. *See page* 239.

gelatinous parts round them are considered a great delicacy. Make an incision down the centre of the back to prevent skin cracking on the white side. Rub this side with cut lemon. Measure off cold water and add salt in the proportion of 6 oz. to 1 gallon water. Bring water to boil. Place turbot on rack, white side upwards. Lower into boiling water. Simmer very gently until cooked through, in about 15 to 20 minutes—a large turbot will take 20 to 35 minutes. Remove carefully. Drain well. Slip, white side upwards, on to a hot dish covered with a folded napkin or paper doily. Garnish with cut lemon, sprigs of parsley, or shredded horseradish. Serve with anchovy, Hollandaise, lobster or shrimp sauce. If liked, you can garnish with lobster coral, crawfish or prawns. Medium-sized turbot for 4 to 6 persons ; middle cut for 4 persons. *To Fry Chicken Turbot:* Flour and fry in boiling oil to cover for ¼ hour. Garnish with fried parsley and slices of lemon. Serve with anchovy, mayonnaise or Tartare sauce and cucumber or tomato salad.

Whitebait (Blanchailles) (*Seasonable, March-August*) : Fry of herring and sprat. Small silvery-looking fish. Must be perfectly fresh for cooking. If not to be cooked at once, place in iced water. *To Clean:* Wash in very cold water. Drain well. Dry on a cloth. *To Cook:* After leaving whitebait on cloth to dry, sprinkle another cloth with flour. Lay fish side by side on cloth. Shake them lightly, till evenly coated. Separate each from the other. Lay, a few at a time, in a frying basket. Plunge in deep smoking hot lard or oil. Fry for about 15 seconds. Drain on paper in oven. Reheat fat and repeat till all are ready. Heat fat again then turn all the fish into basket and plunge into fat for a moment or two until crisp. Serve at once piled up on a hot dish lined with a napkin. Season with salt and cayenne pepper to taste. Garnish with fried parsley. Serve with cut lemon and brown bread and butter. *Devilled Whitebait;* Sprinkle the fish, just before the second cooking, with freshly ground black pepper and cayenne pepper to taste.

Whiting (Merlan) (*Seasonable, May-February, obtainable all the year*) : One of the commonest of sea fish. Flesh tasteless, but most digestible. In olden days, fish was skinned and the tail twisted round and put through its teeth. *To Cook:* Should be cooked perfectly fresh. Usually cooked whole, but can be filleted. Best fried or grilled, but can be baked. *To Fry:* Wash, skin and remove eyes. Leave on head. Dry thoroughly. When ready to fry, insert tail of each whiting between its teeth. Egg and crumb. Fry in deep smoking hot fat until golden brown. Drain on absorbent paper. Dish up. Garnish with fried parsley and lemon. Serve with anchovy, Hollandaise, shrimp or tomato sauce.

CREAMS OF WHITING (Timbales de Merlan)

1 large whiting
½ pint milk
Salt and pepper to taste
3 oz. chopped onion
1 sprig parsley
1 teaspoon chopped celery
Pinch crushed herbs

Clean, wash and fillet whiting. Place head, skin, tail, and bones in a saucepan. Add milk, and salt and pepper to taste. Cover. Bring slowly to boil. Add onion, parsley, celery and herbs. Cover. Cook very gently for ½ hour, then strain liquor into a shallow saucepan. Add fillets. Cover.

3 oz. butter
1¾ oz. flour
2 eggs
3 tablespoons cream
1 teaspoon lemon juice
1 teaspoon minced chervil or parsley

Simmer till soft enough to mash. Remove. Drain and place on a sieve. Add 1 oz. of the butter, mixed to a paste with 1 oz. flour. Add another ounce butter. With a wooden spoon mix the butter with the flour paste and fish as you rub all through a sieve into a basin. Beat and add eggs. Mix well. Season to taste with salt and pepper. Stir in cream. Divide between 5 buttered small plain moulds. Cover with greased paper. Steam for 20 to 25 minutes. Melt remainder of butter. Add remainder of flour. Stir till frothy. Stir in fish stock. When smooth and boiling, flavour with the lemon juice. Turn moulds on to a hot dish. Coat with the sauce. Sprinkle lightly with minced chervil or parsley. *For 5 persons.*

WHITING QUENELLES (Quenelles de Merlan)

3 large raw whiting
2 egg whites
2 tablespoons thick white sauce
Salt and pepper to taste
¼ pint thick cream

Skin whiting. Remove all flesh from bones. Place in a mortar with the egg whites and cold sauce. Pound well. Rub through a hair sieve. Return to mortar. Add salt and pepper to taste and pound well. Lightly stir in cream. Shape like small eggs with 2 dessertspoons dipped in hot water. Place them in a buttered shallow frying-pan containing just enough boiling, salted water to cover them. Simmer very gently for about ¼ hour. Drain on a fold of muslin. Serve with shrimp or lobster sauce. *For 4 persons.*

To Serve Quenelles: Mix 2 tablespoons boiled rice with 2 tablespoons picked shrimps, 2 tablespoons chopped hard-boiled egg, salt and pepper to taste, 2 tablespoons white sauce and 1 tablespoon cream. Stir lightly over moderate heat till piping hot. Arrange quenelles in a circle on a hot dish. Pile rice mixture in centre. Sometimes I substitute fluffy mashed potatoes or a mound of creamed spinach for the rice.

Witches (Carelet) (*Obtainable all the year round*) : A member of the plaice family. Treat like plaice.

TO USE UP LEFT-OVERS

When buying fish for boiling or steaming, you should decide before choosing, whether you want any left over or not to make up for a second meal. There are many appetising ways in which you can utilise boiled or steamed fish. In any recipe where I have mentioned " mashed potato," *the potato must be seasoned and beaten with butter or margarine and a little hot milk before using.*

AMERICAN FISH PIE (Poisson au four Américain)

1 lb. cooked mashed potatoes
2 oz. grated cheese
1 egg yolk
Salt, pepper and mustard to taste
½ lb. cooked fish

Heat potatoes in a saucepan with milk to moisten. Stir in half the cheese and egg yolk. Season to taste with salt, pepper and mustard, then line a greased fireproof dish with two-thirds of the mixture. Fill centre with fish mixed with the sauce

1 cup parsley sauce
Grated nutmeg to taste
½ oz. butter

and seasoned with nutmeg. Cover with remainder of potato. Ornament with a fork. Sprinkle with cheese. Dab with butter. Bake for ½ an hour in a moderate oven, 350° F. *For 4 or 6 persons.*

CURRY OF FISH (Kari de Poisson)

1 lb. boiled fish
1 tablespoon butter
1 small onion
1 peeled clove of garlic
2 teaspoons curry powder
1 teaspoon flour
½ pint milk
Salt to taste
Juice ½ lemon

Break fish into large flakes. Melt butter in a saucepan. Peel, slice and add onion and garlic. Fry till pale brown. Sprinkle in curry powder and flour, and mix smoothly, then add milk, or half milk and half white stock. Boil for 5 or 6 minutes. Season to taste with salt. Stir in lemon juice and fish. Cook till piping hot. Serve garnished with boiled rice. Sometimes, I substitute 1 pint prawns, roughly chopped, for the fish. *For 4 persons.*

FISH AND RICE BALLS (Boulettes de Poisson)

1 pint cooked fish
1 pint boiled rice
2 beaten eggs
Salt, pepper and paprika to taste
1 tablespoon lemon juice
1 tablespoon minced parsley
1 tablespoon minced chives

Flake fish. Place in basin. Stir in rice, eggs, salt, pepper and paprika to taste, lemon juice, parsley and chives. If eggs are small, add a tablespoon or two of milk. Shape into balls about 2 inches across with floured hands. Dip in top milk, then in crushed corn flakes. Place side by side in a well-greased baking tin. Bake in a moderate oven, 350° F., for about 20 minutes. Serve with cheese, Hollandaise, or tomato sauce. *For 6 or 7 persons.*

FISH CAKES (Gâteaux de Poisson)

1½ cups cooked fish
3 cups hot mashed potato
1 tablespoon melted butter
Salt and pepper to taste
Dash anchovy essence, if liked
1 beaten egg
1 teaspoon minced parsley

Divide fish into fine flakes. Stir in potato, fat, and salt and pepper to taste, anchovy essence and as much of the egg as is needed to moisten mixture. Add parsley. Beat well. Divide into equal-sized portions. Roll with floured hands into balls, then flatten into cakes. Egg and crumb. Fry in smoking hot fat to cover until golden brown. Drain on absorbent paper. *For 6 persons.*

FISH CROQUETTES (Croquettes de Poisson)

8 oz. cooked fish
1 teaspoon crushed herbs
1 teaspoon minced parsley
8 oz. stale breadcrumbs
1 tablespoon minced onion
Salt and pepper to taste
1 oz. butter or margarine

Use any cooked white fish, smoked haddock or salmon. Remove any skin and bone from fish. Flake fish finely. Mix with herbs, parsley, breadcrumbs, onion, and salt and pepper to taste. Melt butter or margarine and stir into mixture. Beat egg and add. When blended, divide into 8 or 10

1 egg
Fried parsley and cut lemon

equal portions. With floured hands, roll into small balls. Egg and crumb. Place a few at a time in a frying basket and fry until golden. Drain on absorbent paper. When all are ready, serve on a hot dish lined with a paper doily. Garnish with fried parsley and cut lemon. Serve with tomato or any piquant sauce. *For 4 or 5 persons.*

FISH RISSOLES (Rissoles de Poisson)

Use the ingredients as given for Fish Croquettes, but, instead of making mixture into balls, place lightly in the centre of rounds of very thin shortcrust 2½ to 3 inches across. Brush edges of the rounds with cold water and fold over. Press edges together with prongs of a fork. Brush with beaten egg. Dip in crushed vermicelli. Fry in smoking hot fat until golden. Drain and serve like croquettes. Good hot or cold. *For 4 or 5 persons.*

FISH HOLLANDAISE (Poisson, Hollandaise)

1½ lb. spinach
Salt and pepper to taste
¾ cup stale breadcrumbs
¼ cup milk
½ teaspoon grated onion
1 tablespoon melted butter
1 egg yolk
1 tablespoon lemon juice
1 egg white
1½ cups flaked boiled fish
1½ gills Hollandaise sauce
Paprika to taste

Wash spinach in several waters, then drain and place in a saucepan. Stir frequently till soft. Season with salt and pepper to taste. Place breadcrumbs in a basin. Add milk. Cover and stand for 10 minutes. Stir till smooth. Add onion, butter and egg yolk. Beat till well blended. Add spinach and salt and pepper to taste. Strain in lemon juice. Mix well. Beat egg white until stiff and fold into mixture. Pack into a well-buttered round border mould, 6 inches in diameter and holding about 2½ gills. Place in a tin containing hot water to the depth of 1 inch. Bake in a moderate oven, 350° F., for about 20 minutes, till set. Meanwhile, flake fish. Heat in the well-buttered top of a double boiler. Cover and steam over boiling water till piping hot. To dish up, loosen edges of mould and turn out into a rather shallow hot dish. Stir half the sauce into the hot fish. Pour into the centre of spinach ring. Dredge lightly with paprika. Serve remainder of sauce in sauce boat. *For 3 or 4 persons.*

FISH SOUFFLE (Soufflé de Poisson)

2 oz. butter
1 oz. flour
1½ cups milk
1 teaspoon grated onion
Salt and pepper to taste
6 oz. flaked cooked fish
3 separated eggs
½ pint caper sauce

Melt butter in a saucepan. Remove pan from stove. Stir in flour. Gradually add milk, stirring constantly. Return to stove. Cook until smooth, stirring constantly. Add onion, salt and pepper to taste, and fish. Beat egg yolks and stir into mixture. Beat egg whites until stiff. Fold gradually into mixture. Grease the bottom of a shallow fireproof casserole. Add mixture. Place in a baking tin containing warm water coming half-way up the sides. Bake in a moderately hot oven, 425° F., for about

¼ hour, until cooked through, or until inserted knife comes out quite clean. Serve with caper sauce. *For 4 persons.*

SCALLOPS OF FISH (Coquilles de Poisson)

2 cups cooked flaked fish
2 cups diced cooked potatoes
1 cup cooked diced celery
2 cups grated cheese
1½ cups white sauce
Salt and pepper to taste

Mix fish with vegetables. Add 1½ cups of the grated cheese, sauce, salt and pepper to taste. Place in 4 greased scallop shells. Sprinkle with remaining cheese. Bake for about 10 minutes in a moderately hot oven, 375° F. Serve with a green salad. *For 4 persons.*

STEAMED FISH PUDDING (Pouding de Poisson)

2 cups cold boiled or steamed fish
Dash anchovy essence
1 tablespoon lemon juice
2 tablespoons melted butter
Salt and pepper to taste
1½ cups hot milk
1 cup stale breadcrumbs
2 eggs

Flake fish into a basin. Stir in anchovy essence, lemon juice, butter and salt and pepper to taste. Pour milk over crumbs. Leave till cool. Mix with fish. Separate yolks and whites of eggs. Beat yolks. Stir into mixture. Beat egg whites till stiff, and fold into mixture. Three-quarters fill an oiled pudding basin. Cover tightly with greased paper. Steam for 1½ hours. Serve with caper sauce. *For 3 persons.*

SHELLFISH

There are two groups of shellfish : (1) Crustacea ; (2) Molluscs, which include bivalves and univalves.

This class of fish offers little nutriment and the fish is usually indigestible when cooked, especially if over-cooked. The molluscs, which include clams, cockles, mussels and oysters, can be served raw with lemon or a piquant sauce and thin brown bread and butter, or in the form of a savoury cocktail, which can also be made with a crustacean, such as crab, crawfish, crayfish, lobster, prawns, scallops and shrimps. The univalves, such as limpets, periwinkles, whelks, etc., must be boiled before eating. The limpet is considered poisonous eaten raw. Almost every shellfish has an inedible part which is sometimes only indigestible and sometimes poisonous. These parts are usually removed before cooking, for example, the beard of the oyster, though sometimes this is eaten. The gills of the crab are poisonous but they are not removed until after cooking.

Clams (Clovisses) (*Seasonable, September-April*) : Clams are a variety of cockles. Very popular in America, but, though found off the coasts of Devon and Cornwall and off the west coasts of Ireland and Scotland, they are little known in Britain. Sold in their shells by the dozen or quart. They can be eaten raw like oysters when bought. Open like oysters or steam open when required. *To Clean:* Remove the hard neck and take out the dark part, which is the stomach, before serving. *To Cook:* Usually stewed or made into soup. In the United States, they make a very popular first course arranged raw on their half shells. Garnish with wedges of lemon. Serve with a small glass or other container of cocktail sauce placed in centre. Can also be treated by any recipe given for oysters or mussels. *To Steam:* Place shells in a basin of fresh water. Scrub thoroughly. Change water several times so as to remove all traces of sand. Place in a large saucepan. Add hot water, allowing 2 tablespoons to 1 quart clams. Cover closely. Steam for about 10 to 15 minutes until shells are slightly opened. Arrange on a hot flat dish, covered with a napkin. Serve with melted butter, flavoured with lemon juice, and salt and pepper to taste. *Allow 3 to 6 per person.*

Cockles : Belong to scallop family. *To Clean:* Wash in three or four waters, soaking for 1 hour in each change of water, then place in a basin. Cover with cold water. Add 1 teaspoon salt to each quart water used. Stand overnight, to allow them to discharge their sand. *To Cook:* Cockles are usually eaten boiled, but they can be pickled, scalloped or made into a sauce. *Allow 1 pint per person. To Boil:* Drain cockles. Pour 1 tablespoon water into a shallow saucepan. Place shells on top. Cover with a folded clean cloth. Shake saucepan over heat for about 5 minutes, until the shells open when they are ready. Dish up on to a folded napkin. Strain remaining stock in pan through muslin, use in a fish soup or stew, or for making sauce to serve with boiled cockles. *Cockle Sauce:* Melt 1 tablespoon butter in a saucepan. Add 1 tablespoon flour. When frothy, stir in ½ pint strained cockle liquor, ground mace and pepper to taste as well as grated nutmeg, if liked. Stir till thick, but do not allow to boil. Serve with boiled cockles. Sometimes, the liquor is simply strained through muslin and reheated and poured over cockles, without any addition. Mock oyster sauce can be made with cockles when oysters are out of season. *To Scallop:* Line greased scallop shells, allowing 1 per person, with breadcrumbs. Half-fill with shelled boiled or steamed cockles. Cover with cockle sauce. Repeat layers. Sprinkle with breadcrumbs, then with melted butter to moisten. Bake in a moderately hot oven, 400° F., until golden brown on top. Serve with cayenne pepper and cut lemon.

Crabs (Crabes) (*seasonable, April-October*) : Caught in traps like lobster pots on rocky coasts. Usually sold ready boiled, but can be boiled alive at home. *To Boil Alive:* Scrub and wash crab thoroughly. Pour water, salt and vinegar into a saucepan in the proportion of 1 tablespoon salt and 2 tablespoons vinegar to 1 quart water. Drop crab, head first, into water. Cover and boil for about 20 minutes. Plunge into cold water when cold enough to handle.

Crabs (Crabe farcis) : *To Dress:* Place the crab on its back. Twist off large and small claws, and remove flaps or aprons. Holding the shell firmly in your left hand, and the body in your right, pull the under section out of the shell. Remove gills, intestines and stomach which lie just under the head. Carefully scrape out the meat from the shell which is known as " brown meat." Place in a basin. Trim the edge of the shell on the under side as far as the dark line at the edge by tapping with a hammer. Wash and dry shell. Polish the outside with cooking oil. Add to brown meat a rounded tablespoon fresh breadcrumbs, if liked, which makes it go further. Season with salt and pepper to taste. Flavour with lemon juice or vinegar and a little minced parsley.

Pack this mixture into shell, leaving a hollow in the middle. Now remove the "dead men's fingers," or "gentlemen's beards" from the body, as they are inedible, with a small knife, scooping out any flesh from the crevices of the body, taking care not to include any shell splinters. Crack the large claws with nutcrackers and remove the flesh. Chop and add to the meat. Season with salt and pepper to taste, and a little lemon juice or vinegar, made mustard and olive oil, allowing, for a medium-sized crab, 1 tablespoon each of lemon juice or vinegar and oil and ½ teaspoon made English or French mustard. Pile into middle of shell. Garnish with small crab claws and sprigs of parsley.

CRAB CAKES (Gâteaux de Crabe)

2 cups flaked cooked crab
¼ teaspoon salt
Pepper to taste
1 beaten egg
Flour as required
Frying fat or oil

Mix crab in a basin with salt and pepper to taste, and egg. Divide into small, equal-sized portions. Shape into small cakes, and dredge with flour. Fry in enough hot fat or oil to cover until golden brown, in 2 or 3 minutes. Drain on absorbent paper. Serve with mayonnaise or Tartare sauce. *For 5 or 6 persons.*

CRAB FRITTERS (Beignets de Crabe)

5 oz. flour
½ teaspoon baking powder
½ teaspoon salt
Pinch grated nutmeg
Pepper to taste
3 eggs
1½ gills milk
1 teaspoon lemon juice
½ teaspoon minced parsley
1 lb. flaked crab
3 tablespoons butter or lard
Fingers of lemon and parsley
  to garnish

Sift flour into a basin with baking powder, salt, nutmeg and pepper. Make a hollow in centre. Break in eggs. Add milk, lemon juice and parsley. Beat with an egg whisk for 2 minutes. Stir in crab flakes. Melt fat in a large frying-pan. Beat mixture again. Fry in tablespoons like round scones, placing them about 2 inches apart, for 3 minutes on each side. Serve on a hot dish lined with a lace paper doily. Garnish with 6 fingers of lemon and parsley. *For 6 persons.*

CRAB NEWBURG (Crabe à la Newburg)

2 oz. butter
3 oz. flaked crab
Salt and cayenne pepper to
  taste
1 cup cream
2 beaten egg yolks
1 tablespoon sherry
4 baked patty cases

Melt butter in a saucepan. Add crab. Stir lightly till hot, then season to taste. Mix 1 tablespoon of the cream with egg yolks. Stir in remainder of cream, then stir into crab mixture. Add a little egg yolk and sherry alternately until both are incorporated, then stir over boiling water until thick and hot, stirring constantly, but don't allow to boil. Divide equally between hot patty cases. Sometimes I serve mixture on rounds of fried bread or hot buttered toast instead of in cases. *For 4 persons.*
  To Vary: Fry 1 finely chopped shallot in the butter before adding crab. Stir in a pinch of grated nutmeg with salt and cayenne pepper.

CRAB SCALLOPS (Coquilles de Crabes)

2 tablespoons melted butter
1 heaped tablespoon flour
1 cup chicken or veal stock
1 medium-sized crab
4 oz. peeled mushrooms
2 tablespoons Madeira or sherry
2 beaten egg yolks
Salt and pepper to taste
1 teaspoon minced parsley
4 tablespoons stale bread-crumbs
1½ tablespoons melted butter

Melt butter in a saucepan. Stir in flour and when frothy, stir in stock. Bring to boil. Flake crab. Slice mushrooms. Stir in crab and mushrooms. Boil 3 minutes, stirring constantly. Draw pan to side of stove and stir in wine, egg yolks and salt and pepper. Add parsley. Butter 3 scallop shells. Pile up with the mixture. Sprinkle with the bread crumbs, then melted butter. Make three crosses with the back of a knife on top of each. Bake in a moderate oven, 350° F., till brown. *For 3 persons.*

DEVILLED CRAB (Crabe à la Diable)

¼ pint white sauce
1 teaspoon lemon juice
1 teaspoon chilli vinegar
1 teaspoon chopped chutney
1 teaspoon Worcester sauce
½ teaspoon French mustard
Salt and pepper to taste
1 medium-sized crab
1 tablespoon breadcrumbs
Minced parsley as a garnish

Heat sauce in a saucepan. Stir in lemon juice, vinegar, chutney, Worcester sauce, mustard, salt and pepper, then flake and add crab. Pile into crab shell. Sprinkle with crumbs. Bake in a moderately hot oven, 400° F., for 10 minutes. Serve on a dish lined with a lace paper doily. Garnish with parsley. *For 2 or 3 persons.*

MOUSSE OF CRAB (Mousse de Crabe)

1½ tablespoons powdered gelatine
1 cup cold water
1 cup boiling water
1 cup thick cream
2 teaspoons minced parsley
1 cup mayonnaise
2 cups flaked cooked crab
Salt and pepper to taste
Crisp lettuce leaves

Place gelatine in a basin. Add cold water. Cover and stand 5 minutes, then stir in boiling water. Stir till dissolved. Chill till slightly thick. Whip cream. Stir parsley into mayonnaise and fold into jelly. Fold in cream, then lightly stir in crab. Add salt and pepper to taste. Fill individual moulds rinsed with cold water. Leave till set and chilled. Turn out on to a dish lined with shredded lettuce leaves. Garnish with cucumber jelly. *For 7 persons.*

Crawfish (*Seasonable all the year round*): A large species of crayfish found in the sea. Very popular in France, where it is known as *langouste*. In Britain, it is frequently possible to buy crawfish in the summer time and South African crawfish tails throughout the year. *To Cook:* Large crawfish are best boiled the day before they are to be served. Can be prepared by any recipe given for lobster, but they require slightly longer cooking. If bought in cans, treat as suggested for cooked crab or lobster. *To Prepare:* Medium-sized shellfish are best, heavy in proportion to size. They should all be thoroughly cleaned, or some will retain grit or sand. It is a good idea to boil them in sea-water when possible. Try not to obtain shellfish to be served raw until just before it is to be eaten, and shellfish, such as crab, crawfish, crayfish, lobster, etc., that is cooked before you buy them, while still hot, so as to make certain they are absolutely fresh.

Crayfish (*Seasonable, June-March*) : A tiny lobster found in fresh water. A great delicacy. Very popular in France, where they are made into a bisque. In Austria, they are most popular shelled and grouped into a crown or coronet and served coated with mayonnaise as a salad. Small crayfish are used extensively in France for decorating dishes. Shells become bright red when boiled. Sometimes larger crayfish are served boiled and cold as a first course with brown bread and butter. *Allow 1 to 3 crayfish per person, according to size.*

Limpets : Can be obtained in some parts of Britain. Not unwholesome. Are poisonous raw. *To Cook:* Boil for a few minutes in salted water.

Lobster (*Seasonable, March-November, but obtainable all the year round*) : Nutritious, but not very digestible. They have a bad effect on some constitutions, occasionally causing skin eruptions, and are very unwholesome if at all stale. Finest caught round Jersey and amongst the islands off the North Scottish coast. *Allow 1 small or ½ large lobster per person. To Cook:* Boil, dress or serve with salad or as a mayonnaise. Devil, scallop or turn into lobster cutlets, soufflé, stew, etc. *To Boil:* The following is the most humane way : Have a saucepan large enough to hold the lobster and add cold water or cold court bouillon to cover lobster well when inserted. Measure water or court bouillon and allow 1 oz. salt to each quart required. Place lobster in liquid in pan. Cover pan. Bring to boil. Cook for 10 minutes, then lower heat and simmer for 10 to 20 minutes, according to size. Skim well. Remove pan from stove. Leave lobster in water or court bouillon until cold. Remove and place on claws to drain. If a female lobster is not boiled long enough, the coral will not be red. If any lobster is boiled too long, it will be thready and tough. *To Dress:* Place lobster on its back on a board. Separate tail from body. Holding it in your left hand, cut a slit lengthwise in the thin part under the shell with a sharp knife. Remove flesh from tail in one portion. Remove the dark spinal cord. Break off large claws and the 4 pairs of small ones. Crack large ones with nutcrackers through the centre and at the joints. Remove flesh. Reserve small claws for garnishing. Split the shell in two equal portions. Remove lungs, stomach, etc., leaving in the coral, in the case of a female lobster, as well as the green part and the pocket to which the legs were attached. *To Serve:* Stand head portion upright on serving dish with half of the tail on either side. Garnish with claws and sprigs of parsley. Sometimes it is served in this way on a napkin. Pass oil and vinegar with it. To improve the colour of the shell, rub, before serving, with a little olive oil and polish with a soft cloth.

AMERICAN LOBSTER STEW (Ragoût d'Homard, Américain)

1 boiled lobster	Choose a medium-sized lobster. Cut it in small
3 tablespoons butter	pieces. Melt butter in a stew pan. Add lobster.
2 pints milk	Cook gently in fat for 5 minutes, but don't allow
1 slice onion or 2 peeled shallots	to brown. Bring milk to boiling point with onion

Paprika to taste
Pinch ground mace
1 teaspoon salt

or shallots. Strain over lobster. Season with paprika, mace and salt. If liked, rub coral or liver through a sieve and stir into stew. Serve in soup bowls with salted crackers. *For 6 persons.*

DEVILLED LOBSTER (Homard au Diable)

1 medium-sized boiled lobster
1 teaspoon dry mustard
2 teaspoons curry powder
Salt and pepper to taste
2 teaspoons tarragon vinegar
1½ tablespoons butter

Remove meat from lobster. Mince and mix with the mustard, curry powder, and salt and pepper to taste. Place in a saucepan. Add just enough water to prevent mixture browning. Boil up twice. Stir in vinegar and butter. Boil up once again. Pile into half shells. Serve at once, with thin brown bread and butter. *For 2 persons.*

LOBSTER À LA NEWBURG (Homard à la Newburg)

1 medium-sized boiled lobster
1 large walnut butter
1 tablespoon minced onion or shallot
1 glass brandy
1 glass sherry
4 egg yolks
½ pint cream
1 heaped teaspoon minced chives or parsley

Cut lobster into pieces about ½ inch thick. Melt butter in a saucepan. Add onion or shallot. Fry slowly for 2 or 3 minutes, stirring constantly. Remove from stove. Add brandy. Set a match to it. When it stops burning, stir in sherry. Beat egg yolks with cream. Strain into lobster, stirring constantly over slow heat until mixture thickens. Do not allow to boil. Stir in chives or parsley. Serve in a circle of boiled rice, or on canapés of fried bread or hot toast, or piled into hot puff pastry cases. *For 4 persons.*

LOBSTER AU GRATIN (Homard au gratin)

1 medium-sized boiled lobster
1 oz. butter
1 shallot
Juice of ¼ lemon
½ cup white sauce
½ teaspoon chopped tarragon
1 teaspoon minced parsley
Salt, pepper and paprika to taste
Breadcrumbs and melted butter
Minced parsley as a garnish

Clean lobster shell and cut it down the back. Remove gills from lobster. Remove and chop meat and coral. Melt butter in a saucepan. Stir in chopped shallot and, when brown, add lemon juice, sauce, lobster meat, tarragon, parsley, salt, pepper and paprika to taste. Mix well and fill half shells with the mixture. Sprinkle with crumbs and then with melted butter. Bake in a moderate oven, 350° F., for 10 minutes. Serve shells on a dish. Garnish with parsley. *For 2 persons.*

LOBSTER BORDELAISE (Homard, Bordelaise)

1 medium-sized lobster
1 glass white wine
1 sprig parsley
1 clove garlic
½ bay leaf

Halve lobster. Remove meat from shell and claws. Divide meat into 8 portions. Place in a saucepan. Add wine and parsley. Peel and chop garlic and add with bay leaf and thyme. Cover

1 sprig thyme
1 tablespoon butter
1 tablespoon finely chopped shallot
1 tablespoon flour
¼ pint tomato sauce
Cayenne pepper to taste

and boil for 5 minutes, then drain well. Reserve the liquor. Place on a hot dish. Melt butter in a saucepan. Add shallot. Fry slowly until soft but not discoloured, then stir in flour. Strain in wine sauce, stirring constantly. Stir till boiling, then add tomato sauce and cayenne pepper to taste. Stir till piping hot. Coat lobster with sauce. *For 2 persons.*

LOBSTER CUTLETS (Côtelettes d'Homard)

1 lb. chopped freshly boiled lobster
½ cup breadcrumbs
1 teaspoon lemon juice
2 teaspoons minced parsley
Salt and pepper to taste
½ pint thick white sauce
2 beaten eggs
Crumbs for coating

Stir lobster, crumbs, lemon juice, parsley and salt and pepper to taste into white sauce. If liked, season also with paprika and cayenne pepper to taste. Mix well and leave until quite cold and stiff enough to handle. With floured hands, shape into cutlets. Egg and crumb. Fry in deep smoking hot fat, 385° F., for about 2 minutes, or until golden brown. Drain. Serve on a hot dish lined with a paper doily. *For 6 persons.*

LOBSTER MOULD (Pain d'Homard)

¾ oz. butter
¾ oz. flour
3 tablespoons milk
Squeeze lemon juice
Salt, pepper and cayenne pepper to taste
1 medium-sized boiled lobster
1 tablespoon cream
1 egg white

Melt butter in a saucepan. Stir in flour and, when frothy, the milk. Stir till smooth, then bring to boil. Cook for 2 or 3 minutes, stirring all the time. Stir in lemon juice, salt, pepper and cayenne pepper to taste. Remove lobster meat from shell and chop finely. Stir in sauce, then add cream and stiffly frothed egg white. Pack mixture into a well-buttered loaf tin. Cover with buttered paper. Steam for 45 minutes, then turn out and serve with Béchamel or shrimp sauce. *For 2 persons.*

LOBSTER THERMIDOR (Homard, Thermidor)

3 boiled lobsters
2 oz. button mushrooms or champignons
½ pint Béchamel sauce
½ pint cream
4 dessertspoons grated Gruyère cheese
Brandy to taste
2 eggs
Salt and pepper to taste
1 chopped truffle
Butter as required

See that each lobster is large enough for 2 persons. Halve lengthwise. Remove all flesh from shells and claws, and cut into tiny cubes. Wash shells and polish with olive oil. If using fresh mushrooms, cut into cubes and stew until tender in boiling water flavoured with vinegar. If using bottled champignons, simply slice. Make the Béchamel sauce very thick. Gradually stir in cream, cheese and brandy to taste. Stir until hot. Remove from stove. Beat eggs and stir into mixture. Add salt and pepper to taste, lobster, mushrooms or champignons, and truffle. Pack lobster mixture into shells. Sprinkle with a few sieved breadcrumbs, if liked. Dab with bits of butter. Bake in a moderately hot oven, 375° F., or under a grill, until brown on top. Sometimes I fry a chopped shallot in butter before making Béchamel sauce. *For 6 persons.*

Mussels (Moules) (*Seasonable, September-March*) : A delicious shellfish not served often enough in Britain. Found on the rocks round our coasts. They do not agree with everyone, but they are not poisonous to eat from September to March, if properly chosen and cleaned.

To Clean: Brush under running water and in several changes of water. Remove all traces of weed ; this is very important. Remove the small crab often found inside before serving, and remove beards. *To Cook:* Mussels are usually treated in what is known in the United States as the " sailor way," and in France as " à la marinière." This is the simplest and most famous way of cooking mussels. They can also be stewed and made into a sauce, fried, pickled, scalloped, etc., and sometimes they are substituted for oysters, when oysters are not obtainable, for making oyster sauce. Again, they are often added to other fish dishes and also used as a garnish. *To Fry* (Moules frites) : Clean. Place in a deep saucepan. Sprinkle with a little salt. Cover them with a napkin, then with lid. Shake them briskly over stove until the shells open. Remove at once and strain liquor into a basin. Shell. Carefully remove the weed under the black tongue and beard. There are 3 ways of preparing them for frying : (1) Flour, egg, then flour. Fry in deep hot oil or butter. Drain. (2) Dip in milk. Coat with seasoned breadcrumbs. Fry in shallow hot butter or oil. Drain. (3) Strain the liquor from 1 quart mussels into a basin. Add 2 beaten eggs, 1 oz. melted butter, and enough flour to make a batter. Season with salt, pepper, and grated nutmeg to taste. Add grated lemon peel and minced parsley to taste. Stir mixture in the top of a double boiler over boiling water until smooth and thick. Spear each mussel with a fork and dip in batter. Place each on a board side by side. When cold and firm, dip in sieved breadcrumbs. Fry in hot oil or deep fat till light brown. Drain. *For 3 persons. To Hustle:* Clean. Place in a basin. Cover with cold water. Soak overnight. Place in a dry saucepan. Cover. Toss over stove. Keep tossing or " hustling," as tossing is called, to the top of pan, so that all get evenly heated. If you don't toss them, the bottom ones will burn, and the top ones won't be cooked. As soon as the shells open, they are ready. If you cook them any longer, they will be leathery. Shell. Remove black weed and any crabs, and beard. Place on a hot dish. Either strain liquor over, or coat with equal quantity of liquor and melted butter, seasoned with pepper and flavoured with vinegar. Add chopped chives or parsley and ground mace to sauce, and bring almost to boil before using.

HUSTLED MUSSELS WITH SAFFRON SAUCE
(Moules, Italiennes)

Make 1 pint white sauce, half with milk and half with strained mussel liquor. Season to taste. Flavour with saffron to taste. Stir in 4 beaten egg yolks over boiling water. Cook till thick, but don't allow to boil. Serve with 3½ pints to 2 quarts unshelled mussels. *For 6 persons.*

HUSTLED MUSSELS WITH TOMATO SAUCE
(Moules aux Tomates)

Strain the liquor from $3\frac{1}{2}$ to 4 pints mussels after hustling. Add tomato purée to taste. Rub through a sieve. Return to saucepan. Stir in 2 or 3 pats unsalted butter or margarine. Serve with mussels. *For 6 persons.*

SCALLOPED MUSSELS (Coquilles de Moules)

Brush 4 individual fireproof dishes or scallop shells with melted butter. Boil, hustle or steam 3 dozen mussels, until open. Remove black weed and any crabs. Beard. Season 4 heaped tablespoons breadcrumbs with salt and pepper to taste. Sprinkle 1 tablespoon of the crumbs over dishes or shells. Divide half the mussels equally and place in dishes or shells. Cover with a layer of breadcrumbs. Dab with butter or margarine, then add remainder of mussels and top with remainder of crumbs. Sprinkle fully half a tablespoon of seasoned mussel liquor over top of each, then coat with melted butter. Bake in a moderately hot oven, 375° F., for about $\frac{1}{4}$ hour, until golden brown. *For 4 persons.*

STEAMED MUSSELS (Moules à la Française)

Clean mussels. Place in large shallow saucepan. Add $\frac{1}{4}$ cup hot water to 2 quarts mussels. Cover closely. Steam for about 15 minutes till shells are half-opened. Serve with melted butter. Season to taste with pepper, flavoured with garlic, and mixed with minced chives or parsley to taste, or with sauce suprème. *For 6 persons.*

STEWED MUSSELS (Ragoût de Moules)

Clean, then boil, hustle, or steam 1 pint mussels. Remove from shells. Strain liquor into a basin. Melt 2 tablespoons butter. Add 2 tablespoons flour. When frothy, gradually stir in liquor. Season with pepper, salt, if necessary, then add minced chives or parsley to taste, and 3 or 4 drops lemon juice. Add to mussels. Serve piping hot on rounds or squares of buttered toast or fried bread. *For 2 persons.*

MOULES MARINIERE

1 quart mussels
1 pint court bouillon
1 peeled onion
1 small carrot
1 clove garlic
3 or 4 peppercorns
Minced parsley to taste

Clean mussels. Pour court bouillon into a saucepan. Chop onion and carrot and add. Chop garlic and add with peppercorns. Bring to boil. Simmer gently for $\frac{1}{2}$ hour. Strain into another saucepan. Add mussels. Cover closely. Shake over stove until shells open. Remove them as they open, but keep the pan covered as much as possible to prevent liquor evaporating. When ready, dish up. Strain liquor over. Sprinkle with minced parsley and a little grated shallot if liked. In France, housewives sometimes boil the strained liquor down till reduced to a third, then dilute 2 egg yolks with ½ gill cream, and stir this into the liquor till it thickens, without allowing to boil. Pour over the mussels. *For 3 persons.*

TO DRESS BOTTLED OR CANNED MUSSELS

Add a jar or can of mussels to ½ pint thick parsley sauce. Flavour with lemon juice and season with tobasco. Beat 1 egg yolk and stir into mixture. Reheat over boiling water, stirring constantly. If liked, add a tablespoon cream. Serve on rounds or squares of fried bread or buttered toast, or in a border of boiled rice or mashed potatoes. If preferred, place in greased scallop shells. Sprinkle with crumbs. Dab with butter and bake till brown. Sometimes I add 1 tablespoon sliced bottled or fried mushrooms to mixture before " shelling."

Oysters (Huîtres) (*Seasonable, September-April*): A highly nutritious mollusc. Good for invalids and convalescents. When cooked, often used as a garnish. Sometimes added to meat puddings and pies or made into a sauce to serve with beef steak. Occasionally used in stuffings. " Natives " considered the best, whether they come from Essex or Kent. Breton, Dutch, Marennes Vertes and Portuguese are usually obtainable in England during their season. *To Clean:* Scrub thoroughly with a stiff brush, then rinse in cold water. To remove sand, place in cold water to cover. Sprinkle with a handful of oatmeal and leave for 2 hours. *To Open:* Take a kitchen cloth in your left hand and then pick up oyster, and, with a strong sharp knife in your right hand, force the point below the edge of upper shell at the joint of the thick end. Press the knife in and twist to prise open, then run it round the surface of the under shell to cut the muscle holding the shells together. Lastly, cut the muscle under the oyster and turn out oyster with its liquor into a basin. Pour liquor through a fine strainer and inspect oyster very carefully in case any pieces of shell adhere which must be removed. To remove, hold under running water. Allow 6 to 12 small oysters per portion, if serving as an hors d'oeuvre. If to be cooked, such as fried or grilled, 3 large oysters are sufficient per portion. " Native " oysters should always be served raw as a first course, but other oysters mentioned and the large American oysters, such as the Cape Cod, should be cooked, and the very large ones may be cut before cooking. *To Cook:* The favourite method of cooking oysters is to simmer or stew them in their own liquor until the edges curl. This process must be watched carefully, for if cooked too long they will become tough. The alternative method of cooking is to drain liquor from oysters and place them in the bottom of a pan. Stand until they plump out and the edges curl. Serve them topped with mushroom sauce, in patty cases or on buttered toast, or add to parsley sauce flavoured with paprika and serve in hot pastry cases, buttered croustades, or on toast. *To Fry:* Clean and dry. Either dip in frying batter, or season with salt and pepper, then dip in flour, and egg and crumbs. Fry in deep fat, 375° F., till golden brown. Drain on absorbent paper. Serve with Hollandaise or tomato sauce. *To Grill:* Clean and dry. Dip in melted butter, then in seasoned crumbs, allowing 3 tablespoons butter and about ¾ cup crumbs to a pint of large oysters. Brush grill rack with melted butter. Lay the oysters on top. Sprinkle with melted butter. Grill till the juice flows, under moderate heat in about 1 minute, then turn. Sprinkle with melted butter and grill for 1 minute longer. Serve on toast. Garnish with lemon and parsley. *To Roast:* Scrub thoroughly with a brush. Place shells in a baking tin, hollow side downwards. Bake in a hot oven, 425° F., until shells split. Open. Season with salt and pepper. Sprinkle with melted butter. Serve in hollow shells. *To Saute:* Drain and dry. Roll in seasoned, sieved breadcrumbs. Fry in a frying-pan containing just enough melted butter to cover bottom of pan for 1 minute, then turn and fry on other side for another minute, till browned on both sides.

BAKED OYSTERS (Huîtres cuit au four)

1 pint large oysters
1 tablespoon olive oil
1 tablespoon lemon juice
Salt and paprika to taste
Pinch curry powder
1 teaspoon grated horseradish
1 cup sieved breadcrumbs
Melted butter as required
Parsley, or lemon, or grilled
    bacon as garnish

Open, clean and drain oysters thoroughly. Mix olive oil with lemon juice, salt, paprika, curry powder and horseradish. Add oysters. Soak for ½ hour, turning at the end of 15 minutes. Dry on absorbent paper. Mix crumbs with melted butter to moisten. Roll oysters in crumbs. Place side by side in a shallow greased baking tin. Bake in a fairly hot oven, 425° F., for about ¼ hour, till crisp and puffy. Serve garnished parsley or lemon, or with tiny grilled curls of bacon. *For 3 persons.*

OYSTERS À LA PARISIENNE (Huîtres à la Parisienne)

½ pint oysters
½ pint white sauce
1 tablespoon butter
½ lb. diced cooked veal
1 tablespoon Madeira or sherry
½ cup cream
Cayenne pepper to taste
Salt to taste

Clean oysters. Add to sauce. Stir over slow heat till edges curl and oysters plump out. Remove from stove. Melt butter in another saucepan. Stir in veal and wine. Bring to boil, then add to oysters. Stir in cream gradually. Bring almost to boiling point, stirring constantly. Season with cayenne pepper and salt to taste. Serve in a hot mashed potato border or in a hot vol-au-vent case. *For 3 persons.*

OYSTERS AU GRATIN (Huîtres au gratin)

1 cup breadcrumbs
1½ cups cracker crumbs
¾ cup melted butter
1 quart canned oysters
2 tablespoons minced parsley
Black pepper, grated nutmeg
    and salt to taste
4 tablespoons oyster liquor
4 tablespoons milk

Mix breadcrumbs with cracker crumbs. Stir in butter. Place half the mixture in the bottom of a shallow greased baking dish. Add half the oysters. Mix parsley with a good dash black pepper, nutmeg and a level teaspoon salt. Sprinkle half the seasonings over oysters, then add remainder of oysters. Sprinkle with remainder of seasonings. Mix oyster liquor with milk, and pour over oysters. Cover with remainder of crumb mixture. Bake either in a fairly hot oven, 425° F., for about ½ hour, or in a moderate oven, 350° F., for about ¾ hour till pale golden brown. *For 6 persons.*

OYSTER PUDDING (Pouding d'Huîtres)

3 cups stale breadcrumbs
Salt and pepper to taste
Dash of paprika
½ cup melted butter
1 pint drained canned oysters
⅓ cup oyster liquor
½ cup cream

Season breadcrumbs with salt, pepper and paprika. Lightly stir in butter. Grease a shallow fireproof dish. Sprinkle with a third of the crumbs. Cover with half the oysters. Sprinkle with a few crumbs. Add remainder of oysters. Mix oyster liquor with cream. Pour over oysters. Sprinkle with remainder of crumbs and paprika. Bake in a moderately hot oven, 400° F., for about ½ hour. *For 8 persons.*

RAMEKINS OF OYSTERS (Huîtres, Louisiana)

2 dozen oysters
½ gill white wine
Salt and cayenne pepper to taste
1½ tablespoons butter
1 green pepper
2 tablespoons flour
2 tablespoons sherry
¼ pint milk
½ gill cream
Pinch grated nutmeg
1 tablespoon grated Parmesan cheese

Open oysters. Beard and quarter. Strain liquor into an enamel saucepan. Stir them in wine and salt and cayenne pepper to taste. Bring to boil. Melt butter in another saucepan. Chop pepper and add. Fry slowly for 5 minutes, then stir in flour. Cook for a moment or two, stirring constantly, then add oyster liquor, sherry, milk, cream, nutmeg and seasoning to taste. Stir till boiling, then add oysters. Reheat. Pile up in buttered ramekins. Sprinkle with grated Parmesan cheese. Place on a baking sheet. Bake in a moderate oven, 350° F., for about 10 minutes. Serve each on a hot dish lined with a lace paper doily. *For 6 persons.*

Periwinkles (Bigorneaux) (*Seasonable, September-January*): Small sea snails or fish contained in small round black shells. Abundant on the coasts of Britain. *To Clean:* Wash in several waters to get rid of the sand. Soak in plenty of fresh water to cover for 30 minutes, then wash again so as to remove any mud and sand that usually adheres to them. *To Cook:* Place in a saucepan. Shake to make them withdraw into their shells. Cover with boiling salted water. Boil rapidly for about 20 minutes. Serve with brown bread and butter. *Allow 1 pint periwinkles for 3 or 4 persons.*

Prawns (Crevettes) (*Seasonable all the year, but best February-October*): Delicate little shellfish. Greyish colour when alive, but lobster-red when cooked. Usually sold ready boiled. *To Boil:* Wash prawns well. Place in a saucepan. Cover with boiling salted water, allowing 2 oz. salt to 2 quarts water. Boil rapidly for several minutes, skimming frequently. Remove and drain on a sieve. *Allow 1 pint for 4 persons.* Be careful not to over-cook prawns, or they will be tough and indigestible. *To Prepare for Dressing:* Hold each prawn in your left hand, and remove the shell first from the back, and then from underneath. Press tail to force out body. Now remove the black cord at the back of prawn. *To Cook:* Curry, pot or scallop, or use as a garnish.

PRAWNS À LA NEWBURG (Crevettes, Newburg)

1½ dozen prawns
2 tablespoons melted butter
Salt, pepper and paprika to taste
1 tablespoon brandy, sherry or lemon juice
1 tablespoon flour
1½ cups milk
1 beaten egg

Cut prawns into three or four pieces. Melt butter, add prawns. Make piping hot. Season to taste with salt, pepper and paprika. Add wine or lemon juice. Strain liquid into a saucepan. Stir in flour, made to a paste with a little of the milk, then add remainder of milk. Cook till slightly thick, stirring constantly, then add egg and prawns. Stir for 1 minute over stove. Serve on croûtes of buttered toast or in hot pastry cases. This is best made in the top of a double boiler. *For 4 persons.*

PRAWN CURRY (Crevettes à l'Indiennes)

1 oz. butter
1 tablespoon minced onion
1 apple
1 dessertspoon curry powder
½ oz. flour
½ gill stock
1½ gills milk
Salt and pepper to taste
1½ pints prawns
1 dessertspoon lemon juice
4 oz. Patna rice

Melt butter in a saucepan. Add onion. Fry till clear, in 2 or 3 minutes. Add peeled, sliced apple, curry powder and flour. Stir till well mixed, then add stock and 1 gill of the milk. Bring to boil, and boil, stirring all the time, for 2 minutes. Gradually thin with remainder of milk, stirring constantly. When boiling, cover and simmer for 20 minutes. Season to taste with salt and pepper. Shell and add prawns. Heat, then stir in lemon juice and a tablespoon or two of cream, if available. Serve in the centre of a hot entrée dish. Boil rice in usual way and arrange round prawn mixture. Cover and serve at once. *For 4 persons.*

Dublin Bay Prawns (Langoustines) : Best of all prawns. Much larger than the usual variety. Like small crayfish, and similar to Italian scampi. (1) If bought alive, prepare and cook like crayfish. Remove from shells and remove black cord along back. Serve cold with sauce Tartare or mayonnaise and salad, or hot with Béchamel sauce. (2) Egg and crumb. Fry and serve with sauce Tartare.

Scallops (Pétoncles) (*Seasonable, October-April*) : Best in January and February, when roe is full and a bright orange. Resembles an oyster in shape. Live in deep waters and are brought to the surface by dredging. When preparing scallops, do not throw away the deep shells. Washed and scrubbed, they can be used again and again in place of china scallop shells. *To Clean:* If not opened, place on top of stove over slow heat, when the shells will soon open by themselves. Loosen them from shells with a flexible knife, then trim away the gristly fibre known as the beard, and the black portion, as only the white and orange parts of the scallop should be cooked. Rinse in 2 or 3 changes of water, then drain well and dry. *To Cook:* Serve, boiled, with sauce Tartare, or in any of the following ways. *To Boil* (Pétoncle) : Drop into salted cold water. Bring to boil. Boil for a minute or two until scallops begin to shrink, then remove and use in any of the following recipes. If boiled too long, they will be tough and indigestible. In France, they are usually boiled in their own liquor or in white wine, then returned to their shells and sprinkled with grated Parmesan cheese and browned in the oven. Sometimes, when boiled, they are served with Béarnaise sauce or Hollandaise sauce flavoured with saffron. *To Fry* (Pétoncles frits) : Dip prepared scallops in slightly beaten egg, then in breadcrumbs, seasoned with salt and pepper to taste. Repeat egging and crumbing, or you'll find the frying fat or oil sparking, as scallops shrink a little and emit a little juice, so they must be well coated before frying. Fry in fat hot enough to brown a piece of bread in a minute, and deep enough to cover from $2\frac{1}{2}$ to $3\frac{1}{2}$ minutes, until golden brown. Drain on crumpled soft paper. Garnish with lemon fingers and parsley sprigs, and fried curls of bacon, if liked. Serve with sauce Tartare. *Allow 2 per person. To Scramble* (Pétoncles hachés) : Beat 2 eggs with 2 tablespoons milk and salt and pepper to taste. Place 1 cup chopped parboiled scallops in a greased saucepan and add egg and milk mixture. Cook, stirring constantly, over heat, until egg sets. Pile on buttered toasts. *For 4 persons.*

DEVILLED SCALLOPS (Pétoncles au Diable)

8 scallops
½ cup water
2 tablespoons butter
¼ teaspoon made mustard
Salt and cayenne pepper to taste
4 or 5 tablespoons stale breadcrumbs

Prepare scallops and place in saucepan. Add water. Heat to boiling point. Boil for a minute or two until they shrink, then drain and reserve liquor. Chop scallops. Beat butter until creamy in a basin. Add mustard, salt and cayenne pepper to taste. Strain in 4 tablespoons of the liquor. Add scallops. Turn in the dressing and leave for ½ hour, turning once at half-time. Place in 4 greased scallop shells. Divide crumbs between the shells. Sprinkle enough melted butter over them to moisten. Bake in a moderately hot oven, 400° F., for 15 minutes, until crisp and golden brown on top. *For 4 persons.*

SCALLOPS À LA POULETTE (Pétoncles à la Poulette)

¼ pint water
½ gill white wine
½ teaspoon salt
9 prepared scallops
1 oz. butter
6 peeled shallots
1 oz. flour
¼ pint milk
2 tablespoons sherry
Cayenne pepper to taste
1 teaspoon minced chives or parsley
¼ lb. champignons
2 egg yolks
2 tablespoons cream
Juice of 1 lemon

Pour water and wine into a saucepan. Add salt and scallops. Cover and simmer very gently for 5 minutes. Melt butter in another saucepan. Chop shallots and add. Fry slowly for 5 minutes, stirring frequently until shallots are clear ; they must not turn colour. Add flour. Stir for 1 minute over slow heat, then draw pan to side of stove. Drain off scallop liquor into the saucepan, then stir in milk, sherry, cayenne pepper and chives or parsley. When boiling, add scallops and sliced champignons. Cook for 5 minutes over slow heat, stirring constantly. Dilute egg yolks with the cream and lemon juice. Stir into scallops. Cook over slow heat, stirring constantly, for 3 minutes, but do not allow to boil. Serve on a hot dish, with boiled rice or new potatoes, if liked. *For 6 persons.*

Shrimps (Crevettes) (*Seasonable, April-September*) : There are two well-known varieties : the brown and the pink. The brown is the more plentiful, netted in large numbers round our sandy coasts. The pink or rose shrimps are caught farther out. These are the finer of the two and have a more delicate flavour. All shrimps are very indigestible when stale. *To Boil:* Throw into boiling water and boil for 5 minutes, but shrimps are frequently sold boiled and picked or shelled. *To Prepare Shelled Boiled Shrimps:* To shell shrimps, hold head between right forefinger and thumb, and, with the left forefinger and thumb nail, raise the shell of the tail on each side, then pinch tail and the body will come out. Remove black cord along back. *To Cook:* Most usually made into fillings for patty cases, into omelets, or potted and served as an hors d'oeuvre or savoury. Shrimps must not be confused with the American shrimps, which are larger than our prawns, and can be dressed by any recipe suggested for prawns.

Whelks (Buccin) (*Seasonable, September-March*) : Small whelks can be treated like periwinkles, but they need to boil for a long time, or they will be leathery. Soak in fresh water to cover for 3 or 4 hours, then throw into boiling salted water and boil for about 45 minutes. Do not attempt to cook large whelks. The small ones can be shelled, and dipped in seasoned flour or breadcrumbs, and fried in hot fat to cover. Season with pepper and moisten with vinegar. Sometimes a maigre soup is made from whelks, and they are often used as a garnish. Follow recipe given for scalloped mussels, substituting whelks for the mussels.

CURRIED WINKLES

3½ pints boiled winkles
¾ pint white sauce
Curry powder to taste
3 tablespoons cream

Rinse winkles in 12 changes of water. Drain. Place in saucepan. Cover. Cook over heat until shells open. Remove pan from heat. Throw away the shells. Rinse the winkles in cold water. Strain the liquor. Make white sauce with liquor and enough milk to make ¾ pint. Flavour with curry powder. Add winkles. Simmer very gently for 10 minutes, then stir in cream. Reheat, but do not allow to boil. Serve in a circle of boiled rice.

SALT AND SMOKED FISH

Salt Fish : Salt fish is not as popular in Britain as on the Continent, where you find it cooked to perfection. The only time salt cod is conspicuous in our menus is during Lent. Salt herring, again, is rarely seen except in the shape of salads in foreign delicatessen shops and restaurants, whereas it is in general use all over Europe.

To Prepare Salt Cod: Remove any rusty-looking bits and thin membrane. Soak in fresh water, flesh side downwards, for 24 to 48 hours, unless otherwise suggested. Change water 3 or 4 times.

To Boil Dried Salt Cod (La Morue bouillie) : Place in a saucepan, flesh side down. Cover with cold water. Bring slowly to the boil, then test water. If very salt, drain it off, cover with fresh cold water and bring again to boiling point. Simmer fish very gently until tender. Drain well. Place on a hot dish. Coat freely with egg and parsley sauce. Garnish with sprigs of parsley or watercress. Serve with boiled potatoes and spinach when possible. Allow 5½ to 8 oz. per portion. Half a pound fish yields 1 cup flaked boiled dried salt cod.

BAKED SALT COD (Morue cuit au four)

1 lb. boiled salt cod
Caraway seeds to taste
4 boiled onions
4 boiled carrots
1 head celery
½ pint cheese or parsley sauce

Butter a fireproof dish generously. Flake cod. Place a layer in bottom of dish. Sprinkle with caraway seeds. Slice onions, carrots and celery. Arrange a layer of the mixed vegetables on top of fish. Repeat layers until fish and vegetables are all used up. Pour sauce over. Sprinkle with breadcrumbs, then with enough melted butter to moisten. Bake in a moderate oven, 350° F., for about ½ hour. Serve with additional cheese or parsley sauce in a sauce-boat, and mashed potatoes. *For 4 persons.*

To Cream Salt Cod (Morue à la Crème) : Flake 1 lb. boiled salt cod. Slice 1½ lb. boiled potatoes. Butter a fireproof dish lavishly. Place half the potatoes in the bottom. Cover with the cod, then with remainder of potatoes. Stir 2 tablespoons melted butter into ½ pint thick cream. Flavour to taste with grated Gruyère cheese. Pour over potatoes. Bake in a moderately hot oven, 375° F., for ¼ hour.

LYONNAISE COD (Morue, Lyonnaise)

Soak and boil 1 lb. salt cod. Cut a medium-sized onion into thin slices. Fry in 3 tablespoons butter till brownish. Add flaked cod and 2 cups sliced boiled potatoes. Fry gently, turning frequently, for 20 minutes. Sprinkle with parsley. *For 4 persons.*

SALT COD, NEW ORLEANS (Morue, New Orléans)

2 cups shredded boiled salt cod
1 heaped tablespoon butter
1 heaped tablespoon flour
1½ pints cream or top milk
Cayenne pepper to taste
1 egg yolk

To make this dish successfully, soak fish overnight, then boil for 40 minutes. Drain. Place in cold water. Bring again to boil and drain. Repeat, allowing it to stand this time for 10 minutes before draining. Drain thoroughly. Melt butter in a shallow saucepan. Add flour. When blended, stir in cream, top milk or half cream and half milk. Stir constantly till boiling. Add fish. Season highly with cayenne pepper to taste. Simmer for 10 minutes, stirring frequently, then remove from stove. Beat egg yolk. Stir in gradually. Serve with boiled potatoes coated with melted butter and minced parsley. *For 4 persons.*

SALT COD CAKES (Gâteaux de Morue)

1 lb. salt codfish
3 cups hot mashed potatoes

Place fish in a basin. Cover with cold water. Soak for 2 hours. Remove fish to a stewpan. Cover

1 heaped teaspoon butter
Pepper to taste
Pinch ground mace
1 beaten egg

with fresh cold water. Bring to simmering point. Simmer for about ¼ hour. Drain well. Cut into shreds. Add to potato. Stir in butter. Season with pepper and mace to taste. Add egg. Beat till well blended. Drop by spoonfuls into a pan of hot fat or oil (365°- 380° F.). Fry till golden brown, in 1½ to 3 minutes, depending on size. Drain well on soft crumpled paper. *For 6 persons.*

To Prepare Salt Herring: Don't buy salt herring until wanted, unless you can store them as stored by retailer in a barrel, covered with brine. This fish soon turns rancid if it comes into contact with air. Skim off fat if necessary. Wash thoroughly, then remove head and fins. Soak in cold water for at least 12 hours. Skin after soaking, then dress as required. Sometimes served in Scotland boiled, and drained, with boiled potatoes in their jackets. Bring to boil and drain twice before serving in this way.

To Prepare Salt Mackerel: Rinse well under cold water tap to remove brine and salt. Soak, skin side downwards, in cold water to cover, for 12 hours, changing water every 3 hours. *Before baking,* remove, after soaking, to a clean basin. Cover with boiling water. Stand for 2 minutes. *Before boiling,* rinse soaked fish in fresh water. *Before frying,* clean and soak all day, changing water every 2 hours. Drain, then soak in fresh water overnight. Drain and wipe next morning. *Before grilling,* rinse and soak, skin side up, in cold water for 12 hours, changing water every 3 hours.

To Bake Salt Mackerel in Milk: Drain off boiling water. Rinse and place in a greased or oiled baking tin. Dredge lightly with flour. Season with black pepper. Cover with top off milk. Add a pat or two butter. Bake till brownish in a moderate oven, 350° F. Serve with boiled or mashed potatoes for lunch, dinner or supper, or with toast for breakfast.

To Boil Salt Mackerel: Drain after rinsing, and wrap each in a piece of cheesecloth or butter muslin. Place in a fish-kettle. Cover with cold water. Simmer gently for ½ hour. Unwrap carefully and remove backbone from each. Season with pepper. Coat with egg sauce.

To Fry Salt Mackerel: Drain off soaking water. Wipe dry. Dip in seasoned flour. Fry in a little hot butter. Garnish with parsley.

To Grill Salt Mackerel: Drain off soaking water. Wipe dry. Place, flesh side up, on a greased or oiled griller without the trivet. Brush with melted butter. Grill from 10 to 15 minutes, turning twice, and basting each time with the fat used. To serve, spread with butter or margarine, and sprinkle with minced parsley.

Smoked Fish (Poisson Fumé) : Very appetising. Bloaters, Arbroath haddock, Finnan haddock and Moray Firth haddock, in short, all smoked haddocks, are generally served at breakfast and sometimes at high tea. Bueckling, smoked eel, smoked fillets of halibut, smoked salmon, smoked sprats and trout are usually served as a first course at lunch or dinner. Smoked haddock and smoked fillet are used for making savoury fish cakes, pies, puddings, soufflés, etc.

Bloater : Herring cured while fresh. Yarmouth bloaters considered best. Best fried, but good grilled. *To Prepare:* Soak overnight in cold water, or in boiling water for 1 to 2 minutes. Drain thoroughly. If to be cooked like kippers, remove fins and head. Split open and bone, if liked. *To Boil:* Place in a saucepan. Cover with cold water. Boil for 15 to 20 minutes, then drain well. Toss in a little melted butter. *To Grill:* Place split, boned bloater, folded back into its original shape, on a grill rack brushed with melted butter. Grill for 3½ minutes on either side. Open and brush inside with melted butter, then fold halves together again. If there are any roes, brush with melted butter and grill alongside. If liked, make two or three gashes equal distance apart across either side. Baste well with melted butter while grilling, or put a little water in grill pan to keep them moist. Allow ½ oz. butter to each bloater, and 1 bloater per person.

DEVILLED BLOATERS

6 bloaters
2 tablespoons chutney
2 dessertspoons French mustard
½ teaspoon lemon juice
Salt and pepper to taste
Melted butter as required

Trim, split and bone bloaters. Mix chutney with mustard, lemon juice, salt and pepper to taste, and ½ teaspoon caster sugar, if liked. Brush insides with melted butter, then spread evenly with paste. Sprinkle with dried breadcrumbs. Bake in a fairly hot oven, 425° F., for about ¼ hour. Arrange round a hot flat dish lined with a lace paper doily. Place a bunch of well-washed and picked watercress, tossed in French dressing, in the centre.

Bueckling : Serve as an hors d'oeuvre or cold luncheon dish with brown bread and butter.

Smoked Eel : Serve cut in slices as an appetiser or first course at lunch or dinner.

Haddock (Arbroath, Finnan, Moray Firth, Smoked) : *Arbroath* is cured without splitting. Seldom met with outside Scotland. Delicious stewed in milk with a little butter and seasoned with black pepper. *Finnan* is called after a village, Findon, 6 miles from Aberdeen. Lovely flavour, due to process of smoking. Many smoked haddocks falsely called Finnans. *Moray Firth* is a delicate dried haddock of the split variety, seldom found outside Scotland. Finnan, Moray Firth and ordinary smoked haddock can be cooked by the same recipes.

SCOTCH KEDGEREE (Kedgeree de Poisson fumé)

3 tablespoons rice
1 lb. smoked haddock
1 heaped tablespoon butter
Squeeze lemon juice
Pinch grated nutmeg
Salt and cayenne pepper to taste
1 hard-boiled egg
1 teaspoon minced parsley
4 slices lemon

Cook rice in boiling salted water in usual way, then hold under tap for a moment or two to separate grains. Keep hot. Remove skin and bone from fish, then break up into flakes. Melt butter in a saucepan. Add fish, rice, lemon juice and nutmeg, salt and cayenne pepper to taste. Chop egg white and add too. Heat gently, stirring lightly with a fork. Pile on a hot dish. Garnish with sieved egg yolk and parsley on top, and slices of lemon round. *For 4 persons.*

SMOKED HADDOCK CROQUETTES (Croquettes Écossaises)

1 large smoked haddock
2 oz. butter
1½ oz. flour
½ teaspoon salt
¼ pint milk
Pepper and paprika to taste
2 beaten eggs
1 teaspoon minced parsley
Breadcrumbs to coat
Fried or minced parsley as garnish

Place fish in a pan. If you have not a large enough pan, cut in four before cooking. Cover with cold water. Bring to boil. Simmer till tender. Drain off water. Skin, bone and flake finely. Melt butter in pan. Stir in flour. When smooth, add salt and milk by degrees. Stir till boiling. Season to taste with pepper and paprika. Cook for 3 minutes, stirring constantly, then remove from heat. Stir in fish, 1½ eggs and parsley, and turn on to a plate. When cold, divide in 12 portions. With floured knives, shape into equal-sized oblongs. Egg and crumb, using remainder of egg. Drop gently into deep, smoking hot fat or oil. Fry till crisp and golden. Garnish with parsley. *For 6 persons.*

Kipper : Split, salted and smoked herring, the variety varying according to the process of curing and smoking. Loch Fyne are paler than other varieties. *To Choose:* Select oily glistening kippers, ignoring all that look dried up. Small and plump ones are better than larger ones. *To Cook:* Usually fried or grilled. Do not boil, as this reduces their oil content and dulls their flavour unless they are very salt. Cooked kippers are useful for snacks and sandwich spreads. If salt, place in frying pan. Cover with hot water. Bring to boil. Boil for 1 minute, then cook to taste. *To Fry:* Melt enough butter in the bottom of a frying-pan to cover bottom. Place kippers in pan, skin side downwards. Fry slowly until skin wrinkles, then turn and fry on other side. Turn once again and finish cooking. *To Grill:* If kippers are dry, soak for 10 minutes in sardine oil, if available. One tablespoon is enough for 2 or 3 kippers. Grill from 3 to 6 minutes, according to thickness, very slowly, turning frequently or at half-time. Serve with a pat of butter melting on top.

Halibut Fillets : Sold in tin. Include in an hors d'oeuvre.

Red Herring : Type of smoked herring. *To Choose:* Choose a plump fish, not too full of roe, with a firm body. If very salt, soak in warm water for 2 or 3 hours. To test condition, pull a fin or two out of the back to taste, then you will know how long to soak them. *To Prepare:* Bone and skin fish, then cover with boiling water. Soak for 5 minutes. Drain well. Cook like kippers. *To Cook:* Usually boiled or grilled.

Old Fashioned Red Herring : Remove head and tails. Split open and bone. Beat 1 egg. Stir in a teaspoon melted butter. Dip fish in this, then sprinkle rather thickly with sieved breadcrumbs. Season with pepper and other herbs to taste. Grill very slowly for 2½ minutes, then turn and grill on other side for 2½ minutes.

Smoked Fillet : Boil in unsalted water to cover until creamy. Serve with egg and parsley sauce and mashed potatoes, or make into fish cakes, kedgeree, fish pies, puddings, etc.

Smoked Salmon : Scotch variety considered best. Serve as a first course. Sometimes included in hors d'oeuvre.

Sprats : Serve as a first course at lunch or dinner with brown bread and butter. Garnish with lemon.

Smoked Trout: Serve as a first course at lunch or dinner with brown bread and butter. Garnish with lemon.

TO CARVE FISH

The important point to remember when carving fish is that the divisions must be made without breaking the flakes, otherwise the effect will be ragged and untidy. The method of carving differs according to whether you have flat or round fish, and according to size of fish. It is not easy to carve fried fish neatly. To get over this difficulty, either fillet before cooking, or only fry small fish so that one is served per person.

Equipment : Silver fish servers, or silver or stainless steel dinner knife and fork.

To Dish up for Carving : Arrange large boiling fish, such as cod, haddock or salmon, on a flat dish on table with the thin part towards carver. Place middle cuts or any thick pieces of large fish, such as cod, halibut or salmon, skin downwards.

Gashed or Gored Fish : If fish was gashed or gored before cooking, slip carver or knife along between each of these portions in turn and the backbone, and lift fillets out neatly.

To Carve Large Flat Fish (Grilled and Steamed) : Carve in fillets not with bone. Sometimes the head is left on fish, particularly in the case of John Dory, and sometimes it is removed. This is a matter of taste. If the head is not removed before cooking, remove it together with the tail and bones along either side before carving. Now make an incision down centre of fish and slip the server or knife under each fillet on either side of the bone, and serve if a whole fillet is wanted. If not, divide into oblongs as illustrated under Turbot, *facing page* 224. Next remove backbone and divide the lower portion down the centre and serve fillets. If very large, fillets can be cut in two crosswise or slantwise before serving. Never turn fish over on dish in order to carve underside. Remove backbone in order to get at underside.

Halibut and Turbot : The best part of turbot is the white skin side. Serve placing white skin side uppermost and carving it first in this way. Make an incision down centre of fish from head to tail, as illustrated. If large, cut into squares. (See A of illustration of turbot, *facing page* 224.) Now divide fish into fillets or oblongs, as illustrated. If the underside of turbot is also required, neatly remove backbone to side of serving dish and carve underside in the same way you did white side. If small, carve slices across from fin to fin, remembering that the fin is a delicacy. (See B.) The width of the portion should depend on the thickness of fish.

John Dory : Follow method given for turbot, remembering that the skin is a delicacy. The head should be left untouched on the dish.

Small Flat Fish (Plaice, Sole, etc.) : Remove head and tail. Make an incision along spine from head to tail. Insert fork in between fin bones, holding other sections with knife, then pressing the fish sideways. Loosen and remove the whole of the spinal bone. (See illustration given for sole, *facing page* 217.) To remove fin bones, make an incision along the edge. (See A.) Now hold the fish back with the fork, and, with the knife, press out all the small bones, so that now the double fillet is served without bones. If fish is large enough for more than two persons, serve single fillets.

To Carve Large Round or Thick Fish : The usual way to carve round or thick fish is to make an incision along the centre of the back all along fish, running the knife from head to tail. Do not cut through the backbone. Now remove skin, if liked, before carving portions. This is usual when carving for a number of persons. If carving for one or two, it is a good idea to turn the skin back so that, when the meal is over, the skin can be drawn together over the carved portion to keep fish below the bone moist. Now carve narrow portions at right angles to the backbone, that is, across fish, either removing skin first, as I suggested, or leaving it on. When portions are removed from the upper side, slip your fish-slice or knife between the backbone and the lower portions, and remove bone, then carve the lower half like the upper. As the fish narrows towards the tail of both halves, portions should be cut wider than when carving towards the head. When carving gurnet or haddock, remember the thickest or shoulder end is the best part. When mullet is so large that it does for 2 persons, carve like mackerel, but be sure to divide the liver, which is usually just visible under the opening of the gills, fairly, as it is a choice morsel. If you have occasion to carve a cod or a large fresh haddock that has had the portions marked off before the fish was cooked, then you must carve according to the markings.

Mackerel : When a large boiled mackerel has to be carved, slide the fish slice or knife from the tail upwards to its gills, and serve. The tail part is considered the best, and the roe is a delicacy. Now remove head and backbone from the lower side, which can then be served.

Salmon : There is more than one way of carving salmon. It is easy to carve a large salmon, if you follow the illustrations, *facing page* 217; cut right across the fish from A to B with a stainless steel knife or fish carver, then in slices or portions, as marked from C to D, starting from the head. If you carve in this way, flesh will not break. When all the upper portion is served, carefully insert knife or server between bone and lower portion, then carve lower portion in the same manner, without turning fish over. If fish is large, it can be carved like cod, so that portions of the belly (which is the thin part) and portions of the back (or thick part) are given to each person. Some carvers prefer to carve salmon in this way : they slice across, as illustrated from C to D, a portion of the thick part, and cut the thin part crosswise so as to be able to give both thick and thin per person.

To Serve Small Split Fried or Grilled Fish (Herring, Trout, etc.) : Place on serving dish with spine upwards, then remove heads. Carefully press the flesh away from the small bones, holding bones back with fork. In this way the spine with the small bones attached will come away in one piece. (See illustration of herring, *facing page* 224.)

To Carve Shellfish, Crawfish and Lobster : Place fish on a board with the back upwards. Hold down firmly, then insert pointed knife into the back of the body and make a cut forward into the head to split it. Now run your knife backwards to split the tail. You then remove the stomach, which lies in the body near the head, and take out the intestines running along the tail. The claws, when to be served with the fish, should be broken first with crackers. Lobster picks should be provided to remove all the flesh from claws.

Meat

Meat, a vital food, is one of our chief sources of protein. High in nutritional quality, it supplies us with easily digested fats of energy value and is an important source of iron. It also furnishes us with a certain amount of phosphorus and some of the vitamins essential to good health. The offal of animals, such as kidneys, liver and other organs, is even richer in iron and vitamins than meat itself. When meat and offal are in short supply, the additional protein required to keep the body in perfect health can be obtained by using more eggs, fish, milk, pulses and whole-grain cereals in our diet.

TO CHOOSE MEAT

When choosing a cut of meat, the following points should be kept in mind :
1. Cuts vary in tenderness according to the age and condition of animal, and to the part from which cuts are taken.
2. The flesh of very young animals—kid, lamb, sucking pig and veal—has a more delicate flavour than flesh of mature animals, but it is deficient in fats and minerals. It also loses a larger proportion of weight while cooking, as it is more watery than mature meat. If a more pronounced flavour is preferred, then choose mature meat.
3. The most tender portions of meat are found on either side of the backbone. It is worth remembering, when choosing meat, that the farther the cut from the backbone, the coarser the fibres.
4. Choose cuts from small-bodied animals when possible, as they have more tender flesh and finer fibres than large animals.

187

5. It is incorrect to think that high-priced cuts are more nutritious than the flank, round, and shoulder, for example. Lower-priced cuts are also rich in food value when properly cooked.

6. If meat is clammy, it is not fresh.

7. Remember the butcher may not be able to cut exactly the weight you want, so be sure you have allowed for enough when ordering.

HOW MUCH MEAT TO BUY

The following is the minimum that should be allowed per person, when meat is required for an average-sized meal. If possible increase quantity of meat with bone to 8 oz., and allow 2 lamb cutlets.

$\frac{1}{4}$ lb. boneless.   1 cutlet, if large.
6 oz. with bone $\frac{1}{4}$ lb. heart, liver or sweetbreads.
$\frac{1}{2}$ lb. tripe.

TO JUDGE MEAT

Generally speaking, the best meat should be firm-fleshed with a fine grain and free from an unpleasant smell. It should be moderately fat and slightly moist. Do not consider buying cuts of flabby meat containing small glands, known as " kernels."

TO STORE MEAT

The moment the meat comes from the butcher, examine carefully in case of any fly-blows. Wipe meat with a damp cloth. Place on a clean china or enamel plate without any chips or cracks, or in a shallow basin. Cover lightly with waxed paper. Place on lowest shelf of refrigerator below freezing unit, or, failing a refrigerator, in coolest part of larder. If solid meat needs to be kept for two days before cooking, store at 45° F. If not able to use fresh meat within a day or two after purchase, it is better to freeze meat in the freezing compartment of refrigerator. Don't defrost it until ready to cook it. Chops, roasts, steaks and stewing steak should be used within three days of purchase.

Ground Meat: This does not keep fresh as long as solid meat. Either use within a day or two of purchase, or freeze it. This also applies to hearts, kidneys, liver and other by-products of meat which should be cooked as soon as purchased, if possible.

Smoked Bacon and Gammon: Remove shop wrappings and rewrap in cellophane or waxed paper. Store in coldest and darkest part of larders When you wish to cook any, only remove what is required. Rewrap and store remainder away at once. Mildly cured ham should be stored like fresh meat.

Cooked Meat: Cover with cellophane or waxed paper or it will dry out. Use within 3 or 4 days. If to be ground, grind only when required. If to be served as a cold cut, remove from refrigerator to larder for at least $\frac{1}{2}$ hour before serving.

Frozen Meat: Store in freezing compartment till time to thaw it out.

If meat is stored at too high a temperature, or left in the larder or refrigerator in the wrappings it came in from the butcher, it will soon decompose. You can always store it in the freezing compartment. If this is impossible, sear on the outside in a hot frying pan, or partly cook it, then cool as quickly as possible, and store in refrigerator or larder.

To Protect Meat Temporarily without a Refrigerator: Hang a leg of lamb or mutton, or large cut of meat, from a sterilized hook in larder, in a free current of air, protected from flies by a wire gauze window. The meat must be protected from flies and other insects, but the screening must not touch meat nor interfere with circulation of air. When you protect meat in this way, you will notice that a dry film forms on the surface of meat to prevent an attack from bacteria. If you haven't a refrigerator, or some cold place in which to store fresh meat satisfactorily, buy meat only as required. How long it will keep fresh depends on its state when you receive it and how cold it can be kept.

CHILLED AND FROZEN MEAT

There is quite a difference between chilled meat and frozen. The former is packed and brought over here under the strictest regulations. Sometimes it is found to be higher in quality than some of the meat produced in this country. The best grade of beef is imported from the Argentine, and the best grade of lamb and mutton from New Zealand. Canterbury lamb, which is so good that it can be easily mistaken for the best English, is at its best from March to September. As chilled meat is never allowed to freeze, but is kept at a temperature sufficiently low to prevent spoilage, it does not lose its flavour nor does it exude its juices when thawed. As a rule, chilled meat is only kept for a week or two. It is sold as fresh meat.

Frozen meat, again, is stored at a temperature slightly below freezing point. It has to be defrosted very gradually. You can tell frozen meat by its solidity and its ice crystals, and by the drips from the cut surfaces. If it has to be stored for a short time, be careful not to place it with cut surfaces downwards or the dripping which continues may result in dry meat. Thaw meat at room temperature when required in a hurry, otherwise cover it lightly with waxed paper and allow it to thaw out. Don't try to hurry the process by placing it near a fire or hot stove, or by standing it in hot water. Frozen meat should be cooked the moment it has thawed out.

TAINTED MEAT

If meat becomes tainted through temperature storage, wash it in cold water, acidulated with vinegar, allowing 8 tablespoons to a gallon of water, then dry thoroughly and cook. If preferred, wipe with a cloth dipped in equal quantity of malt vinegar and water, then soak in a marinade if not required to be cooked at once. If meat has to be kept for a day or two without refrigeration, remove any kernels from the fat and the spinal cord from backbone or neck of lamb or mutton, then sprinkle all over with ground pepper. Cover loosely with butter muslin, and hang up in your larder, keeping cut surface uppermost.

TO BONE MEAT

To Bone a Chop, Cutlet or Steak: Holding the bone end in your left hand, scrape away the meat from that end. When the boning is complete, you should have a piece of solid meat and a clean bone. This is how I bone small loin lamb or mutton chops, when I wish to roll the meat round into flat cakes. Then I encircle cakes with a strip of bacon and bake or grill them. Sometimes I roll the meat round a kidney or sausage before encircling it with bacon.

TO PREPARE MEAT FOR COOKING

Trim meat. Remove any superfluous fat, sinews, etc. Weigh if cuts are for boiling, braising, roasting or steaming. Wipe with a clean damp cloth wrung in cold water. (If any parts show signs of taint, cut them off before weighing.) Skewer or tie into shape if cut demands this. If strong smelling, as sometimes happens if it has been kept wrapped up too long, treat as for tainted meat. Do not wash fresh meat unless absolutely essential on account of strong smell. Wipe it with a damp cloth.

Meat that Must Be Washed; Salt beef, ham, pork, tongue and all the offal such as heads, feet, hearts, kidneys, liver, etc. Soak the offal for $\frac{1}{4}$ hour in tepid salted water, then dry. Blanch sweetbreads.

TO COOK MEAT PERFECTLY

1. You must be able to recognise cuts.
2. You must know which cuts are prime and which inferior.
3. You must know which to choose for boiling, frying, grilling, stewing, etc.
4. You must know how to prepare, season and cook each different cut so as to make it tender and appetizing.
5. You must know how to garnish meat and what are its best accompaniments.
6. Remember that only tender cuts can be fried, grilled or roasted. Less tender require to be steamed, stewed, braised or pot-roasted, according to cut.

HINTS ON COOKING MEAT

1. Beat chops and steaks before cooking to break the tissues.
2. To tenderize tough meat, soak in a marinade for 2 hours, unless a different length of time is specified in recipe, basting or turning meat occasionally.
3. To increase number of portions when cooking a quantity of meat intended for a smaller number, add dumplings, macaroni, noodles or spaghetti to stews or casseroles of meat; make meat into savoury puddings or roly-polys with suet crust, or into pies with flaky or rough puff pastry; curry and serve with boiled rice. Stuff joints. Turn stewing steak into beef olives, etc.
4. If you sprinkle joint with flour before starting to roast it, flour will brown and colour gravy. If preferred, add 2 lumps of sugar to roasting pan before starting to cook meat.

MEAT COOKERY

The purpose of cooking meat is to soften connective tissue so as to render meat tender, destroy bacteria or other organisms, develop flavour, and make it appetising in appearance. There are 7 basic methods of cooking meat : Baking or roasting, boiling, braising, frying, grilling, steaming, and stewing.

BAKING OR ROASTING

This is cooking with dry heat, suitable for prime, tender joints, such as :
Prime Joints: Beef—Chump end of rump and sirloin. *Lamb*—Fore and hind quarters when very young, crown, leg, loin, saddle, shoulder and best end neck. *Mutton*—Loin, saddle, best end neck. *Pork*—Loin (fore and hind), fillet, crown roast and leg. *Veal*—Fillet, loin (best end), and " oyster."
Economical Joints: Beef—Rolled ribs, wing rib, part of chuck rib (called " leg of mutton piece "), topside (pot roast), and buttock when a very large joint is wanted. *Lamb*—Breast and leg. *Mutton*—Boned and stuffed breast and shoulder, haunch, leg, and loin. *Pork:* Fore end and spare ribs. *Veal*— Boned and stuffed breast, shoulder and calf's heart.
Nowadays, an oven is generally used for roasting meat.

THREE MODERN METHODS OF ROASTING

There are three methods of baking or roasting meat. The first is to cook meat on a rack or trivet in a roasting pan at a fairly high temperature, 450° F., for $\frac{1}{4}$ hour to seal in the juices. The temperature is then reduced to moderate, 350° F., and kept there till meat is tender and ready to serve. The second method (a slower one) is better, as it minimizes shrinkage, but some claim that the flavour is not so good. Cook at a low temperature, 325° F., throughout the time required, all joints except fresh pork, which needs moderate heat, 350° F.
The third, which I do not advocate, is to place meat in a cold oven, let it heat to 350° F., a moderate temperature, and continue cooking at this temperature till ready. By this method much of the food value escapes into the roasting pan. It enriches the gravy while impoverishing the meat, but the meat shrinks less by this method of roasting than by the other two. No matter which method you follow for baking or roasting meat, place pan in centre of oven. Do not prick joint with a fork at any time during baking or roasting. Serve with gravy, using unthickened for plain joints and thickened for stuffed. If you follow the second or third methods, you will not be able to get perfect roast potatoes either by cooking them along with the meat or in a second pan in dripping, because of the low temperature. You will have to finish the crisping and browning on top of the stove.

HINTS ON BAKING OR ROASTING

1. Wipe meat. Trim. Place on a rack or trivet in roasting pan. If lean, smear with softened fat, unless caul is sent with meat, when cover joint with it, instead of applying fat. If using a self-basting pan, cover before starting

to cook by first method, or after searing by second method, or after tempera-ture rises to 350° F. by third. Uncover for last ½ hour to crisp joint.

2. If you prefer to roast in a double-roaster, pour water into bottom tin to prevent fat burning in upper tin, and be sure to allow enough fat in upper tin, or smear joint with enough fat so as to have plenty for dripping and for basting with. If roasting in an open tin and meat has enough fat, it is not necessary to add any fat or water to roasting pan. If joint is lean, smear thickly with fat, top with pieces of fat, or add a little dripping, and a little water to pan to serve for basting. Turn twice during cooking, using spoons to help you in the process, not forks. Baste frequently.

3. If there is a layer of fat on any joint, always start roasting with fat side uppermost.

4. Season with pepper before roasting. You can either season with salt before roasting or at half time, according to taste.

POT-ROASTING

This is a good way to cook a piece of meat, such as topside, that is inclined to be tough when roasted in the usual way in the oven. Take, say, 4 lb. of topside. If lean, lard it with salt pork or bacon before cooking. Choose an iron saucepan with a closely fitting lid. Rub meat lightly with seasoned flour. Melt 2 or 3 tablespoons of dripping in saucepan. Add meat. Fry, turning frequently, until a rich brown all over. Slip a lower rack below it. Add stock or water, or equal quantity of stock and tomato juice, to the depth of ½ inch in pan. Cover closely. Cook very slowly over low heat, turning occasionally until tender, in about 3 hours, or more, according to thickness of cut. If liked, add vegetables to pan, such as carrots, turnips and potatoes, about ½ hour before dishing up. Dish up. Make gravy by stirring 1 dessertspoon flour, creamed with stock or water, into the gravy in pan. Stir until boiling, adding more liquid if necessary, and seasoning if required. Some cooks prefer to cook a pot-roast in a casserole or hot-pot jar in a slow oven to cooking on top of stove. If you prefer the oven method, heat oven to 300° F.-325° F. and cook meat in a tightly-covered vessel for 2½-3½ hours, according to size and thickness of meat.

BOILING MEAT

To " boil " meat is rather an erroneous way of talking about cooking meat in water. To boil fresh meat correctly, weigh it, then wipe all over with a damp cloth. Tie firmly, if necessary, to hold meat together. Remove any superfluous fat. Place in a saucepan, large enough to hold meat and water to cover. Cover with boiling salted water, allowing 1 teaspoon salt to each lb. of meat. Add 1 onion, stuck with 2-4 cloves (according to weight of meat), 1 blade of mace, 5 or 6 black peppercorns and a bouquet garni. Bring again to boil. Boil quickly for 5 minutes. Skim and cover, then reduce heat as fast as possible, so that the meat only simmers or " poaches," as it is sometimes called, till tender. That is at 186° F. If allowed to boil, the meat will be tough. Add simmering water as necessary as the meat must be covered with

HAM
Cold Baked Ham garnished with orange slices and sprigs of mint. *See page* 228.

PHEASANT
Garnish hot Roast Pheasant with fried crumbs if liked. *See page* 277-278.

water and the pan must be covered with its lid during the whole period of cooking. If the lid does not fit tightly, weight it down.

Time Required: Allow from 15 to 30 minutes per pound, according to kind, thickness and weight of meat.

To Boil Salt Meat: Cook bacon, calf's head, ham, ox tongue, salt beef, salt pork, etc., by the same method used for fresh meat, but substituting cold, unsalted water for boiling water. If meat is known to be very salt, as bacon and ham frequently is, soak in cold water to cover for 3 to 4 hours, or overnight if necessary, before boiling. If only a little too salt, drain off water when it comes to boil, and replace with fresh unsalted cold water.

Meat Suitable for Boiling: Beef—Aitchbone, brisket, heel, thick and thin flank and silverside. *Lamb*—None. *Mutton*—Breast, knuckle end of leg. *Pork*—Belly or spring (pickled), hand (usually salted), cheek (salted), leg and head (for brawn). *Bacon*—Gammon, cushion, collar and forehock. *Ham*—Knuckle end, cushion, butt end and whole ham. *Veal*—Fore knuckle, breast and head.

HINTS ON BOILING MEAT

1. When boiling a fairly large joint, tie it firmly with boiled string or strong cotton to ensure it keeping its shape.
2. Use stock in which meat has been boiled for making sauce or soup.
3. Add prepared vegetables to taste, if liked, about 40 minutes before meat is ready to serve. Dumplings can also be added 20 minutes later, if required.

BRAISING MEAT

If you have a cut of meat that is not quite tender enough to roast, nor tough enough to put through a meat grinder and make into Hamburg steaks, loaf or slice, and cook in a casserole, or stew, then braise it. Braising is an economical method of cooking meat. It is really a combination of pot-roasting, steaming and stewing, generally used for the less tender cuts of meat which require long slow cooking by moist heat to bring out their full flavour, and make them digestible and tender. In olden days, to braise meat meant to cook it on a mirepoix in a braisière, which was a closed stew pan, so shaped that live charcoal could be placed in the hollow cover. The result was that the meat in the braisière was being cooked by heat both above and below. Nowadays a casserole or strong shallow saucepan with a closely fitting lid and two handles is generally used. Braising is done either on top of the stove or in the oven, or it can be done partly on top of the stove and partly in the oven.

Meat Suitable for Braising: Beef—Thin brisket, clod, flank, short ribs, rump, shank, shin, shoulder, beef olives, ox cheek and heart. *Lamb*—Boned and rolled breast, leg, loin, neck shank and heart. *Mutton*—Boned and rolled breast, small leg, boned as far as the knuckle, loin, scrag end of neck, shank, shoulder and heart. *Pork*—Chops, spare-ribs, steaks, heart, liver, tail, ham, tongue, etc. *Veal*—Stuffed breast, fillet, knuckle, loin, neck and shoulder chops, thick steaks, sweetbreads, calves' hearts, liver, tongue, etc. Any boned and stuffed joints of meat.

METHOD OF BRAISING

As meat chosen for braising is usually lean, the fat deficiency should be supplied by larding. If this is not done by your butcher, you need a set of larding needles, and some larding bacon for making into lardoons which you insert by means of a larding needle in the meat.

To Make Lardoons: Place larding bacon or any firm bacon on chopping board, rind downwards, cut in slices between an eighth and quarter inch thick, parallel with the vein. If you slice crosswise, the lardoons will break when you insert them. Cut slices into strips, $1\frac{1}{2}$ to 2 inches long. Chill before inserting. When preparing, you must consider size of meat you want to lard. If a joint, make lardoons 2 inches long. If a small cut, such as fillet, then cut $1\frac{1}{2}$ inches long. The ends of each lardoon must be even and square.

To Lard Meat: Choose a larding needle to suit size of lardoon. Place a lardoon in the split end of needle. Insert point of needle in meat across the grain. Now take a stitch about $\frac{3}{4}$ inch wide and about $\frac{1}{3}$ inch deep, and draw needle quickly through meat until you have the same length of lardoon projecting at each end of stitch. Arrange lardoons in parallel lines about an inch apart, and be sure to insert next row of stitches exactly below the first. Continue in this way till meat is larded to taste.

To Cook Meat: Place larded meat on a mirepoix in a shallow saucepan or casserole. Cover with a greased paper, cut to fit, then with a tightly fitting lid. Cook very gently on top of stove, or in the oven for about two-thirds of the time required to make meat tender, basting frequently. Remove pan or casserole to a slow oven, 325° F. Baste and cover again with paper and lid until almost tender, then remove lid and paper. Make oven fairly hot, 425° F., and bake for about 20 minutes till the lardoons are crisp. If you find when basting, some time during cooking, that most of the stock has evaporated, add a little more. To dish up, arrange meat on a hot dish. Strain stock into a saucepan. Boil quickly down to a demi-glaze. Skim well. Glaze meat with a brush. Pour remainder round. Garnish with freshly cooked vegetables, such as green peas and pieces of carrot and serve with brown, Espagnole or tomato sauce.

MIREPOIX

½ oz. bacon
1 oz. butter
1 scraped carrot
1 small peeled turnip
1 medium-sized peeled onion
1 stick celery
Stock as required
1 peeled clove garlic, if liked
½ teaspoon black peppercorns
1 blade mace
1 bouquet garni
Salt to taste

Remove rind from bacon and cut bacon into small pieces. Melt butter in braising pan. Add bacon. Fry lightly. Cut all vegetables into thick slices, and arrange on top of bacon. Cover closely. Fry slowly for 10 minutes. Pour in just enough stock to cover vegetables. It should be about an inch deep in pan. Add garlic, peppercorns, mace, herbs and salt to taste. As much of the aroma and flavour that characterizes braised meat comes from the mirepoix, it must be made carefully.

HINTS ON BRAISING MEAT

1. If dry or lean, lard.
2. If to be braised in a casserole, use a casserole with a metal base.
3. If you want a very succulent braise of meat, marinade meat from 2 to 4 hours before cooking.
4. Weigh meat. Allow 25 to 30 minutes per lb., according to kind, and ½ hour over.
5. If stock from meat is not rich enough to impart a good glaze, add a teaspoon of glaze to stock, and dissolve before using.
6. If to be stuffed, bone, stuff, and tie in shape before braising.

SCOTCH BRAISED BEEF (Boeuf Braisé à l'Ecossaise)

¼ lb. carrot
½ lb. celery
¼ lb. turnip
½ lb. Spanish onions
¼ lb. raw streaky bacon
2 oz. butter or beef dripping
1½ lb. topside of beef
4 allspice berries
10 peppercorns
1 blade mace
1 sprig parsley
1 sprig marjoram
1½ pints stock
2 oz. flour
½ oz. glaze
Salt and pepper to taste

Cut washed and prepared vegetables into inch-square dice, then the bacon. Melt the fat in saucepan you use for braising. When smoking hot, add bacon and vegetables. Fry all to a light brown. Lift out. Drain off some of the dripping and fry meat in what remains. The piece should be very thick. When brown on each side, take it out of pan. Pour off remainder of dripping, leaving only the meat essence in pan. Lay all vegetables, bacon, spices and herbs tied in muslin in pan and place meat on this bed. Pour in stock. Cover with greased paper as tightly as possible. Place pan in a slow oven, or on top of the stove. Simmer very gently till meat is tender. The braize can be transferred, if preferred, to a casserole when everything is prepared, but in that case, it may take longer to cook. Mix flour smoothly with a little of the stock. Remove spices and herbs. Strain in thickening. Stir till sauce comes to boil, adding more stock if too thick. Add glaze. Season gravy very carefully. When ready, serve turned out on a hot dish with gravy strained over, and heaps of vegetables round. Sometimes I add a few green peas, boiled separately, to the garnish when serving. A little wine can be added to the gravy before straining, if liked. *For 4 persons*.

CASSEROLE COOKERY

Casseroles are generally used for cooking tough cuts of meat which need long, slow braising or stewing. Cooked, *en casserole*, the fibres of the meat soften and meat becomes tender. This is an excellent form of meat cookery for the following reasons :

1. As the meat can be served from casserole all meat and vegetable juices are retained.
2. Little watching is required.
3. The casserole can be placed either on top of an asbestos mat on top of stove, or in the oven, according to which method of cooking is more convenient. *If casserole has a metal base, no asbestos mat is necessary*.

4. If meat is a tough cut, cook in a slow oven, at 300° F., otherwise, at 325° F., in a moderately slow oven.

5. By serving from casserole, no serving dish or platter is required, which minimizes dish-washing. If all the vegetables to be served are cooked with the meat, there are no vegetable dishes to wash up.

Meats Suitable for Casserole Cookery: Beef—Top and bottom round, neck, chuck, flank, minced and sliced shin, etc. *Lamb or Mutton*—Breast, neck, shoulder, etc. *Pork*—Fillet, fore-end, shoulder and spare ribs. *Veal*—Breast, flank, neck, shoulder, etc. *Miscellaneous*—Calf, ox or sheep's hearts ; calf, ox or pig's kidneys ; lamb or calf's livers ; ox tail ; tripe.

CASSEROLE OF MEAT (Casserole de Viande)

BASIC RECIPE :
2½ lb. meat
1½ tablespoons dripping or butter
3 tablespoons flour
3 or 4 medium-sized peeled onions
2 or 3 scraped carrots
2 teaspoons salt
Pepper to taste
Boiling water or stock

Cut meat into suitable pieces for serving. Melt the fat in a saucepan. Dip meat in flour and brown on both sides in the smoking hot fat. Turn into a casserole. Slice onions and fry for 2 minutes. Place in casserole. Slice in carrots. Add salt and pepper. Pour boiling water or stock into pan. Boil up. Pour into casserole. Add 2 turnips or parsnips if liked. Cover and cook gently in a slow oven, 300° F. to 325° F., letting it simmer until tender. Serve with boiled, steamed, mashed or riced potatoes. *For 6 persons.*

MEAT CURRIES

Some British housewives think that all that is necessary to make a meat curry is to add some curry powder to meat before stewing. This is quite wrong. To make a perfect meat curry, you must adapt the seasoning to suit the meat, and, of course, to your own taste. The same seasoning should not be used, for example, for curry of fish, game, poultry and meat. Some prefer curry made of fresh meat. It is impossible to make real eastern curries, as the spices have to be imported in dried form, but that is no reason why we should not make and serve a good curry. Tamarinds can be bought in jars. When they are not obtainable, and you wish to follow a recipe containing tamarinds, substitute a teaspoon of red currant jelly and a dash of lemon juice. When coconut milk is not available, coconut water made by infusing desiccated coconut in boiling water, or almond milk can be substituted. Given good stock, suitable flavouring, spices and other seasonings, slow cooking and properly boiled rice, it should be possible for every housewife to become expert at curry making and serving.

HINTS ON MAKING CURRY OF MEAT

1. To keep curry a good colour and preserve its flavour, cook in the white-lined top of a double boiler.
2. Cut meat, fresh or cooked, into small pieces fully an inch square.

3. When green ginger is included, it should be sliced very thinly then pounded in a mortar with a pestle, to a paste, before adding.

4. To achieve the sweet-sour flavour of a perfect curry, add the strained juice of a lime, or, failing that, a dessertspoon of vinegar and 1 dessertspoon of light brown sugar. If preferred, substitute a tablespoon of sweet chutney for the sugar.

5. If making a curry of cooked meat, soak it in hot curry sauce for at least ½ hour to allow it to become impregnated with the flavour of the sauce before serving. Don't cook cooked meat in the sauce or meat will harden.

To Serve: Arrange curry in a deep hot dish, in a border of rice, if liked. It should be eaten with a spoon and fork.

Accompaniments : Boiled rice, Bombay duck, chapatties (chapatis), chutney, lentil croquettes, poppadums, etc.

Bombay Duck: If sold flattened, brush them with melted butter, and bake them in the oven or grill them. If not flattened, beat them with a rolling pin before cooking. Sometimes maldive fish, a species of dried shark, is served out East with curries. If you have acquired a taste for this, substitute strips of fried or grilled red herring.

CHAPATTIES

1 lb. wholemeal flour
¼ lb. clarified butter
½ pint warm milk and water
Pinch salt

Sift flour. Melt fat in milk and water. Stir salt then liquid into flour. Turn on to a lightly floured pastry board. Roll out very thinly. Cut into round cakes. Heat enough oil to grease the bottom of a large frying pan. Fry. When brown below, turn and brown on other side. Serve at once.

COCONUT MILK (Lait de Coco)

Sometimes called coconut essence and sometimes coconut water. This is not the milk from the coconut, but an infusion made with boiling water and grated coconut flesh. There are two methods of making it: Place 3 oz. grated coconut in a small basin. Cover with 1 or 1½ gills boiling water. Leave until cold. Strain through muslin and use. The other method is to halve a very fresh large coconut. Scrape off the whole of the white flesh and grate it into a basin. Cover with ½ pint boiling water. Stand for 15 minutes, then strain through muslin and use. In India this infusion is not added to the curry until just before serving.

DRY MEAT CURRY (Kari de Viande)

2 oz. butter
1 sliced peeled onion
2 lb. fillet steak
1 tablespoon curry powder
2 chopped small gherkins
½ tablespoon mango chutney
1 saltspoon salt
Juice of ½ lemon

Melt butter in a shallow saucepan. Add onion. Fry slowly for 3 or 4 minutes. Cut meat into inch squares and add. Sprinkle curry powder over meat. Cook over slow heat for 5 minutes. Add gherkins, chutney and salt. If liked, add a chopped peeled clove of garlic, and a heaped teaspoon curry paste. Cover closely. Cook very slowly for about 1 hour, stirring occasionally. Add lemon juice. Serve with boiled rice. If not able to watch this curry, it is better to cook it in the top of a double boiler, rather than in an ordinary stew pan, to avoid burning.

WET MEAT CURRY (Kari de Viande)

1 lb. meat
1/2 oz. grated fresh coconut
1/2 gill boiling water
1 oz. butter
1 tablespoon chopped onions
1 oz. flour
1/2 oz. curry powder
2 tablespoons finely chopped apple
1/2 pint meat stock
1/2 teaspoon curry paste
1 teaspoon lemon juice
Salt as required

Remove any fat from meat as well as gristle and skin before weighing. Fillet of beef, pork or veal, or shoulder of mutton can be used. Cut meat into inch squares. Soak the coconut in boiling water for 15 to 20 minutes, then strain. Melt butter in shallow saucepan. Add meat. Fry lightly on both sides, then remove to a plate. Fry onions slowly till clear, then stir in flour and curry powder. Fry for 1 to 2 minutes, stirring frequently, then add apple, coconut milk and stock. Use white stock for veal, mutton stock for mutton, beef stock for beef or pork. When blended, stir in curry paste, lemon juice and salt. Bring to boil. Skim thoroughly. Return meat to pan. Cover closely. Simmer for about 1½ hours until tender, the time depending on the kind of meat curried. Skim as required. *For 4 persons.*

FRYING

Thin cuts of only the best parts of meat, such as fillet and rump steak, lamb or mutton cutlets, lamb or mutton loin chops, loin pork chops, cutlets, veal chops, cutlets and fillets, bacon and gammon rashers, calf's brains and sweetbreads, and liver, are all suitable for frying. Deep-fried meat is more digestible than shallow-fried.

Meat for Shallow-Frying: Cook chops and steaks, calf's brains and sweetbreads, and pricked sausages, by this method, in ½-1 inch of hot fat or oil, till brown on one side, then turn and brown on other. Fry slowly, turning frequently, until tender.

Meat for Deep-Frying: Place chops, cutlets, or fillets and small cuts of meat dipped in batter or egged and crumbed, and pre-cooked meaty mixtures, such as croquettes, fritters, kromeskies, etc., in a frying basket, a few at a time, and cook in deep fat, heated to a temperature between 360° F. and 400° F. Fry meat till delicate brown in 5-8 minutes. Drain on unglazed paper.

HINTS ON FRYING MEAT

1. Use clarified fat or beef dripping, lard, or olive or other cooking oil for deep frying. Use bacon or chicken fat, beef dripping, butter, lard or any cooking oil for shallow-frying.

2. Fry bacon very slowly in a dry pan as it has enough fat of its own to prevent burning.

3. See that all meat to be fried is perfectly dry before starting to cook it. If not free from moisture, the drying fat or oil will splutter.

4. Use steak tongs for turning meat. Do not spear with a fork or juices will escape.

GRILLING OR BROILING

This method of cooking calls for quick dry heat. It is most suitable for pieces of small, juicy, tender meat, such as bacon, chops, cutlets, fillet of beef, kidneys and sausages. In days gone by, meat was grilled or " broiled," as it was then called, on a hot greased grid iron in front of or over a clear fire. The ideal fire for grilling over is now usually made of coal and a little charcoal or coke.

In modern days, it is more usual to grill or broil on the grill rack beneath the glowing deflector of an electric or gas griller. When the griller forms part of the oven, be sure to keep the door open whilst grilling. Some experts hold that to grill properly, you cook the meat for half the time on one side, then turn it and cook it on the other. The other method is to keep turning meat with steak tongs until you get it done to taste. The meat is more likely to get burnt by the first method.

To Grill or Broil Meat: Wipe meat with a damp cloth. Cut into portions, if bought in a piece. When possible, cut it so that there is a rim of fat round each portion. Gash fat with a knife to prevent curling. Season meat with pepper. Brush with melted butter or oil on both sides, to prevent surface charring. Grease or oil grill rack. Pre-heat for 5 inches below the deflector when cuts are $1\frac{1}{2}$-2 inches thick. If 1-$1\frac{1}{2}$ inches thick, place so that the meat is only 2 inches below. Now grill by one of the following methods :

1. Grill for half the period required, until nicely brown, then turn and grill on other side till cooked according to taste.

2. Grill quickly for 1-2 minutes to seal in juices, then turn. Cook quickly for 1-2 minutes, then turn again. Season with salt. Cook for another minute or two, then turn and season with salt. Keep on grilling and turning until you get the meat grilled to your taste.

Turn meat with steak tongs, two spoons or a spatula. Do not use a fork on any account or the juices will escape. Perfectly grilled meat should have a puffy appearance and be elastic to the touch. Serve at once with a pat of Maître d'Hôtel butter melting on each portion. Garnish with sprigs of watercress. Serve with potato crisps, chips or straws, and grilled tomatoes or mushrooms.

HINTS ON GRILLING

1. Marinate rump steak for 1 hour before grilling, or beat it well with a meat mallet to break down some of the meat fibres, or treat with a tenderiser.

2. Brush egged and crumbed cutlets with melted butter before grilling.

3. If you find your grilling compartment is not deep enough to allow a 3-inch space between the top of the meat and the deflector, when grilling meat $1\frac{1}{2}$-2 inches thick, either turn electric switch so that it gives you a moderate heat throughout the operation, or adjust gas flame in the same manner, or brown meat quickly on both sides under the deflector, then transfer to a roasting pan and roast on a rack in a slow oven, 250°-300° F.,

turning when half ready until rare, medium or well-done as you prefer. This is a good method when you have to cook a very thick steak for people who prefer it well-done.

4. If able to grill over coal or charcoal, hold grid iron in a slanting direction so that the dripping does not drop on the cinders, causing flame and smoke.

MIXED GRILLS

A mixed grill usually consists of two or more varieties of grilled meat with grilled mushrooms or tomatoes, or both. It is served with the same accompaniments as a grilled chop or steak.

1. Rump steaks or fillets of steak, sausages, mushrooms and thick slices of tomato.
2. Lamb chops, rashers of bacon, and lambs' or sheep's kidneys.
3. Gammon steaks, sausages and tomato or pineapple slices.
4. Slices of calf's liver, sausages, bananas wrapped in bacon.
5. Lambs' or sheep's kidneys, rashers of bacon and tomato slices.
6. Ground meat cakes, rashers or curls of bacon and mushroom or tomato slices.

To Cook a Mixed Grill: You have to plan a mixed grill very carefully so that all its components are ready to serve at the same time. Place the item that takes the longest time on the grill rack first. Grill for 1-2 minutes. Draw out grill rack and turn meat. Add the next item which grills in slightly less time, and so on. If meat is lean, baste with melted butter or oil when you turn it.

TO PAN-GRILL

This is a convenient way to cook a few chops, cutlets or small steaks. Use a strong, heavy frying-pan for this operation. Pre-heat pan. If meat to be pan-grilled is very lean, smear pan lightly with fat. Brown meat quickly on both sides, then lower heat below pan and continue cooking in this way, turning frequently, and pouring off fat as it accumulates until evenly cooked. It is impossible to give exact time required for pan-grilling various cuts. Allow about same time required for grilling.

STEAMING

This is the method of cooking meat by moist heat, either by direct contact with steam from boiling water or stock, or by indirect contact. By the second method, the meat is cooked in the steam of its own juices in a covered pan, over steam from boiling water, or in a covered container surrounded by boiling water. The latter method ensures the full flavour and food value of the meat being preserved. Steamed meat is lighter and more digestible than meat cooked by any other method. I recommend it for invalids who are allowed meat, and for all those who suffer from indigestion and similar troubles.

To steam meat, you need a double boiler, tiered steamer, pressure cooker, or waterless cooker. Given a tiered steamer or waterless cooker, you can steam a 3-course meal over a single burner or hotplate, which means great economy in fuel. If you steam in a pressure cooker, you save time as well. You can also steam meat on a rack or trivet in a saucepan of stock or water, but the legs of the rack or trivet should be long enough to keep the meat above the liquid. Meat may be steamed in a covered basin placed in a saucepan containing boiling water coming half-way up the side of basin. Meat for an invalid, *e.g.* a thin slice of fillet, when steak is wanted, or a lean chop, may be done between two enamel plates. Stand the plates on top of a saucepan of boiling water with the cover on top.

HINTS ON STEAMING

1. Chops, cutlets, mild-cured ham, steaks and tongue can be steamed, as well as beef when making beef tea.
2. Cover small pieces of meat with greased paper to prevent meat from becoming sodden through condensed steam.
3. Allow half as long again as you do for boiling meat.
4. Never let the water or stock in the saucepan boil away. Replenish as required.

STEWING

This is one of the most economical methods of treating meat. It is a process of cooking over slow heat in a covered saucepan, in a small quantity of stock or water which is ultimately served as gravy. The difference between boiling and stewing meat is that you boil at 212° F. in plenty of water, and stew at a gently poaching or simmering point, at between 160°-180° F. in a small quantity of liquid. A stew boiled is a stew spoiled. Stewing is an ideal method of cooking cheap and tough cuts of meat, but prime cuts can also be stewed. Some stews are made of meat only, and some of meat and vegetable. There are two kinds of stews, brown stews and white stews, but the latter is usually called a " fricassée." The difference between them, generally speaking, is that the meat in a brown stew is fried lightly before stewing, while the meat in a white stew is stewed unfried.

Meats Suitable for Stews: Beef—Cheek, chuck, clod, cushion, flank, leg, neck, thin brisket, skin, etc. *Lamb*—Breast, flank, loin, neck, shank, shoulder, etc. *Mutton*—Breast, neck chops, cushion, head, loin, ribs, scrag and end of neck, shoulder, and small leg, boned as far as the knuckle. *Veal*—Breast, fillet, flank, knuckle, neck, shoulder and heart, etc.

HINTS ON STEWING MEAT

To Prepare Meat: If fat, trim off fat and melt down for dripping. Cut meat into suitable portions, sometimes in slices, again in cubes, according to recipe.

If tough, soak in a marinade for at least ½ hour, to soften the fibres, or treat with a meat tenderiser. Drain well before stewing, and use cold water or stock.

Seasonings Required: Cayenne pepper, celery salt, curry powder, freshly-ground black or white pepper, gravy spice, ground cloves, mustard, soy sauce, tobasco, and, or, Worcester sauce, adding according to taste.

Herbs Required: Bay leaf, chives, marjoram, parsley, rosemary, sage, tarragon, thyme, etc.

Vegetables Suitable for Stews: Carrots, cauliflower, celery, Jerusalem artichokes, onions, parsnips, peas, potatoes, turnips, etc. (Mushrooms and tomatoes are also suitable for stews.)

Time Required: Allow 2-3 hours, according to variety and age of meat. If to be cooked in oven, heat to 300°-325° F., unless otherwise stated.

If Gravy is Greasy, skim carefully during cooking, if necessary, and before dishing up.

BROWN STEW OF MEAT (Etuvé de Viande, brune)

1 lb. lean meat
1 oz. flour
Salt and pepper to taste
1 oz. dripping
1 medium-sized onion
2 medium-sized carrots
1 small turnip
¾ pint cold stock or water

Trim off superflous fat before weighing. Wipe meat with a damp cloth. Cut into suitable portions for serving, either in slices ¾ inch thick, or in 2 inch squares, according to taste. Mix flour with salt and pepper to taste. Dip meat in flour. Heat fat in a shallow saucepan till smoking hot, then fry meat till light brown, turning frequently till equally brown all over. Remove to a plate. Peel and cut onion into rings. Fry slowly till beginning to shrivel. Add stock or water. Return meat to pan. Bring to simmering point. Skim well. Cover closely. Simmer gently for 1 hour. Scrape and slice in carrots and peel and slice in turnip. Simmer gently till quite tender and vegetables are cooked, skimming occasionally, if necessary. Arrange meat in centre of a flat hot dish. Skim sauce. Re-season if necessary. Strain over meat. Garnish with vegetables, cooked with meat, or reserve them for flavouring stock, and garnish with vegetables cooked in salt water. *For 4 persons.*

WHITE STEW OF MEAT (Etuvé de Viande, blanche)

BASIC RECIPE :
1 lb. fillet of veal
About ½ pint tepid water
Bouquet garni
1 small peeled onion
6 peppercorns
4 button mushrooms
Salt to taste
1 oz. butter
1 oz. flour
¼ pint hot veal stock
¼ pint hot milk
½ teaspoon lemon juice
GARNISH :
Crimped lemon,
4 rolls bacon.
Crescents of fried bread
Minced parsley

Wipe veal with a damp cloth. Cut into pieces about 9 inches square. Place in a white-lined saucepan. Add water. (The veal should be barely covered with water.) Bring to boiling point. Skim well. Add bouquet garni. Peel and slice in onion. Add peppercorns, mushrooms and salt. Cover. Simmer gently for 1 hour or till tender, then strain off stock. Melt butter in another saucepan. Add flour. When frothy, stir in stock and milk. Stir till smooth and boiling, then add lemon juice. Re-season if necessary. Place meat and mushrooms in sauce and heat over boiling water till piping hot. Arrange on a hot flat dish. Garnish with lemon, bacon, fried bread and minced parsley. *For 4 persons.*

To Vary : (1) If a more highly flavoured and seasoned stew or fricassée is wanted, add after mushrooms, 1 tablespoon sliced carrot, 1 sliced celery stick, a small blade of mace and a clove. If a richer dish is desired, stir 2 tablespoons thick cream into sauce before serving.

(2) *Blanquette* : Follow basic recipe, but beat an egg yolk with the lemon juice and with 2 tablespoons of the cream. Stir into sauce before serving.

MARINADE FOR MEAT (Raw)

2 tablespoons salad oil
1 tablespoon lemon juice or vinegar
2 saltspoons salt
1 teaspoon minced parsley
Freshly ground pepper to taste
1 teaspoon minced onion
½ clove garlic if liked

Mix all ingredients together. Pour over meat. Baste occasionally with the marinade. Soak for 1 hour, turning once or twice. This is a simple marinade for softening the fibres of soft meat. If required for veal, add, if liked, a pinch of crushed herbs and ½ teaspoon grated lemon rind. For other meat, a little curry powder, ½ bay leaf, 1 clove and 1 small blade mace can be added as well. Flavour your marinade to your own taste. Sometimes I add a sprig of chervil or tarragon. What I add, depends to a certain extent on the method of cookery. Increase quantities according to amount of meat to be marinated.

BEEF

Beef is always in season, but is at its best during the winter. The finest is said to come from a heifer about 4 years old.

TO CHOOSE BEEF

Lean, bright red and finely grained, mottled with firm, creamy fat and elastic to the touch ; there should be very little gristle between the fat and the lean. Beef of high quality should have firm white suet. When exposed to the air, the lean darkens, so that you cannot always judge whether it comes from a young or an old animal by its colour. Avoid beef with deep purple flesh. If doubtful when choosing, examine the bones ; choose meat with porous and red bones, and not flinty white ones.

BEEF CHART

This cooking chart will give you some idea of the time required to cook the different cuts of beef. The times given are only approximate as the cuts vary in thickness. The time allowed for roasting is for medium rare beef, but if you prefer yours rare, or well done, you must shorten or lengthen the time required according to taste.

Oven Temperature : 300° F.-325° F., *slow.*

CUTS	METHOD	TIME REQUIRED
Aitchbone	Boil (salted)	2½ hours for 10 lb.
	Roast	25 minutes per lb.
Brisket	Boil	20-25 minutes per lb. and 20 minutes over
	Braise	4-5 hours for 6 lb.

CUTS	METHOD	TIME REQUIRED
Flank	Braise (stuffed)	$2\frac{1}{2}$-$2\frac{3}{4}$ hours
	Roast (stuffed)	About $1\frac{3}{4}$ hours
Heart	Braise (stuffed)	About 4 hours
	Braise (stuffed)	About 4 hours
	Roast	About 3 hours
Ribs (Fore and middle)	Roast	22-25 minutes per lb. (Medium-rare)
	Roast (boned and rolled)	28-33 minutes per lb. (Medium-rare)
Ribs (Chuck)	Braise	25-30 minutes per lb. and 30 minutes over
Rump	Braise	25-30 minutes per lb. and 30 minutes over
	Roast	20 minutes per lb. and 20 minutes over
Silverside	Boil	25 minutes per lb. and 25 minutes over
Sirloin	Roast	20 minutes per lb. and 20 minutes over
Steaks :		
$\frac{1}{4}$-$\frac{1}{2}$ inch thick	Fried	4-5 minutes
$\frac{3}{4}$ inch thick		8 minutes
1 inch thick		10 minutes
1-$1\frac{1}{2}$ inches thick	Grilled	About 15 minutes
$\frac{1}{4}$-$\frac{1}{2}$ inch thick		4-6 minutes
$\frac{3}{4}$ inch thick		8-10 minutes
1 inch thick		10-15 minutes
$1\frac{1}{2}$ inches thick		15-18 minutes
Tongue	Boil (salted)	30 minutes per lb.
Topside	Pot roast	About 3 hours for 3-4 lb.
Undercut (Fillet)	Roast	20-23 minutes per lb. and 20-23 minutes over

ACCOMPANIMENTS TO BEEF

Baked or Roast Beef (hot)	Thin brown gravy, Yorkshire pudding, horseradish sauce or grated horseradish. Red currant jelly for heart.
Baked or Roast Beef (cold)	Pickled beetroot or walnuts, chutney, salad, jacket or scalloped potatoes.
Boiled Beef (hot)	Suet dumplings, caper or parsley sauce, carrots and turnips, and boiled potatoes.
Boiled or Steamed Beef (hot)	Suet dumplings, caper or parsley scalloped potatoes and salad.
Braised Beef	Cooked green peas and young carrots, braised onions, and turnips.
Fried or Grilled Beef	Fried or grilled mushrooms or tomatoes, Maître d'Hôtel butter, and fried potatoes.

STEAKS

If steak has been stored in a refrigerator, allow it to return to room temperature before cooking.

Fillet Steaks : Considered most tender when fried or grilled. Usually cut $\frac{1}{2}$-1 inch thick ; but in America, from 1-2 inches thick, according to taste. Known in France as *filet mignon.* A Chateaubriand usually means a large thick steak about 3 lb. in weight, cut from the centre of fillet, flattened, seasoned, brushed with olive oil and grilled for about 20 minutes, or fried in $\frac{1}{2}$ lb. butter.

Minute Steaks : Cut $\frac{1}{2}$-inch-thick steaks from any cut of beef suitable for frying or grilling.

Porterhouse Steaks : Steaks consisting of slices of sirloin, including upper and lower parts. Popular in the United States. Cut 1, $1\frac{1}{2}$ or 2 inches thick.

Rib Steaks : Thin steaks considered second to the fillet in France, where it is known as *entrecote.*

Rump Steaks : 1-$1\frac{1}{2}$ inches thick. Have to be beaten with a rolling-pin or meat mallet to break down the fibres to help tenderise meat. Many epicures consider rump better flavoured than fillet.

Sirloin Steaks : Steaks taken from the top part of the sirloin. Usually $1\frac{1}{2}$ inches thick.

HINTS ON FRYING STEAK

1. If thin steaks are wanted, beat with a mallet before cooking.
2. Add a dash of mushroom or Yorkshire Relish when making gravy in pan in which meat was cooked, when gravy is wanted.

FRIED STEAK

BASIC RECIPE :
1 lb. fillet or tender rump steak
Salt and pepper to taste
1-2 oz. butter or clarified fat
Maître d'Hôtel butter
Béarnaise sauce as required

Wipe meat. Trim off any skin or tendon. If frying in portions, cut in slices about $\frac{3}{4}$ inch thick. Flatten slightly. Before frying, prepare Maître d'Hôtel butter, and Béarnaise sauce, in the proportion of $\frac{1}{2}$ oz. butter and $\frac{1}{2}$ pint sauce to 1 lb. steak. Garnish with fried button onions, mushrooms or tomatoes. Season steak lightly. Heat frying-pan. Add fat. Heat till smoking, then add steak or steaks. Fry quickly for a minute, then lift meat a little to allow fat to run below. Fry for 5 minutes, then turn with steak tongs and finish cooking in 2-3 minutes. The right time to turn it is when you see tiny drops of juice breaking through top of steak. When frying, keep moving meat about over pan, so that it absorbs fat which might otherwise burn.

Turn only once. Some epicures prefer not to season until steak has cooked for 5 minutes. This is a matter of taste. When ready, serve on a hot dish and sprinkle with minced parsley. Reduce temperature. If frying with butter, melt an additional large " nut " and pour over, or top with Maître d'Hôtel butter. If frying with other fat, melt butter in another pan and be sure to allow other fat to drain out before dishing up. Arrange on whole steak enough slices of tomato, seasoned and fried, to serve four persons. If steak is cooked in portions, place 1 slice on each portion. Top tomato with Maître d'Hôtel butter when using it. Garnish with mushrooms in same way, but if using button onions, arrange them round, allowing 3 or 4 per person. Serve with potato straws or chips. *For 4 persons.*

TO GRILL STEAK

Steak should be cut from 1-1½ inches thick, according to taste, from tender fillet or rump. If grilling rump, flatten it with meat mallet or rolling-pin to tenderise it. Grease or oil the rack. Brush steak with melted butter or oil, and sprinkle with a few drops of lemon juice, if liked. Season with salt and pepper before cooking, or place rack under hot grill and grill for 2 minutes till seared, then season. In any case, after grilling for 2 minutes, turn with steak tongs and grill for 2 minutes on other side. Season if not seasoned before cooking. Lower heat. Continue grilling, turning frequently, until cooked to taste, allowing from 8-12 minutes or 15 minutes, according to whether rare, medium or well-done steaks are liked, as well as according to thickness.

To Serve Grilled Steaks:

1. Serve as described under " Fried."

2. Serve with Hollandaise sauce. Garnish with Maître d'Hôtel butter, soufflé potatoes, grilled mushrooms or tomatoes and asparagus tips and green peas.

3. Garnish with watercress. Serve with chip potatoes, and green peas or grilled tomatoes.

BAKED OR ROAST BEEF (Boeuf rôti)

Sirloin of beef
Salt and black pepper to taste
Flour as required

Weigh and wipe meat with damp cloth. Allowing ½ teaspoon salt to each lb. of meat, rub salt all over joint, either before roasting or at half time. Season with black pepper to taste, then rub lightly with flour. Place, fat side up, on a rack in an open shallow greased roasting tin. Roast in oven heated to 300° F., allowing 18-20 minutes for rare, 22-25 minutes for medium rare, and 27-30 minutes for well-done, per lb.

To Roast Rolled Ribs: Place ribs, prepared as above, lean side up, on rack. Plaster beef dripping all over top, and put a little dripping in baking tin. Roast, basting occasionally with hot dripping in pan, as for sirloin, allowing 10 minutes more per lb. If possible, substitute a layer of beef fat obtained from the butcher, for the dripping, as this will dispense with the basting.

To Roast Fillet of Beef: Fillet of beef, if properly larded, makes a prime joint. Place on rack in baking tin. Season with salt and pepper. Dredge with flour. Add enough melted beef dripping to cover bottom of tin. Bake, allowing 20 minutes per lb. for rare, 24-25 for medium rare, and 30 minutes for well-done beef. If requiring a moderately hot oven for any dish to be baked or roasted, allow 1 hour for fillet, basting 3 times during roasting. Remove skewer before dishing up, if two short fillets have been skewered and larded in place of the long or loin fillet usually roasted.

BAKED MEAT LOAF (Pain de Viande au four)

BASIC RECIPE:
1 lb. ground beef
1 beaten egg
2 dessertspoons minced parsley
½ oz. bacon fat or margarine
2 tablespoons breadcrumbs
1 tablespoon minced onion
Salt and black pepper to taste

Mix all the ingredients together, in order given. Pack down in a greased loaf tin. Cover with thickly greased paper. Bake in a moderate oven, 350° F., for 1 hour. Uncover and baste twice with tomato juice or boiling meat or vegetable stock, enriched with 2 tablespoons bacon or beef dripping. Drain liquid into a small saucepan. Thicken with flour creamed with cold stock. Turn out meat loaf. Serve hot with gravy, new potatoes and green peas, or cold with crisp lettuce leaves and tomato slices. *For 4 persons.*

Balmoral Loaf: Stir ½ lb. ground bacon and ½ teaspoon Worcester sauce in with the onion, and add another beaten egg. Press into a buttered mould. Cover with greased paper. Steam slowly for 3 hours. Turn out. Serve with green peas and fried potatoes. If preferred cold, dredge with toasted breadcrumbs or glaze. Garnish with devilled eggs, beetroot and lettuce hearts. *For 6 or 7 persons.*

Beef and Banana Loaf: Increase quantity of beef to 1½ lbs. and breadcrumbs to 1 cup. Add cup ground pork. Bake for about 1½ hours. Turn out loaf. Place 4 sliced bananas on top. Brush with melted butter. Bake till slightly browned. *For 6 persons.*

Ring of Meat: Bake in a greased ring mould. Turn out and chill. Fill centre with mayonnaise of peas, or with potato and green pea salad.

BOEUF A LA MODE

4 lb. rump steak
2 tablespoons dripping
4 medium-sized onions
1 lb. sliced carrot
2 cloves garlic
3 peeled shallots
1 calf's foot
1 lb. meaty bones
½ wineglass brandy
2 wineglasses graves
Salt and pepper to taste

Ask butcher to lard steak for you or lard it yourself with tiny " matches " of bacon fat. Melt dripping in a saucepan. Rub meat all over with seasoned flour. Brown for ¼ hour, turning occasionally. Remove meat. Add sliced onion, carrot, garlic, and peeled shallots. Stir occasionally till onions begin to brown, then replace meat in pan. Add calf's foot and bones. Pour brandy over meat and set it alight. When flame burns out, add wine. Season to taste with salt and pepper. Cover. Simmer for 4 hours, turning occasionally. When tender, arrange in a hot dish. Skim sauce. Remove bones and thin sauce, if desired, with water or stock. Arrange calf's foot and vegetables around meat and pour sauce round. If wanted cold, place meat in a mould. Arrange calf's foot on top. Cover with sauce and carrot. Weight and stand for 12 hours, then remove fat and turn out. Serve with salad. *For 12 persons.*

BOILED SALT SILVERSIDE

2 lb. silverside
Cold water as required
2 medium-sized scraped carrots
1 small peeled turnip
2 medium-sized onions
6 black peppercorns
12 small dumplings

Wash meat well. (If very salt, soak for a few hours in cold water, then wipe.) Tie into a neat round with a piece of string or tape. Place meat in a flat-bottomed pan. Cover with cold water. Bring to boiling point. Simmer gently for 1½ to 2 hours. Skim. Add sliced carrots, turnip, peeled onions and peppercorns. Cover and simmer for ¼ hour. Add dumplings and cook for ¼ hour. To serve, place meat on a hot dish, and arrange vegetables and dumplings round. *For 6 or 7 persons.*

DEVILLED STEAK (Boeuf au Diable)

2 tablespoons butter
1 large sliced onion
1½-2 lb. stewing steak
2 tablespoons flour
1 teaspoon salt
½ teaspoon pepper
¼ teaspoon paprika
1 teaspoon mustard
3 tablespoons vinegar
2 cups stock or hot water

Melt fat till smoking hot in a frying-pan. Add onion. When brown, remove from pan and cook steak, cut in strips and dipped in flour, in remaining fat. Remove meat from pan. Add seasonings, remainder of flour and the vinegar. Stir well for a moment or two, then add stock or hot water. Return steak to pan. Cover closely and simmer till tender from 2½ to 3 hours. Serve meat on a hot dish. Pour gravy over. Arrange boiled potatoes round. *For 6 persons.*

EXETER STEW (Ragoût à la Exeter)

1 lb. lean steak
2 oz. dripping
2 peeled onions
2 tablespoons flour
2 pints cold water
2 tablespoons vinegar
Salt and pepper to taste
½ lb. tomatoes
8 suet dumplings

Wipe and cut steak in neat pieces. Melt dripping and when smoking hot, brown steak. Lift on to a plate. Brown sliced onions lightly. Add flour. Stir well, then stir in water, vinegar and seasonings. Boil up and add steak and peeled tomatoes. Cover. Cook till steak is tender, in about 2 hours. Add dumplings. Stew for 20 minutes. Dish up meat. Arrange dumplings round. Pour gravy over. Serve with mashed or new potatoes. *For 4 persons.*

FRIED PORTERHOUSE STEAK
(Filet de Boeuf, Porterhouse frit)

2 lb. thick fillet of steak
Salt and pepper to taste
2 oz. butter
6 chopped shallots
¼ pint claret
½ gill aspic jelly
½ pint tomato sauce

Have the steak cut 1½ inch thick. Trim and beat till of even thickness. Season to taste with salt and pepper. Melt butter in a frying-pan and fry steak for about 12 minutes. Remove to a hot dish. Add shallots to butter. Cook for 2 or 3 minutes, stirring occasionally, then add claret. Cook till

1 clove garlic
½ teaspoon minced parsley
½ teaspoon minced chives

sauce is reduced to half its quantity, then add aspic jelly, tomato sauce, chopped garlic, parsley and chives. Stir till boiling. Simmer for 8 minutes. Pour over meat. Serve with chip potatoes. *For 7 or 8 persons.*

GRILLED MINUTE STEAKS, FLORIDA

2 chicken livers
3 tablespoons butter
4 very thin minute steaks
Salt and pepper to taste
Paprika to taste
2 or 3 tablespoons boiling water
Meat extract or cube
Vegetables to garnish

Wash, dry and cut livers into small pieces. Melt 2 tablespoons of the butter in a frying-pan. Add liver and fry slowly while grilling the steaks. Grill steaks first on one side, then on the other until brown, then cook slowly till tender. Season with salt, pepper and paprika to taste. Arrange on a hot flat dish. Cover with liver. Add remainder of butter to butter in frying pan. Stir in boiling water and meat extract to taste. Pour over steaks. Garnish with buttered runner beans, or green peas, and potato croquettes, or with sprigs of buttered cauliflower and potato straws. *For 4 persons.*

GRILLED STUFFED STEAK (Entrecôte de Boeuf grillé)

2 oz. mushrooms
1 small peeled onion
1 sprig tarragon
1 oz. butter
Salt and pepper to taste
2 tablespoons breadcrumbs
1 lb. rump steak
Sprigs of parsley

Choose small mushrooms. Wash, dry, peel and chop. Mince onion with the tarragon. Melt butter in a small saucepan. Add mushrooms and onion. Fry for 5 minutes. Stir in salt and pepper to taste and breadcrumbs. Mix well and leave till cold. Spread over steak. Fold steak and tie securely with string. Grill till brown on both sides, then grill for about 10 minutes, turning every 2 or 3 minutes. Serve on a hot dish garnished with parsley, potato chips and tomatoes. *For 3 or 4 persons.*

HAMBURG STEAKS (Médaillons de Boeuf, Américain)

BASIC RECIPE :
1½ lb. ground beef
1 cup breadcrumbs
1 teaspoon onion juice
1 teaspoon salt
Pepper and paprika to taste
1 egg yolk
Flour as required

Place meat with crumbs, onion juice, salt, pepper and paprika to taste in a basin. If lean, add a little minced, fat salt pork. Add the egg yolk. Mix with a wooden spoon till well blended, then divide into 6 equal portions. Shape with floured hands into flat round cakes about 1¼ inches thick. Handle them lightly and dip lightly in seasoned flour. If wanted grilled, brush with melted butter, and grill quickly on each side for 2 minutes, then grill slowly, turning occasionally, for 6 or 7 minutes. If wanted fried, melt 1 tablespoon of bacon fat, butter or dripping till smoking hot and fry till brown first on one side, then on the other. Cook all together from 7-10 minutes, according to taste. Arrange round a hot oval or round dish. Fill the centre with buttered peas or beans. Garnish each cake with shredded horseradish and arrange potato chips round the outside. They can also be garnished with fried or grilled tomatoes, watercress and potato straws. Serve with brown gravy, and tomato sauce. *For 6 persons.*

To Vary: (1) Omit onion juice from mixture, and serve garnished with fried onion rings, or haricot beans, etc. (2) Serve with a poached or steamed egg on top if a more substantial dish is wanted.

POT ROAST OF BEEF (Boeuf braisé, Anglais)

3 lb. round of beef
Flour as required
1 tablespoon beef dripping or lard
Salt and pepper to taste
¼ pint water or tomato juice
2 medium-sized peeled onions

Wipe meat with a damp cloth, then dredge with flour. Melt dripping or lard if preferred, in a heavy saucepan with a tightly fitting lid. Add beef, and turn frequently while it fries till equally brown all over. Season with salt and pepper to taste. Add water or tomato juice, then slice onions over meat if you have any available. Cover closely. Simmer gently for about 3 hours, till tender. Do not baste meat on any account. The steam rises and falls on the meat constantly. (If you like a highly flavoured pot roast, add a bay leaf and 3 or 4 whole cloves, and substitute 1 tablespoon vinegar for part of the quarter pint of liquid.) Again, you can add potatoes and carrots or turnips that you wish to serve with meat to the pan just long enough before dishing up to cook them. Baste them with liquor in pan when you insert them. Remember, too, that as the liquid cooks away you should add more, a little at a time, as required. Serve on a hot dish with vegetables round. Baste them with the gravy from pan. Serve with horseradish, grated or creamed, and mustard. *Serves 6 persons twice.*

STEWED BEEF, BURGOYNE (Boeuf Bourguignon)

1½ lb. stewing beef
4 thin rashers bacon
2 medium-sized onions
1 tablespoon flour
2½ cups Burgundy
1 blade mace
½ bay leaf
1 sprig parsley
½ wineglass brandy

Cut meat into squares 1 to 2 inches thick. Remove rind from bacon. Chop and fry lightly in a saucepan. Add meat. Brown well. Remove to a hot dish, then add chopped onion. Cook for a moment or two. Sprinkle in flour. Cook till frothy, then stir in wine. Return meat to pan. Add mace, bay leaf and parsley, then cover. Stew very slowly for 3 hours. When ready to serve, set brandy aflame. Add to stew and boil for a moment or two. *For 6 persons.*

STEWED STUFFED STEAK (Ragoût de Boeuf farci)

1½ lb. round of beef
1 heaped cup stale bread-crumbs
A little hot water
¼ cup shredded suet
2 oz. chopped boiled ham
Pepper to taste
Beef bone stock as required
4 young carrots
¼ lb. mushrooms
1½ tablespoons flour
Tomato catsup to taste

Wipe and pound meat on a board with a wooden mallet, or potato masher. Spread evenly with stuffing made in this way : Place crumbs in a basin. Add hot water to cover. Cover and stand for 5 minutes. Turn into a sieve. Drain off all water. Turn into basin. Stir in suet, ham and pepper to taste. (Add a pinch of crushed herbs or a teaspoon of minced parsley if liked). Roll up steak. Tie securely with string. Place in a casserole. Barely cover with hot bone stock. Cover. Cook in a slow oven for about 2 hours. After cooking for ¾ hour, add prepared carrots and peeled mushrooms. When ready, dish up carefully. Remove string. Mix flour with 2 or 3 tablespoons cold water. Pour into a saucepan. Stir in hot stock from casserole. Stir till boiling. Flavour to taste with tomato catsup. Pour over steak and spoon carrots and mushrooms round. Serve with mashed potatoes. *For 6 persons.*

SWISS MEAT ROLL (Roulade de Viande à la Suisse)

½ cup stale breadcrumbs
2 tablespoons stock or gravy
1 beaten egg
Dash Worcester sauce
Pinch crushed herbs
2 medium-sized onions
Salt and pepper to taste
¾ lb. ground beef
½ lb. ground pork
2 tablespoons dripping
1½ cups chopped boiled carrots
Pinch dry mustard

Soak crumbs in stock or gravy in a basin for 10 minutes. Stir in egg and Worcester sauce. Stand for 5 minutes. Beat till smooth. Add herbs, 1 peeled chopped onion or 3 tablespoons minced leek, and salt and pepper to taste. Add beef and pork. Mix well. Turn out mixture on to a sheet of waxed paper. Shape into an oblong about ½ inch thick. Lay a piece of waxed paper on top and press with a rolling pin to even firmness. Melt dripping in a frying-pan. Add remaining onion, peeled and chopped, or 2 tablespoons chopped leek. Cook, stirring frequently, till onion or leek changes colour. Add carrot and mustard. Mix well. Remove waxed paper from top of meat. Spread carrot filling on top. Roll up like a swiss roll, and right on to a greased baking sheet. Bake in a moderate oven, 350° F., for 1¼-1½ hours. Serve with mushroom sauce or brown gravy. *For 6 persons.*

VIENNA STEAKS (Médaillons de Boeuf, Viennoise)

1 lb. finely chopped steak
1 teaspoon crushed herbs
Salt and pepper to taste
1 beaten egg
1 tablespoon flour
1½ oz. butter
2 peeled large onions
½ pint hot brown sauce

Place steak in a basin. Stir in herbs and salt and pepper to taste. Mix well and bind with egg. Divide into 4 equal portions. Shape into 4 or 5 flat cakes, about an inch thick. Dip in flour and shake. Melt 1 oz. of the butter in a frying-pan. Add steaks, and fry rather quickly until brown below, then turn and brown on other side. Fry slowly, turning once or twice, till cooked through. While cakes are frying, melt remainder of fat. Slice and divide onions into rings and fry slowly till soft, stirring occasionally. Arrange steaks on a flat hot dish. Top each with a dab of brown sauce. Serve remainder in a hot sauceboat. Garnish round with onion rings. Serve with fried chips and green peas. *For 4 or 5 persons.*

LAMB

Lamb is seasonable from March to September, but prime when 6-12 weeks old, from May to July, when mint is at its best. It is on the market from the end of December to March, but it is scarce and expensive. Canterbury and other imported lamb is available all the year round. Canterbury lamb, which comes from New Zealand, is considered the best. More delicately flavoured than mutton, lamb is not so nourishing, but it is more digestible than veal.

TO CHOOSE LAMB

Choose fine, firm-grained flesh, light pink in shade, with brittle creamy-white fat. If fat is yellow and lean, flabby and red, lamb will not keep. When buying, inspect the leg. In a young animal, the joint is rather jagged ; later on it becomes smooth. The bones of young lamb should be pink or slightly streaked with red. Decide before buying whether you want to grill, roast or stew meat. All cuts, except the neck and shank, are tender enough to be grilled or roasted. If you want chops, choose between loin, rib and shoulder. Young lamb is usually sold in hind and forequarters. The forequarter consists of the breast, neck and shoulder, and the hindquarter of the loin and leg. Both the forequarters and the hindquarters are usually roasted whole. When catering for a large family, you'll find the forequarter of an older lamb an economical buy. When buying lamb for roasting, see that the " caul " or " fell," the thin papery covering of the internal organs, which is semi-transparent and interlaced with fat, comes with the meat. It protects any joint while cooking and helps the leg retain its shape.

LAMB CHART

This chart will give you the time required to cook the different cuts of lamb. The time is only approximate as the cuts vary in thickness and size according to the age and size of the animal. As lamb is immature, it should be thoroughly cooked, though if you like Continental cooking, you may prefer your joint " rosé," which means cooked until the flesh is only a pinkish, grayish brown, or in other words, medium done. A joint of lamb should have plump and juicy flesh, and a crisp golden brown skin.

Oven Temperature : Slow, 300° F.

CUTS	METHOD	TIME REQUIRED
Breast	Roast stuffed	About 2 hours.
Chops	Fried	10-15 minutes, 5-7$\frac{1}{2}$ on each side according to thickness.
	Grilled	$\frac{3}{4}$-1 inch thick—8-12 minutes.
		1$\frac{1}{2}$-2 inches thick—20-25 minutes.
Fillet (part of leg)	Fried	10-15 minutes.
Forequarter	Roasted	1$\frac{1}{2}$-2$\frac{1}{2}$ hours, according to size.
Hindquarter	Roasted	20 minutes per lb. and 20 minutes over.
Leg	Boiled	15 minutes per lb.
	Roasted	30 minutes per lb.
	Roasted, boned and stuffed	35 minutes per lb.
Loin	Roasted	30-35 minutes per lb.
Neck	Stewed	1-1$\frac{1}{2}$ hours.
	Roasted	$\frac{3}{4}$-1 hour (2 lb. in weight).
Shank	Braised	1-1$\frac{1}{2}$ hours.

CUTS	METHOD	TIME REQUIRED
Shoulder	Roasted	30 minutes per lb.
	Roasted and stuffed	35 minutes per lb.
Tails	Stewed	About 2 hours.

ACCOMPANIMENTS TO LAMB

Baked or roast lamb (hot)	Mint sauce, red currant or apple and rowan jelly, mint sauce or currant jelly, brown gravy, roast potatoes.
Baked or roast lamb (cold)	Mint or red currant jelly, pickles or chutneys and salad.
Roast Saddle (hot) (Do not use garlic with saddle of lamb)	Béarnaise or onion sauce, macedoine of vegetables tossed in melted butter, and Pommes Rissolées.
Boiled	Caper or onion sauce, boiled or mashed potatoes, green peas, carrots and turnips.
Chops (Fried or Grilled)	New potatoes. Garnish with fried or grilled tomatoes and mushrooms, Maître d'Hôtel or herb butter. Serve with demi-glace sauce.

ROAST LAMB

Saddle is a party joint. Leg, loin, best end neck and shoulder all make excellent joints. The breast, boned and stuffed, is an economical and appetising joint, easy to carve. The shoulder and leg can also be boned and stuffed before roasting. If you like the flavour of garlic, rub joint with a peeled clove of garlic, or make tiny slits here and there in the skin and insert slivers of garlic before roasting.

ROAST LEG OF LAMB (Agneau rôti)

BASIC RECIPE :
1 leg of lamb (5-6 lb.)
Salt and pepper to taste
Flour as required if liked

Weigh and wipe lamb with a damp cloth. Season with salt and pepper to taste. Rub with flour if liked. The shank bone can be removed by the butcher if desired. Don't remove the " caul " or " fell." Place, fat side up, on rack in an open baking tin. Roast joint in usual way in a slow oven, 300°-325° F., and 35 minutes extra for well-done meat.

To Vary: (1) Insert slivers of garlic in the skin, or a clove in the joint of leg. If the latter, remove before serving. (2) Baste lamb with melted butter flavoured with lemon juice, before cooking, at half-time and shortly before dishing up. (3) Brush with melted red currant jelly 3 or 4 minutes before serving, or baste ½ hour before serving with equal quantity of red currant jelly and boiling water to glaze.

To Roast Saddle of Lamb: Follow directions for roast leg of lamb, but allow ½ hour less time. Roast, smooth side up, for 30 minutes before serving.

ROAST CROWN OF LAMB (Coronet d'Agneau rôti)

Get the butcher to prepare a roast containing from 12 to 15 ribs, or two " racks," each containing 6 or 7 ribs taken from opposite sides of the lamb. Slice half-way down bones and scrape rib ends. With your hands, bend the two pieces round into the shape of a crown or coronet, joining them together at each side with skewers. Now tie string round to keep them in position. Place in a roasting pan. Season with salt and pepper. Pack stuffing into centre, if liked. Tie on to the top of each bone a little piece of salt pork or fat bacon to prevent ends charring. Roast in a slow oven, 300° F., allowing 35 minutes per lb. If using stuffing, either cover with greased paper and remove shortly before serving, or cook uncovered, and cover with paper only when stuffing shows signs of drying out. Remove fat from each bone and slip a paper frill over each one. Serve with red currant jelly and brown gravy. *Allow 2 ribs per person.*

Roast Candle of Lamb (Côtes d'Agneau, Américain) : This is only one " rack " or set of rib chops prepared for roasting in the same manner as the roast crown, except that the chops are not shaped into a crown.

ROAST SHOULDER OF LAMB WITH SPINACH STUFFING
(Epaule d'Agneau, rôti aux Epinards)

1 scraped carrot
1 peeled onion
2 sprigs parsley
2 oz. fat bacon
2 cloves
18 peppercorns
1 bay leaf
1 sprig thyme
1 boned shoulder of lamb
Salt and pepper to taste
1 lb. picked spinach
2 egg yolks
½ teaspoon sugar
2 saltspoons grated nutmeg
½ gill cold water
Melted lard as required
¼ pint jellied stock
½ teaspoon meat glaze

Slice carrot and onion and chop parsley. Remove rind from bacon. Cut rashers into 6 or 7 pieces. Mix well. Stir in cloves, peppercorns, bay leaf and thyme, and spread on bottom of a greased roasting tin. Season boned shoulder with salt and pepper to taste. Boil spinach for 10 minutes in salted water, then drain well on a sieve. Mince and place in a saucepan with egg yolks, sugar, nutmeg and salt and pepper to taste. Stir till well mixed and piping hot. Spread on inside of shoulder. Fold shoulder neatly and roll up. Tie carefully into shape, and place on top of vegetable mixture. Add water. Spread lamb with melted lard. Roast for 1¾ hours, basting frequently with the liquor in tin. When ready, arrange on a hot dish. Remove ties. Skim fat from gravy in tin. Stir in jellied stock and meat glaze. Bring to boil. Simmer for 5 minutes. Strain over lamb. *For 8 persons.*

BAKED STUFFED LAMB CHOPS (Côtes d'Agneau rôties)

BASIC RECIPE :
6 lamb chops
Salt and pepper to taste
3 tablespoons melted butter
1 tablespoon minced onion
1 cup chopped peeled mushrooms
1½ tablespoons flour

With a sharp, pointed kitchen knife, cut meat of chops, which should be 1½ inches thick, through to the bone. Fry or grill till brown on both sides. Season to taste with salt and pepper. Melt butter in frying-pan. Add onion and mushrooms. Cook slowly until onions are pale brown. Stir in flour, water, and tomato catsup to taste. Keep stirring

1 dessertspoon water
Tomato catsup to taste

until thick, then pack into "pockets" of chops. Secure in place with skewers. Place side by side in a buttered fireproof dish. Bake in a moderately hot oven, 375° F., for about 25 minutes. *For 6 persons.*

To Vary: Bone neck or rib chops. Starting at the thick end, tuck half a sheep's kidney, or a mushroom, seasoned to taste, into the thick part of meat, then curl the narrow meat round it so that you have a flat cake with kidney or mushroom in centre. Remove rind from enough streaky rashers of bacon to encircle cakes. Draw a rasher around each and secure with skewer or tie. Now you have meat cakes, each inside a ring of bacon. Place side by side on a rack in a baking tin. Brush each with melted butter and lay rind on top of each cake. Bake in a moderate oven, 350° F., turning at half-time, for about 20 minutes. If liked, lay a slice of peeled seeded orange on top of each, 5 minutes before finishing cooking, otherwise serve each with a pat of herb or Maître d'Hôtel butter melting on top. Remove skewers or ties. Dish up. Garnish with sprigs of watercress, potato ribbons, straws or chips and green peas.

BOILED LEG OF LAMB WITH PARSLEY SAUCE
(Gigot d'Agneau bouilli)

1 5-lb. leg of lamb
Slices of carrots
Slices of turnips
Sprigs of cauliflower
Salt and pepper to taste
1 pint white sauce
2 tablespoons minced parsley

Boil lamb slowly for 1¾ hours, in water to cover. When tender, dish it up and garnish with slices of boiled carrots, turnips and cauliflower sprigs. Season white sauce to taste with salt and pepper. Add parsley. Pour half of the sauce over the leg. Serve remainder of it in a sauceboat. Put a frill on the bone and serve leg with boiled potatoes. *For 6 persons.*

BRAISED LAMB (Agneau braisé)

1 boned leg of lamb
Salt and pepper to taste
¼ cup dripping
1 medium-sized onion
2 young carrots
1 small white turnip
1 sprig parsley
1 sprig thyme
1 bay leaf
1 pint boiling stock or water

Stuff cavities in lamb with herb stuffing, if liked, otherwise season with salt and pepper to taste. Melt dripping in deep stew pan. Peel and slice in onion. Scrape and slice in carrots and peel and slice in turnip. Add parsley, thyme and bay leaf. Cook all slowly together for 5 minutes. Turn into a deep fireproof dish. Add lamb, skewered or sewn in shape, then water and salt and pepper to taste. Cover. Bake in a moderate oven, 350° F., for 2 hours. Remove cover. Bake for ½ hour. Serve with new or mashed potatoes. *For 6 persons.*

BRAISED STUFFED BREAST OF LAMB
(Poitrine d'Agneau, farcie braisée)

½ lb. cleaned spinach
1 tablespoon chopped green pepper

Wash spinach thoroughly. Cut finely and place in a pan with pepper, onion and half the butter. Cook long enough to wilt spinach slightly—about

1 tablespoon chopped onion
4 tablespoons butter
2 cups dried breadcrumbs
2 tablespoons chopped celery
Breast of lamb
Salt and pepper to taste

2 minutes. Stir constantly. Push spinach to one side of pan. Melt remainder of butter in other part of pan. Mix with breadcrumbs so that butter is absorbed. Add celery. Stir till rather dry. Simmer breast of lamb till tender in water to cover. Remove from broth. Remove bones from lamb. Allow to cool. Spread out the breast. Cover with a thin layer of prepared stuffing and roll. Tie at both ends with clean white string. Place rolled meat in a baking tin. Sprinkle lightly with flour, then pour $\frac{1}{4}$ cup of broth round it. Brown in a hot oven, 425° F. When serving, slice meat from end to end of roll. The green pepper can be omitted from stuffing, if preferred. *For 6 persons.*

GRILLED LAMB CHOPS (Côtes d'Agneau, grillées)

3 lamb chops
Salt and pepper to taste
Butter as required

Remove outer skin and excess fat from chops. Place on greased rack in grill pan. Sear one side quickly, then turn and sear on other side. Continue cooking according to taste, allowing about 10 minutes altogether for chops about an inch thick. Season with salt and pepper to taste. Smear with butter. Arrange on a bank of mashed potatoes. Pour brown or tomato sauce round. Garnish with sprigs of parsley and green peas. *For 3 persons.*

GRILLED STUFFED LAMB CAKES
(Médaillons d'Agneau, grillées)

6 rib chops
6 peeled mushrooms
1 tablespoon butter
Salt and pepper to taste

Carefully remove meat from each chop, then trim any skin from meat. Tuck a mushroom at long end and wrap end round to form a flat circular piece. Skewer in place. Brush with melted butter. Grill for 3 minutes on each side, then continue to cook, turning often, until grilled to taste. Remove skewer. Sprinkle on both sides with salt and pepper. Serve each with a pat of parsley butter melting on top. *For 6 persons.*

LAMB HOT-POT (Hochepot d'Agneau)

1½ lb. stewing lamb
1 quart water
2 tablespoons dripping
1 onion or chopped spring
  onions
½ cup diced carrot
½ cup diced turnip
6 peeled medium-sized
  potatoes
8 dumplings
1 teaspoon salt
¼ teaspoon pepper

Trim meat. Cut into cubes, 2 inches square. Place meat trimmings with bones, if any, in a stew-pan. Add water. Cover and cook over a low heat till boiling. Simmer for $\frac{1}{4}$ hour. Meanwhile dredge meat cubes with flour. Melt dripping in a frying pan. Add meat cubes and fry till brown, turning occasionally. Add meat to stew. Cover and simmer gently for 1 hour. Peel and slice onion. Add carrot and turnip to fat in frying pan. Fry till all remaining fat is absorbed, then add to stew, rinsing frying pan with a little of the liquid from stew. Cover and simmer gently for $\frac{3}{4}$ hour. Remove bones, if there are any. Add potatoes, par-boiled for 10 minutes, then drained. Cover. Simmer for 5 minutes. Add dumplings. Season with salt and pepper. Cover and cook rapidly for about ¾ hour. *For 8 persons.*

MUTTON

Seasonable all the year round. Southdown is of the highest quality. It has a distinctive flavour on account of the sheep having been reared on the salt marshes or near the sea coast. Sheep reared on mountainside and moorland also produce fine mutton, with a slightly " gamey " flavour. Most nourishing mutton is said to come from sheep 3-6 years old.

TO CHOOSE MUTTON

Prime mutton should be dark coloured with firm flesh. Younger mutton is flabby. Small boned mutton is generally sweeter and finer in texture than large boned. Choose short plump legs and shoulders rather than " leggy " ones. You can be sure of the age of sheep by looking at the breast bones. When about 4 years old, the red breast bone of the lamb will have become white, and all bones smooth and dry. New Zealand mutton, available all the year round, when of high quality, is scarcely distinguishable from British mutton.

MUTTON CHART

This chart will give you some idea of the time required to cook the different cuts of mutton. The times are only approximate as the cuts vary in thickness and size according to the breed of sheep.

Oven Temperature : Slow, 325° F.

CUTS	METHOD	TIME REQUIRED
Breast	Boiled, boned and stuffed	About 2 hours.
Leg	Boiled	20 minutes per lb.
	Braised and stuffed	3 hours on stove or in slow oven, 275° F. uncovering last half hour.
	Roasted	30-35 minutes per lb.
Loin	Roasted	About 30 minutes per lb.
Neck	Braised	About 2 hours.
	Roasted	About 30 minutes per lb.
Shoulder	Braised and stuffed	About 3 hours.
	Roasted and stuffed	35 minutes per lb.

ACCOMPANIMENTS TO MUTTON

Baked or roast mutton (hot)	Currant or mint sauce, brown gravy, and roast potatoes, etc.
Baked or roast mutton (cold)	Currant or mint jelly, pickles and salads, jacket or scalloped potatoes.

Boiled mutton (hot)	Caper, olive or parsley sauce, boiled carrots and turnips and mashed potatoes.
Boiled mutton (cold)	Pickled onions : potato or Russian salad. Garnish with watercress.

ROAST MUTTON (Mouton rôti)

Mutton is never cooked rare, and is usually roasted until well-done. If you prefer your joint faintly pink, allow a minute or two less per lb. Before roasting you must weigh joint and allow time for roasting according to taste. In Scotland, roast mutton is sometimes rubbed all over with flour and seasoned with black pepper before roasting. If you like the sophisticated flavour garlic gives to mutton cooked on the Continent, peel a clove of garlic, halve it and rub it over the lean part. Now cut the halves into slivers and insert them here and there in slits in the skin. When roasting a leg of mutton and you find the shank too long for your baking tin, remove it, and roast joint with the curved side uppermost. The shank can be turned into soup. As the loin and neck are difficult joints to carve, have them both well jointed by the butcher. When you want to roast neck without boning, have the butcher saw the rib bones 3 inches down, then fold this part under and secure with string or cotton before roasting.

ROAST STUFFED LOIN OF MUTTON (Longe de Mouton rôti)

Boned loin of mutton
3 tablespoons stale bread-crumbs
2 tablespoons minced bacon or ham
2 tablespoons shredded suet
2 teaspoons minced parsley
1 teaspoon crushed herbs
Salt and pepper to taste
Milk or stock to moisten

Weigh and wipe meat with a damp cloth. Trim off any superfluous fat. Flatten with a rolling pin. Mix crumbs with bacon or ham, suet, parsley, herbs and salt and pepper to taste. Add ½ teaspoon grated lemon rind or paprika if liked. Moisten with milk or mutton stock or add a beaten egg and milk as required. Spread over the inside of the meat to within an inch of the edge and tie with tape. Weigh. Bake in a slow oven, 325° F., allowing 30 minutes per lb. Serve with brown gravy and onion sauce.

ROAST STUFFED NECK OF MUTTON
(Carré de Mouton farcie rôtie)

3 tablespoons stale bread-crumbs
1½ tablespoons shredded suet or margarine
½ teaspoon minced parsley
½ teaspoon crushed herbs
Salt and black pepper to taste
1 beaten egg
1 clove garlic or tablespoon minced onion

Mix bread crumbs with the suet or margarine, parsley, herbs, salt and pepper to taste, and enough of the egg to make a moist stuffing. Add a minced clove of garlic before the egg if you like, or a tablespoon minced onion. Bone mutton and stuff. Roll up and tie. Place dripping in roasting pan. Melt in oven. When hot, place meat in tin with peeled potatoes round. Baste both well with

2½—3 lbs. neck of mutton
2 oz. mutton or bacon dripping
3 lb. potatoes

fat. Bake in a slow oven, 325° F., allowing 3c minutes per lb. *For 8 persons.*

BOILED MUTTON A LA FRANCAISE
(Mouton bouilli, Française)

6 pints cold water
1 bay leaf
1 sprig thyme
1 blade mace
2 cloves
1 pinch curry powder
1 teaspoon salt
4 oz. carrots
3 oz. turnips
5 lb. leg of mutton

Turn water, bay leaf, thyme, mace, cloves, curry powder, salt and sliced vegetables into a large saucepan or fish-kettle. Bring to boil and boil 1 hour. Meanwhile, trim mutton and wipe over with a damp cloth. Place mutton, thick side downward, in seasoned water. Cover and simmer from 1½ to 2 hours, allowing 20 minutes to the pound. Remove mutton from pan and place on serving dish. Serve with caper sauce. *For 8 persons.*

BREDEE

3 tablespoons butter or margarine
2 medium-sized onions
1½ lb. mutton
4 cups sliced peeled tomatoes
1 tablespoon chopped green or red pepper
2 teaspoons sugar
¼ teaspoon pepper
½ cup water

Melt butter or margarine in a shallow saucepan. Peel and mince onion and add. Fry till golden brown, turning frequently. Add mutton. Cut into small pieces suitable for serving. Fry quickly for a minute or two, stirring frequently to prevent onion burning. Add remaining ingredients. Cover. Simmer gently for about 2 hours, till tender, stirring occasionally, and adding more water if necessary. When dish is ready, there should only be about ½ cup of liquid left. Serve with mashed potatoes and boiled rice. *For 6 persons.*

CASSEROLE OF MUTTON CHOPS
(Côtes de Mouton en casserole)

1 tablespoon butter
4 chump chops
1 cup sliced carrots
½ cup diced turnip
½ cup diced celery
½ cup chopped onion
1½ tablespoons flour
Salt and pepper to taste
1¾ cups stock or water

Melt butter in a frying-pan. Brown chops on both sides. Place mixed vegetables in a casserole. Arrange chops on top. Pour off the fat into a saucepan. (If chops are fat, use only half the dripping.) Add flour and salt and pepper to taste, then stock or water. Boil up. Pour over chops. Cover closely. Bake in a slow oven, 325° F., for 1½ hours. Skim before serving. *For 4 persons.*

CURRIED MUTTON (Kari de Mouton)

2 oz. butter
1 dessertspoon chopped onion
1 small apple
¾ oz. flour

Melt half the butter in a saucepan. Chop onion and apple. Add and fry lightly for 2 or 3 minutes. Stir in flour and curry powder. Cook for about 2 minutes. Stir in stock, lemon juice, desiccated

½ oz. curry powder
½ pint chicken or veal stock
1 dessertspoon lemon juice
2 teaspoons desiccated coconut
Salt to taste
1 lb. lean mutton
1 teaspoon chutney
½ gill milk
1 tablespoon cream
1 pint boiled rice
1 teaspoon white vinegar
Minced parsley and lemon to decorate

coconut and salt to taste. Stir well together. Continue to stir sauce till boiling. Skim and simmer while you are preparing meat. Cut meat into blocks 1 inch square. Melt remainder of butter in a large saucepan. Add meat. Fry for 2 or 3 minutes. Stir occasionally. Add curry sauce. Cover and simmer for 2 hours. Re-season if necessary. Add chutney, milk and cream. Stir till boiling. Boil rice in salted water containing 1 teaspoon white vinegar to whiten. Arrange curried mutton in centre of a hot dish and spoon rice round in a border. Decorate with minced parsley and lemon slices. *For 4 persons.*

HARICOT OF MUTTON (Haricot de Mouton)

2 lb. best end of mutton
1 oz. butter or dripping
2 medium-sized carrots
2 peeled onions
2 small turnips
1 oz. flour
¾ pint stock or water
Salt and pepper to taste

Wipe mutton with a damp cloth. Divide into chops. If very fat, trim off some of the fat. Melt butter, dripping, or the fat from meat in a saucepan. Add meat and brown. Remove to a plate. Slice and add carrots, onions and turnips. Fry for 2 or 3 minutes. Stir in flour then stock and meat. Turn into a casserole. Season to taste. Cook in a moderate oven, 350° F., for 2 hours. Serve with mashed potatoes. *For 4 to 6 persons.*

IRISH STEW (Ragoût de Mouton, Irlandaise)

1½ lb. neck of mutton
3 large peeled onions
¾ pint cold water
2 lb. peeled potatoes
Salt and pepper to taste

Wipe and divide neck into suitable portions. Trim off any skin. Place a layer of meat in the bottom of a shallow saucepan. Cover with sliced onions, then with remainder of meat. Add water. Cover. Bring to boil. Uncover and simmer for ½ hour. Place half the meat and onions in bottom of another saucepan. Season. Slice and add half the potatoes. Sprinkle with salt and pepper to taste. Cover with the remainder of the meat and onions and then with the potatoes. Season again. Add all the stock from first pan. Cover and simmer for 1 hour, stirring occasionally. Remove from stove. Stand for 5 minutes, then serve. *For 4 to 6 persons.*

LANCASHIRE HOT-POT (Hochepot, Lancashire)

2 lb. best end neck of mutton
1 peeled onion
2 lb. potatoes
3 sheep's kidneys
12 oysters, if liked
Salt and pepper to taste
½ pint stock or gravy
1 oz. butter

Divide meat into cutlets and trim. Put trimmings, short rib bones and onion into a stewpan. Make into stock with cold water. Put a layer of potato in the bottom of a fireproof dish. Arrange cutlets slightly overlapping on top. Cover with sliced kidney and oysters. Oysters can be omitted, or ½ lb. peeled mushrooms and 2 oz. diced ham can be used instead. Season well and repeat layers, ending with a layer of halved potatoes. Pour stock down the side. Dab with butter, then cover and bake from 2 to 3 hours in a moderate oven, 350° F. Remove cover, and brown before serving. This hot-pot may require the addition of a little more gravy before serving in the dish in which it was cooked. *For 6 persons.*

MUTTON PILAFF (Pilau de Mouton)

¾ lb. mutton (shoulder meat)
2 medium-sized onions
2 oz. cooking fat
2½ cups stock
1 cup rice
Pinch allspice
Pinch mace
Salt and pepper to taste

Cut meat into small pieces and chop onions coarsely. Fry meat and onion in fat till browned. Pour off fat. Add boiling stock to meat. Cover and simmer for 1 hour. Meanwhile, fry washed and dried rice in remaining fat, adding a little more if necessary. Add rice, meat with spices and seasoning. Cover and cook gently about 20 minutes, till rice is soft. Uncover pan and stir frequently till liquid is absorbed. Turn on to a hot dish. If you like, press mixture into a greased basin and heat in oven for a few moments, then turn out. *For 4 persons.*

SHASHLYK

This is a form of Kebabs, popular in Russia, sometimes made with calf's kidney instead of mutton.

1½ lb. lean mutton
2 oz. bacon
Salt and pepper to taste
3 tablespoons butter
2 spring onions
½ cup rice
1 peeled onion
1½ cups stock

Wipe mutton. Cut into 1½ inch squares, about ⅛ inch thick. Cut bacon to fit. Season mutton with salt and pepper to taste. Run mutton and bacon alternately on to thin skewers. Place skewers of meat side by side in a frying-pan. Fry slowly, turning frequently, until half ready. Pour off dripping and add a heaped teaspoon of butter. Chop spring onions and place in pan alongside meat. Baste with fat in pan. Cover and cook for about 20 minutes, then uncover and fry slowly until mutton is tender. Meanwhile, rinse rice and place in saucepan with remainder of butter and salt to taste. Chop onion finely and add. Stew over slow heat, stirring contantly until rice begins to turn yellow, then add stock. Cover pan and steam slowly for 15-20 minutes, or transfer to a casserole and cook in a slow oven, 300° F., for the same period of time. Arrange in a mound or border on a hot dish. Lay skewers of meat on top. Pour in gravy from meat. *For 6 persons.*

PORK

Seasonable from September to April, it is more difficult to digest than any other meat as it is more fatty, but it is high in food value. Pork should always be thoroughly cooked. If not it is unpalatable.

TO CHOOSE PORK

The flesh should be pale pink in colour and the tissues finely grained. Choose with clear skin and fat and see that the flesh yields when pressed. The best pork has a thin delicate rind.

PORK CHART

This chart will give you some idea of the time required to cook the different cuts of pork. The times are only approximate as the cuts vary in thickness, size and amount of bone.

Oven Temperature : Moderate, 350° *F.*

CUTS	METHOD	TIME REQUIRED
Belly	Boiled	20 minutes per lb.
Chine	Boiled	30 minutes per lb.
Foreloin	Roasted	25 minutes per lb. and 25 minutes over.
Hand	Boiled	30 minutes per lb.
Head	Boiled	3½ hours.
	Roasted	1-1½ hours.
Leg	Roasted	35-40 minutes per lb.
Loin—4 lb.	Roasted	35-40 minutes per lb.
Shoulder (boned and rolled)	Roasted	4-6 lb. 40-45 minutes per lb.
Spare Ribs	Roasted	About 1½ hours.
Tenderloin	Roasted	About 1 hour.

ACCOMPANIMENTS TO PORK

Baked or Roast Pork (hot)	Apple sauce or apple and onion sauce, but not when pork has apple stuffing, new or roast potatoes, braised celery or chicory, buttered Brussels sprouts, or baked or breaded tomatoes.
Baked or Roast Pork (cold)	Apple chutney and potato salad garnished watercress, or mango chutney and Waldorf salad.
Boiled Pork	Parsley sauce and boiled carrots or parsnips, and pease pudding.
Fried and Grilled Chops	Maître d'Hôtel butter, fried potatoes and green peas, string beans or braised endive and chestnut purée.
Sucking Pig	Chestnut or herb stuffing, brain sauce, roast potatoes and cabbage or green peas. Garnish with watercress and strings of cranberries. Place an apple or orange in its mouth.

ROAST PORK (Porc rôti)

BASIC : See that the butcher cracks the bones so that the meat can be carved in slices between the ribs. Wipe joint with a damp cloth. Season with salt and pepper to taste and rub with flour. Score skin. Place loin, fat side up, and ribs downward, on a rack in an open baking tin. Bake in a moderate oven, 350° F., allowing 40 minutes per lb. Serve garnished with glazed apple rings, or serve with apple sauce, and decorate with parsley or watercress. Serve with roast potatoes.

To Vary: (1) Rub pork lean with a cut clove of garlic before roasting. (2) Baste with cider at half-hour intervals while cooking.

Stuffing for Pork : Apple, apple and prune, celery, celery and olive, herb, onion, orange, sausage.

A PIG WITHOUT A HEAD (Cochon sans Tête)

Streaky pork
Salt to taste
3 medium-sized onions
2 medium-sized cooking apples
¾ teaspoon crushed sage
1 saltspoon pepper
¾ teaspoon caster sugar
Dripping as required
1 cup boiling water
Fried apple slices to garnish

Choose a thin piece of the streaky pork, about 6 inches wide and 10 inches long. Salt it well and cover. Stand for 24 hours. Peel and chop onions and apples. Stir in sage, pepper and sugar. Dip pork in cold water. Wipe dry. Place on a board, with skin downwards, then cut out all the bones and remove loose fat below. Spread stuffing equally over. Roll up pork as tightly as possible. Sew it up with fine white string. Rub skin well all over with dripping. Place on a rack in a baking tin. Roast, basting frequently, for 2½ hours. Dish up pork. Cut twine in the middle. Pull out from each end. Pour off fat into a bowl. Stir boiling water into the essence in baking tin and season. Strain into hot sauceboat. Garnish meat with fried apple slices. Serve with roast potatoes. *For 4 or 5 persons.*

CROWN ROAST OF PORK (Coronet de Porc)

2 sets back ribs of equal size
1¼ pints stuffing
Salt and pepper to taste

Method: Prepare and roast like " Roast Crown of Lamb." See page 214. Roast, uncovered, in a slow oven, 325° F., for 2½-3 hours. Baste stuffing occasionally with fat in pan. Serve with brown gravy, and apple sauce. Garnish round base with an overlapping wreath of fried apple wedges. *For 6 persons.*

ROAST STUFFED SHOULDER OF PORK
(Epaule de Porc rôti)

BASIC RECIPE :
3-4 lb. shoulder of pork
Salt and pepper to taste
2 cups stale breadcrumbs
3 tablespoons minced celery
2 tablespoons melted butter
1 tablespoon minced onion

Have butcher bone shoulder. Wipe meat with a damp cloth. Place shoulder, fat side down, on a board. With a sharp knife, make 1 or 2 gashes in the flesh where thickest to provide pockets for stuffing. Sprinkle pockets and rest of shoulder with salt and pepper. Mix crumbs and celery

½ tablespoon minced parsley
1 teaspoon minced chives
¼ teaspoon crushed herbs
1 saltspoon celery seed
Flour as required

with butter. Add onion and parsley. Cook gently for 3 or 4 minutes, stirring occasionally. Add chives, herbs and celery seed. Stir till blended. Pack into pockets. Sew edges of shoulder together to form a large pocket, and fill lightly with remainder of stuffing. Sew up or skewer opening. Season a tablespoon or two of flour with salt and pepper and rub all over outside of shoulder. Score, if liked. Place on a rack in an open roasting pan. Bake in a moderate oven, 350° F., until tender, allowing 35-40 minutes per lb.

To Vary : (1) Substitute 1 cup chestnut purée for 1 cup crumbs in stuffing. Add ½ teaspoon grated lemon rind. (2) Substitute ½ cup chopped mushrooms for ½ cup of the crumbs. (3) Substitute a square cut piece of boned shoulder for the joint. Sew up on three sides, then stuff and sew up fourth side.

ROAST SUCKING PIG (Cochon de Lait rôti)

1 sucking pig, about 3 weeks old
6 oz. breadcrumbs
2 medium-sized onions
1 teaspoon crushed sage
Salt and pepper to taste
¼ pint thick cream
Slices of lemon

See that the butcher scalds, scrapes, draws and removes the toes from the pig. Wash in plenty of warm water, then in 2 or 3 rinses of cold water to remove all traces of resin flavour. Take off the feet at the first joint very carefully so that enough skin is left to fold neatly over them. Dry pig thoroughly. Rub all over with seasoned flour. Sieve crumbs into a basin. Peel onions and bring to boil in cold water, then drain and mince finely. Add to crumbs with sage, salt and pepper to taste, and cream. Mix well. Stuff pork. Sew up paunch with fine string. Truss. Wrap in greased paper. Roast, when possible, in front of the fire, keeping it well basted with cream, for 2 hours, or bake in a very hot oven, 450° F., for ¼ hour, then lower to moderate, 350° F., and bake from 2-2½ hours. If you like crackling, rub skin all over with oil or fat instead of flour before roasting, and baste frequently with dripping when roasting. *For 10 persons.*

ROAST TENDERLOIN OF PORK (Filet de Porc rôti)

BASIC : There are two ways of preparing tenderloin, or fillet. You can either split one, and flatten it out with a cutlet bat or rolling-pin, stuff and roast it, or you can split and flatten two tenderloins the same size, and sew or skewer the edges together with stuffing between, before roasting. In either case, rub split tenderloin with a cut clove of garlic, if liked, then brush with melted butter. Stuff with 1 cup of herb, potato or celery stuffing. Sew up the one or sew the edges of the two together. Rub all over with seasoned flour. Place on a rack in an open roasting tin and bake in a moderate oven, 350° F., allowing 30-35 minutes per lb. Allow for 6-8 ozs. per person when purchasing.

To Vary: (1) Fry stuffed tenderloin in a little hot lard till brown all over. Remove to a fireproof dish. Pour ¾ pint sliced tomatoes over. Cover and bake in a moderate oven, 350° F., for 1 hour. (2) Cut tenderloin into fillets lengthwise. Flatten. Spread with stuffing. Roll each up. Dredge with seasoned flour. Fry carefully in a little hot dripping till brown all over. Place in a

VEGETABLES

Platter of boiled Vegetables, coated with melted butter. Garnish cauliflower also with paprika. *See page* 444.

SALADS

Jellied Tomato Salad and Tomato Sandwich Salad. *See pages* 477 *and* 461-462.

fireproof dish. Pour ¼ pint sour cream over. Cover closely. Bake in a slow oven, 325° F., for about ½ hour.

BAKED PORK CHOPS (Côtes de Porc rôties)

5 peeled onions
Salt and pepper to taste
4 medium-sized cooking apples
4 pork chops
Flour as required
4 medium-sized potatoes
½ pint boiling water

You want a very wide dish or a baking tin for cooking pork chops in this way. Grease it well. Halve the onions and arrange halves in bottom of dish or tin. Sprinkle with salt to taste. Peel and core apples. Cut each apple into 4 rings and slip the end of each chop through rings. Arrange chops and apple rings on top of the onions. Dredge lightly with flour. Peel and slice potatoes and arrange slices in between the chops. Sprinkle again with salt and pepper to taste. Pour in boiling water. Cover. Bake in a moderate oven, 350° F., till tender. Uncover and bake till a rich golden brown. *For 4 persons.*

BRAISED PORK CHOPS (Côtes de Porc braisées)

Basic : Dredge pork chops, cut 1 inch thick, with flour. Melt enough fat in a heavy frying pan to cover bottom. Add chops. Brown on both sides. Season with salt and pepper to taste. Transfer to a fireproof dish. Add 2 tablespoons water. Cover tightly. Simmer very slowly, or bake in a moderate oven, 350° F., for 30-40 minutes. *Allow 1 per person.*

To Vary : (1) Substitute tomato juice for the water, and cover chops with sliced onions. (2) Have 4 pork chops cut 1 inch thick with a pocket in each. Fill with celery stuffing. Brown on each side in a little hot fat or salad oil in a heavy shallow saucepan. Add ½ cup hot apple juice. Cover. Braise in a slow oven, 325° F., for 1 hour or until so tender you can cut meat with fork.

FRIED FILLETS OF PORK (Filets de Porc frits)

6 fillets pork
1 tablespoon minced onion
2 tablespoons lemon juice
1½ tablespoons salad oil
¾ teaspoon salt
½ teaspoon paprika
Frying fat and flour
Beaten egg and breadcrumbs

Ask your butcher to divide 1½ lb. tender lean pork into 6 fillets, then trim them. Mix onion with lemon juice, oil, salt, paprika and a good dash of pepper if liked, on a dish. Dip each fillet in the marinade, then soak, basting every half hour, for 2 hours. When required, drain, dip in flour, shake a little, dip in beaten egg and then in breadcrumbs. Shake lightly. Fry in a little hot fat until golden brown and tender, turning continually. *For 6 persons.*

FRIED PORK CHOPS (Côtes de Porc frites)

4 lean pork chops
Frying fat if required
Salt and pepper to taste
2 tablespoons flour
1 cup boiling brown stock

Place chops side by side in a hot frying-pan. Fry till brown below. Turn and brown on other side, then add a little fat if required. Fry slowly until the meat is cooked, seasoning when half-done. Arrange on a flat, hot dish and keep hot in the

1 dessertspoon sherry
Sprigs of watercress

oven. Strain off 2 tablespoons of the fat into a saucepan. Stir in flour. When it froths, stir in stock by degrees. Stir till boiling. Season with salt and pepper to taste. If too thick, add a little more stock, then add sherry. Serve in a hot sauceboat. Garnish chops with sprigs of watercress. *For 4 persons.*

GRILLED STUFFED PORK CHOPS (Côtes de Porc grillées)

6 thick pork chops
Salt and pepper to taste
1 tablespoon minced onion
1 tablespoon butter
1/4 cup chopped mushrooms
1 1/2 tablespoons flour
1/4 cup stock or water
1 teaspoon minced parsley

Split the chops lengthwise to the bone and sprinkle with salt and pepper. Cook onion in butter until it begins to colour. Add mushrooms, flour and stock, or water in which you have dissolved part of a meat cube. Cook until boiling. Add minced parsley, salt and pepper. Divide into 6 portions and place in the hollow of each chop. Fasten together with small wooden toothpicks. Grill and serve with brown gravy. *For 6 persons.*

LEICESTER HOT-POT (Hochepot, Leicester)

6 small pork chops
1/2 lb. onions
1 1/2 lb. potatoes
2 pig kidneys
1 small cored peeled apple
1 teaspoon powdered herbs
Salt and pepper to taste
1 cup stock
1 tablespoon tomato sauce or mushroom ketchup

Trim chops. Peel and slice onions and potatoes. Scald, core, skin and slice kidneys. Place a layer of potato in the bottom of a greased hotpot dish or casserole. Cover with a layer of onion and kidney then with half the chops and sprinkle with half the apple, cored and finely minced. Repeat layers, then season with herbs and salt and pepper to taste. Cover with remainder of potatoes. Add stock flavoured with tomato sauce or mushroom ketchup. Cover closely. Bake in a slow oven, 325° F., for 2 1/2-3 hours. *For 6 persons.*

BACON AND HAM

Prime bacon and ham should have a smooth thin rind. The lean should adhere to the bone and the fat should be firm, pinky-white and free from black specks or yellow streaks. The lean should be finely grained. If properly cured both bacon and ham should have a pleasant smell. Choose short thick plump hams in preference to elongated.

To Cook Bacon: The time required to fry or grill bacon will depend on the thickness of the rashers and whether it is liked lightly cooked or cooked till crisp. To boil bacon, allow 30 minutes per lb.

To Cook Gammon: Remove rind from slices, and gash edges of fat here and there to prevent curling. Grill under moderate heat, allowing time according to thickness, and turning frequently : 1/4 inch thick, 10 minutes ; 1/2-3/4 inch thick, 15-20 minutes ; 1 inch thick, 20-30 minutes. To fry gammon rashers, grease a heavy frying-pan with ham fat. Fry slightly till brown below, then turn and brown on other side. Lower heat and cover. Fry slowly till tender, turning several times : $\frac{1}{4}$ inch thick, 10 minutes ; $\frac{1}{2}$-$\frac{3}{4}$ inch thick, 15-20 minutes ; 1 inch thick, 20-30 minutes. To boil gammon, allow 30 minutes per lb.

To Cook Ham : If no directions are given with ham, cook in the following way : To bake in a slow oven, 300° F., allow $\frac{1}{4}$ hour per lb. for ham 12 lb. and over, and 18 minutes per lb. when under 12 lb. If baking half a ham, allow 22 minutes per lb. If you want to glaze it, bake in a slow oven, 300° F. until $\frac{3}{4}$ hour before ham is ready, then carefully remove rind. With a sharp knife, cut all the fat on top into diamonds or squares. Spread with glaze to taste. Fix a clove in each diamond or square. Increase temperature to 325° F., and finish baking.

Glazes for Hams: (1) Before inserting cloves in fat, you can spread fully $\frac{1}{2}$ lb. of brown sugar all over fat, rubbing it well in, then insert cloves and sprinkle with 3 or 4 tablespoons of cider or orange juice. Baste twice with ham dripping and bake for $\frac{1}{2}$ hour. (2) Smear fat with 1 cup extracted honey.

To Bake Ham in a Pastry Case: Cover with a paste made of flour and water, stiff enough to keep in the juices. Place on a rack in a baking tin. Bake in a moderately hot oven, 375° F., for about 4 hours. Remove crust, then rind. Cover with bread raspings and trim knuckle with a paper frill.

To Boil: Cover ham with boiling water, rind side up, in a partly covered saucepan, allowing 25-30 minutes per lb. If ham is to be served cold, leave overnight in liquid, then remove rind. If to be served hot, remove rind and drain well. Glaze, if liked, $\frac{1}{2}$ hour before ready to serve. (See *Baked Hams.*) To boil ham successfully, see that water is kept at a simmering temperature, about 180° F., while cooking.

ACCOMPANIMENTS FOR BACON AND HAM

Fried or Grilled Bacon: Fried or grilled mushrooms or tomatoes.

Boiled Bacon: Usually served as an accompaniment to roast chicken or turkey.

Baked Ham (Hot) : Cider or raisin sauce and corn fritters, or candied sweet potatoes. Garnish with pineapple.

Baked Ham (Cold) : Potato salad, chutney and pickles.

Boiled Ham (Hot) : Spinach, or green peas, or sprouting broccoli, and a savoury wine sauce.

Boiled Ham (Cold) : Potato salad, chutney and pickles.

BAKED GAMMON (Jambon rôti aux Pommes)

2lb. 1 inch thick, sliced lean gammon
1½ cups light brown sugar
10 cloves
6 peeled cooking apples
½ cup water
Parsley as a garnish

Remove rind from gammon. Rub $\frac{1}{2}$ cup sugar into ham. Place in a fireproof dish. Sprinkle with cloves. Core and halve apples. Place round gammon. Sprinkle apples with remainder of sugar, then add water. Bake in a moderate oven, 350° F., for $\frac{3}{4}$ hour. Garnish with parsley. Serve with a green salad. *For 6 persons.*

BAKED HAM (Jambon rôti)

10—12 lb. ham
½ cup vinegar
½ cup water
1 cup brown sugar
Cloves as required

Scrub and trim ham. If very salt, soak overnight in cold water. When ready to cook, plunge into boiling water. Boil quickly for 10 minutes, then simmer for 2 hours. Stand in water till cool. Drain and remove rind. Place on a trivet in a roasting pan. Baste well with vinegar and water. Bake for 1 hour in a rather hot oven, 425° F. Remove from oven. Score fat. Rub with sugar and a cut clove of garlic, if liked. Prick thickly with cloves. Bake until brown.

To Vary: After placing ham in roasting pan, spread to ½ inch thickness with 1 cup brown sugar mixed with 2 tablespoons flour. Prick with cloves, 1 inch apart. Baste with cider or pineapple juice. Cover and roast in a slow oven, 325° F., allowing 25 minutes to the pound.

BOILED HAM (Jambon boulli)

1 trimmed ham
2 scraped carrots
1 peeled white turnip
12 peppercorns
1 sprig thyme
1 bay leaf
Thin rind 1 orange
1 pint white wine
1 glass Madeira or sherry

Soak in cold water to cover for half a day, changing water 3 times. Drain and cover with boiling water. Add all other ingredients. Cover and barely simmer until the skin shows signs of coming away from the meat, about ½ hour per lb., then remove and drain well, if to be served hot. (If cold, allow to cool in the liquid.) Remove from pan when nearly ready. Skin. Rub fat with Demerara sugar, and lean with a cut clove of garlic, if liked. Either bake till crisp, or prick fat with cloves before baking. Serve with champagne, Madeira or port wine sauce.

BRAISED YORK HAM (Jambon d'York braisé)

2 oz. shredded beef suet
1 sprig marjoram
1 sprig thyme
1 sprig parsley
1 bay leaf
1 blade mace
2 oz. butter
1 sliced carrot
1 sliced head of celery
4 sliced peeled onions
2 pints stock
1 York ham
1 pint cider

Soak ham overnight in water to cover. Place in a saucepan. Add cold water to cover. Cover and boil for 20 minutes. Place suet in a saucepan with herbs, mace, butter, carrot, celery and onions. Cover with stock. Cover and cook slowly for 30 minutes. Turn into a pan large enough to take ham. When ham has boiled for 20 minutes, remove from pan. Carefully, take off the rind and trim. Place on vegetable braise. Add cider and stock. Cover closely. Cook very gently in a slow oven, 300° F., for about 4 hours. The time depends on the size of ham. Trim and glaze when ready. Serve with braised celery, if wanted hot.

CASSEROLE OF HAM (Casserole de Jambon)

4 large peeled potatoes
1 peeled onion

Cut potatoes into thin slices. Chop onion, parsley and carrots. Put a layer of potatoes in bottom of

1 sprig parsley
2 scraped carrots
Salt and pepper to taste
2 slices ham
¾ pint milk

casserole. Sprinkle with salt and pepper to taste, then with half the onion and carrot. Sprinkle with half the parsley. Cut one slice of ham in 3 or 4 pieces. Arrange on top of vegetables. Cover with remainder of vegetables and parsley. Sprinkle with salt and pepper to taste. Cover with remaining slice of ham, cut into pieces. Add milk. Cover and cook in a slow oven, 325° F., for 1¾ hours. Uncover for last 15 minutes to brown. *For 6 persons.*

FRIED GAMMON WITH ORANGE SAUCE
(Jambon frit aux Orange)

1 thick slice gammon
2 dessertspoons flour
1 cup orange juice
2 seedless oranges
Sprigs of parsley

Choose a slice of gammon about 1 lb. in weight. Fry till brown on both sides, and cooked right through. Place on a hot serving dish. Remove and measure fat. Return 1 tablespoon to pan. Stir in flour, then orange juice. Stir till boiling, and cook for 5 minutes, still stirring, until sauce is thick. Pour round ham or serve in a sauceboat. Peel and cut oranges into equal-sized slices. Arrange slices overlapping each other down the centre. Place a sprig of parsley at each end, if liked. Serve with scalloped potatoes. *For 3 or 4 persons.*

GAMMON RASHERS OPORTO (Tranches de Lard, Oporto)

Place trimmed rashers in a casserole. Cover with port wine. Add 2 peppercorns for every ½ lb. ham. Cover and cook in a slow oven, 300° F., till tender. Add the strained juice of ½ orange or 1 tangerine for every 4 tablespoons of wine left. Drain into a saucepan. Boil up and serve as gravy. *Allow 1 rasher per person.*

VEAL

The flesh of young calves, from 8-12 weeks' old, is obtainable throughout the year, but best from March-September. As it does not keep well, it should be cooked within 2 days in warm weather, and 4 days in winter. Bull calf flesh is best for joints as it has a firm grain. Use flesh of the cow calf for made-up dishes.

TO CHOOSE VEAL

Flesh of a very young calf is very savoury, but rather indigestible. It is a delicate greyish-pink colour. The flesh of an older calf is redder, more digestible and nourishing. Prime veal is light pink and finely grained, with little fat. Fat should be semi-transparent, and bones porous and red. The fat round the kidney should be sweet smelling and plentiful. The connective tissues should have a blistered appearance. If the fat is soft and moist, and the lean bluish-tinged, the veal is not fresh enough to eat.

VEAL CHART

The times given in the following chart are only approximate, as the **cuts** vary according to size and age of the animal. As veal is immature, it should be thoroughly cooked.

Oven Temperature: Slow, 300° F.

Cuts	Method	Time Required
Best end of neck - - -	Stewed	$1\frac{1}{2}$ hours.
Breast (2-3 lb.) - - - -	Braised	$1\frac{1}{2}$-2 hours.
Breast (3-4 lb.) - - - -	Stuffed and roasted	About 2 hours.
Breast (2 lb.) - - - -	Stewed	About $1\frac{1}{2}$ hours.
Fillet - - - - -	Roasted	30 minutes per lb.
Flank - - - - -	Stewed	25 minutes per lb.
Knuckle (fore) - - -	Stewed (3 lb.)	2-3 hours.
Loin - - - - -	Braised (3 lb.)	1-$1\frac{1}{2}$ hours.
Loin (well done) - - -	Roasted	35 minutes per lb.
Shoulder - - - -	Roasted	35 minutes per lb.
Shoulder (5 lb.) - - -	Stuffed and roasted	40-45 minutes per lb.
Shoulder (3-5 lb.) - - -	Pot roast	2-$2\frac{1}{2}$ hours.
Chops ($\frac{1}{2}$-$\frac{3}{4}$ inch thick) - -	Braised	45-60 minutes.
Chops (1 inch thick) - - -	Grilled	15-18 minutes.
Cutlets ($\frac{1}{4}$-$\frac{1}{2}$ inch) - - -	Fried	10-12 minutes.
Cutlets and Steaks ($\frac{1}{2}$-$\frac{3}{4}$ inch thick)	Braised	45-60 minutes.

ACCOMPANIMENTS TO VEAL

Baked or Roast Veal (Hot) : Rolls of bacon ; cut lemon ; brown or sour cream gravy, and mushroom or onion sauce, if liked. If not stuffed, garnish with forcemeat balls.

Baked or Roast Veal (Cold) : Salad, or a mixed French salad, pickled gherkins.

Boiled Veal (Hot) : Parsley sauce ; boiled bacon ; diced boiled carrot and onion, and forcemeat balls, if liked.

Braised or Stewed Veal: Forcemeat balls or baked curled rashers of bacon ; slices of lemon ; green peas or mushrooms, or purée of spinach or sorrel.

Fried or Grilled Veal Chops or Cutlets: Madeira, mushroom or tomato sauce ; fingers of lemon ; forcemeat balls, or grilled curls of bacon, or curled anchovies ; parsley or watercress ; chips, and fried or grilled mushrooms or tomatoes.

ROAST VEAL (Veau rôti)

The best joints for roasting are the fillet from the top of the leg, the loin, and the best end of neck. The shoulder is second quality, and the breast third. Most veal joints are boned and stuffed before roasting. Veal is always roasted until well done. Serve with thickened gravy.

ROAST FILLET OR LOIN (Longe ou Filet de Veau rôti)

Wipe meat with a damp cloth. Brush with bacon dripping, or lard with strips of bacon or salt pork. Season with salt and pepper. If using a meat thermometer, insert so that the bulb is in the thickest part of the meat. Place with the fat or larded side up on a rack in a shallow baking tin. Roast, uncovered, in a slow oven, 300° F. Allow 30-35 minutes per lb. Not necessary to baste if larded. If not, baste every 20 minutes with bacon dripping for preference.

ROAST STUFFED SHOULDER OF VEAL
(Epaule de Veau rôti)

Bone 5 lb. shoulder of veal. Wipe with a damp cloth. Stuff. Roll up and tie in place. Place on rack, join downwards, in an open baking tin. Roast in a slow oven, 300° F., allowing 40-45 minutes per lb. Baste lavishly twice while roasting, with bacon dripping for preference.

ROAST STUFFED BREAST OF VEAL (Poitrine de Veau rôtie)

3-4 lb. breast of veal
½ lemon
Salt and pepper to taste
½ pint stale breadcrumbs
2 tablespoons margarine or shredded suet
¼ teaspoon grated lemon rind
2 teaspoons minced parsley
¼ teaspoon crushed herbs
Cayenne pepper to taste
1 beaten egg

Wipe veal carefully with a damp cloth. Bone and remove any gristle. Spread out on a chopping board, skin side downwards. Trim neatly into an oblong. Arrange trimmings over thinnest part. Rub over with cut lemon. Sprinkle with salt and pepper to taste. Mix crumbs with fat, lemon rind, parsley, herbs and cayenne pepper. Stir egg into crumb mixture. Place stuffing in centre of veal, leaving a wide rim uncovered. Roll up like a Swiss roll. Sew up opening with a needle and strong cotton or fine string. Weigh. Rub seasoned flour all over roll. Melt enough beef or veal dripping to cover bottom of roasting pan. Place roll on rack. Baste with melted dripping. Roast in a moderate oven, 350° F., allowing 25 minutes to the lb. and 25 minutes over. Remove cotton or string before dishing up. Serve with brown gravy. *For 6 persons.*

BLANQUETTE OF VEAL (Blanquette de Veau)

1¼ lb. boned shoulder of veal
5 tablespoons butter
Salt and pepper to taste
1 scraped carrot
1 teaspoon minced parsley
1 slice onion
½ bay leaf
2 cloves
1 sprig thyme
¾ pint stock from veal bones
3 tablespoons flour
2 egg yolks
½ cup cream

Wipe and cut meat into pieces about 2 inches square. Melt 2½ tablespoons of the butter in a frying pan and add veal. Fry slowly until a delicate brown. Place in a casserole. Season with salt and pepper. Place carrot in a cheese-cloth or muslin bag wrung out of boiling water, with parsley, onion slice, bay leaf, cloves and a sprig of thyme if liked. Place on top of veal. Add stock made from bones to water in which a chicken cube has been dissolved if stock is not available. Cover and cook in a slow oven for

12 small boiled onions
1 pint fried potato balls

about $1\frac{1}{4}$ hours, until veal is tender. Add remainder of butter to the butter left in pan after frying veal. Stir in flour. When frothy, stir in $1\frac{1}{4}$ cups of stock drained from the veal and strained. Stir constantly until boiling, then remove pan from heat. Cool slightly. Beat egg yolks in a basin. Stir in cream. Stir egg mixture into pan, and keep stirring over slow heat until cooked. *On no account allow to boil.* Remove bag from casserole. Arrange veal in the centre of a hot flat dish. Stir sauce into remainder of the veal essence in casserole. Pour over veal. Serve remainder in a sauceboat. Arrange boiled onion and fried potato balls round. *For 4 or 5 persons.*

BRAISED NECK OF VEAL (Collet de Veau braisé)

3 lb. best end of neck
2 medium-sized carrots
2 medium-sized onions
3 slices turnip
2 celery sticks
1 bouquet garni
1 blade mace
10 peppercorns
2 cloves
1 oz. butter
1 pint veal stock
2 oz. flour
Glaze as required
1 tablespoon capers
1 teaspoon lemon juice
Salt and pepper to taste

Wipe neck with a damp cloth. Saw the bones across as you do when preparing lamb cutlets, then remove short pieces of rib bones, and fold meat flap under. Season to taste. Prepare and slice vegetables. Place them in a shallow saucepan with bouquet garni, which should include 1 sprig marjoram and 2 of thyme, mace, peppercorns, cloves and half the butter. Add stock, enough to cover vegetables. Arrange veal on top. Cover with a greased paper, then with lid. Simmer gently for 1 hour, then add remainder of stock. Continue cooking slowly for about 2 hours. When nearly ready, melt remainder of butter in a small saucepan. Add flour. Stir gently over low heat, until it turns a nut brown shade. Remove from stove. When veal is ready, dish up, and brush it with glaze. Strain a little of the stock on to the butter and flour. Stir till smooth and boiling, then add remainder of stock as required. Stir till boiling, then add capers, lemon juice and salt and pepper to taste. Serve in a hot sauceboat. *For 6 or 7 persons.*

FRICASSEE OF VEAL (Fricassée de Veau)

2 lb. cubed veal
2 tablespoons flour
Salt and pepper to taste
2 tablespoons butter or lard
1 small peeled onion or 4 chopped spring onions
1 cup hot stock or water
1 cup green peas
¼ pint single cream

Toss veal in flour, seasoned with salt and pepper to taste. Melt butter or lard in a stewpan. When hot, add veal. Fry slowly till brown, turning frequently. Add onion and water, or stock. Cover tightly. Simmer gently for $\frac{1}{2}$ hour. Add peas. Cover and simmer till tender (about $\frac{1}{2}$ hour). Add cream. Stir till hot. *For 6 to 8 persons.*

FRIED VEAL CUTLETS (Côtelettes de Veau frites)

1½-2 lb. veal cutlets
1 egg yolk
2 tablespoons milk
Salt and pepper to taste
2 cups stale breadcrumbs

If cutlets are sold with bone, buy 2 lb. for 6 persons. If sold without bone, $1\frac{1}{2}$ lb. will be sufficient for 6 persons. Beat egg yolk and dilute with milk. Dip cutlets in egg and milk. Sprinkle

Bacon fat as required
Fingers of lemon

with salt and pepper to taste, then dip in bread-crumbs. Melt bacon fat in a frying-pan. Fry cutlets till golden brown on both sides. Garnish with fingers of lemon on a hot flat dish. *For 6 persons.*

LARKS WITHOUT HEADS (Alouettes Sans Têtes)

1¼ lb. fillet of veal
½ lb. pork sausage meat
1½ oz. bacon fat or butter
¾ pint beef or veal bone stock
Pinch crushed herbs
Salt and black pepper to taste
1 rounded dessertspoon plain flour
1 heaped teaspoon minced parsley

Cut veal into thin strips. Spread with sausage-meat to within ½ inch of the edge. (If liked, sprinkle each with ½ teaspoon finely chopped onion.) Roll each strip up. Tie with white thread. Melt fat in a shallow saucepan. Add veal olives, and brown, turning carefully. Add stock, herbs, salt and black pepper to taste. Cover. Simmer gently for about 1 hour. Dish up olives. Remove threads carefully. Cream flour with cold water or stock. Add to boiling stock. Stir till blended. Add parsley and more seasoning if required. Pour round olives. *For 6 persons.*

OSSI BUCHI

2 knuckles of veal
3 tablespoons olive oil
3 tablespoons butter
1 heaped tablespoon chopped carrot
¼ cup chopped celery
1 heaped tablespoon chopped onion
Salt and pepper to taste
1½ tablespoons tomato paste
1 cup sherry
1 teaspoon minced parsley

Get the butcher to saw the knuckles into 3 inch portions. Heat oil and butter in a large shallow saucepan. Add veal. Fry, turning frequently until brown all over, in about 10 minutes. Add carrot, celery, onion and salt and pepper to taste. Cover. Simmer gently until carrots are soft in about 10 to 20 minutes. Blend the tomato paste with the sherry. Stir into vegetables. When well blended, cover closely. Simmer slowly for about 30 to 45 minutes until veal is tender. If gravy is wanted, add water to taste at half-time. Serve with rice boiled in veal stock. *For 6 persons.*

SCALLOPINO

1½ lb. veal cutlet
Salt and pepper to taste
Flour as required
2 oz. butter
¼ cup white wine
½ pint boiled peas

Wipe meat with a damp cloth. Cut in pieces about 2 inches square. Pound on a board until flat. Mix 2 or 3 tablespoons flour with salt and pepper to taste and coat veal. Fry slowly in butter until delicately brown on both sides. Add wine. Reduce heat. Continue to cook until wine has almost evaporated and gravy thickened. Remove meat to a hot dish. Heat peas in the gravy, then pour round meat. Sometimes freshly cooked asparagus tips are substituted for the peas. *For 5 or 6 persons.*

SCALLOPS OF VEAL MILANAISE
(Escalopes de Veau, Milanaise)

1 cup rice
2 rashers of bacon
1 tablespoon chopped onion
2 oz. chopped peeled mushrooms
3 tablespoons olive oil or butter
2 scallops of veal
Flour as required
Tomato purée to taste
Salt, pepper and paprika to
taste
3 tablespoons grated cheese

Boil rice in salted water till tender, then hold in a colander under cold water tap to separate grains. Drain well. When half boiled, chop and put bacon in frying-pan. Add onion, mushrooms and 2 tablespoons of the oil or butter, or 1 tablespoon of each. Fry till mushrooms, onion and bacon are cooked. Meanwhile, beat veal scallops till flat and thin. Dip in seasoned flour. Melt remainder of butter or olive oil in a frying-pan. Fry till brown on each side, then continue to fry slowly until tender. If ½ inch thick, they take about 10 minutes. When veal is tender, add tomato purée to taste to the bacon and mushrooms. Stir in rice. When well blended and piping hot, season to taste with salt, pepper and paprika. Stir in 2 tablespoons of the cheese and sprinkle remainder over. Serve veal with the risotto and any green vegetable. *For 2 persons.*

VEAL CHOPS (Côtes de Veau)

Beat and trim chops neatly. Season lightly with salt and pepper. Brush with melted butter or olive oil, and grill, or melt 1½ tablespoons butter in a frying-pan and fry quickly for 3 minutes on each side, then lower heat, and fry slowly for 3 minutes on each side.

VEAL CHOPS A LA CLOTILDE : Season chops on both sides with salt and pepper. Brush both sides with olive oil and grill. Serve topped with a neat round of paté de foie gras covered with a large peeled mushroom, smeared with butter and grilled and lightly seasoned with salt and paprika.

VEAL MARENGO (Ragoût de Veau, Marengo)

1½ lb. shoulder of veal
4 tablespoons olive oil
2 medium sized onions
2 peeled shallots
2 peeled cloves of garlic
5 tomatoes
Salt and pepper to taste

Wipe veal with a damp cloth. Cut into small pieces about 1½ inches square. Heat oil in a covered saucepan. Add veal. Fry till light brown all over. Do not place one piece on top of another. If the pan is not broad enough to take them all, side by side, fry a few at a time. Chop onions, shallots, garlic and add to meat. Stir till blended. Cook over moderate heat for 5-10 minutes. Wash, scald, peel and slice tomatoes into pan. Cover closely. Simmer slowly till tender, in about ½ hour. If preferred, 2 oz. butter can be substituted for 3 tablespoons of the oil. If meat is fried too quickly, more oil or butter might be required. *For 4 or 5 persons.*

VEAL AND SAUSAGE ROLL (Roulade de Veau)

3½ lb. breast of veal
12 oz. pork sausagemeat
1 cup stale breadcrumbs
1 teaspoon minced onion
1 teaspoon minced parsley
2 tablespoons melted butter
3 tablespoons stock
Salt and pepper to taste
Flour as required
6 rashers fat bacon

Ask butcher to bone veal. Flatten it out on a board. Spread with sausage meat. Mix crumbs with onion, parsley, butter, stock and salt and pepper to taste. Spread over sausage meat. Roll up tightly. Tie neatly with string. Dredge with flour. Remove rind from bacon. Place 3 rashers in the bottom of a casserole. Stand roll on top. Cover with remainder of bacon rashers. Cover casserole. Bake in a hot oven, 450° F., for 20 minutes, then reduce heat to moderate, 350° F., and cook for 1¼-1½ hours. If to be served hot, serve with gravy made with stock from the bones of veal and the liquor in the casserole. *For 8 or 9 persons.*

VEAL SCALLOPS WITH SOUR CREAM SAUCE
(Escalopes de Veau aux Champignons)

6 scallops veal
3 tablespoons flour
Salt and pepper to taste
Dripping as required
Paprika to taste
2 sliced peeled onions
½ cup thick sour cream
Stock or water to taste

Have scallops cut barely ½ inch thick. Dip each in flour, seasoned with salt and pepper to taste. Melt fat in a frying-pan. Add enough paprika to make fat red. Fry onions then add scallops. Brown scallops on both sides. Stir in cream, a little at a time. Add fried onions. Cover. Cook slowly for ½ hour, or till tender. Thin sauce to taste with stock or water. Serve scallops on a hot dish, overlapping each other. Garnish with fried or grilled mushrooms. Pour sauce over scallops. *For 6 persons.*

WIENER SCHNITZEL (Escalopes de Veau, Viennoise)

2 lb. scallops of veal
Salt and paprika to taste
Flour as required
Beaten egg and crumbs
1 tablespoon butter
1 lemon
6 anchovies
Minced parsley as garnish

Flatten slices evenly. Sprinkle both sides with salt and paprika. Dip lightly in flour, then egg and crumb. Melt butter in a frying-pan. When smoking hot, add slices of veal. Fry for 8 minutes on each side. Serve, arranged on a hot dish with a slice of lemon, topped with a curled anchovy, on top of each. Garnish with parsley. *For 6 persons.*

TO CARVE MEAT

To be a perfect meat carver requires knowledge of the position of the bones and joints, and a considerable amount of practice. It is also important to have a sharp carving knife, from 10-12 inches long, and a two-pronged fork with a guard. The carving knife should have a blade about 1 inch across, curving gradually to a point, and the edge of the knife should be very keen and fluting upwards. The experienced carver usually has 2 carving knives at hand, as carving hot meat expands the blade and the edge loses its keenness.

There ought to be a second knife, as a knife should never be sharpened at the table. Although different joints demand different techniques for carving, here are a few rules all carvers should observe.

1. See that the joint is dished up on a platter large enough to allow cut portions to be laid alongside joint. If a large enough one is not available, provide a second heated platter or plate to take portions as they are cut.

2. Make certain that the fork guard is in position before starting to carve.

3. The knife should be so sharp that no pressure is required while carving. The hand should only direct the knife, either towards or away from you as the case may be. If the knife is so blunt that you have to use pressure, the portions will not be smooth. Never use a blunt knife which necessitates "sawing" the meat, as this results in frayed, unsightly slices.

4. Cut beef (except fillet), ham and tongue in very thin slices, veal medium thick, and lamb, mutton and pork in rather thick slices.

5. Carve all meat across the grain, except a saddle of mutton.

6. Never pour gravy around the joint, if you want to keep your table cloth or mats clean ; always serve gravy in a hot sauceboat.

7. See that the carver has joint placed in correct position in front of him.

8. To carve successfully and economically, draw each stroke of knife the full length of the blade. If part of the joint is choice, and part of secondary quality, as in the case of the sirloin with its undercut, and there is not enough undercut to serve everybody, a portion of the undercut and of top of the sirloin should be served to each person.

To Sharpen Carving Knife: Steels, stones and patent knife sharpeners will all sharpen a knife, but use a patent knife sharpener for a stainless steel blade. To sharpen non-stainless steel knives with a steel, placing the blade flat against the steel, draw blade smoothly downwards in a circular movement until tip reaches base of steel. Repeat this movement, first on one side of blade, then on other, until knife is sharp enough.

TO HELP THE CARVER

See that the butcher divides the rib bones from the back bones of joints like loin or neck of lamb, mutton, pork and veal. If he saws through the ribs near to the backbone, it will be simple to carve joint into chops. If rolled joints are secured with string, cooking and slicing will be made simpler.

TO CARVE BEEF

Aitchbone and Round of Beef: Slice across evenly and thinly including fat with lean.

Fillet: Carve rather thickly across the grain.

Rolled Ribs: Place meat on platter with the smaller cut surface upward. With guard of fork up, insert fork firmly into left side about 2 inches from top. Slice across grain, from right to left, towards fork. Lift each slice to side of platter with the blade of the knife, supporting it with the fork. Don't cut the strings binding the roast till you reach them when carving. When you do so, let the string drop on to the platter.

Sirloin: (*See illustrations facing page* 328). Remove the bone at the back as illustrated. Turn joint on its back with the fillet or undercut upwards, then cut away the fat. Carve the fillet first, holding knife slightly slanted outward, and cut slices fully one-sixth of an inch thick. When all the fillet has been carved, reverse joint and carve the top, beginning always at the rib end. (Please note that if the joint has been taken from the right side of the animal, the bone end will be away from you when carving, but if taken from the left side, the bone side will be towards you.) Carve slices about one-eighth inch thick with a knife slanted outward as before. This will enable you, when you reach the bone, to remove the flesh easily. When you reach the end part, where the slices become smaller, cut first slice almost through, but not quite, and then cut the next right through. When serving, open these two slices, and they will form a large slice. Always serve a little fat with the lean.

To Carve Boned Roasts and Pot Roasts: Carve thinly across the grain from right to left.

To Carve Crown Roast: Insert fork firmly between ribs. Cut downwards, allowing 1 rib per person. Serve slices on knife blade, supporting with a fork.

TO CARVE LAMB

Leg: Place joint on serving dish with thickest part of leg upwards. Carve in moderately thin slices, straight down at right angles to the bone, beginning at the thick end. When all the meat is removed from the top, turn joint upside down and carve the underside in the same way. As some people prefer the knuckle end, it's a good idea to ask if anyone has a preference, as this part is better " done " than the remainder.

Loin: Beginning at the outer chop, carve right through downwards between chops, serving fat and lean together. This is easy to do if the butcher has " jointed " the loin properly.

Neck (Best End): Carve this joint downward, in the direction of the bones, into cutlets. This is only possible if the butcher has removed the scrag and chine bone.

Saddle: Place the thin end of the saddle, which consists of 2 separate loins, on the right of the carver, though in front. Carve meat on one side of the backbone in long, $\frac{1}{2}$ inch thick slices, until the prime parts are removed. Some carvers carve the slices in slanting curves from the centre of joint downwards. Before beginning to carve, raise saddle with a fork and remove the kidney fat. Carve the other side of the back in the same way. Now reverse joint and carve underside as you carved the top.

Shoulder: This is a most difficult joint to carve, as there are three bones in the shoulder : the knuckle, middle bone and the blade bone. Parts of the shoulder are lean and parts are fat, which means that the carver has to divide the portions so that the lean and fat are evenly divided for those who want both. Arrange joint so that the blade end points away from carver. Inserting fork firmly into meat, lift far side of joint very slightly, then carve vertically up to the bone through centre of meat. This will result in the joint gaping slightly. Carve further slices from each side of this opening as far as the knuckle on one side, and the blade bone on the other. Though the meat around the knuckle is slightly coarser than the remainder of the joint, it should be carved and given to those who prefer the meat better done than the rest of joint. Now turn joint so that the blade bone is towards carver, and carve meat on the top of it downwards in thin slices parallel with the centre of the bone. Lastly, reverse joint and carve meat in horizontal slices. Some carvers contend that rather thin wedge-shaped slices should first be carved and served with slices from the back of the blade bone with a little thinly sliced fat, in which case, the meat will have to be carved horizontally instead of vertically, as already described.

Stuffed Breast: Beginning at one end, carve fairly thick slices downwards to the bottom of the joint.

Target: This consists of the ribs from the best end with the breast and scrag. It is a cheap cut. Before cooking it, the bones should be sawn through from the back and the breast, so that when roasted the portions can be easily separated. Always serve a piece of breast with a cutlet.

TO CARVE MUTTON

Haunch: Leg with loin attached. Place serving dish on table so that the knuckle is furthest away and the loin nearest carver. Carve as you would for a leg and loin, but, to enable you to do this, the chine of the loin should be carefully sawn through before cooking. Start carving near the knuckle end, making a slit from a little above knuckle down the side, then make a slanting cut from where you started to carve to opposite end in front of you. Now carve each successive slice slanting or sloping, so that the gravy drains into the hollow that remains. Serve with each portion of mutton a small piece of fat carved from the left side.

Leg: (*See illustrations facing page* 321). Place on serving dish with shank at left hand. Hold the knuckle bone either by its frill or with a napkin or a holder screwed on to the bone. It is not possible to carve leg of mutton successfully lying flat on a dish. First make an incision above the knuckle A, then, with knife slanted towards knuckle bone, cut 2 or 3 slices B, according to the size of the leg. Now begin to cut from two directions C, as illustrated, thus obtaining two slices instead of the one right across. If the slice becomes too large, it can be divided into three sections. In this way the whole of the cushion is removed, leaving us with meat only at the bottom of the bone on the smaller side of the leg D, illustrated. Finally cut away flesh around bone, so that all meat is removed and every slice taken off neatly, leaving no trimmings at all.

Loin: To carve a loin of mutton successfully, its bones should have been sawn through. Place joint on serving dish with thick part away from carver. Carve chops, starting at the right outer chop, serving fat and lean together. If loin is very large, carve in slices the whole length of the joint. Run knife round chine bone and under meat along ribs. Cut downwards in slices as with a saddle.

Saddle: (*See illustrations facing page* 289.) There are three methods of carving a saddle of mutton. (1) Cut along spine bone (as illustrated, A-B), but do not go right down. When knife touches bone, bear it towards flesh, lift it slightly, and then cut straight down. Now cut slices lengthwise downwards slightly cutting towards spine. (See cut C, and lift these as shown in second illustration.)

Four slices from each side can then be cut. Serve with each slice a little fat from sides (see cut D). (2) Make incision along spine as in first method. For the right side, incline blade of knife slightly towards this bone and progress forward. This gives you long slices with lean and fat. (See cut E.) For the left side, cut outwards, as shown in third illustration. When the long saddle is served with the chump, a slice of the chump can be served with the first and second slices which are small. (3) Another good method is to carve this joint cross-wise on the slant, which gives a good slice of fat and lean, as illustrated. (See cut F.) The chump, if left on the saddle, should be carved with the knife inclined slightly inwards to meet the curve of the chump bone. In this way the whole of the meat is easily removed.

Shoulder: (*See illustrations facing page* 344). Usually served with skin side uppermost, but the underpart, known as the " oyster cut," and considered more delicate and juicy than the upper, is usually carved first. In that case, turn joint over after inserting fork in fleshy part, and carve underpart slantwise, right to the bone (as illustrated in sketch, from A-B and C-D). Now insert knife at bone and loosen meat. Serve a small piece of crispy roasted fat with each portion of meat. I am illustrating another method of carving a shoulder of mutton or lamb. The shoulder is taken from the left side. Naturally a shoulder from the right would be reversed. There are three bones to deal with. The knuckle is marked A, the middle bone or clod, B, and the blade bone C. As the shoulder consists of lean and fat parts, a clever carver should divide the portions so that both are evenly distributed. Now look at the diagram in the first photograph. On the underside of the blade bone is the lean portion, which should be first cut off and sliced outwards with the knife slanted. This particular joint produces three or four slices. (See second illustration.) From the clod or middle bone, cut four slices of fat meat. (See cut D in first picture.) The carver, in serving a slice of each of these portions, easily disposes of these parts. The best part of the shoulder is from the blade end towards the middle bone. Carve this portion in slices, shaping the cut so as to reach the curve created by the blade bone (see cut E). This part of the shoulder has an almost equal division of fat and lean. When all this part has been carved, turn the shoulder so that the round side of the blade bone is uppermost. This will give you a projection (see F in first illustration) resembling the breast bone of a chicken. Cut away the meat from each side of this ridge, slanting knife outward in a similar manner to that in which meat is cut off saddle. (See cut G.) Note that the bone is situated not in the centre but slightly to one side. This meat is fairly lean, so the fat which lies in the outer part of the shoulder can be utilised along with it (see cut H), but remember to remove the gland in this fat before carving it.

Stuffed Breast of Mutton: Carve downwards in fairly thick slices right through joint.

TO CARVE PORK

The leg and loin of pork can be carved like leg and loin of mutton, but the loin must be well jointed and the skin which provides crackling well scored. The butcher or cook must attend to this before cooking. If the leg is stuffed, a portion of stuffing must accompany each helping.

Leg: (*See illustration facing page* 321). Follow method given for leg of mutton, cutting slices rather thick, or adopt this simpler method : Arrange joint on dish with shank at left hand. Now take hold of the bone by its frill, or holding it with a napkin, make an incision at the knuckle marked A, then carve from mark B down to the centre bone, as illustrated in sketch. Continue carving even slices slantwise, as shown in sketch from B-A, and loosen slices by passing point of knife along centre bone. This is the best way to carve a leg when you want the joint to look neat at a second serving, as the underside is not touched. If serving a large number, it is better to carve slices alternately from the left and the right, then reverse joint and carve the underside in a similar manner.

Loin: (*See illustrations facing page* 320.) It is impossible to carve a loin of pork unless loin has been properly jointed by butcher. Starting at the right chop, with the thick part of joint away from carver, insert knife between bones and cut down between each chop. This is only possible if the rind was properly scored before cooking, in order to secure equal-thick slices, see B. Serve a piece of crackling with each portion, and a piece of kidney as well if you come to it.

Sucking Pig: Cut head in two, and use with ears and sprigs of rosemary as a garnish. Carve joints as illustrated. If joints are long, separate them. Divide ribs also if sucking pig is fairly old.

TO CARVE HAM

Frill shank. Place a whole ham on a serving dish with the shank end to the carver's right, and the decorated side upwards. The thin side will then be either nearest or furthest away from carver, depending on which side of pork ham comes from. There are different ways of carving a whole ham. You can serve it like a leg of lamb or mutton, or you can carve it in a more economical way by beginning at the knuckle end and carving thin slices straight across from thin to thick side, or *vice versa*, till you come to the thick end. Some experienced carvers claim that the correct way to carve is to give a thin slice, cut slantwise, from both the thick end and the knuckle end to each person.

Another method is to insert fork, then carve two or three slices from the thin side, parallel to the length of ham. Reverse ham so that it rests on cut surface, then, holding it firmly with a fork, cut a small wedge from shank end. This makes it easier for the carver to cut the following slices away from bone. Now cut thin slices, still steadying ham with fork, right down to leg bone until you reach the aitchbone. To release slices from bone, carve along bone at right angles to slices. Lastly, reverse ham to its original position and carve at right angles to bone.

To Carve Half a Ham (*Shank End*): Remove cushion part. Turn upside down so that ham rests on cut side, and carve, beginning at the thick end. Separate remaining section from shank by cutting through the joint, then bone and turn and slice.

To Carve Gammon: Carve in thin slices, starting at the thick end, working gradually along to the knuckle bone.

TO CARVE VEAL

Breast: Carve like stuffed breast of lamb, if boned and stuffed. If not boned, separate ribs from brisket.

Fillet (Boned and Stuffed): Carve across in thin even slices as you would carve round of beef.

Loin: Carve as you would sirloin of beef, but, before doing so, reverse and remove the kidney and fat. Now turn back into original position and carve in diagonal slices moderately thick. Serve a little kidney and fat with each portion.

Neck: Slice diagonally in moderately thick portions. Do not try to carve into chops unless the meat is already jointed.

Shoulder: Arrange on dish with the underside uppermost. Carve, starting at the knuckle end, and serve like shoulder of mutton.

Calf's Head: Usually cooked unboned, but halved. Arrange on serving dish with nose to right. First remove eye socket, then make a cut lengthwise from under the ear across cheek to the nose, cutting through to the bones. Cut nose away. When carving, keep dipping the knife in the liquor in the dish between each cut, so that the gelatine from the head is kept liquid, otherwise the knife will stick and the slices will not be clean. At the fleshy part of the neck is a sweetbread, known as the " throat sweetbread." Serve a part of it with each portion of meat. Now remove jaw bone below, and you'll find more lean meat. The titbits from a calf's head are the ears, the flesh round the eyes and under the jaw, and the palate. A slice of brain and tongue, if left in head when cooked, can be served with each portion, together with a small portion of boiled ham.

TO CARVE TONGUE

Before serving a boiled ox tongue, trim off any cartilage or ugly tissue from the root end. Starting at this end, carve in thin parallel slices, unless a preference is given for slices $\frac{1}{4}$-$\frac{1}{2}$ inch thick, leaving the root end untouched. This will give you long slices from the small end.

To carve a *Pressed Tongue,* cut horizontally in thin slices from right to left, holding tongue in position with fork inserted on left side.

FROM HEAD TO TAIL

This section includes recipes for all the edible parts of calf, lamb, ox, pig and sheep not usually classified as meat. With a little trouble, each one of them can be turned into an appetising dish.

CALVES', LAMBS', AND SHEEP'S BRAINS (Cervelles)

Should be cooked as soon as possible after purchasing. If not convenient, partially cook in the following way and store in the refrigerator when they can be dressed according to taste, when required.

To Prepare for Cooking: Wash thoroughly. Carefully remove arteries and membrane. Place in a basin. Cover with water. Soak for 1 hour. Drain well.

To Partially Cook: Cover with boiling acidulated water, allowing 1 teaspoon salt and 1 dessertspoon lemon juice or vinegar to 1 quart water. Cover and simmer for ¼ hour.

To Cook: Cover with boiling acidulated water, as for partially cooked meat, or substitute court bouillon, as prepared for fish. Simmer until tender for 20-25 minutes. Chill in cold water till firm. Drain well. Serve separated into small pieces or slices, with Béchamel sauce, black butter, or mushroom or tomato sauce, for lunch or supper, or fry slowly in a little hot bacon dripping until pale brown, and serve with bacon for breakfast.

To Vary: (1) Brush with melted butter or oil and grill.

CALF'S BRAIN CAKES (Crêpes de Cervelles)

1 set calf's brains
2 tablespoons breadcrumbs
2 teaspoons minced parsley
Salt, pepper, and cayenne pepper to taste
1 egg yolk

Wash brains well. Soak in cold salted water for 4 or 5 hours. Place in a saucepan of cold salted water. Bring slowly to the boil and simmer for 20 minutes. Remove from the saucepan. Drain well. Chop finely. Mix chopped brains with breadcrumbs, parsley, salt, pepper and cayenne pepper to taste. Bind with beaten egg yolk. Drop in spoonfuls into deep smoking hot fat and fry till light brown. Drain on absorbent paper. Serve garnished lemon. *For 2 persons.*

HAGGIS (Hachis)

If you wish to be initiated into the mysteries of a haggis, take the stomach bag of a sheep. Wash it till perfectly clean with cold water. Turn it outside in. Scald and scrape it with a knife, then steep in salted water until required. Now parboil heart, lights and liver of sheep. Grate liver. Put other parts through a meat grinder with ½ lb. of mutton suet. Toast 1 lb. of pinched oatmeal before the fire, or in the oven. Mix ingredients together with 3 chopped onions. Season to taste with salt and pepper, then fill the bag and, before sewing, add a little water in which you have parboiled the onions before chopping. Some cooks add only the onion water for flavouring and throw away the onions. Sew up bag, taking care it is not too full, so as to allow oatmeal to swell. Prick the bag all over with a long needle to prevent bursting. Put on an enamel plate in a saucepan with enough boiling water to cover. Boil for 4 or 5 hours, keeping the haggis constantly covered with water.

HAGGIS PUDDING (Pouding de Hachis)

Boil the lights and half the liver of a sheep, then mince lights and grate liver. Mix with 5 oz. shredded suet, 2 chopped onions, 2½ handfuls of oatmeal, salt and pepper to taste, 1 cup of the liquor in which the lights and liver were boiled, and a little milk. Pour into a buttered pudding basin or mould, filling it $\frac{3}{4}$ full. Cover with greaseproof paper. Steam from 3 to 4 hours. Turn out on to a hot dish and serve.

Haggis can be hung up in a dry place after boiling and then be boiled again when required, but only long enough to make piping hot right through.

HEADS (Têtes)

Calf's: Generally used for making mock turtle soup, or brawn. Very good, collared. Can be roasted.

Hog's: Bake and serve with fried brains, or boil and serve with cabbage or spinach, or turn into potted head, or brawn.

Sheep's: Very appetising boiled and served with parsley or Béchamel sauce, or made into brawn or broth. In Scotland, sheep's head is often made into broth, then the head removed and served as a separate dish coated with parsley sauce.

TO PREPARE HEADS

Calf's: Remove brains and tongue. Wash head carefully. Soak in cold water to draw out all the blood. *To Bake $\frac{1}{2}$ Boiled Calf's Head*—Drain well. Brush lavishly with melted butter. Sprinkle thickly with grated Parmesan cheese. Bake in a moderately hot oven, 375° F., until nicely browned.

Hog's: Scald and clean head, then split open and remove ears, snout, brains and eyes. If not salted by the butcher, soak it for 24 hours, before pickling.

Sheep's: Split head in two and remove brains. Soak in tepid water for 1 hour to get rid of all blood. If to be baked, or boiled, tie halves together.

BOILED CALF'S HEAD WITH VINAIGRETTE SAUCE
(Tête de Veau, Vinaigrette)

½ calf's head
1 large scraped carrot
1 peeled medium-sized turnip
1 large peeled onion
½ bay leaf
Salt and pepper to taste
1 dessertspoon minced parsley

Clean head. Remove brain and tongue. Wash with salted water and bone head. Wrap in a piece of muslin with the tongue. Place in a saucepan. Slice in the carrot, turnip and onion. Add bay leaf, salt and pepper to taste, and parsley. Cover and simmer for 1½ hours, then skin tongue. Serve along with the head and vegetables. Pour Vinaigrette sauce round. *For 4 persons.*

CANADIAN HEAD CHEESE (Pâté de Tête de Porceau)

1 small hog's head
Ears and tongue
1 tablespoon salt
1 sprig thyme
2 sprigs parsley
2 sprigs sage
2 cloves
1 peeled medium-sized onion

Ask the butcher to scrape and clean the head for you. Split it and remove eyes and brain. He can also scrape the ears. Now scrub the tongue yourself with a small stiff brush. Rinse it with the other parts in a large colander, under the cold water tap. Place all in a saucepan. Cover with cold water. Add salt, thyme, parsley and sage.

243

Salt, pepper, celery salt and paprika to taste
½ cup vinegar

Stick cloves in onion and add to pan. Bring slowly to boil. Skim, then cover. Simmer gently from 2 to 3 hours, till very tender. Uncover and stand till cool. Remove from stock to a colander and drain well, then strip meat from bones. Slice ears and tongue into 1½ inch squares, or triangles and oblongs, about an inch long. Place in a basin. Season to taste with salt, pepper, a dash celery salt and paprika. Stir in vinegar. Add, if liked, a dash of allspice. Mix well. Pack tightly into small wet moulds or bowls, using layers of meat from head, and bits of tongue and slices of ears alternately. Cover with a rinsed plate. Weight down. Leave for 2 to 3 days in a cool place, or chill in a refrigerator. Serve cold, cut in thin slices, if liked.

HEARTS (Coeur)

A calf's heart is considered most choice, but lamb's, ox's and sheep's hearts can all be made into appetising dishes. Soak in warm water containing a little vinegar, allowing 1 tablespoon vinegar to 1 quart water, for 2-3 hours, depending on size, to get rid of all blood, changing water at half-time. Drain well. Remove valves and any coarse fat and hard parts, and cut the two holes into one without damaging the skin to simplify stuffing. A calf's heart is enough for 2 or 3 persons, lamb's for 1, ox's for 6, and a sheep's for 2.

Calf's or Lamb's Hearts: Stuff and roast, or cut into slices ¼ inch thick. Fry in butter or dripping.

Ox Heart: Parboil. To do this, soak in cold water for 1 hour, then stuff. Tie in a cloth. Place in a saucepan of boiling water to cover. Simmer gently for 2 hours. Remove cloth and roast, basting lavishly with melted dripping for about 2 hours. Serve with brown gravy and red currant jelly. Can also be braised.

Sheep's Heart: Stuff. Skewer firmly. Wrap in fat bacon. Place in a deep fireproof dish. Add an onion stuck with 2 cloves and enough meat stock to come half-way up the hearts. Bake in a moderate oven, 350° F., for 2 hours. Thicken gravy. Season, and flavour with mushroom or walnut ketchup. Dish up. Pour gravy over. Serve with red currant jelly.

BRAISED SHEEP'S HEARTS (Casserole de Coeur de Mouton)

2 sheep's hearts
1 tablespoon seasoned flour
1 oz. margarine or mutton dripping
½ cup chopped carrot
¼ cup chopped onion
½ cup chopped celery
Salt and pepper to taste
½ cup stock

Trim hearts carefully. Wash thoroughly in salt water. Drain and dry. Dip in seasoned flour. Melt fat in a frying-pan. Add hearts and brown all over, then transfer to casserole. Add vegetables to remaining fat in pan. Cook till all fat is absorbed, then place with hearts. Season to taste with salt and pepper. Add stock. Cover and cook in a moderate oven, 350° F., for 2½ to 3 hours. *For 4 persons.*

ROAST STUFFED OX HEART (Coeur de Boeuf rôti)

1 young ox heart
2 cups stale breadcrumbs
1 minced onion
2 tablespoons melted butter
1 tablespoon minced parsley
½ teaspoon crushed herbs
Salt and pepper to taste,
  paprika to taste
Dripping as required

Clean and remove arteries, clotted blood and veins of heart if not already done by butcher. Mix crumbs with onion, butter, parsley, herbs, salt, pepper and paprika to taste. Stuff heart. Rub with dripping mixed to a paste with flour. Bake in a moderately hot oven, 400° F., for about 2 hours until tender. *For 6 persons.*

ROAST STUFFED SHEEP'S HEARTS
(Coeur de Mouton Rôti)

3 sheep's hearts
2 cups stale breadcrumbs
2 tablespoons melted butter
1 minced onion
2 teaspoons minced parsley
Dash mixed herbs
½ teaspoon crushed sage
Salt and pepper to taste
Milk or stock to moisten
2 tablespoons flour
Little dripping
1 cup water

Allow 1 heart between 2 persons. Remove all clotted blood and veins. Wash well, trim and drain. Mix crumbs in a basin with butter, onion, parsley, herbs, sage and salt and pepper to taste. Moisten with milk or stock. Stuff hearts. With floured hands, shape remainder of stuffing into tiny balls. Sew up " pockets " with strong needle and linen thread. Mix flour to a paste with dripping and season to taste. Rub over the hearts. Place on a trivet in a baking tin. Pour water into tin. Cover. Bake in a moderately hot oven,

400° F., till tender. Remove threads. Fry balls in a little of the dripping from the baking tin. Serve hearts with forcemeat balls and brown gravy. *For 6 persons.*

CALVES' KIDNEYS FLEURETTE (Rognons de Veau, Fleurette)

3 calves' kidneys
1 cup stock or water
1 tablespoon butter
1 teaspoon minced parsley
1 bay leaf
1 wineglass sherry
Pinch crushed thyme
1½ teaspoons butter
1 teaspoon flour

Trim and blanch kidneys in boiling water for a moment. Remove to a saucepan. Add stock or water. Cover and simmer for 10 minutes. Remove, cut into thin slices and place slices back in liquid. Add parsley, bay leaf, sherry and thyme. Cover and simmer until kidneys are tender. Melt butter in a frying-pan. Add flour. Strain in kidney liquid, and bring to boil. Arrange kidney

in centre of a hot dish. Pour sauce over. Serve as a luncheon dish with mashed potatoes. *For 6 to 8 persons.*

DEVILLED SHEEP'S KIDNEYS
(Rognons de Mouton à la Diable)

4 sheep's kidneys
1 dessertspoon flour
1 teaspoon curry powder
Salt to taste
1 dessertspoon Worcester sauce
A few drops of vinegar

Wash kidneys and split them open. Do not separate them. Skin and remove cores. Mix flour with curry powder and salt. Dip kidneys in the mixture. Run a skewer through two, so that they are quite flat. Skewer second pair in

Mustard to taste
1 tablespoon stock or diluted gravy
3/4 oz. margarine or bacon dripping
2 slices hot toast

the same way. (If you don't skewer them, they'll curl up and be raw in the centres.) Heat Worcester sauce with vinegar and from $\frac{1}{2}$ to 1 teaspoon made mustard according to taste, and stock or undiluted gravy. Melt fat in a small frying-pan. Add kidneys when fat is smoking hot, placing them cut side downwards. Brown quickly for 1 minute, then turn and brown quickly for another minute. Cook slowly for $1\frac{1}{2}$ minutes, then turn for the last time and cook slowly on other side for $1\frac{1}{2}$ minutes. Have toast piping hot. Drain off any fat from kidney pan into pan containing Worcester sauce. Reheat quickly, and pour over toast. Arrange two kidneys side by side on each. *For 2 persons.*

FRIED SHEEP'S KIDNEYS (Rognons de Moutons frits)

4 sheep's kidneys
1 beaten egg
1 cup sieved stale breadcrumbs
Butter for frying
4 rounds buttered toast
Salt and pepper to taste
1 teaspoon minced parsley
1 tablespoon butter

Wash, skin and cut kidneys nearly in two. Remove all the fibre. Close kidneys. Egg and crumb. Melt enough butter to cover a small frying-pan. Fry kidneys for 4 minutes on each side, turning once or twice, then place each on its toast. Open. Season inside with salt and pepper to taste. Mix parsley with butter to a paste. Stuff kidneys. Close up and serve. *For 4 persons.*

GRILLED CALVES' KIDNEYS (Rognons de Veau grillés)

2 calves' kidneys
$\frac{1}{2}$ pint brown stock
3 rashers bacon
$\frac{1}{4}$ lb. mushroom caps
1 oz. butter
Salt and pepper to taste
2 tablespoons Madeira wine

Wash, skin, core and slice kidneys into a small saucepan. Add stock. Cover and stew gently for 10 minutes. Drain and arrange alternate slices of kidney and bacon on skewers. Skewer a peeled mushroom cap at each end. Grill and gently remove to an oblong of fried bread or buttered toast. Melt in a saucepan. Add kidney stock. Season with salt and pepper to taste. Add wine. Boil up and pour sauce over. *For 6 persons.*

GRILLED SHEEP'S KIDNEYS (Rognons de Mouton grillés)

4 sheep's kidneys
1 tablespoon melted butter
4 tomatoes
4 rashers bacon
Maître d'hôtel butter
4 rounds fried bread

Slit kidneys in two without halving. Skin, core and remove any fat. Keeping them flat, run them on a skewer. Dip in melted butter. Grill for 4 or 5 minutes, turning frequently. Halve and grill tomatoes and bacon rashers. When all are ready, slip a pat of Maître d'Hôtel butter into each kidney. Place rounds of fried bread on a hot dish. Lay a kidney on top of each. Garnish with tomatoes and bacon. *For 4 persons.*

STEWED OX KIDNEY (Rognons de Boeuf en Ragoût)

1 oz. kidney
Salt and pepper to taste
Cayenne pepper to taste
1 tablespoon flour
1 tablespoon butter
1 small peeled onion
1 dessertspoon vinegar
Boiled macaroni and toast
Minced parsley to garnish

Trim kidney, and remove any skin and core. Wipe and cut into pieces about $\frac{1}{2}$ inch thick. Soak in cold, salted water for $\frac{1}{2}$ hour. Dry. Add salt, pepper and cayenne pepper to flour. Dip pieces of kidney in flour. Melt butter in a stewpan. Add kidney and fry slowly for 3 minutes. Chop onion and add with from $\frac{1}{4}$ to $\frac{1}{2}$ pint water, according to taste. Cover and simmer gently for 45 minutes, stirring occasionally. Add vinegar. Dish up. Arrange boiled macaroni round dish. Garnish with parsley and snippets of toast. *For 4 persons.*

LIVER (Foie)

Calf's liver is the choicest and most expensive, but beef, lamb and pig's liver are all used. When choosing liver, see that it is a bright red and has very little smell. As beef liver is strongly flavoured, though cheaper and more nutritious than the others, be sure to soak in water to cover, mixed with 2 tablespoons vinegar for $\frac{1}{2}$ hour, then drain and thoroughly dry before cooking.

To Prepare Livers for Cooking: Wash and dry with a damp cloth, and peel off the thin outside skin. Remove any veins. If beef (ox) liver is tough, parboil for 20 minutes before cooking whole, or 5 minutes if slicing before cooking.

To Fry Liver: (1) Roll slices, cut $\frac{1}{2}$-$\frac{3}{4}$ inch thick, in seasoned flour. Fry in a little melted butter or margarine until browned on both sides. Lower heat, and fry till cooked through. (2) Cut in 5-inch strips. Soak for $\frac{1}{2}$ hour in French dressing, using 2 parts oil to 1 vinegar. Egg and crumb. Fry in deep hot fat or oil till brown.

To Grill Livers: Wash. Slice $\frac{1}{2}$ inch thick. Brush with melted butter or cooking oil. Grill for 5 minutes, turning frequently. Season with salt and pepper and smear with butter.

To Roast Liver: Wash and dry liver. Dip $\frac{1}{2}$-$\frac{3}{4}$ inch thick slices in seasoned flour. Place in a buttered fireproof dish. Cover with strips of bacon. Bake in a moderate oven, 350° F., for about $\frac{1}{2}$ hour.

BAKED STUFFED LIVER (Foie de Veau rôtie)

$\frac{1}{2}$ lb. calf's liver
1 tablespoon bacon dripping
1 tablespoon minced onion
$\frac{1}{4}$ lb. stale breadcrumbs
1 tablespoon minced parsley
Pinch crushed herbs
Salt and pepper to taste
Milk, stock or water as required
2 rashers bacon

Wash and dry liver. Cut into 4 equal-thin slices. Place in a greased fireproof dish. Melt bacon dripping. Add onion and cook gently till soft. Add crumbs, parsley, herbs and salt and pepper to taste. Moisten with milk, stock or water. Spread on liver. Remove rind from bacon. Chop bacon and sprinkle over liver. Pour in just enough stock or water flavoured with beef extract, to prevent liver sticking to dish; $\frac{1}{4}$ pint should be enough unless dish is very large. Cover. Bake in a slow oven, 325° F., for 1¼-1½ hours, till liver is tender. Serve with potatoes and sliced carrots. *For 4 persons.*

BRAISED LIVER (Foie de Veau braisé)

1 lb. calf's liver
3 tablespoons seasoned flour
3 oz. butter or margarine
½ cup shredded celery
½ cup chopped onion
1 chopped clove garlic
6 rashers bacon
½ pint stock
Salt to taste
1¼ lb. potatoes
6 small carrots

Wash, dry and cut liver into ¾ inch-thick slices. Coat with seasoned flour. Melt fat in a heavy frying-pan. Add liver, celery and onion. Fry slowly, turning occasionally, until browned, then place in a greased casserole. Add garlic. Place bacon with rinds removed on top. Pour in stock at the side. Season with salt. Cover. Bake in a moderate oven, 350° F., for about 30 minutes. Peel and halve potatoes and add. Scrape carrots and add. Cover, and continue baking in a moderate oven, 350° F., until vegetables are tender, in about ½ hour. Remove cover. Draw vegetables away from bacon. Bake till bacon is crisp. Dish up. If gravy is not thick enough, thicken with flour creamed with stock. *For 6 persons.*

LIVER FRITTERS (Beignets de Foie)

2 oz. flour
1 tablespoon olive oil
1 egg yolk
¼ lb. steamed calf's liver
Salt and cayenne pepper to taste
1 teaspoon lemon juice
Onion juice to taste
1 tablespoon liver gravy
1 egg white

Measure flour into a basin. Add oil and egg yolk. Stir in enough water to make a stiff paste. Beat well with a wooden spoon, then thin with more cold water to a creamy batter. Put liver through a meat grinder. Mash in a basin with salt, cayenne pepper, lemon juice and onion juice to taste. Add liver gravy to moisten. Leave till cold and set. Fold stiffly frothed egg white into batter. Dip slices of liver mould in batter. Fry in deep smoking hot fat till crisp brown. Drain well. *For 3 or 4 persons.*

STEAMED LIVER PUDDING (Pouding de Foie)

1 lb. calf's liver
½ cup breadcrumbs
Stock to moisten
1 tablespoon minced onion
2 well-beaten eggs
Salt and pepper to taste
½ teaspoon minced parsley
1 tablespoon butter

Mince liver. Stir in breadcrumbs and stock. Mix pulp with onion, eggs, salt, pepper, parsley and melted butter. Grease a pudding mould. Add mixture. Cover with a buttered paper. Steam for 45 minutes. Unmould. Serve with tomato sauce. *For 5 persons.*

SWEETBREADS

Sweetbreads usually on sale are the glands of calves and lamb. The calves' are considered the more delicate. As they are easily digested, and are not so stimulating as meat, they are invaluable for invalids. There are two kinds of sweetbread : the " heart," which is round, firm, white and compact, is the more desirable as it is more delicate than the other which is known as the

" throat." The " heart " is more suitable for serving whole. The " throat " is less compact and is of a darker shade, and somewhat membraneous. It is more suitable for using in recipes in which sweetbreads are cut in small pieces. They are a great delicacy, and specially useful for making into entrées. Sweetbreads are usually sold in a pair, though sometimes separately. As they spoil quickly, they should be cooked as soon as possible. If this is not practical, wash thoroughly and place in a basin of cold water. Soak for 1 hour, then cook. They can also be pre-cooked when it is not possible to cook and serve them at once, in which case, weight them down between two plates, then store them in a refrigerator until you are ready to dress them. Before braising, creaming, frying, grilling or dressing sweetbreads in any way, boil them by the following method :

TO COOK SWEETBREADS

Wash, then place them in a saucepan. Cover with acidulated salted water, allowing 1 teaspoon salt and 1 dessertspoon vinegar to each quart of water. Cover. Simmer for $\frac{1}{4}$ hour. Drain quickly and plunge into cold water to whiten and firm them. Now remove the membrane and tubes, then, allowing $\frac{1}{2}$ to 1 pair per portion, dress them.

NOTE : Use this method of cooking when sweetbreads have to be stored in a refrigerator for some time before dressing.

To Braise Sweetbreads: Cut 2 pairs pre-cooked sweetbreads in slices lengthwise about $\frac{1}{4}$ inch thick. Melt $1\frac{1}{2}$ tablespoons butter a in shallow saucepan. Fry till delicately browned, turning once or twice. Add 1 cup rich brown stock, 2 teaspoons chopped shallot and parsley, salt, pepper and paprika to taste, and a dash of mushroom ketchup and Worcester sauce. Cover and cook slowly for 5-10 minutes. Add a tablespoon of sherry. Bring to boil. Serve on a bed of spinach. *For 6 persons.*

To Cream Sweetbreads: Separate 3 pairs of sweetbreads, pre-cooked, into small pieces, about the size of a walnut. Add 1 pint well-flavoured hot Béchamel sauce. Stir in 1 heaped teaspoon finely chopped parsley or chives. When ready to serve, beat 1 egg yolk slightly, and stir in slowly. When nearly boiling, serve in hot patty cases, on buttered toast or fried bread, or in little nests of mashed potato put through a forcing pipe. Dredge lightly with paprika.

FRICASSEE OF SWEETBREADS (Fricassée de Ris de Veau)

1 pair calf's sweetbreads
$\frac{1}{2}$ oz. buutter
$\frac{3}{4}$ oz. flour
$\frac{1}{4}$ pint stock
$\frac{1}{4}$ pint milk
$\frac{1}{4}$ pint cream
Salt and pepper to taste
2 yolks eggs

Blanch and trim sweetbreads. Press them between two plates. When cold, cut in slices. Melt butter in a saucepan. Stir in flour, and, when mixture froths, gradually stir in warm stock, then warm milk, stirring all the time. When smooth and at boiling point, stir in cream. Boil, still stirring, for a minute or two, then season to taste with salt and pepper. Add sliced sweetbreads. Put lid on pan, and simmer for 20 minutes, then stir in egg yolks and serve when hot and thick. Do not boil again. This is best cooked in a double boiler. Garnish with fleurons of puff pastry or serve in a puff paste *vol au vent* case, garnished with a criss-cross design of thin strips of pimiento, heated in boiling water. *For 4 persons.*

FRIED SWEETBREADS (Ris de Veau, frit)

1 lb. sweetbreads
¼ cup shredded celery
1 sprig parsley
1 small teaspoon salt
1 teaspoon lemon juice
Cold water as required
1 slightly beaten egg
1 cup stale sieved breadcrumbs
1 tablespoon butter

Wash and soak sweetbreads in salted water to cover for ½ hour. Drain. Place in a saucepan with celery, parsley, salt, lemon juice and enough cold water to cover. Bring to boil. Simmer gently for ½ hour. Remove membrane and any fat from sweetbreads. Split lengthwise. Egg and crumb. Melt butter in a frying-pan. Add sweetbreads. Fry quickly till brown below, then turn and fry on other side. Serve with tomato sauce or Tartare sauce. *For 4 persons.*

TONGUE (Langue)

Tongue can be bought fresh or pickled. Calf's, lamb's, ox, and sheep's tongues are all sold fresh or pickled, and canned tongues are always available when fresh are not.

To Choose Tongue: A good tongue should be plump in shape with smooth skin when young and tender. If fresh from pickle, it requires 2-3 hours' soaking, according to size.

To Prepare for Cooking: Scrub tongue well in lukewarm water with a small brush.

BOILED LAMBS' TONGUES (Langues d'Agneau bouillies)

4 fresh lambs' tongues
1 teaspoon salt
1 in. cinnamon stick
1 thick slice onion, stuck with
  3 cloves
½ bay leaf
Boiling water as required
3 tablespoons lemon juice

Scrub tongues, then rinse well. Place in a shallow saucepan. Add salt, cinnamon stick, onion, bay leaf and boiling water to cover. Bring to boil. Skim, then cover again and simmer gently for ¾ hour. Add lemon juice, or vinegar, if preferred. Cover and simmer again for about ½ hour or until tender. Leave in stock till cool. Remove tongues. Skin them and take off root ends. When quite cold, place on serving dish, garnished with hearts of lettuce. Serve with sauce Tartare. *For 4 persons.*

BOILED OX TONGUE (Langue de Boeuf bouillie)

Wash tongue thoroughly. If fresh, soak in cold water to cover from 1-2 hours. If pickled, soak in cold water to cover for 3-4 hours. Place in a large saucepan. Cover with tepid water. Bring slowly to the boil. Skim thoroughly. Add 1 sliced carrot, 2 or 3 slices turnip, 1 sliced medium-sized onion, 6 peppercorns, and a bouquet garni. Bring again to boil. (If you have any beef stock to spare, you can substitute the stock for the water.) Cover tightly. Simmer gently, allowing ½ hour per lb., and ½ hour over. When ready, remove to

250

a board and skin carefully. There are two ways of shaping the tongue : (1) Stick a fork or skewer through the tip to straighten it and put another through the root. Leave until cold, then brush with glaze and decorate with flowers of savoury butter piped through a forcing pipe, and encircle root with a paper ruffle. Garnish with parsley. (2) Twist it into a round in a basin, bowl or cake tin, and weight it down. Leave overnight or until cold, then turn out. Garnish with a piping of savoury butter and parsley.

CREAMED CALF'S TONGUE (Langue de Veau à la Crème)

1½ oz. butter
3 tablespoons flour
¾ pint hot milk
2 teaspoons minced onion
Salt and pepper to taste
8 oz. cold diced tongue
1½ teaspoons minced pimiento
1½ teaspoons minced parsley
1 pint boiled green peas

Melt butter in a saucepan. Add flour and when mixture froths, stir in milk. Bring to boil. Boil for 5 minutes, stirring constantly. Add onion and salt and pepper to taste. Boil for 2 minutes, stirring constantly. Add tongue and pimiento. Heat till piping hot, then stir in parsley. Serve on a hot dish in a border of dressed green peas. *For 4 persons.*

TRIPE

Tripe is the muscular inner lining of the ruminant stomach of an ox. Generally partially cooked before it is sold. Wash very thoroughly before dressing it. There are many varieties of tripe, such as blanket, book, honeycomb, monk's hood, etc. Blanket and honeycomb are most often on sale. Honeycomb is the more delicate of the two varieties. Easily digestible, tripe is most nourishing and very suitable for invalids.

To Choose: See that it is perfectly fresh with a sweet smell and white in colour.

FRIED TRIPE (Tripe frite)

Wash and remove fat from tripe. Place tripe in a pan. Cover with boiling water. Simmer very gently for 4 to 5 hours, till tender. Turn into a basin. Leave for 24 hours. Drain. Cut into oblongs. Egg and crumb. Fry in a little smoking hot dripping for about 10 minutes, till light brown. Serve with onion sauce. *Allow 6 oz. tripe per person.*

TRIPE AND ONIONS (Tripe à l'Anglaise)

2 lb. tripe
1 oz. flour
1 pint milk
4 to 6 onions
Salt and pepper to taste

Buy tripe ready cleaned. Place it in a saucepan. Cover with cold water and bring to boil. Pour into a colander. Drain well, then cut into 3-inch squares. Place in a saucepan. Cover with cold water. Bring to boil, and simmer gently for 2 or 3 hours, until tender. Turn again into the colander, and, when well drained, place in a clean saucepan. Mix flour to a paste in a basin with a little of the milk. Stir in remainder of milk, then add milk and flour to tripe. Stir over fire till boiling. Add boiled peeled onions, finely minced, and salt and pepper to taste. Cover and simmer for 15 minutes. *For 4 to 6 persons.*

TRIPE PROVENCALE

1 oz. butter
2 or 3 medium-sized carrots
6 medium-sized onions
1 pint stock
½ pint Madeira, sherry or white wine
Salt and pepper to taste
2 lb. tripe

Melt fat in a saucepan. Add scraped and sliced carrots, and peeled and sliced onions, and fry till brown, then turn fat and vegetables into a casserole. Rinse saucepan out with a little of the stock. Pour liquid into casserole with remainder of stock and wine. Add salt and pepper to taste, and tripe cut into pieces about 2-2½ inches square. Cover closely, and cook very slowly for 4 or 5 hours, either over a low heat with an asbestos mat, or in a slow oven, 275° F. Serve from casserole. *For 4 persons.*

FAGGOTS

1 lb. pig's fry, including caul
3 medium-sized onions
3 oz. breadcrumbs
½ teaspoon salt
½ teaspoon dried crushed sage
½ teaspoon crushed herbs

Soak the caul in salted water. Wash the fry. Peel onions. Place fry and onions in a saucepan with just enough water to cover. Simmer for ¾ hour. Remove from stove. Drain off liquid. Pour a little on the crumbs. Keep the remainder for making gravy. Chop fry. Add minced onion, crumbs and seasonings. Beat till smooth with a fork. If too dry, add a little of the liquid to make mixture bind. Cut caul in pieces about 4 inches square. Put 2 tablespoons of mixture in each. Fold caul round to form balls. Place in a greased baking tin or fireproof dish. Brown quickly in a moderately hot oven, 400° F. If mixture is reheated just before making into balls, it can be browned under the grill. To make the gravy, use 1 oz. flour to 1 pint liquid. Mix flour to a cream with a little cold water. Add liquid in which fry was cooked and seasoning to taste. Bring to boil and boil for 3 minutes, stirring all the time. Pour a little of this round the faggots before browning in the oven. Pour the remainder round just before serving. *For 5 or 6 persons.*

LAMB'S FRY

1½ lb. lamb's fry
3 thin rashers bacon
1 small peeled onion
1 small scraped carrot
1 bouquet garni
2 tablespoons boiled macaroni
3 oz. butter
1 oz. flour
Salt and pepper to taste
1 teaspoon minced parsley
Egg and crumbs

Wash fry. Remove rind from bacon. Slice onion and carrot thinly. Place fry in a shallow saucepan. Add onion and carrot slices, bouquet garni and cold water to cover. Bring slowly to boil. Skim and simmer slowly for about 1 hour. Turn into a basin. Leave till cold, then strain gravy into a jug. Cut meat in two equal portions, then cut 1 portion into small dice. Chop macaroni. Melt 1 oz. butter in a shallow saucepan. Add flour. Stir till frothy, then stir in strained liquor from fry. Stir till boiling. Season to taste with salt and pepper. Add diced meat, macaroni and parsley. Cover. Keep hot, but do not allow to boil again.

252

Halve rashers of bacon. Roll each portion up and run on 2 skewers. Bake in a moderate oven, 350° F., for about 20 minutes, turning at half-time, so that rolls are cooked through and equally crisp. Cut remainder of fry into thin slices. Season with salt and pepper and egg and crumb. Melt remainder of butter in a frying-pan. Cook fry quickly until light brown on both sides. Pile macaroni mixture in centre of a hot dish. Arrange slices of fry against macaroni. Garnish round base with bacon rolls and cooked green peas alternately. *For 6 persons.*

STEWED OX TAIL (Queue de Boeuf en ragoût)

1 ox tail
½ lb. onions
2 cloves
1 teaspoon minced parsley
6 peppercorns
Salt and paprika to taste
Water as required
½ lb. diced carrot
½ lb. cubed turnip
2 oz. diced parsnip
1 oz. butter
2 teaspoons flour

Wash ox tail thoroughly, then cut into joints. Peel onions. Stick cloves in 1 onion. Place in saucepan. Add parsley, peppercorns, salt and paprika to taste, ox tail joints, and just enough cold water to cover. Bring to boil. Skim if necessary. Simmer gently for 3 hours. Strain stock into a basin. Stand for 5 minutes, then skim. Return to pan. Peel and slice remainder of onions and add with carrot, turnip and parsnip. Cover and simmer gently till vegetables are tender. Mix fat and flour to a paste. Stir into stew. Bring to boil and simmer for about 7 minutes. Dish up. *For 4 persons.*

PIG'S FRY

1 pig's fry
Crushed herbs to taste
1 oz. flour
4 rashers bacon
½ pint stock or hot water
Salt and pepper to taste

Wash and dry the fry well. Scald, skin and core kidney. Slice kidney, heart and liver. Season with herbs to taste. Dip in flour. Remove the rinds from bacon rashers. Cook bacon in a frying-pan, turning once until fat is clear. Remove rashers to a hot dish. Keep hot while you cook " fry " in bacon fat for about 10 minutes. Arrange on top of rashers. Sprinkle remainder of flour into fat. Stir till frothy, then stir in water or stock. Season to taste. Bring to boil and simmer for 3 or 4 minutes. Pour over fry. Serve with mashed potatoes. *For 4 or 5 persons.*

GRILLED DEVILLED PIGS' TROTTERS
(Pieds grillés à la Diable)

3 cooked pigs' trotters
Salt and white pepper to taste
½ oz. butter
1 teaspoon white wine vinegar
1 teaspoon Worcester sauce
1 egg yolk
Mustard to taste
Cayenne pepper to taste
Breadcrumbs as required
Minced parsley as garnish

Split trotters in two. Season with salt and pepper to taste. Place butter in a basin. Stir in vinegar, Worcester sauce, egg yolk, salt to taste, mustard and cayenne pepper to taste. Mix to a smooth paste. Spread on both sides of the trotters. Roll in breadcrumbs. Place on a rack in grill pan. Grill for 4 to 5 minutes. Garnish with parsley. *For 6 persons.*

BOILED SHEEP'S TROTTERS (Pied bouillis)

2 sheep's trotters
½ pint milk
½ pint water
1 peeled Spanish onion
Salt and pepper to taste
½ oz. flour
1 teaspoon minced parsley

Place trotters in a large basin. Cover with boiling water. Stand for 1 minute. Scrape off all wool with a knife, but be careful not to remove any skin. Take away the little bag between the hoofs. Place the trotters in a saucepan. Cover with water, then cover and simmer for 2 hours. Remove, scrape, and take away any shell or horn from each hoof. Split prepared trotters in three lengthwise. Place in a saucepan. Add milk and water. Slice in onion. Add salt and pepper to taste. Cover and simmer for 2 hours. Remove trotters. Place on a hot dish. Dissolve flour in 2 tablespoons cold milk. Stir in hot stock, then return to the saucepan and boil for 5 minutes, stirring constantly. Season to taste. Add trotters, Reheat. Arrange on a hot dish. Sprinkle with parsley. *For 2 persons.*

BAKED FRANKFURTERS (Saucisses de Frankfort au four)

8 frankfurters
French mustard as required
3 cooking apples
2 tablespoons sugar
½ cup grated cheese

Arrange frankfurters side by side in a greased fireproof dish. Spread lightly with mustard. Peel apples, then core and cut them into thin slices. Place apple over frankfurters. Sprinkle with sugar. Bake in a moderate oven, 350° F., for about 20 minutes. Sprinkle with grated cheese. Bake for a few minutes till cheese melts. *For 4 persons.*

BAKED STUFFED FRANKFURTERS
(Saucisses de Frankfort au four)

8 frankfurters
Mashed potatoes as required
1 heaped teaspoon chopped fried onion
3 or 4 fried mushrooms
Grated cheese as required

Make a slit down side of each frankfurter. Mix potato with onion. Chop mushrooms and add, then pack this mixture into sausages. Lay side by side in a shallow greased fireproof dish. Bake in a moderate oven, 350° F., for about 20 minutes. Sprinkle with cheese. Bake for a few minutes longer until cheese melts. *For 4 persons.*

PORK SAUSAGE LOAF (Pain à la Fermière)

1 lb. beef sausage meat
1 lb. pork sausage meat
½ cup stale breadcrumbs
1 teaspoon salt
Pepper to taste
Crushed herbs to taste
½ teaspoon chopped parsley
2 fresh eggs
¼ cup thin cream

Mix sausage meats with crumbs. Add seasoning and herbs. Beat eggs. Stir in cream. Add to meat mixture and mix well together. Press into a greased loaf tin, or shape into a loaf and place in a greased loaf tin. Bake, without a cover, in a moderate oven, 350° F., for about 1 hour. Serve, turned out, on a hot dish, with celery. *For 6 persons.*

LEFT OVER AND CANNED MEAT

AMERICAN CHOP SUEY (Chop Suey Américaine)

2 tablespoons meat dripping
1-2 cups minced onion or shallots
2 cups shredded celery
2 cups meat stock or thin gravy
1 tablespoon cornflour
Cold water as required
2 cups chopped cooked beef, lamb, mutton or pork
2 cups sliced raw young carrots or radishes
Salt and pepper to taste
Yorkshire relish or soy sauce
Boiled rice
Minced chives or parsley

Melt dripping in a shallow saucepan. Add onion according to taste. Fry gently for 5 minutes, stirring occasionally, then add celery and stock or gravy gradually. Cover. Simmer for 5 to 7 minutes. Thicken with the cornflour creamed with cold water. Cook, still stirring, till smooth and thick. Add meat and carrots or radishes. When Jerusalem artichokes are available, these can be substituted for carrots or radishes. Season to taste with salt and pepper. Flavour with a few drops of Yorkshire relish or soy sauce. Heat thoroughly and stir well. Serve in a circle of boiled rice, sprinkled with minced chives or parsley. *For 5 or 6 persons.*

AMERICAN CORNED BEEF HASH (Hachis de Boeuf Salé)

3 tablespoons beef dripping
2 tablespoons chopped onion
2 cups chopped corned beef
2 cups cubed boiled potatoes
1 cup beef stock or water

Melt fat in a frying-pan. Add onion. Fry slowly till clear. Mix the beef, potatoes and liquid. Stir into onion, then spread evenly over bottom of pan. Fry slowly. As base turns brown, keep lifting and stirring in crusty bits, then when cooked to your taste so that the hash is speckled with brown and browned below, fold over like an omelet. Serve with fried apple rings and cabbage or savoy. Sometimes hash is topped with a fried or poached egg. *For 4 persons.*

BEEF CROQUETTES (Croquettes de Boeuf)

2 tablespoons margarine
1 tablespoon minced onion
1 heaped teaspoon minced parsley
2 cups minced cooked flank
1 cup mashed potato
3 tablespoons left-over gravy
Salt and pepper to taste
1 tablespoon stock or water
1 beaten egg
Egg and crumbs

Melt fat in a frying-pan. Add onion and parsley. Cook gently for 5 minutes. Stir in meat, potato, gravy and salt and pepper to taste. Turn on to a plate. Leave till cold. Stir stock or water into egg. Divide mixture into 12 equal portions. Shape with lightly floured hands into croquettes. Dip in egg, then in crumbs. Fry in deep smoking hot fat, deep enough to cover three at a time, until golden brown, in 4 or 5 minutes. Drain on paper. Serve on a hot dish. Garnish with parsley. *For 6 persons.*

BUBBLE AND SQUEAK (Hachis de Boeuf, Anglais)

8 oz. cooked beef or canned sausage meat
8 oz. cooked cabbage
2 oz. beef dripping

Remove all fat, gristle and skin from meat. Cut meat into thin slices. Chop cabbage on a board. Melt dripping in a frying-pan. Brown meat a

Salt and pepper to taste

little on both sides, then remove to a hot dish. Place cabbage in pan. Sprinkle with salt and pepper to taste. Fry slightly and brown here and there. Pile in the centre of a hot dish and arrange meat round. If liked, any left-over boiled potatoes can be fried with the cabbage. Any remains of corned beef, ham or tongue can be substituted for part of the beef. *For 2 or 3 persons.*

COLCANNON

1 lb. boiled silverside
1 medium-sized cabbage
Salt and pepper to taste
2 oz. butter

Cut meat in rather thin slices. (Under-done roast beef can be used, if preferred.) Trim and shred cabbage. Rinse and boil in boiling salted water to cover, in a covered saucepan, till tender. Drain thoroughly. Season with salt and pepper to taste. Melt fat in a frying-pan. Fry meat lightly on each side, but only for a few minutes. Arrange in overlapping slices round a flat hot dish. Toss cabbage in remaining fat in frying-pan until piping hot, then turn into centre of meat. Serve at once with mustard pickle. *For 4 or 5 persons.*

CURRIED COOKED MEAT (Kari de Viande)

1 oz. butter
1 apple
2 teaspoons curry powder
1 peeled onion
2 peeled tomatoes
1 teaspoon chutney
1 dessertspoon desiccated coconut
1½ dessertspoons rice flour
½ pint white stock
1 tablespoon cream
Salt to taste
1 lb. cooked meat
½ teaspoon lemon juice

Melt butter in a saucepan. Add apple and curry powder. Slice in onion and tomatoes. Add chutney, coconut and rice flour to stock, then Stir into other ingredients. Stir till boiling, then simmer for 20 minutes. Rub all through a wire sieve. Return to a saucepan. Add cream, salt to taste and a lump of sugar. Cut meat into 1-inch squares, and add to sauce. Draw pan to side of stove and, when meat is hot, stir in lemon juice. Serve surrounded by boiled rice. *For 4 persons.*

GOLABKI (Choux farcis, Polonaise)

6 large cabbage leaves
1 cup rice
1 lb. minced beef
1 beaten egg
1 chopped onion
Salt and pepper to taste
Tomato juice as required

Parboil cabbage leaves for 10 minutes, or till pliable. Rinse rice in a colander under cold water tap, and drain well. Throw into a pan of boiling, salted water and boil for 20 minutes. Drain rice. Stir in meat, beaten egg, onion and salt and pepper to taste. Divide mixture equally between cabbage leaves, and roll up each leaf. Tie gently with narrow tapes to keep their shape. Place side by side in a shallow baking dish or casserole. Half cover with tomato juice. Cover and bake in a hot oven, 450° F., for about 1 hour, basting occasionally. *For 6 persons.*

When carving a Target of Lamb, a cutlet and bits of breast should be served together. *See page* 238

Roast Loin of Pork marked for carving. *See page* 240.

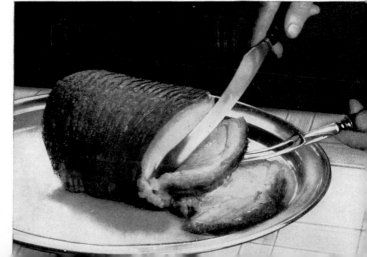

Cut Pork through the rind, then carve in regular slices. *See page* 240

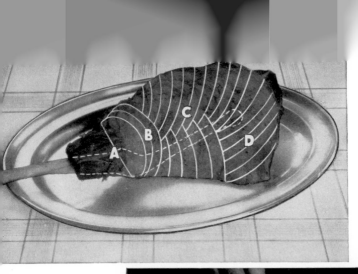

Roast Leg of Mutton marked for carving. (Follow same method for leg of lamb.) *See page* 238.

With a knife slanted towards knuckle bone, cut two or three slices according to size of leg. After removing all the cushion, carve the meat from the other side. *See page* 238

Lamb or Mutton carved and arranged ready for serving. *See page* 238-239.

KROMESKIES (Kromeskies de Viande)

3 oz. minced cooked veal
1 oz. minced cooked ham or tongue
3 chopped button mushrooms
Salt and pepper to taste
Pinch grated lemon rind
½ oz. butter
½ oz. flour
5 tablespoons milk

Mix veal with ham or tongue, mushrooms, salt and pepper to taste and lemon rind. Melt butter in a small saucepan. Add flour. Stir in milk gradually. Stir till smooth and boiling. Add enough of this panada to veal to bind mixture. Leave till cold. Divide mixture into 6 equal portions, and shape like a cork. Wrap each in a small, very thin slice of bacon. Dip in coating batter. Fry in deep fat till crisp and golden. Drain on absorbent paper. Garnish with lemon and parsley. *For 3 persons.*

LAMB FRITTERS (Beignets d'Agneau)

½ lb. sifted flour
2 teaspoons baking powder
1 teaspoon salt
1 dessertspoon caster sugar
Pepper to taste
Pinch celery salt
1 beaten egg
1½ cups milk
2 tablespoons meat gravy
5 oz. minced cold lamb
1 rasher bacon
Sprigs of parsley for garnish

Sift flour with baking powder, salt, sugar and seasonings into a basin. Beat egg till honey-coloured, and stir in milk and gravy. Make a hollow in centre of flour. Pour in egg mixture. Stir until all flour has been gradually incorporated with the liquid, and you have a smooth batter. Stir in lamb. Remove rind from bacon. Grill bacon lightly, then chop and add to batter. Mix well. Drop from a tablespoon into deep, smoking hot fat and fry till brown, in 2 or 3 minutes. Drain on soft paper. Serve piled on a hot dish lined with a lace paper doily. Garnish with sprigs of parsley. *For 6 persons.*

LAMB AND MACARONI CROQUETTES
(Croquettes d'Agneau, Italienne)

1 cup chopped cooked lamb
1 cup cold boiled macaroni
1 cup thick hot parsley sauce
Salt and pepper to taste
1 dessertspoon grated onion
Dash of mushroom ketchup
Eggs and crumbs as required

Mix lamb with macaroni, sauce, salt and pepper to taste, onion, and ketchup. Spread on a plate to cool. With floured hands, shape into equal-sized balls. Dip each in crumbs, then in beaten egg, then in crumbs again. Fry a few at a time in as much smoking hot fat as possible for about a minute, till golden. Drain on crumpled paper. Pile in centre of a ring of green peas. Serve with tomato sauce. *For 4 persons.*

LAMB OR MUTTON BATTER (Pouding de Viande, Yorkshire)

3 tablespoons flour
Pinch of salt
1 beaten egg
½ pint milk
8 oz. cooked minced lamb or mutton
1 teaspoon baking powder

Sift flour with salt into a basin. Mix egg with half the milk. Stir into flour to make a creamy mixture. Beat well. Stand for ½ hour. Stir in meat, baking powder and remainder of milk, and mix well. Add herbs, onion, parsley and more salt and pepper to taste. Melt ½ oz. dripping in

Pinch crushed herbs
1 dessertspoon minced onion
1 teaspoon minced parsley
Pepper to taste

baking tin. Pour in batter. Bake in a hot oven, 450° F., from ½ to ¾ hour. *For 4 persons.*

MOUSSES OF HAM (Mousses de Jambon)

1 lb. lean cooked ham
2 egg yolks
1 saltspoon grated nutmeg
1 saltspoon cayenne pepper
1 tablespoon sherry
¼ pint cream
3 egg whites

Mince ham finely. Place in a mortar with egg yolks. Pound to a paste. Press through sieve into a basin. Season with grated nutmeg and cayenne pepper. Add sherry. Mix well with a spoon. Gradually stir in cream, mixing continually. Beat egg whites to a stiff froth. Fold lightly into ham mixture. Pile up in 6 small greased ramekins. Place them in a baking tin containing hot water to the depth of 1 inch. Bake for about 15 minutes in a moderate oven, 350° F., till set. Remove and serve on a hot dish lined with folded napkin. *For 6 persons.*

SHEPHERD'S PIE (Pâté à la Bergère)

1 lb. cold beef, mutton or whale meat
2 small peeled onions
1½ oz. mutton or beef dripping
½ pint gravy
½ teaspoon minced parsley
Salt and pepper to taste
1½ lb. cold potatoes
¼ cup hot milk
2 tablespoons butter or margarine

Remove any fat, gristle and skin from meat before weighing. Cut meat into dice. Chop onions. Melt mutton dripping in a saucepan if using mutton, or else beef dripping. Fry onion till pale brown, then stir in meat, gravy, parsley and salt and pepper to taste. Simmer for 5 minutes, then turn into a buttered pie dish. Mash potatoes. Season to taste. Add milk and fat. Mix well. Pile up over meat. Decorate with a fork. Bake in a moderate oven, 350° F., for about ½ hour. *For 4 persons.*

TOAD IN THE HOLE

BASIC RECIPE :
½-¾ lb. cold roast beef
¼ lb. flour
¼ teaspoon salt
Pepper to taste
½ pint milk
1 egg
1 oz. dripping

Cut meat into small squares. Sift flour, salt and pepper into a basin. Add enough milk to make a thin cream, then beat in egg. Beat till smooth, then beat from 5-10 minutes to aerate batter. Stir in remainder of milk. Stand for 1 hour. Melt dripping in small baking tin, or shallow fireproof dish. When hot, add meat. If there is no fat attached, add 2 or 3 tablespoons left-over gravy. Place in oven till meat is heated through, then pour in batter. Bake in a hot oven, 450° F., for about ½ hour. *For 4 persons.*

To Vary: (1) Substitute left-over stewed steak and kidney for the cold roast beef. (2) Substitute ½-¾ lb. beef sausages. Slit and skin, then cut in halves. Shape each half with your hands into a roll. Brush with tomato catsup, if liked. Follow method given for Toad in the Hole, but add ¼ teaspoon crushed herbs to the batter before pouring over sausages. Bake in a fairly hot oven, 450° F., for about ½ hour.

COLD MEATS

There are many ways of treating cold meat besides serving with salad. Set in aspic, turn it into a mousse, or make into a brawn, galantine, loaf or mould.

To Use up Cold Boiled or Roast Meat : Cut in thin slices and arrange slices overlapping either round a flat dish or down the centre. If round, fill centre with sprigs of watercress, curly endive or parsley. If down the centre, arrange watercress, endive or heart of lettuce leaves round meat with small boiled beets or tomatoes, stuffed with Russian salad, nestling in foliage. To make a more substantial dish, tuck as well in the greenery, whether in centre or round the meat, half devilled egg per person. If an assorted meat platter is required, alternate boiled or roast meat with brawn, liver sausage, ham or tongue, salami, etc.

Galantines : Brush with glaze when cold. Decorate with savoury butter squeezed through a forcing pipe.

Moulds and Mousses : Ring base with heart of lettuce leaves, curly endive or watercress. Garnish with ornaments of pimiento, radish roses, etc. If liked, make a small hole in centre and insert celery foliage or watercress.

Moulds of Meat in Aspic : Garnish round base with chopped aspic, decorated chopped green or red pepper or pimiento or minced parsley.

Garnishes for Cold Meats : Chopped aspic, black, green or stuffed olives, fans of pickled gherkin, ornaments of boiled beetroot and pimiento, radish and tomato roses, devilled eggs, sprigs of chervil, fennel or parsley, heart of lettuce leaves, curly endive, etc.

AYRSHIRE BEEF GALANTINE (Galantine de Boeuf, Ayrshire)

½ lb. breadcrumbs
Pinch black pepper
½ teaspoon salt
¼ teaspoon ground mace
¼ teaspoon ground nutmeg
1 lb. ground steak
1 lb. chopped fat bacon
2 raw eggs
¼ pint stock
3 hard-boiled eggs

Mix breadcrumbs and seasonings together. Add steak and bacon. Beat eggs with stock and add. Mix well. Form meat mixture into a roll with the halved hard-boiled eggs in centre, end to end. Roll up in a buttered cloth. Tie securely. Place in a pan half-full of hot stock, or water, flavoured with 1 teaspoon meat extract. Bring to boil. Add a small piece of carrot, turnip, 1 onion and a sprig of parsley. Simmer for 2 hours. Drain. Press between 2 plates. When cold, brush with brown or tomato glaze. *For 8 persons.*

BOLSTER OF VEAL (Galantine de Veau)

1 breast of veal
1 lb. sausage meat
2 hard-boiled eggs
¼ lb. lean ham
2 oz. boiled tongue
Salt and pepper to taste
Meat glaze as required

Remove bones from breast, taking care not to break the outer skin. Spread breast with sausage meat. Arrange slices of egg down centre. Cut ham and tongue in strips and arrange on meat, according to taste. Season with salt and pepper to taste. Roll up. Tie firmly in a pudding cloth, wrung out of boiling water. Sew up along sides. Place in a saucepan of boiling bone stock. Cover and simmer for 3 hours. Drain. Unroll and roll up again tightly. Place between two plates or boards. Cover with a weight. Leave till quite cold. Remove boards and cloth. Brush galantine with melted meat glaze. Chill. Garnish with ornaments or slices of beetroot and heart of lettuce leaves before serving. *For 6 to 8 persons.*

CALF'S HEAD BRAWN (Tête de Veau en Gelée)

Remains of a calf's head
Cold ham or bacon
2 hard-boiled eggs
1 teaspoon minced parsley
1 grated lemon rind
Salt and pepper to taste
½ teaspoon ground mace
⅛ teaspoon ground nutmeg
⅛ teaspoon ground cloves
½ pint jellied stock

To every pound of calf's head, allow ½ lb. cold ham or bacon. Cut meat into dice. Slice hard-boiled eggs. Butter a large mould and arrange some of the slices of egg in the bottom. Mix together parsley, lemon rind and all the seasonings. Cover bottom of mould with a layer of diced meat, then arrange a few slices of egg on top. Cover with another layer of meat, then with egg and so on till the mould is full. Heat jellied stock, which should consist of the liquor from calf's head reduced to a thick jelly, and pour over till mould is full. Cover with a buttered paper and bake in a slow oven, 275° F., for about 2 hours. Add a little more hot stock as soon as you take the mould from oven. When required, turn out from mould on to a dish. Garnish with parsley. Serve with potato or Russian salad.

GALANTINE OF SHEEP'S TONGUE
(Galantine de Langues de Mouton)

6 fresh or salt tongues
3 hard-boiled eggs
½ oz. powdered gelatine
¾ pint stock
Salt and pepper to taste
1 teaspoon minced parsley
Coralline pepper
Lettuce and tomato to garnish

If fresh tongues are to be used, cook them very gently for about 2 hours until skins come off quite easily. When skinned, cut in half lengthwise. Shell eggs. Soften gelatine in 2 tablespoons of the cold stock, then heat remainder of stock until nearly boiling and add to gelatine. Stir till dissolved. (If stock is very weak, you'll need 1 oz. gelatine.) Season stock with salt and pepper to taste. Ornament bottom of a wet mould with a slice of hard-boiled egg. Sprinkle a ring of parsley round, then a ring of coralline pepper. Season tongues and place a layer on top. Add enough of the remaining stock to set tongue. Cover with four slices of hard-boiled egg, arranged side by side, then add another layer of tongue and more stock to set. Repeat layers until all tongue and eggs are added, then pour over remainder of stock. Leave till set and chilled. Turn out carefully. Garnish round base with shredded lettuce slices and tomato slices. *For 6 persons.*

LAMB OR MUTTON JELLY (Aspic de Viande)

1 tablespoon beef aspic jelly
½ pint boiling water
¼ pint mint sauce
2 cups canned peas
1 cup chopped cooked lamb or mutton
1 heaped teaspoon minced chives or parsley
Salt and pepper to taste

Dissolve jelly in boiling water. Add mint sauce and cool. Rinse a mould and stir in ¾ gill of the liquid jelly. Leave till set, then cover with a layer of peas, or sliced cooked French beans. Sprinkle with 2 tablespoons of the liquid jelly, and leave till set. Mix all but a tablespoon of the remaining peas or beans with the meat and chives or parsley, and season with salt and pepper to taste. Place in mould and fill with remaining liquid jelly. When set and chilled, turn out on to a dish lined with crisp lettuce leaves. Garnish with remaining peas or beans and radish roses. *For 3 or 4 persons.*

MOUSSE OF HAM (Mousse de Jambon)

1 lb. lean boiled ham
2 oz. white sauce
1 saltspoon mustard
Salt and white pepper to taste
½ pint beef aspic jelly
4 sheets gelatine
2 or 3 drops cochineal
½ pint whipped cream
Truffle as required

Good flavoured York ham makes the best ham mousses. First prepare mould. Place it on crushed ice, rub it well with olive oil, then rub oil off again. Decorate according to taste with diamonds or other ornaments cut from truffle. To do this, pour a very little aspic jelly into the bottom of mould. Leave till set, then add a very little more and turn mould round and round on ice until well coated with jelly. Now take each piece of truffle and dip into liquid jelly. Arrange in any form you like. To make mousse, pound ham in a mortar with white sauce until blended, then rub through a fine wire sieve and pound again. Gradually beat in mustard, salt and pepper, and then stir in aspic jelly and gelatine dissolved in a little of the jelly. Stir till blended, then stir in cochineal and lightly fold in cream. Gently place in prepared mould. Leave until set. Dip quickly in hot water and unmould. Garnish with crisp lettuce leaves and radish roses. *For 6 persons.*

MOUSSE OF TONGUE (Mousse de Langue)

1 tablespoon powdered gelatine
2 tablespoons cold water
½ pint chicken or veal stock
2 egg yolks
Paprika and cayenne pepper to taste
½ teaspoon salt
Good pinch mustard
1 slice onion
½ pint milk
10 oz. chopped cooked tongue
1 teaspoon vinegar
1 tablespoon minced parsley
¼ pint whipped cream

Soak gelatine in the cold water for 5 minutes, then dissolve in ¼ cup of the stock. Place egg yolks in a basin. Add paprika, cayenne pepper and salt. Stir in mustard, onion, remainder of stock and milk, both heated. Turn into top of a double boiler and cook, stirring constantly, over hot water, for about 5 or 6 minutes, or until slightly thickened, then stir in gelatine. Remove onion. Allow to cool, then add tongue, vinegar and parsley. When beginning to thicken, fold in cream. Turn into a wet mould. Leave till firm and chilled. Unmould on to a flat dish. Garnish with sprigs of watercress. Serve with mayonnaise. *For 6 persons.*

MOUSSE OF VEAL (Mousse de Veau)

2 egg yolks
1 cup canned milk
1 tablespoon powdered gelatine
¼ cup cold water

Beat egg yolks. Stir in milk. Turn into the top of a double boiler. Stir till thick over boiling water. Allow to cool. Dissolve gelatine in water. Stir in stock, then add to custard and meat.

½ cup hot white stock
1 cup minced veal
½ teaspoon grated onion
Salt and pepper to taste
2 egg whites
2 peeled tomatoes

Season to taste with onion, salt and pepper. Leave till beginning to thicken. Fold in stiffly-whisked egg whites. Place in a wet mould. Stand in a refrigerator till well chilled. Turn out when required. Garnish with sliced tomatoes and small heaps of Russian or potato salad. *For 4 or 5 persons.*

NORFOLK PORK ROLL (Roulade de Porc, Norfolk)

2½ lb. pickled pork
3 oz. breadcrumbs
2 oz. chopped cooked veal
3 oz. finely chopped ham
1 teaspoon chopped onion
2 teaspoons minced parsley
Salt and pepper to taste
1 beaten egg
Sprigs of parsley and water-cress
Slices of hard-boiled egg or tomato

Remove any bones from pork. Wash meat in tepid water. Wipe dry. Mix breadcrumbs in a basin with veal, ham, onion, parsley and salt and pepper to taste. Bind with egg. Spread stuffing down centre of pork. Roll up neatly. Tie in a cloth. Place in a saucepan. Cover with boiling water. Boil for 2 hours. Remove from pan. Tighten cloth. Leave till cold. Remove cloth. Trim off ends. Roll in lightly browned bread-crumbs. Arrange on a cold dish. Garnish with sprigs of watercress and parsley, and slices of hard-boiled egg or tomato. *For 6 persons.*

OXTAIL BRAWN (Queue de Boeuf en Gelée)

1 ox tail
1 lb. shin of beef
Salt and pepper to taste
1¼ pints water

Remove fat and joint tail. Cut beef in dice. Place in a casserole. Add salt and pepper to taste and water. Cover. Cook slowly for 4 hours. Uncover. Remove meat. Bone tail. Strain gravy, then season to taste and let all get cold. Remove fat from gravy. Cut up meat from tail into neat pieces, and arrange all the meat in a mould rinsed out with cold water. Melt gravy and strain over. Serve, turned out when set on a dish garnished with parsley or lettuce and tomato. *For 6 persons.*

PRESSED BEEF (Boeuf Salé)

7 lb. salt brisket
1 peeled onion
12 allspice
6 cloves
12 peppercorns
1 teaspoon mixed herbs
Glaze as required

Scrape meat well, and place in a pan of warm water with onion, allspice, cloves, peppercorns and mixed herbs (tied in muslin). Cover and simmer gently for 4 hours, till tender when tested with a skewer. Remove from pan. Take out bones, which should slip out easily. Trim and place between 2 small pastry boards. If a large piece is needed, boil two briskets like this, remove bones and place one on top of the other to press. When cold, they will look like one piece. Leave liquor in which meat was boiled to get cold, then remove fat from top and strain liquor. Boil rapidly to consistency of thin glue, skimming well. Brush top of cold brisket with this glaze.

SCOTTISH POLONI

1 lb. stewing steak
½ lb. sausage meat
6 oz. stale breadcrumbs
2 eggs
¼ pint beef stock
Salt and pepper to taste
Dash Worcester sauce

Wipe meat and remove any gristle. Put twice through mincer. Mix with sausage meat, crumbs, eggs and stock, water flavoured with meat or vegetable extract, or vegetable water. Season to taste. Stir in sauce. Pack into a large greased jam jar with straight sides, or use two smaller ones. Cover tightly with greased paper. Steam for 2 hours. Turn out while hot. Slice when cold. *For 6 persons.*

VEAL BRAWN (Veau en Gelée)

2 lb. knuckle of veal
3 oz. bacon
2 pints water
1 bay leaf
1 clove
1 large blade mace
6 white peppercorns
½ teaspoon salt

Choose the meaty end of veal knuckle. Wipe. Cut up and place in a saucepan. Remove rind from bacon and chop. Add bacon to veal. Add water, bay leaf, spices and salt. Bring to boil. Skim. Cover and simmer for $1\frac{1}{2}$-2 hours, or till tender. Remove veal. Cut it in small pieces and lay aside. Return bones to stock. Cover and simmer for 2 to 3 hours, when stock should be reduced to about a pint. Strain into a basin. Add veal. Re-season if necessary. Pour carefully into a wet mould. When set and chilled, turn out into a serving dish. Garnish with slices of peeled tomato and heart of lettuce leaves, or with devilled eggs set in a border of mustard and cress. *For 5 or 6 persons.*

Game

"Game" is the term usually applied in the culinary world to all wild birds and animals that are edible.

On the whole, game is easier to digest than meat. Some varieties are more digestible than others, such as partridge, pheasant, quail and wild rabbits. Wild duck should always be avoided by those with delicate digestions on account of its close-textured, oily flesh.

Only young birds should be chosen for roasting, but old birds which are not so expensive can be cooked in a casserole, stewed, made into soup, or turned into an entrée. When purchasing any kind of game, avoid birds, hares and rabbits shattered by shot or that are bruised or wet, through being badly packed. The better the plumage of birds, the better their condition.

GAME IN SEASON

The following table only gives the seasons for home birds. They are generally more expensive at the beginning of the season than towards the end. Game dealers are allowed two weeks' grace after the dates given in which to dispose of game. When British game is out of season, imported game is generally available : black game, hazel hen, pheasants and ptarmigan are in season from December to June, and partridge from February to May. As air transport develops, there is no reason why, in the future, we should not be able to have game all the year round.

BIRD				SEASON
Black Game	-	-	-	-	August 20th-December 10th.
				Prime from end of October.
Capercailzie (Capercaillie)			-	August 20th-December 10th.
Grouse	-	-	-	-	August 12th-December 10th.
Hare	-	-	-	-	September-March.
Ortolan	-	-	-	-	November-February.
Partridge		-	-	-	September 1st-February 1st.
Pheasant	-	-	-	-	October 1st-February 1st.
				Prime, November-January.
Pigeon	-	-	-	-	August-April.
Plover	-	-	-	-	August 1st-March 1st.
Ptarmigan	-	-	-	-	October 1st-May 1st.
Quail	-	-	-	-	All year round.
				Prime, May-September.
Rabbit	-	-	-	-	September-March.
				Prime, September.
Snipe	-	-	-	-	October-February.
Teal	-	-	-	-	October-February.
				Prime, December.
Venison : Buck		-	-	-	July 1st-October 1st.
Doe		-	-	-	End October-January 1st.
Wheatear	-	-	-	-	July-October.
Widgeon -		-	-	-	August 1st-March 15th.
				Prime, October-November.
Wild Duck	-	-	-	-	August 1st-March 15th.
				Prime, October-November.
Wild Geese	-	-	-	-	August 1st-March 15th.
Woodcock	-	-	-	-	August 1st-March 15th.
				Prime, October-November.
Wood Pigeon -		-	-	-	All year round.

BUYING BIRDS

You should always consider how many you wish a bird to serve, and whether you wish to serve it cold as well as hot, before choosing.

Bird for 1	-	-	Golden plover, ortolan, pigeon, quail or snipe.
Bird for 2	-	-	Young grouse, hazel hen, partridge, ptarmigan, teal, woodcock or wood pigeon.
Bird for 2 or 3	-	Old grouse, hen pheasant or widgeon.
Bird for 3 or 4	-	Grey hen, hen pheasant, pin tail or wild duck.
Bird for 4 or 5	-	Black cock or cock pheasant.
Bird for 6 or more		Hen capercailzie (6), or cock capercailzie (8-10).

TO CHOOSE GAME

Birds: You can generally tell by the feel of the end of a breast bone of a game bird whether it is fit for roasting or not. When young, the end breaks easily; when old, it is quite firm when pressed. Now hold the bird up by

265

the lower beak. If bird is young, beak will bend in the middle ; if old, it will remain stiff and straight. All young birds have soft, even feathers, smooth, pliable legs, supple toes and short spurs. Hens are more juicy and tender than male birds, but the latter have the stronger flavour. Ducks and other water fowl should have supple, moist feet.

Hares: Should have smooth claws, supple ears, so tender that they are easily torn, and a narrow cleft in the lips. The ribs ought to be well covered with flesh. Young hares also have short stumpy necks and long joints, and the hair on their bellies is whitish. If you look under their paws, you'll find a small nut in young hares. Choose young hares for roasting. Old hares, which have fawn-coloured hair on their bellies, are tough, so should be jugged or made into soup. Young hares for roasting should be well hung, but hares to be jugged or made into soup cannot be too fresh.

Rabbits: Choose like hares.

Venison: There are three kinds of venison available in Great Britain. Flesh of the buck is said to be finer than that of the doe. The varieties are red deer (peculiar to Ireland), roebuck (only found in the north of Scotland), and fallow deer (in England). The flesh of the latter is the finest. To obtain a good joint of venison, it should be cut from a deer less than 3 years old. The finest venison comes from deer $2\frac{1}{2}$-3 years old. The fat should be firm and white, and the lean very finely grained, and rather darker than mutton. The cleft of the hoof should be close and smooth. The haunch, liver and kidneys are highly prized in the roebuck and fallow deer, but the haunch is the best part of the red deer.

TO HANG GAME

All game should be hung in a current of air. Do not draw it till required for cooking. The time required will depend on the weather. If dry, frosty or windy, it can hang for two or three weeks or longer, but if the weather is muggy, keep a close watch on it, for it may require to be cooked within a few days. If game is brought to you, freshly killed, write the date on a label and tie it to leg, so that you know how long to keep it for cooking. Game birds should be hung by the neck, tied tightly with string, and ground game by their feet. If any game is badly shot, examine frequently as it doesn't keep well. The time of hanging depends on whether the bird is liked slightly " high " or not. If liked slightly high, hang until the breast or tail feathers can be easily plucked. If not hung as suggested under the name of each species, the flesh is likely to be tasteless and tough. These instructions don't apply to game bought from a game dealer who sells birds hung only long enough to tenderise, or until " high," as you prefer.

TO STORE DRESSED GAME

Wipe with a damp cloth, inside and out. Wrap in cellophane or greaseproof paper. Place on bottom of refrigerator. Game should never be stored more than 2 days, or 3 if absolutely fresh, as it loses its flavour and is apt to become smelly. Take care not to freeze it, as frozen game is as tasteless as game that is cooked the moment it is killed.

TO PREPARE FEATHERED GAME

The following only applies to birds not already plucked, singed, drawn and trussed.

To Pluck: Holding bird in your left hand, breast downwards, and grasping the wing farthest away from you where it joins the body, start to pluck off the feathers from under the wing. When all the feathers are plucked on that side except the down, pluck the other wing, and then proceed with the body, taking care not to tear the skin. Remove pin feathers with tweezers. If wing tip feathers are difficult to pluck, immerse tips in boiling water for 2 or 3 minutes, then pull out feathers. Cut wing tips off and use them for stock with the giblets.

To Singe: Holding bird by neck with your left hand, either expose all its surface bit by bit, to a gas flame, or move a lighted paper quickly all over it. No hairs nor fuzz should be left on bird. If you find after trussing that some remain, singe again. Take care when singeing not to scorch skin.

To Draw and Clean: Leave the feet on birds, but remove the toes and scald, and skin feet. Lay bird on its back on a table or large board. Chop off ends of the pinions (wing tips). Turn bird, breast downwards, and cut a cross-wise slit in the back of the neck. Now, passing your knife under the skin, cut off the neck and head where neck joins body, but be careful not to cut through the under skin of the neck. Next slit through the skin of the back of the neck at the place where you first made the cut and through the skin below about 8 inches from the breast, leaving the front and back flap of skin to fold over each other. Now remove the crop. Loosen the entrails of *large birds* by working the forefinger round inside the body. *To remove entrails:* Make a deep cut across body between tail and vent and cut out vent, making the opening large enough to allow you to insert your finger. With a piece of kitchen paper between your fingers, you can then pull out the whole of the inside in one motion, but when doing so, take care not to break the gall bladder. With fingers, remove all the lung tissue from each side of the back bone. *To remove entrails from small birds:* After loosening the inside at the neck, gently squeeze the bird until the inside comes out on to a piece of paper. *Quails:* Draw from neck end or leave in entrails. *Exceptions:* Ortolans, plover, snipe and woodcock are not usually drawn, but the gizzards must be removed. The entrails are considered a great delicacy. The heads and necks of these birds are skinned and left on, and their long beaks are used like a skewer when trussing. Pass them through the legs and body to keep birds shapely. Wipe inside and out with a clean kitchen cloth dipped in warm soda water, allowing $\frac{1}{2}$ teaspoon baking soda to 1 quart water. Never wash inside of game birds unless you happen to break any part of the inside when drawing.

To Prepare Giblets: Slit gizzard and remove membrane with all the contents. (*See also* Poultry Giblets.) Separate gall bladder carefully from liver, and cut off any liver that is tinged with green. Wash all giblets thoroughly.

To Truss: There is more than one way of trussing game birds. If in a hurry, just tie wings close to the body, then tie legs in the same way. Otherwise truss like this :

Large Birds—Black Game, Capercailzie and Pheasants: Run a trussing needle and string through the centre of the two leg joints, then turn, breast downwards, and carry the string in a slanting direction between the two centre bones of the wing, catching the underneath part of the pinion. Now draw string over bird, through the pinion and wing at the other side, when it will meet the other end of the string. Tie ends together. Turn bird, downwards, and, holding it in the left hand, run the needle and string through the back beside the thigh bones. Now pull legs straight out. Turn bird on its back and tie string over legs, then through breast over other leg and tie ends together. If preferred, truss as you would a chicken for roasting.

Small Birds—Grouse, Hazel Hen, Partridges, Ptarmigan, Quail, etc.: Place bird flat on board with its head end towards you. Turn back wings, and, with your left hand, force legs suddenly down level with the sides of the body while, with the right hand, you run a skewer through the wing, thigh and body, seeing that you pierce both thigh and wings. Now run a smaller skewer through the body close to the tail and over the legs. The skewers can be made fast with string.

Plovers, Snipe and Woodcock: Remove wing tips at first joint, then, pressing wings close to the body, push a small skewer through the right wing, the body and the left wing. Next, holding the legs of the bird firmly down to the sides, truss them in place with the beak of the bird. To finish trussing a plover and woodcock, turn bird with breast towards you, then draw its head down to the left and catch it with skewer that keeps the legs firmly down to the sides.

Wild Ducks: Truss like small birds, but leave feet on and twist backwards close to thighs.

Wood Pigeon: Before trussing, cut off head and neck close to body when cleaning, and chop off toes at first joint. Cross legs by cutting a slit in the skin of one and passing the other through it. Pass a trussing needle and string through the pinions and legs and bring it out at the other side. Pass it back again, and bring it out near where it first entered, then tie the two ends of string firmly.

To Bard: As game is lacking in fat, though a nutritious and palatable food, it is necessary to bard with slices of fat bacon before roasting. This means covering the breast with the bacon and tying or skewering it on.

ACCOMPANIMENTS

All birds, except members of the wild duck family, can have the same accompaniments : bread sauce ; brown or sour cream gravy ; potato chips, crisps, straws or new potatoes ; fried breadcrumbs ; watercress garnish or salad ; red currant jelly, if liked. Oiled butter, flavoured with lemon juice and seasoned with cayenne pepper to taste, can be served in place of gravy with grilled birds. Pheasant can be served at Christmas with chestnut gravy.

Wild Ducks: Wine or orange gravy and watercress salad, or wine gravy and orange and mint or orange and watercress salad ; potato crisps, chips or straws.

TO PREPARE HARES AND RABBITS

Hares should not be paunched until just before cooking. Rabbits should be paunched as soon as killed. Don't skin either until just before cooking, or the flesh will become dry. Place a bowl beneath a hare to catch the blood for the gravy.

To Paunch: Cover table with three or four layers of paper. Cut a small slit with a pair of scissors at the fork, then snip right up to the breast bone through the pelt, taking care to cut the pelt only. Draw the pelt away from the skin on each side of the stomach. Slit up the skin as you slit up the pelt. Remove the intestines and stomach and burn them. Remove the kidneys, heart and liver with gall bladder, then carefully detach liver from gall bladder, so as not to puncture it. Throw it in fire. Draw out and throw away lungs. Wash out thoroughly and trim away flesh on which the gall bladder rested, as it might be bitter. If the blood of the hare is wanted for soup or to add to jugged hare, strain it into a jug or basin before washing hare. Dry hare thoroughly.

To Skin: Chop off the ears. If preferred, leave them until you come to skinning the head, then ease off skin and leave them on head. Cut off feet at the first joint. Now you can either skin a hare or rabbit on a board, or make a slit in one of the legs and suspend it from a hook or nail. If skinning on a board, loosen skin round back legs, then holding end of a leg, bend it at the joint and pull it through skin. Now pull off the skin up the back, taking care not to tear the flesh. Skin the second hind leg in the same way. Holding the hind legs of hare or rabbit firmly, pull as much of the skin as possible firmly away from body towards the head, bringing your hand a little higher as you proceed, so as to keep body in position while skinning. Turn skin of first one foreleg over leg and pull stump of leg through it, then repeat with other leg. Now pull skin over head. If head is wanted, cut skin through at the ears, mouth and round the eyes with a sharp-pointed knife, then pull off skin. If head is not required, cut it off without skinning. If to be skinned, remove eyes, nose and lips. When skinning the head of a hare for roasting, take great care not to tear the ears, as they should be left on. If the hare or rabbit is suspended from a hook for skinning by the head, ease off skin at the opening at the fork, and pull it away towards the hind legs, then turn the skin of the legs over and pull off. Now ease the hind legs and continue skinning body as already described.

To Truss: Wipe inside of rabbit or hare with a damp cloth, then stuff. Sew up opening. Cut the sinews in the hind legs at the thigh. Draw forelegs towards the back flat against the sides, and skewer them in place. Bring hind legs forward, pressing them close against the body and flat against the front ones, and skewer. Press head well back towards the shoulder, and run a skewer down the mouth, and into the back to keep head in position. With a small skewer, curl tail up on to back of hare, when trussing a hare, and fix it there. Fix a piece of string round the end of each skewer and tie on top of the back, so as to keep all the legs well pressed to the sides of the body. Now grease a piece of greaseproof paper and tie it over the head like a hat to protect ears from burning. When trussing a rabbit, the ears may be cut off, if preferred.

Boiled Rabbit : Baked curls of bacon or boiled pickled pork, boiled dumplings and parsley sauce.

Roast Rabbit or Hare : Thick brown gravy, chestnut, mushroom, or savoury stuffing, forcemeat balls, baked curls of bacon and watercress.

GAME MARINADE

Certain kinds of game, such as black game, capercailzie, ptarmigan and other birds of this species, and venison, which also has a rather dry flesh, are improved by soaking in a marinade.

MARINADE

2 peeled medium-sized onions
2 tablespoons olive oil
2 sprigs parsley
½ gill white wine
½ pint water
2 sliced carrots
1 tablespoon vinegar
3 bay leaves
Salt and pepper to taste

Slice onions into a saucepan. Add remaining ingredients. Bring to boil. Simmer for ½ hour. Strain and leave till cold. If liked, port wine can be substituted for white wine. Soak chops and steaks of venison, to be fried or grilled, for ½ hour, turning at half-time. Soak birds for 2 hours, turning every half-hour. Soak joints of hare or rabbit for 1 hour, turning at half-time.

TIME FOR ROASTING

BIRD	TIME
Black Game	45-50 minutes.
Capercailzie	1 hour or longer, according to age.
Grouse	½ hour. If wanted well-done, 35 minutes.
Hare (medium-sized)	1¼ hours. (large) 1½-2 hours.
Ortolan	10 minutes.
Partridge	½ hour.
Pheasant	35-45 minutes, according to size.
Pigeon	20 minutes-½ hour.
Plover	10-15 minutes.
Ptarmigan	About ½ hour.
Quail	About 20 minutes.
Rabbit (young)	35 minutes. (old) ¾ hour.
Snipe	¼ hour.
Teal	9-15 minutes.
Venison (buck)	4-5 hours.
(doe)	3¼-3¾ hours, if covered with paste, otherwise less time.
Wheatear	12-15 minutes.
Widgeon	About 20 minutes.
Wild Duck	20-25 minutes.
Woodcock (underdone)	15-20 minutes. (well-done) 20-25 minutes.
Wood Pigeon	20-30 minutes.

GRILLED GAME (Gibier grillé)

Grouse, partridges, baby pheasants, pigeons, ptarmigan, quail and woodcock can all be grilled. Singe, clean and split birds down back. Do not skin them. Wipe carefully all over with a wet cloth. Brush both sides with melted butter or olive oil. Season with salt and pepper. Place, skin side downwards, on greased or oiled grill rack. Slip grill pan under grill bars from 3-4 inches from bars. Baste well while grilling at a moderate heat, 350° F., for about 15 minutes, turning at half-time. Cover each bird, if liked, with a rasher of bacon. Grill till bacon is crisp. Smear with butter. Season. Serve each on a slice of hot buttered toast.

TIME TO ALLOW

BIRD	TIME
Grouse	25-30 minutes.
Partridge	20-25 minutes.
Baby Pheasant	40-50 minutes.
Pigeon	30-40 minutes.
Ptarmigan	25-30 minutes.
Quail	10-12 minutes.
Wild Duck (rare)	15-20 minutes.
(well-done)	About 25 minutes.
Woodcock	About 15 minutes.

BLACK GAME (Coq de Bruyère)

Belongs to grouse species. Male known as " black cock " or " heath cock," and females as " grey hen " or " brown hen." The thighs of black game are considered the choicest morsels.

ROAST BLACK GAME (Coq de Bruyère, rôti)

Prepare bird. Bard breast with fat bacon. Place on a rack in a baking tin. Roast black cock in a hot oven, 450° F., for about $\frac{3}{4}$ hour, or in a slow oven, 325° F., for about $1\frac{1}{4}$ hours. Roast grey hen in a hot oven, 450° F., for about $\frac{1}{2}$ hour, or in a slow oven, 325° F., for about 1 hour. Dip a slice of toast in lemon juice. Place under bird for last 10 minutes. Dish up bird on toast. Serve with game gravy, and bread sauce. *For 4 persons.*

To Vary: Bard bird. Slip a pat of butter in its inside. Season with salt and pepper. When half-done, cover with $\frac{1}{2}$ pint sour cream and finish cooking at 350° F. Dish up on toast, if liked. Stir $\frac{1}{2}$ pint stock into liquor in baking tin. Boil rapidly, stirring slowly, until quite thick. Strain over bird.

CAPERCAILZIE (Capercaillie)

Largest European member of grouse family. Sometimes called " Cock o' the Wood " or " wood grouse." The male bird, equal in size to a small turkey, is sometimes buried for 24 hours before cooking, or it can be steeped overnight in new milk, and then in vinegar for 10 hours before cooking, to remove the turpentine taste it acquires through living largely on pine needles. Wash and dry thoroughly. Skin and bard it well with fat bacon. Some gourmets contend that a cock capercailzie is not worth eating, but if, when it is very young, you bard it well with fat bacon and roast it or stuff it with chestnut or sausage stuffing and boil, braise or stew it, it is worth your attention. Never choose an old bird. Select the hen when possible.

ROAST CAPERCAILZIE (Capercaillie rôti)

1 young hen capercailzie
Salt and pepper to taste
Flour as required
Softened butter as required
Chestnut or sausage stuffing, if liked
1 cup chicken stock

Rub bird all over with salt and pepper. Dredge with flour. Rub with softened butter. Stuff if liked. Skewer opening. Place on a rack in a baking tin with a cover. Bard breast with fat bacon. Place stock in bottom of tin. Cover. Roast in a fairly hot oven, 425° F., for 10 minutes, then lower to 300° F. Baste well with stock and dripping. Cover. Cook till almost tender, then remove lid of pan and fat bacon. Baste well and roast till breast is brown. Total roasting time should be 20-25 minutes per lb. Serve with game gravy and bread sauce. Garnish with watercress and little bundles of asparagus dipped in seasoned melted butter. *For 6-10 persons.*

GROUSE (Coq de Bruyère)

By " grouse," the red, or Scotch, grouse is indicated. Many gourmets consider grouse the finest game bird. Choose young grouse for grilling or roasting, or split and fry. This bird is equally delicious served hot or cold after roasting. Grouse can also be stuffed and braised or stewed, and made into a galantine, pie, soup or salad, etc.

BRAISED GROUSE (Coq de Bruyère braisé)

1 brace grouse
2 medium-sized onions
2 medium-sized carrots
1 small turnip
1 bouquet garni
6 black peppercorns
¾ pint stock
Salt and pepper to taste
¾ pint Espagnol sauce

Truss grouse as for roasting. Peel onions. Scrape carrots. Peel turnip. Cut vegetables into dice. Place in a large shallow saucepan with the bouquet garni and peppercorns. Lay grouse on top. Add stock. Simmer very slowly, or cook in a casserole in a slow oven, 325° F., for 1 hour, basting occasionally with the stock. Remove lid and bake for ¼ hour to allow to brown. Dish up. Strain the " braise " thoroughly into another saucepan. Skim off any grease. Boil quickly for 5 minutes. Season to taste, then stir in sauce. Bring to boil, stirring constantly, and simmer gently for 5 minutes. Pour over the bird. Serve with boiled or mashed potatoes and braised celery. *For 6 persons.*

ROAST GROUSE (Coq de Bruyère rôti)

Wipe inside and outside of bird with a damp cloth. Season inside with salt and pepper and sprinkle with a squeeze of lemon juice. Slip a pat of butter inside. Bard breast with fat bacon. Place on a trivet in roasting tin, breast upwards. Bake in a moderate oven, 350° F., for about ¾ hour, basting thrice while cooking with melted butter, or bake in a hot oven, 450° F., with ½ cup boiling water in tin for ¼ hour, then quickly lower temperature to slow, 325° F., and bake for 25 minutes. Remove bacon. Brush with melted butter. Dredge with flour. Baste again and bake until brown. The latter method is for well-cooked grouse, and the former for under-done grouse. Garnish with watercress. *For 2 persons.*

To Vary: Simmer liver for 10 minutes in salted water. Drain and pound with a small pat of butter and salt and cayenne pepper to taste. Spread on a slice of hot toast after removing crusts. Place toast on the rack and lift bird on top. Leave for 5 minutes to allow drippings of bird to go into toast.

HARE (Lièvre)

To Joint a Hare for Jugging or Stewing: Remove legs. Divide back into several joints with a sharp knife. As soon as you have cut through the flesh, tap the back of the knife with a hammer, or you won't be able to cut through the bone. Remove the head, then divide ribs in two longways. Split head in two if wanted for soup or stock.

HARE AU VIN (Lièvre au Vin Rouge)

1 fresh young hare
2 tablespoons butter
1 tablespoon flour
½ pint beef stock
½ clove garlic
2 cloves
½ bay leaf
1 sprig thyme
1 pint claret or port wine
Squeeze lemon juice
12 stoned olives
1 teaspoon capers

Prepare and joint hare. Reserve ribs for stock. Strain blood into a jug. Remove liver. Melt half the butter in a saucepan. Stir in flour. When frothy, stir in half the stock. Stir till boiling. Melt remainder of butter in a frying-pan. Dip joints in seasoned flour. Place in frying-pan. Add garlic. Fry joints, turning occasionally, till brown all over. Transfer to a casserole. Add sauce and remainder of butter, cloves, bay leaf and thyme. Rinse out frying-pan with remainder of stock. Strain into casserole. Add wine and lemon juice.

Cover and cook in a slow oven, 300° F., for 1½-2 hours. Dish up. Slowly stir blood and liver, pounded to a paste, into sauce in casserole. Stir until it comes to boiling point. Add olives and capers. Pour over hare. Serve with riced or mashed potatoes and green peas. *For 6 persons.*

JUGGED HARE

1 fresh hare
1 peeled onion
½ small turnip
1 scraped carrot
¼ lb. streaky bacon
1 oz. butter
12 small button onions
1 pint beef stock
1 bouquet garni
6 black peppercorns
1 pint Espagnol sauce
½ gill port wine
2 tablespoons red currant jelly
Salt and pepper to taste

Skin and cut hare into neat joints. Wash and dry them. Slice onion. Peel and slice turnip. Slice carrot and dice bacon. Place the bacon and butter in a shallow saucepan. Cook till the fat begins to flow, then add button onions. Fry slowly for 5 minutes, stirring occasionally, then add remainder of vegetables and joints of hare. Fry slowly till light brown, in about 10 minutes, stirring constantly. Add stock, bouquet garni and peppercorns. Skim well, then add sauce. Cover tightly. Simmer *very* gently for about 1 hour, then remove the joints of hare and place them in an earthenware jar. Strain sauce into a small saucepan. Stir in wine and jelly. Season. Pour over hare. Add button onions from braise. Cover tightly. Simmer in a slow oven, 300° F., for about 1 hour, till tender. Dish up. Pour sauce over. Garnish with forcemeat balls. *For 6-8 persons.*

ROAST HARE (Lièvre rôti)

1 young hare
Veal forcemeat as required
½ pint milk
1 oz. butter
Flour as required
Salt and pepper to taste

Paunch and skin hare, but do not remove ears or tail. Wipe outside and inside with a damp cloth. Stuff, then truss, curling the tail over the back and fixing it with a small skewer. Lard with fat bacon. Roast in a hot oven, 450° F., allowing 1 hour for a leveret and 1¼-1½ hours for a full-grown hare. Baste frequently, using the milk and melted butter. When nearly ready, remove bacon. Dredge with seasoned flour. Baste again and continue to roast until back is brown. Dish up. Make gravy with fat and essence in pan, and thicken to taste with flour creamed with milk. Skim well. Remove from stove. Gradually stir in ½ gill port wine, then reheat, stirring constantly, but do not allow to boil. Strain a little round hare, and serve remainder in a hot sauceboat. Garnish with baked rolls of bacon and fried forcemeat balls. Serve with red currant jelly.

HAZEL HEN (Gélinotte)

A small game bird with tender, white, good-flavoured flesh. Imported from Scandinavia and Russia, chilled or frozen.

ASTRAKHAN OF HAZEL HEN (Gélinotte à la Russe)

1 hazel hen
Olive oil as required
2 tablespoons melted butter
Cream as required
2 tablespoons caviare

Rub hazel hen with olive oil and place on a rack in a baking tin. Roast in a slow oven, 325° F., basting occasionally with the butter, then with the dripping until tender, in about ½ hour. Dish up. Stir cream into the essence in tin, until you get a yellow sauce. Rub through a strainer, then reheat, but do not allow to boil. Stir in caviare. Again reheat, stirring constantly, but do not allow to boil. Coat bird with this sauce. *For 2 persons.*

SOUFFLE OF HAZEL HEN (Soufflé de Gélinottes)

6 hazel hens
2 tablespoons breadcrumbs
1 pint cream
12 mushrooms
1½ oz. butter
5 egg yolks and 4 egg whites
Salt and pepper to taste

Remove meat from raw hazel hens. Put through a meat grinder. Pound in a mortar with fully ¼ pint of the cream and rub through a sieve. Mix crumbs with remainder of the cream. Peel and chop mushrooms. Melt butter in a frying-pan and fry mushrooms. Add to purée. Separate yolks and whites of eggs and gradually beat in yolks. Season to taste. Butter a charlotte mould or soufflé tin. Beat egg whites till stiff, and fold into mixture. Three-quarter fill mould. Cover with greased paper. Steam for 1½-2 hours, till set, then unmould. Garnish, if liked, with 4 chopped truffles. Serve with Russian cream sauce made in this way : Melt 2 tablespoons butter. Stir in 2 tablespoons flour. When frothy, stir in 2 cups tepid cream. Add salt and pepper to taste. Stir till thick. Simmer 1¼ lb. mushrooms in 1 tablespoon chicken or veal stock and salt and pepper, till tender. Add ½ tablespoon flour, and stir till boiling. Stir in ½ lb. chopped boiled sweetbreads, and add to cream sauce. Re-season if necessary. Pour half into a hot sauce-boat and pour remainder over the soufflé.

ORTOLAN (Ortolan)

European bunting very rare now. Used to be caught in nests, fattened up and prepared like quail. Usually served roasted.

ROAST ORTOLAN (Ortolan rôti)

Pluck, singe and truss like quail, but do not draw, except to remove gizzard. Brush with melted butter. Place a bay leaf or vine leaf on the breast of each, then cover with thin rashers of bacon. Tie on securely. Place on a rack in a baking tin. Bake in a hot oven, 450° F., for 20-25 minutes, basting frequently with melted butter. Dish each up on an oblong of toast, placed under them 5 minutes before finishing roasting. Garnish with watercress. The bacon can be removed or left on according to taste. If left on, brush with warm gravy before serving. Serve with orange gravy and fried crumbs. *Allow 1 per person.*

PARTRIDGE (Perdreau et Perdrix)

There are several kinds of partridge. The usual one found in Britain is known as the " grey " or common partridge, which is at its best when young. The other species, occasionally found on the east coast of Britain, is the French or " red-legged partridge," which is prime when mature. You can recognise the old birds by a horseshoe-shaped mark in the breast plumage. Grill or roast young birds, and braise, stew or cook older birds in a casserole.

CASSEROLE OF PARTRIDGES (Casserole de Perdrix)

2 partridges
2 oz. butter
¼ pint diced carrot
¼ pint diced turnip
¼ pint diced mushrooms
White stock as required
1 truffle
¼ pint gravy
¼ pint brown sauce
Salt and pepper to taste
Celery salt to taste

Wipe and truss partridges. Melt butter in a shallow saucepan. Add partridges and fry till brown all over, then transfer to a casserole. Parboil carrots, turnips and mushrooms separately, then drain and finish cooking together in stock. Drain again, but reserve stock for soup. Add vegetables and mushrooms to partridges. Chop truffle and sprinkle over then add gravy and brown sauce. Season with salt and pepper and celery salt. Cover tightly. Cook in a slow oven, 300° F., for about ½ hour. If liked, coat birds with 1 tablespoon melted glaze. Dish up. Pour sauce round and serve. *For 4 persons.*

GRILLED PARTRIDGES (HALVED) (Perdreaux grillés)

2 young partridges
Salt and pepper to taste
3 oz. butter
6 oz. breadcrumbs

Wipe and halve birds lengthwise. Season with salt and pepper. Melt butter. Coat partridge halves with the butter, then with the crumbs. Grill slowly, cut side up, for about 5 minutes on each side. Garnish with watercress. Serve with Madeira sauce. *For 2 persons.*

GRILLED PARTRIDGES (WHOLE) (Perdreaux grillés)

2 young partridges
1 tablespoon olive oil
1 teaspoon salt
½ teaspoon pepper
1 tablespoon Worcester sauce
1 teaspoon French mustard
1 teaspoon lemon juice
½ oz. butter

Split partridges open through backs. Remove spinal bones, then draw. Wrap in a strong towel. Flatten each with a meat mallet. Mix the oil with salt and pepper on a plate. Brush birds with this marinade. Grill for 10 minutes on each side. Stir Worcester sauce, mustard and lemon juice into butter. Spread over partridges. Garnish with watercress. Serve with potato straws. *For 2 persons.*

ROAST PARTRIDGES (Perdreaux rôtis)

BASIC RECIPE:
4 young partridges
Salt and pepper to taste
Fried bacon as required

Wipe cleaned birds inside and out with a damp cloth. Season inside with salt and pepper. Wash and dry livers of birds and replace. Truss. Cover breasts with fat bacon. Tie on securely. Place on a rack in a baking tin. Roast in a hot oven, 425° F., basting every 5 minutes with melted butter, for ¼ hour, then baste with bacon fat in tin. Allow 25 minutes altogether. Untruss and dish up. Keep hot. Stir white stock into drippings in pan. Boil for 2 minutes. Season if necessary and skim off fat. Strain into a hot sauce-boat. Garnish birds with watercress and lemon fingers.

Serve with bread sauce, fried crumbs, potato chips, crisps or straws and lettuce salad. *For 4 persons.*

PHEASANT (Faisan)

Pheasants should be well hung. Allow at least 12 days in cold weather unless birds have been badly wounded. In warm, muggy weather, 3 days is sufficient. Pluck the day before cooking. Boil, braise, stew, cook in a casserole or make all old birds into pie or a soup. Roast, quarter and grill, or fillet and fry young birds. Keep the tail feathers as a garnish for roast pheasant.

BOILED STUFFED PHEASANT (Faisan Farci bouilli)

1 hen pheasant
1 tablespoon shredded suet or butter
¼ pint breadcrumbs
Salt, pepper and celery salt to taste
Pinch grated lemon rind
Beaten egg
1 pint Béchamel or parsley sauce

Remove head and neck, taking care to leave enough of the neck skin to turn over and skewer behind. Mix the suet or butter with the breadcrumbs. Add salt, pepper and celery salt and a pinch of grated lemon rind. Moisten with beaten egg. Stuff bird. Skewer openings. Place in a pan of boiling water to come to below the breast. Bring to boil. Skim. Simmer gently for ½ hour. Skim as required while cooking. When ready, dish up and unskewer.

Coat with a little of the sauce. Serve remainder in a hot sauce-boat. Garnish, if liked, with button mushrooms, fried in butter. *For 4 persons.*

BRAISED PHEASANT AUX MARRONS
(Faisan braisé aux Marrons)

2 oz. butter
¼ lb. bacon
1 sprig parsley
1 bay leaf
1 young pheasant
¼ pint white wine
½ pint white stock
1 lb. peeled chestnuts
Salt and pepper to taste

Melt half the butter in a casserole. Remove rind from bacon. Line bottom of casserole with bacon. Add parsley and bay leaf. Cook in moderate oven, 350° F., for 3 minutes. Place pheasant on bacon. Roast till golden brown all over. Add wine and stock. Cover and continue to cook in a moderate oven, 350° F., for ½ hour. Place chestnuts in a saucepan. Add white stock to cover. Cover and simmer till soft. Rub through a wire sieve. Melt remainder of butter. Add purée. Season with salt and pepper and reheat. Pile on hot serving dish and place pheasant on top. Boil pheasant gravy quickly for 5 minutes. Skim and strain over bird. *For 4 persons.*

ROAST PHEASANT (Faisan rôti)

1 young pheasant
Fat bacon for barding
Butter for basting
Salt and pepper to taste

Wipe outside and inside with a damp cloth. Season inside with salt and pepper. Stuff with a walnut of seasoned butter, or with a tablespoon of diced juicy steak. (The latter is not supposed to be eaten.) Truss. Bard with the bacon. Place on a rack in a baking tin. Roast in a fairly hot oven, 425° F., for 5 or 6 minutes, then season with salt and pepper and baste with melted butter. Continue to roast, basting occasionally with butter, then with the drippings, until tender, in 35-45 minutes. When ready, baste again. Dredge with flour and baste once more. Roast for a moment or two to brown the surface, then untruss and dish up. Fix the tail feathers in place. Garnish with watercress. Sprinkle with seasoned vinegar. Serve with brown gravy or gravy made with sour cream, instead of water or stock, bread sauce, fried crumbs, potato chips, crisps or straws. *For 4 persons.*

Roast Pheasant à la Russe : Place a trussed young pheasant in a basin. Cover with milk, then with a cloth. Leave for 4 days, changing the milk each day. Remove and drain. Dry thoroughly. Bard breast with fat bacon. Place in a deep fireproof dish with enough of the milk that it was soaked in to cover bottom of dish. Roast in a moderately hot oven, 375° F., for 40-50 minutes, according to size. Baste every 10 minutes with a tablespoon or two of cream. Untruss and dish up. Stir a little more cream into the liquor in dish. Use 1 cup altogether. Heat up to boiling point. Strain over bird. *For 4 persons.*

PIGEON (Pigeon)

The only pigeons used as a food in Britain are the wood pigeons. Bordeaux pigeons, a favourite variety from the Continent, are in season from March to October. Young pigeons of any kind of about a month old are known as squabs. Home-bred pigeons are most delicate, but wood pigeons are largest. Pigeons should not be hung, but eaten as soon as possible.

To Grill Pigeons : Wipe, truss and beat birds, wrapped in a coarse towel, without breaking the skins. Brush generously with melted butter. Season with salt and pepper, then dredge each with ½ cup of stale breadcrumbs. Grill till tender, in about ½ hour, turning frequently. Serve with sauce Tartare. *Allow 1 bird per person.*

To Grill Squab: Choose plump, short, fat young pigeons, ¾-1 lb. in weight, with soft legs and feet and pink flesh. Split them down the back. Bard with fat bacon. Place on a buttered grill, flesh side up, then grill slowly for 15-20 minutes. Season when half-cooked, then grill till brown on skin side. Remove bacon and brown below. Untruss. Serve each on a round or square of buttered toast. Garnish with watercress. Serve sprinkled with melted butter, or with mushroom or tomato sauce. *Allow 1 per person.*

ROAST PIGEONS (Pigeons rotis)

2 young pigeons
Fat bacon for barding
Salt and pepper to taste

Make a slit in one leg of each bird, and thread the other through. Tie bacon over the breasts. Place on a rack in a baking tin. Roast for 20-30 minutes in a rather hot oven, 425° F. Dredge with flour. Baste with dripping and leave in oven till brown. Garnish with watercress. Serve with bread sauce. *For 2 persons.*

ROAST STUFFED PIGEONS (Pigeons farci rôti)

4 plump young pigeons
6 tablespoons olive oil
Salt and pepper to taste
1 cup stale breadcrumbs
1/4 teaspoon crushed marjoram
1 tablespoon chopped onion
1 teaspoon chopped parsley
2 tablespoons butter
Salt and pepper to taste
4 rashers bacon

Remove wing tips. Wash and dry pigeons. Brush with olive oil. Sprinkle inside and out with salt and pepper to taste. Mix crumbs with marjoram, onion and parsley. Melt and add butter. Stuff pigeons. Skewer. Tie a slice of bacon round each. Pour remainder of oil into a fireproof dish. Place pigeons in dish. Roast in a moderate oven, 350° F., till brown and tender, in about 20 minutes, basting occasionally. Add ½ cup hot water or white stock. Roast for 10 minutes. Untruss, and remove bacon. Dish up. Serve garnished lemon slices. *For 4 persons.*

PLOVER (Pluvier)

The plover family is a large one, but the golden and the grey plovers are the ones usually cooked. The plover should not be drawn, except when split, or stuffed but always remove gizzard.

ROAST PLOVERS (Pluviers rôtis)

Wipe and truss plovers without drawing, but remove gizzard. Bard with fat bacon. Place on a rack in a baking tin with an oblong of toast below each to catch the drippings and gravy. Roast in a hot oven, 450° F., for 20 minutes. 5 minutes before they are ready, remove bacon to allow breasts to brown. Untruss. Place each on a piece of toast. Serve garnished with lemon and watercress. *Allow 1 plover per person.*

ROAST STUFFED PLOVERS (Pluviers farcis rôtis)

3 plovers
Stuffing to taste
1 beaten egg
1 teaspoon flour
Pinch of salt
Pinch cayenne pepper
Pinch grated nutmeg
1 tablespoon minced parsley
1 tablespoon sieved breadcrumbs
1 oz. butter
Juice 1 lemon
½ pint port wine

Wipe and draw plovers. Discard gizzard. Stir remainder of entrails into the stuffing chosen, then close vents. Mix egg with flour, salt, cayenne pepper, nutmeg, parsley and breadcrumbs. Brush birds with mixture. Place butter, lemon juice and port wine in a fireproof dish. Heat in oven till butter melts, then arrange birds in dish. Roast in a hot oven, 450° F., for 20 minutes, basting occasionally with the sauce or gravy. Dish up. Strain sauce over. *For 3 persons.*

PTARMIGAN (Perdrix blanches)

A member of the grouse family, this is the only bird in Britain to don a white coat in winter. Occasionally shot in Scotland, the ptarmigan is usually imported from Norway and Sweden. Cook like grouse, if liked. If freshly killed, hang like grouse.

BRAISED PTARMIGANS (Perdrix blanches braisées)

2 ptarmigans
2 rashers fat bacon
1 medium-sized carrot
2 medium-sized onions
1 oz. butter
6 black peppercorns
2 cloves
Salt and pepper to taste
Small blade mace
½ pint white stock
¼ gill white wine

Wipe and bard each bird with bacon. Cut carrot and onions into thick slices. Melt butter in a shallow saucepan. Add carrot and onion. Fry for 3 or 4 minutes, stirring occasionally. Add peppercorns, cloves, salt and pepper, mace and stock. Lay ptarmigans on top. Cover with buttered paper, then with the lid. Stew gently for ½ hour. Remove. Untruss and dish up. Keep hot in oven. Strain liquor into another saucepan. Skim off fat. Add wine, boil rapidly for 3 or 4 minutes till well reduced, then pour over birds. *For 4 persons.*

ROAST PTARMIGAN (Perdrix blanches rôties)

Wipe and truss ptarmigan. Bard with fat bacon. Place on a rack in a baking tin. Roast in a fairly hot oven, 425° F., for 30-35 minutes, basting frequently with melted butter. When almost ready, remove bacon, then dredge with flour. Baste with hot dripping. Dish up on a bed of fried breadcrumbs or on a slice of toast placed under the bird before roasting so as to catch the drippings. Serve with bread sauce, brown gravy and fried chips, crisps or straws. Garnish with watercress. *Allow 1 large bird for 2 persons.*

QUAIL (Cailles)

Usually imported from Egypt. As they are sometimes spoken of as " a kind of dwarf partridge " and are in season in the summer, they are a good substitute for partridge when it is out of season. Do not hang unless necessary ; if hung, the bird will keep for several days. They can be drawn from neck end or roasted without drawing according to taste, but you must remove the gizzard.

GRILLED QUAIL (Cailles grillées)

(1) Wipe with a damp cloth. Open all down the backbone with scissors. Cover with a piece of muslin and flatten with a meat mallet. Sprinkle with lemon juice and salt and pepper to taste. Dip in melted butter. Roll in sieved breadcrumbs. Grill for about 10 minutes, turning at half time. Garnish with watercress.

(2) Wipe and slit through the back without separating the breast. Break leg bones. Season with salt and pepper. Brush with melted butter. Grill under moderately slow heat for ¼ hour, allowing 7½ minutes on each side and turning frequently. Serve each on a slice of buttered toast. Coat with Maître d'Hôtel sauce. Decorate with sprigs of watercress and grilled rolls of bacon.

(3) Prepare as for (2). Brush with melted butter flavoured with lemon juice, or with olive oil. Season with salt and pepper to taste. Grill under moderate heat for 5 minutes on each side, turning frequently. Serve, garnished watercress, with mushroom cream sauce.

(4) Wipe and brush birds with seasoned melted butter. Skewer a strip of thin bacon round the body of each. Grill from 10-35 minutes, according to size, turning frequently. Dish up on hot buttered toast. Melt butter in grill pan so that it mixes with the dripping. Add minced parsley and lemon juice to taste and pour over. Garnish with quarters of lemon and sprigs of parsley.

ROAST QUAIL (Cailles rôties)

Draw birds or leave undrawn, removing gizzard, according to taste. Remove neck close to the back and cut off the wings at the first pinion. Truss legs as close as possible to the body, then pass a skewer through the pinions and thighs. Bard with bacon. Better still to cover with a vine leaf before barding. Roast in a hot oven, 425° F., for 12-15 minutes. Dish up. Garnish with watercress. Serve with brown gravy, poured round but not over the birds.

To Vary:

(1) Place a pat of butter inside each bird, then season insides with salt and pepper. Stuff each with a chopped truffle, and bind round with bacon. Melt a tablespoon of butter for 6 quail in a fireproof dish. Cover and roast from 20-30 minutes according to size. Dish up birds on a slice of buttered toast.

(2) Wipe birds. Smear with butter. Wrap in vine leaves. Place in a covered, buttered fireproof dish. Roast from 20-30 minutes, basting every 5 minutes with melted butter. Untruss. Serve each on a croûte of fried bread. Strain the gravy from the dish over birds. Serve with grape sauce in a hot sauceboat. Garnish with quarters of lemon and sprigs of parsley.

NOTE: To make roast quail more delicate, wipe with a damp cloth inside and out and place in a saucepan. Cover with milk. Simmer gently for 6 or 7 minutes. Place on a rack in a baking tin. Smear lavishly with melted butter. Roast for about 4 minutes till nicely browned. Serve with sour bean gravy.

RABBIT (Lapin)

There are two kinds of rabbit usually available. Tame rabbits have delicate white flesh and are larger than the wild ones, the other class, but the wild, sometimes referred to as "warren rabbits," are supposed to have the finest flavour on account of their food. Rabbits should be cooked when perfectly fresh. Fry, grill or roast young rabbits, and boil, braise or stew older ones, or make them into broth. If wanted very delicate, or to take the place of chicken in a dish, always be sure to scald in boiling water and dry before cooking.

BOILED RABBIT (Lapin bouilli)

1 jointed rabbit
Boiling water to cover
Few drops of vinegar
Salt and pepper to taste
2 large onions
¾ pint onion sauce

Place rabbit joints in a basin. Cover with the boiling water. Add a few drops of vinegar. Stand for 5 minutes. Drain off water. Place joints in a stewpan. Add salt and pepper. Peel and add onions. Barely cover with boiling water. Simmer very gently till tender, for about 1-1½ hours, depending on age of rabbit. Drain joints, reserving the liquor and onions. Arrange rabbit on a hot dish. Coat with the onion sauce, made of equal quantity of hot milk and strained rabbit stock. In Scotland, we often serve boiled rabbit with boiled oatmeal puddings, allowing 1 per person. *For 4 persons.*

CASSEROLE OF RABBIT (Casserole de Lapin)

1 jointed rabbit
2 oz. fat bacon
1 oz. flour
Salt and pepper to taste
1 peeled onion
2 sliced carrots
1 slice turnip
1½ pints beef stock or water
½ teaspoon crushed herbs
Pinch ground mace
½ pint boiled peas

Place joints in a basin. Cover with boiling water. Stand for 5 minutes. Cut bacon into dice. Fry for 5 minutes, then remove to a casserole, leaving fat in pan. Dry rabbit joints. Fry in bacon fat till brownish all over, then transfer to the casserole. Slice and fry onion with carrots and turnip until all the fat has been absorbed. Sprinkle round rabbit. Pour stock or water into pan. Stir till boiling. Season with salt and pepper again. Add herbs and sauce. Pour over rabbit. Cover and cook in a slow oven, 300° F., for about 1½ hours till tender, then add peas. *For 4 persons.*

CURRIED RABBIT (Lapin à l'Indienne)

3 tablespoons butter or margarine
2 tablespoons chopped onion
1 tablespoon curry powder
1 teaspoon flour
1 cup water or beef stock
Meat from 1 rabbit
1 cooking apple
1 teaspoon chutney
1 teaspoon desiccated coconut
1½ teaspoons salt
1 tablespoon sultanas
4 oz. rice

Melt fat in a stewpan. Add onion and fry till pale brown. Stir in curry powder and flour. Cook for 3 minutes, stirring constantly. Gradually stir in water or stock. Add meat from rabbit, cut in small chunks, and chopped, peeled apple. Simmer slowly till rabbit is tender. Add chutney, coconut, salt and sultanas. Cover and cook till tender. Meanwhile boil rice in usual way. When curry is ready, stir in 6 drops lemon juice. Serve piled in a hot dish. Scoop rice round. *For 4 persons.*

FRIED RABBIT (Lapin frits)

To Prepare for Frying: Disjoint legs at body and second joints. Split down centre back through breast and divide each half in two pieces.

1 rabbit
1 tablespoon salad oil
2 tablespoons vinegar
1 teaspoon lemon juice
Ground mace to taste
1 teaspoon minced parsley
1 egg and crumbs
½ sliced onion
1 small sprig parsley

Joint and blanch rabbit, discarding ribs. Wipe dry. Stir oil, vinegar, lemon juice, ground mace and 1 teaspoon parsley together, then soak rabbit joints in this mixture for about 1 hour. Remove joints. Wipe dry. Egg and crumb. Fry in deep smoking hot fat or oil, with onion, till golden. Pile up in a dish. Garnish with parsley. Serve with Tartare sauce. *For 4 persons.*

JUGGED RABBIT (Civet de Lapin, Créole)

1 young rabbit
2½ oz. butter
Salt to taste
1 medium-sized onion

Wash, dry and joint rabbit. Melt 1½ oz. of the butter. Add joints and fry until well browned, turning occasionally. Transfer to a casserole or

282

2 cloves
1 blade mace
1 bouquet garni
6 black peppercorns
1 pint beef stock
2 teaspoons lemon juice
½ gill port wine
1 oz. flour
Forcemeat balls

"hot-pot" jar. Season with salt to taste. Peel onion and stick with cloves, then add. Add mace, bouquet garni and peppercorns. Heat stock in pan. Strain over rabbit, with lemon juice and half the wine. Cover closely. Bake in a slow oven, 300° F.-325° F., for about 2 hours. Twenty minutes before serving, pour gravy from rabbit into a saucepan. Knead the flour with remainder of butter. Stir into gravy. Stir until boiling. Add remainder of wine. Re-season if necessary. Dish up. Strain gravy over. Garnish with forcemeat balls. Serve with red currant jelly. *For 4 persons.*

ROAST RABBIT (Lapin rôti)

Remove head, legs and neck. Lard remainder, then pickle it for 24 hours in white wine with 3 or 4 slices of onion, 1 chopped carrot, 1 sprig parsley, 1 bay leaf, 1 sprig thyme, 6 black peppercorns, 1 inch cinnamon stick, and a pinch of grated nutmeg. There should be enough wine to come half way up the rabbit. Turn rabbit occasionally in this marinade. Remove at the end of 24 hours and dry thoroughly. Smear all over with butter or margarine. Place on a rack in a baking tin. Bake in a moderate oven, 350° F., till brown, turning so that it browns evenly, and basting occasionally with melted butter. Season with salt. Dish up and keep hot. Meanwhile, boil the marinade till reduced to almost half its quantity. When rabbit is required, cream ½ oz. flour gradually with about 1½ gills cream. Remove marinade from stove. Strain. Stir in cream. When blended, stir over stove till boiling. Serve rabbit with roast potatoes and red currant or rowan jelly. *For 4 persons.*

ROAST STUFFED RABBIT (Lapin farci rôti)

1 pint stale breadcrumbs
Salt and black pepper to taste
¼ teaspoon crushed herbs
½ minced medium-sized onion
2 oz. melted margarine or bacon dripping
2 or 3 tablespoons milk or stock
1 young wild rabbit

Mix crumbs with seasonings and onion. If liked, substitute ¼ pint minced celery for ¼ pint of the crumbs. Stir in fat and milk or stock, then rub inside of rabbit lightly with salt. Fill with the stuffing. Sew up and truss. Place in a roasting tin. Brush with bacon or beef dripping. Season with salt and black pepper to taste. Turn on side. Roast, uncovered, in a moderately slow oven, 325° F., for 1½-1¾ hours, basting every ¼ hour with melted fat and turning when half done. *For 6 persons.*

SNIPE (Bécassines)

Hang only for a short time. Clean and remove gizzard only. Truss. Fry, grill or roast young birds. Make old birds into a pie or soup, or cook in a casserole or stew.

To Fry Snipe (Bécassines frites) : Roll snipe, trussed as for roasting, in seasoned flour. If preferred, dip in sieved crumbs, then egg and crumb. Fry in hot oil to cover until crisp and light brown, in about 2 minutes. Drain on absorbent paper. Garnish with watercress. Serve with orange salad.

To Grill Snipe (Bécassines grillées) : Split snipe without separating them. Stick their bills in their breasts. Brush with olive oil. Season with salt and pepper to taste. Grill for 3-4 minutes on each side. Dish each up on a slice of toast. Coat birds with Maître d'Hôtel butter. Garnish with watercress.

To Roast Snipe (Bécassines rôties) : Truss without drawing but remove gizzard. Bard with fat bacon. Place each on a piece of toast in a baking tin. Coat with melted butter. Bake in a moderately hot oven, 375° F., for 10-15 minutes, according to taste, basting frequently with butter. Serve on toast with thin brown gravy, fried crumbs and potato chips. Garnish with lemon and watercress. *If small, allow 1 per person.*

Austrian Way with Roast Snipe (Bécassines, Autrichienne) : Season, bard and roast in a quick oven, 450° F., basting frequently with equal quantity of melted butter and white stock. Wash and chop liver and heart, 3 peeled shallots and 1 sprig parsley. Mix together with 1 tablespoon finely minced lemon peel, 1 heaped tablespoon breadcrumbs, and salt and pepper. Stir in ½ gill red wine, and a few drops of sour cream. Melt ½ oz. butter, and cook mixture till liver and heart are tender. To serve snipe, dish up. Coat with heated sour cream. Garnish with small croûtes of bread, fried in butter and topped with the liver and heart mixture. Sometimes diced pineapple or thin slices of pineapple cooked in butter till clear is passed round with this dish.

SNIPE AU VIN (Bécassines au Vin)

6 snipe
6 oz. butter
Seasoned flour to taste
1 tablespoon chopped onion
Pinch ground mace
1 tablespoon breadcrumbs
½ gill sherry
Juice 1 lemon
Dash cayenne pepper

Truss birds. Melt butter in a shallow saucepan. Dip birds in seasoned flour, then place in pan. Add onion, mace, 1 bay leaf, if liked, and cook, tossing frequently, for 12 minutes. Remove from pan. Stir crumbs, wine and lemon juice into essence in pan. When blended, return snipe. Cover. Simmer very gently till tender, in about ½ hour. Season with cayenne pepper. Dish up each bird on a croûte of fried bread. Garnish with watercress. *For 6 persons.*

SWAN (Cygne)

Very rarely on sale. Only young cygnets are fit for roasting. Pot old swans.

ROAST CYGNET (Jeune Cygne rôti)

1 cygnet
2 lb. rump steak
2 minced shallots
1 dessertspoon minced onion
Salt and pepper to taste
Grated nutmeg or ground mace to taste

Truss cygnet as you would a goose. Put steak through a meat grinder. Add shallot, onion, salt and pepper and grated nutmeg or ground mace. Mix till blended. Stuff bird and sew up or skewer vent. Wrap in well-buttered paper. Place on a rack in a baking tin. Pour 1 cup beef stock into tin and add a tablespoon of butter or beef dripping.

Roast in a slow oven, 325° F., for about 2 hours. Remove paper. Dredge with flour. Baste well. Dish up. Make a thick gravy with the liquor in baking tin. Flavour to taste with red currant jelly. Garnish with watercress. *For 6 persons.*

TEAL (Sarcelle)

Highly prized water fowl. Prime during winter months, after frost has set in. Grill like snipe, but for 7 minutes on each side. Do not hang for more than one day. Cook like wild duck or in any of the following ways.

ROAST TEAL (Sarcelle rôtie)

Brush trussed teal lavishly with hot melted butter. Place on a rack in a baking tin. Roast in a hot oven, 450° F., for about 20 minutes, basting frequently with drippings. If liked under-done, roast only for ¼ hour. Before serving, dredge lightly with flour and baste again. Garnish with cut lemon and watercress. Serve with thin brown gravy and orange salad. Allow 1 teal for 2 persons, if bird is large.

To Vary:
(1) Bard with fat bacon. Coat with orange or Bigarade sauce.
(2) Roast barded bird for 10 minutes. Remove bacon fat. Baste and leave till brown. Heat 3 tablespoons white wine and 3 tablespoons rich white stock in a stew pan. Add bird. Cover. Simmer gently for 4 or 5 minutes. Untruss and dish up. Pour sauce round.

REINDEER (Renne)

Reindeer can be cooked by any methods given for beef or venison, or by one of the following methods. Before cooking, soak it for 24 hours in milk to cover, then rinse in cold water and wipe dry with a cloth. You can then marinate it, see page 38, or cook it without marinating.

GRILLED REINDEER STEAKS OR CHOPS (Renne grillé)

Dip steaks or chops in seasoned flour. Shake gently. Brush tops with melted butter or olive oil. Heat grill. Place steaks or chops on rack and cook about 2 inches from heat for 3-5 minutes, according to whether you want steaks rare or well done, then turn. Brush second side with fat or oil, and grill for the same length of time. Arrange on a hot dish. Place a pat of maître d'hôtel butter on each. Garnish with fried mushrooms or tomatoes. Serve with potato chips and green peas.

ROAST REINDEER (Renne rôti)

Soak a rib joint, carefully boned, of reindeer in milk to cover for 24 hours. Drain. Wipe with a damp cloth and spread out flat on a board. Season with salt, pepper and paprika. Spread with stuffing to within an inch of edges, allowing $1\frac{1}{2}$ cups of apple or mushroom stuffing to a $3\frac{1}{2}$-4 lb. joint, weighed before boning. Roll up like a Swiss roll. Tie securely with boiled string. Place on a rack in a baking tin. Season the outside with salt, pepper and paprika and brush with melted bacon or pork fat. Roast in a slow oven, 325° F., allowing 35-40 minutes per lb., according to taste. Serve with roast potatoes. *For 6-8 persons.*

VENISON (Venaison)

The flesh of deer. The buck meat is finer than the doe. To be able to serve a good dish of venison, the meat must be properly preserved and dressed. As soon as it is divided into joints, it should be hung up in a cool dry larder, or stored in a refrigerator at a temperature which will only keep it chilled. If it has to be stored in a larder, dry joints with a cloth and hang up in a current of air. If to be kept for any length of time, sprinkle lightly with ground ginger and pepper to keep off flies, and examine, wipe and re-pepper every day. In cold weather, keep it for a fortnight before cooking. If the weather is close or muggy, a few days will be long enough. Venison should never be served except when in season. To tell whether it is in perfect condition, run a fine skewer or knitting needle into the haunch close to the bone, then remove. If it comes out clean with only a gamey smell, it is in perfect condition. If there is the slightest musty smell, cook at once.

Before cooking, sponge it with a cloth dipped in tepid water, then lave it with equal quantity of tepid milk and water, and dry thoroughly with a clean cloth. As venison is a rather dry meat, it is wise to soak it in a marinade before cooking. Before frying or grilling, beat well with meat mallet, and coat thoroughly with melted dripping or olive oil flavoured with grated onion. When ready to cook, wash venison well with tepid water and dry thoroughly, then marinate as suggested when cuts for frying or grilling are concerned.

ABC OF VENISON

Breast : Braise, roast, stew or cook in a casserole.
Haunch : Prime roast.
Loin : Prime roast ; can also be braised or divided into chops and fried or grilled.
Neck : Divide into chops and fry, grill, stew or make into a casserole.
Saddle : Prime roast.
Shoulder : Braise, stew or make into a casserole. Can also be roasted.
ACCOMPANIMENTS : For fried, grilled or roast venison : Brown gravy, cranberry, red currant, or rowan jelly ; roast potatoes for roast meat, and chips, crisps or straws for fried or grilled. Garnish latter with watercress.

BRAISED VENISON (Venaison braisée)

5 lb. venison
$\frac{1}{4}$ lb. dripping
$\frac{1}{2}$ cup beef stock

Choose a cut of venison from the lower end of the leg or shoulder. Wipe with a damp cloth. Lard with fat salt bacon. Rub with well-seasoned flour.

1 tablespoon red wine
½ cup chopped celery
1 sliced carrot
1 chopped onion
1 chopped cooking apple
½ tablespoon lemon juice
Salt and pepper to taste

Melt fat in a large saucepan. Add venison. Fry till well browned, turning frequently. This process will take about 30 minutes. Add beef stock and wine. Cover closely. Cook gently for 2-2½ hours, or till tender, turning frequently, and adding small amounts of beef stock from time to time when necessary. Half hour before meat is ready, mix the remainder of ingredients together and sprinkle over venison. Serve on a hot platter. Season gravy if necessary. If the gravy is cooked down too much, thin with a little beef stock. Serve with rowan or red currant jelly. *For 9 or 10 persons.*

FILLET OF VENISON ST. HUBERT
(Filet de Venaison, St. Hubert)

2 lb. fillet of venison
2 oz. butter or margarine
1 oz. flour
½ pint beef stock
½ pint Burgundy or claret
Salt and pepper to taste
1 teaspoon red currant jelly

Wipe fillet with a damp cloth and cut into equal-thick slices. Lard each with strips of bacon. Melt butter in a shallow saucepan. Add fillets. Fry quickly till lightly browned all over. Remove to a plate. Stir flour into fat. When frothy, gradually stir in stock and wine. Stir till boiling. Season with salt and pepper. Return venison to pan. Cover closely. Simmer gently for about 20 minutes, or till tender. Dish up. Skim fat from sauce. Stir in jelly. Pour over fillet. If liked, garnish with sliced gherkins to taste heated in beef stock. *For 6 or 7 persons.*

FRIED VENISON CAKES (Dormés de Venaison)

1½ lb. lean venison
3 tablespoons breadcrumbs
Salt and pepper to taste
Paprika to taste
2 peeled medium-sized onions
Maître d'Hôtel butter

Put venison through a meat grinder. Stir in crumbs, salt, pepper and paprika. Divide into 6 equal portions. Shape into round cakes, 1-1¼ inches thick. Fry in a little smoking hot butter or bacon fat till brown on both sides, then fry slowly till cooked through. Slice and fry onions. Dish up. Garnish cakes with pats of Maître d'Hôtel butter and sliced onions. Serve with brown or chestnut gravy and potato chips. *For 6 persons.*

GRILLED VENISON CHOPS (Côtelettes de Venaison grillées)

6 loin venison chops
1 oz. butter
Salt and pepper to taste
2 tablespoons red currant jelly
¾ lb. fried peeled mushrooms

Wipe chops. Melt butter. Brush each chop with the butter. Grill, turning frequently, for about 25 minutes. Season with salt and pepper. Add the jelly to the remainder of butter in a saucepan. Heat till piping hot. Arrange chops in a circle on a hot dish. Coat with the gravy. Fill centre with fried mushrooms. Garnish with potato chips and watercress. *For 6 persons.*

ROAST HAUNCH OF VENISON (Cuisse de Venaison rôtie)

Remove the chine bone and knuckle from a well-hung haunch of venison. Trim. Wash if necessary, or wipe with a damp cloth, then with a dry one. Season with salt and pepper. Roll in a sheet of well-greased paper. Make a stiff paste with flour and water and knead till smooth. Roll out till large enough to cover joint. Wrap joint in the paste, then cover with another greased paper. Tie securely with string. Bake in a moderate oven, 350° F., for 3 or 4 hours, according to size, basting well while cooking with beef dripping. When nearly ready, remove paper and chip off paste. Dredge with flour. Baste well, and bake till brown. Dish up. Serve with brown venison gravy flavoured with port wine and with red currant jelly.

WIDGEON (Canard Siffleur)

Species of Wild Duck. Should be eaten fresh. Usually roasted, but can be treated by any recipes given under " Wild Duck."

ROAST WIDGEON (Canard Siffleur rôtis)

2 widgeons
1 oz. butter
Juice ½ lemon
Salt and pepper to taste
1 tablespoon flour

Truss birds. Place on a rack in a baking tin. Melt butter. Baste birds with the butter. Roast in a moderately hot oven, 400° F., for about 20 minutes, basting frequently with remainder of butter, then with the drippings. Sprinkle with lemon juice and salt and pepper. Dredge with flour. Baste well. Dish up. Serve with orange gravy. Garnish with watercress. Allow ½ bird per person.

To Vary: Rub the breasts of widgeons with their livers until the breasts look red. Dredge lightly with flour and baste well before roasting. Roast at 450° F., for about 20 minutes. Garnish with watercress. Serve with fried crumbs and wine and orange gravy.

WILD DUCK (Canard Sauvage)

Highly esteemed. Duck preferable to drake. Leave the feet on, but turn them close in to body, and truss like a domestic duck. Do not stuff unless with quartered oranges, carefully skinned. Do not hang for more than one day. Mallard and pintails, the latter known as " Sea Pheasant," are the most delicate.

FRIED BREASTS OF WILD DUCK

2 wild ducks
2 oz. butter
½ gill white wine
¼ pint brown sauce
1 oz. meat glaze
Juice ½ lemon

Carefully remove the breasts. Skin and trim. Melt butter in a frying-pan. Fry quickly until brown on both sides, but underdone. Strain off the butter into a saucepan. Add wine. Boil quickly till reduced to half its quantity. Stir in

Remove the bone at back of Roast Sirloin of Beef, then turn joint on its back, with fillets upwards, and remove fat then start to carve fillet. *See page* 237.

Holding the knife slightly slanting outwards, cut off slices from one-sixth to one-eighth inch thick. *See page* 237.

When all the fillet has been removed, turn joint upside down, and beginning at the rib end, carve in slices, with knife slanting outwards, about one-sixth inch thick. *See page* 237.

White Turkey.

Serve Roast Chicken, garnished bacon rolls, with Duchesse or roast potatoes and brown gravy. *See page* 307.

Creamed Chicken can be served in a circle of mashed potato, ornamented with a fork. Garnish with parsley. *See page* 319.

Juice 1 orange
Fried croûtons

sauce, glaze and lemon and orange juice. Add par-boiled, shredded rind of the orange, if liked. Arrange fried heart-shaped croûtons on a hot flat dish. Place the breasts on top. Garnish with skinned sections of 2 oranges. Pour sauce over. *For 4 persons.*

GRILLED WILD DUCK

Choose young plump birds. Halve if large. Flatten breast bones. Rub with a cut lemon. Brush with melted butter or olive oil ½ hour before cooking. Grill under moderate heat, allowing from 15-25 minutes, if liked rare, or 20-35 if liked well done. Season with salt and pepper. Dish up. Brush with melted butter. Garnish with quarters of lemon and sprigs of parsley or watercress. Serve with orange salad and wine gravy. *Allow 1 breast per person.*

ROAST WILD DUCKS (Canards Sauvage rôtis)

2 wild ducks
2 oz. butter
Salt and pepper to taste

Wipe and dry birds. (If liked, they can be stuffed with carefully skinned and quartered oranges or clementines.) Place half the butter inside each. Season inside with salt and pepper to taste. Truss. Place on a rack in a baking tin. Roast in a hot oven, 450° F., for 25-30 minutes. They must not be overcooked. Baste frequently with the drippings. Dredge with flour and baste again with drippings, or substitute ½ gill claret or Burgundy for the fat. Dish up. Serve with the wine gravy, and an orange salad. *For 4 persons.*

WILD GOOSE (Oie Sauvage)

Wild geese are rarely obtainable in shops. If you should be given one, it is a good idea to scrub it with soda water, and rinse thoroughly to get rid of the fishy taste before cooking, as some wild geese taste very fishy. Another way to get rid of the taste, is to bring it to the boil in cold salt water containing a pinch of bicarbonate of soda. Drain, and dry before roasting. They average in size from 8 to 13 lb.

ROAST WILD GOOSE (Oie Sauvage rôtie)

Prepare, stuff and truss like a domestic goose, except that it is not necessary to prick them to extract their fat, as they are not fat. If preferred, stuff only with 2 or 3 onions, 2 cloves, a sprig of sage and a rasher of fat bacon. Place goose on a rack in a baking tin. Dredge with seasoned flour. Brush with melted fat, or bard with slices of fat bacon. Roast in a slow oven, 300° F., allowing 20 minutes per lb., basting occasionally with equal quantity of melted butter or margarine and stock. Serve with thick brown gravy, orange salad and red currant or rowan jelly. *For 6 to 10 persons.*

C.F.C.—10

WOODCOCK (Bécasse)

Considered a great delicacy by experts. Only cooked when plump. Legs and intestines are the most delicate parts. Usually roasted or made into a salmi, but can be prepared in any way suitable for young partridges. Should not be kept too long. Ready to cook when they turn black between the legs, and the feathers are easily plucked. Truss without drawing, only removing gizzard. Pluck carefully as skin is tender.

ROAST WOODCOCK (Bécasse rôtie)

Skin head and neck and skewer with the long beak through legs and body. Brush with melted seasoned butter. Bard with fat bacon. Place on a rack in a baking tin with toast below to catch the gravy and drippings. Roast in a hot oven, 450° F., for about 20 minutes if wanted well done, or 15 if preferred slightly under-done. Remove bacon 5 minutes before dishing up. Baste and brown breasts. Serve on the toast. Garnish with watercress and lemon slices. Serve with brown gravy, fried crumbs and chips. *Allow 1 bird for 2 persons.*

To Vary: Hang birds for a week, then roast as described. Cut a piece of bread for each bird large enough to take a quarter of bird and about $\frac{1}{4}$ inch thick. When birds are almost ready, fry croûtes in butter till golden brown on each side. Remove to a hot dish. Carve each open and scrape out the insides with a spoon. Spread this trail on the croûtes. Sprinkle each with brandy and set a match to it, then quarter birds, and lay each quarter on a croûte. Garnish with watercress. Serve with gravy and potato straws. *Allow 2 quarters per person.*

SALMI OF WOODCOCK (Salmis de Bécasse)

Quarter 2 roasted woodcocks. Place carcases in a saucepan. Add $\frac{1}{2}$ pint claret or Burgundy, salt and pepper to taste, 1 bouquet garni, 1 dessertspoon chopped chives, $\frac{1}{2}$ bay leaf. Cover. Simmer very gently for $\frac{1}{2}$ hour. Remove carcases to a mortar. Pound with a pestle. Return to pan. Simmer gently for $\frac{1}{2}$ hour. Strain sauce and re-heat with birds without boiling. Dish up each quarter on a croûte fried in butter. *Allow 2 quarters for each person.*

MISCELLANEOUS GAME RECIPES

Any kind of game can be used in the following recipes :

DEVILLED GAME (Gibier à la Diable)

(1) Carefully remove all bone and skin from any cooked game. Carve flesh into slices. Season highly with cayenne pepper and paprika, then with salt. Sprinkle with lemon juice. Melt a little butter until oiled, and coat slices with this. Dip in dried breadcrumbs. Shake lightly. Place on a greased baking sheet. Bake in a hot oven, 450° F., till heated through. Arrange in overlapping slices in a circle on a dish covered with a paper doily. Fill centre with watercress salad.

(2) Three or four hours before " devil " is to be served, score underdone game rather deeply over the meaty parts. Mix equal quantity of cayenne pepper, curry powder and salt with powdered mushrooms, then knead into a paste with butter. Smear game with this savoury butter. Grill till well browned, turning frequently. It can be baked in the oven if preferred, but in that case baste with the melted paste occasionally. Usually only joints are devilled.

GAME SAUSAGES (Saucissons de Gibier)

1 lb. cold game
6 oz. lean ham
6 oz. butter
Salt and pepper to taste
Ground mace to taste

Remove all skin and sinew from game before weighing. Put game through a meat grinder, with the ham. Place in a mortar. Pound with butter, adding a small piece at a time. Season with salt, pepper and mace. Tie in sausage skins. When required, fry slowly in a little hot butter or lard for ¼ hour, turning frequently. *For 3 or 4 persons.*

GAME SOUFFLE (Soufflé de Gibier)

Breasts of 2 grouse, or 3 hazel hens
2 oz. butter
1 slice onion
4 egg yolks
Salt and cayenne pepper to taste
4 egg whites

Pound game in a mortar with butter and finely-minced onion. When into a paste, rub mixture through a sieve. Beat egg yolks and season. Stir into paste. Beat egg whites till stiff and fold into mixture. Pour into a buttered soufflé dish. Stand in a baking tin containing hot water, coming half-way up the sides. Bake in a moderate oven, 350° F., for 20-30 minutes till puffy. Serve at onec. If breasts of birds are large or eggs small, you'll need more eggs, one egg or two whites. *For 2 or 3 persons.*

SALMI OF WILD DUCK (Salmi de Canard Sauvage)

1 wild duck
2 oz. butter
1 sliced carrot
1 sliced onion
1½ oz. flour
1 pint stock
Salt and pepper to taste
Rind 1 orange
¼ pint port wine
Juice ½ lemon

Roast duck till half-done. Remove from pan and, when cold, joint neatly. Put chopped carcase of bird into a saucepan. Cover with cold water. Stew gently for 30 minutes. Melt butter in a stewpan. Add carrot and onion. Fry till dark brown. Stir in flour. Add stock and stir till sauce boils. Season to taste. Add shredded or grated orange rind, then the pieces of duck and any essence remaining in pan in which bird was cooked. Stew gently till duck is ready, in about 30 minutes, according to age and size of bird. Ten minutes before that time, add port wine and lemon juice. Serve on a hot dish with skimmed sauce strained over. *For 2 persons.*

COLD GAME DISHES

There are many ways of treating game to be served cold, besides offering part of a cold roast bird salad. Set it in aspic jelly. Make it into a galantine. When time allows, coat it with Chaudfroid Sauce, then apply melted aspic jelly.

ASPIC OF GAME (Aspic de Gibier)

1 quart well seasoned stock
2 wineglasses cooking Marsala
2 wineglasses tarragon vinegar
2 oz. leaf gelatine
2 egg whites
Left-over game

Turn stock into a saucepan. Flavour with any good meat extract. If you haven't any stock, use water and flavour it with meat extract, after adding to water any left over gravy. Stir in Marsala and vinegar, gelatine, softened in a little cold water, and the egg whites. Whisk with an egg whisk till mixture nearly comes to the boil. Boil up and strain through a scalded jelly bag. Set a little of this in the bottom of a wet mould. Decorate mould with one or two peas, strips of pimento, or bits of hard-boiled egg white, or chopped pickled gherkin or parsley. Cover decorations with a little of the aspic. You can add a little diced cold ham or tongue as well as the game, if short of game. Keep on adding the layers, allowing each one to set before adding another, till mould is full. Leave till set, then turn out on to a cold dish, or on to a bed of heart of lettuce leaves. Garnish with tomatoes or hard-boiled eggs. *For 6 or 7 persons.*

BRAWN OF RABBIT (Lapin en Gelée)

1 wild rabbit
1 hard-boiled egg
¼ lb. lean ham
1 pig's trotter
Salt and pepper to taste
½ teaspoon grated lemon rind
Pinch grated nutmeg or ground mace
1 teaspoon minced parsley
½ oz. powdered gelatine
½ pint stock

Soak rabbit in salted water for ½ hour. Shell and slice egg. Cut ham into strips. Thoroughly wash trotter and place in a saucepan. Simmer gently for ½ hour, then add rabbit. Add salt and pepper, lemon rind, nutmeg or ground mace, parsley and 1 stick of celery, if in season. Cover and simmer gently till flesh comes away from bones. Remove rabbit when tender and cut flesh into small pieces. Strain stock. Soften gelatine in 2 tablespoons cold water for 5 minutes, then stir in hot stock. Strain. Pour a thin layer in the bottom of a plain wet mould. Decorate with slices of egg and a little chopped parsley, and allow to set. Mix the ham with the rabbit. Pack lightly into mould till half-full, then place remainder of egg in centre. Fill up with remainder of rabbit mixture, till nearly at the top. Add stock to fill. Chill and unmould. Serve with potato salad. *For 5 persons.*

CHAUDFROID OF PHEASANT (Chaudfroid de Faisan)

1 roast pheasant
1 pint brown chaudfroid sauce
1 hard-boiled egg
Aspic jelly as required
1 lettuce
Mayonnaise as required

Take care not to overcook pheasant for this dish. Carve bird into neat joints. Place on a wire tray. Brush gently with a thick layer of the chaudfroid sauce. Leave till set. Garnish with fancy shapes of egg white, and with sieved yolk. Coat very lightly with melted aspic jelly. If too heavy-handed, you may disturb the garnish. Prepare lettuce as for a salad. Moisten with mayonnaise or French dressing as preferred. Place in the centre of a dish. Arrange the pheasant on top. Garnish with clusters of watercress, and chopped aspic jelly. *For 4 persons.*

CHAUDFROID OF QUAIL (Chaudfroid de Cailles)

4 quail
1/4 lb. chicken or guinea fowl forcemeat
Foie gras to taste
Meat glaze as required
1 or 2 champignons
Aspic jelly as required
1/4 lb. rice
1 1/2 pints chicken stock

Bone quail carefully without removing claws or drumsticks. Place forcemeat in a basin. Sieve 1-1$\frac{1}{2}$ tablespoons foie gras and stir into forcemeat. Stuff quail with this. Tie each bird in a small piece of butter muslin. Place in a pan of boiling stock or water to cover. Simmer gently for 20 minutes. Remove and drain. Press lightly until cold, then remove muslin. Halve birds lengthwise. Place on a wire tray. Coat with melted meat glaze. When set, coat again. They need from two to three coats according to taste. Cut champignons into fancy shapes, such as elongated diamonds. Garnish quail with them. Brush lightly with half-set aspic jelly to keep decorations in place. Leave till set. Rinse rice in cold water and put in a saucepan containing boiling stock. Boil till thick, stirring occasionally. Turn into a wet border mould. When set and chilled, turn out on to a round or oval flat dish. Fill centre with crisp lettuce, lightly coated with mayonnaise or salad cream. Arrange quail side by side with claws upwards on rice border, claws resting against the lettuce. Garnish between each quail with chopped aspic jelly, then garnish round border with chopped aspic and with four roses of heart of lettuce leaves equal distance apart. Garnish centre of lettuce with sprigs of chervil or parsley, or with tomato roses. *For 8 persons.*

GALANTINE OF PHEASANT (Galantine de Faisan)

1 roasting pheasant
8 oz. veal stuffing
Salt and pepper to taste
3 oz. boiled tongue
2 truffles
Meat glaze as required
Aspic jelly as required

Bone pheasant, taking care not to break the skin. Carve through the skin and flesh down backbone of bird. Place flat on a pastry board. Draw skin out into a square. Season with salt and pepper to taste and a little celery salt, if liked. Cover with a thin layer of stuffing. Season. Cut tongue up into matches and truffles into short sticks. Place alternately over stuffing, in even rows. Cover with another layer of stuffing, then roll up like a Swiss roll. Tie tightly in a piece of butter muslin. Lower into a pan of boiling stock or water. Cover. Simmer gently for 1$\frac{1}{4}$ hours, then remove. Drain well. Press lightly till cold. Remove cloth. Coat with melted meat glaze. Remove a thin slice from each end of galantine. Place on a long flat dish. Garnish with piped savoury butter down the centre. Garnish round galantine with chopped aspic jelly and chervil, parsley or watercress. *For 6 persons.*

GALANTINE OF RABBIT (Galantine de Lapin)

2 young rabbits
1 stick celery
5 cloves
1 onion
1 carrot
Salt, pepper and cayenne

Joint and blanch rabbits. Place in a shallow saucepan with celery, cloves, sliced peeled onion, sliced carrot and salt, pepper and cayenne pepper. Add water. Cover and simmer for 1 hour or till tender. Strain $\frac{1}{2}$ pint of the liquor and colour slightly

293

pepper to taste
1 pint water
1 tablespoon powdered gelatine
1 teaspoon lemon juice
1 hard-boiled egg
A few slices of beetroot
Minced parsley to taste

with carmine. Add gelatine, softened in cold water, and lemon juice. Line a wet loaf tin with slices of hard-boiled egg, beetroot and with minced parsley, in a pattern. Pour over some coloured liquor and allow to set. Bone and arrange meat neatly in lined mould. Pour over remainder of liquor and stand till firm. Turn out on to a serving dish. Garnish with green salad and radish roses. *For 6-8 persons.*

QUAIL IN ASPIC (Cailles en Aspic)

3 oz. liver paste
2 tablespoons sifted bread-crumbs
4 quails
1 packet aspic jelly

Beat liver paste till creamy, then mix with the breadcrumbs. Stuff birds equally with the liver mixture. Roast in usual way, but very lightly. Rinse four oval ramekin moulds with cold water. Line each with melted aspic, flavoured, if liked, with Madeira or sherry to taste. When set, place a bird in each. Fill up with aspic. When set and chilled, turn each out on to an individual plate. Serve with heart of lettuce salad. *For 4 persons.*

TO CARVE GAME AND POULTRY

To be able to carve game and poultry slickly, you need to know the position of the bones and joints, just as you do when carving meat. A careless carver can spoil the most succulent of birds. It is also advisable to have a pointed knife with a short, stiff, straight blade and a fairly long handle, but this is not absolutely necessary. An ordinary " carver " can be used. When a large bird, particularly a goose or turkey, is to be carved, which requires the legs to be divided into portions, poultry shears can be used to cut through the bones.

Place the bird on its back on a hot serving dish, with the legs to the left, then fix the fork firmly across the breast bone and proceed.

If the whole bird, such as a goose or turkey, is not required at one meal, there are two methods of carving : (1) Carve one side only. (2) Remove wing joints and leg joints, including the thigh, and carve only the breast. Smallish birds, like grouse, partridges, pigeons, ptarmigans and spring chickens are generally carved in half. It is a good idea to halve them in the kitchen before dishing up.

TO CARVE GAME

Grouse, Partridge, Pigeon, Ptarmigan, Woodcock: Halve. Inserting point of knife at the neck end of the breast, carve firmly through the centre of the bird.

Hare: Place dish before carver with legs to the right. Insert knife at neck end and cut along the backbone to the tail end. Now cut crosswise through the middle of the fillet and you have the choicest portion of one side. Divide according to size. Carve other side in the same way. Remove forelegs and hindlegs, and take the meat from the bones. It is not usual to serve roast hare legs whole. Divide each in two portions at joint.

Pheasant: Carve like chicken, remembering the breast and the wing are the choicest parts. If you have to serve a leg, give a slice of the breast along with it.

Rabbit: Place serving dish with the head of the rabbit to the left of the carver. Insert knife in the centre of the neck end and remove the fillet from the side of the backbone nearest to you, and then from the other side. Cut in two or three portions crosswise. Now remove the legs and then the shoulders, running knife under blade bone to cut off shoulders.

Venison: To carve the haunch, place it on the table so that the knuckle is farthest away from the carver and the loin is nearest. Cut crosswise from about the centre of the knuckle end down the right side, then make a slanting cut from the centre of the knuckle where you inserted the knife along right side almost to end of loin. Continue carving slanting slices to allow the gravy to remain in the hollow. Carve, for those who like fat, a portion of fat from the left side.

Wild Ducks and Widgeons: Carve breasts in slices parallel with the breast bone. This is usually done in the kitchen and the slices replaced on carcase. If joints are to be served, carve like domestic duck.

Plover, Quail, Snipe, etc.: Do not carve. Serve all small birds whole, like Petits Poussins.

TO CARVE POULTRY

Chicken and Fowl: Place on a large flat dish with the legs to the left of the carver. Holding bird firmly by fixing the fork across the breast bone, insert carving knife between the leg and side next to you, and press joint away from body, when you will be able to cut through the skin, around the thigh. To do this, bend the leg over with your knife, and sever the sinew which holds the leg to the body, then with the fork, pull the joint off. Do not cut it. Now carve the wings. When the joint is reached, insert the fork to find the position of the connection, then cut the wing away next to the fork. When both legs and wings have been removed, carefully remove wishbone, then cut all along the breast bone on either side, in order to remove the breast meat. Only remove whole, when carving young chicken. Slice breast when carving older birds. If the wishbone wasn't removed before the breast, then cut across the front of the breast bone. Lift up towards the front, then remove the two pieces of flesh from breast bone. Sometimes breast bone is broken. In this case, be very careful when carving to see that no splinters of the bone have been left in the flesh.

When carving chicken, serve dark meat with a small portion of the breast. The oyster, a small mussel-shaped piece of flesh that lies in a hollow on each side, is considered the choicest portion. Turn bird upside down. Remove oysters with the point of a knife. To make a roasting fowl serve for 4 persons, carve in four, two wings each with a piece of breast, and two legs also with breast. If bird is large, it can be carved into eight portions. This is done by cutting the thighs lengthwise, and serving them with a small slice of breast. The drumsticks accompanied by breast gives two more portions, and the wings with remainder of breast make up the eight. If bird is stuffed before cooking, serve a tablespoon of stuffing with each portion, except when carving the front of the breast when the stuffing is carved along with the flesh.

Petits Poussins: Serve whole.

Capon and Guinea Fowl: Carve like chicken.

Turkey: A turkey can be carved like a chicken, but, as the joints are too large to be served individually, the meat from them should be carved in slices. Most carvers prefer to remove the wings to the side of the dish and carve the breast and stuffing together in long thin slices, but this is a matter of taste. To carve a turkey, do not remove the legs first of all. Begin by cutting off the leg meat from the top in two slices, then under the drumstick, slicing inwards towards the joint. Next carve the flesh off the thigh, and then slice the breast beginning at the thin end, and afterwards proceed onwards towards the wing. This is the ideal method of carving for a party, as in this manner a slice of leg and a slice of breast can be served together and, if turkey is stuffed in the breast, stuffing will also be included. When one side of the bird is carved, turn bird round so that the legs are towards you, in order to carve the other side. This is not the usual method, but I find it much better, as in this way you can obtain equal portions of the white meat for each person.

When carving for a small family, you can follow the method given for carving a chicken, or remove legs and then carve off slices from the breast. Only carve the legs if someone prefers dark meat. They can be devilled for another meal.

Duck: Place on serving dish with feet to the left of carver. First remove legs, and divide at the joints. Remove foot before serving leg, which is the choicest portion together with the thigh, then cut off wings. Now carve breast in thin slices, holding knife slightly inclined outwards. If bird is very young, it is better to remove the wishbone before carving breast.

Goose: Place the bird with the neck to the left of carver. Carve slices from each side of breast the whole length of the bird, though the breast can be cut crosswise, Continental fashion, if liked. Separate the wings from the body and remove, then remove the legs and divide the drumsticks from the thigh. If serving only a small number, only breast need be carved at first meal, but if the party is large, serve slices of breast and leg at the same time.

Poultry

All domestic birds suitable for the table are classified as "poultry." Flesh of chicken, fowl and turkey is more digestible than the flesh of duck or goose, and the white meat is finer textured and more digestible than the dark. Poultry is usually sold dressed for cooking. Poultry is ready for cooking six hours after it is killed. If kept in a refrigerator for any length of time, its flavour suffers.

All poultry should be fresh. If any birds have an unpleasant odour or show signs of a bluish or greenish tinge, which sometimes can be seen round the vent, they should not be chosen. Eyes will be clear if freshly killed, if stale they will be sunken. If freshly killed, feet should be pliant and soft, if stale, they will be more or less rigid. Skin should be smooth and moist, but not wrinkled. The breast bone should be straight and the breast plump, rounded and white. Birds that have been kept in cold storage are usually darker skinned and the flesh slightly shrunken. If very young poultry is wanted, see that the breast bone is pliable.

Frozen Poultry: To thaw poultry quickly, place in a dish under running cold water. Remove it from the water and drain and dry the moment it is thawed. Cook at once. Never re-freeze. If chicken or guinea fowl is left in its original wrapping, it is usually defrosted enough to cook in 12 hours.

SIZES OF BIRDS

Weight to allow per person when buying birds dressed but undrawn : $\frac{3}{4}$-1 lb. of chicken, guinea fowl or turkey, and 1-1$\frac{1}{2}$ lb. duck or goose.

No. of Persons	Birds
For 1 person - -	Poussin.
For 2 persons - -	Broiler, guinea chick, duckling broiler.
For 3 persons - -	Frying chicken, small guinea fowl.
For 3 or 4 persons -	Turkey poults.
For 4 persons - -	Roasting chicken, large duckling, large guinea fowl.
For 5 or 6 persons -	Duck, gosling, turkey poults for roasting.
For 6 persons - -	Roasting chicken, boiling fowl.
For 6 or 8 persons -	Capon.
For 8 or more - - (according to weight)	Goose, turkey (allowing $\frac{3}{4}$-1 lb. per person).

TO HANG POULTRY

Poultry can be cooked on the day it is killed. If this is not possible, hang up by the feet in a cool larder in a cross-current of air, without drawing. Ducks and geese must not be hung for more than 2 days, but turkeys can be hung from 3-5 days, if liked, and turkey poults about 2 days. If you leave bird until a greenish tinge appears round the vent, the bird has hung too long. The weather must dictate the length of time. Birds soon lose their freshness in warm or muggy weather. They can either be hung plucked or with their feathers on. Tie butter muslin securely round bird before hanging to protect it from insects.

TO GROOM POULTRY

To Pluck : Holding bird in your left hand, breast downwards, and grasping the wing farthest away from where it joins the body, start to pluck off the feathers from under the wing, pulling always towards the head. When all the feathers are plucked on that side except the down, pluck the other wing, and then proceed with the body, taking care not to tear the skin. If wing tip feathers are difficult to pluck, immerse tips in boiling water for 2 or 3 minutes, then pull out feathers.

To Singe : Hold bird over the flame from a burning paper, or over a gas flame, so that the surface will be evenly singed all over. Take care not to scorch the skin. With a sharp-pointed knife, cut out the oil sack at the top of the tail.

To Draw : If the tendons and feet are still on, remove. Cut off the head. Make an incision through the skin around the lower joint or drumstick about 1½ inches beneath the joint connecting the legs and feet, but take care not to cut the tendons. Put one leg at the edge of the table and press downwards so as to break the foot joint. Now, holding bird by your left hand, twist foot and pull it off with the tendons. Extract tendons from other leg in the same way. Remove tendons from any old bird with the assistance of a skewer. Pull out the windpipe and crop. To do this, feel under the skin near the neck with your first two fingers and draw out windpipe with the crop, which is attached to skin near the breast. Now make an opening through the skin below the breast bone, but only large enough to allow you to get your hand in. Remove intestines and giblets consisting of the gizzard, heart and liver. Take great care that the gall bladder, which is in the liver, is not broken. Cut it carefully away from the liver at once. If broken, it will impart a bitter flavour to any part of the bird it touches. Next scoop out the lungs, small red spongy pieces lying between the ribs in the hollows of the backbone. The kidneys, which lie in a hollow near the bottom of the backbone, must next be removed. Turn back skin and cut neck off, quite close to body, leaving a long enough piece of the skin to skewer over the back.

To Prepare Giblets : Remove arteries, thin membrane, veins, and any clotted blood around the heart, and any part of the liver which has a greenish tinge. Trim fat and membrane from gizzard, then cut through the thickest part till you come to the inner lining. Take care not to pierce the inner lining. Spread gizzard open and peel the inner skin away from gizzard. Throw it away. Wash giblets thoroughly in cold salted water, then rinse in fresh water. Use for making stock for gravy or soup, or make into a pie.

TIME FOR COOKING GIBLETS

Simmer:	Chicken	- - -	1-$1\frac{1}{2}$ hours (boiler) ; $\frac{3}{4}$-1 hour (roaster).
,,	Duck	- - -	About $1\frac{1}{2}$ hours.
,,	Goose	- - -	2-$2\frac{1}{2}$ hours.
,,	Guinea fowl	- -	About 1 hour.
,,	Turkey	- - -	2-$2\frac{1}{2}$ hours.

Wash thoroughly before cooking. Add cold water to cover. Bring quickly to boil. Simmer gently till tender. If feet are to be cooked with gibletts scrub and soak in boiling water for 2 or 3 minutes, then skin and remove nails before adding.

TO CLEAN POULTRY

Hold bird under cold water tap, and let water run all over and through inside, then dry with a cloth. To clean a goose, add a tablespoon of soda to a basin of warm water. Place bird on a board. Scrub inside and out with soda water. Rinse in fresh cold water and dry with a cloth.

TO STORE DRESSED POULTRY

To store dressed poultry, wash thoroughly inside and out with cold water. Dry with a cloth. Wrap in greaseproof paper. Store at once on lowest shelf of refrigerator or in coldest part of larder.

TO BONE POULTRY

When a boned bird is wanted for boiling or braising, you only partially bone it. When wanted for a galantine, all bones should be removed, and the boned legs and wings turned inside. Do not draw till after boning. There are three ways of boning :

1. (a) Remove wings at second joint.
   (b) Break drumstick halfway down.
   (c) Make an incision with a sharp knife through the skin down the length of the back.
   (d) Pull the skin and flesh off one leg and wing as you would pull a glove off your hand.
   (e) Bone second side in the same way.
   (f) Remove breast flesh from breast bone.
   (g) Turn skin and flesh from wings and legs inside.
   (h) With a palette knife, spread stuffing over flesh side, then roll up carefully. If you wish to re-shape bird after boning, do not turn the wing and leg flesh inwards, stuff the cavities, then sew up the back, and tie or skewer in shape.

2. After singeing bird, break feet and remove tendons. Cut neck, leaving about 3 inches of skin, then remove crop and windpipe. Cut through the joint of the wing nearest the body, then gradually work the flesh off the bones with the fingers and a pointed knife. Dislocate legs when you reach them, then work off flesh till you come to the tail, then cut the bone part away. This leaves the outer part complete with tail attached. Do not remove wing bones, but take out first bone from each leg. This is a good method for boning a bird required for boiling or braising. Truss as for roasting.

3. *To Bone a Boiling Fowl or Turkey:* Pluck, singe and behead bird. Remove gullet, crop, neck and windpipe, then the tendons of the legs. Cut off wings at second joint, distant from body and legs, at hock joints. Give a sharp twist to the leg and wing joints where they join the carcase so as to dislocate them.

   (a) Make an incision from neck to tail with the point of a sharp knife, keeping it close to the carcase as you cut.
   (b) With knife, work flesh gently away from ribs, breast bone and below breast bone.
   (c) Turn and bone other side in the same way, then remove carcase.
   (d) Cut away tail.
   (e) Spread bird flat out on table, skin downwards.
   (f) Sever ligaments attaching body and thighs. To do this, gently push leg inwards from the hock joint, then work flesh downwards from where it was dislocated towards hock. Sever joint.
   (g) Remove thigh bone, then work flesh off drumstick and turn leg inside out.
   (h) Bone second leg in the same way.
   (k) Bone wings, then turn skin of legs and wings inside.
   (l) Trim off any discoloured part or any gristle, etc. before stuffing and cooking.

To Joint : Cut off a leg and divide at the joint into drumstick and second joint. Remove the wing from the same side, cut off the tip and then divide the wing at the middle joint. Joint the other leg and wing in the same way. Neatly separate the wishbone, with the meat on it, from the breast. Cut breast in half lengthwise and the back through the middle crosswise, then hack the side bones apart with a meat chopper. Every large bird should give 12 joints. Use tips of the wings with giblets for stock or gravy.

To Fillet: Skin breast. With a small, sharp-pointed knife, cut through flesh beginning at end of collar bone, and keep close to the wishbone and breast bone as you cut off the meat. Now, with your fingers, raise the flesh from the bone and prise the meat away from the bones below. Lastly, cut meat away from wing joint. If filleting a large bird, such as a capon or a poularde, a goose or a turkey, separate fillet into two. The upper fillet is known as the " large fillet " and the lower as the " mignon." If you want to decorate fillet with a frill, leave an inch of wing bone attached to meat. Remove the skin of the large fillet and the tendons from the mignon. If difficult to skin the large fillet, place it on a board, skin downwards. Now cut through the flesh at top of fillet and continue to cut along its length, keeping knife as close to fillet as possible.

TO TRUSS POULTRY

It is necessary to truss poultry to make the birds keep their shape and to simplify carving. You need a needle for the purpose called a trussing needle, and fine string, but trussing can be done with the aid of a skewer and string. If bird is to be stuffed, stuff before trussing.

To Truss Chicken, Guinea Fowl and Turkey for Roasting: Place, breast downwards, on a board. Draw neck skin over back to close the opening. Fold wings backwards and inwards over flap. Turn bird, back downwards. Slip tail through slot in skin above vent to close opening. Push legs, backwards towards the wings, and press them well into the sides and down. This is to make the breast look plumper. With a trussing needle, threaded with fine string, pierce through the wing and leg at one side, through the body and the leg and wing on opposite side. Turn bird upside down (that is breast downwards), and run needle through wing tips and flap of skin. Remove needle and tie two ends of string loosely. Draw the ends together down to parson's nose and tie around it. Lastly, press the legs together, shanks upwards and tie string tightly round. A quick way of trussing is to tie a piece of string to the end of the neck skin with the middle of the string, leaving two long ends. Draw them down over the back. Turn wings backwards and leg to the front, pressing them close to the body. Draw string up on either side over the legs. Cross ends, then tie legs down, under and around the tail. Always untruss before dishing up.

To Truss Duck and Goose for Roasting: Follow first method given for chicken, guinea fowl and turkey, but do not fold the wings back. Remove ends of wings, then secure them with the legs to sides as described under trussing chicken, guinea fowl, and turkey. When trussing, leave ducklings' feet on, but remove the feet of duck and geese at the first joint. To fix ducklings' feet, dislocate them by a sharp twist at the joint above, then turn back and cross above the tail after drawing the latter through the vent. Gently press down the breast bone with a rolling pin.

To Truss Chicken and Turkey for Boiling: Follow method given under trussing for roasting in general except that the legs have to be trussed inside the body. If you truss them outside, you would not have a smooth surface for coating with sauce. Take dressed bird and cut the skin round the leg joints without severing the tendons. Twist shanks sharply and remove with the tendons and the feet. Now slip a finger into the opening at the vent, and, passing it between the flesh of the thighs and drumstick, and the skin, free the leg from the skin in order to push the leg into inside of bird, or " pocket " it, as this operation is called. Place right thumb against the hock joint and force leg upwards and backwards into the body. Pack in behind the leg the skin that covered the drumstick. Treat the other leg in the same way. Now draw the skin over to enclose the tail and close the opening. To finish trussing, draw the ends of string forward, as in trussing for roasting, twist tightly round the parson's nose twice, then over the whole hock joint. This prevents the legs slipping out of place and breaking through the skin. Tie ends tightly.

HINTS ON STUFFING POULTRY

Chickens, guinea fowls and turkeys are frequently stuffed only at the breast end, but many people prefer to stuff the body as well. In the latter case, choose a different stuffing for the body, especially when stuffing a turkey. Ducks and geese are generally stuffed at the tail end. To stuff a bird, place enough stuffing in the neck end to make bird look plump when cooked, but do not stuff too tightly or skin will burst during cooking. Do not use hot stuffing unless bird is to be cooked at once. Sprinkle inside of bird with salt before stuffing. Always fix the flap of skin at the back of the neck over the stuffing before proceeding to fill the body. If stuffing is too tightly packed in body, it may become soggy. If stuffing a guinea fowl, it is a good idea to slip a layer of stuffing about $\frac{1}{4}$ inch thick between the breast flesh and skin before filling the neck and fixing the flap.

Stuffing Suitable for Chicken and Turkey : Almond, chestnut, mushroom, oatmeal (boiled fowls or turkeys), oyster, rice, sausage and savoury.

Stuffings Suitable for Duck and Goose : Apple, apple and prune, chestnut, onion, orange, sage and onion, sausage, etc.

Stuffings Suitable for Guinea Fowl : Mushroom, orange, etc.

The general rule is to allow 1 cup stuffing for 1 lb. of bird to be stuffed.

CHICKEN AND FOWL

Chicken is the most digestible of all birds, so is particularly suitable for invalids and convalescents. White-skinned chickens and fowls are best for boiling, and those with black legs and yellow skins for roasting, but both can be boiled or roasted. The white meat, the breast and the wing, is more digestible and delicately flavoured than that of the legs. The " oysters," situated in a hollow on either side of the back bone are considered a " bonne-bouche."

To Choose a Chicken: Make up your mind what kind of chicken dish you want to have and choose a suitable bird. When selecting chickens for roasting, or fowls for boiling, you should avoid all birds that are long and bony with coarse skin, long hairs and scaly legs, as well as birds of all ages with blemished skin. Do not be led into buying a cock over a year old unless wanted for stock, but a hen of that age can be made into a succulent stew.

I must mention the poussins, or baby chickens which gourmets consider such a delicacy. Though tender and suitable for frying or grilling, they are tasteless, so are very often stuffed and cooked in a casserole or roasted.

TO HELP YOU CHOOSE

BIRD						AGE	WEIGHT
Poussin	-	-	-	-	-	6-8 weeks	$\frac{3}{4}$-lb.
Spring Chicken		-	-	-	-	8-13 weeks	1-2$\frac{1}{2}$ lb.
Frying Chicken		-	-	-	-	3$\frac{1}{2}$-5 months	2$\frac{1}{2}$-3$\frac{1}{2}$ lb.
Roasting Chicken		-	-	-	-	5-9 or 10 months	3$\frac{1}{2}$-5 lb.
Capon	-	-	-	-	-	6-10 months	6-10 lb.
Boiling Fowl	-	-	-	-	-	Over 9 or 10 months	4-6 lb.
Cock	-	-	-	-	-	Over 10 months	3-6 lb.

Chicken for Made-up Dishes: 4 lb. boiling fowl yields about 1 pint cooked diced meat (2$\frac{1}{2}$ cups).

BOILED FOWL (Poulet bouilli)

1 boiling fowl
Lemon juice as required
Salt to taste
4 peppercorns
1 bouquet garni
1 blade mace
1 clove
1 sliced carrot
1 sliced celery stick
1 sliced onion
Water as required

Prepare bird for boiling. Rub all over with cut lemon. Place in a saucepan. Add 1 teaspoon salt, peppercorns, bouquet garni, mace, clove, carrot, celery stick and onion, and a peeled clove of garlic, if liked. Pour in enough boiling water to come to below the breast. Cover. Simmer till tender. Time will depend on age of bird. A young bird takes only about an hour, but an old fowl might take up to 4 hours. Remove chicken to serving dish. Serve with egg or egg and parsley sauce, made with part milk and part chicken stock, and with boiled ham. *For 4-6 persons.*

TO USE UP BOILED FOWL

Accompaniments : Béchamel, cream, egg, parsley, Suprème or white sauce ; boiled rice, if not filled with oatmeal stuffing ; boiled new potatoes or mashed or riced potatoes ; buttered spinach, peas or French beans. Garnish with watercress.

1. Add to curry sauce. Serve in a border of boiled rice.
2. Make into a cottage pie with Béchamel sauce.
3. Flavour parsley sauce with chopped fried mushrooms to taste. Add diced fowl. Serve on rounds of fried bread or toast, or in patty cases.
4. Mix with shredded celery, allowing 1 tablespoon celery to each 3 tablespoons shredded fowl. Coat with mayonnaise. Serve as a salad or use as a sandwich filling.

TO BOIL AND ROAST AN OLD HEN (Poulet bouilli rôti)

1 old hen
½ teaspoon salt

Dress, clean and joint hen. Rub all over with salt, ground ginger and pepper. Stand overnight. Place

½ teaspoon ground ginger
Pepper to taste
Boiling water as required
5 tablespoons melted butter or margarine
1 teaspoon made mustard
1 teaspoon vinegar
Paprika to taste
¾ cup breadcrumbs

in a saucepan. Cover with boiling water. Simmer for 3 or 4 hours till tender. Drain. Place in a baking tin. Stir 2 tablespoons of the butter into the mustard and vinegar. Season with paprika and a pinch of salt. Rub all over with this mixture. If jointed, coat with mixture before placing in tin. Mix breadcrumbs with remainder of butter. Sprinkle over hen. Bake in a hot oven, 425° F., till crumbs are golden. *For 6 persons.*

TO BRAISE A FOWL

The orthodox way of braising a fowl is to stew it slowly in a casserole or pan tightly closed, on a bed of vegetables, herbs, etc., with a little liquid. Another method is to brown it first of all in a shallow saucepan in a little bacon fat, butter, dripping or hot oil, then transfer it to a bed of vegetables in a casserole. It should then be tightly closed and cooked in a slow oven. The third way, only suitable for cooking old fowls, is to steam it for about half the time, then cook it in a casserole on a bed of vegetables. See also " Entrées."

To Braise a Roaster (American Fashion): Prepare bird as for roasting. Stuff, truss, brush with melted butter, bacon fat or dripping, and dredge with seasoned flour. Place on a rack in a covered roaster. Cover. Cook without any liquid, in a moderate oven, 350° F., turning occasionally to secure even browning. A 4 lb. roaster will take about 2 hours, and a 5 lb. about 2½ hours.

To Braise a Boiler (Prairie Style): Place, breast up, on a rack in a saucepan with boiling water coming up to below the rack. Cover. Simmer gently for 1½ hours. Replenish with boiling water from time to time so as to keep it just below the rack all the time. Remove bird to a board. Stuff and truss it as for roasting. Coat with melted butter, bacon fat or dripping. Season to taste with salt and pepper. Place on a rack in a covered roaster. Add ½ pint of the chicken stock. Cover. Cook in a moderate oven, 350° F., for about 1½ hours or till tender, turning occasionally. If not brown enough when tender, uncover and brown.

BRAISED FOWL (Poulet braisé, Américaine)

1 boiling fowl
1 dessertspoon tarragon vinegar
2 peeled medium-sized onions
Salt and pepper to taste
6 slices pickled pork
1 cup sliced carrot
2 or 3 slices turnip
1 pint chicken stock or water
6 black peppercorns
1 blade mace
1 sprig parsley
½ cup sliced celery
1 tablespoon melted fat
½ pint cooked peas

Wipe bird with a damp cloth. Brush all over with tarragon vinegar. Stuff with one of the onions. Sprinkle inside with salt and pepper to taste. Truss as for boiling. Place half the pork in the bottom of a casserole. Slice remaining onion and place with the carrot and turnip on pork. Lay bird on top. Cover breast with remainder of pork. Pour stock or water in at the side, then sprinkle into it the peppercorns, mace, parsley and celery. Cover with a greased paper, then tightly with lid. Cook in a slow oven, 300° F., for 2½-3 hours, depending on age. When tender, remove to a rack in baking tin. Brush with melted fat. Increase oven heat to moderate, 350° F., and brown. Meanwhile add peas to braised vegetables. Cover. Cook for 5 minutes in oven. Dish up bird and spoon vegetables and gravy round. *For* 6 *persons.*

STEAMED FOWL (Poulet cuit à la Vapeur)

Prepare fowl as for boiling. Place on top of a low rack in a saucepan. Add enough hot water to come up to below rack. Add salt and pepper to taste, 2 slices onion, ½ carrot, 2 sprigs parsley, 3 or 4 celery leaves, ½ bay leaf, 3 black peppercorns, and ½ clove garlic. Cover closely. Simmer very slowly for 3½-4 hours according to weight, replenishing the water as it must always be just below rack. Leave in pan to cool if to be served cold, or to be used in any made-up dish. The breast should be downwards while it cools. When quite cold, place in a covered container in the coldest part of your refrigerator, or, failing that, in larder. Strain stock into a jar or basin and cover. Remove fat when chilled. Use it for frying or making pastry. A fowl, 4-4½ lb. in weight, yields about 4 cups of roughly chopped meat and skin.

TO STEW A CHICKEN OR FOWL : A chicken can be stewed whole when young, but when it becomes a fowl it is better to cut it up before stewing.

STEWED CHICKEN (Poulet étuvé)

2½ lb. chicken
½ tablespoon butter
Salt and pepper to taste
1 button onion
6 new potatoes
1 sprig thyme
½ bay leaf
2 oz. lean ham
2½ gills stock

Prepare and truss bird for boiling. Melt butter in a saucepan. Add bird. Fry slowly till brown all over. Add salt and pepper to taste. Peel onion and potatoes and add with thyme, bay leaf, diced ham and stock. Cover. Bring to boil. Boil rapidly for 5 minutes. Skim if necessary. Simmer very slowly till tender in about 1 hour. Turn on to a hot dish. Untruss. Serve with cream, mushroom or parsley sauce made with the stock. *For* 3 *persons.*

TO FRY CHICKEN

To fry chicken for 4 persons, choose 2 spring chickens or a bird about 3 lb. in weight. Prepare and split spring chickens or quarter the 3 lb. bird. Wash and dry. Put ½ cup flour into a paper bag. Add salt and pepper. Shake the portions of bird in bag. Melt 3 oz. bacon dripping, butter or margarine, or 1 oz. butter and 2 oz. lard or margarine, till moderately hot. (If you prefer, fry in deep fat). (Use a heavy frying-pan with fairly deep sides.) Add chicken to the fat or oil. Fry till brown, turning frequently. (If you like chicken with a tender crust, cover after browning and finish cooking, turning occasionally. If you prefer a crisp crust, cover after browning and fry very slowly for ¼-½ hour, then uncover and finish cooking.) The time for cooking depends on the size of the portions. There is a third way of cooking fried chicken. That is to transfer it to a casserole or covered roaster along with the fat after frying, then cook it in a moderately slow oven, 325° F., for $\frac{3}{4}$-1 hour, according to size, till brown.

FRENCH FRIED CHICKEN (Poulets frits, Français)

2 spring chickens
1 cup flour
1 egg
1 cup milk
1 tablespoon melted butter

Cut chickens in quarters. Dip each piece in batter made in the following way : sift flour into a basin. Beat egg slightly. Stir in half the milk. Beat thoroughly, then add remainder of milk. Melt butter. Add to batter. Stir rapidly till blended. Fry chicken in deep fat, 375-385° F., until brown. Place in a covered fireproof dish. Bake in a moderate oven, 350° F., for about $\frac{1}{2}$ hour. If preferred, use poussins, about 8 weeks old, but only halve them before dipping in batter. Garnish with watercress. Serve with Beurre Noisette or cream gravy. *For* 4 *persons.*

To serve Fried Chicken: If gravy is wanted, drain off fat until only 2 tablespoons are left. Stir in 2 tablespoons flour. When frothy, stir in $\frac{3}{4}$ pint chicken stock, or cream, according to taste. Stir till smooth and boiling. Season. If liked, tomato juice can be substituted for the stock, or 1 cup of stock can be diluted with $\frac{1}{2}$ cup of cream and used.

Accompaniments to Fried Chicken: Browned butter, maître d'hôtel butter or piquant or Tartare sauce ; potato crisps, chips or straws, or corn fritters.

GRILLED CHICKEN (Poulet grillé)

Spring chickens are excellent for grilling. You can grill either halved or jointed birds. They should not weigh more than $2\frac{1}{2}$ lb. One bird of this weight is enough for 2 persons.

Clean and halve or joint birds. To halve, split along the middle of the backbone, then either split again through the middle of the breast, or flatten out the whole bird with a rolling pin. This means that it can be grilled split and flattened, or divided into two halves. If liked, the rib bones and the breast bone can be taken out. To make bird lie quite flat if to be grilled, split and break the hip, knee and wing joints from the inside. By doing this, the bird will be more evenly grilled. Brush on both sides with melted butter or bacon fat. Season with salt and pepper. Place on a well-greased heated rack, skin side downwards. Cook till richly browned on both sides, turning frequently, and cooking mostly on the flesh side, as skin scorches quickly. Baste frequently with melted butter. They will take 20-35 minutes. When almost ready, mix 1 tablespoon butter witn 1 teaspoon minced parsley and $\frac{1}{2}$ teaspoon lemon juice and use this for basting. Dish up. Garnish with watercress and grilled tomatoes or mushrooms.

To Vary: (1) Joint, wash, then simmer, covered, in $\frac{1}{2}$ pint boiling water for $\frac{1}{4}$ hour. Remove and season. Brush with melted butter or bacon fat, and grill very slowly till tender. (2) If liked, birds can be grilled till golden brown, then transferred to a rack in a covered roaster. Cover with strips of bacon or smear with melted butter. Add enough chicken giblet stock to cover bottom of roaster. Bake in a very slow oven, 275 ° F., for about $\frac{1}{2}$ hour.

To Devil Grilled Chicken : Grill as described for 7 minutes. Cream 2 oz.

butter with 1 teaspoon made English or French mustard, 1 teaspoon lemon juice, ½ teaspoon salt and ½ teaspoon paprika. Smear this over the chicken, then sprinkle with ¾ cup sieved breadcrumbs. Melt enough butter to moisten crumbs and sprinkle over. Bake in a greased fireproof dish in a moderate oven, 350° F, till chicken is tender and crumbs are crisp and golden.

TO ROAST CHICKEN

BASIC: When you want a chicken for roasting, choose a bird from 5-9 months old, according to size required, weighing from 3½-5 lb. If a larger bird is needed and capons are available, choose one from 6-10 lb., according to your requirements. Prepare bird for cooking. Wash inside and out. Dry thoroughly. Season inside with salt and pepper, then stuff the neck opening to plump out. Whether you stuff the body or not is a matter of taste. You can use the same stuffing for neck and body or different ones as you please. After stuffing neck, draw the flap of skin over the back and sew to the back with string, or skewer and lace with string, then stuff body and sew up or skewer vent. If the vent opening has been made too large, cover the stuffing with a crust of bread to prevent any escaping, when you intend to skewer opening. Now truss bird for roasting. Weigh bird. Brush body all over with melted butter, bacon fat or olive oil. Place, breast downwards, on a rack in a roasting oven. Roast in a moderate oven, 350° F., until tender, allowing ½ hour per lb. for birds up to 4 lb., and 23-25 minutes per lb. for birds over 4 lb. Melt 2 oz. butter or bacon fat, or heat oil. Baste with this 10 minutes after starting to cook, and every 20 minutes until ready. When finished, use drippings in tin. Turn breast upwards at half time, lifting bird with a towel in your hands. To test whether a bird is ready or not, insert a skewer into the thigh. If there is any trace of blood when the juice runs out, continue to cook and test again. If there is no trace, the bird is ready to dish up. Remove to a hot dish. Take out any skewers and string used in trussing. Slip back into oven whilst you make the gravy so as to keep the bird hot. Garnish with parsley or watercress. A 3½ lb. bird is enough for 4 persons; a 4-5 lb. for 6 persons.

To Roast a Half Chicken: Stuff hollow in body and cover with a greased paper. Turn chicken carefully upside down into a well-greased roasting tin. Smear with melted butter or bacon fat. Roast in a moderate oven, 350° F, for about ¾ hour. Turn bird upside down. Wet the top of the paper with a damp cloth and carefully peel off paper, helping with a knife if necessary. Turn upside down on to a hot dish.

To Pot-Roast an Older Chicken: Place in a moderately slow oven, 325° F., and roast until lightly browned. When half cooked, pour ¼ cup boiling chicken stock into a covered fireproof dish, put chicken in dish. Cover. Bake until tender. If a crisp crust is wanted, uncover for last ½ hour. If wanted glazed, spread 4 tablespoons red currant jelly thickly over bird 10 minutes before serving. Roast for 5 minutes. Baste again with jelly. Finish roasting.

Accompaniments for Roast Chicken: Brown or cream gravy and bread sauce. Garnish to match accompaniments. Fried chipolatas or crisp baked or grilled curls of bacon.

STEWED STUFFED FOWL (Poulet farci étuvé)

1 boiling fowl
6 small carrots
3 medium-sized onions
Salt and pepper to taste
Pinch crushed herbs
¾ lb. minced steak
½ pint stale breadcrumbs
1 minced shallot
2 egg whites

Prepare fowl and rub all over with a cut lemon. Place in a shallow saucepan. Peel and slice onions. Scrape, wash and cut carrots into 2-inch pieces. Add onions and carrots to pan. Season to taste with salt and pepper. Add herbs. Cover. Stew gently from 2-3 hours, according to age and size, in enough chicken giblet stock to cover the thighs.

Mix meat with the crumbs, shallot and egg whites, till thoroughly blended. With floured hands, shape into 8 balls. Twenty minutes before bird is ready to serve, drop balls one by one into the boiling stock. Cover. Simmer gently till ready. Serve with Hollandaise sauce. *For 8 persons.*

FOWL BAKED IN MILK (Poulet au Lait)

Joint an old hen. Place in a buttered baking dish. Smear each joint with creamed butter. Dredge with flour, then pour a quart of milk over. Cover tightly. Bake in a moderate oven, 350° F., until tender, the time depending on age. Uncover and brown a little before serving. Serve either from dish or on a hot flat dish with gravy in a hot sauceboat. *For 4 or 5 persons.*

CHICKEN DUMPLINGS (Pommes de Volaille)

½ lb. flour
4 teaspoons baking powder
1 teaspoon salt
½-¾ teaspoon curry powder
2 tablespoons butter or margarine
1½ cups diced boiled chicken
Milk as required

Place flour in a basin. Stir in baking powder, salt and curry powder. Sift into another basin. Rub in fat. Add chicken. Stir in ¾ cup milk, and more if necessary to make a thick, dropable batter. Drop from a dessertspoon into a shallow saucepan containing enough boiling chicken stock to cover dumplings. Cover closely. Cook for 12 minutes without uncovering pan. Serve coated with parsley or mushroom sauce. *For 6 persons.*

CHICKEN WITH MUSHROOMS (Poulet en Cocotte)

2 tablespoons chopped onion
2 tablespoons diced carrot
1 oz. butter
1 bay leaf
1 sprig thyme
1 pint chicken stock
1 roasting chicken
1 tablespoon Marsala
1 lb. mushrooms

Place onion, carrot and butter in a casserole. Add bay leaf and thyme. Cook slowly for 10 minutes, stirring frequently, then add stock and trussed chicken. Cover closely. Cook in a slow oven, 300° F., for 1 hour. Add wine. Peel and slice mushrooms and add. Cover. Continue to cook for ½-¾ hour, till chicken is tender. Serve untrussed on a hot dish with vegetables and mushrooms round. Pour gravy over. *For 4 or 5 persons.*

CHICKEN WITH RICE (Poulet au Riz)

1 boiling fowl
1 bouquet garni
Salt to taste
3 peeled onions
1 slice fat bacon or salt pork
1 clove
1 blade mace
6 peppercorns
2 cups rice

Place fowl in a large saucepan. Cover with boiling water. Add bouquet garni and salt to taste. Slice and add onions with bacon or pork, clove, mace and pepper corns. Bring to boil. Cover. Simmer gently till half cooked, then sprinkle rice into stock. Lay bird on top. Simmer very slowly till rice is tender, removing fowl and stirring occasionally to prevent burning. If preferred, the bird can be browned in butter before boiling and a chopped clove of garlic can be added to the onion. *For 6 persons.*

HAMBURG CHICKEN (Poulet à la Hamburg)

1 spring chicken
2 oz. butter
1 oz. minced parsley
Salt and pepper to taste

Prepare chicken as for roasting. Beat butter till softened, then beat in parsley. Season with salt and pepper. Slip parsley butter into chicken, then truss. Rub bird all over with additional softened butter, or use margarine. Season with salt and pepper. Place on a rack in a roasting tin. Roast in a hot oven, 500° F., for 10 minutes. Baste with melted butter in tin. Cover. Lower heat to moderate, 350° F. Roast till tender in 30-45 minutes. Dish up. Garnish with watercress. Strain butter from tin into a small saucepan. Stir till thick with a little thick cream, but do not allow to boil. Pour into a hot sauceboat. *For 3 persons.*

SPATCHCOCK OF POUSSIN (Poussin grillé)

1 petit poussin
Salt and pepper to taste
Squeeze of lemon juice
1½ tablespoons melted butter

Split prepared poussin in two through middle of backbone. Flatten, then wipe with a damp cloth. Fix flat with skewers. Remove wing tips and feet. Season with salt and pepper. Sprinkle with lemon juice. Brush with the butter. Grill for about 15 minutes, turning frequently, and brushing with melted butter each time you turn it. Remove skewers. Dish up. Garnish with watercress and crisply fried bacon. Serve with fried chips and Hollandaise or Tartare sauce. *For 1 person.*

DUCK

There are many kinds of edible ducks, but the most popular for cooking is the famous large white Aylesbury duck. Rouen ducks, not so often available, are richer than Aylesbury ducks. Ducks are available all the year round, but are at their best in summer. Ducklings are usually obtainable from February until August, and ducks from August to February. If a duck is wanted for roasting, choose one from 6-9 or 10 months old. After 12 months, ducks are too tough for roasting and should be braised.

To Choose : Fresh prime ducklings and ducks should have fine pink flesh, pliable feet, firm thick breasts, firm full vents, and their livers should be pale in colour. Young birds are free from hair, and their bills snap easily. If doubtful about the age of a bird, feel the windpipe, and examine the neck. If the windpipe is hard and the neck long and lanky, the bird is old. The windpipe of a young duck should yield when pressed gently with the thumb.

BRAISED DUCKS (Canards braisés)

1 pair young ducks
3 rashers bacon
1 scraped carrot
1 peeled onion
2 cloves
Sprig of thyme
Sprig of parsley
Salt and pepper
Paprika to taste
Broth or stock

Prepare ducks as for roasting. Place them in a stewpan with the bacon and carrot. Prick onion with the cloves and add with thyme, and parsley to pan. Season with salt, pepper and paprika. Cover with broth or stock. Simmer ducks till tender, basting frequently after some of the liquid has evaporated, then remove from pan. Place where birds will keep hot. Strain and thicken gravy. Dish up ducks. Garnish with slices of carrot. Pour gravy over. (Joint birds if preferred before cooking and cook in a casserole.) *For 6 persons.*

ROAST DUCK (Canard rôti)

BASIC : Clean, singe, draw and wash inside of bird. Wipe outside with a damp cloth. Season inside and out with salt, pepper and ground ginger. Rub with a cut clove of garlic if liked. If you choose a very young bird, do not stuff it ; just tuck an onion or 2 sliced apples inside and remove before serving. Weigh. Truss and place on its side on a rack in a roasting tin. (If duck is very fat, prick all over with a fork.) Roast in a moderately slow oven, 325° F., allowing 25 minutes per lb. Baste every 10 minutes with the dripping or strained orange juice. When brown on one side, turn and brown on other. Roast until the meat on the breast and legs is tender. Dredge with flour. Baste well. Dish up. Drain off all the dripping except 1½ tablespoons. Add 1½ tablespoons flour. Stir till frothy, then stir in 1 cup hot, white stock or water. Season. Stir constantly till boiling. Serve in a hot sauce-boat. Garnish bird with fried thick apple slices, or with apples, stuffed with pork sausagemeat and baked. Serve with apple sauce if apple stuffing is not used, in which case, serve with Bigarade, olive, orange or cranberry sauce.

ROAST STEAMED DUCK

Prepare and truss bird for roasting. Steam for ½ hour, then place on a rack in a roasting tin. Season with salt and pepper. Smear bird with butter, then cover with buttered paper. Place 2 tablespoons butter in roasting tin. Roast in a moderately slow oven, 325° F., basting every 10 minutes with the drippings in tin, till tender, in 1-1½ hours, depending on size. When almost ready, peel and cut 2 seedless oranges into ¼ inch thick slices, and 2 slices of pineapple into cubes. Melt 2 tablespoons of butter in a frying-pan. Add fruit. Cook slowly for 4 minutes, turning after 2. Carve duck. Arrange portions on a hot dish, overlapping each other. Arrange orange slices round. Top slices with pineapple cubes. Garnish with watercress. *For 4 or 5 persons.*

DUCK A L'ORANGE (Canard à l'Orange)

Melt ¼ lb. butter in a heavy saucepan. Season a young duck and add. Fry slowly, turning frequently, till brown all over. Add ¼ pint chicken or duck giblet stock, the juice of an orange, and 2 or 3 snippets of orange rind. Cover pan. Cook slowly till tender, in about ½ hour.

DUCK AUX CHOUX (Canard aux Choux)

Melt ¼ lb. bacon fat in a heavy saucepan. Add a young trussed duck. Fry, turning frequently, till well browned. Add ¼ pint chicken or duck giblet stock. Chop and rinse a cabbage, throw into plenty of boiling salted water. Boil rapidly for 2 minutes, then remove duck. Place cabbage in bottom of pan with duck on top. Season with salt and pepper to taste. Cover. Cook slowly for 30-35 minutes.

Duck aux Petits Pois (Canard aux Petits Pois) : Follow recipe for Duck aux Choux, but substitute ¾ or 1 pint green peas for cabbage.

Duck au Vin (Canard au Vin) : Follow recipe for Duck aux Choux, but substitute any dry white wine for the stock, allowing ½ pint wine, for ¼ pint stock. Cook slowly, turning frequently without covering pan, for 30-40 minutes. Dish up. Garnish with crisply fried bacon and watercress.

DUCKLING A LA BIGARADE (Caneton à la Bigarade)

2 oz. fat bacon
1 small peeled onion
1 stick celery
1 scraped carrot
1 duckling
Salt and pepper to taste
2 oz. butter
¼ pint white stock
¼ pint white wine
1 teaspoon lemon juice
Juice of 1 orange
½ teaspoon shredded lemon rind
½ teaspoon shredded orange rind

Cut bacon into small squares, and place in a casserole. Chop onion and celery. Dice carrot. Place prepared vegetables in casserole. Lay duckling on top. Season with salt and pepper. Smear with the butter. Cover closely. Cook for 20 minutes on top of stove. Uncover. Bake in a moderate oven, 350° F., till brown, turning frequently. Dish up. Strain off fat. Add stock and wine to braise. Bring to boil. Boil for 10 minutes. Strain in lemon and orange juice. Meanwhile, cook the lemon and orange rind in boiling water for 6 minutes, then strain off water. Strain sauce into pan containing rind. Dish up duck. Pour sauce over. *For 4 or 5 persons.*

DUCKLING AUX POMMES (Caneton aux pommes)

Joint a duckling, and fry in 3 oz. butter in a shallow saucepan. Peel and core 2 lb. of apples. Cut each in 8 wedges. Remove duckling to a plate. Place apples in pan. Season with salt, pepper and a dash of ground cinnamon. Stir till blended with the butter. Lay joints on top. Cover closely. Stew gently for about 40 minutes, or till tender.

GOOSE (Oie)

Some gourmets consider goose to be the King of Poultry, others associate it only with Michaelmas, when it becomes prime. Most British housewives, however, ignore it completely except to consider it as an alternative to turkey at Christmas time. Up to 6 months old, both the male and female are known as " green geese " or goslings. Geese are in their prime, in Britain, from September to February.

TO CHOOSE :

For roasting: Green geese or goslings, and geese up to 10 months old.
For boiling, braising or stewing: Geese from 10-12 months old.
A young goose should have a pliable yellow bill and soft, fat pliable feet. As a goose grows older, the bill becomes darker. The webbing of the feet should be easily torn, and the under side of the bill easily broken when bent. The skin should be smooth and white and the breasts plump with a straight breast bone. Young birds have an abundance of pin feathers. Avoid birds with stiff quills.

To Cook: Green geese or goslings can be split and grilled. Do not use sage and onion stuffing when goslings are to be roasted, and do not apply any fat to geese of any age when roasting.

TO ROAST A GOOSE (Oie rôtie)

Choose a young bird, 8-12 lb. in weight. Singe off any down and remove any pin feathers. Cut off tips of wings, both feet, and the neck at body, unless you wish to stuff the neck, when leave enough skin to form a flap to fix to back. Wash thoroughly with hot water, scrubbing the outside if necessary, then carefully draw bird, taking care not to break the gall bladder. Wash again inside and out and dry the outside. Rub inside with salt and outside with salt and pepper, and with ½ teaspoon ground ginger if liked. Fill body loosely with stuffing and neck cavity if wanted. Sew up vent, or cover the stuffing with a crust of bread and skewer vent. If stuffing neck, fold the skin back and sew to back, or fix with a skewer. Truss. If bird is fat, prick skin well with a sharp fork or skewer. Weigh. Place on a rack in an open roasting tin, one side downwards. Bake in a slow oven, 325° F., allowing 18-20 minutes per lb. If bird is heavier, add a cup of hot chicken stock or water to pan after roasting for ½ hour. Turn on opposite side every half hour. It is not necessary to baste it. Untruss and dish up. *For 10 persons.*

HINTS ON ROASTING

1. If you want goose to have a Continental flavour, rub outside with a cut clove of garlic before stuffing.
2. If you wish breast to be richly browned, dredge breast with flour when nearly ready, and baste well with the hot dripping.

3. If you like to introduce the flavour of bacon to a goose, bard breast with 6 thin strips of fat salt pork or bacon, but remove $\frac{1}{2}$ hour before dishing up to allow breast to get as brown and crisp as the rest of the bird. Dredge with flour before basting for the last time.

4. If using a covered roaster, no basting is required.

Stuffings suitable for Goose : Apple, apple and prune, chestnut, liver, mushroom, onion, orange, sage and onion, sausage and savoury, etc.

Garnishes: Baked apples or fried apple rings, if apple stuffing is not used ; parsley or sprigs of watercress, etc.

Accompaniments: Brown gravy, apple sauce (unless apple stuffing or garnish is used) or cranberry jelly or sauce, roast potatoes, Brussel sprouts, green peas, stewed red cabbage, or savoy.

DEVILLED GOOSE (Oie à la Diable)

1 roasting goose
Stuffing to taste
4 tablespoons pure malt vinegar
2 dessertspoons made mustard
½ teaspoon black pepper
1 dessertspoon salt

Prepare, stuff and truss goose for roasting. Place in a large saucepan. Cover with boiling water. Simmer gently for 1 hour. Drain well. Wipe dry. Stuff body and neck. Sew up and truss. Place on a rack in a baking tin. Roast in a slow oven, 325° F., allowing 20 minutes per lb., and basting occasionally with the vinegar mixed with remaining ingredients. Serve with goose giblet gravy. *For 7 or 8 persons.*

GUINEA FOWL (Pintade)

Guinea fowls are in season from January to June when game is scarce. The flesh is digestible and very similar to pheasant in flavour. They can be cooked by any recipe given for pheasant or chicken, but are better pot-roasted than roasted as the flesh is rather dry. The chicks are delicious split and grilled like chicken. All guinea fowls can be braised, pot-roasted, roasted or stewed in a casserole, but only young ones can be grilled. If you breed guinea fowls, remember that these birds should hang well like a pheasant before cooking. Guinea chicks for frying or grilling should weigh from $\frac{3}{4}$-$2\frac{1}{4}$ lb., guinea fowls from $2\frac{1}{2}$-3 lb.

ROAST GUINEA FOWL (Pintade rôtie)

Thin rasher of bacon
1 guinea fowl

Tie some thin slices of fat bacon over breast of guinea fowl. Place it in a self-basting roaster, for the flesh of guinea fowl is dry. Roast in a moderate oven, 350° F., 50 minutes to $1\frac{1}{4}$ hours, according to size. When ready, untruss. Place on a hot dish. Garnish with picked and well-washed watercress. Serve with fried crumbs, bread sauce and potato crisps. *For 4 persons.*

Stuffings suitable for Guinea Fowl: Mushroom, olive, orange, etc.

Garnish: Sprigs of watercress.

Accompaniments: Brown or sour cream gravy, bread sauce ; chips, crisps or straws ; orange or orange mint salad.

TURKEY (Dinde or Dindon)

For some time past, the black-plumed Norfolk turkey has been the most popular in this country. Now this excellent bird has to compete with the white turkey, bred in order to give us a turkey which, when dressed, supplies the maximum of breast meat. The latter is usually more compact, and has a less prominent breast bone than other varieties. Seasonable, September-March, and prime in December and January.

TO CHOOSE

Examine the breast, flesh, legs and neck. The breast should be plump, rounded and broad, the flesh snow-white, the legs smooth and black with plump spurs, with supple moist feet, and the neck short. The hen is more tender than the cock. Avoid all birds with sharp spurs, or with rough hairy legs. If a turkey is wanted for frying or grilling choose a turkey poult (Diudonneau). If wanted for roasting, a poult can be chosen for a small family and a hen turkey (dinde) from 9-12 lb. for a medium-sized one. When a turkey is wanted for a large party, choose a cock (dindon) from 15-18 lb. Do not allow the feet to be cut off until the tendons have been drawn.

BOILED TURKEY (Dindonneau bouilli)

1 turkey (9-10 lbs.)
Sausagemeat as required
2 medium-sized onions
3 cloves
2 medium-sized carrots
3 sticks celery
8 black peppercorns
1 sprig parsley
1 sprig thyme
1 bay leaf
1 teaspoon salt

Wipe inside and outside of bird with a cloth. Truss for boiling. Stuff skin at neck with sausagemeat, then turn flap of skin over back and sew up or skewer. Place in a large saucepan. Cover with turkey giblet stock or water. Bring to boil. Skim if necessary. Peel onions and insert cloves. Scrape, wash and slice carrots. Slice celery sticks. Add vegetables to pan with peppercorns, parsley, thyme, bay leaf and salt. Bring again to boil. Skim again if necessary. Cover. Simmer gently from 2-2½ hours. Dish up. Remove skewers or stitches and string. Coat with celery or mushroom sauce. Garnish with forcemeat balls. Serve with hot boiled ham or tongue if liked. *For 10-12 persons.*

BRAISED TURKEY (Dindonneau braisé)

1 turkey (8 or 9 lb.)
Stuffing as required
8 oz. fat bacon
½ cup sliced carrot
½ cup sliced celery
¼ cup sliced turnip
¼ cup sliced parsnip
2 sliced medium-sized onions

Wipe bird inside and out with a damp cloth. Sprinkle inside with salt and pepper to taste. Stuff body and skin at neck with the same stuffing, or use different ones. Truss. Cover breast and legs with half the fat bacon or use salt pork, then cover turkey with a piece of muslin dipped in oil. Tie on with string. Mix the vegetables

Salt and pepper to taste
1 quart turkey giblet stock
   or water

and place in the bottom of a covered roaster. Place remainder of fat bacon or salt pork over the vegetables, and lay turkey on top, breast upwards. Season with salt and pepper to taste. Cover roaster tightly. Roast in a moderate oven, 350° F., allowing 25 minutes per lb., but add stock or water at the end of the first ½ hour. Thirty minutes before bird is ready to dish up, uncover and remove muslin and bacon or pork to allow bird to brown lightly. Strain liquor into a saucepan. Thicken to taste with flour or chestnut flour. Season and serve in a hot sauce-boat. Garnish with watercress. *For 10 persons.*

Stuffings Suitable for Braised Turkey: Mushroom, oyster, sausage, sausage and chestnut, etc.

TO ROAST A TURKEY (Dinde au four)

There are several methods of roasting turkeys. One is to place in a hot oven, 450° F., for 10 minutes, then lower to moderate, 350° F. I prefer roasting a turkey at a slow temperature throughout the cooking period, for it shrinks less in this way and is not apt to scorch. You can roast at an even temperature, no matter the weight of bird, if you like. In that case, roast at 300° F., allowing 25 minutes per lb. for birds under 12 lb., and 20 minutes for larger birds, or you can roast according to the following table :—

TIME-TABLE FOR ROASTING TURKEYS
(Weight of Stuffed Bird)

Weight		Temperature	Time
Turkey Poult,	5-7 lb. - - -	325° F.	25 minutes per lb.
Young Turkeys,	7-10 lb. - -	300° F.	23 minutes per lb.
Turkeys,	10-13 lb. - -	300° F.	3½-4½ hours
	14-17 lb. - -	275° F.	5-6 hours
	18-23 lb. - -	250-275° F.	6½-7½ hours
	24-30 lb. - -	250° F.	8-9 hours

BASTING TIME TABLE

Unless instructions are given to the contrary in recipes, baste according to the following table ; turning from side to side when basting :

5-12 lb. - - - - - -	every ½ hour
12-20 lb. - - - - - -	every ¾ hour

TO ROAST TURKEY (Dinde rôtie)

Dress, clean, stuff, truss and weigh bird. Roast in one of the following ways :

1. Rub bird all over with 2-3 oz. of butter according to size of bird, mixed to a paste with flour. Place on back on a rack in a roasting tin. Tie strips of fat bacon over breast and legs, then cover with thickly buttered greaseproof

paper. Roast in a hot oven, 450° F., for ¼ hour, then lower to moderately hot, 375° F. Pour 1 cup chicken or turkey giblet stock into tin. Add a lump of sugar. Roast, basting frequently, till tender, allowing 20 minutes per lb. (a 10 lb. bird takes from 2-2½ hours ; a 12 lb. bird 2½-3 hours). About 15 minutes before dishing up, remove paper and bacon. Baste well and leave in oven till breast is browned.

To Vary: Smear bird thickly over with bacon dripping and roast on its side in a moderately slow oven, 325° F., allowing 25 minutes per lb. for birds under 10 lb., and 18-20 minutes for larger birds, according to weight. Turn from side to side every ½ hour.

2. Rub bird all over with salt and pepper. Mix 2½-3 oz. bacon fat or margarine, or half and half with ¼ cup flour. Rub this all over the breast, legs and wings. Dredge bottom of roasting tin with flour. Place bird on side on rack. Roast in a moderate oven, 350° F., till tender, allowing 20 minutes per lb. up to 10 lb. in weight, and 18-20 minutes over 10 lb. Baste every ¼ hour with 3 oz. fat melted in ½ cup boiling water. When this is finished, baste with dripping in tin. If cooking in a covered roaster, do not baste, but add before starting to cook ½ cup giblet stock or water to prevent flour browning too much and spoiling flavour of gravy. Turn frequently while cooking so that it browns evenly. If cooked in an open tin and it browns too fast, cover with greased greaseproof paper.

To Roast Half a Turkey (Demi-dinde rôtie) : You can roast a half turkey stuffed or unstuffed. Prepare half as you would a whole bird. Tie the tail piece and leg end together. Draw wings back against the breast. Stuff neck skin, then draw flap on to back and skewer. Stuff hollow in body. Cover with a sheet of greased paper, and tie down at both ends. Brush bird with melted butter. Cover with butter muslin or cheesecloth dipped in melted fat. If roasting unstuffed, prepare for oven in the same way. Bake in a slow oven, 300° F., split side downwards on a rack. Allow half the time used for cooking a whole bird. Baste every ½ hour with melted fat. Remove cloth ½ hour before dishing up to allow top to brown evenly.

Stuffings for Roast Turkey : Almond and celery ; celery ; chestnut ; chestnut and oyster ; cranberry ; liver ; mushroom ; sausage, and savoury.

Garnishes for Roast Turkey: Baked or grilled sausages or baked bacon rolls ; watercress.

Accompaniments for Roast Turkey: Bread sauce ; brown or chestnut gravy ; cranberry jelly or sauce.

TO COOK SMOKED TURKEYS

Smoked turkey can be boiled, sliced and fried or roasted when young. If boiled or roasted, it should be cut in thin slices and served hot or cold. It makes an appetising hors d'oeuvre, or first course, when cold, but if roasted, can be served as a main course.

To Boil: Cook like a fresh turkey, but add 3 or 4 sticks of celery and a sliced onion to the stock or water in which it is cooked. Simmer very slowly for 4 hours, if about 10 lb. in weight, and let bird cool in stock. If bird is older or larger it will take longer.

To Fry: Remove the breast meat of a raw young smoked turkey, cutting it into slices about ½ inch thick across the grain. Dip lightly in seasoned flour. Fry slowly in butter. Serve with green peas and new potatoes.

To Roast: Rinse thoroughly inside, then hold under the cold water tap and rinse all over. Soak in cold water to cover for 12 hours, then wipe dry inside and out. Stuff if liked, but omit salt. Truss bird, with legs and wings close to body. Place on one side in a shallow roasting tin. Bake in a very slow oven, 250° F., turning bird every ½ or ¾ hour, but do not baste with dripping. Use vinegar instead, sweetened to taste with brown sugar and flavoured with a pinch of ground cloves or dry mustard. Baste with this every ½-¾ hour when turning. Young turkey, about 10 lb., will take about 4½ hours. Serve with mushroom sauce.

STUFFED TURKEY LEGS (Pattes de dindonne aux étuvées)

2 young turkey legs
2 oz. boiled ham
6 lightly fried mushrooms
¼ teaspoon grated lemon rind
¼ teaspoon crushed herbs
2 tablespoons breadcrumbs
Salt and pepper to taste
1 beaten egg
1 pint turkey stock

Bone and trim legs. Cut enough bacon into thin strips for larding legs. Chop ham and mushrooms. Mix with lemon peel, herbs, crumbs and salt and pepper to taste. Mix to a paste with the beaten egg. Stuff cavities in legs. Flatten the stuffings at the ends with a wet knife. Pat legs back into original shape. Place in a shallow saucepan. Add stock. Cover. Simmer gently for about ½ hour. To serve, place a bed of braised or stewed celery on a flat hot dish and arrange legs on top. Serve coated with about 1½ gills Velouté sauce. *For 4 persons.*

STUFFED GOOSE'S NECK (Cou d'Oie farci)

1 neck of a goose
2 oz. raw goose
Herb stuffing as required
1 medium-sized onion

Skin, wash and dry neck. Make stock of neck for gravy. Wash and dry skin. Tie up the narrow end. Put goose through a meat grinder. Add enough herb stuffing to give you the necessary amount to fill skin loosely. Sew up opening securely with coarse thread. Place in a shallow saucepan. Add ¾ cup stock or water. Peel and slice onion. Add to water. Bake in a slow oven, 325° F., basting occasionally with liquid, until crisp and brown. Serve with brown gravy. *For 3 persons.*

CHICKEN LIVER WITH SPAGHETTI
(Foie de Volaille, Italienne)

¼ lb. spaghetti
2 chicken livers
2 tablespoons butter or bacon
    dripping
2 medium-sized tomatoes
Grated cheese to taste
Salt and pepper to taste

If the spaghetti is not of the cut variety, break it up. Throw into boiling salted water to cover. Boil from 15-20 minutes till tender, then drain in a strainer and hold it for a moment under the cold water tap to separate pieces. Meanwhile, rinse, dry, lightly flour and fry livers slowly in the bacon fat or butter. Scald and peel tomatoes. Chop and fry till soft. Press with livers through a sieve. Place purée in a saucepan.

Add grated cheese and salt and pepper to taste. When spaghetti is ready, toss in this mixture. *For 2 persons.*

Turkey Liver (Foie de Dindon, Italienne) : Follow above recipe, but use only 1 liver.

FRIED GOOSE LIVER (Foie Gras frits)

1 goose liver
Hot goose fat as required
Salt and pepper to taste
4 fried mushrooms
2 fingers of lemon

Carefully remove gall bladder. Soak liver in cold water for 3-4 hours. Drain thoroughly. Sprinkle place where gall was attached with sugar. Place in a saucepan. Add enough hot goose fat to come half-way up liver. Fry slowly till brown, then turn and brown on other side. Drain. Season with salt and pepper to taste. Arrange on a hot dish lined with a lace paper doily. Garnish with mushrooms and fingers of lemon. Serve with potato straws or chips. *For 2 persons.*

LIVER AND KIDNEY DEVIL (Kebabs à la Diable)

4 chicken or duck livers
4 rashers streaky bacon
2 sheep's kidneys
2 oz. butter
Salt and pepper to taste

Wash and halve livers. Remove rind from bacon. Skin and split kidneys in two, then core and cut again in two. Cut bacon into as many pieces as there are kidneys, and the same size. Melt butter in a saucepan. Dip each piece of bacon, kidney and liver in butter, then in sieved seasoned breadcrumbs. Spike slices of liver and kidney alternately on a skewer with a piece of bacon between each. Grill slowly till cooked to taste, turning occasionally to secure even cooking. Sprinkle lightly with cayenne pepper. Divide equally between 4 persons, serving if liked on hot buttered toast or fried bread. Garnish with fried mushrooms. Serve with French mustard and green peas, devil sauce, and potato straws if liked. *For 4 persons.*

LEFT OVER POULTRY

CHICKEN LOAF (Pain de Volaille)

2 cups chopped cooked chicken
1 medium-sized onion
1½ tablespoons butter
1 cup stale breadcrumbs
½ cup hot milk
½ cup green pea purée
Salt, pepper and paprika to taste
2 eggs

Measure chicken free from skin and gristle. Peel, slice and chop onion. Melt butter in a small saucepan. Add onion. Fry slowly till clear. Place crumbs in a basin. Add milk. Stir in pea purée, salt, pepper and paprika, onion and butter in pan. Beat eggs. Stir into mixture. Pack into a buttered fireproof dish. Bake in a moderate oven, 350° F., with lid on top for first half hour. Uncover, bake till brown in 15-20 minutes. Serve hot or cold. *For 4 persons.*

CREAMED CHICKEN (Poulet à la Crème)

1 pint diced cooked chicken
1 pint white sauce
Salt and pepper to taste

Stir chicken into the sauce. Add salt and pepper to taste, and paprika or celery salt. Heat in the top of a double boiler till piping hot. *For 6*

1 saltspoon paprika or celery salt

persons. *To Vary:* Add 3 or 4 tablespoons cooked green peas or fried sliced mushrooms, or 1 dessert-spoon minced parsley.

FRENCH CREAMED CHICKEN (Poulet, Parisienne)

1 pint medium white sauce
1/4 pint cream
1 pint diced cooked chicken
6 oz. sliced mushrooms
2 tablespoons butter
Salt and pepper to taste
Pinch of ground mace
2 tablespoons Madeira or sherry

Use white sauce made with 1 part hot chicken stock to 3 parts hot milk. Gradually stir in cream. Stand pan in another pan containing hot water. Stir in chicken. Fry mushrooms slowly in the butter, and add with the butter, salt and pepper to taste and mace. When required, add Madeira or sherry.

CREAMED CHICKEN WITH ITALIAN PASTES
(Poulet à la Crème, Italienne)

Cream 1 pint diced cooked chicken with white sauce made with ½ pint milk and ½ pint stock. Add 2 tablespoons cooked green peas, or sliced fried mushrooms. Serve either in a ring of boiled or fried noodles, or boiled spaghetti or macaroni.

CREAMED CHICKEN WITH VEGETABLES
(Poulet à la Crème, Chez Moi)

Cream 1 pint diced cooked chicken with white sauce, made with ½ pint milk, ¼ pint cream and ¼ pint chicken stock. Stir in 1 beaten egg, chicken, and either 1 pint cooked asparagus tips, or ½ pint tips and 1½ gills mixed diced cooked vegetables. Serve on canapés or turn into a greased fireproof dish. Cover with stale breadcrumbs. Fleck with butter. Bake in a moderate oven, 350° F., until golden brown.

TO SERVE ANY CREAMED CHICKEN : Serve in hot patty cases, on rounds or squares of hot toast or fried bread, in nests of mashed potato, or use as a filling for pancakes, then cover with cheese sauce and brown under grill.

SHORTCAKE OF CHICKEN (Gâteau de Poulet)

3/4 lb. flour
6 teaspoons baking powder
1 teaspoon salt
2 oz. butter
Milk and water as required
4 cups diced cooked chicken
1¾ cups Velouté sauce
2 heaped tablespoons chopped pimiento
2 tablespoons cooked green peas

Sift dry ingredients into a basin. Rub in butter. Moisten with equal quantity of milk and water, usually about a cup. The dough should be soft enough to handle. Divide into 2 equal portions. Shape into flat, equal-sized rounds with hands, or roll lightly into shape. Press one portion into an oiled sandwich tin. Brush lightly over with melted butter. Place second round on top. Bake in a moderately hot oven, 425° F., for about ½ hour. When ready, gently separate the two layers. If not quite dry in centre, return to oven, placing top one upside down on another tin, till both are dry. Place chicken and sauce in the top of a double saucepan. Stir frequently over boiling water till boiling. Add pimiento and peas. Place between shortcake layers, reserving a little to place in the centre of top layer. Garnish with minced parsley or paprika. Serve cut in wedges. *For 6-8 persons.*

SCALLOPS OF CHICKEN (Coquilles de Volaille)

1 cup mashed potato
½ oz. butter
Hot milk as required
Salt and pepper to taste
½ cup left-over gravy
1 heaped teaspoon minced parsley
Pinch ground mace
1½ cups white sauce
2 cups diced cooked chicken or turkey
2 tablespoons grated cheese

Mash potato with butter and milk. Season to taste. Beat till fluffy. Stir gravy, parsley and mace into the sauce, then the chicken or turkey. Season again, if necessary. Divide equally between 6 greased scallop shells. Pipe mashed potato round inside edge. Sprinkle with grated cheese. Place shells on a baking sheet. Bake in a hot oven, 450° F., for about 10 minutes. *For 6 persons.*

CASSOULET OF GOOSE (Cassoulet)

1¾ pints haricot beans
1 lb. bacon fat
1 pint white wine
Cold water as required
Salt and pepper to taste
1 bay leaf
1 sprig thyme
1 clove of garlic
2 lb. shoulder of mutton
¼ lb. fat bacon
¼ lb. sliced onion
10 pieces goose confit
2 tablespoons goose fat
1 sliced smoked sausage

Soak beans overnight in cold water to cover. Line the bottom of a heavy saucepan with the bacon fat or fresh pork fat. Drain beans well and add with the wine, and enough cold water to cover the beans by about an inch. Season with salt and pepper to taste. Add bay leaf, thyme and garlic. Cut mutton into suitable pieces for serving. Fry bacon slowly, till all the fat is extracted, then strain fat into a heavy shallow saucepan. Add mutton. Fry slowly, turning frequently till brown. Transfer to pan containing the beans. Add onion to fat and fry slowly till clear, stirring frequently.

Sprinkle over the mutton any fat remaining as well as essence of mutton. Cover closely. Cook very slowly until mutton is tender, and the beans soft. Now add the goose, with its fat. Place in a hot pot jar. Cover closely. Cook in a fairly hot oven, 425° F., until the skin forms on top. Stir cassoulet carefully. Continue to cook and skim every 5 minutes, for ½ hour, then add sausage. Cover and reheat in oven till sausage is heated through. Serve from hot pot, sprinkled with minced parsley. In France, where this dish is very popular with the peasants, a Toulouse sausage is used in this recipe. *For 10 persons.*

SECOND THOUGHTS (Petits Pains de Volaille)

2 tablespoons powdered gelatine
½ cup cold water
1½ cups chicken or turkey stock

Soak gelatine in cold water for 5 minutes. Bring stock to boil. Add to gelatine. Stir till dissolved. Cool slightly. Stir in salt and pepper to taste, onion, celery and chicken or turkey. Pour into

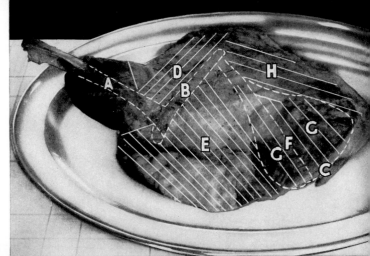

Shoulder of Lamb marked for carving.
See pages 237-239.

Turn shoulder upside down and carve the slices off the under section of the blade with the knife slanted. See pages 237-239.

When all the meat has been carved off the shoulder, remove the gland from the fat on the outer side of shoulder before serving the fat with the lean. See pages 237-239.

Garnish Boiled Frankfurters with fried potato straws and fried tomato slices, topped with parsley.

Arrange a border of boiled shell macaroni, and boiled Frankfurters round Fried Sausagemeat Cakes, topped with grilled mushrooms.

Garnish drained boiled noodles, tossed in parsley sauce, with sliced boiled Frankfurters or Vienna sausages. *See pages* 50 502.

Salt and pepper to taste
1 teaspoon minced onion
¼ cup minced celery
1 cup diced cooked chicken or turkey

6 wet individual moulds. When set and chilled, unmould each on to a bed of lettuce. Garnish with crescents of cold boiled beetroot. Serve with mayonnaise. *For 6 persons.*

DEVILLED TURKEY LEGS (Pattes de Dinde à la Diable)

2 cooked turkey legs
1 saltspoon white pepper
Pinch of cayenne pepper
1 saltspoon salt
1 mustardspoon made mustard
½ clove garlic
Strained juice of ½ lemon
1 oz. butter

Score meat of legs ½ inch apart with a sharp knife, making the scores ¾ inch deep. Mix pepper, cayenne pepper, salt and mustard. Peel and mince garlic. Add to seasoning with the lemon juice. Rub this paste into the gashes, and all over the legs. Grill slowly for 15-20 minutes, turning frequently until nicely browned all over. Arrange on a hot dish. Melt the butter. Brush legs over and pour remainder of butter round. Garnish with sprigs of parsley or watercress. *For 2 or 4 persons according to size of legs.*

COLD POULTRY

In this section, cold poultry dishes are grouped together, except salads, which can be found in the salad section. Guinea fowl and turkey can also be treated by any recipe given for chickens, and vice versa, and any recipes for duck or goose are also interchangeable.

CHAUDFROID OF CHICKEN (Chaudfroid de Poulet)

1 plump roasting chicken
2 sliced carrots
1 sliced onion
1 sliced leek
1 calf's foot
Salt and pepper to taste
1 blade mace
White stock as required
Water as required
2 tablespoons butter
3 tablespoons flour
½ gill boiling milk
1 beaten egg yolk
1 dessertspoon gelatine
1 canned pimiento
½ oz. blanched pistachio nuts

Truss, singe and clean chicken. Place in a saucepan. Add carrot, onion, leek and foot. Season with salt and pepper. Add mace. Cover with equal quantity of stock and water. Cover closely. Bring to boil. Skim. Simmer for 1 hour, or till tender, then remove bird. Boil stock quickly to jellying stage. Cool and strain. When cold, carefully remove any fat. Melt butter in a saucepan. Stir in flour. When it starts to brown, stir in milk gradually and ½ pint of the stock. Stir till boiling. Boil for a few minutes, then cool slightly. Add beaten egg yolk, stirring constantly, and cook for 2 or 3 minutes, still stirring, but do not allow to boil. Remove from stove. Soak gelatine in 2 tablespoons of cold water. When sauce is cool, stir in dissolved gelatine. Stir till blended. Place chicken on a rack with a dish below, and coat with the sauce. When set, garnish with ornaments, cut from pimiento and with chopped blanched pistachio nuts. Put a frill on each leg. Serve with lettuce salad. *For 6 persons.*

CHAUDFROID OF DUCK (Chaudfroid de Canard)

2 cold roasted ducklings
½ pint brown sauce
½ gill chicken or veal stock
½ gill aspic jelly
½ gill sherry or Curaçao
Juice of 1 orange or 2 tangerines
Grated rind of 1 orange or 2 tangerines
2 truffles
2 hard-boiled egg whites

Cut ducklings into neat joints. Skin and trim neatly. Heat sauce in a shallow saucepan. Stir in stock and jelly. Cook till reduced to ½ pint, then stir in sherry or Curaçao and orange or tangerine juice. Par-boil rind, then shred finely and add to sauce. Pour into a basin. When almost cold, place ducklings' joints on a rack over a dish and coat with the sauce. When set, decorate each portion with slices of truffle, and diamonds or crescents of egg whites. Brush lightly with additional aspic jelly about to set. Arrange like a pyramid. Garnish with chopped set aspic jelly and watercress. *For 6 persons.*

CHAUDFROID OF GUINEA FOWL (Chaudfroid de Pintade)

1 boiled guinea fowl
2 oz. butter
2 oz. flour
1½ gills strained chicken stock
1½ gills milk
Salt and pepper to taste
¾ level teaspoon powdered gelatine
1½ gills liquid aspic
Ornaments of pimiento

Carefully skin bird. Melt butter in a saucepan. Stir in flour. Cook till frothy. Add stock to milk. Stir into butter and flour. Cook over slow heat, stirring constantly, until smooth and boiling, then turn into a basin. Season. Dissolve gelatine in liquid aspic. Stir into sauce. Stir over ice until beginning to set, then coat bird all over with sauce. Decorate with ornaments of pimiento and minced chives or parsley. Cover with liquid aspic. Garnish round base with aspic set with a few green peas. (If liked, substitute tomato juice for half the stock.) *For 4 persons.*

CHICKEN ASPIC (Aspic de Volaille)

Rind of 1 lemon
1 sliced medium-sized carrot
1 sliced small turnip
Shells and whites of 2 eggs
1½ pints chicken stock
1 sliced onion
1 sliced celery stick
1½ oz. powdered gelatine
¼ gill tarragon vinegar
¼ gill chilli vinegar
½ gill lemon juice
6 white peppercorns
Salt to taste

Grate lemon rind. Place in a saucepan with carrot and turnip. Wash and crush egg shells and add with remaining ingredients. Whisk slowly over stove till mixture comes to boiling point. Allow contents to rise to the top, then withdraw from stove at once. Cool slightly, then pour into a scalded jelly bag, and allow to strain into a basin below. Allow to set if wanted for decorating cold dishes. If wanted for setting fish or meat, it can be used while liquid for lining the bowl, and when beginning to set, can be poured over fish or meat.

CHICKEN, HAM AND TONGUE LOAF (Pain, Smithsfield)

½ lb. cold chicken
2 tomatoes
2 oz. butter
2 oz. flour
½ pint stock

Mince chicken. Peel and mince tomatoes. Melt butter in a small saucepan. Add flour. Stir till frothy, then stir in stock by degrees. Stir till smooth and boiling, then till mixture shrinks from

2 eggs
2 oz. minced ox tongue
2 oz. minced boiled ham
Salt and pepper to taste
Celery salt to taste
1 grated onion

side of pan. Remove from stove. Beat eggs. Add to slightly cooked mixture, then beat till smooth. Stir in remaining ingredients. Pack into a deep buttered loaf tin or mould. Cover with buttered paper. Bake in a slow oven, 300° F., for about $1\frac{1}{2}$ hours. Cool. Turn on to a flat dish. Garnish with watercress and devilled eggs. *For 6 or 7 persons.*

CHICKEN RING MOULD (Coronet de Volaille)

1 lb. boiled fowl
$\frac{1}{2}$ oz. powdered gelatine
$\frac{3}{4}$ pint chicken stock
A few canned peas
1 teaspoon minced parsley
$\frac{1}{4}$ lb. boiled ham
Salt and pepper to taste

Weigh chicken free from skin and bones. Dissolve gelatine in the stock. When cool, strain, then pour a thin layer into a wet ring mould. When almost cold and set, place a ring of boiled or canned peas round mould. Mix stock with the parsley. Dice chicken and ham and add to stock. Season to taste with salt and pepper. When beginning to set, stir well and pour into ring mould. Turn out when cold and jellied. Pile green peas, coated with mayonnaise, in centre. Garnish base with devilled eggs or slices of hard-boiled eggs, each arranged on a lettuce leaf, on top of a round of beetroot. *For 6 persons.*

CREAMS OF CHICKEN (Crèmes de Volaille)

$\frac{1}{2}$ oz. butter
2 oz. flour
$\frac{1}{4}$ pint milk
$\frac{1}{2}$ lb. cold boiled chicken
2 tablespoons cream
Juice of $\frac{1}{2}$ lemon
Salt and pepper to taste
$\frac{3}{4}$ oz. powdered gelatine
$\frac{3}{4}$ pint hot chicken stock

Melt butter in a saucepan. Add flour. When frothy, stir in milk. Stir till boiling. Boil for 3 minutes, stirring constantly. Mince chicken finely. Stir into white sauce, then stir in cream. Strain in lemon juice. Add salt and pepper to taste and stir till blended. Dissolve gelatine in stock and allow to cool. When beginning to set, line 6 individual moulds with a little of the jellied stock. Strain remainder of jellying stock into chicken mixture. Stir till blended. When cool, divide between the moulds. Leave till set and chilled. Turn each out on to a bed of mustard and cress or lettuce leaves. Garnish with rings of boiled beetroot and chopped aspic. *For 6 persons.*

GALANTINE OF CHICKEN (Galantine de Volaille)

1 boiling fowl
1 lb. sausagemeat
Salt and pepper to taste
$\frac{3}{4}$ lb. ox tongue
2 hard-boiled eggs
Stock and meat glaze

Prepare fowl for boiling, but remove wings at second joints. Cut down middle of back and remove flesh from the bones by filleting. Lay out flat on a pastry board. Spread with sausage meat. Season with salt and pepper. Cut tongue into strips and arrange over the meat. Place eggs, point to point, down the centre. Roll up and sew skin. Tie very tightly in a pudding cloth. Cook in chicken or chicken giblet stock to cover for 3-4 hours, depending on size and age. Remove from stock. Leave in cloth till cold. Remove cloth. Brush galantine with glaze. Decorate to taste with a design

323

piped in creamed savoury butter, and with chopped pistachio nuts if liked. *For 6 or 8 persons.*

MOUSSES OF CHICKEN (Mousses de Volaille)

1 tablespoon powdered gelatine
¼ cup cold chicken stock
¾ cup hot chicken stock
½ teaspoon grated onion
Salt and paprika to taste
1 cup cream
1½ cups cooked chopped chicken
Lettuce and mayonnaise

Soften gelatine for 5 minutes in the cold stock. Dissolve in the hot stock. Add onion, salt and paprika. Cool until beginning to thicken. Beat cream till stiff. Fold in the gelatine mixture, then the chicken. Dip 6 individual moulds in cold water. Pour the mixture into them. Chill. When required, unmould each on to a plate lined with crisp lettuce leaves. Garnish with sieved egg yolk. Serve with mayonnaise. *For 6 persons.*

Entrées

This French term is sometimes applied to all made-up savoury dishes, sometimes only to savoury dishes served with a sauce. They may be hot or cold, light or substantial. In a formal menu, the entrée is always served between the fish and the " remove." If a substantial entrée is wanted to take the place of the " remove," which is the main dish in the menu, a light entrée can precede it. All entrées should be artistically garnished. Dish them so that they are easy to serve. This is important when the entrée is passed round the table. Guests should find it easy to help themselves. The substantial entrée can be served as a main course at a party if the remainder of the menu is suitably planned round it.

NOTE: See "From Head to Tail," Cold Meat, Game, Poultry, Salads, Savoury Pastry, etc., for further recipes for entrées.

Light Entrées: Bouchées, boudins, cannelons, cassolettes, coquilles or scalloped dishes, crêpinettes, croquettes, croûstades, fritters, quenelles, soufflés, or vol-au-vents made of cooked or raw game, meat or poultry, etc.

Substantial Entrées: Cutlets, fillets, chartreuse of hare, chaudfroid of chicken or pigeon, galantines of poultry and game, jugged hare, noisettes, tournedos, and certain elaborate game or poultry pies, etc.

Fish can also be served as an entrée during Lent if desired. See Fish Section. If a hot and a cold entrée are wanted, see that the hot one is lighter than the cold and served first. *The first entrée should always be simpler than the second.*

BOUDINS OF PHEASANT (Boudins de Faisan)

1 hen pheasant
¼ lb. panada
2 oz. butter
2 beaten eggs
Salt and pepper to taste
1 tablespoon rich brown sauce
2 truffles
2 oz. tongue
¼ lb. mushrooms
¾ pint creamed artichoke bottoms

Remove skin from pheasant. Carefully cut off a the meat, and put it through a meat grinder. Plac in a mortar. Add panada and butter. Pound wit a pestle until into a smooth paste, then graduall pound in the eggs and salt and pepper to taste Rub through a wire sieve into a basin. Add sauce made from the carcase of the pheasant. Stir ti blended. Cut truffles and tongue into dice. Fr mushrooms gently and dice. Moisten all thre with a little additional salt, and season with sa and pepper. Shape some quenelles in tablespoons from the pheasant forcemea and place a little of the truffle mixture in the centre of each. Poach in boilin water for ¼ hour. Drain thoroughly. When cold, egg and crumb and fry i deep hot fat. Arrange up against a ring of mashed potato. Pour artichoke into the centre, and some brown sauce round the edge. *For 5 persons.*

BRAISED GOSLING (Oison braisé)

1 gosling
Salt and pepper to taste
2 medium-sized onions
1 medium-sized carrot
¼ lb. butter
1 clove
1 bouquet garni
1 pint white stock
Vegetables for garnish
½ cup sherry
1½ oz. flour

Wash and dry goose. Cut up into meat joint: Season lightly with salt and pepper to taste. Pre pare and slice onions and carrot. Melt half th butter in a shallow saucepan. Add joints, vege tables, clove, ½ bay leaf and 1 sliced clove of garli if liked. Fry till brown, turning frequently, the add bouquet garni and stock. Cover closel Simmer very gently for ¾ hour. Meanwhil prepare the vegetable garnish. Boil ½ pint pea Peel 12 button onions or shallots. Prepare 1 doze olive-shaped balls from carrots and turnips. Parboil separately in boilin water till almost tender. Drain well. Place onions or shallots and carrot an turnip balls in a shallow saucepan. Add enough melted glaze to coat then Cover and cook gently until tender, shaking frequently. Dish up goose. Kee hot. Strain stock into a small saucepan. Stir in sherry. Mix flour to a past with remainder of butter and add. Stir till smooth and boiling. Cover. Simme gently for 8 minutes. Season to taste. Skim off fat. Pour over goose. Arrang glazed vegetables and cooked peas alternately round goose. *For 6 persons.*

BRAISED PIGEONS (Pigeons à la Bourgeoise)

2 plump pigeons
½ pint brown sauce
5 tablespoons claret
Carrot and turnip as required
6 button onions
1½ oz. meat glaze
1 tablespoon butter
6 mushrooms
Salt and pepper to taste

Braise trussed pigeons as in above recipe for abou 40 minutes, then halve. Heat sauce. Add clare then pigeons. Cover and simmer for 10 minute Cut the carrot and turnip into neat shapes. Tos in butter to coat for 2 or 3 minutes. Cover wit stock and stew gently till tender. Parboil onion Strain off water. Add meat glaze. Stir gentl until glazed and occasionally until tender. Me butter. Add mushrooms. Fry slowly. Season to taste. Dish up pigeons. Coat with sauce and pour remainder round. Garnish with vegetables and mushrooms arranged alternately with groups of green peas in between. *For 4 persons.*

BRAISED WILD DUCK (Canard Sauvage braisé)

1 wild duck
Salt and pepper to taste
Chopped bacon as required
½ oz. butter
1 cup sliced onion
1 cup diced carrot
Pinch crushed herbs
½ pint brown sauce
¼ pint rich stock
½ gill red wine
Juice ½ lemon

Wipe and truss duck. Season with salt and pepper. Line a casserole with bacon. Place bird in casserole. Add butter, onion, carrot and herbs. Roast in a hot oven, 450° F., till brown all over, then lower heat to moderate, 350° F. Drain off any fat. Add sauce and stock. Cover and cook for 20 minutes, then add wine and lemon juice. Remove bird and joint. Bring sauce to a quick boil. Arrange joints on a hot dish. Spoon sauce and vegetables over. Usually only the breast of the bird is served. Make remainder into stock or a salami. *For 2 persons.*

CASSEROLE OF CHICKEN (Casserole de Poulet)

1 roasting chicken
3 oz. butter
Salt and pepper to taste
½ oz. flour
½ pint chicken stock
Juice ½ lemon
Minced parsley to taste

Wipe and joint chicken neatly. Melt 2 oz. of the butter in a frying-pan. When hot, add the joints. Season with salt and pepper. Fry till light brown all over. Transfer to a casserole. Mix flour into a cream with a little of the stock, then stir in remainder of stock. Pour over chicken. Cover closely. Bake in a slow oven, 325° F., for about ¾ hour. When tender, arrange joints on a hot dish. Stir remainder of butter into sauce with the juice of the half lemon. Return chicken to casserole. Cover and heat for 2 or 3 minutes in oven. Dish up. Sprinkle with parsley. Garnish with triangles of toast. *For 4 or 5 persons.*

CASSEROLE OF DUCK (Casserole de Canard)

1 duck
Seasoned flour as required
½ pint chopped mushrooms
¾ pint white stock
½ teaspoon onion juice
1 teaspoon minced mint
Salt and pepper to taste
½ pint green peas

Clean, singe and joint duck. Dip joints in seasoned flour. Fry till brown in a little hot butter, and pack into a casserole. Add mushrooms, then cover with stock. Add onion juice and mint. Season. Cover and bake in a slow oven, 300° F., for 1 hour, then add peas. Cover and cook till tender, about 1 hour longer. Re-season if necessary. *For 4 persons.*

CASSEROLE OF GROUSE (Casserole de Coq de Bruyère)

1 brace old grouse
1 oz. flour

Joint birds. Wipe joints with a damp cloth. Dip them in the flour. Melt butter in a large

2½ oz. butter or margarine
1 pint beef stock
Salt and pepper to taste
¼ lb. mushrooms
1 medium-sized carrot
1 medium-sized onion
2 tomatoes
Fleurons of pastry

frying-pan. Add joints. Fry slowly till lightly browned, turning frequently. Transfer to a casserole. Add remainder of flour to fat left in pan. Stir over low heat till brown. Remove pan from heat. Add stock, made with beef cubes if necessary, and salt and pepper. Wash mushrooms in salted water. Peel and steam. Add to casserole with peeled carrot and onion, left whole. Scald, peel and chop tomatoes and add. Strain in gravy. Cover casserole. Place in a slow oven, 300° F., and cook till tender, in 1-1½ hours, depending on age of birds. Remove carrot and onion. Dish up. Garnish with fleurons of pastry. *For 6 persons.*

CASSEROLE OF GUINEA FOWL (Casserole de Pintade)

1 guinea fowl
¼ lb. bacon
12 button onions
6 oz. mushrooms
Salt and pepper to taste
½ pint white stock
12 small new potatoes

Wipe bird with a damp cloth, inside and out. Rub with seasoned flour. Remove rind from bacon. Chop bacon and place in the bottom of a casserole. Arrange bird on top. Peel onions and mushrooms and arrange alternately round bird. Season with salt and pepper. Add stock. Cover. Cook in a slow oven, 300° F., for ¾-1 hour. Peel and add potatoes. Cover and continue cooking till potatoes are tender. If liked, the bird can be jointed and browned in the fat before cooking, when it will take about 40 minutes unless old. *For 4 or 5 persons.*

To Vary: Stuff with ½ lb. seasoned pork sausagemeat.

CASSEROLE OF PIGEONS (Casserole de Pigeons)

2 plump young pigeons
1 tablespoon chopped onion
2 oz. butter
½ cabbage
6 thin rashers bacon
¼ pint brown sauce
¼ pint white stock
½ gill white wine
Salt and pepper to taste

Wipe and joint pigeons. Place onion and butter in a casserole with a metal base. Melt butter. Add joints of pigeons. Fry slowly till brown all over and onion is clear. Strain off butter. Divide cabbage into leaves. Wash thoroughly, then drain off water. Remove rind from bacon. Fry bacon lightly, then roll each piece in one of the cabbage leaves. Place side by side in casserole. Lift joints on top. Add sauce, stock and white wine. Season with salt and pepper. Cover closely. Cook slowly for fully half an hour. If liked, cook in oven, at 300° F. for the same amount of time. Remove fat from surface. Serve from casserole. *For 2 or 3 persons.*

CASSEROLE OF QUAIL (Casserole de Cailles)

6 quails
2 oz. butter
Flour as required
1½ gills white stock
½ gill port wine
Rind of ½ orange

Wipe and truss quail without drawing. Melt butter in a saucepan. Dip quails in flour. Fry till brown all over, turning frequently. Place in a casserole. Strain butter over from pan. Cover. Cook in a slow oven, 300° F., for ½ hour. Dish

2 tablespoons red currant jelly
Juice of ½ lemon
Salt and pepper to taste

up. Cover and keep hot. Drain off fat. Pour stock and wine into casserole. Add orange rind. Turn into a saucepan. Simmer slowly for 10 minutes. Stir in jelly, then add quails and lemon juice. Season with salt and pepper. Bring to boiling point. Dish up quails again. Strain sauce over. *For 6 persons.*

CASSOLETTES OF FISH (Cassolettes de Poisson)

Croûtes of bread
2 oz. anchovy or bloater paste
3 soft roes of bloaters
6 quartered oysters
1 oz. butter
2 drops lemon juice
Cayenne pepper to taste
1 scrambled egg

Cut 6 croûtes of bread, 3 inches long and 1 inch wide, then carefully scoop out the centres with a sharp knife so as to leave 6 cases of bread. Fry in butter or bacon dripping till golden brown. Mix the paste with the soft roes and oysters. Melt the butter in a small frying-pan. Add the oyster mixture and fry slowly for 2 or 3 minutes until the roes are cooked. Add the lemon juice and cayenne pepper to taste. Divide filling equally between the cassolettes. Cover the filling with scrambled egg, allowing about a teaspoon per case. *For 6 persons.*

CASSOLETTES OF GAME (Cassolettes de Gibier)

8 oz. shortcrust or rough puff pastry
8 oz. cooked game
¼ lb. cooked ham
4 mushrooms
1 oz. butter
1 chopped peeled shallot
¼ pint brown sauce
Salt and pepper to taste
Mashed potatoes as required

Roll pastry out thinly. Line 6 small plain timbale moulds. Prick well with a fork. Bake in a hot oven, 450° F., for about 15 minutes. Put game and ham through a meat grinder into a basin. Chop mushrooms and add. Melt butter in a small saucepan. Add shallots. Fry slowly till soft, then stir in game, mushrooms and sauce. Season. Cook for 3 or 4 minutes, stirring constantly, then pack into pastry cases. Spread mashed potatoes over the top. Ornament with a fork. Bake in moderate oven, 350° F., for 10 minutes, till potatoes are golden. Garnish with parsley. *For 6 persons.*

CHARTREUSE OF HARE (Chartreuse de Lièvre)

1 hare
3 oz. butter
2 oz. flour
¼ pint stock
3 eggs
Salt and pepper to taste
1 pint brown sauce
4 mushrooms
Cayenne pepper to taste
1 peeled onion
1 peeled carrot
1 bay leaf
1 sprig thyme

Remove the meat from the bones of hare. Reserve 1 fillet. Weigh out 1 lb. of hare. Put through a meat grinder, then into a mortar. Pound thoroughly. Melt 2 oz. butter in a shallow saucepan. Stir in flour. When frothy, stir in stock. Boil till thick, stirring constantly until mixture shrinks from the sides of the pan. Leave till cool. Add to hare in mortar. Pound to a smooth paste. Add eggs one by one, beating between each addition. Season with salt and pepper. Rub through a wire sieve. Stir 2 table-

329

Squeeze of lemon juice
1 teaspoon red currant jelly
¼ pint Port wine

spoons of the brown sauce into purée. Brush charlotte mould with melted butter. Pack the forcemeat all over the bottom and round the sides leaving just enough to cover filling. Melt enough butter in a small frying-pan to cover bottom. Add reserved fillet of hare. Fry slowly until tender. Cut into dice. Peel, chop and fry mushrooms. Add to diced hare. Season with salt and cayenne pepper to taste. Bind mixture with brown sauce. Pack this into the centre of the lined mould. Cover the top with remainder of forcemeat Cover with a piece of buttered paper. Steam for 1 hour. Meanwhile, break up the bones of hare. Melt the remaining 1 oz. of butter in a saucepan. Add the bones. Slice in onion and carrot. Add bay leaf and thyme. Fry slowly for 5 minutes, then add remainder of brown sauce, squeeze of lemon juice, jelly salt and cayenne pepper to taste, and Port wine. Bring to boil. Boil for 7 or 8 minutes. Remove chartreuse from saucepan. Stand for a minute or two then turn out on to a hot dish. Strain sauce over. *For 6 persons.*

CHICKEN A LA KING (Poulet, Royale)

1 pint diced cooked chicken
3 tablespoons chicken fat or butter
½ cup shredded green pepper if liked
¼ lb. sliced mushrooms
3½ tablespoons flour
1 cup hot chicken stock
¾ cup scalded milk
¾ cup scalded cream
4 tablespoons sliced pimiento
Salt and pepper to taste
2 egg yolks
4-6 tablespoons sherry
1 tablespoon minced parsley

Measure chicken free from gristle and skin. Melt fat in a saucepan. Add green pepper and mushrooms. Simmer about 5 minutes, till soft. Add flour. Stir till blended. Slowly stir in hot stock and milk. Stir over low heat till smooth and thick and boiling. Draw pan to side of stove. Stir in cream, pimiento, salt and pepper and then chicken Beat egg yolks slightly. Stir in a little of the hot sauce. Stir slowly into remainder of sauce, then stir in sherry. Serve on a hot flat dish. Garnish with minced parsley, hot triangles of puff pastry and little groups of heated asparagus tips or green peas when wanted for a party. Serve if preferred in hot patty cases. *For 6-8 persons.*

CHICKEN BEAULIEU (Poulets, Beaulieu)

2 roasting chickens
Salt and pepper to taste
3 tablespoons melted butter
1 rasher bacon
¼ cup shredded carrots
1 tablespoon minced onion or shallot
1¼ cups brown stock
2-3 cups potato balls
3 tablespoons Madeira or sherry

Remove joints and breasts from chickens. Season with salt and pepper, then brush with melted butter. Place in a casserole. Bake in a hot oven, 425° F., for 12-15 minutes, turning once. Meanwhile, remove rind from bacon and cut bacon into strips. Place carrot in a saucepan of boiling water to cover. Boil for 5 minutes, then drain. Place bacon strips, onion and carrot in frying-pan. Fry slowly, stirring frequently for 5 minutes. Add stock and potato balls. Bring to boil. Pour vegetables and stock round joints. Add wine. Season. Cover. Bake in a moderate oven, 350° F., for about ½ hour, till tender. Serve from casserole. *For 6 persons.*

CHICKEN BONNE FEMME (Poulet, Bonne Femme)

1 plump roasting chicken
3 tablespoons melted butter
3 oz. sliced carrot
3 oz. onion rings
Salt and pepper to taste
½ lb. button mushrooms
1 tablespoon flour
1 pint chicken stock
5 oz. sliced tomatoes
½ tablespoon minced parsley

Joint chicken neatly. Rinse in tepid water, then dry. Melt butter in a shallow saucepan. Add carrot and onion rings. Fry gently for 10 minutes, stirring frequently, then add joints and salt and pepper. Simmer for another 10 minutes, stirring occasionally. Add mushrooms, flour, stock and tomatoes. Stir until boiling. Simmer for ½-¾ hour, or till tender, then add parsley. Dish up. Garnish with triangles of flaky or puff pastry. *For 6 persons.*

CHICKEN MARYLAND (Poulet, Maryland)

There are several versions of Chicken Maryland, depending in what part of the United States it is served. The chickens usually treated in this way weigh from 2½-3½ lb.

Californian Chicken Maryland : Joint a 3½ lb. chicken. Wash and dry joints. Dip in flour seasoned with salt, pepper and paprika to taste. Melt 2 tablespoons butter in a deep frying-pan. When smoking hot, add joints. Cover closely to prevent steam escaping. Fry slowly for ¾ hour, basting and turning several times during that period. Remove joints to a hot dish. Stir 2 tablespoons flour into butter in pan. When frothy, stir in about a pint of milk. When smooth and boiling, season to taste. Boil for a minute or two, stirring constantly, then pour over the chicken. If liked, less milk can be used and cream added to taste, but do not allow to come to the boil after adding cream. Serve with banana or corn fritters. *For 4 persons.*

New York Chicken Maryland : Joint 2 birds about 2½ lb. each. Wash and dry. Dip joints in seasoned flour, then in egg, beaten with water till blended, allowing 2 tablespoons to 1 egg. Roll in coarse dry breadcrumbs. Place joints in a lavishly greased baking tin or fireproof dish. Bake, uncovered, in a moderately hot oven, 375° F., till tender, in 45-50 minutes, turning occasionally and basting when turning with the following :— Melt 2½ oz. butter with 2 tablespoons water or chicken stock and 1 teaspoon lemon juice. Dish up. Garnish with watercress. Serve with cream gravy. *For 6 or 7 persons.*

Washington Chicken Maryland : Joint a chicken about 4 months old. Wash and dry joints. Dip in seasoned flour, then " egg and crumb." Place joints in a lavishly greased baking tin. Bake for 5 minutes in a hot oven, 450° F., then baste thoroughly with ⅔ cup of melted butter. Lower heat to moderately hot, 375° F., Bake for 20-30 minutes, basting every 5 minutes with butter in tin. Dish up. Garnish with slices of orange, and sprigs of water-cress. Place a coffee spoonful of red currant jelly on the centre of each orange slice. Serve chicken with cream mushroom sauce. *For 4 persons.*

331

CHICKEN MARENGO (Poulet, Marengo)

1 roasting chicken
Salt and cayenne pepper
2 tablespoons flour
1 oz. butter
2 tablespoons olive oil
1½ pints rich white stock
½ gill Madeira or sherry
2 tablespoons tomato purée
1 peeled medium-sized onion
2 cloves
1 bruised clove of garlic
1 sprig parsley
1 sprig thyme
Juice of 1 lemon
12 fried mushrooms

Skin and divide bird into 6 or 8 joints, according to size of bird. Season with salt and cayenne pepper, then dip joints in flour. Melt butter in a saucepan. Add olive oil. (If preferred, omit butter and use ¼ pint olive oil.) When hot, add joints, and fry, turning frequently, till golden brown all over, in about 10 minutes. Drain fat into another pan and add stock, wine and purée. Peel onion and stick with cloves. Add to stock mixture with garlic, parsley and thyme. Bring to boil. Pour over chicken. Cover. Simmer gently for ¾ hour. Dish up. Skim sauce. Remove onion and herbs. Boil up quickly for 2 or 3 minutes, then add lemon juice and season if necessary. Pour over joints. Garnish with mushrooms and fried croûtons of bread, or baked triangles of puff pastry. The dish may be garnished with fried egg as well as the garnishes given. *For 6-8 persons.*

CREAMS OF GAME (Crèmes de Gibier)

6 oz. cold game
3 oz. stale breadcrumbs
¼ pint milk
1 oz. butter
2 beaten eggs
¼ pint whipped cream
Salt and pepper to taste

Put game through a meat grinder. Add crumbs. Bring milk to boil. Stir into game, and add butter, then stir in eggs. Lightly fold in cream and salt and pepper. Three-quarter fill buttered dariole moulds. Cover each with buttered paper. Tie down securely. Steam for 10-15 minutes till risen and set. Remove from pan. Turn out on to a hot dish. Serve with hot tomato sauce poured round. *For 4 persons.*

CREAM OF TURKEY (Dindon à la Crème)

3 tablespoons butter
2 tablespoons flour
1 cup milk
Salt and pepper to taste
Cayenne pepper and celery salt
1½ cups diced cooked turkey
2 hard-boiled eggs
3 tablespoons Madeira or sherry

Melt butter. Stir in flour. When frothy, draw pan to side, and stir in milk. Return to stove. Stir till boiling. Season with salt, pepper, cayenne pepper and celery salt. Add turkey and stir till boiling. Separate eggs. Mince yolks and chop egg whites. Add gradually with Madeira or sherry, stirring constantly. (If preferred, substitute cream for half the wine.) Serve on croûtes of fried bread or hot buttered toast, or in hot pastry cases. *For 3 or 4 persons.*

CREPINETTES OF CHICKEN (Crêpinettes de Volaille)

2 oz. boiled fowl
1 oz. boiled ham
2½ tablespoons thick white sauce
Salt, pepper and celery salt

Mince chicken and ham. Place in a basin. Stir in white sauce, salt, pepper and celery salt to taste. Cool. Shape into 6 equal-sized balls. Wrap each in a piece of the caul. Join the caul with egg white.

Pig's caul as required
1 beaten egg white
3 mushrooms
2 tablespoons brown sauce

Place in a greased fireproof dish. Pour enough hot stock into the dish to cover the bottom. Cover with greased paper. Bake in a moderately hot oven, 375° F., until thoroughly heated, in 10-15 minutes. Brush with melted glaze. Peel, chop and fry mushrooms in a dessertspoon of melted butter. Stir in brown sauce. Season. Divide equally between 6 ramekins. Place a crêpinette on top. Pipe a border of green pea or potato purée round. Serve with ½ pint tomato sauce in a hot sauce-boat. *For 6 persons.*

CROQUETTES OF CHICKEN (Croquettes de Volaille)

½ lb. minced cooked chicken
½ pint Béchamel or Suprême sauce
¾ lb. minced ham or tongue
3 or 4 chopped mushrooms
Pinch of grated nutmeg or ground mace
Salt and pepper to taste
1 minced truffle if liked
1 tablespoon cream

Carefully remove all skin and gristle from chicken before mincing. Heat sauce. Add chicken, ham or tongue, mushrooms, nutmeg or ground mace, salt and pepper, truffle and cream. Mix lightly till blended. Turn out on to a plate. When cool, divide into 10 equal portions. With lightly floured hands mould each into the shape of a large cork. Beat an egg with a tablespoon of water, then egg and crumb croquettes. Stand for 1 hour or longer in a cold place till coating is dry. Fry till brown in deep fat. Drain on absorbent paper. Arrange in a hot dish covered with a paper doily. Garnish with fried parsley. Serve with mushroom sauce. *For 5 persons.*

CROUSTADE OF PARTRIDGES (Croûstade de Perdreaux)

2 partridges
2 oz. butter
½ pint Espagnole sauce
Salt and pepper to taste
8 oz. shortcrust

Remove breasts from birds. Halve lengthwise. Trim neatly. Lard with thin strips of fat bacon. Place on a buttered tin. Cover with buttered paper. Roast partridges. Leave till cold, then carefully remove all the meat from the bones. Pound in a mortar with half the butter. Work in 5 tablespoons of the sauce, then rub through a wire sieve. Heat remainder of sauce. Stir in essence from the roasting tin and boil down till reduced by a third. Stir into forcemeat. Season with salt and pepper. Line a pie plate or flan ring with the shortcrust. Prick well. Bake in a hot oven, 425° F., for about 25 minutes. While the pastry is cooking, cook the fillets in the oven for about 12 minutes, then remove and brush with melted glaze. Pile the forcemeat into the pastry case, making it high in the centre. Arrange fillets on the forcemeat. Cover with buttered paper. Reheat in oven. *For 6 persons.*

CURRY OF CHICKEN (Kari de Volaille)

1 (4 lb.) chicken
1 clove
1 blade mace
1 sprig parsley
1 tablespoon chopped onion
2 oz. butter
1 chopped apple

Prepare chicken and cut into joints. Carefully remove breasts. Place joints in a saucepan. Add spices and parsley. Cover with boiling water. Simmer for at least 1 hour, then add breasts. Continue to simmer till joints and breasts are tender. Remove from saucepan. Place onion

1 firm tomato
1 oz. curry powder
½ oz. flour
1 dessertspoon chutney
Squeeze lemon juice
Salt to taste
¾ pint chicken stock

and butter in a large frying-pan. Fry onion slowly till pale gold. Remove to a plate. Add chicken joints. Fry, turning occasionally, till pale brown then place with onion. Add apple and sliced peeled tomato to fat. Fry gently till apple is soft. Add onion, curry powder and flour. Fry slowly for 2 minutes, stirring constantly, then add remainder of ingredients. Cover tightly. Simmer gently for 20 minutes. Place in the centre of a ring of boiled rice. Serve with chutney and chapatties, or poppadums. *For 6 persons.*

LAMB CUTLETS

A lamb cutlet is a trimmed chop from the best-end neck of lamb. To prepare stand the neck of lamb with the chine end on the board, and the ends of the ribs upstanding. Saw away the chine bone, taking care not to damage the meat. Saw off the top of the rib bone very carefully so that the chops are equal in length, and the bones 3½-4 inches long, depending upon the size of the fillet of meat in each case. With a sharp knife, slice through the flesh half-way between each bone in order to have cutlets of equal thickness. Beat cutlets lightly with a wet cutlet bat or side of a rolling pin. Trim fat on each so as to leave only a narrow rim. Lastly, with a small sharp knife, scrape off skin underneath bones, then scrape off skin and fat from tips so as to leave each tip quite clean ¾ inch down. This is to make room for the frills. Mutton cutlets are also trimmed in this way.

TO COOK CUTLETS

They can be dipped in seasoned flour, but are usually floured and egged and crumbed. Fry or grill.

To Fry: Pour in enough dripping to cover bottom of a frying-pan to the depth of about ¼ inch. Arrange cutlets in fat when smoking hot, placing the side of each cutlet which is to be served uppermost, in the fat. Fry till golden brown for about 3½ minutes, then turn and fry on the other side. If wanted well-done, allow 5 minutes on each side. Arrange cutlets in a semi-circle with the bones to the inside, leaning, if liked, up against a mound of mashed potatoes, or arrange them down centre of a flat oval dish. Garnish with green peas, or mushrooms and green peas, alternately. Serve with Madeira or tomato sauce.

To Grill: Brush prepared cutlets with melted butter or olive oil. Grill for 8-10 minutes according to thickness, turning 3 times, seasoning lightly with salt and pepper. Slip a frill on the end of each bone. Dish up like fried cutlets. Serve with same accompaniments.

CUTLETS OF LAMB AU BEURRE
(Côtelettes d'Agneau frites)

6 lamb cutlets
Salt and pepper to taste

Trim cutlets, and season on both sides with salt and pepper. Melt butter in a frying-pan. Fry

334

1½ oz. butter
1 teaspoon meat glaze
1 tablespoon white wine
½ teaspoon minced chervil or tarragon
½ teaspoon minced parsley
1 teaspoon lemon juice
Sprigs of watercress

lightly on both sides. When nearly ready, dish in a circle or oval on a hot dish. Strain off butter. Add glaze and wine, herbs and lemon juice, and a large pat of butter. Heat. Pour round cutlets. Fill centre with fried potato balls. Garnish round edge with buttered carrot straws and fried mushrooms, and watercress. *For 3 persons.*

CUTLETS OF MUTTON, BONNE FEMME
(Côtelettes de Mouton, Bonne Femme)

8 mutton cutlets
2 oz. butter
16 small onions
½ pint stock
3 large potatoes
1 teaspoon meat extract

Trim cutlets. Remove most of the fat. Melt butter in a frying-pan, and when smoking hot, fry cutlets till light brown. Remove cutlets while you fry onions. Turn meat and onions into a casserole. Drain off butter for future use. Add stock and potatoes, scooped into small balls, then cover and cook in the oven for about 30 minutes. Dish up cutlets in a circle. Place onions and potatoes in centre. Skim fat from gravy. Thicken and flavour with extract. Pour round cutlets. Decorate each cutlet bone with a paper frill. Serve at once. *For 4 persons.*

FRIED MUTTON CUTLETS (Côtelettes de Mouton frites)

2 lb. best end neck of mutton
1 egg
3 tablespoons breadcrumbs

Prepare the cutlets (page 334). Egg and crumb. Drop into shallow smoking hot fat and fry for 5 minutes on each side. Drain well. Serve with tomato sauce round a mound of mashed potatoes. *For 4 persons.*

CUTLETS OF MUTTON, REFORME
(Côtelettes de Mouton, Réforme)

6 mutton cutlets
Egg and crumbs
Butter as required
1 croûte of fried bread
Glazed truffles

Wipe trimmed cutlets. Egg and crumb. Pat them flat with a palette knife. Melt enough butter to cover bottom of frying-pan. Add cutlets. Fry for 4 minutes on each side. Fry round slice of bread till golden brown. Brush one side of croûte with flour moistened with egg white. Place croûte, floured side downwards, in the centre of a hot serving dish. Garnish with fancy skewers, each spiked with a glazed truffle. Sprinkle over the edge shredded hard-boiled egg white if liked. Arrange cutlets round. Coat dish with Réforme sauce. *For 6 persons.*

DARIOLES OF CHICKEN (Darioles de Volaille)

1 pint liquid aspic jelly
Breast of 1 cooked chicken
1 truffle

Line the bottom of 6 dariole moulds thinly with the aspic. Leave till set. Cut chicken into neat slices, then truffle into tiny fancy shapes. When

335

1 heaped teaspoon minced parsley
Chervil or tarragon leaves
Sprigs of chervil or parsley

jelly lining is firm, arrange pieces of truffle in the bottom of each mould. Sprinkle lightly with parsley, and finish designs with chervil or tarragon leaves. Carefully pour in a little more jelly to set garnish. Leave this till set, then place 2 or 3 pieces of chicken in each mould, standing upright, not flat. Fill up mould with aspic jelly when beginning to set. Chill. When required, dip each mould quickly in warm water and turn out on to a serving dish, arranging them in an oval. Decorate with remainder of aspic jelly, finely chopped, and sprigs of chervil or parsley. *For 6 persons.*

DEVILLED BROCHETTES OF LAMB
(Brochettes d'Agneau à la Diable)

1½ lb. leg of lamb
Salt and pepper to taste
½ teaspoon paprika
1½ lb. lean raw bacon
½ oz. butter
1 teaspoon white vinegar
1 teaspoon Worcester sauce
1 egg yolk
1 saltspoon dry mustard
Stale breadcrumbs
Watercress to garnish

Cut lamb into squares, an inch thick. Season with salt, pepper and paprika. Cut bacon into equal-sized pieces. Arrange alternately on 8 skewers. Turn lamb and bacon in the oil, then grill for 12 minutes, turning frequently. Mix on a plate the butter, vinegar, Worcester sauce, egg yolk, mustard, with more salt and pepper to taste. When brochettes are ready, turn them in the devilled butter. Roll in crumbs. Grill for 2 minutes on each side. Arrange skewers on a hot dish. Garnish with watercress. *For 8 persons.*

DEVILLED FOWL (Poule à la Diable)

1 cold cooked fowl
1 teaspoon Worcester sauce
1 teaspoon French mustard
1 teaspoon English mustard
1 dessertspoon chutney
Dash of cayenne pepper
½ teaspoon salt
2 oz. butter
½ pint gravy
1 teaspoon flour, rice or potato

Cut fowl into neat joints and score them well, making deep cuts in the meat so that the sauce can soak right in. Mix together the Worcester sauce, mustards, finely chopped chutney, cayenne pepper and salt. Melt half the butter. Stir into mustard mixture, and mix together thoroughly. Spread joints with this, rubbing it well into the cuts. Grease the bottom of a skillet. Put pieces of fowl in and lay a buttered paper on top. Bake in a moderate oven, 350 F, for 10 minutes. Take it out, remove the paper and place pan on the top of stove. Sauté briskly for 5 minutes. Arrange joints on a hot dish. Pour gravy into pan. Cream flour with a little cold gravy and stir in. Bring to the boil, stirring constantly. Strain round joints. Sprinkle with finely chopped parsley. *For 6 persons.*

DEVONSHIRE LAMB PATTIES (Médaillons d'Agneau, Devonshire)

1¼ lb. lean lamb
Salt and pepper to taste
6 rashers bacon
Melted butter as required

Choose lamb from shoulder. Put through a meat grinder. Season with salt and pepper. Shape into round cakes about one inch thick. Remove

6 slices tomato
Potato straws
Watercress to garnish

rind from bacon, and wrap a rasher round each. Fasten with a cocktail stick. Brush grill rack with melted butter, and grill cakes quickly on each side until beginning to brown, then continue grilling slowly until cooked right through. When almost ready, place a slice of tomato on top of each. Brush with melted butter, and grill until brown. Arrange round a hot, flat dish. Pile the straws in centre. Garnish with watercress. *For 6 persons.*

DORMES DE VOLAILLE

1 oz. butter
1 chopped shallot
1 oz. flour
¼ pint stock
¼ lb. cooked chicken
1 oz. boiled ham
4 hard-boiled eggs
1 teaspoon minced parsley
Salt and pepper to taste
Squeeze of lemon juice
Breadcrumbs
1 egg

Melt butter. Stir in shallot and fry for a minute or two without browning. Add flour. Stir in stock and boil till sauce thickens, stirring constantly. Mince chicken and ham finely. Add to sauce. Halve eggs lengthwise. Remove yolks carefully and chop. Add to meat. Mix in parsley, salt and pepper to taste and lemon juice, and stir all well together. Stuff whites of eggs with this preparation, shaping them so that the stuffed halves look like a whole egg. Dip in breadcrumbs, then egg and crumb. Fry dormés till golden brown in deep smoking hot fat. Serve on a hot dish lined with a lace paper doily. Garnish with parsley. *For 4 persons.*

FILLETS OF BEEF (Filets de Boeuf)

This is a popular entrée. Have the fillet cut from ½-1 inch thick according to taste. Fry or grill as described under Steaks, page 205-206.

Fillets with Creamed Cucumber (Filets de Boeuf au Concombre) : Cook fillets. Peel and slice a medium-sized cucumber into a small saucepan. Add 1 tablespoon butter. Cover. Simmer slowly for 10-15 minutes, shaking occasionally. Season. Arrange each fillet on fried bread to fit. Top with cucumber. Garnish with green peas and potato chips.

Fillets Dauphinoise (Filets de Boeuf, Dauphinoise) : Fry ½ lb. chopped mushrooms in 1 oz. butter. Cook till liquid evaporates, then lower temperature. Cream ⅓ oz. flour with ¼ pint thick cream. Stir into mushrooms. Cook over hot water till thickened. Fry fillets. Arrange each fillet on fried bread cut to fit. Dish up mushrooms in a circle and place fillets on their croûtes in centre. Pour a glass of port wine into the frying-pan. Add a walnut of butter creamed with as much flour as it will take up, and beef stock as required to give you a sauce that will coat. Top each fillet with a slice of fried peeled tomato, and pour sauce round the dish, arranging sauté potatoes also round.

Fillets with Mushrooms (Filets de Boeuf aux Champignons) : Cook fillets. Arrange each fillet on a croûte of fried bread cut to fit. Drain a small can of champignons or mushrooms. Place in a saucepan. Toss till warm over low heat. Coat the mushrooms with cream and place one on top of each fillet. Garnish with green peas and carrots alternately.

Fillets à la Parisienne (Filets de Boeuf à la Parisienne) : Fry a croûte of bread to fit each fillet in butter till golden brown on both sides. Cover each with a thin slice of foie gras. Sprinkle lightly with grated Gruyère cheese. Flatten cheese with a broad-bladed knife. Bake in a moderate oven, 350° F., for 5 minutes. Fry fillets. Place fillets on a hot dish. Cover each with a croûte. Add 2 or 3 tablespoons of beef stock of jellying consistency to the butter in which the steaks were cooked. When boiling, add brandy to taste, not more than a liqueur glass. Pour round steaks. Garnish with a ring of creamed mushrooms, then with small tomatoes fried in butter.

COQUILLES OF SWEETBREADS (Coquilles de Ris de Veau)

1 large braised sweetbread
8 sliced mushrooms
5 tablespoons Velouté sauce
5 tablespoons tomato sauce
Salt and pepper
½ gill cream
Crumbs and melted butter

Cut sweetbread into cubes. Add mushrooms. Pour Velouté sauce into a saucepan. Stir till piping hot, then stir in tomato sauce. Cook, stirring constantly, until reduced to about a third of its quantity. Season with salt and pepper. Stir in cream. Stir till hot, then add sweetbread and mushrooms. Fill 6 buttered shells lightly with the mixture. Sprinkle with crumbs, then with melted butter. Bake in a hot oven, 450° F., for 7 or 8 minutes, until light brown. *For 6 persons.*

FRICASSEE OF CHICKEN (Fricassée de Poulet)

1 (4 lb.) chicken
2 heaped tablespoons chicken fat or butter
Salt and pepper to taste
1¼ pints boiling water
1 oz. flour
½ pint milk

Prepare bird as for boiling. Cut into suitable pieces for serving. Melt butter in a shallow saucepan. When hot, add joints. Fry slowly till brown, turning occasionally. Add salt and pepper to taste and water. Cover closely. Simmer gently till tender in about 1½ hours. Dish up bird. Cream flour with a little of the milk, then stir in remainder of milk. Stir in stock. Stir till smooth and boiling. Season if necessary. Pour over chicken. Serve with mashed or riced potatoes, or boiled new potatoes and green peas. *For 5 persons.*

NOTE : If you want a white chicken fricassée, do not brown joints. Stew in the water with salt and pepper to taste till tender, then melt fat and make sauce.

Fricassée of Turkey: Follow above recipe but substitute turkey for chicken.

FRIED GAME CAKES (Dormés frits)

1 lb. cold game
Salt and pepper to taste
¼ lb. mushrooms
1 oz. butter
¼ lb. breadcrumbs

Put game through a meat grinder into a basin. Season highly with salt and pepper. Peel mushrooms. Melt butter in a small fireproof dish and add mushrooms. Bake in a moderate oven,

Milk as required
2 eggs

350° F, turning once or twice, until tender. Remove and mince. Place breadcrumbs in a basin. Add milk to moisten. Soak for 10 minutes, then drain. Stir mushrooms and crumbs into game. Beat 1 egg. Add to mixture. Shape into small round cakes about ¾ inch thick. Egg and crumb cakes. Fry in hot fat until crisp and golden. Arrange down centre of a flat hot dish on heated artichoke bottoms if possible. Garnish with fried parsley and green peas. Serve with brown sauce. *For 5 persons.*

FRIED GUINEA CHICK BREASTS (Pintade frites)

Allow 1 breast per person. Skin breasts and carefully remove from carcase. Dip in seasoned flour. Melt enough butter or bacon dripping to cover bottom of a heavy frying-pan or shallow saucepan. Add breasts. Fry very slowly for 15-20 minutes, turning frequently, until tender and light brown. Serve in a circle on a flat hot dish. Fill centre with green peas. Arrange boiled new potatoes and fried mushrooms alternately round.

FRITTERS (Beignets)

This term usually applies to anything coated in batter and fried till crisp and golden brown. The addition of oil adds crispness to batter. The consistency should be of thick cream so that it does not run off the coated food. You will find recipes for other fritters besides those suitable for light entrées in the other sections. See index.

To Fry Fritters: Use clarified fat or cooking oil for frying. Make a bath from about 2½-3 inches deep, just deep enough to fry fritters. Heat fat to 370° F., and oil to 375-385° F., or drop an inch square of bread into hot fat or oil and when it browns in 1 minute, the temperature is correct. The temperature should be hot enough to make the batter expand before the outside becomes crisp and starts to colour. If making fritters from coated cooked fish, game, meat or poultry, dip one piece at a time into the batter. If making fritters from flaked fish, or diced game, meat or poultry, dip in a tablespoon. Turn when the fritters rise to the top so that they brown evenly all over. Allow superfluous batter to drain back into basin before frying, and do not add too many at once to the fat. Remove with a skimmer or fish slice, and drain on absorbent paper.

To Serve Fritters: Arrange on a hot dish lined with a paper doily as soon as cooked. Do not cover them or they will lose their crispness. Garnish with fried parsley.

BRAIN FRITTERS (Beignets de Cervelles)

Calf's or sheep's brains
1 peeled small onion
6 peppercorns
1 dessertspoon vinegar
1 tablespoon olive oil
Salt pepper to taste

Wash and soak brains in cold water. Skin. Place in a saucepan. Add onion, peppercorns and a squeeze of lemon juice or dash of vinegar. Cover with cold water. Bring to boil. Simmer gently for 10 minutes. Drain and throw into cold water.

339

1 teaspoon minced parsley — Leave for a minute or two, then drain thoroughly and slice. Mix the vinegar and oil on a plate. Add salt and pepper, then parsley. Marinate the brains in this for 30 minutes, turning at the end of ¼ hour. Drain. Dip each slice in frying batter. Fry in deep hot fat or oil till golden brown. Drain on absorbent paper. Arrange on a hot dish lined with a paper doily. Garnish with fried parsley. Serve with Tartare sauce. *For 2 or 3 persons.*

CHICKEN FRITTERS (Beignets de Volaille)

1 cup minced cold chicken
1 tablespoon butter
2 tablespoons flour
½ teaspoon salt
Celery salt and pepper to taste
½ cup chicken stock
Frying batter

Measure chicken without any skin or gristle. Melt butter in saucepan. Stir in flour, salt and celery salt and pepper to taste. Cook till frothy, stirring constantly, then gradually add chicken stock. Keep on stirring and cooking till smooth and thick. Spread half the sauce in a greased soup plate. Lay chicken on top. Cover with rest of sauce. Leave till firm, then cut into pieces, 1 x 2 inches. Dip pieces in batter, then fry in deep smoking hot fat till golden brown. Drain on absorbent paper. Garnish with fried parsley. *For 3 persons.*

MEAT FRITTERS (Beignets de Viande)

½ lb. flour
2 teaspoons baking powder
¾ teaspoon salt
1 beaten egg
1½ cups milk
1½ tablespoons tomato juice
¾ cup diced cooked game, meat or poultry
1 minced rasher of cooked bacon
1 dessertspoon minced celery
Salt, pepper and paprika

Sift flour, baking powder and salt into a basin. Stir egg into the milk, then gradually stir in tomato juice. When blended, stir into flour mixture. Beat till smooth. Add meat, bacon, celery, salt, pepper and paprika to taste. Beat till blended. Drop in tablespoonfuls in hot, deep fat or oil. Fry for about 2½ minutes, till golden brown. Drain on absorbent paper. Serve with mushroom or tomato sauce, green peas, and potato straws. *For 4 persons.*

OYSTER FRITTERS (Beignets d'Huîtres)

7 oz. flour
1 teaspoon baking powder
¼ teaspoon salt
1 egg
½ cup milk
1 dessertspoon melted butter
1 pint small oysters

Sift flour, baking powder and salt into a basin. Beat egg slightly. Add milk and melted butter. Stir till blended. Pour into flour mixture. Stir until smooth. Dry and drop in the oysters. Fry a few at a time in boiling hot lard or oil till brown below, then turn and fry till brown on the other side, allowing about 4 minutes. Do not pierce them when turning or the fritters will be heavy. Drain. Garnish with sprigs of fresh or fried parsley and asparagus tips if liked. Serve with Tartare sauce, and creamed cucumber. *For 4 persons.*

NOTE : If using fresh oysters, drain and pick them over carefully so as to remove any pieces of grit and shell that may adhere. Chop rather finely. If using quick-frozen, drain and chop 1 packet for above amount of batter.

PRAWN FRITTERS (Beignets de Crevettes)

¼ lb. flour
1 teaspoon baking powder
1 saltspoon salt
Pepper to taste
1 beaten egg
½ cup milk
Dash of Worcester sauce
1 cup chopped prawns

Sift flour with baking powder, salt and pepper. Add egg to milk. Stir in sauce. Make a well in centre of flour. Pour in liquid. Gradually stir in flour from the sides. When blended, add prawns. Stir well. Drop from a teaspoon into deep hot fat, 370° F. (Before dipping spoon in batter, always dip it in the hot fat.) Fry till golden brown in about 3 minutes, turning frequently. Drain on absorbent paper. Serve with horseradish or Tartare sauce. *For 3 or 4 persons.*

SALMON FRITTERS (Beignets de Saumon)

1½ lb. fillet of salmon, ½ inch thick
Seasoned flour as required
½ teaspoon minced shallot
Pinch of crushed herbs
French coating batter

Cut the fillets up into 2 inch squares. Dip in seasoned flour. Add shallot and herbs to the batter. Season with cayenne pepper to taste. Coat squares. Fry in hot fat or oil till crisp and golden. Serve, hot or cold, garnished with fried parsley. *For 5 or 6 persons.*

SWEETBREAD FRITTERS (Beignets de Ris de Veau)

1 large calf's sweetbread
1 oz. butter
¼ lb. mushrooms
2 button onions
1 teaspoon minced parsley
½ pint Madeira sauce
½ pint frying batter
Fried parsley to garnish

Blanch, braise and trim sweetbread, then press it. When cold, cut in slices. Melt butter in a saucepan. Add sliced mushrooms, onions and parsley, also ½ teaspoon each of chopped chervil and tarragon if you have any. Cook Madeira sauce till well reduced, then stir into the mushroom and onion butter. Dip sweetbread in this mixture, and stand in refrigerator until required. When wanted, dip each slice in the batter and fry in deep smoking hot fat till crisp and golden. Serve on a hot dish lined with a lace paper doily. Garnish with fried parsley. *For 4 persons.*

HAM PYRAMIDS (Pyramides de Jambon)

2 cups ground ham
2 cups mashed potatoes
1 teaspoon minced parsley
1 teaspoon onion juice
Pinch crushed herbs
Dash of cayenne pepper
2 tablespoons cream
2 tablespoons butter
2 egg yolks
Dried breadcrumbs as required
Frying fat as required

Place ham in a basin. Add potato, parsley, onion juice, herbs, cayenne pepper and cream. Mix well with a wooden spoon. Melt and stir in butter. Beat and add enough of the egg yolks to make a paste that will mould. Now with floured hands, divide each into small equal portions, and mould into pyramids about 2½ inches high. Dip in beaten egg yolk, then in crumbs. Fry in deep smoking hot fat for about 1-1½ minutes, until golden brown. Serve arranged on a hot dish with buttered peas or string beans in the centre. *For 4 or 5 persons.*

KROMESKIES OF CHICKEN (Kromesquies de Volaille)

½ lb. minced cooked chicken
2 oz. minced ham or tongue
4 diced mushrooms
1 diced truffle
Salt and pepper to taste
White sauce as required
Thin rashers of bacon
2 oz. flour
2 separated eggs
1 tablespoon olive oil
2 tablespoons milk

Mix the chicken, ham or tongue, mushrooms and truffle in a basin. Season with salt and pepper. Stir in enough sauce to make a paste. Turn on to a plate. Leave till cold. Divide into 8 or 9 equal parts. Shape into " corks." Wrap each in a thin piece of bacon or ham. Sieve flour with a pinch of salt into a basin. Separate yolks and whites of eggs. Add the yolks to the flour, then the oil and milk, beating till blended. Beat till light. Beat egg whites to a stiff froth. Fold lightly into batter. Coat each kromesky with the batter. Fry in deep smoking hot fat till golden brown. Drain on absorbent paper. Garnish with fried parsley. Serve with brown, mushroom or tomato sauce. *For 4 persons.*

LAMB EN BROCHETTE (Kebabs d'Agneau à l'Ananas)

About 1½-2 lb. shoulder of lamb
6 slices pineapple
1½ cups sieved breadcrumbs
Salt and pepper to taste
2½ oz. butter
Watercress as a garnish

Remove bones, etc., and trim meat into neat squares, 1 inch in size. Cut pineapple to fit. Season crumbs with salt and pepper. Dip meat and pineapple in melted butter, and coat with the crumbs. Run alternate squares on skewers. Grill under moderate heat for about 10-15 minutes, or till tender, turning often. Serve round a hot flat dish with buttered peas in the centre and potato balls round the outside. Garnish here and there with watercress. *For 6 persons.*

NOISETTES OF MUTTON (Noisettes de Mouton)

BASIC RECIPE:
1 lb. best end neck of mutton
2 tablespoons clarified butter
Salt and pepper to taste
Glaze and mashed potato
½ pint tomato sauce
¼ lb. cooked green peas

With a sharp knife, carefully cut away the mutton from the bones in one fillet, then divide in slices, half an inch thick. Trim. Melt butter in a frying-pan. Season mutton to taste. Fry slowly on both sides, for about 4 minutes on each side, till cooked to taste. Coat with liquified glaze. Arrange overlapping on a border of piped mashed potato. Pour sauce round. Garnish with peas, or string beans if preferred. *For 6 or 7 persons.*

As an alternative, stew ¼ lb. chopped peeled mushrooms gently in liquified glaze to moisten, until tender. Season to taste. Spread on a plate. When cold, cut out into neat sections. Place each noisette on a croûte of fried bread. Top with a mushroom square and heat for a moment or two in the oven, then arrange down the middle of a hot flat dish. Garnish along each side with fried slices of tomato. Top each with a cube of Maître d'Hôtel butter. Pour rich brown sauce round.

À l'Espagnole : Marinate noisettes in 2 tablespoons olive oil mixed with 1 tablespoon vinegar, 1 chopped shallot, 1 bay leaf, salt and pepper to taste, and 2 teaspoons minced parsley, for 5 hours. Dry gently, then dip first in breadcrumbs, then egg and crumb. Melt 2 oz. butter or dripping in a frying-pan. Fry noisettes quickly on both sides till brown, then fry very gently for 5 minutes on each side. Arrange in a row on a narrow border of piped mashed potatoes, or creamed spinach. Pour ½ pint Espagnole sauce round. Garnish with 4 halved tomatoes slightly scooped out, and filled with chopped cold ham, moistened Espagnole sauce and baked in a moderate oven, 350° F., for about 7 minutes. Allow 1 oz. ham.

Aux Champignons : Fry and glaze noisettes as in basic recipe. Mix ¼ pint thick white sauce with 2 large chopped mushrooms fried in ½ oz. butter, 2 dessertspoons cream, and salt and cayenne pepper to taste. Fill 4 patty cases equally with mushroom sauce, and lay a noisette on top. Crown each with a cube of Maître d'Hôtel butter. Dish up. Garnish with potato croquettes or pommes rissollées and sprigs of watercress.

Savoyade : Trim and fry noisettes as for the Espagnole method. Dish each up on a canapé of fried bread. Top each with a cooked artichoke bottom, heated in stock and crown these with one or two green peas. Pour sauce round, made by mixing ¼ pint mutton gravy with ½ pint Espagnole sauce. If preferred, substitute 5 tablespoons liquified meat glaze for the gravy. Simmer for 20 minutes, then skim and strain round noisettes.

NOISETTES OF PHEASANT (Noisettes de Faisan)

1 large young pheasant
1 beaten egg
Sieved breadcrumbs as required
Butter for frying
Salt and pepper to taste

Joint bird, then bone joints, taking care not to break the flesh more than you can help. Flatten with a meat mallet. Trim neatly. Fold skin under each portion. Season egg with salt and pepper, then coat noisettes with egg and breadcrumbs. Fry slowly in enough hot butter to cover bottom of frying-pan, until well browned on both sides, then drain well. Serve with Tartare, or Espagnole sauce. *For 6-7 persons.*

PARTRIDGES A L'ESPAGNOLE (Perdreaux à l'Espagnole)

2 young partridges
1 large onion
Salt and pepper to taste
¼ pint olive oil
½ pint tomato sauce
Croûtons of fried bread

Wipe and joint partridges. Slice onion. Season joints with salt and pepper. Heat oil in a shallow saucepan. Add onion, and partridge joints. Fry slowly, turning occasionally, till the onion is clear and the joints are brown all over. Drain off oil. Stir in tomato sauce. Bring to boil. Cover. Simmer gently till tender in about ¾ hour. Dish up. Strain sauce over. Garnish with croûtons and stoned olives or green peas. *For 4 persons.*

TO MAKE PATTY CASES

Roll out pastry to ½ inch thickness on a floured board. Cut into rounds 2½ inches in diameter with a cutter dipped in hot water. With a 1 inch diameter cutter, make a ring in the centre of each round to about half the depth of the pastry. Brush rounds with beaten egg yolk. Bake on a baking sheet brushed with cold water in a hot oven, 450° F., until risen and pale gold. Cut out centres, then carefully scoop out any soft inside pastry. Fill and reheat. Arrange on a hot flat dish lined with a lace paper doily. Garnish each to taste.

To Make Patty Cases for Buffet Parties, known as " Bouchées " : Roll to ⅛ inch thickness, and cut out 1½-2 inches in diameter. Here is an example :

BOUCHEES A LA REINE

1 roasting fowl (3½ lb.)
1 tablespoon butter
1 tablespoon sifted flour
½ pint milk
Salt and pepper to taste
Grated nutmeg to taste
Chopped champignons to taste

Roast or grill chicken, then remove all the meat from the bones. Mince. Melt butter in a shallow saucepan. Add flour. Stir till frothy, then gradually stir in milk. When smooth and boiling, season with salt, pepper and nutmeg, then stir in champignons. Stir constantly till boiling. Remove from stove, and use. Enough for 18 patty cases.

QUICK FILLINGS FOR PATTY CASES

Creamed Fish: Heat 1½ cups flaked cooked fresh or smoked or canned fish in 1½ cups medium-thick white sauce, flavoured to taste with minced parsley or chives and ground mace.

Creamed Green Peas: Mix 1 cup left-over cooked green or canned peas with ⅛ cup medium-thick parsley or cheese sauce. If liked, use half green peas and half diced boiled carrot.

Creamed Macaroni: Mix 1 cup boiled macaroni with 1 cup medium-thick white sauce, 2 tablespoons cooked green peas, salt and pepper to taste and 2½ tablespoons grated cheese. Stir till cheese is dissolved.

Size of patties to serve: 1. As a main course at lunch or supper, 3-3½ inches across ; 2. As a first or second course at dinner, 2½ or 3 inches across ; 3. For an apéritive party, 1½-2 inches across.

CHICKEN PATTIES (Bouchées de Volaille)

1 cup cold, boiled fowl
1 tablespoon butter
1½ tablespoons flour
¼ pint hot chicken stock
Cayenne pepper and salt
Grated nutmeg and ground mace to taste
1 egg yolk
1 dessertspoon cream
6 baked patty cases, 3 inches across

Cut fowl into ¼ inch pieces. Melt butter in a saucepan. Stir in flour. When frothy, stir in hot stock gradually. Bring to boil, still stirring. Season sauce with cayenne pepper, salt, grated nutmeg and ground mace. Turn into the top of a double boiler. Cook over hot water for 10 minutes, stirring constantly. Add chicken to sauce. Mix well. Cook for 10 minutes, stirring occasionally. Beat egg yolk with cream and stir into mixture for 1 minute. Fill hot patty cases with the mixture. Decorate each with a sprig of parsley. *Yield :* 6 patties.

CHICKEN LIVER PATTIES (Bouchées à la Chasseur)

10 chicken livers
2 oz. butter
¼ pint Chasseur sauce
Salt and cayenne pepper
8 patty cases

Wash and dry livers thoroughly, then cut into small squares. Melt butter in a frying-pan. When hot, add livers. Fry quickly, turning occasionally, then strain off the fat and stir in the sauce. Season with salt and cayenne pepper. Cook until hot, but do not allow to boil. Fill cases and garnish with sprigs of parsley. *Yield :* 8 patties.

CRAB PATTIES (Bouchées de Crabe)

1 oz. butter
1 oz. flour
½ pint milk
¼ teaspoon French mustard
Salt, pepper and paprika
2 oz. grated cheese
3 oz. cooked crab
6 baked patty cases

Melt butter in a saucepan. Stir in flour, then dilute with milk. Cook, stirring constantly till smooth, then season with mustard, salt, pepper and paprika. Add the cheese, then crab. Season to taste again if necessary. Make piping hot and pile into hot patty cases. Either replace top or plant a prawn or a sprig of parsley in the centre of each. *Yield:* 6 patties.

Lobster Patties: Follow above recipe, substituting lobster for crab.

OYSTER AND VEAL PATTIES (Bouchées d'Huitres, Helston)

½ pint canned oysters
½ pint white sauce
1 tablespoon butter
½ lb. chopped cooked veal
1 tablespoon sherry
½ cup cream
Salt and pepper to taste
Paprika to taste
About 12 patty cases

Use canned or sauce oysters. Beard oysters after draining off liquor. Heat white sauce. Add oysters. Heat, stirring constantly, until edges curl. Melt butter in another pan. Stir in veal and sherry. Stir till boiling, then mix with oysters. Stir in cream by degrees, and bring almost to the boil, stirring constantly. Season to taste with salt, pepper and paprika. Fill patty cases. Garnish with minced parsley or chives. *Yield :* About 12 patties.

PRAWN PATTIES (Bouchées de Crevettes)

1 pint cooked prawns
1 oz. butter
¾ oz. flour
1 cup hot milk
Salt and pepper to taste
Paprika to taste
Pinch of ground mace
2½ tablespoons cooked green peas or sliced fried mushrooms
1 tablespoon cream
Squeeze of lemon juice
12 patty cases, 2½ inches across

Shell prawns carefully, then chop. Melt butter in a saucepan. Stir in flour. When frothy, stir in milk gradually. Season with salt, pepper, paprika and mace. Stir until smooth and boiling. Add peas or mushrooms, prawns, cream and lemon juice. Stir until blended and use. Garnish each patty when filled with a prawn head. *Yield :* 12 patties.

Shrimp Patties: Follow above recipe, substituting shrimps for prawns.

345

SHRIMP AND MUSHROOM PATTIES
(Bouchées de Crevettes aux Champignons)

2 tablespoons butter
1 small onion or shallot
1½ teaspoons minced parsley
1 cup roughly-chopped peeled mushrooms
1 tablespoon minced pimiento
2½-3 tablespoons flour
2½ cups milk
2 cups freshly boiled shrimps
2 beaten egg yolks
Salt, pepper and cayenne pepper to taste
10-12 patty cases

Melt butter in a saucepan. Add minced onion or shallot, parsley, mushrooms and pimiento. Simmer for 10 minutes. Add flour. Mix and stir in 2 cups of the milk by degrees. Add shrimps. Simmer, stirring occasionally, for 10 minutes. Cool slightly. Beat egg yolks. Add remainder of milk, salt, pepper and cayenne pepper. Stir into shrimp mixture. Stir till piping hot, but do not allow to boil. Pile at once into hot patty cases. Decorate with sprigs of parsley. *Yield:* 10-12 patties.

SWEETBREAD PATTIES (Bouchées de Ris d'Agneau)

1 pair cooked lamb's sweet-breads
1 cup chicken or veal stock
1 tablespoon butter
1 dessertspoon lemon juice
Pinch of ground mace or grated nutmeg
1 saltspoon paprika
¾ teaspoon salt
2 egg yolks
¼ cup cream
About 9 patty cases

Cut sweetbreads into small pieces. Place in the top of a double boiler. Add stock, butter, lemon juice, spices, paprika and salt to taste. Beat egg yolks. Gradually beat in the cream. Stir into the sweetbread mixture. Cook over boiling water, stirring constantly, until rich and creamy, but be careful not to allow the mixture to come to the boil or it will curdle. Pile at once into hot cases. Decorate each with a celery tip. *Yield:* About 9 patties.

POUSSINS A LA PORTUGAISE

3 poussins, 6-8 weeks
Seasoned flour as required
2 oz. butter
1 pint brown sauce
3 medium-sized tomatoes
½ gill Madeira or sherry
Salt, pepper and paprika

Halve birds. Dip each half in flour. Melt butter in a shallow saucepan. Add poussins. Fry till brown all over, turning frequently. Add sauce. Stir occasionally till boiling. Cover and simmer till ready in about ½ hour. After cooking for 20 minutes, peel, slice and add tomatoes, with Madeira or sherry. Cover and finish cooking. Season. Dish up. Coat with sauce. *For 6 persons.*

GRILLED AYLESBURY DUCKLING
(Caneton grillé, Aylesbury)

1 Aylesbury duckling
Salt and pepper to taste
2 oz. butter
4 croûtes of fried bread
Sprigs of watercress
Tarragon vinegar
Potato straws

Draw and singe a duckling. Cut it down the back. Flatten it well, securing it in place with a skewer. Sprinkle with salt and pepper. Melt ½ oz. of the butter. Sprinkle over duckling. Place on a trivet in a baking tin. Bake in a hot oven for 10 minutes. Remove from oven. Melt half the

2 large seedless oranges
4 tablespoons mint sauce

remainder of the butter and sprinkle over duckling. Season to taste with salt. Grill for 8-10 minutes, or till tender, turning twice or thrice. Divide into 4 equal portions. Arrange on croûtes of bread on a hot dish. Melt remainder of butter in grill pan. Strain over duckling joints. Garnish with sprigs of watercress, washed, dried and moistened with tarragon vinegar, and potato straws. Peel oranges. Slice and arrange in a salad bowl. Dress with the mint sauce. Serve with duckling. *For 4 persons.*

QUENELLES OF CHICKEN (Quenelles de Volaille)

¼ lb. cooked chicken breast
1 oz. butter
¼ pint stale breadcrumbs
2 egg yolks
¾ pint Béchamel or white sauce
Salt and cayenne pepper

Weigh chicken free from skin and bone. Put through a meat grinder. Melt butter. Soak crumbs in milk to moisten for 3 minutes, then squeeze dry in a cloth. Add egg yolks and butter. Stir in chicken with a few drops of sauce if required. Season with salt and cayenne pepper. Mix well, then turn on to a plate. When cool, take a dessertspoon. Fill up with mixture. Mould into an egg shape with a knife, then remove with the other spoon to a shallow saucepan or frying-pan, well buttered, and half-filled with boiling chicken or veal stock. Simmer quenelles very gently for 10 minutes, then drain on a cloth. Serve arranged on a circle of mashed potatoes. Coat with sauce. Sprinkle with parsley. Fill the centre with cooked green peas or spinach. *For 3 or 4 persons.*

GRILLED PIGEONS (Pigeons grillés)

3 fat young pigeons
½ teaspoon salt
¼ teaspoon white pepper
1 dessertspoon salad oil
3 oblongs buttered toast
6 curls of grilled bacon
Watercress to garnish

Remove heads and cut off feet at the first joints, then split pigeons open through their backs, without separating. Draw, then remove their breast bones, and wrap each in a coarse towel. Flatten neatly with mallet or hammer. Mix salt, pepper and oil on a plate, then unwrap birds and roll them over and over in this seasoning. Arrange on a grill and grill for 6 minutes on each side. Serve each on a piece of buttered toast. Decorate with grilled bacon and watercress. *For 6 persons.*

QUENELLES OF GAME (Quenelles de Gibier)

1 lb. cold game (without bone or sinews)
3 oz. butter
Salt and pepper to taste
Grated nutmeg to taste
6 or 8 button mushrooms
1 dinner roll
Gravy as required
1 egg yolk
Egg and crumbs

Put meat through grinder. Pound purée in a mortar with butter, salt, pepper and nutmeg. Mince mushrooms and add. Pound again. Crumble the roll into a small basin. Moisten with gravy. Soak for 5 minutes, then drain off all moisture, squeezing crumbs with a wooden spoon. Place crumbs in a shallow saucepan with as much game gravy as they will absorb. Stir over stove till it turns into a smooth mass and comes away from sides of pan. Remove from stove. Stir in yolk without

347

beating. Leave till cool. Pound with meat mixture till thoroughly blended. Chill. Mould into quenelles. Egg and crumb. Fry in hot fat to cover till bright brown. Drain on absorbent paper. Serve coated with brown or mushroom sauce. *For 6 persons.*

RABBIT MARENGO (Lapin, Marengo)

1 rabbit
Salt and pepper to taste
1 oz. butter
2½ tablespoons olive oil
½ gill white wine
½ pint brown sauce
¼ pint tomato sauce
12 mushrooms
Fried croûtons

Wipe rabbit with a damp cloth. Cut into joints. Discard ribs. Season joints with salt and pepper. Melt butter in a shallow saucepan. Add oil. When hot, add rabbit. Fry till golden all over, then drain off fat. Add wine. Stew for 5 minutes, then gradually stir in the brown sauce and tomato sauce. Cover. Simmer very gently for ¾ hour. Peel and wipe mushrooms with a damp cloth. Place in a greased baking tin. Season with salt and pepper. Sprinkle with melted butter. Bake in a moderate oven, 350° F., for about 10 minutes. Dish up rabbit on a border of mashed potato. Skim sauce and strain over. Garnish alternately with groups of fried croûtons and mushrooms. *For 4 persons.*

SALMI OF PLOVERS (Salmi de Pluviers)

2 plovers
Melted butter as required
3 minced shallots
½ teaspoon flour
2 tablespoons rich white stock
¼ pint Madeira
Salt and pepper to taste

Remove breasts, legs and wings from birds. Brush with melted butter. Mix shallot with the flour. Dip joints in mixture. Grill till brown. Place in a shallow saucepan. Add stock and wine. Season with salt and pepper. Bring to boil. Dish up plovers. Rub sauce through a sieve and reheat. Pour over birds. Serve with mashed or riced potatoes and green peas. *For 2 persons.*

STEWED GOOSE (Oie étuvée à la Reine)

2½ lb. young goose
1 lb. chopped mushrooms
¼ pint cream
½ oz. flour
Salt and pepper

Buy or cut up enough goose to give you the amount required. Place joints and pieces in a large frying-pan. Fry very slowly to start with till fat flows, then fry more quickly, turning frequently, till equally brown and tender, placing lid on pan after browning stage is reached. When tender, add mushrooms and continue frying till mushrooms are cooked and the water that comes out of them has evaporated. Mix cream with the flour and stir into goose and mushrooms. Stir till boiling. Season with salt and pepper. *For 6 persons.*

SCALLOPS OF PHEASANT (Coquilles de Faisan)

1 boiled pheasant
2 tablespoons butter
4 tablespoons flour
¾ pint white stock

Skin pheasant and remove meat. Cut into ½ inch dice. Melt butter in a saucepan. Stir in flour. When frothy, stir in stock. Stir till boiling. Cook,

½ gill cream
1 egg yolk
6 sliced mushrooms
Salt and pepper to taste
Grated nutmeg to taste
4 tablespoons grated Parmesan
cheese

stirring occasionally, for a few minutes. Stir cream into egg yolk and add, stirring constantly. Stir over low heat for a moment or two, then add diced pheasant and mushrooms, fried lightly in melted butter. Season with salt, pepper and grated nutmeg. Cook slowly for 5 minutes, stirring constantly. Pile into buttered scallop shells. Sprinkle with cheese. Brown under the grill. *For 5 persons.*

SHEEP'S TONGUES WITH SPINACH
(Langues de Moutons braisées)

4 sheep's tongues
1½ pints good stock
1 medium-sized onion
1 bouquet garni
1 dessertspoon potato flour
2 tablespoons cold water
Salt and pepper to taste
Spinach for 4 persons

Wash tongues and place in a shallow saucepan. Cover with boiling water. Simmer gently for 1 hour, then remove and drain. Skin and trim neatly. Pour stock into a shallow saucepan. Peel, slice and add onion with bouquet garni. Bring to boil. Skim if necessary. Cream potato flour with cold water, and stir into stock. Stir till boiling. Add tongues. Season with salt and pepper, and add a drop or two of browning if necessary. Cover with a greased paper then with lid. Braise very gently for 1 hour. Make a pyramid of cooked spinach in centre of flat hot dish, then arrange tongues round. *For 4 persons.*

SOUFFLE OF CHICKEN (Soufflé de Volaille, Fermière)

2 rashers of bacon
¼ lb. cold chicken
2 egg yolks and 3 egg whites
4 tablespoons thick white
sauce
Salt and pepper to taste
Stale breadcrumbs as required

Remove rind from rashers. Put bacon and chicken through a meat grinder. Pound in a mortar till into a paste. Put yolks in a basin. Beat well. Stir in the sauce. Mix with chicken paste by degrees until perfectly blended. Season with salt and pepper. Brush 1 large soufflé mould or individual moulds with melted butter. Sprinkle thickly with stale breadcrumbs. Beat egg whites till stiff. Fold lightly into mixture. Fill mould or moulds only three parts full. Bake in a moderate oven, 350° F., for 15-20 minutes, if small, until well risen and browned. If large, bake for about 40 minutes. *For 4 persons.*

SOUFFLE OF PARTRIDGES (Soufflé de Perdreaux)

2 partridges
2 oz. panada
2 oz. butter
Salt and pepper to taste
4 egg yolks
¼ pint brown sauce
½ gill glaze
2 egg whites

Carefully remove all meat from partridges, then take away any skin and sinews. Put meat through a grinder. Place in a mortar. Add panada, butter and salt and pepper to tast. Pound to a smooth paste, then rub through a wire sieve into a basin. Gradually stir in egg yolks, brown sauce and glaze. Beat egg whites till stiff. Fold into mixture. Three quarters fill a greased soufflé dish or tin. Bake in a moderate oven, 350° F., with dish or tin set in a baking tin containing hot water coming half

349

way up the sides, for about 1 hour, till firm in the centre when tested with a knife. *For 4 persons.*

STEWED BLACK COCK (Ragoût de Coq de Bruyère)

1 black cock
2 tablespoons butter
1 clove garlic
1½ gills beef stock
¼ pint port wine
Salt and black pepper to taste
2 snippets lemon peel

Cut bird into joints as you would a chicken. Melt butter in a shallow saucepan. Add joints. Fry slowly, turning occasionally with a fork, until light brown all over. Remove joints to a plate. Peel, slice and fry garlic for 2 or 3 minutes, then remove and throw away garlic. Pour stock into pan. Add wine, salt and pepper to taste and lemon peel. Heat to boiling point. Place joints in a clean saucepan. Strain sauce over. Cover. Simmer very gently for 25-35 minutes, depending on size of bird, or till tender. Pile joints in centre of a hot dish. Pour gravy round. Garnish with snippets of toast or fried bread. *For 4 persons*

STEWED CHICKEN LIVERS (Foie de Volaille au Ris)

3 or 4 chicken livers
1 dessertspoon minced onion
1 tablespoon butter
Salt and pepper to taste
Pinch of paprika
½ cup chicken stock

Wash and dry livers. Cut into slices. Dredge lightly with seasoned flour. Fry onion slowly in butter till light brown. Add liver. Shake pan over stove till liver is seared, then add seasonings and stock. Bring to the boil. Simmer for 2 or 3 minutes. Serve in a border of boiled rice. *For 2 persons.*

SPANISH DUCKLINGS (Canetons, Espagnole)

2 ducklings
Salt and black pepper to taste
Paprika to taste
1 oz. butter
Seasoned flour as required
1 medium-sized onion
¼ pint water
½ pint tomato juice
¼ pint white wine
2 sprigs parsley
1 lb. shelled peas
4 sliced young carrots

Joint birds. Season with salt, black pepper and paprika. Melt butter in a frying-pan. Dip joints in flour. Fry till golden all over, then lift into a saucepan. Mince and add onion. Stir in water, tomato juice and wine. Cover and simmer for 30 minutes. Add parsley, peas and carrots. Cover and simmer for 30 minutes, or till tender. Remove parsley. Serve in a hot dish with the joints in centre and vegetables round. Skim grease off sauce. Thicken if liked. Pour over joints. *For 8 persons.*

STEWED PIGEONS (Ragoût de Pigeons)

2 plump tame pigeons or 2 wood pigeons
Salt and pepper to taste
1 oz. butter
1 tablespoon flour
White stock or water to cover

Wipe and season inside and out of pigeons with salt and pepper. Melt butter in a saucepan. Dredge birds with flour. Fry for 5 minutes on each side, turning frequently. Add stock or water. Cover. Simmer till tender, from 1-2½ hours, depending on age, size and variety. *For 4 persons.*

350

To Vary: 1. Fry 12 peeled button onions in the butter with the pigeons. Follow basic recipe but add after stock a dash of mushroom ketchup, 1 teaspoon vinegar, 1 saltspoon anchovy sauce and 2 tablespoons port wine.

2. Joint pigeons. Season, flour and fry as in basic recipe. Add 3 tablespoons diced bacon, 1 minced shallot and stock as in basic recipe.

STUFFED QUAILS TOSCA (Cailles à la Tosca)

3 quails
Liver stuffing as required
White stock as required
Meat glaze as required
1 lettuce or curly endive
Mayonnaise as required

Bone quails without removing the drumsticks. Stuff. Wipe with a damp cloth. Tie each in a piece of butter muslin. Place in a saucepan. Cover with boiling white stock. Cover and simmer for $\frac{1}{4}$ hour. Remove and drain well. Press lightly and leave until cold. Halve quails. Place side by side on a flat dish. Coat with melted meat glaze. Place side by side on a wire rack. Coat with chaudfroid sauce. When set, coat the other side with mayonnaise. Sprinkle lightly with melted aspic. When set, cut each out carefully. Serve on a border of aspic, the white side upwards with any green salad in the centre. Decorate border with mustard and cress and radish roses. *For 4 persons.*

STUFFED TURKEY DRUMSTICKS (Jambes de Dindon, farcies)

2 large drumsticks
1/4 lb. sausagemeat
Salt and pepper to taste
1 sliced carrot
2 slices onion
1/2 pint chicken stock
2 cloves

Remove drumsticks from bird, leaving a large flap of skin for folding over. Break bones just above first joints. Now bone legs and remove tendons without breaking the skin. To do this, begin at the thighs, and scrape the meat from the sinews to remove them all together. Season sausagemeat if necessary with salt and pepper to taste. If liked, add 2 minced mushrooms. Stuff into legs, but do not fill too full or the skin will burst during cooking. Either close opening at end of each with cocktail sticks or fold flap of skin over and sew with a needle and cotton, making join on under-side. There are two ways you can cook stuffed drumsticks :

1. Place vegetables, stock and cloves in a shallow saucepan. Add legs. Cover tightly. Braise slowly from $1\frac{1}{2}$-2 hours, turning at half time. Remove legs to a baking tin. Brush with melted butter. Bake in a hot oven, 450° F., till brown. Meanwhile, boil stock rapidly down to $\frac{1}{4}$ pint. Remove stitches or cocktail sticks. Serve garnished with watercress, with gravy in a hot sauceboat. *For 2 persons.*

2. Place stuffed legs in a greased fireproof dish. Add enough boiling chicken stock to come $1\frac{1}{2}$ inches up side of dish. Bake in a moderate oven, 350° F. till tender in about 1 hour. Serve whole or thickly sliced. *For 2 persons.*

SUPREME OF SWEETBREADS (Suprême de Ris de Veau)

1 lb. sweetbreads
3 cups chicken stock
1 peeled and sliced onion

Soak sweetbreads in cold water to cover for 1 hour. Drain and place in a saucepan. Cover with cold water. Bring to boil. Simmer for 2 minutes.

1 scraped carrot
1 tablespoon butter
1 tablespoon flour
1 tablespoon minced onion
A few grains of ground cloves
2 teaspoons cream
1 egg yolk
1 teaspoon lemon juice

Remove and plunge in cold water. Trim off all fat and gristle. Place in a saucepan. Add 2 cups of the stock and sliced onion. Slice in carrot. Cover with a greased paper. Simmer very gently for 1 hour. At the end of 50 minutes, melt fat in a saucepan. Stir in remainder of stock. Add minced onion and cloves. Cook for 5 minutes, stirring constantly. Stir in cream, diluted with egg yolk. Cook for 1 minute, stirring constantly, then stir in lemon juice and strain. Arrange sweetbreads on a hot dish. Cover with the sauce. Serve garnished with green peas. *For 4 persons.*

SWEETBREADS A LA KING (Ris de Veau, Royale)

1 cup cream
1 tablespoon butter
Salt and pepper to taste
2 egg yolks
1½ cups boiled cubed sweetbreads
¾ cup quartered fried mushrooms
¼ cup boiled green peas
1 teaspoon minced parsley
1 tablespoon minced pimiento
Triangles of baked puff pastry

Heat ¾ cup of the cream in the top of a double boiler. Add butter, salt, pepper, and egg yolks mixed with remainder of cream. Cook over boiling water, stirring constantly, until thick. Stir in hot sweetbreads, mushrooms and peas. Pile at once in the centre of a hot dish. Sprinkle with parsley and pimiento. Garnish with triangles (fleurons) of pastry. *For 3 or 4 persons.*

TIMBALES OF GAME (Timbales of Gibier)

¼ lb. cold game
6 mushrooms
2 oz. butter
Salt and pepper to taste
½ pint Béchamel sauce
1 lb. mashed potato
2 egg yolks

Remove skin, bone and sinews from game before weighing. Cut meat into fine dice. Peel and mince mushrooms. Melt ½ oz. butter in a small saucepan. Add mushrooms. Fry slowly for 2 or 3 minutes, stirring constantly. Add game, and salt and pepper, then enough of the sauce to moisten. Mix till blended. Rub mashed potatoes through a fine sieve. Melt 1 oz. of remaining butter in a shallow saucepan. When hot, add potato purée. Season with salt and pepper to taste. Stir over stove till heated through, then add 1 egg yolk. Stir till blended. Turn on to a plate. Leave till cool. Butter some dariole or timbale moulds. Line thinly and smoothly with potato purée, pressing it well into the moulds. Fill centre with game mixture. Spread potato purée over the top of each. Smooth with a knife to make them all level. Brush over with remaining egg yolk well beaten. Place in a greased baking tin a little apart. Bake in a moderate oven, 350° F., till pale gold. Heat remainder of sauce. Add remainder of butter, bit by bit. Heat till almost boiling. Turn out moulds on to a hot dish. Pour sauce round. *Yield*: 6 or 8 timbales.

TOURNEDOS OF BEEF

BASIC : A tournedo is a small medallion or round of fillet of beef, cut ½ inch, 1 inch, or 1½ inches thick, according to requirements of recipe. To make them,

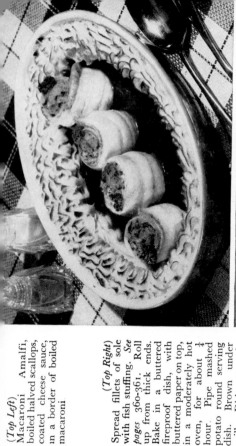

(Top Left)
Macaroni Amalfi, boiled halved scallops, coated cheese sauce, in a border of boiled macaroni

(Top Right)
Spread fillets of sole with fish stuffing. *See pages 360-361.* Roll up from thick ends. Bake in a buttered fireproof dish, with buttered paper on top, in a moderately hot oven, for about $\frac{1}{4}$ hour. Pipe mashed potato round serving dish. Brown under grill. Dish up sole with mushroom sauce.

(Bottom Left)
Serve Chestnut Croquettes and fried potato cakes with sauce and a green salad *See page* 507

(Bottom Right)
Serve Corn Souffles at lunch, high tea or supper. *See page* 517.

Scoop centres from Braised Onions. Fill hollows with creamed chicken or turkey. Serve with mashed potato and mushrooms or tomato sauce.

Vegetable Platter of buttered boiled vegetables. Serve with **Hollandaise Sauce** if preferred to coating with butter. *See page* 444.

cut the fillet into slices of the necessary thickness, then cut out a round from each slice with a plain cutter 2 inches across. Season with salt and pepper to taste. Fry in melted clarified butter, allowing 2 tablespoons to 1 lb. of fillet. When browned on both sides, and cooked rare, medium-done, or well-done, according to taste, dress according to recipe. When placing each on a croûte of fried bread, let the croûte be about ¼ inch wider in diameter. If preferred, tournedos can be grilled.

Tournedos à la Béarnaise : Fry tournedos prepared from 1½ lb. fillet of beef, sliced 1½ inches thick, quickly. Dish each up on a fried croûte. Arrange in a circle on a hot dish. Brush each tournedo with hot meat glaze. Pour ½ pint Béarnaise sauce into a hot sauce-boat. Arrange sprigs of watercress in centre of tournedos. Garnish round edges between each tournedo with Julienne potatoes or potato straws. *Yield; 8 tournedos, 2 per person.*

Tournedos à la Chasseur : Fry 6 tournedos, cut an inch thick, quickly in 1½ oz. butter. Dish up in a circle. Drain off the butter. Add ½ gill white wine to pan. Boil up for 2 or 3 minutes, then stir in ½ pint Chasseur sauce. Simmer for 10 minutes. Pour over fillets. Top each with a slice of fried onion or with a fried mushroom. Arrange Pommes Duchesse round.

Tournedos à la Drexel : Cut 5 tournedos from 2 lb. fillet, sliced 1 inch thick. Fry quickly until nicely browned. Season with salt and pepper. Place each on a fried croûte cut the same size as the fillet. Top with a slice of fried tomato crowned with a teaspoon of thick Béarnaise sauce. Garnish each with a slice of truffle. Arrange potato straws around the outside.

Tournedos au Foie Gras : On the Continent, tournedos are often served garnished with foie gras : make a small horizontal cut at the top of each with a sharp knife, then slip the knife round so as to make a pocket. Rub foie gras through a fine sieve. Pipe quickly on to each tournedo when dished up. 1 small tureen of foie gras is enough for 2 lb. of fillet.

VOL-AU-VENTS

To make a large vol-au-vent case, allow 1 lb. puff pastry. After it has had 6 turns, roll to about ¾ inch thickness. Chill. To cut out, use an oval or round cutter sold for shaping a vol-au-vent case. It is deeper than the average cutter. Dip cutter in hot water and cut out a round or oval. Brush with beaten egg. Dip a smaller cutter of the same shape in hot water and shake. With it, mark a smaller round or oval inside the large one, to about half the depth of the pastry, leaving a margin of 1 inch. Make a hole in the centre with a fine skewer right to the base of the pastry. Place on a baking sheet covered with two thicknesses of brown paper. Bake in a very hot oven, 500° F., for 5 minutes, then gradually reduce heat to 350° F., and finish baking in about 20 minutes. Remove the lid and scoop out any soft inside. Add hot filling. Put on cover again. Serve at once.

CHICKEN VOL-AU-VENT (Vol-au-vent de Volaille)

6 oz. cubed or diced chicken
2 oz. cubed or diced cooked
  ham or tongue
6 champignons
2 truffles
½ pint hot Béchamel sauce
1 vol-au-vent case, 7″

Mix the chicken, ham or tongue, champignons, truffles, with the sauce. Season. Add a few drops of lemon juice or sherry if liked. Stir till blended and piping hot. *For 3 persons.*

OYSTER VOL-AU-VENT (Vol-au-vent d'Huîtres)

2 dozen oysters
2 oz. butter
1 oz. flour
5 tablespoons oyster stock
About 5 tablespoons milk
½ teaspoon lemon juice
2 egg yolks
Salt and cayenne pepper
½ gill cream
1 heaped teaspoon minced
  parsley
1 vol-au-vent case, 8″

Remove oysters from shells. Strain their liquor over them and turn into a saucepan. Bring to boil. Strain off the liquor. Remove beards from oysters and halve oysters. Melt butter in a small saucepan. Add flour. Cook slowly for 3 or 4 minutes, stirring constantly, then add oyster liquor made up to ½ pint with milk. Stir till boiling. Simmer gently for 8 or 9 minutes, then add lemon juice, egg yolks, salt and pepper, cream and parsley. Continue to cook, stirring constantly, until thick, but do not allow to boil. Rub through a fine sieve. Reheat over boiling water, stirring constantly. Add oysters. Stir till piping hot. *For 4 persons.*

WILD MUSHROOM VOL-AU-VENTS
(Vol-au-vents à la Russe)

1 lb. wild mushrooms
2 tablespoons butter
1 minced onion
Salt and pepper to taste
1 teaspoon flour
1 tablespoon sour cream
6 small vol-au-vent cases

Throw mushrooms into boiling, salted water. Stir for a moment or two, then drain thoroughly and mince. Melt butter in a small saucepan. Add onion, mushrooms, salt and pepper, and flour. Stir in cream and a teaspoon of the mushroom water. Stir till boiling. Remove from stove. Cool. Use for filling individual vol-au-vents, 2½ inches square. Cover with little tops and re-heat for 5 minutes.

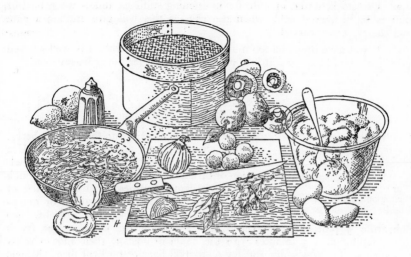

Stuffings

Stuffings are very important. They serve two functions. They add piquancy to baked fish, a roast bird or a joint, certain birds suitable for boiling, and vegetables to be baked. They also make a dish go farther.

AMOUNT OF STUFFING REQUIRED

The amount of stuffing needed cannot be exactly estimated here. It depends not only on the kind to be used, as some swells more than others, but on the structure of the bird for which it is required, or on the type of joint, not on the weight.

Pack such stuffings loosely into birds and fish and into cavities or pockets in joints. If you wish to stuff both body and neck of birds, allow approximately $1\frac{1}{2}$ cups per pound of bird, weighed fully drawn. If you only wish to stuff body, allow :

Fish (About 5 lbs. boned) :	About 1 pint
Chicken (4 to 5 lbs.) :	$1\frac{1}{4}$ to $1\frac{3}{4}$ pints
Duck :	About $1\frac{1}{4}$ pints
Goose (About 10 lbs.) :	About 2 pints
Turkey (About 10 lbs.) :	4 to 5 pints
Small Birds :	2 to 4 tablespoons

HINTS ON STUFFINGS

1. Use two-day old bread for bread stuffings.
2. If a game bird has a strong flavour, or is slightly high, fill with celery or

355

onion stuffing to absorb and lessen flavour. Remove this stuffing before dishing up birds.

3. Use stock, water, or milk for moistening stuffings, unless when bird or joint is to be served cold, when use egg, as this will give stuffing a paté consistency, easily carved.

4. If you have prepared too much stuffing, bake or steam it in well-greased individual moulds, or turn it into croquettes or use for filling bacon rolls.

SAVOURY STUFFING (Basic)

2 pints stale breadcrumbs
½ cup melted fat
½ teaspoon salt
½ teaspoon crushed herbs
3 tablespoons chopped onion or shallot
1 saltspoon pepper
2 tablespoons milk or stock

Mix the crumbs in a basin with the fat, salt, herbs, onion or shallot, pepper and milk or stock. Use with fish, game, meat, chicken, guinea fowl, pigeon or turkey. Do not use with wild fowl, duck or goose. Adapt quantities given to suit size of bird. *To Vary :* (1) Add a bruised or finely-minced peeled clove of garlic to crumbs. (2) Substitute ½ pint shredded celery, for ½ pint of the crumbs, but fry it in the fat for 2 or 3 minutes with the onion or shallot, then add to other ingredients. (3) Wash, dry and fry or parboil liver of bird till firm. Mince. Stir into crumb mixture. NOTE : Both Celery and Liver Stuffing have been mentioned in the recipes for birds.

ALMOND STUFFING (Farce d'Amandes)
(*For* 10 *lb. Turkey*)

8 cups breadcrumbs
1 cup hot top milk
½ cup melted butter or margarine
2 beaten eggs
1 tablespoon grated onion
1 cup shredded celery
1 teaspoon crushed herbs
Salt and pepper to taste
½ pint minced roasted almonds

Place crumbs in a basin. Stir in milk, fat and eggs. Stand for 10 minutes. Stir in onion, celery, herbs, salt, pepper, a dash of paprika if liked and the almonds.

APPLE STUFFING (Farce de Pommes)

1 tablespoon minced onion or shallot
2 tablespoons melted butter
½ pint breadcrumbs
1 pint finely chopped apple
White stock as required
Salt, pepper and paprika to taste

Cook the onion or shallot in the fat till slightly browned. Add crumbs, and ½ cup finely minced celery, if liked, apple, stock to moisten, and salt, pepper and paprika to taste. Stir till blended. Use with duck, goose or pork.

CHESTNUT AND OYSTER STUFFING (Farce à la Gauloise)
(For a 10- or 12-lb. Turkey)

2 lbs. chestnut purée
1 pint small oysters
1 teaspoon grated onion
White sauce as required
Salt and paprika to taste
1 teaspoon Marsala
1 heaped teaspoon minced chives or parsley

Place purée in a basin. Add oysters, onion, and sauce as required made with 1½ gills milk, and either ½ gill chicken stock or oyster liquor. Season with salt and paprika and cayenne pepper, if liked, to taste. Add Marsala and chives or parsley and a pinch of ground mace, if liked.

CHESTNUT AND VEAL STUFFING (Farce à la Voisin)
(For a 10- or 12-lb. Turkey)

50 boiled chestnuts
1 pint minced cooked veal
1 teaspoon minced parsley
Pepper to taste
¼ teaspoon crushed thyme
3 tablespoons butter
Salt to taste
1 minced truffle
1 teaspoon grated onion

Mix with remaining ingredients. This stuffing is also suitable for a chicken or capon. Adapt quantity of ingredients to suit size of bird.

CHICKEN STUFFING (Farce de Volaille)

8 oz. raw chicken breast
1 oz. butter
1 oz. flour
5 tablespoons chicken stock
1 beaten egg
Salt and cayenne pepper to taste
2 tablespoons cream

Put chicken through a meat grinder. (It should be weighed free from skin and sinew.) Melt butter in a saucepan. Add flour. When frothy, stir in stock. Stir till smooth and boiling. Remove from stove. When cool, place in a mortar. Pound the minced chicken with a little of the sauce, then gradually pound in remainder of sauce. Stir in egg, and salt and pepper to taste, then cream. Rub through a wire sieve. Use for stuffing vegetables, patty cases, etc.

KIDNEY STUFFING (Farce de Rognons)

¾ oz. butter or bacon fat
8 oz. calf's kidney or sheep's kidneys
1 tablespoon minced shallot
2 cups breadcrumbs
2 beaten eggs
3 tablespoons chicken or veal stock
5 tablespoons cream
Salt and pepper to taste
1 tablespoon minced chives
¼ teaspoon paprika
Squeeze of lemon or lime juice

Melt butter in a shallow saucepan. Skin and chop kidney or kidneys and add. Fry slowly with the shallot for 3 or 4 minutes. Stir in remaining ingredients. Substitute parsley for chives, if liked, and add a tablespoon of Madeira or sherry, according to taste. Use for stuffing chicken, guinea fowls, or turkey. *Yield:* About 3 cups.
To Vary Kidney Stuffing: Add 2 oz. lean minced ham or ½ cup chopped walnuts.
Liver Stuffing (Farce de Foie) : Follow recipe for kidney stuffing, but substitute calf's liver or the equivalent in chicken livers for the kidney in foregoing recipe.

357

MUSHROOM BREAD STUFFING (Farce à la Grandmère)

1 pint breadcrumbs
4 tablespoons melted butter
1/2 cup chopped mushrooms
Salt and cayenne pepper to taste
1 teaspoon minced chives or parsley
1/4 teaspoon crushed herbs

Mix crumbs with butter, mushrooms, salt and cayenne pepper, chives or parsley and herbs. Add a dash of celery salt, if liked. *Yield :* 3 cups. Use for stuffing chicken or turkey crop.

ONION STUFFING (Farce d'Oignon)
(*For* 10- *to* 12-*lb. Goose*)

6 cups breadcrumbs
2 cups giblet stock
2 beaten eggs
1 teaspoon salt
1/2 teaspoon grated nutmeg
2 teaspoons crushed sage
1/2 teaspoon crushed thyme or marjoram
1/4 lb. goose, chicken or bacon fat
4 chopped medium-sized onions
1/2 cup chopped raisins
3 tablespoons chopped parsley
1/2 cup chopped celery tops
Black and cayenne pepper to taste

Place crumbs in a basin. Add stock. Stand for 5 minutes. Stir in eggs, seasoning, herbs. Melt fat. Add onion. Fry slowly till pale brown. Add raisins, parsley, and celery tops. Mix with the crumbs and egg. Stir in pepper to taste. *Yield:* About 7 cups. *To Vary :* Add minced fried or parboiled goose liver or 2 tablespoons minced green pepper with the celery tops. Omit raisins if liked.

ORANGE STUFFING (Farce d'Orange, Delmonico)
(*For Duck or any Wildfowl*)

3 cups breadcrumbs
1/4 cup orange juice
1/4 cup mandarin juice
2 teaspoons grated orange rind
1 orange
2 oz. butter
2 cups minced celery
1 beaten egg
Salt and pepper to taste

Dry crumbs lightly in the oven. Mix with orange and mandarin juice and orange rind. Peel orange. Separate and peel fingers and remove any pips. Add to crumb mixture. Melt butter. Stir into mixture with remaining ingredients. *Yield:* About 5 cups.

OYSTER STUFFING (Farce d'Huîtres)
(*For Turkey Crops, and Rump Steak*)

1 1/2 dozen sauce oysters
1/2 pint stale breadcrumbs
1 1/2 oz. butter
Grated nutmeg to taste
1 teaspoon minced chives
1 teaspoon minced parsley
Salt and pepper to taste
2 beaten eggs

Beard and chop oysters. Mix the crumbs with the creamed butter, nutmeg, chives, parsley and salt and pepper to taste. Add grated rind of 1/2 lemon if liked. Knead till blended. Stir in eggs and a dash of tobasco, if liked.

PRUNE AND APPLE STUFFING (Farce de Fruits)
(For a Duck or Goose)

6 tart apples
1/4 lb. prunes
2 oz. caster sugar
1 cup breadcrumbs
1/2 teaspoon crushed herbs
Salt and pepper to taste

Choose medium-sized apples. Wash prunes. Cover with cold water. Stand for 12 hours. Turn prunes and water into a saucepan. Cover. Simmer gently till soft. Add sugar. Simmer for 5 minutes, then turn into a dish. When cool, stone and quarter. Peel, quarter and core apples. Stew in 2 tablespoons of the prune juice until half-cooked. Stir in prunes and remainder of ingredients. Double quantity for a goose.

RICE STUFFING (Farce au Riz)
(For Chicken, Guinea Fowl or Beef Olives)

4 tablespoons minced bacon
2 tablespoons shallot
2 cups boiled rice
1 minced green pepper
1/2 cup stale breadcrumbs
1/2 cup minced celery
1 saltspoon ground mace
Salt and pepper to taste
1/2 cup white stock

Fry bacon lightly for 5 or 6 minutes with the shallot and a minced clove of garlic if liked. Drain off all but 1 tablespoon of the fat. Stir into it remaining ingredients. If liked, substitute tomato juice for the stock. *Yield :* About 3 cups. *To Vary :* Substitute 1/4 lb. pork sausage-meat for the bacon and add 1/2 teaspoon crushed herbs.

SAGE AND ONION STUFFING (Farce à l'Anglaise)
(For Duck, Goose or Pork)

8 large peeled onions
Salt and pepper to taste
1/2 teaspoon sugar
1/2 pint breadcrumbs
1 heaped tablespoon sage leaves
2 oz. butter

Place onions in a saucepan. Cover with cold water. Bring to the boil. Add a pinch of salt and pepper. Cover. Simmer till half tender. Drain thoroughly. Mince finely. Add salt and pepper to taste, 1/2 teaspoon made mustard, if liked, sugar, breadcrumbs and sage. Melt butter in a saucepan. Add mixture. Stir till blended, then cool and use. Enough for a goose, a brace of duck, or crown roast of pork.

SAUSAGE STUFFING (Farce aux Saucissons)
(For Game or Poultry)

2 lb. pork
6 tablespoons breadcrumbs
1/2 teaspoon minced parsley
1 minced clove of garlic
Salt and cayenne pepper to taste
Pinch of grated lemon rind
1/2 teaspoon crushed herbs
1/2 teaspoon minced sage
2 tablespoons gravy or stock
Parboiled liver of bird

Use equal quantity of lean and fat pork. Put through a meat grinder into a basin, then grind once again. Add crumbs, parsley, garlic, salt and cayenne pepper, lemon rind, herbs, sage, gravy or stock, then the minced liver of bird. Mix lightly till blended, then use. *Yield:* About 10 cups. Enough for a 10-lb. goose or turkey. *To Vary :* Substitute sausage-meat for pork.

SCOTTISH OATMEAL STUFFING (Farce d'Avoine)
(*For Boiled Fowl or Rabbit*)

3 oz. medium oatmeal
1½ oz. butter or shredded suet
1 dessertspoon minced onion
Salt and black pepper to taste
1 teaspoon minced parsley, if liked

Toast the oatmeal spread out in a baking tin in a slow oven till crisp. Remove from stove. Leave until cool. Melt butter and add or stir in suet. Add remaining ingredients. Use for filling neck of fowl and stuff body with sausage meat, if liked. Use in body of rabbit. In Scotland this stuffing is sometimes used in a deer's or ox heart.

TRUFFLE STUFFING (Farce de Truffes)
(*For Chickens or Capons*)

½ lb. truffles
¾ lb. knuckle of veal
1 chicken's liver
Salt and pepper to taste
1 beaten egg

Scrub, dry and peel truffles, reserving the peelings. Mince the knuckle of veal with the chicken's liver and the peelings. Make several slits in the chicken's skin and insert in them thin slices of truffle. Cut remainder in dice. Stir into veal mixture with salt and pepper to taste and the egg.

To Use Truffle Stuffing: Stuff prepared bird. Wrap in muslin. Chill for 2 days, but do not freeze. Turn twice daily. Spread freely with butter, and roast, basting with melted butter diluted with equal quantity of water, thrice during roasting.

VEAL STUFFING (Farce aux Fines Herbes)
(*For Poultry*)

2 cups breadcrumbs
1 dessertspoon minced onion
2-3 ozs. butter
½ teaspoon crushed herbs
1 dessertspoon minced parsley
Grated rind of ½ lemon if liked
Salt and pepper to taste
Beaten eggs or milk to taste

Mix the crumbs in a basin with the onion, butter and herbs. Knead with finger tips till blended. Moisten thoroughly with beaten egg or milk, or stock if preferred. If stuffed joint or chicken is to be served cold, use egg which gives a firmer stuffing. When stuffing chicken, I often omit the lemon rind, and add the lightly fried liver of bird. Again, I sometimes substitute ½ cup shredded celery, lightly fried with the onion, for ½ cup of the crumbs. *Yield:* About 2½ cups.

STUFFINGS FOR FISH

LOBSTER STUFFING (Farce d'Homard)

1 newly boiled hen lobster
1 large whiting
¼ lb. butter
6 oz. panada
4 egg yolks
2 egg whites
Cayenne pepper to taste

Remove meat, coral and spawn from lobster. Divide tail flesh into small pieces. Place in a small saucepan with lobster and butter to moisten. Put remainder of flesh through a wire sieve, then place in a mortar. Scrape flesh from whiting. Rub through a wire sieve. Place in mortar with

Grated nutmeg to taste
1 teaspoon anchovy paste

sieved lobster. Pound with a pestle, then gradually pound in remaining butter, panada, egg yolks and whites. When smoothly blended, pound in pepper, nutmeg and anchovy paste. Pound till perfectly blended. Use for stuffing turbans of sole or for filling halibut steaks or a fish gateau.

ROE STUFFING (Farce de Laitance)

2 oz. chopped mushrooms
1 tablespoon breadcrumbs
1 dessertspoon minced chives
1 dessertspoon minced parsley
Juice of ½ lemon
Salt and pepper to taste
1 teaspoon butter
1 large soft herring roe

Mix the mushrooms with the crumbs, chives, parsley, lemon juice and salt and pepper to taste. Melt butter in a small saucepan. Add mixture. Stir till blended. Remove from stove. Bind with soft roe or substitute 2 small hard roes. Use for stuffing herring or mackerel.

SHRIMP STUFFING (Farce de Crevettes)

½ pint picked shrimps
6 oz. breadcrumbs
1½ oz. butter
1 dessertspoon minced parsley
Salt and cayenne pepper to taste
Pinch of ground mace
1 beaten egg
1 to 2 tablespoons cream
Grated rind ¼ lemon

Mix shrimps with the crumbs. Melt fat. Add with remaining ingredients. *Yield:* About 1 pint. Use for stuffing turbans of plaice or sole or any thick fish to be baked, such as haddock or sea bream, as well as for fish steaks to be paired and baked.

Savoury Sauces

Sauce-making is considered by experts to be one of the most important branches of cookery, so I have made a special feature of sauces in this book. Some sauces furnish additional richness to a dish, or impart more flavour. Others contribute actual nutriment. There is a third type of sauce served to counteract the richness of a particular food, such as apple sauce with roast pork.

CLASSES OF SAUCES

There are many hot savoury sauces, but only three main classes. They are :
(1) *White:* This is the basis of many simple appetising white sauces.
(2) *Brown:* This is the basis of Espagnole, from which in turn, is derived Bigarade, Italian, Poivrade sauce, etc.
(3) *Cooked Egg Sauces:* Hollandaise, Mousseline, etc.
To make a simple sauce, you require good stock and a suitable thickening. To make an elaborate sauce, you also require savoury essences or extracts for flavouring, such as essence or juice of fish, meat, game or poultry, or rich stock. A combination of fish stock and milk is the usual foundation of fish sauce. Milk, or chicken or veal stock and milk, is the foundation of a good white sauce. Brown stock is the foundation of a good brown savoury sauce.

WHITE SAUCE

There are three kinds of white sauce : pouring or flowing, coating, and binding or panada. The first is an accompaniment served in a hot sauceboat. The second is used with additions for coating boiled or steamed chicken or turkey, fish loaves, boiled or steamed vegetables and for creamed dishes. The third is required for binding mixtures such as croquettes. The basis of all three is what is known as a " roux." This is a mixture of flour and melted fat. Do not let it brown when required for white sauce. Allow it to brown slightly for blonde sauce, and to become darker for brown sauce."

BASIC INGREDIENTS

POURING (Flowing)	COATING	BINDING (Panada)
¾ oz. butter	1 oz. butter	2 oz. butter
¾ oz. flour	1 oz. flour	2 oz. flour
½ pint liquid	½ pint liquid	½ pint liquid
Salt and pepper to taste	Salt and pepper to taste	Salt and pepper to taste

Melt butter in an enamel-lined saucepan. Draw pan to side. Stir in flour with a wooden spoon. Cook over slow heat for about 3 minutes, stirring constantly, till a smooth roux is formed. Draw pan again to the side, to allow roux to cool slightly, then gradually add liquid, stirring constantly, to keep a smooth texture. If you don't the mixture will " lump." Return pan to heat. Stir till boiling, then boil for about 6 minutes, so as to get the right consistency. Season with salt and pepper to taste.

NOTES ON MAKING WHITE SAUCE

(1) There is less chance of curdling if the liquid used is slightly heated.

(2) If sauce seems too thin, boil rapidly, stirring constantly, till thickness is as you require. If it seems too thick, dilute with a little of the same liquid used, stirring constantly until boiling again.

(3) To prevent a skin forming on top, cover closely with a round of kitchen paper dipped in cold water, cutting the paper so that it fits over the sauce— not the pan—then cover with pan lid.

(4) To enrich sauces, allow ½ oz. more fat in each case, or dissolve it in sauce after removing from stove. To do this, break up the butter into small pieces and beat them in one at a time to prevent the fat floating on the surface.

(5) To flavour sauces, add ½ a bay leaf, a blade of mace, a slice of onion or a clove of garlic to liquid. Soak for 1 hour, then bring to boiling point and strain before adding to roux.

(6) If cream is to be added, before using, stir it in gradually and do not allow sauce to boil again or it will curdle. If lemon juice or vinegar need to be added, add sparingly, drop by drop, stirring constantly, or the sauce will curdle.

BROWN SAUCE

1 oz. butter or margarine
½ slice onion
2 slices carrot
1 slice turnip
1 oz. flour
¾ pint brown stock or water
Salt and pepper to taste

Melt fat in a small saucepan. Add onion, carrot and turnip. Fry slowly until vegetables shrivel and onion is slightly brown. Stir in flour. Fry slowly, stirring constantly, until the roux is a rich brown shade, then draw pan to side of stove and stir in stock or water gradually. When blended, stir till boiling, then slip pan over boiling water and cook sauce for about 20 minutes, stirring frequently, and skimming as required. Season to taste. Skim again if necessary, then strain and reheat. If too thick for your taste, thin with more stock. If too thin, cook a little longer, stirring constantly. If you have to use water, flavour sauce with meat or vegetable extract to taste. Colour if necessary. *Yield:* Fully ½ pint.

COOKED EGG SAUCES

These sauces require great care. On no account must they be allowed to boil, or they will curdle.

HOLLANDAISE SAUCE (Sauce Hollandaise)

4 dessertspoons vinegar
Salt and pepper to taste
3 beaten egg yolks
2 oz. butter

Bring vinegar, salt and pepper to the boil. Boil till reduced to 2 dessertspoons, then allow to cool. Gradually beat in egg yolks, then melt and beat in butter. Stir over boiling water till sauce is smooth and thick. *Yield:* About ½ cup.

FRENCH HOLLANDAISE SAUCE
(Sauce Hollandaise à la Française)

2 egg yolks
2 oz. butter
2 tablespoons cold water
1 teaspoon lemon juice
¼ pint thick white Velouté sauce
Salt and white pepper to taste

Place egg yolks, butter, water and lemon juice in the top of a double boiler. Beat with a rotary beater over boiling water till light and thick, then gradually stir in Velouté sauce, prepared for fish. Season with salt and white pepper to taste. *Yield:* ½ pint.

To Use Hollandaise Sauce : Serve Hollandaise sauce with boiled or steamed fish, fish moulds, or with boiled asparagus, cauliflower, scorzonera, etc.

To Vary :

Anchovy: Beat in anchovy essence to taste. Serve only with fish.

Cucumber: Stir ½ pint drained chopped cucumber into French Hollandaise sauce. Serve with boiled or steamed fish.

Horseradish: Slowly stir in 3 tablespoons grated horseradish and 1½ tablespoons thick cream, whipped, into half quantity French Hollandaise sauce.

ALLEMANDE SAUCE (Sauce Allemande)

1½ oz. butter
1 oz. flour
½ pint chicken stock
Salt and white pepper to taste
Grated nutmeg to taste
1 or 2 egg yolks
1 tablespoon cream
1 teaspoon lemon juice

Dissolve 1 oz. butter in an enamel-lined saucepan. Add flour. Stir only till frothy. Do not allow to brown. Gradually stir in chicken stock. Stir till smooth and boiling. Add salt, pepper and nutmeg. Cover and simmer gently for 20 minutes over boiling water. Skim. Beat egg yolks with the cream. Gradually stir into the sauce. Divide remainder of butter into small " nuts." Add one at a time and beat till blended. Stir over boiling water till sauce thickens, but do not allow to boil. Gradually stir in lemon juice. Either put through a fine strainer or a tammy cloth. *Yield:* About 1½ gills.

BEARNAISE SAUCE

4 peeled shallots
½ gill tarragon vinegar
½ gill wine vinegar
¼ pint Béchamel sauce
3 egg yolks
2 oz. butter
Salt, pepper and mustard to taste

Chop shallots. Place in a small enamel-lined saucepan with the vinegars. Add 6 crushed white peppercorns. Bring to boil. Boil till reduced to 1 tablespoon, then strain into top of a double boiler. Stir the sauce gradually into vinegar. When blended, beat in egg yolks, one at a time, but on no account allow to boil. Stir over hot water for about ¼ hour. Remove pan from heat. Divide butter into " nuts," Whisk in one at a time, until thoroughly blended, before adding the next, or the sauce will curdle. Strain and reheat. Serve in a hot sauceboat with fried or grilled steak. *Yield :* Fully 1½ gills.

MOUSSELINE SAUCE (Sauce Mousseline)

2 egg yolks
½ gill thick cream
1 tablespoon chicken or veal stock
Pinch of grated nutmeg
Salt and pepper to taste
½ oz. butter
1 teaspoon lemon juice

Place the egg yolks in the top of a double boiler. Add cream, stock, nutmeg, salt and pepper. Whisk over boiling water till blended. Divide butter into small pats. Whisk in one at a time. Stir in lemon juice drop by drop. Serve with chicken or fish. *Yield:* Fully ½ cup.

HOT SAVOURY SAUCES

ADMIRAL SAUCE (Sauce Amiral)

½ pint melted butter
1 teaspoon chopped capers
3 chopped shallots
2 anchovy fillets
1 strip lemon rind
Juice 1 lemon
Salt and pepper to taste

When the butter is hot, add capers and shallots. Pound anchovies into a paste. Stir in a little of the butter, then stir the anchovy mixture into remainder of butter. Add lemon rind. Stir till boiling. Simmer gently until shallots are boiled down, then add lemon juice and salt and pepper to taste. Serve with boiled or steamed fish. *Yield:* About 1 pint.

APPLE SAUCE (Sauce de Pommes)

1 lb. cooking apples
2 tablespoons water
½ oz. butter
1 tablespoon brown or caster sugar

Peel, core and slice apples thinly. Place in a saucepan with the water. Cover closely. Simmer gently, stirring occasionally, till into a pulp. Beat in butter and sugar. Serve in a hot sauce boat with roast duck, goose or pork. *Yield:* About ½ pint.

ASPARAGUS SAUCE (Sauce d'Asperge)

2 dozen green asparagus sticks
¾ oz. butter
½ pint Béchamel sauce
Pinch of salt
Pepper to taste
½ teaspoon lemon juice
1 large lump of sugar

Trim and wash asparagus. Place in a saucepan. Cover with boiling salted water. Cook till tender. Throw into cold water. Soak for a moment or two, then drain well. This is best done on a kitchen cloth. Melt butter in a saucepan. Add asparagus. Fry quickly for 6 minutes. Add sauce, salt and pepper to taste. Cook over boiling water for ¼ hour. Rub through a fine sieve or tammy cloth. Reheat with sugar, stirring constantly. Remove from stove. Stir in lemon juice and a few drops of green vegetable colouring. Serve with baked, boiled or steamed fish, or use for coating fish, chicken or turkey loaves. If liked, 4 spring onions can be cooked with the asparagus. *Yield:* About ½ pint.

AURORA SAUCE (Sauce Aurore)

¾ pint Bechamel sauce
1 small peeled onion
1 mushroom
Dash of cayenne pepper
1 tablespoon anchovy essence
1 tablespoon lobster butter
½ teaspoon lemon juice
½ teaspoon tarragon vinegar

Use Béchamel sauce made with veal stock. Pour into an enamel-lined saucepan. Add onion. Peel mushroom and add only the white outside, not the brown inner lining. Stir in cayenne pepper and anchovy essence. Cover. Simmer gently for about 20 minutes, till reduced to about 1½ gills, then strain. Return to saucepan. Bring to boil. Tammy. Return to saucepan. Stir in lobster butter, lemon juice and vinegar. Stir till piping hot, but do not allow to boil. Serve hot with red mullet, soles, trout, etc. *Yield:* About 1½ gills.

SAUCE FOR REHEATING LAMB OR MUTTON: Pour 1 tablespoon vinegar into an enamel-lined saucepan. Add 2 oz. butter, ½ gill red-currant jelly, and made mustard to taste. Season with salt. Stir till boiling. Add slices of meat and reheat. *Yield:* Enough sauce when heating meat for 3 persons.

BECHAMEL SAUCE (Sauce Béchamel)

This French white sauce is called after the Marquis de Béchamel, who was Maître d'Hôtel to Louis XIV.

½ pint milk
½ stick celery
1 slice carrot
1 peeled shallot
1 blade mace
2 cloves
6 white peppercorns
1 oz. butter
1 oz. flour

Pour milk into the top of a double boiler. Dice vegetables and add with mace, cloves, and peppercorns. Cover. Stand in a warm place for 40 minutes, then strain. (If preferred, heat till nearly boiling without standing, then strain.) Melt butter in an enamel-lined saucepan. Add flour. Cook till frothy, but not brown. Gradually stir in seasoned milk. Stir till boiling, then tammy. Reheat, stirring constantly. *Yield:* About ½ pint.

To Vary: (1) Add a sprig of parsley and thyme with the bay leaf, and use half milk and half white stock.

(2) Make sauce with only ¼ pint milk. Add 2 or 3 sliced mushrooms to

vegetables. Stir in $\frac{1}{4}$ pint thick cream after straining or tammying. Reheat, stirring constantly, but do not allow to boil.

BELGIAN SAUCE (Sauce Belge)

1 set calf's brains
1 dessertspoon vinegar
Olive oil as required
1 tablespoon chopped onion or shallot
1 dessertspoon minced parsley
1 teaspoon chopped tarragon or chervil
Salt and pepper to taste
Wine vinegar to taste

Clean and place brains in boiling salted water to cover. Add vinegar. Simmer gently for about 10 minutes, skimming when necessary. Drain off water quickly. Cover with cold water. Stand for a moment or two, then drain and place in a basin. Mash with a fork, then add olive oil, drop by drop. Stir constantly or the sauce will curdle. When you have a thick smooth paste, add onion, herbs, salt and pepper to taste and from 1 to 2 tablespoons vinegar, according to taste. If wine is not obtainable, substitute chives, and use tarragon vinegar. Serve with hot boiled calf's head or with cold calf's head instead of vinaigrette sauce. *Yield:* About $\frac{1}{4}$ pint.

BIGARADE SAUCE (Sauce Bigarade)

$\frac{1}{2}$ Seville orange
$\frac{1}{2}$ pint Espagnole sauce
1 teaspoon lemon juice
$\frac{1}{4}$ pint claret
Pinch of sugar
Cayenne pepper and salt to taste

Remove rind from orange. Add a strip to the sauce. Simmer for 10 minutes, then strain. Add the juice of the $\frac{1}{2}$ orange, lemon juice, claret, sugar, cayenne pepper and salt to taste. Reheat. Serve with roast duck or goose, pork or ham. *Yield:* About $\frac{3}{4}$ pint.

To Vary: Add $\frac{1}{2}$ pint brown stock to the sauce. Simmer gently for $\frac{1}{4}$ hour. Substitute $\frac{1}{2}$ gill port wine for the claret.

BLANQUETTE SAUCE (Sauce Blanquette)

1 pint Béchamel sauce
3 egg yolks
1 teaspoon sugar
Juice of 1 lemon

Make the Béchamel sauce with the stock in which the meat it has to accompany has been cooked, instead of milk. This sauce is usually served with boiled calf's head, chicken, mutton or veal that has to be reheated before serving. When required, gradually stir in egg yolks, sugar and lemon juice. Stir till piping hot, but do not allow to boil. Pour over meat. *Yield:* About 1 pint.

BLONDE SAUCE (Sauce Blonde)

2 minced mushrooms
1 sliced medium-sized onion
1 teaspoon minced parsley
Juice of 1 lemon
3 tablespoons rich stock
$\frac{1}{2}$ gill sherry
3 egg yolks
Seasoning to taste

Put the mushrooms, onion, parsley and lemon juice in a saucepan with stock and sherry. Simmer gently for $\frac{1}{2}$ hour. Remove from heat. Pour into the top of a double boiler. Beat egg yolks. Gradually stir them into sauce. Stir over boiling water for 5 or 6 minutes until thick. Season to taste. Strain into a hot sauce boat. Serve with boiled fish. *Yield:* About $\frac{1}{2}$ pint.

BORDEAUX SAUCE (Sauce Bordelaise)

½ cup claret or port wine
2 chopped shallots
1 pint Espagnole sauce
½ oz. meat glaze
½ teaspoon minced parsley
½ teaspoon minced tarragon
½ teaspoon minced chervil

Pour wine into saucepan. Add shallot. Bring to boil. Cook rapidly till reduced to half its quantity. Stir in brown sauce. Stir till boiling. Simmer for 15 minutes. Skim well. Stir in meat glaze and herbs. Stir till boiling. Serve with beef, duck, ham or pork. *Yield:* Fully ½ pint.

BREAD SAUCE (Sauce de Pain)

1 small onion
2 cloves
½ pint milk
½ teaspoon salt
Pepper to taste
½ oz. butter
2 oz. breadcrumbs

Peel onion. Spear with the cloves. Place in an enamel-lined saucepan. Add milk. Season to taste. Bring almost to boiling point. Cover. Stand in a warm place for ½ hour, then remove onion. Add butter and breadcrumbs. Stir till blended. Cook slowly over boiling water for 10 to 15 minutes. (If a strong flavour of onion is wanted, do not remove onion until after cooking with the crumbs.) Remove from stove. Stir in a pat of butter and dish up. If a smoother sauce is wanted, knead the pat of butter with a teaspoon of flour. Add and stir till boiling. *Yield:* About ½ pint.

To Vary: Infuse a strip of lemon rind with the milk. Stir in a tablespoon of thick cream before serving.

BRETON SAUCE (Sauce Bretonne)

½ oz. butter
1 tablespoon chopped onion
¾ pint Espagnole sauce
1 tablespoon haricot bean purée
Salt and pepper to taste

Melt butter in a saucepan. Add onion. Stir over low heat till well browned, then stir in half the sauce. Gradually stir in purée, then the remainder of sauce. Bring to boil. Season with salt and pepper to taste. Simmer for 5 minutes. Rub through a fine strainer. Reheat, stirring constantly. (If liked, fry 1 clove of garlic with the butter.) Serve with boiled or braised mutton. *Yield:* About ½ pint.

BROWN MUSHROOM SAUCE (Sauce de Champignons, Brune)

½ gill Madeira, Marsala or sherry
1 tablespoon mushroom stock
1 small bottle champignons
2¼ cups jellied brown stock
Salt and pepper to taste

Pour wine into a saucepan. Add mushroom stock. Mince champignons and add. Bring to boil. Simmer till reduced to half quantity, then stir in stock. Season to taste. Stir until piping hot. Use for braised beef, hare, rabbit or veal. *Yield:* About ½ pint.

BLACK BUTTER SAUCE (Sauce Beurre Noire)

¼ lb. butter
2 tablespoons parsley leaves
2 tablespoons French vinegar
Coralline pepper to taste

Melt butter in a frying-pan, until it becomes pale brown. When it starts to smoke, throw in washed and thoroughly dried parsley. Shake pan over stove till parsley is crisp. Turn into a hot sauce-boat. Pour vinegar into pan. Boil up. Pour over butter. Sprinkle with coralline pepper. Serve with grilled mackerel or fried skate. *Yield:* About ¼ pint.

BLONDE BUTTER SAUCE (Sauce Beurre Blonde)

¼ lb. butter
Salt and pepper to taste
1 teaspoon lemon juice

Melt butter in an enamelled saucepan, but do not let it colour. Add salt and pepper to taste and lemon juice. Serve in a hot sauceboat with boiled asparagus, cauliflower or fish. *Yield:* About ¼ pint.

CLEAR BUTTER SAUCE (Sauce au Beurre)

1 oz. butter
½ oz. flour
½ pint hot water
Salt and pepper to taste
1 teaspoon lemon juice

Melt half the butter in an enamelled saucepan. Add flour. Stir till frothy, then lower heat. Cook butter and flour very slowly, stirring constantly, for 2 or 3 minutes, but remember it must not colour. Gradually stir in the hot water. Stir till boiling. Season to taste. Add lemon juice and strain through a hot pointed strainer into a hot sauce-boat. *Yield:* About ½ pint.

To Vary: When wanted for fish, flavour with anchovy essence to taste. When wanted with boiled poultry, add 2 tablespoons drained capers.

CARDINAL SAUCE (Sauce Cardinal)

½ pint Béchamel sauce
½ oz. minced lobster coral
Pinch of grated nutmeg
1 dessertspoon anchovy essence
Salt and pepper to taste
2 tablespoons thick cream

Stir a little of the sauce into the coral. Stir this into remaining sauce. Add nutmeg. Cover. Simmer gently for ¼ hour, then tammy, or sieve through a fine strainer. Reheat. Stir in anchovy essence, salt and pepper to taste, and cream. Serve with chicken or fish. *Yield:* About ½ pint.

To Vary: Substitute half fish stock for half the milk in the sauce when making cardinal sauce to serve with fish. Flavour sauce to taste with lobster butter and omit lobster coral.

CHASSEUR SAUCE (Sauce Chasseur)

½ pint Espagnole sauce
1 teaspoon lemon juice
2 teaspoons meat glaze

Pour sauce into a saucepan. Stir in lemon juice, meat glaze, and salt and pepper to taste. Stir till boiling. Simmer till reduced to half its quantity,

Salt and pepper to taste
2 tablespoons red currant jelly
1/4 pint claret or port wine
Cayenne pepper to taste
Dash of mushroom ketchup

in about 10 minutes. Add jelly, wine, cayenne pepper and ketchup. Reheat, but do not boil. Serve with hare or venison. *Yield:* About 1/2 pint.

CHEESE SAUCE (Sauce Mornay)

2 oz. butter
1 1/2 oz. flour
3/4 pint milk
1 1/2 oz. grated Gruyère or Parmesan cheese
1/4 pint cream
Salt and white pepper to taste
Dash of mustard

Melt butter in a saucepan. Add flour. When frothy, stir in milk. Stir till boiling. Simmer for 10 minutes over boiling water, stirring constantly, then add cheese. Cook for 4 or 5 minutes, still stirring. Pass through a strainer. Return to saucepan. Stir till piping hot. Remove from heat. Stir in cream, salt to taste, and freshly ground white pepper to taste, as well as mustard. Reheat, stirring constantly. Serve in a hot sauce-boat with boiled or steamed fish. Use for coating boiled cauliflower and other vegetables, and in many cheese dishes. *Yield:* 1 pint.

CHERRY SAUCE (Sauce aux Cerises)

1/2 pint consommé
1 oz. meat glaze
1/2 gill claret
2 teaspoons potato flour
1 tablespoon glacé cherries

Pour consommé into a saucepan. Cut up the glaze and add. Stir in claret. Bring to boil, stirring constantly, then thicken with the potato flour mixed to a paste with cold water. Add cherries. Boil for 5 minutes, stirring constantly. Serve with boiled tongue. *Yield:* Fully 1/2 pint.

CHESTNUT SAUCE (Sauce aux Marrons)

1/2 lb. chestnuts
3/4 pint chicken or veal stock
1 1/2 oz. butter
1 oz. flour
Salt and pepper to taste
Pinch of celery salt
3 tablespoons thick cream

Slit the thick side of chestnuts. Boil in water to cover for about 20 minutes, until the shells can be pulled away easily from the nuts. Shell. Place in a saucepan with stock. Cover. Simmer gently till tender. Mash and rub through a hair sieve. Melt butter. Stir in flour. When frothy, stir in chestnut purée. Bring to boil, stirring constantly. Season with salts and pepper to taste. If too thick, dilute with a little additional stock or milk. Stir in cream. Reheat, stirring constantly, but do not allow to boil. If liked, flavour with a few drops of sherry. Serve with boiled or roast poultry. *Yield:* Fully 1/2 pint. *Brown Chestnut Sauce:* Make with 1/2 pint Espagnole Sauce and 1/4 pint Brown Sauce.

CIDER SAUCE (Sauce de Cidre)

1/2 pint still cider
3/4 pint Espagnole sauce
2 cloves

Pour cider into a saucepan. Add sauce, cloves, mace and bay leaf. Bring to boil. Skim. Simmer, stirring occasionally, until the sauce is reduced to

1 blade mace
½ bay leaf
Salt and pepper to taste

a creamy consistency. Tammy. Reheat, stirring constantly. Serve with braised duck, ham or pork. *Yield:* About 1 pint.

CLARET SAUCE (Sauce Vincent)

1½ oz. butter
3 minced shallots
1 red pepper
½ pint brown stock
¼ pint claret
1 tablespoon chilli vinegar
1 tablespoon chutney
1 teaspoon red currant jelly

Melt butter in a saucepan. Add shallots. Slit pepper and remove seeds, then mince and add pepper. Fry slowly till butter turns brown, then add stock, claret and vinegar. Stir till boiling. Add chutney and jelly. Stir till boiling. Skim. Cover and simmer for ¼ hour, then strain. Chill. Skim again. Use for reheating any cold red meat or game. *Yield:* Fully ½ pint.

CLARET FISH SAUCE (Sauce au Vin Rouge)

6 mushrooms
6 small onions
1 clove garlic
White stock as required
½ gill claret
3 or 4 drops anchovy essence
Brown roux, if liked

Mince mushrooms, onions and garlic. Place in a saucepan. Add enough white stock to cover. Bring to boil. Cover and simmer gently till stock is richly flavoured with mushroom and onion. Strain through a jelly bag, pressing with the back of a wooden spoon as you strain, to extract the full flavour of the vegetables. Return to pan.

Add claret. Bring to boiling point. Flavour with anchovy essence. If a thick sauce is required, thicken to taste with roux before adding claret. Serve with fresh-water fish. *Yield:* About ½ pint.

CRAB SAUCE (Sauce de Crabe)

½ pint fish Velouté sauce
1 boiled medium-sized crab
1 teaspoon anchovy essence
Squeeze of lemon juice

If liked, white sauce can be substituted for the Velouté sauce. Heat sauce. Add all the meat from the crab, finely minced. Stir in anchovy essence and lemon juice. Serve with boiled or steamed white fish. *Yield:* About 1 pint.

CRANBERRY WINE SAUCE (Sauce Canneberges)

1 lb. cranberries
¼ pint water
¼ lb. light brown sugar
½ gill port wine

Pick over berries. Rinse and drain. Place in a saucepan with the water. Cook for about 10 minutes till tender. Rub through a sieve. Return to saucepan. Add sugar. Stir till dissolved.

Add port wine. Serve with roast guinea fowl, turkey or pheasant. *Yield:* About 1 pint.

CUCUMBER SAUCE (Sauce au Concombre)

1 small cucumber
1 oz. butter
½ pint Béchamel sauce

Peel cucumber. If old, remove the seeds. Melt butter in a saucepan. Add cucumber. Cover closely. Simmer gently till tender in about 25

Salt and pepper to taste
Green vegetable colouring to taste
2 tablespoons thick cream

minutes, stirring occasionally. Sieve. Heat sauce. Stir in cucumber. Season to taste. Colour a delicate green with vegetable colouring, or use sieved spinach or sorrel. Stir till piping hot. Remove from heat. Stir in cream. Serve with boiled fish. *Yield:* About ½ pint.

CURRANT SAUCE (Sauce de Groseilles)

½ pint Espagnole sauce*
½ gill red currant jelly
1 tablespoon Madeira or sherry

Heat sauce. Add jelly and wine. Stir till at boiling point. Serve with boiled or roast lamb or mutton, or with venison and other game. *Yield:* Fully ½ pint.

*Use Espagnole sauce made without an onion.

CURRY SAUCE (Sauce au Kari)

1 chopped medium-sized onion
1 chopped cooking apple
1 oz. butter or margarine
½ tablespoon curry powder
½ tablespoon flour
½ pint stock
Salt to taste
1 dessertspoon chutney
1 tablespoon desiccated coconut
1 tablespoon sultanas
½ teaspoon lemon juice
2 tablespoons milk or cream

Place onion and apple in a saucepan. Add butter or margarine. Fry onion and apple, stirring frequently, for about 7 minutes, then add curry powder and flour. Stir till blended, then stir in stock. Bring to boil, stirring constantly. Add salt, chutney, coconut and sultanas. Cover tightly. Simmer for 1 hour. When required, stir in lemon juice and milk or cream. Sieve, if liked, before using in making curries from cold game, meat or poultry. *Yield:* About ½ pint.

DEVIL SAUCE (Sauce Diable)

3 oz. butter
½ teaspoon mustard flour
Salt and pepper to taste
½ gill port wine
Juice ½ lemon
½ gill tomato juice

Melt butter in a saucepan. Stir in mustard, salt and pepper to taste, port wine, lemon juice and tomato juice. Cook till boiling. Pour over grilled beef or venison steaks, or use with meat to be devilled. If used with the latter, let the meat soak in the sauce in the oven for 5 minutes before serving. *Yield:* Fully ¼ pint.

ESPAGNOLE SAUCE (Sauce Espagnole)

1 scraped carrot
1 small peeled onion
1 peeled shallot
6 peeled mushrooms
2 oz. butter
2 oz. lean bacon or ham
1½ oz. flour
1 pint brown stock
¼ pint tomato sauce
½ gill sherry

Dice vegetables and mushrooms. Melt butter. Chop and add bacon or ham. Fry slowly for 3 or 4 minutes. Add vegetables. Fry till rich golden brown. Stir in flour then the stock. Cover when boiling. Simmer gently for ½ hour, then skim. Stir in tomato sauce, sherry and salt and pepper to taste if required. Bring again to boil and skim. Strain through a tammy cloth. Reheat if to be served as Espagnole sauce, or use as instructed in high class brown sauces. *Yield:* About 1 pint.

FINANCIER SAUCE (Sauce à la Financière)

1 oz. butter
½ oz. flour
1 pint rich brown stock
6 stoned olives
12 mushrooms
1 teaspoon lemon juice
Salt and pepper to taste
Cayenne pepper to taste

Melt butter in a saucepan. Add flour. Stir till frothy. Stir in stock. When boiling, add olives, mushrooms, lemon juice, salt and pepper and cayenne pepper to taste. Simmer gently till mushrooms are tender, stirring frequently. Serve in a hot sauce-boat with fried or grilled Hamburg steaks or meat loaves. *Yield:* 1 pint.

GENOA SAUCE (Sauce Génoise)

½ oz. butter
1 sliced onion
2 sliced shallots
½ gill red wine
½ pint Espagnole sauce
1 sprig chervil
1 sprig parsley
1 teaspoon anchovy essence
Salt and pepper to taste

Melt butter in a saucepan. Add onion and shallots. Fry slowly till clear, then add wine. Simmer till reduced to half its quantity. Stir in Espagnole sauce, chervil and parsley. Bring to boil. Simmer for ¼ hour, then strain. Season to taste with anchovy essence and salt and pepper. Serve with boiled, fried or steamed fish. *Yield:* About 1½ gills.

GREEN SAUCE (Sauce Verte)

2 sprigs parsley
2 sprigs chervil
2 sprigs tarragon
2 oz. butter
2 egg yolks
3 tablespoons stock
1 dessertspoon lemon juice
White pepper to taste
Salt to taste
2 tablespoons white sauce

Place herbs in a saucepan. Cover with salted water. Add a pinch of bicarbonate of soda. Bring to boil. Remove from heat. Stand till the herbs are slippery when you squeeze them, then drain thoroughly, squeezing off all water. Place in a mortar. Pound with ½ oz. of the butter. Place egg yolks in the top of a double boiler. Add remainder of butter, stock, using fish stock if sauce is wanted for fish, or brown for meat, and white stock for poultry. Add lemon juice, freshly ground white pepper, and salt. Stir over boiling water till sauce begins to thicken, then stir in herb purée and white sauce. Stir till piping hot, but do not allow to boil. *Yield:* About ½ cup.

HORSERADISH SAUCE (Sauce de Raifort)

½ cup grated horseradish
1½ cups milk
3 tablespoons breadcrumbs
½ teaspoon salt
Pepper to taste
1½ oz. butter

Place horseradish, milk and crumbs in the top of a double boiler. Bring to boil. Cook for 20 minutes, stirring occasionally. Stir in salt and pepper, and the butter bit by bit. Serve with boiled beef, salt or roast beef, ham or tongue. *Yield:* About ½ pint.

LEMON WINE SAUCE (Sauce au Citron)

2 oz. butter
½ pint clear brown stock
½ pint white wine
Juice ½ lemon
Snippet lemon peel
4 egg yolks

Melt butter till pale brown in an enamel-lined sauce-pan, then remove pan from stove. Cool slightly. Stir in stock, wine, lemon juice and lemon peel. Bring to boil. Simmer for ¼ hour. Remove pan from stove. Cool slightly, then stir in egg yolks gradually over boiling water. Cook, stirring constantly, until thick, but do not allow to boil. Serve in a hot sauce-boat with pigeons, widgeons or any small roasted bird. *Yield:* About 1 pint.

LOBSTER SAUCE (Sauce d'Homard)

1 hen lobster
2 oz. butter
½ pint Velouté sauce
1 tablespoon glaze
Salt and cayenne pepper to taste
1 teaspoon lemon juice
1 teaspoon anchovy essence
¼ pint thick cream

Remove flesh from claws and tail. Cut into dice. Pound coral in a mortar with butter till smooth, then rub through a hair sieve. Heat Velouté sauce almost to boiling point, stirring constantly, then add coral paste, glaze, salt and cayenne pepper to taste, lemon juice, lobster, anchovy essence and cream. Serve with boiled or steamed fish. *Yield:* Fully ¾ pint.

LYONNAISE SAUCE (Sauce Lyonnaise)

1 teaspoon meat extract
1½ gills fish stock
½ gill Madeira or sherry
½ bay leaf
6 white peppercorns
1 teaspoon chopped onion or shallot
½ oz. butter
½ oz. flour
½ gill tomato purée

Place meat extract, fish stock and wine in a sauce-pan. Add bay leaf, peppercorns, and onion or shallot. Cover. Simmer gently for 10 minutes. Strain. Melt butter in another saucepan. Stir in flour and tomato purée, then the stock from other pan. Stir till boiling. Rub through a sieve. Reheat. Season with salt to taste. Serve with fried liver, boiled, fried or grilled fish. *Yield :* About ½ pint.

MADEIRA SAUCE (Sauce Madère)

1 pint aspic jelly
½ gill Madeira
½ oz. meat glaze

Melt jelly in a saucepan. Add wine. Bring to boil. Cover and simmer for ¼ hour. Add meat glaze. Stir till dissolved. Use for coating fried scallops of veal, breasts of chicken, pork cutlets, etc., which have been fried without egging and crumbing. *Yield:* 1 pint.

MAITRE D'HOTEL SAUCE (Sauce Maître d'Hôtel)

½ pint Béchamel sauce
¼ lb. unsalted butter
1 teaspoon chopped blanched parsley
Juice ½ lemon
Salt and pepper to taste

Heat sauce to boiling point. Add butter bit by bit, stirring after each addition, until melted. Add parsley, lemon juice and salt and pepper to taste. Serve with fried or grilled fish, boiled calf's head, or veal loaf. *Yield:* Fully ½ pint.

MARROW SAUCE (Sauce Moelle)

1/4 pint white wine
1 small peeled onion
1/4 pint brown stock
1/2 pint Espagnole sauce
Parboiled beef marrow to taste

Pour wine into a saucepan. Chop onion, or use 2 chopped shallots, and add. Cover. Simmer gently till reduced to half its quantity. Stir in stock and Espagnole sauce. Stir till boiling and thick, then strain. Reheat, stirring constantly, then slice in beef marrow to taste. Serve with steaks. *Yield:* About 3/4 pint.

MUSSEL SAUCE (Sauce de Moules)

2 oz. butter
1 1/2 oz. flour
3/4 pint fish stock
Salt and white pepper to taste
12 trimmed mussels
2 teaspoons anchovy essence
1 teaspoon lemon juice
1 or 2 tablespoons thick cream

Melt butter in a saucepan. Add flour. Stir till frothy. Gradually stir in stock. Stir till boiling. Simmer for 10 minutes, stirring constantly, then tammy. Return to saucepan. Season with salt and pepper to taste. Add mussels, freed from beards and weed, anchovy essence, lemon juice and thick cream to taste. Stir till boiling. Simmer for 5 minutes, then serve with boiled, steamed or fried fish. *Yield :* 3/4 pint.

BROWN MUSSEL SAUCE (Sauce de Moules, Brune)

1/4 pint fish stock
1/4 pint Espagnole sauce
1/2 gill Madeira
2 teaspoons lemon juice
Salt and white pepper to taste
1 tablespoon potato flour
12 trimmed mussels

Pour the stock and sauce into a saucepan. Add Madeira, lemon juice and salt and pepper to taste. Cream potato flour with cold stock. Stir into sauce. When boiling, skim well and simmer for 10 minutes, stirring constantly, then add mussels. Serve with boiled, fried or steamed fish. *Yield:* 1/2 pint.

MUSTARD SAUCE (Sauce Moutarde)

2 oz. butter
1 tablespoon flour
1 teaspoon English mustard
1 teaspoon French mustard
1/2 pint water
1 dessertspoon vinegar
Salt and pepper to taste
Pinch of caster sugar
2 tablespoons thick cream

Melt butter in a saucepan. Stir in flour and mustards. When frothy, stir in water and vinegar, salt and pepper to taste, and sugar. Stir till boiling. Rub through a hair sieve. Reheat, stirring constantly, then stir in cream. Serve in a hot sauce-boat with fried or grilled herrings or mackerel, or with pork. *Yield:* 1/2 pint.

NORMANDY SAUCE (Sauce Normande)

2 oz. butter
1 oz. flour
1 pint veal stock
2 egg yolks
1 teaspoon lemon juice

This sauce can either be made with veal stock, or with fish stock made from the bones of the fish which sauce is to accompany, or with oysters or mussel stock, and mushrooms. In that case, use half fish stock and half white stock. Melt half the butter in an enamel saucepan. Add flour. Stir till frothy, then gradually stir in stock. When smooth and boiling, simmer for 10 minutes. Skim well.

Bind with egg yolks. Stir in remainder of butter bit by bit till all is melted, then stir in lemon juice. Tammy. Serve with poached fillets of fish, or use for making sole à la Normande, in which case sole, oyster, mussel or mushroom stock should be used as well as white stock. *Yield:* 1 pint.

OLIVE SAUCE (Sauce aux Olives)

½ pint Espagnole sauce
¼ pint rich brown stock
1½ dozen small olives
1 teaspoon lemon juice

Pour sauce and stock into a saucepan. Peel the olives round and round, so that each gives you a ribbon of olive. Reshape each peeling into an olive. Throw into cold water. Bring to boil. Drain thoroughly. Heat sauce and stock to boiling point. Add olives. Simmer gently for 30 minutes. Stir in lemon juice. Season with salt and pepper to taste. Use when reheating meat or poultry. *Yield:* About ½ pint.

ONION SAUCE (Sauce Soubise)

3 medium-sized onions
½ pint Béchamel or white sauce
Pinch of ground mace or nutmeg
Salt and pepper to taste
Pinch of sugar
¼-½ gill thick cream

Peel and simmer onions in a little water till soft. Rub through a fine sieve. Heat Béchamel or white sauce. Stir in onion purée, ground mace or nutmeg, salt and pepper to taste and sugar. Heat. Remove from stove and gradually add cream. Serve with boiled mutton, chicken, or tripe. *Yield:* ½ pint.

OYSTER SAUCE (Sauce d'Huîtres)

½ pint Béchamel sauce
12 canned oysters
1 teaspoon lemon juice
1 or 2 tablespoons thick cream

Heat Béchamel sauce. Rinse and beard oysters. If large, divide each in three. Add to sauce, and strain in a little of the liquor—just enough to give you a creamy sauce. Stir in lemon juice and cream. Serve with boiled or steamed fish. *Yield:* About ½ pint.

PARISIAN SAUCE (Sauce Parisienne)

1 oz. butter
¼ pint sherry
1 oz. glaze
1 tablespoon chopped mushrooms or truffles
½ pint brown sauce

Place all the ingredients, except for the sauce, in a saucepan. Simmer for 5 minutes. Stir in brown sauce. When boiling, simmer until sauce coats the back of spoon. Strain. Reheat. Serve with fried or grilled steaks. *Yield:* About ½ pint.

PIQUANT SAUCE (Sauce Piquante)

½ pint Espagnole sauce
2 tablespoons wine vinegar
1 tablespoon minced onion or shallot

Put sauce on to heat. Pour vinegar into a small enamel saucepan. Add onion. Boil till reduced to half its quantity, then stir into brown sauce.

1 tablespoon halved capers
1 tablespoon chopped gherkins
Salt and pepper to taste

Add remainder of ingredients. Bring to boil. Simmer gently for 5 minutes, stirring constantly. Serve with fried or grilled pork chops, or use in pork entrées. *Yield:* About ¼ pint.

POIVRADE SAUCE (Sauce Poivrade)

2 sliced carrots
2 sliced onions
1 sliced shallot
2 sliced leeks
3 sliced tomatoes
1 head celery
1 clove garlic
6 whole cloves
1 blade mace
24 black peppercorns
1 bouquet garni
¼ lb. lean ham
1 oz. butter
½ pint vinegar
3 oz. flour
3 pints stock

Rinse vegetables. Trim, scrape, wash and shred celery. Place all vegetables in a large saucepan. Slice and add garlic, spices, herbs, and ham, and butter. Heat slowly till butter melts, then fry gently until vegetables are light brown and fat is absorbed. Add vinegar. Boil till reduced to half its quantity. Stir in flour and stock. When boiling, simmer gently for 1 hour. Tammy. Season with salt and pepper to taste. *Yield:* About 1½ pints.

REFORME SAUCE (Sauce Réforme)

1 small peeled onion
1 tablespoon vinegar
½ pint rich brown stock
2 tablespoons Worcester sauce
2 tablespoons Harvey sauce
2 tablespoons piquant sauce
3 tablespoons red currant jelly
Juice ½ lemon
1 dessertspoon potato flour
1 cup port wine

Slice onion into a saucepan. Add vinegar. Simmer till all the vinegar has evaporated, then stir in stock, sauces, jelly and lemon juice. When blended, cream potato flour with cold water and stir into sauce. Stir till boiling. Simmer for 10 minutes, stirring constantly, then skim and strain. Reheat with port wine, but do not allow to boil. Serve with mutton chops or cutlets. *Yield:* 1 pint.

SALMI SAUCE (Sauce Salmi)

2 peeled shallots
1½ oz. butter
1 lb. cooked game bones
½ gill port wine
¼ pint game stock
½ pint Espagnole sauce
1 teaspoon red currant jelly
Salt and pepper to taste

Chop shallots. Melt butter in a saucepan. Add shallots. Fry till pale brown. Chop game bones. Add to the shallots. Fry for a moment or two, then add wine. Cover. Simmer gently for 5 minutes. Add stock and sauce. Stir till boiling. Pour into the top of a double boiler, and simmer over boiling water from 10 to 15 minutes, stirring occasionally. Skim. Strain. Return to pan. Stir in jelly. Season to taste. Use for reheating left-over game or wild fowl. *Yield:* About ¾ pint.

SEVILLE SAUCE (Sauce Seville)

Bones of a chicken
1 oz. butter
½ tablespoon chopped onion
1 oz. flour
½ bay leaf
Pinch of crushed thyme
1 pint chicken stock
1 tomato
2 oz. mushrooms
6 drops lemon juice
½ gill sherry

Rinse bones. Melt butter in a saucepan. Add onion. Fry slowly for 2 or 3 minutes. Add flour. Stir till frothy, and flour turns pale brown, then stir in bay leaf, thyme and stock. Slice and add tomato. Peel, slice and add mushrooms. Stir till boiling. Cook, stirring frequently, till mixture is reduced to ½ pint. Remove from stove. Stir in lemon juice and sherry. Strain. Reheat, but do not allow to boil. Serve with chicken or game loaf. *Yield:* ½ pint.

SHRIMP SAUCE (Sauce d'Écrevisses)

1 pint Béchamel sauce
½ pint freshly boiled shrimps
1 tablespoon thick cream
Cayenne pepper to taste

Heat sauce to boiling point over boiling water. Pound 8 of the shrimps to a paste. Rub through a fine sieve. Stir into sauce. Add remainder of shrimps. Simmer for 2 minutes, stirring constantly, then remove from heat and stir in cream. Season with cayenne pepper to taste. Serve with any boiled or steamed white fish. *Yield :* 1 pint.

SUPREME SAUCE (Sauce Suprême)

2½ oz. butter
1¼ oz. flour
1 pint white stock
2 oz. mushroom peelings
1 bouquet garni
6 white peppercorns
Salt to taste
½ pint cream

Melt 1½ oz. butter in an enamel saucepan. Stir in flour. When frothy, stir in stock. Cook over stove till boiling, stirring constantly, then add mushroom peelings, herbs, peppercorns and salt. Pour into top of a double boiler. Cover. Simmer over hot water for about 25 minutes. Pour through a fine strainer into another enamel saucepan. Gradually stir in cream. Stir over stove till piping hot, but do not allow to boil, then add remainder of butter, a small bit at a time, allowing each bit to melt before adding the next, or the sauce will oil. Use with chicken or veal. *Yield:* About 1 pint.

VELVET SAUCE (Sauce Velouté)

1½ oz. butter
1½ oz. flour
1 pint white stock
6 white peppercorns
Peelings from a ¼ lb. mushrooms
Small bouquet garni
Salt to taste

Melt butter in a saucepan. Stir in flour. Cook till frothy, but not discoloured. Gradually add stock. Stir till smooth and boiling. Add peppercorns, mushroom peelings, bouquet garni and salt to taste. Simmer very gently for 30 minutes, then strain and use.

Glaze Sauce : Dissolve 1 oz. glaze in ½ pint brown clear stock. Simmer until reduced to about ¼ pint then strain.

TOMATO SAUCE (Sauce de Tomates)

1 small peeled onion
1 small scraped carrot
2 oz. lean ham
1 oz. butter
2 lb. sliced tomatoes
1 sprig parsley
1 sprig thyme
6 black peppercorns
Salt to taste
½ oz. cornflour

Slice onion and carrot. Chop ham. Melt butter in a saucepan. Add onion, carrot and ham. Fry slowly for 5 minutes, then add tomatoes, herbs, peppercorns, and salt. Simmer for 10 minutes. Rub through a hair sieve. Reheat, stirring constantly. Cream corn-flour with cold stock. Stir into sauce. Stir till boiling. Boil for 3 or 4 minutes, stirring constantly. *Yield:* About ½ pint.

COLD SAUCES

CHANTILLY SAUCE (Sauce Chantilly)

1 tablespoon grated horse-radish
¼ pint mayonnaise
¼ pint stewed apple
2 tablespoons thick cream

Stir horseradish into mayonnaise. When blended, stir in apple and cream. Season to taste with salt and pepper. (If liked, cream can be whipped before adding.) Serve with cold fish, asparagus or poultry. *Yield:* ½ pint.

Chaudfroid sauces are used for garnishing or coating cold entrées of game, poultry, tongues, galantines, eggs, etc.

BLONDE CHAUDFROID SAUCE (Sauce Chaudfroid, Blonde)

½ oz. powdered gelatine
¼ pint aspic jelly
¼ pint Velouté sauce
¼ gill Espagnole sauce
1 tablespoon Graves
½ gill thick cream
Salt and pepper to taste

Melt gelatine in the aspic jelly in the top of a double boiler over boiling water. Pour sauces into an enamel saucepan. Heat till nearly boiling, then remove from heat. Gradually stir in melted aspic. Pour through a fine strainer into a basin. Cool slightly, then stir in cream and season to taste. Use for coating galantines of veal, joints of chicken, guinea fowl, etc. *Yield:* 2¾ gills.

BROWN CHAUDFROID SAUCE (Sauce Chaudfroid, Brune)

½ pint brown sauce
¼ oz. powdered gelatine
1½ gills aspic jelly
1 tablespoon Madeira or sherry
Salt and pepper to taste

Heat sauce in an enamel saucepan. Melt gelatine in aspic jelly in top of a double boiler over boiling water. Add Madeira or sherry. Simmer for 5 minutes, stirring constantly, then strain. Add salt and pepper to taste. Use for coating fillets of beef, joints of game, beef and game galantines. *Yield:* 3½ gills.

GREEN CHAUDFROID SAUCE (Sauce Chaudfroid, Verte)

1 tablespoon boiled spinach
½ pint sauce suprême
¼ oz. powdered gelatine

Sieve spinach. Stir in sauce. Melt gelatine and aspic jelly in top of a double boiler over boiling water, then stir into sauce. Return to double

¼ pint aspic jelly
½ gill cream
Green vegetable colouring

boiler. Stir till tepid. Add cream, then colour to taste. Use for coating cutlets, eggs, fish and joints of chicken. *Yield:* 1 pint.

PINK CHAUDFROID SAUCE (Sauce Chaudfroid, Rosé) : Follow recipe for Green Chaudfroid Sauce, substituting Velouté Sauce for the Sauce Suprème, and colouring with paprika instead of spinach and green vegetable colouring. Use for coating lamb or veal cutlets, eggs, fish, joints of game, etc.

WHITE CHAUDFROID SAUCE (Sauce Chaudfroid, Blanche)

½ pint sauce suprème
¼ oz. powdered gelatine
¼ pint aspic jelly
¼ pint thick cream
Salt to taste

Pour sauce into an enamel saucepan. Melt gelatine with aspic jelly. Stir gradually into the sauce. When blended, rub through a hair sieve or fine strainer. Stir in cream. Season to taste with salt. Use for coating joints of chicken, cutlets, cooked eggs, galantines of chicken, rabbit or veal, joints of rabbit, white fish, etc. *Yield:* 1 pint.

CUCUMBER SAUCE (Sauce au Concombre)

½ medium-sized cucumber
¼ pint white sauce
½ gill mayonnaise
½ gill cream
Salt and pepper to taste

Peel and slice cucumber. Place in saucepan. Cover with boiling water. Simmer till tender. Drain well. Rub through a hair sieve. Stir purée into sauce. Simmer till thick, stirring constantly, then turn into a basin. Leave till cold. Stir in mayonnaise, cream, salt and pepper to taste, a dash of celery salt if liked, and green vegetable colouring to taste. Serve with cold salmon or lobster. *Yield:* About ½ pint.

CUMBERLAND SAUCE (Sauce Cumberland)

Rind of 1 lemon
Rind of 1 orange
½ gill water
Juice of 1 orange or mandarin
Juice of 1 lemon
½ teaspoon made mustard
1 tablespoon vinegar
½ gill port wine
2 tablespoons red currant jelly

Wash lemon and orange and pare off rind very thinly. Shred. Place in a saucepan with water. Bring to boil. Boil for 5 minutes. Drain. Return to pan. Add remaining ingredients. Stir till boiling. Simmer for 2 minutes. Chill. Serve in a glass dish with game. *Yield:* About ¼ pint.

CRANBERRY SAUCE (Sauce Canneberges)

1 lb. cranberries
¾ lb. sugar
2 cups water

Pick over cranberries. Rinse in a colander under the cold water tap. Drain. Place berries with sugar and water in a large saucepan. Bring to the boil. Cover. Simmer slowly until skins break, in about 10 minutes. Skim. Pour into a glass dish. Serve with roast turkey. *Yield:* About 4 cups.

To Vary: (1) If wanted to jelly, allow 1 lb. sugar and boil to setting point, in about 18 minutes.

EGG SAUCE (Sauce d'Oeufs)

4 hard-boiled egg yolks
Dash of paprika
¼ teaspoon salt
¼ lb. butter
1½ tablespoons thick cream
1½ teaspoons lemon juice

Rub egg yolks to a paste. Stir in paprika and salt. Beat butter to a cream. Gradually work into the egg yolks with a wooden spoon, then beat in cream and lemon juice. Use for coating boiled asparagus, cauliflower, onions, etc. *Yield:* About 1 cup.

To Vary: Add 1 heaped teaspoon minced chives or parsley.

HORSERADISH SAUCE (Sauce Raifort)

2 tablespoons grated horse-radish
½ teaspoon caster sugar
1 saltspoon dry mustard
Salt and cayenne pepper to taste
1-2 dessertspoons tarragon vinegar
¼ pint whipped cream

Mix horseradish with sugar. Stir in mustard, salt and cayenne pepper to taste, and vinegar. Fold in cream. Whisk very lightly. Chill. Serve with cold boiled or roast beef. *Yield:* About 1¼ gills.

To Vary: Substitute 1 teaspoon lemon juice for the vinegar, and thick sour cream, if liked, for whipped cream.

MINT SAUCE (Sauce à la Menthe)

This sauce can either be made with vinegar or with vinegar and water.

4 tablespoons finely chopped mint
2 tablespoons brown sugar
½ pint wine vinegar

Wash and dry mint before chopping. Mix with sugar and vinegar. Stand for 2 or 3 hours, stirring occasionally, till the sugar is dissolved. Chill. Serve with roast lamb. *Yield:* 3 cups.

MOUSSELINE SAUCE (Sauce Mousseline)

2 hard-boiled egg yolks
2 anchovy fillets
2 tablespoons boiled spinach
1 tablespoon parsley
½ gill cold Béchamel sauce
¼ pint mayonnaise
½ gill cream
Salt and cayenne pepper to taste

Pound yolks in a mortar with anchovy fillets and spinach. Soak parsley in boiling salted water for 2 minutes, then drain thoroughly. When cold, pound with the egg yolks till blended. Rub through a hair sieve into a basin. Stir in sauce and mayonnaise. Beat cream only till fluffy, then fold into sauce with salt and cayenne pepper to taste. Serve with boiled or steamed fish. *Yield:* About ½ pint.

QUICK MOUSSELINE SAUCE: Whip ¼ pint of liquefied aspic jelly till fluffy, then gradually whip in ½ pint cream. When thickened, lightly stir in ½ pint mayonnaise flavoured with tarragon vinegar. Chill. Serve with asparagus or fish.

MUSTARD CREAM (Sauce au Moutarde)

¼ pint thick cream
1½ tablespoons made mustard
1 dessertspoon grated horse-radish

Whip cream till fluffy. Fold in mustard and horseradish. Place in a glass dish. Serve with cold ham or tongue. *Yield:* About ¼ pint.

REGINA SAUCE (Sauce Regina)

1 lb. tomatoes
Salt and white pepper to taste
½ teaspoon caster sugar
½ cup brown stock
½ pint mayonnaise

Wash and slice tomatoes into a saucepan. Add salt, pepper, sugar and stock. Cook over slow heat, stirring frequently, until into a thick purée. Rub through a hair sieve. Leave till quite cold, then gradually beat into thick mayonnaise sauce. Serve with cold meat loaf. *Yield:* About ¾ pint.

SWEDISH SAUCE (Sauce Suedoise)

¼ pint white sauce
¼ pint mayonnaise
¼ pint thick cream
Grated horseradish to taste
Salt and cayenne pepper to taste
Chopped hot pickle to taste

Mix all ingredients together in order given. Chill. Serve with salmon or trout. *Yield:* ¾ pint.
  To Vary: Stir 1 tablespoon grated horseradish and 1 teaspoon mustard into ¼ pint mayonnaise. When blended, fold in 1 to 2 tablespoons whipped cream. Serve at once with hot or cold boiled salmon. If liked, this can be frozen in blocks in an ice tray. Serve with boiled or steamed salmon.

TARTARE SAUCE (Sauce Tartare)

¼ pint mayonnaise
1 teaspoon minced parsley
1 teaspoon chopped gherkins
1 teaspoon minced capers
½ teaspoon minced chervil
½ teaspoon minced tarragon

Use thick mayonnaise. Stir in parsley, gherkins, capers, chervil and tarragon. Serve with boiled or fried fish. *Yield:* Fully ¼ pint.
  To Vary: Stir parsley and capers into ¾ pint mayonnaise flavoured with a dessertspoon of chilli vinegar when mixing. Add 6 diced fillets of anchovy, 1 teaspoon lemon juice, salt and white pepper to taste, and omit gherkins, capers, chervil and tarragon.

VINAIGRETTE SAUCE (Sauce Vinaigrette)

¼ pint olive oil
Salt and pepper to taste
¼ pint tarragon vinegar
2½ teaspoons minced shallot
1 tablespoon minced gherkin
2½ teaspoons minced parsley

Mix oil with salt and pepper to taste in a basin. Gradually beat in vinegar. Stir in shallot, gherkin and parsley. Serve with boiled calf's head, or cold asparagus or French artichokes. *Yield:* About ½ pint.

WATERCRESS SAUCE (Sauce Ruisseau)

4 oz. breadcrumbs
¼ pint thick cream
1 bunch watercress
4 or 5 drops tarragon vinegar

Soak crumbs in cream for 15 minutes. Wash watercress thoroughly in several waters, then pick off leaves. Toss in a cloth till dry. Pound in a mortar with cream and crumbs. Flavour with the tarragon vinegar. Rub through a hair sieve. Chill. Serve with cold roast game. *Yield:* Fully ¼ pint.

GRAVY

There are two ways of making a simple gravy :

1.   Drain off all the clear fat from the baking tin. Add stock or water and salt and pepper to taste, to the meat essence that remains. Stir till boiling. Boil for 2 or 3 minutes, then strain into a hot sauceboat. If forced to use water, add a drop or two of meat extract if the gravy needs more flavour. If any fat remains after boiling, skim with kitchen paper before dishing up.

2.   Drain off fat, then add 1 tablespoon flour to essence in tin. Stir over heat till brown, then draw tin to side of stove, and stir in ½ pint stock or water. Return to stove. Stir till boiling. Simmer for 5 minutes. Season to taste, then dish up. Add meat extract or a meat cube if necessary.

HINTS ON MAKING GRAVY

1.   To be sure of having a richly-coloured gravy, add 1 or 2 lumps of sugar, according to size of joint, before roasting at a slow temperature. (If you prefer to roast at a high temperature, omit sugar as it will burn, and colour with browning or caramel if necessary.)

2.   Serve thin gravies for preference with un-stuffed joints.

3.   Serve thickened gravies with stuffed joints, allowing 1 tablespoon fat and 1 tablespoon flour to ½ pint stock or water, when a very thick gravy is wanted, otherwise dilute with 1 pint stock or water.

4.   Gravy for serving with roast veal can be made with sour or fresh cream in place of stock and thickening.

5.   Arrowroot, cornflour, flour, potato or rice flour can be used for thickening gravies.

6.   When a light gravy is wanted for white meat such as poultry or veal, dilute with white stock, and enrich with cream if liked.

UNTHICKENED GRAVY (For Beef, Mutton or Pork)

2 tablespoons meat essence
 and particles
½ pint boiling stock or water
Salt and pepper to taste

Carefully strain off all fat from baking tin into a basin. Scrape any of the particles into the essence in tin. Gradually stir in liquid. Bring to boil. Season to taste with salt and pepper. Strain into a hot sauceboat. If for roast veal, stir 1 tablespoon flour into the meat essence in pan. When the mixture froths, gradually stir in veal stock or water. Bring to boil, stirring constantly. Season to taste with salt and pepper. Boil for 3 minutes, still stirring. Serve in a hot sauceboat. (If the joint was floured before roasting, only use ½ tablespoon flour.)

Wine Gravy : Stir 1 glass port wine (½ gill), into 1 pint unthickened gravy with a teaspoon of lemon juice and stir till piping hot, but do not allow to boil. Serve with roast teal, widgeon or wild duck.

THICKENED GRAVY (For Stuffed Joints)

1 tablespoon dripping
1 tablespoon flour
½ pint tepid stock or water
Salt and pepper to taste
1 tablespoon chilli vinegar

Drain off all clear dripping until only 1 tablespoon of the dripping remains in roasting tin. Stir in flour. When smoothly blended, stir in stock or water. Stir till boiling. Simmer for 3 minutes, stirring constantly. Season and strain into a hot sauceboat. If a very dark gravy is wanted, fry the flour in the dripping, stirring constantly until brown.

Chestnut Gravy : Omit flour from " Thickened Gravy." Stir in enough sieved, boiled chestnuts to make a gravy of creamy consistency before seasoning. This is approximately ¾ cup purée to 2 cups thin gravy. Serve with chicken, guinea fowl, pheasant or turkey.

Giblet Gravy : Follow recipe for " Chestnut Gravy," but substitute minced stewed giblets for the chestnuts. Serve with chicken or turkey.

Orange Gravy : Flavour " Thickened Gravy " to taste with orange juice in the proportion of the juice from half a large bitter orange to ½ pint gravy. Serve with beef or mutton.

Orange and Wine Gravy : Follow recipe for " Orange Gravy," but substitute 1 tablespoon wine for a tablespoon of the stock or water in " Thickened Gravy." Serve with wild duck.

Tomato Gravy : Stir 2 tablespoons meat essence, into 2 tablespoons flour until flour is pale brown, then stir in ½ pint sieved stewed tomatoes, and ½ pint water. Stir till boiling. Boil for 5 minutes, stirring constantly. Season to taste with salt and pepper. Serve in a hot sauceboat. To vary, substitute 1½ cups tomato juice for the tomato purée. Add minced parsley or green pepper to taste. Serve with hamburg steaks, fried or grilled rump steak or lamb patties, or use for coating baked meat loaf.

Cold diced boiled chicken, fried mushrooms and mayonnaise, garnished with lettuce.

Indian Vegetable Salad, garnished. *See page* 463.

Mint Jellies. *See page* 877.

Garnished Stuffed Tomato Salads, on a bed of watercress. *See page* 462.

(*Top Left*)
Garnish Pork and Vegetable Salad with crisp heart of lettuce leaves. *See page 469.*

(*Top Right*)
Unmould Mousse of Chicken on to a dish lined with crisp lettuce and watercress. Garnish with slices of radish. *See page 324.*

(*Bottom Left*)
Garnish Cider Vegetable Salads with crisp heart of lettuce leaves. *See page 476.*

(*Bottom Right*)
Arrange Russian Salad in a border of curly endive, garnished with slices of hard-boiled egg. *See page 460.*

Savoury Butters

I have given an alphabetical list of recipes for savoury butters, as these butters have many uses. Add a pat of one of them to a savoury sauce after removing the saucepan from the stove, as for example, a pat of crayfish, lobster, prawn or shrimp butter to white sauce to be served with fish. This not only gives you a quick sauce, but colours, enriches and mellows it. Savoury butters are helpful for decorating cold glazed meats, or for garnishing grilled steaks, kidneys and other meats at the moment of serving. The butters can also be used for spreading bread for canapés and sandwiches. When making a choice select a butter that blends with the filling or spread, for example, anchovy or lobster with fish, horseradish with beef, ham with chicken. Store any butter left over in a covered container in the refrigerator.

For Sauces: Always add butter after removing pan containing sauce from stove.

ANCHOVY BUTTER (Beurre d'Anchois)

2 oz. butter
1 teaspoon anchovy paste
Squeeze of lemon juice
Squeeze of onion juice

Beat butter to a cream in a basin. Beat in remaining ingredients.

To Vary: Increase anchovy paste to 1 oz. Omit onion juice and allow juice of $\frac{1}{2}$ lemon. Use for garnishing hot grilled fish, steaks or savoury canapés.

CAMEMBERT CHEESE BUTTER (Beurre de Camembert)

1 ripe Camembert cheese
1 oz. butter
3 dashes tobasco
3 drops Yorkshire Relish
Paprika to taste

Peel and beat cheese in basin with the butter till blended. Stir in tobasco, Yorkshire relish and from ¼ to ½ teaspoon paprika to taste. Rub through fine sieve. Use as a spread for celery, lettuce, radish, onion, olive or watercress sandwiches or canapés.

CAVIARE BUTTER (Beurre à la Russe)

¼ lb. butter
2 to 4 oz. caviar
¾ teaspoon lemon juice
Cayenne pepper to taste

Beat butter to a cream in a basin. Beat in caviare to taste, lemon juice, and cayenne pepper to taste. Sieve, if liked. Enough for 3 dozen small sandwiches or canapés.

CORAL BUTTER (Beurre Rouge)

2 oz. butter
Coralline pepper or 1 lobster coral
Salt to taste

Pound butter till creamy in a mortar with coralline pepper or dried lobster coral and salt to taste, and colour butter pink. Rub through a fine sieve. Use for colouring lobster bisque, lobster cream, soufflé, etc.

DEVILLED BUTTER (Beurre à la Diable)

2 oz. butter
½ teaspoon curry powder
½ saltspoon black pepper
½ teaspoon paprika
Pinch of cayenne pepper

Cream butter. Beat in the seasonings till thoroughly blended. If liked, substitute a third of a teaspoon of curry paste for the powder, and add ½ teaspoon of chutney and a squeeze of lemon juice. Spread on a plate, ¼ inch thick. Chill.

Cut in ¼ or ½ inch squares. Use for garnishing grilled kidneys or meat.

GREEN HERB BUTTER (Beurre Ravigote)

1 oz. parsley
2 oz. tarragon
½ oz. chervil
½ oz. chives
2 oz. spinach
3 peeled shallots
¼ lb. butter
Salt and pepper to taste

Wash the herbs and spinach. Cover with boiling water, then plunge into cold. Drain thoroughly. Pound together with a pestle in a mortar or wooden bowl. Mince shallots. Fry in ½ oz. of the butter till slightly coloured. Turn into the herb purée. Pound well, then gradually pound in the butter and salt and pepper, cayenne, if preferred, to taste.

HAM BUTTER (Beurre au Jambon)

3 oz. lean boiled ham
2 oz. butter
1 tablespoon cream
Pinch grated nutmeg
Cayenne pepper to taste

Mince ham. Pound in a mortar with the butter, cream, nutmeg and cayenne pepper till blended. If liked, with a pinch of mustard as well. Sieve. Use as a sandwich spread or for garnishing. Enough for 2 dozen canapés.

HORSERADISH BUTTER (Beurre de Raifort)

2 tablespoons grated horseradish
2 oz. butter
Squeeze of lemon juice
Salt to taste

Place horseradish in a mortar. Cream butter and add to horseradish with lemon juice and salt to taste. Pound till blended. Sieve. Use as a garnish or as a sandwich spread with a beef or venison filling.

MAITRE D'HOTEL BUTTER (Beurre Maître d'Hôtel)

3 oz. butter
1 tablespoon minced parsley
1 tablespoon lemon juice
Salt and cayenne pepper to
taste

Cream butter. Blanch and mince parsley. Pound it into butter, then beat in lemon juice, drop by drop, adding more if wanted sharper. Season to taste. Spread $\frac{1}{4}$ inch thick on a plate. Chill. Cut in squares.

MINT BUTTER (Beurre de Menthe)

¼ lb. butter
1½ teaspoons lemon juice
Cayenne pepper to taste
Salt to taste
1 tablespoon minced blanched
mint

Cream butter. Gradually beat in lemon juice, seasonings, and mint. With butter hands, shape into balls the size of small marbles. Use for garnishing grilled lamb or mutton chops. Appetizing spread for sandwiches with a lamb or mutton filling.

MONTPELIER BUTTER (Beurre Montpélier)

2 oz. spinach
1 oz. parsley
¼ oz. chives
¼ oz. burnet
¼ oz. chervil
¼ oz. tarragon
6 hard-boiled egg yolks
2 anchovies
1 teaspoon capers
2 gherkins
¼ lb. butter

Blanch the spinach and herbs. Drain thoroughly. Pound in a mortar with the egg yolks. Bone anchovies if not using fillets. Mince with the capers and gherkins and add to herbs. Pound till blended, then gradually pound in butter and salt and cayenne pepper to taste. Sieve. Use for garnishing.

ONION BUTTER (Beurre d'Oignons)

½ cup creamed butter
½ cup minced spring onions

Mix the butter with the onions, taking care that no green part of the stems is included. Pound till blended. Season with salt if necessary, and with cayenne pepper to taste. Use as a garnish for steaks, meat and game cakes, etc.

PERIGUEUX BUTTER (Beurre Périgueux)

5 or 6 truffles
Madeira or sherry when required

Peel, trim and mince truffles. Place in a small saucepan. Add Madeira or sherry. Simerm gently for 5 minutes. Leave till cool. Pound in

1/4 lb. butter
1/2 to 1 fillet of anchovy

a mortar with the butter and anchovy or anchovy essence if preferred.

PROVENCAL BUTTER (Beurre de Provence)

2 oz. butter
1 teaspoon wine vinegar
1 teaspoon made mustard
1 teaspoon anchovy paste
2 teaspoons grated Roquefort cheese

Cream butter in a small basin. Add vinegar, mustard, anchovy paste, and cheese. Pound in, if liked, 2 teaspoons minced parsley, 1 dessertspoon lemon juice and salt and cayenne papper to taste. Use for garnishing grilled fish, or as a spread for salad sandwiches.

SHRIMP BUTTER (Beurre de Crevettes)

2 oz. butter
Salt and cayenne pepper to taste
3 tablespoons minced shrimps
Pinch of ground mace

Beat butter to a cream in a small basin. Beat in salt and cayenne pepper to taste, shrimps, and mace, or substitute grated nutmeg for the mace. Pound till blended. Use for piping on cold fish dishes, or make into balls the size of small marbles for garnishing fried or grilled fish or fillets of fish, or use as a spread for canapés or sandwiches to be used with fish.

SMOKED SALMON BUTTER (Beurre de Saumon, fumé)

1/4 lb. butter
2 tablespoons minced smoked salmon
1/4 teaspoon lemon juice
1/2 teaspoon grated horseradish

Cream butter in a mortar or wooden basin. Gradually pound in salmon, then lemon juice and horseradish. Sieve. Use for garnishing or as a spread for canapés, or for sandwiches to be filled with fish.

TARRAGON BUTTER (Beurre Estragon)

3 oz. tarragon leaves
3 oz. butter
Squeeze of lemon juice
Salt to taste, if required
Cayenne pepper to taste

Blanch and drain tarragon leaves thoroughly. Press out all moisture with the back of a wooden spoon. Place in a mortar. Add butter. Pound till blended. Sieve. Stir in lemon juice, salt if required and cayenne pepper to taste. Use for garnishing cold chicken or turkey dishes.

WATERCRESS BUTTER (Beurre de Ruisseau)

1/4 lb. butter
2 heaped tablespoons minced watercress
1 teaspoon lemon or lime juice
Salt and cayenne pepper to taste

Wash and pick over watercress leaves, then wash again. Drain thoroughly, pressing with the back of a wooden spoon. Mince and measure. Pound butter and cress in a mortar or wooden bowl with a pestle. Beat in lemon juice and salt and cayenne pepper to taste. Sieve. Use for garnishing cold beef, ox tongue, galantines, etc., or use on canapés, or with bread for sandwiches with a beef, veal or game filling.

Garnishes

Garnishes play an important part in the service of food. When arranging a dish, remember that it should appeal to the eye as much as to the palate. Garnishing is really an art, and, like most arts, it needs practice. Here are a few rules to guide the amateur :

(1) Do not use garnishes to cover up badly-prepared food.
(2) Use edible garnishes as they increase the food value of the dish.
(3) Never over-garnish.
(4) When garnishing, see that the garnish is so placed that it will not interfere with the service.

The object of garnishing any dish is to aid the digestion by stimulating the flow of digestive juices.

Breadcrumbs, Fried : Drain on absorbent paper. Use as a garnish for creamed eggs, fish, meat, poultry or vegetables.

Croustades : Cut 24-hour-old bread in slices 2 inches thick. Remove crusts. Shape into oblongs, rounds or squares. Remove centres with a curved knife to the depth of about 1½ inches. Either brush all over with melted butter and bake till golden brown at 350° F., or fry in deep hot fat till golden brown, and drain on absorbent paper. Use in place of patty cases for serving creamed chicken, fish, lobster, meat, mushrooms, oysters, pheasant, poultry or creamed vegetables, such as asparagus tips, and peas.

Shells : Remove crusts from thinly-sliced new bread. Spread both sides with butter. Press each into a well-buttered muffin tin, so that the points come upwards. Bake in a moderately hot oven, 400° F., till golden. Fill with creamed fish, or drop an egg into each, and season it, then float a little melted butter on top and bake till set.

CHEESE

Cheese Balls : For each ball, take a rounded dessertspoon of cream cheese. Season with salt, paprika and pepper. Roll into a ball. Dip either in minced chives or parsley. Roll lightly in chopped walnuts or dust with paprika. Sometime I roll them in poppy seeds. Use for garnishing green salads, or serve with celery or watercress.

Cheese Bonbons : Mix 4 oz. mashed Roquefort or Blue Danish cheese with 2 tablespoons grated Cheddar, 1 teaspoon Worcester sauce or Yorkshire Relish, $\frac{1}{4}$ teaspoon paprika, 1 teaspoon tomato catsup, and $\frac{1}{2}$ oz. creamed butter. When blended, shape into balls the size of large marbles with butter pats. Chill. Use for garnishing salads, or serve with celery or radishes.

Cheese Carrots : Put 8 oz. of fresh Cheddar or Dutch cheese through a potato ricer. Roll a tablespoon of the cheese in the palm of your hand into the shape of a carrot. Insert a sprig of washed parsley in the thick end. Make remainder of cheese into " carrots " in the same way. Chill. Brush with mayonnaise. Roll in minced parsley, chives, or a mixture of parsley and chopped nuts. Use for salads, or serve with celery, radishes or watercress.

Cheese Popcorn : Pop corn in the usual way. (See Savoury Section.) Sprinkle at once with grated Cheddar, tossing the corn in the cheese until it is well covered. Cool. Store in closely-covered tin, lined with greaseproof paper. Use for garnishing clear soup.

EGG

Egg Balls : Mince hard-boiled eggs. Mix to a stiff paste with mayonnaise, curry paste, or Sauce Tartare. Chill. Roll into balls the size of marbles, then in finely minced chives, parsley, green and red pepper, blended, or green pepper. Use for garnishing green salads, beetroot, ham or tongue platters, etc.

FISH

Anchovies : Choose the fillets drained of oil, for garnishing fish loaves ; tomatoes, stuffed with a fish mayonnaise ; beef salads and Wiener Schnitzel. Curve each fillet for garnishing. Use stuffed anchovy fillets for decorating the aspic lining of a mould to be filled with aspic of fish, or a mousse ; and for garnishing mayonnaise of fish and platters, or a tray of appetisers.

Crayfish : For dressed fish dishes and fish salads.

Lobster Claws, Coral and Feelers : Use with any lobster dish or salad.

Mussel Shells : Wash and dry. (1) Fill with devilled crab, lobster or crawfish. Dredge lightly with crumbs. Dab with butter, and brown ; or substitute creamed shrimps and mushrooms, and crumb, butter and brown. Use for garnishing any hot baked whole fish or fillets. (2) Fill with sauce divine or Tartare. Use for garnishing any fish salads, allowing 2 or 3 per salad.

Shrimps : Shell. Moisten with sherry or Madeira. Drain and use for decorating fish salads. Use dry for decorating aspic linings for fish in aspic, or fish mousses. Use a tablespoon of shrimps on a lettuce leaf as a garnish to smoked salmon.

Smoked Salmon : Chop. Flavour with lemon juice and season with cayenne pepper. Use as a garnish to egg mayonnaise, fish salads, fish, etc.

APPLES

Rings : Core red-cheeked apples. Cut in slices $\frac{1}{4}$ inch thick. Fry in deep hot fat, 275° F., until brown, for 2 or 3 minutes. Drain on absorbent paper. Sprinkle with sugar. Use for garnishing roast duck, goose, ham or pork, placing a maraschino cherry in the centre of each.

Shells : Cut a thick slice off the blossom end of each apple. Carefully remove the pulp and core without cutting right through. If your knife slips, cover the hole with a piece of the removed peel. Scallop the edges. Use as containers for Waldorf salad for serving with cold duck, goose or pork.

LEMON

Butterflies : Cut half slices of lemons almost in half again, leaving them joined in centre. Twist the quarters left slightly, and poise on food to be garnished. Sprinkle minced parsley or chives across the " waist." Use for garnishing fried fish or fillets of fish, baked fish, pancakes, etc.

Cross : Cut lemon in slices about $\frac{1}{4}$ inch thick. Cut out a round of paper the size of the lemon slice. Make a cross on it. Place on top of the lemon slice, and fix in position with cocktail sticks or toothpicks. Cut out cross right through the paper with a very sharp-pointed knife. Use for garnishing fish dishes, smoked salmon, potted shrimps, caviare, etc. Dredge each arm of the the cross towards the centre with chopped chives or parsley, and place a caper in the centre.

Curly Cues : Take a slice of lemon, cut crosswise. Make a slit in the rind and through the pith, then remove half the pulp from the slice, scraping it away from the rind very carefully. Now curl the loose piece of rind remaining round, as illustrated.

Quarters : Cut a slit from one point to the middle. Slip through the slit on to the rim of tumblers when required for long drinks. Half quarters can also be treated in the same way.

Shamrock : From a crosswise slice of lemon, cut 4 small wedges out, equal distance apart. Use for decorating fried fish or fish salads. Place a tiny sprig of parsley, a caper, or a little chopped red pepper on the centre of each shamrock.

Shells : If lemons are large, halve crosswise. If small, cut a third of the length from blossom end. Carefully remove pulp with a sharp, curved knife. Drain. With scissors, cut out a scallop all round the edge, or slit the edge about $\frac{1}{4}$ inch apart and $\frac{1}{4}$ inch down. Cut out every alternate piece. Use for serving mayonnaise, sauce divine or Tartare in individual portions for hot or cold boiled salmon, or fill with tomato cocktail sauce and arrange in centre of a plate of oysters in their shells.

Turrets : Cut slices of lemon, cut crosswise, through at the rind about every $\frac{1}{4}$ of an inch, and lift every alternate section right up. Tuck a tiny sprig of parsley or chervil through a hole in the centre. Use for garnishing the centre of a dish of baked, fried or grilled fish, or arrange round a dish of mayonnaise of fish equal distance apart, allowing one per person.

Wedges : Cut a lemon into 4, 5 or 6 wedges from point to point. Cover with strips of pickled gherkin or red pepper boiled for 2 or 3 minutes until pliable, or with pimiento.

ORANGE

Segments : Peel seedless oranges carefully. Cut on either side of each dividing membrane and carefully remove pulp, segment by segment. Use for garnishing blancmanges, creams and jellies with cream, or use on trifles, flan cases covered with cream. Dip in caster sugar and arrange on the top of a dessert cake, or open pie covered with cream, like a large flower.

Shells (for method, see Lemon Shells): Use, scalloped, as containers for individual fruit cocktails, fruit salads, or fruit jellies.

Slices : Use peeled for garnishing a green salad with wild duck. Use unpeeled for garnishing a baked ham, fixing them on with cloves. Bake for 2 or 3 minutes before serving.

PINEAPPLE

Rings : Heat in pineapple juice. Arrange round a baked ham. Fill the centres with a spoonful of red currant jelly, or tuck a maraschino cherry into each.

HERBS

Borage : Wait till it flowers before using. Cut off sprigs, flowers and foliage together. Use for garnishing long drinks and fruit and cider cups.

Chervil : Use sprigs for garnishing hard-boiled eggs dipped in aspic jelly, and for aspic linings for savoury moulds, green salads, a tray of appetizers, sandwiches, etc.

Fennel : Use sprigs for garnishing cooked fish.

PASTRY

Cut flaky, rough puff or puff pastry into fan shapes, crescents or triangles. Place an inch apart on a lightly greased baking sheet. Brush tops lightly with equal quantity of beaten egg yolk and milk. Bake in a moderately hot oven, 400° F., till golden brown. Use while hot for garnishing white entrées, chicken à la king, etc. Use triangles of shortcrust for decorating open fruit pies.

PICKLES

Gherkins : Cut gherkins in thin slices without cutting through the base. Spread out like a fan. Use for garnishing grilled steaks, fish or meat salads.

Olives : *Black :* (1) Arrange in the form of a daisy on the centre of a macaroni or spaghetti dish. (2) Cut in slices lengthwise and arrange in a wreath round. (3) Quarter lengthwise. Use for decorating canapés, making a butterfly on oblong canapés (like the lemon butterflies), a crescent on crescents, and a lazy-daisy on rounds.
Stuffed: (1) Remove ends. Cut in thin slices. Use for decorating aspic in the lining of a mould to contain jellied meat or a mousse, for decorating canapés, sandwich loaves, etc. (2) Chop and use for garnishing crab, lobster or smoked salmon canapés.

VEGETABLES

Asparagus Tips : Use hot boiled asparagus tips piled in a little bundle, tied, if liked, half-way down with a strip of pimiento, as a garnish for creamed fish, meat or poultry, chicken à la king, etc. Use cold boiled asparagus tips with the pimiento band, in bundles equal distance apart, round a meat platter, and for certain salads. If liked, the tips can be slipped through a ring of lemon, onion, green or red pepper.

Beetroot : (1) Cut boiled or pickled beetroot into thin slices, then cut into fancy shapes with vegetable cutters. Use for decorating aspic jelly, linings of moulds for savoury mousses, salads, fish salads, salmon mayonnaise, meat platters, and canapés. (2) Dice and use for garnishing root vegetable salads, canapés, etc.

Carrots : *Blossoms:* Trim roots from young carrots. Halve lengthwise. Make into " curls." Throw into cold water as prepared, to chill. Allow 4 for each blossom. Fix wider ends of each " curl " together with a toothpick. Tuck a tiny sprig of chervil, parsley or watercress in the centre. Place in a bowl of water and chill. Use as a central garnish for a large tray of appetisers or a meat platter.

Curls: Trim roots from young carrots. Halve carrots lengthwise. With a sharp knife, cut in long thin slices. Roll each slice into a pin wheel. Pack close together in a shallow dish of ice-cold water. Leave till cold. Drain. Use for garnishing cold and jellied meats and salads.

Marbles: Scrape young tender carrots and wash well. Cut into little balls with vegetable cutter. Use for garnishing cold meat and salads.

Straws: Wash, scrape or peel young carrots of equal length. Halve, then quarter. Cut in small strips, then into straws, 2½ to 3 inches long. Lay on a plate. Cover with a damp cloth. Chill for 1 hour. Use for garnishing salads.

Celery : To curl or fringe, choose large tender sticks. Cut in 2 to 3 inch lengths. Slit the ends with a sharp knife to fringe them. (If curls are wanted, slit in narrow strips almost to the end.) Throw into ice-cold water. Leave until the ends curl. Use for decorating fish mayonnaise or green salads.

Cucumber : *Boats:* Peel 3 medium-sized cucumbers rather thickly. Halve lengthwise. Scoop out the seeds, leaving a ½-inch wall. Simmer in boiling salted water until tender in 20 to 30 minutes. Drain thoroughly. Use for serving green peas, creamed mushrooms or shrimps, etc. NOTE : If the cucumber isn't pointed at each end, cut each end to a point, making the boats about 4 inches long.

Butterfly: Cut 2 small wedges from a slice of cucumber at opposite sides and place them, points to centre, on top of the larger wedges, so as to give you a butterfly. Sprinkle sieved egg yolk and parsley across the joins. Use for garnishing fried or grilled white fish or salads.

Cones: Peel cucumbers, and slice very thinly across. Make a cut from the edge of each slice to the centre. Draw one cut edge over the other to form a cone. Dip edge in paprika if liked. Use for garnishing salads.

Lily: Wash and cut a cucumber into very thin slices crosswise. Draw one edge over the other of one of the slices, and fix with a toothpick at the bottom. Insert a tiny strip of raw carrot or golden pepper for a stamen. Draw a second slice of cucumber over the open sides, and fix also at the bottom with toothpick, Place gently in ice-cold water and leave till crisp. Use for garnishing the centre of a large salad or meat platter.

Primrose: With a sharp-pointed knife, nick out 6 tiny strips of peel equal distance apart from the sides of a cucumber, then slice. Use for garnishing baked, fried or grilled fish, or arrange a group in the centre of a large root salad or mayonnaise, making the primrose's stems from the cucumber peel removed.

Slices: Wash cucumber. If ridged slices are wanted, use a ridged knife. To make fluted slices, cut with a tiny fluted cutter. Use these slices for garnishing salads, canapés, etc.

Stars: Wash and slice cucumber crosswise. Cut 4 wedges equal distance apart, from each slice, cutting only as far as the seeds. Sprinkle centre with minced chives or parsley when wanted to garnish mayonnaise and salads. When wanted for pancakes, put a tiny blob of jelly in the centre.

Peppers : Remove points and stem ends from peppers. Scrape out the seeds carefully. Cut in rings, or slice and dice.

Use the orange and scarlet or red for garnishing a green salad, and the green for root salads and mayonnaise. Use diced and stripped only for canapés. Pimiento can be used like red pepper.

Shamrocks: Cut prepared peppers into rings 1 inch thick. Arrange 3 in the shape of a shamrock leaf on individual plates. Fill each ring with fish mayonnaise.

Radishes : *Fans:* Choose rather long radishes. Wash well. Cut into thin slices crosswise, almost through the radish. Chill in ice-cold water. Use for garnishing meat salads.

Lilies: Trim round radishes carefully. Wash and dry. Make a vandyke round the middle of each with a small, sharp-pointed knife. Cut in two, crosswise. Use for decorating hors d'oeuvre and meat salads.

Roses: Choose firm, round, equal-sized radishes. Trim carefully. Wash and dry. With a small sharp knife, cut the skin down in 5 sections, almost to the stem end. Place in ice-cold water. As they chill, the petals will unfold and open out. Use for garnishing cold platters, green salads, appetizer trays, etc.

Tomatoes : *Cups:* Cut a small slice from the blossom ends of tomatoes. Carefully scoop out the pulp, leaving a shell of about ⅛ inch thick.

Roses: Peel washed, firm tomatoes thickly as you would an apple. Roll the peel round your finger and coax it into the shape of a rose. Fill centre with a little cress or cream cheese, sprinkled sieved egg yolk. Use as a central decoration on a green salad to be served with cheese.

Sunflower: Divide tomato into 5 wedges without cutting through the base. With a sharp curved knife, gradually draw back each wedge, exposing the centre of pulp. Use as a central decoration for a green salad, or for decorating an appetizer tray. The centre pulp can be carefully removed and the tomatoes filled with a root vegetable salad, allowing it to show in between the wedges.

Vegetables

Vegetables are a protective food. They provide not only starch and sugar for energy, but roughage, vitamins and mineral salts. The green, leafy vegetables in particular are a valuable source of mineral salts and vitamins. In days gone by, vegetables were only considered as an accompaniment to game, meat and poultry. To-day, they play a more important part in the menu. To keep the family in perfect health, at least two vegetables should be served daily, in addition to potatoes, one cooked, the second in a raw form, as salad.

When early fresh vegetables are unobtainable, use frozen vegetables instead. Canned vegetables are a useful substitute for left-over boiled, fresh or frozen vegetables. The following table gives a list of home-produced vegetables in season. It is only approximate, as produce is available according to whether the " season " is early or late.

VEGETABLES IN SEASON

VEGETABLE	SEASON
Artichokes (Chinese)	October—December
Artichokes (Globe)	July—September
Artichokes (Jerusalem)	October—March
Asparagus	April—mid-June
Aubergines	June—November
Beetroots	All the year round
Broad Beans	July and August
Broccoli (hearting)	September—June

396

VEGETABLE	SEASON
Broccoli (sprouting)	March—April
Broccoli (early purple variety)	Available January and February
Brussels Sprouts	September—March
Cabbages	All the year round
Cabbages (colewort)	July—November
Cabbages (red)	October—December
Cabbages (savoy)	September—April
Calabrese	September—October
Capsicums	June—October
Cardoons	November—December
Carrots	All the year round
Cauliflowers	Mid-June—mid-November
Celeriac	October—March
Celery	September—March
Chicory	November—May
Corn-on-the-Cob	Mid-August—October
Couve Tronchuda	September—December
Cucumbers	All the year round
Cucumbers (ridge)	July—September
Endive	September—March
Escarole (Batavian Lettuce)	September—March
Garlic	All the year round
Good King Henry	March—May
Greens	January—April
Greens (Dandelions)	March—April
Hamburg Parsley	September—April
Kale	All the year round
Kohlrabi	Autumn
Leeks	September—June
Lettuce	Late April—October
Mushrooms	All the year round
Onions	All the year round
Onions (spring)	February—September
Orach	July—September
Parsnips	August—May
Peas	Mid-June—October
Pe-Tsai	November
Potatoes	All the year round
Potatoes (new)	March—July
Pumpkins	October—January
Radishes	All the year round
Salsify	October—March
Scorzonera	October—March
Seakale	November—May
Seakale Beet	September—April
Shallots	November—January
Skirret	September and October
Sorrel	May—September

VEGETABLE							SEASON
Spinach	-	-	-	-	-	-	All the year round
Spinach Beet	-	-	-	-	-	-	November—April
Squash	-	-	-	-	-	-	July—September
String Beans	-	-	-	-	-	-	May—October
Sugar Beet	-	-	-	-	-	-	September—December
Swedes	-	-	-	-	-	-	September—May
Tomatoes	-	-	-	-	-	-	March—December
Turnips	-	-	-	-	-	-	June—April
Vegetable Marrow	-	-	-	-	-	-	June—November
Watercress	-	-	-	-	-	-	February—June
Zucchini	-	-	-	-	-	-	July—September

If you grow your own vegetables, gather them early in the morning on the day they are to be cooked. If vegetables have to be kept for any length of time, store in a cool, dark, dry, well-ventilated place. The green varieties should be placed in a covered container and the others in an open vegetable rack.

TO STORE FRESH VEGETABLES

Artichokes (*Globe*) : Cut with long stalks. Insert stalks in a box of damp sand in a frost-proof out-house. If to be kept for more than a day or two, remove a tiny bit of the stalks every day and replace artichokes in sand.

Artichokes (*Jerusalem*) : Lift and store like potatoes, or leave in the ground during winter. Wise to have some always in storage, as they cannot be dug in frosty weather.

Beetroot: Leave in ground till October. Lift carefully to prevent bruising or bleeding. Store indoors in boxes or buckets of sand.

Carrots: Leave main crop in ground till early October, and late carrots till middle of November. Remove leaves $\frac{1}{2}$ inch from the roots. Store in boxes or buckets of slightly moist sand on a slatted shelf so that the air can circulate round the containers in a cool frost-proof shed.

Celeriac: Leave in ground till beginning of November, then trim off foliage and rootlets. Store in dry sand or earth in a frost-proof shed.

Celery: Leave in ground till well frosted and dig up as required. When frost is severe, it should be protected by covering the foliage and the top of the ridges with old bracken, clean straw or straw mats. Can be stored in a refrigerator.

Chicory: Leave in ground till early November. Store in sand till required for forcing. To force, pack roots closely together in boxes or deep pots 21 days before they are required. Bury up to the crown in fine damp soil. Store in a cool dark shed or cellar. Syringe occasionally with lukewarm water.

Garlic: Hang up in the air in a net bag in pantry.

Leeks: Leave in ground. Lift as required. If hard frost is likely, lift a few. Store in vegetable rack.

Onions: Rope the stems together after drying in the sun and suspend from a hook in a cool pantry or frost-proof shed.

Potatoes: Lift when soil is fairly dry so that the tubers are clean. Store in any dark, frost-proof shed or cellar on a bed of straw or on a wooden base in a cold temperature, but not below 32° F. Cover with sacks. Examine every week or two and remove any showing signs of disease. When sprouts appear late in the season, rub off and burn. Do not give sprouts to poultry. To prevent potatoes freezing, stand a pail of water beside them.

Pumpkin: Store on a shelf or in net bags in a cool, dry pantry.

Salsify: Lift in October when soil is dry. Remove tops an inch from roots. Store like carrots.

Shallots: Store like onions.

Squash: Store like pumpkin.

Swedes: Prepare and store like carrots.

Turnips: Prepare and store like carrots.

Vegetable Marrow: Store like pumpkins.

The above notes on storage are chiefly intended for home growers. Those who buy their vegetables should store them as suggested in my introductory note. Where " roots " are concerned, the notes will not only be useful to home-growers, but to others who prefer to buy roots in large quantities and store them.

VEGETABLE TABLE

The quantities in the following table are only approximate.

VEGETABLE	QUANTITY (*Raw*)	YIELD (*Cooked*)	NO. OF PERSONS
Artichokes -	$1\frac{1}{4}$ lbs.		4 persons
Asparagus -	1 lb.	16-20 sticks	3 or 4 persons
Aubergines -	1 (1 lb.) gives $4\frac{1}{2}$ cups diced	$1\frac{3}{4}$ cups	2 persons
Beetroot -	1 lb. topped	2 cups diced	3 or 4 persons
Broad Beans -	2 lb.	1 and $\frac{2}{3}$ cups shelled	For 3 persons
Broccoli— (hearting) -	2 lb.	3 cups	4 or 5 persons
Broccoli— (sprouting) -	2 lb.		4 to 6 persons
Brussels Sprouts -	$1\frac{1}{2}$ lb.	3 cups	4 persons
Cabbage -	1 lb. or $3\frac{1}{2}$ cups finely shredded	1 pint shredded	3 persons
Calabrese -	See Sprouting Broccoli		
Carrots -	1 lb. topped or $2\frac{1}{4}$ cups	2 cups	3 or 4 persons
Cauliflower -	2 lb.	3 cups	4 or 5 persons
Celeriac -	1 lb.	2 cups diced	3 or 4 persons
Celery -	1 head, $1\frac{1}{4}$ lb.	2 cups	2 persons
Chicory -	1 lb.		1 or 2 per persons
Corn-on-the-Cob -	4 medium-sized ears, or 1 cup cut corn		2 persons
Cucumber -	1 ($\frac{3}{4}$ lb)	$1\frac{1}{2}$ cups diced	4 persons
Endive -	1 large		3 persons

VEGETABLE	QUANTITY (*Raw*)	YIELD (*Cooked*)	NO. OF PERSONS
Greens - -	1 lb.	2½-3½ cups	2 or 3 persons
Hamburg Parsley -	1 lb.	1 pint diced	4 persons
Kale - -	1 lb.	2 cups	2 persons
Kohlrabi -	1 lb. (4 medium-sized)	2 cups diced	3 persons
Leeks -	2 large or 4 small		1 person
Mushrooms -	1 lb.		4 persons if baked, fried or grilled. 6 persons if creamed
Onions -	1 lb. small (2-2½ dozen)	1¾ cups	3 or 4 persons
Parsnips -	1 lb.	1 pint diced	4 or 5 persons
Peas -	1 lb.	1 cup	2 persons
Potatoes -	1 lb. (4 or 5 medium-sized)	1 pint raw or cooked, diced, or 2¼ cups mashed	3 persons
Pumpkins, Squashes and Vegetable Marrow -	2 lb.	2 cups mashed	4 persons
Spinach -	1 lb.	1½-2 cups	2 persons
String Beans -	1 lb.	3 cups sliced	2 or 3 persons
Swedes -	1 lb.	2 cups diced	3 persons
Tomatoes -	1 lb. (5 or 6) or 24 slices		3 or 4 persons
Turnips -	1 lb. (3 or 4 medium)	2 cups diced	3 persons

TO COOK VEGETABLES

The usual method of cooking vegetables in Great Britain is by boiling, either by the old method, or by the new, which is a combination of boiling and steaming. You can also bake, fry, grill, " pan," pressure-cook, steam and stew vegetables.

Young fresh vegetables can be cooked rapidly in a small amount of stock or water in a tightly covered pan, so as to retain as much of the food values as possible. This method is usually known as the " Conservative Method," as by using it, the valuable elements in fresh vegetables are conserved or retained. This is suitable for all vegetables except broccoli, Brussels sprouts, cabbage, cauliflower, greens and spinach. The flavour of green vegetables cooked conservatively is rather strong and they are indigestible.

TO BOIL VEGETABLES

Allow enough boiling water to cover vegetables. Add salt, 1 teaspoon to each quart of water, except to delicate vegetables such as asparagus, peas, spinach, etc., which should not be salted until nearly tender. Cover all root vegetables before cooking. Boil green vegetables uncovered. Cook all vegetables until tender, then drain in a colander until every drop of water has run off, and dress to taste. Greens should be boiled quickly and all other vegetables steadily, but not too fast, unless otherwise stated, or they may break. To prevent loss of minerals, you can wrap prepared vegetables in parchment before boiling, but in this case allow a little longer time for cooking.

THE CONSERVATIVE METHOD

If you prefer this method, which is really a combination of boiling and steaming, you must use only fresh young vegetables. Wash thoroughly. If soaking is necessary, keep soaking time as short as possible. Half an hour is the limit. If soaked too long, minerals and water-soluble vitamins dissolve out and thus food value is lessened. Use only enough liquid to prevent burning.

To Boil Vegetables Conservatively: Pour $\frac{1}{4}$ pint boiling water into a saucepan. Add 1 teaspoon salt and 2 lb. diced, sliced or shredded young, fresh vegetables if large. If small, trim and add whole. Cover tightly. Boil briskly for 10-15 minutes, shaking pan occasionally. Length of time depends on age and size of the vegetables. Test with a fork. When tender, but not mushy, drain off any liquid and use for making gravy or sauce for vegetables, or add to stock for soup. If sauce is wanted, thicken vegetable stock with flour after draining vegetables. Season and flavour. Add a teaspoon of butter or margarine, and stir until boiling. Add vegetable. Toss lightly over heat and turn into a vegetable dish. If the liquid is going to be turned into a sauce, you can add the butter or margarine before cooking if preferred.

There is another conservative method worth remembering, and that is to cook all vegetables, except green leaf vegetables, in a very little melted butter in a tightly closed pan, very slowly until almost tender, (about $\frac{1}{2}$ hour), then add $\frac{1}{2}$ cup beef, chicken or veal stock or water, and salt and pepper to taste. Cover again. Stew gently until liquid has evaporated and vegetable is tender. Allow about 25 minutes for young vegetables, and 1-1$\frac{1}{2}$ hours for old.

TO STEAM VEGETABLES

Prepare vegetables as for boiling, unless otherwise stated under recipe. Place in a colander lowered into a saucepan half-filled with boiling water, or on a rack in a saucepan with boiling water coming up to the bottom of the rack, or in a buttered compartment of a steamer or top of a double boiler. Cover tightly. Steam until tender. All steamed vegetables retain most of their nutritive value, but green vegetables lose their colour.

TO DRESS BOILED OR STEAMED VEGETABLES PLAINLY

Greens, Leaves, Pods, Seeds and Stems: Moisten with melted butter. Season with pepper and more salt if necessary.

Fruit Group: Coat with parsley sauce.

Roots and Tubers: Coat with seasoned melted butter, or mash and moisten with butter. Season with pepper and more salt if necessary. Sprinkle with minced parsley.

To Cream Vegetables: Measure cooked vegetables and make a third or half of its quantity of well-seasoned white sauce, according to taste, using liquid in pan, if cooked conservatively, together with milk. Heat together in the top of a double boiler, or better still, have both hot when you lightly mix them together.

To Vary Creamed Vegetables:

(a) Add minced parsley, chives or the green of spring onions to taste. *Potatoes:*—Minced mint can be used instead.

(b) Creamed asparagus, broccoli, cauliflower, new potatoes, runner beans, salsify, scorzonera, and any other vegetable you like, can be crumbed by placing the creamed vegetable in a shallow fireproof dish. Cover with stale bread-crumbs, and sprinkle until moistened with melted butter, or prepare crumbs in this way : Melt butter or margarine, allowing ½ cup melted fat to 1½ cups crumbs. Fry, stirring frequently, until golden brown. Pour over and serve.

(c) Stir egg yolk into white sauce before adding vegetable, allowing 1 yolk to each ½ pint sauce. Stir over boiling water for 2 minutes, but do not allow to boil, then add hot vegetable.

To Mash: Mash, if liked, boiled carrots, Jerusalem artichokes, parsnips, potatoes, squash, swedes, turnips or vegetable marrow, or equal quantity of boiled potato and Jerusalem artichoke or swede. Add butter and seasoning to taste to all these vegetables.

TO COOK VEGETABLES IN MILK

Asparagus, diced string beans, celery, cucumbers, diced onions, peas, diced potatoes, salsify and scorzonera, can all be stewed in milk. Place prepared vegetables in the top of a double boiler with just enough milk to cover, then return to pan. For every cup of milk used, add a small tablespoonful of butter creamed with the same quantity of flour, and salt and pepper to taste. Stir till boiling, then cover and cook for 10 minutes before serving. Add a teaspoon of salt to every quart of milk before starting to cook vegetables.

TO PRESSURE-COOK VEGETABLES

This method provides in the minimum of time perfectly cooked vegetables of a good colour and flavour with little loss of vitamins and mineral salts. As instructions for cooking by this method vary according to the cooker, pay particular attention to the booklet or chart supplied with the cooker. Generally speaking, the vegetable is prepared as for the table. Place in cooker. Add ½ gill boiling water. Fasten on cover securely. Open vent. Wait until the 15 lb. pressure is indicated, then begin counting cooking time. When the vegetables are young and tender, you must stop the cooking process as quickly as possible by standing the pan in cold water the moment the time is finished. Instructions to do this are given under each individual vegetable for which it is necessary. Let the pressure drop gradually when cooking other vegetables. Do not open vent until pressure drops to zero, then open carefully and remove cover. Serve vegetable with the liquid in pressure cooker, adding a little butter if liked, or use liquid in cooker for gravy, soup or stock. When following suggestions for pressure-cooking vegetables, if the time allowed is, for example, 2-3 minutes, or 3-4 minutes, instead of a specified number of minutes, this means that the vegetables when young will take 2 minutes, and when more mature, 3 minutes.

FROZEN VEGETABLES

Ready to cook without de-frosting. Follow instructions on packet. Most varieties take about half as long to cook as fresh. Dress like fresh vegetables.

VEGETABLE ABC

The following alphabetical table of vegetables includes advice upon how to choose, and by what method to boil. The table also tells you how to dress boiled or steamed vegetables and gives suggestions of how many the vegetables will serve. When buying vegetables, purchase roots weekly and greens and other vegetables daily, when possible.

Acidulated Water: Add 1 teaspoon vinegar or 1 tablespoon lemon juice to 1 quart water, when acidulated water is mentioned in any recipe. This is used for vegetables that become discoloured during preparation, and for boiling them.

Artichokes (Chinese) (Artichauts Chinoise): If home-grown, lift. Do not expose to the light if stored.
To Prepare: Wash and remove stringy ends.
To Boil: Plunge into boiling salted water. Cover. Boil till tender (about 20 minutes).
To Steam: Cook in a steamer or on top of a rack in a saucepan with water boiling below, for about 45 minutes, till tender.
To Dress: Drain well. Scrape skins off carefully. Coat with parsley butter or Hollandaise sauce.
To Fry: Par-boil as described under " To Boil," for 10 minutes, then drain. Fry in melted butter, or egg and crumb and fry in deep fat. Serve on thin slices of fried bread or hot buttered toast.
Allow 1-1¼ lb. for 4 persons.

Artichokes (Globe) (Artichauts): Of European origin. Rich in mineral salts and iodine. :*Two varieties:* green and purple. The purple is more prickly than the green. Should be cut with a few inches of stem. Choose with fleshy leaves, clinging tightly together. If with fuzzy centres, they are too old. If home-grown, they should not be cut until wanted for cooking.
To Prepare: If outer leaves are coarse, remove. Remove tips of the prickly variety, then round off leaves. Cut stems even with remaining leaves. Remove inner choke, which is a fuzzy growth on bottoms, sometimes called " hearts." Tie a thread round the thickest part of the leaves. Soak in cold acidulated water to cover for ½ hour to cleanse and free them from insects, then rinse thoroughly under cold water tap. The bottoms are sometimes pickled.
To Boil: Place, head downwards, in boiling, salted, acidulated water to cover or in equal quantity of boiling water and milk to cover. Boil gently in an uncovered saucepan, for about 25-35 minutes, until tender, according to age

and size. When tested, the leaves should pull out easily. Drain upside down, then untie tops. Serve in a hot dish lined with a folded serviette.

To Boil Artichoke Bottoms: Remove all leaves and the choke. If still fuzzy, pull out or scrape off fuzz. Rinse. Throw into boiling, salted, acidulated water to cover. Simmer gently until tender. Drain well. Serve with Béchamel, Hollandaise or Tartare sauce. If any bottoms are left over, fry in a little melted butter until pale brown below, then turn and brown on the other side. Season with pepper to taste, and salt if necessary. Sprinkle lightly with lemon juice.

To Pressure-Cook: Cook at 15 lb. pressure for 10 minutes.

To Steam: Steam from $\frac{3}{4}$-1$\frac{1}{4}$ hours, until tender.

To Dress : Serve hot with oiled butter, cream, Hollandaise or Tartare sauce, or cold with vinaigrette sauce.

Allow 1 globe artichoke per person.

ARTICHOKES FARCITI (Artichauts Farci à l'Italienne)

12 young globe artichokes
¼ lb. ground boiled ham
1 lb. minced boiled chicken breast
2 tablespoons cream
1 teaspoon minced parsley
Pinch of ground mace or grated nutmeg
Salt and pepper to taste
½ pint chicken stock

Boil artichokes until almost tender, then drain well. Pull leaves gently apart and remove chokes. Mix ham with the chicken, cream, parsley, mace or nutmeg and salt and pepper to taste. Either pack the stuffing in between each leaf, or into the centre. Close artichokes as far as possible. Pour chicken stock into the bottom of a casserole. Pack artichokes in side by side. Bake in a moderately hot oven, 375° F., for 20-25 minutes, until the stuffing is set and artichokes tender. Dish up. Serve with cream sauce, made partly with liquid in casserole. *For 6 persons.*

Artichokes (Jerusalem) (Topinambours) : These are rich in carbohydrates and contain vitamin B. They are considered to provide a digestible form of starch. *Three Varieties:* red, white and the old purple-skinned. Choose firm tubers.

To Prepare: Wash and boil in their skins, or wash, scrape, and throw into acidulated water. Rinse in a colander under cold water top.

To Boil: Plunge into boiling, salted water. Cover. Boil for 25-35 minutes, or till tender. Drain well. If boiled in their skins, rub off skins before dressing.

To Pressure-Cook: Cook at 15 lb. pressure for 2$\frac{1}{2}$ minutes.

To Steam: Cook for $\frac{3}{4}$-1 hour.

To Dress: 1. Season with salt and pepper and ground mace or grated nutmeg, if liked. Sprinkle with lemon juice and minced chives or parsley and moisten with melted butter.

2. Re-heat in Béchamel, cheese, egg or parsley sauce.

3. Leave till cold and coat with mayonnaise.

To Fry: Par-boil artichokes. Slice and skin thinly. Fry like potato chips, till golden. Season and sprinkle with minced parsley.

To Par-Boil and Bake: Wash, scrub and par-boil. Rub off skins. Place in a greased fireproof dish. Cover with beef or veal stock. Bake in a moderately hot oven, 375° F., for about 35 minutes, with cover on for 20 minutes. Uncover and finish cooking. Season to taste.

CREAMED JERUSALEM ARTICHOKES
(Topinambours à la Crème)

2 tablespoons butter
2 cups chopped fresh mushrooms
2 tablespoons flour
Salt and pepper to taste
Pinch of ground mace
1 teaspoon minced parsley
1 pint milk
4 cups cubed boiled artichokes

Melt butter in a saucepan. Add mushrooms. Simmer gently for 5 minutes, stirring occasionally. Stir in flour, salt and pepper to taste, mace, and parsley. Gradually add milk, stirring constantly. When boiling, add artichokes. Turn into the top of a double boiler, and heat till piping hot. This makes a delicious filling for little baked cases of pastry or mashed potato. *For 6 persons.*

Asparagus (Asperges) : Rich in mineral salts. A source of vitamins A, B and C. There are several first class varieties of asparagus :
English :
1. Thin and green and full of flavour.
2. Pale and very fleshy.
French:
1. Argenteuil, thick with lilac tips, an improved version of the Dutch.
2. Lauris, grown in Southern France, is a glorified relation of the green English asparagus.
To Prepare: With a sharp knife, cut off tough lower ends, and carefully scrape off scales and coarse outer skin at lower ends remaining. In Central Europe, the stalks are often thinly pared, so that not only the tips but the remainder of the stalks can be eaten. Tie stalks in bundles, keeping the heads even.
To Boil: Place in an open saucepan of boiling salted water, with tips well above water. Cover with a perforated lid. If freshly picked, boil for about 15 minutes till tender, but not broken. If bought, it will take from 20-30 minutes, according to freshness. Drain well.
NOTE : If you wish to boil the tips as well as the stalks, place on a rack in a saucepan of boiling water to cover, and boil, uncovered, for about 15 minutes, till tender, then drain. Useful for garnishing. There is still another way of boiling asparagus. Lay on side. Cook till tender in about 25 minutes or longer, according to age. If white, drain after boiling for 20 minutes.
To Boil Conservatively: Allow about 15 minutes.
To Pressure-Cook: Cook at 15 lb. pressure for $2\frac{1}{2}$ minutes. Place cooker at once in cold water to lower pressure quickly.
To Dress: Arrange on a rack in an asparagus dish, or in a hot dish lined with a folded napkin, or on toast. Serve with melted butter or Hollandaise sauce, or with hot boiled mayonnaise mixed with hot medium-thick white sauce, flavoured lemon juice, allowing 1 tablespoon lemon juice and $\frac{1}{2}$ cup sauce to 1 cup mayonnaise.
To Cream: Cut tender portions of prepared sticks in inch or $1\frac{1}{2}$ inch lengths. Place in a saucepan with boiling water to cover, allowing $\frac{3}{4}$ teaspoon salt to each pint of water used. Cover. Simmer for 10 minutes, then add tips. Simmer with lid tilted for about 5 minutes longer until both are tender. Drain thoroughly. Coat to taste with white or Béchamel sauce.
To Serve Creamed Asparagus: 1. On buttered toast or fried bread. 2. In

405

hot pastry cases. 3. In croûstades. 4. As a shortcake filling. 5. Combined with equal quantity of creamed chicken as a filling for a vol-au-vent case.

To fry Asparagus Tips: Roll each tip in seasoned breadcrumbs. Dip in beaten egg and milk, allowing 2 tablespoons milk to 1 egg, then roll again in crumbs. (If cooked or canned, cut in 3 inch lengths. Season. Dip in melted butter, then in dried breadcrumbs.) Fry in deep, hot fat, 365°-370° F., for about 2 minutes, until the tips are golden brown. Drain on absorbent paper. Serve with Hollandaise sauce. Allow 6-10 sticks per person, according to thickness.

ASPARAGUS WITH VELVA SAUCE (Asperges Velva)

1 large bunch asparagus
2 tablespoons salad oil
2 tablespoons flour
1 cup milk
Salt and white pepper to taste
½ teaspoon paprika
1½ tablespoons lemon juice
2 egg yolks

Boil asparagus and drain well. Serve with sauce. Heat 1 tablespoon of salad oil slightly in the top of a double boiler. Stir in flour and milk by degrees. Stir constantly till thick. Cook for 3 minutes, stirring constantly. (If too thick, stir in another tablespoon of milk.) Stir in remainder of salad oil by degrees. Remove from stove. Season with salt and pepper, and paprika to taste. Stir in lemon juice. When well blended, beat in egg yolks, one at a time. Re-heat slowly, stirring constantly, but do not allow to come to boil or sauce will curdle. Serve in a hot sauce boat. *For 6 persons.*

Aubergine (Aubergine) : Commonly known as " Egg Plant." There are several varieties of this egg-shaped fruit, which is treated like a vegetable, but the deep purple is the best flavoured. Choose sound firm glossy pods, free from bruises and heavy for their size. Avoid if flabby. Does not keep well.

To Prepare: Wash and dry. If wanted for stuffing, par-boil in boiling, salted water to cover.

To Boil: Throw into boiling, salted water. Simmer for 10 minutes. Drain well. Halve, stuff and bake.

To Mash: Peel a large boiled aubergine. Mash. Melt 1 tablespoon butter in a saucepan. Add a minced clove of garlic, 3 or 4 chopped peeled tomatoes, 1 teaspoon minced parsley, and cook slowly, stirring frequently, until tomatoes are soft, then add the aubergine. Stir over heat until thoroughly blended. Season with salt and pepper to taste, then add grated Gruyère cheese to taste. Stir until blended. Pile on a hot dish.

To Prepare for Frying and Grilling : Peel if liked, and slice ¼-½ inch thick crosswise, or, if very small, lengthwise. Sprinkle with salt. Pile on top of each other. Weight down to draw out the bitter juice. Stand for 1 hour, then drain well.

To Fry: Dry well and dredge with flour. Fry slices slowly in a little hot butter or olive oil till crisp. (If tiny, they can be cut into fingers instead of crosswise.) The slices can also be floured, egged and crumbed and fried in deep fat.

To Make Aubergine Fritters (Beignets d'Aubergine) : Prepare 1 aubergine as for frying, then dip in batter and fry in deep fat till golden brown. They can also be cut into ¼ inch thick slices, soaked overnight in cold, salted water, then drained and soaked in fresh water for ½ hour. Drain and dry. Season with pepper, then dip in flour and egg and crumb, or dip in savoury batter, and fry in deep smoking hot fat or oil for about 5 or 6 minutes, until golden brown and tender. Drain on absorbent paper. Season with paprika, pepper and salt to taste. Pile on a hot dish. Garnish with minced parsley or grated cheese. *For 2 persons.*

To Grill (Whole) : Wash and halve small aubergines. Make small gashes along the cut sides with a knife. Season with salt and pepper to taste. Brush with olive oil. Grill slowly, on one side only, until tender, in about 8 minutes, depending on the thickness. Serve with tomato sauce, flavoured with garlic, lemon juice, minced parsley, or a shredded anchovy if liked.

To Grill (Slices) : Cut, unpeeled, into ¾ inch thick slices. Soak in a marinade for ½ hour. Season with salt and pepper to taste. Dip in melted butter or olive oil. Grill slowly, allowing 5 minutes on each side. Serve with parsley butter, or coat with melted butter or tomato sauce, and garnish with fried parsley.

Allow 1 large aubergine for 2 persons.

BAKED STUFFED AUBERGINES (Aubergines aux Champignons)

3 medium-sized aubergines
2 tablespoons butter
1 tablespoon chopped onion
¼ lb. chopped peeled mushrooms
2 tablespoons ground bacon
1 cup breadcrumbs
½ cup boiling stock
Salt and pepper to taste

Wash and halve aubergines lengthwise. Remove part of the flesh, leaving a lining ½ inch thick. Place in a saucepan. Cover with boiling salted water. Simmer gently for 5 minutes. Melt butter in another pan. Add onion. Chop removed aubergine flesh and add with mushrooms and bacon. Cook slowly for 10 minutes, then add crumbs, stock and salt and pepper to taste. Stuff aubergine shells. Sprinkle with extra crumbs. Dab with tiny pats of butter. Bake side by side in a shallow greased fireproof dish, containing just enough stock to cover bottom, for ½ hour in a moderately hot oven, 375° F., *For 6 persons.*

RATATOUILLE PROVENCALE

1 large aubergine
1 small squash or vegetable marrow
6 firm peeled tomatoes
3 tablespoons olive oil
1 heaped tablespoon finely minced onion
1 minced clove of garlic
1 bay leaf
Salt and pepper to taste
¾ tablespoon minced parsley
½ cup grated Parmesan cheese

Wash and carefully peel aubergine. Slice, then cut into pieces. Place in a saucepan. Cover with boiling water. Boil for 10 minutes, then drain thoroughly. Meanwhile, peel squash or marrow. Remove any seeds and cut squash or marrow into dice. Place in a saucepan. Cover with boiling water. Boil till tender in about 10 minutes. Slice and chop tomatoes. When the aubergine and marrow or squash are thoroughly drained, heat oil in a shallow saucepan. Add onion. Fry until clear, stirring occasionally, then add garlic, bay leaf, salt, pepper and parsley, aubergine, marrow or squash and tomato. Fry slowly, stirring occasionally, for 15 minutes, until all the vegetables are tender. Add more salt and pepper if required. Place in a shallow, greased, fireproof dish. Sprinkle with cheese. Brown under grill, or on top of a moderately hot oven, 400° F. *For 4 or 5 persons.*

Beet (Betterave) : This is the name given to a long or round fleshy red or crimson root, but also includes edible leaf beets, such as seakale or silver beet, (sometimes called Swiss Chard), in which the leaves have been developed instead of the roots, and spinach beet, which is an excellent substitute for spinach. Sometimes referred to as perpetual spinach.

To Prepare: Remove only rootlets, but not too close to the skin. Cut off foliage about 2 inches from roots, but don't cut or scratch off any " beards " or skin, or some of the juice will escape during cooking and the colour and flavour will be spoilt. Wash very gently to remove any soil or grit. Can be baked, boiled or steamed.

To Boil: Place in a saucepan of boiling, salted water to cover. Add lemon juice or vinegar in the proportion of 1 tablespoon to 1 quart water to fix the colour. Cover. Simmer gently till tender in $\frac{1}{2}$-1 hour, if young, or 2 or more if old. Plunge into cold water. Rub off skin.

To Boil Conservatively: Slice and allow to simmer for 30 minutes.

To Pressure-Cook: Cook sliced beet at 15 lb. pressure for 5 minutes, placing cooker in cold water at once to reduce pressure quickly. Cook small whole beets for 10 minutes, those weighing about $\frac{1}{2}$ lb. for 20 minutes, and those of about 1 lb. for 35 minutes.

To Steam: Place in a steamer or on top of a rack in a saucepan with boiling, salted water below. Allow $1\frac{1}{2}$-2 hours for young beet, and $2\frac{1}{2}$-3 hours for old. Plunge into cold water. Skin.

To Dress: Gently rub off peel with a kitchen cloth or remove with your fingers, or a very blunt knife. Dice, rice, or slice thickly. Season with salt if necessary and pepper. Moisten with melted butter sharpened to taste with hot vinegar. If liked, cook a slice of onion or a clove of garlic in the butter until well-flavoured before using.

NOTE : If thrown into cold water after cooking, skin will come away easily.

To Bake: Arrange roots in a greased baking dish. Bake in a moderate oven, 350° F., till tender, then rub off outer skin and peel. Slice. Coat with melted butter. Season with salt and pepper.

Allow 1 medium-sized beet for 2 persons.

Beet, Seakale or Silver (Swiss Chard) (Carde Poirée) : A beet which has been cultivated to develop the leaves instead of the roots. Strip off leaves. Boil and dress like spinach. Slice fleshy, delicately flavoured, midribs and boil in salted water. Drain and serve with melted butter or in any other ways suggested for seakale.

CHARD A LA FRANCAISE (Carde Poirée à la Française)

1 peck chard leaves
1 tablespoon butter
3 tablespoons flour
$1\frac{1}{2}$ gills beef stock
$\frac{3}{4}$ teaspoon salt
$\frac{1}{4}$ teaspoon pepper
$\frac{3}{4}$ teaspoon sugar
Dash of grated nutmeg
1 tablespoon vinegar

Wash and cook the leaves in water adhering to them, until tender. Drain thoroughly. Chop finely. Melt butter in a saucepan. Add flour. When frothy, stir in stock, salt, pepper, sugar, nutmeg and vinegar. Cook until smooth and boiling. Boil for 1 minute, stirring constantly, then add chard. Stir until blended and piping hot. *For 6 persons.*

Broad Beans (Fèves de Maris) : Rich in proteins and carbohydrates, they furnish vitamins A, B, and C. Windsors best flavoured. Choose fresh, green pods.

To Prepare: Pod before cooking. If not freshly picked, throw them into rapidly boiling water. Blanch for 2 minutes, and rub off the outer skins before cooking.

To Boil: Throw podded beans into boiling salted water. Add a pinch of brown sugar and a peeled clove of garlic if liked. Cook slowly but steadily, uncovered, until skins begin to crack, if not already skinned, in 20-30 minutes, according to age. If they take longer to boil, they should be made into a purée or soup. Drain well.

To Boil Conservatively: Allow 20-25 minutes.

To Pressure-Cook: Cook at 15 lb. pressure, for 3 minutes. Place cooker into cold water to reduce pressure quickly.

To Dress: Toss in melted or parsley butter, or serve masked with white or parsley sauce, or white sauce flavoured to taste with minced chives.

NOTE : If old, rub boiled beans through a sieve. Moisten purée with butter or butter and cream. Reheat. Season with pepper, and add a dash of lemon juice. Sprinkle lightly with minced parsley.

Allow 1-1½ lb. for 2 persons.

PUREE OF BROAD BEANS : (Purée de Fèves de Maris) : Drain boiled broad beans. Throw into cold water. Drain again and skin. Mash with a fork then with a wooden spoon. Add melted butter, salt and pepper and top milk or cream to taste. Stir constantly until piping hot. Serve with boiled bacon, ham or salt beef.

Broccoli (Hearting) (Chou Broccoli) : Indistinguishable from cauliflower. Choose full, white, compact heads, free from dirt and mildew, with crisp outer leaves.

To Prepare: Trim neatly, removing coarse, outer leaves and thick stalks. Trim stalk remaining, so that broccoli sits flat if serving whole. Cut a cross in remaining stem to facilitate cooking. Place, head downwards, in salted, acidulated water, for a few minutes to draw out any insects, then drain and cook.

To Cook and Dress: See Cauliflower.

To Pressure-Cook: Allow 1½ minutes at 15 lb. pressure, placing pan in cold water at once to reduce pressure quickly.

Broccoli (Sprouting) (Choux de Broccoli) : There are three varieties : Italian sprouting, or calabrese, purple and white sprouting. The green sprouting (Calabrese) is considered a great delicacy. Stalks should be tender and firm, and the buds, in the heads, compact. If showing signs of flower, they are too old. When old, the stalk is tough and stringy.

To Prepare: Cook with at least 6 inches of stem. Peel stems. Soak in salted water for 10 minutes. Dry. Tie, for boiling in bundles, like asparagus.

To Boil: Cook, uncovered, in boiling, salted water for 15-20 minutes, or until tender. Season with pepper. Sprinkle with a few drops of lemon juice and moisten with melted butter, or fry 1½ tablespoons minced onion in 2 tablespoons butter, add 2 teaspoons lemon juice and salt and pepper to taste, then add broccoli and baste with the sauce, while heating, for a minute or two. *For 4 persons.*

To Boil Conservatively: Allow 15 minutes.

To Pressure Cook: Allow 1½ minutes at 15 lb. pressure, placing cooker in cold water at once to reduce pressure quickly.

To Dress: See Asparagus.

Allow 4 or 5 shoots per person, depending on size.

Brussels Sprouts (Choux de Bruxelles) : Introduced from Belgium in the nineteenth century. Rich in carbohydrates and mineral salts. Furnishes vitamins A and C. If home-grown, gather young and small. If bought, choose when possible, young, small, green, tightly closed sprouts in preference to open ones. They should all be of uniform size. Considered better if the frost has touched them.

To Prepare: Remove discoloured, yellow or wilted leaves. Wash well under running water or soak in salted water for ½ hour, then toss in clean water. Trim off stalks level.

To Boil: Throw into fast-boiling water to cover. Cook rapidly, uncovered, until almost tender, then add salt to taste. When tender, in 10-15 minutes, drain thoroughly in a colander.

To Boil Conservatively: Allow 10 minutes.

To Pressure-Cook: At 15 lb. pressure, allow 1½ minutes for young, freshly-picked sprouts, 2 minutes for bought, and 3 minutes for mature sprouts.

To Dress: Toss in melted butter, seasoned with pepper and grated nutmeg if liked, or coat with Béchamel, cheese, Hollandaise or white sauce.

Allow 1½ lb. for 4 persons.

BRUSSELS SPROUTS A LA FRANCAISE (Choux de Bruxelles à la Française) : Melt 2 oz. unsalted butter or margarine in a shallow saucepan. Add 1 lb. well-drained, boiled sprouts, ¼ teaspoon grated nutmeg, 1 teaspoon lemon juice, salt to taste and 1 tablespoon Béchamel or white sauce. Toss sprouts over the stove until blended with the butter, seasoning and sauce. Arrange in a shallow, hot dish. Garnish with a border of sippets of fried bread or toast.

BRUSSELS SPROUTS AU JUS (Choux de Bruxelles au Jus) : Wash 1 lb. trimmed sprouts. Throw into boiling, salted water to cover. Boil, uncovered, for 5 minutes. Drain well. Pour 1 pint veal stock into a saucepan. Add sprouts. Cook until tender in 5-10 minutes, shaking pan occasionally. Dish up. Boil stock rapidly until slightly reduced, then pour round.

BRUSSELS SPROUTS AUX MARRONS (Choux de Bruxelles aux Marrons) :

1. Cook 1 lb. trimmed sprouts in boiling water for 5 minutes. Drain. Melt 1 tablespoon butter in a shallow saucepan. Add sprouts, salt and pepper to taste, and ½ teaspoon minced parsley. Simmer slowly for 15 minutes, shaking pan frequently. When tender, pile 1 pint hot chestnut purée in the centre of a flat dish, and arrange sprouts round.

2. Boil shelled chestnuts in salted water for 20 minutes, then peel. Prepare and boil 1½ lb. sprouts. Drain well. Toss in butter then add to the chestnuts, and simmer over slow heat, tossing frequently until flavours have blended, in about 10 minutes. Serve with chicken, goose or pork.

Cabbage : Valuable source of vitamins A, B and C, and mineral salts.

Choose crisp-leaved cabbages with hard or firm solid heads. Insist on closely trimmed, heavy heads. Only 3 or 4 of the outer leaves should be retained when cabbage is mature. Spring cabbage cannot be expected to have much heart. Do not choose any cabbages with burst heads, or yellowed leaves. Stew or pickle red cabbage.

To Prepare: If any of the leaves should be discoloured or wilted, remove. Soak cabbage in cold, salted water to cover for $\frac{1}{2}$ hour. If very large, chop or shred, or quarter. If medium-sized, halve. If cooking by the conservative method, shred. Soak in cold, salted water to cover for $\frac{1}{2}$ hour. To preserve food value, boil conservatively, but cabbage has a very strong flavour cooked in this way.

To Boil: Place prepared cabbage in a tin-lined or enamel saucepan. Cover with boiling, salted water. Boil, uncovered, very rapidly, till tender in 35-40 minutes. If shredded, allow 10-15 minutes, stirring occasionally. Drain thoroughly in a colander.

NOTE : Add 1 tablespoon lemon juice or vinegar to 1 quart water used in boiling red cabbage to fix the colour.

To Boil Conservatively: Allow 3-10 minutes (shredded). Allow 10-15 minutes (quartered).

To Pressure-Cook: At 15 lb. pressure, allow 1 minute for shredded cabbage, 2 minutes for quartered, freshly picked, 3 minutes for quartered, bought.

To Dress: Moisten with butter and season with pepper and a little grated nutmeg if liked.

Allow 1 large cabbage ($1\frac{1}{2}$ lb.) for 4 persons.

TO CREAM CABBAGE (Chou à la Crême) : Add 1 cup cream or white sauce to 1 well-drained, boiled, shredded cabbage. Season with pepper and either $\frac{1}{4}$ teaspoon grated nutmeg or $\frac{1}{2}$ cup grated cheese, or flavour sauce when making with mustard. Stir until blended. Serve on a hot dish.

BAKED CREAMED CABBAGE : Fry 1 small shredded cabbage in enough bacon fat or butter to cover bottom of the frying-pan for 3 minutes, stirring constantly. Add $\frac{1}{4}$ teaspoon paprika, a dash of pepper, salt to taste, and 1 minced clove of garlic. Stir until blended. Place in a shallow, greased, fireproof dish. Stir in 1 cup cream, using sour or sweet according to taste. Bake in a moderate oven, 350° F., for about 25 minutes. *For 3 or 4 persons.*

TO USE UP LEFT-OVER CABBAGE

Fried: Remove rind from 1 or 2 rashers of bacon, depending on quantity of cabbage left. For 3 cups of cabbage, allow 2 rashers of bacon. Cut bacon into dice. Throw into a dry, hot frying-pan, and fry till crisp. Add cabbage and cook till light brown, stirring frequently. Add a few drops of vinegar to taste, and a pat of butter, and serve at once, garnished with sliced hard-boiled eggs, allowing 2 eggs to 3 cups of cabbage. *For 4 persons.*

Sizzle and Squeak: Place 18 small, pricked sausages in a dry frying-pan. Cook, turning frequently, until brown and crisp, then remove to a hot dish. Drain off some of the fat, leaving 2 tablespoons in pan. Add 3 cups shredded, cooked cabbage, and fry for 5 minutes, stirring constantly. Arrange in centre of a hot dish. Place sausages round. *For 4-6 persons.*

TO COOK SAUERKRAUT (Choucroute) : Wash well in a large basin of water. Drain well. Place in a shallow saucepan.

1. Cover with boiling water. Boil for 30 minutes, uncovered, then drain thoroughly. Moisten with butter and season with salt and pepper to taste.

2. Add goose fat, allowing 4 tablespoons to 3 lb. sauerkraut. (When goose fat is not available, substitute butter or lard.) Add 2 or 3 tablespoons white wine and a slice or two of fat bacon. Cover and cook slowly for 1½ hours, stirring occasionally.

Capsicum (Piments) : Half-hardy South American plants bearing green pods that turn red when ripe ; some turn yellow. Choose firm, sound pods. To keep fresh, cover with cold water and store in refrigerator. Remove seeds and membranes before chopping to use in omelettes, scrambled eggs, salads, stuffings, etc., or cutting into strips for certain salads.

Cayenne Pepper is made from the Chili pepper, a member of the Capsicum family. Chilis, when dried, are used for pickles, etc.

To Deep-Fry Green Peppers: Wash peppers. Cut in thin slices cross-wise. Remove seeds and membranes. Dip in beaten egg diluted with 1 dessertspoon water, then in seasoned breadcrumbs, allowing ¼ pint crumbs to 4 peppers. Throw several at a time into a deep, hot fat. Fry till lightly browned, in about 4 minutes. Drain on absorbent paper. Serve with grilled chops or steaks, or fish.

To Saute: Soak peppers for a minute or two in boiling water to cover. Remove and rub off skins. Halve. Remove stems and seeds and membranes. Fry slowly in a little melted butter, turning occasionally, for about 10 minutes. Add beef stock, chopped shallot or onion, minced parsley, salt, and a dash of paprika. Cover. Simmer very slowly, stirring occasionally, for 30 minutes. Allow 1 shallot, 1 teaspoon parsley, 1 dessertspoon butter, ½ pint stock, salt to taste and a dash of paprika to 6 peppers. Serve on toast or fried bread. Garnish sieved egg yolk.

PEPERONI FRITTI (Fried Green Peppers)

4 large green peppers
2 tablespoons olive oil
½ clove garlic
Salt and cayenne pepper to taste

Remove stems from peppers. Wash and dry peppers. Remove seeds and membranes. Divide lengthwise into short strips, about 1¾ inches long. Heat oil with garlic. Add peppers and salt and cayenne pepper to taste. Fry quickly for 3 minutes, stirring occasionally, then cover, and cook slowly till soft, in about ¼ hour. Serve as a garnish for fried or grilled sausages, or pork chops. *For 3 persons.*

Stuffed Green Peppers: Either cut off stem end, and remove seeds and membranes, and stuff peppers, or, if very large, make a gash down one side, and remove membrane and seeds and stuff lengthwise. Throw into boiling, salted water. Boil, uncovered, for 3 minutes if to be baked, when stuffed, in a little water. If to be baked in a greased, fireproof dish, allow 10 minutes. Another way of preparing them is to place them in a basin. Cover with boiling water and leave in the water till cold before stuffing.

FILLINGS FOR PEPPERS

Asparagus: Halve 1 cup boiled or canned, drained asparagus tips. Melt 1 rounded tablespoon butter or margarine in a saucepan. Stir in 1 rounded tablespoon flour. When frothy, slowly stir in 3 tablespoons of asparagus stock or liquid from can and ¼ cup cream or top milk. Stir till smooth and boiling. Season with salt, pepper and paprika, then add a pinch of grated nutmeg, and the asparagus. Pack into 4 prepared pepper cases. Cover with breadcrumbs. Dab with butter. Bake in a moderately hot oven, 375° F., for about 25 minutes.

Chicken and Rice: Mix ½ pint chopped, boiled chicken with ½ pint boiled rice, 1 dessertspoon grated onion and ½ gill sieved, stewed or canned tomatoes. Pack into 4 prepared pepper cases. Place in a greased baking dish, just large enough to take them. Pour ½ cup chicken stock round peppers. Sprinkle filling with breadcrumbs. Dab with butter. Bake in a moderately hot oven, 375° F., for 20-25 minutes.

Corn: Toss 2 cups cooked or fresh corn in 4 tablespoons rich, white sauce flavoured with onion. Pack into 4 prepared pepper cases. Bake in a moderately hot oven, 375° F., for about 25 minutes.

Ham and Mushroom: Melt 1½ tablespoons butter or margarine. Add 1 tablespoon finely chopped onion or shallot. Fry slowly for 3 minutes. Add 3 heaped tablespoons chopped mushrooms, 2 tablespoons stale breadcrumbs, 2 heaped tablespoons minced or ground lean raw ham, and salt and pepper. Moisten with brown gravy as required. Pack into 4 prepared pepper cases. Cover with breadcrumbs and dab with butter. Bake in a moderately hot oven, 375° F., for about 25 minutes, till crisp and brown.

Italian: Mix 2 tablespoons concentrated tomato paste or purée with 1 cup boiling water. Chop 2 or 3 fillets of anchovy preserved in oil. Stir in 3 tablespoons grated cheese, 1 tablespoon minced parsley, ½ cup each of stale breadcrumbs and boiled rice, and of chopped, cooked chicken, pork or veal. Add 1 tablespoon chopped onion or shallot, ½ minced clove of garlic, 1 beaten egg and salt and pepper. Pack into 5 or 6 prepared pepper cases. Place in a greased, fireproof dish. Sprinkle with 4 tablespoons olive oil or melted butter. Bake in a hot oven, 425° F., for about ¼ hour. Pour the tomato liquid round. Bake till peppers are tender in about 15 minutes. *For 5 or 6 persons.*

Cardoon (Cardon) : A species of European thistle, first cousin of globe artichokes. Blanched ribs are used in salads and soups, and can be cooked by any recipe given for celery. Heads edible and similar in flavour to those of globe artichokes. Prepare similarly.

To Prepare: Remove prickles at the side with a flannel. Blanch in salt water sharpened with vinegar in the proportion of ½ tablespoon vinegar to each pint of water, for 15 minutes. Drain. Scrape off outer skin. As you finish each stalk, cutting it into 2½ or 3 inch lengths, throw it into fresh acidulated water.

To Boil: Throw into boiling acidulated water. Add a croûton of bread to absorb the bitterness. Cover and boil for 20 minutes. Remove with a skimmer. Throw into cold water, then rub off thin skin with a cloth. Place in a saucepan. Cover with white stock. Simmer gently till tender, then drain.

To Dress:
(a)   Serve coated with melted butter or melted butter sauce.
(b)   Dip in seasoned flour and fry till golden.
(c)   Prepare as described, but boil in water with the addition of a walnut of butter kneaded with salt to taste. Drain when tender. Melt enough butter in the bottom of a saucepan to cover bottom. Add cardoons. Cover and simmer gently for 5 minutes. Season with pepper and grated nutmeg.

Carrots (Carottes) : Excellent source of vitamin A. Should be firm and sound, and free from cracks. Usually sold by the bunch in the spring and topped in winter. Reckon on 5 or 6 medium-sized carrots to the lb.
To Prepare: Leave skins on if wanted boiled or steamed whole. Scrape before dressing. Scrape if to be served cubed or sliced. If young, can be cooked whole after gently scrubbing. If very large, quarter or halve lengthwise. Rather tasteless, they are best combined with celery, green or red peppers, mushrooms, onions, etc.
To Boil: Throw into boiling, salted water. If cubed, diced or sliced and young, allow 20 minutes. When old, about $\frac{1}{2}$ hour. If halved or quartered, 30-50 minutes depending on age.
To Boil Conservatively: Allow 30 minutes.
To Pressure-Cook: Allow 4 minutes for young, whole carrots at 15 lb. pressure, and 2 minutes for sliced carrots, when cooker should be placed into cold water at once to reduce pressure quickly.
To Steam: Allow $\frac{3}{4}$-1 hour, according to age and size.
To Dress: Coat with parsley butter or melted butter flavoured to taste with grated cheese, or serve with onion sauce. Young carrots are delicious stewed in butter flavoured with chopped onion.
For 3 or 4 persons, allow 1 lb. topped carrots which equals 1 lb. diced, raw carrot, or 2 cups cooked, diced carrot.
TO GLAZE CARROTS (Carottes glacées) : Scrape and wash young carrots. Cut them into 3-inch lengths, then into thin slices, then each slice into match-like shapes. Drop into boiling, salted water. Simmer gently, till tender, in about 10 minutes. Melt enough butter to cover bottom of a frying pan. When hot, add drained carrots. Dredge lightly with salt, pepper and sugar. Fry till lightly coloured. Sprinkle with minced parsley and serve.
TO STEW CARROTS (Carottes sautées) : Prepare and cut 1 lb. carrots lengthwise in quarters. Place in a saucepan. Add 1 teaspoon lemon juice, 3 tablespoons sugar, $\frac{1}{4}$ cup water, $\frac{1}{2}$ teaspoon salt and 1 tablespoon butter. Cover tightly. Stew gently until carrots are glazed and tender, tossing occasionally.
TO TOAST CARROTS : Cut young or old carrots in slices across or lengthwise. Boil in salted water to cover, sweetened with a teaspoon of sugar, until tender. Drain well. Roll in melted fat, then in cornflakes, or breadcrumbs. Arrange in a shallow well-greased, fireproof dish. Bake in a moderate oven, 350° F., until brown, in about 15 minutes.

BRAISED CARROTS (Carottes braisées)

6 medium-sized carrots
2 tablespoons butter

Wash and scrape carrots. Quarter lengthwise. Place in a basin of boiling water. Stand till

1 cup beef stock
½ teaspoon salt
Pepper and paprika to taste

water is cold, then drain. Melt butter in a frying-pan. Add carrots and fry gently, turning frequently, until well browned. Add stock, salt, pepper and paprika. Turn into a casserole. Cover and cook in a fairly hot oven, 400° F., for ½ hour. When tender, serve from casserole. *For 3 persons.*

CARROTS AND PEAS (Carottes et Pois)

4 oz. sliced young carrots
Salt and pepper to taste
1 tablespoon butter
1 sprig tarragon
1 pint shelled peas
Minced chives or parsley to taste

Place carrot slices in a saucepan with salt and pepper, half the fat and tarragon vinegar. Cover with cold water. Cover and cook quickly for 10 minutes. Add peas. Cover again. Cook gently till peas are tender, when water should be absorbed. Add remainder of fat. Remove tarragon and dish up. Sprinkle with minced chives or parsley. *For 6 persons.*

CARROTS MAITRE D'HOTEL (Carottes à la Maître d'Hôtel)

12 medium-sized carrots
1 sprig parsley
1 small onion
1 clove
¼ teaspoon salt
¼ teaspoon sugar
1 saltspoon white pepper
¼ pint water
¾ oz. butter
Juice of ¼ lemon

Choose new carrots. Scrape, then halve lengthwise. Place in a small saucepan, with the parsley, onion, peeled and stuck with clove, salt, sugar, pepper, water and ¼ oz. of the butter. Cover pan. Boil for 5 minutes. Turn into a greased casserole. Cover and cook in a moderate oven, 350° F., for about 35 minutes. Uncover. Remove parsley and onion. Cook over an asbestos mat till nearly dry. Add lemon juice and remainder of butter. Sprinkle with minced parsley. *For 4 persons.*

Cauliflower : Source of vitamins A, B and C. Choose full, white, compact heads, free from dirt and mildew, with fresh, crisp, green outer leaves.

To Prepare : Trim neatly, removing coarse outer leaves. Trim stalk off level with outer leaves remaining, then make a criss-cross with knife on bottom of remaining stem. Place, head-downwards, in salted, acidulated water. Soak for ½ hour to get rid of any insects and grit. Rinse in fresh water. Drain well.

To Boil: Cook, covered, in a small amount of boiling, salted water, from 20-30 minutes, till tender, or cook uncovered in boiling, salted water to cover, till tender, in 15-20 minutes. Drain well.

To Pressure-Cook (Sprigs) : Cook at 15 lb. pressure for 1½ minutes, placing cooker into cold water at once to reduce pressure.

To Steam: Allow ½ hour.

To Dress:

1. Sprinkle with ¼ cup butter, melted till pale brown.

2. Place drained cauliflower in a greased fireproof dish. Sprinkle with 2 tablespoons fine stale breadcrumbs, fried in 1½ tablespoons butter till crisp.

NOTE : When cauliflower is wanted in a hurry, divide flower into sprigs and boil for 10-15 minutes, till tender. Dress as suggested.

For 4 or 5 persons, allow 2 lb., which yields 3 cups cooked.

CAULIFLOWER AU GRATIN (Chou-fleur au gratin)

1 medium-sized cauliflower
1 oz. butter
½ oz. flour
¼ pint cold water
Salt and cayenne pepper to taste
1 tablespoon thick cream
2 oz. grated Parmesan cheese

Boil and drain cauliflower thoroughly. Place in a greased fireproof dish. Melt butter. Stir in flour. When frothy, stir in water, salt and cayenne pepper, cream and half the cheese. Stir until hot and blended. Pour over cauliflower. Sprinkle with the rest of the cheese. Bake in a moderate oven, 350° F., for 15 minutes, until golden brown. *For 4 persons.*

CAULIFLOWER FRITTERS (Beignets de Chou-fleur)

1 medium-sized cauliflower
1 cup flour
¼ teaspoon salt
Pepper to taste
2-3 cups milk
½ teaspoon melted butter or olive oil
2 separated eggs

Soak cauliflower in salted water for 1 hour, and cook in salted milk and water until just tender, but unbroken. Drain. Chill. Separate into sprigs. Sieve flour with salt and pepper. Gradually stir in milk and butter or oil. Beat egg yolks and add. Beat until honey-coloured. Beat egg whites until stiff. Fold into batter. Dip each sprig into batter, then fry, one or two at a time, in deep, hot fat, until golden brown. Drain on absorbent paper. Garnish with parsley. Serve with fried or grilled meat. *For 4 persons.*

Celeriac (Céleri-rave) : Known sometimes as " turnip-rooted celery," or " knob celery ", is a variety of celery cultivated for its swollen stem base instead of stalks. Valuable for hors d'oeuvres, soups and salads. Sometimes served raw, cut into thin slices and seasoned with salt and moistened with vinegar, as a relish. Choose firm, sound roots. If home-grown, draw the soil well up about the middle of September to cover the bulbous stems. Keep the plants covered with bracken or withered leaves to protect them through the cold weather. If preferred, lift in early October when leaves should be removed and crops stored in sand in a cool, dark shed.

To Prepare: Peel roots and remove green tops, then cut into quarters or slices, or dice. Throw into cold, salted, acidulated water. Drain and rinse.

To Boil: Halve or quarter and cook in boiling, salted, acidulated water to cover in a covered saucepan for ½-¾ hour till tender. Drain well.

To Boil Conservatively: Allow 15-20 minutes.

To Pressure-Cook: Cook at 15 lb. pressure for 2 minutes.

To Steam: Cook for about 1 hour.

To Dress: Serve, masked with white or parsley sauce, hot Hollandaise sauce, or mushroom sauce, or moisten with seasoned butter, or simmer gently for 10 minutes in rich brown gravy, and coat with melted butter or Béchamel sauce.

Allow 1½ lb. celeriac for 6 persons.

CELERIAC A LA CRÈME (Céleri-rave à la Crème) : Cut prepared celeriac into thick slices, then dice. Boil in salted water to cover. Drain well. Coat with cream sauce.

CELERIAC AU GRATIN (Céleri-rave au gratin) : Quarter boiled celeriac, or

Steak and Kidney Pudding

Preparing Steak and Kidney for a Steak and Kidney pudding. *See page* 539.

Lining a greased pudding basin with Suet Crust. *See page* 524.

Rolling out cover for a Steak and Kidney Pudding.

Placing cover on top of pudding.

Serve pudding with a clean napkin pinned round the basin.

Fruit Tartlets, made of shortcrust and fruit set in jelly. *See pages* 560-566.

Raised Veal and Ha Pie. *See page* 540.

Mince Pies ready for reheating. *See page* 568

cut into slices. Place in a greased, fireproof dish. Cover with Mornay sauce, then with raspings. Bake in a moderately hot oven, 375° F., for about 15 minutes.

CELERIAC FRITTERS (Beignets de Céleri-rave): Dip diced celeriac or strips, after boiling, draining and drying, in batter. Fry in deep, hot fat till crisp and golden. Garnish with fried parsley.

CELERIAC PUREE (Purée de Céleri-rave): Place 1 diced large celeriac in boiling, salted water. Boil for 5 minutes, then drain thoroughly. Melt ½ oz. butter in a saucepan. Add celeriac, 1 lump of sugar, salt and pepper to taste, and a pinch of paprika. Cover with white stock. Cover. Simmer very gently till soft. Sieve. Re-heat. Just before serving, stir in a large pat of butter.

Celery (Céleri): Provides vitamin C. There are two types: the self-bleaching and the yellow or green leaf. Choose plump, white, compact heads with crisp stalks and fresh foliage.

To Prepare: Remove leaves. Scrape stalks. Wash thoroughly. Cut in halves, or quarter, or in three inch or inch lengths, according to how you mean to dress it. Scrape and trim only for braising.

To Boil: Throw into fast boiling, acidulated water. Cover. Boil rapidly for ¼ hour, then simmer till tender in about 15 minutes. Drain well.

To Boil Conservatively: Allow 20 minutes.

To Pressure-Cook: Allow 2 minutes at 15 lb. pressure, then place cooker in cold water at once to reduce pressure.

To Steam: Cook for 1-1¼ hours.

To Dress: Mask with melted butter or white sauce, or stew gently for a few minutes in rich stock. Sometimes I boil it only for 10 minutes, then drain it well and stew it in a covered casserole in rich brown stock till tender.

For 2 persons, allow 1 large or 2 small heads celery. 1¼ lb. celery yields 2 cups sliced cooked, or 3 cups when raw.

TO CREAM CELERY (Céleri à la Crème): Prepare, dice and boil celery till tender. Drain well. Measure. Add white sauce, allowing ¼ pint sauce to ½ pint celery. Dish up. Sprinkle with minced parsley.

To Vary: Boil in water only for 5 minutes. Drain. Cover with milk. Add 1 slice onion, 1 sprig parsley, and 1 sprig thyme. Cover. Simmer very gently till tender. Drain well. Finish as described above.

CREAMED CELERY A L'ITALIENNE (Célerialla Crema): Cut 4 heads of prepared celery into 2 inch lengths. Wash and dry thoroughly. Throw into boiling water. Boil for 5 minutes. Drain. Melt 2 oz. unsalted butter in a small saucepan. Add 1 tablespoon flour. When frothy, stir in ½ pint rich clear stock. Add celery. Boil for 20 minutes, stirring frequently. Beat 2 egg yolks. Beat in ½ cup cream gradually. Season with grated nutmeg, and salt and pepper if required. Stir into celery very gradually. Heat, stirring constantly, till piping hot, but do not allow to boil. Dish up. Garnish with fried croûtons. *For 4 persons.*

BRAISED CELERY (Céleri Braisé)

3 or 4 heads of celery
Salt, pepper and grated nutmeg to taste

Trim and wash celery and cut each head into 2 or 3 portions. Tie each up with boiled twine. Place in a shallow buttered fireproof dish. Season with

½ pint rich stock
2 or 3 slices streaky bacon
Melted glaze as required

salt, pepper and nutmeg. Moisten with the stock. Cut bacon into strips. Fry slowly for a few minutes, then place on top of celery. Cover dish and place in a hot oven, 425° F., to cook. Cook for 30 minutes. When done, remove and drain celery. Drain off liquor. Add melted glaze to taste and cook till reduced by one third. Serve celery on a hot dish with sauce poured over. *For 4 persons.*

CELERY FRITTERS (Beignets de Céleri)

3 oz. flour
1 teaspoon baking powder
1 teaspoon salt
Pepper to taste
Pinch of ground mace or grated nutmeg
4 well-beaten eggs
1 pint chopped celery
3 tablespoons hot butter or bacon fat

Sift flour with baking powder, salt and pepper, mace or nutmeg. Stir in eggs and celery. When blended, drop spoonfuls of the mixture into the fat. Fry until golden, turning frequently. If preferred, fry in hot deep fat. Drain on absorbent paper. *For 4 persons.*

Chicory : Sometimes called " Succory ". Most popular type is Witloof. Choose crisp, clean heads. Can be cooked by any methods suggested for celery. Excellent ingredient for winter salads.

To Prepare: Trim off any discoloured leaves and roots. Rinse. Soak in slightly salted cold water for 10 minutes.

To Boil: Throw into boiling, salted water and simmer till tender, for about ½ hour. Drain. Rinse in cold water. If you don't like the bitter taste, boil in salted water for 10 minutes, then drain and re-boil in fresh, salted water for about 20 minutes till tender.

To Pressure-Cook: Allow 3 minutes at 15 lb. pressure.

To Dress: Flavour butter sharply with lemon juice, then season with pepper. For 3 persons, allow 1 lb.

CHICORY A LA FRANCAISE (Endive à la Française) : Wash prepared chicory. If very thick, make a cross-cut in the bottom of each head. Place in a saucepan. Cover with boiling, slightly salted water. Bring to boil. Boil for 5 minutes. Drain well. Place in a shallow saucepan or casserole. Coat with melted butter. Season with pepper. Sprinkle with a pinch of sugar and mustard if liked. Cover with a round of buttered paper, then with lid. Simmer very gently, or bake in a slow oven, 300° F., for about 1 hour. If liked, a few drops of meat extract can be added when almost ready, but baste before continuing cooking.

To Vary: Omit the boiling and cook in a shallow saucepan containing enough butter to cover bottom of pan, with salt and pepper added to taste.

BELGIAN CHICORY (Endive à la Belge)

Boiled heads of chicory
Thin slices of boiled ham
Cheese sauce
Crumbs and butter as required

Wrap each head of chicory in a slice of boiled ham. Pack in a greased fireproof dish. Cover with cheese sauce. Sprinkle thickly with breadcrumbs. Fleck here and there with butter. Bake in a moderate oven, 350° F., till crisp and brown. Allow 2-3 heads per person. If liked, celery can be cooked by same method.

Corn-on-the-Cob (Maïs) : Good source of sugar and starch. Perfect ears have green husks and cobs filled with plump milky kernels. Use freshly picked when possible, as it loses its sweetness if not cooked soon after picking.

To Prepare: Remove outer husks only. Strip down inner layers. Remove silk. Replace inner husks. Use a stiff, small brush for removing silk. Tie inner husks in place with strips of the outer husks if liked. If any tips are undeveloped, cut them off.

To Boil: Throw into fast-boiling water to cover. Cover. Cook from 5-12 minutes, according to age. Lift with kitchen tongs. Remove husks. Arrange on a dish covered with a napkin, and draw the corners over. Serve with salt, pepper and plenty of butter. If liked, place on a rack in a hot vegetable dish accompanied by a dish of hot, melted butter.

To Pressure-Cook: Allow $2\frac{1}{2}$ minutes for young, freshly picked corn, at 15 lb. pressure, or 3 minutes for mature bought corn.

To Dress (Grated Cooked Corn) : Heat for 2-4 minutes, with butter and salt and pepper and its own juice, adding a little milk or cream if necessary.

To Roast: Leave husks on corn. Place on a rack in a baking tin. Roast in a moderately hot oven, 400° F., for about $\frac{1}{4}$ hour till tender. Serve coated with seasoned butter.

Allow 1-2 ears per person. 4 medium-sized ears yield 1 cup cut corn.

TO COOK CORN IN MILK (Maïs au lait) : Place corn cut or grated from cob, in the top of a double boiler. Cover with milk. Cover closely. Cook over boiling water for about $\frac{1}{4}$ hour. Drain. (Reserve milk for cream of corn soup.) Season to taste with salt, pepper and paprika. Toss in butter to coat. Add minced chives, spring onions or green pepper to taste.

TO FRY CORN (Maïs frit) : Melt butter in a frying-pan, allowing 2 table-spoons to 1 pint of corn removed from cobs. Add corn. Fry for about 5 minutes until a delicate brown, stirring constantly. Season with salt and pepper to taste. Moisten with thick cream. Stir until piping hot. Serve at once. *For 6 persons.*

BAKED CORN (Maïs au four)

1 beaten egg
¼ pint milk
3 oz. breadcrumbs
1 pint can sweet corn
3 oz. grated cheese
1 teaspoon minced chives
Salt and pepper to taste
¾ oz. butter

Stir beaten egg, milk and half the breadcrumbs into corn. Add half the grated cheese, chives and salt and pepper to taste. Turn into a buttered pie-dish. Mix remainder of breadcrumbs and cheese together. Sprinkle thickly over corn. Dab with butter. Bake for about 30 minutes in a moderate oven, 350° F. If not brown at the end of that time, finish under grill. *For 6 or 8 persons.*

CORN PANCAKES (Maïs, Maryland)

1 can creamed corn
½ cup flour

Drain corn. Sift flour with baking powder, salt and pepper to taste. Stir into corn with parsley,

1 teaspoon baking powder
Salt and pepper to taste
1 dessertspoon minced parsley
¼ teaspoon crushed herbs
2 beaten eggs

herbs and eggs. Beat till blended. Drop from a tablespoon into a frying pan, just covered with melted butter or bacon dripping, in rounds, a little apart. Fry until crisp and golden brown below, and bubbles appear on top. Turn and fry on second side. Garnish with parsley. *For 3 persons.*

Couve Tronchuda : Sometimes known as "Seakale Cabbage." The thick fleshy mid-ribs are delicious cooked and served like seakale, and the head or "cabbage" at the top is left to the last and cooked like cabbage.

Cucumber (Concombre) : Practically no food value. Rather indigestible if eaten raw. Choose firm large cucumbers for cooking and slender ones for salads. Avoid all that are soft.

To Prepare: Peel thickly because the layer just beneath the skin is bitter. Remove ends. Halve lengthwise. Scoop out seeds if prominent. Cut into neat chunks or slices, about 2 inches thick.

To Boil: Place in a saucepan of boiling, salted water to cover. Cover. Boil steadily till tender in 5-10 minutes. Drain in a colander lined with a cloth.

To Dress: Serve coated with Béchamel or white sauce flavoured with tarragon, or toss in a little seasoned butter flavoured with lemon juice, or re-heat in a rich, white stock.

CREAMED CUCUMBER (Concombre à la Crème) : Peel and slice into double their quantity of medium-thick white sauce and cover closely. Simmer till tender. Add minced parsley or chives to taste and 1 sliced hard-boiled egg for every 2 cucumbers cooked.

STEAMED CUCUMBER (Concombre étouffé) : Rinse and cut in slices 2 inches thick crosswise. Place in a basin. Steam until tender. Arrange on a hot dish, standing upright. Coat with cream, Hollandaise or parsley sauce.

CUCUMBER FRITTERS (Beignets de Concombre)

1 medium-sized cucumber
Frying batter as required

Peel cucumber. Cut into thin slices. Dredge with salt and pepper. Dip each slice into frying batter in turn and fry in smoking hot fat for 2 or 3 minutes until pale gold. Drain on absorbent paper. Serve piled on top of each other on a hot dish lined with a lace paper doily. *For 2 persons.*

Dandelion Greens (Dents-de-lion) : Use only before the plants blossom, otherwise too bitter.

To Prepare: Throw out any damaged leaves. Cut off roots. Wash thoroughly in several waters to get rid of any grit, then drain well.

To Boil: Throw into plenty of boiling water. Boil, uncovered, for 20-30 minutes, until tender, salting when almost tender. Drain very well, pressing out all moisture with the back of a wooden spoon.

To Dress: Turn on to a chopping board. Chop and measure. Allow 1 oz. butter to every pint of dandelions, as well as 1 teaspoon flour and 2 tablespoons cream or gravy. Melt butter. Add flour. Stir till frothy, then stir in cream

or gravy and dandelions. Season to taste, then add another spoonful of cream or gravy and serve at once garnished, if liked, with sieved, hard-boiled egg.
Allow 2 lb. for 4 persons, which yields about 4 cups.

Endive (Curly) (Chicorée) : Choose with crisp, fresh, green outer leaves and yellow heart leaves. Generally used for salads.
To Prepare: Remove roots and any discoloured leaves as well as very dark leaves. Tear leaves apart and wash thoroughly, then drain well.
To Boil: Plunge into boiling, salted water or veal stock. Boil, uncovered, for 30-40 minutes.
To Pressure-Cook: Allow 30 minutes at 15 lb. pressure.
To Dress: Pour off water or stock. Stir in beaten egg yolk gradually. Stir till piping hot, but do not allow to boil. Season if necessary. Pour over endive.
BRAISED ENDIVE (Chicorée braisée) : If large and spread open, blanch in boiling water for about 12 minutes, then drain well. If very young and tender, this is unnecessary. Place heads in a large shallow fireproof dish. Season. Cover with diluted meat glaze or rich, brown gravy, then with a buttered paper. Cover closely. Bake in a moderate oven, 350° F., till tender, in about 15 or 16 minutes. If liked, 2 oz. butter can be substituted for half the gravy or dissolved meat glaze. Turn occasionally while cooking. Garnish if liked with chopped hard-boiled eggs.
CREAMED ENDIVE (Chicorée à la crème) : Boil. Drain. Toss in Béchamel sauce.
Allow 1 endive for 3 or 4 persons.

Escarole (Batavian Lettuce) : Can be cooked like spinach, but is usually braised.

Good King Henry : Sometimes known as " Goosefoot " or " Mercury." Popular in Lincolnshire. The blanched shoots should be cooked like asparagus and the leaves that come later on, like spinach.

Greens : Many leaves of plants can be classified as "greens." They include beetroot, Brussels sprouts and turnip tops, cabbage sprouts, lettuce, kale, etc. Good source of vitamin C and mineral salts. Choose fresh, crisp-looking greens. Discard any that are wilted or discoloured. All greens can be cooked as suggested by the following methods, but recipes for some will be found under their respective headings, such as kale, lettuce and spinach.
To Prepare: Trim off stalks where necessary. Rinse under cold, running water, then toss in a basin of cold water and lift out and drain to get rid of all sand and dirt.
To Boil: Throw all greens into fast-boiling salted water to cover. Cook, uncovered, till soft (usually about ¼ hour). Drain well in a sieve. Boil turnip tops for 5 minutes in fast-boiling water, then drain well and boil in fresh, boiling, salted water till tender. This will lessen the bitter taste.
To Boil Conservatively: Allow 15 minutes.
To Dress: Moisten with melted butter, seasoned with pepper, or coat with white sauce. Garnish if liked with sieved, hard-boiled egg.
NOTE : If very young, chop after draining, and treat like spinach. Flavour

421

boiled greens with a few drops of lemon juice or vinegar if liked, or add a little cream as well as butter. In the United States, small bits of chopped pork or bacon are sometimes cooked and served with greens, or bacon fat is substituted for butter in dressing.

Allow 2 lb. for 6 persons, which yields about 6 cups cooked.

GREENS IN VINEGAR

2 quarts lettuce, kale or spinach
4 tablespoons meat dripping
2 tablespoons chopped onion
1 teacup mild vinegar
Salt and pepper to taste

Pick over, wash and drain vegetable. Heat fat. Add onion. Fry slowly till yellow. Add vinegar. Heat till boiling. Add greens. Cover. Cook till soft. Season to taste. *For 4 persons.*

Hamburg Parsley : Like a delicate parsnip.
To Cook: Treat like carrots and parsnips.

Kales (Choux Navets) : This includes all cabbage without hearts. There are many varieties. Scotch kale best known. Furnishes vitamin C. Choose young crisp sprouts or curly leaves.
To Prepare: Trim off stalks. Wash thoroughly.
To Boil: See Cabbage.
To Pressure-Cook: Allow 4 minutes at 15 lb. pressure, placing cooker in cold water at once to reduce pressure.
To Dress: See Cabbage.
Allow 1 lb. for 2 persons.

Kohlrabi (Knol-kohl) : A curious variety of cabbage with a swollen, turnip-like stem which is edible. The leaves are similar to the leaves of kale. Rather nutty flavour. Choose young and firm.
To Prepare: Cut off leaves about an inch from stem.
To Cook: Steam, unpeeled, for 30-50 minutes, rather than boil, or peel, slice and cut into cubes and soak in acidulated water for 1 hour, then rinse. Cook, uncovered, in boiling, salted water to cover for 25-35 minutes, then drain. Dish up.
To Pressure-Cook: Allow $3\frac{1}{2}$ minutes at 15 lb. pressure, placing cooker in cold water at once to reduce pressure.
To Dress: Stir a beaten egg yolk slowly into 1 pint thin, white sauce for coating six kohlrabi. Season with pepper and paprika and pour over. Can also be creamed or scalloped.
Six medium-sized kohlrabi yields 4 cups cooked, which is enough for 4 or 5 persons.

Leeks (Poireaux) : Useful for substituting for onion when onion is not available. Used mostly in broths and soups. Sold bunched or by the pound. Choose young or medium-sized leeks with fresh, green leaves.
To Prepare: Remove root ends. Peel off outer skin and trim green stalk down according to what leeks are to be used for. When trimmed, should be about 5 inches long. Wash very thoroughly. Tie in bundles for boiling.

To Boil: Throw into salted, boiling water. Bring to boil. Drain. Throw into fresh, boiling, salted, acidulated water. Cover. Boil till tender in 25-35 minutes, according to thickness, then drain well.

To Pressure-Cook: Allow 6 minutes at 15 lb. pressure, placing cooker in cold water at once to reduce pressure.

To Dress: Moisten with butter. Season with pepper or coat with Béchamel, Mornay, parsley or white sauce.

To Braise: Par-boil leeks for about 12 minutes, then drain well. Place in a greased fireproof dish. Add enough stock to cover bottom. Fleck with butter. Season to taste. See " To Braise Vegetables."

Allow 2-4 leeks per person, depending on size.

LEEKS AU GRATIN (Poireaux au gratin)

12 leeks
½ pint hot white sauce
3 tablespoons grated cheese
¼ pint stale breadcrumbs
2-3 tablespoons melted butter

Cut prepared leeks into 2 inch lengths. Boil in salted water to cover, then drain well. Place in a greased fireproof dish. Cover with the sauce. Mix cheese with crumbs, then with fat. Sprinkle on surface. Brown in oven, or under grill. *For 4-6 persons.*

Lettuce (Laitue) : If home-grown, should not be gathered till required. Furnishes us with mineral salts and vitamin C. Two popular varieties ; cos and cabbage. Iceberg lettuce and Arctic lettuce are especially crisp varieties of the cabbage shape. Choose crisp, fresh lettuces. Cabbage varieties should have firm hearts. Generally used in salads, but delicious braised.

To Prepare: Remove wilted leaves. Wash under running water. Quarter heads.

To Boil: Place in a saucepan. Add ¼ pint boiling water and ½ teaspoon salt unless boiling a large quantity, say 2 lb., when you need 1 dessertspoon salt. Cover closely. Cook rapidly for 10 minutes till tender. Drain well. Season with pepper and a little grated nutmeg if liked, then sprinkle with melted butter to taste, or with chopped, crisply fried bacon.

Allow 1 small lettuce per person, or 1 large lettuce for 2 persons.

Mushrooms (Champignons) : Many edible mushrooms found wild in England. Commonest are generally known as " field mushrooms." There are edible mushrooms, such as the Fairy Ring (seasonable May-October), Blewitt (September-November) Shaggy Cap (July-October), Beef Steak (July-October), and Parasol (July-November). The field mushrooms are in season in the summer and autumn. Cultivated are always available. Choose freshly gathered. Never pick dry, rubbery, or black, wet mushrooms.

To Prepare: Wipe with a damp cloth, dipped in salt, unless they are earthy, in which case rinse them, then dry thoroughly. Remove stems. Only peel caps if outer skin is tough. Slice if large.

To Fry: For every cup of prepared mushrooms, melt 2 tablespoons of butter, and fry rather slowly from 5-7 minutes, stirring frequently. If liked, 2 tablespoons of olive oil can be substituted for the butter. On the Continent, a clove of garlic is usually heated with the fat or oil before frying mushrooms, and sometimes removed half-way through. Season with salt and pepper to taste, and a pinch of ground mace if liked.

To Grill: Brush prepared large mushroom caps with melted butter or olive oil and a cut clove of garlic if liked. Season with salt and pepper and a small pinch of ground mace or nutmeg if liked. Place, cup side up, on greased griller. Grill for 8 or 9 minutes from 2½-3 inches below unit. Use as a garnish. Allow 3 per person.

To Dress: Serve on rounds or squares of hot, buttered toast.

Allow 1 lb. for 5 or 6 persons.

CREAMED MUSHROOMS (Champignons à la Crème)

1½ lb. mushrooms
2 tablespoons butter
2 tablespoons flour
Pinch of salt
Pepper to taste
1 cup fresh or sour cream

Prepare mushrooms, washing them quickly in water sharpened with vinegar, then drain and dry in a cloth. Quarter. Throw into a pan of boiling salted water to cover. Boil until tender, then drain well. Melt butter. Stir in flour, and mushrooms. Season with salt. Fry slowly for 5 minutes, stirring frequently, then add pepper and fresh or sour cream. Cook, stirring constantly, until cream begins to thicken. Turn into a hot vegetable dish. *For 6 persons.*

MUSHROOMS AND CHESTNUTS (Champignons aux Marrons)

1 lb. chestnuts
1 lb. mushrooms
Salt, pepper and paprika to taste
2 tablespoons flour
½ pint top milk or cream
1 dessertspoon minced parsley

Peel and boil chestnuts until tender, but unbroken, then drain thoroughly. Fry mushrooms in butter and season. Add flour. When blended, gradually stir in top milk or cream. Add chestnuts. Stir gently until piping hot. Dish up. Sprinkle with parsley. *For 8 persons.*

CEPES : These mushrooms are highly prized in France. In Britain, Cépes are generally obtainable bottled or canned, in high-class delicatessen shops and grocery stores. In Italy and Provence, they are often cooked, cooled, coated with French dressing, and served as an hors d'oeuvre.

To Fry: Egg and crumb and fry in hot olive oil. Drain on absorbent paper. Garnish with fried parsley.

To Grill: Drain and soak in boiling water for 2 or 3 minutes, then dry and coat with melted butter. Grill. Season with salt and pepper to taste. Garnish with minced chives or parsley.

Nettles : Valuable source of mineral salts. Choose young tips before signs of flowering. May be cooked with dandelions, sorrel and watercress, or alone.

To Cook: Wash 2 lb. nettles very, very carefully in several waters, stirring vigorously while washing, as the tips may contain a lot of grit. Boil in a covered saucepan in water that clings to them, stirring once or twice. Ready in about 10 minutes. Drain thoroughly. Rub through a sieve. Add butter or cream, or an egg yolk. Stir till blended, but do not allow to boil. Serve in a hot dish.

Allow 2 lb. for 4 persons.

Okra (Févi) : Sometimes called "Lady's Fingers" or "Gumbo." A tropical bean. Its young pods are edible and mostly used in the United States for making Chicken Gumbo Soup, in curries and vegetables dishes. Imparts a mucilaginous consistency to soups and an unusual flavour. Obtainable in cans.

To Prepare: Wash fresh okras in cold water and drain well. Trim both ends neatly.

To Boil: Place in a saucepan. Cover with boiling, salted water. Simmer gently, uncovered, till tender in about $\frac{1}{4}$ hour. Drain well.

To Dress: Coat with equal quantity of melted butter and cream, allowing 1 tablespoon of each to 12 pods, or with butter only. Season with salt and pepper. Toss over stove till blended.

To Serve Canned Okras: Heat in liquid. Drain and dress as above. Allow 6-8 pods per person.

Onions (Oignons) : There are many varieties of onions. Bermuda and Spanish most commonly used, but Egyptian, potato, Rocambole, and Welsh can all be grown. For cooking choose firm, sound bulbs with thin skins. The Rocambole has a mild garlic flavour. Sometimes called "sand leek." Use Welsh as you use chives either when cooking or in salads.

To Prepare Onions (bulbs) : Peel and remove roots. If small, cook whole. If large, quarter or slice. To quicken the cooking of whole onions, make two gashes at the root end.

To Boil: Throw small, whole or quartered onions into boiling water. Simmer gently, uncovered, for 30-40 minutes, till tender. Salt when three-quarters cooked. Drain well.

To Pressure-Cook: Allow 8 minutes at 15 lb. pressure, placing cooker into cold water at once to reduce pressure.

To Dress: Moisten with butter, or coat with cheese sauce and brown under grill or coat with parsley sauce.

To Bake:

1. Peel and slice $\frac{1}{2}$ inch thick. Place in a shallow, greased baking dish or tin. Add $1\frac{1}{2}$ tablespoons melted butter and enough white stock or water to cover bottom of dish. Bake in a moderate oven, 350° F., until tender, in about $\frac{1}{2}$ hour, basting and turning occasionally, until tender.

2. Peel and cut into thin slices. Arrange in a greased baking dish or tin. Cover with thin cream. Bake in a moderately slow oven, 325° F., until soft, basting occasionally.

To Fry:

1. Peel and slice. Soak in cold water for $\frac{1}{2}$ hour. To every quart allow 3 tablespoons fat. Melt till smoking hot. Add onions. Fry slowly for about 20 minutes, stirring frequently till tender and faintly brown. Season with salt and pepper.

2. Peel. Slice $\frac{1}{4}$ inch thick and separate into rings. Soak in cold water for $\frac{1}{2}$ hour. Drain and wipe dry. Dip in seasoned flour. Fry in deep, smoking hot fat, 365°-370° F., till pale brown. Drain on absorbent paper. Dredge with salt.

To Scallop: Cut whole, boiled onions in quarters. Place in a greased baking dish or tin. Cover with white or cheese sauce, allowing ½ pint sauce to each pint onions. Cover with sieved stale breadcrumbs. Dab with butter or margarine. Bake until crumbs are brown.

Allow 1 lb. onions for 4 persons.

TO GLAZE ONIONS (Oignons glacés) : Peel 1 lb. small, white onions. Throw into a saucepan. Cover with plenty of boiling, salted water. Boil till tender but unbroken. Drain thoroughly. Toss in a cloth until dry. Melt 3 tablespoons butter in a small saucepan. Add 2 tablespoons sugar and onions. Cook slowly over heat, shaking frequently, until onions become glazed. Serve as a garnish to fried or grilled chops or steaks, or Hamburg steaks. *For 6 persons.*

BAKED SPANISH ONIONS (Oignons au four)

3 medium-sized Spanish onions
½ clove garlic
1 oz. butter
1 teaspoon minced parsley
Salt and pepper to taste
Juice of ½ lemon
2 tablespoons breadcrumbs

Peel and cut off a slice at each end of the onions. Cut in two crosswise. Arrange on a buttered baking dish, cut sides up. Mince garlic. Knead butter with garlic, parsley, and salt and pepper. Stir in lemon juice. Spread this mixture evenly over the 6 half onions. Cover. Bake in a moderate oven, 350° F., basting twice at regular intervals, for 35 minutes. Sprinkle with the crumbs. Baste again with liquor in dish. Bake for about 10 minutes, till tender. Serve from dish with cold cuts. *For 3 persons.*

BRAISED ONIONS (Oignons braisés)

1½ lb. equal-sized onions
Salt and pepper to taste
1 oz. Demerara sugar
½ pint stock
1 oz. butter

Peel and cook onions in boiling salted water for 15 minutes. Drain. Dry and place in a shallow buttered fireproof dish. Sprinkle with salt, pepper and sugar. Add stock. Dab with butter. Cover and bake in a moderate oven, 350° F., for 20 minutes then uncover. Bake, basting occasionally with the stock, until onions are tender, in about 20 minutes. *For 6 persons.*

Orach : A decorative, crimson plant, sometimes called " Mexican Spinach." Cook like spinach or in combination with spinach. Makes lovely floral decoration.

Parsnip (Panais) : Source of carbohydrates and phosphorus. Not at their best till after the first frosts. Choose firm, medium-sized young roots, free from cracks. Good for flavouring soups and stews, or cooking in a casserole or stew of beef.

To Prepare: Wash. Scrape if liked. If large, halve or quarter lengthwise, or slice or cube as required. If very small, leave whole.

To Boil: Throw, scraped or unscraped, into boiling, salted water. Cover. Boil from 40 minutes-1 hour, depending on age. Drain. Scrape if necessary.

To Pressure-Cook: Allow 10 minutes at 15 lb. pressure.

To Steam: Allow 1¼-1½ hours, according to age.

To Dress: Coat with melted butter or parsley sauce, or cut into slices length-wise and fry lightly in a little butter.

BOILED PARSNIPS WITH BLACK BUTTER (Panais au beurre noir) : Prepare 1½ lb. parsnips. Cut them into 4 inch pieces. If very thick, quarter. Boil until tender. Drain well. Melt 2 oz. butter. Add 1 teaspoon lemon juice, salt and black pepper to taste. Cook very slowly until a rich brown. Pour over parsnips. Serve with roast beef or fried or grilled steaks. *For 6 persons.*

PARSNIPS A LA MAITRE D'HOTEL : Season 1 quart diced, boiled parsnips with salt if necessary and pepper to taste, and ½ teaspoon paprika. Toss in 2 tablespoons melted butter, flavoured with ½ tablespoon lemon juice. Serve with poultry for preference.

FRIED PARSNIP CAKES : Boil 2 lb. prepared parsnips. Drain well. Mash. Season with salt and pepper and moisten with butter. Add a dash of lemon juice if liked. Shape into small, flat, even-sized cakes. Coat with flour. Fry until brown on both sides in a little smoking hot butter.

TO MASH PARSNIPS (Panais en purée) : Peel, quarter and boil 6 medium-sized parsnips in acidulated water until tender. Drain thoroughly. Mash. There should be about 1 pint pulp. Season with salt, pepper and paprika, 1 tablespoon lemon juice and 3 tablespoons butter. Beat until blended. Dish up. Decorate with the prongs of a fork. Sprinkle with minced parsley.

For 4 persons, allow 1 lb., which yields 1 pint cooked, diced parsnips.

PARSNIP FRITTERS (Beignets de Panais) : Divide peeled, boiled parsnips into sticks about 3 inches long. Dip in frying batter. Fry in deep smoking hot fat until golden brown. Drain on absorbent paper. Serve with tomato sauce.

PARSNIP PANCAKES (Crêpes de Panais)

12 boiled parsnips
1 well-beaten egg
Salt and pepper to taste
1 oz. flour
2 tablespoons melted butter

Mash parsnips, then put through a ricer. Beat in egg, salt, pepper, flour and butter. Melt a table-spoon of bacon fat or dripping in a frying-pan. Drop the batter from a tablespoon in rounds a little apart. Fry until brown below and bubbles form on top. Turn and fry until brown on the other side. *For 6 persons.*

Peas : Source of proteins and starches. There are 3 kinds of peas : Peas that you pod, peas with edible pods, sometimes known as " sugar " or " mange tout " peas, popular in France, and Asparagus peas. Sugar peas should be topped, tailed and cooked like young, green, string beans. Choose fresh, fairly well-filled, medium-sized pods of a bright green colour. If home-grown, gather just before cooking.

To Prepare: Do not shell peas until ready to cook them. Pick over and rinse thoroughly.

To Boil: Throw into boiling water to cover. Add a lump of sugar if liked. Cover. Simmer till peas are tender, in 15-20 minutes, adding salt when nearly tender. Drain well.

To Pressure-Cook: For young, freshly-picked peas, allow ½ minute. For

VEGETABLES

mature peas, allow 1 minute at 15 lb. pressure, then place cooker in cold water at once to reduce pressure quickly.

To Dress: Add butter and pepper. Toss lightly. If liked, combine with young, boiled diced carrots to taste.

For 6 persons, allow 3 lb. peas in the pod, which yields 3 cups cooked peas.

CREAMED GREEN PEAS (Pois à la Creme)

2 lb. green peas
1 tablespoon butter
3 chopped spring onions
1 cos lettuce heart
4 sprigs parsley
1 sprig thyme
½ teaspoon salt
Pepper to taste
¾ gill cream
2 tablespoons green pea stock

Pod. Rinse and drain. Melt butter in a shallow saucepan. Add peas and onion. Wash lettuce leaves and add with parsley, thyme and salt. Add enough boiling water to cover bottom of pan. Cook rapidly for 10 minutes, then lower heat. Cover saucepan closely. Simmer gently until peas are tender, then remove lettuce and parsley. Season with pepper. Dilute cream with 2 tablespoons stock from the peas. Stir until piping hot, but do not allow to boil. Dish up peas and pour sauce over. *For 4 persons.*

PETITS POIS A LA FRANÇAISE

1 pint shelled green peas
¼ pint boiling water
1 sprig parsley
1 sprig mint
1 sliced onion or shallot
Pinch of salt
Pinch of sugar
¼ lb. lean ham
½ oz. butter
¼ oz. flour

Place the peas in a shallow saucepan with the water, parsley, mint, onion or shallot, salt and sugar. Cover. Simmer gently for about 25 minutes until tender. Dice ham. Melt butter in a saucepan. Add ham. Fry slowly until tender. Stir in flour. Add peas. Cook gently for 3 minutes, tossing often. Season. Pile in hot serving dish. Garnish with fleurons of puff pastry. *For 4 persons.*

Potatoes (Pommes-de-terre) : Source of mineral salts, carbohydrates and vitamins A, B and C. Choose medium-sized, even, shallow-eyed, clean-looking, sound potatoes, free from warts and shoots.

To Prepare: Scrub and dry potatoes.

To Bake in their Jackets: Choose kidney-shaped potatoes. If you want potato skins to be soft and tender, brush with melted oil or dripping. Prick with a fork. Place in a baking tin or on a rack in oven. Bake in a fairly hot oven, 425° F., turning once or twice, for ¾-1 hour. To test when ready, lift them with a cloth in your hands. Squeeze gently and if they are soft, they are ready. Serve in a hot dish lined with a folded napkin. If preferred, cut a deep gash crosswise at the top of each potato, and holding it in both hands with cloth, carefully squeeze to allow steam to escape, and force potato into opening. Sprinkle potato with salt and pepper and slip a pat of butter into each. Allow 1 per person.

To Rice: Put boiled or mashed potatoes through a potato masher or ricer into a hot vegetable dish.

BAKED STUFFED POTATOES (Pommes de terre farcis)

BASIC RECIPE:
6 baked potatoes in their jackets
1 tablespoon butter
1 tablespoon hot milk
Salt and pepper to taste

Cut potatoes in half lengthwise. Carefully scoop out potato into a saucepan. Mash until smooth. Add butter, milk, salt and pepper to taste. Beat until fluffy. Divide between potato shells. Ornament with a fork. Bake in a hot oven, 450° F., for about 5 minutes. *For 6 persons.*

To Vary:

1. Stir ½ cup grated cheese into potato before packing into shells. Dredge lightly with grated cheese.

2. Stir ½ cup chopped ham, silverside or tongue and 1 teaspoon minced chives or parsley into potato pulp.

3. Line potato shells with mashed potato, prepared as in basic recipe, then slip an egg, or ½ tablespoon of prawns in cheese sauce, into each shell. Season with salt, pepper and paprika. Bake until egg is set, or fish browns.

HINTS ON BOILING POTATOES

1. Be careful to boil steadily. If you boil quickly, the potatoes will break. If you boil too slowly, they will acquire a strong flavour, become heavy instead of light, and their colour will be affected.

2. If forced to boil potatoes of an unequal size, divide the large ones to equal the small ones in size.

3. If the flavour of onions is liked, boil a sliced, peeled onion with each lb. of potatoes.

4. To make very old potatoes white and mealy, seven minutes before they are ready, add 2 teaspoons vinegar to every quart water used.

5. To boil large, old potatoes perfectly, cook in boiling salted water till outsides are soft, then add 1 pint cold water. The cold water will send heat to the centres and enable the potatoes to finish cooking right through without breaking up.

To Boil New Potatoes: Scrub, scrape and drop potatoes into boiling water to cover. When all are prepared, drain in a colander. Rinse under tap and place in a pan. Add 1 quart boiling water and 1-2 teaspoons salt, according to when you add it. Cover and boil steadily from 20-30 minutes, until tender when tested. Drain quickly. Cover. Shake over moderate heat until dry. When dry, sprinkle with melted butter and parsley, in the proportion of 2 tablespoons butter and ½ tablespoon minced parsley to 1 lb. potatoes. Shake lightly over heat. Substitute minced chives for parsley if liked.

To Boil Old Potatoes: Choose potatoes of a medium and uniform size. Peel thinly. Rinse. Throw into boiling, salted water to cover. Cover. Boil steadily, but not rapidly, until tender when pierced with a fork in about 20 minutes. If very old, start to boil in cold, salted water. Drain thoroughly. Re-cover. Stand for a moment or two, then tilt lid to let out the steam. Another way of drying the potatoes is to place a folded towel on the top as soon as they are drained. This will absorb moisture.

To Boil in Jackets: Place in a saucepan. Cover with boiling water. Boil for 20-30 minutes. Add 1 rounded dessertspoon salt at the end of 15 minutes, then boil until a fork will easily pierce them. Drain quickly. Shake over the stove until dry with lid on pan. Serve in jackets, or scrape off, and coat with parsley butter.

To Boil Potatoes with Onions: Halve 6 large potatoes. Place in a saucepan. Add enough boiling water to come half-way up the sides of pan, and add 1 chopped onion. Cover closely. Boil steadily until tender, in about 15-20 minutes. Drain. Add 1 dessertspoon salt. Shake over stove until dry and mealy looking. Scrape off any peel and coat with parsley butter.

To Pressure Cook: Allow 8 minutes at 15 lb. pressure.

To Steam: Wash and dry medium-even-sized potatoes. Make a cut cross-wise in their skins on one side. Steam till tender when tested with a skewer or knitting needle, in about 30-40 minutes. Season potato in openings with salt and pepper and insert a pat of butter. Can also be steamed skinned.

To Dress: Toss in melted butter, flavoured with minced chives, parsley, or caraway seeds, allowing 1 teaspoon seeds to 2 tablespoons butter, or coat with fennel or parsley sauce, or mash.

To Fry Boiled or Steamed Potatoes (Sauté) : Melt enough dripping to cover the bottom of a frying-pan. Cut potatoes into thin slices. Fry till brown below, then turn and fry on other side. Season with pepper to taste and salt if necessary. Serve, sprinkled with minced parsley or chives.

MASHED POTATOES (Purée de Pommes de Terre)

6 medium-sized boiled or steamed potatoes
2½ tablespoons butter
¼ cup hot milk
Salt and pepper to taste

Mash potatoes till smooth. Stir in butter and enough of the milk to moisten. Season with salt and pepper. Beat till creamy. Pile lightly into a hot vegetable dish. *For 3 or 4 persons.*

DUCHESS POTATOES (Pommes de Terre, Duchesse)

3 oz. butter
2 lb. mashed potatoes
2 separated eggs
Salt, pepper and grated nutmeg to taste

Stir butter into hot potato. Mix well then stir in one yolk at a time. Season with salt, pepper and grated nutmeg or ground mace. Beat egg whites to a stiff froth. Fold in gradually. Place in a forcing bag and squeeze out on a greased baking sheet in snails, roses, pyramids or any shape you want. Brush with beaten egg or melted butter. Bake in a hot oven, 450° F., till brown. Use as a garnish or a vegetable. *For 6 persons.*

POTATO BORDER (Bordure de Pommes de Terre)

3 large potatoes
1 oz. butter
1 egg yolk
Salt, pepper and coralline pepper to taste

Put hot potatoes through a potato masher. Stir in butter. When well mixed, stir in egg yolk and salt and pepper and coralline pepper. Mix till well blended. With well-floured hands, shape into a circle or oblong as desired. Brush with beaten egg. Decorate with a knife. Bake till golden brown on dish on which it is to be served.

NOTE : If wanted green, colour with sieved, cooked or canned peas, or sieved spinach to taste.

To Fry Sliced Raw Potatoes (Pommes de terre, Pont-neuf): Heat oil until smoking hot. Thinly slice potatoes. Place in a frying basket. Fry until golden brown. Drain on absorbent paper. Re-heat oil until smoking hot between each batch. Sprinkle with salt to taste.

Potato Chips (Pommes de terre Liardes) : There are two ways of preparing potatoes for chips : Either cut peeled potatoes into slices $\frac{1}{4}$ inch thick, then cut into strips $\frac{1}{4}$ inch broad, or, if potatoes are plump and stumpy, cut them into eighths. Throw into cold water as prepared. There are two methods of frying chips :

1. Heat fat required, the quantity depending on the number of chips to be fried, in a deep fryer or saucepan, until hot, but not smoking hot. If using a frying thermometer, this is 250° F., for fat and 255° F. for oil. If using a deep fryer, allow from 1-1½ lb. fat. Use clarified dripping, lard or oil for frying. No matter what pan you use, the fat should be at least 3 inches deep. Dry potatoes thoroughly with a cloth. Place a few at a time in frying basket and lower into fat or oil. (If you try to cook too many at once, you will cool the fat or oil too much and the chips may become sodden.) Fry until soft. Drain on absorbent paper. When all the chips are soft, heat fat or oil to smoking hot, 390° F. for fat, and 395° F. for oil, and add chips as before. Watch carefully as they brown almost at once. Drain on absorbent paper. Sprinkle with salt.

2. Throw one chip into hot fat or oil, which is below smoking hot temperature. Fry until it colours lightly in a few seconds. If it takes longer, continue to heat fat or oil, and test with another chip, then place a few chips in frying basket, and fry in fat or oil until golden. Drain on absorbent paper. Keep hot while frying remainder. Sprinkle with salt and pepper.

NOTES ON MAKING CHIPS

1. If you haven't a thermometer, the temperature of the fat or oil can be tested with a small piece of bread instead of a chip. If it browns in less than a minute, fat or oil is ready for use. If not, continue to heat and test again. If testing in oil, it should take 20 seconds.

2. If chips are wanted crisp, soak in very cold water for 1 hour. Drain well and dry before frying.

3. If wanted quickly, par-boil prepared chips for 3 minutes. Drain and dry before frying.

FRIED POTATOES IN OTHER WAYS

Potato Balls: Wash, pare and soak as many large potatoes as you want to turn into balls. With a vegetable cutter, scoop out as many balls as possible. Soak in very cold water for 1 hour. Drain. Dry. Cook like chip potatoes, method 1.

Crisps: Wash, pare and cut medium-sized potatoes into slices crosswise, as thin as wafers. Soak in very cold water for 1 hour. Drain. Dry. Cook like chip potatoes, method 1.

Lattice Potatoes: Wash and pare large potatoes. Prepare with vegetable slicer sold for the purpose. Cook like chip potatoes, method 1.

Saratoga Chips: Prepare like potato crisps. Soak for 2 hours, changing water after 45 minutes, then after $1\frac{1}{2}$ hours. Drain. Throw into a saucepan of boiling water. Cover and boil for 1 minute. Drain in a colander. Throw in a basin of cold water. Stand for 1 minute. Drain in a colander. Dry with a towel. Cook like chipped potatoes, method 1, but stir occasionally to prevent chips sticking together.

Souffle Potatoes: Choose equal-sized potatoes. Cut in even slices almost $\frac{1}{8}$ inch thick, then into rounds with a sharp biscuit or pastry cutter. Dry and throw a few at a time into fat heated only to 250° F. Cook for 5 minutes. Drain off fat. When all are prepared, heat fat to 400° F., and add potatoes. If this recipe is properly followed, potatoes should turn puffy and golden at once. Drain on absorbent paper and sprinkle with salt.

Potato Straws (Shoe Strings or Julienne Potatoes) (Pommes Pailles) : Wash and pare potatoes. Cut in slices almost $\frac{1}{8}$ inch thick, then cut slices into match-like strips the same width. If preferred thicker, cut into $\frac{1}{4}$ inch thick strips. Soak in very cold water for 1 hour. Drain and dry. Cook like chip potatoes, method 1.

Potato Wafers: Slice peeled potatoes as thin as a wafer if you have a potato slicer. Soak in cold water for $\frac{1}{2}$ hour. Toss in a towel until dry. Lay side by side in a shallow, greased baking tin. Brush lavishly with melted butter or margarine. Bake in a hot oven, 450° F., for about 25 minutes, until brown below, then turn and bake until brown on other side. Sprinkle with salt.

To Make Cases or Nests of Potato Straws: After preparing, soak in very cold water for 20 minutes. Drain and dry. Take a strainer with a fine mesh and wire handle, measuring 4 inches in diameter, and line with the strips. Slip a similar strainer, only about $2\frac{1}{2}$ inches in diameter, in the centre of the other strainer. Holding the latter in place with a long-handled spoon, lower into hot fat, 250° F., or oil, 255° F. Cook till soft. Remove from fat. Heat fat to 400° F., or oil to 405° F. Return nests to fat or oil, when they will brown quickly. It is best to have 2 pans of fat or oil going when preparing these cases. Use them as containers for creamed fish, small fillets of fried fish, grilled kidneys, creamed chicken or sweetbreads, etc. Drain and salt before filling.

To Roast Potatoes: There are two ways of roasting potatoes :

    1. Wash and peel equal-sized potatoes. Place them in a saucepan of cold water to cover and bring them to the boil. Boil for 3 minutes. Drain and place in a shallow baking tin. Coat with hot dripping. Bake for $\frac{3}{4}$-1 hour according to size, turning occasionally.

    2. Wash, pare and rinse potatoes about $1\frac{1}{4}$ hours before the roast is ready to dish up. Arrange potatoes in the bottom of the baking tin and baste them with the hot dripping. Roast till ready. Turn occasionally. If not using a self-basting roaster, baste them when you baste the meat. If roasting at a low temperature, roast till soft. Transfer with enough dripping to cover bottom of pan to a shallow saucepan. Toss over heat till golden brown all over.

NOTE :

    1. New potatoes should not be parboiled before roasting.

    2. If not easy to roast potatoes under joint, pour some of the dripping into a baking tin and roast as suggested.

    3. Sprinkle potatoes with salt after dishing up.

To Stew Potatoes: Pare enough potatoes to give you a quart when chopped.

Soak in very cold water to cover for 10 minutes. Drain off water. Place potatoes in a stew pan with a teaspoon of salt, ¼ teaspoon pepper, 1 tablespoon butter, 2 cups milk or stock, or 1 cup milk and 1 cup water. Cover and simmer for 20 minutes. Mix flour to a paste with milk or stock and thin with a little of the boiling liquid. Add to stew. Cover and cook for 10 minutes. Serve in a hot vegetable dish.

Allow 1 lb. for 3 or 4 persons, which yields 1 pint diced, raw or cooked potatoes, or 2½ cups mashed potatoes.

CREAMED POTATOES (Pommes de Terre à la Crème)

8 potatoes
1 cup milk
2 tablespoons butter
1½ tablespoons flour
¼ teaspoon salt, pepper and paprika
Minced parsley to taste

Cut potatoes in cubes. Boil in salted water in the usual way till tender but unbroken. Heat milk. Melt butter in a saucepan. Remove from heat. Stir in flour, and when it froths, thin down with milk, stirring rapidly to prevent lumping. Cook till smooth and mellow to taste, then season with salt, pepper and paprika. Arrange potatoes in a hot vegetable dish. Stir a dessertspoon of minced parsley into the sauce. Pour over potatoes and sprinkle with a little more parsley. *For 4 persons.*

GOLDEN POTATO PUFFS (Pommes de Terre, Italiennes)

Small potatoes as required
2 oz. flour
2 yolks of eggs
1 tablespoon salad oil
¼ pint cold water
2 egg whites

Wash and peel as many small, even-sized potatoes as you need. Boil in the usual way, till tender but unbroken. Sift flour into a basin. Stir in egg yolks, oil and water. Beat till smooth, then fold in stiffly frothed egg whites. Dip potatoes in quickly and fry in smoking hot deep fat till golden. Drain on absorbent paper. Garnish with minced parsley. *For 4 persons.*

JULIENNE POTATOES MORNAY
(Pommes de Terre, Mornay)

2 cups potato, cut in strings
1 small chopped onion
1 teaspoon mixed herbs
2 tablespoons butter
2 tablespoons flour
1 cup milk
1 teaspoon salt
Pepper to taste
Grated cheese as required

Cut raw, pared potatoes into long match-like sticks. Cook in boiling water till tender. Drain and turn into a warmed dish. Brown onion and herbs in the fat. Add flour, stirring thoroughly. Add milk, salt and pepper, and cook in the top of a double boiler for 20 minutes. Strain and pour over cooked potato. Sprinkle with grated cheese. *For 2 or 3 persons.*

DEVILLED NEW POTATOES (Pommes de Terre au Diable)

1½ dozen rather small new potatoes
1½ tablespoons butter

Boil potatoes in the usual way. Drain before they show signs of breaking. Drop a few at a time into hot lard and fry for 5 minutes. Drain quickly.

433

¾ teaspoon made mustard
Salt and pepper to taste
1½ teaspoons vinegar
1 beaten egg yolk

Have butter ready melted in another shallow pan and mixed till blended with the mustard and salt and pepper to taste. As you drain the fried potatoes, slip them gently into seasoned butter. When all are in pan, sprinkle with the vinegar. Cook over moderate heat for 3 minutes, shaking pan constantly. Remove from stove. Strain off liquid into another pan. Stir in egg yolk and potatoes. Re-heat, shaking pan, and serve at once. *For 6 persons.*

O'BRIEN POTATOES (Pommes de Terre à l'Espagnole)

1 quart potato balls
Salt and pepper to taste
2 slices Spanish onion
2 tablespoons butter
2 large canned pimientoes
1 tablespoon minced parsley

Peel potatoes and shape them into balls with a vegetable cutter. Throw into cold water as you shape them, then drain well. Fry in deep, smoking hot fat till golden brown and tender. Drain and sprinkle with salt and pepper. Fry onion in the butter until golden. Remove onion. Add chopped pimientoes, and then fried potatoes. Serve hot, sprinkled with minced parsley. *For 4 persons.*

POTATOES A LA WESTPHALIA (Pommes de Terre, Westphalien)

6 raw potatoes
Salt and pepper to taste
1 beaten egg
3 tablespoons butter

Peel, wash and grate potatoes. Season with salt and pepper to taste. Stir egg into potato. Melt butter in a frying-pan. Drop mixture from a tablespoon in rounds, about 2 inches apart. Flatten each round slightly with a fish slice. Fry for 2 minutes. Turn and fry on other side for about 2 minutes. They should be pale gold. Arrange overlapping in a round on a hot flat dish. Garnish with a sprig of parsley in the centre. *For 3 persons.*

POTATO APPLES (Pommes de Terre à la Royale)

2 cups hot mashed potato
2 tablespoons butter
¼ cup grated cheese
½ teaspoon salt
Cayenne pepper and grated
  nutmeg
2 tablespoons thick cream
2 egg yolks

Mix all ingredients together thoroughly. Beat well. Shape into small " apples ". Flour, egg and crumb, and fry in smoking hot fat till golden. Drain on absorbent paper. Garnish with minced parsley. *For 4 persons.*

POTATO CHAPATTIES (Pommes de Terre à l'Indienne)

1½ lb. boiled potatoes
6 oz. self-raising flour
1 heaped teaspoon salt

Mash potatoes until smooth. Leave until cold. Stir in flour and salt and enough cold water to make a stiff dough. Roll out thinly on a lightly floured pastry board. Cut into rounds the size of a saucer. Fry in deep, hot fat until pale gold. Serve with curries in addition to rice or in place of it. These chapatties can be piled on top of each other and kept for a few days under a covered dish or in an air-tight tin, and fried as required. *For 6 persons.*

POTATO CHEESE ROSETTES (Rosettes de Pommes de Terre)

1 teaspoon salt
2 oz. butter
2 tablespoons milk
Pepper to taste
1 beaten egg
4 cups mashed potatoes
2¼ oz. finely grated cheese

Add salt, butter, milk, pepper and egg to mashed potatoes. Beat well. Force through pastry tube on to a well-greased baking sheet, in large rosettes. Sprinkle each rosette with grated cheese. Bake in a hot oven, 450° F., for about 20 minutes, until brown. *For 6 persons.*

POTATO CROQUETTES (Croquettes de Pommes de Terre)

1 pint mashed potato
2 tablespoons butter
¼ teaspoon celery salt
Salt, pepper and paprika to taste
1 egg yolk
Onion juice to taste
1 teaspoon minced parsley or chives

Put potatoes through a masher, then mix in other ingredients. Beat till light and fluffy. Shape into corks with floured hands. Crumb, egg and crumb. Fry. Drain on paper. Arrange in a hot vegetable dish lined with a lace paper doily. *For 4 persons.*

POTATO DUMPLINGS (Pommes de Terre à la Paysanne)

Boil 6 large potatoes in their jackets, then steam, peel and put them through a masher. Cool and weigh. When prepared, stir in 2 beaten eggs, ½ cup farina, barely a cup of flour and salt to taste. Add a grating of nutmeg if liked. Shape into balls the size of a walnut. Drop into boiling, salted water, allowing a teaspoon salt to a quart of water. Simmer for 20 minutes. Drain. Serve hot, sprinkled with melted butter cooked till brown, then with grated onion. *For 6 persons.*

POTATO PUREE (Purée de Pommes de Terre)

Put boiled potatoes through a ricer. Return to pan. Beat until smooth while still hot. Add butter and milk or cream to taste, allowing 1 oz. butter and 2 tablespoons milk or cream to 1 lb. of potatoes. Season with salt and pepper.

POTATO SOUFFLES (Soufflés de Pommes de Terre)

1½ lb. small potatoes
2 oz. flour
1 separated egg
1 tablespoon olive oil
¾ gill warm water

Wash and peel potatoes. Cut into quarters. Boil gently in boiling salted water to cover, until tender, but unbroken. Steam for a minute to allow potatoes to dry. Sieve flour into a basin. Stir in egg yolk gradually, then the oil and water. Beat until smooth. Beat white of egg until stiff. Fold into mixture. Dip each piece of potato into batter and drop 2 or 3 pieces at a time as prepared in deep smoking hot fat. Fry until each forms a brown coat in 3-5 minutes. Drain on absorbent paper. *For 6 persons.*

SCALLOPED POTATOES (Pommes de Terre en Cocotte)

2 lb. peeled potatoes
Salt, pepper and paprika to taste
2 oz. flour
1½ oz. butter

Cut the potatoes in slices crosswise. Brush a large fireproof dish with melted butter. Place a third of the potatoes in the butter. Season with salt, pepper and paprika. Sprinkle with a third of the flour. Dab with a third of the butter. Repeat layers twice. Pour milk down one side. Milk should just show at the sides, but must not cover them. Bake in a moderate oven, 350° F., for 1 hour, then uncover and bake until brown. *For 6 persons.*

To Vary: Sprinkle each layer with 2 tablespoons grated cheese.

STOVED POTATOES (Pommes de Terre, Bourgeoise)

Cooked roast beef bones or scraps of lamb or mutton cutlets
10 or 12 potatoes
2 or 3 sliced peeled medium-sized onions
Salt and pepper to taste

Boil bones in water to cover for 2 hours. Strain stock into a saucepan. Skim off fat. Add sliced potatoes, onion and plenty of salt and pepper to taste. Cover. Simmer for 1 hour. Draw to side of stove. Stand till liquid is almost absorbed. Serve with cold beef, lamb or mutton. *For 4 persons.*

NEW POTATOES IN GREEN JACKETS
(Pommes de Terre, Maître d'Hôtel)

1½ lb. new potatoes
1½ tablespoons lemon juice
¼ cup melted butter
¼ cup minced chives or parsley

Wash, scrape and boil equal-sized potatoes. Cover with boiling water, salted to taste. Cover and cook till tender. Drain well. Stir the lemon juice into the butter and pour over. Toss gently until potatoes are equally coated with lemon butter, then roll in chives or parsley. *For 5 persons.*

SAUTE NEW POTATOES (Pommes de Terre, sautées)

1½ lb. equal-sized new potatoes
3 oz. butter
Salt and pepper to taste

Scrape, wash and dry potatoes, the size of marbles. Melt butter in a saucepan until smoking hot. Add potatoes. Cook, turning occasionally, until nicely browned. Season, then reduce heat. Cover pan and simmer for 10 minutes. *For 6 persons.*

Pumpkin (Potiron): Nourishing and full of vitamins. Stores well. Can be used for soup, or as a vegetable, but more often for a sweet pie. Choose sound pumpkins and buy quantity required by the pound.

To Cook: Peel and remove any seeds. Cut into thin slices. Throw into boiling, salted water. Cover and simmer gently till quite soft, then mash and flavour like turnip or swede.

Allow 2 lb. for 6 persons.

STEWED PUMPKIN (Potiron à la Créole)

2 pints boiled pumpkin
3 tablespoons butter
Salt to taste
¾ teaspoon ground cloves
¾ teaspoon ground mace
¾ teaspoon ground cinnamon
Sugar to taste

Rub pumpkin through a sieve while hot. Place in a saucepan. Add butter, from ¾-1 teaspoon salt, spices and sugar. Simmer gently for about ½ hour, stirring frequently. *For 6 persons.*

Radishes : There are many varieties of radishes, but only one variety is cooked. That is, Winter Radishes, which include black radishes.
Choose, cook and dress like small turnips.

Salsify (Salsifis) : Sometimes called " Oyster Plant," or " Purple Goat's Beard." Two varieties : black and white. Black is finest. Useful Winter. Has stimulating properties. Choose like parsnips. Scrape, trim and wash roots, throwing them into cold lemon water as prepared, allowing 1 tablespoon lemon juice to a quart of water.
To Boil: Throw into boiling, salted water to cover, containing a tablespoon of lemon juice or vinegar. Boil till tender, in 30-45 minutes, testing with a skewer before removing from pan. Drain thoroughly.
Hints on Boiling: 1. If long, they can be cut into lengths, about 4 inches long, before boiling, or into inch slices.
2. If home-grown, they throw up flower stalks in their second year which can be cooked and dressed like asparagus.
To Dress: Coat with parsley butter, seasoned to taste, or mask with Hollandaise, Maître d'Hôtel, onion, parsley or white sauce. Boiled salsify can also be dipped in batter and fried in smoking hot fat till crisp, then drained and served dusted with grated Parmesan cheese and paprika.

SALSIFY AND CELERY PIE (Salsifis au Céleri)

3 cups boiled sliced salsify
¼ pint minced celery
½ pint parsley sauce

Place a layer of salsify in the bottom of a greased fireproof dish. Sprinkle with ¼ cup celery. Repeat layers till salsify and celery are all in dish. Cover with well-seasoned parsley sauce. Sprinkle with crumbs. Dab with butter. Bake in a moderately hot oven, 400° F., for about 20 minutes, till crisp and golden on top. *For 3 or 4 persons.*

Seakale (Chou-de-mer) : Source of mineral salts. Usually forced and sold during winter months, but if home-grown, this is unnecessary, only it will not be in season until late spring. Choose fresh heads. Wash. Tie in small bundles like asparagus.
To Cook: Steam till tender, in 45-50 minutes, or stew in a covered pan in equal quantity of milk and water or vegetable stock, barely simmering, for about 35 minutes. It can be boiled in a covered pan in boiling, salted water for about 25 minutes, or till tender, but by boiling it loses some of its flavour. Take care not to cook seakale too long or it will toughen.
To Dress: Coat with parsley butter seasoned to taste, or serve like asparagus. Allow 3 or 4 heads seakale per person. One lb. for 3 or 4 persons.

CREAMED SEAKALE (Chou de mer à la Crème)

1½ lb. seakale
1½ oz. butter
1½ tablespoons flour
1½ gills milk
Salt and pepper to taste
3 drops essence of celery
3 tablespoons thick cream

Prepare and boil seakale in boiling salted water till tender. Drain well. Place in a hot vegetable dish. Meanwhile, melt butter in saucepan. Add flour. When frothy, gradually stir in milk. Stir till boiling. Season to taste. Stir in essence of celery and cream. *For 6 persons.*

Shallots : Useful when a delicate flavour of onion is wanted, or chopped for salads. Sometimes substituted for onion in sauce used to accompany mutton.

Skirret : Sweet, white, fleshy tubers with a delicate flavour and fragrance. Very popular in medieval days. Known in Scotland as crummocks. Trim, scrub and wash.
To Cook: Throw, unpeeled, into boiling, salted water. When tender, drain. Carefully remove skins. Cut into 2-3 inch lengths. Coat with parsley butter or Béchamel sauce. The tubers can also be fried in a little melted butter till golden brown.
Allow 1 large bunch for 4 persons.

Sorrel (Oseille) : An acid-leaved vegetable, somewhat similar to spinach. Very popular on the Continent for using in certain sauces, salads and soups. Choose fresh, green, undamaged leaves. If home-grown, do not allow it to seed, or it becomes bitter.
To Cook: Can be cooked as spinach or nettles, but most popular made into a purée to serve with veal cutlets, roast veal, etc.

Spinach (Epinard) : Valuable source of vitamins A, B and C, and alkaline salts. Choose fresh, young leaves.
To Prepare: Pick over and remove any coarse stalks. Wash well in 2 or 3 cold waters. Drain.
To Boil: Place in a saucepan with only the water adhering to the leaves after washing. Cook till tender, stirring frequently, in 10-20 minutes. Add salt when nearly ready. Drain well. Hold under cold water tap to improve the colour, though by doing this you lose some of the valuable salts. Chop and sieve if liked.
To Pressure-Cook: Allow 1½ minutes at 15 lb. pressure then place cooker in cold water at once to reduce pressure quickly.
To Dress: Whether sieved or left " en branche," season with salt and pepper. Add butter to taste. If spinach is old, or strong-flavoured, it can be made more delicate by sprinkling with a little flour, then adding top milk. Stir till boiling. If liked a pinch of ground mace or grated nutmeg can be added with the seasoning. Sieved spinach can also be used as a border for poached eggs, fillets of fish Mornay and creamed fish or chicken.
For 4 or 5 persons, allow 3 lb. which yields 4½-5 cups spinach.

Squash : Hubbard is most popular. Cook like vegetable marrows.

String Beans (Haricots verts) : As French or kidney beans, golden butter (wax pod) and runner beans can all be prepared and cooked in the same way, they are grouped here under " String Beans." They are all a good source of minerals salts and vitamins. Choose crisp, slender, smooth pods. When fresh, they will snap easily. If pods bulge, beans are likely to be tough. If home grown, pick when small and stringless, then they only need to be topped and tailed before cooking, and they will retain all their vitamins. On the Continent, the golden butter or wax-pod bean is generally cooked whole or snapped diagonally.

To Prepare: If young and fresh, top and tail. When older, " string " or remove string thinly with a sharp knife. Slice or cut in diamond shapes. When very old, pod and cook beans like young broad beans.

To Boil: Throw into plenty of boiling, salted water to cover. Add a sprig of savory if liked. Boil, uncovered, till tender, in 20-30 minutes. Remove savory. Drain thoroughly.

To Pressure-Cook: Allow $2\frac{1}{2}$ minutes at 15 lb. pressure then place pan in cold water at once to reduce pressure quickly.

To Dress: Season with pepper. Coat with melted butter. Add a squeeze of lemon juice if liked. The beans must not cook after butter is added.

1 lb. yields 3 cups cooked beans, enough for 3 persons.

BEANS AND CELERY (Haricots verts au Céleri) : Boil 1 lb. French beans conservatively with salt and a pinch of sugar. Add 1 cup sliced, boiled or canned, celery. Season with salt and pepper, and ground mace. Add hot cream to coat.

BEANS AND PEAS (Haricots verts aux Pois) : Melt 1 oz. butter in a frying-pan. Add 3 tablespoons stale breadcrumbs. Toss over a slow heat till a light brown. Arrange $\frac{1}{2}$ pint hot boiled French or runner beans and $\frac{1}{2}$ pint boiled peas in a vegetable dish. Season to taste with salt and pepper. Sprinkle with the crumb mixture. Serve at once. *For 6 persons.*

BEANS AND POTATOES WITH BACON (Haricots verts au Lard) : String 1 lb. French or runner beans, or use stringless beans. Do not slice them. Boil in usual way. Slice 1 lb. peeled potatoes and boil in usual way. Remove rind from 2 rashers of bacon. Cut bacon into small pieces. When vegetables are ready, frizzle bacon till lightly browned in frying-pan. Season beans and potatoes with pepper. Dish up. Garnish with bacon and sprinkle with a few drops of the bacon fat. *For 6 persons.*

CREAMED FRENCH BEANS (Haricots verts à la Crème) : Throw $1\frac{1}{2}$ lb. prepared beans into boiling, salted water. Boil till tender. Drain thoroughly. Melt 1 oz. butter in a shallow saucepan. Add beans and toss in butter. Stir in $\frac{1}{4}$ pint thick cream. Toss again, but do not allow to boil. Serve at once. *For 6 persons.*

STRING BEANS AND MUSHROOMS
(Haricots verts aux Champignons)

2 tablespoons butter 1 cup sliced mushrooms 2 cups boiled string beans	Melt butter in a small saucepan. Add mushrooms. Fry till tender. Add beans, sour cream and salt and pepper. Stir occasionally until piping hot.

439

4 or 5 tablespoons sour cream
Salt and pepper to taste

Dish up. Serve garnished with minced chives or parsley. *For 4 persons.*

Swedes : Usually yellow flesh. Claimed to be unfit to cook till after the first frost. Choose firm roots free from cracks.

To Prepare: Wash or scrub and peel thickly. Cut into equal-sized hunks or cubes.

To Boil: Throw into boiling, salted water to cover. Cover. Boil till tender in $\frac{1}{2}$-1 hour, according to age. Drain well.

To Boil Conservatively: Allow 15-20 minutes for sliced, and 20-30 minutes for halved swedes.

To Pressure-Cook: Allow 4-5 minutes at 15 lb. pressure. Place at once in cold water to reduce pressure.

To Dress: Mash, taking care to smooth out all lumps. Season with black pepper and grated nutmeg if liked. Add butter to taste. If liked, cubed swede can be served without mashing.

NOTE : When cooking a joint of beef, par-boil small hunks of swede, then slip them under joint to finish cooking. Drain and serve round joint. Allow 1 lb. for 2 or 3 persons, which yields about 2 cups cooked cubed swede, or one and two-thirds cups mashed swede.

SWEDE MAITRE D'HOTEL : Cut peeled swedes into dice. Boil until tender. Drain well. Re-heat in sauce allowing for every 1 lb. swedes, $\frac{1}{4}$ pint parsley sauce, flavoured with 1 teaspoon lemon juice, salt and pepper to taste, and grated onion.

GLAZED SWEET POTATOES

1¼ lb. medium-sized sweet potatoes
⅔ cup brown sugar
⅓ cup water
1½ tablespoons butter

Scrub potatoes and place in a saucepan. Cover with boiling water. Cover and simmer gently till tender. Drain off water. Peel potatoes. Halve lengthwise and place side by side in a shallow, greased baking tin. Measure sugar, water and butter into a saucepan. Stir over slow heat, until sugar is dissolved. Bring to boil. Boil for 5 minutes. Pour over potatoes. Bake in a hot oven, 475° F., for about 20 minutes, until a pale brown. *For 4 persons.*

Tomatoes (Tomates) : Source of vitamins A, B and C. Very nutritious. Really a fruit, but classed for cooking purposes as a vegetable. Can also be made into jam, candied and used for garnishing, or used raw in salads. Red most popular, but yellow a very delicate flavour. Choose equal-sized, firm tomatoes, plump, smooth and free from blemishes.

To Prepare: Wash carefully and remove stems.

To Peel: Place one or two in a basin. Cover with boiling water. Stand for 1 minute. Plunge at once into cold water and remove peel. Do not soak too many at once, or, by the time you get the last ones out, they will no longer be firm.

To Bake (Halved Tomatoes) : Wash, dry and halve tomatoes. Place in a greased baking tin. Sprinkle with salt and pepper. Dust lightly with sugar. Sprinkle with stale breadcrumbs. Moisten with melted butter. Cover. Bake in a moderate oven, 350° F., for about 10 minutes, then uncover and cook for about another 5 minutes, till crisp on top.

To Bake (Whole Tomatoes) : Make deep narrow holes with a thick skewer in 6 firm tomatoes. Mix 2 tablespoons brown sugar with 1 teaspoon salt, and a dash of cayenne pepper. Divide equally between the holes. Take 1½ tablespoons butter and divide into 6 portions. Fill each hole with a bit of the butter, then sprinkle with breadcrumbs and melted butter. Bake in a greased pie dish in the bottom of a moderately hot oven, 400° F., for about ¼ hour.

To Fry (Green) : Wash and dry. Remove a thin slice from stem end and cut into slices ¼ inch thick. Season with salt and pepper to taste.

1. Dredge with seasoned flour or egg and crumb. Fry in melted butter or bacon fat to cover bottom of frying-pan till brown below, then turn and brown on other side.

2. Dip in batter. Fry from 2 to 3 minutes in deep, hot fat.

To Fry (Ripe) : Cut 6 medium-sized ripe tomatoes into slices ½ inch thick. Dip in seasoned flour, then egg and crumb, and fry in a small amount of hot fat till crisp and brown.

To Grill: Remove stem ends from 6 medium-sized green or ripe tomatoes. Halve crosswise. Place, cut side up, on a rack in grill pan. Brush with melted butter or bacon dripping. Season with salt and pepper. Grill about 3 inches from flame or electric unit, until tender, allowing from 15-20 minutes for the green, and 10-12 minutes for the ripe. If liked, sprinkle with grated cheese.

To Stew: Peel. Remove stem ends and quarter 6 medium-sized tomatoes. Place in a shallow, enamelled saucepan. Sprinkle with 1 heaped dessertspoon minced onion if liked. Cover. Stew gently in their own juice until tender. Allow about 15 minutes for ripe tomatoes, and 25-30 minutes for green. Season with salt and pepper. Add a teaspoon of sugar if liked, and 1 rounded tablespoon butter. Stir till butter is melted.

To Stew Canned Tomatoes: If adding onion, boil before mincing. Only cook until boiling. Add seasoning and butter, as suggested above. Bring to boil and serve.

For 3 persons, allow 1 lb. tomatoes.

BAKED STUFFED TOMATOES (Tomates farcies)

BASIC RECIPE :
6 large firm tomatoes
Salt and pepper to taste
Filling to taste
Breadcrumbs as required
Butter as required

Remove a thin slice from the blossom end of tomatoes. Carefully scoop out most of the pulp, leaving a thin lining of tomato. Reserve pulp for sauce or soup unless included in filling. Sprinkle insides with salt and pepper. Turn upside down on a rack. Stand for ½ hour. Fill with any of the fillings given below, or with creamed chicken, fish, mushrooms, rabbit, sweetbreads or veal, allowing twice as much of the fish or meat as you have sauce. Sprinkle filling with breadcrumbs. Dab with butter. Pour enough stock or water into a baking dish large enough to take tomatoes. Place tomatoes in pan. Bake in a moderately hot oven, 375° F., for about 15 minutes, until tops are crisp and golden brown. Serve each on a round of fried bread or buttered toast. *For 6 persons.*

FILLINGS

1. *Aux Légumes:* Mix 4½ tablespoons shredded celery with 3 tablespoons breadcrumbs, 1½ teaspoons minced onion, salt and pepper, and 3 tablespoons grated cheese, then pack into tomato shells.

2. *Ham or Tongue:* Mix 1 oz. minced ham or tongue with the sieved pulp from the tomatoes, 1 tablespoon melted butter, 1 teaspoon minced onion, 1 teaspoon minced parsley, 2 minced, peeled mushrooms and salt and pepper. Add a pinch of crushed herbs if liked.

3. *Herb:* Mix 1 dessertspoon minced onion with 4 tablespoons stale breadcrumbs, 1 teaspoon melted butter, a pinch of crushed herbs, 1 teaspoon minced parsley, 1 tablespoon grated cheese, and 1 tablespoon tomato pulp. Season to taste with salt and pepper.

4. *Sardine:* Mix 1 cup mashed sardines with ½ cup stale breadcrumbs. Season with salt and pepper.

SCALLOPED TOMATOES (Tomates à la Mexicaine)

3½ cups sliced tomatoes
¼ cup minced onion or shallot
2 tablespoons minced green pepper
Salt and pepper to taste
½ teaspoon sugar
2 cups stale breadcrumbs
2 tablespoons butter or bacon fat

Mix tomatoes with onion or shallot, green pepper, salt, pepper and sugar. Place in a buttered fireproof dish alternately with layers of breadcrumbs, ending with breadcrumbs. Dab with butter. Bake in a moderately hot oven, 375° F., for about 25 minutes. If liked, sprinkle with grated cheese, allowing ½ cup for this quantity, after baking for 10-12 minutes. *For 6 persons.*

TOMATO FRITTERS (Beignets de Tomates)

1 can tomatoes
3 slices onion
1 teaspoon salt
6 cloves
Cayenne pepper to taste
¼ cup butter
½ cup cornflour
1 tablespoon caster sugar
1 beaten egg

Place tomatoes, onion, salt, cloves and cayenne pepper to taste in a saucepan. Simmer gently for 20 minutes. Rub mixture through a sieve. Season again if necessary. Melt butter. Add cornflour, sugar and tomato purée gradually. Cook for 2 minutes, stirring constantly, then add slightly beaten egg. Pour into a buttered shallow tin and allow to cool. When cold and set, turn out on to a board. Cut into rounds or squares. Roll in breadcrumbs. Dip in beaten egg then in crumbs again. Fry in deep, smoking hot fat till golden. Drain on absorbent paper and serve at once on a hot dish lined with a paper doily. *For 6 persons.*

TOMATO PANCAKES (Crêpes de Tomates)

¾ lb. medium-sized tomatoes
4 eggs
Pinch of crushed herbs
1 teaspoon minced parsley
3 tablespoons melted butter
1 cup sifted breadcrumbs
Salt and pepper to taste

Place tomatoes in a basin. Cover with boiling water, then peel carefully. Chop tomatoes. Stew gently till soft. Leave till cool. Beat eggs till honey-coloured. Stir in herbs, parsley, melted butter, breadcrumbs and salt and pepper to taste. Add tomatoes and mix well. Drop in tablespoons, a little apart, on to a hot, greased girdle or frying-pan. Cook till brown below, then turn and brown on other side. Serve at once. *For 4 persons.*

Turnips (Navets) : Source of sugar, minerals, starches and vitamins B and C. Two main varieties : long and round rooted. Useful in meat casseroles and stews. Choose with fresh green tops, free from cracks, and with very few fibrous roots.

To Prepare: Wash and peel.

To Boil: Throw into slightly salted, boiling water to cover. Cover closely. Simmer till tender, allowing 15-20 minutes for young turnips, and $\frac{3}{4}$-1 hour for old. (If very large, they should be halved or quartered before cooking.)

To Boil Conservatively: Allow 15-20 minutes for sliced or cubed, and 20-30 minutes for halved turnips.

To Pressure Cook: Allow 5 minutes at 15 lb. pressure, then place cooker in cold water at once to reduce pressure quickly.

To Steam: Slice peeled turnips, or cut into 1 inch cubes. Steam for 20-25 minutes, if white, and 25-30 minutes if yellow.

To Dress: Mash thoroughly with a fork, then beat with a wooden spoon until into a paste. Season with pepper and salt if necessary. Moisten with butter and a little thick cream if liked. Stir till piping hot.

To Cream Turnips: Add to 2 lb. cooked and mashed turnips, 1 cup thick white sauce, flavoured with ground mace or grated nutmeg, and mixed with minced parsley or chives to taste.

GLAZED TURNIPS (Navets glacés)

6 small white turnips
2 tablespoons butter
1½ gills beef stock
1 teaspoon caster sugar
Salt and pepper to taste
1 blade mace

Scrub, wash and peel turnips. Cut into chips as you would potatoes. Place in a saucepan. Cover with boiling salted water. Bring to boil. Boil for 5 minutes. Drain. Melt butter in another pan. Add stock, sugar, salt and pepper to taste and mace. Bring to boil. Cover and simmer for about $\frac{1}{4}$ hour, or till turnip chips are tender. Remove mace. Uncover. Continue to cook till sauce is reduced to a glaze. *For 4 persons.*

VEGETABLE CURRY (Kari de Légumes)

3 oz. bacon dripping
1 chopped peeled apple or a stick rhubarb, chopped
2 diced peeled potatoes
½ cup chopped onion
¼ lb. diced carrot
¾ tablespoon curry powder
Salt and pepper to taste
2 or 3 tablespoons bottled tomatoes
1 cup tiny cauliflower sprigs or broccoli
1 teaspoon home-made chutney

Melt bacon dripping in a shallow saucepan. Add apple or rhubarb, potatoes, onion, or substitute 1 cup chopped green stalks of spring onions, and carrot. Fry gently, stirring frequently till onion is clear and apple or rhubarb soft. Add curry powder, seasoning, tomatoes, and enough beef stock to moisten. Lastly, stir in cauliflower or broccoli sprigs, chutney and mushroom ketchup. Turn into the top of a double boiler. Cook over hot water for 15 minutes, stirring once or twice, and adding more stock if required. Meanwhile, boil rice. Strain in a colander and hold under

443

A few drops mushroom ketchup
4 or 5 oz. rice or mashed potato

cold water for a moment or two to separate kernels. Re-heat. Pile in a mound on a flat hot dish. Arrange curry on top. If potatoes are used, mash these and make a ring round dish, arranging curry in centre. *For 3 persons.*

NOTE : If a vegetarian dish is wanted, substitute butter for bacon fat, and vegetable stock for beef.

VEGETABLE PLATTER (Légumes à l'Américaine)

1 broccoli
6 oz. mushrooms
3 oz. butter
Salt and pepper to taste
12 young carrots
1 can asparagus tips
1 can green peas
4 tablespoons sieved bread-crumbs
¼ pint cheese sauce

Wash and trim broccoli, then soak, head downwards, in cold, salted water. Place in saucepan. Cover with boiling, salted water. Boil gently till tender. Drain well. Divide into sprigs. Peel and remove stalks from mushrooms. Melt half the butter and fry mushrooms gently. Season. Boil carrots in salted, boiling water till tender, then drain. Drain and heat asparagus in ½ oz. of remaining butter. Season. Drain and toss green peas in ½ oz. remaining butter. Season. Fry crumbs in remainder of butter. Sprinkle over broccoli. Arrange vegetables, piping hot, on 4 hot plates. Mask carrots with cheese sauce. *For 4 persons.*

Vegetable Marrow : There are many varieties which can be grown, both bush and trailing varieties ; the small, round S. African marrow which can be boiled whole, or halved and baked in its shell, the Argentine, the Avocado (or Avocadello), the Cocozelle, and the custard marrow. Choose young, small or medium-sized marrows free from bruises.

To Prepare: Immature marrows should be peeled and quartered, then steamed till tender, but steam ripe marrows unpeeled. If large, marrows have to be peeled and seeded. Cut up flesh into equal-sized pieces for boiling.

To Boil: Cook in boiling, salted water to cover till tender, for about ½ hour. Drain thoroughly.

To Boil Conservatively: Allow 20 minutes.

To Pressure-Cook: Allow 3 minutes at 15 lb. pressure for sliced marrow, then place cooker in cold water at once to reduce pressure quickly.

To Dress: Serve with parsley or cheese sauce.

To Roast: Peel any variety of marrow and cut into small hunks. Par-boil for 4 or 5 minutes, then slip under rack containing a joint of beef so that dripping falls on marrow, and finish cooking. Custard marrow is particularly good cooked with roast beef.

To Treat Young Marrows: Blanch 6—about the size of young cucumbers—without peeling. Throw into cold water, then cut into slices about ½ inch thick. Fry slowly in melted butter, till pale gold in colour below, then turn and fry on other side with cover on top for first 3 or 4 minutes. Season with salt and pepper. Drain. Pile on hot serving dish lined with a paper doily. Sprinkle with grated cheese.

Allow 1 medium-sized marrow for 4 persons—about 3 lb. in weight, which yields 3 cups mashed marrow.

Watercress : Source of vitamin C. Usually served with cheese or in sandwiches, or as a garnish to salads. Can be boiled and dressed like spinach or turned like spinach into a soufflé.

Yam : Large mealy tubers, sometimes called " Indian Potatoes." Choose firm, smooth-skinned yams. Bake in their jackets. Serve with butter, salt and pepper, or treat like Sweet Potatoes.

Zucchini : Sometimes called Zucchetti, or Italian squash. Treat like young cucumber-shaped marrows. Do not peel.
Allow 1 medium-sized zucchini per person.

Salads

The food value of salads cannot be over-estimated. The green leaves and vegetables used in their composition are rich in minerals and vitamins. They furnish us with some of the water essential to health and help to keep the system cool in hot weather. The dressing supplies us with heat and energy. By contributing bulk to the diet, salads indirectly aid digestion. For these reasons at least one salad should be served daily.

SERVICE OF SALADS

All salads can be arranged attractively in salad bowls or in shallow glass dishes, and some in fruit or vegetable "cups." Garnish green salads to taste, making them attractive with tomato, radish, red peppers or pimiento. Garnish salads dressed with mayonnaise or salad cream with minced herbs, chopped capers or paprika and cover with a lattice-work of strips of pimiento. Sprinkle the salad in between the strips with minced chives, parsley, or capers. Ring salads of this kind with crisp heart of lettuce leaves, watercress or a combination of both. Garnish to taste with radish roses, green peppers or onion rings etc.

CONTAINERS FOR SALADS

1. *Boats:* Cut large, stumpy carrots or firm, short cucumbers in halves, and trim each to 3-4 inches long. Carefully scoop out centres with a curved grapefruit knife, leaving a wall $\frac{1}{4}$-$\frac{1}{2}$ inch thick.

2. *Baskets:* Prepare like boats, using cucumbers, but give each a handle made from a sweet red pepper.

3. *Cups:*

(a) Remove a slice from the blossom ends of apples, grapefruit, lemons, oranges or tomatoes, and scoop out centre, leaving a lining of about $\frac{1}{4}$ inch thickness. Scallop round edges with a sharp knife to give a vandyked effect to grapefruit, lemons or oranges, if liked.

(b) Boil and cut a slice from the top of round beetroot. Scoop out centres, leaving a wall about $\frac{1}{3}$ inch thick.

(c) Use heart of lettuce leaves for chicken and shellfish salads, coaxed into the form of a cup.

SALAD DRESSINGS

There are four well-known varieties of salad dressings, and each of these dressings in turn can be treated as a standard recipe to be varied according to taste, and according to the salad the dressing is to accompany.

1. *French Dressing:* Combination of edible oil, lemon juice or vinegar and seasonings. It is used for coating green salads and for marinating root vegetables, fish and meats for incorporating in other salads.

2. *Mayonnaise:* A combination of raw egg yolk, edible oil and lemon juice or vinegar. It is most often used for dressing salads such as mayonnaise of fish or poultry salad.

3. *Cooked Dressing:* Combination of edible oil, eggs and vinegar or flour, eggs and vinegar. This can be substituted for mayonnaise.

4. *Cream:* Combination of sweet or sour cream and lemon juice or vinegar. Most generally used for salads that incorporate fruit, tomato and cucumber.

TO CHOOSE INGREDIENTS

Oil: When you have a choice, select the finest grade of olive oil, which is " l'huile de Provence." It has a delicate flavour. If a stronger flavour oil is preferred choose Lucca. Do not buy inferior oil which congeals readily, and is usually of a darker colour than the Provence oil.

Vinegar: If you use vinegar in preference to lemon juice, let it be a reliable wine or white vinegar. In the United States, apple vinegar is freely used for salad dressings ; strained grapefruit or orange juice is often substituted for vinegar when making a dressing for a mixed fruit and lettuce salad. Experiment in using part red wine vinegar and tarragon vinegar, or try combining white vinegar and chili.

FLAVOURINGS

Horse-radish: Grate and add to cooked dressings or mayonnaise for dressing cold beef or tongue.

Mustard: French, flavoured with tarragon, is preferable when mixing salad dressings with wine vinegar, or any other vinegar except tarragon. When tarragon vinegar is to be included in dressing, use any mustard you like.

Garlic: The flavour of garlic is sometimes imparted by peeling a clove of garlic and halving it, then rubbing the salad bowl with the cut side of the clove. Again, a " chapon " is used. To make one, dip a large cube of bread or a cube of a roll in salt, then firmly rub all over with a cut clove of garlic. Place in salad bowl, then add and mix salad. Toss chapon well in the ingredients. Stand for a moment or two. Remove chapon before serving.

Herbs: Add to ordinary French dressing, when possible, freshly minced chervil, parsley and tarragon. These add an aromatic flavour to a dressing. Do not add too much flavouring or seasoning to any salad dressing or the flavouring of the salad will be minimized. Be careful not to add herbs to dressing that you have already added to the salad.

SEASONING

Curry Powder: Add 1 saltspoon curry powder to ½ pint French dressing to be used for chicken or turkey salads.

Paprika: Use for garnishing or seasoning.

Pepper: Use cayenne pepper when a highly-seasoned salad is wanted. When black pepper is required, grind peppercorns with a pepper-mill into salad bowl. White pepper can be used if preferred, but it is hotter than the black and lacks the flavour of the black.

Salt: If possible, grind rock salt with a wooden salt mill into salad bowl when seasoning dressing or salad.

Garlic Salt: Use as a salt and substitute for garlic.

TO MAKE DRESSINGS

It is difficult to find epicures who agree about the proportions of olive oil and acid required for a perfect salad dressing. Most people prefer to use twice or thrice as much olive oil as lemon juice or vinegar when making French dressings and mayonnaise. Others like a more acid dressing which consists of a higher proportion of vinegar or lemon juice. Adapt the proportions of oil and lemon juice or vinegar according to taste.

FRENCH DRESSING

BASIC RECIPE :
4 tablespoons olive oil
1 teaspoon salt
½ teaspoon freshly ground black pepper
2 tablespoons lemon juice or wine vinegar

Measure oil into a basin. Add salt and pepper. Gradually stir in lemon juice or vinegar. (It should be added drop by drop.) Beat until blended. *Yield:* Barely ½ cup. For a salad for 4 persons.

VARIATIONS

1. Add 1 teaspoon French mustard or ½ teaspoon dry mustard to seasonings.
2. Add ¼ teaspoon paprika.
3. Add a bruised clove of garlic or season with garlic salt. Add 1 teaspoon of onion juice or 1 teaspoon finely minced shallot.

FRUIT

Strawberry Meringue, Fruit Coupe, and Individual Trifle, topped with whipped cream, and a halved banana, paired and topped with strawberry jam and whipped cream.

FRUIT
A symphony in fruit.

Almond: Substitute almond oil for olive oil.

Anchovy (For fish salads) : Beat ¾ to 1 tablespoon anchovy paste into ½ cup French dressing, or bruise 2 fillets of anchovy preserved in oil, and break them up with a wooden spoon in salad bowl before starting to mix dressing.

Chives: Add 2 tablespoons minced chives.

Cream: Beat 3 or 4 tablespoons thick cream gradually into ½ cup dressing.

Curry: Add 1 saltspoon curry powder.

Mint: Add 1 tablespoon minced fresh mint. Use with salads to be served with cold lamb, mutton or duck.

Parisian: Follow standard recipe, but beat in 2 teaspoons minced parsley, 2 teaspoons minced chives and ½ teaspoon chervil and tarragon.

Piquant: Add ½ teaspoon crushed marjoram and 1 dessertspoon minced parsley to French dressing, made with lemon juice. Season with cayenne pepper. Add a dash of Angostura bitters or Italian Vermouth.

Spanish: Add ½ teaspoon capers, ¾ teaspoon minced parsley, and 1½ table-spoons chopped, stuffed olives to twice the quantity of French dressing given.

MAYONNAISE

BASIC RECIPE :
½ teaspoon French mustard
½ teaspoon salt
Dash of white pepper
2 egg yolks
¼ pint salad oil
1 tablespoon wine vinegar
1 tablespoon lemon juice

Mix mustard, salt and pepper in a basin. Stir in egg yolks, then add oil gradually, drop by drop, stirring slowly and steadily all the time. Keep stirring till the mixture is very thick, then thin with a few drops of vinegar. Now add a little oil and vinegar and lemon juice alternately until all is used up. (If preferred, 1 dessertspoon wine vinegar can be used and 1 dessertspoon tarragon vinegar, unless fresh tarragon is in the salad.) When the weather is hot, chill all ingredients in the refrigerator before blending, and sink basin in a bowl of cracked ice. *Yield:* ¾ cup. If mayonnaise curdles, which sometimes happens if you add the oil too quickly, either beat an egg yolk in a chilled basin and very gradually beat the dressing into it, or try stirring boiling water into the curdled dressing, allowing 1 tea-spoon to this quantity. Do not store left-over mayonnaise next to the ice tray compartment.

VARIATIONS

Celery: Add ½ cup finely minced celery to every cup of mayonnaise required for a fish, meat or vegetable salad.

Russian: Add ½ cup Chilli sauce, 1 heaped tablespoon minced pimiento, 1½ tablespoons chopped green pepper, 1½ tablespoons chopped celery to 1 cup mayonnaise. Use with cooked root vegetables.

White: Add equal quantity of stiffly whipped cream, seasoned to taste, to mayonnaise, before serving with salad made with chicken, lobster, prawn or salmon.

Mayonnaise to Stiffen: Add 1 teaspoon of gelatine moistened with 1 teaspoon cold water to 1 pint mayonnaise. Pour into the top of a double boiler. Stir over hot water until gelatine is melted.

EMERGENCY MAYONNAISE

½ cup lemon juice
¼ cup sweetened condensed milk
½ cup olive oil
1 egg yolk
¾ teaspoon dry mustard
Pinch of paprika
Salt to taste

Place all the ingredients in a screw-topped jar, using from ¼–½ teaspoon salt, according to taste. Screw on top. Shake vigorously and use at once. *Yield:* ½ pint.

POTATO MAYONNAISE

¼ cup mashed potato
1 teaspoon dry mustard
1 teaspoon icing sugar
¾ teaspoon salt
Cayenne pepper to taste
2 tablespoons vinegar
¾ cup olive oil

Place potato in basin. Stir in mustard, sugar, salt and cayenne pepper, then half the vinegar. Mix until blended. Rub through a fine sieve. Beat well. Stir oil in gradually, then beat in remainder of vinegar. *Yield:* 1 cup.

BOILED MAYONNAISE (Sweetened)

1 teaspoon salt
1½ teaspoons icing sugar
1½ teaspoons dry mustard
Dash of cayenne pepper
2 slightly beaten eggs
2 tablespoons olive oil
5 tablespoons vinegar
Cold water as required

Mix salt, sugar, mustard and cayenne pepper together in the top of a double boiler. Slowly stir in eggs and olive oil. Stir until blended, then add to vinegar enough cold water to make ½ cup. Stir into egg mixture. Cook over boiling water, stirring constantly, until mixture begins to thicken, but do not allow to boil, then strain into a basin. Chill. *Yield:* About ¾ cup.

COOKED CREAM DRESSING

1 teaspoon flour
1 teaspoon dry mustard
1 teaspoon caster sugar
½ teaspoon salt
2 tablespoons butter
2 egg yolks
¾ cup cream
2 tablespoons wine vinegar
2 tablespoons lemon juice

Place flour, mustard, sugar and salt in the top of a double boiler. Add butter and melt. Stir in cream, vinegar and lemon juice. Cook over boiling water until thick, stirring constantly. *Yield:* About 1 cup.

SALAD DRESSING THAT WILL KEEP

2 tablespoons sugar
2 tablespoons flour
1 heaped teaspoon salt
Pinch of celery salt
1 dessertspoon mustard
1 pint milk
2 eggs
1½ gills wine vinegar

Mix sugar with the flour, salt, celery salt and mustard in a basin. Gradually stir in a little of the milk until smooth and creamy, then stir in remainder of milk. Beat eggs. Stir gradually into seasoned milk, then add a little of the vinegar at a time to mixture, stirring slowly in one direction only. Turn into the top of a double boiler.

½ gill tarragon vinegar
2 tablespoons butter or olive oil

Melt butter and stir into mixture, or stir in olive oil. Stir over simmering water until the mixture coats the back of a spoon, but do not allow to boil, or it will curdle. Remove from heat. Cool slightly, stirring occasionally. Bottle or pour into bottling jars. Cork bottles or cover jars securely. Shake before using. *Yield:* About 1¾ pints.

BLUE CHEESE DRESSING

3 oz. cream cheese
¼ lb. blue cheese
Juice ½ lemon
¼ teaspoon salt
½ cup mayonnaise
½ cup cream

Mash cream cheese. Rub Blue Danish, Gorgonzola or Roquefort cheese through a coarse sieve. Season cheese with lemon juice and salt. Stir in cream cheese alternately with mayonnaise. Beat till well mixed. Stir in cream by degrees. Serve with any green salads. *Yield:* About ½ pint.

CURRANT CHEESE DRESSING

¼ lb. cream cheese
1½ tablespoons lemon juice
1 tablespoon currant jelly
¾ cup cream

Mash cheese with a fork. Beat till creamy. Stir in remaining ingredients. Beat till smooth. Chill. *Yield:* About ½ pint.

SOUR CREAM DRESSING

1 cup sour cream
1 dessertspoon sugar
1 teaspoon salt
¼ teaspoon pepper
Pinch of paprika
1 teaspoon made mustard
2 tablespoons lemon juice

Beat cream until smooth. Mix sugar with the salt, pepper, paprika, mustard and lemon juice. Beat gradually into the cream. If preferred, tarragon vinegar can be substituted for 1 tablespoon of the lemon juice. *Yield:* About ½ pint.

CUCUMBER SALAD DRESSING

1 small cucumber
½ teaspoon salt
½ cup sour cream
¼ teaspoon mustard
1 tablespoon minced parsley
1 dessertspoon finely grated onion
Pepper to taste
Juice of ¼ lemon

Pare and grate cucumber. Sprinkle with the salt. Stand for 1 hour. Drain well. Beat cream till stiff. Stir in cucumber and mustard mixed with parsley and onion. Season with pepper. Stir in lemon juice. Use as a dressing for any cold flaked fish.

HORSE-RADISH CREAM DRESSING

¼ cup thick cream
1½ tablespoons lemon juice
1½ tablespoons wine vinegar
Salt and paprika to taste
Dash of cayenne pepper
2 tablespoons grated horse-radish

Beat cream until stiff. Beat in lemon juice and vinegar very gradually, then seasonings. When blended, fold in the horse-radish. Use with game and meat salads. *Yield:* Fully ½ pint.

MOUSSELINE DRESSING

3 sprigs of tarragon
2 hard-boiled egg yolks
2 anchovy fillets preserved in oil
¼ pint cold white sauce
½ cup mayonnaise
1 teaspoon made mustard
¼ teaspoon onion juice
¾ tablespoon minced parsley
¼ cup cream

Place tarragon in a basin. Cover with boiling water. Stand for 5 minutes. Drain thoroughly. Remove leaves from stalks. Chop leaves with the egg yolks and anchovies. Rub through a sieve. Stir sauce gradually into the purée, then add mayonnaise, mustard, onion juice and parsley. If liked, stir in a drop or two of green vegetable colouring. Whip cream and fold into sauce. Chill. Serve with boiled halibut or turbot, or with red mullet. *Yield:* Fully ½ pint.

SALAD CREAM

1-3 cups vinegar
½ cup salad oil
2-3 cups evaporated milk
Pinch of cayenne pepper
1 teaspoon dry mustard
½ teaspoon salt
½ teaspoon caster sugar
1 egg yolk

Place vinegar, oil, milk, pepper, mustard, salt and sugar in a screw-topped jar. Add egg yolk. Screw lid down. Shake until thoroughly blended. Bottle and cork tightly. Shake before using. This is a good dressing for making in a large quantity if it can be stored in a refrigerator. Use with fish salads. *Yield:* About 2½ gills.

SAUCE DIVINE

1 cup mayonnaise
¾ cup thick cream

Use highly seasoned mayonnaise. When sauce is required, whip and fold in cream. Serve with hot or cold asparagus. *Yield:* About ¾ pint.

MARINADES

When making a salad of fish, game, meat or poultry, the flavour will be improved if you soak the ingredients in a marinade for an hour or more before using. When more than one vegetable is to be incorporated with the fish, game, meat or poultry, *marinate each one separately*. Drain thoroughly before coating with dressing.

MARINADE FOR FISH, MEAT, OR ROOT SALADS

2 saltspoons salt
Pepper and paprika to taste
1 teaspoon minced parsley
1 teaspoon minced onion
2 tablespoons salad oil
2 tablespoons vinegar

Mix seasonings together with parsley and onion. Stir in oil. Dilute with vinegar. When blended, pour over fish, meat or salad. Baste occasionally. Let fish or meat marinate for several hours, and salad for 1 hour before using.

LEMON MARINADE FOR FISH

3 tablespoons lemon juice
1½ tablespoons olive oil

Mix all the ingredients together. Rub dish in which marinade is to be made with a cut clove of

About ½ teaspoon salt
Dash of pepper
Dash of paprika

garlic before adding ingredients, or add to marinade a bruised ½ clove of garlic or ½ teaspoon grated onion. Use for marinating fish.

TO MAKE A PERFECT SALAD

Vegetables required for salads must be perfectly fresh and very carefully prepared, and all vareties must be thoroughly dried before being dressed.

Cauliflower: Trim off leaves and stalk, then separate sprigs. Soak in salted water to cover for ½ hour to get rid of any insects. Drain in a colander and toss in a towel until dry.

Celery: Trim, then separate sticks. Scrape. Rinse. Chill in humidiser or other covered container in refrigerator, or soak in cold water containing a squeeze of lemon juice for ½ hour, then dry in a towel.

Chicory: Separate leaves from heads. Trim off any discoloured parts. Soak in cold water for ½ hour. Toss in a towel until dry.

Cucumber: Wash. Soak from 20-30 minutes in salted water to cover then drain and dry thoroughly. Pare if liked. Slice, cutting with a grooved knife, if wanted for garnishing, or cut in fancy shapes.

Radishes: Trim off rootlets and most of the foliage, leaving only enough to hold radishes by, if serving with cheese. Wash thoroughly, using a vegetable brush, to get rid of all soil round the base of the foliage. Soak in cold water for ½ hour until crisp. If wanted as a garnish, slice or serve in the form of roses, or tulips (see Garnishes).

Salad Greens: If you grow your own saladings, pick over, then wash all salad greens very carefully under running water until free from all traces of soil and insects. Shake lightly in a wire basket to get rid of surplus water, then toss lightly in a towel until dry. Chill before dressing. On no account must any of the leaves be pressed, or they will be bruised. If greens are required shredded for a salad, use your fingers, not a knife.

When you cannot use salad greens at once, store them in a humidiser or other tightly closed container in the refrigerator until required, and then wash and dry.

If, through circumstances, you have to make a salad from stale salad greens, wash as described, then place in a basin with the water still clinging to them and cover closely. Store in refrigerator or a cold cellar from 1-2 hours to give them time to revive. Dry as described.

POINTS TO REMEMBER

1. All greens and raw vegetables used must be crisp and dry.
2. Chop herbs for flavouring with a silver or stainless steel knife.
3. Chill not only all ingredients and dressings to be used, but the salad bowl and salad plates before mixing salad.
4. Do not dress green salads until ready to serve them.
5. If celery is unobtainable and the flavour of celery is desired for the salad, finely shred a fine white heart of a young cabbage, and season it with celery salt.

6. Do not put fish or meat to be served in a salad through a meat grinder, nor mince with a knife. Flake fish. Cut meat up in uniform pieces, for you must be able to " bite " at the main ingredient. When making a salad of both dark and light meat of a chicken, guinea fowl, turkey, etc., cut the light meat into larger pieces than the dark. When short of poultry for a mayonnaise or salad, the amount required can be made up with cold veal or sweetbreads.

7. Use a bone, horn or wooden spoon and fork for tossing the salad in the dressing.

ARTICHOKE SALAD (Salade d'Artichauts)

1 crisp lettuce
½ pint thinly sliced Jerusalem artichokes
½ pint thinly sliced cucumber
1 teaspoon minced parsley
1 teaspoon minced chives

Crisp lettuce leaves and line a salad bowl. Mix artichoke and cucumber slices together. Sprinkle with parsley and chives. Pile on lettuce. Serve with sour cream dressing. *For 4 persons.*

ASPARAGUS SALAD (Salade d'Asperge)

Boil or steam 1 large bunch of asparagus until tender. Drain well. When cold, serve in one of the following ways :

1. Arrange 6-10 stalks, according to size, on crisp lettuce leaves on individual plates. Serve with French or mayonnaise dressing. *For 1 person.*

2. Cut rings of pimiento ⅛ inch long. Slide through each ring as many stalks of boiled or canned asparagus as it will take. Place one in the centre of each serving plate. Garnish with heart of lettuce or curly endive leaves. Serve with French dressing or mayonnaise.

3. Arrange a small bundle of cooked asparagus on individual plates lined with curly endive leaves. Mix 1 tablespoon minced parsley or chives with 1 tablespoon minced sweet red pepper and a sieved yolk of hard-boiled egg, and the chopped white. Sprinkle this mixture in the shape of a belt over asparagus. Serve with French dressing.

4. Arrange asparagus on crisp lettuce leaves, the tips all one way. Cover lower part of the tips with a broad band of Hollandaise sauce. Garnish with lemon slices and strips of pimiento, or with highly seasoned, sliced, steamed mushrooms.

ASPARAGUS SALAD, DIVINE (Salade d'Asperge Divine)

Allow ½ cup cooked, boiled or canned asparagus tips about 1¼ inches long, to each person. Chill. When required, coat gently with mayonnaise mixed with ⅓ its quantity of whipped cream. Pile in crisp heart of lettuce cups. Garnish lightly with paprika. Serve at once.

ASPARAGUS FAN SALAD
(Salade d'Asperge, Américaine)

1 lettuce
20 stalks boiled asparagus

Line 4 individual plates with crisp lettuce leaves. Cut asparagus stalks 4 inches long. Arrange 5 on

2 red peppers
3 tablespoons cream
¾ cup thick mayonnaise

each plate, placing them so that the tips spread out like a fan. Slice pepper into rings, and if fresh peppers are not available, use pimientoes. Slip a ring over the end of each stalk. Place a heart of lettuce leaf at the bottom of each plate beneath the ends of the stalks. Fold the cream into mayonnaise. Place 1 or 2 tablespoons mayonnaise on the lettuce leaf. Dredge with paprika. *For 4 persons.*

AUBERGINE SALAD (Salade d'Aubergine)

1 large aubergine
½ crisp lettuce
French dressing as required
1 dessertspoon minced onion
1 teaspoon minced chives

Peel aubergine. Cut in cubes. Place in a saucepan with cold salted water to cover. Bring to boil. Drain. Add fresh, salted, cold water. Bring again to boil. Simmer until tender. Drain thoroughly. Chill. Separate leaves of lettuce. Wash and dry. Coat with French dressing. Arrange in a salad bowl. Place aubergine in the centre. Coat onion and chives with 2 or 3 tablespoons of French dressing and pour over aubergine. If preferred, coat aubergine with mayonnaise and garnish with firm wedges of tomato. *For 4 persons.*

AVOCADO SALAD, HAWAIIAN
(Salade d'Avocado, Hawaiian)

1 avocado pear
1 crisp lettuce
3 small firm tomatoes
Mayonnaise as required
3 small pickled onions

Skin the pear, then cut in rings and slip them off the stone. Trim. Wash and dry lettuce leaves and divide between 3 plates. Place a ring on centre of each. Lay a tomato in the centre. Top each tomato with mayonnaise, then with a small pickled onion. *For 3 persons.*

BAKED BEAN SALAD (Salade d'Haricots)

3 cups baked beans
1 cup diced firm tomatoes or celery
2 tablespoons minced green peppers
1 tablespoon chopped gherkin
½ tablespoon grated onion
French dressing as required

Mix beans, firm tomatoes, or celery, with pepper, gherkin and onion, and enough French dressing to moisten. Chill. Mix with enough boiled dressing to blend nicely. Serve garnished with lettuce or watercress. *For 6 persons.*

BEAN AND TOMATO SALAD
(Salade d'Haricots aux Tomates)

1 pint boiled dried beans
4 firm tomatoes
About ½ gill mayonnaise
Salt, pepper, paprika to taste
1 lettuce
6 almonds

Drain beans well. Peel and slice tomatoes. Stir in mayonnaise. Season with salt, pepper and paprika. Serve in a salad bowl or on individual salad plates, lined with lettuce leaves. Decorate with dabs of mayonnaise and slices of tomatoes.

Sprinkle with chopped blanched almonds. Serve with any cold meat. *For 8 persons.*

BOXING DAY SALAD (Salade de Légumes à la Noel)

1 cup cooked carrots
1 cup chopped celery
1 cup canned peas
1 cup canned asparagus tips
French dressing as required
1 teaspoon minced chives

Slice carrots thinly. Mix with other vegetables. Moisten to taste with French dressing. Turn into salad bowl. Garnish with minced chives. *For 4 persons.*

CARROT BOAT SALADS (Salades de Carottes)

4 medium-sized carrots
1 cup left-over cooked cubed vegetables
Mayonnaise as required
Lettuce leaves for garnish

Scrape carrots and cook whole in boiling water for 25-30 minutes till tender. Drain and scoop out a hollow in the side of each to make boats. When cool, fill hollows with the vegetables moistened with mayonnaise. Serve on lettuce leaves. *For 4 persons.*

CARROT AND BEETROOT SALAD
(Salade de Carottes et Betteraves)

1 cup Russian dressing
1 medium-sized raw carrot
1 small boiled beetroot
1 medium-sized onion or 4 spring onions
½ teaspoon salt
1 teaspoon sugar
¼ teaspoon made mustard
½ teaspoon paprika

Place dressing in a basin. Grate in carrot. Mince and add beetroot and onion or spring onions. Season with salt, sugar, mustard and paprika. Place in a salad bowl. Fringe with lettuce or watercress. Serve with cold meat or brawn. *For 4 persons.*

CARROT AND CELERY SALAD
(Salade de Carottes et Céleri)

½ pint chopped carrot
½ pint sliced celery
¼ cup ground peanuts
Lettuce or watercress
Mayonnaise to taste

Put carrot through meat grinder, using a fine knife. Place in a basin. Add celery and nuts. Line a salad bowl with green lettuce. Pile mixture in centre. Coat thickly with mayonnaise. Garnish, if liked, with minced capers or sweet pickled gherkin. *For 3 or 4 persons.*

CELERIAC SALAD (Salade de Céleri-rave)

2 young raw celeriacs
About ¾ pint diced celery
5 tablespoons wine vinegar

Slice celeriacs. Measure. Take equal quantity of diced celery. Mix together. Stir in vinegars, cayenne pepper, salt and almonds. Chill for ½

3 tablespoons tarragon
   vinegar
Dash of cayenne pepper
Salt to taste
3 oz. blanched almonds
½ cup sour thick cream

hour, then stir in the cream. Serve at once. *For 6 persons.*

CELERY SALAD (Salade de Céleri)

3 cups chopped celery
2 tablespoons chopped walnuts
2 tablespoons olive oil
1 tablespoon vinegar
Salt, pepper and paprika to
   taste

Scrape, wash and chop celery. Add walnuts. Moisten with oil and vinegar mixed together and seasoned. (Add a few grains of caster sugar if liked.) Arrange salad in a plate or bowl lined with lettuce leaves. *For 6 persons.*

CELERY AND POTATO SALAD (Salade de Céleri, Américaine)

½ lb. freshly boiled potatoes
⅓ cup chopped celery
½ teaspoon minced parsley
1 tablespoon minced onion or
   shallots
Salt, pepper and paprika to
   taste
Mayonnaise, flavoured mustard, to moisten

Cut potatoes while hot into cubes. Mix with remaining ingredients. If wanted highly flavoured, add a minced gherkin. Serve piled up in a salad bowl. Garnish with chopped capers and paprika if liked. *For 4 persons.*

CHESTNUT SALAD (Salade de Marrons)

1½ pints boiled or baked
   chestnuts
Worcester sauce as required
Pepper to taste
Pinch of salt
Milk as required
Mayonnaise to taste
Lettuce or endive, etc.

Rub chestnuts through a wire sieve. Add Worcester sauce, pepper and salt, and enough milk to bind. Pile high in the centre of a glass dish. Cover with mayonnaise. Garnish with shredded lettuce, endive, and beetroot, radishes, or spring onions. *For 6 persons.*

CHICORY SALAD (Salade d'Endive)

2 dessert apples
Juice of ½ lemon
Salad cream as required
1 beetroot
Salt and pepper to taste
1 tablespoon vinegar
¼ grated onion
½ lb. chicory

Peel and core apples. Cut them into strips. Moisten with lemon juice and salad cream. Cut beetroot into strips. Sprinkle with salt and pepper, vinegar and grated onion. Wash chicory, and cut it into shreds. Arrange the salad on a plate with a heap of apple in the centre. Surround these with a narrow circle of beetroot and put a row of chicory on the outside. *For 3 or 4 persons.*

CLOVER LEAF SALAD (Salade de Piments Verts)

Remove a slice from the stem end of 2 perfect green peppers. Remove seeds and wash and dry peppers carefully. Season cottage or any of the cream cheeses to taste with salt and paprika if liked. Pack solidly into peppers. Chill until hard. Cut into ½-inch slices. Divide between lettuce leaves arranged in the shape of a clover leaf on individual plates. Serve with Russian dressing, or as an accompaniment to the cheese course. *For 4 persons.*

CANADIAN COLE SLAW
(Salade de Cole Slaw, Canadienne)

¼ cup vinegar
1 tablespoon butter
2 eggs
1 teaspoon salt
¼ teaspoon mustard
1 tablespoon caster sugar
¼ cup cream
1 quart shredded cabbage

Heat vinegar in a double boiler. Add butter. Beat eggs. Add seasonings. Stir in vinegar. Return to double boiler. Cook till thick, stirring constantly. Remove from stove. Stir in cream. Pour over cabbage. Toss slightly. Serve very cold with roast beef. *For 6 persons.*

CORN SALAD (Salade de Maïs)

1 pint canned sweet corn
Salt and pepper to taste
1 teaspoon fresh mustard
½ onion
French dressing as required
1 lettuce
2 hard-boiled eggs

Drain corn thoroughly in a colander, then turn into a basin. Season to taste with salt, pepper and mustard. Mince onion and add. Moisten with French dressing. Stand for 1 hour. Drain and serve in a salad bowl lined with lettuce leaves. Garnish with sliced eggs. Serve with any cold meat. *For 6 persons.*

DIXIE SALAD (Salade de Maïs à la Dixie)

1½ cups corn kernels
1 cup shredded celery
¼ cup chopped green pepper
Mayonnaise and lemon juice
4 green pepper cases

Use freshly cooked or canned corn. Soak ingredients in the juice from a jar of sweet pickles. Chill in refrigerator for 1 hour. Drain off excess liquid. Mix lightly with mayonnaise and lemon juice to taste. Fill prepared green pepper cases with the salad. Set each in a heart of lettuce cup. Garnish top of each with a cross of pimiento. Serve with cold chicken or guinea fowl. *For 4 persons.*

EGG AND TOMATO SALAD
(Salade d'Oeufs et Tomates)

12 slices of tomato
6-9 hard-boiled eggs
⅔ cup mayonnaise
2 tablespoons chilli sauce
3 tablespoons diced green pepper
1½ tablespoons minced onion
3 tablespoons diced celery
¼ teaspoon salt
Dash of pepper

Overlap tomato slices on the two long sides of an oblong dish or deep platter. Cut eggs in eighths. Pile in centre. Blend together the mayonnaise, chilli sauce, green pepper, onion, celery with salt and pepper to taste. Pour over eggs. Chill before serving. Garnish with watercress. Serve with cold beef. *For 6 persons.*

FENNEL AND POTATO SALAD
(Salade à la Française)

1 lb. diced boiled new potatoes
1/4 lb. sliced cooked French beans
1 heaped tablespoon minced pimiento
1 dessertspoon minced fennel
Mayonnaise as required

Mix potatoes, beans, pimiento and fennel in a salad bowl. Coat with mayonnaise. Garnish with cayenne pepper. Use as an accompaniment or as an hors d'oeuvre salad. *For 4 persons.*

FRENCH BEAN MAYONNAISE
(Mayonnaise d'Haricots Verts)

1 can French beans
1 tablespoon olive oil
1/2 teaspoon vinegar
1/2 gill mayonnaise
1/2 gill minced celery
1 teaspoon minced onion

Drain beans. Turn into a basin. Mix the oil with the vinegar, and sprinkle over beans. Stand for 1/2 hour, stirring occasionally. Drain. Mix with mayonnaise, seasoned to taste. Stir in celery and onion. Serve in a salad bowl lined with watercress. Sprinkle with 1 tablespoon crisply fried bacon. *For 4 persons.*

FRENCH BEAN AND BEETROOT SALAD
(Salade d'Haricots Verts à la Provençale)

1 lb. French beans
1 small chopped onion
1 shredded anchovy
1 small peeled beetroot
French dressing as required

String and slice beans. Boil and drain well. When cold, place in a salad bowl. Add onion, anchovy and beetroot, cut in thin slices. Toss in French dressing to moisten. *For 4-6 persons.*

LETTUCE SALAD, PROVENÇALE
(Salade de Laitue à la Provençale)

1/2 bunch watercress
1 lettuce
1 bunch radishes
2 anchovy fillets
1 saltspoon French mustard
Salt and black pepper to taste
2 tablespoons salad oil
1 tablespoon wine vinegar
4 spring onions

Soak watercress in salted water for 1 hour. Pick and rinse in 3 fresh waters. Shake in a clean cloth. Trim lettuce, then separate and tear up the leaves. Rinse and toss in a cloth till dry. Trim, wash and slice radishes. Rub anchovy fillets against a bowl with the back of a wooden spoon till broken down. Add mustard and plenty of freshly ground black pepper, and salt to taste. Stir in oil, then vinegar.

Trim, wash and dry onions, then slice in. Add prepared lettuce and watercress, and radishes. Toss lightly with salad spoons till all the leaves are coated. Lift lightly into a salad bowl. *For 4 or 5 persons.*

NASTURTIUM SALAD (Salade d'Antoine)

1 or 2 lettuce leaves
Potato, onion and green pea mayonnaise
Nasturtium leaves and flowers

Place lettuce leaves at bottom of a salad bowl. Place vegetable mayonnaise in the centre. Arrange nasturtium leaves round. Chop gherkin and egg. Pile in 4 separate portions on top of nasturtium

1 pickled gherkin
2 hard-boiled eggs

leaves, equal distance apart. Garnish with nasturtium flowers. Serve with cold ham or tongue. *For 4 persons.*

POTATO SALAD (Salade de Pommes de Terre)

BASIC RECIPE :
1¼ pint diced boiled or steamed potatoes
1 rounded tablespoon finely minced onion or chives
¾ tablespoon minced parsley
French dressing and mayonnaise

Prepare potatoes while still warm. Slice if preferred to diced. Add onion or chives, parsley, and enough French dressing to moisten. Season with pepper to taste. Chill. Pile in salad bowl. Coat potato with mayonnaise. Dredge lightly with paprika. Garnish round the edge with sprigs of watercress. *For 4 persons.*

VARIATIONS

Potato and Celery Salad: Add 1 cup of shredded celery mixed with 3 tablespoons of chilled mayonnaise to salad before serving.

Potato and Egg: Follow recipe for Potato and Celery Salad. Lightly mix in 2 or 3 chopped hard-boiled eggs before serving.

Potato and Ham: Follow basic recipe, adding 1 cup of diced, boiled ham before serving.

RUNNER BEAN SALAD (Salade d'Haricots Verts)

1 tablespoon olive oil
¼ cup vinegar
2 small slices onion
Salt, pepper and paprika to taste
1 lb. cold cooked runner beans

Measure olive oil and vinegar into a saucepan. Bring to boil. Mince and add onion and a minced clove of garlic if liked. Season with salt, pepper and paprika. Pour over the beans. Stand till quite cold. Arrange in a salad bowl lined with lettuce leaves. *For 4-6 persons*

RUSSIAN SALAD (Salade à la Russe)

½ pint cooked peas
½ pint cooked young carrots
½ pint sliced string beans
¼ pint boiled turnip
¼ pint diced boiled new potatoes
French dressing as required
Boiled dressing or mayonnaise

All the vegetables should be cooked in salted water separately and well drained. Marinate each separately in French dressing to coat for ½ hour. Drain. Coat with boiled dressing or mayonnaise. Garnish with minced parsley. *For 8 persons.*

STUFFED AVOCADO SALAD (Salades d'Avocado, farci)

Halve a ripe avocado pear and remove the stone. If liked, scoop out small spoonfuls of the pulp so that the sections are fluted inside. Stuff with any of the following, or fill hollows with French dressing after stoning.

1. Flake crab, shred crawfish or lobster. Moisten with chilli sauce flavoured with a few drops of lemon juice. Chill and serve.

2. Fill each half of pear three-quarters full with tomato catsup or a tomato cocktail sauce. Garnish lettuce round each pear half with 5 prawns or $\frac{1}{2}$ cup diced crawfish or lobster. Chill. Serve with a fork and spoon—the fork for the fish and the spoon to scoop the pear flesh from its skin. *For 2 persons.*

STUFFED BEETROOT SALADS
(Salades de Betteraves farcies)

6 round cooked or canned beetroots
$\frac{1}{4}$ cup French dressing
Minced cabbage heart as
required
2 tablespoons chopped walnuts
Salt and paprika to taste
Mayonnaise as required
1 tablespoon capers

If necessary, cut a slice from the end of each beetroot to make them stand up erect. Carefully scoop the centres out of the stem ends so as to leave thin cases. Sprinkle with French dressing and stand while you prepare the filling. Chop heart of beetroots and measure. Mix with equal quantity of minced cabbage and the nuts. Season to taste with salt and paprika. Moisten with mayonnaise. Pile into the beetroot cups. Arrange each in a nest of crisp heart of lettuce leaves, placed side by side in a flat dish. Sprinkle with chopped capers. Serve with any cold meat. *For 6 persons.*

STUFFED EGG SALADS (Salades d'Oeufs aux Jambon)

4 shelled hard-boiled eggs
4 teaspoons melted butter
Pinch of salt
2 teaspoons minced ham
1 teaspoon minced onion
Pepper or cayenne pepper to
taste
2 peeled firm tomatoes
French dressing as required
Mayonnaise as required

Cut a slice from the large end of each egg. Remove egg yolks. Mash yolks to a paste. Stir in butter, salt, ham, onion and pepper or cayenne pepper to taste. Fill the whites with the yolk mixture. Cut a slice from the top and bottom of each tomato, then halve tomatoes crosswise. Line a flat dish with crisp lettuce leaves, moistened with French dressing. Arrange tomato slices on top, equal distance apart, and the stuffed eggs on top of the slices, placing them stuffed end downwards. Sprinkle lettuce with the remainder of dressing. Pipe a " rose " of mayonnaise on the top of each egg. Garnish each " rose " with a bit of pimiento. *For 4 persons.*

TOMATO SALADS (Salades de Tomates)

There are many other ways of making tomato salads. Choose firm, equal-sized tomatoes, peeled or unpeeled. Before preparing them in any way, wash very thoroughly. As the skin is indigestible, always peel when catering for invalids or for people with weak digestions.

To peel: Scald a few at a time, cold-dip, then slip off skins.

Sliced Tomato Salad: Cut peeled or unpeeled tomatoes into equal-thick slices crosswise. Arrange on dish. Sprinkle with French dressing. Garnish with minced chives, parsley or onion.

Tomato Sandwich Salad: Cut peeled or unpeeled firm tomatoes of equal size in 3 equal-thick slices crosswise. Put slices together again with fish or meat salad, or with mayonnaise stiffened with gelatine. Arrange on individual plates lined with crisp lettuce leaves. Coat with mayonnaise.

Poinsettia Tomato Salads: Divide firm, equal-sized tomatoes in eighths from flower end to stem without severing each portion. Gently pull each section down to form a petal. Arrange each tomato on an individual plate lined with lettuce or curly endive. Fill centre with mayonnaise of crab, lobster or salmon, or with chicken salad, or prawn and pineapple mayonnaise, allowing twice as many prawns as pineapple, and diced cucumber to taste. Coat with mayonnaise or sauce Tartare.

STUFFED TOMATO SALADS
(Tomates, farcies en Salade)

BASIC : To prepare tomatoes, wash and remove a thin slice from the blossom end of medium-sized firm tomatoes. Carefully scoop out centres with a grape-fruit knife. Season insides with salt. Invert. Chill for $\frac{1}{2}$ hour, then stuff. Top filling with mayonnaise. Garnish with chopped parsley, paprika or chopped aspic jelly. Serve on a bed of salad greens. See illustration facing page 448.

MEATLESS FILLINGS

Cucumber: Peel and dice 2 small cucumbers. Season with salt and pepper to taste. Stir in $\frac{1}{4}$ pint mayonnaise. Stuff tomato cups. Coat tops equally with $\frac{1}{4}$ pint mayonnaise. Sprinkle with minced parsley or chives. Serve with cold, boiled salmon.

Egg and Cheese: Chop 5 hard-boiled eggs roughly. Mix with 3 tablespoons mayonnaise. Season with salt and pepper to taste. Thin 3 tablespoons cream cheese with 2 tablespoons top milk. Stir in 1 teaspoon grated shallot and a pinch of cayenne pepper. Line tomato cups with this mixture. Fill up with egg mayonnaise. Chill.

Pineapple: Mix 8 tablespoons diced pineapple with 2 tablespoons mayonnaise and stuff tomato shells.

Pineapple and Walnut: Mix 1 cup well-drained crushed pineapple with $\frac{1}{4}$ cup minced walnuts, 2 tablespoons minced beetroot, 1 minced, peeled and cored apple, and mayonnaise to moisten. Garnish filling with finely chopped mint. *For 5 persons.*

VEGETABLE SALAD (Salade de Légumes)

1 cup shredded cabbage heart
¾ cup cooked peas
½ cup sliced radishes
5 tablespoons grated raw carrot
2 tablespoons minced spring onion
½ cup French dressing
1½ cups diced cooked potato
Lettuce, cress and radish roses
Pickled beetroot to taste

Mix cabbage with the peas, radishes, carrot, onion and French dressing to moisten. Mix potato also with some dressing. Stand for $\frac{1}{2}$ hour in cold plate in refrigerator. Pile cabbage mixture high in the centre of a salad bowl. Ring with potato salad. Sprinkle with minced parsley or chives. Wreath with heart of lettuce leaves and cress. Nestle 6 radish roses in the wreath. Garnish potato here and there with pickled beetroot. *For 6 persons.*

INDIAN VEGETABLE SALAD (Salade de Légumes à l'Inde)

1 cup diced boiled turnip
1 cup diced boiled beetroot
1 cup diced boiled potatoes
1 cup diced boiled carrot
½ cup shredded fresh celery
¾ cup boiled rice
1 teaspoon minced onion
About ¼ pint mayonnaise
½ tablespoon mango chutney
Curry paste to taste
½ cup drained canned peas

Boil each vegetable, except celery and peas, in salted water in the usual way, and in separate saucepans. Drain well. When cold, stir in celery, rice, onion and mayonnaise, mixed with chutney and curry paste to taste. Lastly, add peas. Pile in a salad bowl. Garnish to taste (see illustration facing page 448, with slices of hard-boiled egg, stars of beetroot and chicory tips). Serve with any cold meat or cold savoury pie. *For 8 persons.*

WATERCRESS AND POTATO SALAD
(Salade de Cresson à la Bretonne)

3 bunches watercress
4 or 5 boiled potatoes
1 peeled shallot
½ tablespoon vinegar
4 tablespoons olive oil
1 teaspoon sugar
Small pinch cayenne pepper
Salt and black pepper to taste

Wash watercress well under running water. Drain and dry. Cut potatoes into thin slices and finely mince the shallot. Mix vinegar with oil, a drop at a time, and stir in shallot, sugar, cayenne pepper and salt and black pepper to taste. Add potato and watercress and toss in the sauce. *For 4 or 5 persons.*

CRAB SALAD (Salade d'Ecrevisse)

½ lb. crab meat
3 tablespoons mayonnaise
1 shredded lettuce
½ teaspoon Worcester sauce
½ teaspoon tarragon vinegar
Pinch of mustard
1 chopped hard-boiled egg
½ teaspoon minced chives
2 chopped pimientoes
Salt and pepper to taste

Chill crab and mayonnaise. Wash, chill and shred lettuce. Mix Worcester sauce, vinegar, mustard, egg, chives and pimiento. Stir in salt and pepper, then mayonnaise. When salad is required, lightly mix in crab flakes. Garnish with strips of pimiento and crab claws. Surround with shredded lettuce, coated French dressing. *For 2 or 3 persons.*

CRAB SALAD A LA DIJONNAISE
(Salade d'Ecrevisse à la Dijonnaise)

1 medium-sized crab
1 chopped boiled potato
¼ pint shelled shrimps
2 small bananas
2 tablespoons thick mayonnaise
Salt, paprika and curry powder to taste
1 teaspoon minced parsley

Carefully remove flesh from crab shell. Shred flesh. Mix with potato, shrimps, and sliced bananas. Moisten with mayonnaise. Stir in salt, paprika and curry powder. If liked, add a little minced tarragon, or a few drops of tarragon vinegar, and minced parsley. Pile into the shell. Garnish with the claws. *For 3 persons.*

CRAWFISH SALAD (Salade de Langouste)

6 grapefruit shells
6 cooked crawfish tails

Invert scalloped shells for ½ hour before using, to get rid of any juice. Remove flesh from crawfish

3 tablespoons shredded celery
Mayonnaise as required
Salt, cayenne pepper and
   paprika to taste
1 small jar or tin of shrimps
Paprika or minced parsley
Watercress as required

tails and cut into small pieces. Add celery. Mix with mayonnaise. Season with salt, cayenne pepper and paprika. Chill slightly and divide equally between the 6 shells. Garnish top of salad with shrimps. Shake a little paprika or minced parsley into the centre. Arrange each in centre of a flat plate. Garnish with water-cress. *For 6 persons.*

EGG AND SHRIMP SALAD
(Salade d'Oeufs et Poisson)

3 hard-boiled eggs
1 crisp lettuce
1 can peeled shrimps
1 bunch watercress
Minced chives or parsley

Shell and slice eggs. Line 6 individual salad plates with lettuce leaves. Dividing shrimps equally between the plates, arrange them in the centre of the lettuce. Dividing egg slices in equal quantities, ring them round. Garnish with watercress. Sprinkle egg lightly with minced chives or parsley. Serve with mayonnaise. *For 4 persons.*

FISH MAYONNAISE (Mayonnaise de Poisson)

1 lb. boiled halibut
¼ pint picked shrimps
¼ pint chopped prawns
1-1½ gills mayonnaise
1 crisp lettuce
1 sliced cucumber
Paprika to taste
Mustard and cress as required

Remove any skin and bone from fish and flake. Mix with shrimps, prawns and mayonnaise. Pile up in a glass dish lined with heart of lettuce leaves, and outer leaves shredded. Ring with overlapping slices of cucumber. Dredge with a little paprika. Sprinkle with mustard and cress. *For 6 persons.*

FISH SALAD, WHITSTABLE (Salade à la Whitstable)

1½ lb. cooked fish
2 hard-boiled eggs
¼ pint picked shrimps
¾ pint mayonnaise
1 heart of lettuce
1 tablespoon chopped gherkin
1 teaspoon chopped capers

Remove all skin and bone from fish, then flake and leave till quite cold. Chop eggs. Add to fish with shrimps and ½ pint of the mayonnaise. Pack tightly into a bowl, then place in a glass bowl lined with shredded lettuce. Cover with remainder of mayonnaise. Garnish with heart of lettuce leaves, gherkin and capers. *For 6 persons.*

PRAWN MAYONNAISE (Mayonnaise de Crevettes)

1 lb. prawns
3 tablespoons French dressing
Crisp lettuce leaves as required
½ cup sliced boiled new
   potatoes
1½ gills mayonnaise
1 tablespoon capers
2 hard-boiled eggs

Shell prawns or use glassed ones. Chill and mix with French dressing. Line a salad bowl with lettuce leaves. Halve and pile prawns up in centre with potatoes round. Spread thickly with mayonnaise. Garnish with chopped capers and quartered eggs. *For 6 persons.*

SALMON MAYONNAISE (Mayonnaise de Saumon)

1 lb. flaked boiled or steamed
   salmon
¾ pint drained cucumber
1 teaspoon minced onion
Salt and pepper to taste
Mayonnaise as required
2 hearts of lettuce
French dressing as required
Garnish to taste

Flake salmon into a basin. Drain cucumber on a cloth. Add to salmon. Sprinkle with the onion. Season to taste with salt and pepper. Toss in mayonnaise to coat. Cut hearts of lettuce, moistened with French dressing, into quarters. Arrange the hearts round a salad bowl. Pile "mayonnaise" in centre. Garnish with mustard and cress, chopped capers and paprika, or with thin slices of beetroot and boiled and sliced new potatoes alternately. *For 4 or 5 persons.*

SALMON AND PRAWN MAYONNAISE
(Mayonnaise de Saumon et Crevettes)

2 lb. cold boiled salmon
2½ dozen prawns
½ pint mayonnaise
2 or 3 lettuces
2 small cucumbers
Mustard and cress to taste

Flake salmon. Chop prawns in three. Mix together. Lightly stir in 1½ gills of the mayonnaise. Serve in individual glass plates or scallop shells lined with lettuce leaves. Decorate each with mayonnaise. Dredge lightly with paprika. Garnish with sliced cucumber and mustard and cress. Allow 2½ oz. salmon per person. *For 14 persons.*

SARDINE AND CUCUMBER SALAD
(Salade de Sardines à la Portugaise)

1 diced peeled tomato
½ cup diced cucumber
1 crisp lettuce
French dressing as required
1 large can sardines
1 teaspoon minced parsley
1 teaspoon chopped onion or
   chives
¼ cup mayonnaise

Stir tomato into cucumber moistened with French dressing. Pile up in the centre of a salad bowl, lined with lettuce leaves, moistened with French dressing. Arrange sardines equidistant from each other round dish. Sprinkle with parsley and chives or onion. Serve with mayonnaise. *For 4 persons.*

MAIN COURSE MEAT SALADS

AYLESBURY DUCK SALAD (Salade de Canard)

1 pint sliced cold duck
½ pint chopped chicory
2 tablespoons olive oil
¼ teaspoon salt
Pepper and paprika to taste
1 tablespoon vinegar
2 tablespoons mayonnaise
1 tablespoon capers

Cut cold cooked duck into ½-inch cubes. Cut chicory into pieces twice as large. Mix these together and pour in the oil. Mix well. Sprinkle with salt, pepper, paprika, and vinegar. Chill. Coat with mayonnaise. Sprinkle with the capers. *For 4 persons.*

BRAWN OR TONGUE SALAD (Salade de Viande)

1 pint diced brawn or tongue
1 cup shredded cabbage heart
Salad dressing as required
¼ pint each of diced cooked
   carrot, turnip and peas
1 pint potato salad
1 lettuce or watercress

Mix meat and cabbage with salad dressing to moisten. Moisten cooked vegetables also with this dressing. Chill both for ½ hour. When required, coat meat with salad cream or mayonnaise, and arrange in the centre of salad dish. Place half the potato at each end, and the cooked vegetables in between. Garnish round edge with watercress or lettuce. If liked, sprinkle potato salad with minced chives or parsley, the cooked vegetable salad with paprika or minced capers, and the meat with minced onion or with a little mustard and cress. *For 6 persons.*

CALF'S LIVER SALAD (Salade de Foie de Veau)

1 lb. calf's liver
4 hard-boiled eggs
3 small peeled onions
French dressing as required
Shredded lettuce as required

Fry liver, then coarsely chop. Chop eggs and onions and add. Mix with French dressing to taste. Serve on shredded lettuce. Garnish with rings of green pepper and dried pimiento. *For 4 persons.*

CHICKEN MAYONNAISE (Mayonnaise de Volaille)

8 hard-boiled eggs
3 crisp lettuces
¾ pint mayonnaise
1 peeled beetroot
2 lb. diced cold chicken
1 pint cooked green peas
Mustard and cress and parsley

Halve and quarter eggs. Line individual glass plates with one or two lettuce leaves. Shred remainder of lettuces. Colour the mayonnaise a delicate pink to taste with juice from a boiled beetroot. Mix chicken, lettuce, peas and mayonnaise lightly. Arrange in a dainty heap on each prepared plate. Decorate with quarters of egg, mustard and cress, chopped beetroot and parsley. Allow about 3 oz. chicken per head. *For 8 or 9 persons.*

CHICKEN SALADS (Salade de Volaille)

1 pint minced chicken
½ pint chopped celery
2 tablespoons olive oil
Pepper and paprika to taste
¼ teaspoon salt
1 tablespoon vinegar
1 tablespoon capers
2 tablespoons mayonnaise

Mince chicken. Mix with celery. Add oil. Stir till blended, then sprinkle with pepper, paprika and salt, and lightly stir in vinegar. Stand in refrigerator or on marble for 3 hours, till well blended. Add capers and mayonnaise to moisten. Mould in oiled cups. Stand again in a cold place for 1 hour, then turn each out on to an individual plate lined with heart of lettuce leaves. Half chicken and half veal can be used for this salad. Garnish each with stuffed olives. Pipe a rose of mayonnaise on top of each. Sprinkle it lightly with paprika. *For 5 persons.*

CHINESE MEAT SALAD
(Salade d'Artichauts à la Chinoise)

1 lb. boiled Chinese artichokes
¼ lb. diced boiled chicken
¼ lb. diced boiled tongue
¼ lb. diced boiled ham
2 sliced hard-boiled eggs
Mayonnaise as required
1 heaped teaspoon minced chervil
½ teaspoon minced tarragon

Mix the artichokes in a basin with chicken, tongue and ham. Place in a salad bowl. Garnish with sprigs of watercress, sliced hard-boiled egg and radish roses. Flavour ½ pint mayonnaise with mustard, if liked. Stir in chervil and tarragon. Pour over salad. *For 6 persons.*

DUCK AND ORANGE MAYONNAISE
(Mayonnaise de Canard)

¾ pint chopped cooked duck
Celery salt to taste
1 tablespoon chopped cashew nuts
¼ pint chopped seedless orange or cucumber
1½ gills cooked green peas
¼ pint mayonnaise
Mint and curly endive

Sprinkle duck with French dressing. Cover Marinate for 2 hours. Drain well. Add celery salt to taste, nuts, orange or cucumber, peas and ⅓ cup of the mayonnaise. Season if necessary, with salt and pepper. Divide equally either between 4 salad plates, or 8 half orange shells, vandyked round the edge with scissors. Plant a tiny sprig of parsley in the centre of each. Sprinkle filling lightly with chopped mint. Edge plates or base of oranges with curly endive coated with French dressing. Serve remainder of mayonnaise separately. *For 4 persons.*

DUCK AND ORANGE SALAD (Salade de Canarde à l'Orange)

Heart of lettuce leaves
⅓ cup French dressing
2 cups chopped cooked duck
3 or 4 tablespoons salad cream
4 medium-sized oranges
Boiled green peas to taste

Line a salad bowl with heart of lettuce leaves moistened with French dressing. Heap duck, moistened with salad cream, in the centre. Ring with overlapping slices of oranges, thinly cut and pips removed. Garnish with boiled, drained peas moistened with French dressing. *For 4 persons.*

GAME SALAD (Salade de Gibier)

Cold game for 6
2 peeled shallots
2 egg yolks
Salt and pepper to taste
Caster sugar to taste
Dash of cayenne pepper
1 teaspoon minced parsley
12 tablespoons olive oil
1 tablespoon tarragon vinegar
3 tablespoons chilli vinegar
½ gill cream
3 hard-boiled eggs

Either grouse or partridge, or a mixture of both makes a good salad. Cut meat in suitable pieces. Mince shallots, and add to egg yolks. Stir in salt, pepper and sugar to taste, then cayenne pepper and parsley. Mix well. Add oil by degrees, and when well blended, stir in vinegars. Whip and add cream gradually. Arrange game in the centre of a salad bowl, with slices of hard-boiled egg round. Mask game with sauce. Garnish with watercress and orange fingers. *For 6 persons.*

HAM SALAD, YORKSHIRE (Salade de Jambon, York)

1½ cups chopped boiled ham
1 tablespoon chopped onion
½ cup chopped drained cucumber
1 teaspoon shredded horse-radish
1 cup chopped nippy cheese
Pinch of celery salt
1 cup mayonnaise
2 peeled tomatoes
2 hard-boiled eggs

Mix ham in a basin with onion, cucumber, horse-radish, cheese and celery salt to taste. Stir in mayonnaise, flavoured with mustard. Edge a salad bowl with shredded lettuce moistened with French dressing. Pile the salad into the centre. Garnish with sliced, peeled tomatoes, and hard-boiled eggs alternately. *To Vary:* Substitute boiled kernels of sweet corn for the cucumber. *For 4 persons.*

HAM AND TONGUE MAYONNAISE
(Salade, Wiltshire)

¼ lb. diced cooked tongue
6 oz. diced cooked ham
2 teaspoons shredded celery
2 or 3 tablespoons boiled green peas
Mayonnaise to coat

Moisten tongue and diced ham with French dressing. Soak for ½ hour. Drain well. Add celery and peas. Coat with mayonnaise. Pile on a flat dish. Garnish with lettuce or watercress and sliced radishes. *For 2 or 3 persons.*

LAMB SALAD (Salade d'Agneau)

1 lb. diced cold lamb
Lemon juice, or vinegar
Olive oil as required
Celery salt to taste
¾ pint diced cucumber
½ cup peas
¼ pint mayonnaise
½ lb. sliced champignons
Mustard and cress
Cubes of mint jelly

Cut lamb into ½-inch cubes. Sprinkle with equal quantity of lemon juice or vinegar and olive oil. Add celery salt. Stand for 1 hour. Drain well. Add cucumber, peas and mayonnaise. Arrange in a salad bowl lined with lettuce leaves. Garnish with champignons, mustard and cress and cubes of mint jelly. If the mixture is too dry for your taste, spread with another tablespoon of mayonnaise before serving and decorating. *For 6 persons.*

MEAT AND VEGETABLE SALAD
(Salade de Viande et Légumes)

¾ cup diced luncheon meat
1 cup diced boiled potatoes
1 heaped tablespoon minced onion
½ teaspoon salt
1 cup diced boiled beetroot
½ cup shredded raw celery
Black pepper to taste
1 tablespoon chopped apple
¾ cup cooked salad dressing
Crisp lettuce leaves

Mix all the ingredients together. Pile into a salad bowl edged with lettuce. *To Vary:* Substitute game for meat. Add ½ clove garlic, finely minced. Garnish with green pepper rings and radish roses, and slices of tomato. *For 6 persons.*

PORK AND VEGETABLE SALAD
(Salade de Porc et Légumes)

2 cups diced cold roast pork
½ cup diced drained pineapple
½ cup diced apple
½ cup shredded celery
1 cup chopped cabbage heart
Mayonnaise as required
Salt, pepper and paprika to taste
Crisp lettuce leaves
1 teaspoon minced parsley
Strips of pimento

Mix pork in a basin with the pineapple, apple, celery, cabbage heart, and mayonnaise to taste. Season to taste with salt, pepper and paprika. Arrange in a salad bowl lined with lettuce leaves. Sprinkle with the parsley. Garnish with pimiento. *To Vary:* Substitute cold duck or goose for the pork. *For 4 persons.*

SCOTCH EGG SALAD (Salade, Ecossaise)

1 dessertspoon grated onion
Pinch of grated nutmeg
Salt and pepper to taste
½ lb. pork sausage meat
4 hard-boiled eggs
½ pint diced boiled carrot
½ pint boiled green peas
¼ pint diced boiled beetroot

Mix onion, nutmeg and salt and pepper to taste with the sausage meat. Shell eggs. Dip in seasoned flour. Divide sausage meat into 4 equal portions. Flatten and place an egg in the centre of each. Wrap it smoothly round egg and mould till evenly covered. Egg and crumb twice. Fry in deep smoking hot fat until crisp and golden.

Leave till cold. Halve and place in a shallow dish lined with crisp lettuce leaves. Arrange carrot and peas alternately round eggs. Garnish here and there with the beetroot. Serve with mayonnaise. *For 4 persons.*

SWEETBREAD SALAD (Salade de Riz de Veau)

¾ lb. diced boiled sweetbreads
French dressing as required
½ small cucumber
½ gill mayonnaise
1 heaped tablespoon whipped cream

Dice and chill sweetbreads, then moisten with French dressing. Stand for ½ hour, then drain well. Stir in diced peeled cucumber and mayonnaise mixed with whipped cream. Arrange in a salad bowl. Garnish with sliced tomato and heart of lettuce leaves. *For 3 persons.*

TOMATO CUP SALADS

To prepare tomato cups, see page 462. Stuff with one of the following. Dredge lightly with paprika.

Chicken and Ham: Mix ¼ pint diced, cooked chicken and ham with ¼ cup mayonnaise, ½ cup cooked green peas, salt and pepper to taste, and ¼ teaspoon minced chives. *For 6 or 7 cups.*

Chicken or Sweetbreads: Mix ½ cup cold boiled chicken or sweetbreads with ⅓ cup diced cucumber, ¼ cup cooked green peas, 2 tablespoons finely chopped gherkin, 1 tablespoon chopped capers, 1 teaspoon minced pimiento, salt and pepper to taste, and wine vinegar to moisten. Soak for 10 minutes, then drain thoroughly. Toss lightly in a cloth. Mix with mayonnaise to moisten. *For 6 or 7 cups.*

Corned Beef: Mix ¾ cup diced corned beef with 1 heaped teaspoon minced onion or shallot, 3 tablespoons cooked green peas, and salt and black pepper to taste. Coat with mayonnaise. *For 6 or 7 cups.*

Ham or Tongue: Mix ½ cup chopped, boiled ham or tongue with 4 tablespoons chopped celery and ½ cup mayonnaise or salad cream. *For 6 or 7 cups.*

TONGUE MAYONNAISE (Mayonnaise de Langue de Boeuf)

1 lb. cold tongue
½ cup minced celery
½ cup diced beetroot
Mayonnaise to taste
Sprigs of watercress
3 or 4 hard-boiled eggs

Chop tongue into dice. Mix with celery, beetroot and mayonnaise to taste. Pile up in the centre of a glass dish fringed with watercress. Quarter eggs and arrange them in a ring inside watercress. Decorate with sieved yolk and chopped white of one quarter hard-boiled egg. *For 5 persons.*

VEAL SALAD (Salade de Veau)

1½ lb. cold cooked veal
1 clove garlic
Salt and pepper to taste
1½ tablespoons wine vinegar
2½ tablespoons olive oil
1 teaspoon Worcester sauce
1 medium-sized beetroot
2 peeled bananas
1 crisp lettuce

Remove all skin and fat from veal. Cut veal into small squares. Moisten with French dressing. Rub a salad bowl all over with cut clove of garlic. Place salt, pepper, vinegar, oil and Worcester sauce in a basin. Mix thoroughly. Skin, slice and cut beetroot into small pieces. Place in the dressing. Soak for 15 minutes, then slice the bananas into another basin and drain dressing from beet over them. Drain veal. Wash and dry lettuce. Shred and place in the bottom of a shallow salad bowl. Arrange banana and beetroot alternately round. Dress veal with mayonnaise and pile in the centre. Dredge veal with paprika, or sprinkle with minced parsley or chives. *For 6 persons.*

WATCH NIGHT SALAD (Salade de Poulet à l'Orange)

2 cups minced chicken
2 cups shredded lettuce
1 dessertspoon minced onion
1 tablespoon minced celery
2 teaspoons minced walnuts
About ½ cup mayonnaise
1 teaspoon salt
¼ teaspoon paprika
6 orange shells

When cold, put meat from left over bird through a meat grinder, using the coarsest knife. Place in a bowl with finely shredded hearts of lettuce, onion, celery, walnuts, mayonnaise, salt and paprika. Serve in vandyked orange shells. Plant a small celery tip in the centre of each. (If you prefer, you can line the orange shells with shredded lettuce and omit lettuce from chicken mixture.) *For 6 persons.*

SALAD PLATTERS (Plats de Salade)

Salad platters make popular main courses for lunch, dinner or supper. Here are some suggestions.

1. Sliced corned beef or luncheon meat, cold ham or tongue arranged in overlapping slices down the centre of a flat dish. Arrange a tomato per person stuffed with vegetable salad around, separating them with potato crisps. Garnish with heart of lettuce leaves.

2. Fill centre of a flat dish with potato, celery and green pea salad. Arrange a wreath of overlapping slices of liver sausage round salad. Tuck radish roses in between the sausage and the salad. Fringe with watercress.

3. Line a round salad plate with heart of lettuce leaves. Pile prawn or crab mayonnaise in the centre. Ring with halved devilled eggs. Make overlapping circles of beetroot equal distance apart round edge. Fill centres of circles with boiled green peas. Turn out a cucumber jelly set in an egg cup in between beetroot circles. Serve with mayonnaise.

4. Arrange cold boiled Frankforters side by side down the centre of a flat oval plate. Arrange alternately round : (a) Overlapping slices of hard-boiled egg, garnished with paprika, running from centre to edge. (b) Overlapping slices of peeled tomato running also from centre to edge. Encircle with radish roses nestling in watercress.

BREAD SALAD PLATTER (Plat de Pain, Américaine)

1 cup diced summer celery
1 cup olives
1 tablespoon minced pimiento
1 dessertspoon minced green pepper
2 hard-boiled eggs
3 tablespoons French dressing
1½ cups diced stale bread
1½ oz. butter
Lettuce or endive

Place celery in a basin. Stone and dice olives. Add with pimiento and green pepper to celery. Separate yolks and whites of eggs. Make French dressing with lemon juice. Season with paprika and salt. Pour over celery mixture. Stir till blended. Chill for ½ hour. Meanwhile, fry bread in the butter until golden brown, then drain. Mince egg whites. Add bread and egg whites to salad. Toss till blended. Make a bed of lettuce or lettuce and escarole or curly endive. Arrange salad on top. Sieve egg yolks over. Garnish with radish roses and mustard and cress. Serve with mayonnaise. *For 4 persons.*

CHEESE SALADS (Salades au Fromage)

As a rule, a cheese salad is served with biscuits, rolls or toast in place of biscuits and cheese at luncheon, supper or dinner, but some cheese salads could be served as a main course at luncheon, high tea or supper. Green salads as well as mixed vegetable salads can be made more nourishing by sprinkling with cheese grated on a coarse grater, or by garnishing with Demi-sel cheese.

CHEESE DRESSING

Beat 6 tablespoons French dressing gradually into 3 tablespoons mashed Danish blue, Gorgonzola or Roquefort. Use only with a green salad.

CREAM CHEESE DRESSING

4 tablespoons olive oil
2 tablespoons wine vinegar
½ teaspoon salt
Dash of cayenne pepper
¼ teaspoon paprika
4 tablespoons (level) cream cheese
2 tablespoons thick cream

Place oil, vinegar, salt, pepper and paprika in a screw-topped jar. Screw tightly. Shake till blended. Beat cheese till smooth with a silver fork. Gradually beat in dressing. Beat cream till stiff. Fold into dressing. Serve with lettuce, chicory, endive, or escarole salads, or with young tomatoes. Serve in place of cheese course. *For 4 persons.*

CHEESE BALL SALAD (Salade au Fromage, Américaine)

12 crisp lettuce leaves
1 lb. raspberries or strawberries
2 oranges
¼ lb. cottage cheese
2 heaped tablespoons chopped walnuts

Divide the lettuce equally between 4 salad plates, arranging them so that the stems meet in the middle. Divide berries in 4 portions. Wash, drain and hull. Arrange on one leaf on each plate. Peel oranges. Remove all membrane. Divide into sections and peel sections. Divide equally between the second leaf on each plate. Divide cheese in 4 portions. Make each portion into 2 or 3 balls and roll in walnuts. Serve on third lettuce leaf. Pass a sauceboat of Cream French Dressing round. *For 4 persons.*

To Vary: 1. Make 3 balls of cream cheese for each person. With a sharp knife, cut a large crisp lettuce in thin slices. Divide equally between 4 salad plates. Cut one large head of chicory in fine shreds and make a nest of each portion of lettuce. Tuck balls in centre. Serve with French dressing.

2. Season cheese cream to taste with salt and cayenne pepper, and paprika. Roll into balls 1 inch across, then in cheese biscuit crumbs. Serve on a bed of mustard and cress.

CHEESE AND BANANA SALADS
(Salades au Fromage, Méxicaine)

4 large ripe bananas
1 large crisp lettuce
¼ lb. cream or cottage cheese
Salt and paprika to taste
1 heaped teaspoon minced parsley

Peel bananas. Remove any threads. Cut in quarters lengthwise, then across. Arrange crisp lettuce leaves on 4 individual plates. Divide banana between plates. Season cheese with salt and paprika. Pipe cheese lightly over the banana, in trails. Sprinkle lightly with parsley. Serve with Almond French Dressing.

CHEESE AND CABBAGE SALAD
(Salade de Chou, Américaine)

Place ¼-½ lb. cream or cottage cheese in the centre of a salad platter. Mix ½ pint finely shredded cabbage heart with half its quantity of grated raw carrot. Moisten with mayonnaise and arrange in a ring round cheese. Sprinkle cheese with paprika to taste. *For 4 persons.*

OLIVE AND CHEESE SALAD
(Salade de Fromage, Africaine)

3 oz. cream cheese
1½ tablespoons thick cream
1 saltspoon salt
1 saltspoon paprika
12 chopped olives
1 chopped pimiento
1 crisp lettuce

Mash cheese in a basin. Stir in cream, salt, paprika, olives, black or stuffed, and pimiento. Pack into a straight-sided mould, about 2½ inches across. Chill. Cut into 6 equal-thick slices. Serve each on a slice of firm tomato on a salad dish lined with lettuce, in a ring. Place 6 halved devilled eggs in the centre. Force a rose of thick mayonnaise on each cheese canapé. Plant a prawn in the centre of each egg. *For 6 persons.*

SALADS IN ASPIC

Jellied salads can be served as an accompaniment to cold cuts when you only need jellied vegetables, but when the vegetables are combined with fish, meat, game or poultry, they can constitute the main course at lunch, dinner or supper. Any kind of savoury jelly can be used for setting the ingredients, but if game, meat or poultry is one of them, real aspic jelly is better. Mock aspic, made with stock or with a packet of lemon jelly, can be substituted for setting vegetables to serve with cold cuts.

SAVOURY ASPIC JELLY (Gelée d'Aspic)

BASIC RECIPE :
1 pint jellied white stock
¾ pint water
4 tablespoons wine vinegar
1 tablespoon tarragon vinegar
1 small peeled onion
1 small carrot
1 stick celery
1 sprig parsley
1 sprig thyme
½ bay leaf
1½-2 oz. powdered gelatine
½ teaspoon salt
6 white peppercorns
Rind and juice of 1 lemon
½ gill sherry
2 egg whites
2 egg shells

Remove every particle of fat from stock with tissue paper or a piece of muslin. Pour stock, water and vinegars into a saucepan. Place onion in a saucepan. Cover with cold water. Bring to boil. Drain. Slice into stock with carrot and celery. Add remainder of ingredients. Stir over slow heat until gelatine is dissolved. Whisk while heating, until frothy on top, then remove whisk and allow jelly to boil up. Draw at once to side of stove. Stand for at least 10 minutes, until all the ingredients settle in the bottom of the pan. Strain through a jelly bag. N.B.—Fish stock should be used for Aspics of Fish.

To Mould with Aspic: Rinse mould in cold water. Shake out any superfluous water, but do not dry. Run a spoonful of the cold jelly over bottom of mould, just enough to cover, then decorate with cooked green peas and ornaments of cooked carrot, beetroot, raw celery, pimiento, or truffle if wanted for a party. When set, add a thin film of jelly. When this is set, add a layer of meat and vegetables, then a thin one of jelly. Repeat layers, allowing jelly to set each time, before adding a fresh layer, until mould is full. The last layer must he of jelly. Allow $1\frac{3}{4}$ cups meat, $\frac{1}{2}$ cup peas, and 1 carrot or beetroot, etc., for quantity of jelly given.

To Unmould: When required, gently loosen round edge of mould with your finger tip or a spatula, and turn upside down. Tap the bottom. If the jelly does not unmould freely, then wrap for about $\frac{1}{2}$ a minute in a cloth wrung out of warm water, or place mould in warm water for a moment or two. If you are slow about this, the jelly may begin to melt.

To Garnish: Garnish base with curly endive, heart of lettuce leaves, watercress, radish roses, and sliced or stuffed eggs. Halve eggs and scoop out yolks. Chop yolks and mix with chopped chives. Season and moisten with mayonnaise. Fill whites with this mixture. If preferred, sieve yolks over green salad and garnish with rings of egg white.

To Vary Savoury Aspic: Substitute $1\frac{1}{2}$ pints water for the stock. Increase wine vinegar to 8 tablespoons and tarragon to 2. Increase sherry to $\frac{1}{4}$ pint and add remainder of ingredients as given in basic recipe. Follow method given.

ASPICS OF LOBSTER (Aspic d'Homard) : Melt aspic jelly as required in a saucepan. Line 6 plain or fluted moulds with the liquified jelly. Leave until set. Decorate the bottom of each with a bit of lobster claw. Cover with a thin film of liquid aspic. Leave until set. Fill moulds three-quarters full with pieces of lobster, arranging them with the red parts towards the outside. Fill up with aspic jelly. Chill. Turn out carefully on to individual plates. Garnish with chopped aspic and sprigs of chervil or parsley. *Yield:* 1 lobster should give 6 moulds.

ASPICS OF PEAS (Aspics de Pois) : Drain 1 cup cooked green peas thoroughly. Divide equally between 5 individual moulds. Fill up with melted aspic jelly. Leave until set. Turn each into a nest of shredded lettuce. Pipe a rose of mayonnaise on tops.

MOCK ASPIC

1 tablespoon powdered gelatine
2 tablespoons cold water
$1\frac{1}{2}$ cups boiling water
2 meat cubes
1 teaspoon sugar
Salt to taste
2 tablespoons lemon juice or mild vinegar
$\frac{1}{2}$ teaspoon minced onion

Soak gelatine in cold water for 5 minutes. Add boiling water. Stir till dissolved. Add cubes, sugar and salt to taste. Stir till cubes are dissolved, then add lemon juice or vinegar and the onion. Stand for 5 minutes, then strain and use when cold and starting to thicken. If this quantity is used and $1\frac{1}{2}$-2 cups of flaked fish or diced meat are added, it will give a savoury fish or meat aspic jelly. *For 6 persons.*

SIMPLE ASPIC

$\frac{3}{4}$ tablespoon powdered gelatine
$\frac{3}{4}$ cup cold stock
$\frac{1}{4}$ cup boiling stock
$1\frac{1}{2}$ tablespoons lemon juice
Salt and paprika to taste
Dash of celery salt

Soak gelatine in $\frac{1}{4}$ cup of the cold stock for 5 minutes, then dissolve in boiling stock. Add to remainder of cold stock. Stir in lemon juice, salt, and paprika to taste, and celery salt. Chill. When it is starting to set, you can stir in gradually $1\frac{1}{2}$ cups flaked cooked fish, diced cooked meat, or chicken, or a combination of cooked fish, or chicken and green peas. Pour into a wet mould. Chill until firm. Unmould on to a bed of crisp lettuce leaves. Serve with mayonnaise. *For 5 persons.*

TOMATO ASPIC

1 can tomatoes
2 slices shallot
1 chilli pepper
1 dessertspoon vinegar
1 dessertspoon powdered gelatine

Bring tomatoes to the boil, then strain. Rinse saucepan. Add juice with shallot, chilli pepper, vinegar, and gelatine. Stir over a slow heat until gelatine is dissolved, then remove from stove. When cool, strain into a border mould. Chill. Unmould. Fill with celery. or green pea mayonnaise, or any mayonnaise of fish or meat. *For 4 persons.*

JELLIED MEAT AND VEGETABLES

1 oz. powdered gelatine
1 pint boiling water
2 teaspoons meat extract
1/4 pint stock
1/2 teaspoon salt
White and shell of 1 egg
1 tablespoon wine vinegar
Pepper to taste
1¾ cups diced cooked meat
1 cup prepared vegetables

Soften gelatine in cold water for 5 minutes. Dissolve in boiling water. Place in a saucepan with meat extract, stock, salt, white and shell of egg. Bring to boil very slowly. Beat steadily with an egg whisk while heating until almost boiling, and there is a good froth on top. Draw pan to side of stove. Stand for 2 minutes, then add vinegar and pepper to taste. Strain through muslin or a jelly bag. When about to set, lightly stir in diced cooked meat and prepared vegetables. Set in a wet mould. *For 6 persons.*

To Vary:

1. *Fish:* Add a heaped teaspoon of minced chives or parsley to the jelly. Substitute shredded crab, diced lobster, flaked, boiled salmon or halibut for the meat. Substitute slices of 2 hard-boiled eggs for the carrot.

2. *Game or Poultry:* Add 1 heaped teaspoon of minced chives or parsley to the jelly. Substitute diced cooked game, chicken or turkey for the meat.

ASPIC OF CHICKEN (Aspic de Volaille)

1 boiled chicken (4 lb.)
1 tablespoon powdered gelatine
1/4 cup cold water
Salt and pepper to taste
Pinch of celery salt
Squeeze of lemon juice
Squeeze of onion juice

To impart as much flavour to the chicken as possible, allow when boiled, to stand in the stock until cold. Remove all skin, then remove all meat from bones, and chop meat very finely. Boil chicken stock until it is reduced when strained to 2 cups. Remove any fat. Re-heat. Remove from stove. Soak gelatine for 5 minutes in cold water and add to stock. Stir until dissolved. Add chicken with salt, pepper and celery salt to taste. Strain in a squeeze of lemon and onion juice. Pack into an oiled border mould. Chill. Turn out on to a bed of green salad. Garnish with devilled eggs nestling in watercress or mustard and cress. *For 6 persons.*

ASPICS OF CHICKEN WITH ASPARAGUS
(Aspics de Volaille à l'Asperge)

1 can asparagus
1 tablespoon powdered gelatine
¼ cup cold water
1 cup well-seasoned chicken stock
½ teaspoon lemon juice
½ teaspoon grated onion
1½ cups diced chicken breast
½ cup mayonnaise
2 tablespoons thick cream

Drain asparagus thoroughly. Soak gelatine for 5 minutes in cold water. Heat stock with lemon juice and onion. Remove from stove. Add gelatine and chicken. Stir until gelatine is dissolved. Pour into lightly oiled custard cups. Chill. Unmould on to 4 individual plates lined with heart of lettuce leaves. Arrange 3 or 4 stalks of asparagus on each side of moulds. Garnish with radish roses. Mix mayonnaise with cream. Serve at once with salad. *For 4 persons.*

ASPICS OF SALMON (Aspics de Saumon)

1 lb. boiled salmon
1 packet aspic jelly
Tarragon vinegar as required
2 tablespoons minced cucumber
½ pint boiled peas
Salt and pepper to taste
2 hard-boiled eggs
½ gill mayonnaise
Minced parsley to taste

Divide boiled salmon into 6 pieces. Prepare jelly according to instructions on packet. Flavour to taste with tarragon vinegar. Leave till almost ready to set. Stir in cucumber, peas and salt and pepper to taste. Pour a thin layer of the prepared jelly into the bottom of a wet shallow mould. When set, lay the pieces of salmon on top equal distance apart. Pour remainder of jelly over. Leave till set. When quite stiff, cut out each block surrounded by a coating of jelly. Line individual salad plates with lettuce or endive. Place a block in the centre of each. Slice hard-boiled eggs. Garnish jelly with egg slices and mayonnaise. Sprinkle with minced parsley. *For 6 persons.*

CIDER VEGETABLE SALADS
(Salades de Légumes au Cidre)

2 tablespoons powdered gelatine
1 pint cold cider
1 cup chopped apple
½ cup shredded celery
Pinch of salt
1 dessertspoon minced parsley
¼ cup chopped walnuts

Soften gelatine in ½ cup of the cider for 5 minutes. Bring remainder of cider to the boil. Stir in softened gelatine. When dissolved, chill until beginning to set. Add remaining ingredients. Stir until blended. Pour into 6 wet individual moulds. *For 6 persons.*

CRAB AND CUCUMBER SALAD
(Salade de Crabe et Concombre)

¾ cup diced cucumber
½ teaspoon salt
Pepper to taste
½ teaspoon sugar
½ cup pure malt vinegar
2 tablespoons powdered gelatine

Season cucumber to taste with salt and pepper. Add sugar. Cover cucumber with the vinegar, heated till fairly warm, and stand for ½ hour. Drain off vinegar, keeping back ¼ cup for the jelly. Soak gelatine in the cold water for 5 minutes, then heat the ¼ cup vinegar with boiling

½ cup cold water
1¼ cups boiling water
2 tablespoons lemon juice
2 tablespoons chopped green pepper or parsley
Flaked crabmeat to taste
Crisp lettuce leaves

water and lemon juice. When boiling, pour on to the soaked gelatine. Stir till dissolved. Cool. Add a little green vegetable colouring, if wanted a rich green, and strain on to the cucumber and green pepper or parsley. Spoon a little of the mixture into the bottom of a mould or of individual moulds. Add flaked crab to taste, then the remainder of the jelly. When set, turn on to a dish lined with lettuce leaves. Garnish with radish roses. Serve with mayonnaise. *For 4 persons.*

JELLIED EGGS AND PRAWNS (Gelée d'Oeufs Chez Moi)

2¼ tablespoons gelatine
3½ cups clear stock
½ cup boiling water
2 tablespoons sherry
Salt and pepper to taste
6 hard-boiled eggs
½ cup boiled green peas
¾ cup shelled prawns
1 lemon shell
Mustard and cress

Soak gelatine in ½ cup of the stock till softened. Dissolve in the boiling water. Add remainder of stock and sherry. Season with salt and pepper to taste. Shell eggs when quite cold. Place eggs, pointed end outwards, in a wet ring mould, after setting a thin layer of jelly in base. Strain enough liquid over to cover. Stand till set. Add peas and prawns, then pour over remainder of jelly, taking care that neither peas nor prawns rest on the eggs. When set and chilled, fill lemon shell with mayonnaise and arrange in centre. Garnish with mustard and cress and a few additional prawns. *For 6 persons.*

JELLIED TOMATO SALAD (Aspic de Tomates)

½ tablespoon powdered gelatine
1 tablespoon cold water
Barely ¼ pint hot tomato juice
1 tablespoon vinegar
1 teaspoon sugar
Pinch of salt
1 teaspoon minced onion
2 oz. boiled green peas
2 oz. grated carrot
1 gherkin or small cucumber
4 tablespoons mayonnaise

Soak gelatine in cold water for 5 minutes. Add to tomato juice, allowing 2 tablespoons less than ¼ pint. Stir in vinegar, sugar and salt. Stir till dissolved. Add onion. Stand till flavoured with onion, then strain into a basin. When beginning to stiffen, gently stir in green peas and carrot. Turn gently into a wet border mould. When set, turn out on to a dish lined with shredded lettuce. Peel and put gherkin or cucumber through a mincer. Stir into mayonnaise. Fill into centre of mould. Serve with any cold cut. *For 4 persons.*

STUFFED TOMATOES IN ASPIC
(Aspic de Tomates farcies)

1 lb. small firm tomatoes
Salt and pepper to taste
1¼ tablespoons powdered gelatine
½ cup cold water
2 bouillon cubes
1½ cups boiling water
Sherry or lemon juice
¼ cup minced celery

Remove a slice from the flower end of tomatoes, then carefully scoop out soft centres. Season shells with salt and pepper. Turn upside down on a rack to drain. Soften gelatine in cold water. Dissolve bouillon cubes in boiling water. Add gelatine. Stir until dissolved. Season to taste with salt. Flavour with sherry or lemon juice as preferred. Leave

477

4 tablespoons flaked Finnan haddock
Mayonnaise to taste
Aspic jelly as required

until beginning to set, then pour a thin layer in the bottom of as many individual moulds as you have tomatoes. Mix celery with fish, and moisten with mayonnaise to taste. Stuff tomatoes with mixture, then place topside down in each mould. Fill up with aspic jelly. Set in refrigerator. When required, turn out on to individual glass plates, lined with lettuce or endive leaves. Decorate each with a blob or rose of mayonnaise and minced parsley. *For about 8 persons, depending on number of tomatoes.*

TOSCA SALAD (Salade à la Tosca)

2 large cans asparagus
2 cloves
2 slices shallot
¼ teaspoon salt
¼ teaspoon paprika
3 slices carrot
2 tablespoons powdered gelatine
¼ pint cold water
1 pint whipped cream
2 or 3 hard-boiled eggs

Drain asparagus thoroughly, but reserve the liquid. Take a border mould, round or oval, and cut the stalks just the height of the mould. Reserve enough stalks to arrange round mould, and cook the remainder in the reserved liquid slowly for 20 minutes with cloves, shallot, salt, paprika and carrot. At the end of 20 minutes there should be hardly any left. Rub stalks and any remaining stock through a coarse sieve. Measure. There should be about 2 cups of the purée. If there is more, cook it slowly until reduced to that amount. Soften gelatine in cold water for 5 minutes. Stir over hot water, *but not boiling*, until gelatine is dissolved, then stir into asparagus purée. Leave until cold, stirring occasionally, until starting to congeal, when fold in whipped cream. Dip mould in cold water. Shell eggs, slice and place close together in the bottom of mould. Now place trimmed asparagus stalks round outer edge with the tips downwards, and pour in the asparagus cream. Chill and unmould on to a flat dish. Garnish with a circle of crisp heart of lettuce leaves. Serve with cold chicken, guinea fowl or turkey dredged lightly with paprika. *For 6 or 7 persons.*

SWEET AND SAVOURY SALADS

Sweet and savoury salads, such as a combination of fish or fruit and vegetables can be delicious if a dressing is chosen to suit.

QUICK FRUIT AND VEGETABLE SALADS

1. Equal quantity of diced Avocado pear, chopped apple and shredded cos lettuce. Dress to taste.
2. Equal quantity of shredded celery, diced cucumber and apple.
3. Equal quantity of diced drained pineapple and tomato arranged on lettuce or endive, and coated with French dressing flavoured with pineapple juice.
4. Equal quantity of diced apple or pineapple and shredded cabbage heart mixed with chopped walnuts to taste and coated mayonnaise.
5. Equal quantity of diced, fresh, ripened pineapple and cucumber coated with mayonnaise, served on lettuce or curly endive.

6. Sections of orange, grapefruit or mandarin served on lettuce and garnished with chopped dates. Sprinkle with French dressing.

ALMOND AND BANANA SALAD
(Salade à l'Orientale)

⅛ cup almonds
½ pimiento
¼ Spanish onion
2 sliced bananas
2 tablespoons cold, boiled, flaky rice
About ¾ cup curry dressing

Blanch and chop almonds. Shred pimiento. Mince enough onion to give you 2 teaspoons. Add to almond mixture with sliced banana and rice. Toss ingredients lightly. Coat with curry dressing. Serve with cold chicken. *For 3 persons.*

APPLE, DATE AND WALNUT SALAD
(Salade à la Tunis)

3 oz. chopped walnuts
½ lb. minced dates
1½ cups diced apple
Mayonnaise as required
Celery salt to taste
2 oz. shredded celery

Mix walnuts with dates and apple. Moisten with mayonnaise, flavoured with celery salt. Add celery. Serve on plates, lined with lettuce leaves, with cold roast lamb or veal, or duck or goose. *For 4-6 persons.*

BANANA AND TOMATO SALAD
(Salade de Bananas et Tomates)

1 lettuce
French dressing as required
12 slices of tomato
1 large banana
2 tablespoons whipped cream
2 tablespoons mayonnaise
1 tablespoon chopped walnuts

Line 4 individual plates with lettuce leaves moistened with French dressing. Place 3 slices of tomato on each plate. Peel, slice and divide the banana equally between each portion. When required, fold the cream into mayonnaise. Put a heaped tablespoon of mixture on top. Sprinkle with the chopped nuts. Serve with cheese. *For 4 persons.*

SPANISH BANANA SALAD (Salade de Bananas, Espagnole)

Slice 4 ripe sound bananas lengthwise with a silver knife. Chop 12 walnuts. Arrange lettuce leaves on 4 salad plates, and place a sliced banana on each. Sprinkle with the nuts. Coat with mayonnaise seasoned with cayenne pepper. Serve with cold ham or tongue. *For 4 persons.*

MADEIRA SALAD (Salade à la Madérae)

1 cup minced carrot
½ cup chopped apple
½ cup minced cucumber
½ cup orange fingers
1 cup mayonnaise
1 lettuce

Mix carrot, apple, cucumber and orange together. Coat with mayonnaise. Chill. Serve in a salad bowl lined with lettuce leaves. Garnish with sprigs of fresh mint. *For 5 or 6 persons.*

ORANGE SALAD (Salade d'Oranges)

6 oranges or tangerines
1 tablespoon olive oil
1 tablespoon lemon juice
Cayenne pepper and tarragon vinegar to taste
½ teaspoon caster sugar
Minced mint or parsley as required

Peel and remove white pith from oranges or tangerines, then divide into sections. Carefully remove skin and pips. Arrange sections in a salad bowl. Mix oil and lemon juice together. Season to taste with cayenne pepper and tarragon vinegar. Stir in sugar. Sprinkle with a little minced mint or parsley. Serve with roast duck or goose. *For 6 persons.*

ORANGE AND MINT SALAD (Salade d'Oranges au Menthe)

6 oranges
Juice of ½ lemon
2 tablespoons caster sugar
3 tablespoons finely chopped mint

Remove pulp from oranges. Extract lemon juice and add to pulp with sugar and mint. Chill. Either serve in orange shells or on crisp lettuce leaves with cold duck or lamb.

PINEAPPLE AND STRAWBERRY SALAD (Salade d'Antoinette)

½ crisp lettuce
2 slices canned pineapple
1 tablespoon lemon juice
½ lb. strawberries
½ gill cream dressing

Line 2 salad plates with crisp lettuce leaves. Cover each with a slice of pineapple. Sprinkle with lemon juice. Pick over the strawberries and divide equally between the two portions. Top berries equally with the cream dressing. *For 2 persons.*

CHEESE
Service of Cheese.

CAKES

Angel Food Cake, Betty's Chocolate Gateau, coated with white glacé icing and coconut, and Walnut Star Gateau, coated with jelly frosting. *See pages* 727, 729, *and* 731-732.

Cereals

You have to go abroad to realize how many savoury dishes can be made with cereals, though owing to the price of meat, the British housewife is learning to introduce them more freely to her own table. Most appetising luncheon and supper dishes, snacks for high tea, and even main courses for dinner can, with a little imagination, be evolved from one or two cereals as well as from all the Italian pastas that are only too little known on this side of the Channel. Nuts and lentils can also be made the basis of a number of interesting dishes.

Cereals are the seeds or grains of a number of grasses. The most important cereals are barley, oats, rice and wheat. In the United States, and some parts of Europe and the Middle East, buckwheat and rye also come into this category.

There are other valuable grain products besides the ones mentioned, such as farina and semolina prepared from wheat, and ground rice from rice, but they are seldom used in savoury dishes.

To Cook Cereals: All cereals should be thoroughly cooked. If not, they will be indigestible and their flavour will be impaired. As cereals have a large starch content, it is also important to allow enough water to soften and swell the starch. Coarsely-grained cereals, such as ground rice and semolina, need longer cooking than the finely-grained, crushed ones. To increase the food value of cereals, boil them in milk instead of water, or substitute milk for part of the water.

Quantity to Allow: 1½ oz. per head.

BARLEY

Barley is said to be the most ancient food of mankind. Experts claim that it has a considerably higher nutritive standard than oats, rice and wheat.

There are two kinds of barley : Pot or Scotch barley, and Pearl barley. The former, the coarser of the two, needs longer cooking. It adds nourishment to soups and stews, but takes about $2\frac{1}{2}$ hours to make it digestible. Pearl barley, which is a finer polished barley, is used in the same way, but it takes $1\frac{1}{2}$-2 hours to cook.

To Boil Barley: Bring 4 cups of water to the boil. Add salt. Rinse $\frac{1}{2}$ cup barley in a strainer under the cold water tap, and drain well. Sprinkle into the boiling water. Stir until water again comes to the boil, then cover. Boil slowly until tender in 1-2 or more hours, according to whether you are boiling the pot or pearl barley. When ready, each kernel should be separate, distinct and swollen, as well as soft throughout.

OATMEAL

Oatmeal, which is made of ground, hulled oats, is a highly nutritious grain. It contains both body-building and flesh-forming properties. There are 4 varieties of oatmeal. The coarse is generally made into brose or porridge, or used in the preparation of the famous haggis. The medium is more popular for porridge, though it is also used for oatcakes, oatmeal biscuits, and other Scottish tea-bread. The third variety resembles flour in texture. This is the one to order when you want to make gruel or a very fine porridge. The fourth variety, which takes the form of flakes, can be used for biscuits, flapjacks, oatcakes, porridge, etc.

HAGGIS
(*As made by James Ireland Craig*)

Take the large stomach bag of a sheep, and also one of the smaller bags — the Knight's Hood bag. Clean thoroughly. Soak over-night in cold, salted water, then turn large bag rough side out. Wash the Knight's Hood bag and the pluck. Place both in a saucepan, and draw the windpipe out over the side, then cover the bag and the pluck with cold water. Boil for $1\frac{1}{2}$ hours, then remove and cut off the pipes and any gristle. Mince pluck, using the heart, lights and half the liver, or put them through a meat grinder. Mince Knight's Hood bag as well. Stir in $\frac{1}{2}$ lb. shredded suet, 2 medium-sized finely minced onions, 2 cups of medium oatmeal, salt and black pepper to taste, and a pinch of Jamaica pepper. Moisten with $\frac{1}{2}$ pint of the pluck stock. Fill the large bag nearly full and sew up. Prick it here and there with a large darning needle. Place in a saucepan. Cover with boiling water, or use the pluck stock. Boil for 3 hours, uncovered. If not to be served at once, then boil for 1-$1\frac{1}{2}$ hours, then for the same time just before serving.

Mock Haggis: Wash and boil 1 peeled onion in salted water to cover. Reserve the liquid. Mince onion and $\frac{1}{4}$ lb. cooked liver. Add $\frac{1}{4}$ lb. shredded suet. Toast $\frac{1}{4}$ lb. medium oatmeal in the oven for a few minutes, then add to onion mixture with salt, pepper and allspice to taste. Moisten with the onion stock.

Press into a greased straight-sided jar. Cover with greaseproof paper. Put an enamel plate in the bottom of a saucepan. Place jar on top. Add boiling water to come halfway up the sides. Cover pan. Steam for 2 hours. Turn out. Serve at once with hot mashed potatoes.

PORRIDGE MEAT LOAF (Pain de Viande, Ecossaise)

⅓ pint minced chicken or veal
¾ pint cold porridge
1 tablespoon minced onion
½ teaspoon made mustard
½ teaspoon crushed herbs
Salt and pepper to taste
2 oz. butter
1 beaten egg
¼ pint chicken or veal stock

Place meat in a basin. (You can use half chicken and half veal if you like.) Stir in porridge, onion, mustard, herbs, salt and pepper to taste. Melt butter. Stir into mixture, then add egg and stock. Mix well. Place in a greased loaf tin. Stand it in a baking tin containing warm water to come nearly halfway up the side of loaf tin. Bake in a moderate oven, 350° F, for about 1¼ hours. *For 4 persons.*

WHITE PUDDINGS (Mealie Puddings)

This is the traditional Scottish recipe, and the puddings are usually served alone or added to stewed, minced meat about 10 minutes before dishing up.

2 lb. toasted oatmeal
1-1½ lb. shredded suet
2 or 3 chopped onions
Salt to taste
About 1 heaped teaspoon Jamaica pepper

Wash the pudding skins thoroughly. Soak them overnight in salt water. When required, drain and tie one end with string, then turn them inside out. Mix oatmeal with suet, onion, about a heaped dessertspoon of salt, and the pepper, and black pepper to taste as well. Pack mixture carefully into skins, till half full, then tie in equal lengths, 5-5½ inches apart. Bring a large deep saucepan of water to the boil. Draw pan to side of stove. Stand for a minute. Add puddings. Return to stove and boil for 5 minutes, then prick each pudding once or twice with a fork, and return to pan of water. Simmer for another 55 minutes. In olden days, these puddings were removed from the water and left till cold, then buried in oatmeal, and taken out as required. Scottish housewives claimed that if stored in oatmeal, they kept fresh for several months. When wanted, simmer for 10 minutes, or place in a saucepan of cold water and bring to boil, then brown in a little fat in a frying-pan.

RICE

Rice is the staple food of nearly half the population of the world. More digestible and nourishing than the potato, it is a valuable source of starch.

There are many uses for rice, besides making it into a pudding or boiling it as an accompaniment to curry. It can be used for thickening broths, in place of potatoes, and it can also be turned into a main course for lunch, dinner or supper in combination with fish, meat, poultry, etc.

Polished or White Rice: This is the inner part of the grain or kernel after the husk has been removed by the milling before the rice is polished. When you want rice to accompany curry or risotto, choose Patna when possible, and rice from Carolina or Java for puddings.

Unpolished or Brown Rice: This is a whole-grain rice, rich in minerals and vitamin B. It takes longer to cook, and doesn't keep as well as the polished rice, nor is it always obtainable. This is not suitable for dishes in which dry or flaky rice is required.

Quick-Cooking Rice: No reference to rice would be complete without mentioning the variety that has been treated so that it cooks in a flash. It is not a substitute for rice ; it is a rice that has been processed so as to reduce the cooking time.

To Prepare Rice: Place rice in a sieve or strainer. Hold under the cold water tap and stir rice until the water runs through clear, then drain.

To Boil Rice

There are two methods of boiling rice :
1. In plenty of water,
2. In just enough water required to cook rice so that all the water is absorbed.

¼ lb. rice
1½ pints water
1½ teaspoons salt

1. Prepare rice as described. Bring water and salt to the boil. Drain rice thoroughly. Sprinkle slowly into the water so that it doesn't go off the boil. Boil rapidly uncovered until tender in about 20 minutes. To tell when rice is ready, after boiling for 15 minutes, rub a kernel between your thumb and forefinger. If there is no hard core in centre, the rice is ready, and should be drained at once. To drain, pour into a coarse sieve with a basin below. Pour a kettleful of hot water through the kernels. Drain thoroughly. To dry, either place over a pan of hot water and cover with a cloth, or spread out on a hot plate and dry in a very cool oven. When thoroughly dried, the rice should be fluffy and every kernel separate. *Yield :* 1½-2 cups rice. *For 2 or 3 persons.*

¼ lb. rice
½ pint water
½ teaspoon salt

2. Prepare and place rice in a strong saucepan. Add water and salt. Cover closely. Bring slowly to the boil. Cook over very slow heat until quite tender in 25-30 minutes, when the rice below will have absorbed all the water. Do not stir while cooking unless you allow it to cook too fast, when it is apt to stick, so stir with a fork. Some varieties of rice may require a little more water, so when the water in pan is nearly absorbed, test the rice and if not practically ready, sprinkle a few drops of additional water carefully over it. Rice is now ready to serve. *Yield:* 1½-2 cups rice. *For 2 or 3 persons.*

BROWN RICE : Follow recipe for Method 1, but allow to cook for ½ hour, then lower heat and cover pan. Simmer until tender in 10-30 minutes longer. To shorten cooking time, heat water only till tepid and soak rice for 1 hour before placing in pan together with water and salt.

QUICK-COOKED RICE : Mix 4-5 oz. of rice with 1 pint cold water. Add a pinch of salt. Bring to boil. Simmer for 1-2 minutes. Remove from stove. Cover closely. Keep warm for 10 minutes before serving. Use for curries, risottos, and other savoury dishes.

To Boil Rice in a Double Boiler: Prepare 1 cup rice. Drain thoroughly.

Pour 1½ cups boiling water into top of double boiler. Sprinkle in rice and a teaspoon of salt. Cover. Place pan over direct heat. When rice comes to a boil, lower heat. Cook until all the water is absorbed in 10-12 minutes, then insert pan in top of double boiler and cook over boiling water for 10 minutes. Remove lid and cook for 5 minutes until rice is dry and fluffy.

Rice Reminders

1. To white rice, add ½ or ¾ teaspoon of lemon juice to water with the salt.
2. Substitute stock for water when boiling rice.
3. If water is very hard, add a ¼ teaspoon cream of tartar with the lemon juice, and salt.
4. If any scum should develop on top of water while rice is cooking, skim it off carefully.
5. Use the rice water and the water poured through the rice as the basis for soup or sauce.
6. To prevent rice sticking to pan, grease bottom of pan before adding water.

To Fry Rice

Uncooked rice is usually fried in butter, lard or oil as part of the method of cooking it for a rice dish such as a pilaf or risotto. When fried rice is wanted, use the following recipe, or fry cold boiled rice which has been rinsed after boiling to separate the kernels.

1 cup rice
Butter as required
¼ teaspoon salt
1½ cups cold water or stock

Prepare rice. Drain well and toss in a cloth till dry. Melt enough butter to cover the bottom of a frying-pan and add rice. Fry slowly till a pale brown. Place with salt, cold water and 1 teaspoon butter in a saucepan. Boil, without stirring and without covering, until nearly all the water or stock is absorbed. Cover closely with a piece of cheesecloth or folded butter muslin. Cook over hot water or over a very low heat till all the water is absorbed, then remove lid to allow steam to escape and rice to dry. *Yield:* 3 cups. *For 4 persons.*

To Make a Rice Border or Ring: Stir 4 tablespoons of melted butter into 4 cups of boiled rice. Brush a quart border or ring mould with melted butter. Pack in rice evenly. Lower into a baking tin containing boiling water coming halfway up the sides. Cover. Stand until heated through. Turn out. Fill with any creamed savoury mixture. *For 6 persons.*

To Make Individual Rice Moulds: Pack boiled or steamed rice into greased dariole moulds. Place in a pan of hot water. Cover and stand for 12 minutes. Turn out. Use as an accompaniment to a curry or savoury meat dish such as a ragout.

TO CURRY RICE

½ lb. rice
Cold water as required
1½ pints hot chicken stock
1 medium-sized onion

Prepare rice and drain well. Place in a saucepan. Cover with cold water. Bring quickly to a boil. Drain. Rinse under cold water tap. Drain. Bring chicken stock to the boil, or veal stock can

2 tablespoons butter
2 teaspoons curry powder
2 teaspoons salt

be used if preferred. Add rice. Boil without stirring, for 10 minutes. Meanwhile mince onion. Melt butter. Mix curry powder to a cream with a little of the butter, and add to remainder of butter with the onion and salt. Stir into the rice. Mix till blended, and transfer to a casserole or covered fireproof dish. Cook in a slow oven, 300° F., until rice is swollen and all the liquid is absorbed. Serve with hot poultry or veal.

To Curry Cooked Rice: Mix 3 cups of hot, boiled rice lightly together with a teaspoon of curry powder, 2 beaten egg yolks, 1 dessertspoon anchovy paste, ¼ cup minced green pepper, salt and cayenne pepper to taste. Stir with a fork over boiling water till rice tastes cooked. Add, if liked, 1 lb. boiled, chopped lobster, flaked white or smoked fish, or a mixture of shellfish and white fish.

To Cook Rice in the Oven: Place ¼ lb. prepared rice, tossed in a cloth till dry, in a casserole with a metal base. Add ¾ pint cold water and a teaspoon of salt. Bring to boil. Cover. Bake in a moderately hot oven, 400° F., for about 15 minutes, till tender.

FRENCH RICE BALLS (Boulettes de Riz)

3 cups boiled rice
1 cup grated cheese
1 beaten egg
¾ teaspoon salt
Pepper to taste
Egg and crumbs

Drain rice well after boiling, but do not rinse. Stir in cheese, using a sharp tangy cheese, egg, salt and pepper. Spread out on a plate and leave till cold. Shape into 5 or 6 balls. Roll in stale breadcrumbs, then in a lightly-beaten egg diluted with 2 tablespoons of water. Crumb again. Flatten tops.

Bake a little apart on a greased baking sheet in a moderate oven, 350° F., for about 20 minutes. Place a teaspoon of red currant jelly on the centre of each. Use for garnishing baked ham. *For 5 or 6 persons.*

FRIED RICE WITH MUSHROOMS (Moo-Goo-Chow-Fon)

3 tablespoons olive oil
1 teaspoon salt
Pepper to taste
2 eggs
8 oz. sliced mushrooms
2 tablespoons minced onion
4 cups cold boiled rice
2 tablespoons soy sauce
½ teaspoon caster sugar

Pour the oil into a heavy saucepan about 10 inches across. Add salt and pepper. When hot, fry eggs until firm, then remove and cut into shreds. Add mushrooms to oil with the onions. Cook slowly for 5 minutes, stirring constantly, then add rice. Mix with a fork till blended. Stir in egg, sauce and sugar. Cook, stirring constantly, till piping hot. Serve at once. *For 6 persons.*

STUFFED RICE RING (Roulade de Riz, Méditerranée)

2½ cups long-grained rice
½ lb. grated cheese
2 oz. butter
Chicken and bacon filling
¼ lb. fried mushroom caps
½ pint boiled peas
1 oz. blanched almonds

Prepare and boil rice till tender, then drain in a colander and rinse with boiling water. Place in a hot saucepan. Add cheese and butter. Toss lightly over moderate heat until the cheese and butter are melted, then pack into a greased round border mould, 10 inches in diameter. When required, lower into a baking tin containing boiling water coming halfway up the mould. Bake in a moderate oven, 350° F., for about 30 minutes. Turn on to a round, hot, flat dish. Pile creamed chicken and bacon or tongue in the centre. Arrange mushroom caps equal distance apart on ring, and green peas tossed in melted butter, round. Sprinkle filling with split almonds fried till golden brown. Serve with a hot sauceboat of parsley sauce. *For 8 persons.*

MOCK SOLE (Filets de Semoule)

½ pint milk
2 oz. semolina
1 oz. butter
1½ oz. grated cheese
Pinch of ground mace
Salt and pepper to taste

Heat milk in a saucepan. Sprinkle in the semolina. Bring to boil, stirring constantly. Stir over slow heat for ¼ hour. Add butter, cheese, mace, salt and pepper. Spread on a plate. When quite cold, divide in 4 equal portions. Shape into fillets of fish. Egg and crumb. Fry in deep smoking hot fat till golden. Arrange on a hot dish lined with a paper doily. Garnish with lemon slices and sprigs of parsley. *For 2 persons.*

SEMOLINA FRITTERS (Beignets de Semoule)

½ pint milk
5 tablespoons semolina
1 tablespoon flour
3 tablespoons minced ham
Salt and pepper to taste

Bring milk to the boil. Stir in semolina. Cook until very thick, stirring constantly. Cream flour with cold water. Stir into semolina with ham, salt and pepper. Stir over slow heat for about 5 minutes, then spread out 1 inch thick on a buttered plate. Leave till quite cold. Cut in rounds about 2½ inches across. Dip in beaten egg, then in grated cheese. Egg and crumb. Fry in deep, hot fat till golden brown. Drain on absorbent paper. Serve in a hot dish lined with a paper doily. Garnish with sprigs of parsley. *For 3 persons.*

Eggs

Eggs are more valuable in the diet than any other article of food on account of their versatility. They make an excellent substitute for meat because of their protein content, but as they are lacking in starch, dishes made from them are more nourishing when the eggs are combined with farinaceous foods.

TO CHOOSE EGGS

To get the best results from eggs, you have to know how long they have been laid. This is only really possible when you keep poultry and collect the eggs yourself. If you buy direct from a poultry keeper, you might be equally lucky. On the other hand, should you have to depend on eggs distributed through shops, new-laid eggs are generally out of the question.

New Laid: Choose for boiling, poaching, scrambling, shirring and steaming.

Fresh: (From 3-10 days old) : Choose for baking and frying, for batters, omelets, soufflés and all egg dishes in which the yolks and whites are beaten separately.

Preserved Eggs: Few housewives trouble nowadays to preserve eggs, but for the curious, here is the method.

TO PRESERVE EGGS

The best time to preserve eggs is in the spring or early summer when they are most plentiful. There are several methods of preserving, but I consider the waterglass the simplest. Choose eggs, non-fertile, and from 24-48 hours

488

old. They should have perfect shells. Wipe them with a clean flannel cloth. They should not be washed. Use any cracked or soiled eggs at once.

Waterglass Method: Use preserving pail, with a removable basket in the shape of a lining, or, failing this, an 8-gallon stone crock or jar. The advantage of the former lies in the fact that you can pack all the eggs into the basket and lower it into prepared waterglass. The alternative is that you have a choice between preparing the solution in a large container, packing the eggs into the crock or jar and pouring the solution over gently, or pouring the solution into the crock or jar, and placing each egg into it with your hands. The latter method requires great care or you may crack them. The correct way to place the eggs in the container is in rows, pointed ends downwards. They should be submerged at least 2 inches under the solution.

To Make the Waterglass: Proceed carefully as instructed on tin. If in course of time the solution leaves the top layer of eggs exposed through evaporation, bring it to required level with cold water. If you add more eggs from time to time, you must add enough cold solution to keep eggs 2-3 inches below.

The Coating Method: There are several ways of preserving eggs by the coating method :

1. Rub carefully all over with a paste made of boric powder and lard, or with a special preparation on the market.

2. By a quick dip in solution specially sold for this purpose with a wire dipper to save using the hands. The solvent evaporates, leaving eggs coated. They should be stored in a rack.

To Store Preserved Eggs

Waterglass: Stand container in a cold but frost-free place on a wooden base, not on a brick, cement or stone floor.

Coated: Place containers in a cool, dark cupboard on a shelf or on a wooden base below a shelf in larder. Should not be stored in the light.

Duck's Eggs : Be careful about using duck eggs. They are more liable to infection than hen eggs. It is on account of this, and because the shells of duck eggs are more porous than those of hen eggs, that it is unwise to preserve them.

To make duck eggs safe to eat always cook them thoroughly. For example, boil them for at least 15 minutes, or use them in puddings or cakes which require long baking, such as Yorkshire puddings and fruit cakes. Duck eggs should never be eaten uncooked, nor should they be used in lightly-cooked dishes such as poached eggs, scrambled eggs, omelets, custards, sponge cakes, meringues, honeycomb mould, etc. The result of eating infected duck eggs may be very serious, particularly in cases of young children, invalids and elderly people.

Goose Eggs : Boil for 7-9 minutes, depending on whether you like them soft or medium-boiled, or use in any of the following recipes given for hens' eggs. One medium-sized goose's egg is equivalent to 3 medium-sized hens' eggs, sometimes 4.

EGG PATTIES (Patisserie aux Oeufs)

½ lb. shortcrust
1 tablespoon butter
2 oz. peeled mushrooms
1 oz. chopped lean ham
Pepper to taste
6 eggs
1 beaten egg

Roll out pastry thinly. Line 6 deep patty pans or tartlet tins neatly. Prick the bottoms with a fork. Melt butter in a saucepan. Chop and add mushrooms, ham, and pepper to taste. Simmer gently for 2 or 3 minutes. Remove from heat. Leave till cool. Divide equally between the pastry cases and spread evenly over the bottom of each. Break an egg into a cup and pop into a case. Fill all cases in this way. Season eggs with salt and pepper to taste. Brush edges with cold water. Cover cases neatly with a round of pastry. Cut a slit in the centre of each to allow steam to escape. Brush each lightly on top with the egg. Bake in a hot oven, 450° F., for about ¼ hour. *For 6 persons.*

LENTEN EGGS (Oeufs à la Carême)

1 lb. spinach
4 poached eggs
½ pint Mornay sauce

Wash spinach very thoroughly. Boil in the usual way. Drain thoroughly. Rub through a sieve. Add butter, salt and pepper, and a pinch of grated nutmeg if liked. Divide equally between 4 large buttered scallop shells. Place a neatly and lightly poached egg on top. Divide the sauce equally between the shells. Dredge lightly with grated Parmesan cheese if liked. Bake in a moderate oven, 350° F., for about 10 minutes, until golden brown. *For 4 persons.*

MONK'S PIE (Oeufs, couchés)

½ lb. tomatoes
2 tablespoons butter
3 cups mashed potato
Salt and pepper to taste
1 teaspoon grated onion
3 heaped tablespoons grated cheese
4 or 5 eggs
½ pint parsley sauce

Scald, peel and slice tomatoes. Melt butter in a saucepan. Add tomatoes. Cover and simmer until into a thick pulp. Rub through a sieve. Beat purée into the potato. Season with salt and pepper to taste. Stir in onion and half the cheese. Spread out evenly in a large oval or oblong, shallow, buttered fireproof dish. Make enough hollows with the back of your hand, or a tablespoon, equal distance apart, to take the eggs. Cover with sauce. Sprinkle with remainder of grated cheese. Bake in a moderately hot oven, 400° F., for about 10 minutes, until golden brown. *For 4 or 5 persons.*

POOR WIFE'S EGGS (Oeufs, Pauvre Femme)

6 eggs
Salt and pepper to taste
6 oz. butter
2 oz. diced bread

Crack eggs into a cup, one by one, and place each in a shallow buttered fireproof dish large enough to take them side by side. Season with salt and pepper. Melt butter in a frying-pan. Sprinkle a teaspoon over each egg. Bake in a fairly slow oven, 325° F., for about 12 minutes, till set to taste. Fry bread in remainder of butter, shuffling the pan so that it browns equally. Pour over eggs. *For 3 persons.*

BAKED EGGS IN TOMATO SHELLS

Remove blossom ends from firm tomatoes. Carefully scoop out the pulp and season insides with salt and pepper. Invert for $\frac{1}{2}$ hour. Drop an egg into each. Season with salt and pepper. Sprinkle a teaspoon of melted butter over each egg. Place tomatoes in a shallow, greased, fireproof dish, containing just enough stock to cover bottom of dish. Place in a fairly slow oven, 325° F., and bake till eggs are set, in about 12 minutes.

HARD-BOILED EGGS

To boil eggs until hard so that the whites are tender, not tough, first place a rack in a saucepan of cold water, then add the eggs. Heat water slowly until it starts to simmer, but *on no account* allow it to boil, as the boiling will toughen the whites. Allow it to keep at this temperature for $\frac{1}{2}$ hour.

CURRIED EGGS (Kari d'Oeufs)

1 oz. butter
1 medium-sized onion or 4 spring onions
1 tablespoon curry powder
1 dessertspoon flour
¾ pint hot white stock
1 teaspoon tomato chutney
½ cooking apple
1 clove
Pinch of ground mace
Salt and pepper to taste
A few drops of mild vinegar
4 hard-boiled eggs

Melt butter in a saucepan. Peel, chop and add onion. Fry gently till it turns colour. Stir in curry powder and flour. Cook gently for 3 or 4 minutes, stirring constantly. Add stock. Bring to boil, still stirring. Chop and add tomato chutney and apple, then add clove, mace, salt and pepper to taste, and vinegar. Mix well, then cover and simmer from $\frac{1}{4}$ to $\frac{1}{2}$ hour, stirring frequently. Strain over hard-boiled eggs, halved, and arranged in the centre of a hot dish. Spoon boiled rice round. Garnish to taste with quarters of extra hard-boiled eggs. Serve with chutney. *For 4 persons.*

EGGS A LA KING (Oeufs au Roi)

6 hard-boiled eggs
2 cups medium Béchamel sauce
1 cup sliced fried mushrooms
½ cup cooked green peas
1 dessertspoon minced parsley
Salt and pepper to taste
6 croûtes fried bread or buttered toast

Shell and cut eggs into 8 wedges lengthwise. Heat the sauce. Add mushrooms, peas, and parsley. Season with salt and pepper to taste, and add a pinch of grated nutmeg if liked. Pour the creamed eggs over croûtes of bread or toast. Garnish with minced chives or parsley. *For 6 persons.*

EGGS AU GRATIN (Oeufs au Gratin)

BASIC:
6 hard-boiled eggs
1 tablespoon melted butter
1 teaspoon minced parsley
1 teaspoon grated onion

Shell and halve eggs crosswise while still hot. Remove yolks to a basin. Stir in butter, parsley and onion. Moisten about $1\frac{1}{2}$ tablespoons of the crumbs in a basin with milk. Season. Stand for 3 minutes. Add to yolk mixture. Beat till blended.

5½ tablespoons stale bread-crumbs
Salt and pepper to taste
1 pint Béchamel sauce
¾ cup grated cheese

Pile into egg whites. Place in a shallow buttered fireproof dish. Cover with the sauce. Mix remainder of crumbs with cheese and sprinkle over the top. Fleck all over with butter. Bake in a moderate oven, 350° F., for about ¼ hour, till golden brown. *For 3 or 6 persons.*

To Vary Service: 1. Substitute boiled rice for the moistened crumbs.

2. Place 3 or 4 picked shrimps or a prawn in the bottom of each egg white before adding yolk filling.

EGG NEST (Nid d'Oeufs)

3 oz. butter
1 tablespoon minced onion
2 oz. flour
1 pint milk
1 teaspoon minced parsley
4 hard-boiled eggs
1½ lb. mashed potatoes
Salt and pepper to taste
1 beaten egg yolk
2 oz. grated cheese

Melt 2 oz. of the butter in a saucepan. Add onion. Cook slowly till clear. Stir in flour. When frothy, stir in milk. Stir till smooth and boiling. Add parsley. Shell and quarter hard-boiled eggs. Melt remainder of butter in a saucepan. Add potatoes. Season to taste. Beat till smooth. Place in a flat, greased fireproof dish. Shape into a flan case with straw-like edge. Brush with egg yolk. Bake till pale brown in a hot oven, 450° F.

Season sauce to taste. Stir in cheese. Stir over stove till cheese is melted, then add quarters of egg, saving a few for garnishing. Pour into case. Sprinkle with grated cheese, if liked. Bake for 3 minutes. Garnish. *For 4 or 6 persons.*

ITALIAN EGGS (Oeufs, Italienne)

6 hard-boiled eggs
1 small can tuna fish
1 tablespoon mayonnaise
1 oz. butter
Salt and pepper to taste

Shell and cut a thick slice from the top of each egg. Remove yolks. Reserve two, and pound the remainder in a basin with fish, mayonnaise and butter. Season well. When blended, rub through a sieve with the back of a wooden spoon. Force mixture into 6 whites, after cutting them vandyke fashion round the edges. Arrange on a dish lined with lettuce or mustard and cress. Garnish with fingers or triangles of cold toast spread with remaining yolks moistened with mayonnaise or butter. Garnish with slices of truffle or chopped capers. *For 6 persons.*

SCOTCH EGGS (Oeufs, Écossaise)

3 hard-boiled eggs
½ lb. sausage meat
1 beaten egg
Stale breadcrumbs as required
6 croûtes of fried bread
1 teaspoon minced parsley

Shell the eggs when quite cold. Dip in seasoned flour. Divide the sausage meat equally between them, and carefully coat each egg evenly all over with the meat. Brush with beaten egg. Dip in breadcrumbs. Fry in deep smoking hot fat until rich brown. Halve crosswise. Arrange each on a croûte of fried bread, or buttered toast if preferred. Sprinkle the yolks with minced parsley. If wanted cold, arrange in a bed of cooked green peas, fringed, 2 inches apart, with wedges of tomato. Serve with mayonnaise. *For 3 persons.*

SAVOURY OMELETS

Savoury omelets are just as popular for lunch, high tea or supper as for breakfast. They can be prepared by any of the recipes given in the Breakfast Section, see pages 60-62.

EZE OMELET (Omelette à l'Eze)

4 eggs
½ tablespoon grated Parmesan cheese
¼ gill water
Salt and pepper to taste
1 dessertspoon minced onion
1 tablespoon chopped potato

Break eggs into a basin. Add cheese, water and salt and pepper to taste. Beat quickly for 2 minutes. Place the onion and potato in a frying-pan with 1½ tablespoons butter. Fry slowly till pale gold. Drop in egg mixture. Fry in the usual way. Fold in two. Serve on a hot dish. *For 2 persons.*

MUSHROOM OMELET (Omelette de Champignons)

Follow recipe given for basic English Omelet, in the Breakfast Section, page 61, but add ½ teaspoon onion juice to egg yolk mixture. Fill omelet before folding with 2 oz. sliced fried mushrooms. *For 2 persons.*

PEASANT'S OMELET (Omelette, Paysanne)

2 medium-sized aubergines
2 tablespoons butter
1 medium-sized onion
Pinch of saffron
Salt and pepper to taste
6 eggs

Peel and slice aubergines. Melt butter in a frying-pan and fry slices till tender. Remove to a basin. Peel and slice onion. Fry slowly till clear and soft, but do not allow to brown. Add to aubergine. Mash together. Flavour with saffron and season with salt and pepper. Beat eggs well. Stir into aubergine mixture. Fry in hot butter. See French Omelet, page 62. *For 4 persons.*

SAVOY OMELET (Omelette, Savoyarde)

1½ tablespoons butter
2 rashers bacon
2 tablespoons diced cold boiled potato
4 eggs
2 tablespoons grated cheese
Pepper to taste

Melt butter in an omelet pan. Draw pan to side. Remove rind from bacon. Dice bacon and throw into pan. Add potatoes. Fry lightly till bacon is cooked, stirring frequently. Beat up eggs. Stir in cheese and salt and pepper. Add to bacon and potatoes. Fry like a French omelet, till brown below, then turn and fry on the other side, adding more butter as you turn the omelet, if required. *For 2 persons.*

VEGETABLE OMELET (Omelette de Légumes)

4 separated eggs
1½ tablespoons milk
3 tablespoons butter
Salt and pepper to taste
½ cup cooked drained green peas

Beat egg yolks with milk till blended. Beat egg whites to a stiff froth. Melt 1 tablespoon butter in an omelet pan. Fold egg whites into egg yolks with salt and pepper to taste. Pour into pan. Fry till set below, lifting edges with a palette

493

¼ cup diced cooked celery
1½ tablespoons grated onion
1½ tablespoons sliced champignons

knife to allow liquid to run below and set. When still moist on top, slip in vegetables. Fold and serve at once. *For 6 persons.*

To Prepare Vegetables: Melt remainder of butter in a small saucepan while beating yolks, and add vegetables. Season with salt and pepper to taste, and heat so that they are ready at the same time as the omelet.

WELSH SOUFFLE OMELET (Omelette, Gauloise)

OMELET:
½ oz. cornflour
¼ pint top milk
2 separated eggs
Salt and cayenne pepper to taste
¾ oz. butter

FILLING:
½ oz. butter
1 tablespoon thin cream
Salt and pepper to taste
Pinch of ground mustard
1 oz. grated cheese
Pinch of minced parsley

Mix cornflour to a cream with a little of the milk. Bring remainder to boil. Stir in creamed cornflour. Boil for 3 minutes, stirring constantly, then remove from heat. Beat in egg yolks one at a time. Add salt and cayenne pepper to taste. Place butter in an omelet pan. Heat ingredients for the filling, except the cheese, in a saucepan. Beat egg whites to a stiff froth. Fold into omelet mixture. Cook over low heat until delicately browned below, then under grill or on top of an oven, heated to 350° F., till golden brown. Meanwhile, stir cheese into filling. When omelet is ready and cheese is melted, pour filling into centre and fold in two. *For 2 persons.*

POACHED EGGS

Poached eggs make a more substantial dish if served on croûtes of fried bread or hot, buttered toast, topped with a savoury spread, or on a purée, then coated with sauce.

POACHED EGGS ST. GERMAIN : Rub ½ pint boiled green peas through a sieve into a small saucepan. Add 1 tablespoon cream or top milk, ½ oz. butter, ½ teaspoon salt, ½ teaspoon sugar and pepper to taste. Stir till piping hot. Divide equally between 2 hot individual plates. Top each with a poached egg. *For 2 persons.*

POACHED EGGS ST. JEAN : Prepare and fry 6 fish cakes, ¾ inch thick, made of haddock or smoked fish. Arrange on a hot, flat dish. Crown each with a poached egg, then arrange a cross of pimiento on top of each. Serve with Béchamel sauce. *For 6 persons.*

SPANISH POACHED EGGS : Fry 4 rounds of bread, cut slightly larger than a poached egg, in butter on both sides, till crisp and golden. Spread thinly with anchovy paste, then with fried seasoned tomato. Top each with a poached egg. Dredge lightly with paprika. *For 4 persons.*

POACHED EGGS IN A FOG (Oeufs en Brouillard)

1½ lb. boiled spinach
Butter to taste
Salt and pepper to taste

Drain spinach well. Chop. Add butter with salt, pepper, ground mace and paprika. When piping hot, place in the bottom of a hot, buttered fireproof

Ground mace and paprika to taste
6 eggs
2 tablespoons chopped boiled onion
¾ pint cheese sauce

dish. Poach eggs lightly and arrange on spinach. Sprinkle the onion round the edge. Mask with the sauce. Heat under the grill until golden brown. *For 6 persons.*

SCRAMBLED EGGS FOR LUNCH OR SUPPER

Eggs scrambled with certain savoury additions and served on fried bread or toast make an appetising light snack for high tea or supper.

BASIC RECIPE :
4 eggs
2 oz. butter
4 tablespoons milk
Salt and pepper to taste
4 croûtes of bread

Beat eggs only till blended. Melt butter in a small saucepan. Add eggs, milk and salt and pepper to taste. Stir until thick. Serve on croûtes, fried, or toasted and buttered hot. Sprinkle with minced chives, parsley or paprika. *For 4 persons.*

VARIATIONS

Cheese: Melt 4 oz. sliced Gruyère cheese with ½ oz. butter in the top of a double boiler. Stir in 1 cup hot chicken stock, 1 dessertspoon minced parsley, 1 dessertspoon grated onion, salt, pepper and paprika to taste. Omit milk. Add eggs and follow above recipe.

Corn: Reduce butter to ¾ oz. and melt in saucepan. Add 1 can thoroughly drained corn, or use the kernels from 5 ears of boiled corn. Follow above recipe. Sprinkle with minced parsley and paprika.

Green Pepper: Decrease butter to 1½ oz. Substitute 1½ tablespoons cream for the milk. Add 1 split seeded and chopped green or red pepper, or 1 tablespoon minced pimiento, as mixture begins to thicken.

Rice: Stir 2 cups boiled rice into egg mixture. Add ¼ teaspoon paprika. Beat till blended. Follow above recipe. *For 6 persons.*

Tongue: Chop ¼ lb. cooked tongue. Add to egg mixture with 1 teaspoon minced green pepper. Substitute bacon fat if possible for the butter.

SHIRRED EGGS WITH KIDNEYS (Oeufs aux Rognons)

4 lambs' kidneys
Salt and white pepper to taste
4 eggs
1 dessertspoon melted butter
4 grilled bacon curls

Split, skin, core and wash kidneys. Grill kidneys. Season with salt and pepper. Break eggs and place in a shallow buttered fireproof dish. Sprinkle evenly with melted butter. Season. Bake in a fairly slow oven, 325° F, till eggs are set. Arrange kidneys round eggs and a curl of bacon on top of each kidney. *For 4 persons.*

Pastes

All forms of pastes, whether made in Italy or elsewhere, are boiled by the same method.

Throw into a saucepan containing a large quantity of boiling, salted water. Cook quickly, uncovered, until soft, then drain carefully, unless otherwise instructed. Hold under cold water tap for a moment or two to get rid of the starch. Reheat in the top of a double boiler over hot water if not in a sauce.

ITALIAN SAUCE FOR ITALIAN PASTAS

¼ cup olive oil
3 tablespoons minced onion
2 minced cloves garlic
1 lb. ground beef or steak
1 small can tomatoes
3 teaspoons salt
Dash of cayenne pepper
2 cups white stock or water
¾ teaspoon caster sugar
6 oz. Italian tomato purée
Pinch of basil
1 bay leaf

Heat the oil in a shallow saucepan. Add onion and garlic. Fry slowly for 3 or 4 minutes until clear, then add meat. Stir over a moderate heat until browned. Stir in tomatoes, then salt, cayenne pepper, stock or water, sugar, tomato purée, basil and bay leaf. Stir over moderate heat until blended, then simmer gently, uncovered, stirring frequently, for about 1¼ hours.

To Use: Store in the refrigerator in a covered jar. Use for coating any kind of boiled Italian pastes.

GNOCCHI (Gonoquis)

Gnocchi can be baked, boiled or fried, but it is more generally boiled, then dressed with cheese or tomato sauce. In France, gnocchi paste is usually formed into dumplings, then boiled and dressed.

FARMHOUSE GNOCCHI (Gonoquis à la Fermière)

9 medium-sized potatoes
¾ oz. grated cheese
3 tablespoons flour
Salt to taste
3 beaten eggs
Cheese and melted butter

Wash and bake potatoes in their jackets. Slit and allow steam to escape, then scoop out potato into a basin. Mash till smooth, then stir in cheese, flour, salt and eggs. When blended, knead well. Shape into balls or " corks." Dip in flour. Place in a large saucepan three-quarters full of boiling salted water. Cover. Boil until the dumplings rise to the top, in 5 or 6 minutes. Remove carefully. Drain thoroughly. Place in a large, shallow, greased, fireproof dish. Sprinkle first with grated cheese, then with melted unsalted butter. Place in a hot oven until the cheese melts. *For 4 persons.*

FRENCH GNOCCHI (Gonoquis à la Française)

1 cup milk
¼ lb. flour
2 egg yolks
Salt and pepper to taste
3 cups grated cheese
½ pint thick white sauce

Bring milk to a boil. Cream flour with cold milk and stir into boiling milk, then stir till boiling and very thick. Draw to side of stove. Stir in 1 egg yolk, then another. When blended, stir in salt and pepper and 2 cups of the cheese. With floured hands, shape into little balls of equal size. Throw into a large pan of boiling, salted water. Cook until they rise to the surface, then remove with a slice or perforated spoon. Drain thoroughly. Place side by side on a large, flat, hot dish. Coat with the sauce and sprinkle with grated cheese. Brown under grill or in the top of the oven. *For 4 persons.*

GNOCCHI DUMPLINGS (Boulettes de Gonoquis)

2 lb. potatoes
Salt to taste
10 oz. flour

Peel and boil potatoes in salted water. Put through a ricer. Gradually stir in flour. Knead until smooth. If dough sticks to your fingers, add a little more flour. Roll out into a long rectangle. Cut first into strips ¾ inch thick, then into ¾ inch lengths. Toss in flour. Make dents on each piece with the prongs of a fork. Throw into 4 quarts of salted water at a full boil. Boil for about 10 minutes. Drain thoroughly. Dish up. Coat with tomato sauce. Sprinkle with grated cheese. *For 4 persons.*

SEMOLINA GNOCCHI (Gonoquis de Semoule)

1½ pints milk
1 saltspoon salt
1 saltspoon grated nutmeg
9 oz. semolina

Bring milk to boil. Add salt and nutmeg. Sprinkle in the semolina. Stir till boiling, then cook for about 7 minutes, still stirring. Remove from heat. Stand for 10 minutes. Stir in Parmesan

2 oz. grated Parmesan cheese
3 egg yolks
2 oz. grated Gruyère cheese

cheese and 1 egg yolk at a time. When blended, pour into a large flat dish, making layer from $\frac{1}{2}$-$\frac{3}{4}$ inch thick. Leave till cold. Cut into narrow blocks. Place in a buttered fireproof dish with a tiny pat of butter on top of each. Sprinkle with Gruyère cheese. Brown under the grill or in a hot oven. *For 6 persons.*

MACARONI

Macaroni furnishes us with protein, and ranks high in energy value. It is also a good substitute for potatoes on account of its starch content.

There are many varieties of pastes which come under the heading of macaroni. Generally one looks upon macaroni as long or short tubes of dried paste. Now-a-days one has a great choice not only in form but in type of paste, such as egg macaroni and green macaroni flavoured with spinach. The directions for boiling, except for the length of time, apply to them all.

To Boil Macaroni

2 quarts water and 1 dessert-spoon salt to ¼ lb. macaroni

Bring water to a full boil in a four-quart saucepan. Add salt, then sprinkle in the macaroni slowly, so that the water does not go off the boil. Boil, uncovered, until tender in 12-20 minutes, the length of time depending on the thickness of the type of macaroni being boiled. (If any special instructions are given with the brand, follow them exactly.) After it has boiled for 2 minutes, slip a spatula under the macaroni to loosen it at the bottom, but be careful not to break it. Shake the pan occasionally to prevent sticking. When tender, turn into a colander.

To Get Rid of the Starch: If you want to serve macaroni hot, pour hot water through it from a kettle to get rid of the starch. If to be served cold or in a salad, or to be used in a savoury dish, hold it under the cold water tap instead. Some varieties of macaroni are more brittle than others. When you have boiled a brittle variety, lower the colander into a saucepan or basin of cold water, and let the water swell up over it, then drain away. Allow macaroni to drain well after rinsing before dressing in any way. This is important.

No. cups	Type of Macaroni	Approx. Wt.
1	uncooked broken or elbow macaroni or macaroni shells equals - - - - - - -	$\frac{1}{4}$ lb.
1	cooked broken macaroni - - - - -	$5\frac{1}{4}$ oz.

CASSEROLE OF MACARONI AND BEEF
(Casserole de Macaroni, Canadienne)

1 oz. beef dripping
½ cup chopped onion
1 lb. ground steak
Salt and pepper to taste

Melt dripping in a shallow saucepan. Add onion. Fry slowly till clear but not brown. Add beef. Stir lightly in the fat until brown, then add salt and pepper to taste, tomato soup, macaroni and

1 can tomato soup
3 cups boiled macaroni
½ cup beef stock

stock. Stir lightly till blended. Turn into a 2-quart casserole. Bake in a moderate oven, 350° F., for about ½ hour. *For 6 persons.*

CASSEROLE OF MACARONI AND SALMON
(Casserole de Macaroni, Ecossaise)

1 can salmon
2 separated eggs
2 cups cooked cut macaroni
2 tablespoons minced onion
¾ cup thin cream
Salt and cayenne pepper to taste
Pinch of celery salt
½ teaspoon dry mustard

Choose a tin of salmon 1 lb. in weight. Remove any skin and bone from fish, then flake. Do not drain. Beat and add egg yolks. Place macaroni in a greased casserole, 3 pint size. Turn salmon mixture into a saucepan. Stir in onion, cream, and seasonings, and a heaped teaspoon of minced parsley if liked. Stir till boiling, then simmer for 5 minutes, stirring constantly. Remove from heat. Beat egg whites till stiff. Fold into mixture. Pour over macaroni. Bake in a moderately hot oven, 375° F., for 25-30 minutes. *For 5 persons.*

ITALIAN MACARONI (Macaroni à l'Italienne)

½ lb. macaroni
1 tablespoon butter
¼ lb. grated Gruyère cheese
2 tablespoons grated Dutch cheese
1-2 tablespoons tomato sauce

Boil, drain and rinse macaroni. Melt butter in a saucepan. Add macaroni. Stir until the steam comes from it, then lightly stir in cheeses. When melted, stir in tomato sauce. Pile on a hot dish. *For 6 persons.*

MACARONI AND KIDNEYS (Macaroni aux Rognons)

2 oz. macaroni
4 sheep's kidneys
1 oz. butter
1 teaspoon minced onion
1 teaspoon flour
½ pint white stock
Salt and pepper to taste
¼ teaspoon meat extract

Boil, drain and rinse macaroni. Split, skin and core kidneys. Melt butter in a frying-pan. Fry kidneys till tender in 3 or 4 minutes. Remove and fry onion. Add flour. Stir till frothy, then stir in stock. Stir till boiling. Season to taste with salt and pepper and add extract. Chop kidneys. Add to sauce with half the macaroni. Cover. Heat over boiling water for 10 minutes. Dish up. Garnish with remainder of macaroni tossed in melted butter. *For 2 persons.*

MACARONI AND SPINACH PATTIES (Macaroni aux Epinards)

½ cup boiled macaroni
2 cups chopped cooked spinach
1½ tablespoons melted butter
1 tablespoon minced onion
1 saltspoon ground mace
1½ tablespoons grated cheese
¾ teaspoon baking powder
⅓ cup stale breadcrumbs
2 beaten eggs
3 tablespoons water

Place macaroni in a basin. Add spinach, butter, onion, mace, cheese, baking powder and crumbs, then 1 egg. Season with salt and pepper to taste. Stand for 10 minutes. If the mixture is not stiff enough to handle, add a few more crumbs. When required, divide into 8 equal portions. With floured hands, shape into flat cakes about ¾ inch thick and 2½ inches wide. Mix remaining egg with the water. Dip patties in egg then in crumbs, one at a time. Fry in enough melted butter or bacon fat to cover the bottom of a large frying-pan till brown below, then turn each with a palette knife and brown on other side. Drain on absorbent paper. Dish up round a hot, flat dish. Fill the centre with green peas. Serve with cheese, onion or tomato sauce. *For 4 persons.*

MACARONI CHEESE (Macaroni au gratin)

2 oz. cut macaroni
1 oz. butter
1 oz. flour
½ teaspoon made mustard
¾ pint milk
Salt and pepper to taste
3-4 oz. grated cheese

Boil, drain and rinse macaroni. Melt butter in a saucepan. Stir in flour. When frothy, stir in mustard and milk. Add salt and pepper to taste. Stir till boiling and simmer for 8 minutes, stirring constantly. Add three-quarters of the cheese. Stir in macaroni. When blended, pack into a shallow greased fireproof dish. Sprinkle with remainder of the cheese. Brown under the grill or in the top of a hot oven, 450° F. *For 4 persons.*

MACARONI AND CHEESE CROQUETTES
(Croquettes de Macaroni Ecossaise)

1 oz. macaroni
1 slice boiled onion
1 oz. butter
1¼ oz. flour
¼ pint hot milk
1 saltspoon made mustard
1 oz. grated cheese
Salt and pepper to taste

Boil, drain and rinse macaroni. Chop with the onion. Melt butter in a small saucepan. Add flour. When frothy, stir in milk, mustard, cheese, macaroni and onion, salt and pepper to taste. Turn on to a plate. Leave till cold. Divide in 6 or 7 equal portions. With floured hands, shape each into a cork. Egg and crumb. Fry in deep smoking hot fat till golden brown. Drain on absorbent paper. Pile on a hot flat dish. Garnish with sprigs of parsley or green peas. Serve with onion or tomato sauce. *For 2 persons.*

MACARONI LOAF (Pain de Macaroni)

¾ cup broken macaroni
1 cup hot milk
⅓ cup breadcrumbs
3 tablespoons melted butter
1 heaped teaspoon minced parsley
1 tablespoon chopped onion
1 cup grated cheese
Salt and pepper to taste
2 beaten eggs

Boil, drain and rinse macaroni. Pour milk over the crumbs. Add butter, parsley, onion, cheese, salt and pepper to taste. Stir in eggs, then macaroni. Turn into a well-greased loaf tin. Bake in a slow oven, till firm, in about ¾ hour. Leave in tin till nearly cold, then turn out into a glass dish. When quite cold, coat with thick mayonnaise. Garnish with sprigs of parsley. Decorate with a criss-cross of pimiento over the top. *For 3 or 4 persons.*

MACARONI RING (Roulade de Macaroni)

6 oz. cut macaroni
1½ tablespoons flour

Boil, drain and rinse macaroni. Mix flour to a cream with a little of the milk. Stir in remainder

1½ cups hot milk
½ oz. butter
2 beaten eggs
Salt and pepper to taste
¼ teaspoon celery salt
½ teaspoon made mustard

of milk. Pour into a saucepan. Add butter. Cook till boiling, stirring constantly. Remove pan from heat. Cool slightly. Stir in eggs, salt, pepper, celery and mustard. Add to macaroni. Stir till blended. Pack evenly into a greased round border mould. Bake in a moderate oven, 350° F., for about 35 minutes. Stand for a moment or two. Gently turn on to a hot dish. Fill with creamed Finnan or smoked haddock flavoured with grated cheese and minced parsley. Garnish base of ring with sprigs of parsley arranged about 2 inches apart, or surround with green peas. *For 6 persons.*

TIMBALE OF MACARONI (Timbale de Macaroni)

¾ lb. shortcrust
4 oz. macaroni
8 oz. peeled mushrooms
1 oz. butter
1 oz. flour
½ pint macaroni water
1 tablespoon cream
Salt and pepper to taste
Squeeze of lemon juice
Egg yolk and milk to brush

Roll pastry out thinly and line a greased cake tin smoothly with two-thirds of it, fitting it neatly into the base. Break up the macaroni. Boil and strain it. Stalk mushrooms. Melt butter in a saucepan. Add mushrooms. Fry slowly, turning occasionally, until soft. Remove and chop. Stir flour into remaining butter in pan. Stir till frothy, then add water, stirring constantly until boiling. Add macaroni, mushrooms, cream, salt and pepper to taste, then lemon juice. Mix well. Cook and pack into lined tin. Brush top edge with cold water. Cover with remainder of pastry rolled into a round to fit. Brush with milk, or egg yolk diluted with milk. Bake in a hot oven, 450° F., until pastry has risen and set, then reduce heat to 375° F., and finish cooking. (Should take about 45 minutes to bake.) Turn out on to a hot dish. Serve with any green vegetable. *For 4 persons.*

NOODLES (Nouilles)

Noodles can be served as an accompaniment to meat, particularly stews and casseroles of meat, in place of potatoes, or made into a savoury dish with or without the addition of meat or poultry. Also used for thickening broths and other thin soups. They have the same food value as macaroni. You can make them at home with very little trouble, or buy them loose and in packets. Among the most popular varieties are :

Lasagne: which are obtainable with or without eggs, narrow or wide.
Linguine: Narrow eggless noodles about ⅛ inch across.
Mafalde: Narrow twisted noodles.
Tagliarini: Very narrow egg noodles about ⅛ inch wide.

RICH NOODLE DOUGH (Nouilles au Beurre)

3 eggs
¾ tablespoon melted butter
10 oz. flour
¼ teaspoon salt

Beat eggs lightly. Stir in butter, or olive oil, if preferred. Sift flour with salt. Gradually stir into egg mixture. Turn on to a lightly-floured pastry board. Knead lightly for a minute. Divide dough in two equal portions. Roll each into a sheet as thin as a wafer. Spread out on a clean cloth to dry. Leave for about 1 hour. Roll up like a Swiss roll. Cut into slices $\frac{1}{4}$ inch thick. Unroll. If ribbon noodles are wanted, hang up on a string to dry till crisp. If short, fine noodles are wanted, cut with a very sharp knife into shreds before drying on waxed paper. Store in a tightly-covered jar. *Yield:* $\frac{1}{2}$ lb.

VEGETABLE NOODLES (Nouilles aux Légumes)

¼ cup vegetable purée
1 beaten egg
1 saltspoon salt
½ lb. sifted flour

Mix purée with egg and salt. Gradually stir in flour. Knead till smooth. Cover. Stand for $\frac{1}{2}$ hour. Follow method given for Rich Noodle Dough. (*See page* 501.)

NOTE : If you want green noodles, use asparagus, green pea, or spinach purée. If you want red, use tomato. To make a success, the purée must be pressed until all the moisture is out of it before measuring. It is best to rub it through a fine sieve. Cut the noodles in ribbons $\frac{1}{4}$ or $\frac{1}{3}$ inch wide.

To Make Noodle Balls for Soups: Roll out any of the pastes into a rectangle as thin as a wafer. Fold in two. With a vegetable cutter, cut out tiny circles $\frac{1}{4}$ inch across. Place in a frying basket. Lower into hot fat, 365° F. Fry for about a minute till puffy and pale brown. Drain on absorbent paper. Pass round with soup in place of croûtons.

BOILED NOODLES (Nouilles, bouilles)

Throw into boiling, salted water, allowing 2 quarts water and $\frac{1}{4}$ teaspoon salt to each cup of noodles. (If preferred, boil in the same quantity of chicken stock.) Boil, uncovered, usually from 10-20 minutes, depending on thickness and variety. (The very fine will only take 5 or 6 minutes.) Noodles should be tender, but still firm when ready. Turn into a colander when cooked. Rinse under running water, then drain. *For 3 persons.*

To Dress Boiled Noodles:

1. Season with pepper. Toss in melted butter or thick cream.

2. If to be served with a stew or casserole of meat or poultry, toss in enough rich gravy to coat.

3. Coat with melted butter. Serve sprinkled with grated cheese, or fried breadcrumbs.

Creamed Noodles: Mix 2 cups boiled noodles with $\frac{1}{2}$ pint parsley sauce.

FRIED NOODLES (Nouilles, frites)

Throw thin noodles into boiling, salted water, adding them gradually so that the water doesn't go off the boil. Boil for 5 minutes. Turn into a colander. Hold under the cold water tap. Drain thoroughly. Fry a small amount at a time in a wire basket in deep hot fat about 390° F., until a pale brown. Drain on absorbent paper. Sprinkle with salt if liked. When all are ready, re-heat for a moment or two in a moderately hot oven, 375° F.

LASAGNE (Baked Lasagne Noodles)

2 tablespoons olive oil
2 tablespoons minced onion
1 large can tomato purée
Salt and pepper to taste
Paprika to taste
Pinch of caster sugar
¾ lb. Mozzarella cheese
1 lb. Lasagne noodles
5 quarts boiling salted water
3 oz. grated Parmesan cheese

Heat oil. Add onion. Fry slowly till slightly browned, then add tomato purée, salt, pepper, paprika and sugar. Cover. Simmer gently for ¾ hour, stirring frequently. Meanwhile, cut Mozzarella cheese into thin slices. Throw noodles into water. Boil for about ¼ hour, stirring from the bottom occasionally to prevent sticking. Drain, rinse and drain. Place half the noodles in the bottom of a shallow greased fireproof dish. Cover with half the sauce, then with half the Mozzarella. Sprinkle with half the Parmesan cheese. Repeat layers. Bake in a moderate oven, 350° F., for about ¾ hour. *For 6 persons.*

SPAGHETTI

Spaghetti, which has the same food value as macaroni, can be just as savoury if properly cooked, drained and given an appetising sauce. It can be treated by any of the methods suggested for macaroni.

There are several varieties of spaghetti besides the long, fine tubes to which we are so accustomed. For example, you can buy cut spaghetti just as you can buy cut macaroni.

TO BOIL SPAGHETTI

Pour 2 quarts of cold water into a saucepan. Add 1 teaspoon of salt. Bring to the boil. Slowly sprinkle in ½ lb. spaghetti so that the water does not go off the boil. Boil from 15-20 minutes, according to thickness. Drain in a strainer. Pour 2 pints of cold water through to remove all starch, and then re-heat over boiling water in the top of a double boiler, or use hot water for rinsing.

½ lb. broken spaghetti equals 2 cups.

1 cup uncooked equals 2 cups cooked spaghetti.

ITALIAN SAUCE FOR SPAGHETTI

1 oz. butter
1½ tablespoons olive oil
2 heaped tablespoons minced onion
1½ cups chopped peeled tomatoes
6 minced anchovies
1 dessertspoon minced parsley
¼ teaspoon crushed herbs
2 tablespoons white stock
3 tablespoons grated Parmesan cheese
Salt and pepper to taste

Melt butter in a shallow saucepan. Add oil and onion. Fry slowly until the onion turns pale brown, then add tomatoes, anchovies, parsley and herbs. Cover. Simmer gently for ¼ hour, then stir in stock, cheese and salt and pepper to taste. Use for coating 1 lb. spaghetti, boiled and drained. Pile spaghetti on a hot flat dish. Sprinkle to taste with grated Parmesan cheese. *For 6 persons.*

SPAGHETTI AU GRATIN

1 lb. spaghetti
1 oz. butter
Salt and pepper to taste
Grated cheese to taste
1/4 pint milk
1/4 pint thick cream
3 beaten egg yolks

Boil, drain and rinse spaghetti. Place a third in the bottom of a well-buttered fireproof dish, 3 pint size. Dab with 1 or 2 bits of butter. Season with salt and pepper. Sprinkle with grated cheese to taste. Repeat layers. Bring milk to boil. When cool, stir in cream. Beat egg yolks. Stir in liquid. Pour over spaghetti. Sprinkle with a thick layer of grated cheese. Bake in a moderate oven, 350°F., for about ¼ hour. *For 6 persons.*

SPAGHETTI LOAF (Pain de Spaghetti)

1/4 lb. broken spaghetti
1/2 cup milk
1/2 cup cream
1 large tin canned salmon
Salt and pepper to taste
1 dessertspoon lemon juice
1 teaspoon grated onion
3 beaten eggs
1/2 cup stale breadcrumbs

Boil, drain and rinse spaghetti. Place in a basin. Mix milk with the cream and pour over. Remove any skin and bone, and liquid from salmon. Flake fish and add to spaghetti with salt and pepper to taste, lemon juice, onion and a pinch of celery salt if liked. Beat eggs and stir into mixture. Grease a loaf tin. Coat inside with breadcrumbs. Pour mixture into tin. Bake in a fairly slow oven, 325° F., for ¾ hour. Stand for a moment or two, then turn out on to a hot dish. Garnish with parsley or watercress and wedges of lemon. Serve with egg, mushroom or parsley sauce. *For 6 persons.*

SPAGHETTI POLONAISE

3/4 lb. spaghetti
1 oz. butter
1 oz. grated Parmesan cheese
1 oz. grated Gruyère cheese
Pepper to taste
2 tablespoons stale breadcrumbs
2 tablespoons melted butter

Boil, drain and rinse spaghetti. Place in a dry saucepan. Add butter and cheeses. Season with pepper, and salt if required. Toss till blended. Place in a hot dish. Sprinkle with breadcrumbs, fried till golden in melted butter. *For 5 persons.*

VERMICELLI

Vermicelli is the finest of Italian pastes. It is used mostly for thickening broths and soups, and for making puddings, but it is possible to use it also in savoury dishes.

To Boil Vermicelli: Throw into boiling, salted water. Boil for 5 minutes. Drain and use.

SCRAMBLED VERMICELLI (Vermicelli, brouilli)

1 heaped tablespoon butter
2 tablespoons diced cooked lean bacon
1 cup milk
1 cup boiled vermicelli

Melt butter in a saucepan. Fry bacon till ready. Stir in milk and vermicelli. Heat slowly, stirring frequently. When beginning to simmer, add eggs, salt, pimientoes, olives, and pepper. Stir

6 eggs
¾ teaspoon salt
2 chopped pimientoes
6 olives
Pepper to taste
1 teaspoon minced parsley

till eggs are thick. Serve in a hot dish or en cocotte sprinkled with parsley. *For 3 persons.*

RAVIOLI

Ravioli can be made from the following pastes, or with any noodle dough, and savoury fillings can be used to taste.

1. DOUGH FOR RAVIOLI

6 oz. sifted flour
1 saltspoon salt
3 egg yolks
4 egg whites

Sift flour and salt into a basin. Drop in egg yolks and whites. Mix to a smooth stiff dough with the help of a little warm water. Knead until smooth. Cover with a clean cloth. Stand for ¼ hour. Roll to wafer thinness on a lightly-floured board.

To Vary: Omit egg white and use only 1 egg yolk, and increase water as required.

2. DOUGH FOR RAVIOLI

¾ lb. flour
¼ teaspoon salt
1 oz. butter
2 eggs
About 1 cup tepid water

Sift flour and salt into a basin. Rub in butter. Drop in eggs, then mix to a stiff dough with water as required. Knead till smooth. Cover. Stand for ¼ hour. Cut in two equal portions and roll out thinly on a lightly-floured board.

To Make Ravioli: Cut pastry into strips, 2½ inches wide. Measure each strip out in 2½ inch portions, and mark with the back of a knife. Fill half of the portions each with a heaped teaspoon of filling. Cover with remainder of strips. Press edges together with finger-tips. Mark round the filling with the tip of your thumb to keep the filling from spreading too far. Cut apart with a sharp knife or a pastry jagger.

To Cook Ravioli: Leave for 2 hours to dry out slightly, then place in plenty of rapidly-boiling white stock, or salted water. Simmer for 10-15 minutes till dough is tender, then remove with a perforated spoon. If boiled too long, the layers of pastry will open. Arrange on a flat hot dish. Coat with tomato sauce. Sprinkle with grated Parmesan cheese. *For 6 persons.*

FILLINGS FOR RAVIOLI

Chicken: Beat 2 eggs lightly. Mix 1 cup minced, boiled chicken with 1 cup minced, well-drained spinach, ½ cup stale breadcrumbs, 1½ teaspoons minced parsley, ½ minced clove of garlic, pinch of ground mace or grated nutmeg, pinch of crushed herbs, and salt and pepper to taste. Stir in enough egg to bind mixture.

Meat: Mix ¾ cup minced, cooked meat with ¾ cup sieved, boiled spinach, ¼ cup breadcrumbs, ¼ cup grated cheese, 1 minced clove of garlic, ½ teaspoon crushed basil, and enough beaten egg to bind.

Spinach: Mix ½ cup stale breadcrumbs with 1 cup grated Romano or Parmesan cheese. Stir in ¼ teaspoon grated nutmeg, ½ minced clove of garlic, salt and pepper to taste, 1 lightly-beaten egg, and white stock as required.

Nuts and Pulses

Nuts are commonly regarded as being suitable for salting, serving with port, for adding to tea bread, or for decorating cold sweets and sundaes. They can also be used for making savoury croquettes, cutlets, loaves and other nourishing dishes. Some of the following recipes are intended principally for vegetarians. All can be adapted for vegetarian use by substituting vegetable fat for meat fat, and milk, vegetarian or vegetable stock for any meat stock suggested in the recipe.

There is one point to remember when preparing nuts, and that is the more they are baked or roasted, the more indigestible they become. It is better to boil or steam nut dishes than bake them when catering for people with delicate stomachs.

ANNIE'S NUT ROAST (Noix au Gratin)

1 medium-sized onion
1 tablespoon butter
1 cup stale breadcrumbs
¼ cup water
1 cup grated cheese
1 cup ground walnuts
Juice of 1 lemon
Salt and pepper to taste
Dash of celery salt
2 beaten eggs

Mince onion. Melt butter in a saucepan. Add onion. Cook slowly for 2 or 3 minutes. Cover crumbs with water. Soak for 5 minutes, then drain off water. Add crumbs to onion. Stir till blended, then turn into a basin. Stir in cheese, nuts, and remaining ingredients. When blended, pack into a greased fireproof dish. Bake in a moderate oven, 350° F., for about ½ hour, till mixture is set and golden brown. Serve with tomato sauce. *For 2 persons.*

CHESTNUT CROQUETTES (Croquettes de Marrons)

2 cups hot sieved chestnuts
2 oz. butter
2 beaten eggs
1½ tablespoons grated onion
Pinch of celery salt
Salt and pepper to taste

Place chestnut purée in a basin. Melt and stir in butter. Stir in eggs and seasonings. When blended, shape into croquettes. Mould into cork shapes. Crumb, then egg and crumb. Fry in deep hot fat, about 380°F, for 3-4 minutes, until golden brown. Serve with brown gravy or mushroom sauce. *For 4 persons.*

FRIED WALNUT SAUSAGES (Saucissons de Noix)

1½ cups ground walnuts
1 cup boiled rice
1 cup dried breadcrumbs
1 cup milk
1 teaspoon grated onion
Salt and pepper to taste
½ teaspoon paprika
1 teaspoon crushed herbs
Pinch of celery seed
2 beaten eggs

Mix all ingredients together till thoroughly blended. With floured hands, shape into sausages of equal size. Melt enough fat in a large frying-pan to cover the bottom of pan. Fry the sausages side by side over low heat till golden brown all over. Arrange side by side on a flat hot oval dish. Garnish with lemon wedges and baked rolls of bacon if liked. Serve with brown gravy, mushroom or tomato sauce. *Yield:* 6 sausages.

MARION'S MOCK TURKEY (Dindon, Faux)

2 cups ground peanuts
1 tablespoon minced onion
2 beaten eggs
2 cups brown breadcrumbs
2 tablespoons butter
1 teaspoon meat extract
1 cup milk or vegetable stock
½ teaspoon crushed sage or herbs
Dash of celery salt

Place nuts, onion, eggs and crumbs in a basin. Melt and add butter. Stir in remaining ingredients. Shape with floured hands into a loaf. Grease and flour a loaf tin. Place loaf in tin. Bake in a moderate oven, 350°F, for about ½ hour, till golden brown. Serve with tomato sauce. *For 4 persons.*

NUT CUTLETS (Côtelettes aux Noix)

1 oz. butter
1 oz. flour
¼ pint milk
¼ lb. milled nuts
½ tablespoon minced boiled onion
½ teaspoon minced parsley
2 oz. stale breadcrumbs
Squeeze of lemon juice
Salt and cayenne pepper to taste
Pinch of ground mace or grated nutmeg

Melt butter in a saucepan. Stir in flour. When frothy, stir in milk. When boiling, stir in nuts, onion, parsley, crumbs, lemon juice, salt and cayenne pepper to taste, then mace or nutmeg. Stir over low heat until thick. Turn on to a plate. Leave till cold. Shape into cutlets with floured hands. Egg and crumb twice. Fry in deep smoking hot fat till golden brown. Garnish each with a small piece of macaroni to represent the bone. Arrange overlapping on a hot dish lined with a lace paper doily. Garnish with sprigs of parsley.
Serve with tomato sauce and a green salad. *For 3 persons.*

PULSES

Pulse vegetables are the dried edible seeds of leguminous plants. They are valuable, especially lentils, on account of their high percentage of protein. They also furnish us with minerals, and make a cheap and excellent substitute for meat. Deficient in fat, fat or fat meat should always be used in their cooking. The pulses are dried beans, green and red lentils, dried and split peas.

Buy pulses in small quantities and store in tightly-closed jars. If kept for any length of time, they need longer soaking and take much longer to cook than when fresh. Always wash thoroughly before soaking. Soak, when possible, in soft water. If hard water must be used, boil it and allow it to become cold before pouring over. Soak all pulses, covered, overnight so that the soaking water can be used in cooking if liked. Do not salt pulses until after they are cooked. To prevent pulses sticking to the bottom of pan, use the top of a double boiler for cooking.

TO COOK PULSES

Wash and soak beans, lentils, or peas in cold water to cover, allowing $1\frac{1}{2}$ pints to each cup of pulse. Measure pulse. For each cup or half pint of soaked beans, lentils or peas, you need $2\frac{1}{2}$ cups or 1 pint of water. If there is not enough soaking water, make up this quantity with fresh cold water.

To Boil: Bring 4 cups water to the boil. Add 2 cups soaked, drained beans, lentils or peas. Cover and simmer slowly till tender. Drain. Reserve liquid for soup, or accompanying sauce.

To Improve Flavour of Boiled Pulses:

1. Add a peeled clove of garlic to the water.

2. Add a stick of celery with foliage, or 2 sprigs of parsley, $\frac{1}{2}$ bay leaf, 1 clove and 2 tablespoons minced onion to water. Remove all additions after boiling, but leave onion if liked. Drain.

To Make Purée: When drained, rub while hot through a sieve. If liked, put first of all through a potato ricer and then through a sieve. Measure. Add butter, salt and paprika or pepper, allowing $\frac{1}{2}$ oz. of butter, about 1 teaspoon salt, and a saltspoon of pepper or paprika to each cup of purée. Beat with a perforated spoon or fork until blended. Pile in a mound on a flat, hot dish. Garnish with fried parsley. If not flavoured with onion, garnish also with fried onion rings. Serve with roast pork, pork or sausage loaf, corned beef, or boiled ham. *For 4-6 persons*

To Bake Purée: Stir 2 tablespoons of cream into purée boiled with or without flavourings suggested. Place in a shallow, greased, fireproof dish. Bake in a fairly hot oven, $425°$ F., till heated through and starting to brown on the top.

BOILED DRIED BEANS

Boil beans as described above. Season with salt and pepper. Dress in one of the following ways:—

1. Coat with $1\frac{1}{2}$ tablespoons of thick cream.

2. Add ½ tablespoon butter and toss beans in butter till melted.
3. Coat with brown, cheese or tomato sauce.
4. While beans are cooking, melt ½ tablespoon butter or bacon dripping. Add a tablespoon of minced onion and fry slowly till brown. Add 2 cups of sliced or canned tomatoes. Season with salt and pepper. Stir occasionally till boiling. Add cooked beans. Simmer for about ¼ hour, stirring frequently. Dish up. Sprinkle with minced parsley.
5. Melt ½ tablespoon of butter. Add 1 teaspoon minced parsley, ¼ teaspoon crushed herbs or thyme, salt and pepper to taste, then beans. Cover and simmer for 2 or 3 minutes, then remove from stove. Add the juice of a lemon. Re-heat, tossing beans well, then dish up.

CASSEROLE OF HARICOT BEANS
(Casserole de Fèves)

1½ cups haricot beans
¼ lb. bacon
2 medium-sized onions
Salt and pepper to taste
1 cup milk

Wash and soak beans overnight in a quart of water. Drain well. Measure. Add cold water, allowing 2 cups to each cup of soaked beans. Cover and bring to boil. Simmer gently till soft, then drain. Remove rind from bacon. Fry bacon without colouring. Remove from pan. Peel, slice and chop onions and add to bacon fat. Fry slowly till soft. Chop bacon. Add to beans. Place half the beans in bottom of a buttered casserole. Cover with a layer of onion. Season with salt and pepper to taste. Repeat layers. Sprinkle with the milk. Cover. Bake in a moderate oven, 350° F., for about 20 minutes, then uncover and bake for 10 minutes. *For 4 persons.*

BEAN LOAF (Gâteau d'Haricots)

½ lb. dried beans
1½ oz. butter
2 peeled tomatoes
1 tablespoon chopped onion
2 oz. stale breadcrumbs
Pinch of crushed herbs
Salt and pepper to taste
Grated rind of ¼ lemon
1 beaten egg

Wash, soak and boil beans till soft. Drain and sieve. Melt butter in a shallow saucepan. Slice in tomato. Add onion. Fry lightly. Stir into bean purée with the remaining fat, crumbs, herbs, salt and pepper and lemon rind. Bind with egg. Press into a well-buttered loaf tin. Bake in a moderate oven, 350°F., for about ¾ hour. Stand for a moment or two. Turn out carefully on to a flat hot dish. Garnish with sprigs of parsley. Serve with cheese or onion sauce. *For 4 persons.*

BEAN PIES (Pâtés d'Haricots)

¼ lb. shortcrust
1 cup boiled dried beans
2 tablespoons beef gravy
1 teaspoon minced onion
2 teaspoons minced mushrooms
½ teaspoon Worcester sauce
Salt and pepper to taste

Line 6 patty tins smoothly with shortcrust. Prick bottoms with a fork and trim edge of linings. Mix all remaining ingredients together. Divide equally between patty tins. Knead and roll out remainder of pastry, and cut into 6 rounds to fit tops of tins. Brush the edge of each on one side with cold water and lay, wet side downwards, on top of filling. Press lightly round the edge. Make a hole in the centre of each with a skewer. Brush carefully with milk or beaten egg. Bake in a fairly hot oven, 425° F., till pastry is crisp and golden brown. Serve at once. *Allow 1 per person.*

LENTILS

Both the green and red variety of lentil can be cooked by any of the recipes given for beans. Boiled lentils, which make such a good accompaniment to sausage dishes, can be served with onion, Maître d'Hôtel or Vinaigrette sauce, or they can be turned into a purée and served with roast duck, goose or pork.

To Dress Boiled Lentils:

1. Melt $\frac{1}{2}$ oz. butter. Add lentils. Season with salt and pepper to taste and add a teaspoon of vinegar. Toss over stove till piping hot.

2. Melt 1 oz. butter in a saucepan. Add a dessertspoon of minced onion. Fry slowly till clear. Stir in 1 teaspoon flour. When frothy, add enough boiling, white stock to make a thick sauce. Add lentils and a teaspoon of vinegar. Cover and simmer for 10 minutes, shaking the pan occasionally. Serve in a hot vegetable dish.

LENTIL CROQUETTES (Croquettes de Lentilles)

1/4 lb. lentils
1 pint water
1 blade mace
1 clove
1 small sprig parsley
1/2 oz. butter
1/2 oz. grated Parmesan cheese
1 teaspoon minced parsley
Pinch of crushed herbs
1 teaspoon minced onion
1 oz. stale breadcrumbs
Salt and pepper to taste
1 beaten egg yolk

Wash and drain lentils. Place in a saucepan. Add water, mace, clove and parsley. Cover and simmer gently till tender, then strain. Mash lentils till smooth and dry. Stir in butter, cheese, parsley, herbs, onion, crumbs, and salt and pepper to taste. Add egg yolk. Stir over slow heat till thickened, then spread on a wet plate. Cover with a sheet of buttered greaseproof paper. Leave till quite cold. With floured hands, shape into small equal-sized rolls. Egg and crumb. Fry in deep smoking hot fat till crisp and golden. Drain on absorbent paper. Arrange on a hot dish lined with a lace paper doily. Garnish with sprigs of parsley. *For 2 or 3 persons.*

LENTIL ROLLS (Roulades de Lentilles)

1 cup lentils
1 oz. butter
2 peeled tomatoes
2 oz. grated cheese
1 cup stale breadcrumbs
Salt and pepper to taste
1/2 lb. flaky pastry

Rinse lentils in a colander under the cold water tap. Drain well. Tie loosely in a piece of butter muslin. Place in a saucepan of boiling salted water to cover. Boil until soft then rub through a wire sieve. Place in a saucepan. Add butter. Chop tomatoes and add. Stir in cheese and enough of the crumbs to thicken the mixture. Season with salt and pepper. Roll pastry into a thin rectangular sheet. Cut into squares. Brush with beaten egg. Place a roll of the mixture in the centre of each square. Fold the pastry over. Brush with beaten egg. Bake a little apart on a greased baking sheet in a moderate oven, 350° F., for about 20 minutes. Arrange on a hot dish. Serve with cheese sauce, flavoured with minced parsley. *For 4 persons.*

LENTIL SOUFFLE (Soufflé de Lentilles)

¼ pint lentils
½ pint cold water
½ oz. butter
2 egg yolks
½ gill cream
Salt and pepper to taste
3 egg whites

Wash and drain lentils. Soak overnight in ¾ pint cold water. Drain well. Place in a saucepan with the ½ pint cold water. Cover. Simmer gently till soft. Rub through a hair sieve. Return to saucepan. Stir in butter. When dissolved, beat in yolks, then cream. Season purée with salt and pepper. Beat egg whites till stiff. Fold into mixture. Pour into a buttered soufflé dish. Bake in a moderate oven, 350° F., for about 25 minutes or until set. Serve from dish accompanied by a green salad. *For 2 persons.*

BOILED DRIED PEAS

Dried peas can be bought whole or split. The former are usually boiled and served as an accompaniment to a savoury dish or made into cream of green peas. The latter can be treated by any way suggested for lentils, but they are most popular made into pease pudding or into a purée.

TO BOIL SPLIT PEAS

To Boil in a Cloth: Place peas in a cloth allowing ample room for swelling. Tie securely. Lower them into a pan of boiling water, in the proportion of 3 cups of water to each cup of soaked peas. Cover and simmer gently until starting to "pulp." They usually take 2-2½ hours if soaked for 12 hours. Remove from cloth. Rub through a hair sieve with a wooden spoon. Add salt, pepper and butter to taste. Reheat, stirring constantly. Serve with boiled bacon or ham.

PEASE PUDDING

½ lb. split peas
3 pints cold water
1½ oz. butter
Salt and pepper to taste

Soak peas over night in 3 quarts of water. Drain. Tie loosely in a pudding cloth, allowing them plenty of room to swell. Place in a saucepan. Add cold water. Bring to boil. Cover and simmer for 2-2½ hours, till soft. Turn into a colander. Leave till all the water has drained away, then untie the cloth and place peas in a basin. Mash with a wooden spoon. Stir in butter, salt and pepper to taste. Place in a fresh pudding cloth wrung out of boiling water and floured. Tie up very tightly. Lower into a pan of boiling water to cover. Bring again to boil. Cover and simmer for 30 minutes. Turn gently on to a hot dish. Serve with boiled bacon or pork.

Savoury Batters and Souffles

There is no secret about making a good batter. If you stir the mixture until it is quite smooth, beat it thoroughly, and cook it at the proper temperature, your batter should be a success. Bake in a fairly hot oven, 425° F.; fry in fat heated to 375° F., or in oil heated to 375-385° F.; steam over boiling water.

Batters are all made from a mixture of flour, egg, and usually milk or milk and water for liquid, and sometimes with the addition of melted butter or olive oil. The same batter can be used for pancakes and Yorkshire pudding, but coating batter required for fish, fritters, kromeskies, etc. needs less liquid.

COATING BATTERS

The following batters can be used for coating fish, fritters, kromeskies, etc. They should be creamy yet thick enough to hold to the food they are coating. If too thin they will run off.

ECONOMICAL COATING BATTER

2 oz. flour
½ saltspoon salt
½ gill milk or water
1 saltspoon baking powder

Mix flour and salt to a smooth thin paste with about ½ gill liquid. Beat well. Stir in baking powder and use at once.

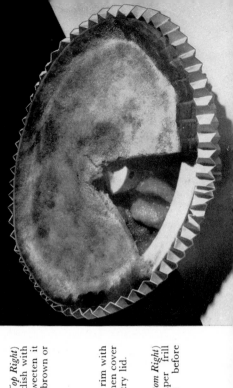

Apple Tart

(Top Left)
To make an Apple Tart, first cover wet rim of pie dish with a pastry strip. *See pages 542-543*

(Top Right)
Half fill pie dish with fruit, then sweeten it to taste with brown or castor sugar.

(Bottom Left)
Brush pastry rim with cold water, then cover pie with pastry lid.

(Bottom Right)
Place a paper frill round dish before serving tart.

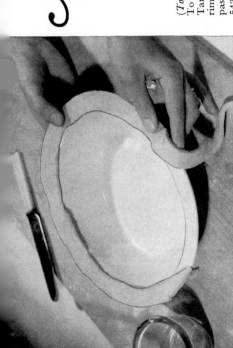

Christmas Pudding decked with sugar and holly. *See pages* 594-595.

Serve Pear Flan with whipped cream. *See page* 557.

Lemon Chiffon Pie. *See page* 553.

Cranberry Puffs. Serve with custard sauce or cream. *See page* 573.

BINDING BATTER

7 oz. flour
2 teaspoons baking powder
½ teaspoon salt
1 lightly beaten egg
1 cup milk
¾ tablespoon melted butter

Sift flour with baking powder and salt. Mix the egg with the milk and butter. Stir into flour mixture. Beat until smooth.

SIMPLE COATING BATTER

¼ lb. flour
¼ teaspoon salt
1 egg
About ¼ pint milk and water

Sift flour with salt into a basin. Make a hollow in the centre. Break egg into a cup to ensure fresh-ness, then drop into hollow. Pour in ½ gill of the liquid. Beat egg and liquid with a wooden spoon, gradually drawing in the flour. Beat from 8-10 minutes, so as to incorporate as much cold air as possible, then stir in as much of the remaining liquid as is required to give you a coating consistency. Stand for ½-1 hour before using.

FRENCH COATING BATTER

2 oz. sifted flour
1 saltspoon salt
1 dessertspoon olive oil
½ gill tepid water
1 egg white

Sift flour and salt into a basin. Make a hollow in centre. Pour in oil then gradually stir in the water. Beat well. Stand for 1 hour. When required, beat egg white to a stiff froth and fold into mixture.

Cheese Fritters : Cut cheese into fingers or squares. Dip in any of the coat-ing batters. Fry in deep hot fat or oil till golden. Drain on absorbent paper. Serve, garnished parsley, as a hot savoury.

Meat Fritters : Cut corned beef, luncheon meat, or tongue in neat slices. Dip in coating batter. Fry in deep hot fat or oil till golden brown. Drain on absorbent paper. Serve garnished with parsley and sauce Tartare.

Fritters : For fritter recipes see Entrée Section pages 339-341.

SAVOURY BATTER
This can be baked, fried or steamed

¼ lb. flour
¼ teaspoon salt
1 egg
½ pint milk

Sift flour and salt into a basin. Make a well in centre of flour. Drop in egg. Stir in half the milk, gradually drawing the flour in from the side with a wooden spoon. Beat for about 10 minutes to incor-porate as much cold air as possible, then stir in enough of remainder of milk to give you a thin cream. Cover. Stand in a cool place for ½-1 hour.
To Vary: Use 2 eggs. Substitute ¾ gill tepid water for the milk. Separate yolks and whites of eggs. Slowly stir 1 tablespoon olive oil into the egg yolks, then the flour alternately with the water. Beat till smooth with a wooden spoon. Cover and stand for 2 hours. When required, beat egg whites till stiff and fold in.

Baked Savoury Batter: Heat 1 oz. dripping in a pie dish. Add 8 oz. left-over meat or balls of sausage meat, chopped boiled ham or tongue. Slowly pour in ½ pint of the Savoury Batter. Bake in a hot oven, 450° F., for about ½ hour.

SAVOURY PANCAKES

BASIC RECIPE :
¼ lb. flour
¼ teaspoon salt
1 egg
¼ pint milk
About ¼ pint water

Sift flour and salt into a basin. Make a hollow in the centre. Drop in egg. Gradually beat in the milk, drawing in the flour from the sides of the basin as you beat. Beat for 8-10 minutes, so as to incorporate all the cold air possible. Stir in remainder of milk and water. Take a frying-pan, the diameter you wish pancakes to be. Melt enough lard in it to cover bottom. Pour in sufficient batter to cover bottom of the pan thinly. Fry over moderate heat till pancake sets and turns golden below. Turn or toss on to the second side. Fry till tinged with gold below. Fill and roll. Keep hot till all are ready, then serve. Garnish with parsley. *For 3 persons.*

To Fill Pancakes: Spread each pancake as fried up to within an inch of the edge with hot creamed fish, chicken, guinea fowl, turkey, or sweetbreads and mushrooms. Roll up. If liked, arrange on a shallow, greased fireproof dish. Coat each with 2 tablespoons cheese sauce. Brown under the grill or on top of the oven.

YORKSHIRE PUDDING

The finest Yorkshire pudding is baked under the joint so that it catches the drippings from the meat. If unable to bake in this way, place in a Yorkshire pudding tin, or in individual tartlet tins.

¼ lb. flour
¼ teaspoon salt
1 or 2 eggs
½ pint milk

If not baking under a joint, heat a baking tin, 10 × 7½ inches, or 12 tartlet tins. Sift flour and salt into a basin. Make a well in the centre. Break egg or eggs and drop into well. Beat thoroughly, then stir in milk. Continue to beat until the surface is covered with bubbles, then stand for 1 hour at least. Heat tin. Pour enough of the beef dripping from the joint into the tin to give you hot fat to the depth of ¼ inch. Pour in batter. It should be a little over ½ inch deep. Either bake in a hot oven, 450° F., for about ½ hour, or bake for 20 minutes in a moderately hot oven, 400° F., then lower heat to moderate, 350° F., and bake from 10-12 minutes, until ready. Cut the large one into squares. Serve at once. *For 4 persons.*

SAVOURY CUSTARD

BASIC :
1 pint milk
½ teaspoon salt
Pepper to taste
¼ teaspoon paprika
1 tablespoon melted butter
2 eggs

Heat milk to boiling point. Stir in salt, pepper, paprika and butter, and a pinch of grated nutmeg if liked. Beat eggs only till yolks and whites are blended. Slowly stir in the milk. Strain into a buttered fireproof dish, 1½ pint size. Lower into a baking tin containing hot water coming half-way up the sides. Bake in a moderate oven, 350° F., until set, in about 45-50 minutes. *For 4 persons.*

VARIATIONS

Cheese: Stir 1 cup grated cheese into mixture before adding to egg.
Fish: Stir 1 cup flaked, boiled, fresh, or smoked fish, or flaked crab into mixture before adding to egg.

CHEESE CUSTARD FLAN (Flan au Fromage)

6 oz. shortcrust
3 eggs
¼ lb. grated cheese
1½ gills canned milk or cream
½ pint milk
Salt and pepper to taste

Roll out shortcrust thinly. Line a greased pie plate, 9 inches across. Prick bottom well with a fork. Trim and ornament edges. Beat eggs till yolks and whites are blended. Stir cheese into canned milk or cream, then into egg mixture. When blended stir in fresh milk gradually, then add salt and pepper. Pour into pastry case. Bake in a hot oven, 450° F., about 10 minutes, then lower to moderate, 350° F., and bake till custard is set in about 25 minutes. *For 6 persons.*

EGG CUSTARD RING (Roulade à la Crème)

4 eggs
¾ teaspoon salt
½ pint hot milk
Pepper and cayenne pepper to taste
½ teaspoon minced parsley
1 saltspoon onion juice

Beat eggs till honey-coloured. Stir in salt, milk, pepper and cayenne pepper to taste, parsley and onion juice. When blended, pour into a small baking tin containing hot water coming half-way up the side. Bake in a slow oven, 300° F., until firm, in about ¾ hour. Garnish alternately round the base with cooked green peas and mushrooms. *For 4 persons.*

SOUFFLES

There are really only two kinds of soufflés : savoury and sweet. They, in turn, can be divided into two classes : hot and cold.

The basis of a standard savoury soufflé is a panada. This is a mixture of fat, flour and milk, enriched with egg yolks, flavouring and seasonings, and lightened with stiffly-beaten egg whites, folded in very carefully just before baking or steaming. If properly prepared and cooked, a soufflé should be delicately flavoured, digestible and nourishing. See Entrée Section, page 349 for further Soufflé recipes.

Soufflé Dishes or Tins: To cook soufflés properly, you need fireproof soufflé dishes or soufflé tins with straight sides. Choose a 3 pint one when making a soufflé from 3-4 eggs, and a 2 quart size for a soufflé made from 4-6 eggs. The mixture should only come half-way up the sides of dish or tin to allow for expansion. If not available, place soufflé mixtures in a shallow, fireproof dish, and steam them in a baking tin.

To Prepare Soufflé Dish for Baking: Brush inside with clarified butter or olive oil, then brush a triple folded band of white kitchen paper with clarified butter, about $4\frac{1}{2}$ inches wide, on one side only. Tie round the top, buttered side inwards, so that it extends $3\frac{1}{2}$-4 inches above the rim. The band is necessary to prevent the soufflé falling "over-board" when it rises above the level of its container.

To Prepare Steamed Soufflé Tin: Brush tin with clarified butter or olive oil. Place a round of greaseproof paper in the bottom of tin. Brush with butter or olive oil. Tie a greased triple-folded band of white kitchen paper $4\frac{1}{2}$ inches wide, buttered side inwards, round tin, so that it extends $3\frac{1}{2}$ inches above the rim. Cut a round of greaseproof paper of the same diameter for the top of soufflé case.

TO MAKE A PANADA

To make a panada, allow 1 oz. butter, and 1 oz. sifted flour to $\frac{1}{4}$ pint milk or stock, according to the type of liquid required, and 3-4 eggs. Melt butter in an enamel-lined saucepan. Throw in the flour. Stir over moderate heat for 5 or 6 seconds, then add all the liquid at once. Beat well with a wooden spoon over the heat until the mixture leaves the sides of the pan clean, as when making choux pastry. Remove from heat at once.

BAKED SAVOURY SOUFFLE

¼ lb. flaked fish, or sieved minced game, poultry or veal
1 oz. butter
1 oz. flour
¼ pint milk or stock
Salt and pepper to taste
3 egg yolks
4 egg whites

Prepare dish or soufflé tin. Pound the meat, fish, game or poultry in a mortar with a pestle, or rub through a sieve. (If preferred, pass twice through a meat grinder.) Make panada as previously described. Add to purée. Season with salt and pepper. Add egg yolks, one at a time, beating thoroughly after each addition. Whisk egg whites until stiff, and fold them in very carefully so as to retain all the air beaten in. Pour gently into prepared soufflé dish or tin. Place in a baking tin containing hot water to come half-way up the side of dish or tin. Bake in a moderate oven, 350° F., for $\frac{3}{4}$-1 hour. Remove paper. Serve at once *For 3 persons.*

HINTS ON BAKED SOUFFLES

1. If baked in a moderate oven, 350° F., always place container in a baking tin containing hot water coming half-way up the side of dish. If to be baked at a low temperature, 300° or 325° F., this is not necessary.

2. If baked in a moderate oven, 350° F., soufflé will be moister and not so firm in texture as when baked at 300° or 325° F.

3. If you want a soufflé to rise higher in the centre than round the edge, make a round slit, about 2-2½ inches from the edge, with a sharp knife just before baking or steaming.

TO STEAM A SOUFFLE

Stand soufflé tin on a plate in the bottom of a saucepan. Pour in enough boiling water to come a quarter up the sides of pan. Cover. Let the water simmer gently for about 35 minutes, until the soufflé is firm in the centre when pressed lightly with fore-finger. Remove papers and string. Stand for 2 or 3 seconds until it shrinks very slightly, then ease it away from the sides gently with a palette knife, and turn out carefully, drawing the tin up from the soufflé. Serve at once.

CORN SOUFFLES (Soufflés de Maïs)

½ oz. butter
1 tablespoon flour
½ cup milk
Salt and pepper to taste
¼ teaspoon paprika
1 minced pimiento
2 cups canned creamed corn
2 separated eggs

Melt butter in a saucepan. Add flour. When frothy, stir in milk. Stir until boiling, then season with salt and pepper and paprika. Rub the pimiento through a sieve and stir into sauce. Drain corn before measuring. Stir into mixture. Cool slightly. Beat egg yolks until blended. Stir into corn. Beat egg whites until stiff. Fold in. Turn into individual, greased, fireproof dishes. Place dishes in a baking tin containing hot water coming half-way up the side. Bake in a moderately hot oven, 375° F., until set in about 25 minutes. *For 4-6 persons.*

HADDOCK SOUFFLE (Soufflé d'Eglefin)

10 oz. flaked cooked fish
2 cups mashed potatoes
Salt and pepper to taste
2 tablespoons butter
1 tablespoon lemon juice
1 teaspoon minced onion
Dash of celery salt
Pinch of crushed herbs
1½ tablespoons minced parsley
1 tablespoon minced pimiento
3 fresh eggs

Stir fish into the potato. Season with salt and pepper. Melt and stir in butter. Add lemon juice, onion, celery salt, herbs, parsley and pimiento. Separate yolks and whites of eggs. Beat yolks well then beat into fish mixture. Beat egg whites to a stiff froth and fold into mixture. Place in a shallow buttered ovenware dish. Bake in a moderate oven, 350° F., for about ½ hour, till set. *For 6 persons.*

MARROW SOUFFLE (Soufflé de Courge)

1 pint mashed boiled marrow
½ pint thin white sauce
2 teaspoons grated onion
Salt and pepper to taste
3 separated eggs

Stir marrow into sauce. Add onion and salt and pepper. Stir in lightly-beaten egg yolks. Fold in stiffly-frothed egg whites. Bake in a buttered pie dish, in a moderate oven, 350° F., for about ½ hour, till firm. *For 4 persons.*

SPINACH SOUFFLES (Soufflés d'Epinards)

2 separated eggs
¾ pint sieved cooked spinach
Salt and pepper to taste
¾ gill grated cheese

Beat egg yolks. Stir into spinach. Heat in a saucepan, stirring constantly, till egg sets. Remove from stove. Season to taste with salt and pepper. Stir in grated cheese. Beat egg whites till stiff. Fold into mixture. Half-fill greased ramekins. Place in a baking tin containing hot water to the depth of 2 inches. Bake in a moderately hot oven, 375° F., for about 20-30 minutes. Serve at once. *For 3 persons.*

517

STEAMED FISH SOUFFLE (Soufflé de Poisson)

½ oz. butter
1 oz. flour
½ gill fish stock
¼ lb. raw fish
2 small eggs
Salt and pepper to taste
½ teaspoon lemon juice
½ gill cream

Prepare a ½-pint soufflé dish. Make panada, and leave until cool. Meanwhile, mince and pound fish in a mortar with a pestle. Add the panada. Pound until blended, then add the eggs, one at a time. Season with salt and pepper. Stir in lemon juice, then the cream. Place in prepared dish. Cover with greased paper. Steam slowly until firm, in about ¾ hour. Turn out gently. Wipe the surface with absorbent paper, then coat with 1½ gills mushroom or parsley sauce. Garnish with lemon butterflies. *For 3 persons.*

Pastry

Perfect pastry needs fine flour and good quality fat, a light touch and careful baking.

Before starting to make pastry, assemble everything you require, remembering that both utensils and ingredients should be cool so as to give you light pastry.

NOTES ON BAKING PASTRY

1. Do not bake pastry at the same time as any food which is steaming in the oven, or it will not rise properly and the crispness will be affected.
2. Open and close oven door very gently to avoid a draught.
3. Always allow pastry, when to be eaten cold, to cool slowly in the kitchen. Do not remove it to a cold room or larder.
4. Cool all pastry cases, baked in tins, on a wire rack.

TO GLAZE PASTRIES

When glazing, take care not to let the glaze run over the edges, or the pastry will not rise evenly. When making economical pastry, I generally glaze with milk.

Fruit Pies, Tarts, Tartlets, etc.: Brush with beaten egg white or water and dredge with caster sugar, or with sweetened milk and water, before pastry goes into the oven, or when half cooked.

Meat Pies and Pasties: Brush with beaten egg yolk diluted with equal quantity of milk, stock or water if liked, or use beaten egg.

FLAKY PASTRY

This pastry is used for meat pies and pasties, mince pies, jam puffs, Eccles cakes, and certain flan cases. Good flaky pastry should be crisp and evenly flaky. To ensure this, the dough must be mixed to the proper consistency and thinly rolled. It is also important to distribute fat of equal thickness equally over the rolled out pastry and anything made of flaky pastry should be cooked quickly in a hot oven, 475° F., until pastry is risen and set.

½ lb. flour
Pinch of salt
3 oz. butter
1 teaspoon lemon juice
About ¼ pint ice cold water
4 oz. lard

Sift flour with salt into a basin. Lightly rub in butter with the finger tips. Mix to a stiff paste with lemon juice and water. Knead lightly on a floured board until free from creases. Place lard on a well-floured pastry board. Press out into thin wafers with a floured rolling pin. Roll pastry into a square ¼ inch thick. Cover with wafers of lard, then fold pastry sides to centre both ways, then over in half again to form a square. Roll. Chill. Roll out and use.

Rich, Flaky Pastry: Use equal quantity of fat and flour.

Yield: Two 8 inch flan cases, or an 8 inch double-crust pie.

HOT WATER CRUST FOR RAISED PIES

Raised pies are useful to serve cold at lunch, supper, to take on a picnic, or to cut up and serve at a buffet party. The professional way of making a raised pie is to shape in a mould specially sold for the purpose. This mould consists of an oval base with an ornamental side which can be opened after the pie is cooked to enable you to remove the pie without damaging. Raised pies can also be moulded by hand, either into a round or oval case, or round a 2 lb. oiled jam jar. These pies are generally filled with game, mutton, pigeon, pork, sausage, or veal, but any combination of meats which are appetising served cold can be used such as veal and ham. A case can be lined with sausage-meat before putting in the meat or game. To make a perfect raised pie, all scraps of bone, gristle and skin must be removed from meat before using, and a rich jellying stock should be used for filling up the spaces, rather than stock in which gelatine is dissolved.

HOT WATER CRUST

BASIC RECIPE :
1 lb. flour
½ teaspoon salt
1½ gills milk
6 oz. lard

Sift flour with salt. Heat milk and lard slowly in a saucepan till the lard melts and the mixture comes to the boil. Stir rapidly into the flour, mixing till you get a pliable dough.

To Vary:
1. Substitute water for milk.
2. Reduce lard to ¼ lb. and use milk or water, or equal quantity of each.
3. Follow standard recipe, but use 2 oz. butter and 4 oz. lard.

TO MOULD RAISED PIES

As soon as you have mixed the dough, knead until quite smooth, adding a few more drops of liquid, if required. If you mix in too much liquid, the paste will be moist and softish when baked, and if you don't add enough liquid, it becomes brittle and is not elastic enough to " raise " which is the term used in shaping the pies. *Mould pastry while still warm.* Divide dough into 2 portions—one quarter and three-quarters. While moulding the larger portion, place smaller one in a warm place over hot water. Cover with a cloth.

1. Hollow out larger portion into a round with the knuckles and draw the sides up to form a case 4 inches in diameter and between $\frac{1}{4}$ and $\frac{1}{2}$ inch thick. Trim edges if necessary.

2. Take a 2 lb. jam jar, if a small pie is wanted, or a tin if a larger one is wanted, Brush the outside with oil, or flour, and mould the larger portion of dough over the inverted jar or tin and down the sides, seeing that the case is of the same thickness all round. Trim edges if necessary. Leave till set, then remove.

3. To line a pie mould, brush inside with melted butter. Divide hot water crust into 2 equal portions, then halve one. Roll one of the half portions into a round or oval shape slightly larger than the base of the mould. Turn up a rim about $\frac{1}{4}$ inch deep all round the edge, and place in bottom of mould. Roll out the large portion into a strip deep enough to cover the sides and long enough to go round. Brush the lower edge with beaten egg white, then press the strip well on to the base, and mould it round the inside base with your fingers. Trim the top edge of lining. Brush the lining with beaten egg white.

NOTE : To prepare a round mould as just described without a tin for the purpose, follow the instructions given in number 3, making the bottom round about 6 inches in diameter and the strip 4 inches wide, and the exact length of the circumference of the round. Brush lower edge of strip and rim of bottom round with beaten egg white. Draw the strip into a round and lay it on top of the rim, pressing it on firmly, then mould the ends of strip securely together. Pin a fold of greaseproof paper round the outside to ensure the case keeping its shape while filling it.

TO FILL AND COVER PIES

Pack the filling into the moulds. Press it down well, making it level with the rim of the case, in the centre, but flatten it slightly all round the inside edge. Brush inside of rim of case with beaten egg. Roll remainder of the pastry to fit the top of the filling closely. Lay on top of filling. Press edges together. If liked, make the sides of the lining a little higher and overlap this on to the lid, then notch all the way round with your thumbs and forefingers. Make a hole in the centre to allow steam to escape. Brush top with beaten egg yolk diluted with equal quantity of water. Decorate with foliage cut from trimmings of pastry. (If a fringed edge is wanted, make the lining half an inch higher than the filling. Cut with scissors $\frac{1}{2}$ inch apart, then draw down each alternate half inch of pastry to the outside, and the remainder inside, or simply scallop pastry all the way round with scissors and draw the points slightly downwards, or leave them upright.) If not baked in a mould, pin a fold of parchment, greased on the inside, round the outside of the case, or use thin cardboard lined with greased paper, to keep the case in shape while cooking.

TO BAKE RAISED PIES

If pie is made in a mould, tie a triple fold of paper round the outside of tin projecting 2 inches above the tin to protect the edges. Place on a baking sheet If pie case is made without a mould, lift pie very gently with a spatula or fish knife on to a greased baking sheet. Bake the moulded pie in a moderate oven 350° F., for 1½ hours, and the pie in a mould in a fairly hot oven, 425° F. for about 20 minutes, until the top is pale gold, then cover with paper, and lower temperature to moderate, 350° F., and bake until filling is cooked through in 1½ hours for a veal and ham filling, or 2 hours for a pork filling. Remove from oven, and place a small funnel in the hole in the centre. Fill up pie with well-seasoned rich stock that will jelly, or use stock in which gelatine has been dissolved, allowing 1 tablespoon powdered gelatine to 1½ gills of boiling stock Soak gelatine for 5 minutes in 4 tablespoons of the cold stock, then bring remainder to boil. Stir in soaked gelatine and use when gelatine is dissolved. Leave till cold before moving if not in a mould. If moulded, leave pie till slightly cooled before removing mould, and filling with the jellying stock. Garnish with parsley. Serve cold.

PUFF PASTRY (Pâté Feuilletée)

This pastry is richest of all. When the fat is available, this is used for all dishes that require a very light pastry, such as French pastries, patty cases, mince pies, vol-au-vents, jam puffs, turnovers, etc.

½ lb. flour
Pinch of salt
½ lb. chilled unsalted butter
1 teaspoon lemon juice
Cold water as required

To make perfect puff pastry, chill all the ingredients and utensils before using, and allow sufficient time for chilling pastry between rollings.

To Prepare: Sift flour and salt into a basin. Rub in about a dessertspoon of the butter. Mix to an elastic dough (about the same consistency as butter) with lemon juice and water. Turn on to an enamel or marble-topped table, if possible, otherwise on to a pastry board. Knead lightly for 2 or 3 minutes, until smooth and glossy and no longer sticky. Roll into a strip, ⅛ inch thick, long and wide enough to enclose butter if in an oblong or square pat. If preferred shape butter into a fat round cake, then roll pastry into a round, large enough to enclose butter. Place butter in the centre. Draw the sides of the dough over the butter to enclose it. Seal joins by patting with a rolling pin. Chill for ¼ hour. Roll into a long strip, taking care not to let the butter break through. (Strip should be 1½ feet long with straight edges and square corners.) Fold in three, a third away from you, and a third from the top towards you. Turn pastry half round so as to bring the folds to the sides. Press edges firmly so as to enclose the air, with a rolling pin. Chill for 20 minutes. Roll out again. Continue folding, chilling and rolling until the pastry has had 7 "turns," as this operation is termed. Wrap in waxed paper. Chill until firm, then use.

To Bake: Bake in a very hot oven, 500° F., for about 5 minutes, until risen and set, then lower temperature 50 degrees every 5 minutes, until down to moderate, 350° F., and finish cooking. *Do not open the door until the pastry is risen and set.* There are other methods of baking puff pastry. One is to place in a hot oven, 500° F., and switch off at once. This is a very successful way of baking flan and patty cases.

ROUGH PUFF PASTRY (Pâté Demi-Feuilletée)

Rough puff pastry is somewhat similar to flaky, but it is easier to make. It can be used like flaky or puff.

½ lb. flour
¼ teaspoon salt
6 oz. butter
About ¼ pint ice-cold water

Sift flour and salt into a basin. Cut butter into tiny pieces the size of an almond and add bit by bit to flour. (If a more economical pastry is wanted, use equal quantity of butter and lard, or margarine and lard.) Mix to a stiff paste with ice-cold water. Turn on to a lightly floured board. Roll out dough into a thin strip about ⅛ inch thick, of equal width, and with square corners. Fold in three, up one third and down one third, then press edges with a rolling pin, to seal them. Chill. Half turn so that the sealed edges are at the sides. Roll and fold three times, chilling 10 minutes between each operation, but for 1 hour at the end before using. Bake in a hot oven, 475° F.

SHORTCRUST (Pâté Brisée)

This is generally used for making fruit and jam tartlet cases, custard and other open flan cases, or pies, pasties, etc. It is more digestible than the flaky group of pastries.

BASIC RECIPE :
½ lb. flour
¼ teaspoon salt
4 oz. butter or margarine
¼ pint ice-cold water

Sift flour and salt into a basin. Rub fat in lightly with the finger tips until as fine as breadcrumbs. Stir in enough of the water to make a firm dough with a fork or knife. Pat lightly into a ball. Wrap in waxed paper. Chill and use. Bake in a hot oven, 425°-450° F.

Yield: Enough for two 7-inch pie shells or flan cases, or for the top and bottom crusts of an 8-inch pie, or for a top crust and a flan case.

VARIATIONS

Economical: Decrease fat to 2½ oz., using lard and margarine, but sift ½ teaspoon baking powder with the flour and salt.

Nut: Stir ¼ lb. ground nuts into the mixture before adding water. Use with butterscotch, caramel and chocolate fillings.

Orange: Add 1 teaspoon grated orange or tangerine rind after rubbing in fat, and substitute orange or tangerine juice for the water.

Rich: Increase fat to 5 oz. Rub in, and add 3 teaspoons of caster sugar. Moisten with 1 egg yolk diluted with 1½ tablespoons cold water. Mix to a firm dough, adding more water if required. Use for open tarts, flan cases, cheese cakes and tartlets.

Spiced: Sift ¼ teaspoon each of ground cinnamon, cloves and ginger with the flour and salt before mixing. Good with apple or quince pie.

SUET CRUSTS (For Boiling or Steaming)

BASIC RECIPE :
1 lb. flour
3 teaspoons baking powder
3/4 teaspoon salt
6 oz. shredded suet
About 1/2 pint cold water
RICH SUET CRUST :
1 lb. flour
2 teaspoons baking powder
1 teaspoon salt
1/2 lb. shredded suet
About 1/2 pint cold water

Sieve flour and baking powder with salt into a basin. Stir in suet. (If using fresh suet, remove all skin and gristle before weighing and chop suet finely with a little of the flour.) Stir in enough of the water to make a light elastic dough, moderately stiff. It should leave the basin clean. Turn on to a floured board. Knead lightly, but only until free from cracks. Roll out quickly to about 1/4 inch thickness, unless otherwise instructed. Use for making savoury meat puddings, meat rolls, steamed fruit puddings, etc.

To Vary:

1. Substitute self-raising flour and omit baking powder.

2. If a fluffier crust is wanted, increase quantity of baking powder in first recipe to 5 teaspoons, and increase to 3 teaspoons in second recipe.

3. To make a lighter crust, substitute stale breadcrumbs for half the flour.

4. *Savoury:* Stir 1/4 teaspoon crushed herbs and 2 teaspoons minced parsley in with the suet.

To Make a Savoury Meat Pudding: Roll out pastry. Cut about a third of the dough off for the lid. Roll remainder of dough to fit the inside of the basin. It should be about twice the size of the lid. Line basin very carefully with rolled side of dough next to the basin, taking care not to stretch it or leave thick creases in lining. If creases are left, the pastry will look holey. Let it overlap rim of basin by about 1/4 inch. Fill. Roll out dough for lid. Brush pastry round the rim of the basin with cold water. Place pastry lid on top. Press gently round the edge, then trim edges. Cover with a greased paper. Tie down securely. Cook in a steamer, or place in a saucepan containing boiling water to come half way up basin. Steam for 3 1/2-4 hours, according to type of meat used in filling. If tender, 3 1/2 hours should be enough ; if a tough cut, it may need 4-4 1/2 hours. Be sure to replenish pan with boiling water when necessary. If to be boiled, filling must be piled high in the centre, but not tightly, to allow for shrinkage. If you haven't enough meat to fill the basin, lay crusts of bread on top, otherwise water may penetrate. Cover also with a floured, scalded pudding cloth. Place in a saucepan. Fill up with boiling water. Boil for 2 1/2-3 hours, according to type of meat.

To Dish Up: Remove cloth, if used, paper and place basin on a flat dish. Tie a folded napkin round. If preferred, stand for a moment or two then unmould to a hot dish.

BAKING POWDER OR BISCUIT CRUST
(Pâté Américaine)

1/2 lb. flour
3 teaspoons baking powder
1/2 teaspoon salt
2-3 oz. butter or margarine
Fully 1/2 cup milk

Sift dry ingredients into a basin. Rub fat in lightly. Mix quickly to a soft dough with the milk. Turn on to a lightly floured pastry board. Knead gently until free from cracks. Roll out lightly into ½-1 inch thickness. Use when a quick crust is wanted for a meat or poultry pie. Bake in a hot oven, 450° F.

CHEESE PASTRY (Pâté au Fromage)

BASIC RECIPE :
4 oz. grated cheese
4 oz. butter or margarine
6 oz. flour
1 small teaspoon salt
Cayenne pepper to taste

Rub cheese through a wire sieve. Beat fat until softened. Beat in cheese. Sift flour with salt and cayenne pepper. Stir into cheese mixture. Blend with a wooden spoon until into a paste. Stand for 30 minutes before using. This pastry is useful when savoury fish pasties are wanted, or for vegetarian pastries. Bake in a hot oven, 450° F.

To Vary:
   1.   Reduce fat to 3 oz. and add 1 beaten egg yolk with about 2 tablespoons of water. Mix to a stiff paste. Knead lightly until smooth.
   2.   Reduce fat to 2 oz. cheese to 2 oz., but use Parmesan, and sift ½ teaspoon mustard with the flour, salt and cayenne pepper. Mix to a stiff paste with egg yolk diluted with equal quantity of water if liked.

CHOUX PASTRY (Pâté Choux)

Choux pastry, sometimes known as " French Pastry," is generally used for cream buns, cream puffs, eclairs, profiteroles, etc. Cases of choux pastry can also be used for filling with savoury creams for buffet parties.

BASIC RECIPE :
¼ lb. butter
1 saltspoon salt
1 cup water
¼ lb. sifted flour
4 eggs

When mixing choux pastry, you must add egg until the mixture is of the required consistency. Place butter, salt and water into a strong, fairly large saucepan, as you have to allow for the eggs being added later on. Bring to a brisk boil. Draw pan to side of stove. Throw in all the flour at once, stirring vigorously with a wooden spoon. Cook over stove, stirring constantly, until smooth and thick, and it forms a smooth ball in the centre of the pan. The sides of pan should be quite clean. Draw pan to side of stove. Stand for 5 minutes. Stir in 1 egg at a time, and beat after each addition until blended. After the last egg is added, beat vigorously until smooth and thick enough to retain its shape when piped. The batter should break off easily when you lift out the spoon. If not to be baked at once, wrap in waxed paper. It can be left for several hours or overnight if liked before baking.

ECONOMICAL VARIATIONS

   1.   Reduce eggs to 3 and increase water to ½ pint.
   2.   Reduce butter to 2 oz. and use ½ pint water, and 2 large eggs or 3 small ones.

To Shape and Bake Choux Pastry: There are different ways of shaping it. Either use spoons or a forcing bag fitted with a pipe or tube. There are also two ways of cooking the cases. They can either be cooked in a moderately hot oven, 400° F., until ready, or the large ones can be cooked in a hot oven, 450° F., for ¼ hour, then reduce temperature to moderate, 350° F., and bake for about 22 minutes longer. The medium-sized need 12 minutes at a hot temperature, then 15-20 minutes longer, and the miniature ones need half the time suggested for the large shells.

Eclairs: With a pastry bag fitted with a plain tube $\frac{1}{2}$ inch across, squirt oblongs, $3\frac{1}{2}$-4 inches long and 1 inch wide, on to a floured or greased baking sheet. Take care to keep the strips even and arrange them 2 inches apart to allow for expansion. As you make each one, pull bag slightly backwards, then with a sharp knife, cut the strip of pastry off close to the tube. Bake in a moderately hot oven, 400° F., for 35-40 minutes. Split and cool on a wire rack. Fill and decorate.

Profiteroles: Use a forcing bag with a $\frac{1}{4}$-inch plain tube. Squirt the paste in tiny balls on to a greased baking sheet about $1\frac{1}{2}$ inches apart. Bake in a moderately hot oven, 400° F., for about 20 minutes, until golden brown. Split and cool on a wire rack. Fill and decorate according to taste.

Yield: About 8 large buns, puffs and éclairs, $1\frac{1}{2}$ dozen medium-sized, or 3 dozen miniatures.

DRIPPING PASTRY (Pâté à la Graisse)

1 lb. flour
$\frac{3}{4}$ teaspoon salt
$\frac{1}{2}$ lb. dripping
Ice-cold water
1 teaspoon baking powder

Sift flour into a basin. Mix salt with the dripping. Beat till creamy. If the dripping is hard, stand in a warm place for several hours before using, or you will not be able to cream it. Sift flour again into a basin. Mix to a soft smooth dough with the water. Roll out. Spread with the dripping to within an inch of the edges. Sprinkle with the baking powder. Taking one third, fold it over a third, then bring the other third on top. Roll out thinly. Repeat folding and rolling twice more. Use for hot meat pies or pasties. Bake in a very hot oven, 500° F.

POTATO FLAKY PASTRY (Pâté aux Pommes de Terre)

2 cups cold mashed potatoes
1 cup flour
$1\frac{1}{2}$ teaspoons baking powder
$\frac{1}{4}$ teaspoon salt
Milk as required
2 oz. butter or margarine

Beat potatoes till smooth. Sift flour with baking powder and salt. Stir into potatoes, then beat in enough milk to give a light, soft but dry dough. Turn on to a lightly floured board. Roll out. Dab one-third of the fat over in flakes to within $\frac{1}{2}$ inch of the edges. Fold in three. Roll into a strip. Repeat flaking the fat over, folding and rolling out twice. Use for covering any meat or poultry mixture. Ornament with a fork. Make one or two holes with a skewer in the top of crust. Bake in a moderately hot oven, 400° F., till light and golden.

POTATO SHORTCRUST (Pâté Brisée aux Pommes de Terre)

$\frac{1}{2}$ lb. flour
$\frac{1}{2}$ teaspoon salt
2 oz. butter or margarine
2 oz. lard
$\frac{1}{4}$ lb. sieved boiled potatoes
Cold water as required

Sift flour and salt into a basin. Rub in butter or margarine, then the lard. Stir potato lightly into the mixture. Mix to a dry dough with cold water. Turn on to a lightly floured board. Knead well. Roll out to $\frac{1}{4}$-$\frac{1}{2}$″ thickness. Use for meat pies and pasties.

TO COVER A MEAT PIE

Flaky or rough puff pastry is generally used for covering a meat pie. To cover a pie large enough for 6 persons, follow either recipe for flaky or rough puff pastry. Roll out on a lightly floured board in an oval strip to $\frac{1}{2}$ inch thickness and about $1\frac{1}{2}$ inches wider than the dish which is to be covered, taking care not to stretch it. Have filled pie dish ready with funnel inserted in centre. Cut a narrow strip of pastry about $\frac{3}{4}$ inch wide, which is long enough to cover rim of the dish. It should be slightly wider than the rim, so that it extends very little over both the outer and inner edge. If too narrow and you have to stretch it, it will shrink, pulling the cover along with it. Brush the rim of the dish with cold water. Cover with the strip of pastry. Brush ends of the strip with water and join them together without overlapping. Brush strip with cold water. Cover with a pastry lid. Press the edge of cover and strip together with a knife, or with your fingers. Now, holding the pie dish up in your left hand, with a sharp knife held obliquely, so that the edge of the pastry slopes away from the dish, trim edges neatly, cutting away from you in short, clean strokes.

TO DECORATE RIM : You can either crimp or notch, flake, or flute edges.

To Crimp or Notch: With thumbs and forefingers, squeeze the paste up into notches, equal distance apart all the way round.

To Flake: This is the simplest way of decorating the edges. Dip first finger of your left hand in flour. Press the back of it lightly down on the rim of the pastry farthest away from you. Then with the back of a floured knife, sharply tap edges all round with a lifting movement. This not only helps the pastry to rise by opening up the edges, but results in a very flaky rim to your pie.

Before decorating the centre of the pie, make a hole with a knife in the centre, so that steam can escape. Brush pastry all over with beaten egg as far as the edge, but take care not to let any run over, or the part moistened will not rise. Decorate round the centre with a tassel of pastry or pastry leaves.

To Make a Tassel: Roll out trimmings of pastry, then cut out a strip 2 inches wide. Cut it with a knife along one side, into a fringe about 1 inch deep. Roll up and place in the centre, taking care not to close the ventilation hole, or the pastry won't be so light nor the pie so wholesome. Brush tassel with beaten egg.

NOTES ON BAKING MEAT PIES : Place in the oven on a baking sheet. Keep it at a hot temperature as given under each pie if meat is raw, until pastry is risen and set, then cook very slowly, until meat is tender. If meat is cooked, same temperature can be used throughout. If the pastry gets too dark, cover with a double fold of greaseproof paper. To test if the meat is tender, when you think the pie should be ready, slip a skewer through the hole in the centre. When cooked sufficiently, insert a funnel in the hole and fill up pie with rich hot stock made from the same meat (or meat bones) as that used in pie. Remove from oven. Wipe dish carefully with a wet cloth. Tuck a sprig of parsley in centre of pie, and slip a pie collar over edge of dish.

TO MAKE A DOUBLE-CRUST PIE : Divide the dough into two parts, one slightly larger than the other. Roll the larger part out for the lining, to fit pie plate. To line plate, grease thoroughly, then fold the larger portion of pastry over your rolling pin, lift on to the plate, and unfold it. This prevents you stretching it as you are apt to do with your hands. Brush the edge of the pie plate with cold water, and pat the pastry over the rim. Prick the bottom well with a fork. Fill. Roll remainder of pastry to fit the top of the plate and the rim. Brush the pastry rim with cold water, then lift the cover with your rolling pin on to the top of the filling. Notch the edges together, or make the cover ½ inch wider than the plate, and fold the overlap under the rim, then ornament the edge with the tines of a fork. Prick the top with a fork. Glaze if wanted. Bake.

ASPARAGUS HORNS (Cornets d'Asperge)

About ½ lb. flaky pastry
1 beaten egg
1 cup diced cold chicken
¼ pint mayonnaise
Salt and pepper to taste
2 dozen cooked asparagus tips

Roll pastry out as thinly as possible. Cut into long strips ¾ inch wide. Wind each carefully round a cornucopia tin, beginning at the bottom and being careful not to stretch the pastry. Brush with egg. Lay slightly apart on a greased baking sheet. Stand for 20 minutes. Bake in a moderately hot oven, 375° F., for 10-15 minutes. Mix the chicken with the mayonnaise. Season with salt and pepper to taste. Remove horns from tins when required. Fill with the mayonnaise. Plant 3 asparagus tips in the end of each. *For 8 persons.*

BERKSHIRE ROLY POLY (Pâté Berkshire)

1 lb. suet crust
6 oz. Berkshire bacon
2 medium-sized onions
½ teaspoon crushed sage
Salt and pepper to taste

Roll out suet crust into an oblong about ¼ inch thick. Remove rind from bacon, and slice thinly, or very thin halved rashers can be used. Place over pastry. Mince onions. Stir in sage and salt and pepper to taste. Sprinkle over bacon. Roll up, pressing the folds tightly together at the ends. Wrap in pudding cloth. Boil for 2 hours. Serve with mashed potatoes and green peas. *For 6 persons.*

CHANNEL BOATS (Bateaux Anglais)

6 oz. flaky pastry
2 hard-boiled eggs
Mayonnaise as required
2 tablespoons grated Parmesan cheese
Salt and cayenne pepper to taste
12 anchovy fillets
3 tablespoons butter
1 teaspoon shrimp paste
Dash of lemon juice
Rice paper

Roll pastry out to ⅛ inch thickness. Line tiny boat-shaped moulds neatly with pastry, then trim the edges. Prick the centres with a fork. Bake in a hot oven, 475° F., till risen and set, then lower heat to moderate, 350° F., and bake till golden brown. Turn out. When cold, chop eggs. Mix to a paste with mayonnaise, cheese, salt and cayenne pepper to taste. Place in bottom of cases. Arrange an anchovy fillet in the centre of each. Beat butter to a cream with the shrimp paste. Stir in lemon juice and salt and cayenne pepper to taste. Pipe round inside edge. Add sails of rice paper. *Makes 12 boats.*

CHEESE ECLAIRS (Eclairs de Fromage)

Choux pastry
½ cup grated cheese
½ teaspoon paprika

Stir grated cheese and paprika into Choux pastry, using basic or a variation. Force this mixture through a plain tube into a buttered baking tin in 4 inch strips. Bake for about 30 minutes in a moderate oven, 350° F. When cooked, split and fill with cheese custard.

To Make Cheese Custard: Melt 3 tablespoons of butter in a saucepan. Add 3 tablespoons flour. Stir till frothy, then add ½ teaspoon salt, ¼ teaspoon paprika and 1¼ cups milk. Keep stirring to boiling point, then draw pan to the side and add 2 beaten egg yolks, mixed with ¾ cup grated cheese. Bring again to boiling point, then remove pan from stove and use.

CHEESE TARTLETS (Tartelettes au Fromage)

4 oz. flaky pastry
½ oz. grated Cheddar cheese
½ oz. grated Parmesan cheese
1 separated egg
1-2 dessertspoons cream
Salt and cayenne pepper to taste

Roll out pastry thinly. Line patty tins neatly with pastry. Mix cheeses with egg yolk, cream, salt and cayenne pepper to taste. Beat egg white to a stiff froth. Fold into mixture. Three-quarters fill cases. Bake in a hot oven, 450° F., for about 10 minutes. Serve hot. *Yield:* 6 tartlets.

CHEESE TURNOVERS (Tricornes de Fromage)

3 rashers bacon
1 cup thick cream
1 cup grated cheese
Pinch of mustard
Salt and cayenne pepper to taste
1 saltspoon curry powder
1 beaten egg
¾ lb. flaky pastry

Remove rind from bacon. Fry bacon slowly till crisp. Beat cream till stiff. Crumble bacon and add to cream. Fold in cheese, mustard, salt, cayenne pepper, curry powder and egg. Roll pastry out very thinly. Cut into rounds the size of a saucer. Place a dessertspoonful of filling in the centre of each. Brush edges with cold water. Fold in two. Notch the cut edges with thumbs and forefingers, or press them together with a fork. Make a slit in the centre of each. Brush pastry lightly with beaten egg. Bake in a hot oven, 450° F., for about 20 minutes. Serve hot for lunch or supper with a green salad. *For 4 or 5 persons.*

CHESHIRE PORK PIE (Pâté de Porc, Cheshire)

5 lb. boned loin of pork
Salt and pepper to taste
Grated nutmeg to taste
Sliced apples as required
Dash of sugar
½ pint white wine
1 tablespoon butter
1 lb. flaky pastry

Skin pork, then remove all the fat from meat. Season meat with salt and pepper to taste, and nutmeg. Place a layer in the bottom of a deep pie dish. Insert pie cup or funnel if required. Peel and core enough apples to cover the top of pork. Lay on top. Sprinkle with sugar. Cover with remainder of pork. Sprinkle with the wine. Dab with the butter. Cover pie in the usual way with pastry. Bake in a hot oven, 450° F., for 10-15 minutes, then lower to 325° F., and bake for 1¾ hours. *For 6 persons.*

CHICKEN PIE (Pâté de Volaille)

1 boiling chicken or fowl
Salt and pepper to taste
3 tablespoons butter
4 tablespoons flour
4 cups strained chicken stock
½ lb. flaky or puff pastry

Place bird in a saucepan. Cover with boiling water. Add a sliced onion, carrot, stick of celery if liked, and salt and pepper. Cover and simmer till tender. Joint or remove meat in large pieces from the bones. Melt butter in a saucepan. Stir in flour, then stock. Season. Place chicken in a pie dish. Cover with the sauce. Leave till cold. Roll out pastry. Place a pie cup or funnel in the centre. Cover with pastry in the usual way. Bake in a hot oven, 450° F., for 15 minutes, then lower to moderate, 350° F., and bake for ½ hour. *For 6 persons.*

CHICKEN AND VEAL PIE (Pâté de Volaille et Veau)

1 young boiling fowl
1 lb. veal
½ lb. mushrooms
1 oz. butter
Salt, pepper and paprika to taste
½ pint jellied stock
½ lb. rough puff pastry

Joint chicken neatly. Dip in a little flour seasoned with salt, pepper, paprika, and celery salt if liked. Cut veal in small pieces, and dip in flour. Place chicken and veal in a pie dish. Place a pie cup or funnel in centre. Fry mushrooms in butter. Arrange them among the chicken joints, alternately with pieces of veal. Fill up with tiny forcemeat balls, or balls of pork sausage meat lightly fried. Sprinkle with a little salt, pepper and paprika to taste. Pour over the stock. Cover with pastry in the usual way. Bake in a hot oven, 450° F., for 15 minutes, then lower to moderate, 350° F., and bake for about 1 hour. Fill up with rich giblet stock through a funnel in centre. *For 6 persons.*

JELLIED CHICKEN PIE (Pâté de Volaille, froid)

1 roasting chicken
¼ lb. ham
2 hard-boiled eggs
½ lb. pork sausages
1 minced onion
Salt and pepper to taste
Pinch of ground cloves
Pinch of ground mace
4 or 5 sheets leaf gelatine
¾ gill water
1½ lb. flaky pastry

Remove skin from bird. Cut bird into joints. Dice the ham. Slice eggs. Skin sausages and make the sausage meat into balls the size of marbles. Arrange the joints in the pie dish. Sprinkle with onion, salt and pepper, cloves and mace. Tuck the sausage balls in between the joints, cover with the egg slices, then sprinkle with the ham. Pack 2 sheets of gelatine in the centre. Add water. Roll out pastry thickly into an oval. Cover pie in usual way. Glaze with beaten egg. Make a hole in the centre of pastry. Bake in a hot oven, 450° F., for 15 minutes, then lower to moderately slow, 325° F., and finish baking. It takes about 1½ hours altogether. When cooked, remove ornament from centre and fill pie up with giblet stock in which you have dissolved remainder of gelatine. Leave till cold. *For 6 persons.*

CORNISH PASTIES

BASIC RECIPE :
½ lb. potatoes
¾ lb. lean mutton or steak
1 tablespoon minced onion
Salt and pepper to taste
2½ tablespoons water or beef
or mutton stock
1 lb. shortcrust

Wash and peel potatoes, then cut into dice. Remove the gristle from meat. Either mince or cut meat into small pieces. Mince onion. Mix the potato with the meat, onion, salt and pepper to taste and water or stock. Roll pastry out to ¼ inch thickness. Cut into rounds with a saucer. Divide filling equally between each. Brush the edges of the rounds with cold water. Draw the sides of the pastry up over the filling and notch across the top to form a frill. Prick here and there with a fork. Brush top with beaten egg yolk, or milk. Make a slit in the centre of each. Bake in a hot oven, 450° F., for 10 minutes, then lower to moderate, 350° F., and bake until meat is tender, in about 50 minutes. *For 8 persons.*

To Vary:

1. Substitute diced chicken, pork or rabbit for the meat given, and add a good pinch of ground sage, mixed herbs or thyme.

2. Clean and fill herrings with herb stuffing. Use as a filling for pasties with the heads sticking out of one end and the tails at the other. These are known as " star-gazing pasties " in Cornwall.

DEVONSHIRE PIE (Pâté Devonshire)

2 lb. pork chops
2 lb. tart apples
2 teaspoons sugar
Ground allspice to taste
2 onions
Salt and pepper to taste
¼ pint gravy
1 lb. flaky pastry

Trim chops and cut them short. Peel, core and slice apples. Put a layer in the bottom of a pie dish. Sprinkle with sugar and ground allspice, then add a layer of sliced onions. Season with salt and pepper, then cover with a layer of prepared chops. Repeat layers till ingredients are used up. Pour in gravy. Cover with flaky pastry. Bake in a hot oven, 450° F., for 10 minutes, till pastry is risen and set, then reduce heat and bake in a moderate oven, 350° F., for about 1½ hours. *For 6 persons.*

EGG AND BACON PIE (Pâté à la Campagne)

6 oz. shortcrust
½ lb. bacon
¼ lb. mushrooms
3 eggs
Salt and pepper to taste

Knead shortcrust on a lightly floured board until smooth. Halve. Roll one half into a round to fit a sandwich tin 7 inches across. Line tin. Trim edges. Remove rind from bacon, using either streaky or back rashers. Pile rashers on top of each other, then cut into strips with a pair of scissors, then into squares. Wash, dry and peel mushrooms. Arrange bacon in the bottom of the tin, so that 3 spaces are left for the eggs. Arrange mushrooms on top of the bacon, then drop eggs into the spaces. Season with salt and pepper to taste. Brush edge of pastry lining with beaten egg. Roll out remainder of pastry to form a lid. Lay on top. Press edges together. Trim and decorate pie round the edge. Make 5 loaves from the trimmings. Brush with egg and arrange in the centre.

Make a tassel from the last of the trimmings. Brush with egg and place in centre. Bake in the centre of a hot oven, 425° F., for about 40 minutes. Serve cold, garnished with sprigs of parsley. *For 6 persons.*

EVESHAM CHICKEN TARTLETS
(Tartelettes, Evesham)

2 tablespoons butter
2 teaspoons minced onion
2 tablespoons flour
¾ cup milk
Salt and pepper to taste
¼ lb. fried mushrooms
1 tablespoon cream
1½ cups diced cold chicken
9 hot tartlet cases
A few heated asparagus tips

Melt butter in a saucepan. Stir in onion. Cook slowly till soft ; then stir in flour. When frothy stir in milk. Stir till boiling. Season with salt and pepper. Stir in mushrooms and cream. Add chicken. Stir gently till boiling. Pile into hot pastry cases. Drain and remove tips from asparagus. Plant the tips equal distance apart in the filling. Serve with a green salad. *Yield:* 9 tartlets.

FISH PASTIES (Pâtés de Poisson)

6 oz. shortcrust
12 oz. boiled or steamed fish
4 oz. cooked green peas
1½ tablespoons minced parsley
Salt and pepper to taste
¼ pint white sauce
1 tablespoon vinegar

Roll out pastry thinly. Cut into rounds about 6 inches across. Flake fish. Stir in remaining ingredients. Put a heaped tablespoon on the centre of each round of pastry. Brush edges with cold water. Fold in two. Press edges together with a fork. Bake a little apart on a greased baking sheet in a moderate oven, 350° F., for 25-30 minutes. Serve hot with sauce such as egg or parsley sauce. *For 4 persons.*

FORFAR BRIDIES

1 lb. steak
Salt and pepper to taste
3 oz. shredded suet
1 medium-sized onion
1 lb. dripping pastry

Pound the steak with a meat bat or rolling pin. Cut into strips, then into inches. Place in a basin. Season with salt and pepper. Add suet. Peel and mince onion and add. Roll pastry out thinly. Cut into 3 ovals. Divide the filling equally between the 3, drawing it up to within 1 inch of the edges. Brush edges with cold water, and crimp on the top. Bake like Cornish pasties. *For 3 persons.*

FRIED MUSHROOM PIES (Pâtés de Champignons)

1 lb. potato pastry
1¼ lb. mushrooms

Roll stiff potato pastry, bound with beaten egg, out to ¼ inch thickness. Cut into rounds about 4½ inches across. Chop and fry mushrooms. Cool. Pile on the centre of each round. Either brush edges with cold water, or beaten egg white, and press together with a fork. Dip in flour. Cook one or two at once in smoking hot fat until golden brown. Drain on absorbent paper. Serve garnished with parsley. *For 4 persons.*

GAME PUDDING (Pouding de Gibier, Anglaise)

4 or 5 small game birds
¾ lb. beef steak
1 teaspoon minced onion
1 teaspoon minced parsley
1 teaspoon crushed mixed herbs
½ tablespoon flour
Salt and white pepper to taste
¾ lb. suet crust

Remove the breasts from 4 grouse or 5 partridges. Old birds can be used for this pudding. Remove any fibre from the breasts. Put steak through a meat grinder. Stir into steak, onion, parsley, herbs, flour, salt and white pepper. Line a pudding basin about 7 inches across with suet crust. Put a layer of meat mixture in the bottom, then a layer of grouse or partridge. Repeat till basin is full. Fill up with game stock made from the carcases. Cover with suet crust in the usual way. Steam for 2-2½ hours.

GIPSY PIE (Pâté de Lapin au Lard)

1 rabbit
1 lb. ham or bacon
¼ lb. pork
½ lb. potatoes
½ lb. flaky pastry
Salt and pepper to taste
Minced parsley to taste
Stock or water as required

Cut rabbit into small joints. Dice the ham, pork and potatoes. Grease pie dish with butter and line it with pastry. Fill up with layers of rabbit, ham or bacon, pork and potatoes, adding seasoning and parsley between each layer. About half fill with stock or water. Cover with a lid and make a hole in top of pastry. Bake in a hot oven, 450° F., for 10 minutes, then lower to moderately slow, 325° F., and bake for 50 minutes. When ready, fill up with boiling stock. *For 8 persons.*

GLASTONBURY PIE (Pâté, Glastonbury)

2 pigeons
1 lb. rump steak
1½ tablespoons flour
½ teaspoon black pepper
1 teaspoon salt
Pinch of grated nutmeg
Beef stock as required
1-1¼ lb. flaky pastry

Wipe and quarter pigeons. Cut up steak. Mix flour with pepper, salt and nutmeg on a plate. Dip meat and pigeon quarters in turn in the seasoned flour. Arrange a layer of steak in the bottom of the dish, then the pigeons. Insert pie cup or funnel in centre. Cover with remainder of steak. Half-fill dish with stock. Cover with pastry in the usual way. Decorate top to taste and make a hole in the centre. Bake in a hot oven, 450° F., for 15 minutes, then reduce to moderately slow, 325° F., and bake until cooked through. The pie should take about 2 hours altogether. Add more hot seasoned, thickened stock as required. If wanted cold, arrange 3 shelled, hard-boiled eggs on the top of the filling before covering with pastry. Add a little gelatine to the stock to make it jelly. *For 6 persons.*

HELSTON PASTIES (Pâtés, Helston)

¼ lb. raw calf's liver
½ lb. raw rump steak
Salt and pepper to taste
Good pinch of curry powder
2 peeled potatoes
1 peeled medium-sized turnip

Chop up liver and steak finely, but don't put through a meat grinder. Mix well. Season to taste with salt, pepper and curry powder. Cut vegetables into thin slices. Stir into meat with salt and pepper. Roll out dough into a thin sheet

533

1 large or 2 small carrots
1 large peeled onion
¾ lb. dripping crust

and cut into 6 inch squares. Place meat mixture equally on the squares. Brush edges of pastry with cold water. Fold in two. Ornament round edges with a fork. Make a slit in the top. Brush with beaten egg. Bake in a hot oven, 450° F., for 10 minutes, then lower to moderate, 325° F., and cook for about 50 minutes, until meat is tender. *For 6 persons.*

LAMB PIES (Pâtés d'Agneau)

½ lb. flaky pastry
1 teaspoon minced parsley
½ tablespoon Worcester sauce
1½ gills lamb stock or gravy
¾ pint minced cold lamb
1 teaspoon minced onion
Salt and pepper to taste
Mashed potato as required

Cover inverted tartlet tins with thin flaky pastry. Prick well with a fork. Bake in a fairly hot oven, 375° F., for about 15 minutes. Stand for a moment or two, then remove from tins. Stir parsley, sauce and stock or gravy into the lamb. Add onion and salt and pepper to taste, then heat in a saucepan. Fill pastry cases with the mixture. Pipe mashed potato on top in rings till filling is covered. Brown lightly in the oven, or under the grill. *For 6 persons.*

LANCASHIRE PIE (Pâté, Lancashire)

1 lb. rump steak
Cold water as required
1 tablespoon grated onion
Salt and pepper to taste
2 lb. potatoes
½ lb. suet crust

Wipe meat. Cut into suitable portions for serving. Place in a shallow saucepan. Just cover with cold water. Add onion. Cover and stew gently until tender. Pour into a pie dish. Season well with salt and black pepper to taste. Leave till cold. Peel, wash and slice potatoes. Arrange over the meat and gravy. Insert a pie cup or funnel if required. Roll out suet crust for baking. Cover pie dish in the usual way. Bake in a fairly hot oven, 425° F., for 10 minutes, then lower to 325° F., and bake for 50 minutes. *For 4 persons.*

MEAT AND POTATO PASTY (Pâté à la Paysanne)

1 lb. flaky or rough puff pastry
6 medium-sized potatoes
3 oz. cooked beef or pork
Salt and paprika to taste
Pepper to taste
1 tablespoon minced onion
3 tablespoons thick cream

Line a shallow pie plate or sandwich tin, 9 inches across, thinly with pastry made with milk instead of water. Prick the bottom with a fork. Peel and slice potatoes, and lay them over the pastry. Chop meat and lay on top of potatoes. Season with salt, paprika and pepper, then sprinkle with onion and cream. (If using pork, sprinkle also with a teaspoon of crushed herbs). Roll out remainder of pastry and cut into a round, the same size as the plate or tin. Lay on top of the fillings. Trim edge of the pastry lining, until it overlaps the plate by about ¼ inch all the way round. Brush overlap with cold water and turn on top of the cover. Ornament this overlap gently all round with the tines of a fork. Bake in a moderate oven, 350° F., for ¾ hour-1 hour, until golden brown. *For 4 persons.*

MEAT ROLLS (Rouleaux de Viande)

1 lb. pork sausages or ground
seasoned steak
½ lb. flaky pastry

Skin sausages. Divide each into 3 equal lengths. Roll pastry into a strip ¼ inch thick, then divide into 1½ dozen equal-sized squares, approximately 3-3½ inches. Brush the edge of each square, before filling, with cold water, then placing a sausage or portion of steak on a square, cover it with one side of the square and roll up, leaving the ends open. Place on a baking sheet with the join below. Brush with beaten egg. Prick with a fork or decorate with 2 or 3 small gashes with a knife crosswise, making them equal distance apart. Bake in a hot oven, 475° F., for about 20 minutes. *Yield:* 1½ dozen rolls.

MELTON MOWBRAY PIE (Pâté, Melton Mowbray)

PASTRY:
10 oz. lard
1 lb. 6 oz. flour
½ teaspoon salt
¾ gill milk
¾ gill water
½ beaten egg

FILLING:
2 lb. diced pork
1 teaspoon salt
½ oz. black pepper

To make the pastry, rub ¼ lb. of the lard into the flour with salt. Put remainder of lard in a saucepan. Add milk and water. Bring to boil. Stir half the liquid into the flour with a wooden spoon, then beat well. Add egg and remainder of hot milk and water. Knead well. Stand in a warm place for 10 minutes. Mould a case as already described. Mix the pork with salt, black pepper and cold water or stock to moisten. Pack into mould. Fleck filling all over with tiny bits of butter. Cover with pastry. Decorate, glaze and bake in a fairly hot oven, 425° F., for 10 minutes, then lower to 325° F., and bake for 2 hours altogether. Remove from baking sheet or unmould when slightly cool. Stand till tepid. Dissolve ¼ oz. powdered gelatine in stock made from the bones of the pork and the trimmings. Pour into hollow in centre of pie. Serve cold. *For 6 persons.*

NEWLYN TURNOVERS (Pâtés de Poisson)

½ oz. butter or margarine
½ oz. flour
¼ pint milk and water
1 cup cold boiled haddock
1 tablespoon minced parsley
2 oz. grated cheese
¾ lb. flaky pastry
1 beaten egg

Melt fat in a saucepan. Stir in flour. Remove pan from stove, and stir in liquid. Return to stove. Stir till boiling. Add haddock, parsley and cheese, stirring constantly. Boil for 1 minute, then turn on to a plate and leave till cool. Roll out pastry thinly on a lightly floured board. Cut into rounds the size of a saucer. Place a spoonful of mixture on centre of each. Brush edge of each round with cold water. Fold over in half. Press edges lightly together. Brush with beaten egg, diluted with equal quantity of milk. Place on a paper, thickly covered with stale breadcrumbs, and toss lightly till crumbed on top as well as below. Shake off loose crumbs lightly. Place in a baking tin. Bake in a hot oven, 450° F., for ¼ hour. *Yield:* 1 dozen.

POT PIES

Popular in certain parts of Canada and the United States. A variation of our sea pie (see page 538).

CHICKEN POT PIE (Pâté de Volaille, Américaine)

BASIC RECIPE :
1 roasting chicken, stewed
2 tablespoons sliced onion
1 sliced carrot
2 sliced celery sticks
1 teaspoon salt
1 whole clove
4 peppercorns
Pinch of ground ginger
About 1¼ pints chicken gravy
Baking powder crust

Cover a chicken, about 4 lb. in weight, with boiling water. Add all remaining ingredients except gravy and dough. Cover closely. Simmer until meat shows signs of coming away from the bone. Remove from stove. Leave in stock until cool. Remove and bone chicken. Strain stock. Skim off fat. Cut large pieces of chicken across the grain. Place in a pie dish, mixing the dark with the light meat. Pour the gravy over. Make a baking powder dough from ½ lb. flour and 5-6 oz. fat. Roll to ½ inch thickness. Cut out enough rounds about 2 inches in diameter, to cover meat. Place side by side on filling. Bake in a fairly hot oven, 425° F., for about 20 minutes. *For 6 or 7 persons.*

To Vary: Substitute ¼ pint cooked green peas for carrot, adding them when filling is cold.

Veal Pot Pie (Pâté de Veau, Américaine): Substitute veal for the chicken in above recipe.

CHICKEN POT PIE WITH BATTER CRUST
(Pâté de Volaille, Bourgeoise)

3 cups diced stewed chicken
3 cups boiling chicken gravy
½ lb. flour
1 teaspoon salt
2 teaspoons baking powder
About 1 cup milk
1½ tablespoons melted butter
2 beaten eggs

Place chicken while hot in a greased pie dish. Add gravy. Sift flour with salt and baking powder. Stir 1 cup of milk less 2 tablespoons with the butter and eggs. Beat only till blended. Pour over filling. Bake in a moderately hot oven, 375° F., till golden brown, in about 35-40 minutes. Serve at once. *For 5 persons.*

MUSHROOM AND BACON PIE WITH BATTER CRUST
(Pâté à la Campagne)

¾ lb. mushrooms
Salt, black pepper and paprika
  to taste
¾ lb. peeled potatoes
6-8 rashers bacon
1 pint beef stock
1 cup flour
2 teaspoons baking powder
¾ cup milk
¼ cup melted butter

Peel stems of mushrooms.

Peel, stem and cleanse mushrooms. Sprinkle with a little salt, pepper and paprika, and fry in a pan without any fat until the juice begins to run. Slice and boil potatoes. Drain. Remove rind from bacon and grill bacon. Cut half the bacon into small pieces. Place in the bottom of a baking dish. Cover with half the mushrooms and add half the potatoes, then remainder of mushrooms and potatoes. Sprinkle with salt, pepper and paprika. Slice and stew in the stock for ½ hour. Strain stock over potatoes. Cover with remainder of bacon. Sift flour with $\frac{1}{4}$ teaspoon salt and baking powder. Mix to a batter with milk and butter. Pour over the bacon. Bake in a hot oven, 400° F., until brown. Serve with a green salad. *For 6 persons.*

RABBIT PIE (Pâté de Lapin)

1 young rabbit
1 lb. veal bones
1 peeled onion
1 blade mace
Salt and pepper to taste
Cold water as required
$\frac{1}{2}$ lb. pickled pork
$\frac{1}{4}$ pint stock
4 sheets gelatine
1 lb. flaky pastry

Wash head, heart and liver in cold salted water. Place in a saucepan. Wash bones and add with onion, mace and salt and pepper to taste. Cover with cold water. Bring slowly to boil. Skim carefully. Cover. Simmer gently for $2\frac{1}{2}$-3 hours. Strain. Joint rabbit. Cover with boiling water and wipe dry. Place joints in a pie dish. Cut up pork into slices, then into squares. Tuck under joints of rabbit. Season with salt and pepper. Add stock. Break up and tuck 2 of the sheets of gelatine in between the joints. Insert pie cup or funnel. If pie dish is not full, the crust will sink. Roll pastry almost $\frac{1}{2}$ inch thick. Cut out lid. Roll remaining pastry to $\frac{1}{4}$ inch thickness. Cut out strip for rim of dish. Cover in the usual way, but make a hole with a skewer at either end of the pie. Ornament with a tassel and foliage. Glaze. Bake in a hot oven, 450° F., for 20 minutes, till pastry is risen and set, and starting to colour, then lower to slow, 325° F., and bake for about $1\frac{1}{4}$ hours. Remove from stove. Take off the tassel, and widen the holes to allow steam to escape. Dissolve remainder of gelatine in a cup of stock. Pour through a funnel into pie, adding more stock if necessary. Cool, till jellied, then replace tassel before serving. *For 6 or 7 persons.*

SAUSAGE PIES (Pâtés de Saucissons, Ecossaise)

$\frac{1}{2}$ lb. pork sausages
$\frac{1}{2}$ lb. veal cutlet
$\frac{1}{4}$ lb. bacon
Salt and pepper to taste
Ground mace to taste
Stock or water to moisten
1 lb. flaky or rough puff pastry
2 hard-boiled eggs

Skin sausages. Remove any skin from veal, as well as rind from bacon. Put veal and bacon through a meat grinder. Stir in the sausage meat. Season with salt, pepper and ground mace to taste. Moisten with stock or water. Roll pastry to barely $\frac{1}{2}$ inch thickness. Stamp into 3 inch rounds. Reserve these for the lids. Gather remainder of pastry together and roll out thinly this time. Stamp out the same number of rounds as before. Line patty tins with the thin rounds of pastry. Prick with a fork. Divide meat mixture equally between each then cover filling in each case with a slice of egg. Brush the edge of the linings with cold water before putting on the lids. Make a hole in the centre. Press edges together with a fork. Decorate each pie with one or 2 tiny leaves of pastry. Brush tops carefully with beaten egg yolk diluted with equal quantity of milk. Bake in a hot oven, 450° F., until the pastry is risen and set, in about 10 minutes, then lower to moderately slow, 325° F., and bake for about $\frac{3}{4}$ hour altogether. Remove from tins. Re-open the centre holes to allow steam to escape if they have closed during cooking. *Yield:* About 12 pies.

SAVOURY ECLAIRS (Eclairs, Paysanne)

1½ dozen baked choux cases
¾ lb. cooked chicken or veal
3 oz. cooked ham or tongue
¼ pint stiff white sauce
Salt and pepper to taste
1 tablespoon mayonnaise

Make the pastry according to instructions given under Choux pastry, into small round balls. When baked, remove from oven. Brush with beaten egg white. Return to oven and bake for another 5 minutes, then remove, slit, and leave until cold. Mince meats. Stir into sauce. Season to taste, then stir in mayonnaise. Stuff choux cases. Serve with garnished watercress, in a dish lined with a paper doily.

SCOTCH MUTTON PIES (Pâtés de Mouton, Ecossaise)

FILLING:
¾ lb. lean mutton
Salt and black pepper to taste
Pinch of grated nutmeg or
  ground mace
1 dessertspoon minced onion
PASTRY:
¼ lb. beef dripping
½ pint cold water
1 lb. flour
½ teaspoon salt

Remove any bone, gristle or skin from mutton. Cut into very small squares an inch thick, keeping lean and fat separate. Season with salt and pepper to taste, nutmeg or mace and onion. Add a tablespoon of minced parsley if liked. Put dripping in a saucepan with the water. Bring to boil. Sieve flour into a basin with the salt. Make a hollow in the centre. As soon as dripping and water come to the boil, pour into flour. Stir till into a dough. Leave till cool enough to handle. Knead lightly for a moment. Turn on to a floured board. Knead lightly until free from cracks. Divide two-thirds of the pastry into 6 equal portions. Place remainder in a covered warm dish to keep warm. Line each small round tin with a portion of pastry, kneading it into the tins to form small, thin cases. If preferred, the cases can be moulded round the bottom of a small, plain tumbler, then placed on a baking sheet. Fill with meat mixture moistened with gravy, lean and fat alternately. Cut rounds from remainder of pastry. Brush edges of one side with cold water and cover pies, wet side downwards. Press edges firmly together. Trim and ornament with a pair of scissors, or notch edges. Make a small hole in the centre of each pie. Brush tops with beaten egg or milk. Bake in a moderate oven, 350° F., for about 40 minutes. When ready, fill, through a funnel, with a little hot, thickened mutton gravy. Serve at once. *Yield:* 6 mutton pies.

SEA PIE (Pâté de Boeuf à la Mer)

BASIC RECIPE:
1 lb. steak
1 medium-sized sliced onion
1 thinly sliced carrot
Salt and pepper to taste
½ lb. suet crust

Use rump steak when possible. Cut steak into thin slices about 3 inches square. Place in a shallow saucepan. Add enough boiling water to cover meat. Bring to simmering point, and simmer for 25 minutes. Add onion and carrot. Season to taste. Continue to simmer gently while rolling out the pastry into a round to fit inside the saucepan. Place on top of meat. Cover closely. Simmer gently for 1½ hours. Divide pastry into 4 or 5 equal portions. Dish up meat, vegetables and gravy. Lay the pastry on top or round the meat. Serve with boiled or mashed potatoes. *For 4 or 5 persons.*

SPINACH TARTLETS (Tartelettes d'Epinards)

¾ lb. puff or rough puff pastry
1½ cups chopped, cooked, or canned spinach
1½ tablespoons butter or margarine
¼ cup grated cheese
½ cup white sauce
1 tablespoon dried bread-crumbs
Salt and pepper to taste
1 separated egg

Line 12 patty tins, about 2½ inches across, smoothly with pastry. Prick insides with a fork. Bake in a hot oven, 475° F., till pastry is risen and set, in about 7 minutes. Lower heat to moderate, 350° F. Meanwhile, heat spinach in a saucepan, stirring constantly. Add fat. Stir till melted. Stir in cheese, sauce, breadcrumbs, salt and pepper to taste, and a dash of grated nutmeg if liked. Beat egg yolk well. Add to mixture. Stir over moderate heat till piping hot. Remove from stove. Beat egg white till stiff. Fold into mixture. Three-quarters fill partly baked pastry cases. Bake in a moderate oven, 350° F., for about 10 minutes, till pastry is golden brown and filling is set. Top with pastry lids, baked alongside. *Allow 1 or 2 per person.*

STEAK AND KIDNEY PIE (Pâté de Boeuf et Rognon)

2 lb. beef steak
½ lb. ox kidney
2 tablespoons seasoned flour
Minced onion if liked
Stock or water as required
¾ lb. flaky, puff, or rough puff pastry

Wipe meat with a damp cloth. Trim off fat. Cut into thin slices about 3 by 1½ inches. Remove skin from kidney and any core. Beat meat slightly, then dip in seasoned flour. Cut kidney into small pieces and place one with a bit of fat on each piece of meat, and roll up. Pack into a pie dish. Insert pie cup if required. Sprinkle with 1-2 tablespoons minced onion if liked. Half fill with stock or water. Cover pie in the usual way. Bake in a hot oven, 450° F., for about 20 minutes, then lower to moderate, 350° F., and bake till meat is tender, in 1½-2 hours, depending on whether rump steak or round steak is used. *For 7 or 8 persons.*

STEAK PUDDING (Pouding de Boeuf à l'Anglaise)

1 lb. suet crust
2 lb. rump or round steak
2 tablespoons flour
1 teaspoon salt
¾ teaspoon black pepper
2 tablespoons minced onion if liked
Stock or water as required

Line a greased pudding basin about 8 inches across with suet crust, using plain, rich or savoury, according to taste. Wipe meat and trim off any fat. Cut into thin slices, about 3-4 inches long or 3 inches square or 2-2½ inches oblong. Beat lightly on a chopping board. Place flour on a plate. Stir in salt and pepper to taste. Dip meat in flour. Roll up each piece of meat with a bit of fat if possible and pack into lined basin. Sprinkle with onion if liked. Add stock to come three-quarters of way up basin. Cover. See basic recipe, page 524. *For 8 persons.*

STEAK AND KIDNEY PUDDING : Follow above recipe, but reduce steak to 1½ lb. and add ½ lb. ox kidney. Skin and core kidney, then rinse and dry. Cut up in small portions about the size of a small walnut. Dip in seasoned flour together with steak. Tuck a bit of kidney in the middle of each piece of meat before rolling up.

STEAK ROLY POLY (Rouleau de Boeuf)

Suet crust
¾ lb. buttock steak
1 medium-sized onion
Salt and pepper to taste
1 egg white

Mix suet crust, using half quantities of rich suet crust with the Savoury variation, into a dough. Wipe steak with a damp cloth. Peel onion. Put steak and onion through a meat grinder. Stir in salt and pepper to taste. Roll crust into an oblong from ¼-½ inch thick. Beat egg white slightly. Brush pastry with egg white. Spread it with meat mixture to within ¾ inch of the edges. Roll up like a Swiss roll, then roll in floured, scalded pudding cloth. Tie securely at each end with string. Lower into a pan of boiling water. Simmer gently for 2 hours. Serve with thick brown gravy, boiled, mashed or riced potatoes, and any green vegetable. *For 4 or 5 persons.*

VEAL AND BACON PIE (Pâté de Veau, froid)

½ cup breadcrumbs
1 oz. shredded suet
½ teaspoon crushed herbs
Salt and pepper to taste
Grated rind of 1 lemon
1 tablespoon minced parsley
1 beaten egg
1 lb. fillet of veal
¼ lb. chopped bacon
2 sliced hard-boiled eggs
½ gill water
¾ lb. flaky pastry
Jellied stock as required

Mix stale crumbs with suet, herbs, seasoning, lemon rind, parsley and beaten egg to bind. Cut veal in strips, about 3 inches long. Spread with the forcemeat. Roll them up. Place the rolls in a pie dish. Insert pie cup or funnel if required. Tuck the bacon in between, then cover with the hard-boiled egg. Sprinkle with the water. Roll out pastry, and cover pie in the usual way. Glaze with remainder of beaten egg. Bake for ¼ hour in a hot oven, 350° F., then lower to moderate, 350° F., and bake for about 1¼ hours, until pastry is golden and meat cooked. Remove from oven. Stand for a few minutes, then pour through a funnel into the hole in centre, about ½ pint of dissolved, jellied beef or veal stock seasoned to taste. Serve cold. *For 4 or 5 persons.*

RAISED VEAL AND HAM PIE (Pâté de Veau, Anglaise)

6 oz. raw streaky bacon
1½ lb. stewing veal
1 teaspoon minced parsley
Salt and pepper to taste
Raised pie crust
2 hard-boiled eggs

Remove rind from bacon. Put through a meat grinder with the veal into a basin. Stir in parsley, salt and pepper to taste. Prepare crust from 1½ lb. flour. Reserve a third for lid. Mould into shape. Half-fill mould with the mixture. Shell and halve eggs. Place equal distance apart on mixture. Fill with remaining mixture. Cover in usual way with pastry and glaze. Bake in a hot oven, 425° F., for about 20 minutes, until the top is pale gold, then cover with paper and lower temperature to 250° F., Bake until filling is cooked through, in about 1½ hours. Fill up with rich stock through a funnel inserted in centre. Serve cold. Garnish centre with parsley. *For 8 persons.*

VENISON PIE (Pâté de Venaison)

2 lb. shoulder of venison
Salt and black pepper to taste

Cut meat into suitable pieces for serving. Trim off any bits of fat. Place the meat in a pie dish.

1/4 teaspoon ground mace
1/4 teaspoon ground allspice
1/4 pint claret
3 tablespoons minced onion
1/2 pint jellying stock
2 or 3 tablespoons vinegar
1 1/4 lb. flaky pastry

Tuck the fat in between. (If there is no fat attached to the venison, cut wafer slices of mutton fat, say 4 or 5, and use instead.) Insert pie cup. Season with salt, black pepper, mace and allspice. Add claret with onion, stock and vinegar. Cover with pastry in the usual way.

Glaze. Bake in a hot oven, 450° F., for 1/4 hour, then lower to moderate, 350° F., and bake for about 1 1/4 hours. *For 6-8 persons.*

SWEET PASTRY

This section starts with recipes for pastry used only with sweet fillings and follows with recipes for fruit tarts, pies and flans, which are sometimes served as a dessert and sometimes for tea.

ALMOND SHORTCRUST (Pâté Brisée aux Amandes)

6 oz. sifted flour
1/4 cup ground almonds
2 oz. caster sugar
1/4 teaspoon salt
1/4 lb. butter or margarine
1 beaten egg
Ice-cold water as required

Sift flour with almonds, sugar and salt into a basin. Rub in fat. Mix to a stiff dough with the egg and sufficient cold water. Use for cheese cakes, tartlet cases, etc., remembering to chill and fold before baking.

Cashou (Cachew): Follow above recipe, substituting ground cachou nuts.

CREAM CHEESE PASTRY (Pâté, Viennoise)

1/4 lb. flour
Pinch of salt
1/4 lb. butter
3 oz. cream or cottage cheese

Sift flour, then sift again with salt. Lightly rub in butter. Stir in cream cheese or very dry cottage cheese. When blended, wrap in waxed paper. Chill in refrigerator for 12 hours. Roll out thinly on a pastry board, covered with waxed paper. Use for turnovers, or crescents with a sweet filling, or for any pastries with a jam or fruit filling. Bake in a hot oven, 450° F., for 12-15 minutes. Dredge lightly with icing sugar.

FLEUR PASTRY (Pâté, Fleur)

6 oz. flour
1 saltspoon salt
3 1/2 oz. butter or margarine
1 oz. caster or icing sugar
1 egg yolk

Sift flour and salt into a basin. Rub in fat. Stir in sugar. Add egg yolk. Knead with hand till pliable. Roll out and use at once. Use for pie, flan and tartlet cases.

MUERBETEIG PASTRY

This pastry is generally used for lining pie plates, and tartlet tins, in cheese cakes, etc.

541

8 oz. flour
1 beaten egg
Pinch of salt
4 oz. butter
¾ 1 oz. caster sugar
Rum or water to moisten

Chill ingredients and make the pastry in a cold room. Sift flour into a basin. Make a hollow in the centre. Add egg, and salt. Divide butter up into tiny flakes, and add. Chop all these ingredients together with a knife, then add sugar, according to taste, and rum or water to moisten. Knead till smooth. Chill for ½ hour. Bake on a floured baking sheet in a moderately hot oven, 400°-410° F.

SPICED SHORTCRUST

½ lb. flour
Pinch of salt
½ teaspoon ground cinnamon
½ teaspoon baking powder
6 oz. butter
½ tablespoon caster sugar
1 egg yolk
Water if required

Sift flour, salt, cinnamon and baking powder into a basin. Rub in butter. Stir in sugar and egg yolk, with a tablespoon or so of ice-cold water if required to make a rather stiff paste. Roll out evenly. Use for mince pies, apple flans and for any sweet pie in which the sweet filling would combine with spiced shortcrust.

TARTS (Tartes)

A tart can be made of any kind of freshly prepared, or bottled fruit, and covered with pastry to taste. Generally a form of shortcrust is used, but flaky or rough puff can be substituted if preferred.

FRUIT TART (Tarte de Fruit)

BASIC RECIPE:
½ lb. shortcrust
Cold water as required
Fresh fruit to taste
Sugar to taste

Chill shortcrust. Roll out pastry to ¼ inch thickness, keeping the pastry the shape of the pie dish, but roll till at least 1 inch larger than dish. Cut off a strip a very little wider than the rim of dish. Brush rim of dish with cold water. Lay strip on top without stretching it. Moisten the ends and mould neatly together with fingers. Prepare fruit. For this amount of shortcrust, you need about 2 lb. of fruit before it is prepared. Pour enough cold water into pie dish to cover the bottom. Place half the fruit in the bottom of a pie dish. Sweeten with sugar. Add remainder of fruit, piling it well up in the centre. This is important. Press the fruit lightly down as it shrinks while cooking so that you can use as much fruit as possible. If the sugar touches the pastry, the pastry will be soggy. Brush pastry strip with cold water. Place rolling pin under the centre of the pastry and transfer pastry to cover the fruit without stretching it. Press lightly with your finger, or with a fork or knife, over the strip. Holding the pie in your left hand, trim edges with short, sharp strokes, then flute edges as illustrated. Glaze if liked. Make small holes equal distance apart on the sides of the cover to allow steam to escape. Place on a baking sheet or tin. Bake in a hot oven, 450° F., near the top of stove, for about 17 minutes, until pastry is set and starting to brown, then either lower temperature to 350° F., or move pie lower down in the oven, and leave it there till fruit is cooked, which you can tell by testing with a skewer, and pastry is crisp and golden brown. Usually takes about 40 minutes from start to finish. Dredge with caster or icing sugar. *For 6 persons.*

Apple Tart : Peel, core and thinly-slice apples. Place half in pie dish. Sprinkle with caster or brown sugar, spiced to taste, allowing 1 cup sugar mixed with $\frac{1}{4}$ teaspoon cinnamon and a saltspoon of ground cloves or grated nutmeg to 2 lb. apples (weighed before preparing). Sprinkle with 2-3 table-spoons water. Dab all over with tiny flecks of butter or margarine, about 1 oz. To cover, follow basic recipe. Bake in a hot oven, 450° F., for 10 minutes. Lower to moderate, 350° F., and bake for about $\frac{3}{4}$ hour. This tart may be served with vanilla ice cream, when it is known as Pie à la Norde.

Apple and Quince : Dissolve 3 oz. Demerara sugar in 1 tablespoon hot water. Pour into a small pie dish. Peel and slice 1 lb. cooking apples. Peel and chop 1 large ripe quince. Mix together. Pile high in dish. Add 1 clove. To cover, follow basic recipe, allowing 6 oz. flaky pastry. Cook in a hot oven, 450° F., for $\frac{1}{4}$ hour, then lower to moderate, 350° F., and cook for about $\frac{1}{2}$ hour till fruit is tender when tested with a skewer. *For 4 persons.*

Apricot : Wash $\frac{1}{2}$ lb. dried apricots in two or three waters. Place in a basin. Cover with cold water to the depth of an inch. Soak for 24 hours. Strain off water into a jug. Place half the apricots in pie dish. Add 2 or 3 tablespoons of caster or Demerara sugar, then remainder of apricots and about 4 table-spoons of the apricot water. To cover and bake, follow basic recipe, allowing only 10 minutes at 450° F., and about $\frac{1}{2}$ hour in a moderate temperature, 350° F. When ready, brush with egg white. Sprinkle with caster sugar. Return to oven for 5 minutes to glaze.

Blackberry and Apple : Allow $\frac{3}{4}$ lb. apple to $1\frac{1}{4}$ lb. blackberries, and the juice and grated rind of a lemon. Prepare the fruit. Mix together. Place half the fruit in a dish. Sprinkle with the lemon juice, grated rind and a heaped cup of sugar. Add remainder of fruit and $\frac{1}{4}$ pint of water. To cover and bake, follow basic recipe.

Blackcurrant, Cherry, Raspberry and Red Currant : Follow basic recipe, but only allow 1 tablespoon of water. Strip stalks from currants. Stem cherries. Stone if liked. Wash and drain. Rinse currants. Hull raspberries and drain. Follow basic recipe, allowing 5 oz. brown sugar to 2 lb. black-currants, and 5 oz. caster to 2 lb. of any of the other fruits. To make a red currant and raspberry tart, allow 1 part red currants to 3 of raspberries.

Gooseberry : Top and tail, then wash 2 lb. gooseberries. Half fill pie dish. Add sugar to taste, 4-6 tablespoons depending on sweetness of the berries, and 3 or 4 tablespoons cold water. If preferred, sweeten with golden syrup. Add remainder of berries. To cover, follow basic recipe. Bake in a fairly hot oven, 425° F., for 20 minutes, then lower to 350°-375° F., and cook till fruit is tender when tested with a skewer. Glaze if liked.

Plum : Use damsons, greengages, or any plums in season. Wipe and stone. Place half of them in a pie dish with 6 blanched and peeled kernels, and ½ cup water, as stoned fruit needs more water than any other fruit. Add sugar to taste, and remainder of fruit. Follow basic recipe for covering and baking.

Rhubarb : Wipe and trim rhubarb stalks. Cut into inch lengths. Follow method given for Apple Tart.

PIES (Pâtés)

There are many varieties of pies. In this section, I am including chiffon pies, cream pies, etc., consisting of fillings placed in crumb cases or baked pastry cases. Some are topped with meringue and baked. Others are topped with whipped cream and decorated. I am also including such Transatlantic favourites as double-crust fruit pies and recipes for other pies equally suitable for serving at dinner or tea.

TO MAKE A TWO-CRUST FRUIT PIE

Use Fleur, Muerbeteig, shortcrust or spiced shortcrust, if no special pastry is suggested in recipes. If you want a thin crust such as is popular in America ½ lb. dough is sufficient, otherwise use ¾ lb. This is why I have suggested " from ½-¾-lb. pastry " in my recipes for two-crust pies.

FRESH FRUIT

½-¾ lb. pastry
1 saltspoon salt
1½ tablespoons flour, or 1 tablespoon cornflour
Sugar to taste
4 cups prepared fruit
½-1 oz. butter

Form pastry into a 9 inch case in the usual way. Mix salt, flour and sugar together. Spread half this mixture over the bottom of pastry case. Cover with the fruit, using sliced, peeled apples, blackberries, cherries, loganberries, plums, raspberries, or a combination to taste. Sprinkle with remainder of flour and sugar mixture, then with a dessertspoon of lemon juice if liked. Fleck with butter before covering with pastry. This method helps to prevent the bottom of the top crust becoming soggy.

BOTTLED, CANNED OR COOKED FRUIT

Pastry to taste
1 pint fruit
About ¾ pint juice
Sugar to taste
Pinch of salt
Flour or cornflour as required
¾ tablespoon butter

Make shortcrust with ½ lb. flour and 5 or 5½ oz. fat, or use Muerbeteig or Spiced Shortcrust, see pages 541-542. Line a 9 inch pie plate. Prick well with a fork. Mix fruit with the juice. If fruit is large, slice before using. Apples, blackberries, cherries, gooseberries, peaches and plums are all suitable. Mix sugar to taste with the salt, flour or cornflour, allowing from 2-6 oz. of sugar according to sweetness

Serve Steamed Castle Puddings with jam or marmalade sauce. *See page* 573.

Serve Ginger Suet Pudding with hot apple sauce. *See page* 593.

Eat Apple Jelly Dumplings with apple jelly. Serve with custard sauce. *See page* 2.

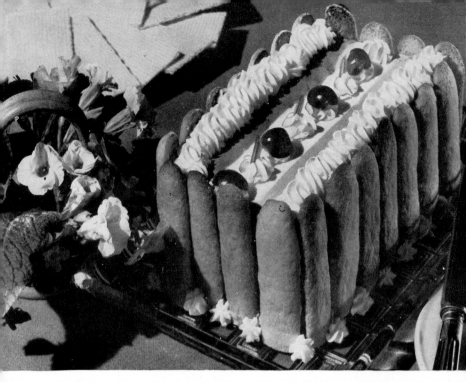

Decorate Carnival Gateau with pieces of glacé fruit and angelica. *See page 622.*

Trim Festival Iced Pudding with festoons of whipped cream and walnuts and berries.
See page 622.

of fruit, and 1-2 dessertspoons of flour or 1-2 teaspoons cornflour, according to juiciness of fruit. Mix thoroughly with the fruit and juice. Pack into pastry case. Dab with butter. Cover with remainder of pastry rolled out to fit, or with a lattice of pastry. Bake in a hot oven, 450° F., for 10 minutes. Lower to moderate, 350° F. Bake for about 25 minutes.

Dried Fruit: Wash, soak and stew apples, apricots, peaches or prunes then follow recipe given for Cooked Fruit Pie, substituting the stewed, dried fruit for the bottled and cooked, and using juice in the same way.

TO COVER TWO-CRUST PIES

There are two ways of covering any of these two-crust pies :

1. Divide pastry in two, making one portion a little larger than the other for the under crust. Roll the larger portion to $\frac{1}{8}$ inch thickness. Fold in two over a floured rolling pin, and line a pie plate 9 inches across. Prick the bottom well with a fork. Trim neatly all the way round, leaving $\frac{1}{2}$ inch overlapping edge of plate. Fill as already described. Brush edge of lining with cold water. Gather up remainder of dough and roll to $\frac{1}{8}$ inch thickness. Fold in half over rolling pin, then place this over half the filled crust. Unfold and finish covering. Trim edge around the rim without cutting into lower crust. Bring the overlap from lower crust over the edge of the top crust. Either crimp or notch edges together, or press lightly together with the floured prongs of a fork.

2. Use larger portion of dough for the cover, and reserve the smaller as a lining for the pie plate. Line as described above, but without leaving an overlap. Prick the bottom. Fill. Gather remainder of pastry and roll out into a round $\frac{1}{8}$ inch thick, $\frac{1}{2}$ inch wider than the edge of the lower crust. Lift up lower crust and tuck this $\frac{1}{2}$ inch underneath. Crimp, notch, flute or press edges together with the floured prongs of a fork.

TO DECORATE PLAIN COVERS OF TWO CRUST PIES
TOOLS REQUIRED

1 pie crimper	Assorted biscuit cutters
Pie tins with fluted or scalloped edges	Ornamental rolling pin
	Sharp knife

To Decorate Rims: Fold overlapping $\frac{1}{2}$ inch of pastry under or over cover, then :

1. Press all the way round with a fork dipped in flour.
2. Decorate round the edge with a pastry crimper.
3. Crimp or notch with your thumbs and forefingers. Use this decoration to give you an upstanding edge when the pie is to be filled with a juicy fruit.
4. Flute or scallop with knife and left thumb.
5. Pat rim all the way round with the flat of a knife, or with the back of a knife, making slanting parallel cuts all the way round, then cross these with parallel cuts in the opposite direction.
6. Make a rope edge by pinching edge of crust between your thumbs.
7. To make a daisy edge, turn the top of a teaspoon, bowl side downwards, and shape all the way round, then mark with the prongs of a fork.

To Decorate Centre of Covers: This must be done before placing cover over filling. If you decorate the cover with "cut-outs" either with a knife or a cutter, it is not necessary to prick the top.

1. With a knife, mark a tree across the centre with a small tree on each side, equal distance apart from central one.

2. With small biscuit or cocktail cutters, stamp design over cover, for example : diamonds, crescents. If wanted for a Valentine party or an engagement party, use a heart-shaped cutter.

TO BAKE TWO-CRUST PIES

Fresh Fruit: Bake in a hot oven, 450° F., on a high shelf, for about 10 minutes until pastry is risen and set, then lower to moderate, 350° F., placing it on lowest shelf to allow lower crust and filling to cook without scorching the upper. Bake from 35-40 minutes longer until filling is ready when tested with a skewer and crust is golden brown.

Bottled, Canned or Cooked Fruit: Bake in a hot oven, 450° F., for about 10 minutes, until pastry is risen and set, then lower to moderate, 350° F., and finish cooking in about 25 minutes, or bake in a fairly hot oven, 425° F., for about 27 minutes.

NOTE : The lower crust of pies browns quicker in a tin pie plate than in a fireproof glass or ware plate.

TO MAKE AN OPEN PIE OR FLAN CASE

Use any form of shortcrust, but not flaky or rough puff pastry, allowing 4-6 oz., according to taste. 6 oz. is necessary when you want an upstanding rim for a pie that is to be baked with a liquid filling such as a custard pie. Roll out pastry on a lightly floured board into a round about $\frac{1}{8}$ inch thick and 3 inches larger than the top of pie plate or tin. Fold over rolling pin and place in plate or tin. Unfold and fit without stretching. Holding plate or tin in your left hand, trim edge with a knife, or a pair of scissors, leaving an overlap all the way round of about 1 inch. Turn $\frac{1}{2}$ inch of the edge under. Crimp or notch, or flute so as to have a firm, upright rim. *This kind of rim is most important when pie or flan is to be filled with a custard or any liquid filling, or is to have a meringue or whipped cream topping.* Chill thoroughly. Glaze rims before baking.

TO BAKE CASES FOR OPEN PIES

Bake in a hot oven, 450° F., for 10-15 minutes, or in a very hot oven, 500° F., for about 12 minutes. Take a quick glance after 4 or 5 minutes to see if there is any sign of blistering or bulging in the pastry case. If there is, prick it again. If the rim of the case is browning faster than the case, place on a lower shelf to finish cooking, or lower temperature when the pastry is risen and set, to moderate, 350° F., and finish cooking. By either of these latter methods, the case should take about 20 minutes. If a fruit filling is going to be used and pie is likely to be left for a little while before serving, it is a good idea to brush the inside of case with beaten egg white and return to the oven for a minute or two to dry before cooling and filling.

NOTE : Many experts advocate placing a piece of greased greaseproof paper, greased side downwards, inside the case, and filling it half full with beans or rice. Others suggest lowering a second pie plate or tin over the paper to prevent the bottom rising. The beans or rice, or pie plate or tin is not removed until rim of case is light brown. If the pastry is well pricked and chilled before baking, neither of these methods is necessary.

TO BAKE FILLED CASES

If you wish the bottom crust to be very crisp, brush it with beaten egg white and leave until set before filling. Bake on the bottom shelf of a fairly hot oven, 425° F., otherwise the pastry will be brown before the filling is ready. For time, see under respective recipes.

TO DECORATE OPEN PIES AND FLANS

Follow suggestions given for Two-Crust Pie Covers, applying them only to the one crust, turning the overlap either under or over according to taste.

1. *Lattice Work:* Roll half the dough to $\frac{1}{8}$ inch thickness. Place in a pie plate, as already described, to line it. Prick well. Fill. Gather remainder of dough and roll into an oblong $\frac{1}{8}$ inch thick. Cut in narrow strips, $\frac{1}{2}$ inch wide with a knife or pie crimper. Trim and brush ends with cold water. Glaze. Arrange half the strips equal distance apart over the filling, pressing the ends into the edge of the pie to seal them. Now either lay an equal number of strips equal distance apart over the top of the first ones, or weave a strip over and under across the centre. Continue to add cross strips equal distance apart, but fold back each alternate one of the strips going in the opposite direction, to avoid contact with the filling when applying. Either method will give you diamond openings through which the filling will peep. Now carefully lift the overlap over the ends of the pastry strips and notch all the way round.

2. *Criss-Cross:* Cut two strips of pastry about 1 inch thick and $\frac{1}{2}$ inch wide of the same diameter as the filling in pie. Glaze strips. After pricking the bottom crust, brush the ends of one of the strips with cold water and place in the centre, drawing the ends lightly against the case to seal them. Brush the ends of the second strip with cold water and cut a tiny piece $\frac{1}{2}$ inch wide out of the centre. Lay this strip across the other one so that the cut portion fits exactly over the top of the first strip. Press ends of strip against the case to seal them. This will give you 4 complete compartments, so that you can have two contrasting fruits or jams arranged alternately in the sections.

3. *Parallel Bars:* Cover filling in pie with glazed, graduated strips, cut $\frac{1}{2}$ inch wide with a pie crimper, placing them about 1 inch apart. Press moistened ends up against case to seal them.

4. Cut out diamonds, leaves or stars of pastry. Glaze. Brush edges with cold water and arrange all over the filling.

5. Make a circle of glazed crescents or rings over fillings, keeping them about 2 inches from the edge of pastry.

6. Follow method given for arranging strips criss-cross, but insert an extra strip between each so as to divide the pie into 8 wedges. Do not cross them in the centre, but put a rose, diamond or star of pastry in the centre.

7. *Meringue:* Beat 3 egg whites with a rotary beater or whisk until they

hold their shape. Gradually beat in 6 oz. caster sugar or 3-6 tablespoons of smooth icing sugar, according to taste. Beat until blended. Stir in 2 or 3 grains of salt and $\frac{1}{4}$ teaspoon vanilla essence, or $1\frac{1}{2}$ teaspoons lemon juice. Cool filling before covering. Spread meringue over thinly, being careful to bring it tight up to the edges, then add remainder of meringue and swirl it with a fork, or force through a forcing pipe in any design you like. Bake in a slow oven, 325° F., for about $\frac{1}{4}$ hour.

8. *Cream:* Chill 1 cup thick cream, bowl and beater. Beat slightly, then gradually beat in a dessertspoon of smooth icing sugar. Beat until cream forms small peaks, then lightly stir in about $\frac{1}{3}$ teaspoon vanilla essence, and a few grains of salt. To keep cream fluffy for a few hours, or in hot weather, beat in $\frac{3}{4}$ teaspoon powdered gelatine, softened in $\frac{3}{4}$ tablespoon cold water, before adding vanilla and salt. Force cream through a pastry tube in parallel trails a little apart across filling, or pipe criss-cross or in large roses over the top. You can also spread it thickly over the top and swirl it with a fork.

ALMOND PIE (Pâté d'Amandes)

½ lb. rich shortcrust
1 oz. almonds
2 oz. butter
3 oz. caster sugar
2 small separated eggs
2 oz. cake crumbs
2 oz. ground almonds
1 oz. flour
2 or 3 drops almond essence

Line a 9 inch pie plate with the pastry. Trim and ornament. Prick bottom well. Blanch, dry and cut almonds into strips. Beat butter until softened. Gradually beat in sugar. Beat until fluffy. Add egg yolks one at a time. Beat until blended. Stir in crumbs, ground almonds, flour and almond essence. Beat egg whites until stiff. Fold in lightly. Pour into pastry case. Sprinkle with almond strips. Make a lattice work of pastry on top from trimmings. Bake in a fairly hot oven, 425° F., for 25-30 minutes. *For 4-6 persons.*

AMERICAN SYRUP PIE (Pâté à la Vermont)

4-6 oz. shortcrust
1 oz. butter
1 cup brown sugar
1 cup maple syrup
½ cup milk
3 beaten egg yolks
½ grated nutmeg
3 stiffly-whisked egg whites

Line a 9 inch pie case with pastry. Prick well. Beat butter till softened, then gradually beat in sugar and syrup. Stir in milk, yolk and nutmeg. Fold in egg whites. Lightly pile into case. Bake in a fairly hot oven, 425° F., until pastry is risen and set, then lower to 300° F., and bake till filling is set and pastry brown, in about 25 minutes. *For 6 persons.*

APPLE KRUNCH PIE (Tourte de Pommes, Parisienne)

6 oz. flaky pastry
2 lb. cooking apples
½ gill water
2 tablespoons apricot or raspberry jam
3 oz. butter
3 oz. caster sugar
1 large separated egg

Roll out pastry and line the sides of a pie dish, taking it over the rim. Ornament edges. Glaze. Bake in a hot oven, 450° F., for 20 minutes. Peel, core, slice and stew apples with the water till soft. Mash. Stir in jam and 1 oz. of the butter. Pour into pie dish. Cream remainder of butter, then beat in sugar, egg yolk, almonds, and cake

1 oz. ground almonds
3 oz. sponge cake crumbs
Juice of 1 lemon

crumbs. Strain in lemon juice. Stir till blended. Beat egg white to a stiff froth. Stir into mixture. Pile on top of apple. Bake in a moderate oven, 350° F., for about 20 minutes. *For 5 persons.*

To Vary: Substitute short or Fleur pastry for flaky, and desiccated coconut for the almonds.

BANANA CREAM PIE (Tourte de Bananes)

¼ cup cornflour
5 oz. caster sugar
Pinch of salt
2 cups hot milk
3 egg yolks
1 oz. butter
¼ teaspoon vanilla essence
1 baked pastry case, 9 inches across
3 sliced bananas

Mix cornflour with the sugar and salt in a basin. Gradually stir in milk. Pour into the top of a double boiler. Cook, stirring constantly, until thick, in 8-10 minutes. Beat egg yolks slightly. Gradually add 2 or 3 tablespoons of the hot sauce to the egg yolks. When blended, stir into the remainder of the hot sauce. Cook over hot water, stirring constantly, for 5 minutes, then remove from heat and cool slightly. Add butter and vanilla essence. Stir until butter is melted. When the pastry case is cold, peel and slice bananas and arrange all over the bottom of the case. Cover with the filling. Garnish round the edge of the filling with large swirls of fluffy whipped cream, sweetened and flavoured with vanilla and decorated with slices of additional banana planted in the cream, not laid flat on top. *For 6 persons.*

BARBARA FRIETCHIE PIE (Tourte à la Barbara)

6 oz. shortcrust
¾ cup caster sugar
¾ cup light brown sugar
½ cup cream
2 egg yolks
2 tablespoons butter
Pinch of salt
½ teaspoon vanilla essence
2 egg whites
Grated nutmeg to taste

Line a 9 inch pie plate with pastry and prick well. Glaze edge. Place the sugars, cream and beaten egg yolks in the top of a double boiler. Stir well till blended, then cook over boiling water, stirring constantly till thick. Remove from heat. Stir in butter, salt and vanilla essence. Beat egg whites till stiff. Fold into mixture. Pour into case. Dredge lightly with grated nutmeg. Bake in a fairly hot oven, 425° F., on a low shelf, for about 10 minutes, then quickly decrease to slow, 300° F. Bake for about ¾ hour, till knife inserted in centre comes out clean.

BAVARIAN FRUIT CREAM PIE (Tourte, Bavaroise)

1 vanilla wafer case
1 tablespoon powdered gelatine
2 tablespoons cold water
1 lb. frozen strawberries
1½ teaspoons lemon juice
Few grains of salt
3 tablespoons caster sugar
½ pint cream

To make case, mix ¼ cup caster sugar with 1½ cups powdered vanilla wafers. Mix to a paste with about 5 tablespoons of hot melted butter. Press mixture all over the bottom and sides of a 9 inch pie plate or tin to give you a neat case with an upstanding rim. Bake in a slow oven, 325° F., for ¼ hour, then cool. Soften gelatine in water for 5 minutes. Drain juice from berries. Stir lemon juice into berries. Heat juice. Pour over soaked gelatine. Stir till

549

dissolved. Add salt and sugar. Leave till cold, then stir in berries. Chill till beginning to thicken, then whip and fold in cream. Turn into cold pie case. Chill. Garnish with whipped cream and extra berries. *For 6 persons.*

BLAEBERRY PIE (Tourte, Ecossaise)

1 lb. blaeberries
½ cup caster sugar
Pinch salt
1 tablespoon flour
Pinch ground cinnamon
¾ tablespoon melted butter
1 tablespoon lemon juice
8-10 oz. Fleur or short pastry

Pick over berries before weighing. Rinse and drain thoroughly. Mix sugar with the salt, flour and cinnamon. Stir lightly into the berries with butter and lemon juice. Line an 8 inch pie plate or tin with pastry ¼ inch thick. Prick well. Fill with blaeberry mixture. Cover in the usual way. Bake in a hot oven, 450° F., for about 20 minutes. Lower to moderate, 350° F., and bake for 20-25 minutes. Dredge with caster sugar. *For 5 or 6 persons.*

BUTTERSCOTCH PIE

1 baked pie shell, 9 inches across
2 oz. butter
¾ cup light brown sugar
2 cups milk
⅓ cup flour
¼ teaspoon salt
2 eggs
⅓ teaspoon vanilla essence

Cool case. Rinse a strong saucepan. Add butter. When it begins to melt, add the sugar. Cook, without stirring, for about 2 minutes, until into a rich, dark caramel syrup. Pour off about a cup of milk, and stir remainder of milk slowly into the syrup. Pour into the top of a double boiler. Stir over boiling water until nearly at boiling point. Cream flour with the reserved milk. Add salt. Stir into hot mixture. Cook over slowly boiling water for about ¼ hour, stirring constantly, then remove from stove. Beat eggs slightly. Stir in one at a time, then return pan to stove. Cook for about 2 minutes, stirring constantly. Remove from stove. Add vanilla essence. Stir occasionally till cold. Spoon into case. Decorate with whipped cream. *For 6 persons.*

BUTTERSCOTCH CREAM PIE

1 pie shell, 9 inches across
¾ tablespoon powdered gelatine
¼ cup cold water
1 rounded tablespoon butter
¾ cup light brown sugar
5 egg yolks
½ cup hot milk
¾ teaspoon vanilla essence
1 cup thick cream

Use a wafer-thin Fleur pastry case, or a crumb case. Soften gelatine for 5 minutes in the cold water. Melt butter slightly in a strong frying-pan. Add sugar. Cook until into a rich, dark syrup without stirring. Beat egg yolks. Gradually stir in hot milk, syrup and soaked gelatine. When blended, turn into the top of a double boiler. Cook over hot water until the mixture coats the back of a spoon, stirring constantly. Remove from heat. Cool, stirring occasionally, then add vanilla essence. Whip cream. Fold into mixture. Leave until thickened, but not set. Turn lightly into case. Decorate with trails or roses of whipped cream sweetened and flavoured with vanilla essence. *For 6 persons.*

CHERRY CREAM PIE (Tourte de Cerises à la Crème)

4-6 oz. shortcrust
Sieved breadcrumbs as required
1 can cherries
½ cup caster sugar
Pinch of ground cinnamon
1 egg yolk
3 tablespoons cream

Line a pie plate or tin, 9 inches across, thinly with the shortcrust. Prick and ornament rim with notching or fluting. Glaze edge. Sprinkle bottom evenly with sieved breadcrumbs. Arrange cherries on top. Mix sugar with the cinnamon and sprinkle over the fruit. Beat egg yolk well. Stir in cream and cherry juice. Pour over fruit. Bake in a fairly hot oven, 425° F., on a low shelf, till pastry is risen and set, in about 10 minutes. Lower heat to moderate, 350° F., and bake for about ½ hour till cherries are soft and pastry golden. Serve hot or cold. *For 6 persons.*

CHOCOLATE CHIFFON PIE
(Tourte de Chocolat, Américaine)

1 baked pastry case, 9 inches across
2 oz. unsweetened chocolate
½ cup strong black coffee
1 dessertspoon powdered gelatine
¼ cup cold water
3 egg yolks
1 cup caster sugar
Pinch of salt
¾ teaspoon vanilla essence
3 stiffly beaten egg whites

Place pastry case on serving dish. Grate chocolate. Heat coffee. Melt chocolate in the coffee. Soak gelatine for 5 minutes in the cold water. Add to coffee. Stir till dissolved. Beat egg yolks with half the sugar. Stir in salt and vanilla essence. Add to chocolate mixture. Stir till blended. Leave till cool. Beat remainder of sugar into egg whites. Fold into chocolate mixture. Turn into cold pastry case. Chill for 3-4 hours till set. Decorate with trails, roses, or swirls of whipped cream. *For 6 persons.*

CHOCOLATE CREAM PIE
(Tourte de Chocolat à la Crème)

1 baked pastry case, 9 inches across
2 oz. grated chocolate
2 cups milk
¼ cup cornflour
Pinch of salt
1 tablespoon butter
3 separated eggs
1 cup caster sugar
1 teaspoon vanilla essence

Bake pastry case only lightly. Melt chocolate in the top of a double boiler over boiling water. Stir milk slowly into cornflour and salt, and add to chocolate. Boil for 2 or 3 minutes, stirring constantly, until thick and smooth, then add butter. Beat egg yolks and sugar in a basin. Stir in hot mixture. Return to double boiler. Cook over boiling water, stirring constantly, for 1 minute. Cool. Stir in vanilla essence. Beat egg whites till stiff. Fold into mixture. Pile into hot pastry shell. Bake in a slow oven, 300° F., until when knife is inserted, it comes out clean, in about 20 minutes. Remove from oven. Cool at room temperature from 3-4 hours. Decorate or serve with whipped cream. *For 6 persons.*

COCONUT CREAM PIE (Tourte de Coco, Américaine)

1 baked pastry case, 9 inches across

Cool pastry case. Mix sugar with cornflour and salt. Gradually stir in milk. When smooth, turn

5 oz. caster sugar
¼ cup cornflour
1 saltspoon salt
2 cups scalded milk
3 egg yolks
1 oz. butter
¼ teaspoon vanilla essence
1 cup grated coconut
Coconut meringue

into top of double boiler. Stir over boiling water till thick in 8-10 minutes. Beat egg yolks slightly. Stir in a little of the hot mixture, then stir this into the mixture remaining in double boiler. Cook over hot water for 4 or 5 minutes, stirring constantly, then remove from heat. Cool slightly. Add butter and vanilla essence. Stir till butter is dissolved, then stir in coconut. Pour into pastry case. Spread with meringue mixture, piling it up lightly. Bake in a moderate oven, 350° F., for about ¼ hour. Sprinkle, if liked, with ½ cup desiccated coconut. *For 6 persons.*

Coconut Meringue: Stir 2 egg whites into ¼ lb. caster sugar. Place in the top of a double boiler. Add a pinch of salt and 1½ tablespoons water. Beat with egg beater till thoroughly blended, then cook over boiling water for about 1 minute, beating constantly. Remove from heat. Beat from 1-2 minutes longer, till mixture holds its shape. If liked, grated fresh coconut can be substituted for desiccated if toasted in a moderately hot oven, 400° F., till it starts to turn golden brown, before sprinkling over meringue.

CUSTARD PIE (Tourte à la Crème)

BASIC RECIPE:
Pastry
4 eggs
2 oz. caster sugar
Pinch of salt
½ teaspoon vanilla essence
3 cups milk

Make case with shortcrust, Fleur pastry or spiced shortcrust, using 5 oz. flour and other ingredients in proportion. See recipes. The rim must be upstanding. Prick well. Glaze edge. Beat eggs thoroughly. Stir in sugar and salt. Gradually stir in vanilla essence and milk. Pour into pastry case. Bake in a hot oven, 450° F., for about 10 minutes, then lower to moderate, 350° F., and bake about 25 minutes longer, till a hot knife comes out clean when inserted in the middle. *For 6 persons.*

Caramel Custard Pie: Melt sugar in a strong, wet frying-pan until into a rich brown syrup. Heat milk. Stir in syrup and 2 oz. more sugar. Mix eggs with salt. Gradually stir in caramel milk and vanilla essence. Follow basic recipe.

EGG NOG PIE (Tourte, Egg Nog)

1 baked pastry case, 9 inches across
1 tablespoon powdered gelatine
2 tablespoons cold water
1 pint thin cream
Pinch of salt
5½ oz. caster sugar
3 beaten egg yolks
1 teaspoon vanilla essence
1 saltspoon almond essence
3 egg whites

Make the pastry case of rich shortcrust, Fleur or nut pastry. Soak gelatine in cold water for 5 minutes. Heat cream nearly to boiling point in the top of a double boiler. Stir salt and half the sugar into egg yolks. Beat till fluffy. Stir in a little of the cream. When blended, stir into remaining cream in double boiler. Cook over hot water, stirring constantly, until mixture coats the back of a spoon in about 8 minutes. Stir in vanilla and almond essence, and gelatine. When blended, remove from heat and chill till beginning to stiffen. Beat egg whites till stiff. Gradually stir in remainder of sugar. Fold into egg cream. Pour into baked case. Decorate with daisies of maraschino cherry petals, and with angelica stems. *For 6 persons.*

GUERNSEY PIE (Tourte, Guernsey)

1 pastry case, 9 inches across
Apricot or raspberry jam
4 sponge cakes
½ gill sherry
3 separated eggs
½ pint tepid milk
Caster sugar as required

Prick the pastry case well with a fork. Spread a thick layer of jam over the bottom. Halve sponge cakes and soak in the sherry. Arrange on top of the jam. Beat egg yolks. Stir in milk. Pour into the top of a double boiler. Stir over hot water until custard coats the back of a spoon, then remove from heat and add sugar to taste. Stir until dissolved. Cool slightly. Pour over cakes. Bake in a moderate oven, 350° F., for about 1 hour. Beat egg whites to a stiff froth. Stir in 4 tablespoons of caster sugar. Spread lightly on pudding. Continue to bake in oven for about 10 minutes until meringue is set and tipped with gold. Chill and serve. *For 6 persons.*

LEMON CHIFFON PIE (Tourte au Citron, Chiffoné)

1 small tablespoon powdered gelatine
¼ cup cold water
4 beaten egg yolks
1 cup caster sugar
½ cup strained lemon juice
¼ teaspoon salt
1 teaspoon grated lemon rind
4 egg whites
1 baked pastry case, 9 inches across

Soften gelatine in cold water for 5 minutes. Beat egg yolks until perfectly blended. Beat in half the sugar and all the lemon juice and salt. Cook in the top of a double boiler over boiling water, stirring constantly, until the mixture coats the back of a spoon. Stir in lemon rind and softened gelatine. When blended, remove to a basin. Leave until beginning to thicken, but not set. Beat egg whites until stiff. Beat in remainder of sugar. Fold lightly into the lemon cream. Pile into pastry case. Chill. Decorate with fluffy spoonfuls of whipped cream, allowing 1 cup cream before whipping, and vanilla essence to taste. Sweeten with 2 tablespoons sifted icing sugar. *For 6 persons.*

Lemon Chiffon Cream Pie: Follow recipe for Lemon Chiffon Pie, but before chilling, fold in 1 cup thick cream stiffly whipped, in which case, omit decorating with cream.

LEMON MERINGUE PIE (Tourte de Citron, Américaine)

2½ tablespoons cornflour
1 tablespoon flour
1 cup cold water
4 tablespoons lemon juice
Grated rind of ½ lemon
¾ cup caster sugar
Pinch of salt
1 tablespoon butter
2 separated eggs

Mix cornflour and flour to a cream with a little of the water. Stir in remainder of water, lemon juice, rind, caster sugar and salt. Pour into the top of a double boiler. Stir constantly till thick and boiling. Cook gently for 8-10 minutes, still stirring, then remove from heat. Cool slightly. Add butter. Stir till dissolved. Beat egg yolks. Stir into mixture. Stir over boiling water for 2

1 thin baked pastry case, 9
inches across
4 tablespoons sifted icing sugar

or 3 minutes. Pile into pastry case. Beat egg whites till stiff. Fold in icing sugar, and a squeeze of lemon juice if liked. Pile roughly over filling. Bake in a slow oven, 350° F., till meringue is set, in about 15 minutes. Cool at kitchen temperature out of a draught. *For 6 persons.*

MINCE PIE (Tourte de Fruit)

There are various ways of making a large mince pie.
1. Fill a pastry-lined pie plate or sandwich tin with mincemeat. Cover with pastry lid. Decorate rim. Prick all over with a fork. Glaze and bake in a hot oven, 450° F., for about 20 minutes.
2. Follow method No. 1, but cover filling with narrow strips of pastry, cut out with a pie crimper, or twisted. Cross with the same number of strips prepared like the first. Bake as above.

FARMHOUSE APPLE OR GOOSEBERRY PLATE PIE

Roll out thinly, shortcrust made with butter and flour, allowing ½ lb. butter to 1 lb. flour. Cut into 4 rounds the size of a dinner plate. Place two of the rounds a little apart on a greased baking sheet. Spread with sliced apples or gooseberries to within 1 inch of the edge. Sprinkle with sugar to taste. Dredge lightly with flour to prevent the juice escaping. Brush edges of filled rounds with cold water and cover each with a second round. Notch edges with thumbs and forefingers. Bake in a hot oven, 450° F., for about ½ hour. Cool. Dust with icing sugar, using vanilla-flavoured when possible. Serve cold. *For 6 persons.*

RASPBERRY CHIFFON PIE
(Tourte de Framboises, Chiffone)

¾ tablespoon powdered gelatine
¼ cup cold water
½ cup hot water
½ cup strained raspberry jam
3 separated eggs
Pinch of salt
1½ tablespoon lemon juice
A few drops of cochineal
1 baked pastry case, 9 inches across

Soak gelatine in cold water for 5 minutes. Add hot water. Stir till dissolved. Stir in jam. Beat egg yolks till blended. Stir into mixture with salt, lemon juice and cochineal. Cool until mixture starts to congeal. Beat egg whites till stiff. Fold into mixture. Pour into pastry case. Chill. Decorate with whipped cream if liked, and berries. *For 6 persons.*

RHUBARB CREAM PIE (Tourte de Rhubarbe à la Crème)

½-¾ lb. Fleur pastry
1 pint stewed rhubarb
1 cup caster sugar
Grated rind of 1 orange
½ oz. butter

Make pastry case 9 inches across. Prick and ornament. Heat rhubarb in the top of a double boiler. Stir in sugar, orange rind and butter. Blend the cornflour with cold water and stir into

1 tablespoon cornflour
1 tablespoon cold water
3 egg yolks

mixture. Stir over boiling water till the sauce coats the back of a spoon. Beat egg yolks. Stir in sauce. When blended, pour into case. Cover with a solid pastry lid or with criss-cross strips of pastry. Bake in a moderately hot oven, 375° F., for ¼ hour, then lower to moderate, 350° F., and bake for about ½ hour. *For 6 persons.*

SHOO-FLY PIE (Tourte, Américaine)

6 oz. shortcrust
1 cup cornflakes
¾ cup golden syrup
¾ cup water
¾ teaspoon baking soda
¼ lb. flour
1 cup crushed cornflakes
¾ cup brown sugar
½ cup butter or margarine

Line a pie plate or sandwich tin, 9 inches across, thinly with shortcrust. Ornament edges with forefinger and thumbs. Prick insides. Sprinkle with the cornflakes. Mix syrup with the water in a saucepan, stirring constantly, over slow heat, until blended, then remove from stove. Stir in soda. Mix flour with crushed cornflakes and sugar. Rub in fat until mixture looks like coarse crumbs. Pour syrup into pastry case. Sprinkle with crumb mixture. Bake in a fairly hot oven, 425° F., for ¼ hour, then lower to moderate, 350° F. Bake until firm, from 20-30 minutes. Dredge with caster sugar. Serve hot or cold. *For 6 persons.*

STRAWBERRY CHIFFON PIE (Tourte de Fraises, Chiffoné)

1 baked pastry case, 9 inches across
4 egg yolks
½ cup golden syrup
Pinch of salt
Juice of 1 lemon
Grated rind ½ lemon
¾ tablespoon powdered gelatine
3 tablespoons cold water
4 egg whites
½ cup caster sugar
1 cup halved strawberries

Leave pastry case till cool. Mix egg yolks with the syrup, salt, lemon juice and rind. When blended, stir in the top of a double boiler for 1 minute, then beat with an egg beater till foamy in about 2 minutes. Remove from heat. Soften gelatine for 5 minutes in cold water. Stir into custard. Leave till cool. Beat egg whites till stiff. Gradually beat in sugar. When stiff, fold gently into the jelly, then fold in strawberries. Pile into pastry case. Decorate on top with large halved berries or with whipped, sweetened cream flavoured with vanilla, and berries. *For 6 persons.*

VEGETABLE MARROW PIE (Tourte de Courge)

4-6 oz. pastry
¼ pint milk
2 oz. caster sugar
¼ teaspoon ground mace
1 teaspoon melted butter
Pinch of salt
1 cup sieved cooked marrow
1 teaspoon ground ginger
¼ teaspoon ground cinnamon
2 eggs

Line a 9 inch pie plate with pastry, and prick bottom with a fork. Brush with beaten egg white. Mix all the ingredients together. Beat well. Bake in a hot oven, 450° F., for 5 or 10 minutes, then reduce heat to 325° F., and bake for about 35 minutes, until set. Decorate with spokes of whipped cream, and crystallized ginger if liked. *For 6 persons.*

555

WINE CHIFFON PIE (Tourte au Vin)

1 small tablespoon powdered gelatine
¼ cup cold water
1 cup milk
1 cup thin cream
3 separated eggs
Caster sugar as required
¼ teaspoon salt
2 tablespoons rum or sherry
1 dessertspoon chopped maraschino cherries
1 baked pastry case, 9 inches across

Soften gelatine in cold water. Heat milk with the cream till nearly boiling. Beat egg yolks slightly. Beat in ¼ cup of caster sugar and salt. Stir in milk and cream gradually. Pour into the top of a double boiler. Cook over hot water until mixture coats the back of a spoon, stirring constantly. Remove from stove. Add gelatine. Stir till dissolved. Cool. Stir in rum or sherry. Chill. Beat egg whites till stiff. Beat in 3 tablespoons caster sugar. When the gelatine mixture begins to congeal, fold in egg whites and cherries. Fill pastry case. Decorate with shaved chocolate or chocolate shot. Chill. *For 6 persons.*

FRUIT FLAN (Flan de Fruit)

BASIC RECIPE:
1 baked pastry case, 7, 8 or 9 inches across
Fresh, bottled or canned or cooked fruit

Prepare plain, or rich shortcrust, Fleur, Muerbeteig or nut pastry, in a quantity according to size of flan required or amount of filling available. See pages 519-541 for recipes. Prepare fruit according to whether it is fresh, bottled, canned or cooked. Cool pastry case. Add prepared fruit. If using fresh fruit such as raspberries or strawberries, trickle hot apricot glaze over, allowing just enough to set fruit, 1 teaspoon to 4 raspberries or strawberries. If using bottled, canned or stewed fruit, set with dissolved gelatine or with arrowroot creamed with cold water added to syrup, stirred till boiling and cooled before pouring over fruit.

Apricot Glaze: Stir equal quantity of apricot jam and water in a pan till boiling.

To Set Fruit with Arrowroot: If using fresh fruit, pour ¼ pint water into a saucepan. Add 1½ oz. sugar and ½ teaspoon lemon juice. (If liked, stir in 1 level dessertspoon apple, gooseberry or red currant jelly to impart flavour and colour.) Stir over heat until sugar is dissolved. Bring to boil. Boil for 5 minutes. Cream 1 teaspoon arrowroot with cold water and stir into syrup. Stir until boiling. Remove from stove. Add a drop or two of cochineal if setting red fruit. If setting apricots, peaches, or yellow fruit, substitute the melted jelly from lemon or lime marmalade for the red jelly, and add green or yellow colouring. Cool slightly. Pour over fresh fruit. If required for setting bottled, cooked or canned fruit, substitute the juice for the water. If necessary, make it up to ¼ pint with water. Leave until cold, then pour over fruit in case.

To Set with Gelatine: Heat 1 teaspoon powdered gelatine in a small saucepan with ¼ pint fruit juice. Stir over slow heat until dissolved, then sweeten with sugar to taste. Stir again over slow heat until dissolved. Cool until ready to congeal, then pour over fruit. Chill until set, before serving.

To Set with Jelly: Arrange fruit in baked case. Dissolve a jelly according to instructions on packet, choosing a jelly that either tones or contrasts with the fruit, such as strawberry jelly with strawberries, lemon jelly with apricots or peaches, or strawberry jelly with pears. Pour over fruit when ready to set.

APPLE FLAN (Flan de Pommes)

1 baked flan case, 9 inches across
¾-1 lb. apples
3 tablespoons water
Demerara sugar to taste
3 tablespoons tangerine marmalade
3oz. macaroon biscuits

Brush bottom of flan case with egg white before baking. Peel, core and slice apples into a saucepan. Add water and sugar to taste. Cover. Stew gently till beginning to soften, but do not allow to become mushy, then drain. Beat marmalade till it thins. Crush macaroons and stir in the marmalade. Spread half of this mixture in pastry case. Cover with the apples, then spread remainder of macaroon mixture on top. Bake for 7 or 8 minutes in a moderate oven, 350° F., till crisp. *For 6 persons.*

BANANA FLAN (Flan de Bananes)

1 baked flan case, 9 inches across
4 bananas
Juice of 1 orange
6 oz. caster sugar
¾ gill water
4 halved glacé cherries
1 cup whipped cream

Cool pastry case. Use large bananas. Pour orange juice into a saucepan. Add sugar and water. Stir till sugar is dissolved. Bring to boil. Boil for 10 minutes. Chill. Peel bananas and remove loose threads. Cut in thickish slices. Arrange overlapping in circles. Pour chilled syrup over. Leave for 10 minutes, then decorate with cherries and whipped cream. *For 6 persons.*

PEACH FLAN (Flan de Pêches)

1 large can peaches
1 baked pastry case, 9 inches across
2 oz. caster sugar
2 tablespoons cornflour
¼ cup orange juice
1 teaspoon grated orange rind
½ oz. butter
Few grains of salt

Drain syrup from peaches. Slice peaches. Arrange in pastry case. Mix sugar and cornflour. Place in a saucepan. Add syrup. Cook till thick, stirring constantly. Remove from heat. Stir in orange juice, rind, butter and salt. Pour over peaches. Chill. Decorate with whipped cream and sliced peaches. *For 6 persons.*

PEAR FLAN (Flan de Poires)

Fingers of cooked pear of equal thickness
1 baked pastry case, 9 inches across
¼ pint pear syrup
¼ oz. powdered gelatine
Cream to decorate

Arrange fingers of pear in the shape of a wheel in pastry case. (If preferred, arrange half pears with stalk ends to centre.) Place half the syrup in a small saucepan. Add sugar if required. Bring to boil. Soften gelatine in remainder of cold syrup. Stir into hot syrup. When dissolved, remove from heat and leave till beginning to thicken, then pour over fruit in case. Decorate with a rose of cream in centre of each. *For 6 persons.*

SWEDISH APPLE FLAN (Flan de Pommes, Suédoise)

1 baked flan case, 9 inches across

Cool pastry case. Peel and core apples. Slice and stew them till soft with 6 oz. of the sugar, then

1 lb. tart apples
½ lb. caster sugar
2 teaspoons shredded orange peel
2 teaspoons minced baked almonds
1 dessertspoon crushed ratafias
2 egg whites

pass through a wire sieve. Add peel, almonds, and ratafias. Fill case with mixture. Beat egg whites to a stiff froth. Lightly stir in remainder of sugar. Pile on top of filling. Bake in a moderate oven, 350° F., for about ¼ hour, till pale gold. Serve hot or cold with custard sauce or cream. *For 6 persons*

APRICOT ROLY POLY (Roulade des Abricots)

PASTRY :
½ lb. flour
½ teaspoon salt
3 teaspoons baking powder
2½ oz. butter
1 oz. caster sugar
1 beaten egg yolk
⅓ cup milk

FILLING :
2 oz. butter
1 can apricots in syrup

Sift flour, salt and baking powder into a basin. Rub in fat. Stir in sugar. Mix to a dough with egg yolk and milk. Roll out on a lightly floured board, into an oblong, about ½ inch thick. Beat 2 oz. butter to a cream. Spread carefully over the pastry to within 1 inch of the edges. Drain syrup from apricots. Cut each apricot in four. Arrange over the pastry. Dredge with a little caster sugar. Roll up. Tie in a pudding cloth. Steam for 1¼ hours. Untie and serve on a hot dish, with heated syrup in a sauceboat. *For 6 persons*.

BAKEWELL TART (Tourte, Bakewell)

½ lb. shortcrust
2 tablespoons jam
¼ lb. butter
¼ lb. caster sugar
3 egg yolks
1 egg white
3 drops almond essence
2 oz. ground almonds or cake crumbs

Line pie plate, 9 inches across, with pastry. Prick well. Ornament edge. Spread apricot, blackcurrant or raspberry jam or lemon curd over the inside. (If you wish to use a pie dish, line only the sides and rim with pastry. Decorate edges.) Sometimes I put a layer of raspberry jam in the bottom and cover it with lemon curd. Beat butter to a cream. Beat in sugar, and egg yolks, one at a time. Beat egg white slightly with the almond essence, and stir in with almonds or crumbs. Mix well. Pour into case. Bake in a fairly hot oven, 425° F., on the centre shelf, for about 20 minutes, then lower to moderate, 350° F., and bake for about 10 minutes. Serve hot for dinner or cold for tea. *For 6 persons*.

EPSOM ROLY POLY (Roulade, Epsom)

¾ lb. suet crust
½ lb. golden syrup
1 oz. currants
½ oz. minced candied peel

Roll pastry on a lightly floured board into an oblong ¼ inch thick. Spread with syrup to within 1 inch of the edge. Sprinkle with currants and peel. (If liked, grate a little nutmeg or sprinkle a little cinnamon over filling.) Roll up. Place, join downwards, in a floured pudding cloth. Tie at both ends. Boil for 2 hours. Untie. Serve with hot custard sauce. *For 6 persons*.

HARVEST FLAN (Tourte Surprise)

1 pastry case, 9 inches across
5 oz. flour
½ lb. butter or margarine
1 cup caster sugar
1 saltspoon grated nutmeg
1 slightly beaten egg
Grated rind of ½ lemon
3 tablespoons lemon juice
½ cup golden syrup
½ teaspoon bicarbonate of soda
½ cup hot water

Sieve flour into a basin. Rub in butter or margarine. Stir in sugar and nutmeg. (This will give you a crumby consistency.) Mix the egg with the lemon rind, lemon juice and syrup. Dissolve soda in the hot water and stir into syrup mixture. Pour filling into pastry case. Sprinkle crumb mixture evenly on top. Bake in a hot oven, 450° F., for about 10 minutes, then lower to moderate, 350° F., for ½ hour longer. When ready, the top of pie should be golden brown, and there should be a layer of jelly between the crust and the top. *For 6 persons.*

JAM TART (Tourte de Confiture)

1 pastry case, 9 inches across
Jam as required

Use Fleur or shortcrust. Prepare pastry case. See page 546. Prick well with a fork. Fill up with jam to taste. If liked, make a criss-cross or lattice-work of pastry over the top. Cover rim with a strip of pastry, so as to conceal the ends of lattice-work. Ornament it with a fork. Brush with slightly beaten egg white or water. Sprinkle with caster sugar. Bake in a hot oven, 450° F., for 20-25 minutes. *For 6 persons.*

KENTISH CURRANT PUDDING (Pouding, Canterbury)

1 lb. self-raising flour
6 oz. shredded suet
6 oz. cleaned currants
Cold water or milk
8 oz. unsalted butter
2 tablespoons light brown sugar
Squeeze of lemon juice if liked

Sift flour into a basin. Stir in suet and currants with a pinch of salt. Mix to a dough with cold water or milk. Roll to 1½ inch thickness. Carefully line a greased pudding basin. Place the butter in the centre. Pack the sugar round. Sprinkle with lemon juice. Brush edge of lining with cold water. Roll remainder of pastry out to fit. Lay on top. Press edges together. Cover with greased paper. Steam for about 3½ hours. Serve with custard sauce. *For 8 persons.*

MANCHESTER TART (Tourte, Manchester)

½ lb. flaky, rough puff or puff pastry
2-3 tablespoons apricot, peach or raspberry jam
½ pint milk
1 lemon rind
2 oz. breadcrumbs
2 separated eggs
2 oz. butter
1-2 oz. caster sugar
1 tablespoon brandy

Roll out pastry very thinly and line a greased pie dish. Decorate the rim. Spread bottom thinly with jam. Pour milk into a saucepan. Add lemon rind. Bring to boil. Pour over breadcrumbs. Soak for 5 minutes, then remove lemon rind. Beat egg yolks. Add to crumbs with the butter and sugar. If liked, add 2 or 3 drops of lemon or dish. Place dish in a shallow baking tin containing a little hot water. Bake in a slow oven, 300° F., for ¾ hour. Beat egg whites till stiff and make into a meringue, with 4 tablespoons additional sugar. Pile on top. Bake in a slow oven, 325° F., for about 20 minutes. Serve cold with cream. *For 6 persons.*

MARZIPAN TART (Tourte, Marie-Antoinette)

½ lb. shortcrust
¼ lb. sifted icing sugar
¼ lb. ground almonds
Juice ½ lemon
1 egg white
Canned cherries or apricot jam
  as required

Roll pastry into a neat round to fit the base of a greased layer cake tin. Mix icing sugar in a basin with the almonds and strained lemon juice, then stir in enough stiffly beaten egg white to make a stiff paste. Dredge pastry board with caster sugar. Roll mixture out and cut into strips. Make 2 strips the width of the pastry in tin and lay across each other with ends equal distance apart, on cake. Cut enough short strips to reach from the centre to the edge, and arrange like the spokes of a wheel in between the crossed strips. Arrange a long strip all round the cake. Bake in a rather slow oven, 325° F., for ¾-1 hour. When ready, fill the spaces between the spokes with canned cherries, or with apricot jam. Dust with icing sugar. *For 4 or 5 persons.*

TREACLE TART (Tourte d'Or)

½ lb. shortcrust
3 oz. fine breadcrumbs
½ cup golden syrup
Grated rind 1 lemon
Strained juice 1 lemon

Make pastry case, 9 inches across. Prick bottom. Mix crumbs with the syrup, lemon rind and juice. Spread evenly in case. If you have any strips of pastry left over, cover filling with lattice-work. Bake near the bottom of a fairly hot oven, 425° F., for about ½ hour. It may be necessary to remove tart at the end of 20 minutes to top of oven to brown. *For 6 persons.*

VATRUSHKI

½ lb. curd
1 beaten egg
2 tablespoons caster sugar
Vanilla essence to taste
1 pastry case, 8 inches across

Place curd in a basin. Stir in egg, sugar and vanilla essence to taste. Make pastry case of shortcrust, Fleur or Muerbeteig pastry. See page 541-542. Spread filling smoothly inside. Bake in a moderately hot oven, 375° F., for about 35 minutes. *For 6 persons.*

SMALL PASTRIES

Pastry for cheese cakes, tartlets and other small pastries to be baked, is generally rolled ⅛ inch thick. Use any pastry you like for cases, but Fleur, Muerbeteig, and shortcrust should be used unless other suggestions are made in recipes. Cases can be rounded, boat-shaped or fluted. When baking a case, prick any blisters which appear as soon as noticed.

Choux Pastry is used for éclairs, cream buns, etc.

Flaky or Rough Puff Pastry can be used for turnovers unless otherwise instructed, mince pies, certain cheese cakes, etc.

Puff Pastry is used for horns, milles feuilles, etc.

Shortcrust is used most generally for small pastries.

To Make Cheese Cakes or Tartlet Cases: Roll pastry ⅛ inch thick. Cut into plain or fluted rounds, or boat shapes, according to taste, slightly larger than the tins, taking into account the depth of the tins.

To Make Cases:

1. Invert tins. Fit rounds or ovals over tins according to shape. Trim edges neatly. Prick all over with a fork. Arrange tins with pastry side upwards, on a baking sheet. Bake in a hot oven, 450° F., for about 13 minutes, until delicately browned. Remove from tins and cool before filling.

2. Line tins neatly with pastry. Press it very gently with thumbs against the bottom and sides of each tin to make certain that all air is excluded. Prick insides thoroughly with a fork. Chill for ½ hour. (If making cases of puff, rough puff or flaky pastry you can line each case with greased paper and half fill with rice to prevent pastry rising.) Bake in a hot oven, 450° F., for about 6 minutes, until pastry is almost cooked and edges have begun to brown. Remove from oven if dry in centres. If not, leave for 4 or 5 minutes to dry before taking out and filling.

To Decorate Filled Tartlets:

1. Cover fillings such as jam, fruit, etc. with a cross composed of very narrow cross-strips of pastry, baked beforehand.

2. Decorate with meringue. Bake in a moderate oven, 450° F., for about 12 minutes.

3. Decorate with whipped cream, sweetened and flavoured with vanilla to taste, then with chocolate shot, or a glacé cherry cut to resemble a flower, with leaves of angelica.

APPLE DUMPLINGS (Pommes de Pommes)

BASIC RECIPE :
¾ lb. shortcrust
6 medium-sized cooking apples
Caster or brown sugar to taste

Roll shortcrust out thinly. Cut into 6 rounds, large enough to cover apples. Peel and core apples. Place one apple on the centre of each round. Pack hollows in each with caster, light brown or Demerara sugar. Brush edge of each round in turn with cold water, and draw up edges over top of apple and twist to the right. Place, a little apart, twist downwards, on a greased baking tin or fireproof dish. Brush lightly with milk. Bake in a moderately hot oven, 375° F., for about 25 minutes. When almost ready, brush each with water and sprinkle with caster sugar, then finish baking. Serve with custard sauce. *For 6 persons.*

To Steam: Substitute suet crust for pastry. Prepare dumplings as described, but tie each one in a pudding cloth lined with greased paper. Steam for about ¾ hour. Serve with custard sauce.

To Vary Fillings:

1. Use light brown sugar mixed to taste with cleaned currants. Flavour with ground cinnamon if liked.

2. Mix brown sugar to a paste with butter or margarine. Allow 1 tablespoon paste per apple. If liked, insert a clove in the filling.

3. Fill with apple, gooseberry, red currant jelly, or honey.

4. Use mincemeat.

APPLE SAUCER PIES (Pâtés de Pommes)

½ lb. shortcrust
½ lb. cooking apples
Sugar to taste

Roll pastry out thinly on a floured board and line and decorate 4 small greased sandwich tins or enamel plates. Peel, core and slice apples. Place half of them on the "crusts." Sprinkle with sugar to taste, mixed with ground cinnamon if liked. Cover with remaining apples, then with a second round of pastry. Press edges together. Ornament. Make holes with a skewer on top of each. Bake on a baking sheet in the centre of a fairly hot oven, 425° F., for about ½ hour. *Yield:* 4 saucer pies.

APRICOT CHEESE CAKES (Talmouses d'Abricots, Anglaise)

6 oz. rough puff pastry
Apricot jam as required
1 egg
Butter, sugar and flour
1 saltspoon baking powder
2 drops almond essence

Line about 15 patty tins thinly with pastry. Prick well. Chill. Place ½ teaspoon apricot jam in the centre of each. Weigh egg, then weigh the weight of the egg in butter, caster sugar and flour. Beat butter till softened. Gradually beat in sugar. Beat egg. Sift flour with baking powder. Add egg and flour alternately to the butter mixture, beating between each addition, then the essence. Place a teaspoon of the batter in each case, covering the jam. Bake on a baking sheet, in a fairly hot oven, 425° F., for about 20 minutes. *Yield:* About 15 cheese cakes.

APRICOT DUMPLINGS (Pommes d'Abricots)

6 oz. flour
3 teaspoons baking powder
½ teaspoon salt
¼ lb. butter or margarine
⅓ cup milk
1 can apricots
2 dessertspoons caster sugar
6 pats of butter

Sift flour, baking powder and salt into a basin. Rub in fat with the tips of the fingers, then stir in just enough milk to make a soft dough. Roll out to less than a ¼ inch thickness. Divide into 6 equal portions or rounds with a cutter. Place 2 apricots, one on top of the other, cup sides together, on part of each piece. Sprinkle with sugar. Brush edges of dough with water and twist together over the top of fruit like apple dumplings. Place, twist downwards, in a greased baking tin. Sprinkle again with sugar and dab a pat of butter on the top of each. Bake in a moderate oven, 350° F., for about 20 minutes. (If you use the trimmings of pastry, you will need 6 more apricots. This will give you 3 more dumplings.) *Yield:* 6 or 9 dumplings.

BALMORAL TARTLETS (Tartelettes, Balmoral)

½ lb. shortcrust
1 oz. butter
1 oz. caster sugar
1 separated egg
½ oz. sponge cake crumbs
½ oz. chopped glacé cherries
½ oz. minced candied orange peel

Roll out and line patty tins thinly with shortcrust. Prick well. Chill. Beat butter till softened. Add sugar. Beat until creamy. Stir in egg yolk, crumbs, cherries, peel and cornflour. Beat egg white until stiff. Fold in lightly. Pile into cases. Cover each with a cross-cut of pastry, sealing the ends to the lining with cold water or slightly beaten egg white.

¾ oz. cornflour

Bake in a moderately hot oven, 400° F., for about 20 minutes. *Yield:* About 20 tartlets.

BANBURY PUFFS (Pouffes à la Banbury)

1 oz. butter
½ oz. flour
1 tablespoon brandy
¼ lb. currants
½ oz. mixed peel
2 oz. moist sugar
Pinch of allspice
Pinch of cinnamon
1 egg yolk
Flaky pastry as required

Melt butter in a saucepan. Add flour and brandy. Cook till thick. Cool, then add washed and dried currants, chopped peel, sugar, spices and egg yolk. Roll pastry thinly. Cut into 5-inch rounds. Spread a dessertspoon of the mixture over half of each round. Wet edges with cold water, then turn other half of round on top. Press edges together. Decorate round the edges with the back of a fork. Prick on top. Dust with caster sugar, or place mixture in the centres of pastry rounds, and draw the edges together over the top. Turn over. Roll each lightly before baking. Place on a wet tin. Cook in a hot oven, 450° F., for about 25 minutes, till crisp and brown.

BRIDESMAIDS (Dames d'Honneur)

¼ lb. Fleur pastry
Raspberry jam as required
2 egg whites
2-3 oz. caster sugar
2 oz. ground almonds
2 drops ratafia essence

Line patty tins thinly with pastry. Prick well. Place a teaspoon of raspberry jam in the bottom of each. Beat egg whites till very stiff. Stir in sugar. Beat again for 10 minutes, then stir in ground almonds and ratafia essence. Place a spoonful of mixture in each lined case. Brush lightly with slightly beaten egg white. Bake in a hot oven, 450° F., for 10 minutes, then lower to moderately slow, 325° F., and bake for about 10 minutes, till crisp and golden. *Yield:* About 6 tartlets, 2½ inches across.

BUTTER TARTLETS (Tartelettes, Canadienne)

4 oz. shortcrust
1 tablespoon butter
¾ cup caster sugar
2 eggs
1½ cups currants or sultanas
1 teaspoon vanilla essence

Line small patty tins with shortcrust. Prick well. Beat butter and sugar to a cream. Drop in eggs and beat thoroughly. Stir in cleaned fruit and essence. Put some mixture in each case, half filling it. Bake in a hot oven, 450° F., for about 15 minutes. *Yield:* About 6 tarts.

BUTTER ALMOND TARTLETS (Tartelettes au Beurre)

1½ dozen baked, small tartlet cases
¼ lb. icing sugar
2 oz. butter
2 oz. ground almonds
½ lemon
Crystallized cherries as required

Cool cases. Beat half the sugar to a cream with the butter. Add remainder of sugar and beat till fluffy. Stir in almonds. Grate lemon rind. Stir into mixture with enough lemon juice to moisten. Place a teaspoon of the mixture into each case. Decorate with a crystallized cherry. *Yield:* 1½ dozen tartlets.

CHOCOLATE TARTLETS (Tartelettes de Chocolat)

6 pricked tartlet cases
¾ oz. sweet chocolate
½ gill milk
½ teaspoon cornflour
½ teaspoon butter
1 large or 2 small egg yolks
1 teaspoon caster sugar
Pinch of ground cinnamon or cloves

Place lined tartlet tins on a baking sheet. Melt chocolate in half the milk. Mix cornflour to a cream with remainder of milk. Stir into chocolate mixture. Boil till thickened, stirring constantly, then remove from heat. Stir in butter, egg yolk or yolks, sugar, cinnamon or cloves, and 2 or 3 drops of vanilla essence if liked. Half fill tartlet tins. Bake in a fairly hot oven, 425° F., for about 8 minutes. Lower to moderate, 350° F., and bake till firm, in about ¼ hour. When cold, swirl each on top with meringue (made with 1 large or two small egg whites and 3 oz. caster sugar), coming to a point on the centre. Decorate with chips of glacé cherries and angelica. Cook in a cool oven, 250° F., for about 40 minutes, till crisp, but not discoloured. *Yield:* 6 tartlets.

COCONUT CHEESE CAKES (Talmouses de Coco)

½ lb. short or Fleur pastry
2 oz. butter
2 oz. caster sugar
1 beaten egg
1 oz. rice flour or ground rice
2 oz. desiccated coconut
¼ teaspoon baking powder
Jam to taste

Line 12 tartlet tins, 2½ inches across, thinly with pastry. Prick well. Beat butter till softened. Gradually beat in sugar. When fluffy, stir in egg and rice flour or ground rice. Beat well. Stir in coconut and baking powder. Place a small teaspoon of apricot or raspberry jam in each case. Half fill with the batter. Bake in fairly hot oven, 425° F., for about 20 minutes. *Yield:* 12 tartlets.

COFFEE CHEESE CAKES (Talmouses au Café)

About ½ lb. short or flaky pastry
1 egg
Butter and sugar as required
1 oz. cleaned sultanas
1½ oz. flour
1 oz. ground rice
Coffee essence to taste
Butter icing as required

Line 15 boat-shaped tins thinly with pastry. Prick well. Put a small teaspoon of apricot, or raspberry jam in the bottom of each. Before beating egg, weigh out its weight first in butter or margarine, then in caster sugar. Beat egg. Beat fat till softened, then gradually beat in sugar. Stir in egg quickly. Beat well. Stir in sultanas. Sift flour and ground rice. Add to fat mixture with coffee essence to taste. Two-thirds fill lined tins. Bake in a hot oven on a baking sheet for about ¼ hour, 450° F. Turn out carefully. Leave till cold. Decorate with butter icing made with 2 oz. butter and 4 oz. icing sugar with coffee or vanilla essence to taste. Sprinkle with chopped nuts. *Yield:* 15 tartlets.

CONGRESS TARTS (Tartelettes, Anglaises)

¾ lb. shortcrust
3 oz. butter or margarine
3 oz. caster sugar
3 oz. ground rice

Line 18 tartlet tins thinly with pastry and prick well. Beat fat till softened. Gradually beat in sugar. When fluffy, stir in ground rice and egg. Add salt and almond essence. Beat well. Put a

1 beaten egg
Few grains of salt
3 drops almond essence

heaped teaspoon of the batter into each case. Fix two strips of pastry across, either parallel or criss-cross, sealing with cold water to lining. Bake on a baking sheet in a moderately hot oven, 400° F., for about 20 minutes. *Yield:* 18 tartlets.

CORONATION TARTLETS (Tartelettes, Royale)

6 oz. shortcrust
1 oz. butter
½ cup caster sugar
1 teaspoon cornflour
1 separated egg
1 tablespoon water
½ teaspoon vanilla essence
½ tablespoon chopped glacé cherries
½ tablespoon chopped glacé pineapple

Line 8 tartlet tins thinly with the shortcrust. Prick well. Beat butter till softened. Beat in sugar. When fluffy, stir in cornflour. Beat egg yolk. Stir into fat mixture with water, vanilla essence, cherries and pineapple. Beat egg white till stiff and fold into mixture. Three-quarters fill cases. Bake on a baking sheet in a hot oven, 450° F., for about ¼ hour. *Yield:* 8 tartlets.

CREAM BUNS (Pâtisserie à la Crème)

Taking 2 round or oval dessertspoons, fill one with choux paste, and with the help of the other, lay the paste in rounds or ovals on a greased baking sheet or on to a baking sheet covered with waxed paper, about 2 inches apart. (If preferred, a forcing bag with a ½ inch plain pipe can be used.) Bake in a moderately hot oven, 400° F., until well risen and golden brown, in 20-25 minutes. Split and cool on a wire rack, then fill with whipped cream, sweetened and flavoured to taste with vanilla, or with confectioner's custard, or with any cream filling you like, see pages 747-751. Cover with chocolate, coffee or any icing to taste. Decorate if liked with chopped nuts.

CREAM HORNS LADY LOCKS (Cornets à la Crème)

½ lb. flaky or puff pastry
1 egg white
Caster sugar as required
Whipped cream as required

Roll pastry out very thinly on a lightly floured board. Cut into strips from ¼-1 inch wide, according to taste, and 6 inches long. Brush one side lightly with water and wind strips, dampened side upwards, round special cone-shaped moulds overlapping edges slightly at each turn. Brush with slightly beaten egg white. Dredge with caster sugar, or brush only with equal quantity of beaten egg and milk. Place a little apart on baking tin. Bake in a hot oven, 450° F., until risen and pale brown in about 12 minutes. Cool very slightly for about 1 minute, then carefully remove moulds. Return horns to baking tin. Bake for about 3 minutes to finish cooking. Place on a wire rack. Leave till cold. Fill with confectioner's custard, or with strawberry or raspberry jam, and whipped cream. *Yield:* About 9 or 10 horns.

CREAM PUFFS (Pouffes à la Crème)

These are also baked, but in their own steam. To cook them, you need a large baking tin with a closely fitting lid. If the lid does not fit closely, the steam will escape and the puffs will not cook properly. (This can be prevented by sealing the edges of the tin and the cover together with flour paste.) Force choux pastry out in small or medium-sized balls about 3 inches apart on a greased tin. Cover. Bake in a moderately hot oven, 400° F., for about ¾ hour. The oven door must not be opened during cooking. When ready, remove carefully with a palette knife and slit each quickly at the side to allow the steam to escape. Cool on a wire rack, then fill with whipped cream, confectioner's custard or any filling to taste. Dredge with icing sugar or decorate to taste.

DERBY CURD CHEESE CAKES (Talmouses, Derby)

½ pint milk
½ teaspoon rennet
2 egg yolks
1 oz. butter or margarine
Grated rind of ½ lemon
1 teaspoon grated nutmeg
2½ oz. caster sugar
1 oz. cleaned currants or sultanas
½ oz. sponge cake crumbs
½ lb. short or rough puff pastry

Warm milk to blood heat. Stir in rennet. Stand in a warm room till the curd sets. Pour curd into a strainer lined with muslin. Leave for at least 6 hours to drip, pressing occasionally with a wooden spoon. When all trace of whey has disappeared, beat egg yolks. Stir into the curd. Melt butter or margarine. Stir into curd with remaining ingredients. When blended, line 12-14 patty tins thinly with pastry. Prick well. Place a heaped teaspoon of the mixture in each case. Place on a baking sheet. Bake in a fairly hot oven, 425°F., for about 25 minutes. *Yield:* 12-14 cheese cakes.

ECCLES CAKES (Pâtisserie, Eccles)

½ lb. flaky pastry
1½ oz. Demerara sugar
3 oz. washed and dried currants
2 oz. chopped, minced peel
1½ oz. melted butter or margarine
Grated nutmeg as required
Water and caster sugar as required

Roll pastry out to ¼ inch thickness. Cut into rounds the size of a breakfast cup. Turn the rounds upside down. Brush edges with a pastry brush, dipped in cold water. Mix sugar, currants, peel, butter or margarine and grated nutmeg to taste. Place a large teaspoonful on centre of each round. Bunch up the edges into the centre of each round, then turn upside down and roll each into a round until the currants just show through. Make 3 shallow cuts alongside each other, down the middle of each cake. Brush with water. Dredge with caster sugar. Bake for about 20 minutes in a hot oven, 450° F., until golden. Dredge with caster sugar. *Yield:* 10 Eccles cakes.

ECLAIRS

To Make and Bake Eclairs: Follow method given under Choux Pastry. When quite cold, carefully insert whipped, sweetened cream flavoured with vanilla to taste, with a small spoon, or pipe it in. (If preferred, confectioner's custard or chocolate or coffee cream can be used instead. Chocolate cream goes well with coffee icing and coffee cream with chocolate icing.) Coat tops with chocolate glacé or coffee icing.

FRUIT ECLAIRS : Crush sweetened, ripe or canned fruit to taste. Measure and stiffen with gelatine. Allow 1 teaspoon powdered gelatine dissolved in 1 tablespoon of the fruit juice to each cup of the pulp or purée. Chill thoroughly before using.

PINEAPPLE ECLAIRS : Follow basic recipe for éclairs, page 525. Whip 1 cup of cream. Sweeten to taste. Flavour with 1 or 2 drops of pineapple essence, then add 1 oz. chopped glacé pineapple. Fill éclairs. Decorate tops with glacé icing flavoured with lemon or tangerine juice. *Yield:* 8 éclairs.

FRANGIPANI TARTLETS (Tartelettes à la Frangipane)

About ¼ lb. rich shortcrust
½ gill milk
1 teaspoon cornflour
2 teaspoons sherry
2 teaspoons brandy
1 teaspoon grated lemon rind
  or minced citron peel
2 small egg yolks

Roll out pastry. Cut out rounds for 6 or 7 tartlet tins. Prick well. Stir half the milk into the cornflour. Bring remainder to boil. Boil for 1 minute, stirring constantly. Stir in sherry, brandy, lemon or citron peel, and egg yolks. Leave till cool, stirring occasionally, then half fill cases. Bake in a hot oven, 425° F., for about 8 minutes, then lower to moderate, 350° F., and bake for about ¼ hour, till filling is set and pastry is pale gold. Make a meringue of 2 egg whites and 3 oz. caster sugar. Pipe in a swirl on the top. Return to oven, cooled to 275° F., and bake for about 30 minutes, till pastry is golden and meringue is set. If liked, decorate meringue, before baking, with chopped blanched almonds or cashew nuts. *Yield:* 6 or 7 tartlets.

JAM PUFFS (Pouffes de Confiture)

½ lb. flaky or puff pastry
Jam to taste
1 beaten egg white

Roll pastry into a square about ⅛ inch thick. Divide into 8 equal-sized squares. Brush each with cold water. Place a teaspoon of jam, apricot, greengage, peach, quince, raspberry or strawberry, on the centre of each. Brush edges with cold water and fold into triangles. Press edges lightly together with a fork. Place on a baking sheet about 1½ inches apart. Brush with egg white. Dredge with caster sugar. Bake in a hot oven, 450° F., for 15-20 minutes, till well risen and golden brown. *Yield:* 8 puffs.

MAIDS OF HONOUR (Demoiselles d'Honneur)

Maids of Honour are little cheese cakes sometimes flavoured with lemon and sometimes with almond and vanilla. They are one of the oldest forms of cheese cakes that you can make.

Method: Line patty tins thinly with flaky or rough puff pastry. Prick well. Three-quarters fill them with mixture. Bake in a hot oven, 450° F., for 10-15 minutes, or in a moderately hot oven, 400° F., for 20-25 minutes.

FILLING :
1 oz. caster sugar
1 beaten egg
1 oz. butter
2 oz. ground almonds
¼ oz. desiccated coconut
½ teaspoon vanilla essence

Place sugar in a basin. Add egg. Beat till fluffy. Melt butter. Stir into mixture. Add remainder of ingredients. Beat till blended. Fill cases. Dredge with caster sugar when baked. *Yield:* 15 tartlets.

MARZIPAN CHEESE CAKES (Talmouses de Marchpane)

½-¾ lb. puff pastry
5 blanched bitter almonds
1 tablespoon rose water
¼ lb. ground almonds
2 oz. butter
¼ lb. caster sugar
Strained juice of 1 lemon
2 stiffly frothed egg whites

Line 24 patty tins thinly with pastry and prick well. Pound bitter almonds with rose water. Stir in ground almonds. Beat butter till softened. Gradually add sugar. Beat till creamy and stir into almond mixture with lemon juice. Fold in egg whites. Three-quarter fill cases with mixture. Bake in a fairly hot oven, 425° F., for 20-25 minutes. *Yield;* 24 tartlets.

MINCE PIES

Roll out flaky, rough, puff or shortcrust. Divide into a third and two-thirds. Roll the third out thinly to about ⅛ inch thickness, and cut into rounds, plain or fluted, 2½-3 inches in diameter. Place a heaped teaspoon of mince meat on the centre of the rounds. Roll out remainder of pastry slightly thicker than the first amount to ¼ inch thickness. Cut into equal number of rounds, plain or fluted. Brush edges of covered rounds with beaten egg white. Cover with the thicker rounds, pressing edges slightly together with a fork. Make a slit in the shape of a cross-cut in the centre of each. Brush with beaten egg, taking care not to let it run down the sides, then dredge with caster sugar. Bake in a hot oven, 450° F., for about 10 minutes, then lower to moderate, 350° F., and bake for about 20 minutes, or bake in a fairly hot oven, 425° F., for 25-30 minutes.

To Vary Mince Pies: Follow above recipe, but fit each base into a rather deep patty tin before filling, covering and glazing. Bake in a hot oven, 500° F., if using puff pastry, 475° F., if using flaky or rough puff, and 450° F., if using shortcrust, allowing 10-12 minutes at 500° F., 12-17 minutes at 475° F., and about 20 minutes at 450° F.

TURNOVERS (Pâtisseries)

BASIC : Roll out 1 lb. flaky, puff or rough puff pastry, to barely ⅛ inch thickness on a floured pastry board. Cut into rounds or squares, 4½ inches across. Place a tablespoon of filling on the centre of each. Brush edge all the way round either with cold water or beaten egg white. Fold in two, or point to point. Press edges gently together with a fork. Bake on a greased baking sheet about an inch apart, in a hot oven, 450° F., for about 10 minutes. Beat 1 egg white till frothy. Brush over turnovers. Dredge quickly with caster sugar. Return to oven with door ajar for a few moments. *Yield:* 12 turnovers.

Apple: Peel, core and slice 1 lb. cooking apples into a saucepan. Add 2 tablespoons cold water and caster sugar to taste. If liked, add also a small piece of cinnamon stick. Cover. Stew gently till tender. Remove cinnamon if used. Mash well. Use when cold.

Tutti Fruitti: Place ¼ cup each of chopped dates, raisins, nuts and figs in a saucepan. Add 1 cup light brown sugar, 1 tablespoon butter, and 1 tablespoon flour. Stir till hot. Remove from stove. Cool slightly. Beat 1 egg. Stir into mixture, then stir over stove again until hot but do not allow to boil.

Cool. Stir in 3 tablespoons lemon juice and 1 dessertspoon grated lemon rind.

Victory: Wash and drain 4 tablespoons currants. Stew gently in a covered saucepan with water to cover till water has almost evaporated. Stir in 1 teaspoon butter, 1 teaspoon honey, $\frac{1}{2}$ teaspoon lemon juice and $\frac{3}{4}$ tablespoon sugar. Cool before using.

VIENNA ROSETTES (Rosettes, Viennoise)

$\frac{1}{4}$ lb. butter
$1\frac{1}{2}$ oz. icing sugar
$\frac{1}{4}$ lb. sifted flour
6 oz. shortcrust
Jam to taste

Beat butter till softened, then gradually beat in sugar. Beat till fluffy. Lightly stir in flour. Roll out pastry thinly and line floured patty tins 2 inches across and 1 inch deep. Prick well. Place $\frac{1}{2}$ teaspoon of jam in the bottom of each. Pack filling into forcing bag fitted with a rose tube. Pipe a rose or roses into cases. Place on a baking sheet. Chill for 1 hour. Bake in a moderately hot oven, 400° F., for about 20 minutes, till pale gold. Dredge lightly with sifted icing sugar. *Yield:* 15 tartlets.

FRIED PASTRIES (Pâtisseries, frites)

Pastries made of baking powder dough and choux pastry can be fried as well as baked.

Baking Powder Dough: Roll dough $\frac{1}{4}$ inch thick. Cut in oblongs, 4 by 2 inches. Place 1 tablespoon of filling on the centre of each, and make into squares. Brush edges with cold water or beaten egg white, then fold over and press together with a floured fork. Drop two or three at a time into hot, deep fat heated to 375° F., if using a thermometer. Fry till light brown in about 3 minutes, turning when they rise to the top so that they brown evenly. If preferred, cut into rounds, or squares, and make into semi-circles or triangles.

Fillings: Sieved stewed, sweetened apples, or quinces, mincemeat, jam or jelly, lightly beaten.

Choux Rings: Force rings of choux pastry (see page 525), on to sheets of buttered paper. Slip one or two at a time into hot fat, 375° F. Fry till crisp and brown. Drain. Dredge with icing sugar. Serve at once.

Fritters: Drop from a round spoon in deep, hot fat, 375° F. Fry till golden brown. Drain on absorbent paper. Slit and fill with apricot, raspberry or strawberry jam. Dredge with icing sugar. Serve at once. If liked, serve with hot white sauce flavoured with vanilla instead of slitting and stuffing.

Desserts

In olden days, when no dinner party menu was complete without an elaborate course of fruit, fruit was called " dessert." Nowadays, it is customary to classify all forms of pudding, including ice cream as well as fruit as dessert. It may appear as a combination of ice cream and fruit or sauce, or of fresh cooked or canned fruit and cream or custard sauce, sweet pastry, or a dessert cake. At a formal dinner, fresh fruit can follow a hot or cold pudding, pastry or a savoury. At an informal dinner, fresh fruit is seldom served at the end of a meal, except when a savoury takes the place of a pudding or pastry.

To Choose Dessert

To choose dessert, consider the other courses of the meal. If substantial, you want a rather light dish. If meal is light or largely vegetarian, prepare a rich or substantial dessert.

BAKED PUDDINGS

This section consists of all the baked puddings except batter, milk and soufflés which are given in their own sections. Cook in suitably-sized ovenware dishes. Grease dish before starting to mix the ingredients.

APPLE BETTY (Pommes, Américaine)

2 tablespoons butter
2 cups breadcrumbs

Melt butter in a saucepan. Stir in crumbs. Grate lemon rind. Mix with the sugar and spices.

Rind and juice of 1 lemon
½ cup caster sugar
¼ teaspoon grated nutmeg
¼ teaspoon ground cinnamon
3 cups chopped apple
¼ cup water

Sprinkle the bottom of a greased pie dish with a quarter of the crumbs. Cover with half the apple. Sprinkle with half the spiced sugar, then add a quarter of the crumbs. Cover with remainder of apple. Sprinkle with the last of the sugar and spice mixture. Strain the lemon juice into the water, and sprinkle over. Top with the remainder of crumbs. Cover closely. Cook for ¾ hour in a moderate oven, 350° F. Uncover and brown quickly. Serve with cream, or custard sauce. *For 4 persons.*

APPLE CHARLOTTE (Charlotte de Pommes)

BASIC RECIPE:
1 lb. peeled and cored apples
2 tablespoons cold water
½ lemon
4 oz. caster sugar
3 oz. butter
Thin slices of stale bread

Slice apples into a saucepan. Add water, grated rind and strained juice of lemon, sugar, and 1 oz. of the butter. Cover. Stew gently until quite soft. Remove crusts from bread. Cut into fingers. Spread one side of bread with butter. Line the bottom and sides of a pie dish or charlotte mould with the fingers, buttered side to the dish. Pour in the cooked apples. Melt remaining butter. Cover the top with bread, dipped in the butter. Bake in a moderately hot oven, 375° F., for about ¾ hour. Remove from oven. Stand for a moment or two, then turn out gently on to a hot dish. Dredge with caster sugar. *For 5 persons.*

To Vary: Cook 3 tablespoons ground almonds, grated rind of ½ lemon and ¼ teaspoon of ground cinnamon with the apples. When soft, stir in 1 heaped tablespoon cleaned currants or chopped, stoned raisins. Sprinkle the lining of mould with brown sugar before filling.

APPLE GINGER PUDDING (Pouding de Pommes au Gingembre)

1 pint thick apple or crab apple sauce
1 egg
1 cup golden syrup or honey
1½ oz. butter
2 teaspoons ground ginger
½ teaspoon ground cinnamon
1 teaspoon bicarbonate of soda
½ teaspoon salt
½ cup hot coffee
7 oz. sifted flour

Grease a baking dish and pour in the apple sauce. Beat egg. Add syrup or honey. Melt butter. Add with ginger, cinnamon, soda, salt, coffee and flour in this order. Beat well. Pour over the sauce. Bake in a moderate oven, 350° F., for about 40 minutes. Serve with hot custard sauce or cream. *For 6 persons.*

To Vary: Substitute sour cream for the coffee.

APPLE KRUNCH (Pommes à la Marie)

2 lbs. cooking tart apples
Sugar as required
4 oz. butter
4 oz. flour

Peel, core and slice apples into a greased, round, ovenware dish. Add sugar to taste, or sweeten with honey or syrup. Flavour with 1 or 2 cloves if liked. Cover and cook in slow oven, 300° F., till almost tender. Rub butter into the flour. Stir in 3-4 oz. caster or light brown sugar. Pour over apples when almost ready. Bake in a moderately hot oven, 400° F., till pale gold and crunchy, in 25 to 30 minutes. Serve with cream, or hot custard sauce. *For 4 persons.*

BAKED APPLES (Pommes au Four)

BASIC RECIPE :
6 large tart apples
¼ lb caster sugar
½ cup water
¾ oz. butter

Wipe and core apples. Place either in a buttered baking tin or fireproof dish side by side. Cook sugar and water in a saucepan for 2 minutes. Add butter. When melted, pour over fruit.
Bake, covered, till tender in a moderately hot oven, 375° F., for about 30 minutes, basting frequently with syrup in tin or dish. Serve with cream, or custard sauce. *For 6 persons.*

Stuffed with Almonds: Remove peel from apples half-way down before baking. Fill each with 1 teaspoon of chopped, blanched almonds. Follow basic recipe. When ready, spike with halved, blanched almonds round the top. Top with a little whipped cream or vanilla ice cream.

Stuffed with Dried Fruits: Stuff apples with 1 cup diced, cooked, dried apricots, figs, peaches or prunes, or use mincemeat.

Stuffed with Marshmallows: Bake apples only with 6 tablespoons water in a covered pan for ¼ hour. Stuff with a quartered marshmallow, then plaster each with a teaspoon of caster sugar mixed to a paste with a teaspoon of butter. Bake, uncovered, till tender in about 10 minutes.

Yule Apples: Mix 1 cup chopped, stoned raisins with ¼ cup chopped walnuts. Stuff apples. Follow basic recipe.

BAKED BANANAS (Bananes au Four)

6 small bananas
2 tablespoons apple or quince jelly
2 tablespoons claret
Caster sugar as required

Peel and cut bananas lengthwise. Place in a shallow buttered fireproof dish. Spread each with jelly, then sprinkle with claret. Dredge lightly with caster sugar. Bake for about 20 minutes in a moderate oven, 350° F. Serve with cream. *For 4 persons.*

BAKED PEACHES (Pêches au Four)

6 peaches
6 teaspoons honey
6 teaspoons butter
Ground cinnamon to taste

Choose sound under-ripe rather than over-ripe peaches. Cut in halves. Remove stones. Arrange in a shallow baking dish. Mix honey and butter to a paste. Flavour with cinnamon to taste. Stuff a teaspoonful into each half peach. Bake in a moderate oven, 350° F., until tender in about ¼ hour. Serve hot with cream. *For 3 persons.*

APRICOT SOUFFLE PANCAKES (Crêpes d'Abricots)

½ pint milk
4 oz. butter
3 tablespoons sifted flour

Bring milk to boil. Remove from stove. Cut butter into small pieces and drop into milk. Leave till cool. Stir flour into egg yolks, then

2 separated eggs
Apricot jam as required

into milk. Beat egg whites till stiff. Fold into batter. Divide between 4 large or 6 small buttered fireproof saucers, or shallow small round tins. Bake in a fairly hot oven, 425° F., for about 15 minutes. Place a little heated apricot jam inside each and fold over. Dredge with sifted icing sugar. Either serve garnished with lemon fingers or Devonshire or whipped cream. *For 2 persons.*

BUTTERSCOTCH APPLES (Pommes au Caramel)

8 medium-sized apples
1 tablespoon butter
4 tablespoons Demerara sugar
2 tablespoons water

Peel and core apples. Mix butter and sugar to a paste. Pour the water into a shallow, greased fireproof dish. Stuff apples with the paste. Arrange apples in dish. Spread remainder of paste over apples. Cover and bake in a moderate oven, 350° F., for 15 minutes. Uncover. Baste with the syrup and bake, basting once or twice, until a pale gold, but unbroken. Serve from dish with custard sauce or whipped cream. *For 4 persons.*

CASTLE PUDDINGS (Poudings Château)

2 oz. butter
2 oz. caster suga.
3 oz. flour
½ teaspoon baking powder
Pinch of salt
1 beaten egg
2 tablespoons milk
Grated rind of ½ lemon

Brush 4 medium-sized dariole moulds with melted butter. Beat butter and sugar to a cream. Sift flour with baking powder and salt. Fold flour and egg alternately into the butter and sugar. Stir in milk and lemon rind. Three-quarters fill moulds with batter. Bake in a fairly hot oven, 425° F., for about 25 minutes. Turn out carefully on to a hot dish. Serve masked with marmalade sauce. *For 4 persons.*

CRANBERRY PUFFS (Poufs d'Airelles)

1 egg
¾ cup milk
3 oz. flour
4 tablespoons golden raising powder
¼ cup caster sugar
¼ teaspoon salt
⅓ cup melted butter
1 cup cranberries
2 tablespoons caster sugar

Beat egg lightly, then stir in milk. Sift together dry ingredients, except the 2 tablespoons sugar. Add milk and egg and butter, alternately to the dry ingredients. When blended, roll cranberries in remaining sugar and fold carefully into the batter. Pour into buttered dariole moulds. Cover with buttered paper. Stand in a baking tin containing a little warm water. Bake in a moderate oven, 350° F., till puffy, in about ½ hour. Top with stewed cranberries when turned out. Serve with custard sauce or cream. *For 6 persons.*

DEVONSHIRE PUDDING (Pouding, Devonshire)

¾ cup breadcrumbs
½ cup shelled almonds
3 separated eggs
6 oz. caster sugar

Stand breadcrumbs in a warm place to dry slightly. Put almonds through a meat grinder with a fine knife. Beat yolks. Add sugar. Beat till

573

½ teaspoon ground cinnamon
1 teaspoon grated lemon rind
¼ pint thick cream
1 cup hot cider

fluffy. Stir in crumbs, almonds, cinnamon and lemon rind. Beat egg whites till stiff. Fold into mixture. Turn lightly into a buttered cake tin with removable base. Bake in a moderate oven, 350° F., from 30-40 minutes, till firm. Remove from oven. Stand for a moment or two, then slip off gently on to a flat, hot dish. Serve with cream, whipped and sweetened, and flavoured to taste, and the hot cider. *For 4 persons.*

FRENCH SAUCER PANCAKES (Crêpes à la Française)

2 oz. butter
2 oz. caster sugar
2 separated eggs
1 oz. flour
1 oz. rice flour
Pinch of salt
¼ teaspoon baking powder
¼ pint milk
Grated rind ½ lemon

Beat butter till creamy. Beat in sugar. When fluffy, stir in egg yolks. Beat till blended. Sift flours with salt and baking powder. Stir into egg yolk mixture alternately with milk. Add lemon rind. Beat till smooth. Beat egg whites till stiff. Fold into batter. Divide equally between 12 well-buttered, small round tins or fireproof saucers. Bake in a hot oven, 450° F., for about 10 minutes, till pale brown. Stand for a second or two. Turn gently on to a sheet of greaseproof paper. Place a little apricot, quince, raspberry or strawberry jam in the centre of each. Either make into sandwiches, or fold in two. Either garnish with lemon or serve with whipped cream. *For 6 persons.*

FRIAR'S OMELET

5 oz. breadcrumbs
8 sliced peeled apples
¼ lb. caster sugar
2 oz. butter
1 grated lemon rind
Juice of 1 lemon
2 well-beaten eggs

Place 2 oz. breadcrumbs in the bottom of a well-buttered pie dish. Stew the apples with the sugar, butter and lemon rind and juice until apples are tender but still whole. Cool slightly. Stir in eggs. Place in pie dish. Cover with remainder of breadcrumbs. Dab with bits of butter. Bake in a moderate oven, 350° F., for about ¼ hour. *For 4 persons.*

GINGERBREAD SPONGES (Poudings au Gingembre, Américaine)

¼ lb. flour
½ teaspoon bicarbonate of soda
¼ teaspoon ground allspice
1 teaspoon ground ginger
1 oz. brown sugar
¼ lb. wheaten meal
¼ lb. golden syrup
2 oz. butter
1 beaten egg yolk
½ cup milk
1 stiffly-beaten egg white

Sieve flour, soda, allspice and ginger into a basin. Stir in sugar, wheaten meal and syrup. When blended, melt butter and stir into mixture, then add egg yolk and milk. Fold in egg white. Three-quarters fill buttered gem tins. Bake in a moderate oven, for 20-30 minutes. Turn out on to a hot dish. Dredge with caster sugar. Serve with hot custard sauce. *For 6 persons.*

GOOSEBERRY ROLL (Roulade de Groseilles Vertes)

½ lb. sifted flour
½ teaspoon salt

Mix and sift dry ingredients, then cut in butter. When well mixed, add enough milk to make a

3 teaspoons baking powder
2 oz. butter
About ¼ cup milk
1 pint topped and tailed
gooseberries
¼ cup firmly packed light
brown sugar

soft but not sticky dough. Turn on to a floured pastry board. Knead just enough to shape into a smooth ball. Roll out lightly to ½ inch thickness. Spread to within an inch of edge with gooseberries. Sprinkle with brown sugar, then roll up like a Swiss roll. Place, join downwards, on a greased baking sheet. Brush with butter. Bake in a moderately hot oven, 375° F., for 25-30 minutes. Serve with lemon sauce. *For 6 persons.*

PEACH COBBLER (Pouding de Pêches, Américaine)

3 cups thinly sliced ripe
peaches
1 crushed peach kernel
2½ oz. caster sugar
1 tablespoon lemon juice
1½ oz. butter
¼ lb. sifted flour
½ teaspoon salt
2 teaspoons baking powder
⅛ cup milk

Scald and skin peaches before slicing. Place in layers in a buttered pie dish, 3 pint size. Add crushed kernel. Sprinkle each layer of fruit with sugar and lemon juice. Dab with ½ oz. of the butter. Sift flour, salt and baking powder together. Add an extra 1½ oz. sugar. Rub in remainder of butter. Add all the milk at once. Beat lightly. Drop the batter by tablespoonfuls on top of peaches. Bake in a fairly hot oven, 425° F., for about ½ hour. Serve with cream. *For 6 persons.*

PINEAPPLE ROLL (Roulade d'Ananas)

½ teaspoon salt
8 oz. flour
3 teaspoons baking powder
2 oz. butter
¼ lb. caster sugar
½ cup milk
2-2½ cups diced canned pineapple

Sift salt, flour and baking powder into a basin. Rub in butter and add half the sugar. Mix to a light dough with milk. Turn out on to a floured board. Roll out to an oblong about ⅓ inch thick. Spread with pineapple and remainder of sugar to within ½ inch of the edges. Wet edges and roll up. Place on a buttered baking sheet, join downwards. Brush with milk. Bake in a moderate oven, 350° F., for about ½ hour. Serve with cream or custard sauce. *For 6 persons.*

SCRAP BREAD PUDDING (Pouding de Pain)

1 lb. scraps of bread
¼ lb. shredded suet
2 oz. flour
½ lb. raisins
2 oz. minced candied peel
2 oz. light brown sugar
1 beaten egg
¼ pint milk

Grease a shallow baking tin, 8 by 6 inches. Soak bread in cold water to cover for 1 hour. Drain in a sieve or strainer. Squeeze dry with a wooden spoon. Turn into a basin. Beat with a fork until perfectly smooth. Stir in suet and flour. Stone and chop raisins. Add to mixture with peel, sugar, egg and milk. Stir until blended. Turn into tin. Bake in a moderate oven, 350° F., for 1 hour. Cut into sections. Place in overlapping slices on a hot dish. Sprinkle with caster sugar. *For 6 persons.*

SPONGE MAPLE PUDDINGS (Poudings à la Victoria)

1 oz. butter
2 oz. caster sugar
1 separated egg
2 oz. flour
1 teaspoon baking powder
Pinch of salt
4 tablespoons milk
¼ teaspoon vanilla essence
3 tablespoons hot maple syrup

Beat butter and sugar to a cream. Beat egg yolk. Stir into mixture. Sift flour, baking powder and salt together. Add alternately to butter and sugar with milk mixed with vanilla. Beat egg white to stiff froth. Fold into batter. Bake in 4 buttered dariole moulds for about 25 minutes in a moderate oven, 350° F. Unmould. Serve with hot maple syrup. *For 2 persons.*

To Vary : Stir in the grated rind of ½ lemon before the egg white, or sift 1 saltspoon mixed spice or ground mace with the flour, etc. When maple syrup is not available, substitute heated golden syrup, or heather honey sharpened with lemon juice. Sometimes I coat the puddings with hot chocolate sauce, then sprinkle each with chopped walnuts.

BATTERS

Batter puddings can be divided into three classes : 1. Baked. 2. Fried. 3. Steamed. When a light pudding is wanted, serve fritters, pancakes or other fried batter sweets. When a more substantial pudding is wanted, a baked or steamed batter pudding should be chosen.

BAKED BATTER PUDDING

BASIC RECIPE :
4 oz. flour
Pinch of salt
2 teaspoons of sugar
2 eggs
½ pint milk
½ oz. butter

Sift flour and salt into a basin. Stir in sugar. Make a hollow in centre. Drop in eggs. Add a little of the milk and stir well, gradually drawing flour from sides into the hollow. Beat thoroughly for about 10 minutes, so as to get as much air as possible into the batter. When perfectly beaten, the surface should be full of bubbles. Stir in remainder of milk. Cover basin and stand for 1 hour. Melt butter in a shallow fireproof dish or baking tin that will take 1-1½ pints. Add batter. Bake in a moderately hot oven, 425° F., for about ¾ hour, until crisp and golden brown. Serve with golden syrup, honey, jam or canned fruit syrup. *For 3 persons.*

Apple Batter: Stand batter for only ¼ hour, then stir in remainder of milk with 3 tablespoons extra. Place 4 heaped tablespoons stewed apples in dish or tin. Add ½ teaspoon baking powder to batter. Stir lightly. Pour over apples. Bake in a moderate oven, 350° F., for about 1 hour. Dredge with caster sugar. *For 4 persons.*

STUFFED APPLE BATTER (Lac de Pommes)

4 large tart apples
4 teaspoons crushed pineapple
2 tablespoons golden syrup
4 tablespoons flour

Peel and core apples. Place in a lavishly greased pie dish or baking tin. Pour a teaspoon of pineapple into the hollow in each, then cover each with ½ tablespoon of the syrup. Sift flour into a

Serve Baked Alaska the moment it comes out of the oven. *See page* 621.

Stud Coffee Walnut Gateau with halved walnuts and maraschino cherries. *See page* 622.

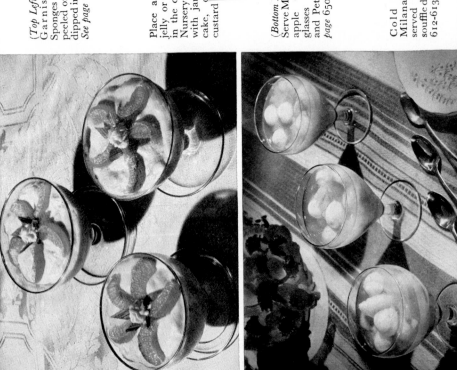

(Top Left) Orange Garnish Sponges if liked with peeled orange sections dipped in castor sugar. *See page 610.*

(Top Right) Place a blob of red jelly or a ripe berry in the centre of each Nursery Trifle, made with jammed sponge cake, covered with custard sauce.

(Bottom Left) Serve Melon and Pineapple Compotes in glasses with cream and Petits Fours. *See page 650.*

(Bottom Right) Cold Banana or Milanaise Souffle, served in individual souffle dishes. *See pages 612-613.*

1 cup milk
1 beaten egg
Grated rind ½ lemon

basin. Make a hollow in centre. Stir half the milk into the egg, then gradually stir into flour. Beat to a smooth batter. Stir in remainder of milk and lemon rind. When thoroughly blended, pour round apples. Bake in a moderate oven, 350° F., for about ½ hour, then uncover and bake till golden in 10-15 minutes. Dredge with caster sugar. *For 4 persons.*

NOTE : Individual batter puddings can be baked in ramekin cases, following basic recipe or any of the variations, allowing only 20 minutes for baking, at 350° F.

FRITTERS (Beignets)

"Fritter" is the term usually applied to food dipped in batter and then fried in deep, hot fat or oil. Oil gives a crisper fritter than fat. The batter required for fritters must be thick enough to cling to the food, and yet not too thick, or the fritters will be tough instead of crisp when fried. Some fritters are made of a thick batter rather like choux pastry.

The fat or oil used for frying should be between 2-3 inches deep, and heated : *Fat,* 370° F. ; *Oil,* 375°-380° F.; If you haven't a frying thermometer to test the fat or oil, watch it carefully until a slight blue smoke curls from the surface, then use at once. To test the temperature, you can drop a teaspoonful of the batter into pan. When temperature is correct, it should rise at once to the top. If not hot enough, it will sink to the bottom. Another test is to drop an inch square of bread into pan. If the bread browns in 1 minute, the temperature is correct.

SIMPLE BATTER

BASIC RECIPE :
4 oz. flour
Pinch of salt
1 egg
¼ pint milk

Sift flour and salt into a basin. Make a hollow in centre. Drop in egg. Gradually add milk, drawing in flour from sides and beating as you add. Use for coating fruit or substitute one of the following batters.

To Vary: Sift 1 teaspoon baking powder with flour and salt. Reduce milk to ¾ cup. Melt ½ oz. butter and add after milk.

RICH BATTER

4 oz. flour
1 saltspoon salt
2 separated eggs
1 tablespoon olive oil
1 teaspoon caster sugar
¾ gill water

Sift flour with salt into a basin. Separate yolks and whites of eggs. Slowly stir oil and sugar into egg yolks. When blended, stir in flour alternately with water. Beat till smooth with a wooden spoon. Cover. Stand for 2 hours. When required, beat egg whites till stiff and fold in. Use at once.

LEMON BATTER

¼ lb. flour
1 saltspoon salt
2 separated eggs
1 tablespoon butter
1½ tablespoons lemon juice
Cold water as required

Sift flour and salt into a basin. Beat egg yolks till honey-coloured. Beat in flour. Beat till very light. Melt butter. Add with lemon juice. When blended, thin with water to a thick starchlike consistency. Beat egg whites till stiff. Fold into mixture. Use at once.

TO MAKE FRUIT FRITTERS (Beignets de Fruit)

BASIC : Any fruit, such as apple rings ¼ inch thick, banana or orange slices, pineapple chunks, halved or quartered pears, drained canned fruits, etc., can be made into puffy fritters. With a skewer, dip the larger pieces of fruit or whole fruit into batter and coat thinly. Hold for a moment or two over a basin to allow any superfluous batter to drain away. (If fruit is diced or in small pieces, dip a dessertspoon or tablespoon of prepared fruit into the batter.) Drop the pieces of fruit or the tablespoons of fruit one at a time into hot fat or oil. Don't try to fry too many at once or you will cool the fat or oil and the fritters may be greasy. If too crowded, they will not be able to expand to their full. Cook until golden brown in 3-4 minutes, turning occasionally to ensure even browning. Remove with a skimmer or fish slice, allowing fat or oil to drain into pan, then drain on absorbent paper. Take out any scraps of batter made from drops with a skimmer. Heat fat or oil again to the right temperature before adding the second batch. Dredge with sifted icing or caster sugar. Garnish with fingers of lemon. Serve at once, with foamy or lemon sauce if liked, or whipped cream.

APPLE FRITTERS (Beignets de Pommes) : Peel, core and slice 3 large apples, from ¼-⅓ inch thick. Sprinkle either with a tablespoon of lemon juice or with the grated peel of ½ lemon, and with 2-3 tablespoons caster sugar. Soak for 5 minutes, then drain. Coat with batter, and fry.

APRICOT FRITTERS (Beignets d'Abricots) : Take 1½ cups diced, fresh apricots. Using the variation of Simple Batter (page 577), add apricot. Fry small tablespoonfuls of apricot batter for about 2 minutes, turning occasionally.

BANANA FRITTERS (Beignets de Bananes) : Peel and remove threads from 3 bananas. Cut them in quarters lengthwise. Coat with lemon batter (see above), and fry. If preferred, they can be cut in slices crosswise when 3 slices must be dipped at a time into the batter and fried.

CHERRY FRITTERS (Beignets de Cerises) : Stone 1 pint of rich dessert cherries. Coat with lemon batter (see above). Drop in tablespoonfuls into fat and fry.

ORANGE FRITTERS (Beignets d'Oranges) : Remove peel and all white pith from 2 large oranges. Cut into slices about ⅛ inch thick, then remove pips. Place in a flat dish. Sprinkle with caster sugar. Soak for 1 hour. Drain off syrup into lemon batter (see above). Coat slices with batter and fry.

PEACH FRITTERS (Beignets de Pêches) : Peel, halve and stone 6 fresh peaches, or use canned. Sprinkle with the grated rind of a lemon and 2 tablespoons caster sugar. Cover. Soak for 2 hours, then drain off syrup. Coat halves with lemon batter (see above), and fry, or dip in equal quantity of crushed macaroons and ratafias before coating and frying.

PINEAPPLE FRITTERS (Beignets d'Anana) : Follow recipe for Apple Fritters, page 578, but substitute for apple, either 1 cup chopped, canned or 5 or 6 slices of canned, well-drained pineapple and omit lemon and sugar.

ALMOND FRITTERS (Beignets d'Amandes)

½ lb. butter
1 oz. caster sugar
¼ lb. ground almonds
4 beaten eggs
2½ tablespoons Sauterne
3 grated sponge fingers

Beat butter until softened. Add sugar. Beat until creamy. Stir in almonds. Strain eggs and stir in gradually, then beat in wine. Beat until smooth. Stir in sponge fingers. With floured hands, shape into balls the size of a chestnut. Fry until golden. Drain. Dredge with caster sugar. Serve with any wine sauce. *For 4 persons.*

PANCAKES (Crêpes)

Ever since the Middle Ages, pancakes have been associated with Shrove Tuesday. The traditional recipe for pancakes is the one used on such occasions, but there are many other versions of pancakes worth passing on.

SIMPLE PANCAKES

BASIC RECIPE :
¼ lb. flour
¼ teaspoon salt
1 egg
½ pint milk

Sift flour and salt into a basin. Make a well in centre. Drop in egg. Add about 1 tablespoon of milk then mix in a little of the flour from the sides with a wooden spoon. Keep on adding milk gradually and stirring in flour until half the milk has been used and all the flour absorbed. Beat vigorously for about 10 minutes until batter is covered with air bubbles. Gently stir in remainder of milk. Cover. Stand for 1 hour in a cool place. Pour batter into a jug.

To Fry Pancakes: Melt a walnut of butter or lard in a frying pan about 6-7 inches across until a thin blue smoke rises. Carefully pour enough batter into pan to cover bottom thinly. Leave cake for about ½ minute to set, then gently shake pan or loosen the cake round the edges with a palette knife while frying quickly until golden brown below. Either toss or turn with palette knife and fry on the other side until tinged with gold. (If you fry pancakes slowly, they are bound to be tough.) Turn on to a paper dredged with caster sugar. Dredge pancakes lightly with caster sugar. Sprinkle with a few drops of lemon juice, or spread with heated apricot jam. Roll up neatly and keep hot. Melt a fresh pat of butter or lard for each pancake to be cooked. Serve very hot. Garnish each on top with a lemon butterfly or finger, allowing 1 to each pancake.

To Vary: Increase flour to 5 oz. Sift with 2 teaspoons baking powder and ½ teaspoon salt. Beat egg yolk, then fold in stiffly frothed white. Rub ½ oz. butter lightly into flour. Stir in 2 tablespoons caster sugar, then 1 cup milk. Fold in egg. Follow basic recipe.

CREPES D'ORANGES

2 oz. flour
1 egg yolk
1 egg
1 dessertspoon Cointreau or Curaçao
1 tablespoon olive oil
¼ pint milk
Few grains of salt
12 lumps of sugar
2 oranges or tangerines
3 oz. butter

Sift flour into a basin. Add egg yolk and egg, Cointreau or Curaçao and olive oil. Beat vigorously till smooth. Gradually stir in milk and salt. (The batter should be like a thin cream.) Cover. Stand for ¾-1 hour. Wash and dry oranges or tangerines, then rub lumps of sugar over the skin till impregnated with the oil. Pound in a mortar with the butter and 1 dessertspoon of Cointreau or Curaçao. Stand in a cool place. Brush a 5-6 inch frying pan with olive oil. Heat. Pour batter into a jug, then pour out enough batter into pan to coat pan thinly. Fry till brown, then toss and brown on other side. When all are ready, reheat in a moderately hot oven, 375° F., for about 5 minutes, then spread each thinly with orange or tangerine butter. Roll up. Arrange on a hot dish. Dredge with sifted icing sugar. Pour ½ gill of flaming brandy or rum over. Serve at once. *For 2 persons.*

Crepes Suzette: Prepare pancake as described above. Cream 2 oz. butter with 5 tablespoons caster sugar. Stir in 1 dessertspoon Cointreau or Curaçao and the grated rind of 2 oranges. Spread crêpes with this butter and keep in a warm place. Bring juice of the oranges to a boil with 2 tablespoons caster sugar. Boil for a moment or two, then add 2 tablespoons Cointreau or Curaçao or one of brandy and one of Cointreau or Curaçao. Pour over crêpes. Light up. Serve at once.

TIMBALE CASES

¼ lb. flour
¼ teaspoon salt
2 eggs
1½ gills milk
¾ teaspoon olive oil

Sift flour and salt into a basin. Beat eggs lightly. Stir in milk and oil. Mix thoroughly. Stir into flour mixture. Beat until smooth. Strain into a basin. Stand for 1 hour. Fill a small basin or cup one-third full with the batter. Place timbale iron in deep fat and heat to about 365° F. Drain iron slightly on unglazed paper. Dip iron into batter in cup or basin, allowing the batter to come almost to the top of the iron. Lower quickly into the fat. Fry until delicately brown and crisp, in 1-1½ minutes. Remove quickly from fat. Ease case off with a fork on to unglazed paper, then turn it upside down to allow fat to drain away. Repeat until all the cases are made. *Yield:* About 3½ dozen. Fill cases, when cold, with fruit compote, or salad, bavarois, or fruit sponge or fluff.

To Make Rosettes: Follow recipe for Timbale Cases but stir ¾ tablespoon caster sugar into the batter before using. Fill with any creamy sweet. *Yield:* About 3 dozen.

HINTS ON MAKING ROSETTES AND TIMBALES

1. Take care not to allow batter to come to the top of iron or the shape will be spoiled, as it will come over the edge.

2. Store in a tightly closed tin and use as required. They will soften if kept too long, but can be crisped in a moderate oven, 350° F., for about 5 minutes. May also be used for savoury fillings.

RICH STEAMED BATTER PUDDING

½ lb. flour
½ teaspoon salt
4 separated eggs
1 pint milk
1 oz. butter

Sift flour and salt into a basin. Make a well in the centre. Drop in egg yolks. Gradually beat into flour, adding a little milk as you beat. When all the flour is incorporated, gradually beat in remainder of milk. Melt and add butter. Beat egg whites to a stiff froth. Fold into batter. Three-quarters fill a hot pudding basin. Cover with buttered and floured cloth. Steam for 1 hour and ten minutes. Turn out gently. Serve with Lemon or Wine sauce. *For 6 persons.*

MILK PUDDINGS

Milk Puddings are generally made of a cereal, but a milk pudding can also be made of bread or some of the Italian pastas, particularly macaroni and vermicelli. Custard puddings are also in this section. Serve with cream or top milk.

Milk puddings contain all the ingredients necessary for body building. They are equally suitable for children, invalids, and adults. Digestible and full of nutrients, properly prepared and cooked, they give the housewife an opportunity of introducing part of the milk necessary in the family diet. In this section, baked and steamed milk puddings only are given. Cold milk moulds are included in the Cold Sweet section.

TO PREPARE CEREALS, ETC. :

Arrowroot and Cornflour: Moisten with cold milk. Bring remainder of milk to the boil. Stir into mixture. When blended, pour into top of a double boiler. Cook for 10 minutes over boiling water. Stir constantly to prevent lumping.

Barley: Rinse in a colander under cold water tap. Soak if liked in the milk for 1 hour to shorten cooking time. Cook with the milk in the top of a double boiler, or place straight in a greased pie dish with sugar and flavourings.

Farina, Ground Rice and Semolina: Follow method given for Arrowroot and Cornflour, allowing 7-10 minutes.

Macaroni: Break into inch lengths. Throw into boiling milk. Cover and cook steadily for 30-40 minutes.

Rice: Follow instructions for Barley.

Sago and Tapioca: Rinse in a colander under the cold water tap. Drain. Stir into hot milk in the top of a double boiler. Cool until clear over boiling water, or soak in milk for 1 hour before cooking to save time.

Vermicelli: Crush vermicelli in your hand. Bring milk to boil. Sprinkle in vermicelli. Cook, stirring constantly, for 5 minutes.

BAKED MILK PUDDING TABLE
ALLOW TO 1 PINT MILK

1½ oz. whole grain : barley, macaroni, rice, sago or tapioca.
1½ oz. ground grain : arrowroot, cornflour, farina, ground rice or semolina.
¾ oz. sugar and 1-2 eggs.

Milk Moulds: If pudding is to be moulded instead of baked, allow 2 oz. of whole or small grain or of a farinacious substance such as macaroni, and 2 oz. ground grain, to 1 pint milk, 1 oz. sugar and 1 egg, with flavouring to taste.

To Sweeten Milk Puddings: Use sugar, honey or syrup, or a combination of honey and syrup.

To Flavour Milk Puddings:

1. Add $\frac{1}{2}$ a bay leaf, or 1 inch cinnamon stick, or 1-2 inch vanilla pod, or 2 cloves, or 1 blade of mace, or the rind of $\frac{1}{2}$ lemon, orange or tangerine, to the milk to be used in making pudding. Heat milk very slowly and remove flavouring before stirring in the grain. These flavourings can be dried, stored and used over and over again.

2. Add any essence, or grated nutmeg to taste when the grain is cooked.

To Prepare Milk Puddings: See respective recipes.

TO COOK MILK PUDDINGS

Baked: When the grain is cooked, remove from stove. Add sugar, beaten eggs and flavouring. Bake in a moderate oven, 350° F., until set and light brown. If preferred, only beat in the yolks, then beat egg whites until stiff and fold into mixture before baking. This gives a delicious crust. Or turn egg whites into a meringue for the top.

Steamed: Pack mixture into a buttered pudding basin or mould, filling it three-quarters full. Cover with a buttered paper. Place in a saucepan with boiling water coming half-way up the sides. Steam for $\frac{1}{2}$ hour. Remove mould from pan. Stand for a minute or two before turning out on to a hot dish.

Moulds: Turn mixture into a wet mould. Leave until set and chilled. Turn out. Serve with canned fruit juice, heated and sharpened with lemon juice, or with melted raspberry or strawberry jam, thinned slightly with fruit juice.

To Serve Milk Puddings: Wipe rim of the pie dish with a damp cloth before baking pudding, and take care not to let any of the milk drop on the rim of dish whilst stirring, or it will be discoloured when baked. Always dredge pudding, not covered with meringue, with caster or sifted icing sugar before serving. Slip a paper collar round dish before taking it to the table.

BREAD PUDDINGS

To make good bread puddings, see that none of the crust is crumbled with the bread and place pie dish in a baking tin containing hot water coming half way up the sides.

BREAD PUDDING (Pouding de Pain)

BASIC RECIPE:
2 cups stale breadcrumbs

Place crumbs in a basin. Add milk and sugar. Stand till cool. Stir in butter, eggs, salt and

4 cups scalded milk
¼ lb. caster sugar
3 tablespoons melted butter
2 beaten eggs
¼ teaspoon salt
1 teaspoon vanilla essence

vanilla essence. Pour into a buttered pie dish. Place in a baking tin containing hot water coming half-way up the sides. Bake in a moderate oven, 350° F., for about 1 hour, until a knife inserted in centre comes out clean. *For 6 persons.*

To Vary: Increase eggs to 3 and add 1 cup drained, stewed and sweetened apricots when the pudding is half ready. Stir well and finish baking.

BUTTERSCOTCH BREAD PUDDING (Pouding de Pain à la Creole) : Omit caster sugar. Add 1 cup light brown sugar to melted butter. Cook slowly till dissolved and syrup is a rich caramel shade. Stir into crumb mixture before the eggs.

CHOCOLATE BREAD PUDDING (Pouding de Pain au Chocolat) : Add 2 oz. chocolate to milk before scalding, then beat well. Reduce vanilla essence to ½ teaspoon, and stir in ½ teaspoon ground cinnamon as well.

RAISIN BREAD PUDDING (Pouding de Pain aux Raisins) : Reduce crumbs to 1½ cups, and milk to 3 cups. Soak only for 5 minutes. Stir well. Omit butter. Add sugar, salt and ¼ teaspoon ground cinnamon, then ½ cup chopped, stoned raisins or cleaned sultanas. Bake in a moderately slow oven, 325° F., for 45-50 minutes, until set. Serve with cream. *For 5 or 6 persons.*

TANGERINE BREAD PUDDING (Pouding de Pain au Tangerine) : Stir 1 cup tangerine marmalade into mixture before baking.

BREAD AND BUTTER PUDDING (Pouding de Pain, Anglaise)

6 slices bread and butter
4 oz. cleaned currants
2 oz. caster sugar
1 pint milk
2 beaten eggs
Grated nutmeg to taste

Remove crusts from thin slices of bread and butter. Cut bread in halves or quarters, and line a buttered pie dish, 1½ pint size, buttered side up. Fill up spaces with small pieces of buttered bread cut from one of the slices. Sprinkle with currants and half the sugar. Cover with remainder of bread, buttered side up, and sugar. Heat milk. Stir into eggs. Strain over bread. Grate nutmeg to taste over the top. Soak for 30 minutes. Bake in a moderately hot oven, 375° F., till set and lightly browned in about ½ hour. *For 6 persons.*

BREAD CUSTARD PUDDING (Pouding de Pain à la Crème)

6 thin slices bread
2 oz. butter
4 eggs
2 oz. caster sugar
½ teaspoon vanilla essence
Pinch of grated nutmeg
2 pints scalded milk

Remove crusts from bread. Butter one side of bread. Beat eggs. Stir in sugar, vanilla essence and nutmeg, then gradually stir in milk. When sugar is dissolved, strain into a buttered pie dish, 2½ pint size. Cover with the bread, buttered side up. Place in a baking tin containing hot water to the depth of 1 inch. Bake in a moderate oven, 350° F., till firm in about ¾ hour. *For 8 persons.*

CHOCOLATE BREAD CUSTARD PUDDING (Pouding au Chocolat, Porto Rico) : Melt 2 oz. chocolate in the milk while heating. Beat till blended.

QUEEN'S PUDDING (Pouding de Pain à la Reine)

½ pint scalded milk
¼ pint sieved breadcrumbs
1 teaspoon grated lemon rind
1 dessertspoon butter
2½ oz. caster sugar
2 eggs
2 tablespoons raspberry or
    apricot jam

Pour milk over crumbs. Add lemon rind, butter and ½ oz. of the sugar. Stand for ½ hour to allow crumbs to swell. Separate yolks and whites of eggs. Beat yolks into crumb mixture. Pour into a greased pie dish, 1½ pint size. Stand in baking tin of hot water. Bake in a moderate oven, 350° F., until set in about ½ hour. Heat jam. Spread carefully over top. Beat egg whites till stiff. Fold in 1½ oz. caster sugar. Pile on top of jam. Sprinkle lightly with remainder of sugar. Bake in a moderate oven, 350° F., for about 15 minutes, till meringue is crisp. *For 3 or 4 persons.*

RICE PUDDING (Pouding de Riz)

BASIC RECIPE:
1½ oz. rice
¾-1 oz. caster or brown sugar
Pinch of salt
1 pint of milk
Grated nutmeg if liked

Rinse rice in a strainer under the cold water tap. Drain well. Place with sugar and salt in a greased quart pie dish. Add milk. Stir well. Bake in a slow oven, 300° F., for about 3 hours, stirring every ½ hour for the first 1½ hours to prevent a skin forming on top. (If liked, grate nutmeg to taste on top, at the end of 1½ hours). *For 4 persons.*

To Vary: If liked, cook the mixture in the top of a double boiler over boiling water for 2 hours, stirring frequently until thick and tender, before baking.

SAGO PUDDING (Pouding de Sagou)

1½ oz. sago
1 pint boiling milk
1 oz. caster sugar
1 beaten egg
Vanilla essence to taste

Rinse sago thoroughly under cold water tap. Drain well. Soak in cold milk to cover for 1-1½ hours, then drain again. Stir into boiling milk. Cook from 6-8 minutes, stirring constantly. Remove from heat. Stir in sugar, then cool slightly. Stir in egg and vanilla essence. Stand in a tin containing hot water to the depth of 1 inch. Bake in a moderate oven, 350° F., for 25-30 minutes. *For 4 persons.*

SEED TAPIOCA PUDDING (Pouding au Tapioca)

1 oz. seed pearl tapioca
¾ pint milk
1 saltspoon salt
1 oz. caster sugar
1 separated egg
½ teaspoon vanilla essence

Rinse seed tapioca in the strainer under cold water tap, then place in a basin. Cover with cold water. Stand for 30 minutes. Drain well. Place in the top of a double boiler. Add milk and salt. Stir until boiling. Cover. Simmer over boiling water, stirring occasionally, until tapioca is clear. Remove from heat. Cool slightly. Add sugar. Stir until dissolved. Stir in egg yolk and vanilla essence. Beat egg white until stiff. Fold into mixture. Turn into a greased 1½ pint pie dish. Bake in a moderately hot oven, 375° F., for about 25 minutes. Serve with cream. *For 4 persons.*

SEMOLINA HONEY PUDDING (Pouding de Semoule au Miel)

¼ lb. semolina
1 tablespoon custard powder
1 quart milk
1 heaped tablespoon clear honey
½ teaspoon vanilla essence

Mix semolina and custard powder to a smooth cream with 2 or 3 tablespoons of the cold milk. Heat remainder of milk to boiling point, then stir into semolina mixture. Pour into saucepan. Stir till boiling. Boil for 10 minutes, stirring constantly, until clear and thick. Remove from stove. Stir in honey and vanilla essence. Mix well. Pour into a greased pie dish. Bake in a moderate oven, 350° F., till brown. *For 6 persons.*

CUSTARD PUDDINGS

It is important to use both fresh eggs and milk for custards. They can also be made with skim milk, but the result is not so good as when made with full-cream milk. A custard can either be baked or steamed. The cooking must be done well below boiling point. When using skim milk add a pat of butter.

HINTS ON MAKING BAKED AND STEAMED CUSTARDS

1. Beat eggs only till blended.
2. Be sure to strain the mixture before cooking to remove the thread from the egg or eggs.
3. If to be steamed, cover either with a greased fireproof plate or paper.
4. Place pie dish or individual custard cups in a baking tin containing water coming about 1 inch up the sides to prevent rapid cooking.
5. Before removing from oven, draw out shelf and test custard in centre with a knife. If the knife comes out clean, custard is ready. If any custard adheres to the knife, cook a little longer.

BAKED CUSTARDS (Crèmes au Four)

BASIC RECIPE:
2 eggs
1 oz. caster sugar
Pinch of salt
1 pint hot milk
½ teaspoon vanilla essence

Beat eggs, sugar and salt. Stir in milk and vanilla essence. Strain into a greased pie dish, 1½ pint size. Place in a baking tin of water coming 1 inch up side of dish. Grate nutmeg on top of pudding. Wipe rim of dish. Bake on the centre shelf of a moderate oven, 350° F., for about 40 minutes, until dry in the centre when tested with a knife. If preferred, steam for about the same length of time in a saucepan of boiling water with a buttered paper or fireproof plate on top.

INDIVIDUAL CUSTARDS (Crèmes au Four) : Follow above recipe, but pour into individual buttered custard cups. Bake as described, but in a slow oven, 300° F., for about 25 minutes.

CARAMEL CUSTARD (Crème au Caramel) : Melt sugar very slowly until into a golden brown syrup, and add to pudding after the milk has been added to egg.

CHOCOLATE CUSTARD (Crème au Chocolat) : Dissolve 1 oz. unsweetened chocolate in the milk when heating.

MOCHA CUSTARDS (Crèmes au Moka)

8-10 lumps sugar
¼ pint strong black coffee
¾ pint boiling milk
2 eggs
½ teaspoon vanilla essence

Dissolve sugar in the coffee. Stir in boiling milk. Beat eggs in a basin till frothy, then stir in coffee milk by degrees when off the boil. Add vanilla essence. Pour into 4-6 buttered ramekins. Place in a baking tin containing water to the depth of ½ inch. Cover with a buttered paper. Bake in a slow oven, 300° F., for about ½ hour, till set. Serve with cream. *For 4-6 persons.*

OMELETS AND SOUFFLES

Omelets and soufflés can be two of the most nutritious desserts one can prepare, and omelets are one of the quickest and easiest to make. There are three kinds of omelets : 1. French ; 2. Puffy, in which the yolk and white are beaten separately ; 3. Soufflé omelets which are sometimes fried below and finished under the grill. The yolks and whites of eggs are beaten separately for a soufflé which can be either baked or steamed according to taste. Most mixtures are suitable both for baking and steaming.

OMELETS (Omelettes)

There are two ways of making a sweet French omelet. One method requires only eggs, sugar, salt and flavouring. The other includes milk or water. The latter claims to be lighter than the former.

(1) FRENCH OMELET (Omelet à la Française)

6 eggs
1 oz. caster sugar
Pinch of salt
1 oz. butter

Break eggs into a basin. Beat well. Add half the sugar and salt and beat again. Melt butter in an omelet pan. When foamy, quickly pour in egg mixture. Cook over moderate heat, lifting the edges towards the centre and tipping the pan to allow uncooked mixture to run below the cooked, and tilting it back and forth until mixture is nearly set on top. An alternative way of frying is to stir mixture with a fork until it begins to set, then allow to brown below. When ready to serve, it should be still slightly " runny " on top. Remove from stove. Loosen round the edge with a palette knife or spatula and fold in two. Sprinkle with remaining caster sugar. Serve at once. *For 3 persons.*

(2) FRENCH OMELET (Omelet à la Française)

6 eggs
2 tablespoons cold milk, water or cream
1 tablespoon sifted icing sugar
½ teaspoon vanilla essence

Beat eggs with liquid, sugar and vanilla essence, only till yolks and whites are blended. Fry as described above. *For 3 persons.*

To Vary French Omelets:
1. If liked, hold omelet under the grill for a moment or two to brown slightly more before sugaring.

2. Place 2-3 tablespoons of hot jelly, jam or lemon curd on half of omelet before folding.

Rum Omelet:

1. Omit liquid. Substitute $1\frac{1}{2}$ teaspoons sifted icing sugar for the tablespoon given in Recipe No. 2., and stir in fully a tablespoon of rum in place of vanilla essence. Fry as described above. Pour 3 tablespoons of rum round omelet when served. Set a match to it. If liked, dredge with sifted icing sugar before adding rum.

2. Follow recipe for French Omelet No. 1., but use only 4 egg whites and 6 egg yolks. When served, strew it with sugar, and pour a wineglass of hot rum over. Set it alight.

PUFFY OMELET (Omelette à l'Anglaise)

4 eggs
$\frac{1}{4}$ teaspoon vanilla essence
2 dessertspoons caster sugar
1 oz. clarified butter

Separate yolks and whites of eggs. Stir vanilla essence into yolks, then add sugar. Rub omelet pan with salt, then wipe and add butter. Melt slowly. Beat yolk mixture till thick. Add a pinch of salt to egg whites. Beat till stiff. Fold in yolk mixture. When butter begins to foam, pour mixture into pan. Shake over moderate heat till mixture begins to set. Slip into a moderate oven, 350° F., and bake for about 10 minutes, till puffy and pale gold. Turn quickly on to paper dredged with caster or sifted icing sugar. Spread 2 tablespoons heated jam, jelly or lemon curd, or any other fruit filling in centre. Fold in two. Dredge with sifted icing or caster sugar. Serve at once. *For 2 persons.*

To Vary: Add 3 tablespoons hot water or cold milk after beating yolks till thick. This is claimed to make omelet more tender.

APRICOT PUFFY OMELET (Omelette d'Abricots): Stir 1 teaspoon grated orange rind, $1\frac{1}{2}$ teaspoons lemon juice and 2 teaspoons orange juice into yolk mixture. Fry as described. Slip 3 tablespoons hot apricot purée into omelet before folding. Dredge 1 dessertspoon sifted icing sugar over the top.

NUT OMELET (Omelette d'Amandes): Stir 3 tablespoons caramel syrup into yolk mixture with $\frac{1}{2}$ teaspoon vanilla essence. When butter in omelet pan melts, sprinkle with 3 oz. shredded almonds, then add omelet mixture. Cook as described. Serve, if liked, with caramel sauce.

SOUFFLES (Soufflés)

The basis of a sweet soufflé is a mixture of fat, flour and milk lightened by stiffly beaten egg whites. Care is needed to mix and bake or steam it perfectly. The egg whites must be thoroughly whisked, and lightly and perfectly blended with the flour mixture which is called a " panada." It should be baked in a properly prepared fireproof china or glass soufflé dish. A soufflé dish or tin, round or oval, should be used for cooking steamed soufflés.

To Prepare Baking Dish: Brush bottom of dish or tin with clarified butter or olive oil, then brush a triple folded band of white kitchen paper, about $4\frac{1}{2}$ inches wide, with clarified butter on one side only. Tie round the top, buttered side inwards, so that it extends $3\frac{1}{2}$-4 inches above the rim. The band is necessary to prevent the soufflé falling " overboard " when it rises above the level of its container. Cut a round of kitchen paper, a little larger than the diameter of the soufflé dish and brush also with clarified butter.

To Prepare Steamed Soufflé Tin: Brush bottom of tin with clarified butter or olive oil. Place a round of greaseproof paper in the bottom of tin. Brush with butter or olive oil. Tie a greased triple-folded band of white kitchen paper 4½ inches wide, buttered side inwards, round tin, so that it extends 4¼ inches above the rim. Cut a round of greaseproof paper a little wider than the top of soufflé tin, and brush it also with clarified butter.

Size of Dish or Tin: Use a 3-pint size dish or tin for the 3 egg soufflé, and a 2-quart one for a 4 egg soufflé.

HINTS ON MAKING SOUFFLES

1. When making a fruit soufflé, fruit juice can be substituted for milk.
2. If you want a soufflé to rise higher in the centre than round the edge, cut a shallow round about 2-2½ inches from the edge with a sharp knife just before baking or steaming.
3. If baking at a high temperature, place dish or tin in a baking tin containing enough water to come 1 inch up the sides. If baking in a slow oven, this is not necessary.

SWEET SOUFFLE (Soufflé au Sucre)

BASIC RECIPE:
(1)
1 oz. butter
1 oz. flour
¼ pint hot milk
1 oz. caster sugar
1 saltspoon salt
3 egg yolks
4 egg whites
(2)
3 tablespoons butter
3 tablespoons flour
1 cup hot milk
2 oz. caster sugar
1 saltspoon salt
4 egg yolks
4 egg whites

Melt butter in large saucepan so as to have room for the egg whites later on. Stir in flour. When frothy, stir in milk gradually. Bring to boil. Stir till smooth, then stir in sugar and salt. Stir till sugar is dissolved and you have a thick paste. Remove from stove. Beat egg yolks till thick and lemon coloured. Gradually stir into paste with flavouring to taste. Beat egg whites to a stiff froth. Fold into mixture. Spoon into prepared dish or tin. It should be three-quarters or two-thirds full. Cover with the round of paper, buttered side downwards.

To Bake: Place dish or tin in a baking tin containing enough hot water to come almost half-way up the sides. Bake in a moderately slow oven, 325°F., for about 35 minutes, or in a moderately hot oven, 400° F., for about ½ hour. Don't open oven door until mixture has set. Serve at once. *For 4-6 persons.*

Steamed Soufflé: Follow above recipes. Scoop into a dish or tin. Cover with prepared paper, greased side downwards, to prevent steam condensing on the top. Cook in a steamer, or stand on a fireproof plate and cook in a saucepan, with simmering water below, for 30-40 minutes, till firm when touched in the centre. Remove paper. Stand for a second or two to allow to shrink. Turn gently on to a hot dish. Slide tin off carefully. This needs great care or you may damage soufflé. Serve with hot sauce to taste, prepared in advance, poured round dish if liked.

To Vary:

1. Bake in individual soufflé dishes, allowing 10-15 minutes in a moderately slow oven, 325° F.

2. If a plain soufflé is wanted, allow 1 teaspoon vanilla or a similar essence, adding it with the sugar.

APRICOT OR PEACH SOUFFLE (Soufflé d'Abricots ou Pêches) : Drain 2 cups of canned apricots or peaches. Quarter or slice. (A) Place in bottom of prepared soufflé dish, then cover with No. 2 mixture, and bake as described, or if wanted crusty-edged, but still soft in centre, bake only for 20 minutes in a moderately hot oven, 375° F. Serve with heated apricot or peach syrup and whipped cream. (B) If preferred, place half the soufflé mixture in dish. Quickly and gently lay fruit on top. Cover with remainder of soufflé, and bake as described.

CHOCOLATE SOUFFLE (Soufflé au Chocolat) : Follow recipe No. 1, but reduce flour to $\frac{1}{2}$ oz. and dissolve 2 oz. grated chocolate in the milk before making the sauce. Add $\frac{1}{2}$ teaspoon vanilla essence to egg yolks. Bake as described.

COFFEE SOUFFLE (Soufflé au Café)

1½ oz. butter
1½ oz. flour
1½ gills coffee made with milk
1 oz. caster sugar
3 separated eggs
½ teaspoon vanilla essence

Melt butter in a saucepan. Stir in flour, then add coffee. Stir over heat till the mixture leaves the sides of saucepan. Remove from heat. Stir in sugar, egg yolks and essence, beating each egg in well before adding the next. Lightly fold in stiffly-frothed egg whites. Turn mixture into a prepared soufflé dish or tin. Cover with buttered paper. Steam slowly for 30-40 minutes in a steamer. When cooked, turn out gently. Serve with $\frac{3}{4}$ pint custard sauce. *For 5 or 6 persons.*

MACAROON SOUFFLE (Soufflé de Macarons)

1 cup hot milk
12 macaroon biscuits
4 separated eggs
Flavouring to taste
1 saltspoon salt

Pour milk over the biscuits. Beat till blended. Add yolks. Beat till blended. Cook in the top of a double boiler until thick, stirring constantly. Remove from heat. Leave till cool. Stir in 1 dessertspoon rum, sherry or any sweet liqueur or $\frac{1}{2}$ teaspoon vanilla essence. Beat egg whites with salt till stiff. Fold lightly into mixture. Place in a buttered soufflé dish, about 8 inches across. Bake in a tin of hot water, in a moderately slow oven, 325° F., for about 35 minutes. Serve from dish with whipped cream. *For 4 persons.*

PRALINE SOUFFLE (Soufflé Praliné)

¼ lb. Jordan almonds
3 bitter almonds
4 oz. caster sugar
5 eggs
½ teaspoon vanilla essence

Blanch and peel almonds. Roast until crisp and golden brown. Melt 1 oz. sugar until it turns pale gold. Stir at once into almonds. Pour into an oiled plate until cold. Pound in a mortar with a pestle until very fine. Beat remainder of sugar with egg yolks until light and fluffy. Gradually beat in the almonds. Stir in vanilla essence. Beat egg whites to a stiff froth. Fold into mixture. Scoop into a large prepared soufflé dish. Bake in a moderate oven, 350° F., for 15-20 minutes, then increase heat to 450° F., and finish cooking in about 10 minutes. *For 5 or 6 persons.*

STEAMED PUDDINGS

There are many types of steamed puddings. The most popular are :
1. *Sponge Puddings.*
2. *Suet Puddings,* made either with flour or with a combination of flour and breadcrumbs.
3. *Steamed Dumplings and Layer Puddings.*

HINTS ON MAKING STEAMED PUDDINGS

1. *To make light sponge puddings,* cream fat and sugar thoroughly. Add remaining ingredients. Beat egg whites till stiff. Fold into mixture.

2. *To make a light suet pudding,* use part breadcrumbs and part flour—equal quantity if liked.

3. When suet is not available for suet puddings, butter or margarine can be substituted. Rub into flour mixture. Allow a little less time for cooking.

4. *To make a Rich Steamed Pudding turn out Whole:* Cut a round of greaseproof paper to fit the bottom of basin. Place in bottom of greased basin. Brush paper with clarified fat.

5. Fill basin to within an inch of the rim to allow for rising.

6. Cover with greased paper. Tie down tightly under rim with string, then cover with a pudding cloth if liked and knot ends over the top to provide a handle.

7. Stand basin for a minute after removing from pan to allow pudding to shrink from the basin, then turn out gently on to a hot dish.

SPONGE PUDDING (Pouding, Blanc Savoie)

BASIC RECIPE :
¼ lb. flour
1 saltspoon salt
½ teaspoon baking powder
¼ lb. butter
¼ lb. caster sugar
2 eggs
¼ teaspoon vanilla essence
2 tablespoons milk

Grease a 1½-2 pint basin, and a greaseproof paper cover cut to fit. Sift flour, salt and baking powder into a basin. Beat butter till softened. Gradually beat in sugar. When creamy, beat in 1 egg at a time with a dust of the flour, beating after each addition. Stir vanilla essence into the milk. Add alternately with remainder of flour. Beat well. Two-thirds fill basin with mixture. Cover with greased paper. Tie on securely under rim. Place in a steamer or on a rack in a saucepan containing boiling water coming half-way up the side of the basin. Cover closely. Steam for 1½ hours. Replenish when necessary with boiling water, as the water must not be allowed to boil away, or the pudding will stick to basin. Remove from pan. Stand for a moment or two to allow pudding to shrink from basin or mould. Turn out on to a hot dish. Serve with jam sauce. *For 4 persons.*

INDIVIDUAL SPONGE PUDDINGS : Divide batter equally among 5 greased fireproof cups. Steam for ¾ hour. Turn out carefully. Decorate each with a grape or glacé cherry.

CANARY PUDDING (Pouding au Serin) : Place 4 rounded tablespoons of apricot, raspberry or strawberry jam in the bottom of basin before adding mixture.

CHOCOLATE PUDDING (Pouding au Chocolat) : Sift 3 rounded tablespoons of cocoa with the flour. Stir 1 teaspoon vanilla essence into 2 tablespoons additional milk and add to milk given in basic recipe. Serve with chocolate sauce.

COFFEE PUDDING (Pouding au Café) : Add 2 oz. chopped almonds or 1 oz. chopped almonds and 1 oz. chopped walnuts to batter, and flavour milk with 1 tablespoon coffee essence.

GINGER PUDDING : (Pouding au Gingembre) : Sift, if liked, ½ teaspoon ground ginger with the flour. Stir 3 oz. roughly-chopped ginger, preserved in syrup, into the batter before the second egg.

ALMOND CARAMEL PUDDING (Pouding d'Amandes au Caramel)

3 tablespoons caster sugar
½ cup milk
½ tablespoon flour
1½ oz. ground almonds
3 separated eggs
2 oz. butter
½ oz. caster sugar
Pinch of salt
½ teaspoon vanilla essence

Melt the 3 tablespoons sugar in a frying-pan until caramel brown, then allow to cool. Stir in milk slowly. Stand till caramel re-dissolves. Smooth flour to a cream in caramel milk. Add almonds and beaten egg yolks. Melt and add butter. Stir in remainder of sugar, salt and vanilla essence. Beat egg whites to a stiff froth. Fold into mixture. Butter a pudding mould.

Sprinkle with extra sugar. Pour in mixture very gently, filling three-quarters full. Cover with a round of buttered paper. Tie on securely. Steam for ¾ hour. Turn on to a hot dish. Serve with whipped cream. *For 3 persons.*

APPLE ROLY POLY (Roulade de Pommes)

½ lb. sifted flour
3 teaspoons baking powder
1 teaspoon salt
2 oz. butter or margarine
About ¼ pint cold milk
2 cups sliced cooking apples
3 oz. light brown sugar
½ teaspoon ground cinnamon
Pinch of ground cloves
2 teaspoons grated lemon rind if possible
2 tablespoons melted butter

Sift flour, baking powder and salt into a basin. Cut fat into tiny pieces. Rub lightly into flour. Add enough milk to make a soft but not sticky dough. Knead for a second or two on a lightly floured board. Roll into a rectangle, about ¼ inch thick. Mix apples with light brown sugar, cinnamon, cloves and lemon rind, or moisten with golden syrup and use only 1 tablespoon sugar. Spread dough with fat, then with fruit mixture. Roll up like a swiss roll. Brush edges with cold water. Press together to keep in the

juice. Tie loosely in a pudding cloth, wrung out of boiling water and floured. Steam for 1½ hours. Remove from cloth. Dish up. Slice. Serve with custard sauce. *For 6 persons.*

COCONUT PUDDING (Pouding au Noix de Coco)

4 oz. butter
4 oz. sugar

Cream butter and sugar in a basin. Add egg yolk, milk, flour, baking powder, flavouring to taste

1 separated egg
½ cup milk
4 oz. flour
1 teaspoon baking powder
Flavouring to taste
2 tablespoons desiccated coconut

and coconut. Beat well. Fold in stiffly-beaten egg white. Three-quarters fill a greased mould. Cover with greased paper. Steam for 2 hours. Unmould. Serve with jam sauce. *For 4 persons.*

PINEAPPLE PUDDING (Pouding d'Ananas)

¼ lb. butter
¼ lb. caster sugar
¼ lb. flour
1 teaspoon baking powder
Pinch of salt
3 heaped tablespoons diced pineapple
2 tablespoons pineapple syrup
Lemon juice to taste
2 beaten eggs
Milk as required

Beat butter and sugar to a cream. Sift flour with baking powder and salt. Stir pineapple and syrup, and a squeeze of lemon juice into butter and sugar, then add flour and beaten eggs alternately. Stir in enough milk to make mixture drop easily from a spoon. Three-quarters fill a buttered basin or mould. Cover with a buttered paper. Steam for 2 hours. Turn out on to a hot dish. Serve with cream. *For 4 persons.*

STEAMED SUET PUDDING (Pouding à la Graisse)

BASIC RECIPE:
¼ lb. flour
½ teaspoon bicarbonate of soda
½ teaspoon salt
¼ lb. stale breadcrumbs
¼ lb. shredded beef suet
¼ lb. brown or caster sugar
2 eggs
About ½ gill milk

Grease a 1½-2 pint basin, and a round of grease-proof paper for the cover. Sift flour, soda and salt into a basin. Stir in crumbs, suet and sugar. Beat eggs. Make a well in the centre of dry ingredients. Add eggs and ½ gill milk by degrees, beating constantly. Stir in enough additional milk to give you a dropable consistency. Pack into basin, filling it two-thirds full. Cover with the greased round of paper. Tie securely under rim. Place in a steamer or on a rack in a saucepan with boiling water coming half-way up the sides. Cover pan closely. Cook for 2 hours. Replenish when necessary with boiling water. Remove from pan. Stand for a moment or two to allow pudding to shrink from basin or mould. Turn out on to a hot dish. Serve coated with heated honey, golden syrup, jam or any sweet sauce. *For 6 persons.*

To vary;
1. Omit eggs and use about ¼ pint of milk.
2. Substitute 1 teaspoon baking powder for the soda.

APPLE JELLY DUMPLINGS : Sift ½ teaspoon ground cinnamon with the flour. Follow basic recipe. Divide mixture equally between 6 greased individual pudding basins. Steam for 1 hour. Turn out carefully. Coat each with apple jelly. Serve with custard sauce.

APPLE AND FIG PUDDING (Pouding de Pommes aux Figues)

¼ lb. shredded suet
¼ lb. minced figs

Mix suet with figs. Pare, chop and add apples with brown sugar. Mix together in a basin.

2 cored sour apples
¼ lb. brown sugar
¼ lb. breadcrumbs
¾-1 cup milk
2 separated eggs
¼ teaspoon ground mace
Grated rind ½ lemon
3 oz. flour
Pinch of salt

Place breadcrumbs in another basin. Add milk then beaten egg yolks, rinsing out the egg basin with a tablespoonful of milk. Stir this into suet mixture, then add mace, lemon rind and flour sifted with salt. Lightly fold in stiffly-frothed egg whites. Three-quarters fill a greased basin. Cover. Steam for 4 hours. Unmould. Serve with lemon sauce. *For 6 persons.*

APRICOT JAM PUDDING (Pouding aux Abricots)

2 separated eggs
1 tablespoon apricot jam
1½ gills milk
2 tablespoons caster sugar
2 oz. flour
¼ lb. breadcrumbs
¼ lb. shredded suet

Place egg yolks, jam, milk, sugar, flour, crumbs and suet in a basin. Beat well, then lightly fold in stiffly-frothed egg whites. Three-quarters fill a buttered pudding mould. Cover with buttered paper. Steam for 2 hours. Turn on to a hot dish. Serve with hot apricot sauce. *For 4 or 5 persons.*

DATE PUDDING (Pouding de Dattes)

½ lb. stoned dates
¼ lb. flour
1 cup stale breadcrumbs
½ cup light brown sugar
½ lb. shredded suet
1 teaspoon ground ginger
1 teaspoon ground cinnamon
Pinch of salt
2 eggs
½ cup milk
¼ teaspoon bicarbonate of soda

Put dates through a meat grinder into a basin. Add flour, breadcrumbs, sugar, suet, spices and salt. Beat eggs. Stir in milk. Dissolve soda with a tablespoon of the egg and milk. Add to remainder. Stir into dry ingredients. Beat well. Three-quarters fill a large greased basin or mould. Cover. Steam for 3 hours. Unmould. Serve with custard or sweet white sauce. *For 6 persons.*

FIG PUDDING : Follow recipe for date pudding but substitute dried figs for the dates.

GINGER SUET PUDDING (Pouding de Gingembre à la Graisse)

6 oz. flour
½ teaspoon salt
2 teaspoons ground ginger
½ teaspoon ground mace
2 teaspoons baking powder
½ cup breadcrumbs
1 cup shredded suet
½ cup golden syrup
½ cup treacle
1 beaten egg
1 cup milk

Sift flour, salt, spices and baking powder into a basin. Add crumbs and suet, then syrup, treacle, egg and milk. Beat well. Three-quarters fill a greased mould. Cover with buttered paper. Steam for 2 hours. Unmould. Serve with custard or sweet white sauce or cream. *For 6 persons.*

MARMALADE PUDDING (Pouding de Marmelade)

¼ lb. flour
¼ lb. breadcrumbs

Mix flour with crumbs, spice, sugar, suet, salt and marmalade. Dissolve soda in a tablespoon

½ teaspoon mixed spice
3 oz. light brown sugar
¼ lb. shredded suet
Pinch of salt
¼ lb. marmalade
½ oz. bicarbonate of soda
Milk as required
1 beaten egg

or two of milk. Add with egg to other ingredients with enough additional milk to make a dropable batter. Three-quarters fill a greased pudding basin, dusted with brown sugar. Cover with greased paper. Steam for 2½ hours. Turn out. Serve with custard sauce. *For 4 persons.*

PLUM PUDDINGS

Prepare Plum Pudding mixture when possible about two months before Christmas. Steam for 7 hours when large—for serving 8-12 persons. When small—for serving 4-6 persons, steam for 5 hours. When ready, leave until cool. Remove pudding cloth and paper. Cover with clean dry grease-proof paper, then with a dry pudding cloth. Suspend from cloth handle on a nail in a dry airy cupboard. Re-steam for 2 hours on Christmas day.

To serve Plum puddings;
1. Dredge with caster sugar. Plant a sprig of berried holly on top.
2. Prick all over with blanched split almonds fried lightly in butter.
3. Decorate with holly. Take to dining-room door. Pour a glass of heated brandy or rum over, and set pudding alight. Serve with your favourite custard or hard sauce, or with brandy or rum butter.

PLUM PUDDING (Pouding, Noel)

10 oz. stale breadcrumbs
¼ lb. flour
½ teaspoon ground mace
1 teaspoon ground ginger
1 grated nutmeg
½ lb. Demerara sugar
¼ lb. candied orange peel
1 oz. candied citron peel
2 oz. candied lemon peel
¼ lb. glacé cherries
½ lb. cleaned currants
½ lb. Muscatel raisins
½ lb. Valencia raisins
3 oz. Jordan almonds
1 grated carrot
6 eggs
2 tablespoons treacle
½ lb. shredded suet
About ½ pint old ale

Place crumbs in a basin. Sift in flour and spices. Stir in sugar. Shred candied peels and add. Chop cherries and add with currants. Stone, grind and add raisins. Blanch and chop almonds. Add carrot. Beat eggs. Add treacle and beat well. Add suet to flour mixture. (If preferred, add butter, but in this case, cream it with the sugar, instead of adding sugar to dry ingredients, before stirring into mixture). Add egg and treacle mixture. Stir and stir and stir until thoroughly blended. Cover. Stand for 24 hours. Beat well and stir in enough ale to make mixture rather stiff, but dropable. Divide equally among 3 prepared medium sized basins, filling them two-thirds full. Cover with greased paper and scalded pudding cloths sprinkled with flour. Tie the ends to form a handle. Steam for 7 hours. When required, steam again for 2 hours. Each pudding is enough *for 4-6 persons.*

GRANDMOTHER'S PLUM PUDDING
(Pouding Noel à la Grand'mère)

½ lb. butter
½ lb. Demerara sugar
6 separated eggs

Beat butter and sugar to a cream. Add well-beaten egg yolks. Stir in suet and crumbs. Sift flour, spices and salt together, and add alternately

½ lb. shredded beef suet
½ lb. breadcrumbs
1 lb. flour
1 teaspoon cinnamon
1 teaspoon ground mace
½ teaspoon grated nutmeg
½ teaspoon ground cloves
Pinch of salt
1 cup brandy
1 lb. cleaned currants
2 oz. candied citron peel
2 oz. candied orange peel
2 oz. candied lemon peel
1 cup Maraschino cherries
1 lb. chopped raisins
Juice of 1 lemon

with brandy, using more if required. Stir in currants. Mince peels and cherries and add. Stir in raisins, lemon juice and any liquor that comes away in the cup with the cherries. Lastly fold in stiffly-frothed egg whites. Three-quarters fill 4 well-greased medium sized pudding basins. Steam for 7 hours. When required, resteam for 2 hours. Turn out. Serve garnished with icing sugar, holly and blanched almonds. Each pudding is enough *for* 4-6 *persons*.

SUET LAYER PUDDING (Pouding de Graisse en Surprise)

14 oz. flour
1¾ teaspoons baking powder
Pinch of salt
7 oz. shredded suet
Cold water to mix
1 lb. jam, marmalade, honey, golden syrup or mincemeat

Sift flour with baking powder and salt into a basin. Add suet and enough water to give you a soft dough. Roll out thinly and shape into a round to fit a buttered basin, smoothing out the creases to make pastry even. Put in a layer of jam, marmalade, honey, golden syrup or mincemeat, and divide remaining pastry in four. Fill basin with alternate layers of filling and pastry. Cover with greased paper. Steam for 3 hours. Unmould. Serve with custard sauce. *For* 6-8 *persons*.

DESSERT CAKES

Britain is one of the few countries of the world in which some form of cake is not frequently served as a dessert. Pâtisserie is one of the most popular desserts in Belgium, France and Switzerland. In Central Europe, ' tortes,'— rich layer cakes, take its place ; while Italy provides us with ' tortas.' In Canada and the United States, cake desserts range from chocolate rolls, fruit shortcakes to upside-down-cakes.

CHARLOTTES

The mother of all charlottes is the Charlotte Russe. Old records show that it originally consisted of a round case made of strips of buttered bread, filled with fruit, then covered with buttered bread and weighted down. To-day, we call this type of charlotte either a ' diplomatic,' ' Hydropathic,' or ' summer pudding,' depending on the part of the country in which it is prepared. In olden days, it was baked before serving, and served hot, whereas nowadays the British housewife leaves it for 24 hours, then turns it out and coats it with custard or cream.

Charlotte Russe, to-day, consists of a cake made by lining a round mould or tin with sponge fingers, sometimes known as lady fingers, or strips of sponge cake, then filled with a rich cream flavoured to taste.

CHARLOTTE RUSSE

½ pint packet lemon jelly
1½ gills hot water
Glacé cherries as required
Angelica as required
2 oz. sponge fingers
1½ gills thick cream
3 dessertspoons caster sugar
½ teaspoon vanilla essence
½ gill milk
¼ oz. powdered gelatine
¼ gill cold water
1 egg white

Dissolve jelly in hot water. Leave till cold. Pour a tablespoonful into the bottom of a rinsed charlotte tin, 1¼ pint size, just enough to coat bottom. When set, halve one or two glacé cherries, or cut them into the shape of a four-leaved clover. Dip them in a little of the remaining jelly, and with the help of one or two leaves of angelica, also dipped in the jelly, make a floral design over jelly in bottom of mould. Cover with a thin layer of jelly to set the decorations. Trim biscuits at one end so that they are all of equal length. Place side by side round the inside of tin, so that they fit tightly together and stand firmly on the jelly. (The biscuits, flat sides inwards, should be about the same height as the tin. If preferred, halve biscuits lengthwise and arrange, cut sides inward.) Fill up any cracks between the biscuit with a paste made from crumbled biscuit trimmings and jelly, to prevent filling oozing through cracks. Beat cream till it hangs from the whisk. Stir in sugar and vanilla essence, then gradually add milk. When blended, soak gelatine for 5 minutes in the water. Dissolve over hot water, stirring constantly, but do not allow mixture to get really hot. Cool slightly. Fold into cream. Beat egg white to a stiff froth and fold in. Leave till beginning to thicken, then gently turn into prepared tin. Leave till set and chilled. Dip tin in warm water. Turn upside down on a serving dish, and shake sharply, holding tin and the plate together as you shake. When it loosens, let it slip out carefully to avoid breaking. Chop remainder of jelly on a piece of wet paper. Arrange round the base. *For 4 persons.*

BURNT ALMOND CHARLOTTE (Charlotte à la Josephine)

¾ cup Jordan almonds
½ pint cream
1 packet lemon jelly
1 teaspoon butter
½ lb. caster sugar
¾ cup milk
1 egg yolk
1 teaspoon vanilla essence
Sponge fingers as required

Blanch and chop almonds finely. Whip cream. Dissolve jelly in enough hot water to make ½ pint, including jelly. Melt butter in a saucepan. Add half the sugar. Dissolve until into a caramel syrup, then add almonds. Stir for 2 minutes longer. Turn into a mortar. Leave till cold. Pound into a powder. Place in a saucepan with milk and remainder of sugar. Cook for 10 minutes, stirring occasionally. Remove from stove. Beat egg yolk. Add a little of almond mixture to yolk. Stir till blended, then pour into remainder of almond mixture. Gradually stir into melted jelly. Leave till cool. Beat till mixture shows signs of thickening, then add vanilla essence, and lightly fold in cream. Pour into a charlotte mould lined to taste with sponge fingers. Chill. Turn out. Decorate with roses of additional whipped cream, rings cut from glacé fruit, and chopped pistachio nuts. *For 6 persons.*

CHOCOLATE CHARLOTTE (Charlotte de Chocolat)

10 sponge fingers
1 dessertspoon powdered gelatine
2 tablespoons cold water
1 oz. chocolate
¼ cup boiling water
3 oz. caster sugar
Tiny pinch of salt
1¾ cups evaporated milk
¼ teaspoon vanilla essence or rum

Line a charlotte tin with sponge fingers and lemon jelly. See basic recipe. Soak gelatine in cold water for 5 minutes. Melt chocolate in top of a double boiler, then stir in boiling water. Cook slowly on stove till thick and smooth, stirring constantly. Remove from stove. Stir in sugar, salt and ¾ cup of the milk. Return to stove. Cook for about 2 minutes longer, stirring constantly, then remove from heat. Add gelatine. Stir till dissolved, then leave till cool. Chill remainder of milk. When chocolate mixture starts to thicken, whip chilled milk until stiff. Fold into chocolate mixture. Add vanilla essence or rum. Pour into mould. Chill until firm. Unmould. Decorate with whipped cream and chocolate vermicelli. *For 5 persons.*

EGG NOG CHARLOTTE (Charlotte au Rhum)

1 dessertspoon powdered gelatine
2 tablespoons cold water
6 oz. butter
1 cup sifted icing sugar
4 separated eggs
¼ cup brandy or rum
12 crushed macaroons
Pinch of salt
Sponge fingers as required

Soften gelatine in cold water for 5 minutes. Stir over hot water till dissolved. Cool slightly. Beat butter to a cream, then beat in sugar. Beat in egg yolks, brandy or rum and macaroons. Stir in dissolved gelatine. Whip until stiff. Beat egg whites to a stiff froth with salt. Fold into yolk mixture. Line a round charlotte mould with waxed paper. Cover bottom solidly and the sides with sponge fingers. (If preferred, use slices of sponge cake.) Fill up with egg mixture. Chill. Turn out. Decorate with whipped cream and posies of crystallized violets and angelica. *For 6 persons.*

ORANGE CHARLOTTE (Charlotte d'Orange)

Sponge fingers as required
2 teaspoons powdered gelatine
¼ cup cold water
½ cup boiling water
1 cup caster sugar
1 tablespoon lemon juice
1 cup orange juice and pulp
2 cups thick cream

Line a quart charlotte mould with sponge fingers and jelly. See basic recipe. Soak gelatine in cold water for 10 minutes. Stir in boiling water. When gelatine is dissolved, pour into a basin. Stir in sugar. When dissolved, stir in lemon and orange juice and pulp. Place bowl in a basin of cold water. Leave till mixture is cold, then start whipping. Whip till it begins to foam, then whip cream and fold into mixture. Place in prepared mould or tin. Leave till set. Chill. Turn out on to a serving dish. Garnish with trails of whipped cream between the sponge fingers. Decorate top with whipped cream and crystallized orange and lemon slices. *For 6 persons.*

STRAWBERRY CHARLOTTE (Charlotte de Fraises)

12 sponge fingers
1 tablespoon powdered gelatine
¼ cup cold water
¼ cup boiling water
5 oz. caster sugar
2 tablespoons lemon juice
1 cup sieved strawberries
2 egg whites
¼ pint canned milk or whipped cream

Line a quart charlotte mould with jelly and whole trimmed sponge fingers. See basic recipe, but substitute 12 strawberries large enough to ring the bottom of the mould for the glacé cherries and angelica. Soak gelatine in cold water for 5 minutes. Dissolve in boiling water. Add sugar. Stir till dissolved. Leave till cool. Stir in lemon juice and strawberry purée. When quite cold, beat with an egg whisk till quite frothy. Beat egg whites till stiff. Beat canned milk or cream till stiff. Fold egg whites, then milk or cream into strawberry purée. Pour into prepared case. Leave for 12 hours to chill. Turn out gently. Decorate round the base with the remainder of the jelly, finely chopped, and additional berries. Fill the centre of top with whipped cream. Sprinkle with chopped pistachio nuts. *For 6 persons.*

PINEAPPLE ROYAL (Ananas Royale)

1 can pineapple rings
1 oblong sponge cake
Apricot or raspberry jam as required
Pineapple juice or sherry as required
2 egg whites
2½ oz. caster sugar

Drain juice from pineapple. Turn pineapple into the top of a double boiler. Cook for about 10 minutes over boiling water. Remove from heat. Cut sponge cake into equal slices, ½ inch thick, then neatly cut into rounds. The sponge cake should be wide enough to give you rounds the same diameter as the pineapple slices. Spread sponge rounds with apricot or raspberry jam. Place a slice of sponge cake in the bottom of a round glass fireproof plate. Sprinkle lightly with pineapple juice or sherry. Top with a slice of pineapple. Build up a ' pineapple ' in this way with alternate layers of sponge cake, sherry and pineapple rings. Dissolve a tablespoon of the same kind of jam used in a few drops of boiling water. Brush pineapple and sponge all over the outside with this glaze. Lay a small sponge round on top. Beat egg whites to a stiff froth. Beat in two-thirds of the sugar by degrees, then fold in remainder. Squeeze through a forcing pipe all over the pineapple to suggest " eyes ". Bake in a slow oven, 275° F., until set. Place a tuft of pineapple foliage, made of angelica, on top. *For 6 persons.*

SHORTCAKES

' Shortcake ' is the name given to a layer cake usually filled with fruit and decorated with cream. It is of American origin. In some parts of America, a baking powder mixture, which corresponds to a British oven scone mixture, is used. I prefer shortcake made from a butter sponge batter which is not so common, and seems to make a better combination with the fruit and cream. Occasionally, the American housewife makes her shortcake of a very rich shortcrust.

Fillings for Shortcakes; Sliced fresh apricots, peaches or nectarines ; sliced bananas, stoned cherries ; fresh raspberries or strawberries, which are most popular. Sometimes stewed fruit is used. To stew fruit for a shortcake, allow

$\frac{1}{4}$-$\frac{1}{2}$ lb. sugar depending on type of fruit and sweetness, and about $\frac{1}{2}$ gill of water to $1\frac{1}{2}$-2 lb. fruit. If apricots, peaches or nectarines are not quite ripe, either simmer in their syrup gently for 3 or 4 minutes or scald, peel, slice and sweeten to taste, then stand until sugar is dissolved before using.

FRUIT SHORTCAKE (Gâteau de Fruit)

BASIC RECIPE:
½ lb. sifted flour
3 teaspoons baking powder
½ teaspoon salt
3 oz. butter or margarine
1-2 oz. caster sugar
About ¼ pint milk
Fruit to taste

Sift flour, baking powder and salt into a basin. Rub in fat. Stir in sugar, then add enough milk to make a soft but not sticky dough. The mixture should leave the sides of the bowl clean. Knead lightly on a floured board for about ½ minute. Divide in two equal portions. Turn upside down. Roll each into a round ¼ inch thick, to fit sandwich tin 9 inches across. Grease tin lightly with butter. Pat one round into tin. Brush with melted butter. Cover with second layer. Bake in a hot oven, 450° F., for about ¼ hour, till puffy and dry in the centre. Separate layers. If not quite dry, place on a baking sheet, separated sides upwards, and replace in oven to dry. Place half the prepared fruit on top of one buttered layer, then place other layer on top, buttered side downwards. Cover with remainder of fruit, then with whipped cream. Decorate with fruit to taste. *For 6 persons.*

To Vary: Cut dough into 12 equal-sized rounds, 3 inches in diameter. Place half the rounds in a shallow greased baking tin ½ inch apart. Brush tops with melted butter or margarine. Cover each with remaining rounds, then brush tops with melted butter or margarine. Bake in a hot oven, 450° F., for about ¼ hour. Separate halves, then place prepared fruit on the top of the bottom halves. Cover, insides upwards, with remaining halves. Top with fruit and cream to taste.

BUTTER SPONGE SHORTCAKE (Gâteau Victoria)

¼ lb. butter
¼ lb. caster sugar
2 eggs
1 tablespoon warm milk or water
¼ lb. flour
1 teaspoon baking powder
Flavouring to taste

Grease two layer cake tins, 7 inches in diameter, and dust with flour. Beat fat and sugar to a cream. Add eggs, one at a time, beating after each addition, then add warm milk or water. Sieve flour with baking powder, and stir into egg mixture. Add flavouring to taste or grated rind of ½ lemon and ½ teaspoon vanilla essence. When blended, divide batter equally between the sandwich tins. Spread evenly with a palette knife. Bake in a moderately hot oven, 400° F., for about 20 minutes. Cool on a wire rack. Put layers together with fruit and decorate as suggested. *For 6 persons.*

QUANTITIES OF FRUIT REQUIRED FOR SHORTCAKE

Apricots, Bananas, Nectarines and Peaches: 1½ pints peeled and sliced.
Cherries: About 1½ pints stoned.
Raspberries and Strawberries: Increase quantities for shortcake by half and use 2 pints hulled and crushed.
NOTE: To prepare fruit for filling, sprinkle with caster sugar and lemon juice to taste, omitting lemon juice for raspberries and strawberries.

To Decorate Shortcakes: Top fruit with whipped cream, or with lemon or orange chiffon. Decorate with whole additional fruit similar to filling, if filling consists of sliced bananas, cherries or berries. If filling consists of apricot, nectarine or peach, decorate with glacé cherries and angelica, chocolate shot, chopped nuts, crushed meringue or butterscotch.

STRAWBERRY SHORTCAKE (Gâteau de Fraises)

1½ pints small strawberries
Caster sugar to taste
2 butter sponge layers
Whipped cream to taste

Crush 1 pint berries lightly. Sweeten to taste with caster sugar. Cover and stand for 2-3 hours, until sugar is dissolved, and the juice drawn out. Cover one sponge layer with the crushed berries. (If liked, spread layer thinly with strawberry jam before covering with berries.) Cover with second sponge layer. Decorate as suggested with whipped cream and the remainder of whole berries. (You could butter the sponge layers, and place the buttered side uppermost in each case.) If liked, you can also place small heaps of whole berries and cream alternately round the outside of dish holding shortcake. *For 6 persons.*

TIPSY CAKE (Gâteau au Vin)

8 split sponge cakes
Raspberry jam as required
Madeira or sherry to taste
2 leaves gelatine
2 or 3 tablespoons cold water
1 pint hot custard sauce
2 tablespoons blanched almonds
1 or 2 glacé cherries

Spread half the sponge cakes thickly with jam and pair again. Build them into an oblong 'cake'. Sprinkle with Madeira or sherry, adding a little at a time, until they are soaked through. Soak gelatine for 5 minutes in cold water, then stir till dissolved in custard sauce. Leave till cool. Pour over cake. When quite cold, decorate with whipped cream, almonds and cherries. *For 4-6 persons.*

TOPSY-TURVY CAKES (Gateaux Renversés)

Topsy-turvy cakes, sometimes known as 'Upside-down cakes,' are made from a simple butter sponge, but a plain gingerbread batter is equally suitable for an apple coating. The variety of topsy-turvy cake takes its name from the syrupy mixture placed in bottom of tin.

BATTER FOR TOPSY-TURVY CAKES

2 oz. butter
4 oz. caster sugar
1 beaten egg
6 oz. flour
1½ teaspoons baking powder
¼ teaspoon salt
½ cup milk

Beat butter till creamy. Gradually stir in sugar, then egg. Sift flour with baking powder and salt. Add alternately with milk to butter and sugar. Grease a round or square cake tin, 9 or 10 inches across, or 8 inches square. Add fruit mixture. Pour batter over. Bake in a moderate oven, 350° F., for about ¾ hour. Turn tin upside down on hot serving dish. Stand for a minute or so to allow syrup in bottom of tin to saturate the cake, then gradually ease out on to dish. Serve with whipped cream. *For 6 persons.*

APPLE TOPSY-TURVY CAKE (Gâteau Renversé aux Pommes) : Melt 2 oz. butter or margarine in tin. Add fully ¼ cup light brown sugar, and ¼ teaspoon ground cinnamon or cloves. Stir over slow heat till sugar is dissolved. Place 1 pint fingers of cooking apple in a design over the bottom. Cover with batter and bake.

APRICOT TOPSY-TURVY CAKE (Gâteau Renversé aux Abricots) : Follow method given for apple topsy-turvy cake, but substitute 1½ oz. butter for the 2 oz. given, and omit spices. Arrange 8 halved fresh or canned apricots, cut sides up, in syrup. Cover with batter and bake.

CHERRY TOPSY-TURVY CAKE (Gâteau Renversé aux Cerises) : Follow recipe for apricot topsy-turvy cake, but substitute 2 cups black dessert cherries for the apricots.

TRIFLES

As trifles are composed of a mixture of sponge cake, custard and cream, they are included in Dessert Cakes, rather than in the Cold Sweet section. It is not necessary to flavour the cake for a trifle with wine, but usual. Madeira, Marsala, rum or sherry should be used for this purpose. In days of old, not only was the sponge cake flavoured with wine or rum, but so were any macaroons, or ratafias used in the composition. All trifles should be well chilled.

OLD-FASHIONED TRIFLE (Trifle Anglaise)

8 sponge cakes
Apricot jam as required
¾ gill sherry
2 oz. almonds
3 separated eggs
¾ pint milk
1 oz. caster sugar
½ teaspoon vanilla essence
2 oz. ratafias
1½ gills cream
Cherries and angelica as required

Halve sponge cakes lengthwise, then cut in half crosswise. Spread each piece on one side with jam. Pair. Pile in centre of a shallow glass trifle dish. Sprinkle with sherry. Stand till sherry is absorbed. (Use rum if preferred.) Blanch, peel and split almonds. Make egg yolks and milk into custard sauce with sugar. Pour custard into a basin. Stand for a moment. Beat egg whites to a stiff froth. Fold lightly into custard. Stir in vanilla essence. Leave till cool. Arrange ratafias and half the almonds in a design over the cake. Cover with custard. Whip and sweeten cream. Flavour with vanilla essence. Pile rockily on top, or force through an icing bag in roses or squirls. Decorate with half glacé cherries, foliage of angelica, and remainder of almonds. *For 6 persons.*

Cold Sweets

BLANCMANGE

BASIC RECIPE :
1½ oz. cornflour
1 pint milk
Snippet of lemon rind
1½ oz. caster sugar

Mix cornflour in a basin with enough of the milk to make a cream. Bring remainder of milk slowly to the boil with lemon rind. Strain into creamed cornflour, stirring constantly, till blended. Return to saucepan. Stir till boiling. Boil for 5 minutes, stirring constantly, then add sugar. Stir till dissolved. Pour into a wet mould. Chill. Unmould. Serve with fruit compôte or salad, stewed fruit, or a fruit or chocolate sauce. *For 4 persons.*

To Vary: If preferred, lemon rind can be omitted and ¾ teaspoon vanilla essence added just before moulding. To avoid any chance of scorching, cook in the top of a double boiler instead of in a saucepan. If a richer or more nourishing blancmange is wanted, add 1 large walnut butter before moulding, and stir till dissolved, or cool slightly before moulding, then beat in 1 beaten egg or 2 yolks. If a fluffy blancmange is wanted, fold in the stiffly whipped egg whites after the yolks before moulding.

BUTTERSCOTCH : Substitute 1 cup light brown sugar for the caster. Melt ½ oz. butter. Add sugar. Cook over slow heat until sugar melts and forms a rich syrup, then slowly stir into hot milk before adding to cornflour.

CHOCOLATE : Melt 2 oz. unsweetened or plain grated chocolate in the hot milk before adding to cornflour. Omit lemon rind. Add ¾ teaspoon vanilla essence.

COFFEE : Substitute ½ pint strong black coffee for ½ pint of the milk.
STRAWBERRY : Cover and leave until nearly cold, then stir in ¼ cup crushed
strawberries.

CREAMED RICE (Pouding de Riz à la Crème)

1 quart cold milk
4 tablespoons rice
3 oz. sugar
1 vanilla pod

Cook ingredients in the top of a double boiler,
with the water boiling below, till all the milk is
absorbed. Remove pod. Pour into a basin.
Leave till well chilled, then stir in ½ gill cold
cream to taste. Serve with stewed, dried or canned apricots. For 6-8 persons.

CREAMED SAGO (Pouding de Sagou à la Crème)

½ cup sago
1 pint milk
1 separated egg
2 oz. sugar
¼ teaspoon salt
1 teaspoon vanilla essence

Rinse sago in a colander under cold water tap.
Drain well. Place in a basin. Add milk and soak
for 3 hours. Place in top of a double boiler.
Cover and cook over boiling water, stirring
occasionally, until clear. Beat egg yolk. Stir
in sugar and salt, then hot sago. Stir till blended,
then stir over hot water till like custard. Remove to a basin. Cool slightly.
Beat egg white till stiff and fold in. Leave till cold. Stir in vanilla essence.
Pour into a glass dish. For 4 persons.

FRUIT ANGELINA (Crème de Fruit à la Norvégienne)

1½ pints sweetened fruit juice
4 tablespoons fine semolina

Bring fruit juice to the boil. Stir in semolina.
Simmer gently for a few minutes. Remove from
heat and leave to cool. Whilst cooling, beat with
a rotary whip until light and fluffy. Pile into glasses. Top with a little cream
and sprinkle with caster sugar. For 6 persons.

BAKED CUSTARD (Oeufs au Lait)

7 oz. caster sugar
Pinch of salt
1¾ pints milk
1 teaspoon vanilla essence
6 beaten eggs

Stir sugar and salt into the milk in saucepan.
Bring to boil. Add vanilla essence. Place eggs
in a buttered fireproof dish. Strain milk into the
eggs, stirring constantly. Place in a baking tin
containing hot water coming 1 inch up the sides.
Bake in a slow oven, 300° F., until set in about 1 hour. For 8 persons.

FRENCH CREAM CUSTARD (Crème Renversée au Rhum) : Melt 8 lumps of
sugar very slowly with a teaspoon of water. Simmer until into a caramel syrup,
and line the bottom of a plain charlotte mould. When set, brush the uncoated
sides with melted butter or olive oil. Strain in the custard. Cover with greased
paper. Bake as described. Cool slightly, then turn out gently. Chill. Top with
whipped cream flavoured with rum.

VANILLA CREAM CUSTARD (Crème à la Vanille) : Follow above recipe,
but substitute 2 whole eggs and the yolks of 4 for the 6 eggs given. After adding
milk to eggs, strain into the top of a double boiler and stir constantly over

boiling water until thick, but on no account allow it to start to boil, or it will curdle. When it begins to thicken, remove at once from stove, and pour into serving dish. Chill. If preferred, pour into individual custard glasses.

CUP CUSTARDS (Pots de Crème)

¾ pint milk
1 saltspoon salt
1-2 oz. caster sugar
3 beaten egg yolks
½ teaspoon vanilla essence

Heat milk and salt to boiling point. Beat sugar into egg yolks. Very slowly stir in the hot milk. Stir until blended. Strain into the top of a double boiler. Stir over hot water with a wooden spoon until custard coats the back of spoon. Take care not to allow the custard to boil, or it will curdle. Stir in vanilla essence. Pour into a custard jug. Cover. Stir once or twice while cooling, to prevent a crust forming on top. When cold, pour into individual cups. Decorate each with a rose of whipped cream. *For 4 persons.*

BAKED CUP CUSTARDS : Pour prepared custard into individual buttered or oiled moulds. Place side by side in a baking tin containing hot water coming half-way up the sides. Bake in a moderately slow oven, 325° F., until custard is set in $\frac{1}{2}$-$\frac{3}{4}$ hour. Test with a silver knife before removing from oven. When ready, the knife should come out clean. Chill. Serve with fruit juice or purée, or caramel or chocolate syrup. *For 4 persons.*

CREME BRULEE

2 cups thick cream
4 beaten eggs
2 oz. caster sugar
1 saltspoon salt
2 oz. brown sugar

Heat cream in top of a double boiler to scalding point. Remove from heat. Mix eggs with the caster sugar, and salt. Slowly add the cream, stirring constantly. Return to top of double boiler. Cook over hot water for about 5 minutes, until the mixture coats the back of spoon, beating constantly with a rotary beater. Pour into a buttered fireproof dish. Chill well. Sprinkle evenly with the brown sugar. (The layer of sugar should be about ¼ inch thick.) Place in the top of a cool oven with the oven door open, until the sugar turns into a caramel. Chill. *For 4 persons.*

FLOATING ISLAND (Oeufs à la Neige)

1 pint milk
2 oz. loaf sugar
¼ teaspoon vanilla essence
2 egg whites
¼ lb. caster sugar
5 drops orange essence
4 egg yolks

Heat milk and loaf sugar slowly in a shallow saucepan until sugar is dissolved. Bring to boil. Add vanilla essence. Beat egg whites until stiff. Stir in caster sugar and orange essence. Fill a dessertspoon with mixture and drop into the boiling milk. Repeat. Poach them slowly, turning carefully until evenly coated. Remove carefully. Drain on a sieve. Beat egg yolks. Strain 2 or 3 tablespoons of the milk into egg yolks, then strain remainder of milk into the top of a double boiler. Gradually stir in egg yolks. Stir over almost boiling water until custard coats the back of the spoon. Remove from heat. Leave until quite cold. When required, pour custard into a glass or silver dish, and arrange "eggs" on top. *For 4 or 5 persons.*

FRENCH CHOCOLATE CUSTARDS (Pots de Crème, Française)

½ lb. sweetened chocolate
1 cup hot milk
3 egg yolks
¼ teaspoon vanilla essence

Place the chocolate and milk in the top of a double boiler. Stir over hot water until at boiling point. Remove from stove. Beat egg yolks. Stir in chocolate and milk. Add vanilla essence. Strain into 4 custard cups. Chill. *For 4 persons.*

JUNKETS

A junket is a curd made by adding rennet in liquid, powder or cube form to new milk.

BASIC:
1 pint milk
1 teaspoon rennet
Pinch of salt
Grated nutmeg to taste

Warm the milk to blood heat 98.4° F., then stir in rennet and salt. Stir until dissolved. (Allow 1 teaspoon rennet to 1 pint of milk unless otherwise instructed on bottle, as rennets vary according to the make.) Pour immediately into a glass serving dish or into individual sundae glasses. Leave junket undisturbed in the room in which it is prepared until set. Decorate with grated nutmeg. Serve with thick cream and sugar, or top with whipped cream sweetened and flavoured to taste. *For 4 persons.*

To Vary: If sweet junket is preferred, dissolve ½-1 oz. caster sugar in milk.

YULE JUNKET: Stir 1½ tablespoons brandy, rum or sherry into the milk.

QUICK JELLIES

1 packet fruit jelly
Hot water as required

Place the jelly in a pint measure. Add enough water, just off the boil, to make 1 pint when the jelly is dissolved. Stir until dissolved. Pour into a wet mould. Chill. Turn out. Decorate to taste. *For 4 persons.*

COFFEE JELLY: Dissolve 1 packet of lemon jelly in 1 pint strained coffee, boiling hot and strong. Stir in 4 tablespoons sugar. Chill in a wet mould. Turn out. Serve with whipped cream, sweetened and flavoured to taste with vanilla essence, or fold in 1 cup whipped cream, sweetened and flavoured with vanilla to the jelly when starting to congeal. To vary this, whip jelly until fluffy before folding in cream.

CLARIFIED LEMON JELLY

This can be served as a jelly or used as a coating for moulds to contain rich creams such as bavaroises or a chartreuse of fruit.

1½ pints cold water
4 lemons
6 oz. loaf sugar
2 cloves
1½ oz. powdered gelatine
2 egg shells and whites
1 inch cinnamon stick if liked

Rinse an enamel-lined saucepan. Add the water. Wash the lemons. Remove the rind of 2 thinly and add to water. Strain the juice of the 4 lemons into a half pint measure, and fill up with cold water. Pour into the pan. Add sugar, cloves, gelatine, egg shells and whites and cinnamon stick if liked. Place pan on stove. Stir over full heat until the gelatine is dissolved, then whisk with a rotary egg beater until almost boiling. Remove whisk. Boil up to the top of pan. Withdraw and allow to subside. Boil up once again. Remove and stand for 5 minutes before straining. Place a bowl beneath a jelly bag. Wring the jelly bag out of water as hot as can be borne. Pour in liquid jelly. As soon as about $\frac{1}{2}$ cup has dripped through, remove bowl and slip another bowl into its place. Pour the jelly into the bag again. (If you leave the first drippings in the bowl, the jelly won't be so clear.) Leave until dripping ceases, then until cold. Pour into a wet mould.

NOTE : Be careful to strain jelly in a warm room away from a draught. If strained in a cold room, the jelly may stiffen in the jelly bag before it has all run through. If this should happen, fill a basin with boiling water, and stand it on top of the jelly until it dissolves again.

To Set And Serve Jellies

1. Set in a shallow, wet, oblong tin large enough to give you a jelly about $\frac{1}{2}$ inch thick. Cut in cubes. Serve in glasses alternately with berries or diced pear, sliced banana, or pieces of drained canned pineapple. Decorate with whipped cream.

2. Set a jelly in a basin and another in a tin, $\frac{1}{2}$ inch thick. When the first begins to congeal, whip till spongy. When the other is set, cube and arrange in glasses alternately with teaspoons of the sponge. If liked, berries can be set in the jelly when beginning to thicken.

Guide To Use Of Gelatine

In my recipes for jellies, I have given some quantities of gelatine in ozs., and some in tablespoonfuls, in order to cater for those who prefer to measure by spoon than by weighing.

If you prefer to use French leaf gelatine, allow $\frac{3}{4}$-1 oz. to set 1 pint of liquid, and $1\frac{1}{2}$-2 oz. to set 1 quart, according to the liquid. Ten perfect sheets of French leaf gelatine equals 1 oz. If any are imperfect, you will have to weigh the gelatine.

Hints On Gelatine And Jellies

1. Measure gelatine carefully. If a tablespoon of powdered gelatine is suggested, level the gelatine carefully over the top of the spoon with the blade of a knife.

2. If a recipe suggests the use of $\frac{3}{4}$ oz. powdered gelatine to 1 pint liquid, increase amount of gelatine to 1 oz. in hot weather unless a refrigerator is available.

3. Some recipes call for softening gelatine in cold water or fruit juice before dissolving it in hot liquid, in which case allow 4 tablespoons cold liquid to $\frac{3}{4}$ oz. gelatine unless otherwise instructed. If a recipe calls for dissolving powdered gelatine in liquid, measure the gelatine and the liquid into the top of a double boiler, or into a basin lowered into hot water, allowing 8 tablespoons

liquid to $\frac{3}{4}$ oz. gelatine, and stir over hot water until dissolved, then stir into remainder of ingredients given, according to instructions.

NOTE : Never stir boiling water into any dry gelatine.

4. When dissolving gelatine in milk, do not allow to come to the boil, or the milk will curdle.

5. When making creams, allow 1 oz. powdered gelatine to $1\frac{1}{2}$ pints cream or fruit purée unless otherwise instructed in recipe.

6. Allow a jelly from 2-4 hours to set if you haven't a refrigerator.

7. If wanted quickly and no refrigerator is available, set in individual moulds. Jelly can be prepared more quickly still if only a small amount of the liquid required is heated to dissolve it, and the remainder is stirred in cold, and then set in individual moulds. Stand moulds in cold water. Cover to prevent dust or insects settling on top.

8. If using fresh pineapple juice when making jelly, heat juice to boiling point, or the jelly will not stiffen.

9. Do not stir in any fruit, nuts or other solid ingredients until the jelly shows signs of congealing, otherwise the ingredient added will not be evenly distributed throughout.

To Prepare Moulds for Jelly: Rinse first with boiling water, and then with cold. If using copper moulds, clean and dry thoroughly, then rub over with a piece of tissue paper dipped in salad oil, but take care not to use too much oil or it will cloud jelly.

To Unmould Jellies: Dip mould quickly in a basin of warm water. Wipe it dry with a cloth. Shake very gently. Place dish on which mould is to be served over the top, and turn them over together. If jelly still refuses to unmould, rub mould with a cloth wrung out in hot water.

To Decorate a Mould: Rinse with hot water. Tuck in a bowl of cracked ice. Pour about 3 tablespoons of liquid lemon jelly in mould. If only the bottom is wanted decorated, there must be enough jelly to give you a layer from $\frac{1}{8}$-$\frac{1}{4}$ inch thick. If you wish to mask the whole of the mould, revolve the mould slowly in the ice until the whole of the inside is evenly coated. Leave until set. If you want a thick layer, repeat. The ideal thickness for the whole mould is $\frac{1}{8}$ inch. Do not attempt to decorate until lining is set.

To Decorate: Use a contrast to the jelly, such as angelica glacé cherries, and cut in small fancy shapes ; halved seeded grapes ; sliced bananas ; and chopped or sliced blanched pistachio nuts. You can also use thoroughly drained pieces of canned fruit, cut in fancy shapes. Now make a pretty design on the bottom of the mould in this way :

Dip underside of each decoration into liquid jelly with two fine knitting needles or hat pins. Place in position in the bottom of mould. Leave until firmly set, then pour a very thin layer of liquid jelly over the decorations. If you wish to decorate the sides of the mould, continue in the same way, pressing each piece into position. The process of decorating a mould is much quicker if you have a refrigerator to quicken the setting.

LEMON JELLY (Gelée au Citron)

BASIC RECIPE :
1 oz. powdered gelatine

Soak gelatine in $\frac{1}{4}$ cup of the cold water for 5 minutes. Add hot water. Stir until dissolved.

3½ gills cold water
1½ gills boiling water
5-6 oz. caster sugar
Few grains of salt
¼ pint lemon juice

Stir in sugar, salt, lemon juice and remainder of cold water. Strain into a wet mould. Chill. Unmould. Decorate with whipped cream and fruit. *For 6-8 persons.*

ORANGE JELLY : Reduce lemon juice to ½ gill and cold water to ¼ pint. Add 2½ gills orange juice and allow ½ pint boiling water.

FRUIT JELLY : Follow quantities given for Orange Jelly, but substitute canned fruit juice for the orange juice. Fold in 1½ gills small berries or diced apricots, peaches or pears. Allow 1¼ oz. gelatine.

CUSTARD JELLY (Gelée à la Crème)

1 packet jelly
½ pint hot water
1 pint custard sauce

Turn jelly into a basin. Add water. Stir occasionally till dissolved. Leave till nearly cold. Stir in custard sauce. When cool, beat with an egg whisk till well blended. Turn into a wet mould.

Leave till set. Unmould. Garnish with fruit to taste. *For 4 persons.*

JELLIED CUSTARD (Crème en Gelée)

3 egg yolks
⅓ cup sugar
¼ teaspoon salt
2½ cups hot milk
1 tablespoon powdered gelatine
½ cup cold milk
1 teaspoon vanilla essence
Few drops of almond essence

Beat yolks lightly. Add sugar and salt. Stir in hot milk. Cook over boiling water, stirring constantly, until mixture coats a silver spoon. Remove from heat. Add gelatine soaked in cold milk. Add flavourings. Pour into a mould, or into individual moulds, and leave till chilled, and set. *For 6 persons.*

WINE JELLY (Gelée de Vin)

1½ oz. powdered gelatine
1½ pints water
8 oz. loaf sugar
¼ pint strained lemon juice
Washed rind of 3 lemons
2 shells and whites of eggs
¼ pint brandy
¼ pint sherry
¼ pint Madeira

Put the gelatine, water, sugar, lemon juice and thinly pared rinds into a saucepan. Wash and crush egg shells. Add with the whites. Whisk over the stove until the mixture almost comes to the boil, then remove whisk. Bring to boil. Draw pan to side of stove. Stand for a minute or two until mixture subsides, then bring again to boil. Repeat this once, then simmer for 3 or

4 minutes. Pour slowly into a jelly bag wrung out of hot water. Strain. Strain twice again, then stir in wines. Leave until cold, then pour into a wet mould. *For 8 persons.*

JELLIED FRUIT SALAD (Fruit en Gelée)

1 packet strawberry jelly
¾ pint hot water

Dissolve jelly in hot water. Add salt. Cool. When slightly thickened, stir in pear, apple and

Hawaian Heyday. *See page* 621.

Sweetheart Pudding. *See page* 623.

Serve Drop Scones tucked in a folded napkin. See *page* 687.

Serve Baking Powder Biscuits with butter a any meal. *See page* 689.

Heat Doughnuts and toss in castor sugar. *See pages* 701-702.

Serve Pinwheel Scones hot. *See page* 690.

Pinch of salt
1 cup diced dessert pear
1 diced peeled apple
3 chopped maraschino cherries

cherries. Pour gently into a wet mould. Chill. Turn out. Garnish with whipped cream. *For 6 persons.*

FRUIT SOLID (Gelée de Fruit, Solide)

1 quart sweetened stoned cherries, diced dessert pears, or plums, and syrup
2 tablespoons powdered gelatine
2 tablespoons cold water

Press fruit through a sieve fine enough to retain the skins. Mix this purée with the juice. Heat ½ pint to boiling point. Soak gelatine for 5 minutes in cold water. Add to scalded juice. Stir till dissolved. Stir into fruit purée and juice. Stand until nearly cold, then stir and turn into a wet mould. Chill. Turn out into a glass dish. Serve with cream or cold custard sauce. *For 6 persons.*

MILK JELLY (Gelée au Lait)

1 pint new milk
1 oz. caster sugar
¾ oz. powdered gelatine
½ gill water
Coffee or sherry for flavouring

Measure the milk and sugar into an enamelled saucepan. Stir till sugar is dissolved but do not allow to boil. Soften gelatine in water and add. Stir till dissolved. Flavour to taste with coffee, sherry or an essence. Pour into wet mould. When set, turn out into a glass dish. Pour orange sauce over or round dish. *For 4 or 5 persons.*

QUICK MILK JELLY (Gelée au Lait)

1 packet any fruit jelly
Between ¾ and 1 pint cold new milk

Place jelly in a basin. Stand in hot water. Stir occasionally till dissolved. Leave until almost cold, then stir in milk very slowly. Pour into a wet mould. Chill. Unmould. Decorate to taste. *For 4 persons.*

CHOCOLATE MILK JELLY (Gelée au Lait de Chocolat)

1 pint milk
1½ teaspoons powdered gelatine
1 tablespoon cold water
4 tablespoons sugar
1 oz. plain chocolate
1 teaspoon vanilla essence

Heat milk in top of a double boiler. Soak gelatine for 5 minutes in the cold water. Add with sugar and chocolate to milk. Cook over hot water for ¼ hour, stirring constantly. Add vanilla. Strain into a wet mould. Chill. Turn out. Decorate with whipped cream and chocolate shot. *For 4 persons.*

EAST WIND (Gelée d'Ananas au Lait)

Pineapple juice 2 cups
Cold water as required
1 teaspoon lemon juice
1 packet lemon jelly

Make the pineapple juice up to 3 cups with cold water. Add lemon juice. Bring almost to boiling point. Pour over the jelly. Stir until dissolved. When beginning to set, add evaporated milk and

3 tablespoons evaporated milk
1 ring of pineapple

whisk until stiff. When ready, it should triple its bulk. Place in a glass dish. Decorate with whipped cream and the pineapple ring, cut in 6 pieces. *For 4 or 5 persons.*

SPONGES AND WHIPS

Jellies to be turned into sponges should be cooled until about to thicken, whether made from a packet or from gelatine, then whipped. Whip with a rotary egg beater until fluffy, or of the consistency of whipped cream. Stand until firm, then pile in a shallow glass dish, or in fruit glasses and decorate to taste. Sometimes, sponge recipes are given under the name of " Snow ". Again, half a jelly can be melted in the usual way and the remainder whipped into a sponge, and added.

CHOCOLATE SPONGE (Nuage au Chocolat)

1 ¼ tablespoons powdered gelatine
⅓ cup cold water
2 ⅔ cups milk
¼ cup caster sugar
3 oz. melted chocolate
3 separated eggs
Pinch of salt
¼ teaspoon vanilla essence

Soak gelatine in the water for 5 minutes. Heat milk in the top of a double boiler. Stir in soaked gelatine. Cook over hot water until gelatine is dissolved, stirring constantly, then add sugar. When sugar is dissolved, stir in melted chocolate. Beat egg yolks and stir in chocolate mixture. Mix well, then return to top of double boiler. Cook over boiling water, stirring constantly, until slightly thickened. Remove from pan. Stir in salt and vanilla. Cool slightly. Beat egg whites to a stiff froth. Fold in. Turn into a wet mould. Chill. Unmould. Decorate to taste with whipped cream and chocolate shot. *For 4-6 persons.*

ORANGE SPONGES (Nuages d'Orange)

1 packet orange jelly
½ pint hot water
¼ pint orange juice
1 can evaporated milk

Dissolve jelly in the water, then stir in orange juice. Allow to cool but not set. Whip evaporated milk until thick. Whip thickened jelly to a foam. Fold into whipped milk. Pile into sundae glasses. Decorate with 5 orange fingers. Fill each centre with a rose of whipped cream nestling in foliage made of angelica. *For 6-8 persons.*

STRAWBERRY FLUFF (Fouettée de Fraises)

12 marshmallows
½ pint thick cream
1 egg white
Few grains of salt
½ pint crushed strawberries

Cut each marshmallow into 8 pieces. Beat the cream until stiff. Beat white of egg with salt. Fold in marshmallows, then cream. Chill. Just before serving, fold in berries. Pile in sundae glasses. Top each with a luscious strawberry, and sprinkle with caster sugar. *For 6 persons.*

CREAM DESSERTS

There are many varieties of cold sweets classified under the name of " cream." Some are made of custard, dissolved jelly or gelatine and thick cream and flavouring. For others, the cream is whipped, and again some include both whipped cream and beaten egg white. Others are set in a lining of fruit jelly decorated with glacé fruits and sometimes angelica or pistachio nuts.

To Mould Creams: It is better to brush the inside of the mould with oil before adding the cream, rather than dip mould in cold water to unmould when cream might melt slightly.

ASH GREEN CHESTNUT CREAM (Crème de Marrons, Ash Green)

2 lb. chestnuts
½ pint milk or water
Vanilla essence to taste
6 oz. caster sugar
½ pint double cream
Vanilla essence to taste

Slit chestnuts. Place in a saucepan. Cover with boiling water. Boil for about 20 minutes until tender enough to slip off both inner and outer skins. Rub through a sieve into a clean saucepan. Add milk or water with vanilla essence to taste, and sugar. Stir over slow heat until the moisture is quite absorbed. When perfectly dry, rub through a wire sieve. Press through an icing tube in a circle in a glass dish. When cool, fill the centre with whipped, sweetened cream flavoured with vanilla essence. *For 6 persons.*

NORWEGIAN CREAM (Creme à la Norvégienne)

3 separated eggs
½ gill water
3 sheets gelatine
½ gill sherry
2 tablespoons caster sugar
Strawberry jam as required
Whipped cream to taste

Beat egg yolks. Pour the water over the gelatine. Stir until dissolved. Add sherry and sugar. Stir until sugar is dissolved then stir in egg yolks. When blended, strain. Beat egg whites until fluffy, and stiff, then lightly stir into mixture. Gently pour into a glass dish. When set and chilled, spread thinly with strawberry jam. Cover with swirls of whipped cream. *For 4 persons.*

STONE CREAM

Juice of 1 lemon
½ gill sherry
1 pint cream
2 oz. caster sugar
1 teaspoon vanilla essence
½ oz. powdered gelatine
½ gill cold water
½ gill hot milk

Spread the bottom of a glass dish with apricot jam. Mix lemon juice and sherry. Strain over jam. Bring cream to boil. Stir in sugar and vanilla essence. When sugar is dissolved, cool slightly. Soften gelatine in cold water. Add hot milk. Stir till dissolved. Add cooled cream. When nearly cold, pour carefully over jam. *For 6 persons.*

SHERRY CREAM (Crème au Vin)

1 packet jelly
1½ oz. caster sugar

Dissolve the jelly according to instructions on the packet. Flavour with a few drops of wine.

½ pint thick cream
½ gill sherry
½ teaspoon grated lemon rind

Thinly coat the bottom of a wet mould with jelly. Leave until set. Dissolve sugar in remainder of jelly. Whip cream until fluffy. Stir in sherry, lemon rind and remainder of liquid jelly. Beat until fluffy. Pour into lined mould. Chill. Turn out. Decorate with whipped cream. *For 6 persons.*

COLD SOUFFLES

A cold soufflé is a fluffy, spongy cream made with eggs, dissolved gelatine, cream and flavouring. It is set in a prepared soufflé case, decorated on top to taste, and served from the case. The mixture can be set, if preferred, in individual soufflé dishes made of china or silver, or in paper soufflé cases. If using a dish, always prepare it before the mixture. To do this, tie a stiff paper collar round the top, made of foolscap or a similar paper, so that it stands two inches above the top of the mould or moulds. This must be done very carefully to ensure that the soufflé, when ready, is perfectly round. Prepare mixture and pile into case or cases. It should come 1-2 inches above the rim. Chill until set, then carefully remove string and paper. You may have to run a knife dipped in boiling water round the outside of paper to melt the soufflé very slightly round the edge so that the paper comes away easily without any of the mixture adhering to it. If liked, sprinkle the outside edge with finely chopped nuts or ratafia crumbs, pressing them on with a palette knife.

BANANA SOUFFLE (Soufflé de Bananes)

2 eggs
2 oz. caster sugar
½ lemon
¼ pint mashed banana
¼ pint evaporated milk
¾ oz. powdered gelatine
¼ gill water
½ gill thick cream
Rum or vanilla essence to taste
1 small banana
9 ratafias

Separate yolks and whites of eggs. Beat yolks with sugar, grated lemon rind, and strained lemon juice, over hot water till thick. Remove and cool. Stir in mashed banana and evaporated milk, beaten till frothy. Add gelatine softened and dissolved in the water. Lastly, fold in stiffly-frothed egg whites. Pour into a wet soufflé dish. Decorate when set, with whipped cream, sweetened and flavoured to taste with rum or vanilla, and with banana slices and ratafias. *For 6 persons.*

CHOCOLATE SOUFFLE (Soufflé de Chocolat)

3 separated eggs
1½ oz. caster sugar
½ oz. almonds
2 oz. chocolate
½ pint cream
½ oz. powdered gelatine
3 tablespoons cold water
1 tablespoon white wine
A few drops of vanilla essence

Place egg yolks in the top of a double boiler with sugar. Whisk over heat till like thick cream. Blanch and chop almonds finely and bake on a tin in the oven till light brown. Chop chocolate finely and melt it in a little milk over a stove. Whisk egg whites to a stiff froth, and whip half the cream lightly. Melt gelatine with water over hot water. Stir almonds and chocolate into custard. When cool, fold in egg whites, cream and dissolved gelatine. Stir in wine and vanilla essence. Stir mixture over ice till beginning to set. Turn into prepared soufflé case. Chill. Remove paper before serving. Decorate with roses of whipped cream. Serve remaining soufflé in a silver dish lined with a lace paper doily. *For 6 persons.*

MILANAISE SOUFFLE (Soufflé, Milanaise)

3 separated eggs
6 oz. caster sugar
2½ lemons
½ pint whipped cream
½ oz. powdered gelatine
3 tablespoons water

Put egg yolks, sugar and grated rind and juice of lemons in the top of a double boiler. Whisk till nearly boiling over simmering water. Strain into a basin. Allow to get cold, and when cold, fold in whipped cream. Melt gelatine in water. Strain into mixture. Fold in stiffly-frothed egg whites. Let mixture set creamily. Pour into prepared soufflé case. *For 5 or 6 persons.*

BERRY FLUMMERY (Flummery de Fruit)

1½ lb. berries
3 pints water
3 oz. caster sugar
3 tablespoons cornflour

Pick over and rinse berries. Drain well. Stew in the water until into a mash. Strain. Pour berry juice into the top of a double boiler. Bring to the boil. Add sugar. Stir till dissolved. Cream cornflour with cold water, then slowly stir in a little of the syrup. Stir this into the remaining syrup in double boiler. Cook for 5 minutes, stirring constantly. Pour into a wet mould. Chill. Unmould. Garnish with whipped cream. *For 8 persons.*

CHESTNUT RAIN (Pluie de Marrons)

1 lb. chestnuts
1 oz. grated chocolate
2 hard-boiled egg yolks
1 oz. caster sugar
1 tablespoon cream
1 banana

Slit chestnuts and boil in water to cover till tender. Drain. Peel, and rub through a sieve. Soften chocolate in a saucepan and sieve. Stir into chestnut purée. Add sieved egg yolks, then sugar. Mix thoroughly with cream. Press through a wire sieve into the centre of a glass dish lined with a layer of baked meringue. Decorate with overlapping slices of banana or halved grapes. Edge with roses of whipped cream. *For 6 or 7 persons.*

CHOCOLATE MARIE (Délice de Chocolat)

¼ lb. chocolate
2 tablespoons hot water
4 separated eggs
1 tablespoon brandy, rum or sherry

Prepare this sweet the day before it is wanted. Grate chocolate into the top of a double boiler. Place over boiling water. Add hot water. Stir occasionally until melted. Remove from heat. Beat in egg yolks. Return to heat. Cook for 3 or 4 minutes, stirring constantly, but do not allow to boil. Remove from heat. Cool slightly. Beat egg whites until stiff. Fold into mixture, then stir in brandy, rum or sherry. Serve in glasses. *For 6 persons.*

613

DUTCH FLUMMERY (Flummery à l'Hollandaise)

Rind and juice of 2 lemons
6 oz. caster sugar
½ oz. powdered gelatine
¼ pint Madeira or sherry
¾ pint water
3 egg yolks

Place the rind and juice of lemons, sugar, gelatine, Madeira, or sherry, and water in the top of a double boiler. Stir over hot water until gelatine is dissolved, then remove from heat. Stand for 10 minutes. Beat egg yolks. Gradually stir in liquid. Rinse top of double boiler and strain custard in. Stir over hot water until custard coats the back of spoon. Pour into a bowl. When cold, turn into a wet mould. When set and chilled, unmould. Decorate with whipped cream and chocolate shot. *For 6 persons.*

HONEYCOMB MOULD (Crème Anglaise)

2 large or 3 small separated
  eggs
1 pint milk
Sugar to taste
½ teaspoon vanilla essence
½ oz. powdered gelatine
2 tablespoons water

Beat egg yolks. Stir in milk. Pour into the top of a double boiler. Cook over boiling water until liquid begins to heat, then add 1½ or 2 oz. caster sugar according to taste. Stir until dissolved, and the custard is thick enough to coat the back of spoon. Stir in vanilla essence. Remove from heat. Soften gelatine in the water for 5 minutes, then stir into the custard. Stir until dissolved. Beat egg whites until very stiff. Fold lightly into the mixture. Pour into a wet mould. Chill. Unmould. Serve with chocolate sauce, thick cream or stewed or bottled fruit. *For 4 or 5 persons.*

ROTHE GRUETZE

2 pints red currants
2 pints raspberries
4 cups cold water
Sugar to taste
⅓ cup cornflour
Cold water as required
Whipped cream and red
  currants

Place the currants and berries in a saucepan. Add water. Bring to boil. Simmer for a minute or two until the juice is extracted from the fruit, then strain. Add sugar to taste. Stir until dissolved. Bring to boil. Cream cornflour with cold water. Stir in a little of the fruit juice, then pour the cornflour mixture into remainder of fruit juice, gradually, stirring constantly. Cook until thick, stirring constantly, then pour into custard cups. Chill. Decorate with whipped cream and perfect red currants. *For 8 persons.*

NOTE : Sometimes arrowroot, sago or tapioca is used in place of cornflour to thicken this famous Continental cold sweet.

SUMMER PUDDING (Pouding d'Eté)

½ loaf stale bread
¾ lb. raspberries
¾ lb. blackcurrants
¼ pint water
½ lb. granulated sugar
¾ pint custard sauce

Line bottom and sides of a pudding basin with the bread, cut into slices ¼ inch thick. Hull berries. Pick currants. Place in a saucepan. Add water and sugar. Cook slowly till fruit is tender but not mushy. Cut remainder of bread into slices ¼ inch thick. Fill lined basin or mould with fruit. Cover with a slice of bread, size of top of basin. Stand mould in a soup plate. Place another soup plate on top and weight it down. If any juice should run out, return it to basin or mould. Chill for 24 hours. Turn out very carefully into a shallow glass dish. Cover with the custard sauce. Serve with thick or whipped cream. *For 6 persons.*

SYLLABUB WHIP

2 egg whites
Juice of 1 lemon
½ gill brandy
½ gill sherry
2 oz. caster sugar
1 pint cream

Beat egg whites to a stiff froth. Mix lemon juice with brandy and sherry. Stir in sugar, then the cream. Add egg whites, and ½ teaspoon finely grated lemon rind if liked. Whisk thoroughly, and remove the froth as it rises. Drain on a hair sieve. Fill custard glasses two-thirds full with the cream. Top with remaining froth. *For 6 persons.*

FROZEN DESSERTS

If you like to feature ice cream often in your menus, it would be good to have a "regulation pail" type of freezer in addition to the refrigerator trays so that you can use one or the other according to the type of mixture you want freezing, and the time available. The difference between using a refrigerator for freezing as opposed to the ice cream pail or tub is that you require no ice for freezing in the refrigerator trays, whereas you need cracked ice and salt to freeze in a pail or tub freezer, whether hand or electrically operated. There are many types of ices :—

1. Ice cream made with custard and cream.
2. Ice cream made with custard, cream and evaporated milk.
3. Ice cream made with sweetened, flavoured cream.
4. Ice cream made with thin cream and eggs.
5. Ice cream made with rennet.
6. Ice made with water.

HINTS ON MAKING ICE CREAM

Flavouring and Sweetening: Remember when sweetening and flavouring ice cream that you want the mixture flavoured and sweetened slightly stronger than you like it on account of the fact that both the flavouring and sweetness seem to lose their strength during the process of freezing. If you don't remember this, the ice cream will be slightly tasteless when frozen. Take care not to add too much sugar, or the mixture won't freeze satisfactorily ; ½ lb. sugar is the usual amount to allow for 1 quart of ice cream mixture.

Colouring: As the colouring is not affected by freezing, use very sparingly. Pastel shades are the best.

1. Do not try to make ice cubes while making ice cream or any iced desserts.
2. Sugar must always be thoroughly dissolved before starting to freeze ice cream mixture. When freezing uncooked mixtures, substitute sifted icing sugar for granulated or caster.
3. Always chill mixture before starting to freeze. The temperature should be between 40° and 50° F. If put in a warm freezing tray, it may curdle.

4. To avoid all chance of curdling, see that all the ingredients, bowl and beater, are chilled.

To Make Ice Cream in a Tub Freezer

The mixture must be cold. Place it in the can, filling it until two-thirds full. (Never fill can more than two-thirds full as the mixture increases its bulk by nearly half in the process of freezing.) Adjust dasher and cover in place, and make certain that each part is properly adjusted before you pack ice and salt round can. Holding can straight, with the pivot in the socket of the pail, pack round it broken ice and freezing or rock salt, in the proportion of 3 parts broken ice to one part of salt. Fill pail with the ice and salt. Stand for 3 or 4 minutes to let the mixture become quite cold, then turn the dasher slowly and regularly till mixture begins to freeze. (Do not freeze too rapidly, or the ice cream will have a coarse texture.) You can tell when it reaches this stage by the resistance it offers, then stir more rapidly till stiff. Now remove the crank and dasher. Scrape the cream solidly into the can. Cover and fill the hole in the cover with a cork or plug of soft paper.

NOTE : If fruit is to be added to ice cream, stir in when you feel cream is thickening, about half-time. (Ice cream usually takes about 20-25 minutes to freeze.) Pour off brine in pail and repack with ice and salt, using salt and ice in proportion of 1 to 4. Cover with sheets of newspaper (two or three thicknesses) or a blanket, then with ice. Stand in a cool place for 2 or 3 hours to ripen.

ICE MOULDS

Moulds for ices used to be made of pewter, but nowadays tin moulds with tinned copper tops are more generally used. Some are tall to take varying quantities from $\frac{1}{4}$ to 2 pints ; others are oval and flat with a pineapple top to take $1\frac{1}{2}$ pints. There are also individual moulds in different sizes, and copper-bottomed moulds lined with tin. They are usually obtainable in pint and two pint sizes. If you should come across any old-fashioned pewter moulds with closely-fitting lids, such as a melon mould, it is wise to invest in them. Always chill moulds before using.

To Mould Ice Cream

As soon as ice cream is stiff in the can, remove it and pack well down into a chilled mould, taking care that no air spaces are left in the mould. Fill to overflowing. Cover with a paper greased with butter, then cover tightly with mould cover. Seal round the edge with a strip of muslin dipped in melted butter. Pack in ice and salt, 4 parts ice to one of salt, for 1-2 hours, according to the consistency of the ice. When moulding different ice creams, either arrange in layers in a mould, or line mould with one variety, fill centre with another and top with the first mixture.

A simpler way of moulding ice cream is to pack it into a refrigerator tray. You can line the tray with one variety, making the lining $\frac{3}{4}$ inch thick, then put another in the centre, and top with the first mixture to overflowing. (If liked, you can fill centre with stiffly-whipped cream, flavoured and sweetened to taste, instead of ice cream.)

To Unmould Ice Cream

Remove mould from pail or refrigerator, and take off the paper. Wipe mould carefully. (If frozen in an ice pail, salt might get into it when the mould is opened, if not wiped dry.) Dip for a moment into cold water to loosen the ice, then turn gently and quickly on to a dish.

OLD-FASHIONED VANILLA ICE CREAM
(Glace à la Vanille)

1 teaspoon flour
2¾ oz. caster sugar
1 beaten egg yolk
1 cup scalded milk
1 cup cream
1 teaspoon vanilla essence

Sift flour and sugar into a basin. Stir in egg yolk diluted with milk. Cook in the top of a double boiler over hot water for ¼ hour, stirring constantly, then strain. Leave till cold. Stir in cream and vanilla essence. Pour into a freezing can. Adjust dasher, cover and crank. Pack crushed ice and rock salt alternately round can, allowing 1 part salt to 3 of ice. Turn handle slowly at first, then gradually increase speed until cream is frozen. Lift dasher. Pack cream solidly in can. Cover, and cork opening in lid. Repack freezer with 4 parts ice to one of salt, then cover with folded newspapers. Freeze for 1 hour. *Yield:* About 1½ pints ice cream.

CUSTARD ICE CREAM (Glace à la Crème)

BASIC RECIPE :
1 pint milk
6 egg yolks
½ lb. caster sugar
1 pint cream
1 tablespoon vanilla essence

Bring milk to boil. Beat yolks and sugar in a basin till light and honey-coloured. Stir milk slowly into beaten yolks and sugar. Pour into the top of a double boiler. Stir constantly over hot water until thick enough to coat back of spoon. Remove from heat. Stir frequently until slightly cool. Stir in cream and vanilla essence. Chill. Strain, then freeze as usual. *Yield:* 8 portions.

CANTALOUP BERGNER : Prepare and chill half the quantity of vanilla custard cream. Cut 2 small Cantaloup melons in half. Remove seeds and spongy parts. Scoop out flesh. Cut into dice. Place in a basin with 1 oz. caster sugar, and 2 tablespoons Curaçao. When sugar is dissolved, stir well into ice cream. Divide equally between the 4 shells. Smooth into dome-like shapes. Freeze. To serve, pour 1 tablespoon loganberry or raspberry syrup over each. Sprinkle with shredded coconut.

COUPES DELYSIA : Prepare half the quantity of vanilla ice cream according to standard recipe. Peel, halve, core and slice 2 ripe peaches. Place in a basin. Add fingers of 1 seedless orange, cut in two, and a peeled and sliced banana. Stir in 1 oz. caster sugar, and 2 tablespoons rum. Mix well. Divide fruit equally between 6 sundae glasses. Cover with ice cream. Garnish each with whipped cream and a maraschino cherry.

CHESTNUT ICE CREAM : Prepare 1 pint vanilla custard ice cream according

617

to recipe given. When nearly ready, uncover, and stir in 2 oz. chopped marrons glacés, and 2 tablespoons maraschino. Finish freezing.

PISTACHIO ICE CREAM : Stir ¼ lb. finely minced, blanched pistachios into mixture when slightly cooled. Follow recipe until almost ready, then remove cap and stir in ½ teaspoon almond essence, 1 teaspoon kirsch, 1 teaspoon brandy and ¾ tablespoon maraschino. Finish freezing.

GELATINE ICE CREAM

2 cups thin cream
1 tablespoon powdered gelatine
2 tablespoons cold water
1 pint milk
6 oz. caster sugar
Pinch of salt
1 dessertspoon vanilla essence

Chill cream slightly. Soak gelatine in cold water for 5 minutes. Bring milk almost to boiling point. Add gelatine, sugar and salt. Stir till dissolved. Cool. Stir in cream and vanilla essence. Freeze as usual. *Yield:* About 1½ quarts.

RENNET ICE CREAM

3 cups tepid milk
1 cup thick cream
6 oz. caster sugar
1 saltspoon salt
1 rennet tablet
1 tablespoon cold water
¾ tablespoon vanilla essence

Mix milk and cream in the top of a double boiler. Add sugar and salt. Heat slowly over hot water, until tepid. Meanwhile, dissolve tablet in the cold water. Stir into milk and cream, then stir in vanilla essence. Leave until set. Freeze in usual way. *Yield:* About 1½ quarts.

TO MAKE ICE CREAM IN A REFRIGERATOR

Always follow instructions given in the book issued by the manufacturers of your refrigerator before making ice cream, and if any advice is given contrary to instructions in this book, follow it, as, although the principle is the same, the timing may be different.

Set control for fast freezing. Pour mixture into a chilled refrigerator tray. Pour a little cold water on the shelf before slipping in the tray containing mixture. Always freeze in the bottom of the compartment, not on the top or in the middle. Chill thoroughly. Remove to a chilled bowl. Beat well with an electric or a rotary egg beater, then slip back into freezing compartment. When the mixture begins to freeze round the edges, remove and beat again. Return to compartment. Freeze until solid. When beating, be careful not to allow the ice to melt so that liquid forms. To hasten freezing, brush the bottom of refrigerator tray with cold water. Ice cream mixtures usually take about 3 hours to freeze properly. The moment the ice cream is frozen, change the temperature of the refrigerator to half-way between fast freezing and normal, and leave the ice cream in the tray to ripen properly before serving. If you are fortunate enough to have a small electric freezer, which is made in the United States, to fit into the ice cube tray of refrigerator, you will have smoother ice cream than by making it as described, and removing to beat. In this case, you can also use recipes given for making ice cream in a tub freezer.

(1) REFRIGERATOR ICE CREAM

BASIC RECIPE:
1/4 lb. caster sugar
3/4 tablespoon cornflour
1 1/2 cups milk
2 separated eggs
1 saltspoon salt
1 1/2 teaspoons vanilla essence
1 cup thick cream

Mix sugar and cornflour in top of a double boiler. Gradually stir in milk. Cook over boiling water, stirring constantly, until thick. Cover and cook for 10 minutes, stirring occasionally. Beat egg yolks slightly. Stir in a little of the sauce, then stir this into the white sauce. Cook over hot water, stirring constantly, for 3 minutes.

Remove from hot water. Leave till cool. Beat egg whites with salt, till stiff. Fold into cooled custard. Add vanilla essence. Pour into chilled refrigerator tray. Leave until firm. Beat cream until it turns into peaks. Break up ice cream with a wooden spoon. Beat with a rotary or electric beater until crumbly. Fold cream into mixture. Freeze in refrigerator tray in your refrigerator. *Yield:* About 1 1/2 pints.

BANANA ICE CREAM (Glace de Bananes): Slice and mash enough bananas to give you 1 cup, beating in 3/4 tablespoon lemon juice as you mash. Stir into custard before adding egg whites.

BUTTERSCOTCH ICE CREAM (Glace au Caramel): Reduce sugar to 1 oz., and add 3-4 tablespoons caramel syrup to the hot sauce before adding egg yolks.

STRAWBERRY ICE CREAM (Glace de Fraises): Stir sugar into 1 1/2 cups chopped strawberries instead of into the milk. Add 1 1/2 teaspoons lemon or grapefruit juice. Stir over hot water till sugar is dissolved, then stir into hot milk or custard. Omit vanilla and follow basic recipe.

(2) REFRIGERATOR ICE CREAM

BASIC RECIPE:
2 teaspoons powdered gelatine
1/4 pint cold water
3 1/4 gills evaporated milk
5 oz. caster sugar
2 teaspoons vanilla essence
3/4 pint thick cream

Soak gelatine in cold water for 5 minutes. Heat milk to boiling point. Remove from heat. Add soaked gelatine and sugar. Stir till both are dissolved, then add vanilla essence. Cool. Turn into chilled freezing tray. Chill in refrigerator until thickened round the edges. Whip cream.

Fold into mixture lightly. Pack into tray. Freeze till mushy. Turn into chilled bowl. Beat with a rotary or electric beater till smooth then return quickly to freezing tray. Freeze till firm. *Yield:* About 1 quart.

VARIATIONS

CHOCOLATE (Glace au Chocolat): Melt 2 oz. unsweetened chocolate in milk while heating. Beat till blended. Increase sugar to 7 oz.

ORANGE (Glace, Orange): Use orange juice instead of evaporated milk and increase cream to 1 pint. When frozen mushy, fold in 1 cup minced walnuts.

RASPBERRY OR STRAWBERRY (Glace de Fraises ou Framboises): Stir 1 cup mashed, sweetened berries into chilled mixture before adding cream.

NEAPOLITAN: This is made with three varieties of ice cream, usually vanilla, chocolate or coffee, and raspberry or strawberry, but you can choose any varieties you like, so long as vanilla is included. Pack the half-frozen ice cream in layers in a square, or oblong mould. The brick-shaped mould is generally used. Cover. Chill in the freezing compartment of a refrigerator for several hours, then serve cut in slices.

619

CHOCOLATE ICE CREAM (Glace au Chocolat)

1 oz. chocolate
¼ cup icing sugar
½ cup milk
1 teaspoon powdered gelatine
2 tablespoons cold water
2 oz. caster sugar
1 teaspoon vanilla essence
¾ cup cream

Melt chocolate in the top of a double boiler. Stir in icing sugar and milk by degrees. Stir till almost boiling, then add gelatine soaked in the cold water till soft, and then dissolved. Add caster sugar and vanilla essence. Strain into a basin, containing some cracked ice. Stir over ice until mixture begins to thicken, then beat cream until stiff and fold in. Freeze in usual way. *For 6 persons.*

COFFEE ICE CREAM (Glace au Café)

¼ cup soluble coffee
1 cup milk
½ lb. sugar
3 egg yolks
1 saltspoon salt
3 cups cream

Place coffee and milk in a saucepan. Stir till blended and at boiling point. Stir in half the sugar. Beat egg yolks with salt and remaining sugar. Stir in hot coffee. Pour into the top of a double boiler. Stir over hot water till coffee coats the back of a spoon. Remove from heat. Cool slightly. Stir in 1 cup of the cream. Stand for ½ hour. Cool, then stir in remainder of cream. Freeze in a tub freezer. *Yield:* 1½ quarts.

HOKEY POKEY ICE CREAM (Glace, Hokey Pokey)

1 pint thin unsweetened custard
½ cup warm water
2 teaspoons gelatine
2 rounded tablespoons sweetened condensed milk
1 dessertspoon vanilla essence

Make custard with custard powder in the usual way, except do not sweeten. Place water in a cup. Add gelatine. Stir till dissolved, then stir into custard. Add condensed milk and vanilla essence. Whisk with an egg whisk two or three minutes then pour into a refrigerator tray. Freeze for 2 hours. Remove to a chilled basin. Beat till creamy, but not melted. Replace in tray. Freeze for 1 hour. *For 4-6 persons.*

JUNKET ICE CREAM

1¼ cups caster sugar
2 or 3 grains of salt
1 quart tepid milk
1 teaspoon rennet
2 teaspoons vanilla essence
1 cup thick cream

Stir sugar and salt into milk. Pour into freezer container. Stir in rennet. Add vanilla essence. When mixture is thick, stir in cream and freeze as usual. *For 6 persons.*

MARSHMALLOW ICE CREAM (Glace Guimauvée)

BASIC RECIPE:
2 dozen marshmallows
1½ cups hot milk
1½ teaspoons vanilla essence
1½ cups cream or evaporated milk

Dip scissors in warm water and cut up marshmallows in small pieces. Stir in hot milk. When dissolved add flavouring. Stand till firm. Beat cream, or evaporated milk, till stiff, and fold into mixture. Place in chilled refrigerator tray. Stand till it holds its shape. *For 6 persons.*

MARSHMALLOW COFFEE ICE CREAM
(Glace de Café, Américaine)

1 cup strong black coffee
16 halved marshmallows
1 cup thick cream
½ teaspoon vanilla essence

Heat coffee to boiling point. Add marshmallows. Stir till blended. Remove from heat. Leave till cool. Chill in refrigerator till firm. Whip cream till stiff. Flavour. Fold into coffee mixture. Place in chilled refrigerator tray and freeze. *For 4 persons.*

To Vary:

CHOCOLATE : Melt 3 oz. chocolate. Add to hot milk. Stir till blended. Follow basic recipe.

PINEAPPLE : Stir 1 cup crushed pineapple into ice cream before folding in cream or evaporated milk.

FROZEN SWEETS

Home-made or bought ice cream can be turned into fascinating frozen sweets :

APPLE QUICKIES : Garnish strawberry ice cream brickettes with grated raw dessert apple.

APPLE SLICES : Cut a family brick of ice cream into 6 equal portions. Serve with stewed apples. Garnish with maraschino cherries.

CATHERINE WHEELS : Sandwich thin slices of Swiss roll with ice cream.

HAWAIIAN HEYDAY : Arrange slices of pineapple on individual dishes. Sprinkle with caster sugar. Pour a dessertspoon of Kirsch over each. Just before serving, top with a large spoonful of vanilla ice cream. Decorate with sliced peaches, and halved, stoned black grapes.

ICE CREAM BALLS : Scoop out ice cream in balls. Dip in freshly-grated coconut, or in chopped pistachio nuts or walnuts. Serve in a dish lined with geranium or strawberry leaves.

SNOW CAP TARTLETS : Turn tubs of ice cream into jam tartlets. Coat with whipped cream. Garnish with glacé cherries and angelica.

BAKED ALASKA

Sponge cake as required
1 family brick chocolate or strawberry ice cream
2 egg whites
4 oz. caster sugar

Prepare a very hot oven, 475° F. Stand sponge cake, 1 inch thick, and cut to the shape of an ice cream brick, in a fireproof dish. When ice cream is firmly frozen, place on top. Quickly whisk egg whites till stiff. Lightly fold in sugar with a metal spoon. Cover ice cream and sponge cake completely with this meringue. Dredge with caster sugar. Bake in a hot oven, 500° F., for 2-3 minutes only, until tinged with gold. Serve at once. *For 6 persons.*

CARNIVAL GATEAU (Gâteau à la Fête)

1 firm Neapolitan brick ice cream
About 2 dozen savoy biscuits
Whipped cream as required

Stand ice cream brick on a flat glass dish. Trim savoy biscuits to the height of brick. Spread lightly with whipped cream. Arrange closely in upright position to completely cover sides and press on lightly. Pipe the top and bottom with whipped cream. Decorate with pieces of glacé fruit and leaves of angelica. *For 6 persons.*

COFFEE AND WALNUT GATEAU (Gâteau à la Glace)

3 oz. butter or margarine
4 oz. caster sugar
2 beaten eggs
4 oz. flour
2 oz. cornflour
1 rounded teaspoon baking powder
2 tablespoons coffee essence
1 oz. chopped walnuts
1 family brick vanilla ice cream

Cream fat and sugar till light and fluffy, then beat in eggs by degrees. Sieve flour and cornflour with baking powder. Fold lightly into fat and sugar with coffee essence and a little milk if necessary, to give you a soft dropping consistency. Stir in chopped walnuts. Bake in a lined and greased 7 inch square tin for about 40-45 minutes, in a moderate oven, 350° F. Just before serving, split cold cake in half. Cover with slices of ice cream. Replace top. Cover with remaining ice cream and stud with walnuts. *For 4 persons.*

FESTIVAL PUDDING (Pouding à la Glace)

¼ lb. butter or margarine
¼ lb. caster sugar
2 eggs
6 oz. self-raising flour
Vanilla essence to taste
Milk as required
Sliced peaches and raspberries
1 family brick ice cream

The day before required, prepare sponge base as follows : Cream fat and sugar until light and fluffy. Lightly beat eggs, and add to mixture by degrees, beating well after each addition. Fold in sieved flour with a metal spoon. Add vanilla essence and sufficient milk to give a soft dropping consistency. Bake in a lined and greased swiss roll tin, 9 × 14 inches, in a moderate oven, 350° F., for 35-45 minutes. When cooked, turn on to a wire tray. Remove paper and leave until cold. Build up a hollow sponge case round a 5 inch diameter cake tin as follows : Cut a circle of sponge the size of tin for the base, and cut fingers 3 inches long and ½ inch wide from remaining cake. Brush sides of the base and both edges of fingers with sieved apricot jam. Stand the tin on base and build up the sides with vertical sponge fingers placed closely together. Fix a band of greaseproof paper around the case and leave until set. When ready to serve, remove cake tin carefully and fill case with alternate layers of fruit and ice cream. Decorate top and bottom with whipped cream, walnuts and fruit. (Peaches and raspberries can be fresh, frozen or bottled.) Tie a narrow red ribbon around centre. *For 8 persons.*

PEACH MELBA (Pêche Melba)

5 ripe peaches
¼ lb. caster sugar
¾ pint vanilla ice cream
¾ gill raspberry syrup
Whipped sweetened cream
Vanilla essence to taste

Plunge 1 peach at a time into boiling water. Remove at once, and plunge into ice cold water, then peel carefully. Halve and stone. Sprinkle thickly with caster sugar. Chill until required. (When peaches are not quite ripe, poach them in a little syrup until tender, but not broken. Lift out carefully. Drain on a sieve. Chill.) To serve, arrange a mould of vanilla ice cream in a cut crystal or round silver dish. Cover with raspberry syrup. Arrange peaches round the ice cream. Decorate quickly with whipped, sweetened cream flavoured with vanilla essence. Sprinkle with chopped, blanched pistachio nuts if liked. If individual " Melbas " are wanted, divide peaches equally between 5 sherbet glasses, then top with the ice cream and spoon sauce over each. Decorate with whipped cream and nuts. (If using canned peaches, allow only half a peach each.) If a very elaborate " Melba " is wanted, fill the hole made by removing the stone from each peach with chopped marrons glacés or preserved ginger. *For 5 persons.*

SOUFFLE EN SURPRISE

Genoese pastry as required
1 egg yolk
1 oz. caster sugar
¼ teaspoon vanilla essence
3 egg whites
1 pint vanilla ice cream

Cut the cake into an oval about 1½ inches thick. Carefully scoop out a case from the oval, leaving an edge about 1 inch wide. Beat egg yolk with sugar. Beat in vanilla. Beat egg whites until stiff. Lightly fold them into egg yolk and sugar. Quickly turn vanilla ice cream into centre of the cake, rounding it so as to suggest a soufflé. Cover rapidly with meringue mixture. Dredge thickly with caster sugar. Place in a hot oven, 425° F., for 10 minutes. Garnish quickly with glacé cherries and strips of angelica. Serve immediately. *For 4 persons.*

SWEETHEART PUDDING (Pouding à l'Amour)

2 eggs
6 oz. caster sugar
2 tablespoons warm water
A few drops of vanilla essence
3½ oz. self-raising flour
2 egg whites
1 family brick strawberry ice cream

Whisk eggs and half the sugar together lightly, then stand basin over a saucepan of hot water and continue whisking until thick and creamy. Remove from heat. With a metal spoon, lightly fold in water and vanilla essence followed by the flour. Bake in a greased and floured heart-shaped tin (or a square tin, afterwards cutting the cake to heart-shape) for about 20-30 minutes, in a moderate oven, 350° F. When cold, whisk egg whites until stiff and dry, then add a tablespoon of remainder of sugar and whisk again. Lastly, fold in remainder of sugar lightly. Pipe on to sides of sponge with a star pipe and return to a hot oven, 450° F., for a few minutes to set and tinge meringue with gold. When cold, soak sponge with fruit juice flavoured with sherry. When ready to serve, pile strawberry ice cream into the centre and decorate with whole strawberries and angelica. *For 6 persons.*

WATER ICES

All water ices are based on fruit juice, sugar and water. In some recipes for water ices, instructions are given to dissolve sugar and water and boil to a syrup. A real water ice should be made with cold water, extracted fruit juice and sugar. Water ices made with syrup and fruit juice are really sherbets. Both are made by the same recipe, except that one has cold water, and the other is water sweetened with sugar and usually boiled to a syrup. To obtain the fruit juice, you mash the sieved fruits with sugar to taste, then strain the mash through muslin to retain the seeds. To extract juice from stoned fruit, wash and stone fruit, then pound into a moist consistency. Strain through a fine sieve. Water ices can be frozen in a refrigerator, but no matter how much they are beaten, they are lighter frozen in the regular freezer where they are churned all the time. Serve in small glasses.

To Make Water Ices, Frappés and Sherbets in a Refrigerator: Dissolve sugar in water. When making water ices with syrup, dissolve sugar in water. Bring to boil. Simmer for 5-10 minutes, until into a thin syrup, then cool. Add fruit juice and any other ingredients suggested under each recipe. Turn into refrigerator tray. Place in freezing compartment with the control set at its coldest point. Leave until mushy. Remove from tray to a chilled bowl. Beat until light with an electric beater for preference, or with a rotary egg beater. Quickly fold in stiffly beaten egg white. To prevent water ices melting quickly when served, add before the egg white, 1 teaspoon powdered gelatine soaked for 5 minutes in 2 tablespoons cold water and dissolved over hot water.

To Make Water Ice Quickly: Stir mixture well before freezing. Freeze until set, then whip with a fork before serving in glasses.

Water Ices Made with Fruit Syrup: Allow 4 tablespoons syrup to ½ pint water. Deepen the shade if necessary with colouring, then freeze.

If a Smoother Ice is Wanted: Dissolve a teaspoon of powdered gelatine in ½ pint water and add to remainder of mixture before freezing.

To Serve Water Ices: Decorate with a ring of sliced berries, tangerine sections, or diced pineapple, or serve with rum or sweet liqueur passed round in a jug, allowing 1 teaspoon per portion ; or top with a rose of whipped cream sprinkled with chopped angelica or pistachio nuts. Serve all water ices in small glasses.

SYRUP FOR WATER ICES

8 oz. loaf sugar
1 pint water
½ large lemon

Dissolve sugar in the water in an enamel saucepan. Bring slowly to the boil. Simmer gently for 10 minutes without stirring. Add strained lemon juice. Cool, then strain in a strainer lined with butter muslin. Bottle, cork and store in refrigerator or larder.

APRICOT WATER ICE (Glace à l'Eau d'Abricots)

½ lb. dried apricots
2 oranges
2 lemons
1 tablespoon strained grapefruit juice
½ lb. caster sugar
4 cups cold water

Wash and halve apricots. Place in a basin. Cover with cold water. Soak for 12 hours. Turn apricots and soaking water into a saucepan. Cover and simmer till soft. Rub through a sieve. Stir juice of oranges and lemons and grapefruit juice into purée. Dissolve sugar in the water.

Bring to boil. Boil to a syrup, in about 10 minutes. Leave till cold. Stir into purée. Freeze. *For 12 persons.*

LEMON WATER ICE (Glace à l'Eau au Citron)

6 tablespoons lemon juice
2 tablespoons orange juice
6 oz. caster sugar
1 pint water
½ saltspoon salt
Grated rind ½ lemon

Place lemon and orange juices in a basin. Pour sugar and water into a saucepan. Cook over slow heat till sugar is dissolved, and bring to boil. Simmer slowly for 10 minutes. Pour into a basin. Add salt and lemon rind. Leave till cool. Add to fruit juice. Strain into refrigerator tray. Freeze until firm. Beat in chilled bowl with an electric or rotary beater till light and creamy, but not until it starts to melt. Return to tray and freeze. *For 9 or 10 persons.*

COFFEE FRAPPE (Café Frappé)

2 pints fresh hot coffee
10 oz. caster sugar

Pour coffee into a basin. Add sugar. Stir until dissolved. Chill and freeze to a mush. Serve in tall narrow glasses. Top with whipped cream flavoured with vanilla essence. *Yield:* 1½ quarts.

FRUIT JUICE FRAPPE (Frappé au Fruit)

¼ cup fruit juice
¼ cup water
Sugar to taste
1 stiffly-beaten egg white

Mix fruit juice with the water. Add sugar to taste. Stir till dissolved. Pour into a small refrigerator tray. Place in chilling compartment. Stir every 10 minutes until partially frozen. Stir in egg white. Freeze without stirring for about another 20 minutes until mixture holds its shape. Serve in a tall narrow glass. *For 1 person.*

GINGER ALE FRAPPE (Frappé au Gingembre)

Pour a small bottle of ginger ale into a small container in a refrigerator. Slip into freezing compartment. Leave for ¼ hour. Stir well. Leave till ready in about 20 minutes. Serve in a tall narrow glass. *For 1 person.*

SHERBETS (Sorbets)

Sherbets are simply water ices to which egg white or dissolved gelatine, or both, are added. Any recipe for water ice can be turned into a sherbet by beating in egg whites after first freezing. They can be made of milk or water. At a banquet, sherbet precedes the roast in order to clear the palate. Nowadays, the sherbet or sorbet is usually served as a dessert ; in this case, it can be decorated with fresh fruit or fruit sauce.

SHERBET (Sorbet)

BASIC RECIPE :
½ lb. caster sugar
1 quart tepid water
Strained juice of 3 lemons
Grated rind of 1 lemon
1 egg white

Add sugar to water that has been brought to the boil and allowed to become tepid. Stir till dissolved. Add lemon juice and rind, and egg white. Stir rapidly for about 5 minutes. Freeze for 35 minutes. Serve in small sundae glasses. *For 12 persons.*

To Vary:

1. Stir 2½ tablespoons Aurum, Ceresella, Cointreau, Curaçao, Grand Marnier, Maraschino or Parfait Amour into ice just before serving.

2. Stir 2 tablespoons Benedictine, Cordiale Médoc, Chartreuse, Kummel, or Kirsch into ice before serving.

MAYFAIR : Rub 1 pint hulled strawberries through a fine sieve. Stir 2 tablespoons rum into the purée, then stir this into the lemon ice after it has been freezing for 35 minutes. Freeze for ¼ hour.

FANCY ICED DESSERTS

This section includes some varieties of fancy iced desserts. Simple iced puddings, which require to be moulded, should be half-frozen before moulding. Mousses and parfaits should be chilled only. Freeze the former in a refrigerator tray or in a tub vacuum freezer till mushy, then place in a chilled mould. *Freeze without stirring.*

TO MOULD MOUSSES AND PARFAITS

If frozen in an ice tub, bury in ice and salt, allowing 1 part ice to 1 part freezing salt. Leave for 4 hours. Mould should only be three-quarters full, and sealed as previously described. Freeze in a refrigerator for 3-4 hours in the coldest part of the freezing compartment.

BOMBES OR MOULDS

APRICOT BOMBE (Bombe d'Abricots)

2 cups thick cream or evaporated milk
1 egg white
1 cup apricot purée
½ cup orange juice
1½ cups caster sugar

Measure cream or milk into a basin, then add egg white. Beat till mixture is stiff. Sieve enough stewed dried apricots to give you a cup of purée. Strain in orange juice and sugar. Stir until blended and sugar is dissolved, then fold into cream. Turn into an ice mould. Pack in ice and salt, allowing two parts ice to one of salt. Stand till frozen, in about 4 hours. Turn out and serve at once. *For 6 persons.*

ICEBERG (Mont Glacé)

½ oz. peeled almonds
1 glacé apricot
1 cube glacé pineapple

Cut almonds into squares. Chop apricots and pineapple. Quarter strawberries and cherries. Place in a basin. Add sultanas and rum. Mix

2 glacé strawberries
3 glacé cherries
1 tablespoon washed dried
   sultanas
1½ tablespoons rum
¼ pint cream
¾ pint vanilla ice cream
½ gill strawberry syrup
1 tablespoon maraschino syrup

well. Cover and infuse for ½ hour. Whip and fold cream into ice cream. Add fruit. Mix well. Place in a pint ice-cream mould. Cover with buttered paper, buttered side up, then cover mould. Place in a tub or pail with broken ice and rock salt round. Freeze for 2 or 3 hours, or till firm. Remove. Unmould on to a chilled dish. Serve coated with strawberry syrup, flavoured with maraschino. Arrange wafers round dish. Garnish with a crystallised cherry if liked. *For 4 persons.*

NESSELRODE PUDDING (Pouding, Nesselrode)

1½ cups milk
6 oz. caster sugar
3 egg yolks
1 saltspoon salt
½ cup chopped marrons glacés
¼ cup almond paste
2 tablespoons marron syrup
1 cup thick cream
2 oz. chopped glacé fruits

Heat milk to boiling point. Stir the sugar into egg yolks, slightly beaten. Add salt. Gradually stir in milk. When sugar is dissolved, pour into the top of a double boiler. Cook over hot water for about 7 minutes, stirring constantly, until mixture coats the back of a spoon. Remove from heat. Leave till cool. Sieve half the marrons glacés. Stir in almond paste and marron syrup.
When blended, stir into custard. Mix thoroughly, then whip and fold in cream. Turn into a chilled refrigerator tray. Freeze for 2 hours till into a mush. Carefully line a chilled quart melon mould with half the mixture. Add remainder of marrons and chopped glacé fruits to remainder of mixture. Pack into mould. Cover with waxed paepr, then cover tightly with mould cover. Freeze for 3 hours in a tub freezer. *For 8 persons.*

SPUMONE (Italian Iced Bombe)

COATING:
4 tablespoons cornflour
1 quart milk
10 oz. caster sugar
5 beaten egg yolks
2 tablespoons chopped blanched
   almonds
1 saltspoon salt

FILLING:
½ pint thick cream
¼ lb. caster sugar
7 maraschino cherries
2 tablespoons minced candied
   orange peel

Cream cornflour with ½ cup of the milk. Stir in remainder of milk. Stir sugar into cornflour mixture. When thoroughly blended, pour into the top of a double boiler. Cook very slowly over hot water, stirring constantly, for about 10 minutes, until the mixture comes to the boil. Remove from heat at once. Cool slightly. Gradually stir in egg yolks, then return to top of hot water. Cook for 1 or 2 minutes, stirring constantly, until mixture thickens, but do not allow to boil. Stir in almonds and salt, then leave until cool, stirring occasionally while cooling. Pour into the chilled tray of a refrigerator. Freeze till firm, but do not allow to become too hard. Meanwhile, pour the cream into chilled basin. Whip until stiff. Whip sugar in, a little at a time. When very thick, chop cherries and mince peel. Blend gradually into the cream. Chill. Chill individual moulds with covers. Line to the depth of 1 inch with the partly frozen custard. Fill the hollow with cream. Cover with custard. Freeze

627

in freezing compartment of refrigerator, set at its coldest. (If moulds with covers are not available, cover each portion closely with two layers of waxed paper.) *For 10 or 12 persons.*

MOUSSI S

VANILLA MOUSSE (Mousse de Vanille)

3 cups thick cream
4 oz. sifted icing sugar
1 teaspoon vanilla essence
3 egg whites

Beat cream till thick, but it must not be stiff. Stir in sugar and vanilla essence. Beat egg whites till stiff. Fold into mixture. Freeze in a chilled refrigerator tray. *For 8 persons.*

BANANA MOUSSE (Mousse de Bananes)

½ pint cream
2 oz. caster sugar
2 large peeled bananas
1 teaspoon vanilla essence
2 egg whites
Pinch of salt

Beat cream till thick. Place sugar in a basin. Slice in bananas and mash till blended. Fold in cream and vanilla essence. Beat egg whites till stiff with the salt. Fold into mixture. Pour into a chilled refrigerator tray. Chill till stiff. *For 6 persons.*

CHOCOLATE MOUSSE (Mousse de Chocolat)

2 oz. unsweetened chocolate
1 cup milk
6 oz. caster sugar
1 teaspoon powdered gelatine
1 teaspoon vanilla essence
2 cups thick cream

Place the chocolate in top of double boiler. Add milk and 2 oz. of sugar, and gelatine. Stir and beat over hot water till blended and smooth. Remove from heat. Add vanilla. Strain into chilled refrigerator tray. Chill. When starting to thicken, beat until light. Beat cream till stiff, with remainder of sugar and fold into chocolate mixture. Chill in refrigerator tray. *Yield:* 4 cups.

CARAMEL MOUSSE CAKE : Cover bottom of a chilled refrigerator tray with sponge cake cut ¼ inch thick. Spread a layer of sweetened condensed milk, boiled in can for 4 hours, on top, when cool. Beat 2 egg whites till stiff. Stir in 3 tablespoons sifted icing sugar and 1 teaspoon vanilla essence. Fold into 2 cups of whipped cream. Spread over top. Freeze for about 4½ hours without stirring.

STRAWBERRY MOUSSE CAKE : Line the bottom of a refrigerator tray with sponge cake cut ¼ inch thick. Stem, wash and crush 1 pint small fresh strawberries. Sprinkle with 3 oz. icing sugar. Soak ¾ tablespoon powdered gelatine in 5 tablespoons cold water for 5 minutes. Melt over hot water. Stir into strawberry mixture. When about to set, spread it over the cake, then cover with a layer of banana or vanilla mousse. Freeze for 2 hours without stirring. Serve, cut in squares, garnished with berries.

BISCUIT TORTONI

3 cups thick cream
3½ oz. sieved icing sugar

Whip cream until thick. Whip in sugar and sherry to taste. Lightly stir in macaroon crumbs.

Sherry to taste
3/4 cup macaroon crumbs
3 stiffly-beaten egg whites

Fold in egg whites. Pack into paper cases. Sprinkle with additional macaroon crumbs. Freeze in refrigerator tray. *Yield:* 1 quart.

SWEET SAUCES

SWEET WHITE SAUCE (Sauce Blanche)

BASIC RECIPE:
1 oz. butter
1 oz. flour
½ pint milk
½-1 oz. caster sugar
Flavouring to taste

Melt butter in an enamel-lined saucepan. Draw pan aside. Stir in flour with a wooden spoon. Cook until frothy, stirring constantly, then draw pan to side and lightly stir in milk. When smooth, return pan to stove. Stir till boiling and boil for 5 minutes, still stirring. Remove from heat. Add sugar. Stir till dissolved. Cool slightly. Stir in flavouring to taste. Serve in a hot sauceboat.

To Enrich: Divide 1 oz. butter into small knobs and stir each in separately after removing pan from stove, or stir in 1-2 tablespoons whipped cream or evaporated milk.

CUSTARD SAUCE (Crème Cuite)

BASIC RECIPE:
½ pint milk
2 or 3 grains of salt
2 egg yolks
1 oz. caster sugar

Bring milk to boiling point in the top of a double boiler, but do not allow to boil. Add salt. Beat egg yolks. Gradually stir in milk. Return to top of a double boiler. Cook over hot water, stirring constantly, until sauce coats the back of spoon. Remove from heat. Add sugar. Stir until dissolved. Flavour to taste. Pour into a hot sauceboat. If wanted cold, stir occasionally until cool, then flavour. Stir and leave till cold. Serve in a glass dish or in custard cups.

To Vary:
1. Substitute 1 or 2 eggs for the yolks.
2. Add ½ teaspoon almond essence, brandy, rum, sherry, or vanilla essence.
Rich Custard Sauce: Allow 3 eggs or 5 egg yolks.
Fluffy Custard Sauce: Reduce milk to ½ cup and bring to boiling point. Place egg yolks in the top of a double boiler. Increase sugar to ¼ lb. Add to yolks. Beat till creamy. Stir in milk. Stir over hot water till thick enough to coat back of the spoon, then remove from stove. Stir in 1 teaspoon vanilla and ¼ teaspoon almond essence. Fold in 2 stiffly beaten egg whites. Serve at once in a hot sauceboat.

CUSTARD SAUCE WITH CORNFLOUR

½ teaspoon cornflour
½ pint milk
1 beaten egg
1 dessertspoon sugar
Pinch of salt

Blend cornflour with a little of the milk to a cream. Stir in egg, sugar, salt and remainder of milk. Pour into a saucepan. Stir till thick. Keep on stirring over slow heat for about 3 minutes, but do not allow to boil. Remove from heat. Cool slightly. Add flavouring to taste. Serve in a hot sauceboat.

GERMAN CUSTARD SAUCE

¼ pint Madeira or sherry
2 egg yolks
Strip of lemon rind
1 dessertspoon caster sugar

Place all ingredients in the top of an enamel-lined double boiler. Beat over hot water with an egg whisk till thickly frothy. Remove lemon rind. Serve at once in a hot sauceboat.

APPLE SAUCE (Sauce de Pommes)

2 lb. cooking apples
5 tablespoons water
4 pats butter
Caster or Demerara sugar to taste

Peel, core and slice apples into a saucepan. Add water. Cover and stew till tender. Add butter and sugar to taste. Beat to a pulp. If preferred, flavour before cooking with ground cinnamon to taste. Serve in a hot sauceboat with ginger-bread or any steamed spiced pudding. *Yield:* about ¾ pint.

APRICOT WINE SAUCE (Sauce aux Abricots)

1 tablespoon apricot jam
2 oz. caster sugar
¼ pint cold water
1 teaspoon lemon juice
¼ pint sherry

Place jam and sugar in a small saucepan. Add cold water. Stir over low heat until sugar is dissolved, then bring to boil. Add lemon juice and bring again to boil. Stir in sherry. Heat for a moment or two, then strain into hot sauce-boat. *Yield:* Fully ½ pint.

CHOCOLATE CREAM SAUCE (Sauce de Chocolat, Royale)

¾ lb. caster sugar
1½ oz. butter
¼ lb. chocolate
1 cup cream
¼ cup sherry
¾ teaspoon vanilla essence

Beat sugar and butter to a cream. Melt choco-late. Stir into mixture. When blended, stir in cream. Place in the top of a double boiler. Stir over boiling water until boiling. Cover. Simmer over boiling water without stirring for 6 or 7 minutes, then gradually stir in sherry and vanilla essence. Serve in a hot sauceboat. *Yield:* About ¾ pint.

COFFEE CUSTARD SAUCE (Sauce de Café à la Crème)

2 eggs
½ cup strong boiling coffee
2 oz. caster sugar
Few grains of salt
½ cup thick or whipped cream

Beat eggs. Slowly beat in the coffee. Add sugar and salt. Cook in the top of a double boiler, stirring constantly until sauce coats the back of a spoon. Chill. When required, fold in thick or whipped cream. Serve in a glass dish, with any milk mould. *Yield:* Fully ½ pint.

GOLDEN SAUCE (Sauce d'Orée)

1 tablespoon cornflour
½ cup water
½ cup golden syrup

Mix cornflour to a cream with a little of the water, then add remainder of water. Add syrup. Stir till well blended, then bring to boil. Cook for 5 minutes, stirring constantly. Add 1 or 2 tablespoons minced dates or cherries. Serve in a hot sauceboat with steamed puddings. *Yield:* Fully ¼ pint.

LEMON SAUCE (Sauce de Citron)

1 tablespoon cornflour
½ cup caster sugar
1 cup boiling water
1½ tablespoons butter
1½ tablespoons lemon juice
Grated nutmeg to taste
Salt to taste

Mix cornflour with sugar. Place in a saucepan. Stir in water by degrees. When it is added, stir till boiling, then boil for 5 minutes, stirring constantly. Remove from stove. Add butter, bit by bit. Stir in lemon juice, nutmeg and salt to taste. Serve in a hot sauceboat with steamed puddings. *Yield:* Fully ½ pint.

MARMALADE SAUCE (Sauce de Marmelade)

1 dessertspoon cornflour
Rind and juice of 1 lemon
½ pint water
1 tablespoon marmalade
1 tablespoon caster sugar

Cream cornflour with lemon juice. Pour water into a small saucepan. Add lemon rind. Bring to boil, then remove the rind and stir in creamed cornflour. Stir till smooth and boiling, then boil for 5 minutes, stirring constantly. Add marmalade and sugar. Stir till sugar is dissolved, then use. Serve, in a hot sauceboat with butter, sponge or marmalade pudding. *Yield:* Fully ½ pint.

PEPPERMINT MARSHMALLOW SAUCE
(Sauce à la Menthe, Américaine)

6 oz. caster sugar
½ cup water
1 dessertspoon butter
3 chopped marshmallows

Dissolve sugar in water in a saucepan. Bring to boil. Boil for 5 minutes. Add butter and marshmallows. Stir until dissolved. Flavour to taste with essence of peppermint. Serve in a hot sauceboat. *Yield:* About ½ pint.

WINE SAUCE (Sauce de Vin)

1 snippet lemon peel
¼ pint cold water
1½ oz. caster sugar
1 teaspoon arrowroot
1 oz. butter
½ gill brandy
½ gill sherry

Cut the lemon peel very thinly. Place in a saucepan with the water. Boil for 5 minutes, then remove peel. Add sugar. Stir until dissolved. Mix arrowroot to a cream with an additional tablespoon of cold water. Stir into boiling syrup. When boiling, add butter bit by bit, stirring between each addition until melted. Stir in brandy and sherry. Stir until piping hot, but do not allow to boil. Serve in a hot sauceboat. *Yield:* Fully ¼ pint.

UNCOOKED SAUCES

HARD SAUCE

BASIC RECIPE:
1/4 lb. butter
2 cups sifted icing sugar
2 teaspoons boiling water
Few grains of salt
Vanilla essence to taste

Beat butter to a cream. Beat in sugar gradually. Stir in boiling water drop by drop. Beat in salt and from 1-1½ teaspoons vanilla essence according to taste. Beat till fluffy. Pile in a small glass dish. Chill. Serve with Christmas Pudding.

GINGER HARD SAUCE: Substitute for water given 2 teaspoons ginger syrup from a jar of ginger, and 2 tablespoons of minced ginger.

LONDON HARD SAUCE: Use 2 oz. butter and 1 cup sifted icing sugar. Flavour with 2-3 teaspoons vanilla essence and 5 or 6 drops lemon essence.

BRANDY BUTTER (Beurre de l'Eau de Vie)

1/4 lb. unsalted butter
1/2 lb. sifted icing sugar
3 teaspoons brandy

Beat butter till softened. Gradually beat in icing sugar. Beat till creamy. Beat in the brandy drop by drop. Pile in a glass dish. Chill. Serve with Christmas or steamed batter pudding. *For 6-8 persons.*

RUM OR SHERRY BUTTER: Follow recipe for Brandy Butter, substituting rum or sherry for the brandy.

FRUIT SAUCE (Sauce de Fruit)

1 egg white
1 cup fruit purée or mashed fruit
1/2 lb. caster sugar

Use any fresh or canned fruit for this sauce, but bananas, peaches, raspberries, and strawberries are most popular. Beat egg white till frothy, then beat in purée and sugar. Serve in a glass dish with milk moulds. *Yield:* About ¾ pint.

ICE CREAM SAUCES

APRICOT SAUCE (Sauce d'Abricots)

1 pint jar apricots in syrup
1 lemon
Rum to taste

Sieve apricots with the syrup. Strain in lemon juice. Flavour to taste with rum.

BUTTERSCOTCH SAUCE (Sauce à la Caramel)

1/4 lb. butter
1 lb. light brown sugar
1/4 tablespoon lemon juice
1/2 cup thick cream

Place all the ingredients in the top of a double boiler. Cook until sugar is dissolved, stirring constantly, then for 1 hour, stirring occasionally.

CARAMEL SYRUP (Sirop à la Caramel)

1/2 lb. caster sugar
1 cup boiling water

Melt sugar in a thick frying-pan over slow heat until slightly brown, stirring constantly. Slowly stir in water. Boil for 6 minutes.

CHOCOLATE VELVET SAUCE
(Sauce de Chocolat, Américaine)

1 oz. chocolate
3 tablespoons boiling water
½ oz. unsalted butter
6 oz. caster sugar
½ cup chopped marshmallows

Melt chocolate in the water in the top of a double boiler over hot water. Add butter. Stir constantly until a smooth paste. Add sugar. Stir till dissolved and the sauce is slightly thick. Add marshmallows. Stir till melted and smoothly blended.

MARSHMALLOW SAUCE (Sauce de Guimauve)

¼ lb. caster sugar
3 tablespoons water
12 halved marshmallows
1 egg white

Dissolve sugar in the water in the top of a double boiler. Boil to a syrup in about 5 minutes. Add marshmallows. Leave for 2 minutes without stirring. Beat egg white till stiff. Gradually pour in marshmallow syrup. Beat till smooth. Serve with chocolate or coffee ice cream.

MELBA SAUCE (Sauce Melba)

½ pint raspberries
¼ pint red currant jelly
1 tablespoon boiling water
5 oz. caster sugar
1 teaspoon cornflour

Place berries and jelly in the top of a double boiler. Add water. Heat to boiling point, stirring occasionally. Mix sugar with cornflour. Add to berries. Cook for 9 or 10 minutes over boiling water until clear and thick. Sieve and leave till cool. *Yield:* 1½ gills.

MOCHA SAUCE (Sauce Mocha)

1 cup strong black mocha coffee
4 tablespoons cognac

Add boiling hot coffee to cognac. Serve with vanilla ice cream.

CHANTILLY CREAM (Crème Chantilly)

1 pint thick cream
3½ oz. caster sugar
3 egg whites
Vanilla essence to taste

Chill cream. Stir in sugar. Beat till fluffy, then add egg whites. Beat till fluffy. Stir in essence. (As an alternative, keep 2 vanilla pods in a 2 lb. jar of caster sugar covered tightly, and use this vanilla sugar for sweetening when omitting vanilla essence.)

MOCK CREAM

2 teaspoons cornflour
¼ pint milk
1½ oz. unsalted butter
3 teaspoons caster sugar
5 drops vanilla essence

Mix cornflour to a cream with a little of the milk. Heat remainder of milk. When boiling stir it into the creamed cornflour. When blended, return to the saucepan. Bring to the boil. Cook for about 2½ minutes, stirring constantly, then remove from heat and leave till quite cold. Beat butter till softened. Add sugar. Beat till fluffy. Whisk in cornflour mixture, a little at a time, beating well with a whisk. Stir in vanilla essence.

SAINT HONORE CREAM (Crème Saint-Honoré)

4½ gills milk
3 separated eggs
2½ oz. caster sugar
⅓ oz. flour
2 leaves gelatine
Vanilla essence to taste

Heat milk till tepid in top of a double boiler. Beat egg yolks with the sugar. Stir in flour. When smoothly blended, stir in half the milk. Dissolve gelatine in remainder and stir into yolk mixture. Cook over boiling water, stirring constantly until thick but do not allow to boil. Beat egg whites to a very stiff froth. Fold gently into cream. Flavour. Chill and use in gâteaux.

Fruit

To Choose Fresh Fruit: Fruit should be fresh and free from bruises and decay. Usually at its best when most plentiful, and therefore at its cheapest. Buy the most perishable fruit, such as berries, currants and peaches, in limited quantities. Fruit may be cheaper bought in bulk, but if part of it " spoils " before it can be cooked or served, the saving you made by buying in bulk is lost.

To Clean: Wash fruit carefully before using. Soft fruits, berries, and currants should be placed in a colander and gently lowered into a basin of cold water, so as to wash it without bruising. Washing is necessary on account of sprays sometimes used on fruit bushes and trees.

To Prevent Discoloration: Certain fruits such as apples, pears and quinces darken when pared. To avoid this, dip at once as peeled in grapefruit, lemon or pineapple juice.

To Store Fruit: Store all fruit, except bananas and lemons, in a covered container in a refrigerator, or in a cool dark place if you haven't a refrigerator, such as under a shelf in your larder. Before storing melons in a refrigerator, wrap closely in greaseproof or waxed paper or in aluminium foil. Store lemons covered with water in a jar.

CANNED, DRIED AND QUICK-FROZEN FRUIT

With the assistance of canned, dried and quick-frozen fruit, it is now possible to have fruit of every kind all the year round.

Canned: Don't choose cans of fruit with bulging sides. A No. 2 can of fruit is enough to fill a 9 inch pie case.

Dried: Be sure that the dried fruit is fresh and is not starting to deteriorate. If it is speckled with white, reject it. Wash in three or four changes of lukewarm water, then soak before cooking. Cook in soaking water otherwise a certain amount of mineral and vitamin value will be lost.

Quick-Frozen: To de-frost quick-frozen fruit, leave in carton in a warm room for an hour or two, depending on variety, before serving.

Apples (Pommes) :
Seasonable: Home-grown: July-April. *Imported:* September-July.
Cooking: Bramley's Seedling ; Lane's Prince Albert ; Lord Derby ; Monarch ; Newton Wonder ; Victoria ; etc.
Dessert: Allington Pippin ; American Mother ; Beauty of Bath ; Blenheim Orange ; Cleopatra ; Cox's Orange Pippin ; Ellison's Orange ; Golden Russet ; James Grieve ; Jonathon ; Laxton's Superb ; Newton Pippin ; Worcester Pearmain ; etc.
All-Purpose: Northern Spy ; Wealthy ; Wine Sap ; etc.
Good cooking apples become fluffy when cooked. If you want apple for an apple cake or flan, that keeps its shape when cut in wedges and cooked, use dessert apples.
2 lb. cooking apples yields 3 cups stewed apples.

Apricots (Abricots) :
Seasonable: August-September.
Imported: September-July.
Should be fairly firm, plump and uniformly golden yellow with juicy flesh. Delicious raw or cooked. Suitable for using in compôtes, salads, pastry cases, etc. Before peeling, stand in boiling water for about 20 seconds, then plunge into cold water, and peel. Can be crystallized, bottled or made into jam, etc.
1 lb. (8-10) apricots yields $\frac{3}{4}$-1 pint sliced fruit, *for 4 persons.*

Avocado or Alligator Pear : Tropical. *Imported* April-May, and September-December inclusive. Rich in proteins and vitamin B. Variety usually imported is a dark green fruit with a large pear-shaped stone in centre.
To Choose: Choose bright, fairly firm fruit. When ready to serve, it should show signs of beginning to soften when lightly pressed.
Usually served cut into rings, coated with French dressing. Some gourmets claim that it is best sprinkled with salt and eaten with a spoon. Others like it sprinkled with lemon or fresh lime juice and sugar as a first course. In the United States, it is served in cocktail form and in shellfish and vegetable salads.
To Prepare: Peel when ripe and halve, removing stone, then brush with grapefruit, lemon or lime juice to prevent discoloration.
Yield: 1 medium-sized avocado yields $1\frac{1}{2}$-$1\frac{3}{4}$ cups diced.

Banana : Available all the year round. Two varieties : 1. The Canary Banana : Aromatic and more delicate than 2. Jamaica Banana. There is a

636

third most popular in the United States, known as the " Red Banana." It is the richest variety. All bananas are rich in vitamin C.

To Choose: Select firm fruit, slightly speckled with brown. If greenish at the tip, place in a warm room until they turn a deep yellow or become slightly speckled, before serving as a dessert. Good bananas are plump. If not to be used at once, choose fruit without specks. Can be served raw or cooked. If required peeled before serving, as for a garnish, dip in any citrus fruit juice.

1 lb. (3 medium-sized) bananas yields 2 cups sliced banana.

Bilberries (Airelles) : *Seasonable:* July-August. *Imported:* July-September. Sometimes known as "blue berries", "blaeberries", "whinberries" or "whortleberries". Grow wild on English, Scottish and Welsh moors. Sometimes imported from Czechoslovakia and Eire.

To Prepare: Stem, rinse and sugar to taste. Chill. Serve as a fruit course at breakfast or with cream, ice cream, custard sauce or milk jelly as a cold dessert, or make into jam. In Wales, bilberry tarts are a great delicacy.

Yield: 1¼ pints enough for 4 persons.

Blackberries (Mûres Sauvages) : *Seasonable:* Mid-August-October. Cultivated varieties include Himalayan and Parsley-leaved.

To Prepare: Pick over carefully, then place in a colander. Dip colander of fruit in cold water, then drain, and stem or hull.

Perfect fruit served as dessert, but blackberries usually made into jam, jelly and tarts in combination with apple which furnishes the acid and pectin lacking in the berries. Delicious cooked, sieved and made into fools.

Yield: 1¼ pints berries for 4 persons.

Black Currants (Cassis) : *Seasonable:* June-August. *Imported:* April-May. Valuable source of vitamin C. Cooling and beneficial to the blood.

To Prepare: Wash and stem. Use in pies, tarts, or summer puddings, or for jam.

Cape Gooseberries : (Edible berry of *physalis peruviana edulis*). Can be grown in England. Makes a delicious accompaniment to ice cream, when crystallized. Generally allowed to remain on stem, and sold in bunches for decoration.

Cherries (Cerises) : *Seasonable:* June-August. *Imported:* April-May. Two main classes : Sour, for cooking, and sweet for dessert. The Mayduke and the Morella are most popular varieties for cooking. (Ripe in August and early September). Used for jam and pies. Black Heart and White Heart, Black Tartarian, Early Rivers, and Governor Wood are some of the most popular dessert cherries.

Yield: 1 lb. when stemmed yields about 3 cups. When stoned and cooked, about 2 cups.

Crab Apples (Pommes Sauvages) : *Seasonable and Imported:* July and August. Dartmouth and John Downie best known. Chiefly used for jams and jellies.

Cranberries (Canneberges) : *Seasonable:* Late Autumn. Mainly imported, when available from September-February. Chiefly used for making cranberry sauce or jelly to serve with turkey or game.

Custard Apples : Tropical fruit. Flavour suggests a combination of banana and pineapple. *Imported: Argentine:* February-July. *California:* March-April. *Madeira:* March-May. *Mexico:* All the year round. Sugar Custard Apple is considered the most delicate.

Damsons (Prunes de Damas) : *Seasonable:* August-September. Deep blue small plum. Related to sloes. Use for dumplings, pies, puddings and tarts, as well as for fools, etc. Makes excellent jams, jellies and cheese. Not to be confused with the Damson Plum which is slightly larger, but inferior in taste.

Dates (Dates) : Fruit of the Date Palm. Imported from *Algeria* and *Tunisia* in February and March, and from *Iran* in September and October. Sometimes imported from *California.* Use for dessert, in steamed puddings and cakes, etc. *Dessert:* sold in boxes, unstoned. *Cooking:* Usually sold in bulk.

Figs (Figues) : *Hothouse: Seasonable* May-September. *Imported: Guernsey*, May-September. *Italy:* June-September. Nourishing as they contain albumen, fat, pectose, salts, sugar and water. Two varieties. *Home-Grown:* Green and Purple. Serve as a dessert, or in a compôte.
Dried Figs: Imported from *Algeria, California, Greece* and *Italy*, as well as *Portugal* and *Turkey.* Use for stewing and in puddings.

Gooseberries (Groseilles) : *Seasonable:* May-September. There are two classes : Culinary and dessert, and many varieties—Hairy and smooth, oval and plump. Pick green for pies, tarts and jelly. Ripe used for dessert and stewing. Careless, Downing, Gunner, Keepsake, Lancashire Lad, Leveller and Whitesmith all fine flavour. Top and tail before cooking.

Granadillas (Passiflores) : Tropical fruit. Sometimes called " Passion Fruit." 2-3 inches long and deep purple when fully ripe. Imported from *South Africa* from December-April, then in August ; from *Madeira* from September-November. Exotic dessert. Imparts delicious flavour to fruit salad.

Grapes (Raisins) : *Seasonable:* All the year round, (Hothouse). *Guernsey :* July-November. *Imported: S. African:* December-July. *Australian:* March-May. Also imported from *Belgium, Holland, Italy, Madeira, Spain*, etc. Black, green and red. Alicante, Black Hamburgh, Gros Colmar, Muscat Hambro, Royal among the best known. Muscat of Alexandria, one of the finest of the amber green variety. Waltham Cross also popular. Hanepoot, both the white and red strain, imported from *S. Africa*, February-April. One of the most delicious varieties. Cannon Hall Muscat considered finest of the muscats—yellowish white. Chiefly used as dessert, and in compôtes, fruit cocktails and salads. The thinnings make delicious jelly.

Grapefruit : *Imported: Jamaica:* October-May. *Palestine:* November-April. Also imported from *U.S.A., Brazil, S. Africa* and the *West Indies.* Known as " Brights " when golden yellow, and " Russets " when splotched with russet.
To Choose: A good grapefruit has thin, fine-grained skin. Is heavy for its size, and free from marks of decay.
Popular for breakfast and first course at lunch or dinner, either as a fruit or in the form of juice.
Yield: 1 small grapefruit yields ¾ cup strained juice. 1 large fruit yields about ½ pint diced pulp and juice.

Greengages (Prunes de Reine-Claude) : *Seasonable:* July-September. Delicious dessert plum varying in shade from green to golden depending on variety. Used for fools, tarts, and preserves, etc. About 15 to the pound.

Guava : Tropical fruit. Imported from *India, Florida* and the *West Indies. India:* November-January. *Florida and West Indies:* September-November. Sweet musky flavour. Highly aromatic variety known as " Strawberry Guava." Not so musky as Guava ; flavour suggests strawberries. Usually made into jelly and cheese.

Lemons (Citrons) : *Seasonable:* All the year round. Rich in citric acid, and contain vitamin C. Rind and juice used in flavouring. Thin, fine-textured skinned preferable as they yield more juice than the thicker skinned. Frequently used for salad dressing in place of vinegar. Essences made from the oil in the skin.
Yield: 1 average-sized lemon gives about 3 tablespoons juice and 3 teaspoons grated rind.

Limes (Limons) : *Seasonable:* All the year round. Imported from March-September from *West Indies.* Best are green and heavy. Juice used for cocktails, long drinks, etc. Rind and juice make a delicious marmalade.

Loganberries : *Seasonable:* Mid-July-August. Cross between blackberry and raspberry. Larger than either. Deep red with luscious flavour. Good for dessert and preserving.

Lychee : Tropical fruit. White, juicy, translucent flesh covering a small seed. Imported from *South Africa,* from January-April. Sometimes dried when it is called " lychee nuts." Usually sold canned in Britain. Treat fresh as a dessert or canned as a compôte.

Mandarin (Mandarine) : Small orange with a loose rind. Very sweet and vinous. Available all the year round except for September. South African fruit known as " Naartjes." Used as dessert and for flavouring ice puddings. Best from December-February.

Mango : Tropical fruit. Many varieties. Large and smooth-skinned fruit with apricot-coloured flesh. Delicious flavour and very aromatic. When green slice and use in chutneys, curries, pickles, preserves and jellies. In the Tropics, they are stoned and served like melon. Imported from *South Africa* : January-April, and from *Jamaica* in May, June and September.

Medlars : *Seasonable* : September-November. Like a large rose-hip, but golden brown. Pick when ripe and leave for a fortnight until they become quite soft, before serving. Use as dessert, or turn, when picked, into jelly.

Melons (Melons) : *Seasonable* (Hothouse) : May-August. *Imported:* All the year round. There are two main varieties :

1. *Musk Melons:* Some have a rough rind or netted surface. Others are smooth-skinned, sometimes known as " winter melons ". Cantaloup is the best example of the former. Honeydew is a good example of the latter.

2. *Water Melons:* Round and oval-shaped. Imported in the summer.

To Choose:

Cantaloup: Segmented. Do not keep well. Choose fully ripe when of a silvery-yellow colour, with a deep musky aroma and a smooth softening at the blossom end. Discard any that are bruised or flabby.

Honeydew: When ripe, the rind is creamy yellow and smooth, and yields to pressure at the blossom end.

Tiger: Segmented. Green and yellow striped. Choose as above.

Water Melon: Rather insipid, large egg-shaped melon most common, but round also available. Choose heavy fruit with a velvety bloom on the rind. Very refreshing. To test for ripeness, thump melon. When ripe, it will give out a dull, hollow sound.

To Serve: Cut all but water melons in balls or cubes for fruit cocktails, or in rings to serve as a first course. Garnish centre of each ring with 4 half slices of peeled orange to form a cup, with 2 halved, seeded grapes dipped in ginger syrup in the middle. Chill melon before preparing. Serve large ones in wedges as a first course, and use halved, small melons as cups for fruit salad, or ice cream. If to be cut in wedges, remove a small portion from the stem end. Pour in 3 tablespoons Madeira, rum or sherry, or 1 tablespoon Cointreau or Curaçao. Replace wedge of melon. Wrap carefully in a cloth and chill. To serve : Cut in wedges and remove seeds. Pass icing or caster sugar with it. See also Appetiser Section. Serve water melons chilled, sliced crosswise or lengthwise in sections, peeled or unpeeled.

Monstera : Cone-like fruit, like a rough honeycombed small, green cucumber. Delicious flavour reminiscent of banana and pineapple. Imported from *Madeira* from October-December.

Mulberries (Mûres) : *Seasonable* : August. Fruit of the black mulberry tree. Makes a delicious dessert, but must be eaten as soon as picked, as they develop mould. Also good for pies, tarts, fools, and for making into syrup, jam or jelly with apple juice as they are low in pectin.

Nectarines (Nectarines) : *Seasonable:* July-October. *Imported:* December-October. Somewhat like a peach, but with a smooth skin and a deeper glow, and firmer flesh. Serve like peaches, but best as dessert.

(*Top right*) Waffles, baked and ready to serve. (*Bottom left*) Waffles, served and ready to eat. *See page* 693.

Filling the Biscuit Barrel.

Fruit Drops go equally well with coffee or tea. *See page* 740.

Dredge Almond Shor Biscuits with casto sugar. *See page* 735.

Olives (Olives): Imported in brine and in pickled form from *Algeria, California, Greece, Italy, Spain, Palestine* and *Turkey*, etc.

Oranges (Oranges): Obtainable all the year round. Sweet and bitter oranges. *Sweet* oranges are used for dessert, in fruit cocktails, salads and cold sweets. The juice is popular for breakfast; full of vitamin C. *Bitter* oranges used for marmalade, jelly in combination with apple, for salads and sauces to serve with all kinds of duck. Varieties of sweet oranges include Jaffa (few or no seeds), Navel (seedless) but rather coarse flesh, Valencia (very juicy), and blood oranges (fine-grained, rich, sweet flavour and vinous.)
To Choose: Choose heavy, firm fruit with a fine-textured skin.
Yield: Most varieties give about ½ cup juice and 1 tablespoon grated rind.

Peaches (Pêches): *Seasonable* (Hothouse): May-October. *Imported:* December-October. There are two general types: Yellow and white-fleshed. As easily bruised, and so very perishable, buy in small quantities. Delicious for desserts, compôtes, for serving with ice cream and for preserving.
To Choose: Choose fresh fruit with firm, solid flesh. Avoid any with spots or bruises.
If to be cooked, dip each peach as prepared in lemon, grapefruit or pineapple juice to prevent discoloration.
Yield: 1 lb. peaches (4-7 according to size) yields ¾-1 pint sliced fruit.

Pears (Poires): *Seasonable:* August-December. *Imported:* All the year round. Bon Chrétien, Conference, Doyenné du Comice and Williams finest dessert pears. Pitmaston Duchess excellent at Christmas. Of the culinary pears, seckle pears are good for bottling and canning while all firm-fleshed russet-skinned pears store well and are good for cooking and bottling.
Yield: 1 lb. (3 or 4) pears yields 1 pint sliced fruit.

Persimmons (Kakis): Imported from *France* from October-December. Considered by the Japanese as one of the best fruits. Large, round shiny fruit (about the size of a dessert apple) of a bright orange which turns almost brown when ready for eating. Slight chocolate flavour. Sometimes used for flavouring iced sweets.

Pineapple (Ananas): Imported all the year round. Hawaiian most celebrated. The riper the fruit, the richer the flavour. Avoid pines with decayed spot at the base around the eyes. Perfect dessert, and a delicious ingredient in fruit cocktails, cups and salads.
Yield: 1 medium-sized pineapple (about 2 lb. in weight) yields about 1¼ pints of diced fruit, for 5 or 6 persons.

Plums (Prunes): *Seasonable:* July-October. Imported all the year round, but scarce in November. Many varieties from blue, green and purple to red and yellow. There are also many varieties of both culinary and dessert plums.
Culinary: Belle de Louvain, Pond's Seedling, and President are well known.
Dessert and Culinary: Monarch, Orleans and Victoria can be cooked before

they are ripe, and used as dessert when ripe. Two of the best culinary plums are the Pershore Yellow, and the Purple Pershore.

To Choose: Select plump, clean plums equally ripe all over.

Yield: 1 lb. (about 15 medium-sized) plums yields 2 cups cooked plums.

Pomegranate (Grenade) : Eastern fruit. Imported from *South Africa* in April, and from *Spain* in September-December inclusive. Like a large irregular orange, but with a ruddy brown, leathery rind. Full of seeds. Use juice for fruit cocktails, in salads and drinks, and for syrup.

Prunes (Pruneaux) : Dried plums imported from *France* and *Portugal*, etc. Usually stewed, but can be made into many attractive cold sweets. Dessert varieties are Carlsbad and Elvas.

Yield: 1 lb. cooking prunes yields 4 cups cooked fruit or 2 cups cooked, stoned fruit.

Quince (Coing) : *Seasonable:* September and October. Yellowish pear-shaped fruit, acid-flavoured. Not suitable for dessert, but usually turned into jam, jelly or cheese. Quince should be firm, greenish-yellow or a golden-yellow colour and free from blemishes. They combine well with apples and oranges. The yellow flesh turns pink when cooked. To prevent discoloration when preparing, dip each portion in any citrus fruit juice.

Raspberries (Framboises) : *Seasonable:* June-November. Three varieties : Red, yellow and white. Popular for dessert, and also for making sauce to serve with ice cream, and for adding to fruit cocktails, compôtes and salads. Use for filling flans and tartlets. Make delicious jam. Wild raspberries are the sweetest. Lloyd-George variety has the longest fruiting season.

Red Currants (Groseilles Rouges) : *Seasonable:* July and August. *Imported:* May and June. Useful for garnishing cold sweets, for making jelly to serve with roast lamb or mutton, and for providing the necessary acid and pectin when making preserves from cherries, raspberries, strawberries, etc.

Rhubarb (Rhubarbe) : *Seasonable:* April-July. *Forced:* December-April. Excellent for purifying the blood. Best steamed.

Yield: 1 lb. sliced rhubarb gives about $3\frac{1}{2}$ cups raw and 2 cups when steamed without water.

Rowans : Fruit from the Mountain Ash or Rowan tree. Orange berries. Used with apple for making jelly for serving with game.

Sloes (Prunelles) : *Seasonable:* Autumn. Fruit of the Blackthorn. Used chiefly for sloe gin, but makes delicious jelly, in combination with apple or quince.

Strawberries (Fraises) : *Seasonable:* May-July ; *Forced:* March-April. There are two common varieties : the garden variety and the wild Alpine strawberry which can also be cultivated. The latter is the Fraise de Bois of

rance. Ranks with raspberries as one of the most delicious dessert fruits.
lso popular for garnishing fruit cocktails, mousses, and cold soufflés, and for
dding to fruit salads and turning into fruit fools and delicious jam.

Tangelo (Ugli) : A citrus fruit. Cross between the grapefruit and tangerine,
ometimes known as " Ugli ". It is larger and more irregular in shape than the
rapefruit. Can be used as a breakfast fruit, but chilled, it makes an excellent
essert. The fruit can also be added to cocktails and salads.

Tangerine (Tangerine) : A variety of small orange. *See* Mandarin.

Wineberries : Sometimes called " Japanese Wine Berry ". *Seasonable:*
eptember. Fruit of a species of bramble. Bright orange red berry. Used as
essert with cream.

TO PREPARE FRUIT FOR DESSERT

Grapes: If wanted for a family party, place bunches in a colander. Sprinkle
old water over from the tap. Drain. Serve. If wanted at a formal dinner,
nd finger bowls are not to be provided, pass a beautiful cut-glass vase filled
vith water round with the grapes so that guests, after cutting off the grapes with
rape scissors placed alongside the fruit, can dip the grapes in the water before
ating them.
Greengages and Medlars: Wipe with a dry or damp cloth as required.
Mandarins and Oranges: Polish with a dry cloth. If liked, cut a cross at
he blossom end of these fruits, that penetrates the flesh. With the point of
he knife, raise one of the four divisions, then another until you have lifted them
ll, when press back slightly so that all that remains to be done is to pull off
ach quarter of skin when served.
Melon: Wipe with a damp cloth. Cut in wedges. Remove all seeds and
ith. Decorate along the top with one or two berries. If small, halve melon
nd remove the seeds and pith. Fill with sugared berries, sliced peeled peaches
r fruit salad.
Persimmon: Cut off flower end, then cut in half. Serve a whole or half to
ach person. Tuck a tiny sprig of mint or borage in the centre of each half if
ked. Serve persimmon with a spoon, as the flesh has to be scooped out.
Pineapple: Stand upright on a chopping board. Remove rind with a sharp,
ong-bladed knife, beginning at the top and slicing to the bottom. With a small,
ointed knife, remove each eye. Cut in slices crosswise, from $\frac{1}{2}$-$\frac{3}{4}$ inch thick,
hen with a small, round cutter, remove the hard core from each.

APPLES IN BLOOM (Pommes en Fleurs)

red apples
cup caster sugar
rated rind ½ lemon
uice of 1 orange

Place apples in a saucepan. Cook in boiling
water coming half-way up their sides in a covered
pan until soft. Skin carefully so that you do
not remove their red cheeks when skinning. Add
ugar, lemon rind and orange juice to the water. Simmer until reduced to 1

cup. Chill and pour over the apples. Serve, ice cold, with cream and macaroⁱ
biscuits. *For 6 persons.*

BANANA BOATS (Bateaux de Bananes)

6 bananas
1 tablespoon lemon juice
Grated chocolate to taste

Remove one section of skin from each banan
Scoop out fruit. Scrape skins, and, holding ba⁰
one banana, cut remainder of fruit into dic
Sprinkle with lemon juice. Stand in a cool pla

for 2 hours. Fill skins with prepared fruit. Decorate with whipped cream aⁱ
sliced remaining banana, and grated chocolate. Serve at once. *For 5 persoⁱ*

CANTALOUP COUPES (Coupes de Cantaloup)

1 ripe chilled cantaloup
¾ cup sherry
¼ cup sloe gin
A grain or two of salt
Grenadine syrup to taste

Cut out the centre of cantaloup melon. Remo
any seeds. Cut pulp into inch cubes. Place
basin. Mix sherry with sloe gin, salt and grenadiⁱ
syrup to taste. Add melon. Chill. Serve
champagne or sherbet glasses. Decorate wiⁱ

sweetened whipped cream. Sprinkle with crushed meringue. *For 6 or*
persons.

JAMAICA APPLES (Pommes à la Jamaïque)

6 large cooking apples
3 tablespoons caster sugar
6 teaspoons butter
1½ cups canned pineapple
    juice

Core, peel and halve apples crosswise. Place ⁱ
a buttered flat baking dish. Mix caster sugar ⁱ
a paste with butter, and spread over apples. Po⁰
pineapple juice over. Cover and bake in a slo⁰
oven, 325° F., for 15 minutes, basting frequentⁱ

Uncover. Bake for about 10 minutes, till tender. Chill. Serve with whippⁱ
sweetened cream or with custard sauce. *For 6 persons.*

MANDARIN DREAMS (Rêves aux Mandarines)

2 sliced bananas
2 diced pears
6 mandarins
6 sponge cakes
3 slices canned pineapple
    (chopped)
6 stoned dates

Mix the banana and pear together. Squeeze juiⁱ
from mandarins. Split and put halves of spong
cakes together with apricot jam, flavoured ⁱ
taste with ground almonds and vanilla essenc
Place one cake, cut in three, crosswise, in tⁱ
bottom of a sundae glass. Divide mandarⁱ
juice between each. Stand for 1 hour until tⁱ

cakes have absorbed all the juice. Sprinkle with banana and pear mixtur
pineapple and chopped dates. Cover with whipped, sweetened cream. *For*
persons.

PEAR PORCUPINE (Porc-épics de Poires)

10 oz. caster sugar
2¼ cups water

Dissolve sugar in the water in a saucepan, thⁱ
bring to boil. Add lemon rind and boil for

Rind of ½ lemon
6 large dessert pears
1 tablespoon butter
Cochineal to colour
1 tablespoon rum
3 oz. blanched almonds

minutes. Peel and core pears, and place them in the syrup. Cook gently till soft, but unbroken, then remove to a baking dish. Add a little lemon juice, if too sweet, to the syrup. Stir in butter, cochineal and rum. Cut almonds lengthwise in strips. Stick into pears. Bake in a moderate oven, 350° F., until the tips of the nuts are brown. Cool. Strain a little of the syrup over each. Decorate with whipped cream and angelica. *For 6 persons.*

STRAWBERRY COUPES (Coupes de Fraises)

1 lb. ripe strawberries
½ lb. loaf sugar
½ pint water
Whipped cream or ice cream as required

Fill 8 sundae glasses two-thirds full with the fruit. Dissolve the sugar in water. Bring to boil. Boil for 10 minutes. Chill. Divide equally among the berries. Top with whipped cream or ice cream. Serve with vanilla wafers. *For 6 persons.*

WHITEHOUSE COUPES (Coupes, Whitehouse)

½ lb. black grapes
¼ lb. Muscat grapes
6 dates
3 ripe pears
2 peeled bananas
½ cup diced canned peaches
1 cup dessert cherries
Caster sugar to taste
Dash of Kirsch or Maraschino
6 quartered marshmallows
Whipped cream as required

Halve and seed grapes. Chop dates. Peel, core and dice pears. Slice bananas. Stir in peaches and cherries. Mix these fruits gently in a basin. Sprinkle with sugar and Kirsch or Maraschino. When sugar is dissolved, chill. Strain off juice. Reserve for a fruit drink or a cocktail. Stir in marshmallows and cream to coat. Pile in sundae glasses. Decorate with chopped blanched pistachio nuts. *For 6 persons.*

STEWED FRUIT, COMPOTES AND SALADS

The methods to be used for stewing fruit should vary according to the use to which the fruit is to be put. If wanted for a fool, mousse or any other sweet that demands sieved fruit, it can be stewed in a saucepan until tender and it will not matter if it becomes mushy. To keep stewed fruit whole, stew very gently and don't add the sugar until nearly tender. If you haven't time to watch it, you can steam it in the top of a double boiler over boiling water until tender.

If Wanted for a Compote, or Fruit Salad: Stew, as suggested, in the top of a double boiler, or prepare a syrup and cook it gently in the syrup until tender. Allow from 3-4 oz. sugar to 1 lb. fruit, depending on the sweetness and ripeness. Green gooseberries, for example, need more sugar than ripe gooseberries. The amount of water depends on the juiciness of the fruit.

STEWED APPLES AND PEARS : Dissolve ¼ lb. caster sugar in ½ pint cold water. Add 2 cloves, 1 inch cinnamon stick or ¼ teaspoon each of ground cloves and ground cinnamon. Bring to the boil. Draw pan to side of stove. Prepare 1 lb. apples or pears. Add to syrup as prepared. Add thinly peeled lemon rind. Cover and simmer gently until tender. Lift out fruit with a draining spoon. Remove lemon rind, cloves and cinnamon. Boil syrup for 3 or 4 minutes. Pour over fruit. *For 2 persons.*

STEWED BLACKBERRIES, COOKING CHERRIES, DAMSONS, GOOSEBERRIES, GREEN-GAGES AND PLUMS : Follow method given for apples and pears, omitting the spices. Simmer until tender in a covered pan, or cook in a covered fireproof dish in a slow oven, 300° F., until tender. (Damsons, if very sour, may require a little more sugar.) If fruit is very ripe, decrease sugar according to taste.

TO STEW RHUBARB : Prepare, cutting into inch slices. Measure. Allow ½ lb. caster sugar to 4 cups sliced rhubarb, or use only ¾ cup sugar and add syrup to taste just before dishing up. Rinse top of a double boiler with water. Add rhubarb, then sugar. Cover closely. Steam over boiling water till sugar and juice form a syrup and rhubarb is tender but unbroken. Chill before serving.

TO PREPARE FRUIT FOR COMPOTES AND SALADS

Apples and Pears: Wash, pare, core and cut into fingers or rings. Dip as prepared in lemon or grapefuit juice.

Bananas: Peel, remove threads and slice crosswise. Sprinkle with lemon juice to prevent discoloration.

Berries and Currants: Pick over. Place carefully in a colander. Sink in a pan of cold water. Gently lift colander up and down in cold water, then change water. Repeat once more and drain thoroughly. Hull berries ; stem currants.

Cherries: Wash, stem, slit and stone if liked.

Damsons: Wash and drain.

Grapes: Wash in a colander like berries. Drain carefully.

Greengages and Plums: Wash and drain. Halve and stone if liked.

Mandarins and Oranges: Peel and remove all white pith. Cut away sections from membrane. Lift out and remove pips.

Peaches: Peel. If skin is too tough to come off, place in boiling water for 30 seconds, then slip off skins.

Rhubarb: Remove roots and foliage. Wipe stalks with a damp cloth. Cut in 3 inch sticks, or 1 inch slices, according to taste.

DRIED FRUIT

Place dried fruit, i.e. apple rings, apricots, bananas, figs, peaches, pears, prunes, and any other dried fruit, in a colander. Wash in several changes of lukewarm water until the water runs clear. (If any adhere to each other separate them.) Remove stems from figs. Soak ½ lb. apple rings overnight in 1½ pints cold water. Soak other dried fruits in 1 pint water to ½ lb. fruit, for 12 hours. Strain off water, reserving it. By soaking dried fruit, you shorten the cooking time.

To Cook Soaked Dried Fruit: Place in a saucepan. Add sugar, allowing ¼ lb. to 1 lb. fruit, and soaking water. Bring to boil. Simmer until tender, allowing ½ hour for apricots, and 25-30 minutes for figs and prunes.

To Cook Unsoaked Dried Fruit: Wash and place in a saucepan. Cover with cold water. Bring to boil. Boil rapidly until puffy, in ½ hour. Add sugar, allowing ¼ lb. to 1 lb. fruit, using caster for apricots, and caster or brown sugar for figs and prunes. Stir gently until dissolved. Cover and simmer apricots for 5 minutes, and prunes and figs for ¾-1 hour.

APRICOT AND PEACH SALAD (Salade de Fruit Séché)

4 oz. dried apricots
4 oz. dried peaches
1 quart cold water
¾ cup caster sugar
Juice of 1 lemon
¾ pint custard sauce

Wash and drain apricots and peaches. Halve, if liked, and place in a basin. Cover with water. Stand for 24 hours. Pour fruit and water into a saucepan. Cover and bring to boil. Simmer till soft. Add sugar. Cover and simmer till sugar is dissolved. Add strained lemon juice. Pour into a glass dish. Chill. Serve with custard sauce. *For 5 persons.*

FIGS IN AMBER SYRUP (Figues Ambrées)

1 lb. dried figs
Cold water as required
2 tablespoons lemon juice
1 snippet lemon rind
Sugar as required
¾ tablespoon Madeira or sherry

Wash and stem figs. Place in a saucepan. Add cold water to cover by about 1 inch. Add half the lemon juice, lemon rind and a small piece of ginger if liked. Cover. Heat gently until puffy and soft. Remove figs with a draining spoon so that all the liquid runs back into pan. Measure. Add half as much sugar as juice. Stir over slow heat until sugar is dissolved. Bring to boil. Simmer gently until syrup is thick. Add remainder of lemon juice and the figs. Simmer for 1 minute, then remove from heat and cool. Add wine. Stir lightly, then chill. Serve with whipped cream. *For 4 or 5 persons.*

FRUIT FOOLS

A fool is a simple old English sweet made by mixing a purée of fresh or cooked fruit with thick cream. When cream is unobtainable, substitute thick custard sauce. Part cream and part custard sauce can also be used.

FRUIT FOOL (Foule de Fruit)

BASIC RECIPE:
½ pint sweetened fruit purée
½ pint whipped cream
Garnish to taste

Chill the purée and the cream. Stir purée gradually into cream or into part cream and part custard sauce. Chill either before or after mixing. Pour into individual glasses or into a glass bowl. Garnish with fruit to match the purée, or with halved maraschino cherries and angelica, crushed meringue, or blanched pistachio nuts. *For 4 persons.*

NOTE: If using canned or stewed fruit, be sure to drain fruit well through a hair sieve, otherwise, if the fruit is at all liquid, the fool may be too thin. It is not necessary to add any water to raspberries or strawberries; simply rinse, drain, hull and rub through sieve, then sweeten to taste. When sugar is dissolved, proceed as described.

APRICOT, PEACH OR PEAR FOOL: Follow basic recipe, but flavour with a few drops of almond essence. Decorate with whipped, sweetened cream and chopped glacé apricots, peaches or pears.

BANANA AND RHUBARB FOOL (Foule Muscovado)

7 bananas
½ pint stewed rhubarb purée
1 cup thick custard
Barbados Muscovado sugar to taste

Peel and sieve 6 bananas. Stir in rhubarb purée and custard. Sweeten to taste and colour with a little cochineal. Serve in a glass bowl or in individual glasses. Decorate with the remaining banana cut in slices. *For* 6 *persons.*

CHESTNUT FOOL (Foule de Marrons)

1 pint chestnut purée
Orange juice as required
6 tablespoons whipped cream
1 tablespoon caster sugar

Boil, shell and pound chestnuts in a mortar or strong basin, moistening them from time to time with orange juice. Mix purée with cream and sugar. Chill. Serve in sherbet glasses. Garnish each with a half marron glacé. *For* 6 *persons.*

JELLY FOOL (Foule en Gelée)

1 pint set strawberry jelly
½ pint strawberry juice
1 or 2 bananas
1 pint custard
Few canned strawberries

Chop jelly in a basin. Heat strawberry juice to boiling point. Stir into jelly. Stir occasionally until jelly is dissolved. Arrange slices of banana in the bottom of a wet mould. Pour in enough jelly to set the fruit. Make and cool custard, then beat gradually into remainder of jelly with an egg whisk. Beat for a few minutes, then pour gently into mould. Chill. Turn out into a glass dish. Decorate with slices of banana and strawberries. *For* 6 *persons.*

JUNE FOOL (Foule au Juin)

4 sieved bananas
¼ pint cream
¼ pint custard sauce
¾ tablespoon rum
1 can pineapple
4 dessertspoons pineapple juice
Glacé cherries

Mix bananas with three-quarters of the whipped sweetened cream, then stir gradually into the custard sauce. Add rum gradually. Stir till thoroughly blended. Cut 2 pineapple slices in halves. Chop each half and divide equally among 4 sundae glasses. Cover each with a dessertspoon of pineapple juice. Divide chilled custard equally among the glasses. Decorate with glacé cherries and remainder of whipped cream. *For* 4 *persons.*

COMPOTES

SYRUP FOR FRUIT COMPOTES

The syrup in which fruit compote is served is sometimes made by sugaring the fruit and allowing it to stand until the sugar is dissolved and some of the juice is extracted, but this method is only suitable for fruit that is ripe and ready to eat such as berries and ripe peaches. Fruit such as apricots, apples, peaches, that are not quite ripe, cherries, excepting the fully ripe dessert cherries, pears, etc., require to be cooked in a syrup to give you a compote.

SYRUP FOR FRUIT COMPOTES

½ lb. loaf sugar
1 pint cold water
1 snippet lemon peel

Place sugar in a saucepan. Add water. Stir over low heat till sugar is dissolved, then bring to boil. Wash and add lemon peel. Simmer for ½ hour. Strain over 2 lb. prepared fruit, such as hulled berries, grapes and other dessert fruit ripe enough for dessert. Chill. Serve with cream. *For 6-8 persons.*

APPLE AND PINEAPPLE COMPOTES
(Compotes de Pommes à l'Ananas)

8 medium-sized apples
½ lb. caster sugar
1 teaspoon vanilla essence
3 cups water
1 large can pineapple
Whipped cream as required

Peel and core apples without breaking them. Place in a large, wide-topped pan. Add sugar, vanilla, water and pineapple juice to cover. If there is not enough juice in can of pineapple, add more water. Cook slowly for ½ hour, uncovered, stirring occasionally, then remove with a draining spoon to hot serving dish. Arrange an apple on every slice of pineapple. Keep warm while you boil the pineapple juice and water to a syrup, then pour over. Serve cold, decorated with whipped cream. *For 8 persons.*

APRICOT COMPOTE (Compote d'Abricots)

9 oz. caster sugar
1 pint water
2 lb. apricots

Place sugar in a saucepan. Add water. Stir occasionally over slow heat until the sugar is dissolved, then bring to the boil. Simmer for 5 minutes. Stalk apricots and place in the top of a double boiler with boiling water below. Add syrup. Cover and simmer till fruit is tender. Cool. Pour into a bowl. Serve with cream. *For 8 persons.*

BANANA COMPOTE (Compote de Bananes)

12 bananas
½ lb. sugar
½ cup water
Juice of ½ lemon

Peel and halve bananas. Put sugar and water in a saucepan. Stir till sugar is dissolved. Bring to the boil. After 10 minutes, add lemon juice, then bananas, a few at a time. Stew gently for ½ hour. Remove from heat. Remove bananas. Arrange on a dish, and pour hot syrup over. Chill. Serve with cream. *For 6 persons.*

CHERRY AND CURRANT COMPOTE
(Compote de Cerises aux Groseilles)

½ lb. caster sugar
¾ cup water
1½ pints stoned cherries
¼ pint currant juice

Measure sugar and water into a saucepan. Heat slowly till sugar is dissolved, then boil till a thick syrup is formed. Remove pan from stove and allow to stand for ¼ hour. Add fruit and return to stove. Simmer gently for a moment or two, then boil up and remove fruit to a serving dish with a fruit skimmer. Add currant juice to the syrup, and pour over fruit. Chill. Serve with cream and sponge cakes. *For* 4 *persons.*

COMPOTE OF CHESTNUTS (Compote de Marrons)

1 lb. chestnuts
½ lb. caster sugar
1½ gills water

Boil, shell and blanch the nuts. Dissolve sugar in the water in a saucepan. When syrup comes to the boil, drop in the prepared chestnuts, and let them simmer gently at the side of the stove till tender. Flavour with rum to taste. Serve cold with cream or custard. *For* 4 *persons.*

CURRANT AND RASPBERRY COMPOTE
(Compote de Fruit à l'Été)

6 oz. red currants
¾ lb. raspberries
1 teaspoon lime juice
4 tablespoons water
Sugar to taste

Rinse and drain fruit. Pour lime juice and water into a saucepan. Simmer gently for ¼ hour. Add sugar to taste. When dissolved, chill. Place fruit in salad bowl. Cover with the syrup. *For* 3 *persons.*

JUNE COMPOTE (Compote au Juin)

2 tablespoons caster sugar
1 cup water
2 teaspoons lemon juice
½ lb. grapes
1 cup stoned cherries
1 cup sliced strawberries
2 sliced bananas
2 tablespoons curaçao

Dissolve sugar in water. Add lemon juice. Bring to the boil. Boil for 5 minutes. Chill. Halve and seed grapes. Add with fruit and liqueur to syrup. Cover and chill for 2 hours. Serve with cream. *For 6 persons.*

MELON AND PINEAPPLE COMPOTE (Compote de Fruit)

Diced ripened pineapple
Cubes of cantaloup or honey-
    dew melon

Trim, peel and remove eyes from pineapple. Remove flesh from core. Cut into dice. Squeeze all juice over the fruit. Sprinkle thickly with caster sugar. Stand for 24-36 hours, until the flesh is transparent and all the sugar dissolved. Chill. Mix with equal quantity of melon balls in tall glasses. Cover with the pineapple juice and any melon juice. Serve with cream and petits fours. *Allow* ¼ *pint per person.*

MICHAELMAS COMPOTE (Compote à l'Automne)

1 lb. sugar
½ pint water
2 peeled lemons
2 peeled oranges
1 diced apple
¼ grapefruit
4 sliced bananas

Dissolve sugar in water. Bring to the boil. Boil for 5-8 minutes with the thinly pared rind of ½ lemon. Skim if necessary. Remove lemon rind. Add lemon juice to the syrup. Slice oranges into a salad bowl. Add apple, pulp from grapefruit, banana slices, pear and grapes. (Skin

1 diced pear
¼ lb. green grapes

and stone grapes before adding.) Pour the syrup, whilst hot, over prepared fruit, and allow to cool. Chill before serving with cream or custard. *For 6 persons.*

PEACH COMPOTE (Compote de Pêches)

¾ cup peach juice
½ cup orange juice
3 tablespoons lemon juice
Caster sugar as required
½ tablespoon minced preserved ginger
1 tablespoon grated lemon rind
1 tablespoon grated orange rind
12 halves of canned peaches

Measure peach juice into a saucepan. Add orange and lemon juice and sweeten to taste. Stir over a low heat till the sugar is dissolved, then add the ginger and rinds. Bring to simmering point. Add peaches. Simmer gently for 8 or 9 minutes. Turn into a fruit salad bowl. Chill. Serve with whipped cream. *For 6 persons.*

Peach Compote the French way: Follow the recipe given for Apricot Compote, substituting peaches for the apricots.

STRAWBERRY COMPOTE (Fraises au Marasquin)

2 lb. strawberries
2 teaspoons caster sugar
2 glasses claret
2 liqueur glasses Maraschino

Hull berries, and place in a glass bowl. Sprinkle with sugar. Stand for 1 hour in a cool place. Mix claret with Maraschino. Pour over berries. Serve alone or as an accompaniment to vanilla ice cream. *For 6-8 persons.*

FRUIT SALADS

Fruit salads, which are similar to compotes, can be prepared in 3 ways : by sugaring dessert fruit and leaving it until the juice is extracted and the sugar is dissolved ; by moistening fruit with a syrup ; by coating with a fancy dressing or cream. In the latter case, it is usually served in sundae glasses.

DRESSINGS

FRUIT CREAM

½ lb. caster sugar
3 small tablespoons cornflour
1 cup water
Juice of 1 orange
Juice of 1 lemon
2 separated eggs

Measure the sugar and cornflour into a saucepan. Add water and fruit juices by degrees. When smoothly dissolved, bring to boil and simmer for 5 minutes, stirring constantly. Remove from stove. Stir in beaten egg yolks. Beat well, then fold in stiffly-frothed egg whites. Cool, then pour over 2 lb. prepared fruit. *For 8 persons.*

HONEY DRESSING

½ pint thick cream
2 tablespoons strained honey
Few grains of salt

Whip cream until stiff. Gradually beat in the honey and salt. *For 6 persons.*

To Serve Fruit Salad

Fruit salad can be served in a salad bowl, or in dessert sets, which usually consist of a salad bowl and 6 individual bowls ; in grapefruit or sundae glasses ; in orange or grapefruit skins with a slice cut from the blossom end, and the fruit and membrane scooped out. When using the latter, wash and dry shells, then scallop them round the edge with a sharp knife.

ICED FRUIT SALAD (Salade de Fruit, Glacée)

1 tablespoon lemon juice
¼ cup orange juice
2 sliced bananas
¾ cup diced canned pineapple
¾ cup peeled and seeded grapes
1 cup cream
Chopped nuts as required

Mix lemon juice, orange juice and fruit together in a basin. Stand for 2 hours. Stiffly whip cream, then stir in prepared fruit. Pour mixture into the freezing tray of refrigerator. Freeze until stiff. Serve on individual plates, sprinkled with chopped nuts, accompanied by ice wafers. *For 4 persons.*

PINEAPPLE SALAD
(Salade d'Anana à l'Afrique)

2 small South African pineapples or 1 large pineapple
Caster sugar to taste
Juice of 1 lemon

Remove leaves and stems from pineapples. Peel. Cut out every eye. Cut pineapple or pineapples in halves lengthwise. Remove the fibrous core from the middle of each half. Squeeze all the juice from the discarded parts into a bowl. Strain over pineapple. Cut pineapple in slices ½ inch thick. Arrange neatly overlapping each other in serving dish. Sprinkle lightly with sugar. Cover. Stand for 12 hours. Chill. Sprinkle with strained lemon juice, also with a few drops of brandy or rum if liked. *For 6 persons.*

SOUTH AFRICAN FRUIT SALAD (Salade de Fruit à l'Afrique)

5 oz. caster sugar
½ pint water
2 tablespoons sherry
Juice of ½ lemon
1 South African melon
2 South African peaches
2 South African pears
3 slices South African pineapple
12 South African grapes
12 South African lychees
2 tablespoons maraschino cherries

Place sugar and water in a saucepan. Stir over slow heat till sugar is dissolved, then bring to boil. Measure and boil till mixture is reduced to half its quantity. Add sherry and lemon juice. Allow to cool. Remove a slice from the melon lengthwise, about one third the thickness of the melon. Scoop out seeds. With a potato ball cutter, scoop out as many balls as you can get from the remainder of the flesh or cut into small squares. Place balls or squares in a basin. Add syrup. Peel, halve, stone and dice peaches. Core peel and dice pears. Cut each slice of pineapple into eight equal-sized pieces. Rinse and drain grapes. Peel lychees. Add all the fruit to the syrup. Cover and chill for ½ hour. Stir in maraschino syrup from the cherries. While chilling, vandyke the edge of melon shell with a pair of scissors. When required, fill up with the fruit salad. Make a cross in the centre with the cherries. Serve with cream. *For 6 persons.*

YULETIDE FRUIT SALAD (Salade de Fruit à la Noël)

1 lb. grapes	Skin and seed grapes. Mix in a bowl with
Juice of 2 mandarins	strained mandarin juice. Halve and add cherries,
2 tablespoons maraschino cherries	with diced pineapple and juice, bananas, peaches
1 can pineapple	and pear. Pour maraschino syrup over. Chill for
2 sliced bananas	$\frac{1}{2}$ hour. Place in a salad bowl. Serve with whipped
2 diced peeled peaches	cream. *For 8 persons.*
1 diced peeled pear	
1 tablespoon maraschino syrup	

FROZEN FRUIT

To Freeze Canned Fruit: Canned apricots, berries, peaches, pears and pineapple, if frozen, will give you a delicious sherbet-like iced sweet.

1. Choose fruit preserved in medium-sweet syrup for freezing, or if syrup is sweet and thick, dilute with water or ginger ale, and then freeze. Leave fruit whole, or slice or mash. Turn fruit together with the syrup into the freezing tray. Freeze for 1-2 hours, until the syrup is mushy, stirring once or twice so that the mixture freezes evenly. Pile in glasses. Decorate with whipped cream.

2. Stoned fruits in rich syrup can be frozen in their cans. Pack in ice and salt. Freeze for $2\frac{1}{2}$-3 hours, then open cans. Slice and serve fruit with whipped cream or ice cream.

To Freeze Crushed Fruit: Mash fresh or canned fruit. Sweeten to taste. Freeze in chilled refrigerator tray until mushy in 1-1$\frac{1}{2}$ hours. Pile in tall glasses. Decorate with whipped cream if liked.

To Freeze Fresh Fruit:

1. Prepare and mince 1 lb. fruit. Stir in 1 lb. sugar. Leave until sugar is dissolved, then stir in 2 cups water. Place in chilled refrigerator tray and chill, stirring once or twice, or chill in a tub freezer.

2. Weigh fruit. Allow $\frac{1}{2}$ lb. caster sugar to every lb. of fruit. Crush or mash fruit. Sprinkle with sugar. Stir till sugar and juice form a syrup. Pour into chilled refrigerator tray. Freeze, stirring occasionally.

TO FREEZE FRUIT IN REFRIGERATOR

Ripe apricots, blackberries, loganberries, raspberries, strawberries, diced melon, peaches, pears, and grated pineapple can all be frozen in refrigerator trays. So can canned apricots, all berries, peaches and crushed pineapple, and dried apricots if soaked, steamed, sweetened and sieved. Allow $\frac{3}{4}$ cup icing sugar to 4 cups berries or other prepared fruit. Mash sugar with the fruit. Leave till dissolved. Place in chilled refrigerator tray. Stir about every 20 minutes, until frozen, in about 1$\frac{1}{2}$ hours. Serve in tall glasses. Top with whipped cream. If using sweetened canned fruit, reduce quantity of sugar to taste.

NUTS

Nuts which are rich in oil and a source of proteins and starch, make a valuable substitute for meat. They can be turned into croquettes, au gratin. dishes, loaves, etc., and they play an important part in vegetarian diets. Serve nuts for dessert, piled in a dish like fruit, decorated with or without foliage round the edge. Ground almonds and desiccated coconut, for using in confectionery, are generally obtainable all the year round.

To Prepare for Serving: Wipe almonds and Brazil nuts with a soft cloth. Leave cob nuts and filberts with the outer skins or husks on. Wipe walnuts with a damp cloth, then rub with a dry cloth.

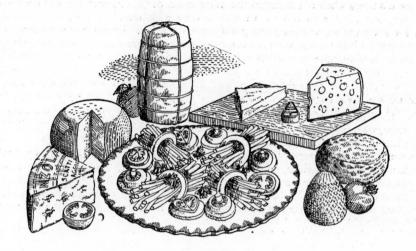

Dinner Savouries

When preparing all savouries, remember two points:

1. They should be " au revoir " morsels that will tickle the palate and yet put a full stop to dinner.

2. They must be made to look specially tempting to appeal to the appetite at the end of a meal.

CHEESE

The service of cheese like the service of dessert, should be a rite. If content to offer cheese when a savoury is wanted, or before the sweet, which the French frequently do, don't be satisfied to provide only one variety. Offer a contrasting choice. Serve in a cheese dish or on a cheese board.

To Serve Camembert Cheese: Slip cheese into a silver container sold for this purpose. Any cheese about the size of a Camembert, can be served in the same way.

To Serve Stilton Cheese: Place in a large cheese dish with a cover. Serve with a scoop. All large cheeses of the Stilton texture can be served in this way.

NOTE : Before serving cheese that has been stored in a refrigerator, remove it long enough before the meal so that it will be at room remperature when required.

To Keep Cheese Fresh

Cover all forms of cream cheese and store in a refrigerator. This cheese is very perishable. Other kinds of cheese should not be tightly covered. Wrap hunks of cheese and whole cheese in a piece of butter muslin wrung in vinegar or cold water before placing in the refrigerator, or the cut portions will become very hard. Alternatively rub the cut portions with butter. If only to be stored for a short time, wrap in greaseproof paper, then in a piece of butter muslin, or in two folds of waxed paper, and store in larder. If you wish to store cheese in a dish, it must have a ventilation hole in the lid.

CHEESE GARNISHES FOR SALADS

1. Cut any soft variety of cheese into small squares. Dip each in mayonnaise, then in crushed potato crisps. Use for garnishing green salads. Serve in place of the usual cheese course.

2. *Cheese Carrots:* Press ½ lb. chopped yellow cheese through a potato masher, or coarse sieve, or put through a meat grinder. Season to taste with paprika. Take a heaped tablespoonful at a time. Place it in the palm of your hand and roll it until it becomes the shape of a carrot. When all are prepared, plant a sprig of parsley in the stem of each, and serve with biscuits or toast and salad.

TABLE OF CHEESES

APPETITOST : Semi-hard Scandinavian cheese made from sour butter-milk.

BEL MILANO : Semi-hard Italian cheese, similar to Bel Paese.

BEL PAESE : Semi-hard Italian cheese made of whole milk. It is pale yellow in colour and noted for its delicacy.

BLUE DANISH : Popular blue-veined, semi-hard cheese from Denmark. It is made from cow's milk.

BLUE VINNY : Hard cheese made from skimmed milk. Comes from Dorset.

BONDON : Small French cheese, of the soft unripened type, made of whole milk.

BRIE : Soft ripened French cheese. Make certain that it is really ripe before serving at table.

CAERPHILLY : One of the finest semi-hard English cheeses, originally Welsh, and too rarely seen. It is also made in Devonshire, Dorset, Somerset and Wiltshire.

CAMEMBERT : Soft ripened cheese from Normandy. Must be really ripe.

CHAMBOURCY : Delicious soft unripened cheese manufactured in the Ile de France.

CHEDDAR : The national all-purpose cheese. It belongs to the hard type.

CHESHIRE : Hard, crumbly, red-tinged cheese, resembling Cheddar, but with a sharper flavour.

CHEVRET : Semi-hard French goat's milk cheese.

COTTAGE CHEESE : Cheese made from soft curds. This soft unripened cheese can be used for canapé and sandwich spreads, as well as in the cheese course.

COULOMMIERS : Rich, double cream cheese. This soft ripened cheese is prepared from fresh milk and enriched with cream. Serve really fresh.

CREAM CHEESE : Soft rich cheese delicately flavoured. Made from pasteurized rich cream usually soured naturally or with rennet.

DEMI-SUISSE : Soft unripened cheese served in France with "fraises du bois," and in America with strawberry jam.

DOUBLE GLOSTER : Delicious hard whole milk cheese made in Gloucestershire.

DUNLOP : A Scottish version of Cheddar.

EDAM : Small, round, hard, Dutch cheese with a brilliant red skin. Rather crumbly, with a mild flavour. *To serve:* Either slice, or remove top and scoop out the inside.

GERVALS : Soft, unripened cream cheese.

GIETOSTE : Coffee-coloured, hard, Norwegian goat's milk cheese with an unusual searching sweet flavour. Serve wafer-thin slices, sprinkled minced chives, on beaten biscuits as an appetizer.

GORGONZOLA : Popular green-veined or marbled cheese from North Italy. This semi-hard cheese is used only at table.

GOUDA : Hard Dutch cheese made of full-cream milk. Similar to Edam. Use like Cheddar.

GRUYERE : Originally Swiss. Now also made in the French Alps and in Italy. Of the semi-hard type. For table use when fresh, and for delicate savoury dishes when stale. This name is also applied to Emmenthaler cheese, usually sold in cartons, which is equally suitable for table service or for cooking.

HARZ KAESE : German soft, unripened cheese made from skimmed milk.

LANCASHIRE : Similar to Cheshire.

LEICESTERSHIRE : Similar to Cheddar.

LIMBURGER : Strongly-flavoured, semi-hard Belgian cheese for table use.

MOZZARELLA : Smooth, white, unsalted Italian cheese. Can be used in cooking as well as at table.

MYSOST : Scandinavian semi-hard, light brown cheese. Rather sweet flavour. Popular as a snack or for table use.

NEUFCHATEL : Small, soft unripened cheese from France. It is used at table and for spreads. Similar to cream cheese.

PARMESAN (Parmigiano) : Dry, hard Italian cheese with a sharp flavour, generally used only for cooking. It will keep indefinitely.

PASTORELLA : Italian, semi-hard cheese. See BEL PAESE.

PETIT SUISSE : Rich, French, soft, unripened cream cheese for table use and for cheese whips.

POMMEL : Unsalted, soft unripened French cream cheese for table use.

PONT L'EVEQUE : French cheese. Similar to Brie, but of stronger flavour.

PORT SALUT : Mild, semi-hard French cheese, originally manufactured by the Trappist Monks at Port du Salut.

PROCESSED : Made of a blend of various types of cheese without rind. Semi-hard, it is usually sold in the form of a brick and in cartons. Suitable for using for cocktail savouries, sandwiches, and in the cheese course.

PROVOLONE : Light yellow Italian cheese made from cow's milk. It is frequently used in cooking but may be served at table.

RICOTTA : This Italian soft unripened cheese is fresh and unsalted and is similar to Cottage cheese. It can be used in cooking and for sandwich fillings as well as in pastries.

RICOTTA SALATA : Dry, hard form of Ricotta, mildly flavoured. Grate and use in cooking.

ROMANO : Hard, dry, salty Italian cheese. Made from cow's and goat's milk. Sharp, tangy flavour. Use in cooking.

ROQUEFORT : Semi-hard, blue-veined French cheese made of ewe's milk. For table use or spreads.

SAGE : An American Cheddar made from a curd flavoured with sage leaves or sage extract.

STILTON : The king of British cheeses. A semi-hard, blue or green-veined whole milk cheese, made in Huntingdonshire and Leicestershire of cow's milk with the addition of cream.

STRACHINO : Sharp-flavoured light yellow Italian cheese made of goat's milk. For table use only.

WENSLEYDALE : Blue-veined, semi-hard, whole milk cheese from Wensleydale and Yorkshire. Exclusively for table use.

COTTAGE AND CREAM CHEESE

There are two varieties of cheese that can be easily made at home without any special equipment. Curd of sour or soured milk is the basis of the first, and cream is the basis of the second. In Britain the first is generally called " sour milk cheese," but it better known in the Americas as " cottage cheese." The second is known as " cream cheese " wherever it is made.

TO MAKE COTTAGE CHEESE : Use sour or soured milk, either whole or skimmed. Pour 1 quart milk into an enamel-lined saucepan. Heat slowly over hot water until lukewarm, about 95° F. It can be heated to 100° F., but not above that. Draw pan to side of stove. Leave there for a few minutes, until the curd collects, then gently strain through a strainer smoothly lined with cheese cloth or butter muslin. Sprinkle with 1 teaspoonful of salt. (If the milk has been left until very sour before using, pour 1 pint of cold water over the curd in strainer.) Draw the ends of cheese cloth or muslin together so that no dust can get to the curd, and leave suspended for at least 6 hours. Leave it entirely untouched until you have a thick dry curd in the strainer. Beat lightly with a wire whisk till smooth and creamy, or mash it with a wooden spoon. It is now ready to prepare for the table. *Yield :* 1 cup cottage cheese.

To Sour Naturally : Pour into a bottling jar. Cover. Stand in a warm place, but not a hot one, until the whey starts to separate from the curd, then proceed as instructed.

To Sour Milk Quickly : Add rennet or rennet tablets to lukewarm fresh milk. Follow the instructions given with the rennet or tablets as to the amount of rennet required. Follow instructions given for making cottage cheese.

To Prepare for the Table : Weigh and stir in sour or sweet cream and melted butter in the proportion of $\frac{1}{2}$ tablespoon of each to $\frac{3}{4}$ lb. of the cheese.

LIPTAUER CHEESE : Mix cottage cheese to taste with Continental mustard, chopped onion, capers, and enough paprika to colour pink. Sometimes a few caraway seeds are also added.

CREAM CHEESE

2½ quarts cream
Salt to taste

Skim cream off milk, and place in cheese-cloth or butter muslin. Gather the corners together and suspend from a hook over a basin to let any milk drain away from the cream into the basin below. Draw aside the corners of the cloth every 5 hours, and scrape any stiff dry cream from the sides into the moist centre. Leave for 24-28 hours, then scrape into small basin and season with salt if liked. Line a small, fancy mould with butter muslin and press in the creamed curd with a knife. Turn out on to serving dish. *Yield :* 1 cheese, 5 oz. in weight.

To serve Cottage and Cream Cheeses : Arrange in a heap or a mould on a dish lined with heart of lettuce leaves.

CHEESE BALLS

¼ lb. cream cheese
Salt and pepper to taste
Paprika to taste

Divide cheese into small spoonfuls. Season each with salt, pepper and paprika, and roll into a ball. Press lightly between two halves of walnut. If preferred, roll in chopped walnuts, or chopped chives or celery. Serve with biscuits or toast.

CHEESE PUZZLE

6 oz. cream cheese
2 tablespoons melted butter
Salt and cayenne pepper to taste
2 tablespoons capers
Stuffed olives

Place cheese in a basin. Stir in butter, salt and cayenne pepper, then well-drained capers. Line a round or oblong mould with slices of stuffed olives. Press cheese into mould. Harden in the refrigerator, and turn out on to a pretty glass dish for serving. Garnish with mustard and cress, or watercress, and young radishes made into roses. Serve with cream crackers or toast.

CHEESE SAVOURIES

Among the most popular after-dinner cheese savouries are canapés spread with cheese enlivened with seasonings and relishes, and garnished to taste, or canapés topped with an appetizing cheese spread and cooked under the grill or in the oven. If more substantial savouries are required, take your choice from the other sections devoted to savouries. I am starting with cheese spreads specially designed for occasions when a quickly prepared savoury is wanted.

CAMBRIDGE CHEESE SPREAD (Fromage à la Cambridge)

2 oz. Stilton cheese
¼ lb. cream cheese
1 tablespoon butter
1 teaspoon salt
1 tablespoon lemon juice
½ teaspoon minced chives

Grate Stilton cheese. Stir into cream cheese. Beat butter until softened. Beat in salt, then add to cheese. Beat till blended, then slowly beat in lemon juice and chives. When blended, spread on freshly-made cold canapés of fried bread, or serve in a cup made of heart of lettuce leaves, with biscuits or toast and celery or watercress.

CHEESE AND TOMATO SPREAD
(Beurre de Fromage aux Tomates)

½ lb. grated cheese
1 cup sieved fresh tomatoes
½ cup stale breadcrumbs
Salt and pepper to taste

Place all the ingredients in a saucepan. Stir over slow heat till thick and smooth. Pile on hot, freshly-made toast or fried bread. Serve at once.

MOCK CRAB (Fromage Piquant)

4 heaped tablespoons grated cheese
Salt and cayenne pepper to taste
1 saltspoon wine vinegar
1 saltspoon anchovy sauce

Rub the inside of a small saucepan with a cut clove of garlic. Place the cheese, salt and cayenne pepper and anchovy sauce in pan. Stir over heat till piping hot, then divide equally among 4 rounds or squares of hot buttered toast about 3 inches across. Sprinkle lightly with minced parsley. If preferred, this can be served cold.

ANCHOVY CHEESE FINGERS
(Bâtons de Fromage, Balnaboth)

4 oz. sifted flour
Salt and cayenne pepper to taste
2½ oz. butter
1 oz. grated Parmesan cheese
2 egg yolks
½ teaspoon anchovy essence
1 egg white

Sift flour into a basin with salt and cayenne pepper to taste. Rub in butter with tips of fingers. Stir in cheese. Mix to a soft dry dough with 1 beaten egg yolk and cold water. Roll on a lightly-floured pastry board into an oblong strip. Divide in two. Spread one half with half the second beaten egg yolk, then with anchovy essence. Brush second strip with remainder of egg yolk and sandwich two neatly together. Beat egg white to a stiff froth. Stir in ½ teaspoon anchovy essence and spread over pastry. Mark into small oblongs. Bake for 20 minutes in a hot oven, 450° F. Cut out fingers. Serve at once as savouries or with apéritifs. *Yield :* About 15 or 16 fingers.

BAVAROIS OF CHEESE (Bavarois au Fromage)

½ pint milk
3 egg yolks
¼ oz. powdered gelatine
1 tablespoon cold water
2 oz. grated Parmesan cheese
½ gill cream
Salt and cayenne pepper to taste

Heat the milk. Beat yolks. When milk is almost boiling, stir into yolks. Return to pan. Stir over boiling water till thick, but do not allow to boil. Cool in a basin. Meanwhile, soak gelatine for 5 minutes in the water, then stir over boiling water till dissolved. Strain into custard, stirring constantly. Stir in cheese. Whip cream, seasoning it with salt and pepper to taste as you whip, then fold into mixture. Cool slightly, then fill 6 wet dariole moulds. Chill. Turn out on to a dish covered with a lace paper doily. Garnish with sprigs of chervil or parsley. *For 6 persons.*

CHEESE AIGRETTES (Beignets au Fromage)

2 oz. flour
¾ oz. butter
¼ pint water
1 beaten egg
1 beaten egg yolk
1½ oz. grated cheese
Salt and cayenne pepper to taste

Sift flour. Place butter and water in a small saucepan. Bring to boil. Add flour. Beat over the stove until the mixture forms a ball in the centre, leaving sides of pan clean. Remove pan from stove. Continue to beat until slightly cooled then add egg. Beat till blended. Add egg yolk. Beat also till blended. Stir in cheese and salt and cayenne pepper to taste. Drop from a teaspoon into deep hot fat. Fry till crisp and golden brown in about 12 minutes. Drain on absorbent paper. Serve at once on a hot dish lined with a lace paper doily. Sprinkle with grated Parmesan cheese. *For 6 persons.*

CHEESE BISCUITS (Biscuits au Fromage)

4 oz. cheese pastry
½ gill thick cream
1 teaspoon minced celery
1 teaspoon grated cheese
Salt and cayenne pepper to taste

Cut out rounds of pastry the size of a half-crown. Prick well. Bake in a hot oven, 450° F., till golden brown. Cool on a wire rack. Beat cream till thickened. Stir in celery, cheese, salt and cayenne pepper to taste, with a dash of paprika if liked. Pile on each biscuit. Serve on a cold plate covered with a lace paper doily. Garnish with cress. *For 4 persons.*

CHEESE CREAM TARTLETS
(Tartelettes de Fromage à la Crème)

4 oz. flaky pastry
1 oz. grated cheese
1 separated egg
1-2 dessertspoons cream
Salt and cayenne pepper to taste

Roll pastry out thinly and line patty tins. Mix cheese with egg yolk, cream, salt and cayenne pepper to taste. Beat egg white to a stiff froth, and fold in. Put into cases. Bake in a hot oven, 450° F., for about 10 minutes. *For 4 persons.*

CHEESE CROQUETTES (Croquettes de Fromage)

6 oz. grated cheese
Salt and cayenne pepper
1 beaten egg
2½ oz. sieved breadcrumbs

Mix cheese with the salt and cayenne pepper to taste. Moisten with part of the egg. Shape into small equal-sized balls. Dip each in beaten egg, then in crumbs. Fry until golden brown. Serve piping hot with celery. *Allow 3 per person.*

CHEESE FLUFFS (Croûtes Cheddar)

¼ lb. yellow Cheddar cheese
¼ lb. red Cheddar cheese
½ teaspoon baking powder
2 separated eggs
6 canapés of bread

Grate cheese. Mix in baking powder. Separate eggs, and stir in lightly-beaten egg yolks. Whip egg whites stiffly, and fold in. Toast one side only of bread, and spread untoasted sides with a thick layer of the mixture. Cook under grill until puffed up and light brown. Serve at once. *For 6 persons.*

CHEESE FRITTERS (Pouffes de Fromage)

¼ lb. Cheddar cheese
Cayenne pepper to taste
1 teaspoon olive oil
Frying batter

Cut cheese in fingers 1 inch wide and about 1½ inches long. Season with cayenne pepper. Brush with olive oil. Dip each piece in batter. Drop into hot fat. Fry till golden brown in about 5 minutes. Drain on absorbent paper. Sprinkle with grated Parmesan cheese. Arrange on a hot dish lined with a lace paper doily. Garnish with sprigs of fried parsley. *For 6 persons.*

CHEESE AND FINNAN CANAPES
(Croûtes de Fromage Finnan)

4 oz. Finnan haddock
½ oz. butter
1 tablespoon milk
2 oz. grated cheese
1 beaten egg
Salt and cayenne pepper to taste
4 canapés of buttered toast

Measure haddock free from bone and skin. Flake it into a saucepan. Add butter and milk. Simmer for 5 minutes. Stir in cheese, egg and salt and cayenne pepper to taste. When thick, pile on canapés. *For 4 persons.*

CHEESE RISSOLES (Rissoles de Fromage)

¼ lb. puff pastry
2 oz. grated cheese
Salt and cayenne pepper to taste
½ gill thick cream
1 beaten egg
Sieved breadcrumbs as required

Roll out puff pastry thinly. Cut into rounds about 1½ inches across. Mix cheese with salt and cayenne pepper to taste. Whip cream. Stir in cheese. Place ½ a teaspoon of filling on the centre of each round. Brush edges with cold water. Fold in two. Press edges lightly together. Ornament with a fork. Brush with beaten egg. Dip in crumbs. Fry in hot fat till golden brown. Drain on absorbent paper. Pile up on a hot dish lined with a lace paper doily. Garnish with sprigs of parsley. *For 6 persons.*

CHEESE SOUFFLES (Soufflés de Fromage)

½ oz. butter
¼ oz. flour
½ gill milk
1½ egg yolks
1½ oz. fine-grated Parmesan cheese
Salt and cayenne pepper to taste
2 egg whites

Grease small ramekins made of fireproof china. Melt butter. Stir in flour. When frothy, stir in milk. Heat till smooth, then remove from heat and cool slightly. Beat in yolks. Stir in cheese and salt and cayenne pepper to taste. Beat egg whites till stiff. Fold into mixture. Three-quarters fill ramekins. Bake in a moderately hot oven, 400° F., for 12-15 minutes, until nicely brown and puffy. Serve at once. *For 4 persons.*

ICED CHEESE SOUFFLES (Soufflés Frappés au Fromage)

½ pint cream
1 teaspoon made mustard
3 oz. grated Cheddar cheese

Whip cream till fluffy with the mustard. Fold in the cheeses. Beat the jelly. Fold into cream. Season with salt. Pour into small prepared soufflé

1 oz. grated Gruyère cheese
¼ pint stiff aspic jelly
Salt and paprika to taste

cases. Leave until set. Coat tops with aspic jelly. Remove paper band. Decorate with a little paprika mixed with a little grated Parmesan cheese. Serve on a cold plate. *For 6 persons.*

CHEESE STICKS (Bâtons de Fromage)

5 oz. flaky pastry
1½ oz. grated cheese
Pinch of celery salt
Pepper to taste

Roll pastry into a very thin oblong. Turn it upside down. Brush with beaten egg. Dab either with anchovy essence, Worcester sauce, gentleman's relish or Yorkshire relish, just here and there. Sprinkle with half the cheese and celery salt, and black or cayenne pepper to taste. Fold in two. Press edges firmly together. Roll again to same size. Egg, dab with relish or sauce, and sprinkle with cheese, then season as before. Roll out and fold again. Roll out to fully an eighth of an inch in thickness. Cut into sticks 5½ inches long and ½ inch wide. Place in a shallow baking tin. Bake in a hot oven, 450° F., for about 10 minutes. Serve piping hot. *Yield :* About 15 sticks.

CHEESE STRAWS (Pailles de Fromage)

5 oz. flour
1 oz. stale breadcrumbs
Salt and cayenne pepper to taste
3 oz. butter
4 oz. grated cheese
1 egg yolk
1 tablespoon cold water

Sift flour into a basin. Stir in breadcrumbs and salt and cayenne pepper to taste. Rub in butter lightly with the finger tips. Stir in cheese and a pinch of dry mustard if liked. Stir in egg yolk diluted with cold water. Mix to a stiff dough. Knead lightly till smooth. Turn on to a lightly-floured board. Roll out pastry into an oblong about 4 inches wide. Trim edges so that strip is equally wide all the way along. Cut into narrow strips about ½ inch wide. Place straws a little apart on a greased baking sheet, and bake in a fairly hot oven, 425° F., till golden. Serve hot or cold. There should be about 30 cheese straws.

CHEESE AND WALNUT BISCUITS (Biscuits au Fromage)

3 oz. cheese pastry
½ oz. grated Parmesan cheese
1 oz. minced walnuts
½ gill thick cream
Salt, pepper and cayenne pepper to taste

Roll out pastry. Prick and cut into small biscuits. Bake a little apart on a greased baking sheet in a moderate oven, 350° F., till golden brown. Cool. Mix the cheese and walnuts with cream. Season to taste with salt, pepper and cayenne pepper. Pile mixture neatly on top of biscuits and garnish with watercress. *For 4 persons.*

DEVILLED CHEESE CANAPES (Croûtes de Fromage, Diablés)

2 or 3 tablespoons cream
1 small cream cheese
1 tablespoon tomato catsup
Salt and cayenne pepper to taste

Whip cream stiffly and beat into the cheese. Stir in tomato catsup, then season to taste. Use less catsup, if preferred. Chill and spread any cheese biscuits with the mixture. Sprinkle lightly with

663

Cheese biscuits as required
2 teaspoons minced olives

cayenne pepper and minced olives. *For 4 persons.*

MONKEY RABBIT (Croûtes, Yorkshire)

1 cup milk
1 cup stale breadcrumbs
1 cup grated cheese
¼ teaspoon salt
¼ teaspoon paprika
Cayenne pepper to taste
Pinch of dry mustard
½ teaspoon Yorkshire Relish
1 lightly beaten egg
4 slices hot buttered toast

Place milk, crumbs and cheese in the top of a double boiler. Cook over boiling water, stirring constantly, till cheese is melted. Add seasonings, sauce, then egg. Cook for a minute until thick, stirring constantly. Pour over toast. Dredge lightly with cayenne pepper. Serve at once. *For 4 persons.*

PARMESAN BOATS (Bateaux au Parmesan)

4 oz. cheese pastry
1 tablespoon aspic jelly
1 tablespoon whipped cream
1 dessertspoon grated Parmesan cheese
Salt and cayenne pepper to taste
1 teaspoon minced pistachio nuts

Roll pastry out thinly on a lightly-floured board. Neatly line 6 small round patty tins. Prick insides well. Bake in a hot oven, 450° F., till pale gold. Cool on a wire rack. Heat the aspic only till it liquefies. Gradually stir in cream, cheese and seasonings. Leave till about to set, then fill cases. Sprinkle filling in each with chopped pistachio nuts. Chill. Pipe a little aspic jelly round the edges. *For 3 or 6 persons.*

SAVOURY DATES (Dattes au Fromage)

1 oz. grated cheese
1 teaspoon butter
2 drops of Worcester sauce
Pinch of minced onion
Salt and cayenne pepper to taste
1 teaspoon minced walnuts
6 large dates

Mix cheese with butter to a paste. Stir in sauce, onion, salt and cayenne pepper, and walnuts. Stone dates if necessary. Divide mixture in 6 portions. Stuff a portion in each date and close dates. Dip in beaten egg, then toss in breadcrumbs. Fry in hot fat till golden brown. Serve in hot dish lined with a lace paper doily. Garnish with sprigs of watercress. *For 6 persons.*

SWISS BATONS (Bâtons à la Suisse)

¼ lb. flaky or puff pastry
2 separated eggs
1½ oz. Gruyère or processed cheese
1½ oz. grated Parmesan cheese
2 oz. butter
Salt and cayenne pepper to taste

Roll pastry out thinly on a lightly-floured board. Cut into the shape of a rectangle. Cut in two equal portions. Place egg yolks and 1 egg white in a basin. Beat till honey-coloured. Grate the Gruyère or processed cheese and add to Parmesan. Melt and stir in butter, then season to taste. Fold in eggs. Spread evenly over one portion of the pastry. Place the other on top. With a very

sharp knife, cut in fingers 2½ × ¾ × 1 inch. Brush with remaining egg white, lightly beaten. Bake side by side on a floured baking sheet in a hot oven, 450° F., for about 8 minutes. Serve stacked on top of each other, piping hot. Garnish with sprigs of watercress. *For 6 persons.*

WELSH RAREBIT

3 slices of bread
2 large tablespoons old ale
¼ lb. grated Cheddar or
    Cheshire cheese
1 oz. butter
1 teaspoon made mustard
Salt and pepper to taste

Cut slices about ½ inch thick. Toast lightly on both sides, and keep hot. Pour ale into a small saucepan. Add cheese. Stir till melted. Add butter, mustard, and salt and pepper to taste. Stir till piping hot. Pour over hot toast. Brown quickly under grill. Serve at once. *For 3 persons.*

SAVOURIETTES

I am starting with a selection of suggestions for savouries, and following with recipes for hot, and then for cold dinner savouries.

ALLUMETTES : Cheese straws cut the size of small matches.

CLYDE CANAPES : Spread rounds of toast 2 inches across with anchovy paste, then with highly-seasoned, mashed fried soft roe. Garnish with chopped parsley.

IVANHOE CANAPES : Mix sieved, boiled Finnan or Arbroath haddock with cream to moisten. Stir over slow heat till piping hot. Serve on rounds of hot toast, 2 inches across. Garnish each with a small grilled mushroom.

MUSHROOM CROUTES : Place a large grilled mushroom on top of rounds of buttered toast. Top each with a fried soft roe. Sprinkle with melted butter flavoured with lemon juice and seasoned with cayenne pepper.

PAILLETTES A L'ANCHOIX : Roll cheese straw paste out to one-eighth inch thickness. Cut in two equal portions. Spread one thinly with anchovy paste. Place the other half on top. Cut in strips as fine as straws, and bake.

PATE DE FOIE GRAS : Serve pâté from the pot arranged on a fancy plate with watercress fringing it. Serve with crisp or Melba toast, or dry biscuits, and celery, radishes or watercress.

POTTED SHRIMPS : Place the pot on a small fancy plate. Decorate round the base if liked, with sprigs of watercress, or fringe it with ivy leaves. Serve with crisp or Melba toast, and radishes or celery.

ANCHOVY CROUTES (Croûtes d'Anchoix)

2 or 3 thin slices of bread
Anchovy paste as required
2 egg yolks
1 teaspoon butter
1 dessertspoon tarragon
    vinegar
Salt, pepper and paprika to
    taste

Toast and butter bread, and remove crusts. Cut into narrow strips about 3 inches long. Spread each evenly with anchovy paste. Keep warm in the oven, while you stir egg yolks, butter and vinegar in a saucepan over the fire till creamy. Season with salt, pepper and paprika to taste. Spread anchovy croûtes with the mixture. Decorate with strips of pimiento. *For 2 persons.*

ANGELS ON HORSEBACK (Les Anges Cheval)

Bacon
Oysters

Cut a thin square of bacon, or half a small streaky rasher in two, for every oyster wanted. (If using

665

Crushed herbs
Pepper to taste
Lemon juice to taste
Fried canapés

canned oysters, drain well before using.) Sprinkle oyster with crushed herbs, pepper and lemon juice to taste. Roll up in bacon and run rolls on a skewer. Grill slowly till bacon is crisp in about 10 minutes. (If preferred, poise skewers on a rack in a baking tin. Bake in a moderate oven, 350° F., only till edges of oysters curl.) Serve each on a fried canapé, made of oblongs of bread cut to fit " Angels." Garnish with sprigs of parsley and lemon slices. *Allow 1 or 2 per person.*

BENGAL CANAPES (Croûtes a la Bengal)

¼ lb. ham
¼ pint thick cream
Chutney to taste
1 oz. grated Parmesan cheese
Dash of cayenne pepper

Chop ham, then pound in a mortar until into a paste. Gradually stir in the cream. Cut 12 rounds of bread, 1½ inches across. Fry till golden brown in hot fat or oil. Leave till cold. Cover each with a layer of ham cream. Dab lightly with chutney, then sprinkle with grated Parmesan cheese and cayenne pepper to taste. Make piping hot. *Allow 2 per person.*

CHEVEUX DE DIABLE

2 oz. flour
1½ oz. butter
1½ oz. grated Parmesan cheese
Cayenne pepper to taste
1 beaten egg yolk
A little water
12 anchovy fillets

Sift flour into a basin. Rub in butter. Add grated Parmesan cheese and cayenne pepper to taste. Mix well. Stir in egg yolk diluted with water, using only enough to make a stiff dough. Turn on to a lightly-floured board. Roll out thinly. Cut into strips, 3½ inches long and ½ inch wide. Cut each fillet in two. Pair half a fillet and a strip of paste. Twist into a corkscrew. Place a little apart on a greased baking sheet. Bake in a moderate oven, 350° F., for about 10 minutes. *Yield : 24 corkscrews.*

CHICKEN LIVER CANAPES (Croûtes de Foie de Volaille)

2 oz. mushrooms
3 chicken livers
1 tablespoon butter
1 teaspoon chopped chives
1 teaspoon minced parsley
1 teaspoon flour
Salt, pepper and paprika to taste
2 tablespoons cream
6 canapés of fried bread

Peel and chop mushrooms. Scald, chop and flour livers. Melt butter in a small saucepan. Add mushrooms. Fry for 2 minutes, then add livers. Fry till tender. Stir in chives, parsley, flour, salt, pepper and paprika to taste. When blended, add cream and cook slowly for 2 or 3 minutes. Pile on canapés, using buttered toast if preferred. *For 6 persons.*

CURRIED PRAWN CANAPES (Croûtes Colchester)

2 oz. butter
4 teaspoons chopped onion
3 tablespoons chopped watercress
2 teaspoons curry powder

Melt butter in a saucepan. Add onion and watercress. Cook over slow heat, stirring constantly, for 3 or 4 minutes. Sift curry powder with the flour, and stir into mixture. Add prawns.

1 teaspoon flour
1 cup minced prawns
Slices of bread

Keep hot while you prepare the bread. Cut slices of bread into fingers, 1½ inches wide and 3½ inches long. Fry in any hot fat or frying oil until crisp and golden on both sides. Drain on paper. Pile prawn mixture equally on top. Decorate each canapé with strips of pimiento, chopped fried mushrooms, or with a slice of fried tomato if liked. *For 4 persons.*

DEVILLED MUSHROOMS (Champignons à la Diable)

¾ lb. mushrooms
2 tablespoons butter
¾ teaspoon minced parsley
1 teaspoon minced onion
Salt, pepper and cayenne pepper to taste

Wash, drain, stalk and peel mushrooms. Melt butter in a frying-pan. Add mushrooms and cook gently for 3 or 4 minutes. Place in a flat fireproof baking dish, cups upwards. Add parsley, onion and 2 or 3 more mushrooms finely chopped, to butter in frying-pan, and fry. Season to taste with salt, pepper and cayenne pepper. Place a little heap of this mixture in each cup. Sprinkle with breadcrumbs, then with a little melted butter. Bake in a moderate oven, 350° F., till brown. *For 4 persons.*

DEVILS ON HORSEBACK (Les Diables à Cheval)

2 chicken livers
3 rashers of bacon
Pepper and paprika to taste
6 fingers of buttered toast

Wash, dry and cut each liver into three. Remove rind from bacon, cut each rasher in two and wrap each piece of liver, seasoned with pepper and paprika to taste, in half-rasher of bacon. Fry or grill for 2 or 3 minutes, or run on skewers, and place on a rack in a baking tin. Bake in a moderate oven, 350° F., for 10 minutes. Turn and bake for 10 minutes longer. Serve each on an oblong of hot buttered toast. Cut to fit. Garnish, if liked, with halved fried tomatoes. *For 2 or 3 persons.*

KIPPER TOASTS (Croûtes Ecossaises)

Flesh of 1 fried kipper
Thick cream as required
Salt and cayenne pepper to taste
3 tomatoes
1 tablespoon melted butter
4 squares hot buttered toast
4 fried mushrooms
1 fried rasher of bacon

Remove the flesh of a fried kipper to a basin. Mash till smooth. Mix with thick cream to taste, then season highly with salt and cayenne pepper to taste. Peel the tomatoes, chop or slice, and fry in 1 tablespoon of melted butter till soft. Prepare the toast. Spread with the tomatoes. Divide the kipper cream equally between the canapés. Top each with a fried mushroom. Chop and pile the bacon into the centre of each. *For 4 persons.*

MARROW BONES

Choose marrow bones from the middle of a round of beef or leg or shin bones. Have them sawn in two crosswise, and the thick ends shaped by chopping them so that the bones will stand upright. Mix a little flour to a paste with cold water and plaster this paste over the open end of each. Stand upright in a deep saucepan containing enough hot water to come half-way up the bones. Cover closely. Simmer gently for about 30 minutes. Carefully remove the paste. Season marrow. Decorate each bone with a paper frill made from a large decorated paper serviette or wrap in a napkin. Serve at once with hot crisp or Melba toast. *Allow 1 or 2 per person.*

MUSHROOM AND BACON CANAPES
(Croûtes à la Campagne)

½ lb. mushrooms
1 tablespoon butter
Pinch of salt
Pepper to taste
4 rings of fried bread
2 rashers of bacon

Wipe and peel caps and stems of mushrooms Melt butter. Chop mushrooms roughly and add. Cover and cook for 10 minutes very slowly, tossing occasionally, then season to taste, adding a pinch of ground mace too, if liked. Finish cooking. Fry the bread in bacon fat or butter and fry the bacon rashers after removing rinds. Chop bacon. Spread mushrooms on rounds of bread. Place a ring of fried bread on the top of each. Fill centres with chopped bacon. *For 4 persons.*

MUSHROOMS ON TOAST (Croûtes de Champignons)

½ lb. mushrooms
2 oz. butter
Salt and pepper to taste
Pinch of ground mace
4 slices of buttered toast

Remove stems level with the flaps of mushrooms. Wipe with a damp cloth. Peel carefully, if wild. Melt butter in a frying-pan, rubbed if liked with a clove of garlic. Add mushrooms, salt, pepper and mace to taste. Fry slowly, turning occasionally, for 5 minutes. Remove crusts from toast. Divide mushrooms equally among the slices. (If preferred, use fried bread and slice mushrooms before frying.) *For 4 persons.*

PRAWN CANAPES (Croûtes d'Ecrevisses à l'Indienne)

12 prawns
1½ oz. butter
Salt and cayenne pepper to taste
6 canapés of fried bread
½ gill curry sauce
Sherry to taste

Shell prawns. Melt butter. Add prawns. Season with salt and cayenne pepper to taste. Cook till piping hot, then divide equally among canapés. Flavour sauce with sherry to taste. Coat the prawns with the sauce. Garnish with chopped green pepper, minced parsley or chervil. *For 6 persons.*

ROE SAVOURIES

Herring roes, and mackerel roes, as well as smoked cod's roe all make appetising savouries. Before using smoked cod's roe, soak it in milk overnight, then drain well.

SMOKED COD'S ROE RAMEKINS
(Ramaquins de Laitance Fumée)

¼ lb. smoked cod's roe
Melted butter as required
3 tablespoons cheese soufflé mixture

Brush 6 ramekins with melted butter. Sprinkle all over the bottom and sides with sieved bread-crumbs. Remove any skin from roe. Mash in a saucepan with enough melted butter to make a thick paste. Add a few drops of lemon juice or sherry. Divide equally among ramekins, then divide soufflé mixture in the same way. Sprinkle soufflé mixture with grated Parmesan. Bake in a moderate oven, 350° F., till soufflé is set, in about 15 minutes. *For 6 persons.*

DEVILLED HERRING ROES : Season soft herring roes with salt and cayenne pepper to taste. Egg and crumb and fry. Serve on oblong canapés of hot buttered toast or fried bread, cut to fit.

HERRING ROES A L'INDIENNE : Place soft roes in a lavishly-buttered baking tin. Sprinkle lightly with lemon juice. Bake in a moderate oven, 350° F., for 5 or 6 minutes. Arrange on fingers of toast. Sprinkle with minced parsley and cayenne pepper to taste. Serve at once.

HERRING ROES A LA MEUNIERE : Dip soft roes in seasoned flour. Shake lightly. Fry in a little hot butter, turning once. Sprinkle lightly with lemon juice. Serve on fingers of fried bread or hot buttered toast. Garnish with minced parsley.

HERRING ROE CANAPES : Follow recipe for Herring Roes à la Meunière, but spread the fried bread or toast fingers lightly with anchovy paste before putting the roes on top.

HERRING ROES EN SURPRISE : Season soft roes with salt and pepper to taste. Roll each in a thin case of puff pastry. Egg and crumb and deep fry. Serve garnished with parsley and lemon butterflies.

HERRING ROES AND MUSHROOM CANAPES : Cut rounds of toast to fit mush-rooms. Divide each roe in two pieces. Fry lightly in a little hot butter. Season lightly with salt and cayenne pepper. Place a mushroom on each round of toast, and tuck a piece of roe into each mushroom. *Allow 1 or 2 per person.*

HERRING ROES, SENORA : Season soft roes with salt and pepper. Fry in a little hot butter, allowing ½ oz. to 3 roes, then add a pinch of crushed herbs and white wine to moisten. Dish up in hot ramekins. Place a saltspoon of caviare on the top of each.

SARDINE CANAPES (Croûtes de Sardines)

1 can large sardines
1 oz. butter
½ teaspoon dry mustard
Dash of Worcester sauce
Sieved stale breadcrumbs as required

Drain sardines. Mix butter to a paste with the mustard and Worcester sauce. Spread sardines with paste. Dip in crumbs. Grill quickly till golden brown. Serve on strips of fried bread or toast. Garnish with parsley and lemon slices. *For 4 persons.*

SARDINE FRITTERS (Beignets de Sardines)

1⅓ cups flour
¼ teaspoon salt
1 beaten egg
½-¾ cup milk
1 can sardines

Sift flour and salt into basin. Add egg, then milk gradually. When smooth, beat well. Have sardines drained free from oil, and tails removed. Dip into batter, and fry in smoking hot fat till golden. Dry on absorbent paper. Serve coated with hot tomato sauce. *For 4 persons.*

SCOTCH NIPS (Croûtes Ecossaises)

6 oz. cooked Finnan haddock
¾ pint thick cream
2 egg yolks
Salt and pepper to taste
4 fried canapés

Chop cooked, dried haddock up finely and place it in a saucepan. Add cream, egg yolks, salt and pepper to taste, and stir over moderate heat till the mixture thickens. Pile it on fried canapés. Sprinkle with a little paprika. Dish up in a circle on a hot plate covered with a lace paper doily. Serve at once. *For 4 persons.*

SHRIMP TOASTS (Croûtes de Crevettes)

¾ oz. butter
¾ oz. flour
1½ gills milk
½ teaspoon anchovy essence
½ saltspoon ground mace
Salt and pepper to taste
Grated nutmeg to taste
½ pint picked shrimps
12 canapés of fried bread

Melt butter in a saucepan. Stir in flour and, when frothy, add milk. Stir till smooth and boiling. Add anchovy essence, mace, salt, pepper and grated nutmeg to taste. Stir in shrimps, then heat till smoking hot. Serve on the canapés. *For 6 persons.*

SMOKED SALMON, DELICE (Délice de Saumon, fumé)

6 oz. shortcrust
Anchovy paste
3 tablespoons cream
2 beaten eggs
Salt and pepper to taste
Minced smoked salmon
Rice paper

Line 10 tiny boat-shaped moulds thinly with shortcrust. Prick the bottoms well. Bake in a fairly hot oven, 425° F., till crisp and golden. Put a dab of anchovy paste in the bottom of each. Measure cream into a saucepan. Stir in eggs, salt and pepper to taste. Stir till thick. Fill up boats. Top each with a teaspoon of salmon. Sprinkle with a little finely-minced onion if liked. Garnish each with a 'sail' of rice paper. *For 5 persons.*

COLD SAVOURIES

ANCHOVY ECLAIRS (Eclairs d'Anchoix)

4 tablespoons butter
1 teaspoon anchovy paste
2 or 3 drops of lemon juice
½ teaspoon minced onion or a few drops of onion juice
1½ dozen small eclair cases

Beat butter till soft and creamy. Stir in anchovy paste, lemon juice, onion and pepper to taste. Slit the eclairs, about 1¼ by ½ inch, on one side only. Fill with anchovy cream. If you want a very delicate filling, fold in a little whipped cream, but serve eclairs immediately after filling. *Yield:* 1½ dozen.

ASPARAGUS CANAPES (Croûtes d'Asperge)

12 bridge rolls
12 anchovy fillets
24 boiled or canned asparagus tips

Split bridge rolls in two. (If the tops are very round, shave a thin slice off them so that they will sit properly on a plate.) Butter cut sides sparingly. (If liked, substitute 12 fingers of fried bread for the rolls.) Arrange a fillet of anchovy preserved in oil down the centre of each. Place an asparagus tip at each side of it with the tips lying in opposite directions. *Yield :* 12 canapés.

BLOATER CANAPES (Croûtes Yarmouth)

3 soft bloater roes
1 teaspoon lemon juice
6 croûtes of fried bread
3 tablespoons mayonnaise

Simmer roes in boiling water and lemon juice very slowly until ready. Let them cool in the water. When required, lift carefully out. Drain well and halve. Place each on a canapé of fried bread. Mask with mayonnaise flavoured to taste with paprika, French mustard and celery salt. *For 3 persons.*

CAVIARE CANAPES (Croûtes de Caviare)

8 fingers of bread
Fresh caviare as required
1 oz. Maître d'Hôtel butter
½ gill cream
Lemon and parsley

Have the fingers cut 2½ inches long and 1 inch wide. Fry in hot clarified butter or fat till golden brown. Drain on absorbent paper. Leave till quite cold. Spread each with caviare. Divide Maître d'Hôtel butter and spread equally over the top. Whip cream. Season with salt and cayenne pepper to taste. With a forcing bag fitted with a plain pipe, make dots of the cream right down the centre of the fingers. Arrange side by side on a flat dish lined with a lace paper doily. Garnish with lemon butterflies and sprigs of parsley. *For 8 persons.*

CHANNEL BOATS (Bateaux à la Manche)

6 oz. cheese pastry
2 hard-boiled eggs
Mayonnaise as required
2 tablespoons grated Parmesan cheese
Salt and cayenne pepper to taste
12 anchovy fillets
1½ oz. butter
1 teaspoon shrimp paste
Dash of lemon juice

Roll pastry out to ¼ inch thickness. Line tiny, boat-shaped moulds neatly with pastry, then trim edges. Prick centres with a fork. Bake in a hot oven, 500° F., till risen and set, then lower heat to moderate, 350° F., and bake till golden brown. Turn out carefully on to a wire rack to cool. When cold, chop eggs. Mix to a paste with mayonnaise, Parmesan cheese, and salt and cayenne pepper to taste. Place in bottom of cases. Arrange an anchovy fillet on centre of each. Beat butter to a cream with the shrimp paste. Stir in lemon juice and salt and pepper to taste. Pipe round inside edge. Add sails of rice paper. *Yield :* 12 boats.

CRAB A LA NEWLYN (Crabe à la Newlyn)

1 cup flaked crab
1 tablespoon minced onion

Mix crab with the onion and French dressing. Cover and stand for 10 minutes. Mix with the

671

1 tablespoon French dressing
2-3 tablespoons thick mayonnaise
6 canapés of fried bread

mayonnaise. Pile on to fried canapés. Garnish with paprika, minced parsley or chives to taste. *For 6 persons.*

FINNAN SOUFFLES (Soufflés de Merluche)

6 oz. Finnan haddock
¼ pint white sauce
Salt and cayenne pepper to taste
¼ pint thick cream
½ oz. powdered gelatine
1 hard-boiled egg
¼ pint aspic jelly

Poach the haddock in boiling water to cover till the flesh is creamy, then drain and leave till cold. Remove bones and skin. Mince and weigh flesh. Put 6 oz. in a basin. Add sauce, salt and cayenne pepper to taste. Stir till blended. Whip cream. Stir into the fish mixture. Melt gelatine in 2 tablespoons of water over boiling water. Cool slightly. Strain into mixture. Stir till blended. Three-quarters fill 7 ramekin cases with the mixture. Place a slice of hard-boiled egg on the top of each. Melt jelly only till it runs, then coat the top of each with the jelly. Garnish each on the centre with a tiny sprig of chervil or parsley. Chill and serve. *For 7 persons.*

HAM CREAMS (Mousses au Jambon)

3 oz. lean ham
½ gill tomato purée
½ gill stiff aspic jelly
¾ gill cream
Salt and cayenne pepper to taste
1 beaten egg white

Line 8 small dariole moulds thinly with aspic jelly. Decorate the bottom of each with a sprig of chervil, or an ornament of truffle. Put the ham twice through a meat grinder, then pound in a mortar until into a paste. Gradually beat in the purée, then stir in aspic jelly. Fold into the cream. Add salt and cayenne pepper to taste, and colour delicately with cochineal. Fold in egg white. Leave until about to congeal. Divide equally among the moulds. Chill. Turn out. Garnish with chopped aspic jelly. *For 8 persons.*

TOMATOES IN ASPIC (Aspic de Tomates)

1 lb. small firm tomatoes
Salt and pepper to taste
1¼ tablespoons powdered gelatine
½ cup cold water
2 bouillon cubes
1½ cups boiling water
¼ cup minced celery
4 tablespoons flaked Finnan haddock
Mayonnaise to taste

Remove a slice from the flower-end of tomatoes, then carefully scoop out soft centres. Season insides with salt and pepper, and turn tomatoes upside down on a rack to drain. Soften the gelatine in cold water. Dissolve bouillon cubes in boiling water. Add gelatine. Stir till dissolved. (If preferred, use aspic jelly.) Season to taste with salt and flavour with a little sherry or lemon juice as preferred. Leave until begining to set, then pour a layer in the bottom of as many individual moulds as you have tomatoes. Mix celery with fish, and moisten with mayonnaise to taste. Stuff tomatoes with mixture, then place topside down in each mould. Fill up with aspic and set in refrigerator. When required, turn out on to individual plates lined with mustard and cress.

(Top Left)
Vanilla Cookies in varying moods. *See page* 736

(Top Right)
Russian Biscuits, good for tea or packed luncheons. *See page* 739.

(Bottom Left)
Serve Butter Biscuits with the Cheese Course. *See page* 737

(Bottom Right)
Arrowroot, Cheese, Water and Digestive Biscuits. *See pages* 736, 737, *and* 739.

(Top Left)
Orange Layer Cake.
See page 733.

(Top Right)
Rolling up a Swiss
Roll *See page 727.*

(Bottom Left)
Dredge Marble Cake
with castor sugar. *See page 730.*

(Bottom Right)
Chocolate Peppermint
Layer Cake. *See page 732.*

Breads

"Give us this day our daily bread."

Bread is a cheap source of carbohydrates and vegetable proteins. It also furnishes us with minerals and vitamin B, some varieties more than others. When bread is leavened with yeast the vitamin content is increased. A good loaf of bread should have a rich golden brown crust when ready, and show signs of shrinking from the sides of the tin. If you tap the loaf, it will sound hollow.

RULES FOR MAKING YEAST BREAD

Utensils and Ingredients : Warm all utensils and ingredients to blood heat, 98° F. This is most important.

To Knead : To knead the dough so that it is smooth and elastic, full of bubbles and springy when pressed with your finger, fold the edges towards the middle, then press it down and away from you with the palms of your hands, or your knuckles, turning it round and round, and continuing to bring the edges to the centre and working it as lightly as possible until it is kneaded so that a dent can be made with the finger which disappears almost as soon as made.

To Raise : Cover dough with a clean cloth and leave it to rise at 80°- 85° F., in a place free from draughts, until the dough has risen to double its size. The ideal place for "raising" bread is a warming cupboard or a linen cupboard with controlled heat. Some housewives may object to turning a linen cupboard into a warming cupboard, but to get perfect bread it is important that the temperature given should be maintained throughout. It is not easy to raise bread close to a stove unless you keep turning the container. When you have no warming cupboard, you can raise it on top of a plate rack, or in a pan of warm water, but you will have to keep the water between 80° and 85° F. You can also place the dough in the top of a double boiler with warm water below, covering pan with lid.

To Shape : Weigh and place in lb. or ½ lb. tins, brushed with melted lard, using tins 9″ × 4½″ or 5″ × 3″ for lb. loaves, and 7″ × 4″ × 3″ for a ½ lb. loaf. The dough should be half the depth of the tin. Cover. Raise in a warm place as before until the dough has almost reached the top of the tin and the middle is rounded. In some recipes, the dough has to be kneaded again then shaped into loaves and placed in tins. Allow to rise again before baking. The tins must be heated to blood heat, 98° F.

To Bake : Unless otherwise stated in recipe, bake in a fairly slow oven, 325° F., for about ¾ hour, or till ready, time depending on size of loaf. Remember that if a soft crust is wanted, bread should be wrapped before leaving to cool.

To Cool : Turn on to a wire rack or tray.

WHITE YEAST BREAD (Sponge Method)

3½ lb. flour
3½ teaspoons salt
1 oz. bakers' yeast
4 teaspoons caster sugar
About 1½ pints luke-warm water

To make dough, sift flour and salt into a warmed basin. Set in a warm place. Cream yeast and sugar in a warmed basin, until liquefied, with a wooden spoon, then stir in warm water, which consists of half boiling and half cold water. Make a hollow in the centre of the flour. Strain in yeast and water. Sprinkle a very little of the flour over the liquid. Cover with a cloth. Set to rise in a warm place free from draughts until the yeast mixture is covered with bubbles. This may take 20 minutes ; it may take longer. It entirely depends on the temperature. This process is called " setting the sponge." Stir in all the flour with your hand, adding more luke-warm water if required as some flours absorb more liquid than others. When mixed, the dough should be firm but elastic.

To Knead : Knead lightly but thoroughly on an unfloured board. Some advocate folding the edges over towards the centre, others folding the dough in two. Choose whichever method you like, but push dough lightly away from you with the balls of your hands or the knuckles, using only enough pressure to make the part folded over adhere to the part below. Turn dough a quarter round and repeat folding and kneading. Keep on with this process until the dough no longer sticks to the unfloured board and is smooth and elastic.

To Raise : Return dough to basin, warmed and sprinkled with flour, or warm and grease basin lightly. (It must be large enough to hold twice the bulk of the dough.) Brush the top of dough with melted fat, then make a cross-cut across the top. Cover with a clean cloth. Set in a warm place to rise until double its bulk. It will take from 1½-1¾ hours. Take care not to stand it in too hot a place or the surface will crack and the texture of the bread will spoilt. When it doubles its bulk, fold in the edges and press it down in the ntre, then turn it upside down, brush lightly with melted fat, and cover again. 'ake care not to use too much fat, or it will form streaks in the bread.) Leave rise again as before. This rising is not essential, but improves the texture the bread. It is claimed that it gives you a finely-grained bread.

To Divide and Shape Dough : Warm loaf tins. Dredge lightly with flour, grease them lightly. Divide the dough into portions that will fill the tins out half-full. With your hands round each portion into a ball. (This is seal the cut edges.) Stand for a few minutes. Now flatten each into an oblong d then fold and seal edges together. Repeat this several times, folding a fferent way each time, then bring the sides together in the middle and place, aled edges downwards. Brush top lightly with melted fat. This keeps the rface elastic.

To Raise and Bake : It is better to use rather shallow loaf tins than deep es. For example, when you want to make a 1 lb. or a $1\frac{1}{2}$ lb. loaf, it is much tter to use a tin $8\frac{1}{2}'' \times 4'' \times 3''$, or $8'' \times 4\frac{1}{2}'' \times 3''$, than a tin that is, say, $\times 3\frac{1}{2}'' \times 3''$. The loaf baked in a shallow tin has a crust round all the side d bakes quicker than one in a deep rather narrow tin. Place the shaped ough in warmed greased tins. Cover tins with a clean cloth, and leave to rise til dough doubles its size in a temperature of 80°-85°. Place in a moderate en, 350° F. Bake until well risen and lightly browned. The bread should ntinue to rise for the first $\frac{1}{4}$ hour, then brown for 20 minutes. When the mperature is reduced, the bread will cook through to the centre. The time ll depend on the size of the loaf. A 2 lb. loaf takes from $1-1\frac{1}{4}$ hours. A 1 lb. m $\frac{3}{4}-1$ hour. Turn loaves after they have been baking for about $\frac{1}{4}$ hour, as to secure even browning. When light and well-risen, and nicely browned, u should hear a hollow ring when you tap it with a knife on the side. Cool on side on a wire rack, raised so that the air can circulate.

QUICK YEAST BREAD : Mix liquid with all the flour. Knead thoroughly until ast is incorporated. Shape into a loaf. Place in warmed greased tins. Cover d allow to rise to double its size, then bake.

TO MAKE A COTTAGE LOAF : Divide half the dough into two portions : one ice the size of the other. Shape into rounds. Place small one on top of the rge one. With a thick wooden skewer make a hole right through the centre. ake as described, allowing a little longer.

PLAITED FRENCH BREAD (Pain à la Française)

oz. bakers' yeast
teaspoons caster sugar
pint tepid milk
lb. flour
teaspoon salt
oz. butter
beaten egg

Place yeast and sugar in a warm basin. Stir till yeast liquefies. Stir in milk. Leave in a warm place for about $\frac{1}{4}$ hour till it froths on top. Sieve flour and salt into a warm basin. Rub butter into flour. Stir egg into yeast mixture, then make a hollow in the centre of the flour. Pour in half the yeast mixture. Gradually beat in flour und the edge, then add remainder of yeast mixture by degrees. Beat to a nooth dough with a large wooden spoon, or with your hand, until the dough rinks from the side of the basin. Dredge lightly with flour. Cut it across e top. Cover with a cloth. Stand in a warm place till double its size in about

675

1 hour. Knead lightly with floured hands. Turn on to a floured pastry boar
Roll out slightly. Cut into three equal-wide strips. Roll each strip back a
forth into a narrow roll, then plait. If the plait is too long to bake on yo
baking sheet, cut in two, or shape plait into a ring. Dredge baking she
lightly with flour. Place plait on sheet. Cover and stand in a warm place f
15 minutes, taking care that the cover does not touch the dough. Brush wi
beaten egg or egg white. Bake in a hot oven, 450° F., for about ½ hour.

To Vary : Instead of rubbing butter into flour, melt it. Stir egg into holle
in flour, then the butter.

BROWN BREAD (Pain brun)

2 oz. flour
6 oz. wholemeal flour
½ oz. butter or lard
½ teaspoon salt
¼ oz. bakers' yeast
½ teaspoon sugar
¼ pint lukewarm milk, water or potato water

Stir flour into wholemeal flour. Rub in f
Stir in salt. Cream yeast with sugar. Stir
half the liquid. Make a hollow in centre of flou
Add yeast mixture. Mix with a wooden spo
or your hand, adding more liquid as required
give you a rather stiff dough. Remove spoon
using one. Knead well. Cover with a slight
dampened cloth. Stand in a warm place till double its size in ¾-1 hour. Tu
on to a floured board. Knead well. Shape into a loaf. Warm and grease
loaf tin, 7″ × 4″ × 3″. Place in tin. Cover and stand in a warm place f
10-15 minutes. Prick dough on top with a fork. Bake in a fairly hot ove
425° F., for 10-15 minutes, then lower to 375° F., and finish baking in abo
50 minutes.

To Vary : To make a darker loaf, use 4 oz. each of the flour and wholeme
flour. If wanted malted, dissolve 1 teaspoon syrup and 1-1½ dessertspoo
malt extract into liquid before adding.

LEE MALT LOAF (Pain de Malt)

1 oz. malt
½ gill warm water
5 oz. wholemeal flour
9 oz. flour
½ teaspoon salt
½ oz. margarine
¼ oz. bakers' yeast
1 tablespoon golden syrup or treacle

Stir malt into warm water. When blended, s
into wholemeal flour. Place in the top of a dou
saucepan. Stand in a covered pan of hot wat
140° F., for 6 hours. Sift flour and salt into
basin. Rub in margarine. Cream yeast wi
½ gill tepid water. Mix syrup or treacle wi
another ½ gill tepid water. Stir into yeast, th
stir into flour. Cover. Stand in a warm place t
risen and spongy in about 1¼ hours. Stir in malt mixture, cooled till tep
then knead until well blended. Warm and grease 2 small loaf tins. Place dou
in tins. Cover. Stand in a warm place till double its bulk, in about ½ hou
Bake in a moderately hot oven, 400° F., for about ½ hour.

ROLLS FROM BREAD DOUGH

Rolls should be baked quickly. If baked slowly, they become very dry.
wanted crisp, place from ½-1 inch apart on baking sheet, or bake in individ
bun tins. If wanted with soft sides, place close together and pull them ap

when ready. If a short crust is wanted, brush the tops only with melted butter before baking.

BREAD ROLLS

BASIC : This recipe should be looked upon as a standard recipe for dinner rolls. Once you memorize it, you can quickly turn out at least a dozen varieties of fancy rolls.

2 cups milk
2 oz. butter
½-1 oz. caster sugar
1½ teaspoons salt
1 oz. bakers' yeast
1½ lb. flour

Grease a baking sheet, muffin tins, or any other kind of tins you are using for baking rolls, depending on variety of rolls. Heat milk to boiling point. Add butter, sugar and salt. Leave till tepid. Cream yeast with a teaspoon of additional sugar. Add to milk mixture, then stir in half the flour. Beat thoroughly. (If using electric beater, beat for 2 minutes.) Cover. Stand in a warm place till double its size. Punch down, then add enough of the remaining flour, kneading it lightly in, until you have a soft dough. (If richer rolls are wanted, add 1 or 2 well-beaten eggs, or egg whites, in which case, you will only need to add 10 oz. flour.) Cover and leave in a warm place till double its size, then knead and shape into rolls. Cover again with a cloth. Allow to rise till double their bulk. (This will take about 1 hour.) Bake in a fairly hot oven, 425° F., for about 15 minutes. *Yield :* About 3½ dozen rolls.

BOWKNOTS : Roll dough ¼ inch thick. Cut in strips 1 inch wide and about 6 inches long. Roll crosswise. (If preferred, cut only ½ inch wide and do not roll.) Tie each in a knot. Place a little apart on a greased or oiled baking sheet. Cover. Allow to double its size. Bake as suggested in basic recipe.

BRAIDED ROLLS : Roll to ½ inch thickness. Cut in strips about 7 inches long and ½ inch wide. Arrange three strips together. Press them at one end together, then plait to other end and press. Cover. Allow to double their size. Bake as suggested in basic recipe.

BUTTERFLIES : Roll out dough about ¼ inch thick. Brush with melted butter. Roll up like a Swiss roll. Cut into slices 1½ inches thick. Place about an inch apart on a greased baking tin. With the handle of a wooden spoon, make a slight hollow across the centre of each. Cover and allow to rise to double their size. Bake as suggested.

CINNAMON ROLLS : Roll dough ¼ inch thick. Brush with melted butter. Sprinkle with caster sugar and cinnamon, allowing 1 or 2 teaspoons cinnamon to 1 cup sugar. (Brown sugar can be used if preferred.) Roll up like a Swiss roll. Cut in slices ¾-1½ inch thick, according to taste. Bake an inch apart on a greased baking sheet as suggested in basic recipe.

CLOVER LEAF ROLLS : Divide dough into small pieces the size of marbles. Shape into balls. Dip in melted fat. Arrange three, or four, if larger rolls are wanted, together in greased muffin tins. Cover and allow to double their bulk. Bake as suggested.

CRESCENT ROLLS : Roll dough ¼ inch thick. Cut into 3 or 4 inch squares. Halve each square diagonally. Brush with melted butter. Begin rolling each triangle at the base. Press the point firmly down in each case, then curve the ends towards each other in the form of a crescent or horseshoe. Place, point downwards, a little apart on a greased baking tin. Cover. Stand till double their size. Either brush with an egg white beaten with 2 tablespoons water till blended, and bake as suggested ; or brush with equal quantity of egg yolk and milk when beginning to brown.

CRISP ROLLS : These can be made either with the basic or ordinary bread dough, or with French dough. When risen, divide into small pieces. Knead into rounds 3 inches across and 1 inch deep. Place 2 inches apart in a shallow greased baking tin. Cover and allow to rise till half as big again. Dip the handle of a small knife in flour, then roll it back and forth through the centre to make a deep crease. Allow to rise again for about 15 minutes. Brush tops only with equal quantity of egg yolk and cold water. Bake in a moderately hot oven, 400° F., for about 20 minutes.

FAN-TAN ROLLS : Roll out dough into a very thin oblong. Brush with melted butter. Cut into strips about 1 inch wide. Pile 1 on top of each other until you have 6 layers. Cut into slices about $1\frac{1}{2}$ inches across. Place each slice on its end in a greased or oiled muffin tin. Cover and allow to rise till double its size. Bake as suggested.

PARKER HOUSE ROLLS (POCKET BOOKS) : Increase sugar by 1 oz. Roll dough to $\frac{1}{4}$ inch thickness. Cut into rounds, 2 or $2\frac{1}{2}$ inches across with a floured cutter. Dip the handle of the knife in flour. Make a deep crease across the centre of each round. Brush half of each round with melted butter, then fold in two and press edges together. Place a little apart on a well-greased baking sheet. Brush with melted fat. Cover and stand till double their size, in about 35 minutes. Bake as suggested.

POPPY SEED ROLLS : Follow recipe for Crescents, but sprinkle top of the crescents with poppy seeds before setting to rise to double their bulk. These rolls can also be made with Kuchen Dough.

TWISTS : Divide dough into small pieces. Roll each out with the palm of your hand into rolls about 7 inches long and $\frac{1}{2}$ inch thick. Holding one end of each strip between the thumb and forefinger of each hand, twist in opposite directions. Draw the ends together, making both ends look alike. Place each twist $\frac{1}{2}$ inch apart on a well-greased baking tin. Brush with melted fat or egg yolk, diluted with milk. Cover and leave till double their bulk. Bake as suggested.

BRIDGE ROLLS

½ lb. flour
Pinch of salt
½ oz. bakers' yeast
1 teaspoon caster sugar
5 tablespoons milk
1 egg
2 oz. butter

Sift flour and salt into a basin. Make two " wells ", one at each side. Cream the yeast with the sugar. Add half the tepid milk. Pour into one of the " wells ". Beat the egg. Melt and stir in butter. Pour into other " well." Cover and stand in a warm place for 20 minutes, then mix well together. Add remainder of milk, and a tablespoon or two more if required. The dough should be soft and smooth. Beat it with your hand. Cover and stand in a warm place till double its bulk. Turn on to a lightly floured board. Roll to $\frac{1}{2}$ inch thickness. Cut into narrow strips about 3 or 4 inches long. Roll each with your hands. Place an inch apart on a slightly warmed greased baking sheet. Cover. Leave to rise till double their size. Brush with beaten egg. Bake in a hot oven, 450° F., for about ¼ hour.

FRENCH BRIOCHE

1 lb. flour
½ teaspoon salt
½ oz. bakers' yeast
About 3 tablespoons tepid water
4 beaten eggs
4 beaten egg yolks
6 oz. butter
1½ oz. caster sugar

Sift flour and salt into a warmed basin. Make two " wells " at each side of basin. Cream yeast with half the water. Pour into 1 " well." Mix eggs with yolks. Melt butter and add to eggs with sugar. Pour into second " well." Beat with your hand, adding more water as required to make a soft, rather sticky dough. Cover. Stand in a warm place for 1 hour. Divide dough into 24 large and 24 small balls. Brush 2 dozen fluted slightly warmed bun tins with melted butter. Slip a large ball into each. Place the small balls on top of each of the large ones. Cover and stand in a warm place for about ½ hour. Brush with equal quantity of beaten egg yolk and water. Bake in a hot oven, 450° F., for about 10 minutes. *Yield :* About 1½ dozen.

CROISSANTS

1½ gills scalded milk
1 small tablespoon lard
1 rounded tablespoon caster sugar
½ teaspoon salt
1 crumbled yeast cake
⅓ cup tepid water
10 oz. sifted flour
½ lb. butter

Pour milk into a hot basin. Add lard, sugar and salt. Stir till dissolved. Leave till tepid. Meanwhile, dissolve yeast cake in tepid water. Stir into first mixture. Warm flour slightly. Add to yeast mixture. Knead to a soft dough on a lightly floured pastry board. When ready, the dough should be smooth and elastic. Place in a slightly warmed bowl. Cover with a cloth. Leave until it is double its bulk in a warm place, in about 1½ hours. Cover closely with lid or plate. Chill in refrigerator. Roll into a rectangle ¼ inch thick. Beat butter till creamy. Dab 2 oz. of the butter all over the dough, then fold the left end over the centre, then the right end over the left end, so that you have three layers. Turn dough round so that the left end is towards you. Roll to ¼ inch thickness. Dab again with 2 oz. butter. Fold as before, then turn it a quarter round. Repeat this twice more. Cover and chill for 2 hours. Roll out on a lightly floured board to ¼ inch thickness, in the shape of an oblong. Divide into 3 inch squares. Cut into triangles. Roll up from the base and stretch pastry slightly as you roll, then draw the ends into crescents. Chill for 30 minutes. Bake a little apart on a greased baking sheet in a hot oven, 450° F., for 10 minutes, then lower to moderate, 350° F., and bake for about 10 minutes longer. *Yield :* 6 to 8 Croissants.

REFRIGERATOR ROLLS (Petits Pains, Américaine)

They can be made by the recipe given for basic dough for rolls, or Bridge Rolls. Place dough in refrigerator immediately it is mixed, or after it has risen. To prepare dough that has risen, punch down several times to get rid of the gas, then place in a basin. Grease surface. Cover with waxed paper, then with a

damp cloth. Place in refrigerator. When rolls are wanted, break off only a
much of the dough as is required, shape, and place a little apart on a warme
greased backing sheet, or in warmed greased bun tins. Cover and leave in a warn
place until double their size in 1-2 hours, then bake in a fairly hot oven, 425° F.
for about 15 minutes.

FANCY YEAST BREADS

BARA BRITH

½ lb. stoned raisins
½ lb. cleaned currants
½ lb. cleaned sultanas
½ lb. caster sugar
¾ oz. bakers' yeast
¾ pint milk
3 lb. flour
¾ pint tepid water
½ lb. lard
2 oz. minced candied peel
½ oz. mixed spice
3 eggs

Mash and dry fruit or place it in a colander o
sieve. Dredge lightly with flour, then shak
well. Place a heaped teaspoon of sugar in a
small heated basin. Crumble in yeast. Sti
till liquefied. Heat milk till tepid. Stir int
yeast. Cover. Stand in a warm place till the
mixture rises to the top of the basin. Sift flour
Place in a large heated basin. Make a hollow i
the centre. Pour in yeast mixture. Graduall
draw in the flour and add the water alternately
Cover and stand in a warm place till double it

size. Melt lard slowly, only allowing it to become tepid. Beat into dough
Gradually add the remainder of sugar, fruit, peel, then the spice. Beat in eggs
one at a time. When thoroughly blended, divide in two. Knead each portio
thoroughly on a lightly floured board, then place each in a greased loaf tir
(2 lb. tin), or large cake tins can be used. Cover. Stand in a warm place ti
well risen in about ½ hour. Bake in a moderately hot oven, 375° F., for abou
¾ hour.

CORNISH SAFFRON CAKE (Pain au Safran)

½ teaspoon saffron
2 tablespoons boiling water
1 lb. bakers' dough
¼ lb. cleaned currants
¼ lb. minced candied peel
¼ teaspoon ground allspice
¼ lb. caster sugar
¼ lb. butter

Grease tin. Place saffron in a small basin, and
add water. Stand in a warm place for about
hour. Strain and stir into dough. Add currants
peel, allspice and sugar to dough, and stir ti
blended. Melt butter. Stir in gradually. Bea
dough with your hand or a wooden spoon. Plac
in a greased warm loaf tin, 9 by 4 by 3 inches

Bake in a moderate oven, 350° F., for about 1 hour.

LARDY CAKE (Pain, Wiltshire)

2 lb. bread dough
6 oz. lard or butter
7 oz. caster sugar
¼ lb. cleaned currants

Roll out dough on a lightly floured board int
an oblong fully an inch thick. Dab with flake
of lard or butter until you cover only two-third
of the dough. Sprinkle half the sugar, then ha

the currants, over this part. Fold in three as for flaky pastry, but fold th
remaining third of dough over a third of the pastry, then fold the remainde
carefully so as not to disturb the fat over the top. Seal ends with your rollin

pin. Turn half-way round. Roll once more into an oblong as before. Repeat process of spreading two-thirds with fat, and sprinkling with sugar and currants. Repeat folding and half turning as before, then roll out to fit a greased Yorkshire pudding tin. That is from 1 to 1½ inches thick. Leave in a warm place to rise till it doubles its bulk. Bake in a moderately hot oven, 400° F., for about 50 minutes. When half baked, brush with a thick syrup of sugar and water, flavoured with vanilla essence to taste, or with honey diluted with boiling water to a thick syrup. If preferred, dredge with caster sugar. Serve hot or cold.

YEAST TEA RINGS

1 oz. bakers' yeast
1 cup tepid milk
1 lb. flour
½ lb. butter
¼ lb. caster sugar
4 egg yolks
Grated rind 1 lemon
Almond paste filling

Grease a large cake tin about 10 inches across with a tube in the centre, known abroad as a " Bundt Form ". Some have plain sides, some fluted. Cream yeast with a teaspoon of caster sugar, then stir in milk and a cup of the flour. Cover. Stand in a warm place until mixture rises well. Cream butter. Stir in sugar, then beat in egg yolks, one at a time. Add lemon rind. Beat till very light. Gradually stir in yeast mixture alternately with remaining flour. Cover. Place in refrigerator at normal temperature. Leave overnight. Roll on a lightly floured board into an oblong about ½ inch thick. Spread quickly with almond or honey paste. Roll up like a Swiss roll. Divide in two. Roll each out with the balls of your hands into a roll, one slightly smaller than the other. Twist the long roll round the short one to give you a ring by moistening and moulding ends together. Allow to rise in a cool place for 3 to 4 hours. Bake in a moderate oven, 350° F., for about 1 hour. Beat 2½ oz. vanilla icing sugar with an egg white for 10 minutes, then spread on ring while it is still warm. Serve slightly hot or cold with coffee.

Almond Paste for Ring : Beat 3 egg whites till stiff. Stir in 6 oz. caster sugar, ½ teaspoon ground cinnamon and 1 cup ground almonds.

Honey Paste : Mix thick extracted honey with ground almonds, cashew or hazel nuts until into a thick paste.

RUSKS

1 crumbled yeast cake
1 pint warm milk
Flour to make a batter
¼ lb. butter
½ lb. caster sugar
2 beaten eggs
1 teaspoon salt

Stir yeast into the milk till dissolved, then stir in enough sifted flour to make a thin batter. Cover. Leave in a warm place to rise overnight. Cream butter and sugar. Add alternately with eggs to batter. Beat well. Stir in salt and enough additional flour to make a soft dough. Mould into small balls with floured hands. Set in a warm place to rise till twice their height. Bake a little apart on a warmed greased baking sheet in a moderate oven, 350° F., for about ½ hour.

Quick Rusks : Cut left-over or stale buns in halves crosswise, or stale bread in slices, then in neat pieces, ½ inch thick. Bake on a baking sheet in a slow

oven, 250° F., to 275° F., for ¾ to 1 hour, or until evenly browned right through.
Serve for breakfast or with cheese, or when on a reducing diet.

STALE BREAD

PULLED BREAD : Remove crusts from a freshly-baked loaf of bread. Pull
pieces of bread apart from the loaf with a fork. Place on a baking tin. Bake
in a very slow oven, 250° F., till pale brown and crisp on the outside, turning
occasionally. Serve in place of rolls.

To Toast a Loaf : Remove crust from top and sides of a small loaf. Cut
thin slices all the way along without perforating the bottom crust. Brush melted
butter over top, ends, sides and in between the slices. Place on a baking sheet.
Toast in a slow oven, 275° F., till golden brown in about ¼ hour. Serve at
once in place of hot rolls.

BANANA TOAST : Remove crusts from 4 slices of bread. Mash 2 bananas.
Stir in ¼ teaspoon salt, 1 rounded teaspoon caster sugar, ½ teaspoon lemon juice
and 1 dessertspoon creamed butter. Toast bread on both sides. Spread with
banana paste. Place side by side on a baking sheet. Bake in a fairly hot oven,
425° F., for 4-5 minutes.

CINNAMON TOAST : Toast slices of bread, cut ¼ inch thick, quickly on both
sides. Spread with butter. Sprinkle with cinnamon sugar made by stirring
1 teaspoon cinnamon into ½ cup caster or light brown sugar. If a stronger
flavour is wanted, allow 1 part cinnamon to 3 parts sugar. Heat under grill till
sugar melts and forms a crust.

MELBA TOAST : Remove crusts from a loaf 48 hours old. With a very sharp
knife, slice bread as thin as a wafer. Arrange on a rack over baking sheet.
Bake in a moderately slow oven, 325° F., till dry and delicately brown in about
20 minutes. Cool. Serve in a bread basket. If preferred, it can be very lightly
spread with melted butter, or sprinkled with grated Parmesan cheese and paprika before baking. When only toasted, it can be stored in a tightly-closed tin
when cold until required.

ORANGE TOAST : Toast 6 slices of bread quickly. Spread lavishly with
butter. Mix grated rind of an orange or 2 tangerines with 5 oz. caster sugar.
Stir in juice of orange or tangerines. Spread over toast. Heat under the grill
till the spread starts to fizzle. Serve at once.

FRENCH TOAST

2 lightly-beaten eggs
¼ teaspoon salt
1 cup milk
6 slices bread
2 tablespoons fat or oil

Strain eggs into another basin. Add salt and
milk. (If sweet toasts are wanted, add 1½ tablespoons caster sugar and stir till dissolved.)
Remove crust from bread. Dip bread in egg
mixture. Fry in enough bacon fat, butter, or
oil to cover bottom of a large frying-pan, till brown below, then turn and brown
on the other side.

To Vary : Fry in smoking hot fat, 385° F., for 1-2 minutes. If a sweet
toast is wanted, fry on an oiled girdle till brown on each side. Serve with stewed
fruit, honey or jelly, or use as a base for stewed apples.

To Freshen Stale Bread and Rolls : Dip hunks of bread or rolls in cold milk

r water. Place in a paper bag. Slip into a fairly hot oven, 425° F. Leave
ntil heated through. Serve at once.

QUICK BREADS

Quick bread can be made with flour and baking powder, or bicarbonate of
oda and cream of tartar, or with self-raising flour. Some recipes suggest
tanding for ½ hour before baking but most of the mixtures can be baked at once.
Some are enriched with fruit, or fruit and nuts, and some with eggs as well.
They can be served at breakfast or tea, or used for making sandwiches.

NOTES :

1. If loaves are wanted glazed, brush with milk or equal quantity of egg
olk and milk very carefully before baking. Do not allow the glaze to drip down
he sides of the dough.

2. Remove from tins as soon as baked. Place on sides on a wire rack until
quite cold. Loaves made with nuts are best left for at least 24 hours before
cutting.

BAKING POWDER BREAD (Pain, Américaine)

BASIC RECIPE :
½ lb. flour
½ teaspoon salt
2 teaspoons baking powder
1½ oz. butter
2 oz. caster sugar
1 beaten egg
¼ cup milk

Grease a loaf tin, 7 by 4 by 3 inches. Sift flour,
salt and baking powder into a basin. Rub in
butter. Stir in sugar. Add egg to milk. Stir
into dry ingredients. Pack lightly into tin.
Bake in a moderate oven, 350° F., for about
¾ hour. Cool on a wire rack.

CURRANT : Decrease sugar to 1½ oz. Stir 3 oz. cleaned currants into sifted
dry ingredients.

NUT AND RAISIN : Sift ¼ teaspoon ground mace with the dry ingredients.
When all are blended, stir in 2-3 oz. chopped raisins and ¼ lb. chopped walnuts,
or ¾ cup cleaned currants. Substitute ½ cup brown sugar for the caster.

WHEATEN NUT BREAD : Substitute 6 oz. wholemeal flour for 6 oz. of the plain
flour. Increase baking powder to 2½ teaspoons. Decrease sugar to 1 oz. Stir
in 1 cup chopped walnuts before baking.

WHITE NUT BREAD : Stir 1 cup chopped walnuts into dough. Cover. Stand
for 20 minutes.

DATE AND NUT : Substitute ½ cup chopped dates for half the nuts.

SODA BREAD (Pain au Soude)

BASIC RECIPE :
½ lb. flour
½ teaspoon salt
½ teaspoon bicarbonate of
soda
1 teaspoon cream of tartar
¾ oz. caster sugar
¾ oz. butter
About ¾ cup sour milk or
buttermilk

Grease a baking tin. Sift dry ingredients into
a basin. Rub in butter. Mix to a soft dough with
milk. Shape into a high round. Place in tin.
Bake in the centre of a fairly hot oven, 400° F., for
30-40 minutes. If sour milk or buttermilk is not
available, use fresh milk, but double the quantity
of cream of tartar. If preferred place round in a
round floured tin. Score with the back of a knife
in 4 crosswise, or score thrice across the top in

683

parallel lines. Brush with beaten egg or milk and dredge with sugar before baking.

BROWN SODA BREAD : Substitute 4 oz. wholemeal flour for 4 oz. of the flour Rub ¾ oz. butter into dry ingredients before adding milk.

FRUIT BREAD : Stir 2-3 oz. cleaned currants, picked sultanas and chopped candied peel, or 1 oz. of each into dry ingredients before adding milk.

DATE MALT SODA LOAF (Pain de Dattes au Malt)

¾ lb. self-raising flour
2 oz. brown or caster sugar
½ teaspoon salt
¼ lb. chopped dates
About ½ pint milk
1 tablespoon malt
1 tablespoon black treacle
½ teaspoon bicarbonate of soda

Grease a loaf tin, 8½ by 5 by 3 inches. Mix flour with sugar, salt and dates in a mixing bowl. Heat milk until tepid. Stir in malt, treacle and soda Heat, then stir into dry ingredients. Pour into tin. Bake in a fairly slow oven, 325° F., for about 1¼ hours.

Scones

GIRDLE SCONES

A girdle is a round of iron, slightly convex, fixed with a handle in the form of a half-hoop. Girdle scones can be made just as well in a large, strong, thick frying-pan. Some experts advocate baking them on a hot-plate of an electric cooker. There are many varieties of scones that can be baked on a girdle. Some are equally suitable for baking in the oven, though there is a considerable difference between the result of baking a mixture on a girdle and baking it in an oven.

To Prepare Girdle : Rub vigorously all over with a pad of kitchen paper and a little salt, then with a clean dry cloth. Heat slowly. When you think it is warm enough to use, sprinkle with a little dry flour. If sufficiently heated, the flour should turn light brown in about 2 minutes. Dredge lightly with flour before starting to bake scones that have been rolled out. Rub with a piece of suet held at the end of a fork, or in a wad of paper, until evenly greased all over for scones made from batter (drop scones, girdle cakes, etc.).

If Using a Frying-Pan, which does not heat as evenly as a girdle, place an asbestos mat below when cooking on gas. *When Using a Hot Plate,* heat slowly. Flour or grease both frying-pan or hot plate as you would a girdle.

GIRDLE SCONES

BASIC RECIPE :
1 lb. flour

Sift flour, salt, soda, cream of tartar and sugar into a basin. Make a hole in the centre. Stir

685

½ teaspoon salt
1 teaspoon bicarbonate of soda
1 teaspoon cream of tartar
½ teaspoon caster sugar

in enough buttermilk or sour milk to make a soft dough. Knead lightly. Turn on to a floured pastry board. Divide into four or eight portions. With floured hands, shape each into a round scone, ½ inch thick. Bake on a hot girdle, dredged lightly with flour, till risen and light brown below. Turn with a palette knife and brown on the second side. The scones are ready when the edges are dry. *Yield :* 4 or 8 scones.

To Vary : Follow basic recipe, but divide dough in only two portions. Shape each into a thick round, then cut in four crosswise, cutting right through if liked. Bake as described. If cutting right through, dip cut edges lightly in flour and shake before baking.

BROWN : Follow basic recipe, but use ½ lb. of flour and ½ lb. of wholemeal flour.

CURRANT : Stir 2-4 oz. cleaned currants into ingredients before adding milk.

KELSO : Rub 1, 1½ or 2 oz. butter into flour after sifting. Stir in 1 oz. each of cleaned currants, sultanas and mixed candied peel before adding milk.

POTATO : Substitute ½ lb. mashed potatoes for ½ lb. of the flour.

RICH : Rub 1 or 2 oz. butter into the sifted flour.

LYDFORD POTATO CAKES

½ lb. boiled potato
½ oz. butter
1 saltspoon salt
2 oz. flour

Mash potatoes with butter while hot. When smooth, stir in salt and flour. Turn on to a lightly floured pastry board. Roll out thinly. Cut into rounds about 4½ inches in diameter. Prick each with a fork. Grease a hot girdle or frying-pan. Fry cakes for 3 minutes on each side until brown. Serve hot for breakfast or tea. *Yield :* About 10 cakes.

BROWN POTATO CAKES : Substitute wholemeal flour for flour.

OLD-FASHIONED MUFFINS

1 quart milk
1½ oz. bakers' yeast
Flour as required

Stir milk into the yeast. Add salt to flour in the proportion of ¼ oz. to 1¼ lb. flour. Stir in enough salted flour to the yeast mixture to make a rather soft dough. Cover with a cloth. Place in a warm spot to rise until double its size. Divide in equal-sized portions about 3 inches across. Shape into neat rounds. Place a little apart in baking tins lined with warm flour 2 inches deep. Cover. Allow to rise in a warm place till double their size. Cook a little apart on a hot girdle for about 4½ minutes, until slightly brown below, then turn and cook on the other side for the same length of time. Use a broad-bladed knife or spatula. *Yield :* About 2 dozen.

To Serve Muffins : With a sharp knife slit them slightly all round the sides, then toast on both sides. Pull them open with your fingers and either butter the insides, or slip pats of butter in between the halves.

DROP SCONES AND GRIDDLE CAKES

Drop scones and griddle cakes are cooked on a girdle or in a strong frying-pan like girdle scones, but whereas girdle scones are rolled out and shaped before baking, drop scones and griddle cakes are dropped from a tablespoon or a jug in rounds on to a hot greased girdle. Drop scones and griddle cakes are really one and the same. The former is of Scottish origin, and the latter is the version popular in Canada and the United States. As baked, they should be laid on a clean towel and covered to keep them warm and pliable. They are better eaten hot than cold. Serve with unsalted butter and honey or jam.

HINTS ON MAKING DROP SCONES

1. Only stir batter till smooth. If stirred too much, scones may be heavy or tough.

2. Make certain the girdle, pan or hot plate is sufficiently hot. If not, the scones will be stodgy, but if too hot, they will brown unevenly. To get the right temperature, test with a few drops of batter before starting to bake. If right, the drops will at once start to brown and form bubbles on top.

DROP SCONES

BASIC RECIPE :
½ lb. flour
¼ teaspoon salt
½ teaspoon bicarbonate of soda
½ teaspoon cream of tartar
1 tablespoon caster sugar
1 beaten egg
About ½ pint buttermilk or sour milk

Sift dry ingredients into a basin. Make a hollow in the centre. Break in egg. Add a little of the buttermilk. Mix till smooth with a wooden spoon, then gradually stir in milk till you have a thick creamy batter. Grease a moderately hot girdle slightly with a piece of suet held in kitchen paper. Drop the batter from a tablespoon, or from a jug in rounds about 2 inches apart. Bake until bubbles form all over the top, then turn with a spatula or palette knife, and bake till golden brown on the other side. Slip them into a folded towel. (Do not turn them twice while baking.) Keep covered in towel till they cool if not wanted hot. *Yield :* 16-20 scones.

To Enrich : Rub 1 oz. butter or margarine into dry ingredients. Use 2 eggs, and reduce quantity of milk to about 1½ gills.

Baking Powder : Omit soda and cream of tartar, and substitute 2 teaspoons baking powder. Add 2 tablespoons melted butter after the egg and milk, using fresh milk, and beat until smooth.

Treacle : Heat a tablespoon, and fill it up with treacle. Add to batter. Beat until blended.

CRUMPETS

Crumpets in England are generally white rounds of tough dough which are delicious toasted on both sides, until nicely browned, then buttered generously. In Scotland, a crumpet is like an elegant slender drop scone, golden brown on both sides. It should be **but**tered generously, then rolled up.

ENGLISH CRUMPETS

10 oz. flour
¾ teaspoon salt
2 heaped teaspoons baking powder
1 tablespoon caster sugar
4 tablespoons melted butter
2 beaten eggs
1½ cups milk

Sift flour, salt, baking powder and sugar. Pour butter into a basin. Stir in egg and milk, then flour mixture gradually, beating constantly. Place large greased muffin rings on a large greased girdle, or into a large greased frying-pan, brushed with melted butter. Fill rings three-quarters full with batter. Bake slowly till fluffy, and browned below, then turn and brown on the other side. Serve buttered hot in a muffineer or on a hot dish lined with a folded napkin.

SCOTTISH CRUMPETS

¼ lb. flour
Pinch of salt
½ oz. butter
1¼ gills milk
¼ oz. bakers' yeast
1 teaspoon caster sugar
1 beaten egg

Sift flour and salt into a basin. Melt butter. Stir in milk. Heat till tepid then remove from stove. Cream yeast with the sugar. Stir milk into egg, then into the yeast. Strain slowly into flour. Beat till you have a smooth batter. Cover. Leave in a warm place till double its bulk in about ¾ hour. To bake : see English crumpets.

MUFFINS

Some muffins are baked on the girdle in rings or without them. Others are baked in the oven. In England, a muffin is a large round thick white scone. In Scotland, a muffin is more like the American baking powder " biscuit " and like this " biscuit " it is baked in the oven.

ENGLISH MUFFINS

10 oz. flour
1 teaspoon salt
2 teaspoons baking powder
2 oz. caster sugar
1 teaspoon bicarbonate of soda
1½ cups sour milk

Heat and grease a girdle or strong frying-pan. Sift flour, salt, baking powder and sugar into a basin. Stir soda in the milk until dissolved, Add to flour mixture, stirring until into a smooth batter. Place as many buttered or oiled muffin rings on the girdle as it will take. Fill rings half full of mixture. Bake slowly for about 7½ minutes, until well browned below, then turn with a palette knife and bake for about as long again. Line a hot dish with a folded table napkin, muffin cloth or doily. Pile muffins inside. (If using a muffineer, pour boiling water into lower container.) Cover and serve with butter.

To Serve in Traditional Manner : Pull muffins open to the depth of an inch all the way round. Toast muffins slowly on both sides. When ready, pull halves apart, and put together with plenty of butter. Serve at once.

YORKSHIRE PIKELETS

½ lb. flour
2 oz. caster sugar
1 saltspoon salt
Buttermilk as required
1 teaspoon bicarbonate of soda
½ gill boiling water

Sift flour, sugar and salt into a basin. Gradually stir in about ¼ pint of buttermilk, just enough to make a thick batter. Dissolve soda in the boiling water. Stir into mixture. To bake, pour from a tablespoon in rounds on to a hot girdle or frying-pan, well greased with melted lard, keeping the rounds a little apart. Fry until brown below and bubbles form on top, then turn and fry on other sides. Serve buttered hot. *Yield :* About 16 pikelets.

OVEN SCONES AND TEA CAKES

In Great Britain oven scones and tea cakes are seldom seen except on the tea table. In Canada and the United States, simple oven scones, known there as " baking powder biscuits," are equally at home on the breakfast and dinner tables. Unlike many of our scones, they are nearly always served hot.

BAKING POWDER BISCUITS

BASIC RECIPE :
½ lb. flour
2 teaspoons baking powder
½ teaspoon salt
2 oz. butter or margarine
About ¼ pint milk

Sift dry ingredients into a basin. Rub in the fat. Stir in as much milk as is required to make a soft dough free from stickiness. Turn quickly on to a lightly floured board. Knead gently but quickly, then roll out with a floured rolling pin as lightly as possible into a round from ½ to ¾ inch in thickness, according to taste. In the North of the United States, they are made thicker than in the South. Cut with a floured cutter into rounds, 2 inches across. Place about ½ inch apart on a greased baking sheet. Bake in a very hot oven, 450° F., for about 12 minutes. *Yield :* 1 dozen " biscuits."

Cream Baking Powder Biscuits : Sift 1 rounded dessertspoon caster sugar with the ingredients. Omit fat and sweet milk. Substitute about 1½ gills cream for milk.

Walnut Baking Powder Biscuits : Stir in 3 oz. chopped walnuts before milk.

Wholemeal Baking Powder Biscuits : Substitute ¼ lb. of wholemeal flour for the same amount of flour. Use only 1½ oz. fat.

BARLEY CREAM SCONES

¼ lb. barley flour
¼ lb. flour
½ teaspoon salt
3 teaspoons baking powder
2 teaspoons caster sugar
2 oz. butter
2 eggs
About 2 tablespoons cream

Sift flours, salt, baking powder and sugar into a basin. Rub in butter. Beat eggs and 2 tablespoons of cream. Add to dry ingredients, using more cream if necessary so as to get a soft dry dough. Pat out lightly on a floured board, then roll into a round ¾ inch thick. Cut into rounds about 2½ inches across. Brush lightly with milk.

Dredge with caster sugar. Bake a little apart on a greased baking sheet in a hot oven, 450° F., for about ¼ hour.

DEVONSHIRE SPLITS

½ lb. flour
¼ teaspoon salt
½ oz. butter
1¼ gills milk
¼ oz. bakers' yeast
¾ teaspoon caster sugar

Sift flour and salt into a basin. Heat butter and milk till fat is melted, then leave till tepid. Beat yeast in a slightly warm basin with the sugar till creamy. Make a hollow in centre of flour. Stir fat into yeast and sugar, then into flour. Mix lightly to a soft dough. Cover with a cloth. Stand in a warm place till double its bulk—in about ½ hour. Turn on to a floured board. Knead till smooth. Pinch off equal-sized small portions. Shape each lightly into a round about ½ inch thick. Brush with milk. Place close together on a greased baking tin. Bake in a hot oven, 475° F., for about ¼ hour. Remove to a rack. Cool slightly. Break apart. *Yield :* 8 splits.

To Serve Devonshire Splits : When cold, halve. Spread each half thinly with butter, then with strawberry jam. Top with whipped cream, flavoured with vanilla essence to taste.

PINWHEEL SCONES

BASIC RECIPE :
½ lb. flour
3 teaspoons baking powder
¾ teaspoon salt
1½ oz. butter
¾ cup milk

Sift dry ingredients into a basin. Rub butter into flour mixture. Make a hollow in the centre. Pour in milk quickly. Stir quickly until the flour is all moistened. Turn on to a floured board. Knead for ¼ minute. Roll into an oblong, ½ inch thick. Brush with creamed butter to within ½ inch of edge. Roll up like a Swiss roll. Cut into slices ¾ inch thick. Place side by side, a little apart, on a greased baking sheet. Bake in a hot oven, 450° F., for about ¼ hour. *Yield :* About 14 scones.

Butterscotch : Cream ¼ lb. butter with ¾ cup light brown sugar. Spread two-thirds of this on the dough to within ½ inch of edge. Roll up. Spread remainder of butter and sugar on a shallow layer cake or pie tin, 9 inches across. Brush the sides of each pinwheel with melted butter. Arrange side by side on tin, cut side downwards but close together. Bake as described.

TUTTI-FRUITTI : Follow basic recipe. Spread dough after buttering with ½ cup chopped raisins or cleaned currants, 1½ tablespoons minced citron peel, and ¼ teaspoon ground cinnamon.

WHOLEMEAL SCONES

½ lb. flour
1 teaspoon salt
¾ teaspoon bicarbonate of soda
3 oz. butter
½ lb. wholemeal flour
1 tablespoon caster sugar
Milk as required

Sift flour, salt and soda into a basin. Rub in butter. Stir in wholemeal flour and sugar. Mix to a soft dough with milk as required. Turn on to a floured board. Divide in two equal portions. Roll each into a round about 1 inch thick. Mark a deep cross on back of each with a floured knife. Place each in a greased sandwich tin. Bake in a moderate oven, 350° F., for about 20 minutes until light brown. Break each round into four, and cool on a wire rack. Serve with butter and honey. If smaller ones are wanted, mark each scone into 8. *Yield :* 8 or 16 scones.

NORFOLK TEACAKES

½ lb. flour
2 oz. caster sugar
Pinch of salt
2 oz. butter
2 oz. sultanas
½ oz. currants
1 teaspoon baking powder
2 beaten eggs

Sift flour, sugar and salt into a basin. Rub in butter with the tips of the fingers, then stir in cleaned sultanas, currants and baking powder. Add eggs to the dry ingredients and milk as required to make a soft dough. Turn on to a floured board. Roll to about ¾ inch thickness. Cut into rounds. Bake in buttered tins, ¾ inch apart, in a fairly hot oven, 450° F., for about 15 minutes. Split and spread with butter. Serve hot.

SALLY LUNN

¾ lb. flour
½ teaspoon salt
1½ oz. butter
Fully ¼ pint tepid milk
½ oz. bakers' yeast
1½ oz. caster sugar
1 beaten egg

Grease two cake tins, about 5 inches across and 2½ inches deep. Heat flour slightly, then sift with salt into a basin. Melt butter. Add milk. Remove from heat. Beat yeast and sugar to a cream. When the liquid is tepid, stir into yeast mixture with the egg. Make a hollow in the centre of the flour. Pour in liquid. Mix and knead into a light dough, adding more tepid milk if required. Divide in two equal portions. Knead each slightly on a lightly floured board, then place tins in the oven for a moment or two till warm, before adding dough. Cover. Stand in a warm place to rise to double their height—when the dough should reach the top of the tins. Bake in a fairly hot oven, 425° F., for about 25 minutes. Brush with melted butter before removing from oven, or use equal quantity of caster sugar and milk. Cut in 2 or 3 slices crosswise. Toast and butter, and serve in their original shape.

YORKSHIRE TEACAKES

2 lb. flour
6 oz. butter
5 oz. caster sugar
½ lb. cleaned sultanas
¼ lb. cleaned currants
½ gill warm water
1 oz. bakers' yeast
2½ gills tepid milk
2 beaten eggs
½ teaspoon salt

Sift flour into a basin. Rub in butter. Stir in sugar, sultanas, and currants. Stir water by degrees into the yeast, and when dissolved, add milk, eggs, and salt. Mix into flour and fruit with a wooden spoon. Cover with a clean cloth. Stand in a warm place for about 1¼ hours until dough has almost doubled its height. Turn on to a lightly-floured board. Divide into equal-sized small pieces. Shape with floured hands into round balls. Roll to an inch thickness. Place a little apart on a greased baking tin or sheet. Brush with beaten egg mixed with a tablespoon of milk. Stand in a warm place until half-risen, then bake in a fairly hot oven, 450° F., for about 15 minutes. This quantity should make 15 teacakes. When cold, store in a closed tin, and split, heat and butter when required.

OATCAKES

Oatcakes are made of oatmeal in thin rounds about 8 inches across. When rolled to ½ inch thickness, they are called " Bannocks." Sometimes oatcakes are cut in four quarters, or " farls " before baking. An implement such as a spatula is required to lift the oatcakes from the board to the girdle without breaking them.

HINTS ON MAKING OATCAKES

1. Use medium oatmeal.
2. Handle as quickly as possible.
3. Sprinkle pastry board with plenty of oatmeal before rolling out.
4. Bake in oven on a greased baking sheet if unable to cook on a girdle, or in a strong frying-pan.

OATCAKES

¼ lb. oatmeal
Pinch of salt
1 saltspoon bicarbonate of soda
1 teaspoon butter, dripping, bacon or poultry fat
Hot water as required

Place oatmeal in a basin. Stir in salt and soda. Melt fat. Make a hole in the centre of the meal. Add fat with as much hot water as is required to make a stiff paste. Dredge pastry board with fine oatmeal. Turn paste on to board. Knead into a smooth ball. Roll out as thin as a penny, rubbing with fine oatmeal occasionally. Cut into four triangles. Turn each over and rub other side with fine oatmeal. Cook one side on a hot girdle until the edges curl, then toast the other in front of a glowing fire, or finish off under a grill. Cool on a wire rack.

BERE OR BARLEY MEAL BANNOCKS

1 lb. bere or barley meal
¼ lb. flour
½ teaspoon salt
Buttermilk as required
1½ teaspoons bicarbonate of soda

Place the meal in a basin. Sift flour with salt and add. Stir until blended. Pour 1 pint of buttermilk into a small jug. Add the soda. Stir until it effervesces, then add to meal mixture. Stir in a bare ¼ pint additional buttermilk, just enough to give you a stiff dough. Turn at once on to a lightly-floured board. Roll out lightly into a large round, about ½ inch thick. Cut into rounds the size of a small meat plate, 8-9 inches across. Bake slowly on a hot girdle until brown below, then turn and brown on the other side. *Yield :* 16 bannocks.

WAFFLES

A good waffle is a crisp, golden-brown, honeycomb wafer about 1/3 of an inch thick. Made from batter, it is cooked in a special waffle iron, either electrically heated, or made for using over a coal or gas fire.

To Temper a New Waffle Iron : Heat until warm, in about 5 minutes, unless instructions given with iron are different. Brush all over the inner surface with melted butter or lard. Pour in enough batter to fill the whole of the surface. Close. Bake till brown when steam will no longer come from the sides, then remove and throw away this first waffle. If any surplus grease is floating in the hollow, wipe off with a clean dry cloth.

To Prepare Iron for Cooking : It should not be necessary to grease again if iron is properly tempered. Merely heat thoroughly before pouring in batter. If you find, after testing, a little batter in iron that sticks, brush with clarified butter or lard, very slightly between each baking.

To Test Heat of Iron : Preheat for 8 minutes unless otherwise instructed. If not certain that iron is hot enough for use, pour a drop of cold water into one of the hollows. It is ready to use if the water boils quickly and turns into a small ball. If it fizzles violently the moment it touches the metal, the iron is too hot. Switch off if electric, or remove from coal or gas and test again.

WAFFLES (Gaufres, Américaine)

BASIC RECIPE :
½ lb. flour
2 teaspoons baking powder
1 oz. caster sugar
½ teaspoon salt
2 separated eggs
2 cups milk
3 tablespoons melted butter

Sift flour. (If a rather short waffle is wanted, remove 2 tablespoons of flour and substitute cornflour.) Sift again with baking powder, sugar and salt. (If a crisp waffle is wanted, omit sugar.) Beat egg whites till stiff. Beat egg yolks. Gradually stir in milk, then melted butter. (Don't spare the fat. Waffles will be tough if you use too little fat.) Make a hollow in the centre of flour. Add liquid, and beat quickly, but only enough to blend. Fold in egg whites, this time barely blending. Have iron heated ready. Gently pour the batter into a jug. Pour about 1 tablespoon or a little more of the batter on to the centre of each section, enough to cover each compartment to within an inch of edge. You need enough batter to run over surface, but do not fill up to the rim, or the waffles will not be able to rise sufficiently, and some of the batter will ooze out at the sides while cooking. As soon as you have added batter, close the iron quickly. Cook till the steam stops coming from the sides, in 2-3 minutes. If cooking over a gas ring or coal fire, turn iron at half time. When ready, the waffle should be golden brown and crisp, and easy to remove with a fork or the point of a knife. *Yield* : 6 waffles.

To Serve : Serve as soon as cooked. The ideal way to prepare waffles is to use an electric iron and cook them at the table. Serve hot with butter and maple syrup, or with fried bacon, or use as canapés for creamed savoury luncheon or supper dishes, fried mushrooms or grilled kidneys.

CHEESE : Stir 1 cup grated Cheddar cheese into the batter before folding in egg whites. If liked, sift ¼ teaspoon dry mustard with the flour.

HAM : Sprinkle 1 tablespoon minced boiled ham over the batter in iron before closing and baking.

SPICED : Sift 1 rounded teaspoon ground ginger and ¼ teaspoon mixed spice with the flour mixture, and follow variation to basic recipe.

Buns and Tea Bread

Buns are generally baked on a baking sheet, or shallow baking tin. Grease sheet or tin, then prepare the dough. It should be light, but firm enough to hold its shape when formed into buns. Place about an inch apart to allow for slight spreading. When ready, dredge with vanilla icing or caster sugar. Buns made of a very moist dough should be baked in greased bun tins.

BATH BUNS

1 lb. sifted flour
6 oz. butter
Pinch of salt
1 oz. bakers' yeast
½ teaspoon caster sugar
¼ pint milk
4 eggs
¼ lb. caster sugar
2 oz. mixed peel

Sift flour into a basin. Rub in butter. Add salt. Cream the yeast with ½ teaspoon caster sugar. Heat milk till tepid. Stir into yeast. Beat eggs. Add to yeast mixture. Stir into flour. When blended, cover basin. Place in a warm place till dough rises to double its size—in about 1 hour. Stir in sugar. Mince peel and add. Shape into balls of equal size. Place 1 inch apart on a greased baking sheet. Stand in a warm place for about ¼ hour until they are half as big again. Brush with warm water or beaten egg, and sprinkle thickly with crushed loaf sugar. Bake in a fairly hot oven, 425° F., for about 20 minutes. *Yield :* 10-12 buns.

To Vary : Follow basic recipe, allowing 5 oz. caster sugar, but add 3 oz. sultanas and the grated rind of ½ lemon.

694

CHELSEA BUNS

4 oz. butter
1/4 pint milk
1/4 lb. caster sugar
1/2 oz. bakers' yeast
2 beaten eggs
1 lb. sifted flour
3 oz. cleaned currants
1 oz. candied peel

Melt butter. Add all the milk, except 2 tablespoons, then stir in 3 oz. of the sugar. Remove from heat when sugar is dissolved. Beat yeast to a cream with remainder of milk. Add eggs. Stir till blended. Sift flour. Stir in butter mixture and the creamed yeast and eggs. Beat till blended. Cover. Place in a warm place to rise till double its bulk. Turn on to a lightly-floured pastry board. Knead for a moment or two, then roll out into an oblong about 1/3 inch thick, and about 12 × 8 inches long. Brush with butter or lard, creamed or melted. Sprinkle with remainder of sugar, currants and peel. Roll up like a Swiss roll. Cut into 12 slices of equal thickness. Place side by side, cut sides uppermost, in a greased oblong tin. Allow to rise in a warm place for 1/2 hour. Bake in a fairly hot oven, 425° F., for about 25 minutes. Glaze when almost ready. Remove to a wire rack. Leave till cold before tearing apart. *Yield :* 12 buns.

COFFEE BUNS

2 oz. butter
1/2 lb. flour
1 teaspoon baking powder
1/4 teaspoon salt
2 oz. light brown sugar
2 oz. cleaned currants or ground almonds
1/4 teaspoon vanilla essence
3/4 teaspoon coffee essence
1 beaten egg
Milk as required

Rub butter into flour. Stir in baking powder, salt, brown sugar and currants or almonds. Add vanilla and coffee essence to the egg. Stir into dry ingredients with enough milk to make a stiff paste. Arrange in 8 rocky rounds, about an inch apart, on greased baking sheet. Bake in a fairly hot oven, 425° F., for about 20 minutes. *Yield:* 8 buns.

CREAM COOKIES

1 1/2 lb. flour
3 oz. butter
3/4 pint milk
1 oz. bakers' yeast
1 teaspoon salt
2 eggs
6 oz. caster sugar

Sift flour into a heated basin. Make a hollow in the centre. Melt butter. Add milk. Heat till tepid. Beat yeast to a cream with the salt. Stir into liquid. Strain into the hollow in flour. Beat eggs till fluffy, and add as well. Beat flour into the liquid until you get a smooth, light dough. Cover. Stand in a warm place till double its size, then beat in the sugar and additional heated flour, until you have a stiff dough free from stickiness. Divide in small portions, about 2 oz. each. With floured hands, quickly shape into rounds. Place, about 1 inch apart, on a warmed, greased baking sheet, dredged with flour. Stand in a warm place till they are half as big again. Bake in a fairly hot oven, 425° F., for about 20 minutes. Glaze. Cool. Split and fill with whipped cream, flavoured vanilla. *Yield :* About 1 1/2 dozen.

695

HOT CROSS BUNS

2 oz. bakers' yeast
Tepid milk as required
2 oz. unsalted butter
1 lb. sifted flour
Pinch of salt
2 oz. minced candied peel
1/4 lb. cleaned currants
2 oz. caster sugar
1/4 oz. mixed spice
1 saltspoon ground mace

Crumble yeast into a small heated basin. Cover it with 2 or 3 tablespoons of tepid milk. Rub butter into the flour. Add salt, peel, currants, sugar and spices. Stir the yeast into a smooth paste. Heat 3/4 pint milk till tepid. Stir into the soaked yeast, then strain into a hollow in the flour. When blended, work into a smooth soft dough with your hands. Turn on to a floured board. Divide in 16 equal-sized pieces. Shape into rounds. Place an inch apart on a floured baking sheet. Stand in a warm place till they are half as big again. Mark a cross rather deeply on top of each with the back of a knife, or cross them with bars of shortcrust. Bake in a hot oven, 450° F., for about 1/4 hour. Glaze and return to the oven for a moment or two to dry. *Yield :* About 16 buns.

LONDON BUNS

1 lb. flour
3 oz. caster sugar
1/2 oz. bakers' yeast
2 oz. butter
1/2 pint tepid milk
3/4 oz. minced candied orange
    peel

Sift flour and sugar into a basin, reserving a teaspoon of the sugar. Cream this with the yeast. Melt butter into a saucepan. Add milk. Heat till tepid. Stir in yeast. Make a hollow in the centre of the flour mixture. Pour in liquid and peel. Mix with a wooden spoon into a dough. Cover and rise in a warm place for about 2 hours. Divide in 12 equal portions. Knead and shape into round buns. Place an inch apart on a greased baking sheet. Stand in a warm place to rise till half as big again. Bake in a hot oven, 450° F., for about 1/4 hour. Glaze with equal quantity of caster sugar and beaten egg. *Yield:* 12 buns.

RASPBERRY BUNS

6 oz. flour
Pinch of salt
2 oz. butter
2 oz. caster sugar
1 teaspoon baking powder
1 egg
Milk as required
About 1 tablespoon raspberry
    jam

Sift flour and salt into a basin. Rub in butter. Stir in sugar and baking powder. Beat egg. Stir in 2 tablespoons milk. Add to dry ingredients with enough additional milk to make a stiffish dough. Divide into 6 equal portions. With floured hands, roll each into a ball. Place 2 inches apart on a greased baking sheet. Make a hole with a thimble wrapped in greaseproof paper, on the top of each. Push in a teaspoon of jam. Wet the edges of the hole and pinch them together. Brush lightly with milk. Dredge with caster sugar. Bake in a hot oven, 450° F., for about 15 minutes. When ready, buns should crack, and the jam show through. *Yield :* 6 buns.

ROCK CAKES

BASIC RECIPE :
½ lb. flour
2 teaspoons baking powder
1 teaspoon ground cinnamon
2-3 oz. butter
2-3 oz. caster sugar
¼ lb. cleaned currants
1 egg
¾ gill milk

Brush a baking sheet with melted lard. Sift flour, baking powder, and cinnamon into a basin. Rub in butter. Add sugar, and currants. Beat egg. Add milk. Make a hollow in centre of dry ingredients with the back of a wooden spoon. Add liquid. Mix to a dough. Divide into 15 equal portions. Lift each on to a baking sheet, arranging them 1½ inches apart. Shape into rough heaps with 2 forks. Bake in a hot oven, 450° F., for 10-15 minutes, or in a very hot oven, 475° F., for about 12 minutes. *Yield :* About 12 rock cakes.

CORNISH : Double quantity of butter and sugar. Add 2 more oz. of currants, 1 oz. minced candied orange peel, and grated rind of 1 lemon. Dredge with caster sugar before baking.

NUT : Omit currants. Add 1 cup chopped walnuts and ½ teaspoon vanilla essence.

TEA BREAD

Under this title, I am grouping small cup cakes baked in bun tins and patty tins, gem tins as the Americans call them, doughnuts, pâtisserie, and other cakes which are too few to classify.

To Prepare Tins : Brush insides of tins, usually 2½ inches in diameter and ¾ inch deep, with a pastry brush dipped in melted, clarified or unsalted fat. To make certain that they will not stick, dredge lightly with flour, and shake until coated, then toss out any superfluous flour. If preferred, cooking oil can be used, but the tins must be well drained before filling them two-thirds full with the mixture. If liked, paper baking cases can be used in place of tins. They require neither greasing nor oiling. *Place each in a bun tin before filling.*

To Bake : Bake all small cakes which need a high temperature near the top of the oven, and others that require a more moderate temperature just about the centre. Heat oven, unless otherwise instructed under each recipe, to between 375°-400° F. Most of the varieties will take from 15-20 minutes at this temperature. When ready, cool slightly to allow for shrinkage, then shake gently on to a wire rack. Place right side up. Dredge with sifted icing sugar of any flavour preferred, or ice when cold, and decorate to taste. Store in a tightly-closed tin.

CUP CAKES

QUICK MIX

If you keep a supply of the following mixtures in an air-tight tin, you can turn out cup cakes much quicker. Store in a dry cupboard.

1 lb. flour
2 teaspoons baking powder
½ teaspoon salt
6 oz. caster sugar

Sift flour with baking powder and salt. Stir in caster sugar. To mix batter, rub in butter or margarine, 4-6 oz. according to taste, then stir in flavouring and fruits or nuts to taste, and moisten with eggs and milk.

CUP CAKES (Petits Gâteaux)

BASIC RECIPE :
¼ lb. butter
½ lb. caster sugar
7 oz. flour
1½ teaspoons baking powder
¼ teaspoon salt
3 eggs
½ cup milk
¾ teaspoon vanilla essence

Beat butter till softened. Gradually beat in sugar. Beat till creamy. Sift flour with baking powder and salt. Beat eggs. Add milk. Stir flour and liquid alternately into butter and sugar, beating well between each addition, then beat in vanilla essence. Three-quarters fill greased patty tins. Bake in a moderately hot oven, 375° F., for about 20 minutes. Dredge with caster sugar. *Yield :* 1½ dozen cakes.

BUTTERFLY CAKES : When cakes are cold, remove a thin slice from the top of each. Pipe cream over the tops. Halve each slice and place so that the edges of the slices stand up like the wings of a butterfly. Pipe cream across the bend.

COCONUT : Stir ½ cup desiccated coconut and the grated rind of ½ lemon into batter after the flour.

STRAWBERRY : Place a teaspoon of batter in each patty tin. Cover with a teaspoon of strawberry jam. Add enough batter to three-quarters fill.

TUTTI-FRUITTI : Add 1 oz. minced glacé cherries, and 1 oz. minced citron peel.

COBURG CAKES (Gâteaux, Coburg)

2 oz. butter
2 oz. caster sugar
2 oz. treacle
1 beaten egg
¼ pint milk
1 teaspoon mixed spice
1 teaspoon ground cinnamon
½ teaspoon ground ginger
½ teaspoon bicarbonate of soda
6 oz. flour

Cream butter and sugar. Mix treacle with egg and milk. Sift spices and soda with flour. Add alternately with egg mixture to butter and sugar. Mix well. Lay half an almond in the bottom of each greased patty tin. Place 1 tablespoon of the mixture in each tin. Bake in a fairly hot oven, 425° F., for about 10 minutes. Dredge with caster sugar. *Yield:* About 15 or 16 cakes.

CUPID CAKES (Gâteaux à l'Amour)

1 oz. glacé cherries
1 oz. citron peel
3 oz. butter
3 oz. caster sugar
2 beaten eggs
¼ lb. flour
¼ teaspoon baking powder
½ teaspoon vanilla essence

Chop cherries and citron peel. Beat butter until softened. Gradually beat in sugar. Beat until creamy. Beat eggs. Sift flour with baking powder. Add flour and eggs alternately to the fat and sugar, beating between each addition. Stir in cherries, citron peel and vanilla essence. Mix lightly. Three-quarter fill greased patty tins. Bake in a moderately hot oven, 375° F., for about 20 minutes. Cool on a wire rack. Spread with rum glacé icing. Decorate with silver balls, or with a cherry cut like a flower on top of each, and angelica leaves and stalks. *Yield :* About 12 cakes.

FAIRY CAKES (Gâteaux, Eugénie)

2 oz. butter
2 oz. caster sugar
2 oz. flour
2 oz. cornflour
½ teaspoon baking powder
1 or 2 beaten eggs
Milk as required
Lemon essence to taste

Cream butter and sugar. Sieve flour and cornflour with the baking powder. Stir into fat and sugar alternately with egg and sufficient milk to make a rather soft consistency. Stir in essence. Grease patty tins. Dust with equal quantity of flour and caster sugar. Half-fill with the batter. Bake in a fairly hot oven, 425° F., for about 10 minutes. Decorate with fondant icing and glacé cherries, or with water icing and violet petals. *Yield :* About 10 cakes.

MELTING MOMENTS (Gâteaux Chiffonés)

6 oz. butter
¼ lb. caster sugar
2 beaten eggs
6 oz. cornflour
2 oz. flour
1½ teaspoons baking powder
1 saltspoon salt
1 tablespoon milk
½ teaspoon vanilla essence

Beat butter till softened. Gradually beat in sugar. Beat till fluffy. Add eggs. Beat till blended. Stir in cornflour. Sift flour with baking powder and salt. Add with milk and vanilla essence. Three-quarters fill greased patty tins. Bake in a moderately hot oven, 375° F., for 15-20 minutes. Cool on a wire rack. Dredge with vanilla icing sugar. *Yield:* About 2 dozen cakes.

QUEEN CAKES (Gâteaux à la Reine)

4 oz. butter
4 oz. caster sugar
2 eggs
¼ lb. flour
½ teaspoon baking powder
1½ oz. currants
Grated rind of 1 lemon
2 tablespoons milk

Beat butter and sugar to a cream. Beat eggs. Sift flour with baking powder and add flour and egg alternately to butter and sugar. Stir in washed and dried currants, and grated lemon rind. Add milk. Beat mixture well. Half-fill buttered patty tins. Bake in a fairly hot oven, 400° F., for about 12 minutes. Dredge with caster sugar. *Yield :* About 18 cakes.

SAND CAKES (Gâteaux Sablés)

¼ lb. butter
3 oz. caster sugar
5 oz. cornflour
2 beaten eggs
½ teaspoon baking powder
Dash of vanilla essence

Beat butter and sugar to a cream. Sift cornflour. Stir into butter mixture, then add eggs gradually. Stir in baking powder and vanilla essence. Three-quarters fill greased patty tins. Bake in a moderately hot oven, 375° F., for about 20 minutes. Dredge with caster sugar. *Yield:* About 14 or 15 cakes.

ALMOND SLICES (Tranches d'Amandes)

¼ lb. butter
5 oz. caster sugar

Beat butter until softened. Gradually beat in sugar. Beat until fluffy. Stir in egg alternately

699

2 well-beaten eggs
5 oz. flour
¼ teaspoon baking powder
2 oz. ground almonds
Milk if required

with the flour sifted with baking powder, small amounts at a time. When blended, stir in almonds and a little milk if necessary. Spread in a shallow baking tin, 7 by 11 by 2 inches. Bake in a hot oven, 450° F., for 15 minutes. When cool, cut in squares. Dredge with vanilla icing sugar. *Yield :* About 3 dozen.

BROWNIES

3 oz. butter
3 oz. chocolate
½ lb. caster sugar
2 well-beaten eggs
2 oz. flour
¼ teaspoon baking powder
¼ teaspoon salt
1 cup chopped walnuts
¾ teaspoon vanilla essence

Melt butter and chocolate slowly until blended. Stir sugar into the eggs. Add chocolate mixture. Stir until blended. Sift flour with baking powder and salt. Stir into egg mixture, then stir in walnuts and vanilla essence. Spread evenly in a greased square baking tin, 8 by 8 by 2 inches. Bake in a moderate oven, 350° F., for 25-30 minutes. Leave until cool. Cut into fingers or squares. *Yield :* About 16.

CHINESE CHEWS (Tranches à la Chinoise)

2 eggs
½ lb. caster sugar
2 oz. flour
½ teaspoon baking powder
Pinch of salt
1 cup chopped dates
1 cup chopped walnuts

Beat eggs until light. Stir in sugar. Beat well. Sift flour with baking powder and salt. Stir into egg mixture. When blended, stir in dates and nuts. Pour into a greased baking tin, 9 inches square. Bake in a fairly slow oven, 325° F., for about 25 minutes. When cool, cut into bars or squares. Roll in vanilla icing sugar. *Yield:* 18 bars.

FRUIT FINGERS (Tranches de Fruits)

8 oz. shortcrust
3 oz. picked sultanas
3 oz. cleaned currants
2 oz. light brown sugar
½ teaspoon ground cinnamon
½ teaspoon ground cloves
2 tablespoons melted butter
Beaten egg and caster sugar as required

Divide shortcrust equally in two. Roll each piece out on a lightly floured board to a square ¼ inch thick. Mix sultanas, currants, sugar, cinnamon, cloves and melted butter. Spread over one square to within ½ inch of the edge. Brush round bare edge with cold water. Lay other square on top. Press down lightly. Brush with beaten egg. Bake in a hot oven, 450° F., till pastry is crisp and golden in about 15 minutes. Dredge with caster sugar. Cut into 20 fingers. Cool on a wire cake rack. *Yield;* 20 fingers.

NOUGAT FINGERS

PASTRY:
2 oz. butter
¼ lb. flour

Rub butter lightly into flour sifted with the salt. Stir in the sugar and almonds. Mix to a light smooth dough with milk. Knead lightly. Roll

Pinch of salt
1 oz. caster sugar
1 tablespoon ground almonds
Milk as required
FILLING:
3 oz. desiccated coconut
1½ oz. caster sugar
1 beaten egg
3 or 4 drops orange juice

into an oblong about ¼ inch thick. Cut into strips 3 inches long and 1 inch wide. Mix coconut with sugar, egg and orange juice. Spread over top. Bake in a moderate oven, 350° F., for about ½ hour.

FRIED CAKES

Fried cakes can be made either with a baking powder or a yeast dough. If fat is used for frying, heat to between 360° F. and 375° F. If oil is used, heat to between 375° and 385° F. The fat or oil should be hot enough to cook a cube of bread an inch square, in 60 seconds.

To Fry Cakes: Place one or two at a time into enough fat to cover them. When they come to the top and have browned below, turn them to allow to brown on the other side. When ready, lift with a skimmer. Let the fat drain back into pan, then drain on absorbent paper.

CHOUX RINGS

Follow recipe for Choux Pastry. See Pastry Section. With a forcing syringe or bag, fitted with a suitable tube, force rings out on to a baking sheet covered with buttered paper, then fry immediately, one or two at a time, in hot fat or oil until crisp and brown. Drain on absorbent paper. Dredge with sifted icing sugar. Serve at once.

CRULLERS

1½ lb. flour
1 oz. bakers' yeast
1 teaspoon sugar
1 pint scalded milk
¼ lb. butter
6 oz. caster sugar
¾ teaspoon salt
Grated rind of ½ lemon
½ teaspoon grated nutmeg
1 egg or 2 egg yolks

Heat a basin and add flour. Stir the yeast in a heated cup with the teaspoon of sugar until liquefied. When milk is tepid, stir half into the yeast. Cover and stand in a warm place till bubbles form on top. Stir the butter, sugar, salt, lemon rind and nutmeg into remainder of the scalded milk. When tepid, stir in beaten egg or yolks. Stir in yeast and a little of the flour, then knead in remainder of flour until you have a smooth elastic dough. Cover closely. Stand in a warm place to rise until double its size. Pat and roll to ½ inch thickness. Cut in fingers 8 inches long and ¾ inch wide. Cover and allow to rise in a warm place till double their size. Make into cork screws by twisting the ends in opposite directions, then pinch ends together to form rings. Fry, drain and dip in sugar.

DOUGHNUTS (Pets de Nonnes)

BASIC RECIPE:
¾ lb. flour

Sift flour and salt into a basin. Make a well in the centre. Place the yeast in a small basin. Add

Pinch of salt
¾ oz. bakers' yeast
1 teaspoon caster sugar
1 oz. butter
1½ gills milk
1 beaten egg

sugar. Stir till they liquefy. Melt butter in a saucepan. Add milk. Heat till tepid, then stir into yeast. Stir into egg. Strain into the well in the flour. Mix together with a wooden spoon and beat well. Cover. Stand in a warm place to rise for 2 hours, then turn on to a lightly-floured board. Knead lightly. Divide into 18 equal-sized portions. Shape each into a smooth ball, then flatten them on the top. Drop a little jam on the centre, then shape into balls again, covering jam completely with dough. Place a little apart on a lightly-floured baking sheet. Stand in a warm place till half as big again. Drop one or two at a time into the hot fat or oil. Fry till both sides are golden brown (about 10 minutes.) Drain on absorbent paper. Coat thickly with caster sugar, or use cinnamon sugar, allowing 1 teaspoon ground cinnamon to 2 tablespoons sugar. Serve hot or cold. *Yield :* 18 doughnuts.

To Vary :

1. Cool slightly. Dip in water icing, then in desiccated coconut.

2. Dip in water icing flavoured with rum, then in chopped blanched pistachio nuts.

3. Use apricot jam, flavoured rum, to fill doughnuts. Dip in water icing.

DOUGHNUT PIES : Roll dough ½ inch thick. Cut into rounds 2½ inches across. Place a heaped teaspoon of apricot, raspberry or strawberry jam on the centre of half the rounds. Brush edges with slightly beaten egg white, and cover each with another round. Press edges lightly together. Allow to rise, then fry.

DOUGHNUT RINGS : Roll out dough ½ inch thick. Cut into rings with a round or fluted cutter, then remove the centres with your smallest cutter, or a thimble kept for the purpose. Fry only for 7 minutes. Dredge, after draining, with vanilla icing sugar.

BAKING POWDER DOUGHNUTS (Pets de Nonnes)

1¼ lb. flour
3 teaspoons baking powder
½ teaspoon grated nutmeg
½ teaspoon salt
½ lb. caster sugar
1 beaten egg
3 tablespoons melted butter
1 pint milk

Sift flour, baking powder, nutmeg and salt into a basin. Stir in sugar, egg and butter mixed with the milk. Mix to a light dough. Turn on to a floured board. Roll to ½ inch thickness. Cut into rounds with a doughnut cutter, or a round cutter 2½ inches in diameter. Fry in hot fat or oil till both sides are golden, (about 8 minutes).

Drain on absorbent paper. Roll in lemon or vanilla icing sugar.

CALIFORNIAN ORANGE DROPS (Gâteaux à la California)

1 oz. butter
1 tablespoon grated orange rind
1 tablespoon orange juice
2 teaspoons lemon juice
1 can sweetened condensed milk
½ cup chopped walnuts
⅓ cup cornflakes

Heat fat till soft, then stir in orange rind and fruit juices. Gradually stir in condensed milk, then walnuts and flakes. Drop from a teaspoon on to a dry baking sheet, 2 inches apart. Bake in a moderate oven, 350° F., for about 10 minutes. *Yield:* Nearly 3 dozen.

MADELEINES

2 oz. butter
2 oz. caster sugar
2 eggs
3 oz. sifted flour
¼ teaspoon baking powder
About ½ gill milk

Grease 6 small castle pudding tins. Beat butter until softened. Gradually beat in sugar. Beat until fluffy. Add eggs, one at a time. Beat until light and creamy, in about 10 minutes. Sift flour with baking powder, and add with milk as required. (If the eggs are large, milk may not be necessary.) Fill tins three-quarters full. Bake in a fairly hot oven, 400° F., for about 20 minutes. Cool. Trim bottoms even. Brush with heated apricot jam. Roll in desiccated coconut. Place half a cherry on top of each, nestling in angelica leaves. *Yield:* 6.

MILLES FEUILLES (Vanilla Slices)

½ lb. puff pastry
Confectioner's custard
6 oz. glacé icing

Roll pastry out on a lightly floured board to ¼ inch thickness. Divide into fingers 2½ inches long and 1 inch wide. Bake in a hot oven, 500° F., until pastry is risen and set, then lower to moderate, 350° F., and bake until crisp and golden. When cool, pair with confectioner's custard. Decorate top with glacé icing, and chopped blanched pistachio nuts, or crystallized violets and pistachio nuts.

ROYAL MILLES FEUILLES : Sandwich fingers of baked thinly rolled puff pastry, in 3 or 4 layers, filling one with confectioner's custard, one with raspberry jam, and one with whipped cream.

SNOWBALLS

2 ozs. butter
¼ lb. caster sugar
1 egg
Grated rind ½ orange
¼ lb. sifted flour
1 teaspoon baking powder
Pinch of salt
2½ tablespoons orange juice
Fully 1 teaspoon lemon juice
2½ tablespoons water

Beat fat till softened. Gradually beat in sugar. Beat till fluffy. Beat in egg, then orange rind. Sift dry ingredients thrice. Add alternately with liquids to creamed mixture. Three-quarters fill small round deep bun tins. Bake in a moderately hot oven, 375° F., for about ¼ hour. Turn out on to a rack. When cold, smear glacé icing thinly over top and sides of each, then sprinkle with desiccated coconut. Place a tiny candle in each when firm, if liked. *Yield:* 9 or 10.

HINTS ON MAKING MERINGUES

1. Use cool fresh egg whites. and see that they are entirely free from egg yolk before starting to beat them.
2. Beat in a large bowl. They must be stiff enough so that they stand up in peaks before adding any sugar.
3. Place or pipe at least ½ inch apart on prepared baking sheet. They can also be shaped on a hard wood board, or in hollows in a meringue board, or

you can follow the Continental method :—Pipe mixture round and round wooden moulds, dipped in cold water, and drained and placed on a baking sheet covered with greased or lightly oiled greaseproof paper. Before baking meringues, except those cooked in hollows in a meringue board, dredge lightly with sifted caster or icing sugar.

4. To keep them white, bake in a very cool oven, 200° F., for about 3-3½ hours, depending on size. To make them biscuit-coloured, bake at 250° F. about 1 hour, or at 275° F., for about 45-50 minutes, depending on position in oven.

5. Remove meringues while warm unless otherwise instructed in recipe you are following. If some adhere to paper on baking sheet, draw paper off baking sheet on to a board covered with a wet cloth. Leave for a few moments, then with a spatula, gently ease meringues from paper to a wire rack.

MERINGUE SHELLS

BASIC RECIPE :
4 egg whites
¼ teaspoon salt
½ lb. caster sugar
½ teaspoon vanilla essence
FILLING :
¼-½ pint thick cream
1 saltspoon vanilla essence
1 dessertspoon caster sugar

Prepare the board or baking sheet. Beat egg whites until frothy. Sprinkle with the salt. Beat till stiff, but not dry, until mixture stands in peaks, when you should be able to turn basin upside down without any of the mixture falling out. Sift sugar. Gradually beat in half the sugar in this way : Sprinkle only 2 tablespoons at a time over the egg white, and beat thoroughly before adding next addition of sugar. When half the sugar is incorporated with the egg white, stir in vanilla or other essence, and colouring if desired. Now fold in remainder of sugar.

To Shape Meringues :

1. If oval cases are wanted, shape with 2 dessertspoons or tablespoons, according to size required. Dip one of the spoons into cold water. Shake well. Fill with the mixture. Dip a palette knife in cold water. Draw it first from one side then from the other over the mixture so as to coax it into a ridge along the top, and pointed at each end. Dip second spoon in cold water. Shake it and gently half scoop the mixture out of the first spoon, then slip it on to the board or baking sheet. It's necessary to let the first spoon help you in this so as to preserve the shape.

2. A real meringue board, is about 1½ inches thick with hollows the shape of an oval meringue in which to bake the mixture. Fill hollows then smooth along the top with a palette knife.

3. When you wish to have meringues shaped in spiral rounds, ovals, pyramids, or nests, use a forcing syringe or an icing bag made of a 14-inch square of cotton or greaseproof paper, with suitable tubes.

To Bake : Dredge lightly with caster sugar. Bake in a very slow oven, 250° F., for about 50 minutes, until meringues are crisp and dry in the centre. Slip off baking sheet or board with a palette knife, and press in the soft centres at once. If not perfectly dry in the inside, return to oven and leave with door slightly ajar, until dry. If baking in a hollowed-out board remove very carefully

CAKES
Petits Fours, made of Genoese Pastry. *See pages* 706-707.

CAKES

Russian Gateau. *See page* 730. Trifle in a Meringue Basket, and a Christmas Candle Cake, a marzipan candle, coated with scarlet royal icing in a round of butter sponge, coated with blue royal icing.

ey may break. They can be perfectly white when cooked properly, or
ill faintly coloured if preferred. *Yield :* About 2 dozen large shells, or about
zen small.

Serve: When cold, fill hollows with whipped cream, sweetened and
ured with vanilla essence. Pair if liked. Force stars of whipped cream over
g or sprinkle cream showing with chopped blanched pistachio nuts, walnuts,
ped toasted almonds, poppy seeds, or chocolate shot.

OCOLATE MERINGUES : Fold 1 cup grated sweet chocolate into mixture
re baking. If you want a more economical chocolate meringue, substitute
spoons cocoa for the chocolate, sieving it with the caster sugar.

FFEE MERINGUES : Fold 4 coffeespoons of coffee essence in gradually, a
at a time as you add the sugar.

MAKE A MERINGUE NEST OR NESTS : Make a round flat base for each nest,
her large, or individual. Pipe a double fancy border round of meringue.
lge lightly with caster sugar. Bake in a very slow oven, 250° F., until
and dry in the centre. Fill with fruit. Decorate if liked with roses of
ped cream.

KISSES

hese fragile morsels make a delicious accompaniment to ice cream. They
also suitable for serving with coffee or tea.

KISSES (BAISERS)

or full instructions on baking see " To Bake Meringues," page 704.

CHOCOLATE KISSES (Baisers de Chocolat)

whites
spoon salt
sifted icing sugar
aspoon baking powder
grated sweet chocolate
p chopped walnuts

Beat egg whites until frothy. Sprinkle with salt.
Beat until stiff. Slowly beat in sugar, 2 or 3
tablespoons at a time, then stir in baking powder.
Beat well. Fold in chocolate and nuts. Drop
1½ inches apart from a teaspoon on to a baking
sheet covered with rice paper. Bake in a slow
oven, 250° F., for about 50 minutes.

COCONUT KISSES (Baisers de Noix de Coco)

whites
p sifted icing sugar
ablespoons freshly grated
conut

Beat egg whites till stiff enough to hold their
shape but still shiny. Beat in 3 tablespoons
icing sugar, a tablespoon at a time, then lightly
fold in remainder and coconut. Drop from a
oon in mounds, 1½ inches apart, on to a greased baking sheet covered with
azed paper. Bake in a slow oven, 250° F., for about 50 minutes, the exact
depending on size of kisses.

MISTLETOE KISSES (Baisers à la Nöel)

4 egg whites
1 cup sieved icing sugar
1 oz. minced dates
1 oz. minced walnuts
1 oz. preserved ginger
1 oz. glacé pineapple

Beat egg whites till very stiff. Gradually stir in ¾ cup sugar. Beat till mixture holds its shape. Fold in remainder of sugar, then stir in dates, walnuts and minced ginger and pineapple. Drop mixture from tip of spoon in small piles on to a buttered baking sheet covered with unglazed paper, an inch apart. Bake till very light brown in a slow oven, 250° F.

PAVLOVAS

2 egg whites
1 saltspoon salt
1 large teaspoon coffee essence
2 oz. chopped walnuts
5 oz. caster sugar
1 dessertspoon cornflour

Beat egg whites until frothy. Sprinkle with the salt. Beat until stiff. Lightly stir in coffee essence, nuts, sugar and cornflour. Drop from dessertspoon in mounds on to a baking sheet lined with greaseproof paper, keeping them about 2 inches apart. Bake in a very slow oven, 275° F., for about 1 hour. *Yield:* About 1 dozen.

JAP CAKES (Baisers au Japon)

3 egg whites
6 oz. caster sugar
6 oz. ground almonds
2 oz. fresh butter
2 oz. caster sugar
Coffee essence to taste

Line a baking sheet with greaseproof paper brushed with melted butter. Beat egg whites to a stiff froth in a basin. Stir in 6 oz. of sugar and the almonds. Spread mixture with a palette knife evenly on a baking sheet covered with unglazed paper. Bake in a moderate oven, 350° F., till almost cooked but not quite set, then remove from oven. Cut into rounds with a pastry cutter 1½ inches in diameter. Return to oven. Bake till brown and crisp. Remove from oven, but let trimmings continue to bake to a rich brown, then rub through a sieve. Cool rounds. Spread half with coffee butter icing—made by creaming the butter with remainder of sugar and flavouring to taste with coffee essence. Top each with another round. Coat top and sides thinly with butter icing, then dip in prepared crumbs.

PETITS FOURS

" Petits fours " is the name given to a large variety of tiny fancy cakes highly decorated with bon-bons, icing and crystallized fruits.

GENOESE PASTRY FOR PETITS FOURS

BASIC RECIPE :
2 eggs
3 oz. caster sugar
3 oz. butter
4 oz. flour
Grated rind of ½ lemon
½ teaspoon vanilla essence

Brush a small baking tin with melted butter, then line smoothly with kitchen paper, brushed with melted butter, and 2 inches wider than the tin. Break eggs into a basin. Add sugar. Beat over hot water till thick and creamy in about 15 minutes. Remove from top of saucepan.

Melt butter in another saucepan. Sift flour. Stir butter and flour alternately into the mixture, then lemon rind and vanilla essence. Pour into the prepared tin. Bake in a moderately hot oven 375° F., for about 20 minutes. When ready, the cake should be spongy in the centre. Remove to a wire rack. Carefully skin off the paper. Cut into fancy shapes such as leaves, hearts, diamonds, rings, half-moons, etc., and decorate to taste.

RICH GENOESE PASTRY

oz. flour
fresh eggs
oz. caster sugar
oz. clarified butter

Prepare tin as in basic recipe. Heat flour. Beat eggs and sugar in the top of a double boiler over hot water till thick and fluffy, then remove from heat. Beat until half cooled. Sift in the flour, then fold it lightly into the eggs alternately with the cool liquid butter. Place in prepared tin. Bake in a moderately hot oven, 375° F., for about 20 minutes.

CHOCOLATE GENOESE PASTRY : Follow the above recipe, but when egg mixture is slightly cooled, break up 2 oz. chocolate and dissolve it in a basin in a saucepan of hot water, then beat it into eggs and sugar. Sift flour with $\frac{1}{2}$ teaspoon baking powder. Fold alternately with the butter into chocolate mixture. Bake as above.

To Decorate Petits Fours :

1. Spread with glacé or water icing, then cover with dots of chocolate icing applied through forcing tube.

2. Halve crosswise. Put together with lemon cheese or jam. Brush top and sides lightly with heated apricot jam. Coat with chopped blanched browned almonds. Dab with jam or icing, or place half a glacé cherry on top of each.

3. Split crosswise and put together with strawberry jam and whipped cream. Spread top with pale green water icing. Decorate each with a small marzipan strawberry.

4. Cut into narrow fingers. Put two together with almond paste or butter crème. Cut into short oblongs. Spread tops with chocolate icing. Sprinkle with chopped blanched pistachio nuts.

5. Cut into tiny rounds. Cut in two crosswise. Put together with butter crème. Pipe a circle of coloured icing round. Fill centre with chopped jelly.

(1) ALMOND PETITS FOURS (Petits Fours aux Amandes)

oz. ground almonds
oz. caster sugar
$\frac{1}{2}$ egg whites
drops ratafia essence

Mix almonds with the sugar. Beat egg whites till stiff. Stir in almonds, sugar, and ratafia essence. Pipe roses of the mixture, a little apart, on to rice paper. Decorate with chips of crystallized fruits. Bake in a slow oven, 300° F., for about 15 minutes, until firm.

(2) ALMOND PETITS FOURS (Petits Fours aux Amandes)

egg yolks
$\frac{1}{4}$ lb. ground almonds

Beat egg yolks till blended. Mix almonds with the sugar. Stir into egg yolk. Add $\frac{1}{4}$ teaspoon of

707

1/4 lb. caster sugar
Curaçao, or Cointreau

Curaçao or Cointreau or 3 drops of almond essence if preferred. Roll out on a board dredged with caster sugar. Cut out with tiny fancy cutters into crescents, diamonds, stars, etc. Decorate with glacé cherries, and angelica. Brush with beaten egg white. Bake in a slow oven, 300° F., for about 15 minutes, until firm.

CHERRY CLOVER LEAVES (Feuilles de Fleurs)

1/2 lb. butter
3 tablespoons icing sugar
1/4 lb. sifted flour
1/2 lb. ground almonds
1 teaspoon vanilla essence

Beat butter till softened. Beat in sugar. Add flour. Beat till blended, then stir in almonds and vanilla essence. Turn on to a board dredged with icing sugar. Divide into tiny portions. Roll each into a small " marble." Place in threes in round plain gem tins. Insert a shaving of glacé cherry in the centre of each with a short narrow stem of angelica. Bake in a moderate oven, 350° F., for about 1/4 hour.

DAMES D'AMOUR

Cut flaky pastry into rounds 1½ inches in diameter. Place in a hot oven, 500° F., and turn off heat. The rounds will cook in the residual heat. When cold, pair rounds with raspberry jam or moistened whipped cream. Brush tops and sides with melted apricot jam. Sprinkle jam thickly with lightly fried almonds, except in centre. Drop a small teaspoonful or saltspoonful of white, green or pink icing on centres. When icing is almost set, decorate with chopped blanched pistachio nuts, or with a flower made from glacé cherries.

MACAROONS

Macaroons are sometimes classified as " biscuits," but are often served in a selection of petits fours. They are usually made of ground almonds, or almond paste, but other ground nuts, particularly cashews, can be used as well.

AMERICAN MACAROONS (Macarons Américains)

1/2 lb. almond paste
7 oz. caster sugar
3 egg whites
1/4 teaspoon vanilla essence
1/3 cup icing sugar
1 1/2 tablespoons flour
1 saltspoon salt

Knead almond paste and sugar on a board till blended. Turn into a basin. Gradually work in the egg whites, then the vanilla essence with a wooden spoon. Sift icing sugar with flour and salt. Stir into almond mixture. Force out through a large rose tube into rounds about 2 inches across, placing them an inch apart on a baking sheet covered with rice paper. Chill slightly, or stand in a cold place for 2½ hours. Bake in a slow oven 300° F., for about 30 minutes. Cut out each macaroon when slightly cold. *Yield :* About 2½ dozen.

ASSORTED MACAROONS (Macarons Assortis)

2/3 cup icing sugar
1/4 lb. ground almonds

Cover a baking sheet with waxed paper. Mix sugar and almonds in a basin. Beat egg whites

2 egg whites
1 saltspoon salt

till stiff. Add salt. Stir into sugar and almonds. When smoothly blended, drop in small mounds from a teaspoon or the tip of a dessertspoon, fully 1½ inches apart, on to baking sheet or drop through a forcing pipe in swirls, rings, or any fancy design you can form. Bake in a moderately slow oven, 325° F., for about 25 minutes. When ready, turn carefully upside down on to a baking board. Brush back of paper gently with water. Pull off paper. Cool on a wire rack.

COCONUT : Substitute 1 cup desiccated coconut for the almonds.

COFFEE : Mix ½ lb. ground almonds with 1 lb. caster sugar and 1 tablespoon coffee essence. Stir in 4 stiffly-beaten egg whites.

RASPBERRY FINGERS (Bâtons aux Framboises)

2 oz. flour
1 oz. cornflour
2 oz. butter
3 oz. caster sugar
8 oz. ground almonds
Raspberry jam and icing

Sift flour and cornflour. Beat butter till creamy. Add sugar. Beat till fluffy. Stir in almonds and flours. Mix to a stiff paste with beaten egg or egg yolk. Line a shallow baking tin, such as a Yorkshire pudding tin, with rice paper. Spread paste out evenly in tin. Bake in moderate oven, 350° F., for about 25 minutes. Cut in strips about 3 inches long and ¾ inch wide. Cut each strip in two crosswise. Put halves together with raspberry jam. Cover tops with raspberry or lemon glacé icing.

RUM SLICES (Tranches au Rhum)

2 egg whites
½ lb. icing sugar
½ lb. ground walnuts
¼ teaspoon vanilla essence

Beat egg whites until stiff. Lightly fold in sugar, nuts, and vanilla essence. Divide in 4 or 5 equal portions. Shape each into a roll about ¾ inch in diameter. Chill thoroughly until stiff enough to slice without breaking. With a very sharp knife cut into slices about ½ inch thick. Bake a little apart on a buttered baking sheet in a moderate oven, 350° F. for about ¼ hour. Spread with icing sugar, moistened with rum. Sprinkle lightly with chopped blanched pistachio nuts.

SHERRY CROISSANTS

¼ lb. butter
¼ lb. cornflour
3 oz. caster sugar
1 teaspoon egg yolk
1 tablespoon sherry
1 egg white
1 heaped tablespoon chopped almonds

Beat butter till softened. Add to cornflour. With finger tips lightly blend, then stir in 2 oz. of the sugar. Mix to a stiff dough with egg yolk, beaten into the sherry. Roll out thinly. Prick lightly with a fork. Cut into crescents. Place a little apart on a baking sheet covered with a greased paper. Beat egg white till frothy. Beat in remainder of sugar. Spread this over each crescent. Sprinkle almonds along the middle. Bake in a moderately slow oven, 325° F., for about ½ hour till crisp. Coat ends with chocolate glacé icing when cold.

VIENNESE CRESCENTS (Croissants Viennoises)

6 oz. butter
6 oz. flour
6 oz. cream cheese

Rub the butter into the flour till perfectly blended. Mix to a dough with the cream cheese. Stand for $\frac{1}{2}$ hour. Roll into a rectangle. Cut into pieces, about $3\frac{1}{2}$ inch square. Fill with apricot jam. Turn one corner over the jam, then roll away from you. Keeping the point below, carefully draw the ends into a crescent. Brush with beaten egg, then bake a little apart on a greased baking sheet in a moderate oven, 350° F., for about 25 minutes. Dredge with sifted vanilla icing sugar.

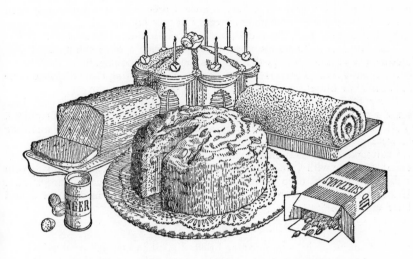

Fruit and Sponge Cakes

There are really only three classes of large cakes :
1. Fruit Cakes, made with fat and eggs.
2. Sponge Cakes, made with eggs and without fat.
3. Butter Sponge Cakes, such as Madeira, made with eggs and fat.

The cakes made with fat and those made without differ in this way : The former are leavened by the carbon dioxide gas released from the raising agent in the batter, namely baking powder or bicarbonate of soda, while the latter, real sponge cakes, are leavened only by the air beaten in with the eggs. All the mixtures are suitable for baking in loaf or round-shaped tins, but the sponges can also be baked in various fancy-shaped tins such as heart and star shaped, as well as in layer cake tins, and in tins manufactured with a tube in the centre.

The Oven : Before heating oven, see that there is a shelf in the centre of oven. You will have to learn from experience how long your particular oven requires to heat to a certain temperature. Study the chart or booklet supplied with your cooker before preparing to bake, and follow the instructions given for heating and baking. Place large cakes in the centre of the oven, standing on the middle of the shelf, unless the batter is very rich when the cakes should be placed slightly lower. Close door gently.

Choosing Cake Tins

Always prepare the tins before mixing the ingredients. It is most important to choose the right-sized tin for a certain amount of batter. The batter should two-thirds fill the tin so that when baked the cake is almost level with the rim of the tin.

Deep Round Tins : When choosing a tin for baking a fruit mixture, one about 3 inches deep with a removable base is always preferable to a tin with a fixed base. The removable base makes it easier to turn out the cake.

Sponge Cake Tins : Use round tins 2″ or 3″ deep or a Balmoral tin.

Tubular Tins : These are most suitable for rich sponge cakes, angel food mixtures, and other batters that require long, slow cooking.

Gateaux Tins : There is quite a variety of interesting shaped tins suitable for sponge or butter sponge mixtures, such as heart, star, etc.

Layer Cake Tins : Select round, plain and fluted tins, buying each in a set of 2 or 3 so that you can use a large, medium-sized, or small tin as required, 9″, 8″ and 7″ in diameter respectively, and make a 2 or 3 layered cake according to taste.

Fruit cakes or gâteaux made with $\frac{1}{2}$ lb. flour need tins 6″ in diameter, and 3″ deep. If made with $\frac{3}{4}$ lb. flour, the cake needs a tin 7″ × 3″, and if made with 1 lb. flour, 8″ × 3″ deep. This only applies to plain fruit cakes and gâteaux. If the cake is very " plummy," choose a tin an inch larger in diameter than I have suggested.

To Prepare Tins

Brush tins slightly with a pantry brush dipped in clarified or unsalted fat, or cooking oil, unless you are using tins made of a metal that requires no greasing. Plain batters can be baked in these tins, but for delicate and rich batters tins have to be lined.

To Line : Cut strips of strong greaseproof or waxed paper long enough to line the inside of the tin and wide enough to extend about 2 inches above the rim. Turn up a " hem " along one edge of the strip to the depth of about 1 inch, and crease it firmly. To enable you to line tin neatly and smoothly, take a pair of kitchen scissors and snip the fold about an inch apart all the way round. Now cut a round to fit the inside base of tin. Brush this as well as the strip with clarified or unsalted fat, or cooking oil. Insert the strip neatly in tin, then fit in the bottom round. If cake is very rich, repeat the layers of paper. When making a wedding cake, you will need 4 or 5 layers for the largest tier. I was taught to stand very rich cakes, such as large Christmas cakes, wedding cake tiers, etc., in a large round baking tin containing a bed of kitchen salt, about an inch deep. I then had to tie a fold of brown paper round the outside of the tin, and finally lap the salt round the sides of the base. The reason for this is to prevent the outside and base of cake becoming hard and sometimes scorched by the time the centre of cake is dry. In some types of stoves, where there is no bottom heat, the base of salt should not be necessary.

Sponge Cake Tins : If cakes are to be baked in deep tins, use dry tins without either greasing or lining.

Layer Cake Tins : If you prefer to line them, neatly cut out a round of greaseproof or waxed paper to fit the bottom smoothly. Grease tin and insert the paper. Otherwise grease or oil and dredge with flour. Shake well.

Swiss Roll Tins : Grease bottom of the tin and line with waxed paper, or with greased greaseproof paper. To do this neatly, see that you cut the paper about 2 inches wider all the way round than the tin. Invert tin on the paper, then slit each corner from edge of paper to corner of tin, so that cut pieces will overlap when paper is inserted in tin.

INGREDIENTS

Flour : Cakes can be made of household flour, but when cake or pastry flour is available, always use it. It will produce a more tender cake than the household flour. This type of flour is known as " soft wheat flour." If not available, use household flour with the addition of a little cornflour. For example : If a recipe calls for ½ lb. of flour, use only 6 or 7 oz., and add 1 or 2 oz. cornflour, or rice flour. Self-raising flour can be substituted for plain flour when making plain cakes, in which case, omit any other raising agent such as baking powder or bicarbonate of soda, and follow directions given for the use of this flour very carefully. All flour used in cakes must be quite dry, and sifted before measuring.

Leavening Agents : The agents generally used for cake mixtures are baking powder and bicarbonate of soda. Sometimes bicarbonate of soda is used in combination with cream of tartar, or with lemon juice or vinegar. If the cake contains a large number of eggs, for example, in a cake with ½ lb. flour, ½ lb. fat, ½ lb. sugar, and 5 or 6 eggs, the addition of any leavening agent is unnecessary.

The third agent which helps in raising a cake, is air. Sponge cakes, in particular, benefit from air incorporated while beating.

Fats : Unsalted butter is preferable for using in light cake mixtures such as mixtures for gâteaux. It imparts a delicate flavour to cakes made with genoese pastry, and other butter sponge mixtures. If salt butter is used, the butter should be washed in cold water and wrung dry in a floured cloth so as to get rid of the salt.

When butter is not available, any fat of a mild flavour, and easy to " cream " can be substituted, such as margarine, but as this contains more water than butter, it is not so good for very light batters. Half butter and half margarine can be used in heavily-spiced cakes such as gingerbread. Margarine and lard or one of the other cooking fats are also suitable. Do not use lard alone, on account of its flavour. Clarified dripping is suitable only for very plain cakes.

Sugar : When a white sugar is wanted, use caster sugar. Either Demerara sugar or fine moist brown sugar is preferable for using in gingerbread or parkin mixtures.

Eggs : Choose as fresh eggs as you can obtain, though preserved eggs, if preserved fresh, can be substituted. Reconstituted dried eggs can also be used to provide food value, but they do not help to lighten the cake. When you are forced to use fewer eggs than the recipe asks for increase baking powder by ½ teaspoon for each egg omitted. The more eggs you add, the lighter and more delicate the texture of the cake.

Fruit : (Currants, seedless Raisins and Sultanas) : It is essential to pick over dried fruit as sometimes tiny bits of stalk remain in it. After picking over, wash and dry. This is unless fruit has been cleaned before packaging.

To Wash : Place in a sieve, and stand the sieve in a basin of cold water. Shake sieve back and forwards so that the fruits float in the water and rub against each other. Change the water twice. When thoroughly cleaned, spread

713

out on flat trays or baking tins. Dry very slowly in a warm place such as a heated linen cupboard, or on a plate rack.

If washed and dried, allow fruit to stand for 12 hours. stirring once or twice before using. If used moist or warm, it may make cakes heavy. If candied peel contains sugar, dip in boiling water to remove it, then dry thoroughly before preparing.

To Prepare Raisins : Clean as described, then remove the stones with the fingers. Keep a basin of warm water beside you while stoning so that you can dip your fingers into the water to get rid of the stones that adhere. Toss raisins, when stoned, in a dry cloth, before using.

Nuts :

To Prepare Almonds : Place in a saucepan. Cover with cold water. Bring to boil. Strain at once, then hold under the cold water tap for $\frac{1}{2}$ a minute. Slip off skins. Toss in a cloth till dry. Split or chop as required.

Brazil and Walnuts : Shell. Be very careful to remove all traces of inner skin from Brazil nuts, and see that the " meat " from the walnuts is free from all traces of shell.

Hazelnuts : Place in a baking tin. Heat in a slow oven for 20 minutes, shaking once or twice, until the skins are dry, then rub off on a clean cloth.

NOTE : To grind nuts either use a nut grater, or a meat grinder with a fine knife.

FRUIT CAKES

There are two methods of making a fruit cake :

1. Creaming.   2. Rubbing-in.

The creaming method is more popular as it gives a finer textured cake than the rubbing in method. The rubbing in method is generally only employed for plain fruit cakes.

To Cream : Place the fat in a slightly warm basin. If hard on account of atmospheric conditions, or because of being stored in a refrigerator, cut up and stand at kitchen temperature until slightly softened. Do not try to soften it in the oven on any account, or it will " oil." Beat with a wooden spoon until softened, and slightly creamy. If using a large quantity of fat, beat with your hand. Sift sugar and add gradually, beating constantly until you have a creamy white texture that will fall fluffily from your spoon or fingers. To make a cake by the creaming method, use the following proportions of flour, fat and sugar. For example, allow to 1 lb. flour, $\frac{1}{2}$-$\frac{3}{4}$ lb. butter, $\frac{1}{2}$-$\frac{3}{4}$ lb. sugar.

To Rub In : Sift flour, with salt, into a basin. Rub in butter with finger tips till the mixture is like fine meal. To make a cake by the rubbing in method, use not more than double quantity of flour to fat. For example, allow to 1 lb. flour, 6-8 oz. fat, and 6-8 oz. sugar.

To Mix Ingredients

By the Creamed Method : There are two methods of adding the eggs :

1. Drop an egg into the creamed fat and sugar. Dredge lightly with some of the flour, then beat till blended. Continue adding in this way.

2. Drop all the eggs required into a basin after breaking each into a cup to make certain the eggs are fresh. Beat well. Add a small quantity at a time to the creamed fat and sugar. Dredge with a little flour each time, and beat until blended after each addition.

If a very light cake is wanted, separate the yolks and whites of eggs. Beat yolks till thick and honey-coloured. Add a little to the creamed fat and sugar but dredge with flour, as with whole eggs, before beating. Beat egg whites till stiff and fold into batter when all other ingredients are added.

Sift flour before weighing, then weigh and sift with baking powder, salt and spices if used. If measuring flour in a cup, sift before measuring. Sprinkle a little of the flour over the fruit and mix well, then gradually add the remainder of flour and any other dry ingredients alternately with milk if used, keeping the batter of the same consistency all the time you are mixing. If moistening only with egg, add all the egg as described, before stirring in the bulk of flour. Stir in any fruit or nuts with flavouring. *Do not beat after adding the flour*, or cake may be heavy. If egg whites are beaten separately, fold in last of all.

By the Rubbing-in Method : Stir any remaining dry ingredients into the flour and fat. Mix to a dropable consistency with the beaten egg diluted with the milk. The batter should be slightly softer than the batter made by the creamed method.

To Bake Fruit Mixtures

Fill prepared tins two-thirds full. Holding each side between your fingers, give a sharp tap on the baking board to allow batter to settle round the bottom of tins, then hollow out the centre of all but the plainest of mixtures, with the back of your hand, to ensure a level top when the cake is baked. Place large cake in the centre of the oven, or slightly lower, standing it on the middle of the shelf. Close door gently.

To Test : When the cake has had the time required to bake, heat a fine skewer and carefully insert it in the centre of cake. If it comes out clean, remove the cake at once to a table. If any batter adheres to the skewer, continue to bake and test again in the same way. Remember that a large rich fruit cake shrinks slightly from the sides of the tin when it is fully baked. Remove from oven. Stand from 5-15 minutes out of a draught before attempting to turn out. Cool on a wire rack, base downwards. Plain cake won't take very long, but always leave rich cakes overnight to make certain they are quite cold in the centre.

To Store : Wrap in 2 layers of greaseproof paper, and place in an air-tight tin.

Faults and Failures

Q. *Why is my cake dry?*
A. For different reasons :
    (a) Over-beating egg whites.
    (b) Over-baking, or baking too long at too low a temperature.

Q. *Why does my cake fall in the centre?*
A. There are many reasons for this :
    (a) Too much fat. Measure carefully.
    (b) Too much raising agent. When this happens, cake rises rapidly, then falls when cooked.
    (c) Too much sugar.
    (d) Not enough raising agent.
    (e) Too much liquid.
    (f) Too slow an oven.
    (g) Moving a cake before the batter is set.
    (h) A sudden drop in temperature before batter is set, caused by opening oven door.
    (i) Removing from oven before perfectly baked.

Q. *Why does the fruit in my cake sink to the bottom?*
A. There are five reasons for this :
    (a) Not enough flour, resulting in too wet a batter.
    (b) Too much liquid.
    (c) Too much raising agent.
    (d) Fruit not properly dried after washing.
    (e) Too low a baking temperature.

Q. *Why is my cake heavy?*
A. It may be because of :
    (a) Too much fat.
    (b) Too much flour.
    (c) Not enough raising agent.
    (d) Not enough sugar, or too much.
    (e) Too much liquid.
    (f) Incorrect baking temperature.
    (g) Beating after the flour is added.

Q. *Why does my cake have a heavy streak at the bottom?*
A. For the following reasons :
    (a) Ingredients not sufficiently mixed.
    (b) Far too soft.
    (c) Flour damp.
    (d) Too much liquid.
    (e) Not enough raising agent.
    (f) Batter allowed to stand in a rather warm place before baking.
    (g) Lower part of oven not hot enough.

Q. *Why does my cake have holes or tunnels?*
A. For four reasons :
    (a) Over-mixing after adding flour.
    (b) Too much flour.
    (c) Too much bicarbonate of soda in soda mixtures.
    (d) Too hot an oven.

Q. *Why doesn't my cake rise evenly?*
A. Because of :
    (a) Too much flour.
    (b) Too much raising agent.
    (c) Baking too quickly.

(d) Placing to one side of the shelf.

(e) Too high a temperature to start with, when the outside forms a crust before cake is cooked in the centre, and then the batter boils through a crack on the top.

BASIS FOR PLAIN FRUIT CAKE

¼ lb. margarine
¼ lb. caster sugar
½ lb. flour
1 teaspoon baking powder
¼ teaspoon salt
2 eggs
Milk as required

BASIS FOR MEDIUM-RICH FRUIT CAKE

6 oz. butter
6 oz. caster sugar
½ lb. flour
½ teaspoon baking powder
¼ teaspoon salt
3 or 4 eggs
Milk as required

BASIS FOR RICH FRUIT CAKE

½ lb. butter
½ lb. caster sugar
½ lb. flour
¼ teaspoon salt
5 or 6 eggs

BIRTHDAY CAKE (Gâteau à la Fête)

1 lb. sultanas
1 lb. currants
¼ lb. raisins
¼ lb. glacé cherries
6 oz. chopped mixed peel
¼ lb. chopped almonds
¾ lb. butter
¾ lb. caster sugar
6 eggs
1 lb. flour
½ teaspoon salt
½ teaspoon mixed spice
¼ teaspoon ground mace
2 tablespoons treacle
2 glasses of sherry

SIZE OF TIN: 9″ × 3½″

300° F., for about 6¼ hours.

Grease cake tin and line smoothly with 3 layers of greased paper. Clean sultanas and currants. Put raisins through a meat grinder, stoning first if necessary. Quarter cherries. Chop peel and almonds. Beat butter and sugar to a cream. Add each egg separately. Beat after each addition till mixture is blended. Sift flour with salt and spices. Stir into batter, then stir in fruit, peel and almonds. Lastly, heat a tablespoon and spoon in treacle. When blended, stir in sherry. Pack into lined cake tin. Give tin a sharp tap on table, then lightly hollow out centre so that cake will rise evenly. Use the back of hand for hollowing out. Bake in the centre of a slow oven, 300° F., for about 6¼ hours. Test with a skewer before removing from oven.

BLACK BUN (Gâteau Noir Ecossaise)

FILLING:
1 lb. stoned raisins

Grease cake tin. Chop raisins. Add currants. Chop and add almonds and peel. Add brown sugar.

2 lb. cleaned currants
1/2 lb. blanched almonds
1/2 lb. mixed candied peel
1/2 lb. light brown sugar
1 lb. sifted flour
1/4 oz. ground cinnamon or cloves
1/4 oz. ground ginger
1 teaspoon Jamaica pepper
1/2 teaspoon black pepper
1 saltspoon salt ⌡
1 small teaspoon baking powder
1 tablespoon brandy
1 tablespoon rum
Beaten egg as required to moisten
PASTRY :
1 lb. sifted flour
1/2 lb. butter
Beaten egg or water as required

SIZE OF TIN : 9″-10″ across

Sift flour with spices, peppers, salt and baking powder into a basin. Add fruit, peel and sugar mixture. Before adding the liquid, prepare the crust. Sift flour into another basin. Rub in butter. Stir in enough beaten egg or water to make a stiff dough. Roll out into a thin sheet. Cut a strip off as deep as the tin, and long enough to go round the inside. Brush the ends with cold water. Fit round inside of tin. Cut a round to fit bottom. Brush the edge with cold water. Insert in tin. Flatten with the back of hand until it joins the side lining and forms a pastry case, so that the edges meet. Prick the bottom of the crust with a fork. Trim edge if necessary. Stir the brandy and rum into flour and fruit mixture for filling, then moisten with beaten egg, or equal quantity of egg and milk. Flatten the filling down with your fingers until it is about $\frac{1}{2}$ inch below rim of pastry. Brush the edge of the pastry with cold water.

Lightly knead and roll out remainder of pastry into a round to fit the top. Press it firmly all round the edge, then trim the edge if necessary. Make 4 holes equal distance apart, right down to the bottom of cake. Brush pastry lightly with equal quantity of beaten egg and milk. Prick all over top with fork. Bake in a moderate oven, 350° F., for about 3 hours.

BOILED FRUIT CAKE (Gâteau, Bourgoise)

1/4 lb. mixed candied peel
2 1/2 oz. dripping, lard or margarine
6 oz. light brown sugar
1/4 lb. cleaned sultanas
1 teaspoon mixed spice
1/2 teaspoon ground ginger
1 1/2 cups hot water
1 lb. sifted flour
2 teaspoons vinegar
1 teaspoon bicarbonate of soda

SIZE OF TIN : 9″ across

Grease cake tin. Chop peel. Place in a saucepan with the fat and sugar, sultanas, spices and water. Bring to boil. Boil for 5 minutes. Remove from stove. Cool. Stir in flour and vinegar, then the soda, dissolved in a tablespoon of hot water. Mix well. Place in prepared tin. Bake in a moderate oven, 350° F., for about 1 1/2 hours till dry in the centre when tested with a skewer. Stand for 5 minutes, then turn on to a wire tray, base downwards, to cool.

CHERRY CAKE (Gâteau de Cerises, Gauloise)

1/2 lb. butter
7 oz. icing sugar
4 eggs
3/4 lb. sifted flour
1/4 teaspoon salt
1 teaspoon baking powder
2 oz. minced candied peel
3/4 lb. halved glacé cherries
Grated rind of 1 lemon

SIZE OF TIN : 8″ round or square

Grease tin and line with 2 layers of buttered paper. Beat butter till softened. Gradually beat in sugar. When fluffy, add eggs, one at a time, beating each in lightly. Sift flour with salt and baking powder. Stir lightly into the batter, then add peel, cherries and lemon rind. Place batter in tin. Bake in a moderately slow oven, 325° F., for about 1 1/2 hours, till dry in the centre when tested.

CHILDREN'S BIRTHDAY CAKE
(Gâteau à l'Anniversaire d'un Enfant)

5 oz. sifted flour
¾ teaspoon baking powder
Pinch of salt
Grated rind of 1 orange
2 oz. desiccated coconut
3 eggs and 1 egg yolk
5 oz. caster sugar
2 oz. butter or margarine
Juice of 1½ oranges
SIZE OF TIN : 7"x 3"

Grease round cake tin. Sift flour with baking powder and salt. Wash and dry orange, then grate rind finely. Extract the juice and add the juice of another ½ orange. Pour over the coconut. Whisk the eggs and yolks with the sugar over a pan of hot water until thick and creamy, and free from dark streaks. Melt butter or margarine slowly, but do not allow it to get hot. When eggs and sugar are ready, remove from water and gradually stir in a little of the flour and fat alternately until both are incorporated. Add coconut and orange mixture. Stir lightly until blended. Pack into tin. Bake in a moderate oven, 350° F. for about ¾ hour, until spongy. When ready, invert tin on a wire rack, and leave until nearly cold, then ease out gently with a palette knife, and cool, base downwards, on a wire rack. Leave till cold, then cover with orange icing. When set, add a little more sugar to remainder of icing. Colour it a deeper orange than the coating icing. Decorate to taste with sugar roses and angelica leaves. Fix candles as required.

CHRISTMAS CAKE (Gâteau Noël)

12 oz. butter
12 oz. brown sugar
6 eggs
1 lb. sifted flour
¼ teaspoon salt
½ teaspoon mixed spice
1 lb. cleaned currants
1 lb. cleaned sultanas
¼ lb. chopped stoned raisins
2 oz. candied citron peel
2 oz. candied lemon peel
2 oz. candied orange peel
2 oz. halved glacé cherries
¼ lb. chopped almonds
2 tablespoons treacle
½ gill brandy or sherry
SIZE OF TIN : 9" x 3¼" inches

Grease tin and line smoothly with 3 layers of greased paper. Beat butter till softened. Gradually beat in sugar. Beat till fluffy. Add 1 egg. Sprinkle with a dessertspoon of the flour and beat till blended. Repeat, adding egg, dredging with flour, and beating, till all the eggs have been incorporated in the fat and sugar. Sift remainder of flour with salt and spice. Stir into egg mixture, then stir in currants, sultanas, and raisins. Chop peels. Stir in with cherries and almonds. Lastly, stir in treacle and brandy, or sherry. Place in prepared tin. Hollow out centre. Bake in a slow oven, 300° F., for fully 6 hours, until dry in the centre when tested with a heated skewer.

SMALL CHRISTMAS CAKE : Halve above quantities and use a tin 7½" × 3", and bake for about 3¼ hours.

To Decorate : See pages 748-755

DUNDEE CAKE (Gâteau Dundee)

6 oz. butter
6 oz. caster sugar
3 eggs
10 oz. sifted flour
½ teaspoon salt
1 teaspoon baking powder
2 oz. chopped candied peel

Line a greased tin with two layers of greased paper. Beat butter till softened. Gradually beat in sugar. Beat till fluffy. Beat eggs. Sift flour with salt and baking powder. Stir flour and egg alternately into butter and sugar, beating well after each addition. Add fruit and ground

4 oz. chopped raisins
4 oz. cleaned currants
4 oz. cleaned sultanas
2 oz. ground almonds
1 oz. split blanched almonds
SIZE OF TIN: 8″ across

almonds. Stir only till blended. Place in tin. Bake in a moderately slow oven, 325° F., for ¼ hour, then place the split almonds on top and continue to bake from 2¼-3 hours, till dry in the centre when tested with a skewer.

EASTER GATEAU (Gâteau de Pâques)

½ lb. sifted flour
2 teaspoons baking powder
1 teaspoon ground cinnamon
½ teaspoon grated nutmeg
½ teaspoon ground cloves
½ teaspoon ground mace
¼ teaspoon salt
¼ lb. cleaned sultanas
¼ lb. minced raisins
2 oz. minced candied peel
4 oz. butter
4 oz. caster or light brown sugar
3 eggs
SIZE OF TIN: 8″ across

Grease tin and line smoothly with greased paper. Sift flour with baking powder, spices and salt. Mix sultanas with raisins, peel, and a tablespoon flour, using your hand for mixing. Beat butter till fluffy. Beat in sugar by degrees. Beat till fluffy. Beat eggs well. Add a tablespoon or two of egg, and a dust of spiced flour. Beat till blended. Continue adding a little egg, and a dust of flour to prevent batter curdling, and beat in after each addition, till all the egg is incorporated. Lightly stir in fruit. Fold in remainder of spiced flour, then stir in enough milk or weak coffee to make batter 'dropable.' Pack into prepared tin.

Bake in the centre of a moderately slow oven, 325° F., for about 2½ hours, till dry in the centre. Stand for 5 minutes after removing from oven. Turn out gently, base downwards, on to a wire rack to cool. Keep for a week wrapped in greaseproof paper, in a tightly-closed tin. Split in two crosswise. Sandwich with marzipan. Coat with white glacé icing. Decorate with trails of icing and marzipan bunnies (see illustration facing page 641), with currant eyes and almond ears.

ETON ROAD CAKE (Gâteau Eton)

½ lb. butter
½ lb. caster sugar
4 eggs
½ lb. sifted flour
Pinch of salt
1 teaspoon baking powder
6 oz. glacé cherries
6 oz. glacé pineapple
6 oz. cleaned sultanas
2 drops lemon essence
SIZE OF TIN: 8″ across

Line greased cake tin with 2 layers of greased paper. Beat butter and sugar to a cream. Beat eggs. Sift flour with salt and baking powder. Rub cherries in a little flour. Chop with the pineapple. Mix cherries and pineapple with the sultanas. Add flour and egg alternately to butter and sugar. Stir in lemon essence with remainder of egg. Stir in fruit. Turn into cake tin. Bake in a moderate oven, 350° F., for about 1½-2 hours, till dry when tested with a skewer. Cool on a wire rack. Ice and decorate to taste.

GENOA CAKE (Gâteau Italienne)

¾ lb. sifted flour
Pinch of salt
½ lb. butter
½ lb. caster sugar
4 eggs
1 teaspoon baking powder

Grease tin and line smoothly with 2 layers of greased paper. Sift flour with salt. Beat butter till softened. Stir in sugar. Beat till fluffy. Add one egg. Sprinkle with a dust of flour. Beat till blended. Add remainder of eggs in the

1/4 lb. cleaned sultanas
3 oz. glacé cherries
6 oz. cleaned currants
Grated rind 1 lemon
1/4 lb. chopped citron peel
2 oz. blanched almonds
2 tablespoons brandy
SIZE OF TIN : 8″ across

same way, then sift flour again with baking powder, and stir into egg mixture. Add sultanas. Halve and add cherries with currants, lemon and peel. Chop and stir in almonds, then brandy, or substitute sherry or milk. Turn into prepared tin. Smooth with a spoon dipped in milk. If liked, the almonds can be omitted from the cake, and split and blanched, then sprinkled evenly over the top. Bake in a moderately slow oven, 325° F., for about 2¾ hours, till dry in the centre when tested.

MEMUS SEED CAKE (Gâteau Memus)

3 oz. butter
4 oz. caster sugar
2 eggs
5 oz. sifted flour
1 teaspoon baking powder
1 tablespoon caraway seeds
SIZE OF TIN : 6″ across

Grease tin and line with a layer of greased paper. Beat butter and sugar to a cream. Beat eggs. Sift flour and baking powder. Add half the egg to the butter and sugar. Dredge lightly with flour. Beat till blended. Repeat till all the egg and flour is added. Stir in half the caraway seeds. Place batter in tin. Sprinkle remainder of caraway seeds on top. Bake in a moderate oven, 350° F., for about 45 minutes, till dry in the centre when tested with a skewer.

SIMNEL CAKE

1/2 lb. butter or margarine
1/2 lb. caster sugar
1/2 lb. sifted flour
1/4 teaspoon salt
3/4 teaspoon baking powder
3/4 teaspoon mixed spice
1/4 teaspoon ground mace
4 eggs
1/4 lb. halved glacé cherries
1 lb. cleaned sultanas
1/2 lb. cleaned currants
2 oz. chopped almonds
2 oz. chopped citron peel
2 oz. chopped orange peel
Grated rind of 1/2 lemon
3 drops of almond essence
1 dessertspoon milk or coffee
Almond paste
SIZE OF TIN : 9″ x 3½″

Grease cake tin. Line smoothly with three folds of greased paper. Beat fat till softened. Gradually beat in sugar. Beat till fluffy. Sieve flour with salt, baking powder, spice and mace. Sprinkle a little of the flour over fat and sugar. Add 1 egg. Beat till blended. Continue in this way until all the eggs are incorporated. Stir remainder of flour into fruit, nuts, peel and lemon rind. Stir into fat mixture. Mix only till blended. Stir almond essence into milk or coffee, and add to batter. Stir only till blended. Lightly pack half the batter into prepared tin. Smooth over the top with a flexible knife. Cover with fully a third of the almond paste kneaded or rolled into a round to fit the inside of tin. Place remainder of batter on top. Press down lightly with the back of a wooden spoon.

Bake in a moderately slow oven, 325° F., for about 3½ hours. Remove from stove. Cool slightly. Mould remainder of paste into a thick ring to fit round top edge of cake. Brush round top edge of cake thinly with melted jelly. Place ring on top. Notch with thumbs and forefingers, or " rough " it up with the prongs of a fork. Smooth side of ring with a palette knife so that it is level with side of the cake. Cover cake in centre with a thick round of paper, then carefully brush top of ring with equal quantity of beaten egg yolk and water. Remove paper. Bake in a slow oven, 325° F. until pale brown, in about 20 minutes. Remove to a wire rack. Stand for ½ hour, then turn out very gently on to rack, base downwards. Run water icing, delicately coloured pale green or lemon, over the centre to form a lake. When almost set, decorate with a nest of eggs (*see illustration facing page* 641), or with other Easter ornaments. *Note:* If preferred, omit almond paste. Leave cake for a week, then split in two crosswise, and sandwich with almond icing. Decorate top as described, using this icing.

TO MAKE ALMOND PASTE FOR SIMNEL CAKE : Mix 6 oz. ground almonds with 4 oz. icing sugar, and 2 oz. caster sugar. Add 3 drops almond essence, the juice of ½ a lemon, and enough beaten egg to make a rather soft consistency. (If preferred, use only egg white.)

SULTANA CAKE (Gâteau aux Raisins)

¾ lb. sifted flour
7 oz. butter
7 oz. caster sugar
3 eggs
2 oz. chopped candied peel
½ lb. cleaned sultanas
1 teaspoon baking powder
Grated rind of 1 lemon
½ teaspoon salt
½ cup milk
1 oz. blanched almonds
SIZE OF TIN : 8″ across

Grease tin and line smoothly with 2 layers of greased paper. Sift flour. Beat butter to a cream. Gradually beat in sugar. When fluffy, beat eggs. Add a little egg to fat and sugar. Sprinkle with a little flour and beat till blended. Repeat till all eggs are beaten in. Stir in peel, sultanas, baking powder, lemon rind, salt and the milk. Place batter in tin. Slightly flatten centre. Shred almonds over top. Bake in a moderate oven, 350° F., for about 1½ hours. Cool on a wire rack.

WEDDING CAKE (Gâteau de Noce)

If you want more than one tier to your wedding cake, it is advisable to bake the tiers at different times. (The cakes ought to be made three months before the wedding.) If too new, the pillars might sink into the layers of cake below them. Now here are the ingredients and method for making a one-tiered cake or the bottom of a two or three-tiered cake :

1 lb. orange peel
½ lb. lemon peel
½ lb. citron peel
2½ lb. currants
1½ lb. sultanas
2 oz. glacé cherries
1¼ lb. butter or margarine
1¼ lb. caster sugar
1½ lb. eggs (in shells)
1 lb. 7 oz. sifted flour
½ teaspoon mixed spice
½ oz. allspice
¼ teaspoon ground mace
½ teaspoon cinnamon
Pinch of salt
1 lb. ground almonds
¼ teaspoon lemon essence

Grease cake tin. Line it with five folds of greased paper and tie a thick band of brown paper around the outside. Shred peels finely. Clean currants well. Clean and pick sultanas. Chop cherries. When all are ready, beat fat and sugar together till softened and creamy, using your hand instead of a spoon. Beat eggs till light and frothy. Sift flour with spices, and a pinch of salt. Add flour mixture and beaten egg alternately to fat and sugar mixture till all the egg is used up, then add remainder of flour alternately with peel, fruits and ground almonds. Remember you should keep on beating with your hand all the time. Lastly, stir in essences, lemon juice, brandy,

¾ teaspoon rose, raspberry or
  banana essence
Juice of ½ lemon
½ wineglass brandy
½ wineglass sherry
SIZE OF TIN : 11½-12″ across

and sherry. Lightly pack cake mixture into prepared tin, filling it half full. Hollow out centre slightly with the back of your hand. Place the cake tin on a bed of kitchen salt in a baking tin, pushing the salt close to the sides. Bake in an oven heated to 300° F., for about 6½ hours. When you think it is ready, test it with a fine knitting needle or skewer. It should not be taken from the oven until the needle or skewer comes out quite clean. Stand for ½ hour in tin to allow cake to shrink, then turn out carefully on to a wire tray. Remove all paper at once. Cool away from draughts. Leave for at least 24 hours to make certain it is quite cold, then wrap in 2 layers of greaseproof paper and store in a tightly-closed tin.

For a Three Tiered Cake, make the same quantity of cake mixture again. Prepare two smaller tins, one 9½ to 10 inches across, and the other 7″, in exactly the same way as the large tin. Half fill the larger of the two tins with cake mixture, and bake in a slow oven, 300° F., for about 5½ hours. When done, treat it in exactly the same way as the larger cake. Now add ½ teaspoon baking powder to the remaining cake mixture. Beat sharply for a moment or two, then turn mixture into the prepared 7″ tin, taking care not to fill it more than half-way. Bake in a slow oven, 300° F., for 3½-3¾ hours. When done, treat it in the same way as the other two cakes.

For a Two Tier Cake, only increase by half the ingredients I have given. Bake the lower tier in a 11½-12 inch tin, following the directions already given. The remaining cake mixture should half fill an 8½″-9″ tin, and this should be baked in a slow oven, 300° F., for about 5 hours. If you make all the cake mixture at once, and bake the bigger tier first, stir 1 teaspoon baking powder into the remaining mixture before putting it into the smaller tin for baking.

Two weeks before the wedding, cover the cakes with almond paste and royal icing. See Icing Section for recipes, pages 751-760.

To Build up the Tiers : If the cake is 2 or 3 tiered, place the second or second and third layers on silver pillars as illustrated.

To Decorate : Decorate layers with ropes and trails of royal icing and ornaments to taste. I used small waxen orange blossoms for the tops of the cakes, and fixed a wreath of larger orange blossoms with foliage around the base. I also used sprigs of white heather, silver lovers' knots, ivy leaves, horseshoes and cupids, and placed a horseshoe on the top to which I fixed fresh white blossoms. If you are expert at icing, perhaps you would prefer to decorate the cakes entirely with piping and trellis work, and introduce only a few ornaments.

SLAB CAKES

Most slab cakes are made from plain batters, sometimes enriched with a little fruit, peel and nuts. These cakes can be eaten fresh, whereas cakes baked in deep tins should be kept for some time before cutting, the time depending on the richness of the cake. Bake the batters in shallow tins. When the cake is ready, turn out on to a wire rack to cool. Dredge with caster sugar, or coat the top with icing. Cut into squares or oblongs as required.

AMERICAN SLAB CAKE (Gâteau Américaine)

¼ lb. butter
½ lb. caster sugar
¾ cup cocoa
3 separated eggs
½ cup cold coffee
6 oz. sifted flour
3 teaspoons baking powder
1 saltspoon salt
¼ teaspoon ground mace
½ teaspoon ground cinnamon
¼ cup chopped stoned raisins
¼ cup candied cherries
¼ cup chopped walnuts
¼ cup chopped candied peel
1 teaspoon vanilla essence

SIZE OF TIN : 8" x 8" square

Brush cake tin with melted fat. Line neatly with three layers of buttered paper. Beat butter and sugar to a cream. Stir in cocoa, beaten egg yolks, coffee, then the flour sifted with baking powder, salt and spices. Mix well, then stir in fruit, nuts and chopped peel. Add vanilla essence. Fold in stiffly-frothed egg whites. Bake in a moderate oven, 350° F., for about 1¼ hours. Turn out on to a cake rack. When cold, coat with water icing. When set, carefully pipe a trellis work of milk chocolate, melted in the top of a double boiler, on top. Decorate with halved walnuts.

APPLE SAUCE SLAB CAKE (Gâteau aux Pommes)

½ pint apple purée
6 oz. sultanas
2 oz. seeded raisins
2 oz. candied peel
2 oz. glacé ginger
2 oz. shelled walnuts
5 oz. butter
6 oz. brown sugar
½ lb. sifted flour
1 teaspoon bicarbonate of soda
1 teaspoon ground cinnamon
½ teaspoon ground ginger
½ teaspoon mixed spice
Rind of ½ a lemon
2 eggs

SIZE OF TIN : 8" x 8" square

Grease and line cake tin. Peel, core and stew enough cooking apples (with just enough water to prevent them burning and sugar to taste) to give you ½ pint purée when sieved. Prepare fruit. Chop peel, ginger and walnuts. Beat butter and sugar to a cream. Sift flour with soda and spices. Add flour by degrees to butter and sugar. Stir in fruit, ginger and walnuts. Grate in lemon rind. Beat eggs. Stir into mixture, then stir in cold apple purée. Beat well. Turn into prepared tin. Dredge the top with caster sugar. Bake in a moderately hot oven, 375° F., for about 1 hour, or till ready when tested. Turn out on to a cake rack to cool.

GINGERBREADS

SLAB GINGERBREAD (Pain d'Epice, Anglais)

BASIC RECIPE :
¼ lb. slightly salted butter
¼ lb. light brown sugar
½ cup syrup
½ cup treacle
1 level teaspoon bicarbonate of soda
½ cup milk
¾ lb. sifted flour
1 teaspoon ground ginger
½ teaspoon mixed spice

SIZE OF TIN : 13" x 8" oblong

Grease tin. Beat butter and sugar to a cream in a basin. Stir in syrup, treacle, and soda dissolved in the milk. Sift flour with ginger and spice. Stir into other ingredients. Pour into prepared tin. Bake in a rather slow oven, 325° F., for about 40-50 minutes. Remove from oven when light and firm. Stand for a moment or two, then turn on to a cake rack. Leave until cold. Cover with water icing, flavoured with rum if liked.

To Vary :

1. Add 1 cup chopped shelled nuts after the flour.
2. Sift ¼ teaspoon each of ground allspice, cinnamon, and cloves, as well as ginger with the flour, then follow basic recipe.
3. Use half margarine or butter, and half lard, and follow basic recipe.
4. Add 1 tablespoon minced walnuts and 3 tablespoons minced crystallized ginger after the flour.
5. Add 1 tablespoon minced candied orange peel and 1 tablespoon chopped stoned dates after the flour.
6. Add 1 cup chopped stoned raisins after the flour.

GINGERBREAD SPONGE (Pain d'Epice, Ecossais)

10 oz. flour
¾ teaspoon mixed spice
½ oz. ground ginger
2 oz. brown sugar
3 tablespoons milk
½ lb. golden syrup
¼ lb. butter or lard
1 teaspoon bicarbonate of soda
2 beaten eggs

SIZE OF TIN : 7″ x 10½″ x 2″

Grease shallow baking tin, and line smoothly with greased paper. Sift flour with spice into a basin. Stir in sugar. Pour 2 tablespoons of the milk into a saucepan. Add syrup and butter or lard. Heat slowly until tepid, then stir till blended with the milk. Dissolve soda in remainder of milk. Stir into eggs. Make a well in the centre of flour. Add fat mixture. Stir in a little of the flour, then add the egg and milk. Beat to a smooth batter with the remainder of flour. Pour into baking tin. Bake in a moderately hot oven, 375° F., for about ¾ hour. Turn on to a wire rack. Cut into fingers when cold.

SPONGE CAKES

There are two classes of sponge cake : one variety is made with eggs, sugar, flour and flavouring ; and the other contains fat, preferably butter. I like to call the former simply " Sponge Cakes," and the latter, " Butter Sponge Cakes." The first needs no raising agent, but the latter requires baking powder, the amount depending on the number of eggs used in the recipe ; the more eggs beaten in, the less baking powder.

Ingredients : The finest flour, finest sugar, and eggs 3 days old, must be used when making sponge cakes. (If Hungarian or Vienna flour is not available, substitute cornflour for flour in the proportion of 1 oz. to 7 oz. flour, in order to lighten the flour.) Keep flour used for sponge cakes in a dry atmosphere.

There are several methods of mixing a sponge cake. If the recipe calls for separation of eggs, beat the yolks until honey or lemon coloured and thick, and the whites until they form peaks or hold their shape, but are not dry.

Tins : It is better not to grease tins for sponge cakes unless the tins are badly worn, when the bottoms only should be greased. Simply put the batter gently into perfectly dry tins. This applies to loaf tins, solid cake tins, tubular tins, Balmoral, gâteau and layer cake tins. If a crisp, sugary crust is wanted, grease tin and dust with equal quantity of caster sugar and cornflour, then shake lightly to remove any surplus before adding batter. Fill tins in each case three-quarters full. Some experts claim that sponge cakes are best baked in a greased tin dredged with flour. Try all the methods of preparing tins, and see which you like best. It is a good idea to tie a double band of paper around the outside of tin in case the mixture rises above the top. See that it extends about 3 inches above the edge of tin.

To Bake Sponge Cakes : Bake in a slow to moderate oven. Place the tin on the centre of a shelf in a moderately slow oven, 325° F., for about 1 hour, for a cake made with 5 eggs, or in an ungreased tubular tin, 9 inches across, and bake in a moderately hot oven, 375° F., for about ½ hour. Bake according to the instructions given on your cookery chart.

To Test : Press the top once very gently with your finger. If the cake is ready, the depression will slowly disappear.

To Cool : When ready, turn the pan upside down on to a rack. Leave for about 1 hour, or at least until cake is cool, then gradually ease it by sliding a palette knife round the side. Turn cake gently on to a wire rack, base downwards. Dredge with caster sugar. Never handle a sponge cake until it is cold.

SPONGE CAKE (Tourte Biscuit)

¼ lb. sifted flour
5 separated eggs
1 teaspoon grated lemon rind
1 tablespoon lemon juice
1 saltspoon salt
½ lb. caster sugar

SIZE OF TIN :
  Round, 9″ x 4″
  Tubular, 9″ across

Leave tin ungreased. Sift flour thrice. Beat yolks till thick and honey-coloured. Add lemon rind and juice. Beat until very thick. Beat egg whites till frothy. Sprinkle salt over the top. Keep on beating until stiff enough to hold their shape, but not dry. Sprinkle 2 tablespoons of sugar over the top. Beat till blended. Continue adding 2 tablespoons of sugar and beating it in until all the sugar is incorporated. Give egg yolks a quick beat. Fold into the mixture. Sift 3 tablespoons of the flour over the batter. Fold in lightly. Repeat until all the flour is folded in. Turn at once into tin. Bake in a moderately slow oven, 325° F., for about 1 hour, then invert tin on a wire rack. Leave for 1 hour, then gradually ease out with a palette knife. Gently place, base downwards, on rack. Dredge top and sides with caster sugar.

COLLEGE SPONGE CAKE (Tourte Biscuit au Collège)

5 oz. loaf sugar
½ gill water
2 eggs
1 egg yolk
½ teaspoon grated lemon rind
¼ lb. sifted flour

SIZE OF TIN : 6″ across, and 3″ deep

Grease tin. Put sugar and water in an enamel saucepan. Bring to boil. Simmer slowly for 5 minutes. Beat eggs slightly with a wire whisk, then pour in the syrup very very slowly, stirring constantly. Whisk steadily for ½ hour till light and frothy. Whisk in lemon rind. Sift flour. Fold in a little at a time very lightly. Half-fill cake tin. Bake in a moderately slow oven, 325° F., for about ¾ hour. Invert to cool on a wire rack, then ease out with a palette knife on to a wire rack, base downwards. Dredge with vanilla icing sugar.

ANGEL FOOD CAKE (Tourte Biscuit, Céleste)

BASIC RECIPE :
1/4 lb. sifted flour
3/4 lb. caster sugar
1/4 teaspoon salt
1/2 pint egg whites
1 tablespoon water
1 dessertspoon lemon juice
3/4 teaspoon cream of tartar
1/4 teaspoon almond essence
1/2 teaspoon vanilla essence

SIZE OF TIN : 9" tubular

Leave tin ungreased. Sift flour. Sift sugar twice. Add 1/4 lb. to the flour, and sift thrice with the salt. Whip egg whites with water and lemon juice until frothy. Add cream of tartar. Beat till stiff and the mixture holds its shape when tested. Sprinkle a dessertspoon of the sugar over the top. Fold in gently. Repeat, then fold in the essences. Stir remainder of sugar into the flour mixture. Sprinkle 2 tablespoons over the top of the egg mixture and fold in gently. Repeat this over different parts of the batter until all the ingredients are blended, using an egg whisk or a spatula. Gently turn into tin. Bake in a moderately slow oven, 325° F., for about 1 hour. Invert cake on a wire rack for 1 hour, then ease out with a palette knife when cold, base downwards, on to rack.

CHOCOLATE ANGEL FOOD CAKE : Substitute 3 tablespoons of cocoa for 3 tablespoons of the flour. Mix with remainder of flour and sift 4 times. Omit almond essence, and increase vanilla essence to 3/4 teaspoon.

NUT ANGEL FOOD CAKE : Increase cream of tartar to 1 teaspoon. Fold in 1 cup thinly sliced toasted almonds or chopped walnuts before baking. Use a 10" tubular tin. Bake in a very slow oven, 275° F., for about 1 1/4 hours.

SPONGE OR SWISS ROLL

BASIC RECIPE :
3 oz. sifted flour
1 teaspoon baking powder
1/4 teaspoon salt
3 eggs
1/4 lb. caster sugar
1/4 teaspoon vanilla essence
3 tablespoons heated jam

1 SWISS ROLL TIN : 12" x 9"

Grease or oil and line tin. Sift flour, baking powder and salt. Beat eggs and sugar till frothy and creamy coloured. Lightly stir in vanilla essence, then fold in flour. When blended, spread evenly with a palette knife in prepared tin, taking care to force batter into corners. Place on an oven shelf near the top, and bake for 7-10 minutes in a moderately hot oven, 400° F.

Meanwhile heat jam in a saucepan. Dredge a kitchen towel with caster sugar. Turn cake quickly out on to towel. Quickly trim off outside edges, and spread with jam. Roll up at once.

NOTE : If you find that it breaks while rolling, turn in about an inch " hem " at one side, and press it nearly flat before rolling up ; it will be easy to roll if you turn it on to a damp kitchen cloth dredged with caster sugar. Roll up quickly away from you, lifting the kitchen towel up as you roll. Place, join downwards, on a wire rack to cool.

To Vary : 1. If a cheaper roll is wanted, use only 2 eggs, 1/4 lb. sifted flour, 5 oz. caster sugar, 1 teaspoon baking powder, and 4 tablespoons cold water. Follow basic recipe, but separate eggs. Beat only yolks with sugar, and fold in stiffly beaten whites after the water.

CHOCOLATE SWISS ROLL : Follow basic recipe, but dissolve 2 oz. chocolate in 2 tablespoons hot water and cool, then stir into egg mixture before folding in flour.

YULE LOG : Use heated apricot or raspberry jam for the filling. When cake is cool, cut a thin slice off each end. Make a knot of marzipan to suggest a short stump, and place it sideways on top of roll. Spread top and sides of roll and stump thinly with chocolate butter icing. When set, force trails of chocolate butter icing in parallel lines along the top and sides of roll, and up the sides of the stump. Decorate ends of log and top of stump with rings of icing piped on with a writing tube. When the coating is almost set, decorate further with a robin and a tiny sprig of artificial holly and mistletoe.

BUTTER SPONGE

6 oz. sifted flour
¼ teaspoon salt
4 oz. butter
4 oz. caster sugar
3 separated eggs
Flavouring to taste
1 rounded teaspoon baking powder

Sift flour with salt on to a piece of paper. Beat butter till softened. Gradually beat in sugar. Beat till fluffy. Beat egg yolks till honey-coloured, then beat into butter and sugar. To avoid curdling, it is a good idea to dredge each addition of egg lightly with about a dessertspoon of the flour. Stir in flavouring. Mix baking powder with a tablespoon of the flour. Stir remainder of flour into egg mixture, then stir in baking powder mixture. Beat egg whites to a stiff froth. Fold into batter. Divide batter equally between two prepared sandwich tins, 8″ across, or place in a gâteau tin, 7″ across, or in a loaf tin, 8″×4″. Bake layer cakes in a moderate oven, 350° F., for about 25 minutes. Bake gâteau in a moderate oven, 350° F., for about ¾ hour. Bake loaf cake in a moderate oven, 350° F., for about 25 minutes. Remove from oven. Stand for a moment or two to allow cake to shrink, then turn on to a wire rack if to be iced. If not to be iced, turn on to a wire rack covered with a kitchen cloth dredged with caster or icing sugar.

SPONGE FLANS

Grease a " flan-pack " tin, about 8 inches across, with melted lard. Beat 1 egg with a few grains of salt till blended. Gradually beat in a small packet of sponge mixture. Beat till into a smooth batter, then stir in ½ oz. creamed butter. When blended, pour batter on to centre raised portion of tin. Spread very evenly over centre with a fork, so that it just begins to run over the edge into the ring beyond. Bake in the centre of a fairly hot oven, 425° F., for about 10 minutes. When well-baked, turn on to sugared paper, or on to a cake sieve, and leave till cool. Sprinkle rim with sifted icing sugar. Fill and decorate to taste. *For 6 persons.*

PEACH OR PEAR SPONGE FLAN : Dissolve ½ packet jelly in enough hot water to make about 1½ gills. When about to set, pour a thin layer into flan case. Arrange sliced peaches in jelly, then cover with remainder of jelly. Decorate with more fruit and roses of whipped cream.

STRAWBERRY SPONGE FLAN : Fill hollow with hulled medium-sized strawberries. Dribble over 3 tablespoons strawberry jam, brought to a boil with 3 tablespoons water, then strained. Chill. Decorate with stars of whipped cream.

CANDLE GATEAU : Cut circles of butter sponge the diameter of a saucer. Coat with water icing, coloured to taste. Ring with shelled walnuts. Insert a real candle wrapped with aluminium foil, or a stick of rock in the centre and fleck it with white icing. Make a handle of angelica, soaked in warm water to make it pliable. Dust with caster sugar.

BETTY'S CHOCOLATE GATEAU (Gâteau de Chocolat, Betty)

¼ lb. butter
¼ lb. sugar
¼ lb. self-raising flour
Tiny pinch of salt
2 beaten eggs
2-4 oz. chocolate
½ teaspoon vanilla essence

2 SANDWICH TINS : 6″ across

Grease tins. Beat butter till softened, then add sugar. Beat till light and creamy. Sift flour with salt. Stir into fat and sugar alternately with eggs. Melt chocolate to taste with vanilla essence. Beat into batter. Divide equally between the tins. Bake in a moderate oven, 350° F., for about 25 minutes. Cool on a wire rack. Put halves together with apricot or raspberry jam or chocolate butter crème. Coat top and sides with chocolate glacé icing. Ornament with shelled walnuts or with a design in dots of piped butter crème.

CRINOLINE LADY (Gâteau à la Crinoline)

5 oz. butter
7 oz. caster sugar
3 eggs
¾ lb. flour
1½ teaspoons baking powder
Milk as required
1 oz. desiccated coconut
3 oz. chopped walnuts
1½ lb. almond paste

SIZE OF TIN : 5½″ across

Grease tin, then line with buttered paper, bringing the paper from 2-3 inches above the sides. Beat butter till softened. Gradually beat in sugar. Beat till fluffy. Drop in each egg separately, and beat well before adding the next. Sift flour with baking powder. Lightly stir into the butter mixture with milk as required, or if preferred, moisten only with egg. Stir in coconut and walnuts. Flavour to taste with rose essence or rose water, and colour a delicate pink with cochineal. Turn into tin. Bake in a moderately hot oven, 375° F., for about 1¼ hours. When cooked, turn out very carefully on to a wire rack. Leave until quite cold.

To Decorate : Make almond paste in the usual way. Divide in two portions. Knead each into a lump. Brush the doll's head below with a little melted jam, and place in centre on top. Form a small piece of almond paste into a roll that will go round the base of cake. Brush the whole of the cake with melted jam, and place roll round the bottom, joining it neatly at the back. Now, cover the cake with strips of paste, becoming thinner as it gets towards the top. Gradually build up the top in the same way till the figure is covered. If you find it easier, coat the whole of the cake with almond paste, then put a roll round the bottom, moulding it to a gradual slope, then build up the top from the edge to get the shape (*see illustration facing page* 673). Leave for 24 hours to dry, in a warm room. Cover almond paste with white glacé icing. When set, cover with royal icing. Decorate, when set, with festoons of pink or blue icing, with cream roses between the festoons, using a suitable forcing pipe, and see that the " under-skirt " shows in front in a large V, ringed with a blue ribbon. Be sure to make the frills of lilac, pink and a delicate blue, alternately.

729

MADEIRA CAKE (Gâteau Madère)

5 oz. butter
6 oz. caster sugar
4 eggs
½ lb. sifted flour
1 teaspoon baking powder
¼ teaspoon salt
Grated rind of 1 lemon

SIZE OF TIN : 7″ across

Grease and line cake tin smoothly with buttered paper. Beat the butter till softened. Gradually beat in sugar. Beat in eggs, a little at a time, to prevent curdling. Sift flour with baking powder and salt. Stir into butter mixture with lemon rind. Turn into tin. Bake in a moderately hot oven, 375° F., until batter is risen and set, then place a broad slice of citron peel on top, and finish baking. Time required about 1¼ hours altogether.

To Vary: If a moister cake is wanted, increase butter to ½ lb., and use only 3 eggs diluted with 1 tablespoon water.

MARBLE CAKE (Gâteau Marbre)

½ lb. flour
Pinch of salt
5 ozs. butter
5 ozs. caster sugar
1½ teaspoons baking powder
2 small beaten eggs
⅛ pint milk
½ oz. cocoa
¼ teaspoon vanilla essence

SIZE OF TIN : 6″ across

Grease and flour tin. Sift flour into a basin with salt. Rub butter into flour with the finger tips. Stir in sugar and baking powder. Make a well in the centre. Add beaten eggs and milk. Stir till blended. Put half the mixture into another basin, and stir in cocoa and vanilla essence. Put alternate tablespoons of the white and chocolate mixture into prepared tin. Bake in a moderate oven, 350° F., for about ¾ hour. When cooked, cool on a cake rack or sieve. Dredge with caster sugar.

RUSSIAN GATEAU (Gâteau à la Russe)

3 oz. butter
3 oz. caster sugar
5 oz. sifted flour
Pinch of salt
½ teaspoon baking powder
1 egg
4 tablespoons milk
Essence to taste
Colouring to taste
Apricot jam as required
Almond paste

1 RUSSIAN CAKE TIN

Line each side of tin with greased paper. Beat butter till softened, then gradually beat in sugar. Beat till fluffy. Sift flour, salt and baking powder. Stir egg into milk, then add flour and egg gradually to creamed mixture. Divide mixture in half. Add 3 drops of vanilla essence and green colouring or cochineal to colour one portion. Add 3 drops of almond essence to the other with 1 tablespoon desiccated coconut if liked, and chocolate colouring. Pack the chocolate mixture into one side of tin, and the green or pink into the other. Press it well into the corners and make it level on top with a palette knife. Bake in a moderate oven, 350° F., for about ¼ hour. Cool on a wire rack. With the loose division, divide each cake in two. Spread one bar of each thinly with the jam. Place a chocolate bar on top of a pink or green bar, then brush one side of this combination with jam. Now place remaining bars together with the pink or green on top this time, and press up against the jammed half. If necessary, trim at ends so that they are perfectly flat. Roll almond paste into an oblong, about 12 × 6 inches, on greaseproof paper. Brush with lightly-beat egg white. Lay the cake exactly in the centre and press on the almond paste with the help of the paper. Mould lightly across the top so that the ends are smoothly joined. Turn upside down. Decorate with glacé cherries, cut in petals, and arrange in a posy on the centre with stalks of angelica ; or coat with top and sides, glacé icing, and decorate with chocolate shot or " hundreds and thousands."

ALMOND PASTE FOR RUSSIAN GATEAU : Mix $\frac{1}{2}$ lb. ground almonds with $\frac{3}{4}$ lb. sifted icing sugar or half icing sugar and half caster sugar, and add a tiny pinch of salt and a beaten egg.

SAND TORTE (Gâteau à la Sable)

6 oz. unsalted butter
$\frac{3}{4}$ cup caster sugar
4 egg yolks
3 oz. sifted flour
3 oz. sifted cornflour
$1\frac{1}{2}$ teaspoons baking powder
1 tablespoon rum
$\frac{1}{2}$ lemon
4 egg whites

1 TUBULAR TIN : 8" across

Grease tin. Beat butter and sugar to a cream. Beat and add egg yolks. Sift flour with cornflour and baking powder. Stir lightly into mixture. Stir in rum, and juice and grated rind of the lemon. Beat egg whites to a stiff froth and fold into mixture. Pour into prepared tin. Bake in a moderate oven, 350° F., for about $\frac{3}{4}$ hour. When cold, spread with chocolate or mocha glacé icing. Decorate with chopped nuts.

VALENTINE GATEAU (Gâteau à l'Amour)

3 oz. butter
$\frac{1}{2}$ lb. caster sugar
2 beaten eggs
$\frac{1}{2}$ teaspoon vanilla essence
7 oz. sifted flour
2 teaspoons baking powder
$\frac{1}{2}$ teaspoon salt
$\frac{1}{2}$ cup milk
1 oz. plain chocolate

1 HEART-SHAPED TIN or ROUND TIN : 9" across

Grease tin. Beat butter till softened. Gradually beat in sugar. Beat till fluffy. Add eggs gradually, then beat in vanilla essence. Sift flour thrice with baking powder and salt. Add alternately with milk to batter, beating after each addition till blended. Remove a third of the batter to another basin. Melt chocolate and stir in. Place a spoonful of the chocolate and a smaller spoonful of the main batter alternately into prepared tin, until all the chocolate batter is added. Add 2 or 3 drops of lemon essence to remaining batter and colour it pink. Spread it lightly over the top. Bake in a moderate oven, 350° F., for 45-50 minutes. Cool on a wire rack. When cold, split carefully across in two and pair with butterscotch filling, if liked. Cover with pale pink glacé icing. Decorate with a wreath of glacé cherries and angelica, or pipe a bow and arrow with white icing on the centre.

WALNUT GATEAU (Gâteau aux Noix)

$\frac{1}{4}$ lb. butter
6 oz. caster sugar
$\frac{1}{2}$ lb. sifted flour
2 teaspoons baking powder
Pinch of salt
2 beaten eggs
$\frac{1}{2}$ cup milk

Grease and line tin smoothly with buttered paper. Beat butter and sugar to a cream. Sift flour with baking powder and salt. Dilute eggs with milk. Beat flour and egg-milk alternately into butter and sugar. Stir in walnuts, lemon rind and vanilla essence. Pour into prepared tin. Bake

731

5 oz. chopped walnuts
Grated rind of 1 lemon
½ teaspoon vanilla essence

SIZE OF TIN : 8″ across

in a moderate oven, 350° F., for about 1¼ hours. When cold, cut in halves crosswise. Put halves together with butter crème. Cover with maple glacé icing. Decorate with halved walnuts, or with rings of piped chocolate dots.

AMERICAN LAYER CAKE

BASIC RECIPE :
6 oz. sifted flour
1 oz. cornflour
7½ oz. caster sugar
2¾ oz. butter
2 eggs
1 saltspoon salt
½ teaspoon vanilla essence
½ cup milk
2 teaspoons baking powder

2 SANDWICH TINS : 8″ across

Grease tins. Sift flour with cornflour. Reserve 2 tablespoons of sugar. Beat butter till softened. Gradually beat in remaining sugar. Beat till fluffy. Beat eggs. Beat in reserved sugar. Gradually beat into butter mixture. Stir in salt and vanilla. Stir in half the flour, then half the milk. Sift baking powder with remainder of flour. Add alternately with remainder of milk. (If a lighter cake is wanted, separate yolks and whites. Beat in yolks in place of 4 eggs, then fold in stiffly-frothed whites before baking.) Divide mixture between tins. Bake in a moderately hot oven, 375° F., for about 25 minutes.

To Vary : Substitute orange, pineapple or tangerine juice for the milk. Add the grated rind of a lemon, orange or tangerine. Coat with glacé icing or Seven Minute Frosting.

COFFEE LAYER CAKE : Substitute black coffee for the milk. Sandwich layers with 3 tablespoons creamed butter mixed with 3 tablespoons cocoa, 3 tablespoons black coffee and icing sugar to thicken. Coat with coffee glacé icing. Decorate with shelled walnuts.

WALNUT LAYER CAKE : Add 1½ oz. chopped shelled walnuts to batter before beaten egg whites. Put together with vanilla butter icing. Coat with Harlequin Jelly Frosting. Decorate with shelled walnuts.

CHOCOLATE PEPPERMINT LAYER CAKE
(Gâteau de Chocolate à la Menthe)

7 oz. sifted flour
1 oz. cornflour
¾ teaspoon bicarbonate of soda
¼ teaspoon salt
2¾ oz. butter
9 oz. caster sugar
1 egg
3 oz. unsweetened chocolate, melted
½ cup thick sour cream
¾ cup milk
¾ teaspoon vanilla essence

2 SANDWICH TINS : 9″ across

Grease tins. Sift flour thrice with cornflour, soda and salt. Beat butter to a cream. Gradually beat in sugar. Beat till fluffy. Add egg. Beat vigorously till blended. Stir in chocolate. Add ½ cup of the flour mixture and beat well, then stir in sour cream and beat well. Stir in remainder of flour alternately with milk, beating after each addition. Stir in vanilla. Divide equally between tins. Bake in a moderate oven, 350° F., for about ½ hour. When cold, put layers together with Peppermint Frosting, and cover to match. Decorate round edge of top with chocolate shot, or with a wreath of chopped nuts.

DEVIL'S FOOD LAYER CAKE (Gâteau au Diable)

BATTER 1
½ lb. caster sugar
½ cup milk
¼ lb. chocolate
1 beaten egg yolk
1 teaspoon vanilla essence

BATTER 2
¼ lb. butter
½ lb. caster sugar
2 eggs
½ lb. sifted flour
1½ teaspoons baking powder
½ cup milk

2 SANDWICH TINS : 9″ across

Grease tins. Place sugar, milk and chocolate in the top of a double boiler. Cook, over boiling water, till sugar is dissolved. Place egg yolk in a basin. Stir in chocolate mixture. When blended, pour into the top of double boiler. Cook over boiling water, stirring constantly, till mixture coats spoon, then remove from heat and leave till cool. Stir in vanilla essence. Beat butter to a cream. Gradually beat in sugar, then beat in eggs, one at a time, beating well after each addition. Sift flour with baking powder. Stir in flour and milk alternately. When blended, stir in the cool batter. Divide equally between tins. Bake in a moderate oven, 350° F., for about ½ hour. When cold, put layers together with American Chocolate Butter Frosting. Coat to match. Mark all over in a hobnail design.

ORANGE LAYER CAKE (Gâteau d'Orange)

10 oz. sifted flour
2 teaspoons golden raising powder
1 saltspoon salt
Grated rind of 1 lemon
Grated rind of 1 orange
2 tablespoons orange juice
5½ oz. butter
½ lb. caster sugar
3 eggs
2 tablespoons strained lemon juice
2 tablespoons boiling water

2 SANDWICH TINS : 9″ across

Grease tins. Sift flour twice with raising powder and salt. Beat lemon and orange rinds, and butter till into a paste, then gradually beat in sugar. Beat till light and fluffy. Add 1 egg, and beat vigorously. Repeat twice. Lightly stir in flour alternately with lemon and orange juice, beating only till smooth after each addition, then quickly stir in boiling water. Divide quickly between each tin. Bake at once in a moderately hot oven, 375° F., for about 20 minutes. When quite cold, sandwich layers with orange crème, and cover with orange glacé icing. Coat with desiccated coconut.

RIBBON LAYER CAKE (Gâteau au Ruban)

10 oz. sifted flour
3½ teaspoons baking powder
½ teaspoon salt
6 oz. butter
½ lb. caster sugar
3 eggs
¾ cup milk
1½ teaspoons vanilla essence
1 oz. plain chocolate
3 or 4 drops almond essence
Sap green colouring

3 SANDWICH TINS: 8″ across

Grease tins. Sift flour. Add baking powder and salt and sift again. Beat butter till softened. Add sugar by degrees. Beat till fluffy. Separate eggs. Beat yolks till blended. Gradually beat into fat and sugar. When blended, add dry ingredients alternately with milk, stirring till blended after each addition. Stir in vanilla essence. Beat egg whites till stiff. Fold into mixture. Divide batter into 3 equal portions. Colour one a delicate pink with cochineal if liked. Pour into a tin. Melt chocolate. Stir into second portion, and pour into second tin. Stir almond essence and a drop or two of sap green colouring to give you a delicate green colour, into third portion. Pour into third tin. Smooth each with a palette knife. Bake in a moderately hot oven, 375° F., for 20-25 minutes. When cool, pair layers with vanilla layer on top, almond next and chocolate at the bottom, with apricot jam between chocolate and almond, and rum butter crème or glacé icing between almond and vanilla. Sprinkle top layer with caster or sifted icing sugar.

VICTORIA SANDWICH

¼ lb. butter
¼ lb. caster sugar
2 eggs
1 tablespoon warm milk or water
¼ lb. sifted flour
1 teaspoon baking powder
Flavouring to taste

2 SANDWICH TINS : 7″ across

Grease tins and dust with flour. Beat fat and sugar to a cream. Add eggs, one at a time, beating well after each addition, then stir in warm milk or water. Sift flour with baking powder into mixture. Add flavouring such as grated rind of ½ lemon, and ½ teaspoon vanilla essence. Divide between tins. Bake in a moderately hot oven, 400° F., for about 20 minutes. Cool. Put layers together with jam. Dust top with icing sugar.

Biscuits

Until recent years, the only biscuits we troubled to make were the kind you roll and cut out. Nowadays, drop biscuits, easier and quicker to make than the former, and biscuits piped through a syringe have come to vary the contents of the biscuit barrel or cooky jar. If very fine biscuits are wanted, substitute ½-1 oz. cornflour for ½-1 oz. of the flour. Cool all biscuits on a wire rack, then store in a tightly closed tin.

SHORT BISCUITS

BASIC RECIPE :
¼ lb. butter
¼ lb. brown or caster sugar
½ lb. flour
1 teaspoon baking powder
Few grains of salt
1 egg yolk

Beat butter and sugar to a cream. Sift flour with baking powder and salt. Stir into fat mixture. Mix with enough egg yolk, slightly beaten, to make a light, soft, rollable dough. Roll out thinly on a lightly floured board. Cut into rounds or fancy shapes with a plain, fluted, or fancy cutter. Place on a buttered baking sheet about an inch apart. Bake in a moderately hot oven, 375° F., for about 12 minutes. Cool on a cake rack.

To Vary : If you wish biscuits spiced, sift either ½ teaspoon ground cinnamon, or ¼ teaspoon cinnamon and ¼ teaspoon ground mace, and ¼ teaspoon ground ginger, with the flour.

ALMOND : Stir in ½ cup blanched minced almonds and ¼ cup minced citron peel after the flour.

CARAWAY : Add 1 or 2 teaspoons caraway seeds after the flour.

CHOCOLATE : Stir 4 tablespoons melted chocolate into butter and sugar after creaming, and add ½ teaspoon vanilla essence to egg yolk.

CURRANT : Add 2 or 3 oz. cleaned currants and 1 teaspoon grated lemon or lemon and orange peel, after the flour.

TO FINISH : Pair the biscuits, using the following fillings :

Butter icing, flavoured with vanilla essence to taste and mixed with a tablespoon or more of minced, blanched almonds, minced walnuts, or glacé cherries.

TO SERVE : Dredge with caster sugar as soon as they come out of the oven, or spread each with a thin layer of water icing when cold, and decorate or top with jam and sprinkle with chopped nuts and desiccated coconut, etc.

VANILLA COOKIES (Biscuits de Vanille)

BASIC RECIPE :
½ lb. butter
¼ lb. caster sugar
1 beaten egg
2 teaspoons vanilla essence
¾ lb. flour
½ teaspoon baking powder
1 saltspoon salt

Cream butter. Gradually beat in sugar. Beat until fluffy. Stir in egg and vanilla essence. Sift flour with baking powder and salt, and gradually stir in egg mixture. Roll out to ⅛ inch thickness on a lightly floured board. Cut into fancy shapes. Bake in a moderate oven, 350° F., for 12-15 minutes. *Yield :* About 4 dozen.

ALMOND COOKIES : Decorate with blanched almonds before baking.

BUTTERSCOTCH COOKIES : Sprinkle with crushed butterscotch the moment they come out of the oven.

ABERNETHY BISCUITS (Biscuits Abernethy)

1 lb. flour
¼ teaspoon salt
1½ oz. butter
1 oz. caster sugar
1 teaspoon caraway seeds
1 egg
¾ gill milk

Sift flour and salt into a basin. Rub in butter. Stir in sugar and caraway seeds. Beat egg. Stir in milk. Make hollow in centre of flour. Add liquid, and enough additional milk to give you a rollable dough. Roll dough on a floured board to ¼ inch thickness. Cut into small rounds. Bake a little apart on a greased baking sheet, in a moderately hot oven, 375° F., till pale gold, in about 12 minutes. Cool. *Yield:* About 2½ dozen.

ARROWROOT BISCUITS (Biscuits d'Arrowroot)

4 oz. arrowroot
4 oz. flour
2 oz. butter
2 oz. caster sugar
Cream or top milk

Sift arrowroot and flour. Rub in butter lightly. Stir in sugar and enough cream or top milk to make a stiff dough. Roll out to ⅛ inch thickness on a lightly floured board. Prick all over with a fork. Cut into rounds 2-2½ inches across. Arrange a little apart on a floured baking sheet. Bake in a moderately slow oven, 325° F., until crisp and brown in about 20 minutes. *Yield:* About 2 dozen.

CHILDREN'S PARTY FARE

Meringues, Birthday Cake, Grape and Strawberry Tartlets, Orange Jelly, and Orangeade. *See pages* 704, 705, 719, 608, *and* 831.

COCKTAIL PARTY
Cabbage Rose, Dates with Cream Cheese Stuffing, Assorted Canapes, and
Luncheon Meat Sticks. *See pages 778, and 786-789.*

BUTTER BISCUITS (Biscuits au Beurre)

4 oz. flour
1 saltspoon salt
2 oz. butter
Cold water as required

Sift flour and salt into a basin. Rub in butter. Mix to a stiff paste with a little cold water. Roll out thinly on a lightly floured board. Prick all over. Cut into rounds 2-2½ inches across. Bake a little apart on a greased baking sheet in a moderately hot oven, 375° F., until crisp in about 10 minutes. *Yield:* About 1½ dozen.

CHEESE BISCUITS (Biscuits de Fromage)

2½ oz. butter
¼ lb. grated cheese
3 oz. flour
1 saltspoon dry mustard
Salt and cayenne pepper to taste
1 beaten egg yolk

Soften butter in the oven for a moment or two, then stir in cheese. Sift flour with mustard and add. Season to taste, then mix to a paste with the egg yolk as required. Roll on a lightly floured board to an eighth of an inch in thickness. Cut biscuits out into squares, 2-2½ inches across. Brush tops with beaten egg. Prick well. Bake a little apart on a buttered baking sheet, for 8-10 minutes in a moderately hot oven, 400° F. Serve hot or cold on a dish lined with a lace paper doily. *Yield:* About 20 biscuits.

CHOCOLATE COCONUT BISCUITS

6 oz. caster sugar
4 oz. ground almonds
1 oz. desiccated coconut
1½ oz. grated chocolate
1 egg white

Mix all the ingredients together. Roll on a pastry board dredged with icing sugar to ½ inch thickness. Cut into fancy shapes. Place each on a tiny piece of wafer paper, then arrange on a baking sheet. Bake in a slow oven, 275° F., for about 45 minutes. Remove from oven. Sprinkle with icing sugar. *Yield:* About 2 dozen.

CRACKNELS

2 eggs
2 tablespoons rose water
¼ teaspoon grated nutmeg
1 lb. sifted flour
Cold water as required
½ lb. butter

Beat eggs with rose water and nutmeg until blended. Stir in flour and enough cold water to make a stiff paste. Roll out into a thin rectangle on a lightly-floured board. Dab here and there with 2 oz. of the butter. Fold in three and roll as you would for flaky pastry. Repeat operation of rolling and buttering until you have incorporated all the butter. Roll out thinly and cut into rounds. Place gently in a saucepan of boiling water. Simmer gently until the cracknels swim to the top. Drain quickly and dry thoroughly. Bake a little apart on a lightly greased baking sheet in a moderate oven, 350° F., for about ¼ hour.

DIGESTIVE BISCUITS (Biscuits Digestifs)

¼ lb. oatmeal
¼ lb. flour

Sift oatmeal and flour into a basin with baking powder, sugar and salt. (Substitute wholemeal

1 teaspoon baking powder
1½ oz. caster sugar
Pinch of salt
2 oz. butter or lard
1 beaten egg

flour for oatmeal when a finer textured biscuit is wanted.) Rub in fat. Mix to a stiff paste with egg. Roll out thinly on a lightly floured board. Prick with a fork. Cut into small rounds. Bake a little apart on a greased baking sheet in a moderate oven, 350° F., for 15-20 minutes, till crisp and golden. *Yield:* About 2 dozen.

FIG NEWTONS (Bâtons de Figues)

¼ lb. butter
¾ lb. caster sugar
1 beaten egg
¾ teaspoon vanilla essence
½ cup milk
¾ lb. flour
¼ teaspoon salt
3 teaspoons baking powder
1 cup chopped figs
1 cup boiling water

Beat butter till softened. Beat in ½ lb. sugar. When fluffy, add egg. Beat till blended. Stir vanilla into the milk. Sift flour with salt and baking powder. Stir alternately with the flavoured milk into the egg mixture until you have a soft dough. Chill for ½ hour. Roll out on a lightly floured board into an oblong, about ⅛ inch thick. Place figs in a small saucepan with remaining sugar and boiling water. Boil for 5 minutes. Cool. Measure off half of the dough and cover it with the fig spread to within half inch of edge. Fold uncovered dough over. Press lightly on top. Cut into oblongs. *Yield:* About 1 dozen.

FROSTED ALMOND CRISPS (Fleurs d'Amandes)

4 oz. unsalted butter
2 egg yolks
7 oz. flour
½ teaspoon baking powder
½ oz. icing sugar
2 stiffly-frothed egg whites
4 oz. caster sugar
¼ lb. ground almonds
Rind and juice of ½ lemon

Cream butter. Add egg yolks and beat till creamy. Sift flour with baking powder and icing sugar. Stir into butter and egg yolks. Mix to a stiff paste, adding a little water as may be required. Roll out thinly. Cut into small rounds. Mix egg white lightly with the caster sugar, almonds and lemon rind and juice. Spread on rounds. Bake a little apart on a lightly-buttered baking sheet in a moderate oven, 350° F., till crisp and brown in about 12 minutes. *Yield:* About 2½ dozen.

JACK FROST FINGERS (Biscuits Jack Frost)

1 oz. grated chocolate
6 oz. caster sugar
5 oz. ground almonds
1 egg white
Royal icing as required

Mix chocolate, sugar, almonds and egg white well together. Roll out on a big pastry board, lightly sprinkled with icing sugar, to ½ inch thickness. Spread with a thin layer of royal icing. Cut into narrow fingers. Place each on a narrow strip of rice paper. Bake for about 45 minutes in a very slow oven, 250° F., until faintly coloured. *Yield:* About 20 fingers.

RICE BISCUITS (Biscuits au Riz)

½ lb. rice flour
½ teaspoon baking powder

Sift flour and baking powder into a basin. Rub in butter. Stir in sugar, egg and milk. Roll out

3 oz. butter
3 oz. caster sugar
1 beaten egg
1 tablespoon milk

thinly on a lightly floured board. Cut into rounds $2\frac{1}{2}$ inches across. Bake a little apart on a greased baking sheet in a moderately hot oven, 375° F., for about 10 minutes. *Yield:* About $3\frac{1}{2}$ dozen.

RUSSIAN BISCUITS (Biscuits à la Russe)

1/4 lb. caster sugar
3 oz. butter
1 egg yolk
1/2 teaspoon vanilla essence
1 tablespoon cream
4 1/2 oz. sifted flour
1 teaspoon baking powder
Jam as required
1 egg white
5 tablespoons caster sugar
1 teaspoon ground cinnamon
1/2 cup chopped nuts

Beat the sugar and butter till creamy, then beat in egg yolk. Stir in vanilla and cream. Sift flour with baking powder. Stir into yolk mixture. Chill for 2 hours. Roll out very thinly on a lightly-floured board. Cut into rounds, 2 inches across. Spread with any tart jam or jelly. Beat egg white till stiff. Add caster sugar. Beat till stiff. Fold in cinnamon and nuts, or chopped dates if preferred. Spread over biscuits. Bake a little part on a greased baking sheet in a moderate oven, 350° F., for about 12 minutes. *Yield:* About 3 dozen.

SAND COOKIES

1/4 lb. butter
1/2 lb. caster sugar
1 beaten egg
7 oz. flour
2 teaspoons baking powder
Pinch of salt
1 egg white
1 tablespoon caster sugar
1/4 teaspoon ground cinnamon

Cream butter. Add sugar, then egg. Stir in flour sifted with baking powder and salt. Leave till quite cold, then roll out on a floured board to $\frac{1}{8}$ inch thickness. Cut into rings. Brush with white of egg slightly beaten, and sprinkle with the tablespoon of sugar sifted with cinnamon. Arrange 4 halved almonds on the top of each, pointing to centre. Bake in a moderately hot oven, 375° F., for about 10 minutes. *Yield:* About 5 dozen.

WATER BISCUITS (Biscuits à l'Eau)

1/2 lb. flour
Pinch of salt
Dash of celery salt
1 1/2-2 oz. butter
Cold water as required

Sift flour with salts into a basin. Rub in butter. Mix to a soft dough with cold water. Turn on to a floured pastry board. Knead thoroughly. Roll out thinly. Beat with a rolling pin. Prick all over. Cut into small rounds. Bake a little apart on a lightly floured baking sheet in a moderately hot oven, 400° F., for about 10 minutes, until crisp and pale brown. *Yield:* About 3 dozen.

ZOO BISCUITS (Biscuits aux Animaux)

1/4 lb. flour
1/3 lb. caster sugar
1/4 lb. cornflour
1 teaspoon baking powder
1/4 lb. butter
2 beaten eggs

Sift dry ingredients into a basin. Lightly rub in butter. Make into a dough with eggs. Roll out thinly on a lightly floured board into an oblong. Cut out with animal cutters. Bake in a moderately hot oven, 375° F., till biscuit-coloured, in

10-12 minutes. When cool, coat with green glacé icing. Fix eyes with currants, or pipe on eyes etc. *Yield:* About 2 dozen.

DROP BISCUITS

BRANDY SNAPS

¼ lb. butter
¼ lb. Demerara sugar
¼ lb. golden syrup
½-1 teaspoon ground ginger
¼ lb. sifted flour
½ -1 teaspoon lemon juice

Place butter, sugar, syrup and ginger in a saucepan. Heat very slowly until just warm. Stir in the flour, then lemon juice. Pour from a teaspoon into rounds about 6 inches apart on to a well-greased baking sheet. Bake in a moderately hot oven, 375° F., for about ¼ hour. Cool for a moment, then lift each off with a palette knife and quickly roll over the handle of a wooden spoon. Slip off carefully. Cool on a wire rack. Fill with whipped cream sweetened and flavoured with rum or vanilla essence to taste.

FRUIT DROPS (Biscuits aux Fruits)

¼ lb. butter
¼ lb. caster sugar
½ lb. flour
½ teaspoon mixed spices
1 teaspoon baking powder
Few grains of salt
1 beaten egg
¼ cup chopped raisins
¼ cup cleaned currants
2 teaspoons minced orange peel
¼ cup minced citron peel
¼ cup minced walnuts

Beat butter and sugar to a cream. Sift flour with spice, baking powder and salt. Stir into butter mixture, alternately with egg. Add fruit, peels and nuts. Drop in teaspoonfuls, about 2 inches apart, on to an oiled baking sheet. Bake in a moderately hot oven, 375° F., for about 10 minutes, till crisp. *Yield:* About 2½ dozen.

SAVOY BISCUITS (Biscuits au Savoie)

3 separated eggs
4 oz. caster sugar
4 oz. flour
Grated rind of ½ lemon

Beat egg yolks until blended, then beat in sugar. Beat until very fluffy. Whisk egg whites to a stiff froth. Sift flour. Add a little of the flour to the yolks. Beat until blended, then fold in a little of the egg white and flour alternately. Lastly, fold in lemon rind. Force through an icing syringe in finger shapes 4 inches long and ¾ inch wide on to a baking sheet covered with ungreased paper. Dredge thickly with caster sugar. Bake in a moderately hot oven, 375° F., for about 8 minutes. When ready, slip off paper with palette knife. Brush the undersides with lightly beaten egg white or whipped cream and pair biscuits. *Yield:* About 1 dozen.

MISCELLANEOUS BISCUITS

BRETTLES

¼ lb. butter
2 oz. caster sugar

Beat butter and sugar to a cream. Stir in egg yolk, fruit rinds and vanilla essence. Beat well.

1 separated egg
Grated rind of ½ lemon
Grated rind of ½ orange
½ teaspoon vanilla essence
¼ lb. sifted flour
1 tablespoon lemon juice
12 glace cherries

Add flour and lemon juice. Mix till mixture is light. Cover and stand in a cool place till firm. Roll into small balls. Dip into beaten egg white. Roll in chopped nuts. Top with half a cherry. Bake in a buttered baking tin about 1 inch apart, in a moderate oven, 350° F., for about 25 minutes. *Yield:* 24 Brettles.

DOMINOES (Dominos)

3 oz. butter
1½ oz. caster sugar
Grated rind of ½ lemon
1 egg yolk
3 oz. flour
¼ teaspoon baking powder

Beat butter and sugar to a cream. Stir in lemon rind and egg yolk. Sift flour with baking powder, and stir into egg mixture. Roll out to ⅛ inch thickness. Cut into 20 equal-sized oblongs. Bake a little apart on a greased baking sheet dredged with flour, in a moderately hot oven, 375° F., till pale brown in about 7 minutes. Cool on a wire rack. Pair with apricot jam. Coat top and sides with pastel glacé icing. Make chocolate glacé icing. Fix a piping tube to your icing syringe and pipe a line across the centre of each biscuit. Now pipe dots on the icing when it is almost set to resemble different dominoes. *Yield:* 20 dominoes.

FALLING STARS (Biscuits aux Etoiles)

½ lb. butter
¼ lb. caster sugar
10 oz. flour
Pinch of salt
1 egg

Beat butter and sugar to a cream. Sift flour with salt. Beat egg. Add flour and egg alternately till all the egg is used up, then mix to a soft dough with remainder of flour. Press through a star tube with a forcing pipe on to a buttered baking sheet 2 inches apart. Bake in a fairly hot oven, 425° F., for about 7 minutes. *Yield:* About 3 dozen.

GINGER NUTS (Biscuits au Gingembre)

½ lb. flour
½ teaspoon baking powder
1 saltspoon salt
2 teaspoons ground ginger
3 oz. butter
1 rounded teaspoon treacle
1 rounded tablespoon golden
  syrup
2 oz. Demerara sugar
1 saltspoon lemon juice
½ egg

Sift flour, baking powder, salt and ginger together. Heat butter, treacle, syrup and sugar very slowly until blended. Cool. Make a hole in centre of flour. Add liquid and lemon juice. Beat and add egg. Stir to a soft consistency. Shape into soft balls the size of a large walnut with your hands. Chill. Place 2 inches apart on a greased baking sheet. Bake in a moderate oven, 350° F., for about 17 minutes. *Yield:* About 2½ dozen.

JUMBLES

3 oz. butter
3 oz. caster sugar

Beat butter until softened. Gradually beat in sugar. Beat till fluffy, then add one egg at a time

741

2 eggs
8 oz. flour
Grated rind of 1 lemon

and beat well after each addition. Sift flour with a grain or two of salt. Grate in lemon rind. Stir into butter mixture. Turn on to a lightly-floured board. Shape into rolls about $\frac{1}{4}$ inch in diameter. Cut off lengths 3-4 inches long, and twist each portion into the definite letter " S." Bake a little apart on a greased baking sheet, in a moderate oven, 350° F., for 15-20 minutes.

MEXICAN BISCUITS (Biscuits, Mexicaine)

$\frac{1}{4}$ lb. butter
Sifted icing sugar as required
$\frac{1}{2}$ teaspoon vanilla essence
$4\frac{1}{2}$ oz. flour
Tiny pinch of salt

Beat butter till softened. Gradually beat in $\frac{1}{4}$ cup sifted icing sugar. Beat till fluffy. Stir in vanilla essence. Sift flour with salt and add to creamed mixture. Mix well. Chill for 3 or 4 hours. Divide dough into tiny pieces, and shape each into a round about an inch across. Bake a little apart on a greased baking sheet in a moderately hot oven, 400° F., for about 15 minutes. Roll at once in sifted icing sugar. Cool on a wire rack, then roll in sugar again. *Yield:* About 15 biscuits.

PERKINS (Biscuits, épicés)

$\frac{1}{4}$ lb. plain flour
Pinch of salt
2 oz. lard, butter or margarine
$\frac{1}{4}$ lb. fine oatmeal
3 oz. caster sugar
$\frac{3}{4}$ teaspoon bicarbonate of soda
$\frac{1}{2}$ teaspoon ground cinnamon
$\frac{1}{2}$ teaspoon ground ginger
$\frac{1}{4}$ teaspoon mixed cloves and mace
3 oz. honey or syrup
Beaten egg to bind

Sift flour into a basin with salt. Rub in fat. Add remainder of dry ingredients. Mix to a firm dough with honey or syrup and egg. Divide into knobs the size of a walnut. Place a little apart on a greased baking sheet. Flatten slightly. Bake in a moderate oven, 350° F., for about 20 minutes, till crisp. If you have almonds to spare, blanch, skin and split enough to crown the centre of each biscuit before baking. *Yield;* 15 or 16 perkins.

PRAIRIE FLAPJACKS

$\frac{1}{2}$ lb. rolled oats
1 saltspoon salt
$\frac{1}{4}$ lb. butter
2 oz. light brown sugar
$2\frac{1}{2}$ tablespoons extracted honey or golden syrup

Place oats and salt in a basin. Melt butter with sugar and honey or syrup in a saucepan. Stir in oats and mix well with a wooden spoon, until blended. Press into a shallow, well-greased oblong tin, pushing it into the corners or the cakes won't be of equal thickness. Bake in a moderate oven, 350° F., for about 25 minutes, until crisp and brown. Cut into oblongs, about 2 inches wide and 5 inches long. Leave in tin till cold, as they are very brittle. When quite cold, store in an airtight tin till wanted. *Yield:* About 9.

RATAFIA BISCUITS (Biscuits, Ratafia)

1 lb. caster sugar
6 oz. ground almonds

Place sugar in a basin. Stir in almonds. (If unable to buy bitter almonds, use $\frac{1}{2}$ lb. ground.

2 oz. ground bitter almonds   Mix thoroughly until blended, then add egg
4 egg whites   whites, two at a time, stirring constantly until the
mixture is into a stiff paste, as the mixture must not run after it is forced out.
Force through a syringe fitted with a round tube in small heaps about 2 inches
apart, either on to a baking sheet covered with rice paper, or dry greaseproof
paper. Bake in a moderate oven, 350° F., until very delicately browned, in
about 10 minutes.

REFRIGERATOR BISCUITS

Refrigerator biscuits are of American origin, but cannot be made perfectly
without the help of a refrigerator, except on frosty days, as the dough has to
be chilled before it is made into biscuits and baked.

VANILLA WAFERS (Gauffres Américaine)

3/4 lb. flour
1½ teaspoons baking powder
1/4 teaspoon salt
6 oz. butter
½ lb. light brown sugar
1 egg
3/4 teaspoon vanilla essence
1 oz. chocolate
1 oz. desiccated coconut

Sift flour with baking powder and salt. Beat
butter till soft. Add sugar and beat till creamy,
then stir in egg and vanilla essence. When
blended, lightly stir in flour mixture. Divide in
3 equal portions. Shape one portion into a roll
about 3/4 inch in diameter. Melt 1 oz. chocolate
and stir into a second portion, then roll up like the
first. Stir 1 oz. desiccated coconut into third
portion. Roll up like the others. Chill all three
until firm, then cut in slices, about 1/4 inch thick. Bake a little apart on a greased
baking sheet in a moderately hot oven, 375° F., for 10-12 minutes. *Yield:*
About 5 dozen.

WHIRLIGIGS

1/4 lb. caster sugar
2 beaten eggs
Juice and rind of ½ lemon
½ teaspoon vanilla essence
7 oz. flour
1/4 cup ground almonds
2 oz. butter
1½ teaspoons baking powder
2 teaspoons cocoa

Stir sugar into eggs. Beat till creamy. Stir in
lemon juice and rind, vanilla essence and 1/4 lb.
of the flour. When mixed, stir in almonds. Beat
butter till softened. Gradually stir in almond
mixture, then remainder of flour sifted with baking
powder. Knead cocoa into half of the dough.
Shape into a neat roll about ½ inch thick. Pat
rest of dough out into an oblong ½ inch thick and
the same length as the roll. Wrap round cocoa dough. Wrap in waxed paper
and chill. Cut in slices 1/8 inch thick. Place on a buttered baking sheet, 1½
inches apart. Bake in a moderately hot oven, 400° F., for 5-7 minutes. *Yield:*
About 3 dozen.

   NOTE : If preferred, roll both out into an oblong exactly the same size and
each 1/8 inch thick. Chill both. Turn plain portion on to a baking board. Cover
with cocoa or chocolate portion. Roll up like a swiss roll. Wrap in waxed
paper. Chill, then follow remainder of above method.

VIENNESE DAISIES (Fleurs de Vienne)

½ lb. butter
2 oz. caster sugar
7 oz. sifted flour
1 oz. cornflour
1 cup ground almonds
¾ teaspoon vanilla essence

Beat butter till softened. Beat in sugar. When fluffy, stir in flour, cornflour, almonds and vanilla essence. Roll out thinly on a board dusted with sifted caster sugar. Cut with a daisy or star cutter dipped in hot water. Bake a little apart on a buttered baking sheet, in a slow oven, 300° F., for about 35 minutes. Cool. Dredge with icing sugar. *Yield:* About 3 dozen.

SHORTBREAD

If you wish to keep up the custom of sending shortbread to friends at Christmas as a token of remembrance, I would omit the icing.

BASIC RECIPE:
½ lb. butter
¼ lb. caster sugar
1 lb. sifted flour

Place the butter on the centre of your pastry board with the sugar on one side and the flour on the other. Gradually knead the sugar into the butter, then knead in flour by degrees. (The dough should look like rich shortcrust.) Divide in 2 or 3 equal portions. Cover baking sheet with greaseproof paper. Lightly knead out cakes, ¾ inch thick, on the paper. Notch edges round with thumbs and forefingers, or ornament them with a fork. Prick centres all over with a fork. Slip on to a baking sheet covered with greaseproof paper. Bake in a moderate oven, 350° F., until firm and delicately browned, in about ¾ hour. Slide carefully on to a wire tray. Dredge with caster sugar.

To Vary: Use ¾ lb. flour sifted with ¼ lb. rice flour.

To Decorate Cakes: Carefully pour 2 tablespoons pink or white glacé icing, flavoured to taste, on to the pricked part of cakes. When almost set, decorate with ornaments made of crystallized lemon or orange slices, or with angelica, or with citron peel. If preferred, pipe a Christmas greeting on icing in a contrasting colour. It is not usual to decorate shortbread except when made at Christmas.

ALMOND SHORTBREAD

6 oz. butter
3 oz. caster sugar
1 oz. ground rice
½ lb. flour
¼ lb. blanched almonds

Beat butter till creamy. Stir in sugar. Sift ground rice with the flour. Stir into fat and sugar. Reserving ¾ oz. of the almonds, chop the remainder and add to flour mixture. Knead into a smooth dough. Pat into a square shape, about ¾ inch thick. Place on a baking sheet covered with greaseproof paper. Notch the edges with thumbs and forefingers or ornament with a fork. Press the almonds lightly in a design over the centre. Prick in between the almonds with a fork. Bake in a moderate oven, 350° F., for 35-45 minutes. Dredge with caster sugar. Cool on a wire rack.

AYRSHIRE SHORTBREAD

½ egg
1 small tablespoon cream
¼ lb. flour
¼ lb. rice flour
¼ lb. butter
2 oz. caster sugar

Beat egg. Add cream. Beat for a moment or two. Sift flour with the rice flour. Rub in butter. Stir in sugar, then the egg and cream. Knead lightly into a soft dough. Roll out on a lightly floured board to ¼ inch thickness. Prick with a fork. Cut with bridge cutters, or into crescents, ovals, bars, etc. Place a little apart on a baking sheet covered with greaseproof paper. Bake in a moderately hot oven, 375° F., for 10-12 minutes, till crisp and pale gold. Dredge with caster sugar. Cool on a wire rack.

PITCAITHLY BANNOCKS

1 lb. sifted flour
½ lb. butter
2 oz. chopped blanched almonds
2 oz. candied citron peel
3 oz. caster sugar

See that flour is perfectly dry. Knead in butter. When smooth, knead in almonds. Chop peel and knead in with the sugar. When dough is free from cracks, knead into one large round or square cake ¾-1 inch thick. Bake on a baking sheet covered with lightly buttered paper, in a moderate oven, 350° F., for about 1 hour. Cool on a wire rack.

Fillings and Icings

The American fashion for using a form of icing known as a frosting, not only as a coating but as a filling has become popular in this country.

In this section, I am following the American habit of giving the name "icing" only to a glacé or form of glacé icing which is uncooked, and reserving the term "frosting" for cooked icings.

When I started to make, fill, and ice layer cakes, the words "butter icing" were used in domestic circles for a mixture of butter and icing sugar with flavouring to taste. Now the term "butter crème" has crept into public use.

HINTS ON FILLING SPONGE LAYERS

1. Layers must be quite cold, or filling will soak in.
2. Brush any loose crumbs off layer to be covered before applying filling.
3. Do not use a moist filling unless cake is to be eaten quickly. If kept for any length of time, a moist filling will make cake soggy. Use a frosting, jam or lemon curd.

CONFECTIONER'S CUSTARD

2 oz. butter
1½ oz. flour
1½ gills milk
2 oz. caster sugar

Melt butter in a saucepan. Stir in flour gradually. When frothy, stir in milk. Stir till smooth and boiling. Boil for 1 minute, stirring constantly. Remove from heat. Cool slightly. Stir in sugar

1 egg yolk
1/4 gill thick cream
1/2 teaspoon vanilla essence or
   1 teaspoon rum

and egg yolk. When blended and thick, fold in cream and flavouring.

CREAM FILLINGS

Cream fillings are ideal for inserting in buns made with choux pastry, cream horns, éclairs, pastry slices, tartlet cases, or any layer cakes made of egg sponge. These fillings contain no cream. The basis of each is a white sauce. This is enriched with eggs or egg yolks, flavourings to taste, etc.

CREAM FILLING

BASIC RECIPE:
5 1/4 oz. caster sugar
1/3 cup flour
1 saltspoon salt
2 cups hot milk
2 lightly-beaten eggs
1 teaspoon vanilla essence

Mix sugar with the flour and salt in the top of a double boiler. Gradually stir in milk. Cook over boiling water until thick, stirring constantly, then cover. Cook for 10 minutes, stirring occasionally. Beat eggs, or 4 egg yolks if preferred. Stir a little of the hot sauce very slowly into egg or egg yolks, then slowly stir this mixture into remaining hot sauce in double boiler. Cook over hot water for 2 minutes, stirring constantly, but take care not to let the water below come to a boil. Remove from heat. Chill, stirring occasionally, then add vanilla essence. Enough for 2 layer cakes or a 3 layered cake, 9 inches across.

To Vary: Stir 1 oz. butter into the filling before chilling, or whip 1/2 cup thick cream and fold in after chilling.

ALMOND CUSTARD: Add 1 cup chopped, blanched almonds when chilled.

BANANA: Omit vanilla. Stir in 1 teaspoon lemon juice, and 1 mashed banana after chilling.

CHOCOLATE: Increase sugar to 1/2 lb. Add 2-3 oz. unsweetened chocolate, grated or shaved, to milk before heating.

COCONUT: Add 3/4 gill freshly shredded coconut after chilling.

COFFEE: Substitute 1/2 cup strong black mocha coffee for 1/2 cup of the milk.

RUM: Omit vanilla. Stir in 1/2 tablespoon Jamaica rum.

SPONGE: Decrease flour to 3/4 oz. Soak 3/4 tablespoon powdered gelatine in 4 tablespoons cold water. Stir into sauce before removing from pan. When dissolved, chill until filling starts to congeal, then add vanilla essence. Beat till fluffy and chill again.

TOFFEE: Substitute 1 cup dark brown sugar for the caster sugar, and stir in 1 oz. butter after the egg. Stir till dissolved. If liked, add 2 oz. chopped fried almonds.

WHIPPED CREAM

1/2 pint thick cream
2 tablespoons sifted icing
   sugar
1/2 teaspoon vanilla essence

Chill cream. Beat until stiff. Gradually beat in sugar and vanilla essence. Beat till firm enough to use as a filling.

To Vary: Reduce amount of cream to 1½ gills. Increase sugar to 4 table-spoons. When stiff and flavoured, fold in a stiffly-beaten egg white. Use and serve at once.

WHIPPED CREAM A LA RUSSE

½ tablespoon powdered
  gelatine
½ gill cold water
1 pint chilled thick cream
4 oz. sifted icing sugar
1 teaspoon vanilla essence
½ gill boiling water

Soak gelatine in cold water for 5 minutes. Whip cream till stiff. Gradually beat in sugar and vanilla. Stir the boiling water into gelatine. Leave till cool. Strain it over the cream. Beat rapidly with a flat whisk, turning the basin all the time while beating so that the beating is uniform throughout, otherwise the gelatine won't blend smoothly with the cream. Chill till nearly stiff, then use as a filling for any sponge layer cakes.

HAWAIIAN CREAM

1 beaten egg yolk
½ cup whipped cream
1½ tablespoons icing sugar
½ cup chopped drained pineapple
½ cup chopped walnuts

Fold yolk into cream. Sift the sugar. Stir in sugar, pineapple and nuts.

NUT CREAM

½ cup crushed nut brittle
1 cup whipped cream
¾ teaspoon vanilla essence

Lightly fold the crushed brittle into the cream. Flavour with vanilla essence.

ALMOND PASTE

Almond paste is usually associated with fruit cakes prepared for festive occasions. It is sometimes referred to as " marzipan," but this term is more generally applied to confectionery. Here we are only dealing with almond paste as a coating and filling.

Almond paste is usually made with ground almonds, but in the olden days, and on the Continent to-day, shelled almonds are sometimes pounded and used in place of ground.

To Pound Almonds: Place in a mortar. Add a few drops of cold water and pound with a pestle. If you don't add the water they are liable to oil.

Ground almonds should always be stored in closely covered jars or tins. If in paper the paper absorbs their oil.

When making almond paste, knead only until smooth and free from cracks. If you knead any longer, the nuts may oil.

Note: To ensure paste keeping fresh if made with egg yolks or whole eggs stir until thick in the top of a double boiler over boiling water before adding any sugar, or whisk with half the sugar over hot water till thickened, then stir into almonds and remaining sugar.

ALMOND PASTE

BASIC RECIPE:
1 lb. ground almonds
½ lb. caster sugar
½ lb. icing sugar
2 teaspoons lemon juice
¼ teaspoon vanilla essence
Beaten egg to mix

Place almonds in a basin. Sift caster and icing sugar. Stir into the almonds. Add lemon juice, vanilla essence, and enough beaten egg to bind ingredients into a paste. Turn on to a board dredged with caster sugar. Knead until smooth.

To Vary:

1. Omit caster sugar and double quantity of icing sugar.

2. Follow basic recipe, but allow ¾ lb. each of almonds, and caster and icing sugar. Add ½ teaspoon additional lemon juice.

3. Substitute beaten egg yolk, if egg whites are wanted for an icing or frosting to top cake covered with almond paste.

4. If a pale or coloured almond paste is wanted, use egg white to bind.

ALMOND PASTE FOR DECORATING A YULE LOG : Mix 1 oz. sifted icing sugar with 1 oz. caster sugar, 1 oz. ground almonds, ⅓ egg white, and rum to taste. Mould into a miniature log. Make rings at the ends with chocolate piping.

COOKED ALMOND PASTE (American Method)

1 lb. caster or loaf sugar
1 cup water
1 lb. ground almonds
1 saltspoon rose water
5 or 6 tablespoons strained orange juice

Place sugar and water in a saucepan. Stir over slow heat till sugar is dissolved. Bring to boil. Boil till syrup spins a thread, 240° F. Stir in almonds, rose water and orange juice. When blended and creamy, remove from heat, and knead on a board dredged with sifted icing sugar. When quite cool, pack in a tightly closed bottling jar. Leave for 6-8 days before using.

COOKED ALMOND PASTE (English Method)

1 lb. granulated or loaf sugar
¼ pint cold water
1 saltspoon cream of tartar
12 oz. ground almonds
2 slightly-beaten egg whites
3 oz. sifted icing sugar

Place sugar and water in a saucepan. Stir occasionally over low heat till sugar is dissolved, then bring to boil. Add cream of tartar. Boil to thread stage, 240° F. Remove from stove. Stir vigorously until syrup turns cloudy, then stir in almonds and egg whites. Cook over very slow heat for 2 or 3 minutes, stirring constantly, then pour on to a marble or enamel slab brushed with oil. Sprinkle icing sugar on the centre, then with a palette knife, turn up the edges into the centre. Press them on to centre with the back of a wooden spoon. When cool enough, knead till smooth, incorporating more icing sugar if necessary to get a smooth workable paste.

ALMOND PASTE REQUIRED FOR

Top and Sides
7-inch Cake: Use quantities given.

Top Only
7-inch Cake: Halve quantities given.

749

Top and Sides	*Top Only*
8-*inch Cake:* Increase by a quarter.	8-*inch Cake:* Use $\frac{3}{4}$ quantities given.
9-*inch Cake:* Increase by a half.	9-*inch Cake:* Use quantities given.

To Apply Almond Paste

Brush top and sides of cake to remove any loose crumbs. As it is important that the surface of the cake should be quite level, examine cake carefully, and either level with a knife, paring surplus off carefully, or allow for additional almond paste to make it level. Some people prefer to apply the paste to bottom of cake which is usually more level than the top. This is a matter of taste. It is important to have a sharp edge round the top if you are going to decorate it with piping of royal icing.

Brush with cooled melted apricot jam, or lightly beaten egg white can be used. Cover the sides first. Divide almond paste into two portions, one slightly larger than the other. Roll larger portion out evenly on a sugar-dredged board into a strip the width of the depth of the cake, and long enough to go round it. Place side of cake on one end, then roll carefully along so that the strip evenly adheres to the surface. Press the edges together with a palette knife, then gently roll the cake over the join so that the edges are moulded smoothly together. Mould and roll the remainder of paste into a round the diameter of cake. Place on top and press lightly with a rolling pin. Cover loosely with greaseproof paper to protect from dust. Stand in a warm room for at least 48 hours to allow it to dry thoroughly if using basic recipe. If short of time, slip the cake, when covered with paste, into a very cool oven, and leave with door ajar till it dries out. If you do not dry almond paste, the oil may penetrate the royal icing. To make certain that this does not happen coat almond paste with glacé or water icing before applying the royal icing.

BUTTER CREMES

Butter crèmes are suitable only for cakes made with butter sponge, egg sponges, or Genoese pastry. The more liquid examples can only be used for fillings, and the dryer, for both fillings and icings. As an icing, butter crème, or " Vienna icing," as it is sometimes called, can be piped on, swirled on top of a cake with a fork, or marked in a hob-nail design, etc.

BUTTER CREME

BASIC RECIPE :
3 oz. unsalted butter
4½ oz. sifted icing sugar

Beat butter with a wooden spoon till softened. Gradually beat in sugar. Beat till soft and white, then add flavouring to taste, and colour if liked.

CHOCOLATE : Melt 1½ oz. chocolate in a basin over hot water, and beat into icing, or dissolve chocolate in 1 tablespoon milk or water, and cool before using.

COFFEE : Flavour with coffee essence to taste, or use soluble coffee creamed with milk.

FLUFFY : Reduce butter to 2 oz. and sugar to 4 oz. Stir in an egg white, beaten to a stiff froth, and ¼ teaspoon finely grated lemon, orange or tangerine rind. Use as a filling for cakes to be eaten at once.

MOCHA : Increase sugar to 5 oz. Sift with 1 teaspoon of cocoa before using. Flavour with $\frac{1}{2}$ teaspoon vanilla essence, and about $1\frac{1}{2}$ tablespoons strong black coffee. Beat well.

ORANGE : Flavour with strained orange juice or essence. Colour yellow.

ROSE : Beat in 1 tablespoon of rose water.

VANILLA : Reduce butter to 2 oz., and increase sugar to 6 oz. Stir in 1 teaspoon vanilla essence. Beat well, then gradually beat in 3 tablespoons thick cream.

WALNUT : Stir in 2 oz. chopped walnuts.

COCONUT BUTTER CREME

1/4 lb. butter
1/4 lb. sifted icing sugar
1/4 teaspoon vanilla essence
1/2 cup desiccated coconut

Beat butter to a cream. Gradually beat in sugar. When fluffy, stir in vanilla essence and coconut. Use as a filling or icing for a butter sponge. If wanted as both, double quantities.

NOBLE BUTTER CREME

2 oz. butter or margarine
1 cup sifted icing sugar
1 dessertspoon cocoa
1 tablespoon hot water
1/2 teaspoon vanilla essence

Beat butter till softened. Stir sugar with cocoa. Gradually beat into butter. Beat till creamy. Stir in hot water and vanilla essence. Use with Betty's Chocolate Cake, or any butter sponge mixture.

THE ART OF ICING

To ice a cake successfully, it must be smooth and free of crumbs. This of course refers more to cakes that have to be coated with royal icing than small cakes and layer cakes coated with glacé, egg, milk, or water icings. As a rule, hard icings are reserved for festive fruit cakes which are not all consumed at one time. In Britain, royal icing is generally used, but in the Americas, boiled icings or frostings are more popular. When it is not possible to make royal icing through shortage of eggs, an icing containing gelatine can take its place. The best foundation for royal icing is almond paste, or almond paste coated with glacé icing.

Soft icings are generally chosen for coating gâteaux, layer cakes, petits fours, small buns, biscuits, etc., though all the boiled varieties make a delicious topping for gâteaux and layer cakes as well.

EQUIPMENT FOR HARD ICINGS

Stand with a flat raised surface, preferably a turntable.
Fairly large basin.   Small Basin.
Palette knife.   Jug of hot water.
Gold or silver cake board, 2 inches larger than cake.
Icing syringe and tubes.   Home-made forcing bag.
Hair sieve.

To Make a Forcing Bag : Cut greaseproof paper into a 9 or 12 inch square. Fold in half diagonally to form a triangle. Press the fold down very firmly to form a crease. Now, holding it in the left hand with the thumb pointing towards the middle, bring the right hand corner up to the middle corner, wrapping the left hand corner round to the back of the middle in the same way as you would make a bag for holding sweets. The result should be a cone shape with the three corners on top of each other and a sharp point at the botton. To complete this, hold the three corners firmly together, then fold them down at this point two or three times to prevent the bag unfolding. Cut off the tip just high enough to enable you to drop in the metal tube so that it goes halfway through the opening. It must fit firmly. (Make two bags when using more than one colour for decorating.) When decorating with several tinted icings and therefore using several bags and tubes, slip those not in use at the moment under a damp towel otherwise the frosting will dry at the tip. If this does happen, be sure to remove a little from the tip before icing, or you will spoil your design. Icing bags can also be obtained made of strong duck or linen which can be washed and dried after use.

Icing Syringe and Tubes : If you prefer to decorate with an icing syringe or " pump " and tubes, or pipes as they are sometimes called, you can buy it in bakelite or metal complete with a selection of tubes. If not an expert, start practising piping inscriptions with a plain tube, then continue with the ribbon and the rose, star or rosette tubes before attempting any elaborate icing with the help of net nails, flower nails, etc.

To Keep Syringe and Tubes Clean : Place immediately after using in a basin of warm water. Soak for 5 minutes, then rinse under warm water tap and dry carefully. Be sure when cleaning the tubes with a skewer, when necessary, that you don't bend the points.

TIPS ON ICING

1. Never fill an icing bag more than two-thirds full.

2. When icing, exert pressure from top of bag to the bottom.

3. To make dots, hold the bag or syringe at right angles to the surface, then press out a dot and release pressure. Quickly withdraw bag or syringe.

4. Don't press the part of the bag containing icing, or it will melt. Keep your two thumbs on the folded-over sides of paper.

5. Always keep basin containing icing covered with a damp cloth and remove it only to fill bag or syringe or it will form a glaze on top.

6. Make icing for piping stiff enough to stand up in peaks by the addition of sifted icing sugar.

ROYAL ICING

The ingredients required to make perfect royal icing are the following :

Icing Sugar: You need a very fine quality of icing sugar. One which requires no sieving unless the packet has been left open for a length of time or has been stored in a damp place.

Egg Whites : See that they are 2 or 3 days old. If too fresh, the icing may not set well. Take care that no trace of yolk is left in the egg white.

Colourings : Use a drop or two of confectioner's blue to impart a pure white shade to the icing that is otherwise " off-white." Any colouring can be added when a delicately tinted icing is wanted, but be sure to add only a drop at a time till you get the shade you want, and always make the icing in the daylight for it is impossible to judge the amount of colouring required when working in artificial light. Coloured icing sugars are now available.

Flavouring : Lemon juice or vanilla essence are most popular, but any flavouring can be added to taste.

To Prevent Icing becoming Brittle : Stir in pure glycerine, in the proportion of 1 dessertspoon to 1 lb. of icing sugar.

To Make Royal Icing (For a cake 9″ across)

You can make royal icing very simply with egg whites, sugar, lemon juice and salt. If you aspire to professional standard as far as colouring is concerned, then you must be able to call upon confectioner's blue. To cut the cake without icing breaking up remember to add the glycerine after remainder of sugar.

ROYAL ICING

2 lb. sifted icing sugar
5 egg whites
1 saltspoon salt
1 teaspoon lemon juice
1 tablespoon glycerine
¼ teaspoon acetic acid
Confectioner's blue as required

Roll and sift sugar if necessary. Beat egg whites slightly with 4 tablespoons of the sugar until the mixture begins to stiffen, then gradually beat in remainder of sugar. Beat in salt, lemon juice, glycerine and acetic acid. Continue to beat until so stiff that when you slash it with a knife the icing holds its shape. Stir in a few drops of confectioner's blue. If the icing is not to be used at once, carefully scrape and stir in any from the sides of bowl into the bulk. Cover with a folded cloth wrung out of hot water, then weight down with a plate to prevent the air penetrating, which would harden the icing. *Yield :* Enough to coat and decorate a 9-inch festive fruit cake unless very elaborate decorations are required.

To Apply Royal Icing

Place cake, coated with almond paste, or with almond paste covered with glacé icing, on a cake board with a dab of icing on the centre. Press down gently. Lift on to turntable. Fill jug with boiling water. When icing is ready, lift enough with a palette knife to cover the surface on the top. Spread roughly over, working from the centre, and bringing the icing right to the edge. To achieve a smooth surface, hold knife upright with the tip of blade on the centre, and the edge resting lightly on the icing. With your left hand, rotate turntable so that the edge of the knife finally completes a circle. This of course needs practice to get perfect results. If too difficult, use the flat of the blade for levelling, dipping it in the water when necessary.

To Coat the Sides : Plaster icing here and there round the sides of cake with knife, then smooth it on with the flat of knife. To obtain a smooth result, hold knife downwards with edge close to icing but keeping knife absolutely upright. Now with your other hand, rotate the turntable, keeping the knife still. If you do this properly, you should not only have a smooth even coating round the sides with a sharp edge where it meets the top, but any surplus icing will be removed at the completion of the circle. If this is too difficult, just spread the icing smoothly over the sides as flat as you can with the blade. Dip the knife in hot water when necessary during icing, but shake it before using again or you will make the icing too wet and it will run. Protect from dust, and leave till dry in 3-4 days. Apply a second coat in the same way so as to get a perfectly smooth coat for decorating, but not until after the first coat is dry and firm. If preferred, you can coat the royal icing with Transparent Icing, or thin royal icing to pouring consistency with lightly beaten egg white, and pour it over to give you a perfect surface. The latter two methods are easier than applying a second coat as described. Leave again till dry.

HINTS ON DECORATION

If you want to decorate in a geometrical design, cut out a paper pattern the exact size of the top of the cake. Draw your design on the paper. Mark it on the cake with a pin through the design. Remove paper, then pipe out design. A very good effect can be given by making a cross on paper, and marking it out on the icing. Remove paper and fill triangles alternately with pink and lilac roses. No matter how you decorate the top of your cake, always give it a firm scroll or wreath of roses round the base where it joins the board. If gifted with patience, you can work out a beautiful design on top of cake through a lace paper doily.

When writing, pipe your inscription, then leave to dry. Repeat on top so as to give a raised effect. Another idea is to pipe with a finer tube along both sides in a pale contrasting shade.

Icicle Icing : When the foundation coat of royal icing or glacé icing is dry, smother cake all over with a thin coat of royal icing, then lift little heaps on your palette knife and place them here and there round the sides or all over the top if wanted. Now, with the flat of your palette knife, or your fingers, slap all over the icing which draws it out in icicles. Tip with silver balls while still wet. Arrange berried frosted holly leaves or any Christmas ornaments on top. You want to suggest not only a rough surface on top, but some snowdrifts. Use your imagination when making this snow-scape.

TRANSPARENT ICING

1 lb. loaf sugar
½ pint water
1 teaspoon lemon juice

Place sugar and water in a thick saucepan. Stand, stirring occasionally, till sugar is dissolved, then bring slowly to the boil. Carefully remove any scum that should rise to the top, and keep inside of the pan above the icing, clean with a damp brush. Boil to 229° or 230° F. Stir in lemon juice. Beat until thick and creamy. Pour at once over cake.

GLACE ICING

The usual version of " Glacé Icing " frequently called " Water Icing " is made of icing sugar and water. The sugar may be moistened with hot water and flavoured with lemon juice. The icing must be soft and shiny, and form a thin coating suitable for applying to a cold cake made of egg or butter sponge. It can also be used for coating biscuits and buns.

Before making icing, rub the sugar through a hair sieve. If at all hard, roll first on a sheet of greaseproof paper with a rolling pin. Mix icing according to instructions. It should be thick enough to leave a fine coat on the back of the mixing spoon.

To ice small cakes, place them on a wire sieve or rack with a plate below. Pour the icing over them from a spoon. Let any surplus icing drip on to the plate below. To ice tiny petits fours that have to be coated all over, dip them in the icing with a skewer, then drain slightly before placing on a rack to dry.

DECORATIONS FOR SOFT ICED CAKES

Keep the following all in separate glass jars each with a screw top.

ALMONDS :

1. Blanch. Bake for 5 or 6 minutes in a hot oven, 450° F. Arrange in daisy designs all over a slab sponge. Fill centres with chopped date, or currants.

2. Coat sides of a gâteau with baked almonds very closely, points upwards.

3. Chop browned almonds. Brush cake all over, or sides only, with melted and cooled apricot jam. Sprinkle thickly with the nuts.

ANGELICA : Use for leaves or stems when a flower or spray of flowers is required, or chop and form an outer ring round the edge of a cake wreathed with glacé cherries.

CHOCOLATE SHOT (Vermicelli) ; or chocolate flakes, obtained by shaving off slices of chocolate from a block with a knife, cutting from above. Useful for gâteaux.

CRYSTALLIZED FLOWERS AND PETALS : Use with angelica for making posies, or wreaths.

CRYSTALLIZED ORANGE AND LEMON SLICES : Use whole for any fancy design, or chopped.

DESICCATED COCONUT: Sprinkle tinted coconut over cakes coated with heated apricot jam. Also effective used in this way all over a layer cake. Another method is to ice the cake with an icing to match the coconut before decorating.

GLACE CHERRIES :

1. Use whole to make clusters with thin stems of angelica, heated and curved.

2. Slit each in four to form a pansy. Arrange in the form of a wreath with angelica foliage on layer cakes, or round gâteaux.

HUNDREDS AND THOUSANDS : Sprinkle over iced petits fours, biscuits, and layer cakes for children's parties.

MIMOSA BALLS : Use for composing a spray of mimosa on a gâteau or layer cake with fine stems of angelica, and for making a wheel design on the centre of a round gâteau or layer cake.

NUTS : *Chopped* : Spread sides of layer cakes, gâteaux, or petits fours thinly with heated apricot jam or red currant jelly, then sprinkle thickly with nuts.

· *Halved Walnuts :* Make a fancy design on gâteaux or layer cakes, or use on the centre of petits fours coated with chocolate or coffee icing.

GLACE ICING

BASIC RECIPE :
¼ lb. sifted icing sugar
2 dessertspoons warm water
Colouring and flavouring

Place sugar in a basin. Stir in water, then colouring, a drop at a time, until shaded to taste. Stir in the flavouring in the same way. Lower basin into a saucepan with hot water coming half-way up the sides. Stir over hot water for a minute or two until sugar is dissolved, but do not allow icing to become hot. Remove from heat. Cool slightly, then stir well and use. The icing should be thick enough to cling to the back of spoon. Enough to top 1 layer cake or 12 small petits fours.

To Apply : Pour the icing quickly on to the middle of a large cake or pour from a spoon on to the middle of a small cake. Spread with a palette knife dipped in hot water from the centre to the edges, and round the sides if desired, then decorate. This method gives you a glossy icing. Don't disturb the icing once cake is covered, or it will not be glossy. The icing will also lose its gloss if the water is too hot. Beat in a little more sugar if wanted for decorating.

To Vary :

1. Allowing ½ lb. sugar to 3 teaspoons warm water, place sugar in an enamel saucepan, then move the pan to the stove. Gradually add water, stirring constantly over low heat. Colour and flavour to taste. Use at once.

2. Substitute milk for the water.

3. Substitute plain fruit juice for the water.

CHOCOLATE : Place 2 oz. plain chocolate in a saucepan with ½ gill water. Boil till the liquid coats the back of a spoon, then quickly add icing sugar and beat well. Stir in ¼ teaspoon vanilla essence when of a smooth coating consistency.

COFFEE : Follow basic recipe, but flavour to taste with coffee essence.

ORANGE OR TANGERINE : Substitute strained orange or tangerine juice for the water, and add grated orange or tangerine rind to taste. Colour with a drop or two of orange colouring.

RUM : Follow basic recipe. Flavour with ¾ teaspoon of rum.

QUICK GLACE ICING

BASIC RECIPE :
10 oz. plain " Easy Icing " sugar
About 2 tablespoons cold milk or water

Sift sugar if necessary. Stir in enough of the milk or water to give you a coating consistency. Add essence to taste or rum or sherry.

CHOCOLATE : Melt 1 oz. chocolate with 1 tablespoon hot water. Stir into 10 oz. chocolate icing sugar, with more hot milk or water as required to make a coating consistency.

LEMON : Use lemon icing sugar. Substitute 3 tablespoons strained lemon juice for 3 tablespoons of the milk or water, and add a pinch of grated lemon rind if liked.

ORANGE : Substitute strained orange juice for liquid, and use plain icing sugar. Add ½ teaspoon grated orange rind if liked.

RASPBERRY OR STRAWBERRY : Use raspberry or strawberry icing sugar. Add 2 teaspoons lemon juice, and strained raspberry or strawberry juice in place of milk or water.

ROSE : Use rose icing sugar. Add 2 teaspoons lemon juice, and enough milk or water to make a coating consistency.

AMERICAN FROSTINGS

The following recipes are for icings suitable for using as a filling as well as icing :

BOILED FROSTING

BASIC RECIPE :
¾ lb. caster sugar
½ cup boiling water
1 small tablespoon golden syrup
2 egg whites
1 saltspoon cream of tartar
1 saltspoon salt
¾ teaspoon vanilla essence

Put sugar, water and syrup in a saucepan. Stir over low heat till sugar is dissolved, then bring to boil. Cover. Boil for about 3 minutes, then uncover. Boil, without stirring, until a few drops of the syrup form a soft ball tossed into cold water—that is to between 238° and 240° F. Remove from heat. Beat egg whites stiffly with cream of tartar until they hold their shape, then rapidly pour syrup over the whites, holding pan with one hand, beating constantly with the other. Add salt and vanilla essence, and keep on beating till frosting is cool and of a spreading consistency. Use at once or it will harden. If making this frosting on a wet day, boil syrup to 245° F. *Yield :* Enough for the top and sides of 2 layer cakes 9 inches across, 2 dozen patty cakes, or a slab cake (butter sponge), 9″ × 9″ × 2″.

AMERICAN GOLDEN FROSTING : Reduce syrup to 2 teaspoons. Omit cream of tartar, and reduce water to ⅓ cup. Place all ingredients but the vanilla essence in the top of a double boiler. Beat with an egg beater for about 7 minutes, till the icing thickens and keeps its shape when dropped from beater. Remove from boiling water. Stir in vanilla essence. Continue to beat till stiff enough to spread, but remember to spread on cake as soon as made.

DIVINITY : Increase sugar to 1½ lb. Double quantity of syrup. Increase water to 1⅓ cups. Double egg whites, and increase vanilla to 1 teaspoon. *Yield :* Enough to cover top and sides of a 3-tiered layer cake 9″ across, or a 2-tiered one 10″ across.

FRUIT : Add ½ cup apricot, peach, raspberry or strawberry purée before using.

GINGER : Reduce sugar to ½ lb., and stir into it 2 oz. light brown sugar. When frosting is ready, lightly stir in 2-3 oz. minced preserved ginger.

Frosting for Piping : When of a spreading consistency, lightly stir in ¼ cup sifted icing sugar. If delicate colouring is wanted, add it before beating. If frosting dries too much for piping while using, thin with egg white.

757

SEVEN MINUTE FROSTING

2 egg whites
¾ lb. sugar
⅓ cup water
2 teaspoons golden syrup
¼ teaspoon almond essence or
¾ teaspoon vanilla essence

Beat egg whites, sugar, water and syrup in the top of a double boiler until blended, then place pan over rapidly boiling water. Beat with a rotary beater, or an electric mixer, until fluffy, and the frosting holds its shape. If beaten by hand, it will take 7 minutes, which gives it its name. If beaten electrically, it will take 3 or 4 minutes. Remove from heat. Stir in essence, then beat till stiff enough to hold its shape. Use at once. Enough for top and sides of a 3-tiered layer cake or for a larger cake 9 inches across.

CARAMEL : Omit essence. Stir in 1½ tablespoons caramel syrup after removing from heat.

CHOCOLATE : After removing from heat, lightly stir in 3 oz. unsweetened chocolate, melted, and ¾ teaspoon vanilla essence. Do not beat. Cool before using.

COFFEE : Substitute strong black coffee for water and omit essences.

MARSHMALLOW : Cut 15 marshmallows in small pieces. Beat into frosting after removing from heat until melted and perfectly blended.

PEPPERMINT : Colour frosting a delicate shell pink before removing from heat, then beat in 7-10 drops of oil of peppermint, and continue to beat until thick enough to spread.

SEA FOAM : Substitute ¾ lb. brown sugar for the caster.

CREAM CHEESE FROSTING

3 oz. cream cheese
1½ cups icing sugar
1 dessertspoon warm water
½ teaspoon vanilla essence

Mash cheese in a basin. Stir in sugar, water and vanilla essence. Beat till creamy.

FONDANT ICING

1½ lbs. loaf or granulated sugar
½ pint cold water
1 dessertspoon glucose

Place sugar and water in a saucepan. Stir till dissolved. Add glucose. Stir till dissolved. Bring to boil. Skim. Place a thermometer in pan. Boil rapidly without stirring to 238° F. Switch or turn off heat. Remove thermometer to a basin of water just off the boil Leave syrup at side of stove for 2 minutes until it settles, then pour into a large rinsed basin. Cool slightly. Stir sides to centre. Beat till stiff. Knead until smooth, either in basin or on a marble slab. If to be used, cover basin with a towel. Stand for an hour, then lower basin into a large saucepan or larger basin containing enough hot water to come half-way up the sides. Stir icing till creamy. Stir in 2 to 3 teaspoons of flavouring essence to taste, 2 dessertspoons coffee essence, or 3 heaped dessertspoons grated chocolate, and colouring to taste. You'll need 10 to 12 drops. When blended, cool slightly and use at once. If not required at once, cover with a damp cloth as you would royal icing. Enough to cover a large cake.

NOTE : Be sure to remove any granules adhering to the inside of pan as you notice them, with a brush dipped in warm water.

JELLY FROSTING

1 egg white
1 cup red currant jelly
½ teaspoon vanilla essence

Beat egg white until frothy, then gradually beat in the jelly. Continue to beat until the mixture holds its shape, adding vanilla essence when almost ready.

HARLEQUIN JELLY FROSTING
(For Petits Fours)

1 tablespoon jelly crystals
3 tablespoons boiling water
½ oz. butter
A few grains of salt
1¾ cup sifted icing sugar

Place jelly and water in top of a double boiler. Stir until crystals are dissolved. Add butter, salt and sugar. Beat rapidly until soft and " pourable."

LEMON : Use 1 tablespoon strained lemon juice, 1 tablespoon jelly crystals and 2 tablespoons water.

PINEAPPLE : Use 1 tablespoon lemon crystals and 3 tablespoons canned pineapple juice.

STRAWBERRY : Either allow 1 tablespoon lemon or strawberry crystals and 3 tablespoons fresh strawberry juice, or 1 tablespoon strawberry jelly crystals and 3½ tablespoons crushed strawberries.

TANGERINE FROSTING

1 tablespoon tangerine jelly crystals
2½ tablespoons tangerine juice
½ oz. butter
1 saltspoon salt
Grated rind ½ orange
1 egg yolk
2 cups sifted icing sugar

Place the crystals and tangerine juice in top of a double boiler. Stir over boiling water until crystals are dissolved. Add butter, salt, orange rind, egg yolk, and sugar. Stir rapidly until blended and spreadable. Use for petits fours. *Yield:* 2-3 cups.

BAKED TOPPINGS

These are very popular in the United States for using on slab cakes.

BROWN WALNUT TOPPING

¼ lb. light brown sugar
1 stiffly whipped egg white
1 saltspoon salt
3 tablespoons chopped walnuts

Sift sugar. Beat egg white with salt till stiff. Beat sugar in slowly. Spread over a slab cake sponge, 8 inches square. Sprinkle evenly with the nuts. Bake in a moderately hot oven, 375° F., for about 25 minutes.

MACAROON TOPPING

1 egg white
4 tablespoons caster sugar

Beat egg white until stiff. Gradually stir in the sugar. Beat until thick, then place basin in a

½ cup desiccated coconut
¼ teaspoon vanilla essence

saucepan of boiling water. Beat over water for 5 minutes. Remove from heat. Stir in coconut and vanilla essence. Spread roughly over baked slab cake when cold.

TIC-TAC-TOE TOPPING

2 tablespoons melted butter
¼ lb. light brown sugar
1½ tablespoons thick cream
1 saltspoon salt
½ cup desiccated coconut

Mix all the ingredients together in order given. Spread over a slab cake 7 inches by 11 inches, when it comes out of the oven. Slip under the grill. Grill over low heat till the icing bursts into bubbles. Remove at once. Cool. Cut into strips.

COATINGS AND GLAZES

Apricot glaze, which can be made in several ways, is most popular.

American Apricot Glaze : Wash and soak dried apricots overnight in cold water to cover. Drain thoroughly. Rub through a sieve. Measure. Allow equal weight of sugar. Stir over low heat till sugar is dissolved. Bring to boil then boil for 5 minutes, stirring constantly.

Chef's Apricot Glaze : Heat equal quantity of apricot jam and water till the mixture runs freely, then rub through a sieve. Flavour to taste with brandy, curaçao or rum.

Use either of the glazes for coating cakes to be decorated thickly with chopped nuts, for spreading on a fruit cake before covering with almond paste, for setting fresh berries in pastry cases, or for coating a large savarin. Store surplus in a screw-top jar, but reheat slightly before using again.

BUTTERSCOTCH GLAZE : Place ¼ lb. light brown sugar in a saucepan with ⅓ cup golden syrup measured in a heated cup and the same quantity of water. Stir over slow heat till sugar is dissolved. Bring to boil. Boil for 2 minutes. Add 1 tablespoon lemon juice. Spread over sweet yeast buns and Danish pastry while warm.

CHOCOLATE COATING FOR FROSTINGS

Melt 2 oz. unsweetened chocolate in a basin over hot water. Gradually stir in 1 rounded teaspoon of unsalted butter. When blended, cool slightly, then pour over frosted gâteaux or layer cakes, or petits fours. Enough for a layer cake, 9″ across, or a gâteau, 8″ × 8″ × 2″.

Invalid Cookery

The food required for invalids can be grouped in two classes : liquid and light (semi-solid).

LIQUID DIET

A liquid diet consists of fruit juices, refreshing and stimulating drinks, meat juices and meat tea, strained broths, gruel, and sometimes egg beaten with milk, or just a simple stock.

CURRANT OR GRAPE JUICE

1½ tablespoons currant or
    grape juice
1 cup cold water
Caster sugar to taste

Mix the juice with water. Add sugar. Stir until dissolved, then chill and serve.

GRAPE COCKTAIL

1 egg white
1½ tablespoons grape juice
Caster sugar to taste

Beat egg white until stiff. Place an ice block in the bottom of a wine glass. Pour in juice. Add egg white. Dredge lightly with caster sugar.

761

PRUNE COCKTAIL

½ cup sweetened prune juice
1 teaspoon lemon or grapefruit juice
¾ cup chilled milk

Stir the fruit juices together. Add milk, gradually, stirring constantly. Serve either first thing in the morning or last thing at night.

ALBUMENISED MILK

1 egg white
½ cup milk

Place egg white in a ½ pint glass. Add milk. Cover closely. Shake thoroughly until blended. Serve at once.

ALBUMENISED WATER

1 egg white
½ cup water

Stir egg white with a silver fork till well mixed. Add water by degrees, stirring constantly. Turn into a glass. Serve at once.

ARROWROOT GRUEL

2 teaspoons arrowroot
2 teaspoons cold water
½ pint boiling milk
Pinch of salt
Caster sugar to taste
Flavouring to taste

Mix arrowroot with cold water to a smooth paste. Add boiling milk, stirring constantly. Boil for 7-10 minutes, stirring constantly. Add salt and sugar and flavouring to taste.

BARLEY WATER

2 oz. pearl barley
Juice of ½ a lemon
1 quart boiling water
1 thin strip lemon rind

Place barley in a jug. Add boiling water to cover. Strain off water. Place barley in the top of a double boiler. Add lemon juice, and lemon rind. Cover. Cook for 2 hours over boiling water, stirring occasionally. Strain through muslin. Sweeten to taste, if liked. (If to be served with milk, omit lemon juice.)

CARRAGEEN LEMONADE

Wash and pick over ¼ cup carrageen (Irish moss). Soak in cold water to cover until soft. Pick over and rinse again. Drain well. Place in the top of a double boiler. Add 2 cups boiling water. Cook over boiling water for 20 minutes, until dissolved, then strain off liquid. Add strained juice of 1 lemon and sugar to taste.

EGG FLIP

1 egg
1 dessertspoon caster sugar

Separate yolk from white of egg. Beat yolk with sugar. Stir in brandy or lemon juice as preferred.

1 dessertspoon brandy or
  lemon juice
½ pint milk

Bring milk to the boil, then add to mixture. Stir well. Beat white lightly and stir in. Serve hot. *For 1 person.*

EGG NOG

Pour barely ½ pint milk into the top of a double boiler. Heat till piping hot, but do not allow to form a skin. Remove from heat. Leave until quite cold. Beat up 1 egg in a ½ pint tumbler with ¼ oz. caster sugar until into a stiff froth. Add 1 dessertspoon brandy. Fill up with milk.

GOAT'S MILK

Excellent for invalids with weak digestions, and for babies. It is rich in minerals, and is also a laxative. It takes 20 minutes to digest, whereas cow's milk takes 2-3 hours.

GRUELS

MILK GRUEL : Mix a dessertspoon of fine oatmeal or patent groats to a cream with cold milk. Stir in ½ pint milk at boiling point. Turn into the top of a double boiler. Boil for 10 minutes over boiling water, stirring constantly. Add sugar or salt to taste, as allowed, and, if necessary, 1 tablespoon of brandy.

OATMEAL GRUEL : Soak 1 tablespoon oatmeal in 4 tablespoons cold water for 10 minutes. Turn ½ pint water into the top of a double boiler containing boiling water below. When boiling, pour in the moistened oatmeal and stir well. Cover and boil for 30 minutes, stirring occasionally. Serve hot in a cup, strained or unstrained as required.

MALTED MILK EGG NOG : Mix 2 tablespoons malted milk to a smooth paste with boiling water in a ½ pint cup. Beat egg thoroughly. Stir into malted milk, then stir in fully ¾ cup hot milk and 2 or 3 drops of vanilla essence. Stir until smoothly blended. Serve at once. *For 2 persons.*

MILK PUNCH

¼ pint milk
1 teaspoon caster sugar
1 tablespoon brandy, rum or
  sherry
Grating of nutmeg

Mix all the ingredients in a screw-topped jar. Screw down tightly. Shake well. *For 1 person.*

MILK TEA

2 teaspoons tea
½ pint milk

Pour tea into a jug. Bring milk to a boil and pour over. Stand for 3-5 minutes, keeping hot. Strain into a cup. *Yield:* 2 portions.

SODA WATER AND CREAM : Stir $\frac{1}{4}$ pint soda water into $\frac{1}{2}$ gill cream. This is frequently served to a patient when milk is not suitable.

SODA WATER AND EGG WHITE : Beat egg white to a stiff froth. Stir in 1 tablespoon brandy or lemon juice. Pour into a $\frac{1}{2}$ pint tumbler. Fill up with soda water.

WHEY

1 teaspoon rennet
1 pint tepid milk

Add rennet to milk. Cover and stand at room temperature until the milk curdles. Strain off whey.

NOTE : If wanted sweetened, allow 2 teaspoons sugar to $\frac{1}{2}$ pint of milk. Dissolve in the whey.

WINE WHEY

1 pint milk
2 wineglasses sherry

Bring milk to boiling point. Stir in sherry. Remove from heat. Cover and stand until the curds settle. Strain off whey.

YOGHOURT

Yoghourt is a fermented milk rich in calcium, phosphorus and proteins as well as the other minerals and food elements contained in the fresh milk from which it was made. It is an excellent addition to the diet of people who have difficulty in digesting fresh milk and fresh milk foods, as well as for those who suffer from intestinal disorders and debility. It is also invaluable for rheumaticky invalids on account of its high alkalinising properties. It can be administered as a drink in place of fresh milk though it is generally eaten with a spoon. Many invalids like it served in place of cream with fresh or canned fruits, or fruit salad. It can also be served in one of the following ways :

1. Serve with any cold packaged breakfast cereal.
2. Substitute for custard when serving berries or cold stewed fruit.
3. Sweeten and use as a filling for a sponge sandwich.
4. Make into a salad dressing by adding 1 tablespoon of lemon juice, a teaspoon of honey and a pinch of salt to a 5 oz. bottle. Shake well before using.
5. Turn it into a pick-me-up when a long drink is wanted : Place 5 tablespoons in a $\frac{1}{2}$ pint tumbler. Dilute with equal quantity of milk or soda water. Whisk well before serving.
6. Turn into cream cheese by suspending it in a small piece of cheese cloth or butter muslin for a few hours. Serve on buttered toast.

Yoghourt can be obtained plain or strawberry-flavoured. It will keep for several days in a cool place, or in a refrigerator for about a fortnight at $45°$ F. It should never be heated as this destroys its valuable bacteria.

LIGHT (SEMI-SOLID) DIET

This diet is planned not only for patients who have graduated from a liquid diet, but also for any invalids for whom a light diet is prescribed. All the recipes given under Liquid Diet can be introduced to the Light Diet. All fruit juices and purées of fruit, sweet and savoury custards and jellies are suitable as well as creamed fish and chicken. *See other sections for recipes for cream soups; creamed chicken and fish, boiled white fish, and fish quenelles; coddled, poached and steamed eggs, simple omelets and custards; jellies; mousses: ice cream.*

SOUPS

BEEF BROTH

2 lb. beef bones
2 lb. shin or shoulder of beef
3 quarts cold water
1½ teaspoons salt

Crack bones. Wipe and cut meat into chunks. Place meat and bones in a saucepan. Cover with cold water. Simmer for 8 hours. If preferred, place in a casserole instead of a saucepan, and cook in a very slow oven, 300° F., for 8-12 hours. Strain through a colander. Season to taste with salt and cool quickly. Skim off any fat when cold. When required, scoop out quantity needed and heat only to simmering point.

BEEF JELLY : This broth can be served as a jelly. If allowed, tomato juice to taste can be added to broth before allowing to set.

(1) BEEF TEA

1 lb. trimmed beef
½ teaspoon salt
1 pint water

Choose juicy meat such as rump, or buttock steak, or topside. Remove any skin, fat and gristle, then shred meat finely, or put through a meat grinder. Turn into a saucepan and add salt and water. Stand for 15 minutes, then place over low heat and stir slowly. Meat will lose colour while the water becomes red then rich red-brown. Do not allow beef tea to become hotter than 130° F. or the albumen will solidify and have to be strained out. This temperature will allow a finger to be dipped into the water without actual scalding. When beef tea is red-brown, skim carefully, removing all fat, and strain. This is a more nutritious beef tea than that usually made, but not as palatable.

(2) BEEF TEA

½ lb. beef steak
1 cup cold water
1 small teaspoon salt
Seasoning

Choose a lean, juicy steak. Place in the top of a double boiler. Add water and salt. Stand for 1 hour. Cook over boiling water for 5-10 minutes, until the juice turns brown. Strain and press meat heavily to extract all the juice. Season to taste with pepper, if allowed, and add a teaspoon of sherry to each cup if allowed. *Yield:* 1 to 2 portions.

CHICKEN BROTH

1 boiling fowl
Cold water as required
1 small onion, if allowed
Boiled rice if allowed

Wash chicken thoroughly inside and out and weigh. Add water in the proportion of 2 pints to every 2 lb. of chicken. Place in a saucepan. Add peel of onion and chopped onion if allowed. Cover and simmer for 3 hours. Season with salt. Strain off stock into a basin. Cool and remove fat. Reheat. Add boiled rice to taste, if allowed.

CHICKEN, BEEF AND VEAL SOUP

½ lb. knuckle of veal
½ lb. shin of beef
½ chicken
3 pints cold water
½ teaspoon salt

Remove all fat from meat, then cut the lean up into small pieces. Put meat with bones into a saucepan with the water and salt. Bring to boil, and skim well. Simmer very gently for 4 hours. When cooked, strain off soup, and as soon as cool, remove fat from the top. Reheat it as required, and serve.

CREAM OF SPINACH

½ pint milk
Salt to taste
¼ cup minced raw spinach
½ tablespoon butter
½ tablespoon flour

Heat milk in the top of a double boiler with salt. Wash spinach well, then drain and put through a meat grinder, but be sure to place a basin beneath grinder to catch any liquid running out. Melt butter in a saucepan. Add flour. Stir till frothy, then stir in hot milk. Stir till boiling and smooth. Heat spinach. Stir in sauce very gradually. Pour into top of double boiler. Cover and cook over boiling water, stirring occasionally, until spinach is soft in about 15 minutes. Rub through a sieve and reheat. Season with salt, and pepper if allowed. Serve immediately.

GRAVY SOUP

½ lb. shin of beef
½ lb. neck of mutton
½ lb. knuckle of veal
Cold water as required
Salt to taste

Break bones and meat into fairly small pieces. Place in a fireproof dish. Cover with water. Cover and place in a slow oven, 300° F., for 3-4 hours. Strain off liquid. Season with salt. Serve hot with thin dry toast, or allow to set.

LIVER SOUP

4 oz. finely-ground liver
1 cup chicken broth
Salt to taste

Add liver to broth, or to tomato soup if preferred. (Broth or soup can be flavoured with onion if allowed.) Heat and season. Serve at once.

VEAL BROTH

½ lb. knuckle of veal
1 quart cold water

Wash knuckle and place in a sauce pan. Add water, salt, carrot, onion, lettuce and chervil.

½ teaspoon salt
1 scraped carrot
1 peeled onion
3 lettuce leaves
Sprig of chervil

Cover and simmer for 1½ hours. Strain and serve in quantity according to doctor's orders. Good for delicate children. (If any indigestion is present, omit onion.)

VEGETABLE BOUILLON

6 small beetroots
1 small potato
1 sprig parsley
4 pints cold water
¼ cup chopped onion
Salt and pepper to taste

Peel and dice beetroots. Throw into a saucepan. Add potato, scrubbed and diced but not peeled, parsley and water. Put in onion, washed, scrubbed and sliced but not peeled. Bring to boil. Simmer gently till vegetables are tender, then strain. Season to taste. Bouillon should be reduced to about 1 quart.

EGGS

See the Egg Section for methods of cookery not given here.

A CODDLED EGG : Use only enough cold water to cover an egg. Bring to boil. Remove pan from heat. Carefully slip each egg into the water with a tablespoon. Cover saucepan. Stand in a warm place for 7-10 minutes, but do not allow to cook.

A LOPPERED EGG : Beat a fresh egg well. Add salt to taste, and pepper if allowed. Melt ½ teaspoon unsalted butter in a saucepan. Add egg. Stir once or twice, then remove pan to a very low heat. Cover and stand until egg is set without further stirring. When firm, lift out by a teaspoon on to thin crisp squares of buttered toast. Garnish with parsley.

ASPARAGUS SOUFFLE

¼ pint cooked asparagus
¼ pint milk
1 tablespoon butter
1½ tablespoons flour
Salt and pepper to taste
2 eggs

Chop asparagus. Place in a saucepan. Add milk. Bring slowly to boil. Rub asparagus and milk through a sieve. Melt butter in a saucepan. Add flour. When frothy, slowly stir in asparagus purée. Stir till boiling. Season with salt, and pepper if allowed. Remove pan from stove. Separate yolks and whites of eggs. Beat yolks till honey-coloured. Cool mixture slightly, then stir in egg yolks. Cool a little more, then beat egg whites till stiff. Fold into mixture. Bake in a small greased fireproof dish in a moderate oven, 350° F., for about 25 minutes. Serve at once. *For 3 persons.*

CHICKEN CUSTARD

3 oz. raw chicken or turkey
¼ pint chicken or turkey stock
    or milk
1 beaten egg
Salt to taste
Pepper if allowed

Shred chicken or turkey finely. Pound in a mortar until into a paste, then gradually stir in stock or milk. Press with the back of a wooden spoon through a fine sieve. Stir egg into the purée. Add salt to taste and pepper if allowed. Pour into 2 tiny ramekin moulds greased with butter. Cover with buttered paper. Steam slowly until set. Serve from dish with white sauce, or turn out and coat with white sauce. *Yield:* 1 portion.

INVALID FISH

White fish is the lightest form of solid food. Do not give herring, mackerel or any oily fish to invalids as they are indigestible. Serve plain boiled or steamed fish with egg, parsley or white sauce, if sauces are allowed. *See the Fish Section for Quenelles, Oyster Stew, and other simple fish recipes made from raw fish, omitting any seasonings, except salt, unless permitted.*

Easily-Digested Fish : Whiting is the most digestible. Next come sole, haddock, plaice, flounder, halibut, turbot, John Dory, and cod, in that order.

Method of Cooking : Bake, boil, grill or steam fish.

To Cook a Fish Fillet : Rinse a fillet of whiting or sole with a damp cloth, then dry. Brush on both sides with melted butter. Season with salt. Place on a buttered plate. Cover with a plate or lid. Stand on top of a saucepan of boiling water. Steam until creamy. Garnish with lemon.

BOILED SOLE

1 prepared sole
2 slices of lemon
Minced parsley to taste
Salt and white pepper to taste
1 onion, if allowed

Clean and skin sole on both sides. Place in a fish kettle. Add lemon, parsley, salt and pepper to taste, also an onion, thinly sliced if allowed. Cover with boiling water. Boil gently for $\frac{1}{4}$ hour. Remove with a fish slice. Drain well. Place in a hot dish lined with a table napkin, or paper serviette. Garnish with cut lemon and sprigs of parsley. Serve with plain hot melted butter, white or egg sauce, as allowed. *For 2 meals.*

FISH SOUFFLE

$\frac{1}{2}$ lb. fillet of fish
1 oz. butter
1 oz. flour
$\frac{1}{2}$ gill fish stock
$\frac{1}{2}$ gill milk
3 eggs
Salt and pepper to taste
$\frac{1}{2}$ gill cream
Ground mace to taste

Brush a soufflé tin with melted butter and tie a fold of greased paper round the top. Flake fish finely. Melt butter in a saucepan. Add flour and when frothy, stir in fish stock and milk, or use all milk. When smooth and boiling, cool then stir into fish with 2 of the eggs, and the third yolk. Pound to a smooth paste. Rub through a wire sieve. Season to taste. Stir in cream and mace, then fold in remaining egg white, stiffly beaten. Pour into tin. Cover with a buttered paper. Steam gently for $\frac{3}{4}$ hour, till firm. Turn out on to a hot dish. Mask with well-seasoned white sauce. Garnish with fingers of lemon and sprigs of parsley. *For 3 persons.*

WHITING MOULDS

1 small whiting
$\frac{1}{2}$ slice of bread

Remove all flesh from fish and pound it to a paste. Soak bread in milk for 10 minutes, then

f this Birthday cake
s wanted for a girl,
oat with pink icing,
ut blue for a boy.
See page 719.

Peach Sponge Flan.
See page 728.

Valentine Gateau. *See page* 731.

A Simnel Cake for Mothering Sunday. *See page* 721.

Easter Gateau. *See page* 720.

¼ pint milk
½ oz. butter
1 egg yolk
½ teaspoon minced parsley
Salt and pepper to taste
1 beaten egg

strain off any superfluous milk. Place soaked bread in a saucepan. Add butter, yolk and parsley. Stir over heat to a thick paste. Add paste to the whiting flesh. Pound till smooth. Season and add beaten egg. Place in small buttered moulds. Steam very slowly for ½ hour. Serve turned out, coated white sauce. *For 1 person (2 meals).*

GAME, MEAT AND POULTRY

All meats are nourishing, but the digestible varieties vary considerably. *Meats that Can be Taken :* Chicken, lamb, mutton or turkey.

TO COOK : Bake, boil, grill or steam, and sometimes stew. *See respective sections for recipes for boiled, creamed or grilled chicken, boiled sweetbreads, boiled or steamed turkey, steamed or grilled loin of lamb or mutton chops and cutlets, chicken and mutton quenelles, chicken fricassee, chicken soufflé, veal quenelles, etc.*

CREAMED SWEETBREADS

Sweetbreads for 1 person
1½ gills veal stock
1 tablespoon cream
1 egg yolk
1 teaspoon lemon juice
Salt to taste

Choose lamb's sweetbreads when possible. Wash well and soak for 2 hours in salted water. Drain well. Place in a saucepan. Cover with fresh, slightly salted, water. Bring to boil, and boil for 5 minutes. Drain and throw into cold water. Stand for 1 minute, then trim off any skin and fat with finger. Cut into small pieces. Place in a saucepan. Add stock. Bring to boil. Skim carefully. Cover and simmer very slowly until tender. Cool a minute. Stir in cream mixed with egg yolk. Stir over low heat till sauce thickens slightly, then add lemon juice and salt to taste. Serve at once. *For 1 person.*

LIVER SOUFFLE

½ cup stale breadcrumbs
2 oz. sieved raw liver
Salt and pepper to taste
1 beaten egg yolk
1 tablespoon cream
1 frothed egg white

Mix crumbs with liver in a basin. Stir in salt and pepper to taste, and a few drops of lemon juice if liked. Beat in egg yolk, diluted with the cream. Fold in stiffly-frothed egg white. Place in a small buttered mould. Cover with buttered paper. Steam for 20 minutes. Serve with sauce if allowed, or vegetable purée. *For 1 person.*

STEAMED FILLET OF CHICKEN

Remove the breast of a chicken from the bones. Season lightly with salt and with pepper if allowed. Coat with melted butter. Place on a fireproof plate brushed with melted butter. Lay on top of a saucepan of boiling water. Cover with lid. Steam very gently until tender in about ½ hour, the time depending on age. Serve with the essence in the plate.

C.F.C.—25

STEAMED LIVER

Wash and dry 3 oz. of calf's liver. Cut into slices $\frac{1}{4}$ inch thick. Remov
any gristle or pipes. Place on a well-buttered enamel plate. Season with sa
and pepper if allowed. Sprinkle with 1 tablespoon veal or chicken stock. Pla
in the top of a pan of boiling water. Cover with a buttered lid or soup plat
Simmer until tender in about 20 minutes. Serve with potato purée, if allowe

STEAMED MUTTON CHOP

1 mutton chop
Pinch of salt
Oil or melted butter as
   required

Wipe chop. Trim off most of the fat. Sha
with a skewer or tie with string. Dredge light
with salt. Brush with oil or melted butte
Stand for $\frac{1}{2}$ hour. Place on a buttered plate
fireproof dish. Cover with greased paper, then with lid. Steam over boilin
water for 40 minutes, turning at the end of 20 minutes. Serve with its gra
poured over it. Garnish with a sprig of parsley. *For 1 person.*

VEGETABLES

The most easily digested vegetables are boiled asparagus, celery, lettuce, s
kale and vegetable marrow. Mushrooms are very digestible baked or stewe
Potatoes, when allowed, should be steamed or cooked in their jackets. Choo
only young vegetables except for potatoes. New potatoes are indigestible.

INVALID DESSERTS

Puddings made with eggs and milk are the most nourishing. Use simp
flavourings for all desserts including grated nutmeg, ground cinnamon, a
lemon juice or the thinly-pared rind of lemon.

ARROWROOT SOUFFLE

1 heaped dessertspoon arrowroot
$\frac{1}{2}$ pint milk
1 oz. sugar
$\frac{1}{2}$ teaspoon grated lemon rind
1 separated egg

Cream arrowroot with a little of the milk. Sca
remainder and pour over creamed arrowroc
stirring rapidly all the time. Return to pan ar
simmer for 8-1 ominutes. Add sugar ar
grated lemon rind. Stir till sugar is dissolve
Cool slightly. Add well-beaten egg yolk. Wh
egg white stiffly. Fold into mixture. Pour into a small greased pie dish. Bal
in a hot oven, 450° F., till well risen and browned—in about 15 minute
Serve at once. *Yield:* 2 portions.

CARRAGEEN MOULD

$\frac{1}{4}$ oz. carrageen
Rind of $\frac{1}{2}$ a lemon
$\frac{1}{2}$ pint milk
1 separated egg
Caster sugar to taste

Soak carrageen for 10 minutes in cold water
cover. Pick over. Place in a saucepan. Add t
lemon rind and milk. Boil for $\frac{1}{4}$ hour till soft a
thick. Strain. Beat egg yolk. Gradually stir
milk and sugar to taste. Add a drop or two

colouring if liked, and flavour with sherry or vanilla essence. Beat egg white until stiff. Fold into mixture. Pour into 2 wet individual moulds. Turn out when set. Decorate or serve with cream if liked.

EGG WHITE CUSTARD

pint fresh milk
oz. arrowroot
tablespoons water
Whites of 2 eggs

Bring milk to scalding point in saucepan. Mix arrowroot and water to a smooth paste in a cup. Whisk egg whites stiffly in large basin. Add arrowroot paste to scalding milk, stirring well. Draw to side of stove, and gradually fold in the egg whites. *Yield:* 2 portions.
(a) Keep hot, with lid on pan, for 8-10 minutes.
(b) Or, as soon as egg whites are added, the mixture may be turned into a basin and put in the oven to set, when it can be served as a semi-solid food.

PEARLY CREAM

tablespoons pearl barley
quart cold water
Pinch of salt
Caster sugar to taste
tablespoons cream or evaporated milk

Rinse barley, then soak in cold water for 12 hours. Place in a saucepan. Add salt. Boil for 5 minutes, then simmer gently on top of boiling water for 4 hours. Stir in sugar to taste and cream or evaporated milk. Strain into wet individual moulds. Chill. Unmould. Serve with sugar or prune juice. Excellent for children and convalescents. *For 6 persons.*

STEAMED CUSTARD

egg
teaspoon sugar
1/4 pint milk

Beat egg and sugar. Stir in milk. Turn into a buttered cup. Cover with buttered paper. Stand the cup in a pan containing 1½ inches of boiling water. Cover closely. Let the water simmer very slowly for about ½ hour. When ready, the custard will be set in the centre. Stand for 2 minutes, then turn out on to a hot plate, or it can be served cold. *For 1 person.*

INVALID JELLIES

Jellies, though digestible, are not nourishing unless made with milk.

CARRAGEEN JELLY

lemon
1/2 orange
1/2 pint water
1/2 oz. carrageen
3 oz. caster sugar
Green colouring to taste

Scrub fruit rinds, then dry. Peel off very thinly. Place in a saucepan. Add water and carrageen. Bring to boil. Boil for 1/4 hour. Extract lemon and orange juice. Strain over the sugar. When dissolved, strain into the boiling liquid. Remove from heat. Add a drop or two of green vegetable colouring. Pour into 2 wet individual moulds. Chill and turn out. Decorate with whipped cream.

EGG JELLY

3 oz. loaf sugar
1 lemon
Water as required
½ oz. powdered gelatine
1 beaten egg

Rub sugar on the lemon rind, till it turns yellow, then extract lemon juice into a ½ pint measure. Add enough water to make up ½ pint. Pour into a saucepan. Add sugar and gelatine. Beat egg. Add to mixture. Whisk over stove till nearly boiling. The moment the gelatine is dissolved, remove from stove. Strain through muslin into two wet individual moulds. Chill. Turn out. Decorate with whipped cream. *Yield:* 2 portions.

FARINACEOUS JELLY

½ oz. pearl barley
½ oz. rice
½ oz. sago
1 pint water
Rind of ½ a lemon
1 oz. caster sugar
Juice of ½ a lemon

Place the barley in a saucepan. Cover with cold water. Bring to boil. Pour into a strainer. Rinse under the cold water tap, then drain well. Place in a saucepan. Hold rice and sago in a strainer under the cold water tap. Drain well. Add to barley. Add water. Wash lemon rind and add. Bring to simmering point. Simmer very gently for 3 hours, removing scum as it rises. Strain through butter muslin. Add sugar. Strain in lemon juice. Stir till sugar is dissolved. Set in small, wet moulds. *For 2 persons.*

PORT WINE JELLY : Dissolve ¼ oz. powdered gelatine slowly in ¼ gill water in the top of a double boiler over boiling water. Add ¼ oz. loaf sugar and ½ teaspoon red currant jelly. Stir over boiling water till sugar is dissolved. Remove from heat. Add ¼ pint port wine. Colour if liked with a few drops of carmine. Strain into 1 small wet mould. Chill. Turn out. Decorate with whipped cream.

CAKES FOR INVALIDS

Simple sponges and cakes made from a Madeira mixture are most suitable for invalids. *See Cake Section.*

BISCUITS FOR INVALIDS

See *Biscuit Section* for recipes for plain short biscuits. The following are also excellent :

CHARCOAL BISCUITS

½ lb. flour
¼ teaspoon salt
Powdered charcoal to taste
¼ lb. butter
½ lb. caster sugar
2 beaten eggs

Sift flour with salt and charcoal to taste. Rub in butter. Stir in sugar. Mix to a dough with eggs. Knead thoroughly. Shape each into a ball the size of a large marble. Flatten in your hand. Prick with a fork. Bake a little apart on a greased baking sheet in a moderate oven, 350° F., for about 15 minutes.

SAVOURY ESSENCES AND JELLIES

The following are equally suitable for invalids on a Liquid or a Light Diet.

BEEF ESSENCE

1 lb. shin of beef
Salt to taste

Remove all fat and skin from meat. Place in a large jam jar. Cover with a closely-fitting lid, then with 2 or 3 layers of greased greaseproof paper. Place in a saucepan of boiling water with cold water coming fully halfway up. Cover. Simmer slowly for at least 3 hours. Strain thoroughly, pressing all the essence from the meat. Season with salt to taste.

CHICKEN ESSENCE

1 boiling fowl
½ teaspoon salt
¼ pint cold water

Skin and bone chicken. Wash skin thoroughly and rinse bones. Break up bones into small pieces. Shred meat coarsely. Place the bones in the bottom of a large preserving jar or fireproof earthenware jar. Fill up with meat, skin and bones alternately. Sprinkle with salt, then with the water. Cover closely. Place in a saucepan. Pour round the side enough cold water to come fully half way up. Cover pan. Simmer very gently for 5-6 hours. Remove jar from pan. Place a hair sieve over a basin, and strain liquid through sieve into the basin. Remove all signs of fat with tissue paper. When cold, the essence will jelly. Serve in small quantities as it is very concentrated. Store tightly covered in a refrigerator.

BEEF JELLY

1 pint clear beef tea
1 oz. powdered gelatine
2 tablespoons hot water
Salt to taste
Pepper if allowed

Pour beef tea into a basin. Stir gelatine in the water till dissolved, then into the beef tea. Add salt to taste, and pepper if allowed. Stir frequently until beginning to set, then pour into small wet moulds.

CALF'S FOOT JELLY

2 calf's feet
5 pints water
¼ pint lemon juice
¼ lb. loaf sugar
Washed rind of 2 lemons
Whites and shells of 2 eggs
1 inch cinnamon stick
3 cloves

Cut each foot up into 4 joints. Wash and blanch. Place in a saucepan. Add cold water. Bring quickly to boil. Drain off water. Rinse feet joints under the cold water tap. Rinse saucepan and add feet. Cover again with 5 pints of cold water. Bring quickly to boil. Cover and simmer gently for 5 hours. Remove scum when necessary. Strain and measure stock. (It should be reduced to 2 pints. If not, bring again to boil and simmer until reduced to this quantity.) Pour into a basin. Leave until cold. Carefully remove every particle of grease.

To Clarify : Pour into a saucepan. Add remainder of ingredients. Whisk with a rotary egg beater over moderate heat until fluffy and beginning to simmer. Draw gently to side of stove. Cover and leave for about 10 minutes, barely simmering. Strain through a scalded flannel jelly bag. If not perfectly clear, pour the liquid back through the bag, letting it drip, into a bowl. Repeat this straining if necessary, several times, until the jelly runs clear. Cover with a clean towel so that no dust can fall on liquid. If it begins to stiffen in the bag before it has all run into the basin, stand a cup in the centre filled with boiling water. Pour into moulds or jars rinsed with cold water. Serve when firm.

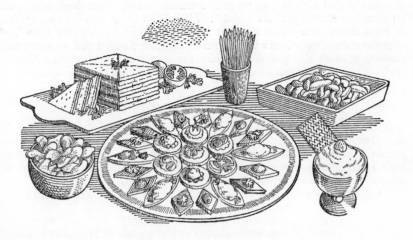

Buffet Fare

A buffet party can take the form of a cocktail or sherry party. It could be a combination of apéritif party and a help-yourself lunch or supper, or it may be a buffet luncheon or supper following a reception in the lounge at which apéritifs and appetisers have been served.

Choose the fare according to the occasion. You can have :

1. *Finger fare :* Canapés, sandwiches and whatnots.
2. *Finger and fork fare :* Canapés, sandwiches, whatnots and fork savouries.
3. *Finger, fork and spoon fare :* Canapés, sandwiches, whatnots, fork savouries, sweets and ice cream.
4. *Knife and fork, and spoon fare :* Sandwiches, fork savouries, cold cuts and salads, galantines, and mousses, trifles, ice creams, etc.

(If liked, canapés and whatnots can be served in addition.)

FOR APERITIF PARTIES

As cocktail and sherry parties are usually a prelude to lunch or dinner, only a few appetisers should be really necessary, but gradually it has become the habit to offer a large variety of savoury whatnots at evening parties. The result of this is that the modern cocktail party is often nothing more or less than a form of buffet party.

If a prelude to lunch or dinner, all that is required is : a dish each of salted nuts, stuffed olives, cocktail onions and potato crisps, and perhaps one or two varieties of savoury canapés such as crab, buttered shrimp or smoked salmon, and mushroom or devilled egg.

If giving a cocktail party, arrange dishes of salted nuts, stuffed olives, cockta
onions and potato crisps here and there about the room, and place canapé
and other cold savouries on a buffet. The hot savouries should be passed roun
in entrée dishes with boiling water in container below. A cabbage rose mak
an attractive centre-piece for a buffet. Flank it on either side with a grapefru
of good shape with a thin slice cut off the stem end. Place each grapefrui
sliced end downwards, on a saucer lined with foliage with a pad of cotton wo
directly beneath the grapefruit. Stab the grapefruit all over with coloure
cocktail onions. Sometimes a cottage loaf is used in place of a grapefruit.

Quantities to Allow

It is impossible to lay down laws about quantities of appetisers required fo
an apéritif party, as some guests who may not have time for dinner for son
reason or other, will make a meal of them, while others will only choose the
with lunch or dinner in mind. I am basing the quantities I am giving on th
assumption that both kinds of guests will be present.

Allow per Person :		4 sandwiches made out of 2 slices of bread, and 2 or canapés.
	or	2 sandwiches and 4 or 5 canapés.
	and	3 cocktail sausages or 2 or 3 slices of Frankforter sausag 1 bouchée, and 1 or 2 other savoury whatnots.

GARNISHES FOR APPETISERS : Sprigs of watercress ; tomato roses ; radis
roses and tulips ; minced green pepper and pimiento ; minced chives or pa
sley ; sieved hard-boiled egg yolk ; minced onion with hard-boiled egg white
caviare ; roses of savoury paste such as caviare and cod's roe, sardine, etc.

To Serve Olives : Black, green and stuffed olives are all suitable. Remov
from bottle. Drain well in a colander or strainer.

1. Chill slightly. Arrange in a crystal or glass dish. Sprinkle with Madei
or sherry just before serving.

2. Place in a bowl rubbed with a cut clove of garlic. Toss in a little oil. Chi
Serve in a glass dish. Sprinkle with minced chives or parsley.

OLIVES WITH CHEESE PASTE

½ oz. cream cheese
Cayenne pepper to taste
Salt to taste
½ teaspoon minced parsley
1 teaspoon anchovy essence
12 large stoned olives

Mix cheese to a smoothly-blended paste wit
all the ingredients except the olives. Stuff olive
Arrange on an appetiser dish.

To Serve Onions : Spear sweet white green, red, and yellow pickle
onions each with a cocktail stick and insert sticks in alternate colours in half
grapefruit, placed cut side down on a fairly large round plate, or in a red c
green cabbage heart. If preferred, they can be served in a glass dish, eac
speared with a cocktail stick.

To Serve Radishes : Make into roses or tulips. See Garnish section. Inclu
in a tray of appetisers, or use for garnishing canapés.

POTATO CRISPS

Both crisps and puffs can be bought in packets. To prepare them for serving, heat in packets in a moderate oven, 350° F. Dish up on a crystal dish lined with a paper doily. Sprinkle with salt or celery salt.

To Make Potato Crisps : There are various forms of potato crisps that can be made at home :

Lattice Potatoes : Slice pared potatoes with a lattice vegetable slicer into a basin of cold water to cover. Stand for 2 hours. Drain well, and dry between two kitchen towels. Fry in deep smoking hot fat until pale brown, keeping " slices " moving all the time with a spoon. Drain and salt.

Potato Curls : Choose kidney potatoes. Pare and cut into curls with a potato curler. Throw into cold water. Stand for 1 hour. Drain dry. Finish off like Lattice Potatoes.

Saratoga Chips : Cut pared potatoes in wafer-thin slices with a vegetable slicer. Throw into a basin of ice-cold water. Stand for $\frac{3}{4}$ hour. Change the water. Stand for another $\frac{3}{4}$ hour. Change water again. Stand for $\frac{1}{2}$ hour. Drain. Plunge in a saucepan of boiling water and boil for 1 minute. Throw into a colander to drain, then in a basin of cold water to cover. Stand for a moment. Remove from water and dry well between kitchen towels. Dry in deep smoking hot fat till pale brown, keeping chips moving all the time with a spoon. Drain on absorbent paper. Dredge with salt.

SALTED NUTS

Shelled almonds, cashews, chestnuts, peanuts, pecans, pistachios and walnuts can all be salted.

To Prepare : Pour boiling water over nuts. Stand for 5 minutes or longer until the skins can easily be removed. (The time depends upon how old the nuts are, and on how long they have been shelled.) Remove skins. Toss in a cloth until dry. Bake or fry.

To Bake : Place in a shallow baking tin with butter or oil, allowing 1 table-spoon to $\frac{1}{2}$ lb. blanched nuts (2 cups). Bake in a moderately hot oven, 400° F., with the door open, stirring frequently with a fork until the nuts are a pale brown all over.

To Fry : Melt butter or oil in a frying-pan until hot, allowing $\frac{1}{4}$ lb. butter or $\frac{1}{2}$ cup of oil to each cup of nuts. Add nuts. Cook over moderate heat until pale gold, stirring occasionally. To deep-fry, heat fat to between 360° and 370° F. Fry for 4-6 minutes until golden brown all over.

To Salt : Throw cooked nuts on to absorbent paper. Sprinkle generously with table salt. Stand for 3 minutes, then drain on absorbent paper. Sprinkle with salt.

To Devil : Sprinkle with cayenne pepper to taste or tobasco, when salting.

DEVILLED JORDAN ALMONDS (Amandes à la Diable)

¾ lb. Jordan almonds
1½ tablespoons table salt
1 tablespoon celery salt
Dash of cayenne pepper

Blanch, peel and dry almonds. Mix salt with celery salt, cayenne pepper and paprika. Heat the olive oil or butter in a strong frying-pan. Add half the nuts. Fry very slowly, turning

1 teaspoon paprika

6 oz. butter or ¾ cup olive oil

constantly, until crisp and pale gold. Remove with a draining spoon to a colander lined with absorbent paper. Sprinkle with half the salt mixture. Remove to a plate lined with greaseproof paper. Fry and devil remainder of nuts in the same way. Transfer to little glass dishes.

CABBAGE POND

Remove the outer and damaged leaves from a firm-hearted pale green cabbage. Cut the stalk level so that it will sit straight on a plate. Carefully cut out a hollow in the centre of the top with a curved knife, deep enough to hold a shallow bowl of mayonnaise level with the top. Wash and dry enough prawns to cover the cabbage from the edge of the bowl to about half-way down the sides. Carefully remove all the shells, but leave on the heads. Spike the cabbage all round with the prawns. Serve with sandwiches spread with anchovy butter and filled with mustard and cress or watercress.

CABBAGE ROSE

Cut a firm-hearted red cabbage level across the base. Remove outer and any damaged leaves. Rinse and drain, then gently pull down the remaining outer leaves—3 or 4 of them—so as to form a large purple rose. Place on a round flat dish. Spike heart with cocktail sticks speared alternately with some or all of the following :

1. Rolled stuffed anchovies.
2. Cubes of Dutch cheese with a slice of pickled gherkin or an onion below.
3. Bits of celery each topped with a peeled prawn, dipped in melted aspic if liked.
4. Halved grilled chipolata sausages.
5. Inch balls of sausage meat coated mashed potato. Egg and crumb twice. Leave for 1 hour to dry out, then fry in deep fat. Serve hot or cold.
6. Tiny pieces of smoked fillet of herring each topped with a stuffed olive.
7. One or two coloured onions.
8. Season cream cheese to taste with paprika. Shape into balls. Chill. Roll in minced olives or chives.
9. Place freshly-picked prawns in French dressing to cover. Stand in a refrigerator for 4 hours.

SLICED BOILED FRANKFORTERS : Spear each slice with a cocktail stick and either serve on a flat dish, sticks upwards, or impale on a cabbage rose.

STUFFED CELERY : Scrape celery stalks hollow enough to stuff. Rinse and dry. Cut in 1½ inch lengths. Mash ¼ lb. cream cheese with 2 minced spring onions, 1 teaspoon finely-minced green pepper or pimiento, and salt and cayenne pepper to taste. Fill celery stalks.

STUFFED DATES : Slit and stone dates. Mash ¼ lb. cream cheese with 1 tablespoon chopped walnuts, 1 oz. finely-minced stem ginger and salt, cayenne pepper and celery salt to taste. Fill dates. Place each in a paper case. Garnish each with minced pimiento or chopped chutney.

DUNKING PLATTERS

Dunking platters are one of the easiest snacks to arrange. You just place the " dip " in a low bowl in the centre of a large round plate or tray, and arrange the " dunks " round. Small potato chips, potato crisps, potato puffs, small pieces of crisp bread and toast as well as unsweetened biscuits of one-bite size, can all be served as " dunks." This type of appetiser can be served before dinner or at any appetiser or buffet party.

AMERICAN DIP

6 oz. cream cheese
3 tablespoons top milk
¼ cup minced walnuts
¼ cup chopped ripe olives
Dash of salt

Mash the cheese with a fork. Slowly stir in the top milk, then remaining ingredients. Pile in a low bowl and arrange in centre of a large round flat dish. Serve with potato puffs and small unsweetened biscuits arranged round alternately in groups. Garnish top lightly with paprika.

AVOCADO DIP

1 Avocado pear
¼ teaspoon any piquant sauce
¾ teaspoon lemon juice
1 saltspoon salt
Cayenne pepper to taste

Choose a ripe Avocado pear. Halve and remove stone. Scoop out pulp and rub through a sieve. Stir in remaining ingredients in order given, and whip until fluffy. Pile in a low glass bowl or arrange on the centre of a round dish or plate. Serve with potato chips, crisps or straws arranged round.

OXFORD DIP

½ lb. cream cheese
1½ teaspoons lemon juice
1 teaspoon Worcester sauce or Yorkshire Relish
1 saltspoon salt
Dash of cayenne pepper
¼ cup mayonnaise
½ cup minced canned shrimps

Rub a small basin with a cut clove of garlic Add cheese with the lemon juice, sauce, salt and cayenne pepper to taste. Stir until blended, then slowly stir in mayonnaise and shrimps. Use as a dip for potato chips, crisps and straws, small biscuits or sprigs of cauliflower, or with an assortment of these arranged round.

WORCESTER DIP

¾ lb. cream cheese
¼ lb. blue cheese
1 dessertspoon finely-minced onion
1 dessertspoon Worcester sauce
Few grains of salt

Mash the cream cheese with a fork. Crumble the blue cheese and add. Stir in onion, Worcester sauce and salt. Whip until blended. Pile in a small bowl. Sprinkle with minced chives or parsley. Serve with any suitable dunks arranged round.

779

SOME DUNKING PLATTERS

1. Heat Frankforter or Vienna sausages in their own brine. Drain. Cut in 1½ inch lengths. Spike each with a cocktail stick. Arrange round bowl. Fill bowl with French mustard.

2. Soak cauliflower sprigs, cut in 2 or 3 pieces, according to size, in salted water for 1 hour. Drain. Dry in a cloth. Place round a bowl of tomato-flavoured mayonnaise.

3. Place cubes of corned beef or luncheon meat on top of cubes of processed cheese. Run cocktail sticks through tiny pieces of sweet pickled gherkin, then through the meat and cheese. Serve with any suitable dip in the centre.

4. Place stuffed olives on top of cubes of canned pineapple. Run a cocktail stick through each, starting from the pineapple. Stoned black olives can be used in place of the green if liked. Serve with any dip you like.

COLD COCKTAIL WHATNOTS

CHEESE NUT BALLS : Pound 6 oz. cream cheese with 2 oz. Roquefort cheese. Add 1½ tablespoons minced onion or shallot, dash of cayenne pepper and thick cream to moisten. Shape into about 1½ dozen tiny balls. Sprinkle 1½ cups of chopped pecans or walnuts on a dish lined with greaseproof paper. Roll the balls in the nuts. Stab each with a cocktail stick of different colour, and arrange on a narrow tray.

DELICES GRIMSBY : Line 10 small boat moulds with shortcrust. Prick with a fork. Bake till crisp and golden. Fill, when cold, with bloater paste mixed to a cream with thick cream and seasoned to taste with paprika. If liked, pipe this filling into cases.

SARDINE TIT BITS : Drain 8 sardines in a piece of muslin. Skin and bone as carefully as possible. Roll each sardine in a thin wafer of smoked salmon. Set a layer of aspic jelly in the bottom of a shallow dish large enough to take all the rolls. Arrange rolls on top. Cover with a thin layer of aspic about to set. When set and chilled, cut each roll out neatly, with an edge of aspic. Serve each one in a paper case.

STRASBOURG SLICES : Roll ½ lb. puff pastry out on a lightly floured board to ⅛ inch thickness. Cut into oblongs 1 inch wide and 2 inches long. Prick with a fork. Place on a baking sheet. Bake in a quick oven, 450° F., till puffy and pale gold. Remove to a cake rack. Cool. Spread each with purée de foie gras and arrange in sets of 3 sandwiched together. Carefully spread the top layer of each with a little aspic jelly about to set. Decorate with ornaments of pimiento or truffle.

HOT COCKTAIL WHATNOTS

BACON ROLLS :

1. Roll small pieces of fresh chicken liver each in a wafer of bacon. Grill on a skewer and serve on canapés of buttered toast.

2. Wrap large stuffed olives each in a wafer-thin slice of mild bacon. Skewer

and grill or crisp in the oven. Serve in a hot dish. Garnish with potato crisps or lattice potatoes.

3. Wrap a thin strip of bacon round an oyster, small piece of chipolata sausage or a champignon. Roll. Skewer each with a toothpick. Grill under fairly slow heat until bacon is crisp, turning once or twice.

CHEESE CRUMB CROQUETTES (Croquettes au Fromage)

1 cup cream cheese
1 beaten egg
¾ cup sieved breadcrumbs
Worcester sauce to taste

Mix ingredients thoroughly together. Shape into marbles. Place in a wire frying basket. Fry in deep smoking hot fat till a golden brown. Drain. Serve at once, each spiked with a cocktail stick.

CHEESE FEATHERS (Plumes au Fromage)

¼ lb. Cheddar cheese
3 eggs
3 oz. flour
½ teaspoon salt
½ teaspoon baking powder
1 tablespoon minced onion

Cut cheese into ¼ inch cubes. Beat eggs till light. Sift flour with salt and baking powder. Gradually stir into eggs. When blended, fold in the onion and cheese. Drip from a teaspoon into smoking hot fat or cooking oil heated to about 380° F. Fry till golden brown. Drain on absorbent paper. *Yield :* About 1½ dozen.

CHEESE STICKS : Remove crusts neatly from a stale sandwich loaf. Cut bread in ⅓ inch slices. Spread thinly with butter. Cut into equal-sized sticks. Sprinkle with grated cheese. Season with salt and cayenne pepper to taste. Place on a baking sheet. Bake in the top of oven till delicately browned.

CHEESE TIDDLYWINKS : Cut 24-hour old bread, sliced ¼ inch thick, into ¼ inch cubes. Beat 1 egg. Stir in 1 tablespoon melted butter, salt, celery salt and cayenne pepper to taste. Roll the bread cubes in this mixture, then in finely-grated Parmesan or Cheddar cheese. Bake a little apart on a greased baking sheet in a moderately hot oven, 375° F., until cheese melts.

CHICKEN TIT-BITS : Skin, joint and bone poussins. Remove breasts. Dip in seasoned flour. Egg and crumb. Fry in hot butter or oil until golden brown. Drain on absorbent paper.

FISH BALLS (Boules de Poisson)

3 medium-sized potatoes
1 cup flaked boiled smoked haddock
1 beaten egg
Salt and pepper to taste
¼ cup milk

Boil potatoes in their jackets, then peel and mash. Add fish and egg. Mix well. Stir in salt and pepper to taste and milk. Beat until fluffy. Drop from a teaspoon into deep hot fat, 375° F. Fry until golden brown in 2 or 3 minutes. Drain on absorbent paper. Impale each on a cocktail stick. Serve hot in an entrée dish with boiling water in the bottom compartment. Place the entrée dish on a tray. Serve balls with Tartare sauce.

HAM KEBABS (Kebabs de Jambon)

1 lb. ground ham
1 cup stale breadcrumbs
1 beaten egg
½ cup milk
3 tablespoons vinegar
3 tablespoons water
½ cup brown sugar
½ teaspoon dry mustard

Mix ham with the crumbs, egg and milk. Shape into tiny balls about the same size as a pineapple chunk. Pour vinegar and water into a basin. Add sugar and mustard. Stir until blended. Brush the balls with this dressing. Impale on skewers alternately with pineapple chunks and maraschino cherries. Place on a rack in a baking tin. Bake in a moderate oven, 350° F., turning occasionally, until the balls are tender in about ¼ hour.

HERB PUFFS : Beat 1 egg white until stiff. Stir in 1 dessertspoon salad dressing, salt and cayenne pepper to taste, 1 saltspoon grated onion, and a tiny pinch of crushed mixed herbs. Remove crusts from 4 slices of bread cut ¼ inch thick. Cut each into 4 triangles. Spread lightly with the dressing. Bake in a moderate oven, 350° F., until pale gold and puffy in 5-6 minutes.

LIVER CROUSTADES (Croustades de Foies de Volaille)

Bread as required
3 chicken livers
1 egg
A little cream
Salt, paprika and cayenne pepper to taste
Squeeze of lemon juice

Cut 3 slices of bread 1½ inches thick. Cut each slice into 4 1½ inch squares. Wash, dry, slice and fry livers in a little smoking hot butter very gently for 5 minutes, till cooked through. Mash with a wooden spoon. Stir in egg and enough cream to make a creamy filling. Stir over stove till thick but don't allow mixture to boil. Season to taste with salt, paprika, cayenne pepper, and add lemon juice. Keep hot over boiling water while you hollow out each bread cube, and fry cubes until golden in butter. Stuff cubes with mixture. Sprinkle to taste with minced parsley or chives. Serve at once. *Yield :* 12 croustades.

SAUSAGES : Grill or fry chipolata sausages slowly until brown and cooked through. Serve each speared with a cocktail stick in entrée dishes containing boiling water in bottom container.

SAUSAGETTES : Fry, skin and pound petit Parisienne or chipolata sausages in a mortar with grated Parmesan cheese, cayenne pepper and minced parsley to taste. Spread on diamonds or ovals of hot buttered toast. Place a fried mushroom on the top of each. Heat in oven. Serve at once.

SAVOURY NEEDLES (Aiguilles au Fromage)

1 oz. butter
¼ pint milk
2 tablespoons flour
2 eggs
1 oz. grated Parmesan cheese
Salt and cayenne pepper to taste

Measure butter and milk into a saucepan. Bring to boil. Sift flour and stir in very quickly. Keep stirring until mixture shrinks from sides of pan. Remove from heat. Cool, then beat in eggs, one at a time. Stir in cheese and salt and cayenne pepper to taste. Chill. Rub mixture through a colander into smoking hot fat. Fry till crisp and dry. Serve piping hot sprinkled with grated Parmesan cheese.

STUFFED CHAMPIGNONS : Drain champignons thoroughly. Place in a small basin. Sprinkle with Madeira or sherry. Soak for 3 hours. Drain. Toss in melted butter until heated through. Dip in lightly fried crumbs. Serve hot, each impaled on a cocktail stick. If liked, quickly stab a cabbage heart or half a grapefruit with the mushroom sticks.

HOT COCKTAIL PASTRIES

ANCHOVY PUFFLETS (Pouffes a l'Anchoix)

1/4 lb. butter
3 oz. cream cheese
1/4 lb. flour
Pinch of celery salt
Anchovy paste as required

Beat butter until creamy, then gradually beat in the cheese. Sift flour with celery salt, and mix with the creamed butter. Wrap in waxed paper and chill. Roll out on a lightly floured board into a thin round. Cut into small rounds with a cutter 2 inches across. Spread almost up to the edge with anchovy paste. Fold in two. Press edges lightly together. Place a little apart on a baking sheet. Bake in a moderately hot oven, 400° F., for about 10 minutes. *Yield* : 4 dozen pufflets.

CHEDDAR FAGGOTS (Fagots au Fromage)

Left-over flaky pastry
1 cup grated Cheddar cheese
1/4 teaspoon dry mustard
Paprika to taste

Roll scraps of pastry out on a lightly floured pastry board. Spread half with the cheese, mustard and paprika. Cover with the other half. Roll out lightly. Cut some into 2 inch strips and remainder into rings. Bake on a baking sheet in a moderately hot oven, 375° F., for 5-8 minutes. Serve the faggots in the rings.

CRAB BOUCHEES (Bouchées de Crabe)

1 oz. butter
1 oz. flour
1/2 pint milk
1/4 teaspoon French mustard
Salt, pepper and paprika to taste
2 oz. grated cheese
3 oz. crab
1 1/2 dozen bouchée cases

Melt butter in a saucepan. Stir in flour, then dilute with milk. Cook, stirring constantly, till smooth, then season with mustard, salt, pepper and paprika. Add cheese, then the crab. Season again if necessary. Make piping hot. Pile into hot bouchée cases (see Pastry Section). Either replace tops, or plant a sprig of parsley in the centre of each. *Yield:* 1$\frac{1}{2}$ dozen bouchées.

DELICES DE MAYFAIR : Line 10 small boat-shaped moulds thinly with short-crust. Prick with a fork. Bake in a hot oven, 450° F., till crisp and golden. Brush the inside of each with anchovy essence. Pour 3 tablespoons cream or top milk into a saucepan. Add 2 beaten eggs, salt and white pepper to taste. Stir till thick. Pile into the " boats." Top each with a teaspoon of chopped smoked salmon heated over boiling water in a double boiler, and sprinkle with cayenne pepper.

PASTRY TIT BITS

7 oz. flour
1 oz. cornflour
½ teaspoon salt
3 oz. butter
About ⅓ cup ice cold water
Seasonings to taste

Sift flour with cornflour, then sift again with salt. Lightly rub in butter. Add a little water at a time, sprinkling only over a little of the flour, then mix and toss aside with a fork. Continue adding water to a little of the flour mixture in this way until all the particles adhere together. Wrap in waxed paper. Chill in a refrigerator. Divide into 4 equal portions. Roll each portion into an oblong ⅛ inch thick. Proceed as follows :

Celery Sticks : Sprinkle half of one of the rectangles with ½ teaspoon celery seed. Fold other half over. Press edges together. Fold in two. Roll out again into a rectangle ⅛ inch thick. Sprinkle with another ½ teaspoon celery seed, then fold in two and roll as before. Cut in strips, 3 × ½ inch. Place a little apart on a baking sheet. Bake in a moderately hot oven, 400° F., for about 10 minutes.

Anchovy Sticks : Spread 1 teaspoon of anchovy paste over half the dough of second rectangle, then fold in two. Follow method given for celery sticks, spreading, when rolled out second time, with another teaspoon of anchovy paste. Bake only for 8 minutes.

Caraway Sticks : Follow method given for Celery Sticks, substituting caraway seeds for celery seed, or ¼ teaspoon freshly ground black pepper for the celery seed.

Cheese Sticks : Follow method as given for Celery Sticks, but sprinkle the dough with 2 tablespoons grated Parmesan cheese, salt, and cayenne pepper or paprika to taste before folding and rolling again. Cover again with the same amount of seasoned cheese. Proceed as for Celery Sticks.

RAGS AND TATTERS : Make flaky pastry with ½ lb. flour. Roll into an oblong about ⅛ inch thick. Spread with beaten egg yolk. Dab here and there with anchovy essence. (If liked, sprinkle half with finely minced Finnan haddock.) Cover half with grated Parmesan cheese. Fold in two. Press gently together. With a pair of sharp scissors, cut in odd, tiny shapes. Place on a greased baking sheet. Bake in a hot oven, 450° F., till pastry is risen and very pale gold. Reheat before serving. Dredge lightly with cayenne pepper.

SAVOURY PUFFLETS : Roll out flaky, puff or rough puff pastry to ¼ inch thickness. Cut into 2 inch rounds with a fluted cutter. Place about a teaspoon of highly-seasoned sausage meat, creamed shrimps, or creamed chicken and mushroom on the centre of each. Brush half the edges with cold water. Fold over. Press edges lightly together. Either fry in deep smoking hot fat, 370° F., until golden brown in about 3½ minutes, or bake in a moderately hot oven, 400° F., until golden brown in about 10 minutes. Serve in an entrée dish with boiling water in the compartment below.

SAVOURY WHIRLS

6 oz. flour
¼ teaspoon salt

Sift flour before weighing, then sift again with salt and baking powder. Cut half the lard and

¾ teaspoon baking powder
2 oz. lard
1 oz. butter
About ¼ cup ice cold water
Savoury filling as required

half the butter into the flour mixture with a pastry blender, or 2 knives. When mixed into a mealy texture, cut in remainder of fat rather coarsely until the particles of flour mixture look like large peas. Sprinkle with 2 tablespoons of the water and stir in lightly. If the dough holds together when you gather it up into a ball, then do not add any more water. Otherwise, add 2 or maybe 3 tablespoons more water. Chill overnight. If this is not possible, chill for ½ hour. Roll out very thinly and cut into oblongs. Spread with filling to taste. Roll up like a Swiss roll. Chill. With a sharp knife, cut in slices ½ inch thick. Bake a little apart on a greased baking sheet in a fairly hot oven, 425° F., until golden brown.

Fillings :
1. Purée of foie gras.
2. Grated cheese seasoned with cayenne pepper and celery salt to taste.
3. Ham paste seasoned with mustard then creamed with thick cream.
4. Cream cheese mashed only until stiff with a little cream or top milk, and flavoured anchovy or bloater paste.

BOUCHEES OF SHELLFISH (Bouchées de Coquillage)

1 cup flaked crab, crawfish, chopped lobster, prawns or shrimps
¼ cup chopped fried mushrooms
1 oz. butter
2 tablespoons flour
½ cup chicken or veal stock
½ cup milk
1 egg or 2 egg yolks
Salt and pepper to taste
Pinch of ground mace
A few drops of sherry
2 dozen hot bouchée cases

Mix fish with mushrooms. Melt butter in a saucepan. Add flour. When frothy, stir in stock and milk. Stir till boiling and smooth. Beat egg or egg yolks slightly. Gradually stir eggs into sauce, then add fish and mushrooms, and salt and pepper to taste. Lastly, add a pinch of ground mace and a few drops of sherry. Stir till piping hot, but do not allow to boil. Remove from heat and fill bouchée cases, made with flaky or rough puff pastry. Dredge filling lightly with paprika, or decorate each with a sprig of parsley. *Yield:* 2 dozen bouchées.

SHRIMP FRITTERS (Beignets d'Ecrevisses)

½ pint frying batter
½ pint picked shrimps
Salt, pepper and paprika to taste
Grated Parmesan cheese as required

Measure batter into a basin. Stir in shrimps and seasonings to taste. Drop by small spoonfuls into a shallow saucepan containing 1 inch depth of smoking hot butter. Fry till brown below, then turn and brown on other side. Serve piping hot in paper cases. Sprinkle with Parmesan cheese.

SOFT ROE TARTLETS (Tartelettes de Laitances)

6 baked tartlet cases
1½ oz. grated cheese
1¼ gills hot white sauce

Keep the cases hot. Stir cheese into sauce in a saucepan, then add salt, cayenne pepper to taste, parsley and egg yolk. Stir over low heat till

Salt and cayenne pepper to taste
1 teaspoon minced parsley
1 egg yolk
6 hot fried soft roes
6 small fried mushrooms
6 asparagus tips

thickened, but do not allow to boil. Place a layer of hot sauce in the bottom of each case. Cover with a hot fried soft roe. Divide remainder of sauce between each. Top each with a mushroom. Decorate each with the point of an asparagus tip. *Yield :* 6 tartlets.

CANAPES

Do not limit your canapés to pieces of toast, unsweetened or savoury biscuits Use bread cut in fancy shapes and fried until golden brown. Other canapés can be baked, rounds of flaky or puff pastry and shortcrust, large potato crisps, bits of crisp bread, short cheese straws, etc.

When giving cocktail parties to celebrate engagements, wedding anniversaries or St. Valentine's Day, use heart and diamond cutters for cutting bread, and make crescents with a round cutter. When wanted for a bridge party, use bridge cutters.

BREAD CANAPES : Cut bread in thin slices, $\frac{1}{4}$ inch thick. Remove the crusts. Cut into any small fancy shapes such as crescents, diamonds, hearts, oblongs, rounds $1\frac{1}{2}$-2 inches across, small triangles, etc. Fry in shallow hot fat or oil until golden brown on both sides, or toast on one side only and dress the untoasted sides.

CRISP-BREAD : Cut or break into small pieces. Top with any savoury spread. Garnish with slices of stuffed or black olive, or with minced onion or chives.

PASTRY CANAPES : Use flaky, rough puff or shortcrust made with fat or fat and cream cheese, or cheese pastry. Roll to $\frac{1}{8}$ inch thickness. Make into shallow pastry cases, like tiny saucers. If liked, the flour can be seasoned with celery salt, cayenne pepper, paprika, or flavoured with caraway seeds before making the pastry.

POTATO CRISPS : Top with pieces of fish in aspic, a piping of any savoury butter, pâté de foie gras thinned with cream, caviare, or with potted shrimps pounded with mayonnaise.

ARTICHOKE TARTLETS : Drain bottled artichoke bottoms thoroughly. Cover each with a ring of hard-boiled egg white dipped in French dressing, then in crisply fried breadcrumbs. Fill centre with chopped fried, thoroughly-seasoned mushrooms. Lay each artichoke in a flat baked case of shortcrust.

CANAPE QUICKIES

There are several spreads than can be quickly mixed for small thin un-sweetened biscuits, or small pieces of crisp bread to provide quick canapés.

DEVILLED BISCUITS : Beat $1\frac{1}{2}$ oz. butter until creamy. Mix 1 teaspoon dry mustard and Worcester sauce to taste to a paste, then beat into butter. Season with cayenne pepper or tobasco to taste. Spread on thin, small, unsweetened biscuits. Bake in a moderate oven, 350° F., until pale gold.

CREAM CHEESE PUFFKINS : Mash 3 oz. cream cheese with 1 tablespoon mayon-naise. Stir in 1 tablespoon minced chives or parsley, salt and cayenne pepper to taste. Beat until blended. Spread on unsweetened biscuits $\frac{1}{4}$ inch thick. Place on a grill rack. Grill until golden brown.

CRABLETS : Mix crab paste to a cream with well-seasoned mayonnaise. Cover small rounds of bread, 2 inches across, with the mixture. Cover thickly with grated Cheddar cheese or grated Gruyère. Grill under fairly slow heat until cheese melts.

MAYONNAISE POUFFES : Beat 1 egg white until stiff with a few grains of salt. Fold in ½ cup thick mayonnaise flavoured slightly with mustard. Spread thickly on small, thin, unsweetened biscuits. Grill under fairly slow heat for 1 minute.

TOMATO AND PRAWN CANAPES : Cover 2 inch rounds of toast with a thick slice of tomato cut to fit. Arrange 3 prawns on top. Dab with mayonnaise.

CRAB CANAPES : Carefully remove any traces of membrane from a can of crab, or use freshly-prepared crab. Moisten with mayonnaise and season to taste. Flavour with lemon juice and season with cayenne pepper to taste. Pile lightly on rounds of bread 1½-2 inches across.

CAVIARE CANAPES :

1. Spread rounds of fried bread, 1½ inches across, with caviare. Place a pickled pearl onion on the centre of each.

2. Mix equal quantity of finely-minced shallot and caviare. Flavour delicately with lemon juice. Pile on rounds of fried bread, 1½ inches across. Centre each with a prawn. Ring finely-chopped egg white round the edge of each canapé.

SMOKED SALMON CANAPES :

1. Chop smoked salmon lightly. Season to taste with cayenne pepper. Flavour with lemon or fresh lime juice. When green pepper is available, add 1 tablespoon minced green pepper to ¼ lb. salmon. Pile lightly on canapés. When green pepper is not available, garnish with minced chives or parsley.

2. Place rings of hard-boiled egg on round buttered cheese biscuits, a little larger in size. Fill rings with chopped smoked salmon.

HOT COCKTAIL CANAPES

ANCHOVY CANAPES (Canapés d'Anchoix)

1 thin pancake—size of a tea-
plate
Salt and cayenne pepper to
taste
½ teaspoon minced parsley
2 anchovy fillets
1 oz. butter
Tomato purée to taste
1 tomato
Buttered toast as required

Make a little batter in the usual way. Season with salt, pepper and minced parsley, then fry in the shape of a pancake. Pound fillets in a mortar with the butter and purée. When pancake is ready, spread with the mixture. Sprinkle with a little cayenne pepper. Roll up. Slice and put each slice on a thin slice of tomato. Slip each savoury on to a tiny round of buttered toast. Make piping hot in the oven. Serve at once.

CHEESE POUFFES (Pouffes de Fromage)

¼ lb. Cheshire cheese
¼ lb. Cheddar cheese
2 beaten egg yolks
Salt and pepper to taste
2 egg whites

Cut bread into slices ⅓ inch thick, then into rounds 2 inches across. Toast lightly only on one side. Grate cheese. Mix with the egg yolks, salt and pepper to taste. When canapés are cool, spread thinly with creamed butter. Fold stiffly-frothed egg whites into cheese mixture. Spread thickly on rounds, making layer higher in the centre than round the edge. Brown under grill.

CHIPOLATA CANAPES (Canapés au Saucissons)

¾ lb. Chipolata sausages
2 tablespoons grated Parmesan cheese
1½ teaspoons minced parsley
Cayenne pepper to taste
Fried mushrooms as required

Fry, skin and pound sausages in a mortar with the cheese, parsley and cayenne pepper to taste. Spread quickly on hot rounds of buttered toast. Garnish each with fried mushroom, filled with crumbled crisply fried bacon.

COLD COCKTAIL CANAPES

AMBER RINGS : Top 2 inch canapés with rounds of ham, tongue or luncheon meat cut to fit. Pipe a trail of tiny dots or roses of chutney, horse-radish, or pimiento butter round the outside edge of each. Pipe devilled egg yolk into the centre of each.

ANCHOVY AND TOMATO CANAPES (Canapés d'Anchoix aux Tomates)

½ lb. firm tomatoes
7 anchovy fillets
Paprika and cayenne pepper to taste
2 tablespoons whipped cream

Scald and carefully peel tomatoes. Mince anchovy fillets. Mix together in a mortar. Pound to a paste and season to taste. Lightly stir in cream. Spread rounds of cold fried bread, 2 inches in diameter, with mixture. Decorate each canapé with mustard and cress.

ANCHOVY STICKS (Canapés d'Anchoix à la Crème)

6 slices buttered toast
Anchovy paste as required
Devonshire cream
Anchovy fillets as required
2 dozen stuffed olives

Remove crusts neatly from toast. Cut toast into inch-wide strips. Spread each strip thinly with anchovy paste, then with Devonshire cream. Lay a fillet on each and sprinkle with a minced olive.

CAVIARE TIT BITS (Canapés de Caviare)

Spread thin rounds of short crust, 1½ inches across (seasoned with salt, cayenne pepper and lemon juice, baked till crisp and cooled), with highly seasoned egg yolk moistened with butter. Top with ice-cold caviare and put a tiny rose of whipped cream on centre of each.

CHICKEN CANAPES (Canapés de Volaille)

Tomatoes
1 large cucumber
Breast of 1 chicken
Mayonnaise to moisten
Minced capers

Cut tomatoes into thick slices and place each slice on a canapé of fried bread cut to fit. Peel cucumber. Cut into thick slices. Scoop out centres with a cutter, large enough to remove almost all but the rim. Place each cucumber ring on a slice of tomato, then fill rings with chopped cooked chicken breast moistened with mayonnaise. Decorate each with minced capers, and parsley, or mustard and cress.

COD'S ROE CANAPES : Boil cod's roe in salted water till cooked. Drain well. Leave till cold. Place in a saucepan. Season to taste with ground mace, pepper, paprika and salt. Add a squeeze of lemon juice. Stir in enough creamed butter to make a thick paste. Spread on canapés of fried bread. Decorate with minced gherkin in centre and minced bacon round.

CREVETTES : Place a prawn or 1 or 2 shrimps, moistened mayonnaise, lightened with a little whipped cream, in each puff cracknel. Allow 1 per person.

EGG CANAPES : Place a thin slice of hard-boiled egg on each canapé. Season lightly with salt and pepper. Place a cold, fried button mushroom on the centre of each. Fill with potted shrimps. Season lightly with cayenne pepper. Pipe a ring of any savoury butter round the base of mushrooms.

EMERALD RINGS : Top 2 inch canapés with a thin slice of processed cheese cut to fit. Top each with a rolled stuffed anchovy.

LIVER SAUSAGE CANAPES : Mash liver sausage to a paste with salt, pepper, minced celery, and parsley to taste. Moisten with a little mayonnaise. Spread roughly on canapés. Garnish each with a narrow cross of pimiento.

MARCH RINGS : Cut rounds of bread, 2 inches across, into rings, removing the centres with a thimble. Fry in butter till golden on both sides. When cool, mix hare paste or pâté to a cream, with thick cream or mayonnaise. Cover rings with this spread. Sprinkle lightly with chopped pimiento or green pepper.

MUSHROOM CANAPES : Fry mushroom caps slowly in olive oil. Season and leave for 24 hours. Place each on a round of fried bread cut to fit before frying. Place half a stuffed olive, cut sides downwards, in centre of each.

NEWHAVEN CANAPES (Canapés, Newhaven)

1 fillet of cooked smoked herring
1 peeled cooking apple
2 cold boiled potatoes
3 tablespoons minced beetroot
French dressing to moisten
12—15 fingers of toast
Paprika as required

Chop the herring fillet, apple and potatoes. Mix with beetroot and French dressing to moisten. Pile neatly on fingers of toast. Dredge lightly with paprika.

OLIVE CANES : Cut strips of bread 1½ × 4 inches, and spread thinly with foie gras paste. Top each with overlapping slices of stuffed or black olive.

PATE DE FOIE GRAS FINGERS : Mash pâté de foie gras with a fork, then lightly beat in equal quantity of thick cream. Season with salt and cayenne pepper to taste. Rub through a sieve. Spread lightly on fingers of freshly-made toast, about ¾ inch wide, and 2 inches long. Sprinkle with minced green pepper.

SAVOURY FACES

Cut French bread in thin slices, or use oblongs or rounds of brown or white bread, cut ¼ inch thick. Cover thinly with savoury spread, made by beating

2 oz. butter or margarine till creamy and mixing with any of the following additions. Garnish to taste.

Chutney : Stir in 1 small tablespoon chutney. Top spread with minced boiled tongue.

Horseradish: Stir in 2 tablespoons grated horseradish. Top spread with a thin slice of brawn.

Mustard : Stir in 1 heaped teaspoon French mustard. Top first with processed cheese sliced thinly, then garnish with crisply curled celery.

Nut : Stir in 2 tablespoons ground nuts. Season with salt. Top spread with shredded celery.

SMOKED SALMON CROWNS : Place thin rounds of smoked salmon on small rounds of buttered toast or fried bread. Pipe mayonnaise round the edge of each canapé. Fill up centres with a teaspoon of minced hard-boiled egg, moistened with mayonnaise. Place half a stuffed olive on the centre of each.

SMOKED SALMON FINGERS : Fry fingers of bread 3 inches long, $\frac{3}{4}$ inch wide, and $\frac{1}{4}$ inch thick, in butter till pale gold. Cool. Cream a tablespoon of butter. Season to taste with salt and pepper. Mix in enough minced mustard and cress to make butter a pretty green. Spread fingers with the butter. Cover with a wafer of smoked salmon, cut to fit the fingers. Decorate with a piping of whipped cream flavoured to taste with minced chives.

SMOKED TONGUE CANAPES : Spread thin rounds of fried bread or toast with diced hard-boiled egg moistened mayonnaise. Top with chopped smoked tongue.

YORK CANAPES (Canapés de Jambon)

3 oz. boiled York ham
1 oz. ox tongue
2 tablespoons butter
½ teaspoon minced parsley
Pepper and paprika to taste
Cayenne pepper to taste

Mince ham and tongue. Beat to a paste with butter and parsley. Season to taste with pepper, paprika and cayenne pepper. Fry rings of bread in deep smoking hot fat till crisp and golden. Spread with the mixture. Sprinkle with minced gherkin.

Aperitifs and Cocktails

Sometimes sherry is offered as an apéritif, sometimes cocktails. When a greater selection is required, gin and Dubonnet are often included. If giving a large party, it is quite in order to offer the following : sherry, gin and orange, gin and French, gin and Italian, and gin and lime. If serving apéritifs before lunch or dinner, a choice of a dry sherry, a Martini cocktail, and a sweet cocktail such as a Bronx or Heart's Delight can be offered. Here is a comprehensive list of apéritifs :

Dry Madeira : Serve slightly chilled.

Dry or Medium-dry Sherry : Serve slightly chilled.

Gin and "French" : Half dry gin and half French Vermouth. (If liked, 2 or 3 drops of Angostura bitters can be added to glass before the gin.)

Gin and Grapefruit Juice, Orange Juice, and Pineapple Juice : Half dry gin and half fruit juice.

Gin and "Italian" : Half dry gin and half Italian Vermouth. (If liked, 2 or 3 drops of Angostura bitters can be added to glass before gin.)

Gin and "Lillet" : Half dry gin and half Lillet.

Gin and Lime : Half dry gin, and half lime juice, with a splash of soda water.

Pink Gin : Pour 2 drops aromatic Angostura bitters into a cocktail glass. Add dry gin to taste, then fill up with chilled water. (If using a sweet gin, allow 3 or 4 drops of the bitters.) Some experts simply swill the Angostura around the glass, then pour it out before adding the gin. This is a matter of taste.

Sherry and Bitters : Allow a dash of Angostura bitters to each glass of dry sherry.

Vermouth : Serve slightly chilled.

Mixed Vermouth : Place ½ a glass of French Vermouth and ½ a glass of Italian in ½ pint wine glasses. Add a tablespoon of cracked ice to each, and a twist of lemon peel, with soda water to taste. Serve with straws if liked.

Bizzy Izzy Highball : Mix equal quantity of Canadian Club whisky with dry sherry and a little lemon juice in a cocktail shaker with cracked ice, allowing a squeeze of lemon juice per person.

Equipment Required for Aperitifs : Cocktail shaker : Measure called a " Jigger " : Sherry glasses : Cocktail glasses to contain about 2 fluid oz.

HINTS ON COCKTAILS

1. Break up ice to suit cocktail shaker. If the ice is not shaken with the ingredients, but is placed in a central compartment it will have to be smaller than if it is put direct into the shaker.

2. If putting ice direct into the shaker, use fresh ice each time you mix cocktails.

3. Never fill shaker full to allow for thorough shaking. Shake as hard as possible.

4. If liked, brush the inside of glass to the depth of ½ inch down the edge, with lemon juice, then dip in caster sugar. When straining cocktail into these glasses, take care not to cover this brushed edge.

TO SERVE COCKTAILS

The majority of cocktails are served in 2½, 4 or 5 oz. glasses. To mix them, you can use any small wine glass containing 1½-2 oz. if you haven't got a jigger, which is equal to 1½-2 fluid oz. When I suggest a cocktail for only 1 person, and a number has to be served, then you must multiply the amount of ingredients in the proportions given. Either prepare gin combinations with ice in a cocktail shaker, or chill the ingredients before mixing. Serve all apéritifs and cocktails on small or large trays, according to the size of party.

To Garnish Cocktails : Add a maraschino cherry impaled on a cocktail stick to a sweet cocktail such as a Manhattan, and a pearl onion or stuffed olive also impaled on a stick, or a twist of lemon peel to a dry cocktail.

COCKTAILS

BACARDI COCKTAIL (Dry)

½ teaspoon Grenadine
Juice of ½ a lime
1 jigger glass Bacardi rum

Place in shaker. Shake well. Strain into a glass.
For 1 person.

BRONX COCKTAIL

Juice ¼ orange
¼ glass French Vermouth
¼ glass Italian Vermouth
½ glass dry gin

Pour into shaker. Shake well. Strain into glass. *For 1 person.*

CHAMPAGNE COCKTAIL

Place a lump of sugar in a champagne glass, or very large glass. Add 1 or 2 drops of Angostura bitters, just enough to saturate sugar, then add a block of ice. Fill up with champagne. Squeeze a piece of lemon peel on top. Garnish with a slice of lemon. *For 1 person.*

Duc de Marne : Place a lump of sugar in a champagne glass. Add 1 dessertspoon South African brandy, then fill up with chilled Duc de Marne Champagne. Garnish with a slice of lemon.

CHING CHING COCKTAIL

¼ pint Jamaica rum
1 sliced orange
4 lumps sugar
Few drops essence of clove
Few drops essence of peppermint
½ pint pounded ice

Shake all ingredients well together. Strain into glasses. *For 6 persons.*

CLOVER CLUB COCKTAIL

⅔ glass dry gin
⅓ glass Grenadine
Juice of 1 lime or ½ lemon
1 egg white

Shake well with ice. Strain into a medium-sized cocktail glass. *To Vary :* Tuck a sprig of fresh mint into each glass. *For 1 person.*

DAIQUIRI COCKTAIL

There are several versions of this popular rum cocktail.

1. Equal quantity of bacardi rum and lime juice sweetened with caster sugar and shaken with cracked ice. Allow 1 teaspoon sugar to ½ glass of rum and ½ glass of lime juice.

2. Shake the juice of ½ a lime with a teaspoon of sugar and a large jigger (2 oz.) of Jamaica rum.

3. Mix a large jigger (2 oz.) of Lemon Hart Rum with the juice of ½ a lemon, 1 teaspoon orange juice, ¾ teaspoon Curaçao, and a teaspoon of caster sugar. Shake well with ice, and strain into glass.

DUBONNET COCKTAIL

1 part Dubonnet
1 part dry gin

Shake well with cracked ice and strain into cocktail glasses.

EDDIE'S EIGHT BELLS

1 glass Lemon Hart Rum
⅓ glass dry Votrix
⅓ glass Vanderhum
⅙ glass orange juice
Dash of Angostura bitters

Shake all ingredients well together with cracked ice. Strain into cocktail glasses, and grate a little nutmeg over each before serving

HEART'S DELIGHT

⅓ Marnique
⅓ French Vermouth
⅓ Jamaica rum
Squeeze of lemon juice

Shake well with cracked ice. Strain into cocktail glasses. Garnish with a maraschino cherry on a cocktail stick.

MANHATTAN (Sweet)

½ glass Italian vermouth
½ glass Bourbon or Rye whisky
Dash of orange bitters
Dash of Angostura bitters

Shake well with cracked ice. Strain into glasses. Garnish each with a maraschino cherry.

MARTINIS

Shake ingredients together with cracked ice. Serve each glass garnished with an olive or a pearl onion.

DRY:

(1)	(2)	(3)
2 glasses gin	⅓ glass French vermouth	1 glass dry gin
1 glass French vermouth	⅔ glass dry gin	½ glass Italian vermouth
Twist of lemon peel	⅔ teaspoon orange bitters	½ glass French vermouth
2 dashes orange bitters		3 or 4 dashes Angostura bitters

* * * * * *

MEDIUM:
1 part French vermouth
1 part Italian vermouth
1 part dry gin

Shake well together with cracked ice. Garnish each glass with a stuffed olive.

* * * * * *

SWEET:
1 glass dry gin
½ glass French vermouth
½ glass Italian vermouth
3 or 4 dashes Angostura bitters
3 dashes of sugar syrup

Shake well with cracked ice. Strain into glasses. Garnish each with a maraschino cherry impaled on a cocktail stick.

JAMAICA ROYAL COCKTAIL

1 glass Jamaica rum
⅔ glass orange juice
Dash of Angostura

Shake well with cracked ice. Strain into glasses. When out of Cointreau, substitute Aurum or Grande Marnier.

MAIDEN'S PRAYER

¾ part Cointreau
¾ part dry gin
¼ part orange juice
¼ part lemon juice

Shake well with cracked ice. Strain into glasses.

OLD FASHIONED

1 lump of sugar
2 dashes Angostura bitter
1 jigger Bourbon or Rye
   whisky
1 slice orange
1 twist lemon peel
1 maraschino cherry

If old fashioned cocktail glasses are not available, use small 7 oz. tumblers. Crush the sugar in the bitters. (If preferred, dissolve it in 1 teaspoon of water mixed with the bitters.) Add whisky. Place 1 or 2 cubes of ice in glass. Add orange, lemon peel and cherry. Pour whisky mixture over. Add a splash of soda if liked. Spear the fruit with a cocktail stick.

To Vary : Add a quarter of a canned pineapple ring with the fruit.

OLD PAL

⅓ part French vermouth
⅔ part Campari
⅓ part Canadian Club whisky

Shake well with cracked ice. Strain into glasses.

ORANGE BLOSSOM COCKTAIL

1 part orange juice
1 part dry gin
1 part Cointreau

Shake well with ice and strain into cocktail glasses.

PLANTER'S PUNCH

2 jiggers rum
Juice of ½ a lemon
Dash of grenadine

Pour the rum, lemon juice and grenadine into a ½ pint tumbler. Add a tablespoon of cracked ice. Fill up with soda water. Decorate with a maraschino cherry. *For 1 person.*

PRINCESS MARY COCKTAIL

⅓ dry gin
⅓ Crême de Caçao
⅓ fresh cream

Shake well with cracked ice. Strain into glasses.

QUEEN ELIZABETH COCKTAIL

½ glass dry gin
¼ glass Cointreau
¼ glass lemon juice
Dash of absinthe

Shake well with cracked ice. Strain into a glass. *For 1 person.*

SIDECAR

¼ part lemon juice
¼ part Cointreau
½ part brandy

Shake with cracked ice and strain into cocktail glasses.

795

WHITE LADY COCKTAIL

¼ part lemon juice
¼ part Cointreau
½ part dry gin

Shake well with cracked ice. Strain into cocktail glasses.

FRUIT JUICE COCKTAILS

When you hear of a cocktail, you imagine it to be alcoholic. It originally was, but nowadays, the word "cocktail" is often applied to chilled fruit juice, and combinations of fruit juices created for those who do not want an alcoholic apéritif or cocktail.

Suitable Fruit Juices : Apricot nectar ; grapefruit ; orange ; papaya ; passion fruit ; pineapple ; tomato. Chill. Allow ½ gill per person.

SUGAR SYRUP FOR FRUIT COCKTAILS

10 oz. sugar
½ pint water

Stir sugar and water in a saucepan over low heat till sugar is dissolved. Bring to boil. Simmer gently for 8 minutes. Cool slightly. Strain into a bottle and cork. Store in refrigerator or larder. Use for sweetening fruit juice cocktails, cups, etc., in place of sugar.

ANGEL'S DREAM

4½ tablespoons pineapple juice
3 tablespoons cream
Chilled ginger ale

Place a cracked ice cube in the bottom of 4 cocktail glasses. Mix pineapple juice with the cream. Divide equally among the glasses. Fill up with ginger ale. *For 4 persons.*

CHERRY COCKTAIL

¼ cup cherry syrup
¼ cup orange juice
3 tablespoons lemon juice
¼ cup ginger ale

Strain the syrup from canned cherries. Pour into a cocktail shaker. Add remainder of ingredients. Shake well. Place a dessertspoon of cracked ice in the bottom of 4 cocktail glasses. Pour in cocktail. Serve at once. *For 4 persons.*

CURRANT AND STRAWBERRY COCKTAIL

½ lb. red currants
½ lb. strawberries
Juice of 1 lemon
2 tablespoons water
Sugar syrup to sweeten

Stem currants. Place in a basin. Hull and add berries, then stir in lemon juice, water, and sugar syrup to sweeten. Mash fruit. Stir till blended. Strain off juice. Pour into a cocktail shaker half-filled with cracked ice. Shake well. For 4 *persons.*

GRAPE JUICE COCKTAIL

¾ pint sweet bottled grape juice
3 tablespoons grapefruit juice
1 pint chilled ginger ale
3 tablespoons lemon juice

Mix grape juice with grapefruit juice in a jug. Chill. Chill ginger ale. When cocktails are required, dip the rims of 6 cocktail glasses in the lemon juice, then in caster sugar. Add ginger ale to the fruit juices. Divide equally between the glasses. Serve at once. *For 6 persons.*

LOVEAPPLE COCKTAILS

1 pint tomato juice
Salt, paprika and pepper to taste
Pinch of celery salt
1-2 tablespoons Worcester sauce
½ teaspoon caster sugar
2 teaspoons lemon juice
3 drops tarragon vinegar
1 tablespoon sherry

Mix tomato juice with salt, paprika, and pepper to taste. Add celery salt, sauce, sugar, lemon juice and vinegar. Pour into a cocktail shaker. Add sherry and ice cubes. Cover and shake till well mixed, and chilled. Serve in cocktail glasses. Pass round with cocktail biscuits or potato crisps. *For 6 persons.*

MINT COCKTAIL

¼ pint strained orange juice
¼ pint canned pineapple juice
1 tablespoon strained grapefruit juice
1 pint sweet cider
6 sprigs of mint

Mix fruit juices with the cider. Chill and strain. Serve with a sprig of mint floating in each. *For 6 persons.*

RHUBARB COCKTAIL : Sweeten juice from steamed rhubarb to taste. Sharpen with lemon juice, allowing a squeeze to each glass. Chill and serve.

TOMATO AND CUCUMBER COCKTAIL

½ pint tomato juice
2 tablespoons cucumber juice
Squeeze of lemon juice
Salt and pepper to taste

Mix tomato and cucumber juice, both obtained by putting cucumbers and tomatoes through a juice extractor. Add lemon juice and salt and pepper to taste. Chill. *For 4 persons.*

Luncheon and Supper Buffets

There are two methods of serving a buffet luncheon or supper. If the dining-room is large, only the food and serving equipment need be laid on the buffet. Two small card tables can be covered with cloths to match, and placed one to the left, slightly in advance of buffet, and the other opposite. On the one to the left, arrange plates, cutlery and paper napkins required. On the other, place liquid refreshments and glasses. If the room is small, then everything may have to go on the buffet. The alternatives are either to have the liquid refreshments passed round on trays, or to arrange a second buffet in another room.

Place behind dishes that need to be served, forks or spoons and forks required, and if everything is to be laid on the buffet, arrange serving plates to the left so that guests can help themselves to savoury dishes, and plates to the right for any desserts. When the buffet is placed in the centre of the room, savouries and sweets can be placed alternately round it with appetizers in the centre, and the liquid refreshment should be served on a small table a little beyond. When arranging food on the buffet, you must see that the dishes are grouped symmetrically. Plates of food ought to stand in front of bowls of salads, trifles, and jellies, etc.

Spring :

MENU FOR COLD BUFFET

* Appetizers

Asparagus Rolls   Smoked Salmon Rolls

** Aspic of Prawns

*** Sliced Meat Platter

New Potato Salad
Tipsy Cake
Macedoine of Fruit
Dominoes
Australian Punch

*   Offer a selection of Savoury " Whatnots " impaled on cocktail sticks, and inserted in a cabbage heart, also a choice of canapés.

**   Set prawns with green peas in sherry-flavoured aspic jelly.

***   Arrange alternately round serving plate overlapping slices of ham and luncheon meat or cold chicken, or turkey. Separate each variety with sprigs of watercress, or with halved eggs, devilled, nestling in heart of lettuce leaves. Serve with pickled beetroot and sweet pickled gherkins.

MENU FOR COLD BUFFET

Summer :

Melon Cocktail
Radishes   Stuffed Olives
Cucumber Sandwiches   Tomato Sandwiches
*   Savoury Aspics
Salmon Mayonnaise
Devilled Egg Canapés
Melton Mowbray Pie
**   Avocado Pear Salad
Milles Feuilles
Strawberry Sundaes
***   Fruit Kisses
Cider Cup

* SAVOURY ASPICS

1 pint Aspic Jelly, see page 473-4

To Make Aspics; Rinse 16 to 18 individual moulds with cold water. Pour into each just enough liquid aspic to cover bottom of each. Chill. Decorate jellied lining of each mould differently. Arrange a cross of champignon strips in the bottom of one, a slice of hard-boiled egg on another, a wheel of pimiento or green pepper strips on a third, and so on. When all are decorated, carefully dribble a thin coating of liquefied jelly over garnishes. Fill moulds up in this way :

1.   Place a firm slice of tomato in mould decorated with champignon. Fill up with diced cooked chicken or guinea fowl, moistened jelly, then with foie gras moistened liquefied jelly.

2.   Place one or two picked prawns or bits of lobster in mould decorated with egg. Cover with green peas. Fill up with savoury liquefied jelly.

3.   Place flaked boiled salmon or canned tunny fish in mould decorated with pimiento or green pepper. Top with chopped hard-boiled egg, then with one or two capers. Fill up with savoury liquefied jelly.

Continue filling moulds in this way until all the ingredients and jelly have been moulded. Chill. Turn out. Fill centre of plate or tray with sprigs of watercress. Place a dish of mayonnaise near by. *Yield :* About 16 moulds.

** Halve and carefully stone Avocado pears. Dress with French dressing. Serve on individual plates lined with crisp lettuce.

*** Force meringue out into ribbon or rose nests on top of rounds of rice paper, and bake. When cold, fill with lemon or orange chiffon. Decorate with small roses of whipped cream and raspberries alternately round inside edge.

MENU FOR HOT BUFFET

Autumn :

Madrilène Soup
Cheese Straws
Steamed Salmon Loaf
Parsley Sauce
Green Peas   Mashed Potatoes
Chicken and Mushroom Patties
* Hot Dough Nuts
** Apple Topsy Turvy Cake
Whipped Cream
Hot Coffee

* Heat dough nuts. Slit. Add more jam. Close. Dip in caster sugar. Serve in a hot dish lined with a folded napkin.

** Serve if liked with vanilla ice cream in place of whipped.

MENU FOR HOT BUFFET

Winter :

Chicken Bouillon
Rags and Tatters
Grilled Chipolatas
* Eggs à la King
** Baked Stuffed Tomatoes
Hot Fish Fritters
Sauce Tartare
Potatoes   Fried Mushrooms
Baked Canary Bananas
Whipped Cream
Mince Pies
Hot Burgundy Punch

* Serve eggs in fried or mashed potato nests.

** Arrange each tomato on a round of fried bread. Garnish with watercress.

MENU FOR HOT AND COLD BUFFET

Spring and Summer :

Fruit Cocktail
Crab Canapés   Mushroom Canapés
* Fried Chicken Tit-Bits
Lobster Salad
Boiled Asparagus
Sauce Hollandaise
** Chocolate Mousse

Snowballs. *See page 703.*

Walnut Gateau, Crinoline Lady, Strawberry Sponge Flan. *See pages* 731-732, 729 *and* 728.

*** Fresh Fruit and Cream
Palm Leaves
Sparkling Wine Cup
Iced Coffee

* Serve each fried chicken tit-bit frilled in an entrée dish with boiling water in container below.

** Serve mousse in glasses, decorated with whipped cream and chocolate shot.

*** Serve fruit in season with cream or ice cream.

MENU FOR HOT AND COLD BUFFET

Autumn and Winter :

* Onion Soup
Sausage Rolls   Devilled Lobster
** Fried Hamburger Steaks
Fried Chips   Fried Mushrooms
*** Pickled Prawn Platter
Stuffed Celery
Butterscotch Tartlets
**** Orange Cradles
Jap Cakes
Claret Cup

* Float an oval or round of fried or toasted bread capped with grated Parmesan cheese on each portion of soup.

** Garnish each steak with a pat of Maître d'Hôtel butter.

*** PICKLED PRAWN PLATTER

1 pint boiled prawns
Sliced shallot to taste
6 or 7 bay leaves
½ pint olive oil
1½ gills white vinegar
1 teaspoon salt
2 teaspoons celery seed
2½ tablespoons picked capers with juice
Dash of tobasco

Carefully remove spinal threads from prawns, then arrange them in a shallow fireproof dish alternately with thin slices of peeled shallot. Place bay leaves on top. Mix the olive oil with the vinegar, salt, celery seed, capers and caper juice, and tobasco. (If liked add a pinch of paprika.) Stir till blended. Pour over prawns. Cover. Chill in refrigerator for about 30 hours. Serve, drained, and arranged on a cold platter. Sprinkle lightly with minced chives or parsley. Place alongside a fancy glass filled with cocktail sticks so that guests can help themselves. Serve with tomato juice and salted crackers. You can prepare them for 4 or 5 days ahead if necessary so long as they are covered and stored in refrigerator.

**** Cut a slice from blossom ends of large, well-shaped oranges. With a sharp, curved knife, remove pulp and membrane. Chill shells in ice-cold water for ½ hour, then dry carefully. Scallop the edge. Fill with drained fruit salad or with cubes of orange jelly. Decorate round inside edge with halved defrosted or canned strawberries, slipping them in between fruit or jelly and skins, cut sides inwards. Pipe a tiny rose of whipped cream on join of each halved berry.

SAVOURY BUFFET PLATTERS

FORK:

1. Boiled cauliflower coated mayonnaise. Arrange alternately round halved green peppers filled with ham or tongue salad, hard-boiled eggs halved lengthwise and devilled, and groups of asparagus tips or boiled baby carrots dipped in French dressing, and sprinkled with minced parsley.

2. Boiled haggis served with mashed potatoes, green peas, pickled onions, and a lettuce salad. Garnish with rings of green pepper, sliced hard-boiled egg and radishes.

3. Creamed chicken, guinea fowl or pheasant and mushrooms in large individual patty cases. Serve with raw vegetables ; tiny cauliflower sprigs ; radish roses ; carrot matches ; celery sticks ; and watercress arranged in a dunking platter with a bowl of mayonnaise or Thousand Island dressing in the centre.

4. Stewed kidneys and mushrooms in a noodle or rice ring. Garnish ring with minced chives or parsley. Serve with green peas, sliced beans or spinach.

5. Aspic of salmon. Serve on a dish edged with heart of lettuce leaves, devilled eggs, cucumber slices and radish roses.

6. Fish croquettes in the centre of a hot dish. Garnish with hot green peas and fried chips. Serve with mayonnaise sauce or sauce Tartare.

7. Poached eggs fried in batter, garnished with grilled chipolata sausages and watercress. Fill centre with buttered sliced carrots and peas. Serve with sliced sandwich loaf.

KNIFE AND FORK:

1. Slices of cold roast veal arranged overlapping each other round a flat serving dish. Sink in centre a round or oval glass bowl of pickled beetroot garnished slices of hard-boiled egg and minced onion, with sprigs of mint, parsley or watercress framing the glass dish. Serve with potato salad and green peas.

2. Fried chicken arranged in centre of a large hot meat dish. Garnish with fried corn fritters. Serve with sauce Tartare.

3. Grilled Frankforters in an entrée dish with hot water below. Serve with potato salad garnished watercress and sliced radishes, and with celery relish and hot buttered rolls.

4. Baked ham loaf garnished with halved pineapple rings edged with minced parsley. Serve with creamed potatoes and sliced beans, asparagus tip and salad.

5. Slices of boiled gammon arranged overlapping each other opposite slices of boiled tongue, with overlapping slices of liver sausage at one side, and brawn or salami at the other. Place an attractive coloured dish of made mustard on the centre. Ring with stuffed tomato salad fringed with overlapping slices of cucumber. Decorate at regular intervals with short stuffed celery sticks in groups of 2, and tuck sprigs of watercress here and there on platter.

6. Place an oblong or oval mould of beetroot or tomato jelly down the centre of a flat, oval meat dish. Arrange round it cornucopias of cold boiled ham filled with boiled asparagus tips or French beans. Ornament each by tucking either a wedge of beetroot or tomato, depending on which jelly is being used, in the

centre of each cornucopia. Serve with potato salad flavoured with minced pimento and onion.

7. Italian sausage " baskets " filled with potato and green pea salad. Arrange round a flat cold plate. Fill the centre with devilled eggs. Garnish each with green salad. Serve with mayonnaise.

8. Thin slices of cold ham spread thinly with foie gras and rolled up. Arrange round a flat dish. Fill centre with jellied hard-boiled eggs coated mayonnaise. Garnish with cress. Serve with pickled gherkins and avocado salad.

9. Slices of luncheon meat paired with cream cheese flavoured grated horse radish. Serve with avocado rings, topping rounds of new buttered bread. Fill rings with tiny round new potatoes, boiled and coated with mayonnaise. Garnish with watercress.

10. Arrange the following tit-bits overlapping each other towards the centre on a large platter :

(a) salted crackers ; (b) slices of salami ; (c) boiled or pickled prawns, points inwards. Repeat.

Arrange devilled eggs in a ring round the centre, one half per person. Fill the centre with a small bowl of mayonnaise. Separate each variety with sprigs of watercress. Arrange radish roses round eggs.

11. Allow 1 hamburger steak per person. Arrange alternately with a group of French or runner beans round a heap of spaghetti or macaroni with tomato sauce. Decorate round the edge with fried mushrooms.

12. Arrange a baked, oblong luncheon loaf in overlapping slices down a hot oval dish. Garnish alternately with butter beans or green peas, and little boiled new potatoes, browned in butter. Serve with pickled gherkins, mustard and hot rolls.

13. Wedges of Melton Mowbray pie, meat upwards, round celeriac or Russian salad. Garnish in between with sweet pickled gherkins, and place a celery stick with foliage outwards, in between each portion.

14. Turn out a can of luncheon meat. Cut in 8 slices. Mix 3 oz. cream cheese with 1 dessertspoon drained horseradish cream. Spread half the cut slices with the cheese mixture and pair. Arrange on a platter, equal distance apart, in the form of a cross. In between the " arms," place 2 or 3 balls of avocado pear, and decorate with sprigs of watercress.

15. Turn out a large oblong can of luncheon meat. Make a diamond design across the top with a knife. Mix ¾ teaspoon made mustard with 3 oz. of light brown sugar. Moisten to a cream with equal quantity of vinegar and water. Spread over the top. Insert a clove in each " diamond." Place in a large flat fireproof dish. Bake in a moderately hot oven, 375° F., for about 20 minutes, basting at the end of 5 minutes, then 10 minutes later, with a tablespoon of stock mixed with a tablespoon of melted bacon fat, and any drippings in tin. Cut into 9 or 10 equal-thick slices. Arrange slices overlapping round a hot flat dish. Frill with overlapping slices of corn fritters, or with pineapple rings fried for 2 or 3 minutes, each covered with a thick slice of fried tomato. Fill the centre with buttered green peas or French beans.

SNACKS

There are many kinds of snacks. There are snacks suitable for a quick luncheon, supper or high tea. Some can be picked up in the fingers. Others need forks and knives. The easiest to make are those served in pastry cases, on squares or rounds of pastry, on fried bread, toast, on bread toasted only on one side, on waffles, unsweetened biscuits, or on halved unsweetened oven scones. Besides the recipes given in this section, there are a few in the savoury section equally suitable for snacks. The quantities can be adapted to suit.

BACON AND CHUTNEY BUNS : Beat 3 oz. cream cheese with a tablespoon of cream. Add a dash of Worcester sauce. Season with salt and cayenne pepper to taste. Remove rinds from 6 rashers of streaky bacon. Halve and grill. Halve 6 unsweetened oven scones crosswise and toast bottom halves lightly on the inside. Divide cheese mixture between these halves. Spread thinly with chutney, allowing 1 teaspoon to each scone. Place 2 half rashers on top of each. Butter remaining halves and place on top, buttered side downwards. Brush tops with melted butter. Slip into the oven for a moment or two, till heated through. Serve at once. *For 6 persons.*

BACON AND LIVER ROLLS : Wash and dry 2 chicken livers. Cut in 4 equal portions. Season with salt and pepper, and crushed herbs if liked. Remove rind from 4 thin rashers of streaky bacon. Cut each rasher in 2. Wrap a piece of bacon round each bit of liver. Run all on skewers. Place in a baking tin. Bake in a moderate oven, 350° F., for about 20 minutes, turning once or twice. Serve each roll on a large finger of hot buttered toast. *Allow 2 per person.*

To Vary : Brush livers lightly with mustard. Dip rolls in melted butter, then in frying crumbs. Bake on a rack in a baking tin in a fairly hot oven, 425° F., for 10-15 minutes.

CAVALRY TROTTERS (Croûtes, Cavaleries)

1 can luncheon meat
5 hard-boiled eggs
1 cup shredded celery
¼ cup chopped green pepper
1 teaspoon minced shallot
¼ cup salad cream
1 dessertspoon vinegar
¼ teaspoon Worcester sauce
Salt and pepper to taste

Cut meat into 6 equal-thick slices. Chop eggs. Place the eggs in a basin. Add celery and remaining ingredients. Stir till blended. Cut 6 slices of bread to fit slices of luncheon meat. Toast on one side only. When cold, butter untoasted sides. Divide the salad between the slices. Cover each with a slice of luncheon meat. Serve garnished with radish roses and watercress. *For 6 persons.*

CHEESE CROQUETTES (Croquettes de Fromage)

2 cups breadcrumbs
2 oz. grated cheese
1 cup boiled rice
Juice of 1 lemon
Pinch of ground mace
2 chopped hard-boiled eggs
1 teaspoon minced parsley
Salt and pepper to taste

Soak crumbs in cold water for ½ hour. Strain and squeeze as dry as possible. Add remainder of ingredients. Shape into small fat sausages. Dip in beaten egg and breadcrumbs. Fry till crisp in deep smoking hot fat. Drain on absorbent paper. Garnish with parsley. Serve with tomato or white sauce. *For 3 or 4 persons.*

CHEESE AND ALMOND TOASTS
(Croûtes de Fromage aux Amandes)

¼ cup chopped blanched almonds
2 separated eggs
¼ teaspoon Worcester sauce
1 dessertspoon minced parsley
½ cup grated cheese
¼ teaspoon salt
4 slices hot buttered toast

Crisp the almonds in the oven, or toss in a little melted butter in a frying-pan till pale gold. Beat egg yolks till thick. Add sauce, parsley, almonds and cheese. Beat egg whites with salt till stiff. Fold into cheese mixture. Pile lightly on the toast. Grill till puffy and golden. Serve at once. *For 4 persons.*

CHEESE AND BACON TOASTS : Allow 1 slice of bread per person. Remove the crusts. Toast on one side only. Spread untoasted side with mayonnaise. Place a slice of firm peeled tomato on top. Season with salt and pepper. Cover with a slice of cheese cut slightly larger than the tomato. For each toast, remove the rind of 2 short rashers of streaky bacon. Fry bacon slightly on each side, then arrange in a cross on each toast. Grill till bacon is crisp and cheese melts. Serve with crisped celery.

CORN SCRAMBLE (Croûtes de Maïs)

1 medium-sized onion
1½ tablespoons butter
1 chopped green pepper
1 small can of sweet corn
1 egg
1 egg yolk
Salt and pepper to taste
4 rounds or squares of fried bread or buttered toast

Peel and finely-mince onion. Melt butter in a saucepan. Add onion and green pepper. Fry till tender and beginning to brown. Drain corn and add. Add egg and egg yolk. Stir over slow heat till scrambled, seasoning to taste when the mixture begins to thicken. Serve on rounds or squares of fried bread or buttered toast with crusts removed. *For 4 persons.*

CRAB TOASTS : Spread rounds of fried bread or toast with flaked crab meat seasoned with salt and cayenne pepper, flavoured lemon juice, and moistened thick white sauce. Stir 1 teaspoon of beaten egg white into 2 tablespoons of creamed butter. Spread lightly over the top of crab. Sprinkle with grated cheese. Brown under the grill. *For 4 persons.*

CURRIED CHICKEN TOASTS (Croûtes de Poulet)

1 cup minced boiled chicken
1 cup minced boiled ham
1 teaspoon curry powder
¾ cup thick white sauce
6 slices of bread

Mix chicken with the ham, curry powder, and sauce. Season if necessary. Toast bread on one side only. Butter the untoasted side. Spread thickly with the chicken, then with sieved breadcrumbs. Place in a buttered fireproof dish. Bake in a hot oven, 450° F., for 5 minutes. *For 6 persons.*

DEVILLED LIVER (Foie, Diablé)

2 tablespoons butter
1 oz. flour
½ teaspoon salt
1 teaspoon dry mustard
Dash of paprika

Melt butter in a saucepan. Stir in flour, salt, mustard, paprika, stock and sauce. When boiling, simmer for 5 minutes, stirring almost constantly. Add liver to sauce. Sieve in egg yolks. Stir till

½ pint chicken or veal stock
1 tablespoon Worcester sauce
½ lb. diced boiled liver
2 hard-boiled eggs

boiling. Chop and add egg whites. Pile on 3 or 4 rounds of hot buttered toast or fried bread. *For* 3 or 4 *persons*.

EGG AND CHEESE CROUTES : Allow for each person 1 egg and 1 round of hot buttered toast. Place a poached or steamed egg on top of each toast. Coat with hot cheese sauce flavoured mustard. Sprinkle lightly with paprika. Garnish with hot asparagus tips, green peas or fried mushrooms.

EGG POUFFES (Pouffes d'Oeufs)

4 beaten eggs
1 tablespoon minced onion
⅓ cup self-raising flour
Salt and pepper to taste
5 oz. snappy cheese

Beat eggs into onion. Stir in flour. Beat till smooth. Add salt and pepper to taste. Dice cheese into ¼ inch cubes. Add to batter. Heat ½ cup fat or oil, fat to 390° F., and oil to 385° F., in a frying-pan. Drop batter from a tablespoon in rounds a little apart. Fry till golden brown on both sides. Dip 8 slices of firm tomato in seasoned flour. Fry lightly till crisp on outside. Arrange pouffes in overlapping slices round a flat hot dish. Garnish with tomato slices and sprigs of parsley. Serve with a green salad. *For 4 persons.*

FINNAN CANAPES : Melt ½ oz. butter in a saucepan. Add 1 tablespoon top milk, and heat slightly. Add ¼ lb. flaked boiled Finnan haddock. Stir gently till smoking hot. Remove from stove. Cool slightly. Stir in 2 lightly beaten eggs, and salt and pepper to taste. When thick, pile on 4 small rounds of hot buttered toast. Garnish with minced chives, parsley, or paprika. *For 2 persons.*

FRANKFORTER ROLLS : Remove crusts from a sandwich loaf. Spread 1 side thinly with creamed butter flavoured with chopped sweet pickled gherkin or stuffed olives. Cut off this slice. Pour boiling water over Frankforters. Soak for 7 minutes. Halve sausages. Place half on slice, and roll up like a Swiss roll. Secure with a cocktail stick. Prepare all slices in this way, then brush each with melted butter and grill carefully until light brown. Serve hot.

FRANKFORTER SANDWICHES : Bring Frankforters to a boil in cold water. Drain and slit each lengthwise. Place a finger of processed cheese, cut thinly almost the length of the sausages, in each slit, then slip each into a buttered split bridge roll. Brush with melted butter. Bake in a moderate oven, 350° F., for about 10 minutes, but only until the cheese melts.

HADDOCK CROQUETTES (Croquettes de Merluche)

2 cups cooked smoked haddock
½ oz. butter
1 teaspoon minced parsley
2 cups hot mashed potatoes
2 teaspoons salt
Pepper and paprika to taste
1 beaten egg
Egg and crumbs

Remove all skin and bones from fish. Flake, then mix with butter, parsley, potatoes, salt, pepper and paprika to taste, then with egg. Leave till cool. Shape into balls or corks. Dip in beaten egg then in stale breadcrumbs. Fry in deep smoking hot fat till crisp and golden brown. Drain on brown paper. Serve with fried mushrooms or baked tomatoes. *Yield :* 16 croquettes.

HAM SANDWICH DE LUXE : Place well-seasoned mashed potatoes between 2 hin slices of gammon. Stick top with cloves. Sprinkle with brown sugar. Bake in a moderate oven, 350° F., for about 1 hour. Cut into 6 equal portions before serving.

LUNCHEON MEAT CROUTES : Allow $\frac{1}{2}$ an unsweetened oven scone made about 3-3$\frac{1}{2}$ inches wide, per person. Split or halve crosswise. Butter each side. Cut rounds of luncheon meat to fit and fry slowly in a little hot fat till brown on each side. Place a slice on the bottom half of each scone and brush it lightly with made mustard. Sprinkle with grated cheese. Place under grill for a few moments until cheese melts and begins to turn brown. Cover with a slice of tomato. Season. Brush the top of the other halves with melted butter and place one on top of each tomato slice. Slip under grill, or into the oven for a moment to reheat.

MUSHROOM SCRAMBLE (Champignons, boulli)

2 oz. peeled mushrooms
1 tablespoon butter
3 tablespoons milk
3 beaten eggs
Salt and pepper to taste

Chop and fry mushrooms. Heat butter and milk together in a saucepan till the butter is melted. Mix eggs with mushrooms and salt and pepper to taste. Add to butter and milk. Cook, stirring constantly, till set. Serve on rounds of fried bread or hot buttered toast. *For 2 or 3 persons.*

PIGS AND WHISTLES (Petits Cochons)

1 can sweet corn
1/4 lb. flour
1/4 teaspoon paprika
Salt and pepper to taste
1 teaspoon baking powder
1 cup minced boiled ham
Pinch of crushed herbs
2 separated eggs

Use creamed corn, not kernels. Drain off any liquid. Sift flour with paprika, salt, pepper and baking powder. Stir into corn. Add ham and herbs. Beat egg yolks. Stir into mixture. Beat egg whites to a stiff froth. Fold in. Drop from the tip of a tablespoon into a deep frying-pan of hot fat or oil. Add 1 or 2 more. Fry till crisp and golden, turning when necessary with a spoon. Drain on absorbent paper. Keep hot while baking remainder. Arrange on a hot dish covered with a paper doily. Garnish with sprigs of parsley. *For 4 or 5 persons.*

SALMON PASTRY FINGERS (Doigts au Saumon)

1 can salmon
2 oz. butter
2 oz. flour
1/2 pint milk
Grated nutmeg or ground mace
Salt and pepper to taste
1/2 lb. rough puff pastry
1/2 beaten egg

Remove any skin and bone from salmon. Flake salmon. Melt butter in a saucepan. Stir in flour. When frothy, stir in milk. Stir till boiling. Add flaked salmon. Season to taste with nutmeg or mace, and salt and pepper, stirring all the time. Leave till quite cold. Divide pastry in half. Roll out one portion into an oblong. Lay on a lightly greased baking sheet. Spread with salmon mixture to within $\frac{1}{2}$ inch of the edge. Roll remainder of pastry to size of first piece and lay on top. Press edges together. Brush top with egg. Mark in a diamond design with a knife, then into 10 fingers. Stand for 20 minutes, then bake in a hot oven, 450° F., for about 20 minutes. Cut out fingers. *For 4 persons.*

SURREY TOASTS (Croûtes, Surrey)

2 cups diced boiled chicken
1½ cups shredded celery
¼ cup boiled green peas
Salt and pepper to taste
⅔ cup mayonnaise
8 rounds of toast or fried bread
8 stuffed olives
Watercress and tomato

Mix chicken with celery, green peas, salt and pepper, and mayonnaise. Spread evenly on the toast or fried bread. Sprinkle with grated cheese. Grill long enough to melt cheese. Garnish each with a stuffed olive, watercress and tomato wedges. *For 4 persons.*

TENBY TOASTS : Grill thin slices of boiled ham, choosing pieces edged with fat. Place each on a round or square of hot buttered toast. Cover with creamed, sliced hard-boiled eggs, flavoured with paprika and grated cheese if liked. Top each with a large fried mushroom.

TOASTED CHEESE

6 oz. Cheddar cheese
1 oz. butter
1 mustard spoon dry mustard
Pepper to taste
2 slices bread

Grate the cheese. Knead the butter and mustard together. Season with pepper to taste. Toast bread. Carefully remove the crusts. Butter the toast. Spread with half the cheese, then dab with half the mustard butter. Spread with the remainder of cheese. Cover with the remainder of mustard butter. Grill till cheese is melted. *For 2 persons.*

SANDWICHES

When sandwiches are called for, you must adapt the cases and the fillings to suit the occasion.

AFTERNOON TEA : Cut bread with small fancy cutters such as fluted, crescent, leaf, etc., and into small triangles and fingers. Use cucumber, foie gras or liver paste, smoked salmon, or tomato, or spread bread with savoury butter and use either watercress or mustard and cress as a filling. Serve also rolled sandwiches filled with asparagus tips or smoked salmon. Use one sweet filling in the assortment.

BRIDGE : Cut bread with bridge cutters (hearts, diamonds, clubs and spades). Choose any savoury filling without onion flavouring.

BUFFET : The type of sandwich served depends entirely on whether the buffet is for a party such as a wedding party, a cocktail party, or for a fork party. If serving only finger fare, sandwiches suggested under the other groups can be used, but if fork fare is served, then more elaborate sandwiches, such as hot sandwiches, sliced sandwich loaves, waffle sandwiches, etc., can be included.

CHILDREN'S PARTY : Use small bridge rolls and bread cut with animal cutters. Fill with slices of hard-boiled eggs ; slices of peeled tomato ; diced cooked chicken or turkey, moistened with white sauce sharpened with lemon juice ; diced ham ; or ham and egg ; etc.

COCKTAIL : Cut bread into dainty triangles, or in small fancy shapes. Use foie gras, crab, ham, smoked salmon, Swiss cheese, etc. Serve as well rolled sandwiches, ribbon sandwiches, etc.

LUNCHEON BOX AND PICNIC : Use bridge rolls, and white, brown or nut bread

Cut whole slices in halves. Choose fillings without salad, otherwise they may be soggy. (Pack any salad separately.)

CASINGS

BREAD : Use 24-hour old bread for all sandwiches except rolled. Bread for rolled sandwiches should be fresh. Slice bread thinly for afternoon tea and party sandwiches. Use sliced bread for picnics and luncheon box sandwiches.

Other Breads Suitable For Sandwiches : 24-hour old brown, malt, milk or rye bread, or 48-hour old nut bread, according to filling available.

TOASTED BREAD : Toast on one side only. Spread untoasted sides with butter or mayonnaise as suggested, then put filling between the untoasted sides. Cut in two diagonally and serve at once.

BRIDGE ROLLS : Choose fresh bridge rolls, small size for afternoon tea or party fare. Choose large ones for picnics and luncheon boxes. Split and butter thinly on both sides, then fill.

CHEESE BISCUITS : Use cream crackers, water biscuits, or other unsweetened and unflavoured biscuits. Spread thinly with butter, and put together with a cheese spread, and celery or watercress.

OAT CAKES : Choose small round or triangular oat cakes :

1. Spread with creamed butter, then with mashed Roquefort or Blue Danish cheese creamed with French dressing. Pair with shredded lettuce.

2. Spread with honey and top with Devonshire cream.

HINTS ON MAKING SANDWICHES

1. Remove crusts from bread before making sandwiches for afternoon tea or for a party. Remove or leave on for lunch box and picnic sandwiches.

2. Before buttering bread, prepare filling.

3. Cream butter or margarine and spread bread before slicing, or applying mayonnaise if used instead of fat. Do not melt fat on any account.

4. If sandwiches are to be made some time before they are required, wrap in aluminium foil, cellophane or waxed paper, then in a damp cloth. Store in larder or a refrigerator. If you have a refrigerator, you can store them in a covered container instead of wrapping them first.

5. Wrap sandwiches for lunch boxes or any packed meal in waxed paper, keeping each variety in a separate wrapping.

6. When making a large number of sandwiches, remove crusts neatly from sandwich loaves. Butter and slice thinly lengthwise, then sandwich the lengths together with the filling. Cut up as required.

7. Allow sandwiches made from 2 slices of bread per person when catering for all parties except picnics, when you want twice or thrice as much as that, depending on the amount of the other fare.

8. Allow 1 lb. creamed butter or margarine to $5\frac{1}{2}$-6 dozen slices of bread.

MINT BUTTER (Beurre à la Menthe)

⅔ cup chopped fresh mint
⅔ cup chopped parsley
Boiling water as required
Salt and pepper to taste

Wash and drain mint and parsley. Chop and measure. Mince well. Cover with boiling water. Stand for 5 minutes. Drain well, and dry in a

Paprika to taste
½ lb. butter

cloth. Mash to a pulp with a fork. Drain again. Season to taste with salt, pepper and paprika. Knead into the butter. Use for bread with cold lamb or chicken filling.

CHEESE SANDWICHES

The simplest cheese sandwiches consist of buttered bread put together with slices of cheese, or diced cheese, such as Edam, Gruyère, or processed. The cheese can be lightly dabbed, or spread with mustard if liked.

BLUE CHEESE SANDWICHES : Beat 2 tablespoons butter or margarine into ½ cup chopped Roquefort or Blue Danish cheese. Grate in a peeled cooking apple. Use with wholewheat bread.

CHEDDAR AND CHUTNEY SANDWICHES : Mix grated Cheddar with chutney to taste. Moisten with mayonnaise or salad cream. Use with brown bread.

CHEESE PASTE

1 hard-boiled egg
1½ tablespoons butter
¼ lb. grated cheese
1 tablespoon vinegar
½ teaspoon salt
¼ teaspoon paprika
Pepper to taste
½ teaspoon caster sugar

Beat egg in a mortar. Add butter and cheese. Beat to a paste, stirring in vinegar by degrees. Season with salt, paprika and pepper, then add sugar. Beat again. Cover with clarified butter to the depth of ¼ inch. Use with brown or white bread.

CHEESE AND ANCHOVY SANDWICHES : Cream 2 tablespoons butter with ¼ cup of grated cheese. Stir in 1 teaspoon vinegar, and salt, paprika, mustard, and anchovy essence to taste.

CHEESE AND CARROT SANDWICHES : Mix ¼ lb. finely grated carrot with 3 oz. grated cheese. Stir in ¼ teaspoon each of made mustard and vinegar. Use with brown bread.

CHEESE AND WATERCRESS SANDWICHES : Mix 3 oz. chopped processed cheese with a teaspoon of margarine, 2 dessertspoons minced watercress and a pinch of salt. Use as a filling between brown and white bread.

COTTAGE CHEESE SANDWICHES

You'll find the recipe for Cottage Cheese in the Cheese Section, page 658. Use any of the following recipes with brown or white bread, or unsweetened biscuits.

COTTAGE CHEESE AND CHIVES : Mix 1 cup cottage cheese with 2 tablespoons minced chives, and salt and paprika to taste.

COTTAGE CHEESE AND GINGER : Mix ½ cup cottage cheese with 4 tablespoons minced preserved ginger, and 2 teaspoons ginger syrup, and 2 tablespoons chopped walnuts if liked.

COTTAGE CHEESE AND RADISHES : Mix 4 tablespoons cottage cheese with 4 tablespoons chopped red radishes, 2 tablespoons minced parsley, 2 tablespoons minced spring onion, salt and pepper to taste, and 2 tablespoons mayonnaise or salad cream.

COTTAGE CHEESE SPREADS : Mix 1 cup cottage cheese with 1 dessertspoon made mustard, and 1 dessertspoon minced parsley. Use for spreading new bread to be rolled, or thin slices of ham to be rolled for an hors d'oeuvre platter.

CREAM CHEESE SANDWICHES

Use Demi-Sel, or any other variety of cream cheese for any of the following recipes.

CREAM CHEESE AND JAM : Measure off equal quantity of cream cheese and strawberry jam. Spread buttered bread first with the cream cheese, then with jam. Top with another slice of bread.

CREAM CHEESE AND WALNUT : Mix $\frac{1}{2}$ cup cream cheese with 2 tablespoons minced walnuts.

DANISH CHEESE SANDWICHES (Sandwiches à la Danoise)

3 oz. Danish Blue cheese
2 tablespoons olive oil
$\frac{1}{2}$ teaspoon salt
$1\frac{1}{2}$ tablespoons lemon juice
3 oz. cream cheese
Paprika to taste

Mash Danish Blue with a fork. Stir in enough of the oil to make a smooth paste. Stir in salt, lemon juice, and cream cheese, then paprika. Use with unsweetened biscuits and shredded lettuce.

EGG SANDWICHES

Egg sandwiches are popular for afternoon tea, children's parties, and packed luncheons. When planning how many you require, remember that 3 medium sized eggs will give you about $\frac{1}{2}$ cup chopped egg. Use with white bread or bridge rolls.

EGG AND ANCHOVY : Chop 6 hard-boiled eggs, yolks and white separately. Rub yolks through a sieve. Add 7 drained anchovy fillets, finely chopped, and mixed to a paste with French dressing to taste. Stir in egg whites and 2 tablespoons finely shredded celery heart. Use with shredded lettuce.

EGG AND BACON : Mix 2 chopped, hard-boiled eggs with 3 rashers cooked bacon, finely chopped, pepper to taste, and a suspicion of salt.

EGG AND CARROT : Mix 2 chopped hard-boiled eggs with 1 cup shredded raw carrot, 1 teaspoon lemon juice, and 6 tablespoons mayonnaise.

EGG AND HAM : Mix 3 chopped hard-boiled eggs with 3 sliced pickled gherkins, $\frac{1}{2}$ cup shredded celery, 4 chopped stuffed olives, $\frac{1}{2}$ cup diced boiled ham, and mayonnaise to moisten.

EGG AND SHRIMP : Soak a tightly packed cup of picked shrimps for 2 hours in French dressing to moisten. Drain thoroughly. Add 3 tablespoons minced spring onions and $\frac{1}{2}$ cup minced watercress. Separate yolks and whites from 3 hard-boiled eggs. Sieve yolks. Mince egg whites. Stir both into shrimp mixture with mayonnaise to moisten. Use between thin slices of brown or white bread, thinly spread with mayonnaise. *Yield :* 12-16 large sandwiches.

EGG AND TOMATO : Mix 1 chopped hard-boiled egg with 1 tablespoon minced shallot, 1 tablespoon minced sweet pickled gherkin, 3 sliced chopped firm peeled tomatoes, salt and pepper to taste, and $1\frac{1}{2}$ tablespoons creamed butter.

EGG AND TONGUE : Follow recipe for Egg and Ham, but substitute chopped tongue for the ham.

FISH SANDWICHES

Make fillings with anchovies, flaked boiled smoked haddock, boiled or canned salmon, sardines, boiled or potted shellfish, and canned tunny fish.

CAVIARE SANDWICHES : Fill thinly-buttered brown or white bread with caviare lightly flavoured with lemon juice.

CRAB PASTE : Mash yolks of 2 hard-boiled eggs to a paste with a tablespoon of melted butter. Stir in 1 tablespoon of lemon juice, and $\frac{1}{2}$ cup minced crab meat. Mix well.

CRAB OR LOBSTER PASTE : Remove the meat from 2 medium-sized boiled crabs or lobsters. Chop finely. Place in a saucepan with 2 oz. butter, and salt, pepper, and cayenne pepper to taste. Simmer gently for 20 minutes, stirring frequently. Remove from stove. Stir in $\frac{1}{4}$ pint thick cream very gradually. Cook over boiling water, stirring constantly, till paste is smooth and fairly thick. Rub through a fine sieve. Press into pots. When cold, cover with clarified butter.

CRAB AND TOMATO SANDWICHES (Sandwiches à la Crabe)

1 cup crab meat
¾ cup minced celery
Mayonnaise as required
3 firm peeled tomatoes
8 slices bread

Chop crab meat. Stir in celery, and moisten with mayonnaise. Spread half the slices of white bread required with mayonnaise. Cover it with the crab mixture. Cut tomatoes into thin slices and lay them on remainder of buttered bread. Top with the other slices. Cut in triangles. *For 6-8 persons.*

POTTED PRAWNS OR SHRIMPS : Shell then chop 1 quart freshly boiled prawns or shrimps. Place in a mortar. Gradually pound in with a pestle, 2 oz. butter. Pound thoroughly. When almost blended, pound in cayenne pepper and ground mace to taste. Pot. Cover with clarified butter.

SALMON PASTE : Remove all skin and bone from a drained can of the best quality salmon. Flake fish. Place in a mortar. Gradually pound in 2 oz. butter, then salt and cayenne pepper to taste. Rub through a fine wire sieve. Pack into small paste pots. Cover with clarified butter.

SALMON AND LOBSTER PASTE : Pound 5 oz. boiled salmon with the meat of a medium-sized boiled lobster in a mortar, then gradually pound in 4 oz. butter. Season with salt, cayenne pepper and ground mace or grated nutmeg. Pound until blended. Rub through a fine wire sieve. Pack into paste pots. Cover with $\frac{1}{4}$ inch thick layer of clarified butter.

SALMON AND CUCUMBER SANDWICHES
(Sandwiches de Saumon au Concombre)

1 cup flaked boiled salmon
½ cup chopped cucumber
2 tablespoons chopped watercress
Salt and pepper to taste
Mayonnaise or salad cream

Mix salmon, cucumber, and watercress with salt and pepper and just enough mayonnaise or salad cream to bind the mixture. Use with thinly-buttered white bread and shredded lettuce.

SMOKED SALMON SANDWICHES : Spread brown or white bread with lemon or

Maître d'Hôtel butter. Top with chopped smoked salmon, and cover with another slice of bread.

SARDINE SANDWICHES : Bone and skin 1 tin of Portuguese sardines. Mash and mix with a minced hard-boiled egg, black pepper to taste, and mayonnaise. Use with white bread and shredded celery or lettuce.

SARDINE AND OLIVE : Mix 1 cup minced sardines with $\frac{1}{2}$ cup minced stuffed olives, 1 teaspoon minced onion, 2 teaspoons minced parsley, 1 tablespoon lemon juice, 1 tablespoon creamed butter, salt and pepper to taste, and salad cream to moisten. Use with white bread.

SHRIMP SANDWICHES : Mix 1 cup shrimps with $1\frac{1}{2}$ tablespoons minced celery, salt and pepper to taste, $\frac{3}{4}$ tablespoon lemon juice and 2 tablespoons mayonnaise.

MEAT SANDWICHES

Every kind of cold meat can be used as a sandwich filling. Chop or dice it, or cut into short small slices when the sandwiches are wanted for a packed luncheon or picnic, or when they are intended for a knife and fork luncheon. Another way of preparing meat is to put it through a meat grinder, and mix it to a paste with seasonings, etc.

CHICKEN AND HAM PASTE (Pâté de Poulet au Lard)

1 boiled fowl
6 oz. cooked ham
Salt and pepper to taste
$\frac{1}{4}$ lb. clarified butter

This paste has the best flavour when, after removing all the meat from the bird, you make glaze from the bones. Place all the bones and skin in a saucepan. Add 1 pint water, 1 sprig parsley, 4 black peppercorns, 1 blade mace, and simmer very gently for about 3 hours. Strain and pot. Mince chicken and ham. Pound to a smooth paste in a mortar. Season with salt, pepper and cayenne pepper to taste. Gradually beat in the butter, then stir in a tablespoon of the glaze. Pack tightly into pots. Cover with clarified butter.

CHICKEN SANDWICHES (Sandwiches de Poulet)

$\frac{1}{4}$ pint diced boiled chicken
$\frac{1}{2}$ gill diced boiled ham or tongue
$\frac{1}{2}$ gill shredded celery
About $\frac{1}{2}$ cup mayonnaise
8 slices of white bread

Mix all ingredients together and divide equally among half the slices of bread. Sprinkle filling with shredded celery, cucumber or lettuce, then pair with remainder of bread.

CHICKEN AND PARSLEY : Mix $\frac{1}{2}$ pint finely minced boiled chicken with 2 tablespoons well-seasoned parsley sauce mixed with 2 tablespoons mayonnaise.

CHICKEN AND WALNUT : Mix $1\frac{1}{2}$ cups diced boiled chicken with $\frac{1}{2}$ cup chopped watercress, 4 tablespoons ground walnuts, and 4 tablespoons mayonnaise. This is enough to fill 12 slices of bread.

CHICKEN AND ASPARAGUS FILLING : Mix $1\frac{1}{2}$ cups diced boiled chicken with 1 cup boiled asparagus tips and $\frac{3}{4}$ cup mayonnaise.

CHICKEN AND CUCUMBER FILLING : Mix 1 pint diced boiled chicken with $\frac{1}{4}$ pint diced cucumber, $\frac{1}{4}$ pint chopped celery, salt and pepper to taste, and $1\frac{1}{2}$ gills mayonnaise.

CURRIED CHICKEN SANDWICHES (Sandwiches au Kari)

1 cup minced boiled chicken
1 cup minced boiled ham
¾ cup thick white sauce or mayonnaise
¾ teaspoon curry powder

Mix chicken and ham. Stir in sauce or mayonnaise flavoured with the curry powder.

CORNED BEEF SANDWICHES : Mix ½ pint chopped corned beef with 1 teaspoon minced shallot, ¼ pint shredded celery, 1 teaspoon made mustard, 1 teaspoon minced parsley, and 2 tablespoons mayonnaise. Use with white bread or bridge rolls.

EPSOM ROLLS (Sandwiches, Epsom)

¼ lb. sliced peeled mushrooms
6 oz. chopped cooked veal
1 teaspoon chopped onion
Mayonnaise to moisten
Salt and pepper to taste
10 large bridge rolls

Fry mushrooms slowly in butter. Leave till cold. Mix with veal and onion. Moisten with mayonnaise. Season with salt and pepper. Split and butter rolls thinly and fill with the mixture. Suitable for lunch, picnics, or buffet parties.

FRANKFORTER ROLLS (Sandwiches de Saucissons)

12 bridge rolls
2 dozen Frankforters
¾ cup piccalilli

Split and thinly butter inside of rolls. Place Frankforters in a saucepan and cover with boiling water. Cover pan. Stand over low heat for 7 minutes, without allowing to simmer. Slip 2 sausages into each roll. Sprinkle with a little of the piccalilli, then close as far as possible. Place each roll on a plate garnished with watercress and spring onion. Serve with mustard.

GAME SANDWICHES : Mix 2 cups diced, cold cooked game, with 1 cup of shredded celery. Season with salt and pepper. Moisten with mayonnaise. Use with white buttered bread. Cut in halves diagonally. Use in luncheon or picnic sandwiches.

HAM SANDWICHES : Mix chopped diced ham with shredded celery, chopped radishes and mayonnaise to moisten. Use with buttered bread thinly scraped with made mustard if liked. When only a ham filling is wanted, chop ham and use with bread spread with creamed butter, and also with mustard if liked.

LAMB AND MINT SANDWICHES : Mix ½ pint minced cold lamb with 1½ tablespoons finely chopped mint and mayonnaise to moisten. Season with salt and black pepper to taste.

LIVER AND BACON SANDWICHES : Mix ½ cup ground cooked liver with ½ cup chopped fried bacon. Season with salt and pepper to taste. Add 1 teaspoon minced parsley and moisten with mayonnaise or thick cream.

LUNCHEON MEAT SANDWICHES : Dice luncheon meat and use as a filling for bread, thinly spread with creamed butter flavoured mustard or chutney.

MUTTON SANDWICHES : Chop meat. Season with salt and black pepper to taste. Use with watercress or shredded lettuce.

STEAK SANDWICHES : Put ½ lb. cooked steak through a meat grinder. Stir in 1 dessertspoon minced onion, and salt and black pepper to taste. Use with shredded lettuce or watercress.

TONGUE AND TOMATO SANDWICHES
(Sandwiches de Langue)

12 slices buttered bread
½ lb. thinly-sliced tongue
½ lb. sliced peeled tomatoes
Mayonnaise as required

Cover 6 of the slices of bread with slices of tongue. Top with slices of tomato. Mix mayonnaise with chopped pickled gherkin to taste, and spread over tomatoes. Pair slices. Cut each in half. Suitable for lunch boxes, picnics, and knife and fork luncheons.

TURKEY AND CHESTNUT SANDWICHES : Mix 1 cup diced cooked turkey with ½ cup chopped boiled chestnuts, 2 chopped hard-boiled eggs, 1 cup shredded celery, and ½ tablespoon chopped pimento. Moisten with ½ cup mayonnaise or salad cream. Use with white bread or bridge rolls.

POTTED SANDWICH SPREADS

Remains of cold meat can be made into savoury pastes for sandwiches with the help of clarified butter, and seasonings. When sieved, pack firmly into sterilized pots and cover with clarified butter to the depth of ⅛ inch. Cover and store in refrigerator or in the coldest part of your larder. See Appetiser Section for other pâtés.

POTTED BEEF (Pâté de Boeuf)

1 lb. cooked beef
4 oz. clarified butter
½ teaspoon grated nutmeg
½ teaspoon pepper
½ teaspoon salt
Pinch of ground mace

Use boiled or roasted cold beef. Mince finely, then pound in a mortar with the butter and seasonings. When thoroughly blended, pot and seal with clarified butter.

POTTED GAME

Remove any skin and bone from cold game, then weigh off 1 lb. game. Put twice through a meat grinder. Pound till smooth in a mortar, gradually beating in 3 oz. of clarified butter. (If liked, reduce butter to 2 oz., and substitute enough rich game gravy or stock to make the game into a buttery consistency, or substitute 1 lb. ground fat ham for butter. Season to taste with salt, pepper and cayenne pepper and ground mace or allspice. Rub through a fine wire sieve. Pot and cover with clarified butter. This also can be packed into a shallow dish and served sliced in an hors d'oeuvre course or when a mixed salad platter is wanted.

POTTED HAM (Pâté de Jambon)

½ lb. lean boiled ham
2 oz. fat boiled ham
Pinch of cayenne pepper
Pinch of ground mace

See that the ham is quite cold before using. Chop and pound in a mortar. Add each seasoning gradually, then the butter. When thoroughly blended, rub through a sieve. Pot up. Cover

Pinch of ground allspice
1 saltspoon made mustard
Few drops Worcester sauce
1½ oz. clarified butter

with melted clarified butter. Use for making sandwiches with brown or white bread, or half-toasted bread.

POTTED HARE (Pâté de Lièvre)

½ young hare
1 lb. streaky bacon
1 bay leaf
1 sprig of thyme
¼ pint stock
¼ pint sherry
6 cloves
1 blade mace
Salt and cayenne pepper to taste

Cut hare into joints. Dice bacon. Fry bacon slowly in a stewpan till fat is extracted, then add hare joints. Remove bacon. Cook slowly till browned all over, turning occasionally, then add bay leaf, thyme, and remainder of ingredients. Simmer gently till hare is tender, either on top of the stove, or in a slow oven. Carefully remove meat from joints. Cut into small pieces. Leave until cold, then pound in a mortar with the bacon and fat skimmed off the stock. Pound till into a smooth paste, and rub through a sieve. Place purée in a basin. Add enough liquor from hare to give a creamy consistency. Leave till quite cold, then pot. Cover with clarified butter.

POTTED TONGUE (Pâté de Langue)

1 lb. cold boiled tongue
3-4 oz. butter
Pinch of ground mace
Pinch of ground cloves
Cayenne pepper to taste

Slice and put tongue through a meat grinder. Pound it well in a mortar, gradually beating in the butter and seasonings. Rub through a fine wire sieve. Pot and cover with clarified butter.

SWEET SANDWICHES

Sweet sandwiches are only served at afternoon tea or children's parties. When required for afternoon tea, the bread should be cut as thin as a wafer, and the sandwiches made small. Use fancy cutters. Arrange sandwiches of the same design on plates covered with a lace paper doily. They can either overlap each other, or be stacked.

BANANA SANDWICHES : Mix chopped banana to taste with mayonnaise flavoured lemon juice and chopped walnuts, or mash 3 bananas with a few drops lemon juice. Spread on thinly buttered bread. Cover thinly with strawberry jam or with whipped cream flavoured apricot jam, and pair.

CHERRY AND PINEAPPLE : Drain the juice from ¼ cup chopped stoned cherries. Mix with 2 tablespoons minced blanched almonds, ¼ cup chopped drained pineapple and mayonnaise to moisten.

CHOCOLATE SPREAD

1 tablespoon cocoa
1 oz. butter
1 tablespoon honey

Place all ingredients except the vanilla essence in a saucepan. Stir till butter is melted, and honey is dissolved. Bring to boil, stirring con-

Christmas Cake. *See page* 719.

Wedding Cake. *See pages 722-723.*

Children's Party Sandwiches. *See page* 808.

Fairy Cakes. *See page* 699.

Milk Jelly. *See page* 609.

Chocolate Sundaes.

(*Top Left*)
Individual Tomato
Aspics. *See page* 475.

(*Top Right*)
Epsom Rolls. *See page*
814.

(*Bottom Left*)
Sausage Dunking
Platter. *See page* 780.

(*Bottom Right*)
Cauliflower Dunking
Platter. *See page* 780.

1 tablespoon chopped dates
1/4 teaspoon vanilla essence

stantly. Remove from heat. Add vanilla essence. Leave till cold, stirring constantly till thick. Use with brown or rye bread, small oatcakes or plain biscuits.

FRUIT FILLING : Chop ½ oz. dates with 2 oz. crystallized ginger and 1 oz. walnuts. Cream a walnut of butter. Mix with fruit and nuts.

PEANUT AND RAISIN : Put ½ cup stoned raisins through a meat grinder. Stir in 1-2 tablespoons honey, a grain or two of salt, the juice of ½ a lemon or orange and ½ cup peanut butter. Use with brown or white buttered bread.

TOASTED CINNAMON : Spread thin slices of thinly buttered bread thickly with cinnamon and light brown sugar, allowing 2 teaspoons of ground cinnamon to ¼ lb. caster sugar. Pair with another slice of bread. Cut in fingers Toast on outside.

VEGETABLE SANDWICHES

There are many other vegetable fillings besides cucumber suitable for sandwiches : Lettuce, mustard and cress, and watercress make an ideal filling for afternoon tea sandwiches or sandwiches to be served with a game or poultry salad at a buffet party. Carrot, cabbage, celery, cucumber, and other salad greens can also be used as sandwich fillings. Grate or shred, and soak for 10 minutes in French dressing, then drain well before using, or coat with mayonnaise.

ASPARAGUS ROLLS : Spread new bread thinly with cream cheese, beaten, if stiff, with creamed butter. Cut slices wafer-thin. Remove crusts and wrap each slice around a boiled asparagus tip. Fix each with a toothpick. Chill. Remove toothpicks and serve garnished with mustard and cress.

CARROT FILLING : Mix grated raw carrot with mashed boiled green peas and mayonnaise to taste, or sprinkle it with lemon juice and use with shredded lettuce tossed in French dressing and well drained.

CELERY : Mix shredded celery with chopped olives and mayonnaise to taste, or with ½ its quantity of chopped apple moistened with lemon juice. Stir in mayonnaise or salad cream to taste.

CUCUMBER : Wash cucumber and slice thinly without peeling. Season with salt and pepper. Use as a filling with white bread.

LETTUCE, MUSTARD AND CRESS AND WATERCRESS : Shred lettuce ; wash and pick over mustard and cress and watercress. Dry. Use as a filling, sprinkled with salt, for brown or white buttered bread.

MUSHROOM : Cream or fry mushrooms. Season and flavour delicately with ground mace. Use as a filling for brown or white bread.

PEPPER : Mix chopped green pepper with half its quantity of chopped onion. Mix with mayonnaise. If liked, substitute chopped olives for onion.

SPANISH : Chop stuffed olives. Mix with mayonnaise. Use with thinly buttered brown bread.

TOMATO AND CHEESE PASTE

1 tablespoon butter
1 small peeled onion

Melt butter in a saucepan. Grate in onion. Cook slowly for 2 or 3 minutes, until soft, then

½ lb. peeled tomatoes
2 oz. grated cheese
¼ lb. breadcrumbs
1 beaten egg
Salt and pepper to taste
Pinch of mustard if liked

add tomatoes. Simmer for 10 minutes, then add cheese, crumbs and egg. Cook for a minute or so stirring constantly until thickened, but do not allow to boil. Add salt and pepper to taste and mustard if liked. Stir until blended. Pack into small jars, unless to be used at once. Store in larder or refrigerator. Will keep for at least a week. Use with white bread.

VEGETABLE FILLINGS :

1. Mix equal quantity of chopped lettuce, grated carrot and wafer-thin slices of radishes, with 1 teaspoon milled nuts and mayonnaise to moisten.

2. Mix equal quantity of shredded celery and picked, but not chopped, watercress. Use with brown bread, spread with cream cheese, mixed with equal quantity of mayonnaise.

3. Mix equal quantity of chopped onion with chopped green pepper and cream cheese.

WATERCRESS AND BEETROOT : Mix chopped boiled beetroot with half its quantity of picked watercress, not chopped. Season with salt and black pepper. Flavour to taste with vinegar or lemon juice. Use with brown bread or split potato oven scones.

HOT SANDWICHES

Hot sandwiches are generally made with bread toasted on the outside, but they can be fried instead. The name " hot sandwich " is sometimes also given to a savoury toast. (See Savoury and Snack Sections.) A hot sandwich makes an appetising main course for lunch, high tea or supper. The usual method of making one is to remove the crusts, and toast the bread on the outside only, then spread the untoasted sides with butter, and put slices together with the filling. If you have a sandwich toaster or a waffle iron, you can make the sandwich in the usual way, cutting the bread to fit one or the other, then toast with the filling inside. This gives you a hotter sandwich.

CHEESE AND BACON SANDWICHES
(Sandwiches Américaine)

8 oz. cheese
8 oz. bacon
1 small peeled onion
2 beaten eggs

Put cheese, bacon, and onion through a meat grinder. Stir in eggs with salt and pepper to taste. Spread on 4 slices of bread, toasted on the other sides. Grill slowly till bacon is cooked. Top each with a slice of bread, toasted on the outside, and buttered inside. Cut in two diagonally. Garnish each portion with a fried mushroom on top. *For 4 persons.*

CRAB AND TOMATO SANDWICHES
(Sandwiches, Baltimore)

8 slices of bread
1½ cups flaked crab
Mayonnaise as required

Remove crusts from bread if liked. Mix crab meat with mayonnaise to taste. Toast 8 slices of bread on one side only. Cover half the slices

1 crisp lettuce
4 sliced peeled tomatoes
Cucumber as required

with the lettuce leaves, then with the crab, then tomato. Cover with remaining slices of bread, toasted sides outwards. Cut in two diagonally. Garnish each with 1 or 2 slices of pickled cucumber. *For 4 persons.*

FINNAN SANDWICHES (Sandwiches de Merluche)

1 small Finnan haddock
1 oz. butter
2 tablespoons top milk
2 tablespoons thick cream
Salt and pepper to taste
Cayenne pepper to taste
1½ teaspoons minced parsley

Scald, skin and fillet haddock. Place in a saucepan. Add butter and milk. Cover. Simmer gently till tender, then remove and flake. Stir in cream, seasonings and parsley. Place between slices of buttered bread, toasted on the outsides only. Cut in triangles. If preferred, thicken fish with a teaspoon of cornflour dissolved in top milk, and use as a filling for sandwich to be toasted either in a toaster or waffle iron. *For 4 persons.*

FRIED EGG SANDWICHES (Sandwiches aux Oeufs)

1 dessertspoon minced onion
1 tablespoon minced green pepper
1 oz. butter
1 cup stewed tomatoes
Salt and pepper to taste
8 slices of bread
4 fried eggs
Grated cheese to taste

Place onion, pepper and butter in a small saucepan. Simmer till tender. Add tomatoes and salt and pepper to taste. Simmer gently until reduced to half the quantity. Meanwhile, toast half the slices of bread. Place an egg on each slice. Sprinkle with grated Gruyère cheese. Toast remaining slices on one side only, then butter the other sides. Meanwhile, melt cheese under the grill, then top with a second slice, toasted side outwards. Coat with the sauce. Garnish each with a fried mushroom. Serve at once. *For 4 persons.*

GRILLED STEAK SANDWICHES : Pound thin slices of fillet steak, then brush with melted butter. Grill, allowing 3 minutes per side. Season with salt and pepper to taste. Slip between slices of white bread thinly spread with horseradish butter. Garnish with grilled mushrooms and tomatoes.

HAM AND EGG SANDWICHES
(Sandwiches de Jambon aux Oeufs)

½ pint chopped boiled ham
3 slightly-beaten eggs
½ teaspoon grated onion
Salt and pepper to taste
20 rounds bread

Mix ham with egg, onion, and salt and pepper to taste. Drop in small teaspoonfuls on to a frying-pan containing enough melted butter or bacon fat to cover pan. Fry till brown below, then turn and brown on the other side. Place between slices of bread, or bread toasted only on the outside. *For 5 persons.*

HOT DOGS : Place Frankforters in a saucepan. Cover with boiling water and stand for 7 minutes. Meanwhile, split bridge or long dinner rolls, and toast lightly on the insides. Drain Frankforters thoroughly. Butter rolls inside. Slip a Frankforter into each. Arrange on a large hot round platter. Garnish in between with stuffed olives wrapped in bacon and grilled. Place a dish of made mustard in the centre. Allow 2 per person. Suitable not only for lunch and high tea, but also for buffet parties.

HURLINGHAM SANDWICHES (Sandwiches, Hurlingham)

4 slices snappy cheese
8 slices hot buttered toast
8 short rashers lean bacon
4 pineapple slices
4 crisp lettuce leaves
Mayonnaise as required

Cut cheese to fit the toast after removing crusts from toast. Place a thin slice of cheese on top of half the slices of toast. Remove rind from bacon. Fry till crisp. Remove and keep hot. Fry the pineapple in the bacon fat. Meanwhile, brown the slices covered with cheese, either under the grill, or in the oven. Place a slice of pineapple on top of the cheese. Cover with a lettuce leaf, then with another slice of toast, buttered side next lettuce. Garnish each with 2 rashers of bacon, and with a curled heart of lettuce leaf filled with thick mayonnaise. *For 4 persons.*

MANHATTAN SANDWICHES : Spread half the slices of bread with hazelnut or peanut butter. Cover with a thin slice of snappy cheese. Top each with another slice of bread thinly spread with creamed butter, flavoured with mustard. Tie in place with cotton. Fry gently in a little butter till golden brown on both sides. Remove cotton and serve.

SARDINE SANDWICHES (Sandwiches de Sardines)

3 large sardines
1 tablespoon mild vinegar
Dash of tomato catsup
Salt and pepper to taste

Skin and bone sardines. Mash with vinegar and catsup. Season with salt and pepper to taste. Place between slices of buttered bread toasted only on the outside. *For 2 or 3 persons.*

SAUSAGE AND APPLE SANDWICHES (Sandwiches aux Saucissons)

12 oz. sausage meat
3 cooking apples
8 slices hot buttered toast
4 curls of bacon

Divide sausage meat into 4 equal portions. Shape into 4 flat squares about $\frac{1}{2}$ inch thick. Fry slowly in a little hot fat until cooked through and brown on both sides. Keep hot. Core apples. Cut into equal-thick slices. Fry in the sausage fat. Arrange a sausage cake on half the toast. Cover each with fried apple. Cover with remainder of toast. Cut in two diagonally. Garnish with grilled bacon. *For 4 persons.*

TONGUE AND EGG SANDWICHES (Sandwiches de Langue)

1 cup minced tongue
1 teaspoon grated onion
2 tablespoons mayonnaise
1 beaten egg
1 cup milk
Pinch of crushed herbs
Salt and pepper to taste

Mix tongue with onion and mayonnaise. Spread on 3 thin slices of bread. Cover each with another slice. Cut in triangles. Beat egg. Stir in remaining ingredients. Dip sandwiches in this mixture. Fry carefully first on one side, then on the other in a little hot bacon dripping till golden brown. *For 3 persons.*

WAFFLEWICHES

The following sandwiches can either be made in a waffle iron, or in a sandwich toaster. Cheese spreads can also be used as a filling. Cut 48-hour-old bread into slices $\frac{1}{2}$ inch thick to fit the sections of either the iron or the sandwich toaster. Pile on the top of a moist cloth and wrap in cloth until the fillings are ready. Brush with melted butter before baking.

CHEESE WAFFLEWICHES : Place $\frac{1}{2}$ cup grated cheese and 2 tablespoons milk in the top of a double boiler. Stir over hot water till cheese is melted. Add 2 sliced, skinned, boiled pork sausages, or Frankforters, and a dash of made mustard. Stir till blended, then remove and leave till cool. Use as a filling for bread, and bake till golden.

CHEESE AND HAM : Mix $\frac{1}{4}$ pint boiled ham, put through a meat grinder, with $\frac{1}{4}$ pint cream cheese. Spread 4 slices of bread thinly with butter, and 4 with the filling. Pair. Brush with melted butter and bake.

CHICKEN : Dice equal quantity of boiled chicken, dark and white meat. Season with salt and pepper to taste. Add shredded celery to taste and mayonnaise. Butter 2 freshly made waffles and spread filling in between.

EGG : Mix 3 chopped hard-boiled eggs with 2 tablespoons chopped green pepper, 2 tablespoons shredded celery and salt and pepper to taste.

MEAT : Mix stewed minced steak and onion, and sliced champignons, allowing 1 oz. champignons to $\frac{3}{4}$ cup steak. Use with buttered bread in a sandwich toaster.

MUSHROOM : Chop $\frac{1}{2}$ lb. mushrooms. Put through the meat grinder. Melt $\frac{3}{4}$ oz. butter in a frying-pan. Add 1 teaspoon grated shallot, mushrooms and salt and pepper to taste. Season if liked with a pinch of ground mace. Fry slowly for 5 or 6 minutes, then remove to a plate. When cold, use as a filling for buttered bread in a sandwich toaster, or bake in a waffle iron.

MISCELLANEOUS SANDWICHES

This section includes recipes for Club sandwiches, pinwheel, plaid, and ribbon sandwiches.

CLUB SANDWICHES

Club sandwiches can either be made from bread cut $\frac{1}{4}$ inch thick, and toasted on both sides, or only on one side, and the untoasted side buttered. In the latter case, the buttered side must always be next to the filling. Remove crusts after buttering. These sandwiches are usually served cut diagonally, or in 4 triangles, and garnished with sweet pickled gherkin cut like a fan, olives and radishes.

TO MAKE A CLUB SANDWICH : Take 3 slices of toast. Spread one side of one slice with creamed butter. Remove crusts. Place, buttered side up, on an individual plate. Cover with a lettuce leaf. Brush with mayonnaise. Top with one filling. Spread with more mayonnaise. Butter second slice of toast on both sides. Place on filling. Cover with second filling. Spread with more mayonnaise. Butter remaining slice of toast on one side only, and place buttered side downwards, on second filling. Cut in two triangles. Garnish to taste.

FILLINGS FOR CLUB SANDWICHES

1. Lettuce with mayonnaise ; crab with mayonnaise ; tomato slices with mayonnaise.

2. Lettuce with mayonnaise ; breast of guinea fowl with mayonnaise ; pieces of crisp bacon with mayonnaise.

3. Lettuce with mayonnaise ; small slices of crisply fried bacon topped with sliced avocado pear, seasoned with salt ; cooked prawns and celery sprinkled minced chives and coated mayonnaise.

4. Lettuce with mayonnaise ; small slices of ham topped Swiss cheese, slices of tomato, topped lettuce, coated mayonnaise.

5. Mix $\frac{1}{2}$ pint chopped boiled chicken with 3 tablespoons shredded celery, 1 teaspoon minced parsley, salt and pepper to taste, and 2 tablespoons mayonnaise. Spread on first layer of buttered toast. Cover with lettuce, coated mayonnaise. Top with second slice of toast. Cover with chopped fried mushrooms seasoned with salt and pepper to taste, then with third slice of toast.

6. Lettuce with mayonnaise. Cover with flaked tunny fish flavoured with French dressing, then with toast. Cover with lettuce, then with egg mayonnaise, then with tomato. Top with toast.

PINWHEEL SANDWICHES

Remove the crusts from a sandwich loaf of brown or white bread. Spread the bottom with creamed butter, then with a smooth filling. With a very sharp knife, cut off a slice from this side. Starting at one end roll up slice as tightly as possible, as you would a Swiss roll. Wrap in a damp table napkin. Chill. When required, cut into thin slices. Serve overlapping each other, or toast under the grill before serving.

Suitable Fillings : Potted fish, game, meat ; cheese spreads ; savoury butter and shredded celery ; etc.

RIBBON SANDWICHES

Remove all the crusts from a sandwich loaf. Spread one side thinly with butter, then with a creamy filling. Cut off a thin slice lengthwise. Repeat. This gives you 2 slices of prepared white bread. Prepare 2 slices of brown bread in the same way. Place a slice of white bread on the bottom of your board, filled side up. Cover with a slice of brown bread, filled side up. Place another slice of white bread on top, filled side up, then a slice of brown, filled side up. Top with a slice of dry white bread. Press down lightly, then chill. When required, slice thinly.

PUMPERNICKEL RIBBONS : Use slices of pumpernickel put together with fillings of a contrasting flavour and colour. Press firmly and chill. Cut into small triangles.

Fillings for Ribbon Sandwiches : Use creamy yet fairly firm fillings that cling to the bread, of a contrasting colour and flavour, such as cream cheese flavoured with finely minced parsley ; liver paste ; egg and pimento paste.

ROLLED SANDWICHES

Remove crusts from very thin slices of new bread. Spread with any cheese filling, or with mashed cheese creamed with mayonnaise. Roll up. Secure with toothpicks, and chill. Remove toothpicks before serving.

NOTE : If liked, these sandwiches can be brushed with melted butter on the outside, and toasted lightly under the grill, turning frequently so that they brown evenly. Serve at once.

ASPARAGUS ROLLS : Prepare bread as described. Place a cooked or canned asparagus tip on the end of each, then roll up. Secure with cocktail sticks or toothpicks, and chill, or toast under grill as described.

DEVILLED ROLLS : Put $\frac{1}{4}$ lb. snappy cheese through a meat grinder. Season with salt and pepper to taste. Stir in $\frac{1}{4}$ teaspoon made mustard and $\frac{1}{2}$ teaspoon of chutney sauce. Spread on bread. Roll and chill or toast as described. If preferred, dip into grated cheese and bake on a buttered rack in a hot oven, till golden brown.

SMOKED SALMON ROLLS : Cover very thin slices of new bread with smoked salmon. Brush with lemon juice. Season with cayenne pepper. Roll. Chill as described.

TOMATO ROLLS : Put 3 oz. processed or snappy cheese through a meat grinder. Stir in 1 tablespoon tomato catsup, 1 teaspoon minced shallot, and $\frac{1}{2}$ teaspoon minced chives. Spread on very thin slices of bread. Roll up. Secure with toothpicks or cocktail sticks. Brush with melted butter and toast under grill.

SANDWICH LOAF

Remove crusts from a sandwich loaf, 24 hours old. Cut off 4 slices lengthwise, about $\frac{1}{2}$ inch thick. Spread 1 slice with creamed butter or a savoury butter to suit filling. Place on serving dish, buttered side upwards. Spread with mayonnaise. Cover with slices of hard-boiled egg. Spread second slice with mayonnaise, and lay on top, mayonnaise side downwards. Spread top with butter, then with diced tongue. Cover with shredded lettuce. Butter third slice of bread, then spread with mayonnaise. Place, spread side downwards, on top of lettuce. Spread top with creamed butter, then with mayonnaise. Cover with slices of peeled tomato. Butter and spread remaining slice of bread with mayonnaise, and place, spread side downwards, on top. Press firmly together. Beat cream cheese till fluffy with a little milk. Spread over the top and sides of loaf. Chill for $1\frac{1}{2}$ hours. To serve, cut in slices crosswise. *Enough for 7 or 8 persons.*

To Garnish Loaf :
1. Sprinkle all over with sieved hard-boiled egg yolk. Decorate down the middle with radish roses.
2. Make a design along the top with sliced stuffed or black olives.
3. Decorate top with daisies made of pimiento, or with sprays of flowers made with pimiento, and leaves of watercress.

Filling Combinations :

1. Chicken salad ; cream cheese and minced pimento ; chopped water-cress mixed with chopped sweet pickled gherkin to taste and mayonnaise.

2. Egg mayonnaise ; grated carrot spread ; shredded lettuce and mayonnaise.

3. Guinea fowl and celery salad ; sliced peeled tomatoes ; cream cheese and green pepper.

4. Salmon mayonnaise ; sliced seasoned cucumber ; sliced hard-boiled egg coated with mayonnaise flavoured with made mustard and Worcester sauce.

5. Ground boiled ham mixed with mayonnaise flavoured mustard and minced pimento, allowing 2 tablespoons pimento and $1\frac{1}{2}$ of mayonnaise to $\frac{3}{4}$ cup of ham ; sliced tomatoes ; slices of liver sausage.

6. Turkey and cress salad ; sliced fried mushrooms ; lettuce and mayonnaise.

Hints on Coating : Allow from 8-10 oz. cream or cottage cheese for an average-sized sandwich loaf. Any cheese spread, sold as such, can be used in combination with cream cheese and cream to moisten. Instead of garnishing coating, you can add a tablespoon of chopped chives or parsley to the cheese or sieved hard-boiled egg before using.

RIBBON SANDWICH LOAVES

Remove crusts from sandwich loaf. Cut bread into slices crosswise, $\frac{1}{4}$ inch thick. Spread bottom slices with diced cold chicken, guinea fowl, pheasant or turkey. Moisten with mayonnaise and season to taste. Cover with a second slice. Mix cream cheese with chopped olives and mayonnaise to taste. Spread on top, then cover with a third slice. Coat top and sides with cream cheese moistened with cream. Decorate top of each with a maraschino cherry, and sprigs of chervil, or with a slice of stuffed olive and foliage of watercress.

Beverages

All drinks containing a large percentage of water can be termed a beverage. Some are intended to quench thirst, such as lemonade, fruit cups and punches ; others to nourish the body, such as chocolate and cocoa ; whilst a third group stimulates, like coffee and tea.

Use water that has just come to the full boil for making all hot beverages, and water fresh out of the tap for making cold. Be sure to serve hot drinks really hot, and cold drinks chilled.

CHOCOLATE

As chocolate contains a certain amount of starch, it needs cooking to make it into a smooth beverage. Chocolate is therefore better flavoured if boiled than if hot milk is added to it after it is dissolved.

TO MAKE CHOCOLATE

1½ oz. plain chocolate
1 saltspoon salt
1 cup boiling water
3 cups hot milk
¼ teaspoon vanilla essence

Melt the chocolate in the top of a double boiler over hot water. Add salt. Stir in the boiling water slowly. When smoothly blended, add the milk brought almost to boiling point. Boil for 1 minute, then beat with a wire whisk till it froths.

Add vanilla essence. Pour into hot cups. *Yield :* 4 cups.

COCOA

Like chocolate, cocoa contains a certain amount of starch. It must be cooked in the making or it won't be smooth. It can either be prepared with equal quantities of boiling water and milk, or with milk only.

COCOA FOR ONE PERSON

1 teaspoon cocoa
1 teaspoon sugar
¼ pint boiling water
¼ pint scalded milk

Mix cocoa with the sugar. Stir in boiling water. Turn into a saucepan. Bring to boil and boil for 2-3 minutes, stirring constantly, then remove from heat. Stir in milk. Serve.

SWISS COCOA : Substitute for the milk and water 2 teaspoons condensed milk diluted with ¾ cup boiling water and ¼ cup scalded milk. Add a grain or two of salt.

COFFEE

To make good coffee, you need freshly-roasted beans. Either grind them as you require coffee, or have them ground at a shop if you haven't a coffee mill. If to be made in a jug, or by the filter method, finely ground coffee is required. If in a percolator, use coarsely or medium-ground coffee. If in a saucepan, use a medium grind. Keep all equipment for making coffee scrupulously clean. Rinse thoroughly with hot water before using. If your coffee-maker has a bag or cloth filter, douse the filter in hot water containing a pinch of bicarbonate of soda after use. Rinse thoroughly in hot water. Leave in a cup or basin of clean cold water when not in use.

To Measure Coffee : Use a coffee measuring spoon sponsored by the Association of Coffee Buyers for measuring. If not available, substitute a dessertspoon for measuring.

1 *heaped dessertspoon coffee — approximately* 1 *level standard coffee measuring spoon of coffee.*

Allow 4 level standard coffee measuring spoons of coffee, or 4 heaped dessertspoons, to 1 pint of water.

½ lb. coffee made with 4 quarts cold water is enough for 20-25 persons.

DRIP COFFEE : Use finely-ground coffee. Place in a strainer, allowing coffee in the proportion of 4 level standard coffee measures of coffee, or 4 heaped dessertspoons, to 1 pint water. Pour freshly-boiled water slowly over the coffee, then cover. Water should take about 5 minutes to drip through into the pre-heated pot below. (It is a good idea to place the pot in a pan of boiling water while coffee is dripping.) If not strong enough, pour coffee into the strainer, and let it drip through once again. When ready, remove filter section, replace lid and serve.

FILTERED COFFEE : A very fine grind of coffee is required. See that the filter paper lies flat and smooth, and spread coffee evenly over it, then follow Drip method.

VACUUM COFFEE : If you have 2 pint vacuum equipment, measure 2 pints fresh water into the lower bowl. Place this over heat. While coming to the boil, place the glass or cloth filter in the neck of the upper bowl which should be perfectly dry. Measure in 8 level standard coffee measuring spoons or 8 heaped dessertspoons of coffee. When water in the lower bowl is boiling briskly, reduce heat. (If electric, switch off.) *Now*, and *not* before, insert the upper bowl into the lower with a slight twist to ensure it fits tightly at the neck. Replace over heat. (If electric, return to ring, but do not switch on heat.) When the water rises into upper bowl, stir gently, taking care not to dislodge the filter. (Some water will always remain in the lower bowl.) In 1-3 minutes, depending on grind (the finer grind requires the shorter time), remove from heat and allow coffee to flow into the lower bowl. Remove upper bowl and coffee is ready for serving. If it has to stand for a little, cover with a small clean cloth. This makes about 8 breakfast cups of coffee. For 1 pint equipment, use 4 dessertspoons of coffee to 1 pint of water.

If you have a vacuum-maker with a vented stem (a small hole in the side of the tube above the water line) the complete apparatus may be completely assembled before placing on heat as the water will not start to rise until it boils. When water rises, remove from heat and follow the procedure given above. (Without this vent water in vacuum rises well below boiling point.)

PERCOLATED COFFEE : Pour cold water into percolator. Bring to boil. Allowing 4 level standard coffee measures or heaped dessertspoons medium-ground coffee to 1 pint of the water, place it in basket. Remove percolator from heat. Insert basket. Cover. Heat rapidly till water begins to percolate, then lower heat, so that it percolates very very gently. From the time the water starts to percolate, you should allow 6-8 minutes before removing pot from heat. (Never allow water to percolate rapidly or the coffee will lose its aroma, and may taste slightly bitter.) When ready, remove basket containing the grounds. Stand for 5 minutes and serve.

THE JUG METHOD : Heat an earthenware jug in the oven or with boiling water and dry. Add medium-ground coffee as required, allowing 4 level standard coffee measures or 4 heaped dessertspoons coffee to 1 pint of water. Pour necessary amount of boiling water over. Stir it briskly. Stand for a minute. Skim off grounds on top with the edge of a spoon. Cover. Stand over very low heat, or over boiling water without simmering from 4-10 minutes, according to strength required. Sprinkle with 2 or 3 tablespoons cold water to settle the grounds. Pour out carefully or strain through muslin into a hot jug or pot. Cover with a cosy. Serve.

ICED COFFEE : Fill ½ pint tumblers half-full with cracked ice or ice cubes. Pour in hot double-strength coffee to within 1 inch of the top. Top with vanilla ice cream, or whipped cream flavoured with vanilla essence. Serve with long-handled spoons.

TEA

To make good tea, you need a teapot, preferably of earthenware, and entirely free from tea stains both inside and in the spout, your favourite tea, and boiling water.

To Make Tea : Use freshly drawn water. Bring it to the boil, and make and infuse tea the moment it comes to a full, rolling boil. If you add the water before it has come to a full, rolling boil, the tea will not be so well-flavoured, nor so stimulating.

1. Fill teapot with boiling water.
2. When water for tea is about to come to a full boil, remove heating water from pot and dry pot thoroughly.
3. Place tea in pot, allowing 1 teaspoon per person, and 1 for the pot.
4. Pour in boiling water. Cover.
5. Slip the pot into teapot nest, then cover with a cosy, or stand pot in a warm place till it infuses. *If you make tea in this way it is not necessary to stir it.*
6. Always clean and dry pot thoroughly after using.

NOTE : 1 lb. tea yields about 200 cups of tea

ICED TEA : Fill a tumbler $\frac{1}{3}$ full with cracked ice. Add sugar to taste, and a slice of lemon. Add more ice if liked. Strain in hot China tea. Garnish with young sprigs of mint if preferred to lemon.

MILK

Though milk is generally classed as a beverage, it is really an important food. It contains all the food value necessary to maintain life. Children should be given Grade A, Tuberculin Tested or Pasteurised milk at every meal. 1 pint milk per day is the minimum, but a quart is not too much. If your child is allergic to milk, supply in the form of soups, puddings, etc. When it is not possible to obtain the type of milk recommended, bring all milk to boiling point for children up to the age of 4.

The allowance of milk for adults should be 1 pint a day. This takes into account milk added to chocolate, cocoa, coffee, or tea, and used in the making of sauces, soups, hot and cold puddings and other dishes in which milk is an ingredient.

TO STORE MILK

As milk left uncovered absorbs odours very quickly, and collects bacteria, it should be properly stored. Do not leave bottles of milk standing in direct sunlight. If exposed to sun for any length of time, the flavour is affected, and also its food value. The moment the milkman delivers your supply, wipe the outside of each bottle with a clean damp cloth, and store on the floor in the larder where there is a current of air, if no refrigerator is available. Do not place it on an upper shelf or on the table. If milk removed from a bottle for some purpose or other is not all used, do not on any account pour the remainder back into the bottle. Cover the container so that no insects or dust can carry germs to the milk, and use it as soon as possible.

The correct temperature for storing milk, whether in the refrigerator or not, is about 40 ° F., but if stored at a temperature between 45° and 50° F., it will not spoil. If you have no refrigerator to keep milk fresh in hot weather, place covered milk bottle in a basin half-filled with cold water. Soak a piece of butter muslin large enough to go over the top and touch the water, in cold water. Place it on top of the bottle. Change the water occasionally during the heat of the day. If the weather is hot, you may find it necessary to scald milk, before protecting it, in this way. Pour into a scalded jug. Cover. Stand in a bowl of cold water, and cool as quickly as possible.

To Scald :

1. Heat carefully in the top of a double boiler until on examining milk, you find tiny bubbles all round the inside edge of pan. Do not let it boil.

2. Place milk in a shallow milk saucepan. Bring rapidly to boiling point, stirring constantly in the shape of a figure eight, to prevent scorching. Remove from stove, and if not to be used, chill as rapidly as possible before storing.

To Sour Milk : When sour milk is wanted in cooking, stir lemon juice or vinegar into sweet milk, allowing 2 standard teaspoons lemon juice or vinegar to 1 cup of milk, or 2 English tablespoons to $\frac{1}{2}$ pint milk. Stir over very low heat for a moment or two, until the milk curdles if wanted in a hurry. Otherwise stand in a warm place until it curdles.

MILK SHAKES

Milk shakes can either be made in a cocktail shaker or in a screw-topped jar. To make, allow $\frac{2}{3}$ tumbler of ice-cold milk, and 2 tablespoons fruit juice or melted jelly to each shake. Sweeten to taste. Add $\frac{1}{3}$ tumbler of cracked ice for each person. Shake until frothy. Pour into tumblers. You can also make milk shakes with milk and ice cream instead of with milk and cracked ice.

BANANA MILK SHAKE : Place a mashed banana in a screw-topped jar. Add 2 cups chilled milk. Screw lid down tightly. Shake well. Pour into a tumbler. Top with whipped cream. Sprinkle lightly with grated nutmeg or chocolate shot if liked. *For 2 persons.*

CHOCOLATE MILK SHAKE : Shake $2\frac{2}{3}$ cups milk with $\frac{1}{4}$ pint chocolate syrup and $\frac{1}{2}$ cup cracked ice in a cocktail shaker. Strain into 4 glasses. Sprinkle if liked with a little ground cinnamon.

COFFEE MILK SHAKE : Mix $1\frac{1}{2}$ cups cold strong coffee in a large cocktail shaker with 2 drops almond essence, 1 cup chilled milk, 1 cup chilled soda water and sugar to taste. Stir till sugar is dissolved, then close and shake well. *For 6 persons.*

ORANGE MILK SHAKE : Chill 2 cups milk. Add 2 cups chilled orange juice, 2 drops of almond essence, and caster sugar to taste. Stir till sugar is dissolved. Shake well. *For 3 persons.*

PINEAPPLE MILK SHAKE : Stir $\frac{1}{2}$ cup chilled sweetened pineapple juice into 2 cups chilled milk. *For 2 persons.*

STRAWBERRY MILK SHAKE : Mix 2 cups chilled milk in a shaker with $\frac{1}{2}$ cup crushed sweetened strawberries. Shake well. Divide equally between 2 tall glasses. Place a tablespoon of whipped cream on top of each. *For 2 persons.*

MILK SHAKES WITH ICE CREAM

ALMOND OR VANILLA SHAKE : Mix 4 drops almond or vanilla essence with $\frac{1}{2}$ pint milk and 1 oz. ice cream. Shake.

CHOCOLATE SHAKE : Melt 1 oz. chocolate, or use a heaped teaspoon of breakfast chocolate creamed with water. Add with a few drops vanilla essence and 1 oz. vanilla ice cream to $\frac{1}{2}$ pint milk. Shake.

ORANGE SHAKE : Add 1 oz. orange syrup and 1 oz. ice cream to $\frac{1}{2}$ pint milk. Shake.

SPANISH MILK SHAKE : Place 3 tablespoons chocolate ice cream in the bottom of a tall glass. Fill up with cold freshly made café au lait.

Drink all these shakes through a straw.

MILK PUNCH

¼ lb. sugar
4 cups milk
1½ teaspoons vanilla essence
1 cup soda water

Dissolve the sugar in the milk. Add vanilla and soda water. Shake either in a cocktail shaker, or in a screw-topped jar with the lid firmly screwed down. Shake well. Pour out from a height into ½ pint tumblers, so that it froths. *For 4 persons.*

BERRY SYRUP (Sirop de Baies)

2½ pints berry juice
2 lb. loaf sugar
1 pint water

Hull and mash enough berries to give you 2½ pints juice, after berries have been allowed to drip through a jelly bag or lined sieve. Place sugar and water in a preserving pan. Stir over slow heat till sugar is dissolved, then boil till clear, and skim. Boil again until a few drops placed in cold water form a soft ball, then remove from heat. Slowly stir in fruit juice. When smoothly blended, bring again to boil and skim. Pour into hot sterilized bottles. Cork and seal with sealing wax over join of cork and bottle.

LEMON SYRUP (Sirop de Citrons)

1 lb. sugar
1 pint strained lemon juice

Add sugar to lemon juice. Stir till dissolved. Pour into small bottles. Store in refrigerator. To use, allow 1 large tablespoon juice to ¼ pint water.

SOFT FRUIT DRINKS

The simplest fruit drinks you can serve are lemon and orange squash and lime soda. If you bruise sprigs of mint, and place one in each glass before adding the squash or lime cordial, you will be amazed at the improvement it makes, if you let it soak for a minute or two. Remove it before adding soda water and ice. When you do this, float a fresh sprig of mint on top of each instead of garnishing with lemon and orange slices.

FRUITADE

¼ lb. caster sugar
1 cup water
Grated rind of 1 mandarin
3 tablespoons lemon juice
2 cups mandarin juice
2 cups strained China tea

Measure sugar, water and mandarin rind into a saucepan. Stir till sugar is dissolved. Bring to boil. Boil for 5 minutes. Remove from stove. Chill. Stir in fruit juices and tea. Strain into tall glasses over cracked ice. *For 3 or 4 persons.*

ORANGEADE

6 oranges
1 lemon
¼ lb. sugar
1 quart boiling water

Scrub rinds of oranges. Remove peel very thinly and place in a jug. Extract orange juice and lemon juice. Add with the sugar. Stir in boiling water. Cover. Leave till cold. Chill. Strain into tall tumblers over cracked ice. Garnish each with a slice of lemon or orange. Serve with straws. *For 4 persons.*

FRUIT AND WINE CUPS

Strictly speaking, a cup is a summer drink prepared and served in large jugs, and consisting of wine diluted with soda water and given fillip and flavour by the addition of brandy and sweet liqueurs. If no special garnish is suggested in a recipe, float a slice or two of lemon and orange on top, and tuck 1 or 2 sprigs of borage, mint or verbena into the cup just before serving. 1 or 2 sprigs of bruised mint impart a delicious tang to non-alcoholic cups if soaked in the fruit juice, and removed from cup before adding remainder of ingredients. Garnish as suggested, with fresh sprigs. If a more elaborate cup is wanted, add slices of peaches, halved grapes or strawberries, or other fruit according to the season.

CIDER CUP

1 quart cider
1 liqueur glass Curacao
1 liqueur glass Brandy
1 liqueur glass Maraschino
½ pint soda water

Place 4-6 blocks of ice in the bottom of a large jug. Add all ingredients. Stir gently till thoroughly chilled. Garnish with slices of lemon, and orange and red-cheeked apples, as well as 2 or 3 sprigs of mint or borage. *For 4 persons.*

CLARET CUP

1 quart Claret
2 liqueur glasses Curacao
1 liqueur glass Maraschino
Peel of 1 lemon
2 tablespoons icing sugar
2 or 3 bottles soda water

Chill all ingredients, but soda water, together for ½ hour. Stir. Add soda water. Garnish with 1 or 2 strips of cucumber and 1 or 2 sprigs of mint.

PIMMS No. 1

Pimms No. 1 makes a delicious long drink specially welcome in summer. It is equally popular at meals, dances, picnics, and at all functions for which cups or punches are required. Always serve it well iced.

PIMMS NO. 1 FOR ONE PERSON : Place a block of ice in a ½ pint tumbler, for preference wider at the top than at the base. Add a whisky measure (3 oz.) of Pimms No. 1. Fill up with a good quality bottled lemonade. Add a slice of lemon and sprig of borage if available, otherwise 1 or 2 small strips of cucumber rind.

A PINT OF PIMMS : Place 1 or 2 blocks of ice in a 1 pint measure. Pour in a measure of Pimms No. 1, as marked on bottle. Fill up with a good quality lemonade. Pour into a 1½ pint glass jug. Decorate with 2 sprigs of borage if available, otherwise mint, verbena, and 1 or 2 strips of cucumber rind, and slices of lemon. Serve in ½ pint tumblers.

SUNDOWNER CUP

3 tablespoons caster sugar
3 bottles Australian Sauterne
½ pint Marnique
1 sliced lemon
3 sliced bananas
1 small sliced cucumber
2 dozen white grapes
3 pints soda water

Stir sugar into the Sauterne. When dissolved, add Marnique. Place 6 ice blocks in a beaker. Add wine mixture, lemon, bananas, cucumber then grapes. When ready to serve, add soda water, one or two maraschino cherries, and one or two fresh sprigs of mint or balm. Serve in tall glasses with straws. *For 24 persons.*

FRUIT PUNCHES

Fruit punch is simply a fruit cup served in a punch bowl instead of in a jug.

FRUIT PUNCH

BASIC RECIPE :
½ lb. loaf sugar
1½ pints water
½ pint orange juice
¼ pint lemon juice
Grated rind of 1 lemon
Grated rind ½ orange

Dissolve sugar in water and bring to the boil. Remove from heat. Leave till cool. Add fruit juice and rinds, then one of the following combinations :

DEVONSHIRE PUNCH : Add 4 cups each of cider, grape juice and ginger ale.

GINGER PUNCH : Add 2 oz. minced preserved ginger, 1 tablespoon ginger syrup and 1 quart ginger ale.

LOGANBERRY PUNCH : Add 2 cups loganberry juice and 1 dessertspoon grated cucumber rind, and sugar to taste if required.

MIDSUMMER PUNCH : Add the strained sweetened juice of 2 cups raspberries and 2 cups strawberries.

PINEAPPLE PUNCH : Add 1 cup grated pineapple and 2 cups soda water.

SUSSEX PUNCH : Add 2 cups cider, 2 cups pineapple juice and 1 quart ginger ale.

To Serve Punch : Place a large block of ice in a punch or deep glass bowl. Strain in punch. Decorate quickly with slices of lemon and orange and sprigs of borage or mint. If liked, 1 or 2 hulled raspberries or strawberries can be added, the sprigs of borage or mint omitted, and a tiny sprig of either inserted in centre of orange or lemon slices. When cherries are ripe, a cluster can be poised on the rim, or small bunches of tiny grapes can be substituted when in season.

WINE PUNCHES

Now-a-days wine punch is only served on special occasions such as at wedding functions, New Year's Eve celebrations, etc. To make it :—

(Top Left) Devils on Horseback. *See page* 667

(Top Right) Aspic Savouries. *See page* 799.

(Bottom Left) Cocktail Sandwiches. *See page* 808

(Bottom Right) Curried Prawn Canapes. *See page* 666.

(*Top Left*)
Meat Rolls. *See page* 535.

(*Top Right*)
Newlyn Turnovers. *See page* 535.

(*Bottom Left*)
Chicken and Walnut Rolls. *See page* 813.

(*Bottom Right*)
Bouchées of Shrimps. *See page* 785.

1. You need a porcelain mixing bowl, a large wide punch bowl, a wooden spoon or fork preferably made of oak, and a ladle for serving punch.

2. When making a cold punch, stir with a wooden spoon or fork. Chill for at least 5 hours.

3. If possible chill any ingredients before mixing rather than pour the punch over the ice, then sink punch bowl in another bowl half-filled with ice, so that the punch is surrounded by ice. To hasten the chilling, sprinkle the ice round bowl with rock salt.

4. When adding sparkling ingredients such as champagne or soda water, pour in just before serving to prevent punch becoming flat.

5. When giving a large party, arrange 2, 3 or 4 punch bowls according to amount required, equidistant from each other on the buffet with a ladle and suitable glasses at the side.

To Garnish Wine Punches : On very special occasions punch bowl can be made very decorative with clusters of green and black grapes, or cherries poised on the rim. Decorate base of bowl with flowers and foliage according to season. At Christmas time, use berried holly and mistletoe, etc.

BAROSSA PUNCH (HOT)

1½ cups apple or prune juice
3 tablespoons honey or sugar
3 inch strips of cinnamon
12 cloves
3 slices of lemon
1 bottle Australian Burgundy

Place fruit juice, honey or sugar, cinnamon, cloves and lemon in an enamel saucepan. Bring to boil. Add wine. Reheat, but do not boil. Serve at once in a heated bowl. *Yield :* About 2 pints.

BAROSSA PUNCH (COLD)

¼ lb. caster sugar
2 bottles Australian Burgundy or Claret
½ pint lemon juice
½ pint orange juice
4 sliced peaches
1 sliced orange
Raspberries or strawberries
2 tablespoons diced pineapple
3 pints soda water

Dissolve sugar in the wine in a mixing bowl. Add lemon and orange juice. Stir well. Place large lumps of cracked ice in a punch bowl. Pour wine mixture over. Add slices of peach and orange, and about 2 dozen halved strawberries, or whole raspberries, and pineapple. Just before serving, add soda water. Serve in tall glasses with a slice of cucumber fixed on the rim of each. *For 24 persons.*

CLARET PUNCH

1 quart Claret
½ pint Sherry
¼ lb. caster sugar
1 liqueur glass Curacao or Maraschino
1 syphon soda water

Mix Claret with Sherry. Add sugar. Stir frequently till dissolved, then add liqueur. Place a lump of ice in a punch bowl. Strain the punch over. Add soda water. Decorate with the peel of a lemon cut in strips. *For 10 persons.*

RUM PUNCH (HOT)

2 lemons
¼ lb. loaf sugar
Juice of 3 lemons
1 teaspoon of ground ginger
1 pint Rum
1 pint Brandy
½ pint Sherry
2 pints boiling water

Scrub and dry lemons. Remove peel as thinly as possible. Place it in a mortar. Pound it to pulp with the sugar. Strain in lemon juice. Add ginger. Stir till blended. Pour into a heated punch bowl. Add Rum, Brandy, Sherry and boiling water. If not sweet enough, sweeten to taste with sugar syrup. Stand for 20 minutes in a hot place. Pour into hot punch glasses. Grate a little nutmeg on top. *For 15 persons.*

MIXED DRINKS

In this section I am including some old favourites and some other mixed drinks which I hope will be just as popular before long. Some are suitable for stirrup cups when you wish to speed the parting guest. Others make good night-caps. A few will provide a change from Gin and Tonic, such as Gin Fizz, Schorle Morle, etc.

INDIVIDUAL EGG NOGS

1 egg
1 tablespoon caster sugar
1 glass Brandy, Whisky, or Rum
Milk as required

Shake egg, sugar, and Brandy, Rum or Whisky in a cocktail shaker. Strain into a tall glass. Fill up with milk. Add a grating of nutmeg.

CHOCOLATE EGG NOG

1 separated egg
1 heaped teaspoon Bournville Cocoa
1 cup milk
1 teaspoon thick cream

Place egg yolk in a small basin. Blend cocoa to a cream with a little of the milk. Add remainder of milk. Stir till boiling. Boil for 2-3 minutes, stirring constantly. Whisk into egg yolk, then whisk in cream. Beat egg white till stiff. Fold into beverage. Serve in 2 glasses (*see illustration facing page* 865).

GIN FIZZ

Juice of ½ a lemon
½ tablespoon caster sugar
1 glass Gin
½ cup cracked ice

Place all the ingredients in a cocktail shaker. Shake well. Strain into a tall glass. Fill up with soda water. Serve at once. *For 1 person.*

HORSE'S NECK

3 or 4 lumps of ice
Long curl of lemon peel
3 dashes Angostura Bitters
Ginger ale as required

Place the ice in a tumbler. Add lemon peel and Angostura Bitters. Fill up with ginger ale. Garnish with a slice of lemon.

MINT JULEP

4 sprigs fresh mint
½ tablespoon caster sugar
1 glass Brandy or Whisky
Cracked ice as required

Rub the lip of a tumbler with a piece of fresh pineapple, then dip in caster sugar. Place mint in tumbler. Add sugar, then Brandy or Whisky. With a long-handled spoon, hold mint to side of the glass, and fill up with finely-cracked ice. Stir gently. Decorate with slices of fruit in season.

SCHORLE MORLE : Half-fill a large, wide-mouthed glass or rummer, with Rhine or Moselle wine. Add cracked ice and soda water to taste. Float a slice of lemon on top. This drink is very popular in the Weserland in the summer. *For 1 person.*

SHANDY GAFF : Mix equal quantity of ginger beer and ale or lager beer, and pour into a large tumbler.

HOME-MADE WINES

There are several points about wine-making, which should be noted :

1. Do not gather fruit or flowers when wet with dew or rain.
2. Use white sugar for sweetening pale wines. Don't substitute golden syrup or treacle for sweetening any kind of wine.
3. Start fermentation in a warm room. If fermenting in bottles, don't seal until all fermentation has ceased. Just cork loosely to keep out the dust. If you seal tightly, and the fermentation is still proceeding, the bottles will explode.
4. Use a flannelette bag when you have to strain wine, fixed in position over a basin or a bag made with a triple layer of muslin.
5. Never mash, stir or squeeze fruit when making wine or it will be muddy.
6. Never leave wine in an enamel or tin vessel. Use earthenware or wooden ones.

BRAMBLE CORDIAL

1 quart Brandy
Blackberries
Port wine as required
Sugar and water as required

Fill wide-mouthed bottles a third full of Brandy. Fill up bottles with blackberries, washed and well drained. Cork and tie down tightly. Store in a dark cellar for 3 months, then strain off the liquor. Place the fruit in a crock. Press and mash it till all the liquor has been extracted, then strain off and add to Brandy. Measure, and to every quart allow 1 pint of Port wine, 1 pint water and ½ lb. crushed loaf sugar. Dissolve sugar in water over slow heat. Cool. Add Port wine and Blackberry Brandy. Strain through a jelly bag. Bottle and cork and seal. Serve in 2 months' time.

ELDERBERRY WINE

1 gallon elderberry juice
3 lb. Demerara sugar
½ oz. allspice
2 oz. ground ginger

Wait until berries are perfectly ripe before picking them. Strip them from the stalks into a tub. Cover with cold water, then cover. Soak for 4-5 days, pressing them two or three times a day with the back of a spoon, then pour the juice through a fine sieve into a large bowl, pressing the fruit with the back of a spoon. Measure off 1 gallon of the juice into an enamel saucepan. Add sugar and spices. Stir over slow heat until dissolved. Bring to the boil. Boil for ½ hour, then pour into an open wine cask. Spread a freshly made slice of toast with baker's yeast, and lay on top. Cover. Allow to work for 4-5 days, then skim. Place in a cask with a vent peg loose to allow for fermentation. When the fermentation has ceased, close vent peg tightly, and close cask. Leave for 4 months then bottle and cork tightly.

RHUBARB WINE

Allow 2 gallons water to 16 lb. sliced rhubarb. Trim and wipe rhubarb with a damp cloth before slicing. Place in a bowl. Add water. Cover. Stand for 10 days, stirring each day. Strain. Measure. Allow sugar in the proportion of 1 lb. to 1 quart of the liquid, and add. Add lemon and bruised root ginger, allowing 1 lemon and 2 oz. ginger to each gallon of the liquid. Stir daily until all the sugar is dissolved, then bottle, but do not fill bottles full. Cork loosely until the wine has finished fermenting, then drive in corks.

HOME-MADE LIQUEURS

Liqueur-making at home is very often confined to cherry brandy and sloe gin. Only recipes that are easy to make at home are given here.

To Serve : When liqueurs are to be served at a party, give, if possible, a choice between Cognac and a sweet liqueur such as Cerasella, Chartreuse, Cherry Brandy, Cointreau, Crème de Menthe, Curaçao, Grand Marnier, Marnique, etc. When you are out of Cognac, substitute Kummel. There are two sweet liqueurs served differently from the others. They are Crème de Cacao and Tia Maria. To serve either, half fill glass with liqueur, then float cream on the top. Liqueur glasses are generally arranged on a tray alongside liqueurs, unless at a very small party when they can go on the coffee tray.

ADVOCAAT

1¼ lb. caster sugar
13 separated eggs
1 pint Brandy

Add sugar to egg yolks. Beat until thoroughly blended, then gradually stir in Brandy. Beat egg whites to a stiff but not dry froth. Fold lightly into yolk mixture. Either stand basin in a saucepan of hot water, or in the top of a large double boiler. Stir over water at boiling point until thick. Do not allow to boil on any account. Serve ice-cold in liqueur glasses with the coffee at Christmas, Hallowe'en, New Year's Eve, or at any other winter parties.

BANANA RUM

About 10 or 12 bananas
1 orange
1 lemon
1 small bay leaf
1 bottle Jamaica Rum

The bananas must be ripe but perfectly sound. Peel and cut each banana in four. Place in a glass jar with a wide mouth. Wash and dry the orange and lemon. Peel thinly and cut peel into shreds. Place shredded peel in jar. Add bay leaf, then

Rum. (There should be enough to cover bananas.) Seal securely and stand for 6 weeks, then strain, bottle and cork tightly.

CHERRY BRANDY

Morella cherries
Rock candy or sugar as required
Bitter almonds as required
Brandy as required

Gather the cherries on a dry day. Wipe with a damp cloth, then toss in a dry cloth, as they must be perfectly dry. Remove stalks to within an inch of the fruit. To every lb. prepared cherries, allow ½ lb. caster sugar, or 3-4 oz. crushed sugar candy. Prick cherries in several places with a fine needle. Place layers of cherries, strewed with sugar or crushed sugar candy, alternately in sweet bottles or jars. When bottles are nearly full, add 6 peeled, blanched bitter almonds, then fill up with Brandy. Cork tightly and seal corks. Leave for at least 4 months in a dark cupboard, then strain off through muslin or blotting paper into smaller bottles. Cork tightly and seal.

DAMSON GIN

2 lb. damsons
1 lb. light brown sugar
1 quart Gin

Rinse damsons and dry on a cloth. Prick each all over with a needle. Place in a large sweet bottle or jar with the sugar. Add Gin. Cork. Shake every day for 2 months, then strain and bottle. Cork tightly. Keep for at least 6 months before serving.

SLOE GIN

3 lb. sloes
2 quarts unsweetened Gin
1½ lb. Demerara sugar
2 oz. bitter almonds

Wipe sloes with a damp cloth and stem, then prick well all over with a needle. Place in large sweet jars or bottles, or in a stone jar. Add Gin and sugar. Blanch bitter almonds and add. Cork tightly. Keep at least until Christmas before serving.

WINE

When buying wine, there are certain points you must bear in mind :

1. Choose your wines to suit the dishes you wish to serve. If you are not an authority on wine, ask your wine merchant to help you, but in that case you must have your menu planned before you call on him.

2. At a family dinner, one wine is sufficient, but at a formal dinner or a banquet, you must serve a wine to suit each course.

3. If you wish to serve Champagne throughout the meal, begin with a young dry Champagne and conclude with a mature wine.

4. Don't offer Burgundy or Claret when shellfish is on the menu.

5. If the weather is hot, choose a white wine or wine cup. If the weather is very cold, a Burgundy.

6. Don't buy only whole bottles. Stock up in half bottles as well so that if

one bottle is not sufficient at a meal, but two bottles are not necessary, you can open a half bottle.

7. Don't serve fine wine with a salad or anything flavoured with vinegar.

TABLE OF WINES

Now here is a table of wines suitable to serve with the different courses in a formal menu :

APERITIFS : Dry Sherry : Amontillado, Fino, or extra-dry Tio Pepe slightly chilled ; or iced dry Champagne ; and the choice of a dry or sweet cocktail.

CAVIARE : Vodka.

EGG DISHES : Dry white Burgundy.

FISH COCKTAILS : Dry white Burgundy or Rhine wine.

FRUIT COCKTAILS, GRAPEFRUIT OR MELON : Light Madeira or Sherry.

HORS D'OEUVRES : Pale dry Sherry, or Italian Vermouth with a dash of Angostura Bitters, chilled Graves or Moselle.

OYSTERS : Chablis, dry Graves, or young dry Champagne.

SMOKED SALMON : Medium-dry Graves or Moselle.

SOUP : Dry Madeira, or a dry Sherry such as Vino de Pasto.

FISH : Chilled Chablis, dry Champagne, Moselle, Rhine wine, or white Burgundy.

ENTREES (Poultry or Veal) : Chilled Chablis, dry Champagne, Moselle, Rhine wine, or white Burgundy.

ENTREES (Game and Meat, excepting veal) : Burgundy, Chianti or Claret at room temperature.

GAME : Full red wine such as Côte de Rhône, or Champagne.

ROASTS : Fine Burgundy, or vintage Burgundy or Claret.

SWEETS : Champagne, Sauterne or any sweet white still or sparkling wine iced.

CHEESE : Brown Sherry, sweet Madeira or Port wine.

DESSERT : Malaga, Port wine, Madeira, brown Sherry or Tokay.

COFFEE : Choice of liqueur Brandy (Cognac) and sweet liqueurs.

When serving a small dinner for a few people, two wines are sufficient. Start with Sherry. Serve it with soup and the fish. Follow with a Claret or Burgundy, Moselle or Rhine wine, whatever is suitable to go with the following course. If serving cheese at a meal in which red wine has been offered, it can take the place of the wines suggested under cheese.

TIPS ON SERVING WINE

1. When serving apéritifs, don't be content to serve merely cocktails. Remember some prefer a dry Sherry or a mixed Vermouth. All cocktails should be well iced. Serve Sherry or mixed Vermouth at a cool temperature. If you store Sherry and Vermouth in a cellar, the temperature will be cool enough for all ordinary occasions.

2. When giving a formal party at which several wines are to be served, place glasses required to the right and at the tip of the knives at each cover. They should be so arranged that each glass is ready to hand as each course comes round.

3. When you serve Sherry with the soup, only half fill glasses.

4. If you have to help your guests to wine, pour a few drops of the newly opened bottle into your own glass and taste the wine, before helping your guests. This is a small point in wine etiquette which dates I am told from the time of the Borgias, if not before.

5. Never fill glasses up to the brim. Fill only a little over half full.

6. Remember to see that the Port decanter is passed from your left hand to the next person's right hand, and so on, " clockwise," and then placed on the table near the host, who will pass it again when another round is wanted.

7. Don't have the Port served until the cheese or dessert appears.

8. Never encourage your guests to smoke between the courses. Only offer cigarettes with Sherry when served as an apéritif.

9. When serving a formal dinner and a red wine is required to go with the roast, choose Burgundy, though a dry Champagne or a Rhine wine is sometimes more popular with roast veal.

10. Serve Champagne with ham and pâté de Foie Gras.

Candies

It is not difficult to make candy when you have the proper utensils. If you only wish to make it occasionally, the following equipment will be sufficient :

Saucepan : Choose a cast aluminium saucepan with a smooth interior, large enough to allow for the mixture to boil up (2-2½ quarts). The pan should be able to hold 4 times the quantity of ingredients being converted into candy.

Setting Tins : Choose small, rectangular tins with straight sides, and about 1½ inches deep. Reserve them only for cooling candy.

Marble Slab : This is necessary if you want to make fondants, but a large heavy platter can be used instead, or an old fashioned marble-topped wash stand. An enamel-topped table will suffice.

Pastry brush for oiling tins or slab.

Broad Spatula for working fondant.

Thermometer (sugar-boiling). Not necessary, but should be available.

Wooden spoons for beating and stirring.

Measuring cup and *spoons.*

Weights and measures.

Cellophane or *waxed paper* for wrapping.

Hair sieve.

Double boiler.

Rolling pin.

Scissors.

EQUIPMENT FOR ADVANCED CANDY-MAKING

Caramel bars and *cutters.*

Dipping forks for coating bonbons and chocolates.

Rubber moulds or mat for shaping chocolates, fondants, jellies.
Funnel and *plug.*
Marzipan moulds.
Crystallizing tray, 10 inches broad and 14 inches long.
Starch tray required when moulding fondants, etc., in starch. A long narrow biscuit tin lid can be used instead.

Ingredients

Sugar : Use caster sugar unless otherwise instructed. If brown sugar is specified, use light brown unless dark brown is suggested. If milk is used in conjunction with brown sugar, and the mixture curdles, beat until smooth again.
Milk : Use fresh milk, or evaporated milk diluted with equal quantity of water.
Cream: When not available, substitute evaporated milk with the addition of butter, allowing $\frac{1}{2}$-$\frac{3}{4}$ oz. butter to each cup of milk used.
Chocolate : Use bitter or unsweetened chocolate, or bittersweet if the former is not available. Otherwise, ordinary sweet chocolate can be substituted.
Cocoa : If this has to be substituted for chocolate, note that $\frac{1}{4}$ cup cocoa, plus 1 teaspoon butter, equals 1 oz. unsweetened chocolate.
Colourings : The most popular are apricot, canary yellow, coffee, pink, green, mauve, orange, yellow and saffron.
Flavourings : Almond, apricot, banana, blackcurrant, cinnamon, clove, coffee, ginger, heliotrope, lemon, orange, peppermint, raspberry, rose, strawberry, violet, etc.

To Colour

Almonds : Blanch and dry almonds. Chop. Spread out on a baking tray or sheet covered with greaseproof paper. Add a drop or two of colouring desired. Stir with a fork till evenly coloured, then toss in a cloth till thoroughly dried. Use for decorating cakes and cold sweets.
Coconut : Sprinkle either desiccated or freshly shredded coconut on a baking sheet or tin covered with greaseproof paper. Add a few drops of colouring to taste. Stir with a fork till evenly coloured. Dry in a warm room. Store in a tightly-closed jar.
Sugar : Spread caster or granulated sugar in a tin lined with thick white paper. Sprinkle with a few drops of colouring to taste. Stir with a fork or spoon till evenly coloured. Dry in the oven with the door open at a very low temperature. While drying, separate the grains occasionally by rubbing with the fingers. Remove, and when quite cold, store in tightly closed screw-topped jars.

To Flavour Sugar

There are two methods of flavouring with vanilla when out of stock of vanilla sugar :—
1. Place 1 lb. caster or icing sugar in a jar with a closely fitting top. Bury two vanilla beans in sugar. Shake occasionally. Leave till flavoured to taste before using.

2. Chop vanilla beans, allowing 1 oz. to each 1 lb. of sugar. Pound in a mortar with the sugar. Rub through a fine sieve. Store in a tightly closed jar.

LEMON OR ORANGE SUGAR : Wash and dry lemons or oranges. Carefully remove all the thin rind, taking care not to cut off any of the white pith. Allow $\frac{1}{4}$ lb. loaf sugar for every 6 lemons or oranges. Dry rind thoroughly in a very low oven with an open door, then place in a mortar. Add loaf sugar. Pound sugar and rind with a pestle and rub through a fine sieve. Store in an airtight jar. Use for coating bonbons and other candies.

SPUN SUGAR

1 lb. loaf sugar
1 saltspoon cream of tartar
1 cup cold water

Place sugar, cream of tartar and water in the top of a double boiler. Stir over low heat till sugar is dissolved. Cover. Place directly on stove. Boil for about $2\frac{1}{2}$ minutes, then uncover. Boil without stirring to very brittle stage, 310° F., wiping down the sides of pan with a fork wrapped in a damp cloth. Remove from heat to a basin of cold water. Leave for 2 minutes, then remove from cold water. Add a drop or two of vegetable colouring, red or yellow according to taste.

To Spin Sugar : Oil the blade of a large knife or rolling pin. Hold it out straight in front of you in your left hand, then dip a warm spoon into the syrup, and shake it back and forwards over knife or rolling pin when the syrup will form long threads that look like silk. The faster you " spin " the sugar, the finer the threads. If the syrup gets too cold, you must reheat to 310° F. Use for decorating desserts, or shape into nests for friandises. Use as soon as possible.

TEMPERATURES

There are two ways of testing the temperature of the syrup. The usual way is to tip a few drops into a cup of cold water, then rub them between your fingers, but the most accurate way is to use a thermometer.

Cold Water Test : Remove pan from stove so as to prevent over-cooking the syrup while making the test. Tip about a teaspoon of the syrup into a cup of cold water. (This will thicken the syrup.) With your fingers, shape into a ball, then test for consistency required.

To Use a Thermometer : Place in a saucepan of cold water. Bring to boil, then plunge into the boiling syrup. Leave until desired temperature is reached, then remove to pan of water in which it was brought to boil. Heat in the water until all traces of the syrup have been removed, then dry thoroughly and store.

TEMPERATURE CHART

Stage	Temperature (Degrees Fahrenheit)	Candy	Cold Water Test
Soft ball	234°-238°	Fudge	Firm enough to form into a pliable ball when pressed between thumb and forefinger.

Stage	Temperature	Candy	Cold Water Test
Soft ball	238°-240°	Fondant	Soft, but does not ooze out when pressed between thumb and finger.
Firm ball	240°-250°	Caramel and Marzipan	Firm, but yields when pressed.
Hard ball	250°-270°	Chewy toffee	Holds its shape. Impossible to pierce it with finger nail.
Firm crack or Brittle	288°-290°	Brittle, Butterscotch, Nougat and hard candies.	Brittle under the water, but is pliable when removed.
Very brittle	310°-320°	Lollipops	Syrup begins to turn yellow. The threads falling from the tip of spoon will snap.

BLACKCURRANT BONBONS

¼ pint blackcurrant jelly
½ lb. sugar
3 tablespoons powdered gelatine
1½ gills boiling water
Few drops of cochineal

Melt jelly in a saucepan. Add sugar. Stir over low heat till dissolved. Boil to 235° F. Add gelatine softened in the water, and cochineal. When dissolved, turn into a rinsed pan. Sprinkle with a little desiccated coconut or chopped nuts. When firm cut into cubes.

COCONUT ICE

1 lb. granulated sugar
¼ pint water
Pinch of cream of tartar
4 oz. desiccated coconut

Put sugar, water and cream of tartar in a saucepan. Heat slowly till sugar has dissolved, then boil to 245° F., (soft ball stage). Remove from stove. Add coconut. Stir till the mixture begins to thicken. Pour half into a tin lined with paper. Colour remainder pink with cochineal, and pour over the white. Leave till cold. Cut into squares or bars.

CREME DE MENTHE

1⅓ cups cold water
3 tablespoons powdered gelatine
1¼ lb. caster sugar
2 tablespoons strained lemon juice
Oil of peppermint to taste
Green vegetable colouring

Measure ⅔ cup of the water into a basin. Add gelatine. Soak for 5 minutes. Place sugar and remainder of water in a saucepan. Stir till sugar is dissolved, then till boiling. Stir in gelatine. Simmer slowly, but steadily, for 20 minutes. Remove pan from stove. Add lemon juice, oil of peppermint to taste, a little grated lemon rind if liked, and enough of the colouring to make mixture light green. Pour into a shallow tin to the depth of 1 inch. Stand till cool and firm, which may take about 12 hours. Turn on to a board. Cut into cubes. Roll in sifted icing sugar.

843

LOLLIPOPS

1 lb. loaf sugar
⅔ cup cold water
1 saltspoon cream of tartar

Place ingredients in a small saucepan. Stir over slow heat till sugar is dissolved, then cook, without stirring, till very brittle, 320° F. Remove at once from the stove. Divide at once into 3 portions : Colour one green. Flavour with peppermint oil. Colour the second yellow. Flavour with orange essence. Colour the third red. Flavour with cinnamon essence. Pour into small, round, flat-based muffin tins, or bun tins. Leave till beginning to cool, then press a stick firmly into each one.

MARSHMALLOWS

2 tablespoons powdered gelatine
½ pint cold water
1 lb. caster sugar
Few grains of salt
Oil of peppermint to taste
Green or red colouring

Soak gelatine in ½ cup of the cold water for 5 minutes. Place sugar in a saucepan. Add remainder of water. Stir until sugar is dissolved, then bring to boil. Boil until syrup spins a thread, about 225° F., then stir into dissolved gelatine. Leave until slightly cold, then add salt, oil of peppermint, and a drop or two of vegetable green colouring, or cochineal, beating until thick and light. Pour into a square dish dusted thickly with sifted icing sugar. Leave in a cold place until firm. Turn out. Cut into squares. Roll again in sifted icing sugar.

CHOCOLATE MARSHMALLOWS : Place ¼ lb. milk chocolate in the top of a double boiler. Heat over hot water until chocolate is melted. Dip 2½ dozen marshmallows in turn in the chocolate. Roll at once in chopped walnuts, desiccated coconut, or chocolate shot. Place a little apart on a buttered tin. Chill.

MARSHMALLOWETTES

1 lb. Barbados sugar
¾ cup water
½ cup butter
2 tablespoons golden syrup
A few grains of salt
Marshmallows as required

Place sugar, water, butter, syrup and salt in a large saucepan. Stir gently till sugar is dissolved. Cook till it reaches 300° F., stirring now and then during the process. Brush starch from marshmallows. Slip them, one at a time, very gently into the toffee, lifting them from saucepan with a candy-dipping fork. Lay them upside down on an oiled plate to cool.

MARSHMALLOWS IN BROWN COATS

2½ cups shelled walnuts
1 cup chopped blanched almonds
½ teaspoon salt
⅔ cup water
2 cups light brown sugar
1½ lb. soft marshmallows

Chop nuts to a medium fineness. Sieve if necessary to be sure the " chop " is equal-sized. Stir in salt. Pour water into a saucepan. Add sugar. Stir over low heat till dissolved. Bring to boil. Boil until syrup threads from spoon, 226° F. Remove pan at once from stove. Place in a basin of hot water. Shake each marshmallow to remove any loose sugar or starch before piercing lightly with a fork, and dipping in syrup. Roll each one immediately after dipping in the nut mixture. Place on paper, brushed lightly with olive oil, to dry.

NOUGAT

¼ lb. chopped blanched almonds
¼ lb. candied angelica
1 lb. glucose
1½ lb. caster sugar
1 cup cold water
2 egg whites
¾ teaspoon almond essence

Dry almonds before chopping. Cut angelica into small pieces. Place glucose and sugar in an enamel saucepan. Add water. Stir over low heat till dissolved, then till boiling. Boil to 290° F. Beat egg whites to a stiff froth. When syrup is ready, gradually beat it into the egg whites. As soon as mixture begins to set, stir in almonds, angelica and almond essence. Turn into a buttered tin. Chill overnight. Cut into bars and wrap in waxed paper.

PENUCHE

½ lb. light brown sugar
¾ cup milk
1 oz. butter
1 teaspoon vanilla essence
2 cups chopped walnuts

Place sugar and milk in a saucepan. Stir over low heat until sugar is dissolved, then till boiling. Boil until a few drops tipped into cold water form a soft ball, 240° F. Remove from stove. Stir in butter, vanilla essence and nuts. Leave till cool. Beat until creamy and slightly thickened. Pour into a buttered tin. Cut into squares when firm.

PEPPERMINT CREAMS

1 lb. caster sugar
⅔ cup water
Pinch of cream of tartar
½ teaspoon essence of peppermint

Place sugar and water in a saucepan. Stir over a slow heat till sugar is dissolved, then till boiling. Add cream of tartar. Boil without stirring to soft ball stage, 240° F. Remove from stove. Place pan in cold water. Add peppermint essence. Stir till thick. Knead into equal-sized rounds. Flatten, and stroke with a fork.

PISTACHIO BALLS

½ lb. sweet chocolate
1 egg
2 tablespoons butter
2 oz. chopped blanched pistachio nuts

Break chocolate in small pieces. Melt in the top of a double boiler over hot water. Stir in egg. When smooth, stir in butter. When butter is dissolved, leave till set enough to handle, then shape into small balls, rolling them in the palms of your hands. Dip quickly in nuts.

RED CURRANT JELLIES

2 tablespoons powdered gelatine
¾ cup boiling water

Soak gelatine in the water. Melt jelly. Add sugar. Stir until dissolved over low heat, then till boiling. Boil till syrup spins a heavy thread,

845

½ cup red currant jelly
½ lb. caster sugar
A few drops of carmine

235° F., then add soaked gelatine and carmine, or cochineal if preferred. Stir until dissolved. Strain into a square wet dish. Chill until set and hard. Cut in squares. Spangle.

SEA FOAM

1 lb. caster sugar
½ cup golden syrup
½ cup water
2 egg whites
1 teaspoon vanilla essence
1 cup broken walnuts

Measure sugar, syrup and water into a saucepan. Stir till boiling. Boil to hard ball stage, 250°-265° F. Beat egg whites till stiff. Slowly add boiling liquid, beating constantly, as you add it, with an egg beater. When beginning to stiffen, stir in vanilla essence and walnuts. Drop in spoonfuls on to waxed paper brushed with oil.

TURKISH DELIGHT

2 lb. granulated sugar
1 quart cold water
10 oz. cornflour
14 oz. icing sugar
3 oz. strained honey
1 teaspoon rose essence
1 teaspoon lemon essence
¼ oz. tartaric acid

Measure sugar into a saucepan. Add 2 cups of the water. Boil to soft ball stage, 240° F. Meanwhile, moisten cornflour with 1 cup of remaining water by degrees. Bring remainder of water to boil. Stir icing sugar into cornflour, then the boiling water. Pour into a saucepan. Stir over heat till thick, then stir in boiling syrup the moment it reaches 240° F. Mix well. Add honey, essences and tartaric acid. Mix well. Pour into buttered tins. Leave till cold. Cut into squares. Dust with equal quantity of sifted icing sugar and cornflour.

SIMPLE CARAMELS

BASIC RECIPE:
½ lb. caster or granulated sugar
1 oz. butter
1 cup milk
Pinch of salt
1 teaspoon vanilla essence

Brush a 10″ tin with melted butter. Place sugar, butter, milk and salt in a saucepan. Stir till boiling, then heat to firm ball stage, 250° F., stirring constantly. Remove from stove. Stir in vanilla essence. Pour at once into tin. When cool, cut in squares with a caramel cutter. Wrap each in a square of waxed paper.

CHERRY : Follow basic recipe, substituting light brown sugar. Stir in ¼ lb. chopped glacé cherries with the essence.

CHOCOLATE : Cook syrup only to soft ball stage. Stir in 3 tablespoons melted chocolate with the essence.

RIBBON : Follow basic recipe. Stir in essence after removing from heat. Quickly pour half the mixture into tin. Cover thickly and quickly with marshmallows. Top with remainder of caramel mixture.

AFRICAN CARAMELS

BASIC RECIPE:
½ lb. caster sugar
½ cup golden syrup

Place sugar in a saucepan. Add syrup and only ½ cup of the cream. Stir constantly over low heat till sugar is dissolved, then simmer gently, stirring

1½ cups thick cream
Pinch of salt
¾ teaspoon vanilla essence

constantly, to soft ball stage, 234° F. Stir in half the remainder of cream, and cook again, to 234° F., then stir in remainder of cream and salt, and cook, stirring constantly, until the syrup turns into a firm ball, 244°-246° F. Stir in vanilla essence. Turn into a buttered or oiled tin, 7″ long. Leave till slightly cooled, then mark into ¾ inch squares. When firm, cut out. Wrap each in cellophane or waxed paper.

COFFEE : Substitute ¾ teaspoon coffee essence for vanilla.

NUT : Stir in 3 oz. chopped cashew nuts, almonds or walnuts after removing from stove.

CHOCOLATE

Chocolates, which usually consist of a nut, fruit, candy or marzipan centre dipped in chocolate, are not easy to turn out. They need practice. They can be made with equipment usually available in every kitchen, but if expert results are wanted, it is better to buy special equipment.

Special Equipment : Chocolate dipping pan with water jacket,
Funnel with a plug,
Starch tray,
Dipping forks,
Sheet of tin.

Centres for Chocolates : Prepare centres before chocolate coating. Caramel, flavoured fondant, fruit, fudge, marshmallows, marzipan, nougat, nut, praline, toffee, truffle, Turkish delight, etc.

RULES FOR MAKING CHOCOLATES

1. Do not attempt to make chocolates on a foggy or muggy day. Choose a dry, warm day for this branch of sweet-making.
2. The temperature of the room should be between 60° and 65° F.
3. See that no draught or steam comes in contact with chocolates.
4. Be careful to have the chocolate at the right temperature. If too cold, chocolates will be streaky. If too hot, they will be grey and speckled-looking.
5. Do not leave chocolates exposed to air. Pack as soon as cold in boxes lined with waxed paper.
6. Before starting to prepare coating, arrange the centres ready on your left, the soft centres cut into any fancy shapes you like. Place a board covered with waxed paper or oilcloth on a table on the right, or a clean sheet of tin kept for this purpose.

CHOCOLATE COATINGS

The chocolate used for coating must be of a high quality. You can buy covering chocolate for this purpose, known as " couverture," which is a good quality plain chocolate mixed with a certain proportion of cocoa butter. The addition of the cocoa butter makes the chocolate harden quickly, prevents stickiness, and helps to prevent discoloration.

To Prepare Chocolate Coating from "Couverture" : Take a double boiler, if you have not a chocolate dipping pan. Heat water in the bottom compartment to 120° F. (It must remain at this temperature all the time the chocolates are being coated.) Shred chocolate. Melt very gently until liquefied, and at blood temperature, stirring constantly. Take care not to allow any drops of water to fall into it while melting. You must also see that the steam from the bottom pan does not come in contact, or it will make the chocolate heavy. When melted, allow to fall to 85° F., or allow it to become quite cold, then remelt it to 85° F.

1. Place pan containing chocolate with water below in between your centres and the prepared board.

2. Lift the centre with your left hand, taking care that no loose particles are attached to it and drop gently into the chocolate.

3. Turn it round with a dipping fork, then lift it out on to a sheet of waxed paper, or oil-cloth, or on to a sheet of tin, kept for the purpose, working as quickly as possible. If the coating looks rough, then the chocolate has become too cool, so increase the heat of the water to bring chocolate to the correct temperature again.

4. Decorate tops or roll chocolates in chopped fried almonds or pistachio nuts.

CENTRES FOR CHOCOLATES

Almonds : Blanch and place on a baking tin. Dry in the oven till pale brown. Dip when quite cold.

Almonds and Raisins : Put ¼ lb. blanched chopped almonds and ½ lb. stoned raisins, mixed with ¼ teaspoon almond essence and ½ teaspoon rose water, through a meat grinder. Roll into small balls. Dry overnight, then dip.

Date Balls : Stone and put dates through a meat grinder, then mix with equal quantity of sifted icing sugar. Mix to a paste with honey. Shape into small balls, and leave until hard, then dip.

Fondants : Knead ¼ lb. grated chocolate into ½ lb. fondant flavoured with vanilla or rum essence. Shape into small balls. Place on a baking sheet lined with waxed paper. Leave in a warm room until dry. Coat with chocolate.

Maraschino Cherries : Drain cherries. Dip each in melted fondant. Place on a baking sheet covered with waxed paper. Stand in a cold place until they become hard. As soon as fondants are hard, dip in chocolate. You must not melt the chocolate till the fondants are almost hard.

Praline Centres: Blanch ½ lb. Jordan almonds. Shred with a sharp knife. Bake in a moderate oven, 350° F., until lightly brown. Melt 10 oz. loaf sugar slowly till into a golden brown syrup in a rinsed saucepan. Pour on to a buttered slab. When cold, pound with a pestle in a mortar. Remove to a plate and pound the almonds. Mix together. Press into small shapes. Leave till dry. Dip in chocolate. Dry on a slab.

CHOCOLATE MALLOWS

4 oz. marshmallows
1 cup pecan or walnuts
8 oz. unsweetened chocolate
4 oz. sweet chocolate

Cut up marshmallows. Chop nuts. Mix with marshmallows in a basin. Melt chocolate slowly in the top of a double boiler over boiling water. Cool slightly. Pour over nut mixture. Stir quickly until marshmallows are dissolved. Leave until almost firm. Shape into balls with a teaspoon. Dip in sifted icing sugar.

CHOCOLATE SCRUNCH

1 cup dates
1 cup raisins
1 teaspoon grated orange rind
1/4 teaspoon ground cinnamon
1/2 teaspoon vanilla essence
1/2 lb. chocolate

Put stoned dates and raisins through a meat grinder. Add orange rind, ground cinnamon and vanilla essence. Mix ingredients well then form into balls. Melt chocolate in top of a double boiler. Dip balls in, one at a time, using a wire chocolate dipper or very fine knitting needle. Place on buttered or waxed paper to cool and harden.

FAIRY TRUFFLES

6 oz. bitter chocolate
1/3 cup and 1 tablespoon condensed milk
Pinch of salt
1/4 teaspoon vanilla essence
3 tablespoons ground almonds or walnuts

Melt chocolate, *without stirring*, in the top of a double boiler. Remove from heat. Stir in sweetened condensed milk, salt, vanilla essence and nuts. Stir only till blended. Turn into a container lined with waxed paper. Press into a block about 1 inch thick. Chill in refrigerator until firm in about 2 hours. Turn out of container. Remove waxed paper and cut into serving pieces. *Yield:* About 1/2 lb.

ROCKY ROAD

1/2 lb. plain chocolate
1/2 lb. milk chocolate
1 tablespoon butter
6-12 marshmallows
1 cup chopped walnuts

Place chocolate and butter in the top of a double boiler. Leave over boiling water for a minute or two, then stir slowly until butter is dissolved. Add marshmallows and nuts. Stir for a moment or two. Pour into a square greased baking tin. When cold, cut into squares.

YULE TRUFFLES

2 oz. grated chocolate
1 oz. sifted icing sugar
1/2 teaspoon vanilla essence
Cream as required
1 tablespoon chopped blanched pistachio nuts
1 1/2 tablespoons chocolate shot

Mix chocolate with icing sugar in a basin. Stir in vanilla essence and enough cream to make a stiff paste. Shape into balls the size of small marbles. Mix nuts with chocolate shot. Dip balls in mixture. Place each in a paper case, or pile up in tiny sweet dishes lined with silver paper doilies.

COOKED FONDANT

1 lb. caster sugar
1/2 pint water
1 saltspoon cream of tartar or 1 dessertspoon glucose

Place sugar and water in an enamel saucepan. Stir over low heat till sugar is dissolved. Wipe down the sides of pan with a pastry brush or fork, wrapped in a piece of damp muslin to get rid of any crystals that might coarsen the fondant. (If preferred, cover pan and cook slowly for 2 or 3 minutes when the steam will dissolve any crystals on the side.) Bring to boiling point, stirring constantly. Add cream of tartar or glucose. Cover. Steam for 3 minutes. Uncover. Boil to soft ball stage, 238°-240° F., without stirring. Remove from stove. Pour immediately on to a slab brushed with cold water, or wiped with a damp cloth. Leave till cool, 110° F. Scrape up mixture, turning it towards the centre with a spatula until the whole mass is creamy white. Knead until smooth. Cover with a cloth wrung out of cold water. Stand for 30 minutes. Cut up into small pieces. Store in an airtight jar with a glass lid. Stand for 2 or 3 days before using.

HINTS ON MAKING FONDANT

1. Be sure that all sugar is melted before syrup comes to boil. If only partly dissolved before boiling, the syrup may " grain." Do not move pan after syrup comes to the boil.

2. Mould in rubber mats or starch.

3. Allow to ripen for 1 hour before making candies, unless otherwise instructed. If to be kept for several days, wrap in waxed paper before storing.

TO SHAPE FONDANTS

There are several ways of shaping fondants. You can knead and work flavouring and colouring to taste into fondant, then shape it, or melt it before shaping.

To Shape Kneaded Fondant : Break off bits. Roll into balls, or shape in rolls ½ inch across, and cut in rounds, or flatten and cut in small bars. Flatten balls slightly if liked. Top with a split almond, half a walnut, or bits of crystallized fruit, or roll in grated chocolate.

Fondant Stuffing : Mould into tiny balls. Press between halves of walnuts or candied cherries, or dip in melted chocolate.

To Shape Melted Fondant : Place the fondant in the top of a double boiler over pan filled as full as possible with cold water. Place over low heat, and heat till the water reaches about 175° F. It must not boil on any account. Remove pan from heat. Stir fondant gently with a wooden spoon until it is pourable. (If too thick, stir in a few drops of hot water.) Then colour and flavour to taste. Stir till evenly blended. Work rapidly. If it becomes thick whilst shaping, reheat water below to 175° F.

1. Drop from the tip of a pointed teaspoon on to a baking sheet covered with wax paper, or very lightly buttered, in rounds.

2. Place melted fondant alongside a rubber fondant mat. Pour into the depressions, or force through an icing bag, or funnel with a funnel dropper, into depressions. If pouring in, let it drip from the side of a spoon. If using a funnel, heat it thoroughly in boiling water before using. When set and cold, bend mat and fondants will pop out.

Centres for Fondant : Bits of marzipan, candied cherries, chopped dates mixed with a little of the melted fondant, chopped walnuts moistened with fondant, pieces of crystallized ginger, etc.

To Coat Centres : Leave fondant over hot water. Pick up one centre at a time with a dipping fork, and drop into fondant. Lift out immediately. Poise the fork over edge of pan to enable surplus fondant to drip back into pan, then lift on to waxed paper, quickly coiling the last drop of fondant on the fork over candies. Stir fondant. Continue in this way until all the centres are coated. If liked, decorate the top of each with a crystallized violet, or rose or lilac petal. If liked, when half the centres are covered, the remainder of fondant can be coloured a delicate pink, green or mauve.

CHERRY AND ORANGE BONBONS

¼ lb. crystallized cherries
1 cup strained orange juice
1 cup cooked fondant

Place cherries in a basin. Add orange juice. Cover. Leave for 12 hours, then turn cherries on to a sieve to drain. Melt fondant till creamy in the top of a double boiler, stirring constantly, then flavour with a few drops of the orange. Gently drop one cherry in at a time. When coated, remove with a dipping fork. Place on a platter lightly oiled. When set, tuck each bonbon into a paper case.

PEPPERMINT WAFERS

1 egg white
1 saltspoon salt
6 drops peppermint oil
1½ cups sifted icing sugar

Beat egg white slightly. Beat in salt and peppermint oil. Sift sugar. Beat in a little at a time until you have a firm paste. Turn on to a platter or slab. Knead until smooth. Roll out into a thin round. Stamp into rounds the size of a penny. Lay on a baking sheet covered with waxed paper. Leave in a cool place before serving or storing, for at least 24 hours.

FUDGE

Perfect fudge must be creamy and smooth. If it turns sugary, then it becomes what is known in Scotland as " tablet."

SIMPLE FUDGE

BASIC RECIPE :
1 lb. caster sugar
1 cup milk
¼ lb. butter
1 teaspoon vanilla essence

Place sugar, milk and butter in a saucepan. Stir over low heat till sugar is dissolved, then till boiling. Boil, stirring constantly, to soft ball stage, 234°-238° F. Remove from stove. Stir in vanilla essence. Cool till lukewarm, 110° F. Beat till creamy and it loses its gloss. Pour at once into a shallow buttered tin, 8″ × 8″ × 2″. Cut into squares when cold.

BUTTERSCOTCH FUDGE : Substitute Barbados sugar for the caster. Pour ¼ pint cocoa made with milk into a saucepan in place of the cup of milk. Add sugar. Stir over low heat till dissolved, then reduce butter to 1 oz. and add. Follow basic recipe. When cooled to lukewarm, beat and stir in 2 heaped teaspoons chopped walnuts.

COCONUT FUDGE : Follow basic recipe. When lukewarm, beat till creamy, then stir in ¼ lb. desiccated coconut and ¼ teaspoon lemon essence.

PINEAPPLE FUDGE : Follow basic recipe till lukewarm. Beat till creamy. Stir in ¼ lb. minced glacé pineapple and ¼ teaspoon lemon essence.

851

RAISIN CREAM FUDGE : Place the sugar in a saucepan. Increase milk to $2\frac{1}{4}$ gills, and butter by 2 tablespoons, and add both. When lukewarm, beat till creamy. Stir in a teaspoon of vanilla essence and a cup of chopped stoned raisins.

CHOCOLATE FUDGE

BASIC RECIPE :
3 oz. unsweetened chocolate
$1\frac{1}{2}$ lb. caster sugar
$\frac{1}{2}$ pint milk
1 oz. butter
Pinch of salt
Pinch of cream of tartar
1 teaspoon vanilla essence

Grate chocolate fine. Place in a saucepan. Add sugar, milk and butter. Stir over low heat till sugar is dissolved. Add salt and cream of tartar Stir till boiling. Boil, stirring occasionally, to soft ball stage, 240° F. Remove from stove. Leave till lukewarm, 110° F. Beat till creamy. Stir in vanilla essence, and 1 cup chopped walnuts if liked. Turn quickly into shallow tin brushed with melted butter or olive oil. Cut into squares before quite cold.

CHOCOLATE PEPPERMINT FUDGE : Omit vanilla essence. Add 2 or 3 drops of peppermint oil. Stir in 1 cup roughly chopped toasted almonds after beating.

CREAMY FUDGE : Stir 3 dessertspoons corn or golden syrup in with the sugar.

MARSHMALLOW FUDGE : Stir in 1 or $1\frac{1}{2}$ cups cut-up marshmallows before pouring out.

MOCHA FUDGE : Substitute $1\frac{1}{2}$ gills strong coffee for $1\frac{1}{2}$ gills of the milk.

DIVINITY

BASIC RECIPE :
1 lb. caster sugar
$\frac{1}{2}$ cup golden syrup
$\frac{1}{2}$ cup water
Tiny pinch of salt
2 egg whites
$\frac{3}{4}$ teaspoon vanilla essence

Place sugar, syrup, water and salt in a saucepan. Stir over low heat till sugar is dissolved, then till boiling. Cook, without stirring, to hard ball stage, 260° F. Keep removing crystals from the inside of pan with a damp cloth wrapped round a fork. When syrup is nearly ready, beat egg whites till stiff so that by the time it reaches 260° F., the egg whites are ready. Pour syrup slowly over egg whites, beating constantly, but do not remove any adhering to bottom of pan. Stir in vanilla essence, and keep on beating till the candy holds its shape when you tip it out of the spoon. (It is best to use an egg whisk for beating.) Drop quickly from the tip of a dessertspoon in round heaps on waxed paper. If preferred, it can be poured into a shallow buttered pan, and cut into cubes when firm.

CHERRY : Add 6 oz. sliced candied cherries and a drop or two of cochineal or carmine while beating.

CHOCOLATE : Melt 1 oz. unsweetened chocolate and stir in just before shaping or moulding.

WALNUT : Stir in $\frac{1}{2}$ cup chopped walnuts when almost ready to shape or mould.

TABLET

Some tablets are very similar to fudge except that the syrup is boiled a little longer. All varieties are slightly granular.

CREAM TABLET

BASIC RECIPE :
1 lb. caster or loaf sugar
1 tablespoon golden syrup
1 cup cream

Place ingredients in a saucepan. Stir over low heat till sugar is dissolved, then till boiling. Add flavouring. Boil rapidly for about 10 minutes, to soft ball stage, 240° F. Remove from stove. Stand for 2 minutes. Beat with a wooden spoon till mixture turns sugary, then pour into a buttered tin. Cut into bars, say 5 inches long and 1½ inches thick. When quite cold, wrap each bar in waxed paper.

CHOCOLATE TABLET : Follow basic recipe, but add 6 oz. grated chocolate after mixture comes to boil.

COCONUT : Add 6 oz. desiccated coconut after mixture comes to the boil.

GINGER TABLET : Add 6 oz. chopped preserved ginger and 1 teaspoon ginger essence after mixture comes to the boil.

WALNUT TABLET : Stir in 6 oz. chopped walnuts and 1 teaspoon vanilla essence after mixture comes to the boil.

COCONUT TABLET

2 lb. caster or loaf sugar
¼ pint milk
¼ pint water
1 oz. butter
1 saltspoon cream of tartar
¼ lb. desiccated coconut

Place sugar, milk, water and butter in a saucepan. Stir over low heat till dissolved, then till boiling. Add cream of tartar. Boil to a firm ball, 245° F., stirring occasionally. Stir in coconut, and boil again to 245° F., stirring occasionally. Cool slightly. Beat with a wooden spoon until creamy and white. Pour into a buttered tin, 8" × 10" × 2". Cut into bars when cool and wrap in waxed paper.

MARZIPAN

There are two kinds of marzipan : Uncooked and cooked. The easiest to make is the uncooked, but you must handle it as little as possible, or the heat of your hands will " oil " it, at which stage it will not mould smoothly. If you wish to make marzipan into fruits, vegetables, etc., that require a certain amount of handling, it is advisable to use boiled marzipan.

UNCOOKED MARZIPANS

Simple :
1. Mix ¾ lb. ground almonds with 6 oz. sieved icing sugar and 4 oz. caster sugar. Stir in the juice of ½ a lemon, 2 drops almond essence, ¾ teaspoon vanilla essence, ¾ teaspoon orange flower or rose water, and enough slightly beaten egg white to make a soft but dry paste.
2. Mix ½ lb. ground almonds with ¼ lb. sifted icing sugar, and ¼ lb. caster sugar. Make a hollow in the centre with the back of a wooden spoon. Drop in 1 egg and a tablespoon brandy. Mix to a stiff paste, adding a little more beaten egg if required.
To Vary : Omit caster sugar. Double quantity of icing sugar. Moisten only with egg yolk if yellow paste is wanted. If a creamy paste is wanted, use only

853

egg whites. Flavour with a few drops of almond essence, 1 teaspoon brandy or rum and $\frac{1}{4}$ teaspoon vanilla essence or orange flower water.

COOKED MARZIPANS

Simple : Stir 1 lb. loaf sugar and $\frac{1}{2}$ cup water over low heat until sugar is dissolved, then stir in $1\frac{1}{2}$ dessertspoons glucose. Boil, stirring constantly, to firm ball stage, 245° F. Pour over $\frac{1}{2}$ lb. ground almonds. Add $\frac{3}{4}$ teaspoon almond essence. Beat with a wooden spoon until creamy. Turn out on a pastry board. Knead till smooth with a little sifted icing sugar.

To Store Marzipan : If not to be used at once, wrap in waxed paper. Tie in a dry towel. Store in a tin with a tightly fitting lid.

TO USE MARZIPAN

You can make marzipan into a variety of sweets in the shape of fruits and vegetables, bars, etc. If too hard when you want to use it, knead in 2 or 3 drops of cold water or lemon juice.

ACORNS : Shape small pieces of marzipan, coloured green, into acorns. Dry overnight. Dip the thick ends first in melted chocolate, then in chocolate powder, or brush first with melted jelly, then dip in chocolate powder.

APPLES : Roll into rounds the shape of an apple. Press a clove in each to suggest blossom end, and a tiny stalk of angelica on the opposite end to suggest a stem. Paint one side reddish, and the other yellowish green with vegetable colouring.

APRICOTS : Use yellow marzipan, colouring it as closely as possible to an apricot shade. Shape into balls like an apricot, with a dent down one side. Dab, if liked, with melted chocolate, to suggest brown specks sometimes found on apricots.

BARS : Prepare two contrasting-coloured pieces of marzipan, such as chocolate and orange, or pink and pistachio. Roll out each into a rectangle, about $\frac{1}{2}$ inch thick. Spread one layer thinly with water icing or glacé syrup. Place another contrasting layer on top. Press lightly all over. Cut into strips, then into small bars, about 1 inch long and $\frac{1}{2}$ inch wide. To vary, roll to $\frac{1}{3}$ inch thickness 2 rectangles of white marzipan. Place a layer, $\frac{1}{3}$ inch thick, of chocolate, pink, flavoured with raspberry, mauve, flavoured violet, or yellow, flavoured orange, fondant on top of 1 layer of marzipan. Cover with remaining layer of marzipan. Cut into bars as suggested.

CARROTS : Roll orange-coloured pieces of marzipan between your hands lightly into carrots. Insert a stalk of angelica in the thick end, after gently fringing it at one end to suggest carrot foliage.

CHERRIES : Flavour some marzipan with kirsch or maraschino. Shape into cherries. Hold each on a skewer in turn, and paint all over with a small brush dipped in carmine. Insert stalks of angelica, or, if to be used for decorating a cake, give leaves of angelica as well. Glaze if liked.

FANS : Colour marzipan to taste. Roll out to $\frac{3}{4}$ inch thickness. Cut out in fan shapes. Decorate with crystallized lilac.

LOGS : Cut out equal-sized bars about 8 inches long, and $\frac{3}{4}$ inch wide, from a light marzipan flavoured to taste. Cut thin sheets of green marzipan and of yellow marzipan, both flavoured differently, and of equal size. Brush green marzipan lightly with beaten egg white, and press round the bars. Trim neatly.

Cover with the yellow marzipan in the same way. Leave for 12 hours to dry. Brush with melted chocolate. Roll in chopped blanched pistachio nuts. When required, cut into short logs, giving each a slanting end.

PEACHES AND PEARS : Shape small equal-sized pieces of pale yellow or cream marzipan into pears and peaches. Paint a greenish shade on the pears. Press a clove at the narrow end to suggest blossom, and a tiny stalk of angelica at the other. Paint a "blush" of pink on peaches after shaping.

POTATOES : Shape small pieces of vanilla-flavoured marzipan into round and kidney potato shapes. Make a few holes for eyes with a skewer. Dip at once into sweet cocoa or chocolate powder. Place on a tin lined with greaseproof paper until dry.

STRAWBERRIES : Shape small equal-sized pieces of marzipan into strawberries. Prick all over with a skewer. Paint delicately with cochineal. Roll in caster sugar. If liked, make " hulls " of green marzipan and place one on the thick end of each strawberry, before inserting very tiny angelica stalks.

To Glaze Marzipan

Glaze for Marzipan : Place 2½ lb. loaf sugar in a saucepan with ½ pint water. Boil to thread stage, 223° F. Stir over slow heat till sugar is dissolved, then till boiling. Boil to thread stage, 223° F., without stirring. Remove from stove very carefully, and leave without disturbing until quite cold. Place the marzipans in even rows in a shallow tin. Cover with the syrup completely. Leave for 7 or 8 hours. Place in a sieve over plate. Drain marzipans on sieve, then dry on a wire rack.

Marzipan Stuffing : Use any coloured and flavoured marzipans for stuffing the following :—

Cherries : Shape into pills. Partly slit glacé cherries and insert a " pill " in each. Mould marzipan round the base. Dip in caster sugar or glaze.

Dates : Slit dates along one side. Stone. Fill with marzipan, stuffed with tiny piece of crystallized ginger. Draw slit sides together. Dip in caster sugar or glaze.

Walnuts : Roll marzipans into balls. Press a ball between two halves of shelled walnuts. Leave till firm, then glaze.

TOFFEE

Toffee, or taffy, as it is sometimes called, is easy to make if you observe the following rules :

1. Choose a large heavy saucepan. Brush round the inside with melted butter before starting to use it.

2. Grease or oil tin, or slab if the toffee is to be set between greased or oiled candy bars.

3. Dissolve sugar before mixture comes to the boil.

4. Do not stir unless instructed in recipe.

5. Reduce temperature after thermometer registers 250° F. by lowering heat.

6. Heat any ingredients such as nuts or candied fruit that are to be added, before adding.

855

7. When toffee is ready, pour at once into prepared tin or on to a slab between greased or oiled bars.

8. Leave till lukewarm. Cut into bars or squares as instructed with a greased or oiled knife.

9. If any grease or oil adheres to toffee, rub with absorbent paper. Wrap or twist each in waxed paper. Store in an airtight jar or tin.

BRITTLE

There are two kinds of brittle : one made from caramelized sugar and the other from pulled candy.

ALMOND BRITTLE

1 lb. caster sugar
1 cup roasted blanched
  almonds

Melt sugar very slowly in a strong wet frying-pan till it turns into a rich golden syrup, stirring only when necessary, which is when sugar is not evenly spread. Quickly stir in almonds. Pour at once into a dry shallow baking tin, 8″ × 8″ × 2″. (If preferred, spread almonds over the tin, and gently pour the syrup over.) Mark into squares if liked before it hardens, then break up, or wait until it is quite cold and crisp, then break here and there with a small hammer. *Yield :* About 1¼ lbs.

BRAZIL, PEANUT OR WALNUT BRITTLE : Substitute ½-1 cup crushed shelled peanuts or coarsely broken walnuts or sliced Brazil nuts, for the almonds in above recipe, and pour into a greased baking tin.

PULLED BRITTLE

1½ cups prepared nuts
1 saltspoon salt
½ lb. loaf sugar
½ cup water
½ cup golden syrup
¾ oz. butter
¼ teaspoon lemon essence

Use slightly roasted, shelled almonds, sliced shelled Brazil nuts, coarsely broken walnuts or pecans, roasted cashew nuts, or shelled peanuts. Spread nuts out in a baking tin. Sprinkle lightly with salt and heat through in a slow oven. When warm, place the sugar, water and syrup in a saucepan. Stir till sugar is dissolved, then until boiling. Brush down the inside of pan with a wet pastry brush, or a fork covered with a damp cloth to get rid of any crystals. Boil till brittle, 290° F. Add butter, lemon essence, and nuts. Pour into a shallow buttered tin and leave only till cool enough to handle, then turn it over on to a hook. Pull and stretch as thin as possible. When crisp, break with a hammer. *Yield :* About 2 lbs.

BUTTER CRUNCH

1¼ lb. caster sugar
1 cup water
¼ lb. glucose
3½ oz. butter
½ teaspoon vanilla essence

Place sugar and water in a saucepan. Stir over low heat till sugar is dissolved, then stir in glucose. Bring rapidly to the boil, stirring constantly. Cover. Boil for 2 or 3 minutes, then remove lid. Boil to brittle stage, 290° F. Remove from stove. Drop in butter, a small piece at a time. Return to stove. Bring to boil without stirring. Boil for 1 minute, add vanilla, then pour into a buttered tin. 8" × 10" × 2". When almost set, mark into squares. Break up when quite cold. If preferred, this toffee can be dropped in small rounds on to a buttered slab, *Yield :* About 1 lb.

BUTTERSCOTCH

1½ lb. light brown sugar
1 cup hot water
Pinch of cream of tartar
¾ lb. butter
1½ teaspoons lemon essence

Place sugar and water in a large saucepan. Stir over low heat till sugar is dissolved, then till boiling. Add cream of tartar. Cover. Boil for 10 minutes. Uncover. Boil without stirring, to very brittle stage, 310° F. Meanwhile, melt butter. When syrup reaches 310° F., pour in butter and lemon essence. Boil up and pour into buttered tins, 8" × 10" × 2", or on to a slab between buttered bars. Mark into bars when nearly cold, and break when quite cold. Wrap in waxed papers. *Yield :* About 2 lb.

CREAM SCRUNCH

1 lb. loaf sugar
1 cup thick cream
1 cup chopped walnuts

Place sugar and cream in a saucepan. Stir over low heat till sugar is dissolved, then till boiling. Boil to soft ball stage, 240° F. Remove from stove. Whip with an egg beater till fluffy. Stir in nuts. Pour into a greased tin. Leave till set. Cut into fancy shapes. Leave till cold. Wrap in waxed or greased paper. *Yield :* About 1¼ lb.

EVERTON TOFFEE

¼ lb. butter
1 lb. golden syrup
1 lb. Demerara sugar

Melt butter in a saucepan. Add syrup and sugar. Stir over low heat till sugar is dissolved, then till boiling. Boil for about 12 minutes, without stirring, to hard ball stage, 250°-270° F. (If liked, stir in a few drops of lemon essence.) Pour into a greased tin, 8" × 8" × 2". Mark into squares when set, and cut up when cold. Wrap in waxed paper. Store in an airtight tin. *Yield :* About 2 lb.

SCOTCH KISSES : Brush off any loose starch from marshmallows. Dip, one at a time, very gently, into the toffee with a candy-dipping fork. Place upside down on a slab to dry.

HELENSBURGH TOFFEE

¼ lb. butter
2 lb. caster sugar
1 cup water
1 can condensed milk
1 teaspoon vanilla essence

Melt butter in a saucepan. Add sugar and water. Stir over low heat till sugar is dissolved, then till boiling. Stir in condensed milk. Boil for about 20 minutes, stirring constantly, to soft ball stage, 240° F. Stir in vanilla essence. Pour into a buttered tin, 8" × 10" × 2". Cut into squares when cold. *Yield :* About 2½ lbs.

857

RUSSIAN TOFFEE

1 lb. caster sugar
1 tablespoon golden syrup
2 oz. butter
1 tablespoon red currant jelly
1 can sweetened condensed milk

Rinse saucepan with cold water. Place sugar, syrup, butter and jelly in pan. Stir over low heat till sugar is dissolved and syrup is almost boiling, then add milk. Stir constantly whilst syrup boils for about 15 minutes, till it reaches hard ball stage, 250°-270° F. Flavour if liked with a few drops of rum. Pour into a buttered tin, 8″ × 8″ × 2″. When almost cold, turn on to a slab and cut into small bars. Wrap in waxed paper. *Yield :* About 1½ lbs.

TREACLE TOFFEE

½ lb. light brown sugar
1 lb. treacle
¼ lb. unsalted butter
2 oz. minced almonds

Place sugar, treacle and butter in a saucepan. Stir over low heat till sugar is dissolved, then till boiling. Boil for 20 minutes, stirring constantly. Remove from stove. Stir in almonds. Pour into a greased tin, 8″ × 8″ × 2″. Leave till set then break up. *Yield :* About 1¾ lbs.

PULLED CANDY

There is an art in making pulled candy. You need a slab or board, a large-sized wardrobe hook, if you haven't a candy hook, and a pair of scissors. Before starting operations, grease all the equipment required. Some candy-makers like to pull candy in rubber gloves. This is a matter of taste. If you have the candy cool enough to handle, gloves are not necessary.

To Pour Candy : Pour candy that has to be pulled out fairly thinly into a shallow buttered tin, or on to a buttered marble slab. Leave there until the edges cool, and become firm, then fold the edges up to the centre. Sprinkle with colouring and flavouring to taste, and turn edges over and inward again, until the candy is cool enough to pull.

To Pull Candy : Brush the hook with melted butter, and grease your hands as well. Pull out candy in a long strip, and place it over the hook fixed at a convenient height—say shoulder level. Pull it down towards you, then fold it over the hook, and pull once more. Keep repeating this process as quickly as possible, until the candy is quite opaque. (If you are too slow, the candy will lose its pliability before it has reached the required state.) As soon as it is opaque, place it on a slab and pull it into a long narrow strip or roll about 1 inch in diameter. With oiled scissors, cut it up in 5 or 6 inch sticks, and twist the sticks, if liked, into corkscrews. If cushions are wanted cut into inch lengths.

BARLEY SUGAR

2 lb. loaf sugar
1 pint water
¾ teaspoon lemon juice
Pinch of cream of tartar
Saffron yellow to colour

Dissolve sugar in the water in a saucepan. Stir till boiling. Boil, without stirring, to between 236° and 240° F., soft ball stage. Add lemon juice, cream of tartar, and a drop or two of essence of lemon if liked. Boil to very brittle stage,

310° F., without stirring. Add a drop or two of saffron yellow colouring to taste. Pour on to a well oiled or buttered slab or platter. Leave till cool. Cut into narrow strips, with oiled scissors. Twist each into a spiral 6 inches long and 1 inch wide, with hands dipped in cold water. Leave till quite cold. Store in an air-tight tin or box.

CINNAMON BALLS

½ pint corn or golden syrup
½ lb. caster sugar
1 dessertspoon water
1 teaspoon butter
1 dessertspoon vinegar
½ teaspoon vanilla essence
½ teaspoon cinnamon essence

Place all the ingredients except the cinnamon essence in a saucepan. Stir over low heat till sugar is dissolved, then till boiling. Boil, without stirring, to brittle stage, 290° F. Remove from stove. Stir in cinnamon essence. Pour on to a buttered tin or slab. When cool enough to handle, pull until creamy and almost hard, then roll into balls in your hands.

GUNDY

3 cups golden syrup
1 cup black treacle
¾ teaspoon bicarbonate of soda
1 teaspoon lemon juice

Place syrup and treacle in a very large saucepan. Stir constantly to brittle stage, 290° F. Stir in soda and lemon juice. Pour at once on to a buttered slab. When partly cold, " pull " to a light yellow. Draw out into sticks 6-8 inches long, and cut up with oiled scissors.

TO CANDY

It is easy to candy fruit rinds, but to candy fruit successfully needs practice. Once it is candied, it can be crystallized or glazed according to taste. Cherries, cranberries, figs, peaches, pears, plums, quinces and canned apricots, peaches and pineapple, etc., can all be candied. As it takes about a fortnight to candy fruit to a commercial standard, I am giving you a simple American method.

SYRUP FOR CANDYING

1 lb. loaf sugar
1 cup water
⅓ cup corn or golden syrup

Place sugar and water in a saucepan and stir over low heat till sugar is dissolved, then till boiling. Add syrup. Stir till blended, then boil without stirring, to thread stage, 232°-234° F. Make fresh syrup for each kind of fruit.

To Prepare Fruit : Stalk figs. Peel and stone peaches and plums. Peel, core and slice pears and quinces, unless small.

CANDIED FIGS AND QUINCES : Simmer in water to cover till tender, but unbroken. Strain and use the water for making the syrup. Prepare syrup. When boiling to 234° F., drop two or three figs or quinces at a time into the syrup. Leave for a moment or two, then remove with a skimmer, allowing surplus syrup to drip back into pan. Spread on a wire rack on a tray to dry. When all stickiness disappears, pack in a glass jar or airtight tin between sheets of waxed paper.

DESSERT PEACHES, PEARS AND PLUMS : Drain off all juice. Add 1 or 2 at a time to boiling syrup. Simmer gently till clear. Lift out with a skimmer, and proceed as for figs and quinces.

CANNED APRICOTS, PEACHES AND PINEAPPLE CHUNKS AND RINGS : Drain off syrup and measure. Make up to 1 pint with water. Add 1 lb. caster sugar. Stir over low heat till dissolved, then till boiling. Place the fruit in a basin. Cover with the hot syrup. Press fruit into the syrup with a small plate or saucer so that it is submerged. Cover with a clean cloth. Leave for 24 hours, then crystallize or glaze.

CANDIED ANGELICA

Pick young, tender stalks in April, before plant flowers. Remove root ends and leaves. Cut in 5 inch lengths. Place in a basin. Dissolve 1 lb. loaf sugar in 1 pint water over low heat. Stir until dissolved, then until boiling. Pour over stalks. Cover with vine or cabbage leaves. Stand for 24 hours, then drain syrup into a saucepan. Throw away the old leaves, and use fresh ones. Bring syrup to a boil. Strain it again over the angelica stems. Cover with fresh vine or cabbage leaves. Stand for 24 hours. Keep on pouring off old syrup and covering with fresh leaves, until the angelica is quite green. Drain. Place on a wire rack in a tin. Dry in a cool oven, 110°-120° F. Store in airtight jars in a dark cupboard.

CANDIED CHESTNUTS

Peel and remove inner brown skin of chestnuts. Prepare syrup in the proportion of 1 lb. sugar to 1 cup water. Add chestnuts to boiling syrup. Bring again to boil. Simmer until tender. Drain. Roll in caster sugar. Place on a slab covered with waxed paper until cold and dry.

CANDIED ORANGE PEEL

Choose oranges with thick skins. Remove peel, either in quarters or in halves, depending on whether you use fresh fruit for candying, or fruit left over. (If using fresh fruit, halve and quarter, then remove membrane and pulp.) Place peel in a basin. Cover with cold water. Add salt in the proportion of $\frac{1}{4}$ teaspoon to 2 large oranges. When dissolved, turn into a saucepan. Bring to boil. Simmer for $\frac{1}{2}$ hour. Drain off water. Cover with fresh cold water, but omit salt. Boil till tender. Drain. Leave till cold. Scrape off any excessive pith from the rind. Cut into strips $\frac{1}{4}$ inch thick. For 3 small or 2 large oranges, allow 1 lb. loaf sugar, 1 cup hot water and $\frac{1}{4}$ cup corn or golden syrup. Place in a saucepan. Stir over low heat till sugar is dissolved, then till boiling. Add peel. Cook till very soft ball stage is reached, 230° F., when syrup should be nearly absorbed by the peel, and the peel transparent. Remove from syrup. Drain. Roll in caster sugar. *3 small or 2 large oranges will yield 6 oz. candied orange peel.*

CANDIED LEMON PEEL

Follow method given for orange peel, substituting lemons.

CRYSTALLIZED FLOWERS

Prepare a heavy syrup. Place ½ lb. loaf sugar and ¼ cup water in a saucepan. Stir over low heat till sugar is dissolved, then till boiling. Boil for 10 minutes, without stirring.

TO CRYSTALLIZE LILAC CLUSTERS : Remove stems from small clusters of purple lilac. Dip in syrup, letting surplus syrup fall back into pan. Place side by side on a slab covered with waxed paper. Protect from dust. Leave in a warm room till dry in several hours. Brush with lightly-beaten egg white. Dredge lightly with caster sugar. Dry in a sunny window.

TO CRYSTALLIZE ROSE PETALS: Dip large scented rose petals in the syrup and follow method for lilac clusters.

TO CRYSTALLIZE VIOLETS : Remove stems from sweet scented violets and follow method given for lilac clusters.

NOTE : Berries and cherries can be crystallized in the same way.

CRYSTALLIZED MINT LEAVES : Choose perfect mint leaves. Follow method given for lilac clusters.

CRYSTALLIZED ORANGE SLICES

¼ lb. caster sugar
2 tablespoons hot water
½ cup golden syrup
3 sliced oranges

Place the sugar, water and syrup in a saucepan. Stir over low heat until sugar is dissolved, and syrup comes to a boil. Boil to brittle stage, 290° F. Place the pan at once in the top of another pan containing boiling water. Impale one slice at a time on a fork. Dip in the syrup. Place in a tin covered with thickly-sugared paper, turning the slices over so as to be completely covered with sugar. Leave until cold, then sugar again.

GLACE FRUIT AND NUTS

Candied, dried, and fresh fruit or dates or figs can all be glacéd. When glazing fresh fruit, take care not to pierce the surface, or the fruit will be spoilt. Glazed fresh fruit should be prepared *only as required*. Do not attempt to glaze fruits except on a cold clear dry day:

SYRUP FOR GLAZING

You can make syrup for glazing either with sugar and water and a pinch of cream of tartar, or with sugar and water, and corn or golden syrup.

Syrup with Cream of Tartar : Place 1 lb. loaf sugar with a cup of boiling water and a saltspoon of cream of tartar in a saucepan. Stir over low heat till sugar is dissolved and syrup comes to a boil. Boil, without stirring, to very brittle stage, 295° F. Remove at once. Dip pan in a basin of cold water, then place it in a pan of warm water to keep it from hardening. Quickly dip 2 or

3 nuts, or 1 or 2 fruits at a time in the syrup with a dipping fork, then transfer to a tin covered with oiled paper.

To Glaze Fruit : Separate oranges and tangerines into sections, and leave to dry overnight before glazing. Stone cherries. Hull strawberries. Seed grapes. Remove stems from figs and stones from dates. Wash and dry clusters of currants, etc. Take 2 forks. Drop fruit, a little at a time, into syrup. Remove one by one with a fork. Drain excess syrup back into pan. Push on to a buttered or oiled slab, or baking sheet, with the second fork. Serve in small paper cases.

To Glaze Nuts : Drop 2 or 3 nuts at a time into syrup. Proceed as for fruit.

MARRONS GLACES

2 lb. chestnuts
Juice of ½ a lemon
1½ lb. loaf sugar
¾ pint water
Pinch of cream of tartar
Vanilla essence or pod
½ teaspoon glucose

Blanch chestnuts. Place in a metal basket in a saucepan of boiling water to cover. Simmer gently till tender. Drain. Transfer to a pan of warm water to cover. Add lemon juice. Leave in water till cold. Lift out and drain. Place on a rack. Leave till dry. Dissolve 1 lb. of the sugar in ½ pint of the water, stirring constantly till boiling. Add cream of tartar. Boil without stirring, to 220° F., thread stage. Add ¼ vanilla pod, or ½ teaspoon vanilla essence. Cool. Add nuts. Bring almost to boil. Keep in a warm place for 24-36 hours, then glaze. To glaze, drain nuts from syrup. Make a fresh syrup with remainder of sugar and water. Add glucose. Bring to boil. Boil without stirring, to soft ball stage, 235° F. Dip each chestnut in quickly, then place on a rack to dry. Serve in paper cases.

TOFFEE APPLES

¼ lb. butter
1 lb. treacle
1 lb. Demerara sugar
1 lb. small sweet apples

Melt butter. Add treacle and sugar. Stir over low heat until boiling, then boil without stirring for about ¼ hour, to hard ball stage, 250°-270° F. Remove from heat. Leave until slightly cool. Meanwhile, wipe apples. Remove stalks. Insert a lollipop stick at stalk end of each apple. Dip in slightly thickened toffee. Stand in a jar until set.

FRUIT AND NUT CONFECTIONS

APRICOT DELIGHT

½ oz. powdered gelatine
2 tablespoons apricot syrup
Juice of 1 lemon
½ lb. loaf sugar
Apricot purée

To make the apricot purée, soak ¼ lb. dried apricots in ¼ pint boiling water overnight. Bring to boil. Simmer gently till soft enough to rub through a hair sieve, then sieve. (There should be ¼ pint of purée.) Soak gelatine in 2 tablespoons of the syrup and the lemon juice for 5 minutes. Heat purée. Add gelatine. Stir over low heat till dissolved, then add sugar. Stir till dissolved. Bring to boil, stirring constantly. Boil for ¼ hour, stirring constantly. Pour into a small shallow wet tin. Leave till set. Cut into squares or rounds. Dip in caster sugar. Place in paper cases.

CARAMEL WALNUTS

1 lb. almond paste
½ lb. shelled walnuts
½ lb. loaf sugar
½ gill water
½ teaspoon cream of tartar

Make the almond paste with egg white and see that it is quite stiff. Shape into little balls. Place half a walnut on each side of each ball. Stand for about 24 hours, till dry. Place sugar in a saucepan. Add water and cream of tartar. Stir till dissolved and boiling, then boil till straw-coloured. Stand pan of syrup in a basin of hot water while dipping to prevent it thickening. Place each walnut, when dipped, on an oiled slab or platter. Leave till set and serve each in a paper case.

Preserving

'All methods of preserving fruit and vegetables are included in this category. Gather all fruit and vegetables for preservation when at their best in dry weather. If picked on a warm damp day, the preserve may mould, or start to ferment if you are not able to make it at once.

TO WASH FRUIT : Rinse all hard fruit in a colander under the cold water tap. Place all soft fruits in a colander. Lower this into a basin of cold water then gently raise and lower the colander in the basin so that the water covers the fruit, then drains away. Repeat this operation twice, then start preserving at once.

TO CHOOSE FRUIT

Fruit slightly under-ripe or just ripe is most suitable as its pectin content is then at its highest. If you want berries to remain whole in jam, choose fruit of equal size.

PECTINS

Perfect jam can be made from certain fruits cooked with a little water, then with sugar. The fruits used in this case are rich in pectin, such as apples, crab apples, cranberries, currants, damsons and gooseberries. Other fruit-which contain little pectin such as blackberries, cherries, peaches, pears, pines apple and strawberries need either the addition of pectin, or must be made with equal quantity of one of the fruits rich in pectin, or with the addition of citrus

Wineglasses Set for Dinner.

Coffee and Liqueur.

Lemon Squash for Buffet Parties.

Whisky and Soda.

Chocolate Egg Nog. *See page* 834.

fruit juice to make their juice thicken. If you have not been successful in making jam from apricots, greengages, loganberries, plums and raspberries add, in future, citric acid, strained lemon juice or commercial pectin. Proportions to 4 lb. fruit :—¼ oz. (1 small level teaspoon) citric acid, juice of 1 lemon, or 1 bottle of pectin.

To Make Pectin

Choose sound, washed cooking apples, gooseberries or red currants. Slice apples without paring. Place fruit and water in the proportion of 3 lb. fruit to 1 pint of water, in a preserving pan. Stew gently until into a pulp, in about ¾ hour if using apples. Mash well. Turn into a jelly bag wrung out of boiling water. Allow to drip into a basin below until the pulp is dry. Remove pulp to saucepan. Add enough water to make a mash. Simmer for 1-1½ hours, then strain as before, and add to the first extract. Bottle and sterilize in this way if not to be used at once : Bring juice to a boil and pour into hot preserving bottles, filling them up to the brim. Seal with hot lids. Place at once on a rack in a sterilizer containing enough hot water to cover jars. Bring to boiling point. Boil for 5 minutes, then remove to a wooden table out of a draught. Store when cold.

TO PREPARE JAM POTS : Wash jars in hot soapy water, then rinse in clear warm water. Place on a rack in a cold oven. Gradually heat to 250° F. Fill while hot.

Sugar

Use refined cane or beet-sugar, granulated or loaf.

Setting Point

The time to start testing for a " set " is generally a minute or two after the sugar has been dissolved and the jam comes to a boil. The two most popular methods are :

Old Fashioned Test : Remove pan from stove. Place a small teaspoon of jam on a cold plate. Cool as rapidly as possible. If ready to pot up, a skin forms over sample. Tilt plate to see if it wrinkles. If it does, it is ready. If it runs, return pan to stove. Bring again to boil and continue boiling then test again.

Thermometer Test : When you add the sugar to fruit, place thermometer in a jug of hot water. When sugar is dissolved, slip in thermometer, and boil until it registers 220° F. If you want a firmer set, boil to 222° F. Remove thermometer to a jug of hot water and pot up jam.

To Pot up Jam : Remove pan from stove the moment the setting point is reached. Quickly take off any scum with a spoon dipped in boiling water. Stir well. Fill jam pots ; place a waxed circle to fit evenly on the surface, waxed side downwards. Wipe rims carefully with a clean cloth wrung out of hot water. Proceed until all the jam is potted. Cover at once with parchment covers or cellophane damped only on the outside, then label.

NOTE : There is one exception to potting up jam in this way and that is jam containing whole fruit such as strawberry jam. It will rise in the jar if potted at once. Leave until a thin skin starts to form on surface, then stir gently, and pot and seal.

TO STORE JAM : Store in a cool, dark, dry, well-ventilated cupboard.

HINTS ON MAKING JAM

1. Remove all damaged or unripened portions of fruit before starting to make jam.
2. Use a preserving pan that, when it contains fruit, water if used, and sugar, is only half-full, so that there is no risk of the jam boiling over.
3. Cook fruit gently until broken down, with acid if included in recipe. Heat sugar slightly in the oven with door ajar. Add when fruit is ready. Stir until dissolved and boiling. Boil rapidly to setting point, stirring occasionally.
4. Do not remove scum until jam is ready.
5. You should be able to get 10 lb. jam from jam made with 6 lb. sugar.

WHY JAM GOES WRONG

1. If jam is runny, it may not have been boiled long enough, or it may be lacking in acid or pectin, or have been made with too much sugar.
2. If jam is syrupy, it has been boiled too long.
3. If jam ferments, it means under-boiling or insufficiency of sugar.
4. If jam crystallizes, this points to over-boiling.
5. If fruit rises to the top of jar, there can be two reasons for this :
    (*a*) Too rapid cooking.
    (*b*) Not cooked sufficiently.
The fruit must be simmered gently until soft, before sugar is added.
6. If jam is mouldy, this is generally caused by excessive heat or damp. Jam should not be stored near a heating system or stove. Damp moistens covers with the result that mould generally develops. Contact with the air also encourages mould. Cover as soon as made to avoid this. Lastly, insufficiency of sugar may result in mould. Allow equal quantity of sugar and fruit.

TABLE FOR SIMPLE JAMS

Apricot : 4 lb. fresh apricots, strained juice of 1 lemon, 4 lb. sugar, and $1\frac{1}{4}$ pints water. Halve apricots. Crack stones and extract kernels. Blanch kernels in boiling water. Place fruit, lemon juice and water in a saucepan. Bring to simmering point, uncovered, and simmer for 20-30 minutes, till broken up. Heat sugar and add. Stir over low heat till boiling. Boil rapidly, without stirring, for about $\frac{1}{4}$ hour, to setting point. *Yield :* 7 lb.

Black Currant : 2 lb. blackcurrants, $1\frac{1}{2}$ pints water and 3 lb. sugar. Wash, top and tail currants. Place in a saucepan with water. Bring to simmering point and cover. Simmer for 30-45 minutes. Heat sugar and add. Stir over low heat till dissolved, then till boiling. Boil rapidly for about $\frac{1}{4}$ hour, to setting point. *Yield :* 5 lb.

Damson : 3 lb. damsons, $\frac{1}{2}$ pint water and $2\frac{1}{2}$ lb. sugar. Wash fruit. Place in a saucepan. Bring to simmering point uncovered. Simmer for about 20 minutes, until broken up. Heat sugar and add. Stir till dissolved, then till boiling. Boil for about 15 minutes to setting point, removing stones while cooking. *Yield :* 5 lb.

Gooseberry : 3 lb. gooseberries, 1 pint water and 3 lb. sugar. Wash, top and tail berries, and place in a saucepan with water. Bring to simmering point, uncovered. Simmer for 20-30 minutes till broken up. Heat sugar and add. Stir over low heat till dissolved and boiling. Boil rapidly for about $\frac{1}{4}$ hour to setting point, stirring rapidly. *Yield :* 6 lb.

Greengage : 3 lb. fruit, $\frac{1}{2}$ pint water, and 3 lb. sugar. Wash fruit. Place in a saucepan with water. Bring to simmering point, uncovered, and simmer for 20-30 minutes. Heat sugar and add. Stir over low heat till dissolved, then till boiling. Boil rapidly for about 15 minutes, to setting point, removing stones while cooking. If liked add 1 oz. split blanched almonds when nearly ready. *Yield :* 5 lb.

Loganberry : 3 lb. berries, and 3 lb. sugar. Remove stalks and hulls. Place in a pan. Bring to simmering point uncovered, and simmer for about 15-20 minutes. Heat sugar and add. Stir over low heat till sugar is dissolved, then till boiling. Boil rapidly for 8-10 minutes to setting point. *Yield :* 4-5 lb.

Plum : Follow recipe for Greengage Jam.

Quince : 2 lb. quinces, 3 pints water and 3 lb. sugar. Peel, core and slice quinces. Place in a pan with water. Bring to simmering point uncovered, and simmer till soft, in $1-1\frac{1}{4}$ hours. Heat sugar and add. Stir over low heat till dissolved, then till boiling. Boil rapidly for about 10 minutes to setting point. *Yield :* $4\frac{1}{2}$ lb.

Raspberry : See Loganberry Jam.

Strawberry : 1 lb. strawberries, 2 tablespoons water, and strained juice of 1 lemon and 14 oz. sugar. Remove stalks and hulls from berries. Place with water and lemon juice in a pan. Bring to simmering point uncovered. Simmer for 15-20 minutes. Heat sugar and add. Stir over low heat till sugar is dissolved, then till boiling. Boil rapidly for 15-20 minutes to setting point. *Yield :* $1\frac{1}{2}$ lb.

BLACKBERRY AND APPLE JAM

4 lb. blackberries
½ pint water
1½ lb. peeled, cored cooking
   or crab apples
6 lb. sugar

Remove any stalks and hulls from berries. Rinse berries. Drain thoroughly. Place in a preserving pan. Add half the water. Stew gently till tender. Meanwhile slice apples into another pan. Add remaining water. Stew apples until soft. Add to blackberries with the sugar. Stir over low heat till sugar is dissolved then till boiling. Boil to setting point. Pot and seal. *Yield :* About 10 lb.

CHERRY AND REDCURRANT JAM

2 lb. cooking cherries
1 lb. picked red currants
¼ pint cold water
3 lb. heated loaf sugar

Wash cherries. Stem and wash currants. Place in a preserving pan. Add water. Bring to boil and simmer for 20 minutes. Heat sugar and add. Stir over low heat till dissolved, then till boiling. Boil rapidly for 10 minutes, then to setting point. Pot and seal.

PEACH JAM

3 lb. peaches
½ pint water
Juice of 1 lemon
2½ lb. loaf sugar

Carefully skin peaches, dipping in hot water for a moment if necessary before skinning. Place fruit, water and lemon juice in preserving pan. Simmer till tender, in about ½ hour, removing stones as they rise. Heat sugar and add. Stir till dissolved over low heat, then till boiling. Boil rapidly for about 10 minutes, to setting point. Pot and seal.

PEAR AND GINGER JAM

4 lb. pears
4 lb. sugar
2 lemons
1 dessertspoon ground ginger

Peel, core and quarter pears. Place in a bowl. Cover with sugar. Leave overnight. Turn into a preserving pan. Add grated rind and juice of the lemons and ground ginger. Stir over low heat till any remaining sugar is dissolved, then till boiling. Boil gently, stirring all the time, till fruit becomes transparent and setting point is reached. Pot and seal. *Yield:* 5-6 lbs.

PLUM AND APPLE JAM

1½ lb. cooking plums
2 lb. cooking apples
½ pint water
3 lb. sugar

Wash plums. Peel, core and slice apples. Place fruit in preserving pan. Tie the plum stones and apple cores in a muslin bag and add with water. Bring to simmering point, uncovered, and simmer for 20 minutes, then remove muslin bag. Heat sugar and add. Stir over low heat till sugar is dissolved, then till boiling. Boil rapidly for 10-15 minutes, to setting point. Pot and seal. *Yield :* 5¼ lb.

QUINCE JAM

Wash, peel and core quinces. Cut into thin slices. Place in a preserving pan. Add just enough cold water to cover. Bring to simmering point uncovered, and simmer gently until soft, stirring frequently. When soft, beat to a pulp with a wooden spoon. Weigh pulp. To each pound, allow ¾ lb. heated loaf sugar. Place sugar in a preserving pan with water, allowing ¼ pint of water to each pound of pulp. Stir over low heat until sugar is dissolved and boiling, then boil rapidly until into a syrup. Add quince pulp. Stir until boiling. Simmer until thick and smooth, and at setting point, stirring frequently as it catches easily. Pot and seal.

RASPBERRY AND REDCURRANT JAM

2 lb. raspberries
2 lb. prepared red currants
3 lb. heated loaf sugar

Pick over raspberries before weighing. Rinse and drain thoroughly. Stem currants before weighing, then pick over and rinse and drain. Place fruit in preserving pan. Add sugar. Stand in a warm place on stove till the juice begins to flow freely, and sugar is dissolved, then

868

move over direct heat, and bring slowly to the boil, stirring frequently. Boil rapidly, stirring occasionally, to setting point. Pot and seal. *Yield :* 4-5 lb.

RHUBARB JAM (MY FATHER'S)

3 oz. preserved ginger
1 large lemon
6 lb. trimmed rhubarb
6½ lb. loaf sugar

Cut up ginger into small pieces. Quarter lemon. Throw away pips. (Use red Victoria rhubarb if possible.) Cut up rhubarb into small cubes about the size of loaf sugar. Place ginger, lemon and rhubarb in a basin with the sugar. Cover closely. Soak for 3 days. Turn into preserving pan. Stir till boiling. Boil rapidly for 35 minutes, then remove lemon pieces and pot and seal. *Yield :* About 10 lb.

STRAWBERRY AND GOOSEBERRY JAM

2 lb. strawberries
1 pint gooseberry purée
3 lb. sugar

Pick over and hull strawberries. Top and tail gooseberries. Wash and drain gooseberries, then place in the top of a double boiler rinsed with cold water. Cover. Cook over hot water till reduced to a pulp, then rub through a hair sieve. Place a pint of the purée in preserving pan. Heat sugar and add. Stir over low heat till sugar is dissolved, then till boiling. Boil rapidly for 10 minutes, stirring occasionally, then add strawberries. Boil rapidly from 10-15 minutes, to setting point. Cool slightly, then stir. Pot and seal. *Yield :* About 4½ lb.

AMBER MARROW JAM

4 lb. peeled marrow
4 lb. loaf sugar
2 oz. chopped glacé ginger
Pinch of cayenne pepper
Grated rind of 2 lemons
Grated rind of 1 orange
Juice of 2 lemons and 1 orange

Cut marrow into small cubes. Place marrow and sugar in alternate layers in a large basin. Cover and stand for 24 hours. Place with ginger in preserving pan. Stir frequently till boiling. Add cayenne pepper, lemon and orange rind and juice. Simmer till marrow is tender, and jam is at setting point. Pot and seal. *Yield :* About 8 lbs.

WHEAL FRANCES TOMATO JAM

4 lb. green tomatoes
4 lb. loaf sugar
4 cups water
2 teaspoons ground ginger
4 sticks fresh angelica

Slice tomatoes. Place in a basin. Heat sugar and add with water and ginger. (If preferred, substitute 7 or 8 lumps of crushed root ginger for the ground ginger.) Cover. Stand in a cool place for 48 hours. Turn into preserving pan. Thinly slice and add the angelica. If preferred, use equal quantity of shredded angelica leaves. Stir till boiling. Boil for 20-30 minutes, stirring frequently, till ready to set. Pot and seal. *Yield :* About 5 lb.

APPLE AND APRICOT JAM

12 cooking apples
Water as required
1 lb. dried apricots
Sugar as required

Roughly slice apples. Place in a saucepan. Add only enough water to prevent burning. Bring to boil. Simmer slowly till into a pulp. Rub through a sieve. Wash, drain and cut apricots in three. Place in a basin. Cover with 2 pints water. Stand for 24 hours. Add to apple pulp and weigh. Place in a preserving pan. While bringing to the boil, weigh out sugar, in the proportion of $\frac{3}{4}$ lb. to each lb. of pulp, and heat in the oven with door open. When fruit is boiling, add sugar. Stir till dissolved, then till boiling. Boil quickly to setting point, stirring frequently. Pot and seal.

APRICOT JAM

(1)
2 lb. mashed dried apricots
4 pints water
4 lb. heated sugar
2 oz. almonds

(2)
2 lb. apricots
7 pints water
7 lb. heated sugar
3 oz. almonds

Soak apricots, in the first case for 24, and in the second case, for 48 hours in the water. At the end of that time, turn apricots and water into a preserving pan. Add sugar. Stir till dissolved, then bring to boil. Boil rapidly for about 45 minutes. Meanwhile, blanch and halve almonds, and add at the end of the 45 minutes. Continue cooking till jam sets when tested. Pot and seal.

JAMS FROM BOTTLED FRUIT

There are two different methods of making fruit bottled in water into jam. One is for making jam with fruit that needs a little cooking such as gooseberries, greengages, plums, as well as rhubarb. The other method is for fruit that requires no further cooking until after the sugar is added. This refers to blackberries, blackcurrants, and raspberries.

Blackberry Jam : Turn a 2 lb. jar of blackberries with their covering water into a saucepan. Add 1$\frac{1}{2}$ lb loaf sugar. Stir over low heat till sugar is dissolved, then till boiling. Boil rapidly for about 25 minutes, to setting point. Pot and seal. *Yield :* About 2$\frac{3}{4}$ lb.

Black Currant Jam : Turn a 2 lb. jar of black currants with their covering water into a saucepan. Add 1 lb. loaf sugar and $\frac{1}{4}$ pint water. Stir over low heat till sugar is dissolved, then till boiling. Boil rapidly for $\frac{1}{4}$ hour, to setting point. Pot and seal. *Yield :* About 1$\frac{1}{4}$ lb.

Gooseberry Jam : Turn a 2 lb. jar of gooseberries with covering water into a preserving pan. Bring to boil. Simmer for 5 minutes. Add 1$\frac{1}{4}$ lb. loaf sugar. Stir over low heat till sugar is dissolved, and till boiling. Boil rapidly to setting point, in about $\frac{1}{4}$ hour. Pot and seal. *Yield :* About 2$\frac{1}{4}$ lb.

Greengage or Plum Jam : Turn a 2 lb. jar of fruit into preserving pan. Bring to boil. Simmer for 10 minutes. Add 1 lb. loaf sugar. Stir over low heat till sugar is dissolved, then till boiling. Boil rapidly to setting point, in about 12-15 minutes. Pot and seal. *Yield :* About 1$\frac{1}{2}$ lb.

Raspberry Jam : Turn a 2 lb. jar of raspberries into preserving pan. Add $\frac{1}{4}$ pint additional water and 1$\frac{1}{4}$ lb. loaf sugar. Stir over low heat till sugar is dissolved, then till boiling. Boil rapidly till jam sets in about 10 minutes. Pot and seal. *Yield :* About 2 lb.

FRUIT CHEESE AND CONSERVES

Fruit cheese and conserves are both a form of jam. Cheese is usually made from sieved cooked berries or plums, sweetened and cooked until thick, while conserves are a cross between jam and marmalade, and are richer than both.

CRANBERRY CHEESE

2 lb. cranberries
2 cups water
1 lb. caster sugar
Pinch of salt

Pick over and wash berries. Bring water to boil. Add sugar and salt. Stir till sugar is dissolved, then till boiling. Boil syrup for 5 minutes. Add berries. Cook, uncovered, without stirring till clear, and at setting point. Skim and pot and seal.

DAMSON AND ALMOND CHEESE

6 lb. ripe damsons
4½ lb. loaf sugar
1 oz. Jordan almonds

Wipe fruit. Place in a preserving pan with enough water to cover bottom of pan. Stand in a warm place on stove but not over direct heat till juice flows, then bring to boil. Simmer till soft, then rub through a sieve. Place in pan. Add sugar. Stir over low heat till sugar is dissolved, then till boiling. Blanch and add almonds. Stir till boiling. Boil for about ½ hour, to setting point. Pot and seal.

CONSERVES

When adding nuts to conserves, stir in just before potting as cooking toughens nuts. If using almonds, dip in boiling water, then drain and shell. Leave whole or chop coarsely. If using walnuts, soak in boiling water for 3 minutes before adding. Bring quickly to boil after stirring in nuts, then pot and seal.

APRICOT CONSERVE

Wash and halve apricots. Stone. Weigh. Allow to every pound ½ cup shredded almonds and ¾ cup stoned raisins, and the weight of apricots, almonds and raisins, in caster sugar. Place apricots and raisins in a preserving pan. Stir almost to boiling. Add sugar. Stir till dissolved, then till boiling. Boil until thick, stirring constantly, then stir in almonds and brandy to taste. Pot and seal.

CHERRY CONSERVE

2 oranges
2 lb. black cherries
4 tablespoons lemon juice
1¾ lb. caster sugar

Peel and cut oranges into very thin slices, discarding any pips. Place in a small saucepan. Add enough water to cover them. Simmer gently until very tender. Stem and wash cherries. Slit

4 cloves
½ teaspoon ground cinnamon

and stone. Place in a preserving pan with orange slices and juice, lemon juice, sugar, cloves and cinnamon. Stir till sugar is dissolved, then till boiling. Boil rapidly, stirring constantly, to setting point. Remove cloves. Pot and seal. *Yield:* About 2½ lbs.

DAMSON PLUM CONSERVE

2 lb. chopped stoned damsons
2 cups water
Pulp and juice of 1 orange
1½ lb. caster sugar
Grated peel of 1 orange
½ cup stoned raisins
2 oz. chopped walnuts

Place plums in a saucepan. Add water. Bring to boil. Simmer for 20 minutes. Turn into a preserving pan. Add orange pulp and juice, sugar, orange peel, and raisins. Stir over low heat till sugar is dissolved then till boiling. Boil till thick, stirring frequently, then add nuts. Stir till boiling. Pot and seal. *Yield :* About 2½ lbs.

PEAR AND GINGER CONSERVE

8 lb. pears
4 lemons
4 lb. loaf sugar
¼ lb. preserved ginger

Wipe pears with a damp cloth, then peel, quarter, core and cut in small slices. Place in a basin. Peel lemons carefully. Cut peel into very thin strips. Strain the juice over the pears. Sprinkle with the sugar. Chop and add ginger and lemon peel. Mix lightly. Cover and stand for 12 hours. Turn into preserving pan. Stir till boiling. Simmer slowly, stirring frequently, till thick and clear in about 3 hours. Pot and seal. *Yield:* About 8 lbs.

VEGETABLE MARROW CONSERVE

5 lb. vegetable marrow
5 lb. sugar
2½ cups lemon juice
2½ gills water
Grated rind of 2 lemons
½ lb. glacé ginger

Halve marrow. Remove seeds and peel. Cut into equal-sized cubes, then weigh. Put alternate layers of marrow and sugar in a deep dish. Sprinkle with the lemon juice. Cover. Stand for 2 days. Turn into a preserving pan. Add water and lemon rind. Stir till sugar is dissolved, then till boiling. Cook slowly, stirring occasionally, to setting point. Boil for ½ hour. Chop and add ginger. When boiling, pot and seal. *Yield :* About 6 lb.

MISCELLANEOUS PRESERVES

ALMACK

3 lb. cooking apples
3 lb. cooking pears
6 lb. plums
12 lb. preserving sugar

Pare and core apples and pears. Stone plums, and cut into small pieces. Mix and cover with the sugar. Stand for 24 hours. Turn into a preserving pan. Bring to boil. Simmer for 20 minutes. Cook quickly for about 15 minutes to setting point. Pot and seal.

APPLE GINGER

7 lb. apples
4 oz. preserved ginger
7 lb. 6 oz. sugar

Wipe, peel and core apples. Place skins and cores in a preserving pan. Cover with water. Boil to a pulp. Chop apples and ginger. Place in a bowl with 6 ozs. of the sugar. Drain pulp. Return juice to pan. Add remainder of sugar. Stir over slow heat till sugar is dissolved. Add apple and ginger, and boil for about 1 hour, to setting point. Pot and seal.

TO BRANDY CHERRIES

5 lb. large black cherries
2½ lb. caster sugar
2 cups cold water
1 pint brandy

Rinse and drain cherries. Dissolve sugar in the water. Bring to boil. Boil, without stirring, till into a clear syrup in about 8 minutes. Place cherries carefully in a crock. Pour syrup over. Stand for 12 hours, then carefully drain off syrup into a saucepan. Bring slowly to a boil. Add cherries. Simmer for about 8 minutes. Remove with a perforated spoon and pack into hot jars. Cover loosely. Bring syrup again to boil. Boil till quite thick, then add brandy, and pour over cherries. Cover and seal.

FRUIT BRANDY

1 quart brandy
1 lb. strawberries
1 lb. cherries
1 lb. blackcurrants
1 lb. gooseberries
1 lb. raspberries
1 lb. sliced peeled apricots
1 lb. sliced peeled peaches
1 lb. sliced peeled pineapple
8 lb. caster sugar

Pour brandy into a stone crock. Add each fruit as it becomes ripe, with a pound of the sugar. Stand for 1 month, then after all the fruit and sugar has been added, strain and bottle. Serve fruit with ice cream. Keep liqueur in a dark cellar for 1 year before serving.

MOCK GINGER

2 vegetables marrows
Sugar as required
Lemon as required
2 tablespoons ginger essence

Wash and dry 2 ripe, but not over-ripe marrows. Cut off the outer peel rather thickly, then remove seeds and pulp. Place peel, seeds and pulp in a saucepan with just enough cold water to cover. Bring to boil. Simmer for ½ hour. Strain off liquid. Weigh marrow. Cut into blocks 2 inches long and 1 inch wide. To each lb., allow 1 lb. sugar and a cup of the marrow liquor. Place in a preserving pan. Stir over low heat until sugar is dissolved, then until boiling. Grate in the lemon rind and strain in lemon juice, allowing 1 lemon to every 2 lb. of sugar required. Add marrow and ginger essence. Stir until boiling. Simmer until marrow is transparent. Pot and seal.

SYRUPED RASPBERRIES

3 lb. raspberries
3 lb. caster sugar

Place berries in a basin. Sprinkle with the sugar. Gently crush fruit and sugar together until every berry is broken. Fill hot sterilized jars to overflowing with berries and sugar. Wipe rims. Cover. Seal. Store in a cool, dry cupboard.

JELLIES

You need the same equipment for jelly as for jam with the addition of a jelly bag with a stand if possible. If you haven't a jelly bag, you can substitute a square of cheese cloth, butter muslin or linen, taped at each corner for tying it to the legs of an upturned chair, or use a large sieve lined with 2 folds of butter muslin. Place a large pudding basin below to catch the drips. To make good jelly, you require fruit rich in acid and pectin, or you must add acid and pectin to the fruit. If pectin and acid are to be added, ripe fruit can be used, but if not, choose under-ripe fruit.

FRUIT FOR JELLIES : Crab apples, currants, gooseberries, loganberries, quinces and red currants. Blackberries, black currants and elderberries also make excellent jelly when combined with cooking or crab apples. Other fruits can also be made into jelly, but it is not advisable, as they will not set unless a large proportion of acid and pectin is added which affects the flavour of the fruit.

TO CHOOSE FRUIT : To get the finest jelly, choose a mixture of ripe and under-ripe fruit in the proportion of ¼ lb. under-ripe fruit to ¾ lb. ripe fruit.

TO PREPARE HARD FRUIT : Prepare as for jam. Slice without peeling or coring, except for quinces which should be cored.

TO PREPARE SOFT FRUIT : Rinse and leave stems on soft fruits. Crush or mash in pan to start flow of juice.

TO PREPARE STONE FRUIT: Wash and halve.

PERFECT FRUIT JELLY should be clear and sparkling, and should have the fresh flavour and colour of the fruit. It must be soft enough to scoop out easily with a spoon yet set enough to hold its shape when turned out.

TO MAKE JELLY

BASIC : Place fruit in preserving pan with water, the quantity depending on the kind of fruit. Juicy berries or red currants require very little water, or none at all. Black currants and hard fruit need more water in order to soften the skins. The general rule for hard fruit is to cover it with water. Simmer very slowly until fruit is quite tender or into a pulp. Pour into a scalded jelly bag, and let the juice drop without squeezing or shaking the bag, or mashing the fruit, until the drips cease. (If you do squeeze or shake bag, or mash fruit, jelly will be cloudy.) Rinse pan. Add juice. Bring to boiling point. Draw pan to side. Add sugar. (Allow ¾ lb. of sugar to every pint of juice unless fruit is very acid, when allow 1 lb. of sugar to each pint of juice. Always heat sugar in a slow oven with door open before adding to juice.) Stir until sugar is dissolved, and syrup comes to a boil. Boil rapidly to setting point, 220°-222° F., depending on how stiff a jelly is wanted. Skim. Pour into heated jars. Cover with waxed circles and seal at once. Do not move jars until jelly is set. Store in a dark, cool airy cupboard.

HINTS ON MAKING JELLY

1.   Juicy fruits such as berries or grapes should be placed in a wet pan. Add no water. Heat slowly until the juice starts to flow, then simmer until soft.
2.   Heat sugar slightly in oven with door ajar before adding to hot juice.
3.   Wash jars in soapy water, then rinse in hot water. Drain quickly, then fill to within $\frac{1}{4}$ inch of the top. Cover and seal at once.
4.   2 lb. fruit yields about 2 cups of juice.
5.   To get perfect jelly, cook only a small quantity at a time, say a quart. Boil this rapidly for 5 minutes. Skim if necessary, then add sugar.

JELLY-MAKING FAULTS

1.   If you boil too slowly after the sugar is added, the pectin may break down and the mixture turn syrupy.
2.   If too little sugar is used, the jelly will not set. If too much sugar is added, it will become syrupy and will not set.
3.   If you squeeze the bag or mash the fruit when extracting the juice, the jelly will be cloudy. It will also cloud if over-cooked.
4.   If it crystallizes, this may be caused by too much sugar or by using over-cooked juice.
5.   Mould is sometimes caused by using damp jars, or by leaving jelly uncovered for some time after it has been potted, or by storing in a damp cupboard.

TO FLAVOUR JELLIES

Apple, crab apple and gooseberry jelly can be flavoured if liked with elderflowers or sprigs of lemon verbena, or rose geranium. Drop 2 or 3 sprigs into the boiling syrup just a minute or two before setting point is reached. Remove before potting.

APPLE JELLY

BASIC RECIPE :
4 lb. cooking apples
2 quarts cold water
Sugar as required

Wash and remove any bruised parts from apples before weighing. Without coring, or peeling, cut into thick slices. Place in a saucepan. Add water. Boil, until mushy, mashing occasionally with a spoon. Pour into a jelly bag. Strain without mashing fruit, until all the juice has dripped into a basin below. Measure juice. Place in a preserving pan. Add sugar, allowing 1 lb. sugar to each pint of juice. Stir over low heat till sugar is dissolved. Bring to boil. Boil rapidly without stirring, for 20-30 minutes, to setting point. Pot and seal.

APPLE AND CRANBERRY JELLY : Follow above recipe, substituting 2 lb. of cranberries for 2 lb. of the apples. Serve for breakfast or with cold lamb, mutton or pork.

APPLE AND ELDERBERRY JELLY : Follow above recipe, substituting 2 lb. elderberries for 2 lb. of the apples. Serve with hare in place of red currant jelly.

APPLE AND ORANGE JELLY : Wash 4 lb. bitter oranges, 3 lb. sweet oranges and

3 lb. cooking or crab apples. Quarter. Remove piths and pips. Place in a preserving pan. Cover with cold water. Simmer gently for 1½ hours, then strain and follow basic recipe.

SPICED APPLE JELLY : Follow basic recipe, but add 6 cloves with the water. Strain before potting.

NOTE : If you want amber-coloured apple jelly, choose pale-coloured fruit. If you want claret-coloured jelly, choose very red apples.

GOOSEBERRY JELLY : Place berries in a saucepan. Cover with cold water. Boil to a mush. Measure juice. Rinse pan. Pour in juice. Add sugar, 1 lb. to each pint of juice. Follow basic recipe.

BAR-LE-DUC : Pour 1 pint of gooseberry juice into a preserving pan. Add 3 lb. loaf sugar. Stir over low heat till sugar is dissolved, then bring slowly to boil. Skim carefully. Boil for 5 minutes. Drop in 1 lb. topped and tailed perfect gooseberries. Simmer for 5 minutes. Remove carefully from syrup without breaking them to hot sterilized small pots. Boil syrup for 5 minutes. Skim well. Strain through a pointed strainer lined with butter muslin. Leave till cold, then cover and seal.

BLACKBERRY AND APPLE JELLY

2 lb. blackberries
2 lb. crab apples
½ pint cold water
Sugar as required

Wash berries. Wash and slice apples, without peeling or coring. Place fruit and water in a preserving pan. Simmer till tender, mashing with a wooden spoon. When into a mush, strain. Measure. Allow ¾ lb. sugar to each pint of fruit. Place juice and sugar in rinsed pan. Stir till sugar is dissolved, then till boiling. Boil quickly without stirring, for about 10 minutes, to setting point. Pot and seal.

CURRANT AND RASPBERRY JELLY

4 quarts red currants
2 quarts raspberries
Sugar as required

Pick over currants but do not stem them. Place with raspberries in a preserving pan. Mash with a wooden potato masher. Cook slowly till currants are almost white, then strain through a jelly bag. Measure juice. Rinse pan and add juice. Weigh out 1 lb. sugar for each pint of juice. Boil for 5 minutes, without stirring. Add sugar. Stir over low heat till sugar is dissolved, then till boiling. Boil without stirring, for 3 minutes, then skim. Pot and seal.

ELDERBERRY JELLY

4 lb. elderberries
½ cup lemon juice
3¼ lb. loaf sugar
1 bottle liquid pectin

Remove large stems from berries. Place berries in a saucepan. Mash with a wooden spoon. Heat slowly till juice begins to flow. Simmer, covered, for ¼ hour. Strain through a jelly bag. Rinse pan. Measure juice and pour into pan. There should be 3½ cups. Strain in lemon juice. Add sugar. Bring rapidly to a boil after sugar is dissolved. Add pectin, stirring constantly, until boiling rapidly again. Boil rapidly for ½ a minute. Remove pan from stove. Skim. Pot and seal. *Yield :* Fully 4 lb.

GRAPE JELLY

4 lb. crushed acid grapes
1 pint water
Sugar as required

Place grapes and water in a preserving pan. (Thinnings of Muscatel grapes make delicious jelly.) Heat to boiling point. Simmer till the seeds are free from the fruit, then strain through a jelly bag and measure. To every cup of juice, allow 5 oz. sugar. Heat juice to boiling point, then add sugar. Stir without boiling till dissolved, then boil to setting point. Skim. Pot and seal.

MINT JELLY

½ peck cooking apples
Cold water as required
Sugar as required
2 oz. fresh mint leaves
2 tablespoons lemon juice
2 or 3 drops sap green

Wipe apples. Remove blossom ends then quarter. Place in a preserving pan. Barely cover with cold water. Simmer gently till soft. Strain and measure juice. Pour into pan. Bring to boil. Boil rapidly for 5 minutes, then add sugar, allowing 1 lb. to 1 pint juice. Stir over low heat till dissolved, then till boiling. Boil rapidly for 2 minutes. Add mint leaves. Boil to setting point. Stir in lemon juice and sap green. Strain into heated pots. Pot and seal.

NOTE : If liked, mince mint leaves finely before adding and do not strain. (*See illustration facing page* 448.) Jellies are topped with slices of hard-boiled egg and radish roses, for serving with cold ham.

QUINCE JELLY

2¼ lb. quinces
4½ cups cold water
2 tablespoons lemon juice
3¼ lb. sugar
½ bottle liquid pectin

Wash quinces. Remove blossom and stem ends. Put fruit through a meat grinder. Place in preserving pan. Add water. Cover. Simmer for ¼ hour. Strain through a jelly bag. Add lemon juice, then measure. (There should be 4½ cups juice.) Place in preserving pan. Add sugar. Stir over low heat till dissolved, then bring quickly to boiling point. Add pectin, stirring constantly. Boil rapidly for ½ minute. Remove from heat. Skim. Pot and seal. *Yield :* About 4½ lb.

RED CURRANT JELLY

4 lb. red currants
½ pint water
3 lb. sugar

Wash fruit only if essential. Strip off coarse stalks from currants with a fork. Crush fruit and add water. Bring to boil. Cover and simmer for 10 minutes until skins are soft. Turn into a jelly bag and allow the juice to drain. Put sugar and 2½ pints of juice in a large saucepan, and stir over low heat till sugar is dissolved. Bring rapidly to a boil. Add a small knob of butter. Bring to a full rolling boil, stirring constantly. Boil hard for 1 minute. Remove from heat. Skim if necessary. Pour into clean, hot, dry jars. Seal at once.

FRUIT BUTTERS

A fruit butter is a sweetened and spiced fruit purée, first cousin to our fruit cheese, usually made of fresh fruit such as apple, peaches, pears, plums, quinces and tomatoes. Apple butter is a great favourite in the United States.

To Make Fruit Butter

Wash fruit and cut off any damaged or unripe portions. Cut up. Place in a saucepan. Add cold water to cover, when making butter of hard fruits. If using grapes, plums or tomatoes, crush and cook in their own juice. Stew slowly until soft, then rub through a fine sieve. Measure purée. To each $1\frac{1}{2}$ cups allow $\frac{1}{2}$ lb. sugar, according to sweetness of fruit. Add flavouring to taste, such as grated lemon rind and juice, or a bag of allspice berries, whole cloves and cinnamon stick. Add 1 saltspoon salt to each quart of butter. Add sugar. Stir till dissolved and boiling. Boil rapidly, stirring contantly, for fruit butter " catches " very easily, until the butter becomes fairly thick, then lower heat and continue to cook, stirring constantly. When ready, there will be no sign of liquid round the edge. To test, lift a spoonful of the butter about a foot above the saucepan, then pour it back into pan. When ready, it starts to pour off the spoon like water, then forms two " streams," which join up in a thin sheet and finally curl away from spoon, leaving it clean. Remove spice bag, if used, and pour into hot sterilized pots. Seal.

Hints on Making Fruit Butter

1. Cider can be used in place of water when making apple butter.
2. Combined fruits, such as apples with grape juice, plums or quinces make good butter.
3. If purée is very thin after sieving fruit, return to pan and cook until thick enough to heap up on a spoon before measuring and adding sugar.
4. Fruit butter can be made from the pulp left over from fruit cooked for jelly. Measure. Allow $\frac{1}{2}$ cup water to each 2 cups pulp. Simmer for 10 minutes. Rub through a sieve.
5. If preferred, substitute ground mixed spice for the whole spices, allowing $1\frac{1}{2}$ teaspoons to 4 quarts of fruit butter.

APPLE BUTTER : Place 4 quarts sliced, peeled cooking apples, and 2 quarts cider in a saucepan. Stir occasionally till boiling. Cook, stirring frequently, till well blended, then add $1\frac{1}{4}$ lb. light brown or granulated sugar, $\frac{1}{2}$ teaspoon ground cloves, and 1 teaspoon ground cinnamon. Stir over low heat till sugar is dissolved, then till boiling. Pot and seal.

APPLE AND GRAPE BUTTER : Place 3 cups sieved, washed grapes, 3 cups sieved, stewed apple and $1\frac{1}{2}$ lb. caster sugar in a preserving pan. Stir over low heat till sugar is dissolved, then till boiling. Pot in hot sterilized jars and seal. *Yield :* About 2 lb.

APPLE AND TOMATO BUTTER : Wipe 2 lb. cooking apples and 4 lb. ripe tomatoes with a damp cloth. Slice without peeling. Place in a preserving pan with 2 pints cider. Stir occasionally till boiling. Simmer till into a pulp. Sieve. Rinse pan. Pour in pulp. Add 1 lb. caster or brown sugar, and ground cinnamon, cloves or ginger to taste. Stir till sugar is dissolved, then till boiling. Stir frequently till mixture draws away from sides of pan. Pack into hot sterilized jars and seal.

PLUM BUTTER : Wash and slice 4 lb. sound plums into a saucepan. Cover with water. Simmer till tender. Sieve. The purée should be thick enough to round up on the spoon. If not, cook till this consistency is reached. Measure. Add sugar, allowing $\frac{2}{3}$ cup to each cup of purée. (If wanted spiced, add $1\frac{1}{2}$ teaspoons ground cinnamon and $\frac{1}{2}$ teaspoon ground cloves.) Bring to boil, stirring constantly, then cook, stirring frequently till mixture shrinks from sides of pan. Pot and seal.

FRUIT CURDS

Fruit curds can be served in place of jam at tea time, or used as a filling for tartlet cases or sponge sandwiches, Swiss rolls, etc. *Do not allow to come to boil.*

APPLE CURD

½ lb. cooking apples
½ lb. caster sugar
2 lemons
2 oz. butter
2 eggs

Wash apples. Peel, core and slice into a saucepan. Cover. Stew to a mush. Sieve. Place in the top of a double boiler. Reheat. Add sugar. Stir till dissolved. Wash lemons. Grate in rind, and strain in juice. Add butter. Beat eggs, and add. Place over hot water. Stir till thick but do not allow to boil. Pot and seal.

APRICOT CURD

1½ lb. fresh apricots
Juice of 2 lemons
Grated rind of 1 lemon
1 lb. loaf sugar
½ lb. unsalted butter
2 beaten eggs
1 beaten egg yolk

Wipe, halve, stone and roughly chop apricots. Place in top of a double boiler, rinsed with water. Cover. Cook over boiling water till soft. Rub through a sieve. Rinse top of boiler. Add purée, lemon juice, lemon rind and sugar. Stir over water till sugar is dissolved. Stir in butter, eggs, and egg yolk. Stir till thick but don't allow to boil. Pot and seal.

BANANA CURD

10 bananas
2 oz. caster sugar
½ a lemon
¼ orange
1 inch cinnamon stick
3 cloves
2 oz. butter
2 beaten eggs

Peel bananas, and remove threads. Place sugar in the top of a double boiler. Grate in lemon and orange rinds, and strain in juice. Tie cinnamon stick and cloves in a tiny piece of boiled muslin and add with butter. Stir over boiling water till butter is melted, then remove pan from heat. Gradually beat in eggs. Return pan to stove. Stir till blended and hot, but not boiling. Mash and add bananas. Cook over reduced heat for 10 minutes, then rub through a fine sieve, or strainer, into dry hot jars. Leave till cold, then seal.

LEMON CURD

2 oz. butter
½ lb. caster sugar
2 lemons
3 beaten eggs

Place the butter and sugar in top of a double boiler. Grate in rind of 1 lemon. Strain in juice of both. Stir in egg. Cook over water at boiling point, stirring constantly, till thick, but do not allow to boil. Pot and seal.

MARMALADES

Marmalade can be made from any fruit. On the Continent and in Central Europe, apricot and peach marmalade are most popular. In Britain and the Commonwealth, marmalades made of citrus fruits are more favoured.

HINTS ON MARMALADE MAKING

1. Wash all fruit thoroughly before using.
2. It is a good idea to soak the peel in the water overnight before starting to cook it.
3. Warm sugar in the oven with door open.
4. Heat the jars, see page 865.
5. Cook the fruit in the water over very slow heat in an open pan, and see that it is absolutely soft before adding sugar.
6. Be sure all the sugar is dissolved before you bring marmalade to the boil.
7. If a dark-coloured marmalade is wanted, substitute Demerara sugar for loaf sugar.
8. Skim. Let marmalade stand for 5 minutes, then stir gently before potting, otherwise the peel may rise to the top of jars. Seal at once.
9. Be sure to store marmalade in a cool, dry, dark airy cupboard. If the cupboard is too warm, marmalade will ferment. If damp, it may become mouldy.

DUNDEE MARMALADE

1 lb. Seville oranges
1 lemon
2 pints water
2 lb. heated loaf sugar

Wash oranges and lemon thoroughly. Place in a saucepan. Add water. Cover. Simmer for about 1½ hours, until the skins are so soft that you can pierce them. Remove oranges and lemon. Leave until cool, then slice neatly. Place pips in the juice. Boil steadily for 10 minutes, then skim out pips and add the fruit pulp. Bring to boil. Stir in sugar. When dissolved, stir until boiling, then boil rapidly without stirring, to setting point, in about 20 minutes (220° F.). *Yield :* About 3½ lb.

GRAPEFRUIT MARMALADE

4 lb. grapefruit
2 large lemons
6 pints water
10 lb. preserving sugar

Remove peel from grapefruit and slice as finely as possible. Remove pips from grapefruit and lemons. Tie in a muslin bag and put to soak in a pint of the cold water for 24 hours. Peel lemons, throwing away peel, and slice up fruit and grapefruit. Place in a pan with the grapefruit peel. Cover with remainder of water, and stand for 24 hours. Place over a low heat. Squeeze water from pips and add to fruit. Simmer for ½ hour, then add sugar. Stir over low heat till sugar is dissolved, then till boiling. Boil until marmalade sets when tested, 220° F. Pot and seal.

JELLIED ORANGE MARMALADE

7 lb. Seville oranges or 6 lb. Seville and 1 lb. sweet
2 lemons
1 gallon cold water
9 lb. loaf sugar

Wash and dry fruit carefully. Peel off rinds very thinly. Take only the rinds of half the oranges, but both the lemons. Either grate them, or peel and then finely shred them. Remove all pith from fruit and throw away. Slice fruit into a large preserving pan. Add pips and cold water, then the prepared rinds tied in a muslin bag. (Throw away the other half of orange rinds.) Bring contents of pan to the boil. Simmer for 2 hours, stirring often with a wooden spoon, then remove muslin bag. Lay it aside in a basin. Pour contents of pan into a jelly bag. Allow liquid to drip through into a deep jar or basin beneath till pulp is dry in bag. If liquid has boiled away too much add boiling water to it to make up the quantity remaining to 8 lb. in weight. Weigh pan, then weigh in liquid. If the liquid has boiled away, pour the boiling water added through the pulp, so as to extract as much of the orange flavour as possible. Now throw away the pulp. Place juice together with contents of muslin bag and any liquid beside it in the basin back in the pan. Add sugar. Stir frequently till sugar is dissolved, then bring to boil. Skim and boil for ½ hour. Pot and seal.

LEMON MARMALADE

10 lemons
Water as required
4-5 lb. sugar

Scrub lemons. Place in a preserving pan. Cover with cold water, and boil for ¾ hour. Change the water twice during this process, replacing with fresh boiling water. Remove lemons and pour the last water into a basin. Quarter lemons. Remove rinds. Pare off pith, and cut the rinds into narrow strips. Cut these again into small pieces. Remove pips from pulp and chop pulp finely. Weigh pulp and the chopped rind, and to every pound, allow 2 lb. sugar and 1 pint of the water in which lemons were boiled. Put water and sugar into pan. When boiling, add pulp and chopped rind. Boil for ½ hour, to setting point, 220° F. Pot and cover.

LIME MARMALADE

6 limes
Water and sugar as required

Wash limes thoroughly. Place in a saucepan. Cover with cold water. Simmer for 2 hours, changing the water thrice during the time. Turn into a basin. When cool, cut into very thin slices and measure. For each ½ pint of fruit, allow 1 pint of water and 1 lb. of loaf sugar. Place the fruit, water and sugar in a preserving pan. Stir over low heat till sugar is dissolved, then until boiling. Cook, stirring constantly, until setting point is reached, 220° F., in about ¾ hour. Pot in hot sterilized jars, and seal. *Yield :* About 3 lb.

ORANGE MARMALADE FROM PULP

1 can of orange pulp (10 lb.)
10 lb. sugar

As the pulp has been thoroughly processed, $\frac{1}{2}$ hour boiling is generally sufficient, that is after the sugar has been added and stirred till dissolved. However, after boiling for $\frac{1}{2}$ hour, test marmalade in the usual way to see whether it is setting properly, 220° F. If marmalade is too bitter, the addition of the juice of 2 sweet oranges will soften the flavour. Pot and seal.

PINEAPPLE AND GRAPEFRUIT MARMALADE

1 Cape pineapple
1 grapefruit
1 lemon
Cold water as required
Sugar as required

Pare and shred pineapple, then cut grapefruit and lemon into quarters, and slice thinly. Measure fruit and cover with water, allowing 3 pints of water to every pint of fruit. Cover. Set aside until the next day, when boil for 3 or more hours, until rind is tender. Leave again until the next day. Measure and add an equal amount of sugar, then boil until thickened. Pot and seal.

QUINCE MARMALADE

Peel, core and slice quinces. Place in a preserving pan with just enough cold water to cover. Bring to simmering point. Simmer gently till fruit is soft, stirring frequently. Beat to a pulp with a wooden spoon, then weigh. To each lb. of pulp, weigh out $\frac{3}{4}$ lb. of sugar. Place the sugar in a preserving pan with water, allowing $\frac{1}{4}$ pint to each lb. of sugar used. Stir over slow heat till sugar is dissolved, then boil rapidly until it becomes a syrup. Add quince pulp, and boil very slowly till thick and smooth. Stir frequently to prevent burning. When at setting point, 220° F., pot and seal.

MINCEMEATS

Though mincemeat is now on sale all the year round, the housewife generally makes her own shortly before Christmas. It should be made at least a month before it is required, to allow the flavour to develop. Prepare all the fruit as you would for a cake.

APRICOT MINCEMEAT

$\frac{1}{2}$ lb. glacé apricots
1 lb. cooking apples
1 lb. currants
1 lb. raisins
1 lb. sultanas
2 oz. glacé cherries
$\frac{1}{2}$ lb. candied peel
2 oz. almonds
1 lb. shredded suet

Chop apricots. Peel, core and chop apples. Clean currants and sultanas and stone and chop raisins. Chop or quarter cherries. Use equal quantity lemon, orange and citron peel. Put with the almonds through a mincer. Mix the fruit, peel and nuts together, then stir in remainder of ingredients. Stir till blended. Cover. Stand for

¼ teaspoon ground mace
1 teaspoon mixed spice
½ lb. Barbados sugar
Grated rind of 1 lemon
Juice of 1 lemon
¼ pint brandy

2 days, then pack tightly into sterilized jars and seal like jam. *Yield:* About 8 lbs.

DUNDEE MINCEMEAT

1½ lb. cooking apples
1 lb. currants
¼ lb. glacé cherries
1 lb. stoned raisins
½ lb. mixed candied peel
2 oz. blanched almonds
1 lb. Demerara sugar
¾ lb. shredded suet
1 saltspoon salt
¼ teaspoon ground mace
½ teaspoon mixed spice
¼ teaspoon ground ginger
½ nutmeg, grated
Juice of 1 orange
1 lemon
¼ pint brandy or rum

Prepare fruit, peel and nuts as described for Apricot Mincemeat. Add sugar, suet, salt and spices. Strain in orange juice. Grate in lemon rind. Strain in lemon juice. Stir in brandy or rum. Stir till thoroughly blended. Cover. Stand for 2 days. Stir and pack tightly in sterilized jars, then seal. *Yield:* About 7 lbs.

Chutneys, Relishes and Sauces

Chutneys and relishes are high-seasoned, highly spiced condiments, usually served with curries and cold meats, but whereas chutneys are of a sauce-like consistency, many relishes set like jam.

EQUIPMENT REQUIRED

Aluminium, enamel-lined, *without chips*, or monel metal saucepan. (Never use brass or copper saucepans for chutneys, relishes or sauces.) Wooden spoon ; hair sieve (do not use a metal sieve, as it imparts a metallic flavour) ; bottles with tightly fitting corks or jars with synthetic skin covers, or jars used for bottling with screwed-down glass lids. Etc., etc.

Corks : When using bottles with cork covers, boil corks first. Line with greaseproof or waxed paper cut to fit, and insert in bottles. When the preserve is cold, dip the necks of bottles in melted paraffin wax so as to make bottles airproof.

Metal Covers : If forced to use metal covers, line them with vinegar-proof discs on sale for the purpose, or pour a layer of melted fat or wax on top of pickle before putting on covers so that the vinegar never comes in contact with the metal.

Paper Covers : They are not very suitable if used like jam covers, unless the preserve is to be eaten quickly. If kept for any length of time, a slight evaporation will occur with the result that the contents shrink. This can be prevented by tying a round of muslin cut to fit and dipped in melted wax, over the top of the paper cover.

Synthetic Skin : Follow instructions supplied with this.

To Prepare Jars : Unless catering for a large family, it is better to use small jars for chutneys and relishes. Wash jars in hot soapy water, then rinse in clear warm water. Place an inch apart on a rack in a cold oven. Heat gradually to 250° F. Fill while still hot.

Vinegar : Use unspiced vinegar of a good quality, for chutneys, relishes and sauces, bottled for preference. Pure malt vinegar and spirit vinegar are best owing to their flavour and greater purity.

To Store : After writing the name of the preserve with the date on each label, label neatly. Store in a cool, dry, dark airy cupboard. Keep preserves for at least 3 or 4 months before using.

CHUTNEYS

You can make chutneys from any kind of acid fruit, or from a combination of acid and dried fruit. Apples, apples and bananas, apples and tomatoes, elderberries, gooseberries, green, and ripe tomatoes, and rhubarb, are all suitable. Choose sound firm fruit, just ripe. Mince or slice finely. Simmer gently in *open* saucepan as long slow cooking is necessary to soften the fruit and other solid ingredients, stirring occasionally at the beginning, and almost constantly towards the end, to prevent burning. If a smooth chutney is wanted rub through a hair sieve, then reheat. Pot and seal.

If you find, on opening a pot of chutney, that the chutney is runny, this means that you haven't cooked it long enough, or you have cooked the fruit or vegetable too quickly. Good chutney should be thick but pourable. The pulp and liquid should not separate when pouring out.

APPLE CHUTNEY

2 lb. cooking apples
1 or 2 lb. onions
1 pint malt vinegar
10 oz. light brown sugar
½ oz. ground ginger
½ oz. mustard seed
2 oz. salt
¼ teaspoon cayenne pepper
¾ lb. cleaned sultanas

Peel and quarter apples. Place in an earthenware casserole. Peel, chop and add onions. Pour in vinegar. Cover. Stew in a slow oven, 300° F., till into a pulp. Stir well. Rub through a hair sieve. Place sugar, ginger, mustard seed, salt and cayenne pepper in a dry crock. Add half the sultanas. Grind and add remainder. Pour in hot chutney. Stir well. Cover. Stir daily for a week. Pot and seal. *Yield :* 4½ to 5 lbs.

APRICOT CHUTNEY

1½ lb. fresh apricots
10 oz. picked sultanas
1 lb. peeled onions
2 teaspoons salt
2 oz. chopped crystallized ginger
1 pint vinegar
1 oz. mustard seed
3 teaspoons ground ginger

Wipe, halve and stone apricots. Wash, drain and either chop sultanas with onion, or put both through a meat grinder if preferred. Place in a saucepan. Add salt, ginger, vinegar, mustard seed, ground ginger, sugar, paprika and turmeric. Stir over low heat till sugar is dissolved, then until boiling. Simmer for ¾ to 1 hour, stirring fre-

¾ lb. Barbados sugar
Dash of paprika
1 teaspoon turmeric

quently, till thick enough. Pot and seal. *Yield :* About 4½ lbs.

BANANA AND DATE CHUTNEY

1 lb. chopped mild onions
½ lb. chopped dates
6 peeled bananas
1½ cups malt vinegar
¼ lb. minced crystallized ginger
1 teaspoon salt
1 teaspoon curry powder
½ lb. chopped raisins
2 cups fruit syrup

Place onion and dates in a saucepan. Remove threads from bananas. Put through a meat grinder and add with vinegar. Stir frequently till boiling. Simmer gently for 20 minutes. Add remainder of ingredients, using the syrup from apricot, peaches or pears bottled in syrup. Stir till boiling. Simmer, stirring frequently, until thick. Pot and seal like bottled fruit. *Yield :* 2 quarts.

GOOSEBERRY AND RHUBARB CHUTNEY

1 lb. green gooseberries
1 lb. trimmed rhubarb
1 lb. cleaned sultanas
3 tablespoons minced onion
1 clove garlic, minced
2 oz. ground ginger
2 lb. Barbados sugar
1 teaspoon salt
1 quart malt vinegar

Top, tail, rinse, drain and halve berries. Remove any strings from rhubarb, and cut in half-inch lengths. Wash sultanas, and drain well. Put through a meat grinder. Place all in a saucepan with remaining ingredients. Stir over low heat till sugar is dissolved, then till boiling. Simmer, stirring frequently, till thick. Pot and seal. *Yield :* About 5 lbs.

GREEN FIG CHUTNEY

¾ lb. green figs
8 oz. green tomatoes
8 oz. cooking apples
4 oz. peeled shallots
3 oz. cleaned sultanas
¼ lb. light brown sugar
½ oz. salt
Dash of cayenne pepper
½ teaspoon ground ginger
¾ pint vinegar

Wash and cut up figs and tomatoes. Peel, core and slice apples. Slice shallots. Place all the ingredients in a saucepan. Stir over low heat till sugar is dissolved, and mixture is boiling. Simmer till thick and tender. Pot and seal. *Yield :* About 2 lbs.

GREEN TOMATO CHUTNEY

3 lb. green tomatoes
1 lb. sliced peeled onions
1 lb. peeled cooking apples
1 lb. light brown sugar
2 peeled cloves of garlic
6 peeled shallots
1 bay leaf
1 sprig parsley
1 sprig rosemary
1 sprig thyme
2 teaspoons ground cinnamon
½ teaspoon ground cloves
Dash cayenne pepper
1 quart vinegar

Wipe and slice tomatoes into a saucepan. Add onions. Core and slice in apples. Add remaining ingredients. Stir over low heat till sugar is dissolved, then till boiling. Simmer gently till the mixture is almost " boiled in," stirring frequently. Remove bay leaf, parsley, rosemary and thyme. Leave till cold. Pot and seal. *Yield :* About 6 lbs.

RHUBARB CHUTNEY

4 lb. rhubarb
¾ lb. raisins
1 lb. apples
1 lb. onions
2 lb. light brown sugar
1 oz. salt
1 teaspoon ground allspice
1 teaspoon ground ginger
1 oz. mustard seed
1½ pints vinegar

Wash and trim rhubarb. Cut into small pieces. Place in saucepan. Stone and add raisins. Peel, core, slice and add apples. Peel, slice and add onions. (If liked onions, apples and raisins can be put through a meat grinder.) Stir in remaining ingredients. Stir over low heat till sugar is dissolved, then till boiling. Simmer, stirring frequently, till thick. *Yield :* About 5 lbs.

CELERY RELISH

1½ cups shredded celery
4 teaspoons caster sugar
1 teaspoon salt
½ teaspoon made mustard
¼ cup vinegar

Mix all ingredients together in order given. Cover closely. Stand in a cold place for 1½ hours. Drain. Serve with cold roast duck, goose, ham, pork or veal. *Yield:* Fully ½ pint.

CHICAGO HOT RELISH

1 peck ripe tomatoes
1 pint chopped onion
1 pint chopped celery
2 green peppers
4 sweet red peppers
1 cup white mustard seed
1 lb. caster sugar
2 dessertspoons mixed spice
⅔ cup salt
3 pints vinegar

Scald and peel tomatoes. Chop and place in a colander. Drain for 2 hours. Place in a basin. Add onion and celery. Slit and remove seeds from green and red peppers. Mince peppers. Add to tomatoes with mustard seed and remaining ingredients. Mix well. Cover. Stand for 12 hours. Stir again. Pack into jars and seal. Store in a very cold place. *Yield :* About 8 lbs.

GREEN TOMATO RELISH

3 lb. chopped green tomatoes
3 tablespoons chopped onion
3 teaspoons black peppercorns
1 teaspoon whole cloves
2½ tablespoons mustard seed
1 blade of mace
6 oz. caster sugar
1 teaspoon salt
1¼ gills hot vinegar

Mix the tomato with the onion in a basin. Cover and stand for 1 hour. Drain. Place tomato and onion in a saucepan. Tie peppercorns, cloves, mustard seed and mace in a small muslin bag and add with sugar, salt and vinegar. Stir over slow heat till sugar is dissolved, then till boiling. Boil for 10 minutes. Remove bag. Pot in hot jars. Seal at once. *Yield :* About 3 pints.

HORSERADISH RELISH

4 cups grated horseradish
2 cups vinegar
¾ teaspoon salt

Use sound sticks of horseradish. Grate into a basin. Add vinegar and salt. Stir till salt is dissolved. Pack up to the rim in small sterilized jars. Seal tightly. Serve with cold beef, corned beef or silverside. *Yield :* About 2¼ pints.

RED CABBAGE RELISH

1 cup shredded red cabbage
1 saltspoon mustard seed
2 tablespoons vinegar
½ teaspoon celery seed
¼ teaspoon salt
1 tablespoon brown sugar

Mix all ingredients together. Keep for at least a week before serving. Serve with cold roast duck or goose or with cold pork or pork pie.

RIPE TOMATO RELISH

8 cups chopped tomatoes
1 cup shredded celery
¾ cup chopped onion
½ cup chopped green pepper
1½ teaspoons salt
2 tablespoons sugar
¾ tablespoon mustard seed
¼ teaspoon grated nutmeg
¼ teaspoon ground cinnamon
1 saltspoon ground cloves
1 cup vinegar

Place all ingredients in a basin. Stir till well blended. Pour into jars and seal. Store in a cold place. Will keep fresh for at least a fortnight. *Yield :* Between 2 and 3 pints.

YULE RELISH

1 lb. cranberries
1 large orange
1 lb. caster sugar

Put cranberries through a meat grinder with the thinly peeled rind of the orange and pulp after removing pips. Stir in sugar. When dissolved, pack into a basin. Cover. Stand for 3 or 4 days, then serve with cold poultry.

SPICED FRUIT

There are two kinds of spiced fruit : one is simply spiced jam, and the other is fruit preserved in a spiced syrup. Both can be served with cold meats, but the jam can also be used as a garnish. Pot in hot sterilized jars and seal like jam.

SPICED APPLES

4 medium-sized cooking apples
2 cups cider
¾ lb. caster sugar
6 whole cloves
2 inch cinnamon stick
4 allspice berries
¼ teaspoon grated nutmeg
¼ teaspoon ground ginger
1½ tablespoons lemon juice

Peel, core and quarter apples. Drop, as prepared, into cold water. Pour cider into a saucepan. Add half the sugar and all the spices. Stir over slow heat till sugar is dissolved, then bring to boil. Boil for 10 minutes without stirring. Drain and add apples, a few at a time. Cook till soft, but not golden. Remove with a skimmer to hot jars. Add remainder of sugar and the lemon juice to syrup. Stir over low heat till sugar is dissolved, then boil till thick. Strain over apple. Serve with fried, grilled or roast pork, boiled or baked ham, roast duck or goose, hot or cold.

SPICED BLACKBERRIES

1 pint cider vinegar
2 lb. sugar
½ teaspoon ground cloves
¼ teaspoon ground allspice
½ teaspoon ground cinnamon
8 lb. blackberries

Pour vinegar into a saucepan. Add sugar and spices. Stir over low heat till sugar is dissolved, then till boiling. Boil for 5 minutes without stirring. Meanwhile, clean and wash berries. Drain thoroughly and add to syrup. Boil for ¼ hour. Pour into hot sterilized jars, filling them up to the rims. Seal.

SPICED CURRANTS

1 pint vinegar
3 lb. caster sugar
1 teaspoon ground cloves
1 teaspoon ground cinnamon
1 teaspoon ground ginger
1 teaspoon ground allspice
5 lb. currants
Pinch of salt

Pour vinegar into a saucepan. Add sugar and spices. Stir over low heat till sugar is dissolved, then till boiling. Add currants and salt. Simmer for 2-3 hours till thick, stirring frequently. Leave till cold. Bottle and cork tightly. Seal with wax.

SPICED GOOSEBERRIES

7 lb. gooseberries
4 lb. light brown sugar
1 pint vinegar
½ teaspoon ground cloves
1 teaspoon ground cinnamon
¼ teaspoon ground mace
½ teaspoon ground allspice

Top, tail and wash berries. Place sugar and vinegar in a saucepan. Add spices. Stir over low heat till sugar is dissolved and boiling. Add berries. Boil for about 20 minutes, till fruit is soft, stirring constantly. Pot and seal.

SPICED PEARS

1½ cups vinegar
1 lb. light brown sugar
1 inch cinnamon stick
½ teaspoon ground cloves
2 lb. pears

Pour vinegar into a saucepan. Add sugar, cinnamon stick and cloves. Stir over low heat till sugar is dissolved, then till boiling. Peel, core and slice pears. Add to syrup. Stew gently till tender, then remove to heated pound pots. Cover with syrup. Seal at once. Serve with cold meats.

SPICED PLUMS

4 lb. plums
1 tablespoon salt
cold water to cover
1 quart vinegar
1 oz. whole cloves
2 blades of mace
1 oz. cinnamon stick
1 oz. allspice berries
1 dessertspoon black pepper-corns
2 lb. light brown sugar

Use firm plums free from blemishes. Place in a saucepan. Add water and salt. Bring to boil, then drain well. Prick fruit with a darning needle. Pour vinegar into a saucepan. Tie spices in a small muslin bag and add with sugar. Stir over low heat till sugar is dissolved, then till boiling. Remove from heat. Cool slightly. Pour over plums. Cover. Stand for 24 hours. Drain syrup into a saucepan. Bring to boil. Boil for 10 minutes. Remove from heat. Add plums. Cover and stand for 4 hours. Remove spice bag. Bring plums and syrup to boiling point. Remove from heat at once. Pack into clean hot jars, and seal.

ENGLISH MUSTARD

½ teaspoon salt
1 teaspoon caster sugar
1 tablespoon olive oil
2 tablespoons ground mustard
2 tablespoons vinegar

Mix salt and sugar together. Stir in oil. Mix mustard to a paste with vinegar and stir mixtures together. Dilute with a little boiling water if mixture is too thick.

SAUCES FOR STORING

Sauces made with vinegar and spices, in contrast to sauces prepared as required, must be properly bottled or they may ferment. The bottles used for sterilizing must be perfectly clean, and the corks should be new.

To Sterilize Corks : Place the corks in a saucepan 5 minutes before they are to be used. Cover with boiling water. Boil for 5 minutes. Remove as required and use.

To Sterilize Bottles : Place bottles on a rack in a saucepan. Cover with hot water, then bring to boil. Cover pan. Simmer for 20 minutes. Remove from stove. Take out and drain each jar as required.

To Fill and Seal : Pour hot sauce through a sterilized funnel into bottles to overflowing. Insert corks. Wipe necks. Either cover with metal caps sold for the purpose, or leave until the bottles are quite cold, then dip the necks in melted paraffin wax.

NOTE : If you make large quantities of piquant sauces use ketchup bottles complete with screw caps and corks for storing.

To make certain that a sauce will keep, allow it to become cold, then bottle it and sterilize. Cork loosely. Place filled bottles on a rack in a preserving pan with hot water coming up to their necks. Heat water gradually to 170° F., and keep at this temperature for ¼ hour, then remove one at a time and seal.

When making sauces, stir with a wooden spoon kept for the purpose, and use a hair sieve, not a wire one. Be careful not to cook too long as sauces thicken as they cool.

APPLE KETCHUP

1 quart apple purée
1¾ gills vinegar
½ lb. caster sugar
2 large minced onions
¾ tablespoons salt
1 teaspoon ground mustard
1 teaspoon ground cloves
2 teaspoons ground cinnamon

To make purée, quarter, core and pare 12 large cooking apples. Cover with cold water. Simmer till soft, and water has almost evaporated, then rub through a sieve. Rinse pan. Add 1 quart purée and remaining ingredients. Stir over low heat till sugar is dissolved, then till boiling. Simmer gently for 1 hour, stirring frequently. Pot and seal in 3 hot small jars. Serve with cold pork, or boiled or baked ham.

CHILLI SAUCE

25 medium-ripe tomatoes
5 peeled medium onions
2 sweet red peppers
1 small head celery
2 cups vinegar
1½ cups light brown sugar
1 teaspoon whole cloves
½ cinnamon stick
1 teaspoon allspice berries
½ nutmeg, grated
¾ tablespoon salt
¾ teaspoon dry mustard

Scald, peel and chop tomatoes. Drain in a colander. Peel and chop onions. Remove seeds from red peppers, and mince or put through a meat grinder. Trim, wash and shred celery. Pour vinegar into a saucepan. Add prepared tomatoes and vegetables. Stir well. Add sugar. Stir till dissolved and boiling, then mix well and boil slowly for 2½ hours. Place whole spices in a small muslin bag. Place in pan with nutmeg, salt and mustard. Boil for 15 minutes. Remove bag. Bottle and seal at once.

ELDERBERRY CATSUP

1 quart elderberries
1 quart boiling vinegar
1 teaspoon salt
Pepper to taste
¼ oz. ground mace
1 teaspoon ground ginger
2 tablespoons caster sugar

Rinse berries carefully, then place in a stone jar. Cover with vinegar, then cover. Place in a cool larder or cellar, then leave for 2 days, then strain. Pour into a sancepan. Add remainder of ingredients. Stir over low heat till sugar is dissolved then stop boiling. Cook over reduced heat very slowly, stirring frequently for about 1 hour, then into sterilized bottles and cork tightly. Seal.

GOOSEBERRY CATSUP

5 lb. green gooseberries
2½ lb. light brown sugar
½ teaspoon black pepper
1 teaspoon salt
1 dessertspoon ground allspice
1 dessertspoon ground cinnamon
1 pint vinegar

Top, tail, rinse and drain berries. Place in a saucepan. Cook slowly till juice begins to flow, stirring frequently, then simmer gently till into a pulp. Rub through a hair sieve. Rinse saucepan. Add purée, sugar and seasonings. Stir over low heat till sugar is dissolved, then till boiling. Boil for 20 minutes, stirring frequently. Add vinegar. Stir till boiling. Pot and seal at once.

HORSERADISH SAUCE

Scrape, wash, dry and shred horseradish. Pack tightly into screw-topped bottles or jars. Boil enough vinegar to cover for 2 minutes. Leave until cold. Pour over horseradish to the depth of ½ inch. Screw on top. This sauce keeps for at least a year. When required, blend a small quantity with salt, pepper, mustard to taste, and thick cream, adding it very gradually.

MINT SAUCE

½ lb. mint leaves
½ pint vinegar
6 oz. caster sugar

Rinse mint leaves. Remove from sprigs before weighing, then drain and toss in a cloth till dry. Mince on a chopping board. Pour vinegar into a small saucepan. Add sugar. Stir over low heat till dissolved, then till boiling. Boil steadily for 5 minutes, then pour at once over mint leaves. When quite cold, bottle and seal.

MUSHROOM CATSUP

5 lb. fresh mushrooms
1/4 cup salt
1 dessertspoon minced onion
1/2 teaspoon ground cloves
1/2 teaspoon ground allspice
1/2 teaspoon grated horseradish
Dash of cayenne pepper
1/2 cup malt vinegar

Wipe mushrooms with a very damp cloth, then chop and place in a basin. Stir in salt. Cover and stand for 12 hours. Mash well with a wooden spoon, then stir in onion, spices, horseradish, pepper and vinegar. Heat till boiling. Simmer slowly till thick in about 1/2 hour, stirring occasionally. (If preferred, rub through a hair sieve, and stir again to boiling point before bottling. If too thick, thin with boiled vinegar to taste.) Seal at once in hot sterilized jars. *Yield :* About 2 1/2 pints.

TOMATO KETCHUP

6 lb. ripe tomatoes
1 oz. salt
1 pint vinegar
1/2 lb. light brown sugar
1 teaspoon ground cinnamon
1/4 teaspoon ground cloves
1/4 teaspoon ground allspice
1/4 teaspoon ground mace
Cayenne pepper to taste

Quarter tomatoes. Place in a saucepan with salt, and vinegar. Simmer till into a pulp. Rub through a hair sieve. Rinse saucepan. Add purée and sugar. Stir over low heat till sugar is dissolved, then till boiling. Simmer till the ketchup starts to thicken, then add spices, one at a time. When fairly thick, pour into sterilized bottles. Seal at once. (If preferred, leave till lukewarm, then pour into hot sterilized bottles, and sterilize for 1/4 hour at 170° F., then cork and seal.)

VINEGARS

APPLE VINEGAR FOR PICKLES

Rinse cores and peelings of ripe apples used in making a batch of apple jelly, then drain well. Place in a stone crock or wide-mouthed jar. Cover with cold water, then cover closely. Stand in a warm place, adding fresh cores and peelings prepared as described from time to time. A scum will form on top and gradually thicken. This is the " mother " or the vinegar plant that makes vinegar. Keep tasting, and when the liquid below the scum tastes strong enough, strain off scum, first through a colander, then through a jelly bag. Cover and stand for a fortnight, then bottle and seal.

BECKENHAM VINEGAR

1/2 lb. light brown sugar
1/2 lb. golden syrup
1/2 pint boiling water
4 1/2 pints cold water
1 vinegar plant

Place sugar, syrup and boiling water in a basin at least 13 inches broad. Leave till sugar is dissolved, then stir in cold water. Place vinegar plant on top. Puncture a piece of brown paper, cut to cover ingredients and overlapping edge of basin, about a dozen times with a skewer, then lay on top of basin. Store in a dark cupboard for 2 months when the plant will have divided into two. Remove the vinegar plant. Bring mixture to a boil in an enamel saucepan. Boil for 5 minutes. Strain through muslin. Bottle when cold.

CHERVIL VINEGAR

Fill a wide-mouthed bottle half-full with chervil leaves. Fill up to the top with a good quality vinegar. Place on a rack in a saucepan. Fill pan to the neck of bottle with warm water, then let the water come to boiling point. Remove from stove. Leave till cool, then cork and seal. It is ready for use in a fortnight.

CIDER VINEGAR

Mix 2 lb. honey soon after it has been extracted from the comb with 2 gallons of good cider in a small cask or large crock. Cover. Leave for 4-6 months. Use very sparingly as it is very strong.

NOTE : You can also make cider vinegar by pouring it into an open jug or pitcher and leaving it for 5 weeks, when it will turn into vinegar.

GARLIC VINEGAR

Place 5 or 6 peeled cloves of garlic in a quart of mild vinegar. Cover and stand for 3 weeks, then strain. Bottle and cork.

MINT VINEGAR

Rinse and dry fresh, young sprigs of mint. Fill up jars with the mint, using as many sprigs as the jars will take, then pour in mild vinegar to overflowing. Cork tightly. Stand for 3 weeks in the sun, then strain. Pour into fresh bottles and cork down. Use for making salad dressing for green salads to serve with cold duck, lamb or mutton.

NOTE : Celery or Dill vinegar can be made by substituting celery or dill blossoms for the mint in above recipe.

RASPBERRY VINEGAR

Pick over and rinse sound raspberries gently in a colander under the cold water tap, then measure. To each lb. of fruit, allow 1 pint mild vinegar. Pour into large jugs, or a ewer. Cover and stand in a cool place for 2 weeks. Strain through a jelly bag then measure. Allow sugar in the proportion of $\frac{1}{2}$ lb. for each quart of juice. Pour sugar and juice into a saucepan. Stir over low heat till dissolved, then till boiling. Pour at once into hot sterilized bottles or jars. Seal.

TARRAGON VINEGAR

Gather enough tarragon to give you $\frac{1}{2}$ pint of leaves. Spread them out on a cloth, and leave them in sun for 3 or 4 days, then place them in a wide-mouthed jar. Cover with a quart of the best cider vinegar. Cover with a cloth. Soak for 2 weeks. Strain through a jelly bag. Bottle, cork and seal. Use for salad dressings, etc.

PICKLES

A pickle is simply a food preserved in brine or vinegar. When we speak of pickles, we are usually thinking of pickled fruit or vegetables, but eggs, fish and meat can also be pickled.

EQUIPMENT REQUIRED

A large aluminium or enamel-lined saucepan. (Brass or copper pans must not be used.)

Long-handled wooden spoon.   A sharp vegetable knife.
Vegetable brush.   Hair sieve.
An aluminium or porcelain basin.   Wide-necked glass jars with corks.

To Choose Vegetables and Fruit

Only firm, sound vegetables and fruit are suitable for pickling, and they must not be over-ripe or green.

Vegetables : Choose freshly picked, crisp vegetables. Beetroot, cabbage, carrots, cauliflower, cucumbers, green tomatoes, Jerusalem artichokes, marrows, onions, ripe tomatoes, shallots and string beans are all suitable.

Fruit : Choose sound fruit free from blemishes. If you grow your own, wait for a dry day, then gather fruit and pickle it right away. Hard and fleshy fruits are most suitable : Apples, apricots, cherries, grapes, peaches, pears, plums, as well as varieties of melon and water melon rind.

To Prepare Vegetables : Wash and scrub. Remove outer leaves of cabbage and cauliflower ; peel beetroot, marrow, onions and shallots ; scrape artichokes and carrots. If red peppers are being added to any pickle, cut a slice off tops and remove any seeds and coarse membrane before preparing according to recipe. String and cut beans into inch slices. Divide cauliflower sprigs into tiny sprigs. Peel onions or shallots. Cube gherkins. Peel and cube marrow and cucumber.

To Prepare Fruits : Wash fruit, and prepare as described under each recipe.

To Brine Pickles

It is necessary to brine certain vegetables in order to draw some of the water out of them. If not brined, they are likely to become shrivelled instead of remaining crisp and firm, and they might become cloudy and not keep well. Other vegetables, particularly cucumber and marrows, should be sprinkled with salt instead of soaked in brine.

To Make Brine : Allow 1 lb. salt to 8 or 9 pints of cold water. If requiring only a small quantity of brine, allow ½ lb. salt to 4 or 4½ pints water. (The first quantity is enough to brine 8 lb. prepared vegetables, the second 4 lb.) To brine, place prepared vegetables in brine, and break them down to make certain they are all submerged. Cover. Stand for 12-24 hours, according to instructions under each vegetable. When brining is completed, remove vegetables to a colander and rinse thoroughly under cold water tap until all traces of salt have been removed. Drain thoroughly then pack into sterilized jars, and add pickle.

Vegetables Suitable for Brining : Cauliflowers, gherkins, onions, shallots.

Dry Salting : Prepare and place vegetables in a deep basin in layers with dry salt sprinkled between, allowing about ½ tablespoon salt to each lb. of vegetables. Cover. Leave for 12-24 hours. Rinse vegetables and finish off as described under Brining.

Vegetables Suitable for Salting: Cucumbers, green tomatoes, marrow, and red cabbage.

NOTE : Beetroot, carrots, Jerusalem artichokes and string beans are all cooked in brine before pickling. See respective recipes.

BASIC METHOD FOR PICKLING VEGETABLES

Prepare brine, or salt, according to variety of vegetable. Rinse thoroughly, then drain thoroughly. Pack into wide-necked, sterilized jars to within 1 inch of the tops. Invert, holding a lid almost over the jars, to get rid of any moisture that may have remained on vegetable. Cover completely with cold spiced vinegar to within ½ inch of the top. Insert corks lined with waxed paper, or use metal covers lined with vinegar-proof discs, or synthetic skin. *On no account must the vinegar come into contact with metal tops if used.*

To Store : Store in a cool, dry, dark, airy cupboard. Keep all pickles except red cabbage for 3 months before serving.

VINEGAR FOR PICKLING

The best vinegars to use are bottled malt vinegar, and spirit vinegar. The vinegar should be added with spices according to instructions in recipes or spiced and prepared beforehand when few or no spices need be added when pickling. Use white vinegar for covering light-coloured vegetables.

SPICED VINEGAR

1 quart pure malt vinegar
½ oz. allspice berries
2 oz. black peppercorns
¼ oz. whole ginger
2 bay leaves
½ oz. salt
2 cloves garlic

Pour vinegar into a large wide-mouthed glass jar, such as a sweet jar. Crush berries, peppercorns and ginger. Place in jar. Add remainder of ingredients. Cover closely. Stand in a warm room for 1 week, then turn into an enamel-lined saucepan. Bring to simmering point. Simmer gently for 1 hour, then cool. Strain and bottle. Cork tightly, using a cork lined with waxed paper. Store in a dry place.

SPICES FOR PICKLES

If using spiced vinegar, be very careful about adding any additional spice. It should not be necessary. If using malt vinegar, or any unspiced vinegar specified under recipe, here is a standard spice mixture that could be added to taste :

STANDARD SPICE MIXTURE

1 tablespoon black peppercorns
1 tablespoon whole cloves
1 tablespoon allspice berries
3 blades of mace
1 tablespoon celery seed
1 inch whole ginger
3 tablespoons grated horse-radish
1 tablespoon chopped peeled garlic
2 tablespoons yellow mustard seed
4 dried chilli peppers

Mix ingredients thoroughly in order given. Allow 2 tablespoons ($\frac{3}{4}$ oz.) of this mixture to each quart jar of pickles. Shake before using.

MUSTARD MIXTURE FOR MUSTARD PICKLES

$\frac{2}{3}$ cup dry mustard
$\frac{3}{4}$ lb. caster sugar
6 oz. flour
1 tablespoon turmeric
2 quarts pure malt vinegar

Mix dry ingredients in a basin. Stir in enough of the cold vinegar to make a smooth paste. Heat remainder of vinegar to boiling point. Stir into paste. Pour into saucepan. Cook till thick, stirring constantly. Pour at once over prepared vegetables. Cover. Stand for 12 hours. Seal in sterilized jars. This quantity is enough for 5 quarts of pickle.

MUSTARD PICKLES (CHOW CHOW)

1 quart gherkins
1½ pints sliced cucumbers
1 quart sliced green tomato
1 quart sliced onion
1½ pints peeled pickling onions
1 pint cauliflower sprigs
4 chopped green peppers
Salt and cold water
¼ lb. flour
¾ lb. caster sugar
4 tablespoons dry mustard
¾ teaspoon turmeric
3 pints vinegar

Place gherkins, cucumber, tomato, onion, onions, cauliflower sprigs and green pepper in a basin. Dissolve a cup of salt in a quart of cold water and add. Stand for 24 hours. Turn into a preserving pan. Heat slowly until vegetables are about to boil. Rinse, then drain. Mix flour to a smooth paste with the sugar, mustard, turmeric and a pint of the vinegar. Heat remainder of vinegar to boiling point and gradually stir into paste. Pour into top of a double boiler. Cook until almost boiling but it must not boil. Add to vegetable mixture. Pack into heated sterilized jars. Cover and seal. *Yield:* About 12 pints.

Hints on Pickling Vegetables

1. To improve the colour of cabbage and cucumber to be pickled, line the bottom and sides of preserving pan with green cabbage or spinach leaves.

2. Cook all pickles in an uncovered saucepan unless otherwise instructed in recipe.

3. Do not let anything metallic come in contact with vegetables, when pickling, packing and covering pickles.

4. Take care that the vinegar completely covers the pickles in jar, or the top layer will eventually become discoloured. This may mean removing a little of the pickle as the *vinegar must only come to within $\frac{1}{2}$ inch of the lid, unless otherwise instructed in recipe.*

5. If you have a choice of jars, choose glass-topped every time.

What Goes Wrong with Pickles

1. *If discoloured.* This might be caused either by using the wrong kind of vinegar or by cooking in the wrong kind of saucepan. If the top layer alone is discoloured, this is due to insufficiency of vinegar.

2. *If tough and shrivelled.* This may mean you have used too much salt, or sugar in the case of sweet pickles, or too strong vinegar.

3. *If slimy and soft.* They have not been properly brined, or dry-salted.

4. *If soft.* Either the brine was too weak or the vinegar was too strong.

SOUR PICKLES

These are what the French call Pickles au Vinaigre. They are unsweetened.

Beetroot : Wash carefully so as not to break the skins. Place in a saucepan of boiling salted water. Simmer for $1\frac{1}{2}$ to 2 hours until tender. When cold, peel and slice or dice. Bottle and cover with spiced vinegar to within an inch of top, and seal.

Red Cabbage : Remove outer leaves from a firm head. Quarter cabbage. Remove centre stalk. Shred cabbage finely. Pile on a platter. Sprinkle freely with salt. Stand for 24 hours. Pour 1 quart pure malt vinegar into a saucepan. Add $\frac{1}{2}$ oz. allspice berries and $\frac{1}{2}$ oz. black peppercorns. Bring to boil. Boil for 3 minutes. Remove. Leave till cold. Place cabbage in an enamelled colander. Drain thoroughly for 1 hour. Pack in jars. Strain in vinegar and seal. Ready for use in 4 days.

APPLE AND BANANA PICKLE

3 lb. cored peeled tart apples
2 lb. peeled bananas
2 oz. minced preserved ginger
$1\frac{1}{2}$ lb. Demerara sugar
1 lb. chopped stoned raisins
$\frac{1}{2}$ teaspoon salt
Dash cayenne pepper
$2\frac{1}{2}$ pints vinegar

Slice apples and bananas into a preserving pan. Add ginger, sugar, raisins, salt, pepper and vinegar. Stir over slow heat till sugar is dissolved, then until boiling. Cook for 2 hours, stirring frequently at first, then constantly when nearly ready. Remove from heat. Cool. Stir and pot and seal. *Yield :* About $7\frac{1}{2}$ pints.

PICKLED BEETROOT

3 lb. sliced cold beetroot
1½ teaspoons salt
1½ teaspoons light brown sugar
1½ teaspoons caraway seeds
Black pepper to taste
1½ pints malt vinegar

Place a layer of the beetroot in a large jar. Mix salt with the sugar, caraway seeds, and black pepper. Sprinkle a little over beetroot. Repeat till all the beetroot and seasoning is used up. Cover with vinegar. Cover closely or else the vinegar will evaporate and the pickle will gradually change colour. If vinegar evaporates, add more. *Yield :* About 4 pints.

PICKLED CAULIFLOWER

Trim and boil perfect heads of cauliflower in salted water for about 20 minutes. Drain. Break carefully into small sprigs. Leave till cold. Pack in sterilized jars. Cover with hot spiced vinegar, sweetened and spiced with mustard, allowing ¼ lb. caster sugar and 2 teaspoons French mustard to each quart of vinegar required. Seal at once.

PICKLED CUCUMBER

Leave ¼ to ½ inch stems on cucumbers. Wash carefully. Dry-salt, or brine if preferred. When cold, submerge cucumbers in this brine. When wanted for pickling, soak in cold water to cover until fresh enough. *Brine suitable :* 2 cups salt to 8 cups cold water. Bring to boil. Skim then leave until cold before using.

Pickled Cucumber : Drain brined cucumbers. Place in a saucepan. Cover with a solution of vinegar and water, 1 part vinegar to 3 parts water. Bring to simmering point. Simmer for 3 minutes. Pack into jars. Cover with boiling vinegar. Seal at once.

MIXED PICKLES

Prepare French or runner beans, cauliflower sprigs, onions or shallots, cucumber, gherkins and marrow in any proportion. Place in a pan of boiling salted water in the proportion of a teaspoon of salt to a pint of water. Bring again to boil. Simmer for 4 minutes. Drain well. Spread out to dry. Bottle and cover with hot spiced vinegar. Leave till cold, then seal.

DILL PICKLES

4 peeled cloves of garlic
24 black peppercorns
4 whole cloves
4 stalks of dill
½ peck small cucumbers
8 cups vinegar
4 cups cold water
1 cup salt

Sterilize 4 quart jars. Place a clove of garlic, 6 of the peppercorns, a whole clove and a stalk of dill in each jar. Scrub cucumbers, about 3 inches long, with water, then rinse and toss in cloths until dry. Pack closely in jars. Pour vinegar into a saucepan. Add water and salt. Bring to boiling point. Fill jars and seal. Keep for at least a week before serving, or turning into a sweet pickle. *Yield:* About 4 quarts.

GREEN TOMATO PICKLE

4 lb. green tomatoes
2 large peeled onions
½ cup salt
1 quart vinegar
1¼ lb. sugar
2 large green seeded peppers
1½ oz. pickling spices

Wash and slice tomatoes into a basin. Slice in onion. Sprinkle with the salt. Cover. Stand for 12 hours. Press down well, then drain off juice. Place tomatoes in an enamel saucepan. Add vinegar and sugar. Chop peppers and add. Tie spice in a small muslin bag and add. Stir over low heat till sugar is dissolved then till boiling. Boil, stirring occasionally, until tomatoes are transparent. Drain and remove bag. Pot and seal. *Yield:* About 5½ pints.

PICKLED MUSHROOMS

2 pints mushrooms
3 blades mace
1 oz. bruised root ginger
3 whole cloves
½ oz. black peppercorns
2 pints vinegar

Wash, dry and peel mushrooms. Trim stalks level with mushrooms. Place mushrooms in a shallow saucepan. Sprinkle with salt. Shake over stove till juice flows, shaking pan occasionally to prevent burning. When most of the juice has evaporated, tie spice in a muslin bag and add with vinegar. Bring to boil. Simmer gently for 10 minutes. Pot and seal.

To Pickle for Immediate Use : Wipe 1 pint button mushrooms with a damp cloth. Place in a basin. Place 1 teaspoon of salt, 1 teaspoon black peppercorns, a sliced peeled clove of garlic, and a pint of vinegar, in an enamel saucepan. Heat with a sprig of tarragon and 2 bay leaves to boiling point. Pour over mushrooms. Cover and stand for 3 days, then serve with any cold meat.

PICCALILLI

½ peck green tomatoes
6 large cucumbers
1 chilli pepper
1 large cabbage heart
¼ peck pickling onions
2 heads celery
5 green peppers
1 stick horseradish
2 teaspoons ground cinnamon
1 teaspoon ground allspice
1 teaspoon ground cloves
2 tablespoons salt
2 lb. light brown sugar
2 quarts malt vinegar

Prepare and chop all vegetables. Grate horse-radish. Place in a basin. Place spices, salt, sugar and vinegar in an enamel saucepan. Stir over low heat till sugar is dissolved, then till boiling. Drain off vinegar. Pack vegetables into heated pickling jars. Bring vinegar to boiling point, and pour over. Cover and seal. If preferred, substitute the same amount of allspice berries and whole cloves for the ground and 2 inches cinnamon stick for the ground. Place in a muslin bag and add to vinegar. When boiling, stand for 5 minutes then remove bag. Cover and seal. *Yield :* About 20 pints.

PICKLED NASTURTIUM SEEDS

2 pints nasturtium seeds
2 pints pure malt vinegar
1 oz. salt
1 blade mace

Gather seeds on a dry day before they show signs of bursting. Rinse, drain and soak in brine for 7 days, changing brine daily. Rinse well. Dry. Pack seeds in bottles. Simmer vinegar, salt, mace,

3 whole cloves
6 black peppercorns

cloves and peppercorns in a saucepan for 15 minutes, then strain over seeds. When quite cold, bottle and cork tightly. Ready for use in 2 months.

SWEET PICKLED ONIONS

4 quarts pickling onions
1 cup salt
¼ cup pickling spices
8 cups mild white vinegar
1 lb. caster sugar

Peel onions under water. Place in a large basin. Cover with boiling water. Stand for 2 minutes. Drain. Cover with cold water and peel. Place in a basin. Sprinkle with the salt. Cover with cold water. Stir till salt is dissolved. Stand for 12 hours. Place in a colander. Rinse under cold water tap and drain. Tie spices in a small muslin bag. Place spice bag, vinegar and sugar in an enamel saucepan. Stir over low heat till sugar is dissolved, then till boiling. Boil for 3 minutes. Remove spice bag. Throw in onions. Bring to full boil. Fill hot sterilized jars to overflowing. Cover and seal. *Yield :* About 8 pints.

PICKLED SHALLOTS

1 quart peeled shallots
1 quart white vinegar
½ oz. salt
1 oz. white peppercorns

Pack shallots, without brining or treating with salt, into jars. Bring vinegar, salt and peppercorns to a boil. Boil for 5 minutes. Pour over shallots. Stand for 12 hours. Strain off vinegar into a saucepan. Bring to boil. Pour over shallots. Repeat process once more, then leave until cold. Cover and seal. *Yield :* About 4 lbs.

SWEET VEGETABLE MARROW PICKLE

1½ lb. peeled vegetable marrow
Salt to taste
½ lb. caster sugar
½ teaspoon pepper
¾ lb. sliced onions
½ oz. ground ginger
¾ pint vinegar

Place marrow in a basin. Sprinkle freely with salt. Leave for 12 hours. Drain well. Place in a saucepan. Add remaining ingredients. Stir over low heat till sugar is dissolved, then till boiling. Simmer till thick in about 2 hours. Pot in hot sterilized jars and seal. *Yield :* About 2½ pints.

PICKLED WALNUTS

Pickle walnuts when young before their shells have formed. Prick them through several times with a large needle. Place in a crock. Cover with brine, allowing 1 lb. salt to 4 quarts water. Soak for at least 14 days, changing brine every 3 days. Drain well. Place on flat dishes. Stand in the sun for a day or two till they turn black. Place 2 oz. black peppercorns, 1 oz. bruised ginger, 1 oz. peeled garlic, 6 allspice berries, and 2 inches scraped horseradish in a small muslin bag. Pour a quart of pure malt vinegar into a saucepan. Add spice bag. Bring slowly to boil. Pack prepared nuts into jars. Strain hot vinegar over. Cover and seal. Ready for use in 6 weeks.

Bottling and Canning

The purpose of bottling food is to preserve fruit or vegetables when in season for using when not in season.

There are two important points to be observed in order to secure perfect packs :

1. All bacteria, moulds and yeasts must be destroyed by heat so as to prevent the action of enzymes. This means that the food concerned must be perfectly processed. If not, the enzymes usually present in fruit, vegetables and meat will cause spoilage. Only sufficient heat will prevent this.

2. The jars or cans must be perfectly sealed to prevent the re-entrance of micro-organisms which will make the food start to decay.

It is safest therefore to use only well-tested methods of bottling and canning. There are other methods that very often give good results, but they are not fool-proof.

EQUIPMENT FOR BOTTLING

Sterilizer.	Wire basket (for blanching).
Bottling Jars.	Long-handled wooden packing spoon.
Bottle Brush.	Pressure cooker.
Measuring Cup.	Wide funnel.
Measuring Spoon.	Pair of tongs for handling jars.

Sterilizer equipped with a thermometer. If you haven't a sterilizer equipped with a thermometer, use a large covered saucepan, wash boiler, or bucket, but it must be deep enough to allow for a rack or a pad on the bottom to take pint or quart jars, and for boiling water coming at least 1 inch over the tops of jars without boiling over. Make a pad $\frac{1}{4}$ inch thick of newspaper or towelling, and lay it on the bottom, for jars must not be placed directly on bottom of any type of sterilizer.

Wide-Mouthed Bottling Jars : There are several types of jars suitable. Most of them are available in 1, 1$\frac{1}{2}$, 2 and 3 lb. sizes. Straight-sided jars are preferable because they enable heat to penetrate evenly to the contents. I prefer the type which has metal covers secured with metal clips. They are sold in 3 sizes :

1. To take 1 lb. fruit or 1 pint of liquid.
2. To take 1$\frac{1}{4}$ lb. fruit or 1$\frac{1}{2}$ pint of liquid.
3. To take 1$\frac{3}{4}$ lb. fruit or 2 pints of liquid.

The next type I prefer is the screw-topped jar with a glass lid. Both these types of jars require rubber rings to make the lids airtight.

Jam jars can also be used with lids and clips, and rubbers specially designed to fit 1 lb. and 2 lb. sizes.

To Prepare Jars : Examine to see they are free from flaws round the rims. If they have any flaws discard them. Buy new rubbers to fit, as rubbers cannot be used a second time. To avoid any food being imperfectly sealed, test jars in this way before filling : Adjust rubber rings on each jar. Fill half full with hot water, then seal and turn upside down. Leave for 5 minutes. If rubber, or rim of jar is faulty, the water will leak.

Before using jars that are required for bottling and sterilizing fruit by the Open Saucepan Method, which is the method generally used for sterilizing jams, jellies, marmalades, preserves, chutneys, pickles and relishes, and other preserves of this nature, thoroughly wash them in warm, soapy water, then rinse well and invert to drain. Place on a rack in a pan of very hot water to cover. Cover. Bring to boil. Boil for 20 minutes, then leave in hot water and take out and drain and use as required.

Wash rubber rings in hot soapy water. Rinse well, then transfer them to a pan of warm water together with any other fittings to be used such as screw tops and glass lids. Use as required.

NOTE : It is not necessary to sterilize jars when fruit is to be processed in a boiling water bath. The jars as well as the fruit are processed during the sterilizing.

METHODS OF PACKING

Cold Pack : Pack prepared product, without heating, in jars, then seal and sterilize. This method is most popular for preserving fruit to be served in solid form, as berries and stone fruit keep their shape better than when pre-cooked. Cover with fruit juice, sugar syrup or water.

Hot Pack : Pre-cook food before packing hot in jars. This method is the best one for certain foods such as apples and pears that need to be pre-cooked before bottling, as well as meats and vegetables. Seal immediately as each jar is packed, and sterilize at once.

Open Saucepan Method : This is only advisable for preserves cooked in a thick syrup and for tomatoes. Cook completely, and pack immediately in hot sterilized jars. Seal at once.

HINTS ON BOTTLING AND CANNING

Before starting to bottle or can, study instructions given with your jars or cans. Get familiar with yours before using them. Some types of jars have lids that have to be turned back a quarter turn, and others $\frac{1}{4}$ inch. Some you seal right away, others you tighten afterwards.

To pre-cook (another name for " blanching ") : do so for the time suggested. This treatment sets the colour and shrinks the food, and you are able to get more of the produce in the jar than if it was not properly pre-cooked. To pre-cook or blanch correctly, place food in boiling water. Bring rapidly to the boil, then start counting time. Use your minute timer. When ready, continue process of bottling or canning at once. Do not leave fruit or vegetables lying about.

To prevent product settling after cooking, be careful to remove all air bubbles, and add more liquid if required to come to $\frac{1}{2}$ or 1 inch from rim, as necessary.

The Water Bath : Be careful when using a water bath to see that the rack, if it is an improvised one, is 1 inch off the bottom, and place jars at least $\frac{1}{2}$ inch apart, and $\frac{1}{2}$ inch from the edge of sterilizer, to allow water to circulate freely. Water should come at least 1 inch above the jars unless you are otherwise instructed. Keep it boiling steadily for amount of time required for sterilizing. Add boiling water if necessary to keep the jars submerged all the time.

Timing : Do not start timing hot water bath until the water comes to a full bubbling boil. Do not start timing in a pressure cooker until the gauge indicates pressure required. If you do, the fruit or vegetables may not be sterilized sufficiently.

Let steam flow from vent or pet cock for length of time given in instructions, usually 10 minutes. Do not attempt to close pet cock until the end of this time, or air left in cooker will result in the pressure reading being inaccurate, and this will mean that the fruit or vegetables are not sterilized sufficiently, and will not keep. Be sure there are 2-3 inches of water in the cooker before inserting jars, unless instructions in your book state otherwise. See that there is a wooden surface handy to the stove, and out of a draught, to which to remove jars after sterilizing, and be sure to complete each seal if only partially sealed as you remove each jar. Leave for 48 hours before testing for seal unless otherwise instructed. Store jars in a dry, cool, airy cupboard with a temperature below 70° F.

WARNING : Boil all bottled or canned *vegetables* for 10 minutes before tasting or using. If you are in any doubt whatever about fruit or vegetables you have bottled, do not taste them. Throw them out.

To Choose Fruit : Choose sound, firm, dry fruit, ripe but not over-ripe. If you grow your own, pick on a dry day. Prepare and bottle at once. Grade according to size, reserving under-sized fruit for jam or jelly, or for bottling in its own juice. Do not prepare fruit until ready to bottle.

To Prepare Fruit : Wash very carefully. Place all soft fruit in a colander. Lower it into a large basin of cold water, and raise and lower it so that water covers fruit and drains away, carrying any dust or grit away with it. Prepare as for steaming or stewing. If bottling fruit so large that only 1 or 2 fit into a jar, such as large pears, peel, halve and core, or quarter if necessary.

To Prevent Certain Fruit Darkening : Apples, apricots, peaches and pears must be dipped in a solution of 1 tablespoon lemon juice or vinegar to 4 cups water, or brined to prevent darkening. To make brine, dissolve common salt in cold water, allowing 2 oz. to 4 quarts water. As you prepare each piece of fruit, place it in the brine, or in lemon or vinegar water solution. Weight down to prevent fruit surfacing. Carefully pack apricots, peaches and dessert pears in jars, and rinse. Drain thoroughly, then add covering liquid. Rinse apples and hard pears in a colander in a basin of cold water.

Pre-cooking in Syrup

It is not necessary to pre-cook most fruits when bottling in syrup, but apples and hard pears must be pre-cooked in light syrup to prevent shrinkage. Use this method for other fruits when intended for fools, pies, tarts, etc. Prepare fruit. Prepare syrup. Add fruit. Simmer for time required. Place fruit in heated jars at once. Cover with the syrup.

APPLES : Prepare and simmer in thin syrup for 1-5 minutes, according to variety of apple. Pack hot in heated jars.

APRICOTS : Simmer in thin or medium syrup for about 5 minutes, according to size.

BERRIES (except strawberries) : Measure, and allow 5-10 oz. sugar to each quart of berries, depending on sweetness of berry. Arrange sugar and berries alternately in a shallow dish. Cover and stand for 2 hours, then cook gently over a slow heat until sugar is dissolved. Pack at once into heated jars.

CHERRIES : Cook for 5 minutes in a medium or thick syrup, depending on whether using dessert or cooking cherries. Or, measure, and for every cup of cherries, allow ½ cup of sugar. Place in layers in a shallow dish. Cover and stand for 1-2 hours. Stir over low heat till sugar is dissolved, then until boiling. Simmer gently for 10 minutes, then pack at once into heated jars.

CRANBERRIES : Cook in thick syrup for 3 minutes, then pack at once into heated jars.

GRAPES : Heat in light syrup to boiling point. Pack at once into sterilized jars.

NECTARINES AND PEACHES : See Apricots.

PEARS : Prepare and simmer in light syrup for 5 minutes. (8 minutes for hard varieties.) Pack hot in heated jars.

PINEAPPLE : For each pineapple, allow ¼ lb. sugar, and place both in a pan. Bring slowly to boiling point, taking 15-20 minutes. Pack at once.

PLUMS : Cook for 2 minutes in boiling medium syrup. Pack at once in heated jars.

STRAWBERRIES : Allow ½ lb. sugar to 4 cups berries. Arrange in layers in a preserving pan. Cover and stand for 2 hours. Simmer for 5 minutes. Cover and stand for 12 hours, then pack, or heat until boiling before packing hot.

To Prepare Syrup

Choose syrup to suit fruit. It can be made either with granulated or loaf sugar with a combination of sugar and honey. Use thick syrup for sour fruit, medium for medium-sweet, and thin for sweet fruit. A syrup suitable for most fruits is made with sugar and water in the proportion of 8-10 oz. sugar to 1 pint of water, or 4-5 lb. sugar to 1 gallon of water.

Bottling with Sugar.	*Bottling with Honey and Sugar.*
Thin Syrup : 6 oz. sugar to 1 pint water.	½ lb. sugar, 1 cup honey to 5 cups water.
Medium Syrup : 10 oz. sugar to 1 pint water.	1 lb. sugar, 2 cups honey to 5 cups water.
Thick Syrup : 1-1¼ lb. sugar to 1 pint water.	2 lb. sugar, 4 cups honey to 5 cups water.

To Make Syrup : Place sugar, honey if used, and water in an enamel saucepan. Stir over low heat till sugar is dissolved, then till boiling. Boil for 4-5 minutes without stirring, then skim. Allow 1 pint of syrup to every quart of large fruit, and ½ pint of syrup to each quart of small fruit. Cool slightly before pouring over fruit in jars.

NOTE : Fruit juice can be substituted for water or part of the water when making syrup.

To Fill and Seal Jars : Place hot jars, just removed from water, on a wooden surface. Remove rubbers from hot water and adjust round neck. Insert a wide sterilized funnel in jar. Pack in prepared fruit as tightly as possible without bruising. Cover with liquid to within ½ inch of the rim, unless otherwise stated under specific fruit, using water or syrup. Fruit bottled in syrup, however, has a tendency to rise to top of jars. If pre-cooked in syrup, fill first with fruit, then pour in syrup to within ½ inch of the rim to prevent fruit breaking. Tap the bottom of each jar on the palm of your hand to help to shake the fruit down. Run a silver knife or packing spoon down the inside of jars to work out any air bubbles. Wipe rim and rubbers with a damp cloth. Adjust lids, removed from hot water, then seal. If using screw-topped lids, screw each down firmly then unscrew about ½ inch. Sterilize.

BOTTLING FRUIT IN ITS OWN JUICE

Cut up prepared large fruit. Place cut-up or whole small fruit in heated sterilized jars, filling them as full as possible, then adjust rubbers. Place a little apart on rack in sterilizer. Add enough warm water to cover the bottom of the rack. Cover sterilizer and heat slowly to boiling point. Boil for 20 minutes, then uncover. The fruit will have shrunk, so fill up one jar from another, then place covers, heated in boiling water, on jar loosely if screw-topped. Pour in enough water at boiling point to cover the jars by an inch, taking care to pour it between the jars. Cover sterilizer, and bring to a slow boil. Boil for 10 minutes. Remove one at a time to a wooden surface and tighten any screw tops. Cool out of a draught at room temperature. This fruit is very useful for making into jam, fruit cheese or jelly, pies, or sauces.

TO PROCESS OR STERILIZE

There are various methods of sterilizing :
1. In a hot water bath. There are two ways of sterilizing in a hot water bath. If you haven't a sterilizer with a thermometer, use the second method.

2. In the oven. This method is asked for often. There are two methods of oven bottling.

3. In a pressure cooker. Follow instructions given with your cooker.

For High Altitudes : The times given are suitable for altitudes up to 1,000 feet. For every additional 1,000 feet, allow 20% more time.

HOT WATER BATH (With a Thermometer)

Place the jars, packed and filled with cold liquid, on rack $\frac{1}{2}$ inch apart and without touching the sides of sterilizer. Pour in at the side enough cold water to cover jars by an inch at least. (If preferred, fill half full before inserting jars, then add remainder.) Cover sterilizer. Bring water very gradually to required temperature. The degrees of temperature vary according to variety of fruit being sterilized. Watch carefully to see that the heat remains at the same temperature during time required for sterilizing. You may need to decrease or increase heat below sterilizer. The water should take about $1\frac{1}{2}$ hours to rise to temperature required. If heated too quickly the fruit is likely to rise to the top of jars. When sterilization is complete, bale out some of the water, then lift out the jars. If you have bottle tongs for removing jars it is not necessary to bale out any water. Place each jar as removed on a wooden surface out of a draught. If screw-topped, tighten each screw as you remove each jar. Leave until cold, continuing to tighten screw tops as they cool. Stand for 48 hours after removing from water bath before testing seal.

TEMPERATURE CHART
(for 1 pint and 2 pint jars)

Fruit	Temperature Reached in $1\frac{1}{2}$ hours.	Time When required temperature is reached.
CLASS 1 :		
Apples	165° F.	10 minutes
Apricots	165° F.	10 minutes
Blackberries	165° F.	10 minutes
Damsons	165° F.	10 minutes
Gooseberries	165° F.	10 minutes
Grapefruit	165° F.	10 minutes
Greengages	165° F.	10 minutes
Lemons	165° F.	10 minutes
Loganberries	165° F.	10 minutes
Mulberries	165° F.	10 minutes
Oranges	165° F.	10 minutes
Peaches	165° F.	10 minutes
Plums, ripe	165° F.	10 minutes
Raspberries	165° F.	10 minutes
Rhubarb	165° F.	10 minutes
Strawberries	165° F.	10 minutes
CLASS 2 :		
Cherries	190° F.	15 minutes
Currants (black, red and white)	180° F.	15 minutes
Grapes	180° F.	15 minutes

Pears	190° F.	20 minutes
Pineapples	180° F.	15 minutes
Plums, under-ripe	180° F.	15 minutes
Quinces	190° F.	20 minutes
Tomatoes	190° F.	30 minutes
Whortleberries	180° F.	15 minutes

1. HOT WATER BATH (Without a Thermometer)

Fill sterilizer with enough water at simmering point to submerge jars by fully an inch. As each jar is filled and closed, lower carefully on to a rack with bottling tongs. Place them ½ inch apart. (If you haven't bottling tongs, fill sterilizer with water to come only half-way up sides.) Work quickly. Fill up with water to fully an inch above jars. When nearly all are inserted, increase heat below sterilizer so as to bring the water rapidly to a full boil : 212° F. Cover sterilizer closely. The moment water is at full boil, start counting processing time. Here is where a minute timer is invaluable. If you have one, set it at time required for processing, and the bell will tell you when to take jars out. If using screw-top jars, screw each down tightly as you remove it.

TIME TABLE

Fruit (Bottled in hot Fruit Juice, Syrup or Water.)	Minutes Required	
	Pint Jars.	Quart Jars
Apples	15	15
Apple Sauce	10	10
Apricots (cold-packed)	20	25
(pre-cooked	15	15
Berries (except strawberries)—		
(cold-packed)	20	20
(pre-cooked)	15	15
Cherries (cold-packed)	20	25
(pre-cooked)	10	10
Figs (pre-cooked)	20	20
Nectarines (cold-packed)	20	25
(pre-cooked)	15	20
Peaches (cold-packed)	25	30
(pre-cooked)	20	20
Pears (cold-packed)	25	30
(pre-cooked)	20	20
Pineapple (cold-packed)	30	30
Plums (cold-packed)	30	30
(pre-cooked)	15	15
Rhubarb (blanched)	20	25
(pre-cooked)	10	10
Strawberries (pre-cooked)	15	15
Tomatoes (cold-packed)	35	45
(pre-cooked)	10	10
Tomato Juice (pre-cooked)	15	15

2. HOT WATER BATH (Without a Thermometer)
(Bottled in Cold Water)

This method is not so satisfactory as when bottling with the thermometer, or without a thermometer with hot covering liquid. The time given is for pint jars. Allow 5 minutes longer for quart.

Place the bottles on rack as described in preceding method. Cover with cold water by fully 1 inch. Cover closely. Heat gently to simmering point, taking 1 hour, so the heat below must be adjusted carefully as necessary. Keep simmering the bottled fruit given in Class 1 for 5 minutes, Class 2 for 15 minutes, and Class 3 for 30 minutes.

CLASS 1 : Apricots, blackberries, damsons, gooseberries, grapefruit, green-gages, lemons, loganberries, mulberries, oranges, raspberries, rhubarb and strawberries.

CLASS 2 : Cherries, currants, grapes, peaches and plums.

CLASS 3 : Ripe pears, quinces and tomatoes.

OVEN BOTTLING

This method is only suitable for fruit and fruit juices. Use screw-topped or metal-topped jars. Pre-heat oven to 250°-275° F., but take care when using electric oven not to switch on top heating element if you have an inside grill.

British Method : Pack required fruit tightly into jars bringing it right up to the top, but do not add any water, and do not fix any of the usual fittings. Cover jars instead with odd lids or patty pans. This is to prevent top layer of fruit being discoloured. Place jars ½ inch apart on a baking sheet on the second or third shelf from bottom of oven. Close door. Keep at this temperature (250° F.) for ¾-1 hour until the fruit starts to shrink and looks cooked, and the juice begins to flow. Meanwhile, heat all the fittings, rubber bands and tops, and screws if screw-topped jars are used, in hot water. When the fruit is ready, remove 1 jar to a wooden surface, and fill up from a second jar, if there has been much shrinkage. When all are filled, cover again, and return to oven. Close door and leave for 7-10 minutes. Remove 1 jar at a time. Fill up with rapidly boiling syrup or water to over-flowing. Fix rubber and lid in position as quickly as possible, and fix at once with clips or screw bands as used. *It is most important that there should be no delay in filling and covering bottles of fruit in this way.* Bring syrup or water again to boil between filling each jar. If using screw-topped jars, keep tightening the screws as the jars cool. Leave all jars for 48 hours before testing seal.

OVEN BOTTLING (American Method)

Pre-heat oven to 250°-275° F. *Don't* switch on top element if you have an inside grill. When the jars are in the oven and being processed, the temperature of the fruit being processed will approximate 212° F. Use only bottles of the screw-top variety, that is bottles that have only to be partially sealed. Otherwise, the steam that forms in other types of jars might break the seal or the jars.

Place jars filled with raw fruit covered with hot fruit juice, syrup or water, and partially sealed, on a rack in the centre of oven 2 inches apart, and 2 inches from the oven walls. Set your minute timer when the jars have been placed in oven, the door closed, and the temperature if it fell slightly when you opened oven door, has reached 250°-275° F. again. When the bell rings, remove one jar at a time, and tighten seals. Continue to tighten from time to time as the jars cool, then leave undisturbed for 48 hours before testing seal.

TIME TABLE

This schedule is for quart jars. If sterilizing pint size, deduct 3 minutes in each case. If sterilizing ½ pint, deduct 4. If sterilizing 2 quart jars, add 3-4 minutes to times given.

Fruit	*Minutes Required* (for quart bottles)
Apples	35
Apricots	35
Blackberries, Bilberries, Loganberries and Raspberries.	40
(NOTE : If pre-cooked, allow only 35 minutes.)	
Cherries	40
Currants	40
Figs	35
Grapefruit	30
Grapes	35
Peaches	35
Pears	35
Pineapple	35
Plums	45
(NOTE : If pre-cooked, allow only 30 minutes.)	
Quinces	60
Rhubarb	30
Strawberries (Generally pre-cooked)	15
Tomatoes	45

TO CAN FRUIT

The only equipment required in addition to equipment used for bottling is a small sealing machine and cans. Follow instructions given with your canning machines.

To Pack and Seal : Prepare fruit as for bottling. Scald cans. Pack fruit carefully into cans as tightly as possible, but take care not to bruise it. Fill up to within ¼ inch of the top with boiling fruit juice, syrup or water. Seal at once. The liquid must not be allowed to cool.

To Process : Place immediately on a rack in a sterilizer large enough to allow boiling water to cover them. Add water. Cover. Bring water quickly to boil. Simmer gently for time required. Time will depend on type of fruit and size of can. (If preferred, sterilize in a pressure cooker at 10 lb. pressure, 240° F.). Cool rapidly to blood heat under cold water tap. Dry and label. Store like bottled fruit.

HOW TO BOTTLE AND CAN FRUIT

The following instructions are given for bottling fruit and processing in a hot water bath *without a thermometer*, in the oven, and in a pressure cooker. The times given for fruit packed in cans, refer to cans processed in a hot water bath *without a thermometer*. The time to be allowed in every case is from the moment the water comes to a full boil, 212° F.

Apples : Wash, peel, core, quarter or slice apples. Place each portion as prepared in brine or in lemon or vinegar water solution. Rinse well. Pre-cook in light syrup or water for 1-5 minutes, according to variety of apple. Pack hot. Cover with its own syrup, allowing $\frac{1}{2}$ inch vacuum when bottling, unless otherwise stated, and $\frac{1}{4}$ inch when canning. Cover and process. $2\frac{1}{2}$ quarts sliced apple *yields* 1 quart bottled or canned.

	GLASS JARS		CANS	
	Pint Jars	Quart Jars	No. 2	No. $2\frac{1}{2}$
Hot Water Bath	15 mins.	15 mins.	10 mins.	10 mins.
Oven	32 mins.	35 mins.		
Pressure Cooker		10 mins.		

Apple Sauce : Make windfalls into sweetened or unsweetened Apple Sauce. Pack hot. Cover and process.

	GLASS JARS		CANS	
	Pint Jars	Quart Jars	No. 2	No. $2\frac{1}{2}$
Hot Water Bath	10 mins.	10 mins.	10 mins.	15 mins.

Apricots : Wash, halve and stone, or leave whole. If wanted peeled, immerse in boiling water for about $\frac{1}{2}$ a minute till skins slip off easily, then plunge immediately into cold water for a second or two and peel. Brine and rinse. Pack in jars and cover with thin or medium syrup, or pre-cook for 4-8 minutes in medium syrup, and cover with the syrup. 2-3 lbs. apricots *yield* 1 quart.

	GLASS JARS		CANS	
	Pint Jars	Quart Jars	No. 2	No. $2\frac{1}{2}$
Hot Water Bath :				
(Cold Pack)	20 mins.	25 mins.	25 mins.	35 mins.
(Pre-cooked)	15 mins.	15 mins.	25 mins.	35 mins.
Oven	32 mins.	35 mins.		
Pressure Cooker		10 mins.		

Berries (Except Strawberries) : Stem and wash firm berries in a colander in a basin of cold water. Drain well. Pack in jars and cover with boiling medium syrup, or pre-cook. Measure and allow 5-10 oz. sugar to each quart of berries, depending on sweetness of berry. Arrange sugar and berries alternately in a shallow dish. Cover and stand for 2 hours, then cook gently over a slow heat till sugar is dissolved. Pack at once into heated jars and cover with their syrup. Cover and process. $1\frac{1}{2}$ quarts raw berries *yield* 1 quart bottled or canned.

	GLASS JARS		CANS	
	Pint Jars	Quart Jars	No. 2	No. 2½
Hot Water Bath :				
(Cold Pack)	20 mins.	20 mins.	15 mins.	20 mins.
(Pre-cooked)	15 mins.	15 mins.	15 mins.	20 mins.
Oven :				
(Cold Pack)	37 mins.	40 mins.		
(Pre-cooked)	32 mins.	35 mins.		
Pressure Cooker		10 mins.		

Cherries : Stem, wash and leave whole or stone using a cherry stoner, as preferred. If left whole, prick them with a darning needle to prevent shrinkage, and save any juice that comes from them to add to syrup. Pack in jars. Cover with boiling medium syrup for sweet cherries and boiling thick syrup for sour. Cold pack whole cherries and pre-cook stoned. Measure, and for every cup of cherries, allow ½ cup of sugar. Place in layers in a shallow dish. Cover and stand for 1-2 hours. Pour just enough cold water into a saucepan to cover bottom and prevent cherries from sticking. Add cherries and sugar. Stir over low heat till sugar is dissolved, then till boiling. Simmer gently for 10 minutes, then pack at once into heated jars. Cover and process. 1½ quarts whole cherries *yield* 1 quart canned or bottled.

	GLASS JARS		CANS	
	Pint Jars	Quart Jars.	No. 2	No. 2½
Hot Water Bath :				
(Cold Pack)	20 mins.	25 mins.	15 mins.	20 mins.
(Pre-cooked)	10 mins.	10 mins.	15 mins.	20 mins.
Oven	37 mins.	40 mins.		
Pressure Cooker		10 mins.		

Cranberries : Wash and stem. Cook in thick syrup for 3 minutes. Pack and process.

	GLASS JARS	
	Pint Jars	Quart Jars
Water Bath	7 mins.	10 mins.
Pressure Cooker		10 mins.

Currants (Black) **:** Wash and stem. Cold-pack. Cover with boiling medium syrup, or pre-cook as for Berries. Pack and process.

	GLASS JARS	
	Pint Jars	Quart Jars
Water Bath :		
(Cold pack)	15 mins.	20 mins.
(Pre-cooked)	5 mins.	5 mins.
Oven :		
(Cold Pack)	38 mins.	40 mins.
(Pre-cooked)	32 mins.	35 mins.
Pressure Cooker		10 mins.

Grapefruit : Peel. Separate into sections, discarding all membrane. Pack in jars. Cover with boiling thin syrup. Cover and process.

	GLASS JARS	
	Pint Jars	*Quart Jars*
Hot Water Bath	6-7 mins.	10 mins.
Oven	27 mins.	30 mins.
Pressure Cooker		10 mins.

Grapes : Wash, stem and pack. Cover with boiling light syrup, or add to syrup and bring to boiling point. Pack hot. Cover and process. $1\frac{1}{2}$ quarts grapes *yield* 1 quart bottled.

	GLASS JARS	
	Pint Jars	*Quart Jars*
Hot Water Bath :		
(Cold Pack)	17 mins.	20 mins.
(Pre-cooked)	3 mins.	5 mins.

Nectarines and Peaches : Choose sound, ripe, uniform fruit. Wash. Dip in boiling water, then dip quickly in cold water, using cheesecloth or a wire basket to hold the fruit as you dip. Slip off skins. Halve and stone. As you prepare fruit slip each one into the following solution : 2 tablespoons each of salt and vinegar to 4 quarts of cold water. Strain boiling medium syrup over, flavoured if liked while cooking, with a few peach kernels, allowing 1 or 2 kernels to each quart of syrup. Cover and process. Or pre-cook, which imparts a richer flavour : Place in boiling medium syrup and simmer slowly for about 5 minutes, depending on size. The fruit must not be cooked until really soft. Pack in hot jars. Seal and process at once. $2\frac{1}{2}$-3 lbs. fruit *yield* 1 quart bottled or canned.

	GLASS JARS		CANS	
	Pint Jars	*Quart Jars*	*No. 2*	*No. $2\frac{1}{2}$*
Hot Water Bath :				
(Cold Pack)	25 mins.	30 mins.	25 mins.	35 mins.
(Pre-cooked)	20 mins.	20 mins.	25 mins.	35 mins.
Oven	32 imns.	35 mins.		
Pressure Cooker :				
(Cold Pack)		10 mins.		
(Pre-cooked)		5 mins.		

Pears : Select Bartlett or Comice pears if possible. Peel and halve. Core and quarter if necessary. Drop each portion in brine or lemon juice or vinegar water solution. Rinse and drain. Cold-pack or pre-cook ripe pears as suggested for nectarines and peaches. Pre-cook hard pears for 6-8 minutes, time depending on the degree of hardness. Cover and process. 2-3 lbs. pears *yield* 1 quart.

	GLASS JARS		CANS	
	Pint Jars	*Quart Jars*	*No. 2*	*No. $2\frac{1}{2}$*
Hot Water Bath :				
(Cold Pack)	25 mins.	30 mins.	25 mins.	35 mins.
(Pre-cooked)	20 mins.	20 mins.	25 mins.	35 mins.
Oven	32 mins.	35 mins.		
Pressure Cooker		10 mins.		

Pineapple : Peel, remove eyes, core, and slice or cut up pineapple. For each pineapple, add ¼ lb. sugar with pineapple to a pan. Cover. Heat very slowly, taking 10-15 minutes to come to boiling point. Remove fruit to hot sterilized jars. Cover with the hot syrup. Cover and process. 2 prepared pineapples *yield* 1 quart bottled.

| | GLASS JARS | |
	Pint Jars	Quart Jars
Hot Water Bath :		
(Cold Pack)	30 mins.	30 mins.
(Pre-cooked)	25 mins.	25 mins.
Oven	32 mins.	35 mins.
Pressure Cooker		10 mins.

Plums : Wash and drain. Prick well. Pack and cover with medium or thick syrup, or pre-cook for 2-5 minutes in syrup, time depending on size. Cover and process. 1½ quarts plums *yield* 1 quart bottled or canned.

| | GLASS JARS | | CANS | |
	Pint Jars	Quart Jars	No. 2	No. 2½
Hot Water Bath :				
(Cold Pack)	20 mins.	20 mins.		
(Pre-cooked)	15 mins.	15 mins.	15 mins.	20 mins.
Oven :				
(Cold Pack)	42 mins.	45 mins.		
(Pre-cooked)	27 mins.	30 mins.		
Pressure Cooker :				
(Cold Pack)		10 mins.		

Quinces : Skin, core and slice. Brine and blanch for 6 minutes. Rinse. Drain. Pack. Cover with boiling syrup. Cover and process.

| | GLASS JARS | |
	Pint Jars	Quart Jars
Hot Water Bath	36 mins.	40 mins.
Oven	56 mins.	60 mins.
Pressure Cooker		20 mins.

Rhubarb : Trim and wash rhubarb stalks. Dry. Cut into short lengths to taste, from ½-2 inches.

1. Pack in jars. Cover with boiling thin syrup, or soak in boiling water for 3 minutes before packing and covering with thin syrup. Cover and process.

2. Measure. Place in a saucepan. Add sugar, allowing 5 oz. to each quart of rhubarb. Sprinkle sugar over the rhubarb. Stand until juice is extracted. Bring to simmering point. Pack and process.

1½ lb. rhubarb will give you 1 pint bottled or canned.

| | GLASS JARS | | CANS | |
	Pint Jars	Quart Jars	No. 2	No. 2½
Hot Water Bath :				
1.	20 mins.	25 mins.		
2.	10 mins.	10 mins.	10 mins.	10 mins
3.	10 mins.	10 mins.		
Oven (as 275° F.)	47 mins.	50 mins.		

Strawberries : Stem berries.

1. Measure. Place in a saucepan. Sprinkle with sugar, allowing $\frac{1}{2}$ lb. to each 4 cups berries. Bring slowly to boiling point, shaking occasionally to prevent fruit sticking. Remove from heat. Cover and stand for 12 hours. Bring quickly to boil. Pack hot in hot jars. Pour in hot syrup to overflowing. Seal and process.

2. Press hulled berries into jars till half-full. Add caster sugar, allowing 2 oz. for pint jars, and $\frac{1}{4}$ lb. for quart. Fill up with berries. Cover and process. $1\frac{1}{2}$ quarts raw berries *yield* 1 quart bottled or canned.

	GLASS JARS		CANS	
	Pint Jars	Quart Jars	No. 2	No. 2½
Hot Water Bath :				
1.	15 mins.	15 mins.	10 mins.	15 mins.
2.	10 mins.	10 mins.		
Oven :				
(Pre-cooked)	12 mins.	15 mins.		

Tomatoes : Scald. Cold dip. Peel. Remove stems, and stem ends if necessary. Leave whole, or cut up. Pack in jars, pressing gently. Add no water, but $\frac{1}{2}$ teaspoon salt to pint jars, and 1 teaspoon to quart. Cover and process. Or pre-cook. Quarter peeled tomatoes. Place in a saucepan. Bring to a full boil, stirring constantly. Pack at once to within $\frac{1}{2}$ inch of top. Add salt, allowing $\frac{1}{2}$ teaspoon for pint jars, and 1 teaspoon for quart. Cover and process.

Tomatoes with Tomato Juice : Scald, cold-dip and peel perfect tomatoes. Pack in clean hot jars. Cover with hot tomato juice. Add salt, allowing $\frac{1}{2}$ teaspoon to a pint jar, or a teaspoon to a quart. Cover and process.

3 lb. tomatoes *yield* 1 quart bottled or canned tomatoes.

	GLASS JARS		CANS	
	Pint Jars	Quart Jars	No. 2	No. 2½
Hot Water Bath :				
(Cold Pack)	35 mins.	45 mins.	45 mins.	55 mins.
(Pre-cooked)	10 mins.	10 mins.		
(Tomato Juice)	22 mins.	25 mins.		
Oven	42 mins.	45 mins.		
Pressure Cooker		10 mins.		

Tomato Juice : Wash ripe, juicy tomatoes. Remove stem ends and cut up fruit. Place in a saucepan. Simmer till softened, stirring frequently. Rub through a hair sieve. Measure. Add salt, allowing 1 teaspoon to each quart of juice. Reheat only till boiling point, stirring occasionally. Pack at once in hot sterilized jars to within $\frac{1}{4}$ inch of the rims. Cover and process. 3-4 lbs. tomatoes *yield* approximately 1 quart juice.

	GLASS JARS		CANS	
	Pint Jars	Quart Jars	No. 2	No. 2½
Hot Water Bath	15 mins.	15 mins.	15 mins.	15 mins.

To BOTTLE FRUIT JUICES

Raw Fruit Juice : Suitable fruits are : apples, berries, sour cherries, ripe grapes, and peaches. Wash and drain fruit. Extract juice in a juice extractor or fruit press. Strain through a jelly bag into a basin. Turn into a preserving pan. Heat to 110° F. Pour immediately into hot sterilized jars. Partially seal. Process for $\frac{1}{2}$ hour in hot water bath, keeping water at about 180° F. Seal completely as you remove each jar.

Cooked Fruit Juices : Suitable fruits are : Bilberries, currants, sour cherries, grapes, loganberries, pineapple, raspberries. Prepare fruit and place in a basin. Mash with a wooden spoon. Turn into a preserving pan. Cover. Heat slowly to simmering point, 185° F. Simmer gently till juice flows. Strain through a jelly bag. Stand for 4 or 5 hours. Carefully pour into clean, hot sterilized jars, taking care not to disturb any sediment. Cover, partially seal, and sterilize in a hot water bath at a steady temperature of 180° F., for 30 minutes. Remove jars one at a time and seal.

NOTE : Any bottled fruit juice can be used for making jelly, but if bottled for any other purpose, the flavour is improved by sweetening. In this case, measure juice, and allow 2-4 oz. sugar to each quart of juice. Stir till dissolved before bringing to simmering point, 180°F.

BOTTLING VEGETABLES

As vegetables, owing to the fact that they are liable to be contaminated by bacteria, need to be sterilized at a higher temperature than 212° F. in order to kill all micro-organisms and bacteria, the only safe way to sterilise them is in a pressure cooker at 250° F. Here are general instructions, but follow instructions given with your cooker.

Greens : Choose only freshly picked tender young greens for bottling, such as beet tops and spinach. Pick over. Wash in several clean waters until free from all signs of grit or dirt. Discard any damaged leaves, and remove any coarse stems. Place in a colander. Lower into boiling water. Cover tightly and steam over water which must not touch greens, for 15-20 minutes. If preferred, place in a cheese-cloth or muslin bag and steam for about 10 minutes, until wilted, without using any water. Pack immediately in scalded jars, but not too tightly. Cut down with a knife. Cover with boiling water to within $\frac{1}{2}$ inch of rim, adding $\frac{1}{4}$ teaspoon salt to pint jars, and $\frac{1}{2}$ teaspoon to quart. Adjust lids. Sterilize in pressure cooker at 10 lb. pressure. Complete seals if not self-sealing.

Canning Times : 60 minutes for No. 2, and 75 minutes for No. 2$\frac{1}{2}$.

Green Peas : Choose young peas. Shell and wash. Place in a saucepan. Cover with boiling water. Bring rapidly to a boil and cold-dip. (If your instruction book says to boil for a certain time before cold-dipping, do so.) Pack into hot jars to within 1 inch of tops. Cover with boiling salted water to within 1 inch of tops. Adjust lids. Sterilize in cooker at 10 lb. pressure. Complete seals if not self-sealing. 2 quarts peas in pod yield 1 pint bottled or canned.

Canning Times : 30 minutes for both No. 2 and No. 2$\frac{1}{2}$ cans.

New Potatoes : Choose young potatoes of equal size and shape, and not too big. Wash thoroughly, scrubbing if necessary, to remove all traces of soil. Stand in boiling water for 1 or 2 minutes, then place in cold water. Leave until cool enough to handle. Rub the outer skin off with a clean cloth. Remove any " eyes." Pre-cook in boiling water for 5 minutes. Pack into hot pint jars. Cover with hot brine. Adjust lids. Sterilize in pressure cooker at 10 lb. pressure for 40 minutes, unless otherwise instructed by the manufacturers of your cooker. Complete seals of jars if not self-sealing.

Canning Times : 35 minutes for No. $2\frac{1}{2}$ cans.

Macédoine of Vegetables : Choose 3 or 4 contrasting vegetables, such as French or runner beans, carrots, green peas, and turnips. This macédoine is useful not only for serving with meat, but for soups. Prepare peas as for bottling, and slice beans in the usual way. Cut carrots and turnip into small equal-sized cubes. If liked, add scraped celery sticks, cut $\frac{1}{8}$ inch thick. Place each different vegetable in a separate saucepan. Add enough water to cover bottom of each pan. Cover and bring to boiling point. Pack at once into heated jars in separate layers. Add salt, $\frac{1}{2}$ teaspoon to each pint. Fill to overflowing with the vegetable stocks mixed in equal quantity, or with boiling water. Adjust lids. Sterilize in pressure cooker at 10 lb. pressure. Complete seal if not self-sealing.

Mushrooms : Grade mushrooms. Wash thoroughly, and peel if mature. Remove nearly all the stalk from each. Prepare in one of the following ways :

1. Place in a casserole. Sprinkle with a little salt and pepper. Cover and stew in a moderate oven, 350° F., till liquid is extracted and they are heated through. Place in heated jars. Cover with their own juice. Adjust lids. Sterilize in a pressure cooker at 10 lb. pressure for $\frac{1}{2}$ hour. Complete seals if not self-sealing.

2. Drop into boiling water containing 2 teaspoons vinegar and 1 teaspoon salt to each quart of water. Leave for a moment or two, then drain thoroughly. Pack into heated jars. Cover with fresh boiling water to within $\frac{1}{2}$ inch of tops. Add salt, $\frac{1}{2}$ teaspoon to each pint. Adjust lids. Sterilize in a pressure cooker at 10 lb. pressure for 35 minutes, for quart jars, and 25 minutes for pint jars. Complete seals if not self-sealing.

TO DRY GARDEN PRODUCE

Fruit, herbs and vegetables can all be dried. The ideal way to dry is in the sun ; the alternative is to dry in artificial heat. Food dried in the sun must be protected from dew, dust and rain, and brought indoors in the evening.

There are three methods of drying indoors :

1. In a cool oven, between 140° and 150° F., but starting at 110° F.
2. In an airing cupboard.
3. On a rack over a solid fuel cooker, or above a radiator.

TO PREPARE FRUIT FOR DRYING

Apples : Pare, core and cut into rings about $\frac{1}{4}$ inch thick with a stainless steel knife. Place each ring for a minute in brine, allowing 3 dessertspoons salt to 1 quart of water. to prevent discoloration, then drain, and dry off surface moisture with cheese-cloth.

Berries, Cherries, Currants and Grapes : Choose sound fruit free from blemishes and damage. Rinse until clean, then drain throughly.

Pears : Use only pears that are almost ripe. Pare, core, halve or quarter. To brine, see Apples. Leave in brine for 5 minutes, then dry with a cheese-cloth.
Quinces : Treat like Apples.
Stone Fruit : Leave whole. If very large, slit and stone.

TO DRY FRUIT IN OVEN

Before starting to prepare fruit, cover oven racks with butter muslin or cheesecloth. If this is not convenient, line large baking tins with it. To cover the oven racks pin the cheese-cloth securely at each corner, for as the fruit dries, it becomes heavier, when the weight will make the material sag. The result is that fruit falls to bottom of oven. About 15 minutes before starting to dry, set your oven regulator at 110° F., and open door 6 inches. As the fruit is prepared, spread it out on trays a little apart, placing slit, stoned fruit, skin side downwards. Insert in oven. Leave for 1 hour. Gradually increase heat to between 140° F. and 150° F. The fruit, when ready, should be dry but pliable, not brittle or burnt. Stir it from time to time, and move the racks or tins in oven from one position to another occasionally. When ready, cool as quickly as possible, but not in a refrigerator. Leave for at least 12 hours, covered with a kitchen cloth, stirring occasionally, then store in paper bags. Tie necks with string. Pack in a tightly closed tin.

TIME TABLE FOR DRYING FRUIT

Fruit	Preparation	Drying Period	Temperature F.
Apples	Pare, core, slice and brine.	4-6 hours	110°-150° F.
Apricots, Peaches	Halve and stone	4-6 hours	110°-150° F.
Pears	Pare, core, halve or quarter and brine	4-6 hours	110°-150° F.
Plums	Halve and stone	4-6 hours	110°-145° F.
Quinces	Pare, core, slice and brine	4-6 hours	110°-150° F.
Berries, Cherries, Currants and Grapes	Wash and dry	6-8 hours	110°-140° F.

To Use Dried Fruit : Soak in cold water, allowing 4 cups water to each $\frac{1}{2}$ lb. of fruit. Stand covered over-night. Stew in soaking water, sweetening when nearly ready, or bake in a covered casserole in a slow oven, 300°-325° F.

TO DRY HERBS

Gather herbs for drying when the dew is off the grass on a fine dry morning well before mid-day. If the leaves are to be used, cut just before the plants blossom. If the seeds, wait until fully developed before picking.

Basil	*Middle of August*
Knotted Marjoram	*July*
Lemon Thyme	*July and August*
Mint	*June and July*
Parsley	*May, June and July*
Sage	*August and September*
Summer Savory	*End of July and August*
Tarragon	*June, July and August*

917

Cut all varieties within 2 or 3 inches from the ground. Discard any withered or insect-eaten leaves. Herbs can be dried in 2-3 days in the open or indoors. The best indoors temperature for drying herbs is about 70° F.

1. Tie by their stems loosely in bunches and hang up to dry in half-shade in the open, or just inside the open door of a shed. If there is any chance of dust getting to them, wrap each bunch loosely in butter muslin before hanging up.

2. Spread them in a single layer on a rack covered with butter muslin or cheese-cloth, and lay them in front of an open window out of the direct rays of the sun, and leave the door of the room open. If drying out of doors, remember to bring in the herbs each evening before the dew begins to fall.

When dry, strip leaves from sprigs or stems, then either pound in a mortar and sieve, or simply rub through a fine sieve. Store in tightly-corked bottles.

TO DRY VEGETABLES

Prepare vegetables as for the table :
Broad Beans : Shell and rinse.
Brussels Sprouts : Trim and rinse.
Green Peas : Pod and rinse.
Greens (Beet tops, cabbage, celery leaves, Swiss chard, spinach, etc.) : Wash thoroughly and drain. Spread them out on prepared oven racks, a leaf at a time. If piled up on the racks, they won't dry.
Leeks : Trim. Wash thoroughly and dry. Cut in thin slices.
Onions : Peel and trim off roots. Cut in thin slices.
Root Vegetables (Beetroot, carrots, celeriac, parsnips, salsify, turnips, etc.) : Scrape or peel and rinse. Cut in thin slices.
Squash and Marrows : Peel. Cut in strips $\frac{1}{2}$ inch thick.
String Beans : String and cut in 1 inch lengths.

Make a large bag of cheese-cloth or butter muslin, or use a large wire basket. Place prepared vegetables in bag or basket. Cover and steam over rapidly boiling water till the vegetables are heated through the centre and limp, then dip in cold water.

TIME FOR STEAMING : Beetroot, carrots, celeriac and parsnips require 8-15 minutes, till three-parts ready. Celery requires 3 minutes. Sliced beans and green peas need 4 or 5 minutes.

TO BOIL FOR DRYING (BLANCHING) : Prepare water bath. Bring 4 quarts water to a boil. Add $\frac{1}{2}$ teaspoon bicarbonate of soda.
Broad Beans : Place in boiling water. Boil for 5-10 minutes. Dip in cold water. Drain and dry between cloths.
Brussels Sprouts : Place in boiling water. Boil for 6 minutes. Cold-dip. Drain and dry between cloths.
Green Peas : Cook in boiling water for 3-5 minutes. Cold-dip. Drain and dry between cloths.
Leeks : Cook in boiling water for 1 minute. Drain and dry between cloths.
Onions : Cook in boiling water for 5 minutes. Drain and dry between cloths.
Root Vegetables : Cook in boiling water for 6 minutes, omitting soda. Cold-dip. Drain and dry between cloths.
Squashes and Vegetable Marrows : Cook in boiling water without soda for 3 minutes. Cold-dip. Drain and dry between cloths.

String Beans : Boil for 6-10 minutes, according to age. Cold-dip. Drain and dry between cloths.

Spread vegetables in thin layers on oven racks covered with butter muslin or cheese-cloth. Heat oven to 110° F. Insert racks. Leave oven door ajar by about 4 or 5 inches. Very gradually increase heat to 140°-150° F., depending on the variety of vegetable. If heated too quickly, the vegetables will harden. Dry from $2\frac{1}{2}$-5 hours as stated, stirring from time to time, and changing the position of the shelves to ensure even drying. The vegetable, when ready, should be dry but pliable, not brittle or discoloured in any way.

If preferred, broad beans and green peas can be left to dry in the sun on the vines, but make certain they are absolutely dry before storing. Spread them out on trays in a sunny room for a day or two after picking before cooling and storing.

TIME TABLE FOR DRYING

Broad Beans	110°-145° F.	3-$3\frac{1}{2}$ hours
Brussels Sprouts	110°-145° F.	2-3 hours
Green Peas	111°-145° F.	$1\frac{1}{2}$-2 hours
Greens	110°-140° F.	3 hours
Leeks and Onions	110°-140° F.	$2\frac{1}{2}$-3 hours
Root Vegetables	110°-150° F.	$2\frac{1}{2}$-3 hours
Squash and Marrows	110°-140° F.	3-4 hours
String Beans	110°-145° F.	2 hours

Remove vegetable from heat. Spread out on trays or platters covered with absorbent paper. Leave for 24 hours, stirring occasionally, till all are evenly chilled. Store in glass jars with tightly fitting covers, or tie in bags. Brush bags with melted paraffin wax, and pack in a large covered tin.

To Cook Dried Vegetables : Soak in cold water to cover for 12 hours. Add bicarbonate of soda to water for beans and peas, allowing 1 teaspoon soda to 1 lb. of the vegetable. Cook vegetable in the soaking water. Bring slowly to boil. Simmer gently till tender, allowing 1-2 hours for beans and peas. Cover onions with boiling water and soak for 1-2 hours before using in place of fresh onions.

To Store Dried Fruit and Vegetables : Keep on a shelf in a dry cupboard, otherwise they may develop mould which also happens if they have not been dried sufficiently. Examine occasionally for insects. If discovered, spread food on trays in thin layers. Place in the sun until insects disappear, then reheat at 160° F. Remove and cool for 24 hours, till evenly chilled.

TO DRY MUSHROOMS

Choose young, tender mushrooms. Peel. Slice if very thick. Remove stalks. Either string on a thread and dry in the shady part of a garden, or at an open window, or dry in the oven.

To Dry in the Oven : Place in a single layer on oven racks covered with butter muslin or cheese-cloth. Place in cool oven, about 140° F., and not above 150° F. Leave oven door 2 or 3 inches ajar to allow steam to escape. Dry, turning occasionally, and changing position of the racks, until of a leathery consistency. Place on trays. Cover with butter muslin. Leave for 12 hours, turning occasionally. Store in airtight tins. Rinse well in cold water before cooking.

To Use Dried Mushrooms : Soak mushrooms in cold water to cover until the water darkens. Use for flavouring savoury dishes in place of fresh mushrooms.

TO SALT VEGETABLES

Allow 1 lb. salt to every 4 lb. prepared vegetables. Use wide-mouthed jars for packing. Place vegetables in $\frac{1}{2}$ inch thick layers, and sprinkle salt evenly over each layer till jars are full. Cover with butter muslin, then with a plate and weight down. Leave vegetables till bubbling ceases, then remove jars to a cold place, and pour melted wax into each, to the depth of $\frac{1}{4}$ inch, or, if preferred, cover with a double thickness of greaseproof paper and tie down.

To Salt String Beans : Choose young, freshly picked beans. If stringless and young, salt down whole. If fairly large, top and tail, string and slice. Wash in a colander under the cold water tap, then drain and dry. Weigh beans. For every 3 or 4 lb., allow 1 lb. kitchen salt. Place a good layer of salt about 1 inch deep into bottom of a large stoneware jar or glass jars, then fill up jar or jars with alternate layers of prepared beans and salt, making the salt layers abour $\frac{1}{4}$ inch thick. Press each layer of beans down well as you fill jars. The last layer must be salt. Cover with a piece of muslin, then with paper, and weight down. In 48 hours, enough brine should have formed to cover beans. If not, add brine to cover made by dissolving 1 lb. salt in 2 quarts cold water. After a few days, when the beans have shrunk, fill jars with more beans and salt. Cover with synthetic skin. If preferred, cover again with the muslin, then with a plate and weight down. Examine occasionally. If scum arises, wash it off the muslin or the skin. Store in a dark, dry, airy cupboard on a wooden shelf, not on a stone floor.

NOTE : Be careful to use the correct amount of salt. If you use too little, the beans will become slimy and unfit for use.

To Cook Salted Beans : Remove from brine quantity required. Wash thoroughly in several waters. Soak for 2 hours in warm water to cover. Cook in boiling, unsalted water to cover till tender in 25-35 minutes.

TO STORE FRUIT

Only apples and pears are stored for any length of time. If storing in any quantity, great care must be taken.

APPLES : Pick sound apples on a dry day between noon and 4.30 p.m., when just ripe. If immature, the fruit will be of poor quality and flavour, and soon shrivel. Bramley Seedling, Newton Wonder and Lane's Prince Albert are all good cooking apples to store. Cox's Orange Pippin, Laxton's Superb are good dessert apples to keep, and Blenheim Orange are suitable for both cooking and dessert, and keep well. Do not attempt to store early ripening apples, for no matter how perfectly they are stored, they will not keep past their normal season for using. Take this into account when buying apples for storing.

If you grow your own fruit, you can tell when apples are ready by taking one gently in your hand. Raise it to a horizontal position. Twist it slightly to the right, and if ready to pick, it will come away in your hand. If it requires to be tugged, it is not ready. When picking, place in a basket lined with 2 or 3 layers of newspaper or straw to prevent them bruising. Do not throw them in. Transfer to a shelf or table covered with newspaper or straw, in a darkish well-ventilated room. Cover with clean cloths. Leave until they stop " sweating " in 3 or 4 days. Wipe one at a time with a clean cloth, then wrap in tissue paper, or in paper sold for the purpose. Pack in 2 or 3 layers on shelves, or in boxes. Label each variety. Keep room at a steady temperature of between 35° and 40° F. If you only wish to store a small quantity, arrange, unwrapped, on shelves covered with 2 or 3 layers of paper without touching each other, in a darkened room. Cover with 3 layers of newspaper.

NOTE : It is most important that the storage room should be well ventilated and airy while the apples are drying out. Do not attempt to store apples until the skins are completely dry, or they will rot. When dry, ventilate only to maintain a steady temperature under the varying weather conditions.

PEARS : Only fully ripened pears should be stored. To pick, lever each off in the palm of your hand. Do not hold them between fingers and thumb, or they will become bruised very quickly. Take care not to break off the spurs with the fruit. Pears are ready when they come away in your hand without any tugging. Gather early varieties a day or two before they are fully ripe, and store in a darkened room for 24 hours. The late pears must be fully ripe before gathering, or they will shrink quickly and decay when stored. Wrap and store like apples, without touching each other, on shelves, not in boxes, in a cool, dark, frost-proof cellar, room or shed, between 40° and 45° F. Place in a slightly warmer room 3 or 4 days before serving.

TO STORE BANANAS : Hang bunches up on a hook.

TO STORE GRAPEFRUIT, LEMONS AND ORANGES : Place in separate nets, and suspend from hooks, so that the air circulates all round them, and prevents them from getting mouldy quickly as they sometimes do if laid flat on a plate or shelf.

TO STORE NUTS

Nuts can be kept for several months if they are mature, perfectly sound and perfectly dry when gathered.

ALMONDS : These are usually ripe in August. They look shrivelled when ripe. Pack them in an airtight box with adhesive tape round the join of lid, and bury them in the garden, if you want to keep them so that they taste freshly picked when served. Otherwise, pick and remove kernel and skin. Dry in a heated linen cupboard, or spread out on a tray in the sun, turning frequently. If stored before they are perfectly dry, they will turn mouldy. Store in airtight tins.

CHESTNUTS : Pack in a box or crock with a layer of dry soil below a layer of nuts. Repeat layers, ending with soil.

COB NUTS AND FILBERTS : Pack tightly in jars to within $\frac{1}{2}$ inch of the tops. Cover firmly with salt, then with lids. Turn occasionally to prevent mildew.

WALNUTS : Walnuts can be packed like almonds in an airtight box if wanted to taste fresh when served. They will keep till Christmas. Another method is to pack them like chestnuts, but use dry sand instead of soil. Again, shell them and place them a little apart on a baking sheet and dry in a cool oven, 110° F., with the door open, or in a heated linen cupboard. Leave for 12 hours, stirring occasionally, then pack in airtight jars.

TO STORE VEGETABLES

BEETROOT, CARROTS AND TURNIPS : Twist off the foliage 2 or 3 inches above the tops. Store in layers of dry sieved sand in a cool, frost-proof cellar or shed.

CELERIAC : Remove foliage and rootlets. Store apart in sieved sand in a frost-proof cellar or shed.

ONIONS : Leave them to dry in a shed, then plait in ropes and suspend from a nail in a cool, dry shed.

PARSNIPS AND POTATOES : Dig up on a dry day, then leave until dry. Place in rows in a cool, dry, light frost-proof shed or attic, on straw shavings, sawdust or sand. Cover rows with straw shavings, sawdust or sand.

SHALLOTS : Lift clumps as soon as the tops begin to wither. Dry in an airy shed. Divide and store like onions.

INDEX

937

Scrap bread pudding, 575
Sea foam, 846
Sea pie, 538
Seaford cocktails, 72
Seakale, 437-8
Seakale, creamed, 438
Sear, to, 40
Second thoughts, 320-1
Seed tapioca pudding, 584
Semi-solid diet, 765-74
Semolina fritters, 487
Semolina gnocchi, 497-8
Semolina honey pudding, 585
Seven minute frosting, 758
Seville sauce, 378
Shad, 151
Shallots, 438
Shallots, pickled, 900
Shandy gaff, 835
Shashlyk, 221
Sheep's hearts, braised, 244
Sheep's hearts, roast stuffed, 245
Sheep's kidneys, devilled, 245-6
Sheep's kidneys, fried, 246
Sheep's kidneys, grilled, 246
Sheep's tongues, galantine of, 260
Sheep's tongues with spinach, 349
Sheep's trotters, boiled, 254
Shellfish, 165-79
Shellfish, bouchées of, 785
Shellfish stuffing, 81
Shells (bread), 389-90
Shepherd's pie, 258
Sherbets, 625-6
Sherry butter, 632
Sherry cream, 611-2
Sherry croissants, 709
Shirr, to, 40
Shoo-fly pie, 555
Short biscuits, 735-6
Shortbread, 744-5
Shortcakes, 598-600
Shortcakes, fillings for, 598
Shortcrust, 523
Shortcrust, almond, 541
Shortcrust, spiced, 542
Shrimp and mushroom patties, 346
Shrimp butter, 388
Shrimp fritters, 785
Shrimp garnish, 391
Shrimp omelet, 63
Shrimp sandwiches, 813
Shrimp sauce, 378
Shrimp stuffing, 361
Shrimp toasts, 670
Shrimps, 179
Shrimps, potted, 77
Shrimps, potted, 665
Side car, 795
Silverside, boiled salt, 208
Simnel cake, 721-2

Sirop à la Caramel, 632
Sirop de Baies, 830
Sirop de Citrons, 830
Sizzle and squeak, 411
Skate, boiled, with black butter, 152
Skate liver, 152
Skewer, to, 38
Skirret, 438
Slab cakes, 723-4
Sloe gin, 837
Sloes, 642
Smelt, 152-3
Smelts à la Meunière, 153
Smelts, Espagnol, 153
Smelts, potted, 153
Snacks, 804-8
Snails, 80
Snipe, 283-4
Snipe au vin, 284
Snoek, 153
Snow cap tartlets, 621
Snow caps, 64
Snowballs, 703
Soda bread, 683-4
Soda water and cream, 764
Soda water and egg white, 764
Soft fruit drinks, 830-1
Soft icing, decorations, 755-6
Sole, 153-7
Sole à la Meunière, 156
Sole à la Portugaise, 156
Sole, boiled, 768
Sole, fillets of, bonne femme, 154
Sole, fillets of, Duglère, 154-5
Sole, fillets of, Florentine, 155
Sole, fillets of, Mornay, 155
Sole, fillets of, St. Raphael, 155
Sole, mock, 487
Sole, scallops, au Parmesan, 156
Sole Véronique, 156-7
Sorrel, 438
Soubise, sauce, 377-8
Soufflé, 61
Soufflé au Café, 589
Soufflé au Sucre, 588
Soufflé de Courge, 517
Soufflé de Flétan, 139
Soufflé de Gélinottes, 275
Soufflé de Gibier, 291
Soufflé de Macarons, 589
Soufflé de Perdreaux, 349-50
Soufflé de Poisson, 164, 518
Soufflé de Volaille Fermière, 349
Soufflé d'Eglefin, 517
Soufflé en Surprise, 623
Soufflé omelet, Welsh, 494
Soufflé Praliné, 589-90
Soufflé, savoury, baked, 516
Soufflé, steamed, 588
Soufflé, sweet, 588
Soufflé, to steam, 516-7

955